IMPORTANT

HERE IS YOUR REGISTRATION CODE TO ACCESS MCGRAW-HILL PREMIUM CONTENT AND MCGRAW-HILL ONLINE RESOURCES

For key premium online resources you need THIS CODE to gain access. Once the code is entered, you will be able to use the web resources for the length of your course.

Access is provided only if you have purchased a new book.

If the registration code is missing from this book, the registration screen on our website, and within your WebCT or Blackboard course will tell you how to obtain your new code. Your registration code can be used only once to establish access. It is not transferable.

To gain access to these online resources

1. **USE** your web browser to go to: **www.mhhe.com/sherrill6e**

2. **CLICK** on "First Time User"

3. **ENTER** the Registration Code printed on the tear-off bookmark on the right

4. After you have entered your registration code, click on "Register"

5. **FOLLOW** the instructions to setup your personal UserID and Password

6. **WRITE** your UserID and Password down for future reference. Keep it in a safe place.

If your course is using WebCT or Blackboard, you'll be able to use this code to access the McGraw-Hill content within your instructor's online course.

To gain access to the McGraw-Hill content in your instructor's WebCT or Blackboard course simply log into the course with the user ID and Password provided by your instructor. Enter the registration code exactly as it appears to the right when prompted by the system. You will only need to use this code the first time you click on McGraw-Hill content.

These instructions are specifically for student access. Instructors are not required to register via the above instructions.

The McGraw-Hill Companies

Higher Education

Thank you, and welcome to your McGraw-Hill Online Resources.

0-07-292240-0 t/a
Sherrill
Adapted Physical Activity, 6/e

Adapted Physical Activity, Recreation, and Sport

Adapted Physical Activity, Recreation, and Sport

Crossdisciplinary and Lifespan

Sixth Edition

Claudine Sherrill, CAPE

Texas Woman's University at Denton
President, International Federation of
Adapted Physical Activity (IFAPA)

Boston   Burr Ridge, IL   Dubuque, IA   Madison, WI   New York   San Francisco   St. Louis
Bangkok   Bogotá   Caracas   Kuala Lumpur   Lisbon   London   Madrid   Mexico City
Milan   Montreal   New Delhi   Santiago   Seoul   Singapore   Sydney   Taipei   Toronto

Higher Education

ADAPTED PHYSICAL ACTIVITY, RECREATION, AND SPORT, SIXTH EDITION

Published by McGraw-Hill, a business unit of The McGraw-Hill Companies, Inc., 1221 Avenue of the Americas, New York, NY 10020. Copyright © 2004 by The McGraw-Hill Companies, Inc. All rights reserved. Previous edition(s) 1998, 1993, 1986, 1981, 1976. All rights reserved. No part of this publication may be reproduced or distributed in any form or by any means, or stored in a database or retrieval system, without the prior written consent of The McGraw-Hill Companies, Inc., including, but not limited to, in any network or other electronic storage or transmission, or broadcast for distance learning.

Some ancillaries, including electronic and print components, may not be available to customers outside the United States.

Domestic   3 4 5 6 7 8 9 0 QWV/QWV 0 9 8 7 6 5

ISBN 0-697-29513-3

Vice president and editor-in-chief: *Thalia Dorwick*
Sponsoring editor: *Vicki Malinee*
Developmental editor: *Carlotta Seely*
Executive marketing manager: *Pamela S. Cooper*
Project manager: *Mary Lee Harms*
Production supervisor: *Enboge Chong*
Design coordinator: *Gino Cieslik*
Art editor: *Jen DeVere*
Supplement producer: *Meghan Durko*
Compositor: *GAC—Indianapolis*
Typeface: *Times*
Printer: *Quebecor World, Versailles*

The credits section for this book begins on page 783 and is considered an extension of the copyright page.

Library of Congress Cataloging-in-Publication Data

Sherrill, Claudine.
 Adapted physical activity, recreation, and sport:
 crossdisciplinary and lifespan /
 Claudine Sherrill.—6th ed.
       p. cm.
 Includes bibliographical references and index.
 ISBN 0-697-29513-3
 1. Physical education for children with disabilities.   I. Title

GV445.S53 2003
371.9'04486—dc22   2003044290

The Internet addresses listed in the text were accurate at the time of publication. The inclusion of a website does not indicate an endorsement by the authors or McGraw-Hill, and McGraw-Hill does not guarantee the accuracy of the information presented at these sites.

www.mhhe.com

Dedicated to my parents, Ivalene and Robert Sherrill, of Logansport, Indiana, and to my adopted family, Rae Allen, Lisa Silliman-French, and Ron French

BRIEF CONTENTS

CONTENTS

PREFACE

Today, 95% of children with disabilities learn sports, dance, aquatics, and health-related fitness in general physical education classes and mainstream sport and fitness programs. In response to this societal change, I have redirected the focus of this sixth edition toward inclusion, adaptation, and accommodation by *general* physical educators and exercise scientists in collaboration with *adapted* physical activity specialists, families, and other resources. Some content, of course, continues to build competencies for working with individuals with severe disabilities who need the expertise of specialists in many settings. Furthermore, I have expanded my ideas on *adaptation theory* as a comprehensive guide to application of our rapidly growing knowledge base.

To help generalists in our profession embrace the diversity now found in job settings, I have infused content from cross-cultural studies, geriatrics, and the new academic area called *disability studies,* which is mainly led by individuals with disabilities. Incorporation of these perspectives contributes to the strengthening of the social science foundations of adapted physical activity and to recognition of the importance of beliefs, attitudes, intentions, and actions in achieving the dream of healthy, active living for all.

The uniqueness of this text continues to be its cross-disciplinary, lifespan, and home-school-community teamwork perspectives. These perspectives have been strengthened by a new chapter on aging and disability and a network of chapter coauthors who have brought fresh, innovative ideas and experiences to the revision. The References section at the end of this book is the most comprehensive of its type.

This edition of *Adapted Physical Activity, Recreation, and Sport* has been revised extensively to stay abreast of the rapidly expanding knowledge base of adapted physical activity as a profession and an academic discipline. It is designed to develop the beginning-level knowledge and skills of both undergraduate and graduate students and of professionals of all ages who aspire to meet individual and societal needs in physical education, recreation, sport, fitness, or rehabilitative settings. The reader can acquire intermediate and advanced levels of knowledge, but real skill can be gained only through direct experience with knowledgeable mentors.

NCPERID Standards and APENS Certification

Study of this text and use of the multiple-choice questions on the Instructor's Resource Guide CD-ROM will enable professionals to meet the personnel preparation standards established by the National Consortium for Physical Education and Recreation for Individuals with Disabilities (NCPERID) in 1995 and to pass the NCPERID National Competency Examination called APENS. This optional examination, which has been widely publicized, was developed to ensure high-quality performance in school-based adapted physical activity service deliv-

ery for individuals from birth through age 21. I am a life member, a past president of NCPERID, and a CAPE.

Comprehensive Resource for Many Courses

This textbook is designed for the basic adapted physical activity course as well as such specialized courses as (a) assessment; (b) curriculum, instruction, and pedagogy; (c) administration, including consulting; (d) disability sport; and (e) introduction to disabilities. The content is purposely broad to afford instructors the freedom to select chapters that meet individual needs and interests. *It is not necessary to cover all chapters in every course.* The Instructor's Resource Guide CD-ROM, developed by Dr. Deborah Buswell and me, explains how the textbook can be used with different course outlines.

The intent is to save the student both money and time by including all the essentials of adapted physical activity in one book that can be kept as a reference for on-the-job use. The content can be surveyed rapidly in beginning courses and read again for in-depth competency development in advanced courses.

Role of This Text in Infusion

Adapted physical activity attitudes, knowledge, and skills must be *infused* into all general education courses. After university students are introduced to the content of this text in a basic course, their competencies should be further enhanced by a personnel-preparation *infusion model* in which individual differences are addressed in every course. *A goal is for this textbook to be used as a resource in every specialization area within kinesiology and sport science.* To achieve this, adapted physical activity proponents must share this text with colleagues in other specializations and encourage infusion of content into their daily lesson plans.

PAP-TE-CA Model Redefined

The content of this text is based on the belief that both general and adapted physical activity personnel need competencies in seven job functions:

P Planning
A Assessment
P Paperwork, Meetings
T Teaching/Counseling/Coaching
E Evaluation
C Consulting
A Advocacy

I call the knowledge comprising these areas the PAP-TE-CA model. It would be helpful if this acronym spelled something meaningful, but we shall have to settle for its spirited rhythm. It is a mnemonic device that effectively ensures memory of the services that guide competency development. The second "P" of PAP-TE-CA has been changed in this edition.

Advocacy (Chapter 4) is the PAP-TE-CA service presented first because this remains our most important professional goal: advocacy at international, national, state, and local levels, and, most essential, advocacy that (a) general physical educators in our neighborhood schools will assume their responsibility for active, healthy lifestyles for all children and (b) fitness counselors and recreation specialists in the community will initiate and facilitate services for all persons.

Organization

Part I, Foundations, prepares physical education generalists, exercise scientists, families, and adapted physical activity specialists to work together in new, exciting roles of support and collaboration. The emphasis is on job functions, competencies, adaptation theory and practice, and new ways of thinking about disability, law, service delivery, inclusion, and empowerment. With practicum or service learning experiences, Part I offers content for an entire course, or it can be combined with Part II or Part III.

Part II, Assessment and Pedagogy for Specific Goals, supports the philosophy of teaching without labels. Each chapter focuses on one physical activity goal and describes assessment instruments and movement activities for practitioners. Part II can be used with Part I in various courses or alone in adapted physical education pedagogy courses or as an infusion supplement for generalist assessment, curriculum, instruction, methods, and exercise science courses.

Part III, Individual Differences, With Emphasis on Sport, teaches that persons with disabilities *do not have shared characteristics or attributes.* Each one is unique! These persons must be assessed individually to determine specific *performance indicators* to guide personalized goals, objectives, supports, adaptations, accommodations, services, and outcomes. Part III can be used to guide courses that emphasize research-based content on disabilities (including those associated with old age), growth and development processes, and physical activity programming; or it can be used in combination with Part I and/or Part II.

New to This Edition

New Chapter

Chapter 28, Aging and Disability, is new to this text and strengthens its lifespan perspective. Written by Claudia Emes, Faculty of Kinesiology at the University of Calgary (Canada), this chapter addresses the various issues confronting the many older persons who have disabilities, such as managing the challenges of chronic diseases.

Revised Chapters

All chapters in Parts I and II have been revised extensively in terms of updated content and emphasis on new directions in adapted physical activity. The following are *90% new:* Chapters 1, 2, 3, 4, 5, 6, and 15.

Practical Knowledge Emphasized

Chapter 2 has been reconceptualized to facilitate enthusiasm for and provide structure for practicum and service-learning experiences. Part II has been extensively revised to focus on physical activity goals and the knowledge that professionals must have to enable individuals of all ages to achieve these goals. Each chapter has been revised to increase the emphasis on assessment and pedagogy specific to a goal. Embedded learning activities in all chapters stress practical applications.

Key Enhancements

- Comprehensive updating to highlight knowledge, attitude, and action changes in the profession and to encourage critical thinking about future trends
- Emphasis on preparation for inclusive, collaborative physical activity services and home-school-community teamwork by professionals in mainstream and special education settings, with supports from adapted physical activity consultants (and/or direct service providers), related services personnel, and family members
- Greater consideration of cross-cultural diversity, including multiethnicity, poverty, and new parenting and family trends
- Increased emphasis on practica, action research, and service learning adapted to different levels of experience. This content is considered *continuing education,* as recommended by APENS
- Addition of case studies, sample assessment and placement forms, and practical applications with emphasis on academic and experiential learning progressing together
- Stronger emphasis on the team approach, especially collaboration between the generalist in the classroom and the specialist as a consultant/advocate to the general physical educator, parents, and others in the community

New Features

Expanded audience. The audience for this text has been broadened to include future exercise scientists and others majoring in kinesiology and physical education who do not plan to teach. Such persons usually obtain jobs in health, fitness, sport, or rehabilitation centers, agencies, or organizations.

Focus on inclusion. Inclusion, in conjunction with new interpretations of IDEA's least restrictive environment (LRE), is the focus of professional preparation. Throughout this book emphasis is placed on inclusion through elimination of barriers and facilitation of enablers through teamwork.

New perspectives on basic concepts. This text emphasizes that disability, adaptation, supports, accommodations, ecological task analysis, intervention, and collaboration demand new ways of believing, feeling, and acting regarding inclusion and person-environment interactions.

Reflective & Critical Thinking Challenges. The challenges presented at the beginning of each chapter emphasize reflective and critical thinking rather than rote memory. They encourage self-evaluation, goal setting, self-determination, and accountability.

Highlighted special activities. Wheelchair icons highlight the many embedded learning activities throughout the book. These activities are designed to encourage personalized involvement and cooperative problem solving and to ensure that practicum experiences, interactions with classmates, and reflective and critical thinking exercises supplement classroom theory.

Optional activities. These activities, which appear at the end of each chapter, can be done anytime: before, during, and after the course(s). Lists of films and videos are presented, and ideas for research, website adventures, field trips, volunteer and service learning opportunities are highlighted. The variety offers something for everyone.

Web resources. Every chapter includes web resources related to the chapter content for further study and exploration. The appendixes have also been updated to include web resources.

Comprehensive reference list. One complete list of references, rather than separate chapter lists, is now included at the end of the book. The most recent publications, as well as primary sources, are included and offer insight into the breadth and depth of our knowledge base.

Glossary. A glossary of new and evolving terms has been added at the end of the text. With the 2002 work of WHO fully incorporated, this tool enhances both service delivery and organizational leadership.

New and Expanded Topics

Chapter 1 Active, Healthy Lifestyles for All: Thinking About Philosophy

- Development of a personal philosophy of adapted physical activity service delivery
- New and emerging concepts of disability, adaptation, inclusion, supports, and job functions
- New emphasis on adapted physical activity supports used by mainstream professionals in collaboration with adapted physical activity consultants
- Update of Adapted Physical Activity Model (Figure 1.1) to include NASPE/AAHPERD standards and emphasize empowerment
- New emphasis on social science, social justice, and academic specialization

Chapter 2 Celebrating Differences, Planning Practical Experience, and Striving Toward Inclusion

- Emphasis on need for lifelong continuing education through practical experiences
- New content on inclusion as a lifestyle, transition needs, and barriers/enablers
- New terminology introduced for disability sport
- Updated disability sport perspectives and growth

Chapter 3 Teamwork, Communication, and Creativity

- Expansion of home-school-community teamwork as basis for service delivery
- New information from IDEA on occupational therapy and physical therapy, artistic/cultural programming, and orientation and mobility
- Added content on cross-cultural complexity, including different communication styles
- Creativity and adaptation theory and practice

Chapter 4 Adaptation, Advocacy, and Law

- First full explanation of adaptation as meta-theory to guide service delivery and empowerment
- New top-down intervention/instructional model as guide to acquisition of functional skills
- Expanded Five Ls Advocacy Model presenting advocacy as a way of life
- Updated new developments in law

Chapter 5 Curriculum Planning and Evaluation Guided by Attitude Change

- Emphasis on importance of relationship between planning and evaluation
- Attitude-behavior link as key to inclusion
- New information about conforming to the Americans with Disabilities Act
- Ways to develop an evaluation protocol

Chapter 6 Assessment, the IEP, and the Accommodation Plan

- PAP-TE-CA tasks of collaborative assessment, decision making, and preparation of individual education programs (IEPs) and accommodation plans in accordance with IDEA and Section 504 legislation
- Information on how general and adapted physical educators can work together in implementing new practices required by No Child Left Behind Act (2001) and related legislation
- Updated information on assessments (Test of Gross Motor Development-2, Brockport Physical Fitness Test, Competency Test for Adapted Physical Educators) and ecological surveys
- Diversity within physical education mainstream highlighted through sample school district forms based on case study data

Chapter 7 Teaching and Consulting

- Teaching styles recommended by APENS
- New information on using personal digital assistant (PDA)
- Additional applied research regarding teaching perspectives and responsibilities

Chapter 8 Self-Concept, Motivation, and Well-Being

- Physical self-concept theory with many new activities related to measurable PE objectives
- Addition of identity theory approaches with applications
- Ideas on mind-body integration

Chapter 9 Inclusion, Social Competence, and Attitude Change

- Expanded discussion of social inclusion, including measurable PE objectives
- Information on multicultural strategies
- Expanded treatment of Hellison's Personal Social Responsibility Model
- New ideas on facilitating attitude change of children with and without disabilities

Chapter 10 Sensorimotor Learning and Severe Disability

- Enhanced discussion of IEP-based sensorimotor interventions
- Numerous additional activities related to measurable PE objectives
- Reflexes and postural reactions in severe disability

Chapter 11 Motor Skills and Patterns

- Assessment and instruction information updated based on Ulrich's Test of Gross Motor Development-2 and other revised tests
- Refinement of content on teaching basic motor skills to children with and without mobility problems

Chapter 12 Perceptual-Motor Learning

- Refined perceptual-motor learning model related to movement skill foundations (MSFs) concept of Allen Burton
- Total number of learning activities, related to measurable objectives, increased to 60
- New information on McCarron Assessment of Neuromuscular Development (MAND) and updated information on other instruments

Chapter 13 Fitness and Healthy Lifestyle

- Recent changes in knowledge
- New directions emphasizing active lifestyles
- Activitygram assessment of physical activity
- Coverage of Brockport Physical Fitness Test

Chapter 14 Postures, Appearance, and Muscle Imbalance

- Expanded discussion of response-contingent auditory feedback
- New information on treatment options for scoliosis

Chapter 15 Sport Recreation and Competition: Socialization, Instruction, and Transition

- Illustrated step-by-step strategies for teaching persons with and without disabilities the basics of wheelchair basketball, indoor soccer (manual wheelchair), and slalom (motorized wheelchair)
- Increased emphasis on uses and benefits of sport

Chapter 16 Adapted Dance, Dance Therapy, and Relaxation

- New coverage on wheelchair dance
- Updated information on dance therapy and adapted dance
- Relaxation techniques to use for stress and with dance-oriented goals

Chapter 17 Adapted Aquatics

- Expanded discussion of aquatic therapy and adapted aquatics
- Stroke techniques for swimmers with disabilities

Chapter 18 Infants, Toddlers, and Young Children

- Expanded information on Individualized Family Service Plan (IFSP)
- Requirements for Individualized Education Program (IEP)
- Additional activities and updates on assessment

Chapter 19 Other Health-Impaired Conditions

- Updated information on all conditions
- Focus on diabetic continuum and all forms of diabetes
- Emphasis on obesity, inactivity, and health risks
- New information on medication management
- Addition of Marfan's syndrome to discussion of aneurysms

Chapter 20 Learning Disabilities, Attention Deficit Hyperactivity Disorder, and Developmental Coordination Disorder

- Updated information on learning disability (LD), developmental coordination disorder (DCD), and attention deficit hyperactivity disorder (ADHD) in relation to physical activity in home, school, and community settings
- New IDEA information on ADD and ADHD

Chapter 21 Mental Retardation, Special Olympics, and the INAS-FID

- New American Association of Mental Retardation (2002) definitions of mental retardation, adaptive behavior, intellectual functioning, and supports
- AAMR revised Supports Paradigm applied to physical activity programming
- New information on programs and curricula

Chapter 22 Serious Emotional Disturbance and Autism

- New content on behavior and disciplinary placement: behavioral intervention plan (BIP), manifestation determination, aquatics adaptations, and daily life therapy intervention
- Expanded information on bipolar conditions in children and on autism spectrum disorder and autistic disorder

Chapter 23 Wheelchair Sports and Orthopedic Impairments

- Updated information on spina bifida, spinal cord injuries, and postpolio syndrome and sport
- Emphasis on *manual* wheelchair activity instruction
- Use of Brockport Physical Fitness Test
- Additional information on winter sports

Chapter 24 Les Autres Conditions and Amputations

- Updated information on diverse *other locomotor impairments* (i.e., muscular dystrophies, dwarfism, childhood growth disorders), and amputations
- Changes in governing disability sport organizations and recommended physical activities
- New information on physical activity programming
- Additional information on prosthetics in sport

Chapter 25 Cerebral Palsy, Stroke, and Traumatic Brain Injury

- Special attention to new sport governing body, National Disability Sports Alliance (NDSA)
- Emphasis on collaboration between schools, communities, and NDSA
- Activities for all: motorized and manual chairs, assistive devices, unique gaits
- Sport classification and rule changes

Chapter 26 Deaf and Hard-of-Hearing Conditions

- Reordered, simplified, and updated information
- Updated and expanded discussions of hearing aid technology and cochlear implants
- The deaf community and its promotion of sport

Chapter 27 Blindness and Visual Impairments

- Updated information on blindness, visual impairments, and deaf-blindness and physical activity
- Role models with demonstrated success in mainstream settings
- Haptic teaching and new directions in sport

Chapter 28 Aging and Disability

- Chronic diseases associated with able-bodied aging: cancer, diabetes, cardiac disease, depression, osteoporosis, Parkinson's disease, and Alzheimer's disease
- Chronic diseases related to the aging of persons with disabilities
- Interactions with older persons

Successful Features

APENS Standards

This new edition features continued support of the Adapted Physical Education National Standards. It offers the complete content that students need to master in order to pass the national APENS examination.

Emphasis on Sports

This text treats sport as an integral part of adapted physical activity. Over 150 pages of text on sport and sport resources are included, as well as outstanding photographs of athletes with disabilities in competition. The revision of Chapter 15 strengthens wheelchair sport coverage. In addition, this text highlights the Paralympics as a source of role models for persons of all ages and as an international movement that everyone should know about.

Pedagogical Aids

Numerous photographs and illustrations. Approximately 250 photographs and 340 illustrations enrich the text. The illustrations, especially those in Part III, show all the important conditions and exercise science concepts. Many chapters include an *introductory unifying figure* that highlights and synthesizes the chapter content.

Use of icons, boldface, and italics. These aids call attention, respectively, to learning activities that promote reflective and critical thinking, definitions, and especially important concepts or applications.

Case studies and assessments. Found in many chapters, the case studies and actual instruments bring realism to the content and offer opportunities for problem solving.

Glossary. Addition of this glossary to the text helps learners identify new and often misused terms and concepts.

American Psychological Association (APA) format. Adherence to APA writing style provides a model for students who wish to acquire research and publication skills.

Subject index. In addition to its standard uses, this index can be used as a testing device. Students can create a card for every word in the index and color-code them by chapter (if desired). These cards can be used for study, tests, and games.

Name index. This index is useful for becoming familiar with authorities in adapted physical activity and related disciplines. It can be used in the same way as the subject index. Emphasis on learning names (i.e., primary sources) is especially appropriate for graduate students.

Appendixes. *Appendix A* presents updated definitions of disabilities as stated in IDEA. The prevalence and incidence statistics in *Appendix B* are helpful in preparing term papers and documenting the need for adapted physical activity service delivery. *Appendixes C, D,* and *E* provide readers with over 100 addresses with websites for obtaining additional information. *Appendix F* presents a chronology of more than 100 events in the history of special education, adapted physical activity, and sport.

Supplements

Instructor's Resource CD-ROM (ISBN: 007252913X)

By Deborah Buswell, Texas State University-San Marcos and Claudine Sherrill

The Instructor's Resource Guide CD-ROM to accompany *Adapted Physical Activity, Recreation, and Sport* is a valuable tool that complements the text. It features an Instructor's Manual, Computerized Test Bank, and PowerPoint presentation.

Instructor's Manual. The Instructor's Manual offers information on teaching adapted physical activity, instructional resources, competencies, sample course outlines for several different courses, lecture notes, and learning activities.

Computerized Test Bank. Brownstone's Computerized Testing is the most flexible, powerful, easy-to-use electronic testing program available in higher education. The Diploma system (for Windows/PC users) allows the test maker to create a print version, an online version (to be delivered to a computer lab), or an Internet version of each test. Diploma includes a built-in instructor gradebook, into which student rosters and files can be imported. A separate testing program, Exam VI, is included for Macintosh users. The Test Bank for *Adapted Physical Activity, Recreation, and Sport* includes more than 1,700 multiple-choice questions.

PowerPoint. This chapter-specific presentation, ready to use in class, corresponds to the content in *Adapted Physical Activity, Recreation, and Sport,* making it easier for you to teach and ensuring that your students can follow your lectures point by point. You can modify the presentation as much as you like to meet the needs of your course.

PowerWeb (www.dushkin.com/online)

The PowerWeb website is a reservoir of course-specific articles and current events. Students can visit PowerWeb to take a self-scoring quiz, complete an interactive exercise, click through an interactive glossary, or check the daily news. An expert in each discipline analyzes the day's news to show students how it relates to their field of study.

PowerWeb is packaged with many McGraw-Hill textbooks. Students are also granted full access to Dushkin/McGraw-Hill's Student Site, where they can read study tips, conduct Web research, learn about different career paths, and follow fun links on the Web.

PageOut: The Course Website Development Center (www.pageout.net)

PageOut, free to instructors who use a McGraw-Hill textbook, is an online program you can use to create your own course website. PageOut offers the following features:

- A course home page
- An instructor home page
- A syllabus (interactive and customizable, including quizzes, instructor notes, and links to the text's Online Learning Center)
- Web links
- Discussions (multiple discussion areas per class)
- An online gradebook
- Links to student web pages

Contact your McGraw-Hill sales representative to obtain a password.

Health and Human Performance Website (www.mhhe.com/hhp)

McGraw-Hill's Health and Human Performance website provides a wide variety of information for instructors and students, including monthly articles about current issues, online articles that celebrate our diversity, downloadable supplements for instructors, a "how to" technology guide, study tips, and exam-preparation materials. It includes information about professional organizations, conventions, and careers. For material related to *Adapted Physical Activity, Recreation, and Sport,* go to www.mhhe.com/hhp. Click on Faculty Support and then Your Text's Ancillaries.

ACKNOWLEDGMENTS

To the many individuals and agencies who shared in this adventure, a heartfelt thank-you. I am especially grateful to *Julian Stein,* who served as major reviewer and adviser for the first edition and who has been my mentor for many years; and to *Janet Wessel* of *I Can* and the *ABC* curriculum, whose work (along with that of *Luke Kelly,* Editor of APENS and NCPERID leader) forms the basis of the PAP-TE-CA service delivery model in this textbook.

To My Coauthors

This was my first experience in coauthoring chapters, and it was enjoyable, motivational, and meaningful. I am extremely grateful for the contributions of the following leaders in adapted physical activity:

Dr. Claudia Emes, University of Calgary, Canada—Author of Chapter 28

Dr. Abu Yilla, University of Texas at Arlington—Coauthor of Chapter 2

Dr. Lisa Silliman-French, Denton Independent School District, Denton, Texas—Coauthor of Chapters 6 and 22

Dr. April Tripp, University of Illinois at Urbana/Champaign—Coauthor of Chapters 8 and 9

Dr. Ronald W. Davis, Ball State University, Muncie, Indiana—Coauthor of Chapter 15

Dr. Gail M. Dummer, Michigan State University, East Lansing—Coauthor of Chapter 17

Dr. James Rimmer, University of Illinois at Chicago and National Center for Physical Activity and Disability—Coauthor of Chapter 13

Dr. Kenneth H. Pitetti, Wichita State University, Kansas—Coauthor of Chapter 13

Dr. Ron French, Texas Woman's University, Denton—Coauthor of Chapter 22

Dr. Patricia Paulsen Hughes, Oklahoma State University, Stillwater—Coauthor of Chapters 24 and 26

Wynelle Delaney, Registered Dance Therapist, Coauthor of Chapter 16

Dr. Deborah Buswell, Texas State University-San Marcos—Author/coauthor of supplements for Instructor's Resource Guide (CD-ROM)

To Creators of Our Knowledge Base

I am indebted to the many persons who are creating the adapted physical activity knowledge base and to the editors of the journals that disseminate this knowledge. Work that appears in the *Adapted Physical Activity Quarterly (APAQ)* and *Palaestra: The Forum of Sport, Physical Education, and Recreation for Those With Disabilities* significantly affects my thought, creativity, and commitment. My thanks to the editors and emeritus editors of these journals for their service and scholarship: *Geoffrey Broadhead,* Kent State University; *Greg Reid,* McGill University; *David Beaver,* Western Illinois University; and *David Porretta,* The Ohio State University. Thank you also to all of the authors and reviewers who motivated my personal best during the years I served as *APAQ* editor. My respect and appreciation to Gudrun Doll-Tepper of Berlin, President of the International Council on Sport Science and Physical Education (ICSSPE), for her futurist thinking, leadership, and tireless advocacy and infusion. Writers who particularly have stimulated my thinking are Terry Rizzo, Samuel R. Hodge, Walter E. Davis, Allen Burton, Dale and Beverly Ulrich, Gail Dummer, A. E. (Ted) Wall, E. Jane Watkinson, Martin E. Block, Karen DePauw, Trevor Williams, Joseph P. Winnick, and Greg Reid.

To the International Community

My deep appreciation to the athletes and leaders in the Paralympic movement who have constructed much of our knowledge about sport potential and goal attainment; also to the leaders in the Special Olympics and Deaf Sport movements. I am grateful also to the members of the International Federation of Adapted Physical Activity (IFAPA) and its regional branches for sharing their research and to the many editors of *IFAPA Proceedings.* A special thanks to the Asian leaders who promoted translation and publication of this book in Chinese.

To My Students

Most important, I thank my students at the Texas Woman's University, who keep me involved in research and practicum experiences, and the parents who trust us with their children. Each edition brings new students as well as memories of past ones who have shared and grown with me and significantly affected the contents of this book. I wish I could mention all their names, but a few will have to do: Karen DePauw, Nancy Megginson, Abu Yilla, Luke Kelly, Jim Rimmer, Sarah Rich, Boni Boswell, Wanda Rainbolt, Jo Ellen Cowden, Garth Tymeson, Jim Mastro, April Tripp, Ellen Kowalski, Carol Pope, Ron Davis, Leslie Low, Lisa Silliman-French, Christoph Lienert, Trish Hughes, Linda Thibault, Leslie Waugh, and Andrea Woodson.

To My Support Network and Photographers

For her photography, assistance with the many aspects of production, and overall support, I thank *Rae Allen.* For their help with photography in this sixth edition, I thank *Abu Yilla, Deborah Buswell, Lisa Silliman-French, Linda Thibault, Leslie Waugh, April Tripp,* and *Trish Hughes.* I am grateful also to the outstanding staff of McGraw-Hill Higher Education, whose editing, production, and marketing excellence makes them the leaders in creating a knowledge base for adapted physical activity. A special thanks to *Carlotta Seely,* my developmental editor, who made this edition possible through her steadfast support, outstanding structure and guidance, and follow-up. I am extremely grateful to have worked with and learned from Carlotta Seely and the entire McGraw-Hill Higher Education staff. A joyous and deeply appreciative thanks to *Mary Lee Harms,* my project manager, who guided the final preparation of the textbook (all of the copyediting, proofing, etc.), for her outstanding expertise, patience, warmth, and marvelous laugh—you helped me manage the stress and perform at my personal best!

To the Reviewers

I would like to thank the reviewers of the sixth edition of *Adapted Physical Activity, Recreation, and Sport.* Their insights, suggestions, and comments have helped to improve this new edition. My appreciation goes to these reviewers: Martin E. Block, University of Virginia; Pamela Buchanan, The University of Texas; Colleen Lewis, State University of New York–Cortland; and Deborah Shapiro, Georgia State University.

To My Role Models

Acknowledgments can be complete only if they extend backward in time to those persons who sparked the initial enthusiasm in teaching and writing: *Dr. Harry A. Scott* of Teachers College, Columbia University, who spoke of competency-based teaching in the early 1950s; *Dr. Josephine Rathbone,* also of Teachers College, who instilled in me a deep concern for the right of all persons to efficient and beautiful bodies; and *Dean Anne Schley Duggan,* Texas Woman's University, who taught me to hear the different drummer and to keep step to the music—however measured or far away.

Claudine Sherrill

PART

I

Foundations

C H A P T E R

1

Active, Healthy Lifestyles for All:
Thinking About Philosophy

Figure 1.1   Adapted physical activity model to guide understanding of philosophy. The acronym NASPE refers to the National Association of Sport and Physical Education.

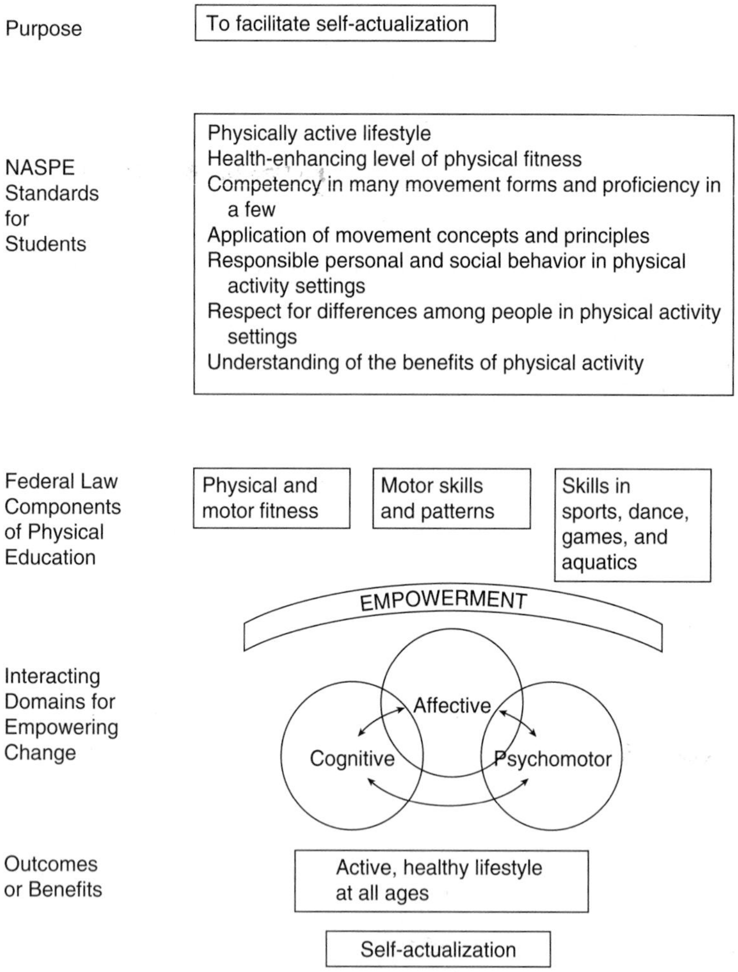

Purpose

To facilitate self-actualization

NASPE
Standards
for
Students

Physically active lifestyle
Health-enhancing level of physical fitness
Competency in many movement forms and proficiency in
    a few
Application of movement concepts and principles
Responsible personal and social behavior in physical
    activity settings
Respect for differences among people in physical activity
    settings
Understanding of the benefits of physical activity

Federal Law
Components
of Physical
Education

Physical and
motor fitness

Motor skills
and patterns

Skills in
sports, dance,
games, and
aquatics

EMPOWERMENT

Interacting
Domains for
Empowering
Change

Affective

Cognitive

Psychomotor

Outcomes
or Benefits

Active, healthy lifestyle
at all ages

Self-actualization

1. Start a journal, with dated entries, that shows you are practicing reflective and critical thinking related to this course. See definitions on p. 14. Write in the journal as often as you want, but no less than once a week.

2. Identify key concepts in this chapter and write your personal beliefs about these concepts in your journal. Do you agree or disagree with them? Why? Indicate the

source of each of your beliefs: knowledge, experience, faith, ethics (moral principles), or opinions of others.

3. Select your strongest beliefs and weave them into a *beginning* philosophy of adapted physical activity. Plan to refine your written philosophy as you progress through the course.

In physical activity, everyone fails at one time or another—by coming in last on the relay team, by missing the basket or field goal that would have tied or won the game, by choking and struggling in the swimming pool, by dropping out of a fitness run or an aerobic exercise class, by letting days go by with no vigorous exercise. Some people, however, fail more than others, and these failures affect all aspects of their lives. Such individuals are often labeled *clumsy, awkward, fat, slow, lazy,* or *disabled* and are treated differently from the **norm** (i.e., average, the social majority). Peers in physical activity settings tend to tease, ignore, or reject them, and professionals are often unsure of how to adapt instructional and environmental variables to facilitate success and foster an active, healthy lifestyle.

An Adapted Physical Activity Model

Figure 1.1 presents a model to guide the understanding of important components of an adapted physical activity (APA) philosophy. This model reflects endorsement of the **abilities-based approach** (Emes, Longmuir, & Downs. 2002), which is favored in the Paralympic sport movement and advocated particularly by adults with disabilities and their close associates. Simplified, the abilities-based approach states, "Look at the person, not the problems. Emphasize abilities, not disabilities." This motto supports *holistic* and *person-centered thinking* (focusing on whole persons rather than their separate parts).

Self-actualization, as used in this text, is the process of a person becoming the best he or she can be; it is assuming responsibility for actualizing one's movement and fitness potentialities, asking for help when needed, and helping others when possible. This term comes from the self-actualization theory of Abraham Maslow (1908–1970), which is part of the humanistic philosophy that strongly influences the helping professions. **Humanistic philosophy** holds that every human being is unique, inherently good, important to the functioning of others, and worthy of help that represents our personal best.

Self-actualization theory and humanistic philosophy are especially important when working with people with disabilities because their real or perceived differences from others often mean that they must find the ego strength to overcome **societal barriers** (e.g., misunderstanding, indifference, prejudice, inaccessible environments). To overcome such barriers, people with and without disabilities follow such mottos as "Become the best you can be" and "Strive for your personal best," which are rooted in self-actualization theory. Both of these mottos imply using your personal best to help others as well as yourself.

The **NASPE standards** in Figure 1.1 can be conceptualized *as long-range goals or desired outcomes.* These standards come from the NASPE of the American Alliance for Health. Physical Education, Recreation and Dance (AAHPERD), the major organization that advocates for our profession and issues policy guidelines. These standards are applicable to all age groups. *Adapted and general physical activity goals are the same, but the objectives (subgoals), time lines, and pedagogy are usually different.*

The federal law components of physical education in Figure 1.1 are goal areas for which specific goals and objectives are written to meet standards. These components come from Public Law (PL) 94-142, the Education for All Handicapped Children Act, which was passed in 1975 but is now reauthorized as **Individuals with Disabilities Education Act (IDEA).** This is the law that mandates physical education services. Volume 20 of the *United States Code* (U.S.C.) includes IDEA, which defines physical education as follows:

(i) The term means development of:
  (A) Physical and motor fitness;
  (B) Fundamental motor skills and patterns; and
  (C) Skills in aquatics, dance, and individual and group games and sports (including intramural and lifetime sports).
(ii) The term includes special physical education, adapted physical education, movement education, and motor development.

All professionals who provide adapted physical education to students classified as disabled under federal law (IDEA) must know this legal definition of the components of physical education. Part II of this text relates specifically to assessment and pedagogy in these and other goal areas. Inclusion, acceptance, self-concept, and motivation (areas of particular importance to people with disabilities) are highlighted also.

The rainbow symbol labeled *empowerment* in Figure 1.1 is included to remind readers that individuals with disabilities, as members of a social minority, generally lack power in the everyday politics that affect their economic, social, and health status. Professionals not only need to provide services but they also must facilitate self-determination, choice-making, and other independent living, work, and play. **Empowerment** is the process by which individuals gain control over their lives, a sense of power equitable with that of others, and a feeling of responsibility for self, others, and the environment. Empowerment occurs through the effort of both self and others. Professionals help individuals to empower themselves.

Figure 1.1 concludes with the interacting domains of human function and a statement of desired outcomes of adapted physical activity. Domains are included to emphasize that all of the goals and objectives of physical education require integrated functioning of the cognitive, affective, and psychomotor abilities. Goals are sometimes classified as primarily **cognitive** (intellectual or thinking function), **affective** (emotional or feeling function), and **psychomotor** (movement, sensorimotor, or perceptual-motor function). Professionals must remember this fact when providing assessment, planning, and other services.

Adapted Physical Activity Versus Adapted Physical Education

Adapted physical activity (APA) is service delivery, pedagogy, coaching, training, or empowerment conducted by qualified professionals to enhance physical activity goal achievement of individuals of all ages with movement limitations and/or societal restrictions (i.e., attitudinal and environmental barriers). In contrast, **adapted physical education** is the term used to describe services delivered to school-aged individuals from birth through age 21. *Services are provided wherever they are needed: in general or mainstream settings, in specially designed classes and programs, and in one-to-one and small-group accommodations.* Adapted physical education is a service delivery system, not a placement.

Regardless of employment site (school, exercise center, recreation setting, rehabilitation or medical facility), professionals must know how to adapt variables so that physical activity is safe for all, appropriate to assessed individual needs, and instrumental in helping individuals become the best they can be. *Virtually 95% of all school-aged students with disabilities in the United States receive their physical education instruction in inclusive (general education) settings.* This means that general physical educators, not specialists, have the major responsibility for accommodating individual differences.

Icons like this, throughout the book, will alert you to special learning activities. Go back to Figure 1.1 and study its contents. In coursework based on this text, it is important to study figures because they highlight the most important facts and often serve as the basis for test questions. Note also that words in bold print indicate that a definition follows or that special attention should be given to the concept being highlighted. Italics are used to indicate learning experiences as well as direct quotes from laws and selected individuals; to introduce or reinforce learning of new, technical, or key terms and labels; and to highlight especially important facts.

Critically think about what you have read so far and write reactions in your journal. Figure 1.1 indicates the components that typically comprise the first part of a philosophy. Do you agree or disagree with the beliefs stated so far in this chapter? Why? What kinds of friendship or other experiences have you had with people with disabilities, their families, and their service providers? What is the importance of physical activity in their lives? Why? What kind of physical education do they receive (or did they receive)? Why? Think about a work setting you are in or want to be in that includes one or more children, youth, or adults with activity limitations. Write your beliefs about the kind of physical activity they need and the benefits they should derive. Think about your beliefs as a guide to present and future actions.

Disability and Individual Differences

The World Health Organization (WHO, 2001) reemphasized that a **disability** is *a limitation in performing activity,* not a medical condition, a different appearance, or a defect of some kind. Minimal amount of activity limitation required for aid is defined differently by each culture, usually for each age group. Thus disability is said to be socially constructed. To professionals, disability *is a legal classification that makes an individual with activity limitations eligible for aid.* The social majority (usually White, middle-class, able-bodied persons) typically constructs the meaning of disability by establishing eligibility criteria that specify how severe a person's limitations in thinking, moving, hearing, seeing, and the like must be in order to access government-funded help (e.g., special education, vocational training, medicare).

When life experiences and/or disability lead to avoidance of physical activity, individuals substantially increase risk for developing heart disease, high blood pressure, and certain kinds of cancer, diabetes, chronic depression, and other conditions that lower quality of life and length of lifespan. Moreover, memory and the learning of new skills at all ages are affected by the amount of oxygen that gets to brain cells. Individuals in their 60s, who look forward to 20 to 40 more years of life, are increasingly aware of the importance of good brain function, facilitated by regular physical activity, as they see peers diagnosed with Alzheimer's disease and other debilitating conditions.

The 20th century brought awareness of the importance of active, healthy lifestyles and an understanding of the adaptations that professionals can use in helping individuals with and without disabilities to achieve physical activity goals. Adapted physical activity (a service delivery area known by many names since the early 1900s) switched from a medical to a crossdisciplinary orientation and matured into a profession. Laws that require free appropriate public education (FAPE) for children with disabilities were passed in many countries. Organizations to advocate physical activity for individuals of all ages, with disabilities, such as the International Federation of Adapted Physical Activity (IFAPA) were formed, and worldwide sports movements like Deaf Sport, Special Olympics, and Paralympics attracted growing numbers of participants and fans. We began to better understand individual differences and to realize that the disability is not exclusively a person-thing (i.e., located within a person) but rather the product of interactions between persons and their social and physical environments.

The 21st century challenges us to better serve the 846 million individuals worldwide who have been identified as having severe activity limitations (disabilities). Of these, an estimated 54 million reside in the United States. This is about one out of every seven persons! In addition to individuals who meet eligibility criteria to be classified as disabled, numerous others have individual differences that merit professional help. **Individual differences** mean person-environment interactions that significantly deviate from the norm and affect goal achievement.

Among the individual differences that most influence American lifestyles is the interaction between eating and exercising. An estimated 60% of Americans are overweight or obese. Both environment and personal variables must be addressed to change the statistic. Almost one in four adults have cardiovascular disease that can be traced to insufficient physical activity that begins in childhood. Clearly, personal reasons why children do not exercise must be examined in relation to the social and physical environment. Cognitive, physical, and sensory limitations complicate person-environment interactions, requiring professional preparation in the art and science of making adaptations to meet unique needs that are identified through skillful assessment.

Uniqueness and Central Themes of This Text

Every textbook on adapted physical education/activity is unique in that authors have different philosophies, beliefs, attitudes, and intentions. This textbook, for instance, places more emphasis on attitudes toward individual differences and toward service delivery and empowerment practices than do most other textbooks (e.g., Auxter, Pyfer, & Huettig, 2001; Block, 2000; Winnick, 2000).

Attitudes are enduring sets of beliefs charged with feelings or emotions that predispose a person to certain kinds of behaviors (see Figure 1.2). The attitudes of teachers determine how they teach. The attitudes of ordinary people determine who they choose as friends. The attitudes of authors determine what content they highlight. The philosophy (or set of beliefs charged with emotion) that guides this book is appreciation of the richness that individual differences, including disabilities and all forms of diversity, bring to our lives. **Adapted physical activity** is first, and foremost, the beliefs and attitudes that enable service providers to embrace individual differences and enjoy the challenge of helping others achieve personal goals in relation to self-actualization through physical activity. Like birthdays and other good things, individual differences are to be celebrated!

The rationale for emphasizing attitudes is the strong belief of many professionals that attitude is the key to changing behaviors that will promote a better quality of life for individuals with disabilities (e.g., Block, 1995b; Folsom-Meek & Rizzo, 2002; Hodge, Davis, Woodard, & Sherrill, 2002; Hodge & Jansma, 1999; Kowalski & Rizzo, 1996; Rizzo, 1984; Sherrill, 1986, 1988; Tripp & Sherrill, 1991). Professionals need to know how to facilitate change in their own attitudes, those of peers, and those of students. Carefully planned, shared, meaningful, satisfying experiences between persons with and without disabilities must supplement traditional professional preparation in order to change attitudes.

*What experiences are you planning for yourself to broaden your contacts? Now is the time to write your goals, dates, and time lines and to start a portfolio to document goal achievement. A **portfolio** is a collection of examples of your best work during the course. The portfolio should contain your best original writing, photographic or video documentation of practical activities, thank you and congratulatory notes from others, and the like. For further information, see Senne and Rikard (2002). Your professor will probably request the portfolio at the end of the course to aid in your evaluation.*

Figure 1.2 "What an individual can be, he must be. He must be true to his own nature. This need we may call self-actualization"—Abraham Maslow (1970, p. 46). This fundamental belief guides service delivery.

Five interrelated themes expressed in the title of this book also contribute to its uniqueness. Following are brief discussions of the key terms in the title.

Adapted physical activity is an umbrella term that has many definitions (DePauw & Doll-Tepper, 2000; Porretta, Nesbitt, & Labanowich, 1993; Sherrill, 1990a; Sherrill & De-Pauw, 1997) but primarily supports theory and practice aimed at all ages as opposed to ages associated only with IDEA and special education. *Adapted physical activity is used in this text because many readers plan to work in sport exercise and science, or to major in physical therapy, as opposed to teaching.*

Recreation is included in the title of this textbook because the professions of physical education and recreation (sometimes called leisure services) are interrelated. *Both professions are guided by the belief that physical activity should be fun, enjoyable, and satisfying.* Only when these conditions are present will individuals develop the intrinsic motivation to engage in physical activity during free time. Both professions strive to enhance **leisure,** defined as "an experience, a process, and a subjective state of mind" (Dattilo, 2002, p. 6). The major difference is that physical education is concerned only with physical activity, whereas recreation encompasses all possible leisure activities. Much collaboration between physical educators and recreators is needed to assure use of community resources and to promote family play. *Recreators do not refer to their profession as adapted recreation or leisure services; neither does this text.*

Sport is included in the title in recognition of the right of all persons to learn and engage in sports of their choice, at an appropriate level (developmental, recreational, competitive, elite), and in the settings of their choice (inclusive or separate; wheelchair, ambulatory, or mixed). Sport is an umbrella term including all forms of structured physical activity designed to provide fun, enjoyment, and satisfaction: sport, aquatics, dance, exercise, and rhythmics. This definition is widely accepted in Europe, whereas in the United States the term *sport* is sometimes used to refer only to competitive physical activity.

This text favors **the sport education model** (Siedentop, 1996, 2002c) with basic movement skills and patterns (as well as physical and motor fitness) taught, whenever possible, in a sport context to facilitate transition from school-based activity to inclusion in family and neighborhood play. To meet NASPE standards, children should be involved in a variety of after-school able-body (AB) or disability sports as early as possible. **Disability sport** is the umbrella term given to training and competition conducted by Deaf sport, Special Olympics, and Paralympics international governing bodies and by affiliated organizations in each country such as wheelchair basketball and sledge (sled) ice hockey clubs. Eligibility for *Special Olympics* is intellectual disability or developmental disability (most countries do not like the term *mental retardation*), whereas eligibility criteria for *Paralympic sports* are (a) any disability except deafness and (b) elite or world-level performance. **Adapted sport** is an umbrella term used primarily in school settings (Winnick, 2000) and by states that have interscholastic athletics for students with disabilities (e.g., the Minnesota Adapted Athletic Conference). Most adult athletes with disabilities favor the term

disability sports, which parallels such concepts as disability rights, disability community, and disability studies.

Crossdisciplinary in the title refers to the integration of knowledge from many disciplines in the creation of a distinct, unique body of knowledge that focuses on adaptation, individual differences, and physical activity. This book, for instance, brings together information from the academic disciplines of kinesiology, exercise and sport science, recreation (leisure studies), social studies, special education, general education, disability studies, counseling, medicine, law, physical therapy, and occupational therapy.

The terms *crossdisciplinary, interdisciplinary,* and *multidisciplinary* can also refer to **types of teamwork.** In this context, *crossdisciplinary* is the highest form of cooperation with members of different professions moving *across* disciplinary boundaries (e.g., physical education, occupational therapy, counseling) to work together as equals on common service delivery goals. *Interdisciplinary* refers to close interactions *between* team members who share freely but preserve disciplinary boundaries. *Multidisciplinary* refers to individuals from *many* different professions addressing common goals, meeting together to share information and decision making, and sometimes working together as partners. *Multidisciplinary is the term used in federal law.* The key to remembering different types of teamwork is knowing the meaning of prefixes: cross or trans (across), inter (between), and multi (many).

Lifespan in the title reflects the inclusion of information on people of all ages. This textbook is the only one, at present, to emphasize adapted physical activity for all ages.

Illustrative Adaptations

Some individuals learn best in one-to-one or small-group situations. Adaptations in class size or in organization of space into stations is helpful. Using partners or peer teachers is another adaptation. When students in the mainstream have movement or learning problems that limit their functional abilities, it is necessary to adapt goals, objectives, pedagogy, and grading practices.

Individualizing warm-up exercises, expectations, and equipment is adaptation. Each student, for instance, should be taught to aspire to a different number of bent-knee sit-ups, depending on his or her abdominal strength. Individuals with low strength execute their sit-ups with hands on their thighs, while the more athletically inclined undertake the traditional sit-up, with hands clasped behind the neck. In learning racket games, awkward students use shorter rackets, while the better coordinated begin with rackets of standard length.

The official rules of such games as volleyball and softball are adapted, and participation for all—not winning—is the main goal. For example, in classes based on the principle of success, all pupils are not required to stand behind the baseline when they serve a volleyball. Each stands at a point on the court where she or he is most likely to get the ball over. Well-coordinated students accept the official rule of hitting the ball one time, while the less athletic may volley it multiple times. In softball, an inning may be played by time rather than by three outs. The pressures inherent in striking out are thereby de-emphasized so that equal turns at bat and optimal skill development are possible.

The well-skilled athlete can learn and practice official rules in after-school athletic programs or in league play. The instructional period in a model physical education program is a time when games and exercises are modified in accordance with individual differences (Siedentop, 2002c). All students are accepted for what they are—awkward, uncoordinated, obese, skinny, or gifted. Students must have no doubt about what is more important to the teacher—the game or the individual. When teaching is based on the concept of individual differences, students seldom fail.

---

*Reflect on a general physical education setting (or the setting in which you work or plan to work). How do you feel about making adaptations? As you read this book, assess your attitudes and determine which underlying beliefs you wish to keep, to change, and to continue thinking about. For example, do you like people, places, things, and behaviors that are different? Or do you prefer similarity? Why? What is your definition of **different**? How much is **too different**? Write your ideas in a journal with the entries dated, so that you can periodically assess how you are changing and the activities that you find most and least meaningful. By reflecting on your attitudes, you will develop competencies helpful in facilitating change in the attitudes of others.*

Adaptation, Modification, Accommodation, and Supports

Adaptation (defined generically in dictionaries as making suitable, adjusting, or modifying) *is the art and science, used by qualified professionals, of assessing and managing variables and services so as to meet unique needs and achieve desired outcomes.* A **variable** is anything that can be changed. Professionals typically assess the interactions among *three types of variables:* **task** (desired action or behavior as in seeing, hearing, moving), **person** (within the learner), and **environment** (outside the learner; may be psychosocial, physical, or temporal). If a task is assessed as too difficult or too easy, the variables that influence the task are adapted. Likewise, if a task comprises a health or safety risk, variables are adapted. Illustrative *person variables* are interest, motivation, previous experience, shortness of breath, perceived competency, and fear. *Person variables can be strengths or weaknesses.* Illustrative *environment variables* include space, class size, the location and intensity of the sun, attitudes of teachers and peers, equipment, lighting, and sound. *Environment variables can be enablers or barriers.*

Adaptation is an umbrella process that encompasses services referred to as modifications, accommodations, and supports in IDEA and other federal laws. Adaptation is thus often used as a synonym for these terms. However, some state guidelines make specific distinctions, as follows:

Modification means to alter or lower the criteria that a student must meet in order to be considered successful (Cali-fornia Department of Education, 2001). For instance, general education (GE) students may be required to throw a regulation softball a distance of 60 feet in 8 out of 10 trials. A student with cerebral palsy might be required, instead, to throw a sponge ball a distance of 10 feet in 6 out of 10 trials. Modifications must be clearly documented in school records because they permit teachers to use different standards for testing and grading students.

Accommodation refers to providing access, removing barriers, or minimizing limitations in order to facilitate a student's achievement of the same goals as GE peers. A student with a limb impairment, for example, might be encouraged to use a wheelchair for endurance activities to achieve the same level of aerobic fitness as the rest of the class. A student who is hard-of-hearing might need a hearing aid or sign language to understand class instructions. A student with blindness might need special sound effects or a sighted peer to guide direction of movement in a sprint or long jump. Accommodations need to be documented but do not influence evaluating student outcomes and assigning grades.

Support services, sometimes abbreviated as *supports,* are supplementary resources and aids that are provided in GE settings to enable students with disabilities to be educated with nondisabled peers to the maximum extent appropriate. **Human supports** include consultants (adapted physical educators), adult aides (paraprofessionals, paraeducators), peer and cross-age tutors, peer helpers, athletes and adult role models with disabilities, coaches and recreators associated with disability sport, special educators, orientation and mobility specialists, and others.

The body of research is growing that shows human supports are valuable in the inclusive setting. For example, Vogler, Koranda, and Romance (2000) described the use of *a people resources model* in facilitating inclusion of a 6-year-old with severe cerebral palsy in the physical education setting with 20 able-bodied (AB) peers. The people resource was an adapted physical educator, who worked full-time with Sammy during daily class periods, helping him perform the same tasks as classmates but "at a different level adapted to his specific needs" (p. 165). More frequently, adapted physical educators, as supports, visit on a regular basis, sometimes dual- or team-teach, and sometimes supply lesson plans with detailed instructions on how to adapt specific activities (Heikinaro-Johansson, Sherrill, French, & Huuhka, 1995; Lytle & Collier, 2002). Research has also documented that peer tutors, with appropriate training, help children with disabilities achieve motor performance goals (Houston-Wilson, Dunn, van der Mars, & McCubbin, 1997) and fitness goals (Lieberman, Dunn, van der Mars, & McCubbin, 2000).

Nonhuman supports are as diverse as the human imagination and the knowledge base. Examples are architectural adaptations like ramps and lowered water fountains, computers, videotape stations for filming and cooperative analysis of movement, hearing aids, communication devices, sport-enabling **prostheses** (artificial limbs) and **orthoses** (braces), wheelchairs, mobility and standing aids, large-print instructional posters or braille materials, and any kind of equipment that enables individuals with disabilities to remain in general physical education classes. There is overlap between the concept of *nonhuman supports* and *assistive technology devices.* An **assistive technology device,** defined by IDEA 1997, is

> any item, piece of equipment, or product system, whether commercially acquired off the shelf, modified, or customized, that is used to increase, maintain, or improve functional capacities of a child with a disability.

Adaptation Theory

Adaptation theory is the grand theory (or metatheory) that enables the synthesis of the many ideas, theories, philosophies, and practices (some old, some new) that guide everyday critical thinking about the beliefs, attitudes, intentions, and actions associated with APA service delivery. This book therefore is about adaptation theory and how to translate it into action. It is about understanding change in ourselves and using knowledge of the change process to facilitate change in others. Consider, for instance, how we adapt or change our beliefs and attitudes as we learn more about disabilities and individual differences. Altered beliefs and attitudes lead to changes in intentions pertaining to the time we will spend with individuals with disabilities and the ways we will treat them in friendship, service delivery, and leadership interactions. Intentions typically result in actions or behaviors that make us more competent and caring. Together, changes in knowledge, beliefs, attitudes, intentions, and actions lead to **learning,** defined by experts *as a permanent change in behavior.*

A **theory,** simply defined, *is a conceptual framework that describes, explains, or predicts.* Service providers use theory, consciously or unconsciously, each time they apply factual and experiential knowledge in their various job functions. Theories are often presented as models and presented in figures that show different components (see Figure 1.3). A **grand theory** is a unified conceptual framework that encompasses many contributing theories. An important decision to be made in organizing a grand theory is which theories are most important to achieving the goals of the profession. Theories pertaining to the following broad areas are especially important: (a) attitudes, (b) individual differences, including disability, (c) physical activity and exercise science, (d) service delivery, and (e) empowerment (Sherrill, 1997a, 1997b). This book emphasizes theories that contribute to these knowledge areas. One such theory, self-actualization, has already been introduced. Sometimes empowerment is considered a theory also.

How Does *Adapted* Differ From *Adaptive?*

Some persons confuse the terms *adapted* and *adaptive.* These words should not be used interchangeably. **Adapted** can be a verb denoting the process of modifying (e.g., they *adapted* the activity, equipment, or facilities) or an adjective referring to a program or service delivery outcome (e.g., *adapted* games were used; the program was *adapted*).

Adapted physical activity is the name of the profession, academic discipline, and system that this book describes. Major organizations that professionals join are the **International Federation of Adapted Physical Activity** (IFAPA) and the **Adapted Physical Activity Council** of the American Alliance for Health, Physical Education, Recreation and Dance (AAHPERD). The major research journal that professionals use is the ***Adapted Physical Activity Quarterly*** (APAQ).

The term *adapted* was first recommended in 1952 by AAHPERD, then called the American Association for Health, Physical Education, and Recreation (AAHPER). This recommendation marked a major policy change in that *corrective and modified* were the predominant terms for individualized assessment and programming at that time. The decision to change terminology to *adapted* was strongly influenced by the widespread acceptance of the work of Jean Piaget (1896–1980), of Switzerland, who was considered the world's greatest child

---

Figure 1.3 **Model of a grand theory (Adaptation) that provides a unifying conceptual framework for critical thinking about the many theories that guide adapted physical activity practices.**

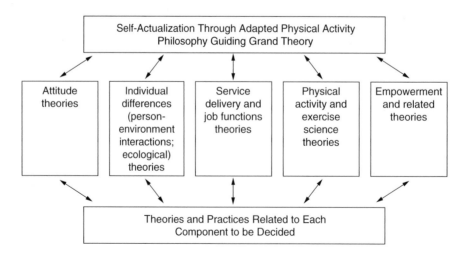

psychologist. Piaget based his developmental theory on the concept that *adaptation* is the fundamental process of change that enables individuals to interact effectively with the environment.

In contrast, **adaptive** is an adjective that describes client behaviors in occupational therapy (Fisher, Murray, & Bundy, 1991; Neistadt & Crepeau, 1998) and appears in the new official definition of mental retardation:

> Mental retardation is a disability characterized by significant limitations both in intellectual functioning and in *adaptive behavior* as expressed in conceptual, social, and practical *adaptive skills*. This disability originates before age 18. . . . *Adaptive behavior* is the collection of conceptual, social, and practical skills that have been learned by people in order to function in their everyday lives. (American Association on Mental Retardation [AAMR] 2002a, pp. 13–14)

Representative adaptive skill behaviors are self-determination, self-esteem, language, and activities of daily living. All helping professions strive to strengthen these and other adaptive skill behaviors.

Deficits in adaptive behavior, now considered a pejorative term, is no longer used. Instead the 2002 AAMR definition refers to **limitations in adaptive behavior** and states that these "affect both daily life and the ability to respond to life changes and environmental demands" (p. 14). Whereas the 1992 AAMR terminology indicated that 10 specific adaptive behavior skill areas should be assessed for diagnosis, *the new system emphasizes three adaptive skill areas: conceptual, social, and practical.* More information on this is included in the chapter on mental retardation in Part III of this book.

In summary, education and service delivery are *adapted,* but behaviors are *adaptive.* Other areas besides mental retardation sometimes use the concept of adaptive behaviors because the concept offers a good framework to guide assessment and programming. Adapted physical educators should determine which adaptive skill behaviors can be facilitated through physical activity and collaborate with special educators in teaching these behaviors.

Service Delivery

Service delivery is the broad term for the job functions that general and adapted physical educators (and many other professionals) perform. A **service delivery system** is a classroom, school, agency, or community collaborative model used to maximize the provision of services to people with different needs. Traditionally we have thought of teachers spending most or all of their time in group instruction in a school gymnasium or outdoor area. Today's professionals, however, are responsible for many job functions or services, some of which demand time outside of a classroom.

Figure 1.4 indicates the job functions typically required of both general and adapted physical educators. The arrows show that these functions are dynamic and interactive; most are performed every day. For example, professionals evaluate their work daily (formative evaluation) as well as periodically

(summative evaluation). An acronym to help remember the job functions is PAP-TE-CA, derived from the first letter of each word, as follows:

P	Planning, including decision making about philosophy
A	Assessment of students and person-environment variables
P	Preparation, meetings, and written work
T	Teaching/counseling/coaching
E	Evaluation of services/programs/models
C	Consultation
A	Advocacy

PAP-TE-CA is a mnemonic (pronounced ni-mon'-ik) device to aid memory. It is illustrative of the games, tricks, or gimmicks that teachers and students can create to adapt instruction and make memory tasks easier. Illustrative other acronyms or first-letter mnemonics that facilitate memory are IDEA for the *Individuals with Disabilities Education Act* and *FIT* for *frequency, intensity, and time* in an exercise plan.

The PAP-TE-CA model emphasizes that the umbrella services of consultation and advocacy are processes necessary to meet the demands of federal laws like IDEA and the No Child Left Behind Act of 2001. **Consultation** is adult-to-adult help, usually through collaborative planning and problem solving, provided to generalists by a specialist. The help is directed

---

Figure 1.4   **Services included in the adapted physical activity delivery system: the PAP-TE-CA Model.**

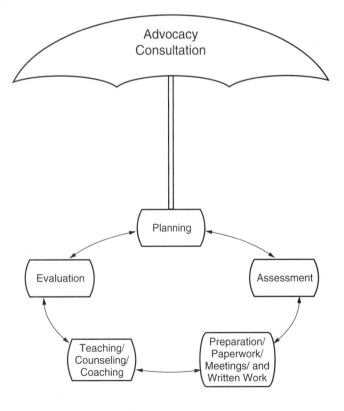

toward increasing the effectiveness of a person who works directly with students. **Advocacy** is the act of working to change the beliefs, attitudes, intentions, and behaviors of others to support a cause. The cause may be broad like diversity or human rights or narrower like a particular individual, service, or law.

The names of the PAP-TE-CA components are slightly different from the last textbook edition. The second P was changed from prescription/placement to *preparation* in order to avoid the medical model term *prescription,* and to recognize a broader job function that includes all kinds of collaborative meetings and paperwork related to individualized programming. The trend today is away from the medical model. The concept of placement was removed from the PAP-TE-CA model because 95% of students with disabilities remain in the general physical education classroom. *Today's emphasis in adapted physical education is on a continuum of services or supports, not a continuum of placements.* The mainstream support continuum contains such options as (a) with a full time paraprofessional, (b) with properly trained peer tutors (1:1 or 1:2 ratio), (c) with student helpers as needed, or (d) with no supports. An adapted physical education consultant is often needed to train, mentor, and supervise people resources.

The PAP-TE-CA model is an adaptation of the original work of Janet Wessel (1977) of Michigan State University in the development of the I CAN Model and the Achievement-Based Curriculum (ABC) Model and Wessel's later collaboration with Luke Kelly of the University of Virginia (Wessel & Kelly, 1986). Both leaders have influenced adapted physical activity practices throughout the world. Kelly was also project director of the team that developed the Adapted Physical Education National Standards (APENS) in the 1990s. APENS is discussed later in this chapter.

Good Service Delivery Is Adapting

Adapting is a desirable practice in all settings: mainstream and nonmainstream, school and nonschool. It is important for both **generalists** and **specialists** to become skillful in adaptation. This is why undergraduates in almost all professional preparation programs take courses in adapted physical activity, engage in practicum experiences that expose them to a wide variety of individual differences, and write journals to encourage reflective and critical thinking (Connolly, 1994).

Today all professionals in the mainstream are expected to address the needs of individuals who formerly were labeled *disabled, handicapped,* or *health-impaired* and placed in separate settings. Likewise, professionals are expected to cope with diversity associated with different cultures, value systems, languages, ethnic groups, and socioeconomic levels.

Often the range of individual differences in mainstream settings is too large for one professional to manage. Schools, agencies, businesses, and industries are therefore increasingly employing specialists to dual- and team-teach and to serve as consultants. Adapted physical activity specialists are typically individuals with master's or doctoral degrees in APA (or education) with particular expertise in psychomotor problem solving.

Generalists must know when to request the help of an APA specialist. One purpose of this text is to familiarize gener-

alists and specialists with ways they can help each other. Some programs lag behind others; when specialists are needed, generalists need to convince administrators to employ them. The future will bring new employment trends, just as the past (legislation and attitude change) has brought new understandings of integration, inclusion, and least restrictive environments.

Good Teaching Is Adapting

Good teaching involves adapting goals, content, and pedagogy to individual needs so as to minimize failure and preserve ego strength. In a sense, *all good physical education is adapted physical education.* The larger the class size and the more varied the abilities of the students, the more adaptation is needed. However, having special education students in class does not necessarily mean additional adaptation demands.

Many students with disabilities participate successfully in general physical education. An individual in leg braces may be able, without adaptations, to engage in swimming, gymnastics, or archery. A pupil with an arm amputation may be a star soccer player or excel in baseball, basketball, or football. Disability therefore should not automatically be equated with adapted physical education services. Any student who routinely performs below average should be provided APA services.

Good teaching requires that generalists and specialists work together. Although all physical educators are expected to practice adaptation, *at least one adapted physical education specialist is needed in every school district or city to supplement and complement the efforts of generalists, to serve as consultants and administrators, and to provide direct instruction for students with severe disabilities who typically require more help than full-time mainstream services can afford.* Of particular importance is providing units of instruction in wheelchair or other specialized sports that will enable students to recreate and compete in nonschool activities designed to challenge abilities different from the norm.

Ecosystems and Ecological Theory

Central to understanding adaptation is the concept of an ecosystem (see Figure 1.5). An **ecosystem** *is an individual in continuous interaction with his or her environment.* This interaction process includes everyone who influences an individual throughout the lifespan as well as the good and bad things in the physical and social environment. Whereas assessment used to focus exclusively on individual needs, the trend is toward **ecological assessment,** the examination of everything in the ecosystem that can contribute to moving, seeing, hearing, thinking, or other observable processes. Whereas the older adapted physical education systems emphasized diagnosis, prescription, and programming for individual change, the newer systems do not use medical terms like *diagnosis* and *prescription* but rely instead on special education and social science concepts associated with ecology.

Ecology is the study of interdependence and interactions of humans (as individuals, groups, and societies) with their psychosocial and physical environment. The concept of ecology evolved in the late 1800s, at the same time that subject matter areas like sociology, psychology, human development,

Figure 1.5 The ecosystem of an individual, showing the influence of persons in the family, neighborhood, community, and school or work site, all interacting within a field of environmental enablers, and barriers and affected by time (i.e., specific situations or contexts).

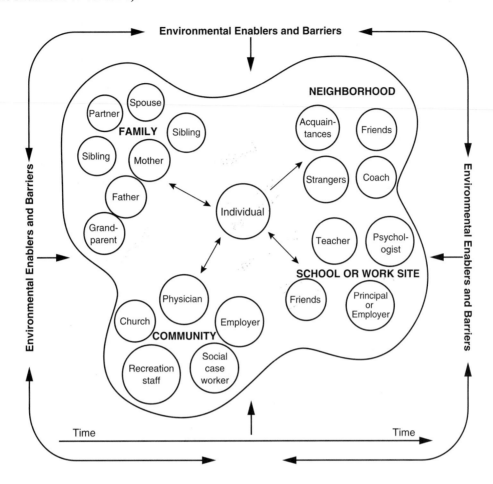

and education began to be taught in universities. The key process in ecological interactions is *adaptation* (a concept that also evolved in the late 1800s) along with *holism* (the belief that wholes rather than parts should be addressed in education, quality of life, and survival). Ecological theory thus drives adapted physical activity practices and the conceptualization of **individual differences** as person-environment interactions that cause persons to be perceived as having unique needs that require special services. Individual differences, remember, is one of the components of adaptation theory.

Ecological task analysis (ETA) is extremely important in adapted physical activity (Davis & Burton, 1991). ETA is a systematic process of brainstorming and critical thinking about all of the variables in the ecosystem that influence success of an individual in learning a particular task. ETA thus determines the adaptations that are chosen. Chapter 3 focuses on ecological task analysis as part of adaptation theory.

Important Concepts From IDEA

Laws important to APA are covered in Chapter 4. However, the Individuals with Disabilities Education Act (IDEA) of 1990, amended in 1997 and expected to be amended in 2003, presents some concepts that must be learned now because they are fun-

damental to understanding service delivery and developing a professional vocabulary.

Person-First Language

IDEA of 1990 changed the way that professionals thought, talked, and wrote about disability. **Person-first language** is placement of the noun (*individual or person*) before the descriptive phrase (*with disabilities*) to conceptualize whole persons first, with many abilities and disabilities, rather than emphasizing the parts that are impaired or the functions that are disabled. This change illustrates *holistic philosophy*. IDEA 1990 also eliminated the terms *handicap* and *handicapped* when referring to human beings. This supported the idea that a handicap is a barrier or a prevention of a barrier as in our reference to *handicapped parking places*. The person-first rule does not apply to deafness, because Deaf people see deafness as a linguistic culture, not a disability. **Deaf** is often capitalized just as other linguistic cultures (English, Spanish) are.

Disability Categories

IDEA uses disability categories to refer to 13 specific activity-limiting conditions that entitle individuals to special education services, including physical education that is specially designed, if necessary (see Table 1.1). Definitions of these special education diagnostic categories from IDEA appear in Appendix A.

Definitions are socially constructed and change with time. Specific conditions included in the categories also change with time. Since the 1997 amendments to IDEA, attention deficit hyperactivity disorder (ADHD) may be served under the category of *Other Health Impairment* or *Emotional Disturbance.* IDEA 1997 also added the option of classifying children, ages 3 through 9, as *developmentally delayed* rather than as having a specific disability.

To be assigned a disability category, individuals must meet criteria that substantiate performance limitations in a particular subject matter area. For example, a student with mental retardation may be categorized as having a disability in reading, writing, or arithmetic, but not in physical education. Thus, the whole child is never considered disabled regardless of whether he or she has an impairment in body structure or in the functioning of one or more organs.

Special Education Services

Special education services refer to instructional services for students with disabilities, *including instruction in physical education,* that are provided in accordance with IDEA regulations. Services are designated as *direct,* meaning face-to-face contact with students, and *indirect,* including such job functions as planning, paperwork, collaboration, and consultation. Services must be provided in settings that are determined during the IEP process to be minimally restrictive.

Related Services

Related services refers to transportation and such developmental, corrective, or supportive services as may be required to assist a student to benefit from special education. *Physical education is not a related service.*

Individualized Family Service Plan (IFSP)

The **IFSP** is a written document that indicates that an infant or toddler (defined as ages birth through 2) has developmental delays in specified functional areas or is at risk for delays and is therefore eligible for direct or related services by qualified personnel in any setting, including the home.

Individualized Education Program (IEP)

The **IEP** is a written document that certifies that a student, ages 3 through 21, meets criteria for assignment to one of the disability categories in Table 1.1. Students ages 3 to 9 may be assigned to a developmental delays category rather than a disability category. Based on multidisciplinary assessment and decision making, and signed by parents to indicate their agreement, the IEP specifies the instructional and related services, as well as sup-

Table 1.1   Disabilities recognized by IDEA listed in order of categories receiving most special education services.

1. Specific learning disability
2. Speech or language impairment
3. Mental retardation
4. Serious emotional disturbance
5. Multiple disabilities
6. Other health impairment
7. Hearing impairment
8. Deafness
9. Orthopedic impairment
10. Autism
11. Visual impairment, including blindness
12. Traumatic brain injury
13. Deaf-blindness

ports, that a student must receive in any school subject in which she or he is found to have a disability. IDEA requires that services be delivered in the least restrictive environment.

Least Restrictive Environment (LRE)

LRE is a legal term used on the IEP to describe the place where instruction must be provided in each school subject in which the student is categorized as having a disability. IDEA indicates that, in most cases, the LRE is the general education setting. Other LRE options include resource rooms, separate classes, separate schools, or homebound/hospital settings. No student can be removed from the general education setting without the school's strict adherence to due process and procedural safeguards.

Transition Services

Both the IFSP and the IEP specify that transition needs shall be written out and implemented. In the IFSP, steps pertain to the transition of children, when they reach age 3, to preschool special education or other appropriate services. In the IEP, steps pertain to adolescents, when they reach age 14, to begin planning the transition from school-based services to community living and working. Actual implementation of transition services must begin no later than age 16. Physical educators should assume responsibility for instruction in lifetime sports and provide experiences in the community that will make transition easier (Krueger, DiRocco, & Felix, 2000). This typically means that adapted physical educators must take students off of the school grounds and give them firsthand practice in using public transportation and community recreation and fitness facilities. *Whenever possible, this is accomplished through collaborative activity with community recreation personnel.*

Individual Differences and Normal Curve Theory

Individual differences in this textbook, and in adaptation theory, are conceptualized as person-environment interactions that deviate significantly from the norm (i.e., the mean, or the 50th

Figure 1.6 A normal curve is a mathematical model that shows where 100 or more students will score if given a standardized test. Along the baseline are standard deviation marks that divide the curve into 3%, 13%, and 68% areas.

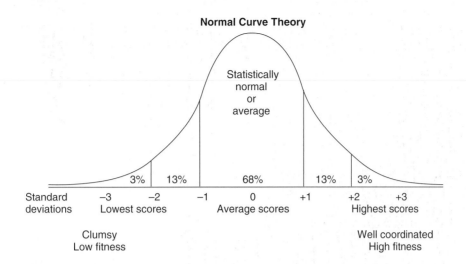

percentile) because we realize that individuals, at all times, are interacting with environment variables that make conditions either favorable or unfavorable to goal achievement. *Individual differences* is a broader term than disabilities because many persons who cannot meet the criteria for services under law can benefit from APA. Individual differences is also a more positive term.

The concept of *deviation from normal* evolved with the creation of the normal curve in the late 1800s and its subsequent use in intelligence testing and classification or categorization of students for appropriate education services (Davis, 1995; Shogan, 1998). Today normal curve theory, although increasingly controversial, continues to be used in educational classification. Figure 1.6 shows that, whenever 100 or more persons are tested, the scores of the middle 68% of this population fall between markers labeled *−1 and +1 standard deviations*. These markers enclose what is called the average or normal performance range. The further an individual's score deviates from the middle 68%, the more different (unique, special, exceptional) he or she is.

The *traditional criterion (or standard) for justifying special education and adapted physical education services has been a score on a standardized test below the −2 standard deviation marker.* Presumably several tests are used in decision making. Only 2 to 3% of the overall population score below this marker on any given test. Although classification into disability categories is meant to be objective and neutral, this practice is increasingly associated with prejudice and discrimination. Many experts insist that classifications in school lead to societal labels that are hurtful and long lasting.

Some cultures and communities choose to serve individuals in the lowest 16% or lowest 50% of the normal curve distribution. Local and state governments, which raise most of the money that supports public schooling, can decide to allocate money for more services than federal laws call for. Citizens help to make decisions that support or do not support provision of disability services each time they vote. Typically, these decisions relate to amount of tax they wish to pay.

Given the tremendous importance of physical activity in lifespan health, quality of life, and longevity, Sherrill recommends that physical educators advocate for special help for any student whose test scores repeatedly fall below the mean (50% percentile), whose performance looks clumsy to an expert observer, or whose body is overweight, obese, or unfit. These are the students likely to make C− or lower on report cards, if teachers grade on performance. They are also the students who find ways to be excused from physical activity and the adults who generally have the most health problems.

Your decision about who should receive APA reflects your philosophy. Do you believe in zero-reject and zero-fail principles? The **zero-reject principle** *emphasizes the right of all individuals to high-quality physical education and recreation programming and to accessibility to the opportunities afforded by community resources. The* **zero-fail principle** *captures the idea of success-oriented instruction, with adaptations so all individuals can fulfill their potentials. These are idealistic principles. Are they too idealistic? Why?*

Qualified Professionals and Professional Preparation

Individuals qualified as **generalists** to deliver APA services in school and nonschool settings have completed one or more courses in adapted physical education that include supervised practicum experiences with individuals with disabilities. Individuals qualified as **specialists** to be employed part- or full-time in APA service delivery or consultation typically have completed undergraduate or graduate degrees with specializations in adapted physical education. Additionally both generalists and specialists should have had knowledge and experience concerning individual differences infused into most or all of their other courses. When this occurs, the curriculum model is called **infusion** (Kowalski & Rizzo, 1996). Once on the job, both generalists and specialists become involved in **continuing education,** which includes in-service training, workshops, conference participation, and independent or small-group learning activities.

Some states like California and Minnesota have developed adapted physical education teacher certifications that personnel must earn to be considered qualified. Most states, however, do not offer certification in adapted physical education. Therefore, there is little control over the quality of professionals employed. To address this weakness, the National Consortium for Physical Education and Recreation for Individuals with Disabilities (NPERID, 1995), with the help of federal grants, involved many experts in the development of the **Adapted Physical Education National Standards (APENS).**

APENS and Voluntary Certification as a CAPE

CAPE, the acronym for certified adapted physical educator, is used to indicate that professionals have passed a voluntary national examination based on the comprehensive content comprising the 187-page book of APENS (NCPERID, 1995). Individuals who pass the APENS examination write CAPE after their name with the same pride that physical, occupational, and recreation therapists write PT, OTR, or TRS after their names. Most service delivery professions offer required or voluntary certification programs to assure quality control of their professionals. The certification examination, rules, and procedures of each profession are subject to periodic review and updating, requiring that service providers engage in continuing education throughout their employment years. Administration of APENS certification is the responsibility of NCPERID, which rotates responsibility for APENS test administration among different universities. For further information, contact www.cortland.edu/APENS, NCPERID officers, Janet Seaman at info@aahperd.org, or Tim Davis, the new APENS coordinator at Cortland State University in New York (davist@cortland.edu).

The APENS book is a useful resource in that it specifies five levels of knowledge for each of 15 standards (see Table 1.2). Levels 1, 2, and 3 are meant for generalists, whereas Levels 4 and 5 are designed for specialists. The APENS content is directed toward school-based service delivery for infants, toddlers, children, and youth through age 21 and is heavily influenced by the requirements of IDEA. *This textbook covers most, if not all, of the content encompassed by APENS.*

Sports Medicine Credentials

The American College of Sports Medicine (ACSM) offers certification opportunities for health and fitness specialists who work with all age groups. Mostly attention is directed toward adults in exercise or rehabilitation centers. Of particular interest in APA are the Clinical Track Credentials that are designed to recognize competence for specialists working with high-risk or diseased individuals as well as those who are apparently healthy. ACSM (2000) provides guidelines for exercise testing and prescription to help professionals prepare for certification exams. Some of the knowledge areas that ACSM assesses are similar to those covered by APENS. For more information, see the World Wide Web: www.LWW.com/acsmere or www.acsm.org.

Table 1.2   Areas covered by the Adapted Physical Education National Standards (APENS).

1. Human development
2. Motor behavior
3. Exercise science
4. Measurement and evaluation
5. History and philosophy
6. Unique attributes of learners
7. Curriculum theory and development
8. Assessment
9. Instructional design/planning
10. Teaching
11. Consultation
12. Program evaluation
13. Continuing education
14. Ethics
15. Communication

History as a Guide to Developing Philosophy

All professions require a knowledge of their history as central to enabling their members to critically think about the past, present, and future of the individuals they serve, the job functions they perform, and the ethics they follow. A proverb, *History is a prophet with its face turned backward,* reminds us that understanding of the past and present facilitates our development of a personal philosophy to guide informed, good decision making in the present and for the future. History also helps us understand why we think and act as we do.

A **philosophy** is the system of beliefs that guide intentions and actions of a person or the purpose (mission, aim) and practices of a profession. This chapter, for example, is meant to expose readers to beliefs that may change their attitudes, intentions, and actions. Readers may agree with some beliefs and disagree with others. A major outcome of studying should be reflective and critical thinking about what is valuable to you in life and in your profession and how to preserve or achieve the things you value most for yourself and others.

Reflective thinking is consideration of the political, moral, and social implications of what we think, feel, and do (Hellison & Templin, 1991). Reflective thinking also involves linking the past to the present and the future, thereby analyzing why we think as we do, and if or how we should change our ways of thinking. **Critical thinking,** often associated with reflection, is analysis or evaluation of beliefs in terms of specific preset criteria (e.g., accuracy, practicality, usefulness, consequences, ethically right or just). Critical thinking while reading is often judgment-making in regard to what is worth remembering and using. Derived from the Greek word *philosophia,* the literal meaning of philosophy is *love of truth and search for what is right, good, and beautiful.* This process is facilitated by both reflective and critical thinking.

Beliefs change as knowledge, experience, faith, and ethics (moral principles about right and wrong) change.

Evolution of Treatment and Education

Attention given to individuals with disabilities varies by time and culture (Kalyanpur & Harry, 1999). Some cultures, in the past, viewed an individual with a disability as a gift from God, a test of religious faith, a punishment for past sins, or a useless family or community property that might interfere with the well-being of others (Leavitt, 1999; Purnell & Paulanka, 1998). These beliefs are still held by many individuals and affect practices. Typically, attitudes are different (harsher) toward infants born with disabilities than for children and adults who acquire disabilities or become ill.

Acceptance Before the 1800s

In ancient Greece and Rome, and probably many other societies, it was common to kill or abandon infants with disabilities. Early tribal cultures abandoned old and unfit persons when they became liabilities to the tribe's survival. Often, however, disability was accepted, and families provided care the best they could. Therapeutic exercise, herbs, climate changes, and rest cures were commonly used before scientific knowledge became available in the 1800s. China is credited with creating the first systems of therapeutic exercise around 3000 B.C.

Throughout most of history, severe disability has not been an issue because medical science and technology were not advanced enough to keep people alive. Individuals with mild disabilities were accepted as part of life, cared for by families with sufficient resources, and abandoned to fend for themselves when families were too poor to offer help. History is full of stories of beggars, hunchbacks, fools, simple simons, monsters, and others (probably all individuals with disabilities) who played various roles in different cultures but usually kept to themselves unless earning livelihoods as jesters, clowns, or freaks in exhibits for the entertainment of others more fortunate. "Freak shows" in traveling circuses continued to be popular until the 1940s (Griffin & McClintock, 1997).

People who were different were thus perceived as interesting oddities unless they posed a threat, as occurred in some forms of mental illness. Evil spirits or the devil were believed to cause mental illness, including the strange behaviors of women persecuted as witches. Of all disabilities, mental illness has been the most misunderstood and thus subjected to the cruelest treatments (whipping, torture, death). Even today, severe mental illness is given little attention by society and is the disability toward which persons express the worst attitudes.

Segregated Placements, Beginning in 1817

The development of the first residential facilities in the United States paralleled the discovery that some persons with disabilities could be helped, and even educated, when brought together for formal training. Sign language and sensory training were the first approaches to be tried, and Deaf individuals were the first to benefit from institutional placement in both Europe and the United States. Sign language, as an educational system, was brought to America from France by Laurent Clerc, a teacher described as a "deaf mute," who helped Thomas Gallaudet to establish an institution for Deaf people in Connecticut in 1817. Deaf education thus was created independently from special education and continues, for the most part, to be separate as does Deaf sport, which originated in France in 1924. The Deaf were therefore the first special population to have their own sport organization and international competitions.

Controversy over the better pedagogy (sign language or oralism) has surrounded deaf education for years, with persons born deaf preferring sign and separate schooling while their hearing parents and teachers preferred oralism and integrated schooling (Jankowski, 1997). Gallaudet College, in Washington, D.C., founded by Gallaudet's son, is the foremost proponent of signing and supports the philosophy that deafness is not a disability but rather a culture.

The Friends Asylum for the Insane in Philadelphia, probably the first for people with mental illness in America, opened in 1817; the Massachusetts Asylum for the Blind opened in 1830, headed by Samuel Gridley Howe; and in 1847, Howe "admitted his first idiot pupils to his school for the blind in South Boston" (Trent, 1994, p. 13). Many other institutions followed, as soon as physicians began to realize that people with disabilities could be trained or educated. Most institutions were created for a single disability, managed by physicians, and emphasized sensory training, exercise, and manual labor as treatment.

Special education for children with intellectual disabilities is generally traced to the sensorimotor training of Victor, a 12-year-old boy found naked, wild, and nonverbal in France around 1800. Jean-Marc Itard (1775–1839), a French physician, assumed responsibility for Victor, "the Wild Boy of Aveyron," and subsequently was recognized as the father of special education.

Edward Seguin, one of Itard's students, who came to America in 1850, is credited with refining Itard's pedagogy and naming it **physiological education.** This approach had three goals: muscular or physical training (the body), education of the senses (intelligence), and moral treatment (the will). Seguin claimed that, in order for "the teacher to push idiots to awaken their senses, their first level of awakening had to be the muscular" (Trent, 1994, p. 46). From Seguin's lectures and books, sensorimotor and perceptual-motor training captured the imagination of educators and dominated the newly developing special education profession until the 1960s (Hallahan & Cruickshank, 1973).

Attitude Changes, Eugenics, and Prejudice

As families began to believe that people with disabilities could be provided a better quality of life, with more services than the home could afford, heads of households sought institutionalization as the best solution to overall family needs. This practice reduced the amount of contact that ordinary people had with peers who looked or acted different, and the separation of society into disabled and nondisabled categories gradually contributed to the development of prejudice and discrimination.

Eugenics, a Western Hemisphere movement in the early 1900s designed to improve the natural gene pool through sterilization of mothers with hereditary defects (e.g., mental retardation, deafness), was embraced as persons were indoctrinated to believe that disability was bad, depleted family resources, and weakened society (Biesold, 1998; Griffin & McClintock, 1997). In 1927, the U.S. Supreme Court upheld a Virginia statute that forbid *feebleminded people* from marrying; *feebleminded* was defined as anyone not able to meet today's third-grade standards (Pfeiffer, 1993). This law also included others who were believed unable to learn (those with vision, hearing, mobility, and speech impairments). A poll in the United States, in 1937, indicated that 45% of the U.S. population favored euthanasia for *defective infants* (the terminology of the times).

Throughout World War II, Nazi Germany conducted sterilization and euthanasia programs to rid Europe of individuals believed to have inferior genes. Less publicized, but nevertheless verified, physicians in the United States frequently performed sterilizations (these were required by 33 states by 1938) and, with the permission of parents, gave newborn infants with severe defects no care. President Franklin D. Roosevelt, esteemed president during World War II, who needed a wheelchair for easy mobility because of polio, let himself be photographed in a wheelchair only one time.

Major Reforms and Placement Options

After World War II, in the 1940s, major reforms characterized the treatment of people with disabilities. War veterans with physical disabilities were visible everywhere, and the nation was proud of these men and women. Polio epidemics and vehicle accidents continued to create wheelchair users, and normal curve testing practices identified more persons with special school needs. Ideas, however, changed about the appropriate placement of children. The National Association for Retarded Children (now ARC) was founded in the 1950s, and families joined professionals in advocating for children to remain home and be educated in nearby schools. Parents also advocated for recognition of new diagnostic categories, like *learning disabilities,* to be addressed by special education. Special day schools opened, still supporting segregation, but enabling most children to live at home while they received high-quality education and therapy in barrier-free environments.

The humanistic philosophy and civil rights movements of the 1960s renewed concerns about *social justice* (i.e., is separate but equal schooling just?), which gradually led to the practice of adding special education wings and classrooms to general education schools. This innovation created the first contact that many children with and without disabilities had ever had with one another. The creation of Special Olympics in 1968 was a strong advocacy effort to make mental retardation visible in the positive light that sport can afford, to increase contact between persons with and without mental retardation, and to improve attitudes. Grassroots efforts led to federal laws in the 1970s that mandated free appropriate public education (FAPE)

in the least restrictive environment (LRE), which was interpreted to be *availability of many placement options* (e.g., special day schools, special self-contained classes and resource rooms within regular schools, integrated classes). Outside the classroom, increasing emphasis was given to nondiscrimination and creation of equal opportunities for all.

Today, the Challenge of Inclusion

The United Nations designated 1981 as the International Year of the Disabled, a recognition that spurred individuals with disabilities throughout the world to increasingly see themselves as a social minority with rights to be fought for. The International Games for the Disabled in New York, in 1984, provided impetus for broadening disability sport (originally conceptualized as wheelchair sport) into a Paralympic movement for all disabilities (except deafness, which Deaf athletes do not consider a disability). Today, in most of the world, the trend is inclusive practices in schools, business and industry, and communities. *The emphasis in school programming has changed from a continuum of placement options to service delivery options, indicating a reinterpretation of the LRE concept.* Much work is needed, however, to materialize the dream of social justice and equal opportunities for all (Adams, Bell, & Griffin, 1997; Kozub, Sherblom, & Terry, 1999).

Today, the Challenge of Cross-Cultural Complexity

Increased racial, ethnic, religious, linguistic, and family style diversity, as well as challenges arising from poverty, make service delivery and empowerment more complex (Leavitt, 1999; Purnell & Paulanka, 1998). According to the U.S. Census Bureau (2000), over 11% of Americans are living below the government-established poverty line; the range, by states, for people below the poverty line is 4.8 to 18%. However, because poor children tend to come from the same neighborhoods and attend the same schools, particularly in large cities, the percentage of poor children in some schools is higher than 90%. This percentage is usually determined by the number qualifying for government-funded school lunch programs.

Ethnic minority groups tend to be overrepresented in special education, probably because most are also poor. In particular, Black Americans are about 2.5 times as likely to receive special education services as White Americans. Reasons for this are unclear, encompassing such factors as bias in testing and classification procedures, disproportionate models of their own race as teachers and administrators to provide encouragement, inappropriate educational opportunities at home and at school, poor living environments, and poor health.

Hispanic children, with the additional challenge of a second language, are the largest growing minority group. Overall, the racial profile in the United States is changing with Hispanic Americans of all ages replacing Blacks as the largest minority group. Racial patterns affect schools in the South and West more than in other regions. In the South, Blacks comprise about 19% of the population. In the West (Texas, New Mexico, Arizona, and California combined), Hispanics comprise about 25% of the population. For our country as a whole, the 2000 census reports that Whites comprise 75% of the population, Blacks

and Hispanics about 12% each, and Asians about 4%. These percentages do not equal 100% because of rounding error.

Family practices also affect percentage of children in special education, also because of the interaction with poverty. Today only 24% of children live with both birth parents (the traditional nuclear family still glamorized on television). Approximately 27% of children reside with one parent in single-parent households; this statistic reflects the influence of both divorce and unwed mothers. These figures, of course, are averages. Percentages are higher among ethnic minorities. Typically, children who live in single-parent households experience more poverty than others, receive less attention, are less likely to engage in after-school sports, and have less good health and fitness. School and classroom diversity caused by these and other factors require changes in professional preparation so that all teachers have cross-cultural understandings to address the tremendous array of unique needs (see Figure 1.7).

Stages of Adapted Physical Activity History

Adapted physical activity has survived many name changes and philosophical differences. In the United States, this service delivery system seems to have evolved through six stages (Sherrill, 1988; Sherrill & DePauw, 1997).

Stage 1, Medical Gymnastics: Before 1905

Prior to the 1900s, all physical education was medically oriented and preventive, developmental, or corrective in nature. The physical education curriculum was comprised primarily of what we know today as gymnastics, calisthenics, body mechanics, and marching or military-like exercise drills. University physical educators were generally *physicians* who applied known principles of medicine to the various systems of exercise. The purpose of physical training (or physical culture, as the profession was called then) was to prevent illness and/or to promote the health and vigor of the mind and body. However, enough professionals had primary interest in therapeutics and correctives that a special interest group was formed within the Association for the Advancement of Physical Education in 1905. Some persons therefore use 1905 as the date of origin for the adapted physical activity profession.

Stage 2, Transition to Sports: 1905–1930

The gradual transition from medically oriented physical training to sports-centered physical education occurred in the early 1900s. Factors influencing this change were (a) the introduction of sports into American culture and, subsequently, into the physical education curriculum; (b) the application of psychological and sociological theory to education, resulting in the conceptualization of the *whole child*; (c) the trend away from medical training as appropriate teacher preparation for physical educators in the public schools; and (d) the advent of compulsory physical education in the public schools.

State legislation making physical education mandatory in the public schools increased the number of students to be taught and brought new problems. What, for instance, would be done if a student were ill or disabled, or lacked the physical stamina to participate in the regular curriculum? The solution was to divide public school physical education into two branches: (a) *regular* (general) and (b) *corrective* or *remedial.* Concurrently, separate curricula were developed for children in the many residential facilities (McKenzie, 1909).

Stage 3, Corrective Physical Education: 1930–1950

Between the 1930s and the 1950s, both regular and corrective physical education served mostly what are known today as ordinary or typical students. Assignment to physical education was based on a thorough medical examination by a physician, who determined whether a student should participate in the regular or the corrective program. *Corrective classes were comprised primarily of limited, restricted, or modified activities related to health, posture, or fitness problems.* In many schools, students were permanently excused from physical education. In others, the physical educator typically taught several sections of regular physical education and one section of corrective physical education each day. Leaders in corrective physical education continued to have strong backgrounds in medicine. Most physical educators completed one university course in correctives.

Veterans returning from World War II were instrumental in initiating a name change. They pointed out that amputations and spinal cord injuries could not be corrected. They also emphasized the potential of sports in rehabilitation and started various wheelchair sports.

Stage 4, Adapted Physical Education: 1950–1970

During the 1950s and 1960s, the population served in public school corrective/adapted physical education broadened to include persons with disabilities. Instrumental in this change was the trend away from residential school placement. This resulted in increased enrollment of students with disabilities, particularly mental retardation, in the public schools. The values that such children and youth could derive from participation in sports, dance, and aquatics adapted to their special needs were increasingly recognized. The following definition (now outdated) evolved in the early 1950s:

> Adapted physical education is a diversified program of developmental activities, games, sports, and rhythmics suited to the interests, capacities, and limitations of students with disabilities who may not safely or successfully engage in unrestricted participation in the vigorous activities of the general physical education program. *(Committee on Adapted Physical Education, 1952, p. 15)*

This definition was viable throughout the next two decades because adapted physical education teaching practices paralleled the special education procedure of segregating students with disabilities in separate classes and/or special schools. During this era, many names were proposed (*special, developmental,* and *remedial*) and used in textbook titles.

Through the efforts of President John F. Kennedy, his sister Eunice Kennedy Shriver, and his brother Senator Edward Kennedy, physical educators became increasingly aware of mental retardation. The Kennedy family was especially concerned with this condition because it affected one of their sisters, Rose. Special Olympics was created in 1968. The human rights movement of the 1960s led to federal legislation that addressed inequities in public school education and prohibited segregation.

Stage 5, IEP-Dominated Service: 1970–1990

Countries throughout the world passed legislation to guarantee rights to persons with disabilities. In the United States, federal law defined **specially designed physical education** as part of special education, and the IEP process dominated eligibility for adapted physical education and pedagogy (see Table 1.3). Public school systems began to employ full-time adapted physical educators and to encourage after-school Special Olympics. Emphasis in adapted physical education changed from meeting the needs of all students to serving those in disability categories.

Physical educators became seriously interested in the development of an APA knowledge base when colleges and universities began offering graduate degrees in APA in the 1970s. The first of these was a master's level specialization created by Joseph Winnick at the State University of New York (SUNY) at Brockport. Professional organizations were created, and the profession (first founded in 1905) was revitalized.

Many individuals provided leadership for this new profession. Chief among these were Julian Stein in the United States and Patricia Austin in Canada. As director of the AAHPERD Office on Programs for the Handicapped/Disabled from 1966 to 1981, Stein influenced teacher education through numerous publications, active involvement in legislation, and extensive consultation and demonstration teaching. At the University of Alberta in Edmonton, Canada, Austin pioneered in establishing exemplary teacher education and service delivery programs.

Stage 6, & Inclusive Physical Activity: 1990s On

From the 1990s on, the IDEA requirement of LRE increasingly has been interpreted as meaning *inclusive general education with as many supports as necessary to enable safe, satisfying, and successful goal achievement.* More attention consequently has been given to meeting the needs of students with severe and multiple disabilities in typical settings (Downing, 2002), preparing adapted physical education consultants (Lytle & Collier, 2002), examining supports (AAMR, 2002a), and complying with federal law (IDEA, 1997) that students with disabilities must be included in general statewide assessment programs, formerly for general education only (Kleinert & Kearns, 2001; Losardo & Notari-Syverson, 2001).

Information about important leaders and developments appears in such sources as Sherrill (1988), Sherrill and DePauw (1997), *Palaestra,* and *Adapted Physical Activity Quarterly.* Appendix F of this text provides a detailed chronology of events important in the history of APA. Photographs of important leaders representing different periods in history appear in Figure 1.8.

Evolution of the Knowledge Base

This evolution of the crossdisciplinary APA knowledge base, or academic discipline, is complex. Specialist training did not begin until the enactment of federal laws that partially funded universities to offer personnel training for physical education and recreation specialists to work with individuals with disabilities. As universities began to confer master's and doctoral degrees in

Table 1.3   Federal laws influencing adapted physical activity.

Rehabilitation Act of 1973

93rd Congress, PL 93-112

Section 504, called the Nondiscrimination clause

No discrimination toward people with disabilities in any program or facility funded by the federal government

Education for All Handicapped Children Act (EAHCA) of 1975

94th Congress, PL 94-112

Free appropriate public education (FAPE)

Special education services for ages 3 to 21, including adapted physical education as a direct service

Diagnostic categories to establish eligibility

Multidisciplinary teamwork and the IEP

Parent involvement and agreement on IEP

Least restrictive environment (LRE), a continuum of options

Amateur Sports Act of 1978

95th Congress, PL 95-606

Governed many amateur activities

Policy and funding for Olympic Games

Established U.S. Olympic Committee (USOC)

Created Committee on Sports for the Disabled (COSD)

EAHCA Amendments of 1986

86th Congress, PL 99-457

Initiated services to infants (ages birth through 2) and IFSP

Expanded services to preschool children ages 3 to 5

Americans with Disabilities Act (ADA) of 1990

101st Congress, PL 101-336

Extended Rehabilitation Act nondiscri͟ programs, facilities, and activities rega͟ source

Afforded civil rights

Removed barriers, changed communit͟

Individuals with Disabilities Educatio͟

101st Congress, PL 101-336

Reauthorized EAHCA with terminology changed to *with disabilities* (person-first concept)

Included ages birth through 21

Introduced transition services for ages 16 through 21

Added autism and traumatic brain injury (TBI) as disability categories

IDEA Amendments of 1997

105th Congress, PL 105-17

Created a developmental delay category for ages 3 through 9

Increased parent involvement in assessment

Interpreted general education as LRE for most students

Emphasized services rather than placements

Required general education teacher in IEP process, when appropriate

Clarified transition services; planning must begin by age 14

Mandated students with disabilities be included in statewide testing

Olympic and Amateur Sports of 1998

105th Congress, PL 105-277

Reauthorized Amateur Sports Act of 1978

Placed Paralympics under USOC

---

these areas in the 1970s, increasing attention was given to the coursework and practicum experiences that specialists needed. *Today's theory and practice come primarily from four sources, thereby supporting the philosophy of a crossdisciplinary academic discipline.*

Medical Roots

Swedish medical gymnastics, an exercise system created by Per Henrik Ling (1776–1839) of Stockholm, is the forerunner of corrective and remedial physical education in the 1920s to the 1950s and adapted physical education thereafter. Ling is therefore recognized as the father of APA. Medical gymnastics was brought from Sweden to the United States by Nils Posse around 1885, introduced into the Boston public schools, and systematically integrated into teacher-training programs.

Physicians, physical therapists, and physical educators with special interest in exercise, posture, and fitness promoted Swedish and other medical exercise systems from the 1900s through the 1930s. Illustrative of textbooks with a medical emphasis that shaped early APA history are *Exercise in Education and Medicine* (1909, 1915, 1923) by R. Tait McKenzie, professor at McGill University in Canada until 1904 and at the University of Pennsylvania thereafter, and *Corrective Physical Education* (1934, followed by seven later editions) by Josephine

Rathbone, who was a professor at Teachers College, Columbia University, in New York City (see Figure 1.8). McKenzie was a physician, whereas Rathbone was a dual PE/PT specialist, a combination popular in the 1920s to the 1950s. Both Canada and the United States give annual R. Tait McKenzie Awards at their national conventions in recognition of McKenzie's leadership. Today, adapted physical educators still refer to medical sources for basic information on disabilities and exercise recommendations. The ACSM (2000, 2001) is a major resource.

Special Education Roots

Special education has multiple roots, one for each type of disability. However, contributions to APA have been particularly strong in the areas of deafness, blindness, and mental retardation. Persons with these disabilities were first served in residential facilities, and pedagogy evolved to meet their special needs out of the sensorimotor training emphasis of the early 1800s.

The Council for Exceptional Children (CEC), which today is the major special education association, was founded in New York in 1922. By then, many individuals formerly educated in residential schools were attending special education classes in their home communities. However, special education did not evolve as a strong profession until federal legislation of the 1970s. Many of the first adapted physical education

R. Tait McKenzie
Stage 2

Josephine Rathbone
Stage 3

Julian Stein
Stages 4–5

Patricia Austin
Stages 4–5

Janet Seaman
Stage 5

Joseph P. Winnick
Stage 6

specialists in the 1970s earned dual certifications in special education and physical education. Because physical education for children with disabilities is defined as special education under federal law, adapted physical education professional preparation continues to incorporate special education knowledge and to follow its service delivery trends.

The new CEC (2002) performance-based standards for beginning special educators is therefore a valuable source. The book also includes the CEC Code of Ethics, Professional Practica Standards, and Mentoring Standards, all documents that are applicable to physical educators.

Physical Activity and Exercise Science Roots

The theory and practice of sport, dance, aquatics, movement education, and fitness that are mastered in order to teach general physical education are essential to adapted physical education. However, professionals must possess additional competencies related to adaptation, sport classification, team balance for fair competition, wheelchair use, and inclusion. For individuals with disabilities, as adults, to participate fully in the community, they must learn participant, spectator, and fan sport roles (i.e., transition skills) and know how to interact with others who love the same sports. The success of the disability sport movement (see Chapter 2) shows us that a sport can be found

for every individual at every age, if positive attitudes are formed early. The disability sport movement itself is the source of much new knowledge as experts create rules, strategies, and techniques for sport success.

The knowledge base of exercise science is also essential to adapted physical education (see Chapter 13). The benefits that ordinary persons derive from physical activity occur in persons with disabilities. The school fitness movement, which began in the 1950s, continues to impact all children in physical education. Adapted physical activity specialists who work with severe disabilities have the additional responsibility for learning as much about the body and its capacity for movement as possible.

Social Science Roots, Including Disability Studies

From the 1980s onward, the **social sciences** (e.g., psychology, sociology, anthropology, human ecology, disability studies) were instrumental in the evolution of APA content on attitude formation and change, inclusive teaching strategies, group dynamics, interpersonal relations, understanding and appreciation of individual differences, social justice, social minorities and oppression, and disability studies. Although attitude theory evolved out of the subject matter of social psychology in the 1930s, it was not widely applied to adapted physical activity until Terry Rizzo (1984; Folsom-Meek & Rizzo, 2002) developed

Figure 1.9 Terry L. Rizzo and Claudine Sherrill have led the initiative to add attitude theory and practice to adapted physical activity professional practice. They believe that attitudes are the key to inclusion and to healthy, active lifestyles. See their many publications in references at end of book.

a survey for measuring teacher attitudes toward inclusion of children in general physical education and Claudine Sherrill began to emphasize attitude change in the third edition of her textbook (1986). *Rizzo, Sherrill, and others strongly believed (and still do) that attitude change theory and practice are the keys to inclusion and social justice* (see Figure 1.9).

The **disability studies** perspective, driven primarily by people with disabilities who have authored textbooks, created university courses, and masterminded political change (Charlton, 1998; Davis, 1995; Mackelprang & Salsgiver, 1999; Oliver, 1990; Wendell, 1996; Yuker, 1988), challenges us to critically think about the many socially constructed meanings of disability, service delivery, empowerment, and oppression. The expression *Nothing about us without us* is perhaps the most succinct summary of the movement to involve people with disabilities in teaching, coaching, politics, and the like where they have the power to change attitudes and practices. This movement, which also emphasizes *holistic learning* concerning everyday life and oppression rather than just physical activity service delivery, has strongly influenced this textbook. The **disability sport movement,** although more concerned with practice than theory, has much to offer the disability studies perspective (see Chapter 2).

Using History to Write Philosophy

History can be written like the pages you have just read, or it can be personal history, the *lived experiences* of each day as you describe them orally to others or write them in your journal. **Phenomenology** is the study of phenomena (things) that "focuses on the lived experience and on the meaning of that experience for the person who lived it" (Connolly, 1994, p. 307). One approach to phenomenology is to reflect on your life experiences (or history) and to weave these together with those of traditional history as a means of clarifying how beliefs evolve. Maureen Connolly (1994) at Brock University, in Canada, gives the best account thus far of using journal writing to understand the value of practicum experiences in enhancing contact, understanding, and appreciation among persons with and without disabilities. Connolly's article provides many examples of journal entries from undergraduate students and how they can be analyzed for themes. The article is also an introduction to qualitative research. A particular strength of Connolly's article is her acceptance of individual differences as natural and good. She states,

> I am claiming that difference *does* make a difference, both to people who are considered different and the people who work with these "different people." I hope to show that physical education, and teacher education, can be enriched by an authentic inclusion of difference. (p. 311)

As you approach the end of this chapter, and maybe other chapters, depending on how fast you wish to go, look back over your journal entries and review the beliefs that you have written as your beginning philosophy of adapted physical education (or activity, depending on your preference) and individual differences, including disability. Group your beliefs into categories (or center headings) that belong in a philosophy. Develop a document that describes the philosophy that will guide work in your chosen field with people with disabilities or differences. Share this assignment with classmates and/or the teacher, as requested. Plan to revise your philosophy periodically. Place your philosophy, with its date, in the portfolio that you are keeping for class.

Roles, Job Functions, and Competencies

This section provides guidance in assessing your present level of knowledge and experience in relation to performing roles and job functions and obtaining the competencies that match job demands. Roles follow:

1. Direct service delivery, meaning face-to-face contact with students or clients or whoever is served in your job setting. This may be in one facility or several.

2. Consultation, usually referring to an adapted physical educator employed to assist several generalists; can also refer to helping parents or others. Work scope varies widely (Lytle & Collier, 2002).

3. Research, the creation of knowledge. This can be **action research,** based on knowledge generated from day-to-day experience, with findings reported in words (i.e., **qualitative research** with interview and observational data subjected to interpretation through special kinds of reflective and critical thinking). Or it can be traditional **scientific research,** aiming to test or generate theory, with most findings reported as statistics that have been used to examine hypotheses (called **quantitative research**).

4. University professor, usually within the adapted physical activity context, means employment in teacher education with obligation to show outstanding performance in the areas of teaching, scholarship, and service.

5. Administration or other, usually encompassing responsibility for guiding and supervising other professionals, grant writing and funding, evaluation of all aspects of program, and all forms of accountability and collaboration.

The terms **job functions** and **services** are generally synonyms. PAP-TE-CA was presented as a model earlier in this chapter to introduce you to job functions. These were planning, assessment, preparation, teaching/counseling/coaching, evaluation, and the umbrella functions of consultation and advocacy.

Competencies *are abilities adequate to perform specific job functions or the tasks comprising these job functions.* The word is derived from the Latin *competere,* meaning "to meet" or "to agree"; this emphasizes that competencies must be linked to specific job functions. Competencies encompass philosophy, attitudes, knowledge, and skills, because these components are all necessary to the performance of specific job functions (see Figure 1.10). Many lists of APA competency guidelines have been developed (see Sherrill, 1988, Appendix). Additionally Porretta, Surburg, and Jansma (2002) have developed competencies to guide doctoral study. However, the PAP-TE-CA model competencies that follow are the first to address **lifespan** service delivery and to include philosophy and attitudes as central to adequate job performance.

Figure 1.10 Competencies include philosophy (beliefs), attitudes, knowledge, and skills that *match* the everyday job functions that professionals perform.

Use the PAP-TE-CA competencies in Table 1.4 to assess yourself and others and to set personal learning goals. Plan to reassess periodically. Use your assessment to set goals and time lines to guide your learning. Balance your goals between theory (book learning) and practice (activities with people with disabilities).

Table 1.4   A checklist for use in assessing PAP-TE-CA specialist competencies.

Competencies Related to Advocacy, Ethics, and Philosophy

1.1 Philosophy that supports
    1.11   The right of all persons to (a) high-quality physical activity, (b) empowerment, and (c) self-actualization
    1.12   Assessment data (not characteristics) as the basis for adapted physical activity
1.2 Attitude of accepting and appreciating individual differences
1.3 Knowledge of
    1.31   Individual differences (person-environment interactions), including disabilities and ecological theory
    1.32   State and local physical education requirements and indicators of high-quality instruction
    1.33   Laws that eliminate barriers and protect rights
    1.34   Opportunities in a variety of settings to enrich health and leisure
    1.35   Theories, models, and strategies relevant to achieving advocacy goals

Table 1.4 **Continued**

Competencies Related to Advocacy, Ethics, and Philosophy (continued)

1.4 Skill in
    1.41 Increasing comfort and communication among people with limited exposure to individual differences
    1.42 Applying attitude theories to promote desired change
    1.43 Using advocacy strategies in the 5 L model (Look at me, Leverage, Literature, Legislation, Litigation)
    1.44 Conducting workshops, focus groups, and in-service education

Competencies Related to Consulting and Continuing Education

2.1 Philosophy that supports
    2.11 Multidisciplinary, interdisciplinary, and crossdisciplinary cooperation
    2.12 Partnerships between persons with and without disabilities in promoting lifespan activity
    2.13 Partnerships between generalists and specialists
    2.14 Partnerships between families, schools, and communities
2.2 Attitude of self-confidence in human relationships
2.3 Knowledge of
    2.31 Supports and resources (e.g., organizations, athletes with disabilities, special educators, related services personnel, parents)
    2.32 Group dynamics and interpersonal skills
    2.33 Consulting, collaboration, and communication
2.4 Skill in
    2.41 Locating, contacting, and establishing rapport with resources
    2.42 Bringing resources together (e.g., planning meetings or introducing people to each other)
    2.43 Communicating and public relations
    2.44 Problem solving and prioritizing

Competencies Related to Planning and Instructional Design

3.1 Philosophy that supports critical thinking about
    3.11 The nature of adapted physical activity (APA); its philosophy, job roles, and functions; eligibility for APA services; multidisciplinary collaboration
    3.12 Diversity and cross-cultural perspectives
    3.13 Desirable family, school, and community interactions and outcomes
    3.14 APA theories, models, principles, and practices
    3.15 Law, government, and ethics
3.2 Attitude of responsibility for critical thinking as the basis for
    3.21 Planning APA services
    3.22 Decision making in all aspects of direct service delivery
    3.23 Evaluating effectiveness
3.3 Knowledge of planning for (a) desired outcomes; (b) classrooms, schools, and school districts; (c) communities; and (d) organizations and agencies
3.4 Skill in
    3.41 Decision making regarding variables to be assessed, procedures to be followed, and resources to be used
    3.42 Prioritizing and establishing goals
    3.43 Writing objectives to achieve goals
    3.44 Matching activities to objectives
    3.45 Calculating instructional time for objectives and activities
    3.46 Writing instructional units and lesson plans
    3.47 Addressing transitional education
    3.48 Creating behavior management plans

Competencies Related to Assessment

4.1 Philosophy that supports assessment as the key to individualizing and adapting
4.2 Attitude of commitment to assessing both individuals and environments
4.3 Knowledge of
    4.31 Instruments and protocols for assessing performance in goal areas as well as environmental barriers and enablers
    4.32 Validity, reliability, and other measurement concepts

Table 1.4   Continued

Competencies Related to Assessment (continued)

4.4 Skill in
    4.41   Using qualitative and quantitative assessment
    4.42   Interpreting assessment data
    4.43   Decision making based on interpretation
    4.44   Making referrals for further assessment

Competencies Related to Preparation, Paperwork, and Meetings

5.1 Philosophy that supports
    5.11   IEPs, IFSPs, and individual physical education programs (IPEPs)
    5.12   Teamwork that requires meetings
    5.13   Lesson plans as means of achieving goals and objectives
5.2 Attitude of accountability
5.3 Knowledge of
    5.31   IEPs, IFSPs, and IPEPs
    5.32   Safety and management of environmental variables
    5.33   Purchase and care of equipment and supplies
    5.34   Exercise indications and contraindications for specific conditions
    5.35   Models that guide lesson planning and school district decision making
    5.36   Support service options
5.4 Skill in
    5.41   Making decisions about continuum of service options
    5.42   Paperwork

Competencies Related to Teaching, Counseling, and Coaching

6.1 Philosophy that supports
    6.11   Adaptation, creativity, individualization, and ecological task analysis
    6.12   Counseling as an integral part of teaching and coaching
    6.13   Self-concept, self-actualization, and empowerment as central constructs
    6.14   Humanistic and behavior management teaching practices
    6.15   Inclusion and least restrictive environment (LRE) strategies
    6.16   Transition services
6.2 Attitude of celebrating individual differences and lifespan ability to learn and change
6.3 Knowledge of
    6.31   Adaptation, creativity, and individualization theories, models, processes, principles, and pedagogy
    6.32   Scientific and psychosocial foundations of adaptation (e.g., biomechanics, exercise physiology, motor learning and control, human development, psychology, sociology, behavior management)
    6.33   Assessment, curriculum, instruction, and evaluation practices that contribute to good teaching
    6.34   Counseling theory and practice related to APA goals
    6.35   Pedagogy related to different teaching styles
    6.36   Pedagogy related to different goals and objectives
    6.37   Pedagogy related to different service delivery and curricular models
    6.38   Coaching and training techniques for wheelchair, Special Olympics, and other sport forms
6.4 Skill in
    6.41   Adapting instruction for person-environment interactions and for achievement of specific goals
    6.42   Using ecological task and activity analysis
    6.43   Motivating students and athletes to personal bests
    6.44   Socializing persons and families into active, healthy lifestyles
    6.45   Applying knowledge in teaching, counseling, and coaching

Competencies Related to Program Evaluation

7.1 Philosophy that supports continuous evaluation as an integral part of service delivery
7.2 Attitude of
    7.21   Striving for personal best while accepting that the best can always be improved
    7.22   Seeking ways to improve and being open to ideas for change

Table 1.4   Continued

7.3   Knowledge of
    7.31   Instruments and protocols for program evaluation
    7.32   Evaluation theories, models, principles, and strategies (formative and summative)
7.4   Skill in
    7.41   Using evaluation instruments and protocol, and, when necessary, developing new ones
    7.42   Applying evaluation theories, models, principles, and strategies

Competencies Related to Research

8.1   Philosophy that supports research as the method of choice for improving service delivery
8.2   Attitude of responsibility for
    8.21   Reading research to stay abreast of new knowledge
    8.22   Conducting research to contribute to the knowledge base
    8.23   Integrating research and teaching
    8.24   Monitoring ethical behaviors in research processes
8.3   Knowledge of
    8.31   Journals and books that publish research
    8.32   Meetings where research is presented
    8.33   Research methods and strategies, including statistics
    8.34   Computer- and hand-search techniques for locating research
    8.35   Topics on which research is needed
8.4   Skill in
    8.41   Locating, reading, understanding, and applying research
    8.42   Reviewing research related to selected topics
    8.43   Planning, conducting, and reporting research

OPTIONAL ACTIVITIES

1. Review one or more of the research studies that serve as primary sources for this chapter. Discuss your review(s) with a partner or small group and consider other research that needs to be undertaken in the same area. Note that only recent research (1995 and beyond) is included in this list. Note some books and position-statement type articles also qualify as primary sources, but they are not targeted in this assignment. What is the value of studying research? Where is most APA research found? What primary sources, providing new knowledge, can you find that have been published later than 2002?

    Full information for the following studies can be found in the **reference list** at the end of the textbook. As you find new studies, add them to the master reference list.

    Block (b), 1995
    Connolly, 1994
    Folsom-Meek & Rizzo, 2002
    Heikinaro-Johanssen, Sherrill, French, & Huuhka, 1995
    Hodge, Davis, Woodard, & Sherrill, 2002
    Houston-Wilson, Dunn, van der Mars, & McCubbin, 1997
    Kowalski & Rizzo, 1996
    Krueger, DiRocco, & Felix, 2000
    Lieberman, Dunn, van der Mars, & McCubbin, 2000
    Lytle & Collier, 2002

    Poretta, Surburg, & Jansma, 2002
    Vogler, Koranda, & Romance, 2000

2. Use the following list to check that you have learned the meaning of abbreviations commonly used in adapted physical activity. As you read future chapters, add to this list of abbreviations.

AAHPERD	CEC	NASPE
AAMR	ETA	NCPERID
AB	FAPE	PAP-TE-CA
ACSM	GE	PL
ADA	IDEA	TBI
APA	IEP	U.S.C.
APAQ	IFAPA	USOC
APENS	IFSP	WHO
CAPE	LRE	

3. Visit websites mentioned in this chapter and learn more about APENS and sport medicine credentials. Learn more about these and other kinds of credentials.

4. Many commercial movies and videotapes feature persons with disabilities. Make a list of some of these and document time spent at a movie or video evening with others.

5. Consider how a portfolio is different from a notebook. When your teachers or others evaluate your portfolio, what criteria will be used?

CHAPTER

2

Celebrating Differences, Planning Practical Experience, and Striving Toward Inclusion

Claudine Sherrill and Abu Yilla

Figure 2.1   **Three models to guide further thinking about personal beliefs.**

PHILOSOPHY COMPONENTS	Categorical, Deficit, or Medical Model	Social Minority or Disability Rights Model	Ecological Model
DISABILITY DEFINITION	Disability is equated with being defective, inferior, or less than.	Disability is equated with being different; different is *not* less than; it is simply being different.	Same, except disability is equated with being different and with person-environment interactions that cause difference.
IDENTITY PERCEPTION	Individuals have common anomalies and deficits that are perceived as personal tragedy.	Individuals have only one commonality (social stigma), and it should be eliminated.	Persons have some common barriers and enablers. Barriers must be eliminated.
TERMINOLOGY USE	Terminology tends to be negative (e.g., *defects, problems*).	Terminology tends to be positive or neutral with person-first emphasized.	Same with person-environment (ecological) variables emphasized.
SERVICE DELIVERY BASIS	Service delivery is based on defects, problems, or characteristics.	Service delivery is based on individual assessment data, personal strengths, and weaknesses.	Same, except assessment encompasses individuals and their ecosystems. Goals focus on barriers and enablers.
SERVICE DELIVERY PURPOSE	Purpose is to give advice, prescription, or remediation.	Purpose is to empower individual to assume active role in self-actualization.	Same as Social Minority Model
APPROPRIATE SYMBOLS	Graphics are passive. 	Graphics are active. 	Same as Social Minority Model

1. Create a personal professional preparation plan (PPPP) that will help achieve the goal of accepting and appreciating differences, including disabilities (see 1.2 on PAP-TE-CA Competencies, Table 1.4).
   (a) Start with your calendar in front of you and determine the time you want to spend on preparation during each 3 weeks of this course.
   (b) Decide also the distance you are willing to drive in order to have desired practical experiences.
   (c) Find out what practical experiences are available, given your time and distance limitations.
   (d) Develop a calendar for each 3-week period and indicate the days and hours that you plan to give to practical experience, to reading, and to small-group or partner discussion outside of class time.

2. Evaluate your personal learning every 3 weeks and revise your PPPP as needed. Consider whether this process is contributing to your self-initiative, self-determination, and thought processes.

3. Turn to the table of contents at the front of the book after you read this chapter, find the topics covered in Chapter 2, and see if you can summarize the essence of each topic.

4. Analyze which topics in Chapter 2 were most meaningful to you and why. Consider putting your analysis paper in your portfolio.

Duncan Wyeth, who is internationally known in the cerebral palsy sport movement, provided the initial ideas for Figure 2.1, which presents old and new ways of thinking about disability. Beginning this chapter with Wyeth's ideas emphasizes the tremendous importance of respecting the knowledge and insight of adults with disabilities and involving them in all aspects of professional preparation, including the content of textbooks. Giving Wyeth a voice in what should be taught also supports the slogan of disability advocates: *Nothing about us without us* (Charlton, 1998). Able-bodied persons (ABs) often have had little contact with peers different from themselves, their sport and physical activity, and their quality of life. Without such experience, how is it possible to think critically about philosophy and practices?

Concurrent with studying this chapter, readers should therefore engage in experiences that will broaden their contacts and maximize their ability to learn from persons with disabilities, especially adults, whose belief systems are based on many years of adapting and coping. This chapter will facilitate your making these contacts optimally interactive, meaningful, pleasant, equal status, and focused on such common goals as understanding diversity, stigma, discrimination, empowerment, and the like. The desired outcome is to progress in understanding, appreciating, and celebrating individual differences, including all forms of disability. Ideally, this will lead to long-standing equal-status friendships and to high-quality service delivery.

Thinking About Disability Models

Figure 2.1 presents three models, each reflecting a particular philosophy in relation to (a) definition of disability, (b) perception of disability identity, (c) use of terminology, (d) basis for service delivery, (e) purpose of service delivery, and (f) appropriate symbols. Each of these models is in use today, and each has many names.

Medical, Deficit, or Categorical Model

The first, originally designated as the *medical or deficit model,* has frequently been called the *categorical model* since the 1970s, when federal law indicated that students had to meet diagnostic criteria for specific disability categories in order to receive special education services, including adapted physical education. The word *categorical* is less pejorative than *deficit* and reflects the changing practices of medical and special education personnel who now try to address both strengths and weaknesses rather than focusing only on deficits.

Consider, for instance, is your adapted physical education course being developed around categories like mental retardation, learning disabilities, and blindness or is it generic (noncategorical) with emphasis on assessment of individual person-environment interactions in specific contexts and programming to eliminate barriers and maximize personal strengths? Perhaps your professor is trying to do both. Is this possible? Jot your thoughts down in your journal.

This textbook allows professors and students to choose content from three philosophical perspectives (see Parts I, II, and III, respectively). Parts I and II provide *noncategorical or generic approaches that avoid labeling people and instead focus on teacher roles, tasks, and competencies. Special attention is given to assessment and pedagogy for specific goals like inclusion and motor performance.* Part III gives a *categorical approach, offering specific information about each disability recognized in IDEA (see Appendix A). It is not possible to cover all three parts in one course. Readers have the opportunity to exercise freedom of choice.*

Social Minority Model

The second model in Figure 2.1 is a more recent development than the first model, which historically is the oldest. The *social minority model, a disability rights perspective,* began in the 1980s and is still evolving. To understand this model, consider the following beliefs of people with disabilities and the work of pioneers like Goffman (1963), Edgerton (1967), and Nixon (1989).

Duncan Wyeth's Beliefs

Duncan Wyeth (see Figures 2.1 and 2.2), who favors the social minority model, advocates that disability is simply difference, neither good nor bad, and only a part of the total person. For example, Wyeth sees his cerebral palsy (CP) speech as simply a CP accent analogous to a Spanish or French accent, and neither

Figure 2.2 Duncan Wyeth (*center*) has been an athlete, coach, and leader in the international cerebral palsy movement.

good nor bad. Wyeth insists that we respect his *personal identity* (biography) and not categorize him, as a whole person, as either able-bodied or disabled. Wyeth believes that he has nothing in common with other persons with disabilities except for *stigma* (others' perception of him as inferior) and *stigmatization* (hurtful actions). Wyeth's strong social science credentials allow him to speak knowledgeably about *stigma as the main experience that separates persons with and without disabilities* (see Figure 2.1). In all other ways, individuals with disabilities (like the rest of us) are unique, different from everyone else, and wanting acceptance for who they are and what they can do. Individual differences are to be celebrated! Diversity enriches! Note that these are Wyeth's beliefs, not facts, and you may agree or disagree with these and the other beliefs presented in this chapter.

Stigma and Stigmatization

Stigma (singular) and *stigmata* (plural) are concepts made meaningful to disability studies by sociologist Erving Goffman (1922–1982) in a classic book entitled *Stigma: Notes on the Management of a Spoiled Identity* (1963). Originally, **stigmata** were tattoo marks cut or burnt into the body by the ancient Greeks to indicate that the bearer was a slave or a criminal; these signs were "designed to expose something unusual or bad about the moral status of the signifier" (Goffman, 1963, p. 1).

Goffman, however, defined **stigma** as the "situation of the individual who is disqualified from full social acceptance . . . an attribute that is deeply discrediting . . . a failing, a shortcom-

ing, a handicap" (p. 3) . . . "an undesired differentness" (p. 5) from what ordinary persons expect that leads to a distancing categorization (i.e., not normal, not like me, not good). Today **stigma** refers to any physical, mental, or social indicator of difference, including labels and assistive devices, *that results in strained one-to-one interactions* (e.g., color of skin, religion, eyeglasses, clothing, crutches, obesity, speech impairment, mental retardation, low socioeconomic status). To better understand stigma, consider these reflections, one from published qualitative research and the remainder (those not cited) from the authors' extensive files of interview data:

> When I lost my arm and leg in the accident, I was really scared about whether anyone would find me attractive again. My boyfriend bagged out, almost immediately. I still have a lot of anger, and I hate the stares in the gym; I go there mostly to keep what body I've got left looking good so that I don't withdraw completely from the public life I used to have. *(Guthrie & Castelnuovo, 2001)*

> You can't understand what it's like. I go into a restaurant with my friends, and does the waitress ask me what I want to eat? No, she asks the guy sitting next to me, "what does your friend want to eat?" as though she thinks I can't talk or hear or something. It's like that everywhere I go. People can't seem to see beyond my cerebral palsy. They hardly ever look me in the eye and say hello. It's like they don't think we have anything in common, that I'm not worth bothering with.

> When I was about 6 or 7, I had warts all over my hands, hundreds of them. You know all of those childhood games where you get in a circle and hold hands. Well, the kids wouldn't hold my hands, wouldn't even touch me, unless the teacher forced them by saying, "hold her elbow." They teased me and nicknamed me "Wart." One day the warts just magically disappeared, but it took a long time before I was able to find a best friend like everyone else.

These reflections offer insight into *stigma* and the *stigmatization that persons with disabilities commonly experience.* **Stigmatization** refers to hurtful actions toward someone perceived as so different from the norm that the personal interactions are strained. **Stigma theory** and its predecessor self-presentation theory (Goffman, 1959, 1963) focus on one-to-one interactions, how individuals with and without disabilities present themselves to one another (e.g., body language, facial expressions, speech, physical proximity), and how persons with stigma manage their "spoiled identity," a self-perception derived from their strained relationships with others.

Illustrative of strategies employed by persons with disabilities to manage stigmata are passing, denial, covering, and withdrawal. Physical educators should recognize these strategies as ways to preserve diminishing self-esteem when feelings of inferiority and shame threaten mental health. For instance, in a mainstream physical education class, one child may say to another: "You're retarded." The response is almost always, "I am not," illustrative of denial and trying to pass, or some form of withdrawal like crying or going to the teacher. Two classic research studies enrich our understanding: a full-length book, *The Cloak of Competence: Stigma in the Lives of the Mentally Retarded,* by Edgerton (1967) and a case study of a partially sighted 9-year-old boy in different kinds of integrated community sport in the *Adapted Physical Activity Quarterly* (Nixon, 1989). These sources are particularly excellent because well-known sociologists conducted the research and gave leisure time and transition issues special attention. Managing stigma is also a major reason given for the ongoing search for a new organizational name by the American Association on Mental Retardation (2002b). The label *mental retardation* is almost universally believed to be stigmatizing.

Passing is hiding and/or denying an invisible disability (e.g., partial sight or learning disability) in an effort to appear like everyone else and thus be accepted. Often persons who are trying to pass think the disability is invisible when it is not, as in mental retardation or hearing loss, and associates may or may not act as enablers in letting them try to hide the stigma. How often, for instance, do people who need hearing aids or glasses refuse to use these accommodations? How often do university students who have signed up with the campus 504 office for instructional accommodations because of dyslexia (reading difficulty) or other specific learning problems share their disability with classmates? Why? French (1994), a partially sighted woman, stated that she felt pressured to pretend to be sighted in order to avoid people's (a) disapproval, (b) anxiety and distress, (c) disbelief, (d) disappointment and frustration, and (e) inability to have fun. French indicated she also used denial to live up to other persons' ideas of normalcy and to *collude* with other people's preferences. **Collude,** a term frequently used in disability studies, means to secretly cooperate for a fraudulent or deceitful purpose, to take the easy way instead of trying to correct misconceptions. Sometimes students collude with teachers when an inappropriate skill is being introduced (see Figure 2.3).

Edgerton (1967) coined the term *cloak of competence* to describe the ways that adults with mental retardation, making the transition into integrated community living, weave many layers of denial together into a cloak that they believe hides their disabilities. Edgerton presents many case studies to show that "the cloaks [denial, excuses] that they think protect them are in reality such tattered and transparent garments that they reveal their wearers in all their naked incompetence . . . like the emperor in the fairy tale who thought he was wearing the most elegant garments but, in fact, was wearing nothing at all" (Edgerton, 1967, p. 218).

Persons who cannot hide their disabilities are often taught **covering** so that the undesired difference is controlled or hidden as much as possible. Examples of *covering* are (a) using a handkerchief to dab the mouth when a disability causes drooling, (b) hiding a spastic or paralyzed hand in the pocket, and (c) wearing oversize clothes to minimize obesity or an unwanted pregnancy. Another strategy is **withdrawal.** Mental withdrawal into one's own world of thoughts occurs when a person remains in the setting but no longer tries to hear or understand. Physical withdrawal may be moving to the sidelines or failure to come to class or a social gathering. Recently, withdrawal of clumsy children from physical activities was partially explained as the

Figure 2.3 Is this boy with multiple disabilities (see Appendix A) in a motorized chair colluding? Why? What clues in this photo tell you that some of his disabilities are blindness and spastic cerebral palsy? What else does the photo tell you?

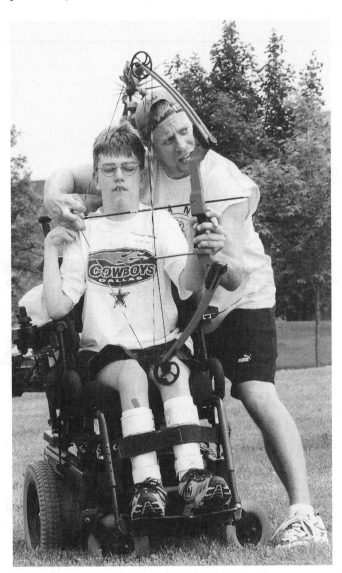

activity deficit hypothesis (Bouffard, Watkinson, Thompson, Dunn, & Romanow, 1996). This hypothesis asserts that physical inactivity, as well as withdrawal from activity, relates to negative social interactions evoked by movement difficulties. Fear of failure in the eyes of significant others (Conroy, 2001) also contributes to withdrawal in sport settings.

Michael Oliver's Beliefs

According to Michael Oliver, the author of *The Politics of Disablement* (1990), which is considered a classic in the disability studies literature, stigma theory is the "dominant conceptual framework for developing an understanding of the experience of disability" (p. 66). Nevertheless, Oliver, who has quadriplegia and leads the emergent British disability movement, criticizes stigma theory as too focused on one-to-one interactions to be useful in promoting social justice. Oliver believes that social minority theory should be expanded so that it describes, explains, and predicts societal change that will enhance social justice.

Oliver posits that disablement is caused, not by the common experience of stigma, but by *discrimination and oppression by the social majority, which has the political and economic power to remove barriers if it so chooses.* Whereas the understanding of stigma theory promotes *bottom-up changes* via one-to-one interactions, Oliver is striving for a transformation of social minority theory that will promote *top-down changes* via organizational and government mechanisms. Regardless of the perspective taken, the purpose is to *empower people with disabilities by changing able-bodied persons, either individually or collectively.* This means that professionals must possess the competencies for *reducing* unfavorable attitudes and practices.

Ecological Model

The ecological or individual differences model (see Figure 2.1) has guided some professionals since the 1950s (Wright & Barker, 1950) but is difficult to implement because of the complexity of assessing and changing person-environment interactions. Nevertheless, both special education and adapted physical education appear to be moving in an ecological direction (American Association on Mental Retardation, 2002a; Davis & Broadhead, in press; Davis & Burton, 1991; Hastie, 1995, 2000; Nihira, Weisner, & Bernheimer, 1994; Siedentop, 2002a).

The ecological model emphasizes that *differentness is the product of interactions between persons and their social and physical environments.* This perspective asserts that persons *with and without* disabilities are responsible for the attitudinal and other barriers that contribute to stigma. Individual, small-group, organization, and government change will occur only through *collaborative and sustained efforts in eliminating barriers and maximizing enablers.* This means that professionals must possess competencies for leading teams composed of diverse individuals in both participatory and directive change cycles (Hersey, Blanchard, & Johnson, 2001). *Participatory change* is bottom-up, whereas *directive change* is top-down (see Figure 2.4). Both forms of change involve understanding of change processes that influence knowledge, attitudes, and behavior.

Empowerment

Empowerment, the ultimate purpose of both the social minority model and the ecological model, is the interactional process by which persons, groups, and societies acquire the vision, motivation, resources, and power to strive toward being the best they can be (self-actualizing). *Among physical educators,* **personal best** is generally delimited to either healthy, active lifestyle or sport competition. Empowerment is complex (Jankowski, 1997; Pensgaard & Sorensen, 2002) and is addressed later in this book. For now, link empowerment with *Nothing about us without us* and *persons with and without disabilities collaborating in local, state, and federal policy making.*

The Meaning of Symbols

Figure 2.1 also depicts the **international symbol of access** and a futuristic rendition that features the access symbol as active rather than passive. The access symbol indicates only that ac-

cessibility standards have been met. It is not meant to accommodate any particular category of disability above others. Many nonwheelchair users require accessible environments (e.g., those with severe conditions that limit strength, cardiorespiratory function, or ease of mobility). The disability community points out that symbols affect perception and attitude. Active graphics more appropriately convey the idea of disability as only a small part of a self-actualizing person than do passive graphics.

Critical Thinking About Models

*Figure 2.1 summarizes three models, each of which reflects a different philosophy. Some persons take components from each model to build an **eclectic philosophy,** while other persons identify wholly with one model. Which are you? Which model do you prefer? Why? If you are eclectic, indicate the model that you identify with the most. State why. Read over*

Figure 2.4 **How do leaders change attitudes and behaviors: by participatory (bottom-up) change strategies, directive (top-down) change strategies, or both? The paths of directional change in both participatory and directive change show that *knowledge changes before attitudes.* Which leader (Wyeth or Oliver) recommends directive change?**

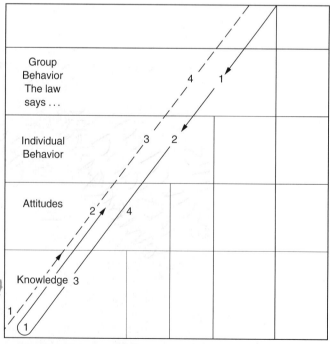

DIRECTIVE
TOP-DOWN CHANGE vIa
Organizational and
Government mandates
POWER, LAW AND POLITICS THEORY

PARTICIPATORY
BOTTOM-UP CHANGE via
one-to-one interactions
CONTACT THEORY

the philosophy that you rough drafted in conjunction with Chapter 1, and consider whether you have adequately addressed the six components included in Figure 2.1. Revise and expand as you wish. Remember philosophy changes as knowledge and experience change; philosophy is thus a work in progress.

♿ *Relate the process of writing your philosophy to the selection of practical experiences that will enhance your understanding of disability and your ability to participate in societal change. How might the information just presented help you avoid misconceptions and inappropriate behaviors? How might the information help you to empower persons with disabilities?*

Planning Practical Experience

Practicum experiences, service learning, internships, equal-status relationships, collaborative teamwork, field trips, and other kinds of contact between people with and without disabilities complement book learning. No matter how advanced one's knowledge is, there is *always* more to be learned through carefully planned experiences. Consider this statement by a university professor:

> I love wheelchair basketball, wheelchair dance, Special Olympics, sled hockey, goal ball, beep baseball. These are a part of my life, a way that I keep learning, my personal choice in how I use my free time. I also try to spend at least one day a week in the schools giving myself field trips to see new things, learn from new people. Likewise, when I plan vacations, I weave in field trips to famous places (e.g., Perkins School for the Blind, Gallaudet

University, Special Olympics headquarters, Lauren Lieberman's Camp Abilities, Courage Center in Minnesota, the Breckenridge Outdoor Education Center in Colorado, the Bob Steadward Centre in Canada . . . and, of course, my life wouldn't be nearly as rich if I didn't get involved in Summer and Winter Paralympics and in the Unified Sports Program of Special Olympics. There's so much to choose from.

Clearly, a number of diverse experiences can be used to acquire knowledge. Most adapted physical activity courses require 1 to 2.5 hr of practicum experience each week (Hodge & Jansma, 1999). Some instructors require experience in on-campus programs, whereas others permit free choice of experiences available in the community (Connolly, 1994; Folsom-Meek, Nearing, Groteluschen, & Krampf, 1999; Hodge et al., 2002).

Types of Practical Experiences

Traditional practicum programs bring school-aged children with disabilities to the university gymnasium and swimming pool one or two times a week. Undergraduates gain awareness-level knowledge and skills by working throughout a semester (or quarter) with one or two children, doing assessments, and developing lesson plans. Sometimes two undergraduates are assigned to a child who requires one-to-one instruction (see Figure 2.5). The professor responsible for the introductory theory class, often with the help of graduate students, mentors the undergraduates and stresses relationships between theory and practice. Public school teachers and aides may also help. Disability types vary, but most children who are bused to the university come from self-contained special education classes. This type of practicum provides comfortable first-level exposure and improves attitudes toward *teaching* movement to children with disabilities, but it is

Figure 2.5   Two undergraduates in a practicum setting work together in teaching this boy with spina bifida (see index) reaching and grasping activities. What other things does this photo illustrate?

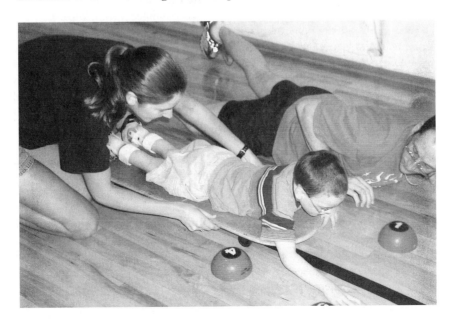

Figure 2.6 Abu Yilla (on the right) was a student athlete funded by the University of Texas at Arlington. Do you have wheelchair users on your campus or in your community who might wish to become friends?

not likely to change attitudes toward *including* children with disabilities in general physical education, a practice called *inclusive teaching* (Hodge et al., 2002). To change attitudes toward inclusion, university students must have successful experiences in inclusive settings. Practica in both self-contained and inclusive contexts are strongly recommended.

When transporting children to the university cannot be arranged, undergraduates travel to a nearby school and assist the physical educator or special educator with a self-contained or an inclusive general physical education class. In off-campus practica, the public school teacher is typically in charge, and the university professor and/or graduate students serve a secondary role in mentoring the undergraduates.

Graduate students develop the competence they will need as university-based teacher educators through experience in mentoring and supervising undergraduates and in planning and conducting action research. Graduate students also often contract for internships with related services personnel (e.g., occupational, physical, or speech therapists) or interdisciplinary instructional teams who can give them new knowledge and perspectives. Clearly, whatever the experience chosen, graduate students are expected to derive different competencies than undergraduates. Often, the graduate student experience is an independent study that affords one-to-one time with a professor in research design, data collection, publication, and preparation of oral or poster presentations. Ideally, such research provides experience with collaborative teams of parents, practitioners, and university-based teacher educators and enhances the adapted physical education knowledge base in classroom pedagogy, disability sport, behavior management, and outcome achievement. In short, graduate students (regardless of past teaching experience) need practicum experiences as much as undergraduates.

In addition to practicum experience with children in physical education settings, many undergraduates and graduates opt for *service-learning* experiences in after-school sport programs for children or adults. The most common of these is Special Olympics and districtwide sport days sponsored by schools, organizations, or agencies. Interscholastic athletics for student-athletes with disabilities is attracting many volunteers also. As of 2002, Minnesota, Illinois, and Georgia were offering such programs (Matter, Nash, & Frogley, 2002), and more states are expected to follow their lead. This type of practical experience is often called **service learning** (Martinek & Hellison, 1997), because volunteers learn while performing services (e.g., conducting events, officiating, scoring, setting up and taking down equipment, observing and writing articles for newspaper and magazines).

Service learning also includes participatory roles at practices, tournaments, and meets for athletes with disabilities (e.g., wheelchair tennis or basketball, quad rugby, goal ball, Deaf sport). This kind of opportunity is discussed later. Observation of such events, and getting acquainted with adult athletes and their families, also provides opportunities to supplement textbook content. Observation, of course, cannot count as service learning or as volunteer work.

Future professionals may enhance their learning by observational or participatory experience in IEP or IFSP meetings; inclusive programs in schools, recreation centers, and other settings; parent and spouse support groups; disability sport events; camps; and the like (see Figure 2.6). The opportunities depend largely on how near the university is to agency and community programs. Many students opt for internships at camps or disability sport programs rather than traditional summer school coursework. The best learning, however, often comes through optional one-to-one experiences that lead to long-standing friendships. *Approximately 11% of individuals with disabilities enroll in higher education,* so it is quite possible to choose new friends from among this population. Initial contacts can be made through incidental meetings on campus or through university offices that pertain to students with disabilities, 504 accessibility, or multicultural affairs. Such offices typically maintain a list of students who have requested volunteer tutors, note takers, readers, or other kinds of support. Sometimes campus activities and projects offer opportunities for students with or without disabilities to work together. For example, research describes such efforts in making campus sports and recreation programs accessible to university students with mobility impairments (Promis, Erevelles, & Matthews, 2001).

Reflective Thinking and Knowledge Construction

To encourage reflective thinking, many instructors require informal writing of journals, logs, case studies, letters, stories, or skits as evidence that students are interpreting and giving personal meaning to new experiences (Connolly, 1994; Tsand, 2000; Xiang, Lowry, & McBride, 2002). Examples of reflective writing about practica appear in Connolly (1994) and on your textbook's website at www.mhhe.com/hhp. For graduate students, helpful references are Clandinin and Connelly (1994) and Brya and Karp (2000). Instructors frequently ask students to select the best examples of their reflective writing to include in their portfolios for midterm and/or end-of-semester course evaluation (Lieberman & Houston-Wilson, 2002; Senne & Rikard, 2002). To better understand why instructors make such assignments, consider this passage from a book on teaching for diversity and social justice:

> Experiential pedagogies usually start from a structured experience and focus the learner's reflections upon that experience. Experience alone is insufficient to be called experiential education, and it is the reflection process which turns experience into experiential education. (Adams et al., 1997, p. 33)

Experiential education has its roots in **constructivist theory,** which can be traced to John Dewey (1859–1952), who created the motto, *We learn to do by doing.* **Constructivism** is a theory on teaching and learning that is based on the belief that students can *actively construct their own knowledge, if given appropriate experience and guidance in learning to reflectively and critically think.* According to Dewey (1933), who is considered the father of the critical thinking tradition, **reflective thinking** is analyzing one's beliefs, examining the effects of one's actions, and acquiring attitudes of open-mindedness. Many contemporary educators use the terms *reflective* and *critical* interchangeably (Fisher, 2001). When prospective teachers engage in active construction of knowledge through searching for personal meaning in new facts and experiences, they are gaining competence needed in the future to teach their own students how to reflectively and critically think (Macdonald et al.,

2002). This skill is a high priority in the public schools (Chen, 1998; Tsangardou & O'Sullivan, 1997).

Research on Practical Experience

Research indicates that hands-on experience for future professionals leads to *greater perceived competence* in working with people with disabilities and/or *better attitudes* toward including children with disabilities in general physical education (e.g., Folsom-Meek et al., 1999; Hodge & Jansma, 1999; Rizzo & Kirkendall, 1995; Rowe & Stutts, 1987; Tripp & Sherrill, 1991). Some research shows improvement in *perceived* competence but not in attitudes (Hodge et al., 2002). Typically, *perceived competence* is measured by response on a 3-point scale to the question "How competent do you feel teaching children with disabilities?" *Attitude toward teaching children with disabilities in a general education class* is measured with an attitude survey by Rizzo (1984), which has been revised several times (Folsom-Meek & Rizzo, 2002). For an example of items on Rizzo's attitude survey, see Table 2.1. As yet, few studies relate perceived competence to actual competence, probably because this variable is hard to define and measure. Therefore, only self-ratings of behaviors have been used (Conaster, Block, & Gansneder, 2002). Much research is needed in all areas of physical education professional preparation and teaching that relate to inclusion of students with disabilities.

Take Rizzo's attitude survey and analyze why you answered each item for the four separate disability groups as you did. How much contact have you had with each group? Why? Do you prefer to work with individuals with some disabilities more than others? Why? Jot your ideas down in your journal.

Some research is **qualitative,** meaning that words instead of statistics are used to convey findings. **Qualitative action research** often involves **participatory observation,** in which the researcher is dually the teacher or coach or someone who participates with (as well as observes) the person or group being studied. Keeping a journal of your participatory observation in a course or practicum can serve as an introduction to **action research** (e.g., weaving together action on the job with systematic reflection about how pedagogy and other action can be improved). Many teachers do action research every day but are unaware that the scholarly world considers their structured, reflective teaching to be research.

Keeping a journal also encourages reflection about inclusive social interaction. For example, the benefits derived from getting to know an adult with a disability are described in detail in *Venus on Wheels: Two Decades of Dialogue on Disability, Biography, and Being Female in America,* by Gelya Frank (2000). This book began as a journal. While teaching an undergraduate class, Frank (a graduate assistant) began a close, lasting friendship with a woman about her own age, Diane DeVries, who had been born without arms and legs. Frank describes her first impressions:

> I watched a blond woman enter the classroom in an electric wheelchair. She looked to be in the fullness

Table 2.1   Illustrative survey items from the Physical Educators' Attitude Toward Teaching Individuals with Disabilities III (PEATID-III) by Terry Rizzo (1995).

Teachers who take the PEATID are instructed to respond to questions like the following according to their understanding of PEATID definitions of disability conditions.

SD = strongly disagree
D = disagree
U = undecided
A = agree
SA = strongly disagree

Students labeled _____ will learn more rapidly if they are taught in my regular physical education class with nondisabled students.

Emotional/behavioral disorder	SD	D	U	A	SA
Specific learning disability	SD	D	U	A	SA
Mild–moderate mentally impaired	SD	D	U	A	SA
Moderate–severe mentally impaired	SD	D	U	A	SA

Students labeled _____ will develop a more favorable self-concept as a result of learning motor skills in my regular physical education class with nondisabled peers.

Emotional/behavioral disorder	SD	D	U	A	SA
Specific learning disability	SD	D	U	A	SA
Mild–moderate mentally impaired	SD	D	U	A	SA
Moderate–severe mentally impaired	SD	D	U	A	SA

As a physical education teacher, I need more coursework and training before I will feel comfortable teaching physical education classes with students labeled _____ with nondisabled students.

Emotional/behavioral disorder	SD	D	U	A	SA
Specific learning disability	SD	D	U	A	SA
Mild–moderate mentally impaired	SD	D	U	A	SA
Moderate–severe mentally impaired	SD	D	U	A	SA

of womanhood, wearing a sleeveless white top with narrow straps. Her tapered arm stumps seemed daringly exposed, and the mysterious configuration of her hips was encased in tight blue jeans that ended where her legs should have begun. She maneuvered her wheelchair with a lever control mounted on one side to face the lectern . . . she took notes holding her pen between arm and cheek . . . As I observed this woman, I imagined that she lived at home with her parents in a sheltered and isolated household. I supposed that she would never marry or have sex. I guessed that she couldn't even masturbate. In a short time I was proved wrong on all of these counts, and perhaps I should not have been surprised. *(Frank, 2000, pp. 1–2)*

When I first noticed Diane, I had no special interest in studying disability. But I was attracted to phenomenology, a branch of philosophy that deals with . . . how people understand one another. My fascination with Diane prompted me to explore the sources in myself that made a woman with no legs so intriguing. Through systematic self-reflection I probed my identification and empathy with her situation, uncovering my own invisible disabilities and then disentangling from the way Diane sees herself. *(Frank, 2000, pp. 3–4)*

These passages are examples of reflective writing. The book provides reflective thinking over a period of 20 years during which Diane married, divorced, finished a master's degree, found employment, and engaged in the struggles common to many women. In her rich description of all of this, Frank weaves sociological theory into her reflective thinking as she strives to maintain a balance in her learning between real-life experience and book knowledge. Thinking back over her personal growth, Frank said,

I was attracted to study Diane's life because of her appearance. My first impressions were of a person with enormous limitations, a victim. With clarification of my own mirroring, I found a survivor. Writing about her life while reflecting on my assumptions helped me to understand my hidden disabilities, come to terms with my own limitations, and grasp how they affected the images I was constructing of Diane. *(Frank, 2000, p. 162)*

The **mirroring phenomenon** referred to in this passage *is seeing parts of one's self in others and thus using reflection about others to think more deeply about yourself.* One of Frank's students, after hearing a speech by Diane, exhibits mirroring in the following reflection:

I could not look at Diane when I first noticed her; of course my emotions were torn between staring and blinding. What was so threatening and appealing at the same time? . . . She is one of us, yet not one of us . . . she has no place, she must be hidden for we cannot place and categorize her . . . it is I who am crippled not she—she can tolerate me but I can't tolerate her . . . Why is she evil then—because she points to my inadequacy. *(Frank, 2000, p. 104)*

This final quotation by one of Frank's undergraduates describes the discomfort, or strained relationship, that many persons feel when they first begin interacting with adults with visible disabilities. Future professionals need many diverse practical experiences to "work through" negative or ambivalent reactions to adults who are different. Within the next decade, they will be collaborating with many physical educators, recreators, and special educators with visible disabilities. Many such persons are currently enrolled in university professional preparation programs. Texas Woman's University, for instance, has a doctoral level federal grant for funding the graduate education of persons with disabilities who wish to specialize in adapted physical education. Some universities give athletic scholarships to elite-level athletes with disabilities (e.g., University of Illinois at Urbana and University of Texas at Arlington). The trend is education of university students with and without disabilities in the same courses and practica (i.e., inclusive teaching).

Equal-Status Relationships

Equal-status relationships are usually friendships or partnerships but may be *any kind of collaboration in which both parties share power, benefit to the same extent (although perhaps in different ways), respect and value one another equally, and experience mutual satisfaction and enjoyment in being together.* Practical experience with children provides many benefits but does not meet the criteria for an equal-status relationship, because power is not shared equally among adults and children, and both parties seldom benefit equally. Likewise, power is seldom shared equally among teachers and students, therapists and clients, or other twosomes where one has the major responsibility for facilitating change.

The concept of equal-status relationships evolved out of **contact theory** *(Allport, 1954), which sets forth the conditions under which contact between two people improves attitudes toward one another and leads to supportive behaviors.* Equal-status relationships, like friendships, generally require a long time to develop and seem to progress best when both persons are about the same age, have common interests and goals, and understand the importance of equalizing leadership and followership, talking and listening, and other elements of shared power. According to Fishbein (2002), most classroom inclusion strategies, as well as research on contact theory, are flawed because the equal-status condition has not been addressed properly. Charlton (1998), who entitled his book *Nothing About Us Without Us,* is building on the equal-status condition of contact theory when he advocates full and equal participation of people with disabilities in events and activities that involve them, including decision making at the managerial and governing levels.

Figure 2.7 shows the author with Abu Yilla, a contributor to Chapter 2 and a coequal friend of many years. Both have

Figure 2.7 Dr. Abu Yilla, university professor and Dallas Mavericks basketball player, celebrating a birthday with Claudine Sherrill. What things make their long-standing friendship equal status?

doctoral degrees, are employed by a university, and teach adapted physical education and sociology of sport. Abu was born in Sierra Leone, Africa, and educated in England and Texas. Claudine was born in Indiana and educated in Texas and New York. Abu had polio at the age of 3, used long-leg braces and crutches for many years, now prefers a wheelchair, and is a wheelchair basketball expert. Claudine had severe asthma at the age of 3, and intermittently for many years; now copes with hearing loss and osteoarthritis; and is a generic adapted physical activity expert. Abu and Claudine bring much rich diversity to each other's thinking and value each other socially as well as professionally. They share interest in exclusion, stigma, prejudice, discrimination, and oppression, and each has experienced these conditions. Each feels passionately about the benefits of sport and physical activity for everyone and the need for everyone to become involved in the politics of change. Can you visualize their equal-status friendship?

Consider how diverse your friends are and the ways that you spend your free time. Do you tend to socialize mostly with persons of your same athletic ability, health status, race, and religion? Why? What efforts do you exert to make new friends? Make a list of your friends and acquaintances with disabilities and chronic health conditions. Do you consider your relationship with these friends to be equal status? Why? Outside of your work or practicum-type experiences, how much contact per week do you have with people with disabilities? Why? Do you wish to set goals to change status quo with regard to your friendships and acquaintances? Why? Respond to the questions in your journal. Discuss your responses with others, and reflect on what they offer. Include illustrative direct quotations from your discussions.

Defining Disability Using the International Perspective

Disability is defined in many different ways by national and international agencies. Most definitions are created by the social majority to determine eligibility for services, insurance, funding, and the like. In the United States, definitions for determining eligibility for special education services, including adapted physical education, come from federal law (see Appendix A).

The DSM and ICD: Sources for Specialists

Definitions used primarily to determine health care needs, insurance, and other sources of money come mainly from two sources. The *Diagnostic and Statistical Manual of Mental Disorders (DSM-IV-TR)* is published by the American Psychiatric Association (APA, 2000). Several definitions in this text come from the *DSM. The International Statistical Classification of Disease and Related Health Problems (ICD-10)* is published by the World Health Organization (WHO, 1993); it is widely used throughout the world except in the United States. "The *ICD-10* is not scheduled for implementation in the United States until 2004" (American Association on Mental Retardation, 2002a, p. 102).

The ICF-World Health Organization: Information for Everyone

Most professionals know by now that the World Health Organization replaced its 1980 definitions of disability, impairment, and handicap in 2001. The new definitions appear in a document entitled *International Classification of Functioning, Disability, and Health (ICF)*, which has been widely disseminated with special attention given to the model in Figure 2.8. The *ICF* model of human functioning and disability conceives **functioning** as an interactive person-environment process, which supports the use of the ecological perspective in this textbook.

The 2001 Definition of Disability

The new *ICF* definitions are as follows:

Impairments: *Problems in body functions and structures, such as significant loss or deviation.* Impairments include intellectual and cognitive dysfunctions that can be discovered or verified through techniques that medical personnel routinely use in diagnosis for treatment and insurance purposes. An individual may look or perform differently from the societal or cultural norm, but this deviance is not considered a disability if the person can benefit from general education services, is employed (as an adult) with a sufficient salary to live without agency assistance, and does no harm to individuals or the environment.

Disabilities: *Activity limitations.* These must be severe enough to interfere with activities of daily living (ADL) like eating and dressing, general education, employment, communication, mobility, and the like. Disabilities are specific to particular areas of

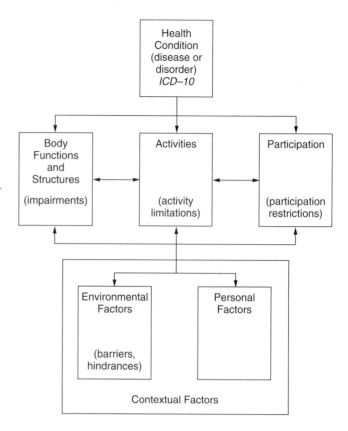

Figure 2.8 The *ICF* model of human functioning and disability. Adapted from p. 18, *International Classification of Functioning, Disability, and Health (ICF)* of World Health Organization (2001).

performance. This interpretation is similar to that of IDEA in which a child can be limited and thus eligible for special education services in some school subjects but not others.

Restrictions: *Barriers to participation caused by person-environment interactions.* Related to accessibility of resources, accommodations, and/or services.

Handicaps: *A term no longer used by the WHO.*

Considering Labels and Contextual Factors

The WHO definitions seem to support medical classification or labeling of impairments by the most specific term available (e.g., severe mental retardation, Down syndrome, spina bifida, muscular dystrophy). The identification of limitations and restrictions is left to individualized, personalized assessment of the person, the environment, and the person-environment interactions. Figure 2.8 shows how contextual factors are broken down into environmental and personal factors that interact (see arrows connecting these two factors). The resulting interactions must be used in relating activity limitations to eligibility for services. According to WHO (2001), *if activities can be changed, or adapted, so that limitations are minimized or eliminated, then the disability no longer exists.* These concepts have formed the basis for much of the revision of this text.

What are the strengths and weaknesses of the model shown in Figure 2.8? What specific activity limitations should (a) make a child eligible for separate, specially designed physical education conducted by an adapted physical education specialist and (b) make an adult eligible to belong to a wheelchair basketball team?

Characteristic: A Frequently Misused Term

Characteristic refers to a highly stable individual quality, a constituent or inborn trait, that is difficult or impossible to change. The opposite of a *characteristic* is a **variable,** something that can be changed, such as a specific behavior or environmental factor. In the educational context, where emphasis is on facilitating change, the focus should be on behaviors, attitudes, and knowledge rather than characteristics.

Historically, the term *characteristic* and its various synonyms (e.g., *attribute, distinguishing feature*) have been misused in much special education and adapted physical activity literature. Teachers have been encouraged to memorize lists of physical, mental, social, and emotional characteristics that presumably capture the uniqueness of specific disability categories, like mental retardation and blindness. Today, this practice is believed to cause misconceptions, prejudice, and discrimination. The trend is away from generalization. Federal law now requires assessment to determine individual strengths and weaknesses and supports service delivery that enables the achievement of personalized goals and objectives.

Technology and pedagogy are becoming increasingly sophisticated, so that, if money is available, almost every aspect of body structure and function can be changed. For example, surgery can modify the facial features of individuals with Down syndrome, cleft palate, and other anomalies; hormone therapy can help dwarfs and others with short stature grow; computers can read words aloud for persons with blindness; and artificial limbs can enable individuals with disabilities to achieve the same speeds and distances as nondisabled peers. The term *characteristic,* as used in the past, is outdated, inappropriate, and dehumanizing. *When describing a disability, think of individuals and specific behaviors that express uniqueness.*

Guidelines for Speaking and Writing

Use the following criteria to guide writing and speaking about persons with disabilities (Research and Training Center for Independent Living, 2000):

1. Do not refer to a disability unless it is crucial to the story.
2. Avoid portraying persons with disabilities who succeed as superhuman. This implies that persons who are disabled have no talents or unusual gifts.
3. Do not sensationalize a disability by saying "afflicted with," "victim of," and so on. Instead, say "person who has multiple sclerosis," "person who had polio."
4. Avoid labeling persons into groups, as in "the disabled," "the deaf," "a retardate," "an arthritic." Instead, say, "people who are deaf," "person with arthritis," "persons with disabilities."

5. Use person-first terminology. Say, "people or persons with disabilities" or "person who is blind," rather than "disabled persons" or "blind person."
6. Avoid using emotional descriptors, such as "unfortunate," "pitiful," and so on. Emphasize abilities, such as "uses a wheelchair/braces," (rather than "confined to a wheelchair"), "walks with crutches/braces" (rather than "is crippled"), "is partially sighted" (rather than "is partially blind").
7. Avoid implying disease when discussing disabilities. A disability such as Parkinson's disease might be caused by a sickness but is not a disease itself; nor is the person necessarily chronically ill. Persons with disabilities should not be referred to as "patients" or "cases" unless they are under medical care.

Many other guidelines are available, but most university students rely heavily on the American Psychological Association's (APA's) *Publication Manual,* which provides guidelines to reduce bias in language with regard to disabilities, age, racial and ethnic identity, gender, and sexual orientation. The only guideline under disabilities not covered in the earlier list recommends avoiding *differently abled, special,* and *challenged* because these "are often considered euphemistic and should be used only if the people in your study prefer those terms" (APA, 2001, p. 69).

Lifespan Concerns

Everyone interested in persons with disabilities must be knowledgeable about physical activity and sport for the different age groups. Lifelong practices for an active, healthy lifestyle typically begin at very young ages. Likewise, heart disease and other conditions previously believed to begin in adulthood are now known to start with childhood inactivity and poor nutrition practices. Exercise scientists and kinesiologists need to join adapted physical educators in the study of relationships between disability and sport.

Individuality and Uniqueness Expressed Through Sports

This chapter now presents accounts of several adults with various psychomotor concerns. The role of physical activity and sport in expressing individuality and uniqueness is explored, as is the personal meaning of feeling different.

Asthma and Health Problems: Case Study 1

• *I was a sickly child, missing approximately 1 week of every 6 weeks of school because of various combinations of asthma, colds, and respiratory illness. My earliest memories center on looking out the windows at the other kids, engaged in fast, wonderful, vigorous games, and wanting desperately to be with them and like them. I was skinny and unfit. Exercise almost always made me wheeze, and I hated my lungs and what I perceived to be an inefficient body that wouldn't let me do and be what I wanted. I read a lot and made good grades, but I didn't feel good about myself.*

By high school, I seemed magically to have outgrown my asthma. Physical education became my favorite class, and the after-school sports program was my life. I felt suddenly alive, really alive. My mind and body were finally working together, and I believed I could do everything. I never achieved the skill level of my friends who had rich, active childhoods, but I made up for this with enthusiasm and extra effort. I felt like my PE teacher liked me for myself, not because I made good grades or was one of her best athletes. She spent a lot of time talking with us kids. We all had a lot of problems, but we would never have gone to the school counselor.

When it was time to enter college, I agonized over whether to major in physical education or medicine. Physical education won. I loved the active life (sports, aquatics, primitive camping), and somehow I felt that PE had made me a happy, whole, integrated person. PE had also helped me to make friends and feel that people cared about me. I worshiped my PE teachers and wanted to be just like them: to help others as they had helped me.

When I got to college, I found out I wasn't as good (skill wise) as other PE majors. I made As on knowledge tests and Cs on skill tests. Amount of effort didn't seem to matter, especially in hand-eye coordination activities. Field hockey provided some success, primarily because I trained so hard I could run longer and faster than my peers. But I wanted to be with my friends and play on the varsity basketball, volleyball, and softball teams!

I discovered that self-esteem is multidimensional. I felt good about myself as a studious, fit individual, but I mourned the highly skilled athlete that day by day I failed to become. It often seemed that I loved physical education more than any of my athlete friends did. They took for granted what I wanted so much. •

These words, from the author of this textbook, illustrate that sports and games can be meaningful to persons who are not well skilled and/or who have health and fitness problems. Physical education can accomplish many goals. Chief among these is the opportunity to share the fun and excitement of the sport setting and to be with peers perceived as popular, healthy, and happy. Persons who miss school frequently and/or lack the stamina to engage in vigorous activities often feel left out. Physical education, if properly conducted, provides an environment in which meaningful contacts are made with significant others. These contacts should lead to shared after-school and weekend experiences in sports. The process of making and keeping friends, and thereby feeling included rather than excluded, is called **social competency** in this text. This goal requires that teachers play an active role in helping students to care about each other and to structure their leisure to include physical activity with friends.

Asthma, diabetes, obesity, cancer, cardiovascular disorders, seizures, and similar problems are called **other health-impaired (OHI)** conditions and are covered in Part III of this book. Federal legislation defines OHI conditions as "Limited strength, vitality, or alertness due to chronic or acute health problems which adversely affect a child's educational performance" (20 U.S.C. 1401(3)(A) and (B); 1401(26)). **Acute** means

rapid onset, severe symptoms, and a short course; **chronic** means of long duration. Asthma, for example, is a chronic condition that is typically *managed* by medication and healthful living practices (e.g., balanced diets and regular eating, sleeping, and exercise practices). Occasionally, however, an acute episode (i.e., an asthma attack) may occur. How individuals cope with acute and chronic OHI conditions varies widely.

Conditions like asthma, diabetes, obesity, and cardiovascular disorders require individualization in regard to exercise. Both perceived and real limitations must be addressed, and students often need extra help in achieving physical education goals and in developing attitudes and habits conducive for lifelong health and fitness. When school district budgets are too limited to classify students with OHI concerns as needing special education, the Americans with Disabilities Act (ADA) may be used to justify support services. Information on procedures appears in Chapter 4. The knowledge and creativity of the general physical educator determine the extent that special needs are met. In such cases, general physical educators are delivering adapted physical education services.

Clumsiness: Case Study 2

• *In about the third grade, I could neither catch nor throw a ball with the proficiency that would enhance my self-concept. By the time I finished third grade, I had come to detest that ball because it was the source of all those feelings of inadequacy, which, at the time, mattered most. One day, after an eternity of missed catches, inaccurate throws, strikeouts, and being chosen last (or being told by the team captain to play in the outfield because the ball seldom got that far), I managed to get that damned ball when nobody was looking. Intent upon punishing that ball for all it had done to me, I took it to the farthest corner of the playground and literally buried it. For a while, I felt good because I knew my spheroid enemy, in its final resting place, couldn't hurt me any more. Unfortunately, our class soon got a new ball. (Eichstaedt & Kalakian, 1987, p. 89)* •

These memories come from Leonard (Lennie) Kalakian, professor emeritus of physical education at Mankato State University in Minnesota, who has coauthored an excellent adapted physical education textbook: *Developmental/Adapted Physical Education: Making Ability Count.* In a telephone interview, Dr. Kalakian said:

> Yes, I was a clumsy child. It took me a long time to find a sport I was really good at, but eventually I became an All-American Gymnast. Obviously, sport and movement were very important to me. When it came time to enter the university, I majored in physical education.

Clumsiness, or physical awkwardness, is the inability to perform culturally normative motor activities with acceptable proficiency (Wall, 1982). The prevalence of clumsiness for general education students who have no sensory, motor, emotional, or learning problems is estimated at 10 to 15%. Prevalence of clumsiness for special education students is much higher.

Clumsiness is related to perceptual-motor function, sensory integration, and information processing. A clumsy individual may demonstrate an acceptable level of proficiency in a **closed skill** (one done in a predictable environment that requires no quick body adjustments) but perform miserably in an **open skill** (one done in an unpredictable, changing environment that requires rapid adjustments). Thus, clumsiness is typically evidenced in activities of balance, bilateral coordination, agility, and ball handling, particularly in game settings.

Clumsiness is caused by both human and environmental barriers (limitations). Among these are insufficient opportunities for instruction and practice; delayed or abnormal development of the nervous, muscular, or skeletal systems; genetically imposed body size and motor coordination limitations; and problems related to space, equipment, surfaces, noise, visibility, weather, allergens, improper clothing, and rules or instructions.

The effect of clumsiness on an individual's mental health depends largely on the personal meaning of sport and movement. How significant others in the ecosystem view sport and value physical prowess affects how clumsy persons feel about themselves. If, for example, the father or mother is an athlete, expectations are probably high that a child will do well in sports. If one's best friend is on a team, achieving similar status may be terribly important. Attitudes toward self, based largely on perceived competence and beliefs about what significant others hold important, predispose individuals toward active or passive lifestyles. This, in turn, may help to decrease or increase clumsiness.

Clumsiness is particularly debilitating because it is a global manifestation that is easily identified but poorly understood. Everyone can pick out "the clumsy kid" in an activity; typically, such persons endure a lot of teasing. No one wants them on their team. The teacher may repeatedly single them out for special help. The ecosystem of clumsy children is different from that of classmates; thus, clumsiness is a psychosocial problem as well as a physical one. Some children, like young Lennie, express their individualities and uniqueness through action. They keep trying new activities until they find one compatible with their body build and motor coordination. Others withdraw and seek success and self-esteem in other areas.

For clumsy students, the development of positive self-concept is an especially important goal. Through individual and small-group movement activities and counseling, students learn to accept limitations that cannot be changed and to adapt the environment so as to make the most of their strengths. Achievement of this goal requires small class sizes so teachers can work individually with students.

Clumsiness is a disability in most physical education classes, yet is not defined as a disability in special education legislation. However, the syndrome of *developmental coordination disorder* (DCD) has been recognized by several organizations (Henderson, 1994; Henderson & Henderson, 2002) and is the theme of Volume 11 (1994) of the *Adapted Physical Activity Quarterly*. Adapted physical activity professionals need to consider what is a disability in a movement setting and should not be governed by eligibility criteria derived by special educators for classroom academic work (Watkinson et al., 2001).

Learning Disabilities: Case Study 3

Learning disabilities (LD) is the special education condition most prevalent in the United States. Over 50% of the students receiving services have a specific learning disability. By definition, these students have average or better intelligence quotients (i.e., they are not mentally retarded). Students with LD are identified on the basis of significant discrepancies between intellectual abilities and academic achievement. Specific problems are diagnosed in the ability to listen, think, speak, read, write, spell, or do mathematical calculations. Typically, students with LD demonstrate an uneven learning profile: They are good in some subjects and bad in others.

Don, a high school counselor, was diagnosed as having a learning disability in the fourth grade. Subsequently, he received individual assistance with math and other problems in a resource room for 3 years. He recalls:

• *I was the fourth boy in a family where education was really important. My father was a university professor, and my mother was a librarian. I don't remember being different until the second or third grade. I loved to read, and it was easy for me, but there were crazy little discrepancies in my learning pattern. Like I didn't memorize the alphabet until I was 7 years old. I just couldn't remember the sequence. My parents thought I would never learn to tie my shoes. I'd watch and I'd listen, but I just couldn't make my fingers do what I wanted.*

But math was what made my life really miserable. In the fourth grade, we started having story problems. You know, things like: "Your car is going 50 miles an hour. It takes 5 hours to drive from Dallas to Austin. How many miles will you drive?" The longer and more complex those sequences got, the more I was lost. In the fourth grade, I brought home a D in arithmetic. Everything else was Bs and Cs, but my parents had a fit. They said my IQ was 125 and I wasn't trying. The school gave me a bunch of tests and assigned me to a resource room 1 hour a day. Although I hated to admit it, I was having trouble remembering and dealing with sequences in my other classes also. Like in gym, this teacher would tell us we were going to work in stations. Then he'd talk on and on about what to do at each station. By the time he finished, I'd have forgotten where to start. I just followed whoever was next to me and copied them.

Everybody kept telling me to try harder, to concentrate, to have a better attitude. I was so humiliated and so hurt, mainly because my parents didn't believe in me. I made up my mind that I would conquer math if it killed me. I quit going out to play after school. All I can remember in junior high and high school is studying. I managed to get dismissed from the special education roll and maintain a C average in math, but only with extraordinary effort.

I used to have terrible migraine headaches and feel so tense all the time. I was so scared I wouldn't have the grades to get into college. Life just wasn't much fun. No, I wasn't very good at PE, but I wasn't bad either, considering I never practiced. I never had a weight problem, so PE just wasn't very important to me. No one in my family cared much about sports. Looking back, I know I missed a lot. •

Analysis of this passage shows that physical education has not been very meaningful in Don's life. As an adult, he has no physical activity leisure skills and interests. He eventually learned relaxation and stress reduction techniques in coursework to become a counselor but remains unaware that this learning could have been part of general PE instruction made available to students with special tension control needs.

The many individual differences among students with LD allow for few generalizations. Although many have average or better intelligence, some have borderline IQs (in the 70 to 90 range) that further intensify learning problems and stress. Some are hyperactive, have attention deficit disorders, and display perceptual-motor problems that can be managed. Others do not. Many are deficient in balance, fine-motor coordination, and agility stunts involving total body coordination. Listening and thinking deficits affect all areas of life, especially social relations. Students with LD often need extra help in developing appropriate play and game behaviors and in acquiring the social competency for acceptance.

Mild Mental Retardation: Case Study 4

• *Eric Tosado is an 18-year-old middle-distance runner from Puerto Rico. Handsome, tall, and slender, Eric easily passes as "intellectually average" as do many persons with mild mental retardation. He reads at about the sixth-grade level, attends high school, works part-time, and has many friends. Eric competes in both able-bodied (AB) track and Special Olympics. He has over 50 trophies from various AB road races and is a gold medalist in the 1,500-m and 3,000-m events of the International Summer Special Olympics Games. Although Eric is a special education student, he has never thought of himself as handicapped in sports. For many years, he avoided Special Olympics because he didn't want to be associated with "the retarded movement." Eric says, "But I love to run so much that I thought, why lose an opportunity to compete? I'm good in able-bodied competition, and I often win local-type races. Teachers kept telling me I could be the best in the world if I entered Special Olympics. It was a way to test myself in international competition, to have opportunities I couldn't find elsewhere. And now I am so glad I made the choice. There's no reason a person can't compete in both AB road races and Special Olympics." Eric's gold medalist times were 4:14.3 in the 1,500 m and 9:38 in the 3,000 m. About the role of sports in his life, Eric says:*

> *It's hard to grow up mentally retarded. A lot of people tease you when you have trouble in studies. Once, when I was little and was upset, a teacher said, "Let's go out and run." He told me I was good at running, and this made all the difference in my life. It's really important to feel good at something. It helps you accept the bad stuff you can't change. Running makes me feel good physically, but competing and winning is what makes me feel good mentally.* •

Eric clearly expresses his individuality and uniqueness in both AB sport and Special Olympics. Strongly motivated to train hard and perform well, he is an excellent role model for persons who aspire to become runners. Like many persons with mild disability, Eric is intensely aware of the *stigma* (i.e., unde-

sired differentness) of mental retardation (MR) and thus reluctant to be associated with activities for the MR population. In sociological terms, he is coping with **role ambiguity:** whether to pass for "normal" or to take advantage of opportunities offered to persons with MR. Good counseling can help Eric to realize that he can be himself and do what he wishes; it is not necessary to choose between roles.

Mental retardation is a condition of impaired intellectual and adaptive behavior function that is diagnosed before age 18 and is documented by a score of 70 or less on a standardized intelligence test and an assessment of personal and vocational independence. Approximately 3% of the world's population has mental retardation, and most of these individuals pass as part of the general population once they have left school. Approximately 90% of all MR conditions are classified as mild. By adulthood, persons with mild MR typically function academically somewhere between the third and sixth grades. Cognitively, their greatest deficits are in the areas of abstract thinking, concept formation, problem solving, and evaluative activity.

Severe Mental Retardation: Case Study 5

• *In the same school with Eric, the same age, and also classified as mentally retarded, is a boy we shall call Juan, who has Down syndrome. Approximately 10% of all persons with mental retardation are born with this chromosomal abnormality, which has distinct physical features (see Figure 2.9). Juan has close-set, almond-shaped, slanting eyes; a flattening of the bridge of the nose; and an abnormally small oral cavity. He is not as tall as other boys of his age and has short limbs with small, stubby fingers and toes. He appears loose jointed because ligaments are lax and muscle tone tends to be poor. Juan has an intelligence quotient of about 45, functions at the first-grade level, and will probably always need to live and work in a sheltered environment. Like Eric, Juan is a special education student and eligible for Special Olympics.* •

In physical appearance, intellectual functioning, and motor ability, however, Eric and Juan are totally different. Whereas Eric can pass as part of the general population, except when called on to read or to do abstract thinking, Juan has been treated as special since birth. There are real problems in assigning both boys the same diagnostic label: mentally retarded. This is why federal law now requires that an individualized education program (IEP) be developed separately for each student. Each person, regardless of label, has distinctly different needs. No two persons with Down syndrome are the same, even though the syndrome causes similar physical appearance. Likewise, no two persons with MR are the same.

Whereas appropriate physical education goals for Eric may be physical fitness, leisure-time skills, positive self-concept, and social competency, Juan probably needs help primarily in play and game behaviors and perceptual-motor function. Special attention will probably be important for him to master the mental operations needed to understand game formations, rules, and strategies and to appreciate the differences between cooperation and competition. He will also need continued guidance on what to watch for during demonstrations,

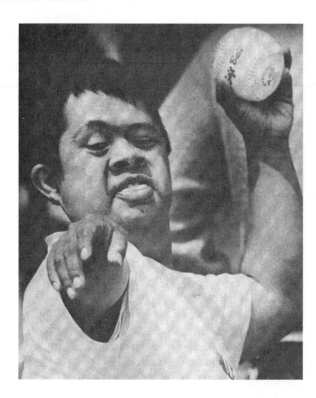

Figure 2.9 Persons with Down syndrome have distinct features.

how to listen to instructions, and how to integrate information from all the senses into meaningful wholes.

Through Special Olympics, many persons have developed good attitudes toward MR. Special Olympics, however, is only one of many sport organizations designed to serve persons who are differently abled. Only persons with MR are eligible to participate in Special Olympics. Therefore, physical educators need to know how to match disabilities with organizations.

Cerebral Palsy: Case Study 6

Cerebral palsy (CP) is a group of neuromuscular conditions caused by damage to the motor areas of the brain. There are many types of CP and many degrees of severity, ranging from mild incoordination to muscle tone so abnormal that a person cannot use a manual wheelchair and must therefore ambulate in a motorized chair. More information on CP is presented in Chapter 25.

CP is the most common orthopedic disability seen in the public schools. Because of the many individual differences within CP, a classification system is necessary for describing persons and assessing their abilities. The National Disability Sports Alliance (formerly the U.S. Cerebral Palsy Athletic Association) uses eight such classifications.

• *Nancy Anderson, a world-class athlete in her middle thirties, is a Class 2 CP, which means that she uses a wheelchair for daily living activities. She can take a step or two, with assistance, to transfer from wheelchair to bed or toilet but is unable to ambulate on crutches. Nancy's motor problems are* expressed largely as **athetosis** *(involuntary, purposeless, repeated movements of head and limbs), but she also has* **spasticity** *(abnormal muscle tightness and exaggerated reflexes). She thus lacks motor control for participation in sports unless rules and equipment are adapted. This combination of motor problems also makes fine-motor coordination like writing difficult, but Nancy uses a word processor and types approximately 24 words a minute. She feeds herself but needs a helper to cut up food. Through speech therapy, Nancy has learned to talk, but experience is needed to understand her speech. Nancy has a bachelor's degree from Michigan State University, lives independently in her own apartment, and writes professionally. Her passion, however, is sports.*

Nancy was introduced to swimming at age 3 by her parents. In the beginning, she simply did exercises in the water to increase range of motion and strength, but eventually, Nancy learned to swim. After introduction to CP sports competition, Nancy began to train seriously, and today she is a top U.S. swimmer in her classification (see Figure 2.10). Illustrative of her times are 1:00.1 in the 25-m free stroke and 1:02.4 in the 25-m back stroke. CP sports rules mandate different distances for swimming and track for each classification. These are the distances appropriate for a Class 2 CP.

Nancy also competes in field events (shot put, club throw, discus) and **boccia,** *a team sport that involves throwing balls at a target ball. She wheels a 60-m dash in 34.01 sec and completes the 100-m dash in 1:00.54. She sees sports as a means of expressing her competitiveness and takes advantage of every opportunity to excel.* •

Paraplegic Spinal Cord Injury: Case Study 7

• *Rick Hansen, a Canadian, is one of the best-known athletes with a spinal cord injury. Not only is he an international-level competitor, but Rick is acknowledged as an outstanding advocate for wheelchair sports. The first to wheel around the world (24,901 miles through 34 countries), he has generated millions of dollars for wheelchair sports, raised awareness levels, and stimulated research and action to enhance the lives of individuals with disabilities (see Figure 2.11).*

Rick was a teenager with three obsessions: fishing, hunting, and sports. His life changed drastically at age 15, when a ride in the back of a pickup truck ended in an injury to the spinal cord at thoracic segments 10 and 12. The result was flaccid paralysis of the hip, leg, and foot muscles, loss of sensation from about the waist down, and changes in bladder, bowel, and sexual function. This condition is variously called a spinal cord lesion, a lower motor neuron disorder, and paraplegia. **Flaccidity** *refers to loss of muscle tone, loss of or reduction in tendon reflexes,* **atrophy** *(wasting away) of muscles, and degeneration of muscle tissue.*

After the accident, Rick spent approximately 7 months in hospitals and rehabilitation centers to learn how to handle all of the changes in his body. This included mastering wheelchair techniques, learning to use leg braces and crutches, and going to the bathroom in a different way. It also included much

Figure 2.10 Nancy Anderson, a world-class swimmer with cerebral palsy, receives last-minute tips from Coach Marybeth Jones, puts on a nose clip, and mentally prepares to win.

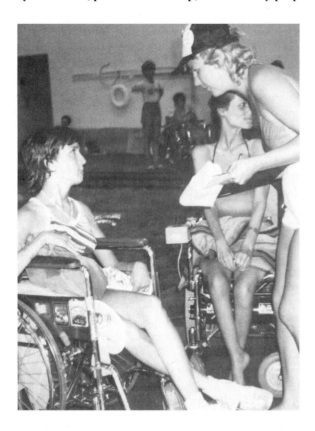 

loneliness, self-evaluation, and periodic depression. Because Rick was younger than the average person who sustains spinal cord injury, there were few persons his age to socialize with in the rehab centers.

Making the transition from rehab center to home also was hard, however. His was the only wheelchair in the small rural town, and he opted to ambulate on crutches and braces for many months. Returning to the gymnasium was the hardest of all. Rick stated:

> *. . . going back into the gym was devastating. I avoided it as long as I could. Then one day I screwed up my courage and peeked through the door. There they were: Bob Redford and the volleyball team. Same coach, same guys, only now I was on crutches and out of it. It was going to be awful. (Hansen & Taylor, 1987, p. 40)*

This first experience ended with Rick rushing out of the gym, jumping into his car, and driving out into the country for a long cry. Looking back, Rick says he underestimated his friends. After initial shyness, his friends were fine. Rick, however, had to learn to cope with new experiences, allow persons to help him with things he couldn't handle, and become creative in devising alternative ways to achieve goals and meet needs. The following passage illustrates his growing acceptance of self and his understanding of the importance of adapting:

> *There's nothing wrong with being carried down a bank by your friends so you can go swimming. What's wrong with taking your clothes off and going in shorts and letting people see that*

you've got skinny legs? It's no big deal. I had to realize that there weren't too many things I used to do that I couldn't do again, but that some of it wouldn't be the same. All I really had to do was adapt. (Hansen & Taylor, 1987, p. 43)

As might be expected, Rick became involved in wheelchair basketball, then track, and later marathoning. He won the Boston Marathon, completing the course in 1 hr, 48 min, and 22 sec, as well as other marathons and races throughout the world. He discarded the crutches and braces (a slow, inefficient method of ambulation for most persons with spinal cord injuries) and made life in a wheelchair adventurous and self-actualizing. He completed a degree in physical education at the University of British Columbia, married a physiotherapist named Amanda Reid, and developed into the mature, creative individual who today serves as a model for thousands of others who are learning to problem solve and move in alternative ways. •

Sport is the way both Rick Hansen and Nancy Anderson express their individuality and uniqueness. These elite athletes both use a wheelchair and have many commonalities: a love of competition, a willingness to train hard, good self-esteem, tremendous perseverance, and a strong commitment to become the best they can be. Their conditions and movement capacities, however, are very different. Nancy has an upper motor neuron disorder that manifests itself in spasticity and athetosis. Rick has a lower motor neuron disorder that manifests itself in flaccidity and loss of sensation. Nancy's total body is involved; Rick has perfect control of his upper extremities. Nancy

Figure 2.11 **Rick Hansen, of Canada, wheeling on the Great Wall of China during his Man in Motion tour.**

is dependent upon others for transportation; Rick can drive anywhere in a car adapted with hand controls and brakes. Rick was socialized into sport before his injury. Because Nancy's condition was congenital, no one expected her to become an athlete and she was not socialized into sport in the ways her peers were.

Is Nancy more like you or Rick? Is Rick more like you or Nancy? On what bases would you make such comparisons: gender, method of ambulation, speech fluency, creative writing ability, amount of travel, interest in basketball versus swimming? Why? Who would you like to spend the most time with? Why?

Deafness: Case Study 8

Persons who are deaf or hearing impaired also demonstrate individual differences in motor performance and fitness. Disability for a Deaf person is primarily environmental and depends on the two-way interactions possible in a given setting. Because most hearing people cannot use sign language, the world is divided for a Deaf person. There is the **Deaf community,** where people share a common language, similar values, and positive attitudes toward deafness; here, one is free of disability. Then there is the hearing world, which is uncertain and unpredictable for a Deaf person; sometimes, one is disabled there and sometimes not.

There is much controversy in educational circles concerning the best school placement for Deaf students or those who are hearing impaired: separate classes where sign language is used, mainstream classes, or some combination. The question is similar to that addressed in bilingual education: Can children be taught better in their native language, or should they be exposed only to English? The issue is complicated for Deaf students because their primary language at home probably depends

on whether or not their parents are deaf. The sensitive physical educator must be aware of this citizenship in two worlds and the inherent problems.

Dr. David Stewart, a professor in the College of Education at Michigan State University and author of *Deaf Sport: The Impact of Sports Within the Deaf Community* (1991), was born deaf (see Figure 2.12). The cause of his deafness is unknown, although genetics is suspected. An operation for otitis media at age 4 improved his ability to hear for a while, but his hearing has progressively deteriorated since that time, and he is now profoundly deaf. Dr. Stewart has written about himself and the importance of sports:

• *I am bilingual in American Sign Language and English and proficient in the use of various forms of English signing. I am culturally Deaf and socialize within the Deaf community. I have a hearing wife and three hearing daughters and spend much time socializing with hearing members of society. I rely heavily on sign interpreting at meetings. In noisy environments with individuals who do not sign, I generally resort to writing or to slow, exaggerated spoken conversations. I have a 95-decibel hearing loss in both ears; yet, I can use the phone with amplification if I am talking about a familiar topic with people I know. My preference is to use a Telecommunication Device for the Deaf (TDD). I empathize with other Deaf individuals dealing with the challenges of a hearing and speaking society. I sympathize with hearing individuals who spend much time trying to understand the various ramifications of deafness. If someone were to ask what my biggest asset in communication is, I would respond that it is my ability to respond to a wide range of communication demands. I do not impose my communication standards on others, and I accord full respect to those with whom I communicate.*

My confidence in deafness as a facilitator of a treasured lifestyle is a result of many years of interacting in both the Deaf and hearing communities. In particular, my involvement in sports has been critical. When I was 14 years old, I had a keen interest in becoming a basketball player because a lot of my friends were interested in that sport. I followed them to my first basketball practice in high school. I didn't have a clue what the coach was saying or what was expected of me. The techniques for doing layups and for following through on a shot went right past me. Because I was a fast learner, I remember saying to myself that, if only the coach would take me aside and explain a few things, then I would fit right into the team picture. I didn't realize at that time that I should have confronted the coach with my own strategies for becoming a good basketball player. Instead, I found other interests and let a chance to obtain a lifelong skill disappear.

Confronting a coach and putting forth my own objectives for learning and playing a game was a skill I learned many years later, when I became involved with other Deaf athletes in various deaf sport activities. Within Deaf sport, communication is not a special consideration, and objectives for participating in sport are clearly focused.

Many Deaf persons gravitate toward Deaf sport activities because communication is restricted in hearing sports. In addition, the bond forged through a commonality of experiences in deafness increases the likelihood of obtaining

social gratification in deaf sport. Hence, the Deaf are a linguistic and cultural minority. •

Many Deaf students participate in integrated physical education. They have a right to full understanding of class instructions, officiating calls, and comments from team members. A certain degree of maturity is required, however, to confront the individual in authority with the idea that he or she is not getting the lesson across. Sometimes, colluding or pretending to understand or somehow fading into the background is easier. The physical educator must create an environment of open, honest, and effective communication. The presence of an interpreter is just as important in physical education as in classroom subjects. To learn, one must understand.

Knowing that opportunities for full participation and socialization in after-school hearing sports may be limited for Deaf students, physical educators should be knowledgeable about Deaf sports and able to provide information about it. The choice of whether to participate during leisure time in Deaf or hearing sports or both belongs to the student, and the decision should be treated with respect and dignity. *Sports are more than motor skills and fitness; they are a vehicle for making and keeping friends.* This requires equal access to communication in all class and after-school activities.

Ideas to Consider About Individual Differences

The preceding case studies were presented to stimulate critical thought about individual differences. Among the ideas you may wish to consider are (a) how the personal meaning of physical activity varies from person to person; (b) how goals of adapted physical activity are illustrated in these accounts; (c) how the persons served by adapted physical education may differ from those served by special education; (d) how misleading it is to lump all persons with disabilities

into a category called "disabled," or "impaired"; (e) how a health impairment like asthma, diabetes, and obesity can be just as disabling as mental retardation and cerebral palsy; (f) how a person with a disability may feel more similar to you and me than to other persons with a disability; (g) how labeling a condition as disabling and providing federal and state monies for special services relates to politics—who decides what condition gets the money and how; (h) how much you can learn by becoming personally acquainted with persons of your own age who have disabilities; and (i) how the persons described in this chapter are similar or different from other individuals with disabilities that you have known.

In this section, you have been introduced to several kinds of individual differences: asthma and other health impairments, clumsiness, learning disabilities, mental retardation, cerebral palsy, traumatic spinal cord injury, and deafness. If you wish to know more about these or other specific conditions, check the **index** *at the end of the book for the page numbers in Part III of the text where the conditions are described in detail. The index can also serve as a spelling aid and guide for assessing your vocabulary in relation to adapted physical activity.*

Disability Sport and Transition Needs

Appreciating disability sport means getting involved as a spectator, fan, coach, athletic trainer, or advocate who helps to raise money for sport programs and to increase others' awareness of and commitment to disability sport. It also means developing the competencies to provide appropriate sport training and competition to children, youth, and adults in school and community programs.

IDEA, from 1990 onward, has required *transition services* in the IEPs of special education students aged 14 and over. This creates the opportunity to prescribe disability sport training as part of public school services (Stewart, 2001). **Transition services** strive to ensure that students have the competencies to become fully involved in community programs when they leave school. In particular, students in wheelchairs or users of canes and crutches need special sport training to participate in community activities like wheelchair basketball and tennis, to make transfers and safely use swimming pools and other community facilities, and to know how to find the resources and programs to enable lifespan sport involvement.

Types of Disability Sport

Disability sport, not *disabled sport,* is correct terminology. It is also appropriate to say *wheelchair sport, Deaf sport, CP sport,* and the like. **Disability sport** originally referred to sport governed by disability sport organizations (DSOs). Today disability sport is any sport (club, community, interscholastic, intercollegiate, or paralympic) conducted primarily for people with disabilities. School-based competitive sports for students with disabilities are sometimes called *adapted sport,* but *disability sport* is preferred by adults.

Mainstream sport refers to activities, events, and settings in which individuals with and without disabilities train, recreate, or compete with each other (Brasile, 1990). In these sports the number of individuals without disabilities is larger than the number with disabilities, whereas in **reverse mainstream sport** the opposite is true. Individuals without disabilities competing in wheelchairs or while wearing blindfolds are examples of reverse mainstream sport.

Able-body (AB) sport originally meant sport exclusively for athletes without disabilities (i.e., able-bodied). Individuals without disabilities are called ABs. Today **able-body sport** means sport *predominantly* for ABs, because laws and human rights policies prevent the exclusion of athletes with disabilities who meet performance criteria.

Special Olympics refers to a worldwide sport movement for athletes with mental retardation (MR). These athletes might have a second disability, but the major eligibility criterion is MR. No one can be a Special Olympian without MR. Special Olympics, founded in Chicago in 1968, is the oldest and largest sport organization for individuals with MR. However, a second organization, founded in the Netherlands in 1986, officially represents the MR condition in the Paralympic movement. Now called the International Federation of Sports for Persons with Intellectual Disability (INAS-FID), it began conducting international competitions in 1989.

Paralympics refers to the worldwide sport movement for elite athletes with disabilities, which parallels the Olympics in that international Summer and Winter Games are held alternately every 2 years. *The Paralympic Games are conducted in the same year and country as the Olympics.* The Paralympics is governed by the International Paralympic Committee (IPC), just as the Olympics is governed by the International Olympic Committee (IOC). The IPC includes representatives from all of the international DSOs that conduct two or more Olympic sports, except for the organization for Deaf sports (CISS), which withdrew in 1994.

Deaf sport refers to sport governed by the Comite International des Sports des Sourds (International Committee of Sports of Silence) and national affiliates for athletes with a hearing loss of 55 decibels or greater in the better ear. Summer and Winter World Games for the Deaf (recently renamed Deaflympics) are held in the year after the equivalent Olympic Games (Stewart & Ammons, 2001). Deaf sport may also be defined as sports offered by the Deaf community, which considers itself a cultural and linguistic minority, not a disability group. The Deaf community does not apply the principle of person-first terminology (e.g., individuals with deafness) because they see *Deaf* as an adjective similar to *American* or *Canadian.* Such phrases as *Deaf sport, Deaf people,* and *Deaf education* are therefore acceptable. The Deaf population was the first to organize an international sport movement.

Wheelchair sports refers to sports conducted in wheelchairs for athletes with spinal paralysis (e.g., spinal cord injury, spina bifida, postpolio) or lower limb amputations. The term evolved out of sports conducted at the **Stoke Mandeville Sports Centre** in Aylesbury, England, the birthplace of international competition for individuals with spinal cord injuries (SCI). The governing body for wheelchair sports is the International Stoke Mandeville Wheelchair Sports Federation (ISMWSF). The Centre was founded in 1944 by Sir Ludwig Guttmann, a neurosurgeon, now called the father of wheelchair sports (see Figure 2.13). The term was also popularized by the wheelchair basket-

Figure 2.13   Sir Ludwig Guttmann, the father of wheelchair sports.

ball movement, which was initiated by World War II veterans in the United States in the 1940s.

The traditional use of the term *wheelchair sport* to encompass only athletes with spinal paralysis and lower limb amputations is confusing in that athletes with CP and other locomotor limitations also compete in wheelchairs. Many sport organizations thus conduct wheelchair sport events and use the term *wheelchair sports* in ways that depart from the traditional definition (Sherrill, 1986).

Paralympic Sport Organizations and U.S. Equivalents

Table 2.2 shows that four international organizations govern Paralympic sports for athletes with physical disabilities:

- *ISMWSF*
- *ISOD*
- *CP-ISRA*
- *IBSA*

Visual impairments are included under the umbrella term *physical disability.* Prior to 1996, those organizations provided all of the athletes for the Paralympics. In 1996, athletes with mental disabilities, representing INAS-FMH, participated in full medal events at the Summer Paralympics in Atlanta. Thus the original meaning of Paralympics (sport only for persons with spinal paralysis, then for persons with other physical disabilities) is gradually changing.

Table 2.2   International sport organizations and U.S. equivalents with dates of founding.

International	United States	Population Served
Comite International des Sports des Sourds (CISS), 1924	USA Deaf Sports Federation (USADSF), 1999	Sports for Deaf athletes (i.e., hearing loss of 55 decibels or greater in the better ear)
International Stoke Mandeville Wheelchair Sports Federation (ISMWSF), 1957	Wheelchair Sports, USA (WS, USA)	Wheelchair sports for spinally impaired
International Sports Organization for the Disabled (ISOD), 1963	No equivalent. The United States has two separate organizations: Disabled Sports/USA (DS/USA) has governed amputee sports since 1989 Dwarf Athletic Association of America (DAAA), 1986	Wheelchair and ambulatory sports for amputees (nine classes) and les autres (six classes)
Cerebral Palsy International Sports and Recreation Association (CP-ISRA), 1978	National Disability Sports Alliance (NDSA), 2001	Wheelchair, ambulatory, and equestrian sports for eight CP classes and others
International Blind Sports Association (IBSA), 1981	U.S. Association for Blind Athletes (USABA), 1976	Sports for three classes of visual impairment
Special Olympics International (SOI), 1968	Special Olympics International SOI), 1968	Sports for athletes with mental retardation
International Federation of Sports for Persons with Intellectual Disability (INAS-FID), 1986	No U.S. equivalent	Sports for athletes with intellectual disability, also called learning difficulties or MR

Note: Disabled Sports/USA, called National Handicapped Sports (NHS) until 1995, is a powerful U.S. sport organization that governs winter sports and other events for several disability groups. Wheelchair Sports, USA, was called the National Wheelchair Athletic Association (NWAA) until 1994. CISS (French) translates to "International Committee of Sports of Silence." USADSF was the American Athletic Association for the Deaf (AAAD) from 1945 to 1999. NDSA was the U.S. Cerebral Palsy Athletic Association (USCPAA) from 1978 to 2001.

The term *les autres* (French, meaning "the others") has evolved to describe locomotor disabilities not served by ISMWSF, CP-ISRA, and IBSA. *Les autres* includes such diverse conditions as dwarfism, muscular dystrophy, polio, and many other low-incidence conditions. In most countries, one organization governs all les autres athletes. In the United States, however, separate organizations have evolved to meet the needs of individuals with amputations, dwarfism, and les autres conditions (see Table 2.2).

As shown in Table 2.2, six national U.S. organizations sponsor two or more sports for athletes with physical disabilities:

- *WS, USA formerly NWAA*
- *DS/USA, formerly NHS*
- *USLASA*
- *DAAA*
- *NDSA, formerly USCPAA*
- *USABA*

Learning these and the international abbreviations is important because the sports world communicates almost entirely through abbreviations. In the United States, each of these organizations is separately incorporated and historically has functioned independently from the others. Since 1979 the United States Olympic Committee (USOC), which has its headquarters in Colorado Springs, has become involved in partial funding of Paralympic teams and in advocacy for disability sport.

Many athletes without the functional capacity to compete in the regular Olympics have achieved recognition as the best in the world compared to others with similar functional capacity. These are the gold medalists at the Paralympics, the Special Olympics, and the Deaf World Games. They also include gold medalists in wheelchair divisions of races like the Boston Marathon. Some persons, however, aspire only to the fun and challenge of competition at the local level.

Recreational Sport and Barriers

Some persons prefer recreational sport. An excellent resource manual by Paciorek and Jones (2001) describes over 50 summer and winter sports in which people with disabilities participate. These sports are available in many settings. Choices include the following:

1. Predominantly AB, also known as mainstream, like general physical education, sport, and recreation
2. Predominantly disability sport conducted by a local DSO
3. **Parallel involvement** in organized events, in which athletes with and without disabilities compete in separate divisions conducted at the same time and place, like running and cycling events and marathons
4. Adaptations that purposively bring individuals with and without disabilities together in interactive training, recreation, and competition:
   (a) **Integrated wheelchair basketball,** which is particularly popular in Canada, and **integrated doubles wheelchair tennis**

(b) **Unified Sport in Special Olympics,** which specifies that 50% of the players on the floor or field must have MR while the other 50% are matched as closely as possible in age and ability

(c) **Challenger Division Baseball,** sponsored by Little League baseball, which uses AB buddies (parents, siblings, coaches, friends, or peer tutors) on the field to assist youth with mental or physical disabilities to enjoy the full benefit of Little League participation in an environment structured to their abilities.

Many individuals with disabilities crave as much sport as possible and want help in achieving inclusion. Others prefer one or two sports. Others dislike sport or feel most comfortable in sports with others "like themselves." A major goal of adapted physical activity, however, is sport for all, which means helping each person develop lifelong commitment to one or more sports of personal choice.

Inclusion is associated with acceptance in AB sport settings, but the issue is much broader (Sherrill & Williams, 1996). *Inclusion is a concern in all kinds of sport settings.* Individuals are not automatically accepted in new social groups and facilities. Professionals must empower individuals with disabilities to take the initiative to include themselves rather than wait passively for someone else to include them. This requires learning specific social competencies, overcoming shyness, and coping with various forms of rejection.

Individuals with disabilities must typically overcome more barriers than AB peers. Among the main barriers are the following:

1. No companion or friend with whom to share sport experiences
2. A lack of money to pay club memberships, buy equipment, etc.
3. A lack of transportation, especially for individuals with blindness
4. Inadequate exposure to sport and lack of socialization into sport
5. A lack of role models

A goal of this chapter is to motivate university students and others to create equal-status relationships with individuals with disabilities that will help overcome these barriers. As university students become professionals, it is hoped that they will continue such relationships and thereby become role models.

Level of Disability Concerns in Sport

Figure 2.14 indicates the level of spinal cord injury used by international organizations to place athletics of more-or-less similar functional ability into sport classifications. The United States uses its own system for basketball rather than the IPC system. Individuals in sport refer to themselves and others either by their numerical sport classification or by the broader terms: quadriplegia, paraplegia, diplegia, or hemiplegia. Knowing these terms allows intelligent spectatorship at sport events.

Following are terms used in disability sport and similar contexts.

Quadriplegia/tetraplegia refers to involvement of all four limbs, the trunk, and many organ functions, like blood pressure, maximal heart response to exercise, temperature regulation, and respiration. When involvement is minimal, the term **walking quads** is used. Involvement is caused by damage to the cervical segments of the spine (spinal paralysis). Athletes with this condition call themselves **quads.**

Paraplegia refers to involvement of the lower limbs and, depending on the level of damage, involvement of the trunk and alterations of organ function as in quadriplegia (see Figure 2.14). Involvement is caused by damage to the thoracic or lumbar spine. Individuals with paraplegia demonstrate a wide range of abilities, depending on whether muscles are paralyzed or merely weakened. Athletes with spinal paralysis call themselves **paras.**

Diplegia and **triplegia** refer, respectively, to conditions in which two (*di-*) or three (*tri-*) limbs are more involved than the others. Usually the legs are more involved than the arms. *The condition is of cerebral origin rather than spinal origin.* These terms, therefore, mostly apply to CP, traumatic brain injury, or stroke.

Hemiplegia refers to loss of sensation and/or movement on either the right or the left side of the body. Athletes with this condition call themselves **hemis.** The origin of this condition may be either cerebral or spinal, so the term is used by all disability sport groups.

Evaluate the kinds of disability sports you have seen in person versus on television over your lifespan. For example, how many times have you seen wheelchair tennis and basketball (the most popular wheelchair sports)? How many times have you seen wheelchair racers in community events, including marathons? How many times have you seen persons using crutches, walkers, or canes as they engage in recreational or competitive sport? What other disability sport events have you seen? What have you learned from these observations?

When planning your practical experiences for the semester, work in as many youth and adult disability sport activities as you can. These are usually conducted in community recreation or private club facilities. Write your reactions in your journal. What did you learn? Did any of your beliefs and attitudes change? Why?

Functional walking refers to ability to walk with assistive devices like crutches, walkers, and canes. Ability to walk is generally divided into **community walkers** (can walk 1,000 yards nonstop and ascend and descend stairs) and **household walkers** (can walk only a few steps). To meet the community ambulator criterion, damage to the spine is at L2/3 or below. Note that this is the criterion for placement in Wheelchair Basketball Class 3. Individuals with CP with Sport Class 5 are community walkers.

Prosthesis (singular) refers to an external artificial body part (e.g., limb or eye). The plural is **prostheses.** See Chapter 24 for more on artificial limbs.

Orthosis refers to a brace or a splint. The plural is **orthoses.**

Figure 2.14 Injury levels associated with DSOs to enable fair competition. C5–8 refers to injury to cervical spinal cord segments; there is one more segment than vertebrae. C5 complete paralysis and above injuries do not permit adequate independent breathing to sustain sport activity. T1–12 refer to thoracic segments. S1–5 refer to sacral segments.

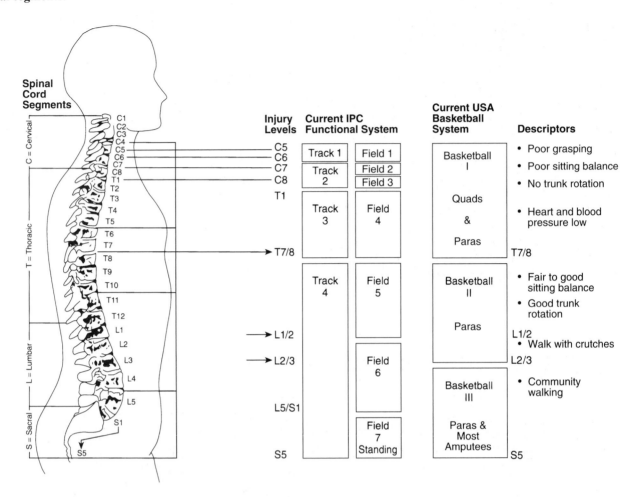

Time-of-Onset Concerns in Sport

Time of onset of disability is typically categorized as congenital or acquired. This variable is extremely important in that it reflects sport socialization and life experiences that influence self-esteem and self-actualization. **Sport socialization** is the process of becoming actively involved in sport and learning how to perform sport roles. This process is facilitated by family, teachers, caretakers, and service providers, but differences in attitudes toward disability often create barriers.

    Congenital refers to a condition present at birth. The most common congenital conditions are mental retardation, cerebral palsy, and spina bifida. The more severe a congenital condition is, the less likely it is that the individual will be socialized into sport and become aware of his or her sports potential.

    Acquired refers to conditions that occur after birth. These are specified by life stage to indicate the amount of sport socialization that occurred before disability. Youth who acquire a disability during or after puberty have the same sport beliefs, interests, and values as AB people.

Learning About Wheelchairs and Ambulatory Devices

Following are the basic facts that beginning APA personnel should know.

Wheelchairs and Cycles

Interactions with individuals with physical disabilities and appreciating disability sport requires a knowledge of wheelchairs. Much sport conversation and interaction pertains to wheelchairs and hand-crank cycles. Figure 2.15 shows that chair styles vary by sport. **Sport chairs** are chairs manufactured specifically for basketball, tennis, and other activities that require maximal maneuverability. **Track and racing chairs** are chairs with three wheels, lowered seat positions, longer wheelbases, and much camber. **Wheelbase** is the distance from front to back wheels. **Camber** is the vertical angle or degree of slant of the big wheels. Knowledge about camber, wheelbase, and other characteristics of chairs enhances communication and inclusion of ABs in the wheelchair community. For more information on manual chairs, see Chapter 23.

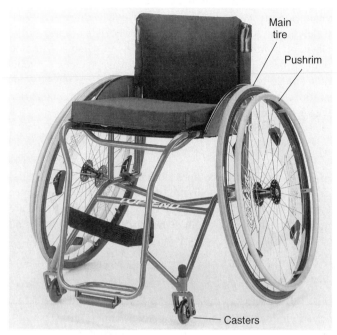

Basketball chair, 4 wheels
Terminator style

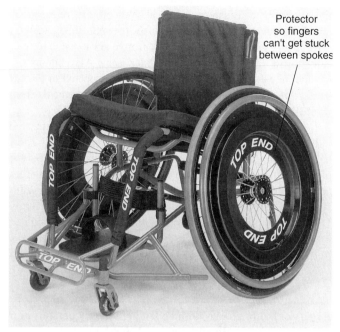

Quad rugby chair, 4 wheels
Offensive play, Terminator style

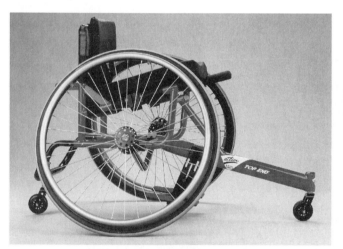

Tennis chair, 3 wheels, with antitip swivel caster option

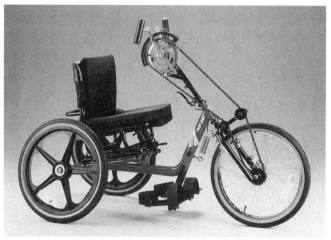

Hand-crank cycle, one of many models

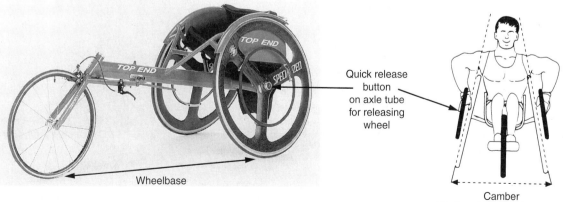

Racing chair, Action model
Note long wheelbase

Racing chair showing wheel camber and diagonal force applied to handrims
Camber

Note that chairs used for sports have low backs with no push handles because the athletes do not need anyone to push them. Sport chairs have rigid frames and do not fold, so a first skill to learn is how to remove the wheels, thereby enabling the chair to be transported by car. Wheels are released by punching down the release button on the axle tube. Athletes drive, make transfers independently from chair to car, and typically throw their chairs into the back seat. AB persons are needed, however, when chairs are to be transported in the car trunk. Athletes can, of course, remove their own wheels from chair frames, but it is thoughtful for ABs to offer help.

Chairs and cycles for individuals with disabilities are individualized, based on personal measurements and sport needs. DSOs for athletes with spinal paralysis do not permit motorized chairs, but these are used by athletes with CP and les autres conditions in Classes 1 and 2 for the most severely involved. The National Disability Sport Alliance (formerly U.S. Cerebral Palsy Association) supports sport recreation and competition for athletes using motorized chairs, manual chairs, cycles, assistive devices, and independent locomotion. Chair styles change frequently as technology improves. *Sports 'N Spokes* is an excellent journal for staying abreast of wheelchair changes. Ron Davis (2002) provides an outstanding, well-illustrated book on how to perform basic wheelchair sport skills. Davis recommends teaching these skills to persons with and without disabilities to promote an inclusive society. All children should be taught wheelchair sport in general physical education, and adults should have in-service and preservice wheelchair opportunities.

Motorized Chairs

Motorized chairs (sometimes incorrectly called electric chairs) give persons with severe disabilities considerable independence (see Figure 2.16). They move at high and low speeds and are generally capable of about 5 mi an hour. Most can climb

Figure 2.16   A recommended activity for persons in motorized chairs is the slalom (an obstacle course) that develops both speed and accuracy. Note the right hand grasping the power control lever and the wide-band strapping above the ankles to prevent falling out of the chair or undesired movements.

inclines of at least 10°. Families/agencies that can afford to do so provide children who have little arm and shoulder strength with motorized chairs at a very young age.

The battery-powered chair is the most common, with two 12-volt batteries mounted on a carrier at the back of the chair below seat level. These batteries must be recharged each night to supply power for approximately 8 hr of continuous use. Regular automobile batteries are used on most chairs.

Motorized chairs, which must have sturdy frames to support the weight of batteries and other special equipment, are very heavy. Without the batteries, a chair typically weighs 75 to 80 lb. Folding the chair is impossible without battery removal. Problems in portability generally lead users of motorized chairs to purchase a second vehicle (manual) for travel.

Medical Model Chairs

For persons with severe disabilities who cannot push their own chair or have minimal arm function, the **medical model chair** is typically prescribed. This model is seen in residential facilities, nursing homes, rental agencies, and schools and recreation centers without the resources to purchase more modern lightweight chairs. These chairs, which have handles so they can be pushed by helpers, are not appropriate for sports instruction and practice.

Skills for Pushing People in Wheelchairs

Competencies for helpers follow. Remember to ask permission of the person in the chair before beginning to push. Introduce yourself and make your intent to help known.

Handling Brakes

Brakes are used to lock the main wheels, thereby immobilizing the chair and providing needed stability for making transfers, engaging in field events, and playing stationary games like shuffleboard. Brakes may be placed partially on to reduce acceleration in going down a steep ramp. Many sport and racing chairs do not have brakes.

Removing Armrests and Foot Plates

Armrests and foot plates should be removed before engaging in sport events and before transfers to and from the wheelchair. Armrests are removed by lifting the tubular frames of the arm out of the tubing on the wheelchair. Removable foot plates are swinging or nonswinging. In the swinging type, the front rigging is released and swung to the side, after which it is removed. In nonswinging foot plates, a button-type or hook-in-place lock is released to permit removal.

Pushing a Person in a Chair

When pushing an individual in a wheelchair, the most important thing to remember is the safest direction for the rider to face. The rest (e.g., the use of the tipping levers) is common sense. Guidelines include the following:

Descending curb or steep ramp: Turn self and wheelchair backward.

Descending stairs: Go down forward with chair tilted backward.

Ascending curb: Go forward.

Ascending stairs: Back up the stairs.

In managing stairs, two adults are best, one in back and one in front. The stronger adult should be in back since he or she has the heavier load. The person in back tilts the chair backward and lifts with the push handles. The person in front lifts the frame (never the foot plates, which might accidentally come off).

Opening and Closing the Chair

To open a wheelchair, *push down* on the two seat rails (outermost surfaces of seat). Do not try to open the chair by pulling it apart because this damages the telescoping parts of removable armrests.

To close the chair, lift up the foot plates. Then grasp the seat at its front and back and pull upward. If you intend to lift the folded chair into a vehicle, remove all detachable parts before closing it. *The best position to stand in while opening or closing a chair is to the side (i.e., facing the wheel).*

Crutches, Canes, and Walkers

Individuals might come to class with assistive devices like crutches, canes, and walkers. Various gaits used with crutches and canes are described in Chapter 11 on motor skills and patterns. The use of crutches requires considerable arm and shoulder strength, and they are often used by persons with amputations or with conditions like mild spina bifida and early stage muscular dystrophy. Canes and walkers are often used by persons who have had strokes or traumatic brain injury.

Note the type of crutches used: (a) axillary, which fit under the armpits, or (b) forearm, also called Lofstrand or Canadian. Individuals with only axillary crutches cannot be programmed for ambulatory track because forceful pressure against the armpits, as in a race, cuts off circulation from the nerves and/or causes other kinds of nerve damage. An orthopedist should be consulted to see if the axillary crutches can be replaced with forearm ones.

Borrow or rent different kinds of wheelchairs and try using them for various activities. Sometimes the university OT, PT, or recreation department has chairs. Otherwise contact someone in a wheelchair for help on locating or borrowing chairs. If you have no previous experience with chairs, find a wheelchair user to help you or see the excellent book by Ron Davis (2002) published by Human Kinetics. See website www.humankinetics.com or call 800-747-4457.

Borrow or rent crutches, canes, and walkers. With a small group, try using these assistive devices for sport activities. What safety rule must be followed when using crutches for racing? Why?

Make photos or videotapes of attempts to use wheelchairs and assistive devices. Study these. What do they show? Place some in your journal or portfolio with an evaluation of what you learned. One person, of course, can take photos of everyone and share.

Inclusion in General Physical Education

Inclusion is a philosophy or an interactional process that facilitates individuals with and without disabilities working, playing, and learning together in positive, meaningful, and satisfying ways. Inclusion thus connotes mutual understanding, acceptance, and appreciation at the one-to-one level as well as the classroom or societal level. Approximately 95% of school-aged individuals with disabilities participate in general physical education classes. Future physical educators should learn about the inclusion process and associated barriers and enablers. The following section is written to increase awareness of how persons with disabilities experience the world. This should lead to greater open-mindedness and empathy.

Barriers to Inclusion (Negative Attitudes)

Barriers to inclusion are mostly human and can be overcome by changing beliefs, attitudes, and behaviors (Lieberman, Houston-Wilson, & Kozub, 2002). Any environmental barrier (physical or social) can be removed if human beings have the vision, commitment, and persistence. Eliminating or reducing barriers begins with a knowledge of the stigmatized social minority, marginization, prejudice, stereotypes, discrimination, oppression, and related topics. Understanding these negative phenomena enables professionals to recognize, manage, or prevent incidents that may be hurtful to one or more parties in interactive relationships.

Stigmatized Social Minority

A **social minority,** in social studies, is any person or group that occupies a stigmatized, disadvantaged, or socially subordinate position within society. A social minority is thus different from a parliamentary or voting minority (i.e., persons of equal status assembled for decision making). The social minority may or may not be a minority in terms of numbers. In schools, minorities are generally the children most often subjected to bullying, harassment, and emotional violence (Garbarino & deLara, 2002). Often these are students with poor movement skills and unfit bodies.

In physical education classes, the social minority is often referred to as a *marginalized group.* Smith and Goc Karp (1998) researched 5 middle-school boys and girls **marginalized** (excluded) by classmates. They noted that marginalization began within the first 2 weeks of class, was initiated by the "power group," which comprised the 4 best athletes (all males), and was reinforced by the other spontaneously formed social groups. The stigmata (discrediting attributes) that promoted the marginalization were poor sports skills or unacceptable social behaviors (e.g., aggressiveness, oversensitivity, withdrawal, or self-isolation). The marginalization process was described as follows:

> As these groups formed, exclusionary tactics were used to protect group membership, maintain group boundaries, establish power, maintain status and friendship, and exclude unwanted persons, those deemed physically inept or socially unpopular. For most groups, these tactics were subtle, and included behaviors such as ignoring certain individuals, or walking or turning away from individuals who were not welcome. For "the power," exclusionary behaviors were more overt and openly displayed. "The power" used both physical and verbal intimidation in order to maintain and protect boundaries. . . . Once marginalized, students rarely changed their status, although a few were able to use strategies that reduced their marginalization temporarily. *(Smith & Goc Karp, 1998, p. 38)*

Students with disabilities in general physical education classes are marginalized unless teachers employ specific strategies to promote inclusion. Social inclusion does not occur without intervention (Nixon, 1989; Place & Hodge, 2001). Moreover, many students experience fear and a sense of alienation in physical education, especially in large urban classes (Ennis et al., 1997). Marginalization seems to come from prejudice, stereotyping, and discrimination, although these phenomena often are not addressed and possible causes are ignored. Children say that teachers generally ignore teasing and bullying (Garbarino & deLara, 2002). Chapter 9 in Part II of this text focuses on the goal of inclusion.

Prejudice

Prejudice refers to "biased attitudes, feelings, and/or beliefs towards particular human populations on the basis of unsubstantiated assumptions and *prejudgments* concerning the nature of members' collective physical, cultural, and/or behavioral attributes" (Kallen, 1989, p. 69). Children born with disabilities such as mental retardation, cerebral palsy, and spina bifida typically grow up in the shadow of the personal tragedy model (still another dimension of the medical model) because families tend to believe that having an imperfect infant is the worst thing that can happen. This belief shows prejudice toward a particular human population (newborn infants with disabilities) because it is based on unsubstantiated assumptions about the infant's potential and the family's consequent quality of life.

By the time that children reach elementary school, their AB classmates and teacher frequently question their sport competence and restrict their participation in class activities, actions that are clearly based on unsubstantiated assumptions and prejudgments. Among both peers and teacher, there is considerable "uncertainty about appropriate performance expectations and activity adaptations" (Goodwin & Watkinson, 2000, p. 152). Comments by fifth- and sixth-grade general physical education students with CP, spina bifida, and amputations follow:

> My teacher won't let me do anything. He's like go pump up balls in the storage room. And they're playing volleyball and I'm like . . . grrr! I think sometimes that they ask you if they want you to participate in sports, like if you want to stay back and do your work or something, like during gymnastics they always ask me and I always tell them NO! I want to be with the group . . . uhmn, baseball uhm, sometimes I can't get the ball like I swing, and I'm slow, so I need a tee and can't get a tee in the big group . . . *(Goodwin & Watkinson, 2000, pp. 152–153).*

Table 2.3   Perspectives of children with physical disabilities in inclusive physical education.

Children's words	Meaning	Subtheme
Bad Days		
They laugh at me	Rejection	Social isolation
They ignore me	Neglect	
They stare at my body	Body object of curiosity	
They think I can't do it	Others judge my ability	Question competence
They think I'm dumb		
Teachers don't let me	Lack of support	Restricted participation
Classmates don't pass to me	Constraints of space	
I can only go on the cement		
Good Days		
Feel good when with the group	Being with the class	Sense of belonging
Teacher says I'm doing a good job	Encouragement and acknowledgment	
They [peers] cheer you on		
Reasons for participation:	Physical education valued	Share in the benefits
- build up my strength	Essential for physical well-being	
- learn new things		
- become faster		
- to stay healthy		
- sportsmanship		
- makes our brain work more		
- cause it's a lot of fun		
I like them to see that I'm good	Skill competence	Skillful participation
	Self-efficacy	

Adapted from Goodwin and Watkinson (2000, p. 150), with permission.

Table 2.3 provides direct quotes from children with disabilities who are in inclusive physical education. They describe their experience as bad days and good days. Qualitative research analysis has been used to categorize these and other direct quotes into the subthemes for bad days (social isolation, question competence, restricted participation) and for good days (sense of belonging, share in the benefits, recognition of skillful participation).

Prejudice spawns all kinds of adult and peer behaviors that convey to a child that he or she is inferior and bad (i.e., a personal tragedy that affects the entire family or a personal tragedy to anyone assigned to the same team). By the time children reach the age that others are socialized into sport, many have internalized beliefs that sport is inappropriate for them and that they are destined to be passive observers of others' athletic achievements. Physical educators must therefore know how to cope with prejudice on the part of both children and their families.

Persons with acquired disabilities likewise experience much prejudice. When these persons are members of minorities, they are subjected to multiple prejudices that tend to exaggerate their negative feelings about self. For example, one of the few female leaders in disability studies, Jenny Morris (1991), entitled her best-known book, *Pride Against Prejudice: Transforming Attitudes to Disability.* Morris engages in multiple roles

that inform her disability activism: single mother, wheelchair user, feminist, PhD in sociology, researcher, writer, and trades union and labor movement leader in England. Morris begins her book with these statements:

Little did I realize that by becoming paralyzed I had become fundamentally different and set apart from the nondisabled world (p. 3) . . . It is very undermining to recognize that people look at me and see an existence, an experience, which they would do everything to avoid for themselves (p. 15) . . . How can we take pride in ourselves, in what we are, when disability provokes such negative feelings among nondisabled people? In order to start to answer this question disabled people have developed an understanding of the nature of prejudice and its effect on us. (p. 15)

According to Allport (1954, p. 9), "a prejudice, unlike a simple misconception, is actively resistant to all evidence that would unseat it . . . prejudgments become prejudices only if they are not reversible when exposed to new knowledge." Consider the following examples of prejudice and what you might do to reduce prejudice:

• At a business meeting of the International Paralympic Committee (IPC, analogous to the International

Olympic Committee) it was announced that, in the future, athletes with intellectual disabilities will be integrated into the Paralympic movement and have events at meets. Several athletes in wheelchairs indicated that they did not want 'retards' affiliated with the Paralympic movement. An athlete with a guide dog stated that people with mental retardation had Special Olympics and the resources of the Kennedy family behind them. Why, several others queried, did retarded athletes need more? One athlete emphatically declared, "If they become part of Paralympics, I'm leaving," as he wheeled out of the room. Several other athletes followed him.

- At a social gathering a new acquaintance asked Mrs. Morales if she worked. Mrs. M said, "Yes, I am an adapted physical education teacher. I teach movement and game skills to children with disabilities so they can be included in general PE classes." The acquaintance replied, "Oh, I could never do that. I think it is so wonderful that you have chosen that career. Oh, you are so courageous to work with children like that." Mrs. M sighed, because she had heard these same sentiments from almost everyone she knows.

- Going out in public so often takes courage. How many of us find that we can't dredge up the strength to do it day after day, week after week, year after year. . . . It is not only physical limitations that restrict us to our homes and those whom we know. It is the knowledge that each entry into the public world will be dominated by stares, by condescension, by pity and by hostility. (Morris, 1991, p. 25)

Prejudice of able-bodied persons is often internalized by persons with disability, causing them to feel inferior and unworthy. Although the concepts of prejudice and stigma are similar, it should be noted that *prejudice* is perception of how the *social majority* judges a difference, whereas *stigma* is perception of how an individual in a face-to-face interaction judges another.

In developing goals to guide the process of changing ourselves and others, readers need to address the elimination of prejudice and stigma as well as the formation of favorable attitudes (i.e., acceptance, inclusion). Both prejudice and its opposite (acceptance) are beliefs interwoven with attitudes. Prejudice is particularly great when people with disabilities belong to racial minorities (Obiakor, 1999).

Stereotypes

Stereotypes are *exaggerated beliefs about the sameness of everyone in a group category* (e.g., all people with disabilities, all people with cerebral palsy, all people older than 60, all people of a certain race, all mothers, all teachers). For instance, when we automatically link characteristics or unique attributes to a particular category of disability, we are **stereotyping** (i.e., indicating a belief that all or most persons in that category have the same traits and behaviors). A common stereotype among physical educators is that all or most children with MR

have motor problems. When persons make comments about athletes like "dumb jock," or observe that Black people have cultural preferences like eating fried chicken or watermelon, or state that women can't throw correctly, this also is stereotyping (Harrison, 2001). Stereotypes can be good or bad; the problem is that they depersonalize. Consider the following comments about stereotyping from three young adults with fairly severe disabilities:

- Oh, stereotyping; that's the worse form of prejudice. ABs don't see us as individuals. It's like the old saying, "All Blacks look the same." Well, to ABs, all people in wheelchairs look the same. All people with Down syndrome look the same. And they think we all have the same characteristics. That's because some textbooks teach about disabilities through lists of common characteristics or attributes. I don't like being reduced to a list or a category.

- One way to get even with ABs is to create a stereotype of them, use it often, and see how they like it. A lot of us use TAB to stereotype ABs. TAB means temporarily able-bodied. That's what they are, and the poor slobs don't even know it. Only 15% of Americans with disabilities were born that way . . . the rest of them become disabled from automobile accidents, or high-risk sports, or disease, or just the degeneration of old age. I really don't spend much time with TABs. They all look the same, act the same . . . they're so damn normal sometimes we call them NORMATES . . . that's the category they seem to want to be in.

- On the stereotype that people with disabilities are sexless, "can't do it," "therefore don't want it," how stupid! Sex is a powerful urge, a universal need . . . we find ways . . . and it hurts or sometimes it really makes me mad when some cute, sexy, little volunteer flirts with me, or hugs me, and acts like she really likes me, and then she is surprised or offended when I hit on her.

Stereotyping is not the same as categorizing; instead it is a learned stimulus-response reaction that prevents open-mindedness and critical thinking about individuality. Generally, stereotypes are learned in childhood from authority and media figures (parents, teachers, textbook authors) and tend to be more rigid than beliefs developed on our own. Stereotypes can be partially true; the flaw is in making a generalization rather than assessing each individual separately. The broader the categories that evoke stereotypes (e.g., disabled, Black, Jew, lesbian), the more likely they are to lead to unfair and hurtful behaviors (see Figure 2.17).

Discrimination

Discrimination is unequal treatment or access, founded in prejudice or ignorance, that devalues persons or denies opportunity on the basis of group membership (e.g., racial, religious, linguistic, disability, poor) or social role (e.g., unemployed, low salaried, elderly). Devalued roles in Western society and negative life experiences, caused by discrimination, are explained in detail by Wolfensberger (2000), who stated that *discrimination*

Figure 2.17 Will these children be stereotyped as physically disabled? as Special Olympians? as Asians? Adapted physical activity emphasizes the elimination of stereotypes.

is a response mainly to ways that people perceive and value social roles, not the way they perceive and value human beings per se. People tend to *treat individuals well* when they are in high, valued social roles like elected public office holder, star athlete, and administrator or boss and to *treat them ill* when they are in low, devalued social roles like garbage collector, chronic invalid, and ineffective or unproductive worker. **Valorization** is the process of increasing the value, respect, and dignity of social roles that are usually assigned to people with disabilities. For instance, valorization is calling persons with MR "athletes" or "Special Olympians" to enhance their social role as participants in sports. Valorization can be enhanced by role-playing or simulating activities that are associated with high and low respect. Often university students are expected to select internships that give them insight into low-status jobs like custodians, factory workers, and migrant laborers. Daily contact generally leads to open-mindedness and new ways of thinking.

It is noteworthy that Wolf Wolfensberger of Syracuse University is the father of both social role valorization theory (1980s through the present) and normalization theory (1970s). His work shows how theories change as new beliefs emerge.

Wolfensberger (1972) achieved international acclaim for his book on **normalization** (i.e., making available to persons with disabilities the educational and living conditions that are as close as possible to those considered "normal or normative" for persons without disabilities). *Failure to do this was considered discrimination.* In the 1980s, however, the concept of *normal* lost favor (Davis, 1995; Shogan, 1998). Wolfensberger (2000, p. 105) abandoned normalization theory because it had become "persistently and massively misinterpreted." To replace normalization theory, Wolfensberger (2000) formulated **social role valorization theory,** a series of beliefs about discrimination and how they can be eliminated.

The Americans with Disabilities Act (ADA) of 1990 extended the definition of discrimination to include failure to make reasonable modification in policies, procedures, and practices when such modifications are needed for equal (although not necessarily identical) access to resources and/or opportunity. Resources may be human or nonhuman (i.e., services, aids, benefits, or facilities necessary to accommodate persons with disabilities).

Like other concepts, the meaning of discrimination is socially constructed and depends, to a large extent, on the resources of a country or culture. An underdeveloped or war-torn country, for example, may prioritize the building of roads or provision of food for the majority before addressing wheelchairs for the mobility-impaired or medicines for people with human immunodeficiency virus (HIV). Discrimination is typically thought of as (a) name-calling, teasing, bullying, and other inappropriate contact, (b) spreading rumors or making generalizations about "those people," (c) avoiding contact, (d) engaging in acts of violence like hate crimes, and (e) failing to make available such basic rights as food, housing, and safety.

Following are some examples of discrimination that persons with disabilities frequently give:

- Every time I go out in public, people come over and ask really personal questions that they would not ask ABs who look different. Like, "Oh, how did you lose your legs?" or "Why don't you use artificial limbs?" or "How do you ever manage? Are you depressed? Do you ever think of suicide? These things simply are no one's business. I wouldn't go up to someone fat, or gay, or really ugly and ask "How did you get that way?" Now, if someone tells me he or she is a student who is preparing for an adapted physical education or therapeutic recreation career, or maybe collecting research data, and then asks for permission to interview me, that is different.

- I get really annoyed when persons assume I need help. So many don't even ask. They just run ahead and push open a door, or grab your arm and start you across the street, or offer advice like "you shouldn't use this escalator; it won't be safe for you." And women make me mad when they stand back and expect me to go through the door or enter an elevator first. They don't treat other men that way. Sometimes I feel a lot of ambiguity. Like at the state fair, they let me bypass the long lines and get on the carnival rides first; they even let my friends on first. I like that. But later when I want to see some exhibit and there is no ramp, that makes me mad. A friend who is blind tells me that restaurants won't let her guide dog in. She tells them about the ADA law, and they say they don't care.

- My PE teacher tells me I have to do the same number of push-ups as everyone else . . . and he's gonna grade me the same way as everyone else . . . I am not certain that that's fair . . . I've got CP and I use crutches. Last year I wanted to train with the able-bodied track team because I qualified to race at the CP Nationals and wanted to get some real coaching. The school told me, "No." I think that violates the law.

Oppression

Social oppression is a relatively new perspective on discrimination that emphasizes the parallels and interconnections among ableism, classism, racism, sexism, ageism, anti-Semitism, and heterosexualism. In the Western world, *able people* (those with the best health and fitness) are traditionally middle to upper class, White, male, younger than 40, English-speaking, Christian, and married to or dating the opposite sex (Adams et al., 1997; Wu, 2002). There are exceptions, of course, but the dominant majority are remarkably similar, interconnected, and desirous of maintaining their privileged status. Generally, they do not realize that their status is privileged. Without sensitivity training, they seldom show much awareness of persons who are oppressed by negative attitudes, polluted air, inaccessible facilities, poorly lighted neighborhoods, insufficient accommodations for sight and hearing losses, inadequate supports to eat and exercise properly, and clothing fashions for the fit and the skinny. Indeed, the world is "right and good" in the eyes of individuals who experience few barriers to their ableness. In particular, people in the middle and upper classes seldom know what life is like for persons who are poor, whose first language is not English, and whose color and facial features are different.

Oppression is the *collective behavior of a dominant majority that consciously or unconsciously devalues or disenfranchises other groups for its own benefit.* The majority controls major political parties and receives recognition as the leaders in American history. In contrast, the rich histories of social minorities, although recently gaining some exposure, have seldom been shared with outsiders. Each minority has functioned apart from the others. *Advocates of oppression theory believe that social minority groups will derive strength by bonding together in the struggle for self-identity, self-determination, and self-actualization* (Adams et al., 1997; Mackelprang & Salsgiver, 1999; Woolley, 1993). Membership on a winning sports team offers a good way to bond with others (see Figure 2.18). Individuals with disabilities are now claiming their right to disability identity and power. In this regard, Morris (1991, p. 17) states:

> But we are different. We reject the meanings that the nondisabled world attaches to disability but we do not reject the differences which are such an important

part of our identities. . . . We can assert the importance of our experience for the whole of society, and insist on our rights to be integrated within our communities. However, it is important that we be explicit about the ways in which we are not like the disabled world. By claiming our own definitions of disability, we can take pride in our abnormality, our difference.

Disability Identity: Good or Bad?

Identity is "the integration of beliefs, values, self-perceptions, and behaviors into a consistent, coherent, and recognizable self-package" (Fox, 1997, p. xii). To achieve this goal, persons with disability *must learn not to internalize society's negative feelings toward them* and instead to claim themselves as good, valued, and necessary human beings. **Disability identity** is multidimensional personhood "that is specific to culture and history, is socially constructed, and is mediated by time of onset, nature of impairment, socioeconomic status, gender, ethnicity, and the multitude of roles, expectancies, aspirations, and perceptions that each individual incorporates into the self" (Sherrill, 1997c, p. 257). Disability identity is a fascinating topic because it explores how persons with disabilities search for and eventually construct a global identity that rejects the tenets of ableism, including society's pressures to become as normal as possible. Through acceptance of themselves and linkage with others who are different also, persons with disabilities make progress toward empowerment.

One way of doing this is to assume a **sporting identity** (Wheeler, Malone, VanVlack, Nelson, & Steadward, 1996; Williams, 1994). Consider the following quotes from Paralympic athletes, all from the Wheeler et al. (1996) qualitative research.

- It was wonderful. When I started swimming, it allowed me the opportunity to find an identity. It brought out a whole bunch of personal strengths that I think might not have come out had I not been swimming . . . I felt great. I felt like I looked good. I had the shape I wanted because I was so fit . . . Yes, I felt wonderful. (p. 388)
- When we're on the track, I think we don't look at ourselves as disabled. When we're in our racing chair it is like putting on a uniform; it's like you are out of it now, you are out of disability. It gives you that. It's like putting a Superman vest on! (p. 388)
- Competing was part of my identity . . . retiring [from Paralympic sport] was a very big decision and I needed a lot of support to make it. . . . But it was difficult because I no longer was going to be a swimmer or an athlete; I needed to regain my identity. (p. 390)

Sometimes athletes with disabilities try to trade a sporting identity for their disability identity or they perceive that their sporting identity is the first positive identity that they have ever had (analyze the preceding quotes for this). **Substitution** is the term for their having internalized feelings of the social majority that disability is inherently bad or piteous and of their experiencing an inner need to get rid of this internalization.

Figure 2.18   Team pictures is one way of bonding. Members of this basketball team dressed up for photos during free time at an out-of-town tournament. This team bonds together athletes of three different ethnic groups, two languages, many different ages, and varied functional abilities. Note that at least four athletes (Class 3s) can stand.

Substitution is another form of passing and denial (see earlier discussion of stigma management). For the best mental health, it is essential to create a positive disability identity and to integrate all of one's separate identities into a positive global self-concept. This is one reason why physical educators need special training in facilitating good self-concepts (see Chapter 8 in Part II).

Privilege and Power

To facilitate empowerment of people with disabilities, physical educators must become aware of all the ways that interpersonal relationships of privilege and power affect them and others (Kozub et al., 1999). White teachers in racially diverse classes need especially to become sensitized. Consider, for instance, this concept:

> White privilege is the concrete benefits of access to resources and social rewards and the power to shape the norms and values of society which Whites receive, unconsciously or consciously, by virtue of their skin color in a racist society. Examples include the ability to be unaware of race, the ability to live and work among people of the same racial group as

their own, the security of not being pulled over by the police for being a suspicious person, the expectation that they can speak for themselves and not for their entire race. (Adams et al., 1997, p. 97)

Many persons have never thought of themselves as privileged or as having more power than others. But persons of color feel strongly that they are treated differently from their White counterparts and that their history of oppression will continue unless extraordinary measures are taken to change the ways that White people unconsciously think and act (e.g., Kennedy, 2002; Wu, 2002). Consider also the trend toward inclusion in general physical education and the privilege experienced by able-bodied, able-minded students (especially those who are gifted athletically) who have unearned access to resources (e.g., equipment, space, teacher's high expectations, teammates' confidence) because of their able-bodied status. How can power be balanced? A first step is for physical educators to understand oppression and to develop strategies for eliminating barriers.

Table 2.4 reveals the forms of oppression commonly operative in today's society. In this table, *agent groups* are those with the most power (agency) and *target groups* are those with

Table 2.4   Forms of oppression and agent/target groups.

Forms of Oppression	Agent Groups	Target Groups
Ableism	People without disabilities	People with disabilities
Racism	Whites	Blacks, Latinos, Asians, Americans, biracial people
Sexism	Men	Women
Classism	Owning class, upper middle class	Lower middle class, working class, poor
Heterosexism	Heterosexuals	Lesbians, gays, bisexuals
Antisemitism	Gentiles, Christians	Jews
Ageism	Young and middle-aged adults	Young people, old people

Adapted from Adams et al. (1997), p. 73, with permission.

less access to resources that enhance life's opportunities. Physical educators must understand all of the isms, because persons with disabilities are subjected to several isms. For example, females with disabilities in a sport setting are considered *doubly disabled* because of unequal opportunities associated with their gender as well as their ability. This implies that greater attention should be given to promoting girls and women in sports. These same females, when nonwhite, nonheterosexual, or living below the poverty line, are triply or multiply disabled. How can we help them?

Narrow Vision

Another barrier is the narrow vision of some professions and some professionals. Physical educators have typically been taught that their major goal is to teach motor skills and fitness. Professional preparation has therefore focused on this goal. The future may show that this goal does not necessarily lead to active healthy lifestyles in a peaceful, inclusive world (or neighborhood), where everyone strives to understand and accept others. When inclusion is a major issue, physical educators should collaborate with family, school, and community teams concerning goals related to acceptance (self and others), positive disability identity, and inclusion. Although physical activity areas have long been considered spaces where much teasing takes place and ableists express dominance in many ways, physical education (properly planned and conducted) can achieve many goals.

What ideas and examples come to mind as you read this section? Have you written these in your journals? Have you discussed them with others? What newspaper articles and TV programs have you seen that address barriers to inclusion?

Strategies to Eliminate Barriers

Mackelprang and Salsgiver (1999, pp. 241–243) offer several strategies for eliminating barriers. Note embedded critical thinking activities in some of the strategies. The strategies are

1. Assume that people are capable or *potentially* capable . . . adopt the *minority view* and work to reject the imposition of the dominant society's views of capabilities on persons

with disabilities . . . [*How do the views of the minority and majority differ? Why?*]

2. Reject the traditional methods of practice that assume that the problem with disability lies with the person and that individuals with disabilities must change or "be fixed" before they can function adequately in society. [*What models does this strategy support? Why?*]

3. Assume that disability is a social construct and that a primary emphasis on intervention must be political in nature . . . [teachers must help children to become self-advocates, to challenge unfair treatment, and to understand politics]. The solutions to problems faced by persons with disabilities rest primarily on access to society's benefits and rewards. Environmental, attitudinal, and policy barriers must be eliminated.

4. Believe there is a disability history and culture. Be highly knowledgeable about political advocacy. . . . Be willing to help consumers [students, clients] help themselves to become politically involved. [*Briefly describe disability history and culture based on content in this chapter and Chapter 1. Does it have personal meaning for you? Why?*]

5. View children with disability as one more panel that makes up the glorious tapestry of human existence. Know that people with disabilities can be happy with themselves and their lives. [*Knowing this, why do so many ABs feel pity for them? How will you respond the next time someone describes a person or condition as sad or tragic?*]

6. Believe that adults with disabilities have, *without question*, the right to control their lives. Service providers must create the experiences for children that will empower them as teenagers and adults to be able to make decisions about work and play that will enhance their quality of life.

Consider each of these strategies in relation to people with disabilities whom you have known, seen, or read about in the media, or can imagine. Construct concrete examples that indicate how you might apply these strategies in different physical activity settings. Write some dialogue in your journal. Include in the dialogue words and actions that you might use in response to the words and actions of others. Which of these strategies is most meaningful to you? Why?

Enablers to Inclusion

Enablers (facilitators) is a term used to specify interacting social and physical environmental variables that *provide opportunities* for achieving outcomes like social inclusion or safe effective movement. Conceptually, enablers are the opposite of barriers (limitations). Enablers and barriers are **contextual** (i.e., they change as the social, physical, and temporal environments change). An uneven surface and holes on a soccer field are seen clearly in bright sunlight but may become barriers when weather or air pollution dims the light unless an enabler like a friend's warning prevents stumbling. Enablers and barriers are perceived differently by each individual, depending on such personal attributes as ability to see or hear and to quickly adapt movement to prevent a fall.

Enablers should not be confused with the more difficult concept of *affordances. Affordances*, a term specific to ecological perception theory, can be either barriers or enablers. Gibson (1979), the creator of affordances theory, stated: "The affordances of an environment are what it offers the animal [human being], what it provides or furnishes, either for good or for ill" (p. 127). **Affordances** are perceptions that enable persons to link the functional utility (good or bad) of an object or event to their capabilities. For example, an affordance may be a ramp perceived by a particular wheelchair user as having the qualities that will make it useful or nonuseful for gaining entrance to a building. The ramp may be perceived as too narrow or too slick or too inclined or just right. Helpers and peer teachers may also be affordances, depending on whether students with disabilities perceive their assistance as positive or negative in terms of interactions that lead to goal achievement (Goodwin, 2001; Goodwin & Watkinson, 2000). Generally, helpers and peer teachers are enablers. Although professionals often talk about *affordances,* this textbook uses the term *enablers* in support of the disability rights slogan, *Disabling Barriers–Enabling Environments* (Swain, Finkelstein, French, & Oliver, 1993).

Most *barriers* have their roots in *negative* beliefs and attitudes. Most *enablers,* in contrast, have their roots in *positive* human beliefs and attitudes. An understanding of these variables enables professionals to afford a social and physical environment that will promote inclusion of one another by persons with and without disabilities (see Figure 2.19). Chapter 3 focuses on enablers.

 Analyze the content of this chapter. Evaluate how it has changed your attitudes and behaviors. What practical experiences have you started? Did you feel comfortable? Why? How do you define comfortable?

Figure 2.19 Children with physical disabilities in presumed inclusive physical education often are left on the sidelines to practice a skill while able-bodied classmates engage in vigorous sports competition. What strategies would you use to promote real inclusion in a mainstream class?

OPTIONAL ACTIVITIES

1. Check that you are using your new vocabulary (the words in bold) and discussing new ideas in your journal and in your everyday speech. Consider how you might use journal writing with students of various ages. Should journal writing be homework or an in-class activity? Why?

2. Make a list of new abbreviations presented in this chapter. Devise two or more games that incorporate physical activity through which you can learn these abbreviations.

3. For graduate students, what ideas has this chapter given you for teaching undergraduates or for conducting in-service and staff development for public school teachers?

4. Check that your journal and the papers in your portfolio have applied the guidelines found on p. 37.

5. Use citations in the text to guide your library and computer browsing. Read at least one book or article listed in the references and discuss it with others.

CHAPTER

3

Teamwork, Communication, and Creativity

Figure 3.1   A model to guide home-school-community teamwork.

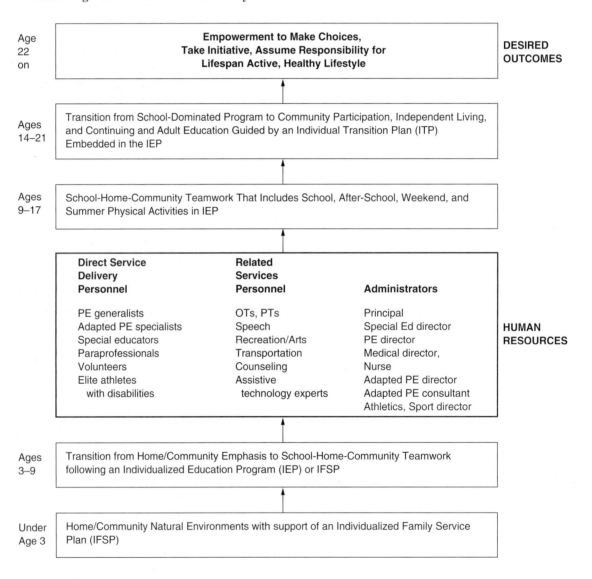

1. How are teamwork, communication, and creativity **enablers to a healthy, active lifestyle?** Give examples of how competence in these enablers by persons with and without disabilities can be used to reduce the barriers explained in Chapter 2. Your examples can be true or imaginary stories.

2. Although service delivery and empowerment are challenges, you are never alone if you know how to build teams, find supports, and/or use the IEP and IFSP systems. Show your understanding of teamwork, communication, and creativity as vehicles to achieving your goals as a good professional.

3. Explain how knowledge gained in this chapter can enable you to meet APENS Standards 11 and 15.

4. How is your understanding of the ecological approach expanded by studying this chapter? Give examples.

5. Show your understanding of possible uses of teamwork, communication, cultural competence, and creativity in establishing and maintaining a home-school-community delivery system that emphasizes active, healthy lifestyles for family members of different ages. Emphasize the role of physical educators in relation to other team members.

The achievement of lifespan active, healthy lifestyles for all is dependent upon families, schools, and communities sharing a common vision and working together to ensure that many physical activity options (both integrated and special) are available. This chapter encourages critical thinking about teamwork, communication, cultural competence, and creativity as **enablers** to active, healthy lifestyles as opposed to the barriers featured in Chapter 2. Remember the motto: disabling barriers, enabling environments. The challenge in adapted physical activity is to use these processes to reduce person-environment barriers and to enhance social, physical, and temporal environments. This is an ecological approach.

A Home-School-Community Teamwork Model

Figure 3.1 presents a model to guide physical educators in helping to shape a community vision. Central to meeting the diverse needs of citizens in any community is teamwork between family members and school and community professionals (Fiorini, Stanton, & Reid, 1996).

Figure 3.1 shows how the emphasis in home-school-community teamwork varies for individuals with disabilities (IWD) during five overlapping life periods: under age 3, ages 3 to 9, 9 to 17, 14 to 21, and age 22 and over. Age ranges were selected to coincide with the availability of special education services (including adapted physical education) that are promoted by IDEA and provided at no cost to families of children with disabilities from birth until age 22.

Figure 3.1 emphasizes that three documents are developed cooperatively by home-school-community team members and guide team interactions: the individualized family service plan (IFSP), the individualized education program (IEP), and the individual transition plan (ITP), which is embedded in the IEP when students reach age 14. Parents or guardians are included on every team and have considerable power in decision making, if they know how to assert their rights (Council for Exceptional Children, 1999; Siegel, 2002). Likewise, the student (if appropriate) is included.

Two boxes in Figure 3.1 are bounded by bold lines. The lower box states categories of human resources that may participate in meetings, in addition to families, friends, advocates, and lawyers. The upper box emphasizes empowerment,

the desired outcome of 22 years of instruction pertaining to physical activity and healthy lifestyle.

The outcome, empowerment, represents formal exit from adapted physical activity service delivery and personal assumption of responsibility for meeting one's exercise and leisure needs. Involvement may be in integrated (inclusive) programs or in disability sport, since both are funded by public taxes or private enterprise and thus can be considered community options. Adults who function at this level do not like their sports to be called adapted; they associate the term *adapted* with *service delivery* and emphasize that adults should have the right to name their sport what they wish.

Empowerment can be process or outcome. It is conceptualized as the outcome of high-quality, team-oriented physical education service delivery, both adapted and general. Empowerment thus is closely associated with self-actualization (see Chapter 1). However, many individuals with and without disabilities either do not progress to this phase or lack resources to remain in it. For these individuals, communities should continue to make available transition and adapted physical activity services, including fitness and leisure counseling, regardless of age.

Figure 3.1 is futuristic in that many communities do not yet have professionals trained in school-community-family teamwork who can provide the leadership for implementation of such models. The trend, however, is toward serving wider and wider ranges of individual differences in inclusive settings. This calls for the involvement of many professionals and team approaches. Of particular importance is the concept of employing physical activity professionals in many settings.

Some of these settings are schools; recreation, sport, and camp facilities; hospitals and rehabilitation centers; fitness clubs; infant and early childhood intervention programs; senior citizen centers; and agencies that provide social, psychological, vocational, and advocacy services (Sayers, Shapiro, & Webster, 2003). These settings may be either integrated or special. The terms *integrated* and *inclusive* are used as synonyms. The law prohibits settings that exclude individuals with disabilities (Block, 1995a).

A first step in teamwork is to learn about the types of human resources who share concerns about lifespan active, healthy lifestyles. Readers should visit as many employment settings as possible and view firsthand the interactions of various professionals, volunteers, and family members. When appropriate, ask individuals for interviews or engage them in small-group discussions about their work, beliefs, and concerns. This will strengthen your communication skills as well as your knowledge base. Describe these experiences with dates in your journal.

Case Study of Teamwork for a Child Under Age 3

Parents of children with developmental delays (or their friends or extended family) often contact professionals for advice and assistance. Consider the competencies that may be needed and ways that physical educators can become involved.

Jean and Joe, both age 36, university-educated, and in the White middle class, greeted their firstborn child, a son with Down syndrome, with ambiguous feelings. They were thrilled to finally have a child but they were concerned about **supports,** "the resources and strategies that aim to promote the development, education, interests, and personal well-being of a person and that enhance individual functioning" (AAMR, 2002a, p. 151). Jean and Joe felt totally inadequate to face the future; none of their friends had a child with a disability and most seemed to perceive the birth as a personal tragedy.

The parents and close friends of Jean and Joe had asked several times why they did not abort the fetus. Jean and Joe had known their infant would probably have Down syndrome (DS) since about the 20th week of pregnancy, when ultrasound procedures and maternal blood screening indicated a high probability of DS (see Figure 3.2). Amniocentesis (done by the physician inserting a long needle through the abdomen into the uterus and withdrawing about an ounce of amniotic fluid to be examined by microscope) confirmed the presence of DS. By the time all lab tests were completed, the couple had less than 3 weeks to make a decision whether to abort or keep the fetus because their state law allowed elective abortions only through the 24th week of pregnancy. Many states use the 24th week to define the time when a fetus legally becomes a living human being rather than a mass of growing cells. Jean and Joe had quickly read everything about DS that books, journals, and websites offered (see Table 3.1) and felt optimistic that their child might have only mild intellectual disability. They particularly liked the book *Choosing Naia: A Family Journal* by Zuckoff (2002) and decided to follow the lead of the couple they read about. They also participated in genetic counseling and parent counseling during the pregnancy.

Even though they had had 4 months to adjust to the idea of an infant with DS, Jean and Joe felt overwhelmed when the birth actually occurred. The family physician knew it was important for Jean and Joe to immediately receive support from other parents who had experienced the birth of an infant with DS. The physician therefore set the team process in motion by telephoning the local office of the ARC (formerly the National Association for Retarded Citizens, but now officially named the ARC). Most local branches of ARC have a parents' committee that provides volunteers to make in-home visits within 2 to 3 weeks of the birth. These volunteers undergo training before qualifying to do home visits, provide information about resources, and give empathy and support.

Figure 3.2 Fetus at age 17 to 20 weeks, the time when most screening for birth defects is complete and prospective parents must make a decision to not abort or to abort.

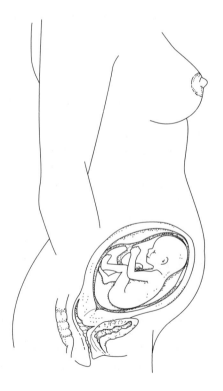

- Uterus is cantaloupe size
- Fetus weighs 3/4–1 pound
- Length is 8–10 inches
- Legs are about the size of adult little finger
- All body parts are formed and beginning to function
- Infant is surrounded by amniotic fluid
- Ultrasound, usually by the 20th week, can indicate sex (penis can be seen)

So Jean and Joe's team began. It was first comprised of *family members, close friends, medical personnel,* and *counselors* and then of *parents with similar experiences and concerns.* These parents introduced Jean and Joe to other parents, to persons with DS of all ages, to Special Olympics, to infant and toddler intervention programs, and to community and organizational resources. (See Sayers, Cowden, and Sherrill [2002] for parents' perceptions of the movement and fitness needs of their infants and toddlers with DS.)

The physician also informed Jean and Joe that community services, mandated and partially funded by federal law, were available for infants with disabilities from birth on and encouraged them to contact the local *special education director* (SED). This led to Jean and Joe's addition of *professionals* in many areas (e.g., speech therapy, occupational therapy [OT], physical therapy [PT], counseling, adapted physical education) to their team. The SED set up a meeting to develop the **individualized family services plan (IFSP)** that would determine free appropriate services needed and the process through which they would be provided. *Jean and Joe were members of this IFSP.* See Chapter 18 for further information on the IFSP and services for children under age 3, because this chapter focuses on teamwork, not the law.

Of particular importance, Jean and Joe lived in New Orleans at the time that the University of New Orleans was offering adapted physical education services for infants and toddlers, ages 6 months and up, who were not yet walking. This university offered an on-campus practicum in which juniors and seniors worked, one or two times a week, with parents and their infants or toddlers with DS. Two adapted physical educators (a professor and a doctoral student) trained and supervised the undergraduates, who did individual assessments and taught the parents how to do pediatric strength exercises in the *natural environment* of the home (Cowden, Sayers, & Torrey, 1998).

The primary goal of this program was independent walking at the earliest possible age. Progressively more challenging homework (pediatric exercises) was assigned each week to the parents, and both the undergraduates and the profession-

als made home visits and telephone calls to provide support. The homework was different for each child, because it was based on individualized assessment week by week. For more information, read Sayers et al. (2002). Jean and Joe joined this program, and their son began to walk independently at about age 30 months. Children without DS walk independently between ages 9 and 17 months.

Had Jean and Joe lived near the University of Michigan, they might have become acquainted with Dr. Dale Ulrich, an internationally known adapted physical education specialist who has been drawing parents of children with DS into his research on teaching walking through use of specially designed treadmills in the home (e.g., Ulrich, Ulrich, Angulo-Kinzler, & Yun, 2001). Ulrich's research is showing that the best way to teach walking is by practice on treadmills rather than the more traditional developmental approach of learning crawling, creeping, standing, and pulling up as lead-ups to independent walking.

Movement programs for infants and toddlers with disabilities are typically conducted by OTs, PTs, and adapted physical educators. These professionals often possess overlapping competencies. Many parents sign their young children up for every service and experience they can afford. Special education services, based on the individualized family service plan (IFSP), are free and may include weekly home visits by OTs, PTs, or adapted PEs (see Figure 3.3). Home visits are best because they take place in the *natural environments* deemed so important in early intervention.

Use your imagination to elaborate on this case study. Try writing some possible dialogue between (a) the mother and father, (b) the parents and their same-age friends, (c) the physician and parents, (d) the parents and others attending the IFSP meeting, and (e) the parents with adapted physical activity professionals and future professionals. Emphasize how professionals can convince parents of the lifespan values of physical activity. Indicate when the dialogue is occurring (e.g., before birth, shortly after birth, at different ages of the child up to age 3). What motor milestones do you think the child will achieve up until age 3? See Chapters 18 and 21.

Use your imagination to create different scenarios (i.e., write a case study of your own). Consider how the evolution of teamwork might develop if the parents were members of social minority groups (ethnic, racial, religious, below poverty line, non-English speaking). What if an unmarried woman (you select her age and determine her supports) was having the child? Brainstorm lots of factors that affect teamwork.

Table 3.1   Selected websites helpful in pregnancy and parenthood.

www.searsparenting.com
    For general pregnancy information, also information on birth defects
www.ndsccenter.org
    National Down Syndrome Congress
www.ndss.org
    National Down Syndrome Society
www.nads.org
    National Association for Down Syndrome
www.thearc.org
    The ARC of the United States
www.aamr.org
    American Association on Mental Retardation

Note. See reference list of Zuckoff (2002) for books.

Case Study of Teamwork for a Child, Ages 3 to 9

Between ages 2 and 3, families are helped to make the *transition* from home/community emphasis to school-home-community teamwork as children prepare to enter preschool programs at age 3 (Council for Exceptional Children, 1999). IDEA uses the term *transition* only for high school students, but many experts note that transition from early intervention to

Figure 3.3   Toddler with Down syndrome (DS) learns walking in the natural environment of the home with the support of the occupational therapist who comes to the home and gives parents lessons on how to facilitate walking. This service is provided under the individualized family service plan (IFSP).

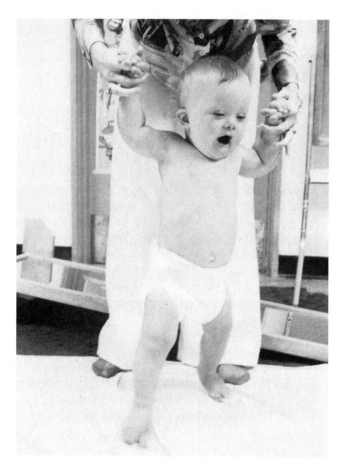

preschool also requires special attention and competencies. For example, Jean and Joe in the previous case study described **transition** as follows:

The services we obtained under the IFSP were absolutely wonderful. But making the transition to the individualized education program is pure hell. The special education people want us to agree to a special education self-contained placement for our son. That would put him in a small preschool class with a lot of kids with behavior management problems. We don't want our son with kids like that. We want him to be placed in an inclusive general education preschool setting so he doesn't feel special. We want him to grow up feeling like a "regular kid." The assessment people came to our house and gave a lot of tests; they concluded that our son has moderate to severe mental retardation. We don't believe his condition is that bad. He can't talk, but he has learned a lot of sign language. He seems to understand language quite well. He's walking good too. We are learning to fight for our rights.

Consider the following case study of a girl at age 3 and age 9 whose mother has completed participation in her first IEP meeting and agreed to a general education placement with pull-out services for speech therapy, creative arts therapy, OT, and adapted physical education. Both Shanika and her mother have beautiful features and well-proportioned bodies. Shanika occasionally gives a smile but mostly appears tired, listless, and withdrawn; she often sleeps in class and, during recess, just sits and watches others. She is thin for her age, has asthma, walks with a pigeon-toed gait, has no age-appropriate ball skills, and misses school more than other children. She seldom talks, is hard to understand, and does not link together more than two or three words. She seems to like drawing even though she sometimes cannot name the things she is drawing. Members of Shanika's household, when interviewed by school assessment personnel who came to their apartment, said she was sick a lot but doesn't cause anyone any bother.

Shanika lives with her grandmother, an adult aunt with an infant, and her mother, age 19, a single parent, in a small apartment in a massive housing project. There are few safe opportunities for outdoor play in this inner-city neighborhood. Shanika is the second child within 3 years; her mother is on welfare and unemployed. School files indicate that the inner city is 97% African American, with 37% of the residents living below the poverty line. Single mothers head 41% of the households, and generally there is no paternal financial support. These statistics parallel those reported in the literature (e.g., Birenhaum, 2002; Irons, 2002). For example, more than 70% of all Black students attend schools that are predominantly Black. This is because poor Black families typically live in segregated neighborhoods and housing projects. Most middle-class White and Black families have moved to suburban or urban areas (Irons, 2002). Throughout the country, up to 46% of working parents have no health insurance and limited access to health services and medical care.

Shanika, at age 3, is considered an at-risk preschool child and is now receiving special education services under the *developmental disabilities option* in IDEA. Shanika's preschool contains mostly children like herself. By providing special education services at age 3, school personnel believe that it is possible that Shanika may "outgrow" the observable, measurable problems in her present level of performance. They recommend that Shanika not be considered for diagnostic labels like mental retardation, orthopedic impairment, and autism until age 9 when specific IDEA categories must be used to meet eligibility for services.

Shanika's mother, grandmother, and aunt attend church regularly, and it was the caretakers for young children during Sunday church service who first recommended that the adults in Shanika's life contact the special education director for evaluation of Shanika's educational performance. Shanika's team developed rapidly from that time on. Table 3.2 indicates the required participants on Shanika's IEP team at age 3 and again at age 9. This table also presents the required participants on an IFSP. Often other professionals, like the speech therapist, attend also, and the adapted physical educator, OT, and others who provide intervention send a written report of their assessments and recommendations to the special education director.

Table 3.2   Required participants in the Individualized Family Services Plan (IFSP) versus the Individualized Education Program (IEP) as specified in the Individuals with Disabilities Education Act (IDEA).

Individualized Family Services Plan for Children Under Age 3	Individualized Education Program for Students Ages 3 Through 21
Parents of child under age 3	Parent(s) or guardian(s)
Other family members or caretakers as requested by parents	Student (if appropriate) who is focus of meeting
Advocate(s) or person(s) outside the family as requested by parents	Principal or principal's designee
	Student's special educator
Two or more professionals from different disciplines (e.g., occupational therapist, speech and language specialist)	One or more general educators, if student receives general education services
Service coordinator	Educational diagnostician or equivalent evaluation specialist

Note. The principal or principal's designee is referred to, in IDEA, as a representative of the Local Education Agency (LEA) or of the school administration.

IEP team members are required by law to hold an annual review of Shanika's program. At this time Shanika's mother and team members discuss whether Shanika and her family are meeting goals; they set new goals and objectives each year, and they revise the program and services as necessary.

Shanika's mother particularly likes the parent component of the preschool physical education program. She and other mothers attend 45-min sessions twice a week with their children. During the first 15 min, mothers learn the lesson plan for the day. During the remaining 30 min the mothers deliver the new lesson plan to their offspring and practice throwing, catching, striking, kicking, and balancing with balls of different sizes and colors at different stations (see Hamilton, Goodway, and Haubenstricker, 1999, for ideas about how the parent-assisted instruction is conducted). The school loans out balls and targets for mothers to take home and conduct ball-handling homework each evening. Mothers are provided with certificates they can give their children after each homework session. Mothers are also encouraged to help their children start a physical education portfolio with these certificates and with photographs that the teacher sends home. Additionally, all children have physical education instruction every day at school.

Consider probable changes in Shanika's movement performance from ages 3 through 9 and the dialogue that might take place between various team and family members before, during, and after IEP meetings. See Chapter 11 for tables that list easy-to-hard movement tasks, the criterion or goal for each task, and the average age that children perform locomotor and object control skills. Do you think that Shanika's family will continue to support physical education skill learning and eventual involvement in sports? Why? How might you, as Shanika's physical educator, encourage family involvement in a physically active, healthy lifestyle?

Do you think Shanika should attend her IEP meetings? Why? Do you believe that you might attend Shanika's IEP meetings? Why? Do you believe that the IEP has the ability to unite family, school, and community as partners? Why? How?

Before age 10, all students receiving special education services must have thorough assessment and be diagnosed as having one or more of the IDEA categorical conditions. Do you believe Shanika will continue to need special education services after age 9? If yes, in what school subjects? Why?

Resources in Service Delivery and Empowerment: The Ecosystem

Professionals, paraprofessionals, volunteers, and family members constitute major categories of adult human resources (Shapiro & Sayers, 2003). Additionally, students may contribute in various ways as peer teachers, tutors, buddies, and partners. One purpose of home-school-community teamwork is to expand the family ecosystem and increase awareness of all of the potential resources and supports.

General Physical Educators

General physical educators teach both general and special education students in the integrated setting, adapting assessment, pedagogy, equipment, and environment as needed. They also may be assigned classes of adapted physical education for students with severe movement problems. Involvement in Special Olympics, cerebral palsy sports, wheelchair sports, and other special events is common.

If the school system does not have an adapted physical education specialist, general physical educators or classroom teachers perform all of the tasks normally expected of a specialist. To fulfill these responsibilities, teachers must often request specific **support services** (i.e., supplementary human and nonhuman resources and aids). Illustrative of these are an adapted physical activity specialist as a dual or team teacher and specially trained paraprofessionals and volunteers. General physical educators may also ask their principals to employ an adapted physical activity consultant to come once or twice weekly and/or to fund participation in such continuing education activities as workshops, conferences, and courses. When a school district has 30 or 40 students with severe disabilities, generalists may band together and ask their administration to employ a full-time adapted physical activity specialist. Generalists are limited only by the breadth and depth of their competencies and their creativity. When adapted physical activity specialists are available, generalists work in close cooperation with them. If such specialists cannot be obtained, physical educators turn to other resources. In this case, physical educators must act as strong advocates in helping non-physical-education people to understand the need to give attention to physical activity, fitness, and leisure concerns.

Research is needed to examine the job functions and tasks of general physical educators in relation to students with disabilities. Recommended readings about inclusion in general physical education are LaMaster, Gall, Kinchin, and Siedentop (1998), Goodwin (2001), Lienert, Sherrill, and Myers (2001), and Place and Hodge (2001). Additionally, Duchane and French (1998) reported that grading practices for students with and without disabilities in general physical education were significantly different and require attention. Barriers specifically to including children with visual impairments in general physical education have been addressed by Lieberman et al. (2002), and Heikinaro-Johansson et al. (1995).

Adapted Physical Activity Specialists

Adapted physical activity specialists usually have a bachelor's degree in general physical education and a master's degree in adapted physical education. Specialists employed as administrators in large or affluent school districts often have a doctoral degree.

Specifically, direct service adapted physical activity specialists (i.e., those who do face-to-face teaching) are responsible for the following:

1. **Planning**—Helping school districts and schools create overall plans, curricula, and programs that maximize the success of all students; finding or developing resources; purchasing equipment; communicating with power figures about needs; writing and directing grants

2. **Assessment**—In-depth testing after a student has been referred for the IEP process or an alternative process if eligibility for special education services cannot be established; writing and presenting comprehensive reports pertaining to different kinds of assessment; assisting general physical educators and others with screening and other kinds of testing; coordinating community-based assessment initiatives

3. **Preparation, paperwork, and meetings**—Serving on IEP committees and interacting with parents and professionals at IEP meetings; sharing in decision making about placement and services; interacting with physical education generalists, principal, parents, and others in planning services, activities, and programs for nonspecial education students who need help

4. **Teaching, counseling, and coaching**—Working with students with disabilities who are assigned full- or part-time to separate adapted physical education or individual tutoring; serving as a resource room dual or team teacher in gymnasium with a general physical educator or in a nearby resource room or station; assisting with crisis management and special problems in large physical education classes; interacting with parents in establishing homework programs; conducting integrated home-school-community fitness and sport programs; initiating and managing sport programs for students not accommodated in general settings; mentoring students with disabilities who are entering integrated programs for the first time

5. **Evaluation**—Evaluating all aspects of adapted physical activity service delivery in both general and special settings; interacting with others on committees and teams responsible for evaluation of architectural, aspirational, and attitudinal barriers and other constraints to inclusive programs

6. **Consulting and coordinating resources**—Helping generalists, families, and others obtain support services and create support networks; fundraising and grant writing; consulting day-by-day as needed; conducting training for physical education paraprofessionals and student volunteers; making individuals aware of needs and rights

7. **Advocacy**—Working in many ways at many levels (local, state, national, international) to change beliefs, attitudes, and behaviors

School systems sometimes assign specific names to overall job roles or positions. The following are commonly used synonyms for direct service adapted physical activity personnel:

1. **Resource teacher** (a teacher who serves a single school, team-teaches with general physical educators, and provides instruction for individuals not in general physical education)

2. **Itinerant teacher** (a teacher who works in several schools, but performs essentially the same job functions as a resource teacher)

3. **Consulting teacher** (a teacher who travels from school to school and does some direct service delivery but mostly provides support services to general physical educators and helps them learn how to adapt instruction)

Administration involves many tasks, most of which center on planning, consulting, conducting in-service training, supervising, evaluating, and conducting research for the entire community. Many adapted physical activity specialists, when employed in administrative capacities, are called consulting teachers although their work includes functions in addition to consultation.

The only national job analysis of adapted physical educators conducted thus far (Kelly & Gansneder, 1998) indicates that most specialists work in urban settings, serve an average of 4.4 schools, and have an average caseload of 104 students. Direct service delivery was provided to about two thirds of the caseload. Other students were served indirectly by the specialist providing lesson plans, consultation, and other supports to general education teachers. On average, specialists divided their time as follows: 52% in direct services, 26% in indirect services, 38% in outside responsibilities, and 15% in travel

Figure 3.4 Andrea Woodson, Class 3 basketball player (tall, minimal disability), teaches ball handling to middle school wheelchair users. Both children had not seen wheelchair sports previously. The girl, in particular, was ecstatic to have a sport model of her own gender.

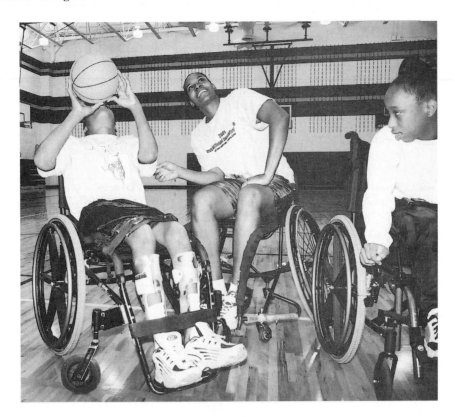

between schools. The most frequently reported outside services were coaching sports for students with disabilities and serving on curriculum committees.

Caseloads vary by states and local school districts. For example, the median caseload for California adapted physical education specialists is 50 students (Lytle & Collier, 2002). Additionally, California and Texas adapted PE specialists spend much time in consultation and collaborative services. Lytle and Collier (2002) reported that adapted PE service delivery is less a matter of choosing among direct services, consultation, and collaboration and "more a matter of dynamically including all three options" (p. 266).

Special Education Personnel

This category of professionals includes administrators, teachers, and paraprofessionals to provide services that benefit students with developmental disabilities or with diagnostic categories defined by federal law (see Appendix A). Typically, a school district employs one or more special education administrators and several special education teachers and paraprofessionals. Specific job functions vary with the school district philosophy. Some teachers work full-time in self-contained classrooms, whereas others work as resource teachers or support personnel. Some teachers serve as educational diagnosticians or full-time in various assessment roles.

Paraprofessionals may be assigned to a classroom or to a particular student. Often, students with severe disabilities are

assigned their own paraprofessional who stays with them all day, accompanying them to mainstream classes. An important competency of both general and adapted physical educators is knowing how to obtain, train, and use paraprofessionals (Pickett & Gerlach, 1997).

Some school districts use special education money to employ adapted physical activity personnel. Such individuals are considered special educators rather than physical educators and typically must have special education certification in addition to adapted physical education preparation.

Athletes With Disabilities: Many Roles

Elite athletes with disabilities can make significant contributions as teachers, coaches, paraprofessionals, and consultants (see Figure 3.4). Specific employment roles vary, of course, with university background and expertise. A growing number of athletes with disabilities are earning graduate degrees in adapted physical activity and/or completing teacher certification requirements. As direct service providers, such individuals are powerful models. As consultants, they can assist general and adapted personnel to make contact with sport organizations and utilize the rich resources that organizations offer. They can also provide information on wheelchair technology, assistive devices, and adapted equipment. Because the rules and strategies of disability sport are continuously changing, athletes with disabilities are more likely to have up-to-date information than published sources are.

Parents and Family Members

In the ecological approach to service delivery, educators not only serve students with disabilities but also work with parents, siblings, and significant others (Hanson & Carta, 1995). The only way to teach the whole person is to understand the total social environment in which she or he lives. Such desired social outcomes of physical education as self-worth, acceptance by others, and life satisfaction depend as much on family and neighborhood interactions as on school training. Thus, the teaching and learning process must be a partnership between school and family.

In planning home-school-community activities, it is important to consider such variables as family composition and size, parent and sibling employment patterns, parental age, socioeconomic level, ethnic group, and cultural background. *The two-parent family no longer is the dominant pattern.* Depending on the ethnic group, between 50% and 80% of all children will live in a single-parent home at some time in their lives (Hernandez, 1994). In most instances, these are mother-only families with male adults absent or frequently changing. This variable and the fact that most mothers now work outside the home strongly affect sport learning and participation. Physical educators must be sensitive to including all kinds of parents (never-married, remarried, gay and lesbian, rich and poor, employed and nonemployed) in after-school programs and in maintaining equity in choice of volunteer helpers.

Both congenital and acquired disabilities affect family life, although in different ways. The incidence of divorce, substance abuse, and health problems (both physical and mental) is greater in families trying to cope with disability concerns than in families without such concerns. Physical educators often have more contact with family members than other school personnel do, because of after-school and weekend sport programs. This contact increases the likelihood that physical educators will be asked to help with family problems in addition to their traditional school responsibilities.

Sports involvement and transition programming typically require additional money, which presumably comes from families. *Physical educators should know that approximately 1 out of every 7 Americans is living in poverty,* and these are the individuals most likely to be coping with disabilities and other developmental risk factors. Families often feel they must make choices about whether to support extraclass activities of siblings with or without disabilities. Siblings are affected in many ways by older and younger family members with disabilities. In summary, many factors must be considered when physical educators seek to form partnerships with families.

Related Services Personnel

Related services personnel are professionals who assist with education, including therapy, of students with disabilities. Federal legislation explains **related services** as

> transportation and such developmental, corrective, and other supportive services . . . as are required to assist a child with a disability to benefit from special education. . . . (Individuals with Disabilities Education Act 34 C.F.R., Part 300, Sec. 300.24)

A brief definition of each government-recognized related service is stated in IDEA. Other services can be justified as a related service if the IEP team agrees that the student needs this service to benefit from special education, including physical education. An outstanding news digest explaining all of the related services was disseminated by the **National Informational Center for Children and Youth with Disabilities** (abbreviated NICHCY) in 2001. NICHCY is perhaps the most useful of all websites in providing information of all kinds about children and youth with disabilities.

 Learn more about this information source. Try this website today and critique it in your journal: www.nichcy.org.

Following are descriptions of related services used most frequently by physical educators.

Transportation Services

Transportation includes—

(i) Travel to and from school and between schools;
(ii) Travel in and around school buildings; and
(iii) Specialized equipment (such as special or adapted buses, lifts, and ramps), if required to provide special transportation for a child with a disability.

See Figure 3.5 for an example of the motorized chairs that are provided through IDEA (if they are agreed on by the IEP team) to students with severe motor coordination difficulties (usually cerebral palsy). Getting such chairs on and off of school and community buses and vans is a challenge that physical educators must meet, because they frequently take students on field trips to community recreation facilities to learn generalization of movement skills practiced in the gymnasium. Transportation to community disability sport events so students will be exposed to role models and future leisure possibilities is also part of the physical educator's job.

Assistive Technology Devices and Services

Assistive devices may be used for mobility, leisure, personal care, communication, and sensory processing of information. Clearly the motorized chair in Figure 3.5 is an **assistive technology (AT) device.** To teach physical education activities to students who are nonambulatory, lightweight wheelchairs are needed as well as sport-assistive devices (e.g., ramps for bowling and boccia, adapted objects for object control practice, adaptive winter sport equipment). These are available from commercial sport companies, but physical educators often need the help of AT service personnel in making wise purchasing decisions. Whether students can use such AT devices at home is determined on a case-to-case basis. Use of AT devices in nonschool settings is determined by the IEP team and written into the IEP.

Recreation Services

Recreation includes—

(i) Assessment of leisure function;
(ii) Therapeutic recreation services;

Figure 3.5 (*A*) A student from Frisco High School (TX) in a brand new Quickie motorized chair is proof that the transportation section under related services in IDEA is enabling better physical education and lifestyle when parents insist on this service at the IEP meeting. (*B*) Hands of student with Class 1 or 2 cerebral palsy are unable to push a regular chair so push stick apparatus is on motorized chair.

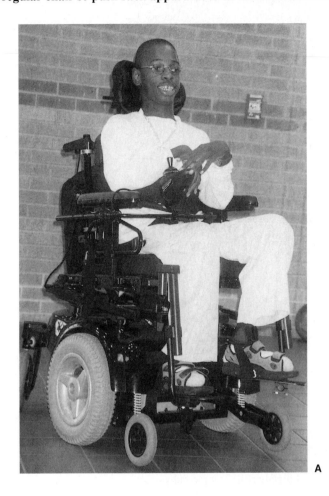

A

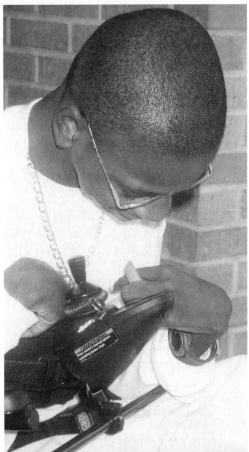

B

(iii) Recreation programs in schools and community agencies; and

(iv) Leisure education

Recreation specialists generally choose to specialize in either community-based recreation (often called *inclusive recreation*) or therapeutic recreation (formerly called *hospital recreation*). The trend is toward **inclusive** facilities and employees who support recreation for all. For example, directors of youth services with city parks and recreation departments are generally expected to serve all children (see Figure 3.6).

Most recreation courses begin with the fundamental difference between recreation, leisure, and free time so that these important terms will be used correctly. **Recreation** refers specifically to activity designed to be fun. However, depending on many variables, recreation may or may not be enjoyable. **Leisure,** defined as "an experience, a process, and a subjective state of mind" (Datillo, 2002, p. 6), involves intrinsic motivation, self-determination, and critical thinking about the meaning of time, environment, and situation in choice of activity or no

activity, (i.e., sleep) during free time. **Free time** is the minutes that remain during each 24 hr when persons decide they have completed their work and **activities of daily living** (ADL). The latter encompass such functions as eating, sleeping, toileting, bathing, dressing, medicating, traveling to and from school or work, and exercising for health reasons.

The greatest difference between certified adapted physical education specialists (CAPES) and certified therapeutic recreation specialists (CTRS) lies in the scope of the program each is qualified to conduct. CAPES are responsible only for physical activities and the state of mind related to such activities. CTRS are responsible for 10 or more widely diverse program activities (i.e., art, music, dance, drama, sports, camping, horticulture, crafts, nature appreciation and conservation) and the state of mind underlying engagement in each. Both professions emphasize carryover values and use of community resources. Leisure education and counseling are performed by both types of specialist, but adapted physical educators delimit their job roles to physical-activity-oriented leisure education and counseling. In short, CTRS and CAPES have much in common.

Figure 3.6   Don Drewry, employee of the Dallas Parks and Recreation Department, works to assure all children equal opportunity to leisure education and recreation activities.

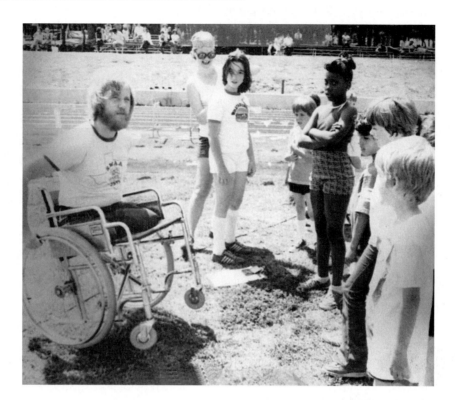

Within both professions, some persons do not take the time to obtain certification, and quality of service delivery varies widely.

Occupational Therapy

The related service that is broadest in scope and most likely to overlap physical education services, particularly in infancy and early childhood programs, is *occupational therapy* (OT). In its early years, OT focused mainly on ADL, particularly on the rehabilitation of arm and hand skills relevant to self-care, work, and leisure. Often, play and arts and crafts activities were the media through which goals were achieved. OT, however, has changed tremendously.

IDEA defines **occupational therapy** as follows:

(i) Means services provided by a qualified occupational therapist; and

(ii) Includes—

(A) Improving, developing, or restoring functions impaired or lost through illness, injury, or deprivation;

(B) Improving ability to perform tasks for independent functioning if functions are impaired or lost; and

(C) Preventing, through early intervention, initial or further impairment or loss of function.

Willard and Spackman's *Occupational Therapy,* first copyrighted in 1947 and now in its ninth edition, is a marvelous textbook of more than 900 pages, designed for use by undergraduate and graduate students (Neistadt & Crepeau, 1998). This text, which includes all of the fundamentals of OT, lifespan service delivery, and disabling conditions, has served as a model for Sherrill's adapted physical activity text since 1976, its first edition. The OT profession elaborates on its job functions by including statements of **three performance *areas*** (ADL, work and productive activities, and play or leisure), **three performance *components*** (sensorimotor, cognitive integration, and psychological skills), and **two performance *contexts*** (temporal aspects and environment). Understanding the breadth and depth of the OT profession's continuous self-study and commitment to excellence helps physical educators to promote cooperation with OTs when assessment tools, goals, and interventions occasionally overlap.

Develop a figure to depict the three performance areas, three performance components, and two performance contexts of OT. Use this figure to explain similarities and differences between OT, physical education, and recreation.

Whereas in the past OT was prescribed and directed by a physician, the American Occupation Therapy Association (AOTA) no longer requires this practice. Occupational therapists now can determine treatment on the basis of their own assessments. Traditionally, OTs worked in hospitals and rehabilitation centers. Today, over one-third of the OTs in the United States work in school settings. Much of their focus is on infants, toddlers, and young children who need assistance in learning self-care activities to benefit from special education instruction. OT has embraced a broad and holistic philosophy that enables its practitioners to do almost anything. Concurrently, the profession has developed high-quality training programs and certification standards.

Physical Therapy

Traditionally, **physical therapy** (PT) has been defined as treatment that uses heat, cold, light, water, electricity, massage, ultrasound, exercise, and functional training. Physical therapists (PTs) devote much of their time to gait training and wheelchair use. Many work in sports medicine and orthopedic rehabilitation. They use therapeutic exercise (including aquatic therapy) to relieve pain, prevent deformity and further disability, develop or improve muscle strength or motor skills, and restore or maintain maximal functional capacities (Bandy & Sanders, 2001; Lockette & Keyes, 1994). **Functional training** refers to teaching the patient to use crutches, prostheses, braces, and wheelchairs.

Most PTs work within a medical model. This means that they carry out an exercise prescription written by a physician. They also work with very sophisticated equipment, like that used in functional electrical stimulation (FES) which enables individuals with paralyzed legs to walk or use limbs, actions previously deemed impossible. State and national certification requirements are changing, however. Some states permit PTs to work without a physician prescription.

IDEA presents only a one-sentence definition: Physical therapy means services provided by a qualified physical therapist.

Corrective Therapy

Corrective therapy is a certification area for persons who are especially interested in therapeutic exercise. Its definition is this:

> **Corrective therapy**—is the applied science of medically prescribed therapeutic exercise, education, and adapted physical activities to improve the quality of life and health of adults and children by developing physical fitness, increasing functional mobility and independence, and improving psychosocial behavior. The corrective therapist evaluates, develops, implements, and modifies adapted exercise programs for disease, injury, congenital defects, and other functional disabilities. (Purvis, 1985, p. 5)

Persons especially interested in corrective therapy affiliate with an organization called the American Kinesiotherapy Association, Inc. (new name in 1988), which publishes *Clinical Kinesiology.* Previously known as the *American Corrective Therapy Journal* (1967–1987) and the *Journal of the Association for Physical and Mental Rehabilitation* (1946–1966), this resource was the first periodical to evolve for adapted physical activity.

Artistic/Cultural Programming

Artistic/cultural programs were officially recognized as related services in IDEA 1997, although the values of art, music, puppets, and dance in special education have been recognized for

Figure 3.7 Private dance lessons, with the promise of performing for family and friends, require much home-school-community teamwork as parents with a child with Down syndrome join forces to integrate her with children without disabilities.

years (Eddy, 1982; Sherrill, 1979). One of the most influential experiences in this author's life was involvement in two federally funded projects that used the arts as the major medium for changing behaviors of young children with severe disabilities; one was at Texas Woman's University (see description of LAMP in Chapter 18), and one was in a satellite program conducted by Very Special Arts (see the wonderful book entitled *The Music Came From Deep Inside* by Eddy [1982] for many activities and documentary photos). **Very Special Arts** (now named VSA Arts) is a national organization founded by Jean Kennedy Smith (the sister of President Kennedy) in Washington DC, where it publishes a newsletter, sponsors VSA arts festivals throughout the country, and advocates for arts in many ways.

Creative teachers often infuse or at least integrate music, dance, drama, chants and nursery rhymes, and the visual/graphic arts into the teaching of movement. Puppets that urge children to move are extremely effective. Encouraging children to explore space and body movements to a variety of sounds and tempos (music, drum beats); colors, shapes, and textures (visual arts); and story telling with puppets and props (drama) stimulates awareness of environment and enhances movement competence. Dance, in particular, teaches mobility, independence, and self-determination. Public performance in any of the arts provides praise and recognition (see Figure 3.7). If a child can be shown to need creative arts therapy (one art or several) to benefit from special education, this service can be written into the IEP and the school system will pay for the specialist. If the arts cannot be provided through school funds, parents should be

Table 3.3   Sources of information on the creative arts.

VSA Arts, John F. Kennedy Center for the Performing Arts, 1300 Connecticut Ave NW, Suite 700, Washington, DC 20036; 1-800-933-8721
American Art Therapy Association www.arttherapy.org
American Dance Therapy Association www.adta.org
American Music Therapy Association www.musictherapy.org
National Information Center for Children and Youth with Disabilities (NICHCY) www.nichcy.org or 1-800-695-0285 (V/TTY)

Figure 3.8   Boy at Lauren Lieberman's CAMP ABILITY learns orientation and mobility skills. The goal is to run between the parallel lines bounding a track lane while maintaining orientation by grasping a "homemade guidewire" that extends downward from the hand to loop around the rope on the ground. The loop should move smoothly forward as the runner advances.

 Get a partner, take turns putting on an eye shade and performing this activity.

made aware of opportunities for free lessons from volunteers and of private lessons by persons with special training in working with children with disabilities.

Acting as proponents of the arts are several professions, each with its own organization: music therapy (founded in 1950), dance therapy (founded in 1966), and arts therapy (founded in 1969). These national organizations, as well the National Dance Association (NDA) of AAHPERD offer many resources to help parents and teachers (see Table 3.3). Chapter 16 provides information on dance activities.

Orientation and Mobility (O and M)

O and M, added to the definitions in IDEA in 1997, offers instruction with goals similar to some physical education goals (see Figure 3.8). O and M is described as follows:

(i) Means services provided to blind or visually impaired students by qualified personnel to enable those students to attain systematic orientation to and safe movement within their environments in school, home, and community; and

(ii) Includes teaching students the following, as appropriate:

(A) Spatial and environmental concepts and use of information received by the senses (such as sound, temperature, and vibrations) to establish, maintain, or regain orientation and line of travel (e.g., using sound at a traffic light to cross the street);

(B) To use the long cane to supplement visual travel skills or as a tool for safely negotiating the environment for students with no available travel vision;

(C) To understand and use remaining vision and distance low vision aids; and

(D) Other concepts, techniques, and tools. (IDEA, Sec. 300.24)

Other Team Members and Supports

Opportunities for home-school-community teamwork are as big as the imagination, the availability of financial help, and the combined energy of the target person and his or her supports. The reflective writings of Christopher Reeve (*Still Me,* 1999, and *Nothing Is Impossible,* 2002), who was paralyzed from C2

(the upper neck) downward in an equestrian accident in 1995, are perhaps the best testimonials to the power of teamwork. Reeve, the longest-living being with a complete C2 spinal cord injury, has attracted every possible support to his own recovery as well as that of all persons who persist in the wish to walk again (see www.christopherreeve.org and www.paralysis.org).

Effective teamwork does not happen automatically or easily. Teamwork can be collaborative or noncollaborative, cohesive or noncohesive. Much of the success of teamwork depends on oral communication skills. Physical educators, like other team members, need extensive training and practice in problem solving around a table. Consider how much expertise a rehabilitation team like that of Reeve requires. Most adults with conditions too severe for self-management must have families with the ability to raise money from independent sources to supplement insurance coverage and to select health care workers who will work well as a team. The alternative is for families to try to do all of the physical work and decision making themselves.

In contrast, in our society, children from birth through age 21 have several laws that act as *enablers* to optimal quality of life. *The major law, IDEA, provides the idea and framework for home-school-community teamwork. The family is the center of the framework, and meetings cannot be held without one parent or guardian present.* Decision making about the student's educational activities over the subsequent 12 months cannot be operationalized without the parent's signature of consent. IDEA is designed to ensure that parents can obtain as much help as they need in arranging for a *free appropriate public education* (FAPE) for their child. IDEA specifies that certain professionals must be represented on the IFSP and the IEP teams, but no limitation is imposed on the number who participate because participation can take many forms (e.g., adviser, mentor, model, advocate, formal contribution as an appointed team member). Table 3.4 lists possible team members and supports. Many of the categories listed are helpful in teamwork designed to improve quality of life as individuals grow older.

Consider teams you have worked on during the past 5 years. Have any of these teams been concerned with life issues instead of sports? For an example, a debate team? What contributions in your chosen career might you make as a member of the IEP team for one of these families? How? Why?

1. *Single-mother family with 2 boys, all living below the poverty line, all bilingual with preferred language being Spanish. Boys both score below average on tests of motor skill but do well in fitness.*

2. *Traditional, long-term father and mother family with one daughter who is legally blind with the condition slowly becoming worse. Parents are urging this 10-year-old to give up sports and spend more time learning new ways to study.*

3. *Wild card situation. Make up your own challenge.*

Multidisciplinary, Interdisciplinary, Crossdisciplinary Teams

Figure 3.9 depicts the multi-, inter-, and crossdisciplinary approaches. Professionals need to understand each approach and think critically about which is best for their situation.

What type of approach would be better in collecting, interpreting, and reporting assessment data for a child's first IEP meeting? Why? Which type would be better in a situation where an OT, PT, and adapted PE are assigned to the same facility during the same hours and told to share a caseload of 80 children with severe motor limitations? Why?

Table 3.4   Possible team members and supports.

Families

Individual with a disability (IWD)
Parents or guardians
Siblings
Caretakers or personal assistants (PAs)
Spouses, partners, offspring of IWD
Parent or student advocates
Interpreter

Direct Service Providers

General physical educators and aides
Adapted physical educators and aides
General education classroom personnel
Special education personnel and aides
Educational diagnosticians

Related Service Providers

Parent trainers and counselors
Recreation professionals
Sports personnel (usually agency)
Occupational therapists (OTs)
Physical therapists (PTs)
Arts professionals (e.g., dance, music)
Orientation and mobility specialists
Speech and language therapists
Audiologists
Transportation specialists and aides
Assistive technology service personnel
School health service personnel (nurse)
Social workers
Psychologists
Transition services personnel
Rehabilitation services personnel
Vocational education professionals

Administrators

Special education directors
Principals
Physical education directors
Athletics directors
Medical directors
Adapted PE director
Other school-based directors
Community-based directors
504 Officer

Peers

Buddies
Partners
Tutors
Helpers

Note 1. Aides are often called **paraprofessionals** or **paraeducators**.
Note 2. Some of the personnel in this table are specified and defined in law, while others are not.

Figure 3.9 Models depicting multidisciplinary, interdisciplinary, and crossdisciplinary approaches.

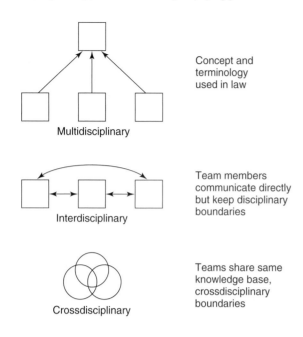

Concept and terminology used in law

Multidisciplinary

Team members communicate directly but keep disciplinary boundaries

Interdisciplinary

Teams share same knowledge base, crossdisciplinary boundaries

Crossdisciplinary

 What other human resources can you think of?

Multi- means "many." **Multidisciplinary** refers to involvement of many disciplines in the service delivery process. Federal law since 1975 has required that many professionals provide input into the evaluation (assessment) of individuals with disabilities and the IEP process. This mandate is implemented in most school systems by having several professionals independently assess a student. Each professional then writes a report of findings and submits it to the chair of the IEP meeting. Sometimes professionals are invited to attend the IEP meeting and present their report, but this is often not the case. The work of each professional tends to parallel that of other team members. According to Klein (1990, p. 56), the multidisciplinary approach is "additive, not integrative." It provides different perspectives, but synthesis and interpretation are left to a responsible individual or committee.

Inter- means "between." **Interdisciplinary** refers to cooperation between two or more persons from different disciplines in a joint project (e.g., conducting assessment, providing service, writing a report, working for consensus on a placement decision). Interdisciplinary teams work together closely, sharing the same space and time, but members are careful to respect disciplinary boundaries. Service delivery is mostly integrated but sometimes constrained by disciplinary defensiveness.

Cross- or *trans-* means "across." **Crossdisciplinary** refers to holistic, multigoal, multilevel sharing in which disciplinary boundaries are crossed, and the coordination of efforts is maximized by team members' helping each other to gain and use the combined, integrated knowledge of all the disciplines. Traditional names of disciplines are seldom used, because emphasis is on the whole rather than the parts. This type of teamwork is far more comprehensive in scope and vision than the

others and requires many years to develop. It often evolves from intensive interdisciplinary sharing in which members begin to learn and use knowledge not traditionally associated with their field. They "cross over" more and more in job performance and eventually become crossdisciplinary as cooperative teaching/learning among members leads to a common knowledge base.

A central theme of this textbook is that adapted physical activity has a crossdisciplinary **knowledge base.** This is different from following a crossdisciplinary *work* approach. Many types of teamwork are used in translating this knowledge into practice.

When applying your knowledge in your work setting and you find you know more about a particular disability than other team members, what situations might occur? How would you handle these?

This chapter emphasizes that general physical educators are expected to provide adapted physical activity services in inclusive settings. These teachers need not feel alone, however, if they understand team approaches. Moreover, an important part of their teaching success is knowing when and how to ask for help from an adapted physical activity specialist.

What Makes Teamwork Collaborative?

Professionals in public schools, universities, and other organizational structures typically spend much time and energy in committee work. One of the components of the PAP-TE-CA 2004 service delivery model is **preparation, paperwork, and meetings** in accordance with research on how adapted physical educators actually spend their work time. It is assumed that their teamwork in preparation, paperwork, and meetings is both cooperative and collaborative.

Cooperation, a component of collaboration, is the full participation of all team members in achieving a common goal: clarifying tasks, listening, paying attention, giving ideas, taking turns, praising, encouraging, evaluating, and other activities related to helping each other (Thousand, Villa, & Nevin, 2002). **Collaboration** goes beyond cooperation; collaboration is broader than its APENS definition by NCPERID (1995, p. 197): "working jointly with others to accomplish a common goal such as making decisions or implementing programs and assessment plans."

*What, for instance, does **working jointly** entail?* Often the hardest part of working jointly is reaching a consensus on the goal of the meeting or project, the time line, the leader, the process, and the specific roles and tasks of each member. **Consensus** is not necessarily agreement; it often is willingness to go along with the majority after all sides of an issue have been expressed and given fair attention. After consensus is reached on these first variables, each group member must totally commit to the goal achievement process and remain on target (or topic) in group discussion until the goal is reached. Collaboration demands that each group member's perspective be listened to and, if necessary, paraphrased to be sure listeners hear what is being said instead of what they may want to hear.

Several attributes, in addition to cooperation, characterize collaboration. One is **positive interdependence,** a process in which the success of every team member is linked to the success of other team members. In true collaboration, everyone feels success when the common goal is achieved. Part of collaboration is helping others feel motivated to give a personal best to the project and to feel good about their contributions. Everyone is considered equally responsible and accountable for achieving the common goal, and group members continuously engage in evaluation of self, others, and the project.

In short, *cooperation and collaboration share five attributes: (a) a common task or activity suitable for group work, (b) small group learning and sharing, (c) cooperative behavior, (d) interdependence, and (e) individual accountability and responsibility* (Thousand et al., 2002). Additionally, collaboration requires a crossdisciplinary perspective. *Collaboration is a more difficult state to achieve than cooperation.* Collaboration implies the involvement of *equal-status experts* in such activities as IEP and IFSP work (Block, 2000; Rainforth & York-Barr, 1997); consultation (Idol, Nevin, & Paolucci-Whitcomb, 1994; Lytle & Collier, 2002); empowerment evaluation (Fetterman, Kaftarian, & Wandersman, 1996); team or partner teaching (Lienert et al., 2001); and learning (Thousand et al., 2002). Perceiving teammates as equal-status experts acknowledges that everyone on a team knows some things better than anyone else and is willing to share; for example, parents (regardless of formal education) know as much about their children as anyone else. Parents may say they *know more* about their children than anyone else, but explicit or implicit competition among team members is avoided.

The concept of collaborative teamwork developed as crossdisciplinary (also called *transdisciplinary*) teams evolved and members were willing to give up disciplinary boundaries in order to work for the common good of the student's education. In the crossdisciplinary model, parents and professionals share knowledge and practice with parents that previously was the exclusive domain of individual disciplines like OT, PT, and adapted PE. Parents share information that previously was the exclusive domain of parenting. Clearly, much parent/professional staff development is needed for team members to achieve collaboration.

Communication

Communication, Standard 15 of APENS (NCPERID, 1995), is the foundation of collaborative as well as other forms of teamwork. It is also the key to good service delivery (remember all of the components of PAP-TE-CA). Success in each of these components depends on the communication competencies of every person involved. APENS divides communication into four areas: parents and families, public relations, understanding job positions of other professionals in order to enhance the probability of mutual cooperation, and the team approach. Several communication strategies are useful in each of these areas.

Facilitating Interpersonal Comfort

Individuals must feel at ease before open and honest sharing can occur. Conversation about mutual interests and concerns therefore serves as a warm-up. Eye contact, dress, postures, position and distance in relation to each other, gestures, and facial expressions all contribute to feeling at ease, but these variables have different meanings in different cultures. For example, White people of middle-class background typically appreciate good eye contact, but people of other cultures may find this disrespectful or threatening. Formal preparation in communication (Littlejohn, 1999) and crosscultural studies (Kalyanpur & Harry, 1999; Leavitt, 1999) is helpful in understanding differences, but skill in observation offers insight into how others are relating to you.

Using Specific Communication Strategies

People tend to communicate best with people they like and respect. Engaging in cooperative activities promotes these feelings, particularly if you are perceived as a good listener. Skills related to listening include appropriate eye contact, head nods, and encouraging verbal cues (e.g., "Uh-huh," "I understand," "Really?"). Also important is **reflective listening,** the spontaneous restatement in summary form of ideas presented by the speaker. Such restatement assures the speaker that his or her message is heard and is viewed as important. Reflective listening also is a technique for encouraging speakers to continue, thereby giving more depth and substance to the shared meaning. **Asking questions** is the joint art of wording and timing so as to obtain the most comprehensive answer possible. This means avoiding questions that elicit yes-or-no answers. Good listening also involves openness, acceptance, and careful avoidance of facial expressions, words, or gestures that might imply bias or discomfort.

Communication strategies should match the purpose of meetings: **consensus** as in IEP meetings or **open sharing** as in focus group meetings. The purpose of a meeting should be clearly stated at the time of invitation and again as the meeting is opened. In **consensus groups,** leadership centers on allowing team members equal opportunity to express their views and on promoting reflective listening by other team members to maximize understanding. When all possible solutions appear to have been listed, the leader guides team members in prioritizing the solutions and reaching a majority agreement. In **focus groups,** leaders engage team members in open sharing of perceptions and concerns on a particular topic in a permissive, accepting environment in which no voting occurs. Reflective listening is used, and the chair avoids expressing her or his views. Focus groups are excellent sources of information to guide decision makers who want to be sure they have heard all sides.

Communication skills differ according to the size of the group. *In general, the ideal size for a focus group is seven.* Little control can be exerted over the size of consensus meetings for IEP and IFSP committees, but the average number attending is five. Seating arrangements are important. First, individuals with visual and auditory impairments must be accommodated (i.e., placed where they can see the most faces or hear the best; where lighting is best). Second, individuals new to the group or shy should be placed opposite the moderator, where eye contact is readily established. Strong leaders or domineering people should be convinced to sit in corner positions at a table (the weak positions) because they will persevere regardless of seating. The moderator should sit at the head of the table.

Meeting Challenges of Cross-Cultural Complexity

Cultural pluralism (also called *multiculturalism*) throughout North America now requires cultural competence. According to Leavitt (1999, p. 3),

> **cultural competence** acknowledges and incorporates—at all levels—the importance of culture, the assessment of cross-cultural relations, vigilance towards the dynamics that result from cultural differences, the expansion of cultural knowledge, and the adaptation of services to meet culturally unique needs.

Cultural competence is the opposite of **ethnocentrism,** the behaviors of persons who have little experience with cultures other than their own and/or who believe that their culture is best and provides the only way to think and live. Many members of the dominant majority, discussed in Chapter 2, exhibit ethnocentrism. Professionals must examine themselves for signs of prejudice, bias, and discrimination in their relationships with families and professionals. A good way to do this is to plan some direct experiences with people from other countries, religions, and family structures. Books, movies, television, and websites can be used as supplementary ways of increasing understandings.

To facilitate understanding, cultures can be classified as individualistic or collectivist. **Individualistic** cultures are traditional achievement-oriented Western cultures (i.e., several generations have lived in a country and become assimilated into democratic ways). There may or may not be strong support of equality within the family (e.g., middle-class families tend to support equal rights of males and females and sometimes of parents and children). In contrast, working-class families may support patriarchal family structures. Regardless of beliefs about equality, members of individualistic cultures tend to focus teamwork on helping individuals with disabilities to achieve self-esteem, self-determination, and independence. Conflict is often considered healthy, a way "to get something off of the chest" and to clear the air. **Collectivist** cultures are those in which family and community concerns take precedence over individual needs, wishes, and rights. There is generally a hierarchy of status among family members, with being older and being male valued most highly. In collectivist cultures, conflict is considered dysfunctional and persons will discuss concerns a long, long time in order to achieve consensus rather than dealing with issues quickly and directly and letting the majority win. "Saving face" and maintaining win/win situations is important in the collectivist culture, and patience and self-discipline in group discussions are extremely important. Members of collectivist cultures may not wish to be singled out for awards or praise; cooperation is stressed so highly that rising above one's peers is frowned on.

Of course, there are exceptions to cultural patterns so acquaintances from other cultures should be carefully observed in an effort to determine which beliefs and practices seem to make them uncomfortable or comfortable. Much time and energy must be planned for interactions with families and team members from other cultures. Additionally, definite differences in communication styles among African Americans, Asian Americans, and Hispanics exist (see Table 3.5) and should be honored.

How can you document that you are becoming more culturally competent as part of your adapted physical education course? What kinds of documents will you put in your portfolio to aid end-of-semester evaluation?

To develop cultural competence, future professionals obviously need many kinds of contact with cultural subgroups (social minorities). In adapted physical education, this means sustained direct and indirect contact with individuals and sport teams with disabilities, their families and friends, and the settings they frequent.

Considering Family Relationships

Family relationships that vary in *cohesion* and *adaptability* affect communication (Leavitt, 1999). **Cohesion** (enmeshment vs. disengagement) is the continuum of family bonding and interdependence, ranging from overprotective to nonexistent. Overprotective parents typically blur personal boundaries and limit opportunities. One of the best examples of this continuum in **APAQ** (*Adapted Physical Education Quarterly*) research identified four forms of parental encouragement and discouragement with regard to sport participation among children with visual impairments: strong encouragers, weak encouragers, tolerators, and discouragers (Nixon, 1989). Results indicated the need for more communication about benefits and dangers with parents who tend to overprotect children in sports. Few parents were strong encouragers of sport in Nixon's study.

Enmeshment is associated with not wanting to share family problems and concerns with professionals. This may occur because of shyness, embarrassment, fear, denial, or a desire to hide neglect and abuse. **Disengagement** is the state when parents no longer care. They are numb or have given up. Often this is because they are living in poverty, have several other children and aging parents whose needs must be met, and have been able to find no concrete help over a long period of time. Clearly it is important for professionals to recognize the reason for communication behaviors representing either extreme of the cohesion continuum.

Adaptability (on a continuum from chaos to rigidity) refers to the ability of a family to meet new demands. Families at the chaotic end exhibit breakdowns in control and structure. Few rules are enforced, and promises (including coming for appointments) are often unkept. Promises are important to parents in chaos; they are simply under too much stress (self or other imposed) to function in an acceptable manner. Rigid families at the other end of the adaptability continuum have too much control and structure, making change difficult. With either the chaos or rigidity extreme, it is better to supplement oral communication with written recommendations. Specific deadlines may be given, with reminders, of the time line for disagreeing with anything in the written document.

Professionals increasingly maintain electronic portfolios on families. What would you put in an electronic portfolio for a family with an 8-year-old boy with attention deficit hyperactivity disorder (ADHD) and concomitant clumsiness? Why? Critically analyze some of the variables that would

Table 3.5   Generalizations about communication styles of ethnic groups.

African American

Eye contact *direct* while speaking, *indirect* while listening
Many dialects, depending on socioeconomic status, education, neighborhood
Some words ("you boys"), a touch or an accidental bump in crowd, and symbols (reminders of slavery) are offensive
Most have preference for name of race (Black or African American)
Sensitivity to potential racial slurs, stereotyping, and "put-downs"
Background noise and interruptions accepted
Conversations considered private, not acceptable to join without permission
Personal questions to new acquaintances not appropriate
Arguments often loud and colorful, verbal abuse infused
Open emotion, body language, and facial expression
Especially intolerant of slurs against mother, grandmother

Hispanic

Eye contact *indirect* when showing respect or attention; a sustained stare challenges authority or shows disrespect
Touching, close distance between speakers common
Public affection among females (sisters, mothers and daughters, girl friends) accepted
Background noise and interruptions accepted
Hissing used to gain another's attention
Gestures with talk, much body language, open emotion
Spanish interspersed with English
Raising one's voice to gain attention accepted
Especially intolerant of slurs against family, especially females
Males often speak for female relatives, feel responsible for welfare of females

Asian American

Eye contact is *indirect* or avoided to show respect and attention; stares are challenges to authority
Close distance between speakers common
Crowded areas, accidental bumps, background noise tolerated
Hierarchies based on social class, age, and gender govern speech; head nods and bows indicate degree of respect
Common to share information about age, order of birth in family, job status, and marital status, even with relative strangers, because these factors determine social status and hierarchy of respect
Facial expression, body language neutral (closed); few gestures or direct indicators of emotion
Giggling indicates embarrassment or uncertainty
Use of "no" and direct conflict is avoided; same questions, responses, explanations, and silent spaces are used repeatedly until consensus is perceived
Public affection (hugging, kissing, hand holding) between members of opposite sex seldom seen
Females (sisters, mothers and daughters, girl friends) may hold hands, hug, or be affectionate in public
Impolite for children to interrupt adult conversation

affect communication between family and professionals. Or do this activity for a child and family of your own description. Or do this activity for an older adult (e.g., over 70) who is increasingly sedentary and beginning to experience memory, sight, and hearing losses. What family members are involved when an older adult needs physical activity and leisure support?

Using Case Studies to Improve Communication Skills

Good communication, based on reflective and critical thinking about knowledge and practice, is essential to all aspects of professionalism. More practice in sharing ideas and negotiating consensus in small-group settings is needed in physical education teacher education (PETE) students. Case studies are wonderful vehicles for this practice. Particularly outstanding is *Case Studies in Adapted Physical Education: Empowering Critical Thinking* by Hodge, Murata, Block, and Lieberman (2003). Most of the 40 case studies in this book are four to five pages long and followed by thought-provoking questions, which typically begin "What is the primary issue in this case? Are there related issues? If so, what are they?"

Discuss one of these cases with two or three classmates. Videotape or audiotape the discussion and then assess your own and others' strengths and weaknesses in communication. Make a plan to guide the assessment process so that there is honest evaluation and yet no one's feelings are hurt. How do you build trust in relation to taking and receiving criticism from others? Is your criticism both positive and negative? Why? What are you learning about discussing children with their parents?

Make plans for improving your listening, speaking, and body language skills. Record plans and give evidence of follow-through in your class portfolio.

The previous edition of this text (Sherrill, 1998) included sections on *persuasive communication theory* and *social cognitive communication theory.* These sections, along with models, are available on the textbook website on the McGraw-Hill website: www.mhhe.com/hhp

Case Study of Teamwork in Sport

Fifteen families bonded together in Arlington, Texas, to create an additional sport option for their children, ages 7 to 16 years. In each family, one or both parents had a strong sports background. Most of the parents described their children as having MR: 6 had mild MR; 4 had moderate MR; 3 had severe MR. Of these 13 children, 3 also had physical disabilities and 2 (twins) had a primary diagnosis of autism. The other children had cerebral palsy or muscular dystrophy. Almost half of these children received their physical education instruction in a general physical education (GPE) setting. Others received adapted physical education services, mainly in separate settings. All children had IEPs on file.

Many of these parents had met each other through Special Olympics and believed that Special Olympics was tremendously important to their families. They were pleased that all six adapted physical educators in Arlington were involved in after-school Special Olympics programming and believed that these teachers should not be asked to take on additional responsibility. However, the parents wanted more sports opportunities for their children.

The story of teamwork begins with a new parent (a mother of a teenage daughter with DS) who came from a city that had Challenger baseball. Mrs. CB told other parents about Challenger baseball, a division of Little League baseball, in which individuals with disabilities, ages 5 to 21 years, participate in baseball in standard team uniforms, compete on community diamonds at peak hours, and use peer buddies to assist players who require individual help in batting or fielding. In Mrs. CB's words,

> One of the greatest joys over the last 5 years has been baseball. When we moved here, it was really important that we find a Challenger team. Baseball gave her something to look forward to. It's made her one of the regular kids. She has a uniform. She has something she does on weekends that lots of kids do on weekends. She has trophies; she has pictures. I think it has been an important part of her childhood. (Castañeda & Sherrill, 1999, p. 383)

Challenger baseball makes available four divisions (prep, minor, major, senior) that have *rule adaptations that are*

ability-appropriate. For example, in the prep division, buddies without disabilities help players; score is not kept; the side is retired when half of the players on the roster have batted. In the prep division, also, players may bat using a tee or a pitch from the coach. Team organizers can choose which division (i.e., which category of adaptation) is most appropriate.

Mrs. CB passed her enthusiasm on to the other parents, and they held numerous meetings to plan team practices and competitions. Mrs. CB contacted the board of directors of the North Arlington Little League, which subsequently approved the formation of the Arlington Challenger Division. Other parents performed chores such as (a) scheduling games with the Arlington Parks and Recreation Department on the same grounds and during the same prime time that persons without disabilities played, (b) designing and ordering uniforms, (c) providing transportation for players, (d) contacting the local newspaper to ensure good coverage of games, and (e) recruiting more players and buddies for the rosters. Parents also served as coaches, dugout managers, pitchers, and team parents. Siblings volunteered as buddies. For the first year, the parents shared all the work of running the sports club. One or more members of these 15 families were present and involved in conducting at least 50% of the practices and competitions.

An outstanding newspaper article about the organization attracted the attention of one of Arlington's adapted physical educators at the beginning of the second season. Mr. C came out to observe a practice, was intrigued, and kept returning "to help out," despite the fact that he coached two afternoons a week for Special Olympics. The parents began to trust him and to want him to be head coach because none of them had had coaching experience. After several weeks, Mr. C accepted the invitation to be head coach, providing the parents would run all other aspects of the organization and continue to help coach (see Figure 3.10). In turn, Mr. C recruited other coaches and assistants from the special education teachers and aides, and the teamwork between teachers and parents developed into collaboration (i.e., equal-status contributions and mutual meaningfulness) that, in time, extended to other home-school-community projects. Mr. C based his master's thesis (action research, qualitative method) on the second season of Challenger baseball and how interactions with parents and siblings enriched his knowledge of adapted physical education and sport.

As part of the interviewing for his thesis, Mr. C asked parents what the most valuable outcomes of Challenger baseball were. In rank order, with the highest first, these were (a) fun and enjoyment, (b) an overall good feeling related to equal opportunities, (c) social networking and emotional support for families, (d) baseball knowledge and skill, and (e) increased social interactions of children with peers. As a result of this experience, Castañeda and Sherrill (1999) came to believe that all future adapted physical educators should be required to take courses in family studies and to have more direct experience with parents as part of graduation requirements. The researchers also noted how teamwork in organizing and planning after-school and weekend sports led to empowerment of parents, who in turn shared their power with the teachers who helped. Mr. C said,

> The parents are wonderful. They would do anything for me. They know that I really care about their

Figure 3.10 Challenger baseball players with parents or buddies providing individual help during games. Parents and siblings, interviewed individually, indicated that fun and enjoyment should be the primary outcome of sport. What message were they giving the coach? Why?

children, that I volunteer extra time just like a family member. In fact, I guess they have made me feel like I am a member of their respective families. Most important, they know I listen to them. I respect their knowledge and experience. If they say the most important outcome of Challenger baseball is fun and enjoyment, they know I will work to make that outcome happen. The parents' caring for me also generalizes to the instructional program. They all believe that adapted physical education is great, and they are strong advocates for anything I need. I can depend on them.

This case study shows that sport, properly conducted and adapted to individual abilities, is an ideal way to promote teamwork and collaboration between teachers and parents. No other school subject facilitates getting acquainted with parents in the same easy, comfortable way as afforded by physical education and after-school sport. A problem to be resolved, however, is that often *only the parents with a sport background* take the responsibility for involving their children in sport.

How can physical educators and parents like those in this case study work together to socialize parents without sport experience to the values of sport participation? **Sport socialization** *is the process of becoming involved in sport,*

learning sport values and roles (e.g., athlete, coach, fan, parent facilitator), and acquiring a sporting identity. Brainstorm ideas and write in your journal or share with others. Consider socialization for the specific sport roles that parents assumed in this story.

Have you ever observed adults without sport interests being socialized into sports because of the needs or interests of their children? If yes, what did you learn from this? How were you socialized into sport? When? Were your other family members socialized into sport?

What experience have you had with parents in Special Olympics, Challenger baseball, and other sport adapted for children with disabilities? How does it compare with the experience reported in this case study? Do you believe that parents should be involved in coaching? Why?

Read the research study that provided findings for this case study and that by Nixon (1989) and find other research on teamwork, outcomes, values, and goals associated with after-school sport. Identify the similarities and differences in sport programs for children with and without disabilities. Give specific examples or anecdotes. What did you learn from this case study? Can you design a similar (parallel) research study focused on another sport or parents of different backgrounds?

Creativity

Creativity is an essential ingredient to adaptation and hence extremely important for physical educators. The outstanding book *Creativity and Collaborative Learning* (Thousand et al., 2002, p. 268), which many universities use as a textbook for pedagogy courses, defines **creativity** as "the production of something new—and in some way useful or 'good'—things or ideas. Second, everyone is creative. Third, creativity skills can be learned."

When defined operationally, so concrete behaviors can be observed and assessed, *creativity is a combination of fluency, flexibility, originality, and elaboration* with such affective behaviors as acceptance of new ways and people, imagination, curiosity, caring, and courage. These behaviors can be seen in movement activities, sport strategies, social interactions, children's play, and adults' leisure activity.

Table 3.6 presents cognitive and affective behaviors that are important in adapted physical education. The table's four cognitive creative behaviors have a well-established knowledge base (Guilford, 1952; Torrance, 1962; Williams, 1972). Less attention has been given to affective domain components (Williams, 1972). The five affective behaviors in Table 3.6 reflect the author's beliefs about the attitudinal-behavioral composites that are essential in working with individual differences.

As we shall see in Chapter 4, adapting, as an approach to service delivery, is largely dependent upon creative thought and action. The body of knowledge being developed on creative behaviors is called *creativity theory*. Much research is needed in this area.

Cognitive Creative Behaviors

Cognitive creative behaviors are *f*luency, *f*lexibility, *o*riginality, and *e*laboration (FFOE). These four behaviors act as a "foe" to boredom and burnout and are important for professionals to develop.

The illustrations of FFOE that you are about to read may seem far-out, by adult standards, but they work with children—not just those with problems, but all children. Most students need many more repetitions to learn skills than their interest and concentration can sustain. Part of adapting is trying enough different ways, with abundant enthusiasm, to maintain student interest.

Let's think of a third-grade boy named Bob in relation to FFOE. The IEP goals for Bob, to be met within 9 months of instruction and homework practice, are (a) to demonstrate *ability to throw (using overarm pattern) a baseball* the distance between first and second base, with sufficient accuracy for a skilled player to catch the ball (8 out of 10 trials) and (b) to demonstrate *ability to catch a baseball* thrown accurately so it arrives within an arm's length of him and between knee and chest height from the distance used in his class between second and third base (6 out of 10 trials). Let's say that the distance between bases used in Bob's class is 40 feet, but that Bob can throw accurately only about 15 feet, and he almost always misses balls thrown to him. Bob needs a lot of practice, but he is likely to experience boredom and burnout if the teacher has him practice the same tasks every day. What creative strategies can the teacher use to act as a "foe" to boredom and burnout?

Fluency

Fluency is the generation of a large number of relevant, workable ideas directed toward achieving a goal. Fluency is measured as the number of ideas generated. For instance, lots of changes can be made in relation to such variables as *nature of the ball*—weight, size, texture, color; *wording of instructions*—best cue phrases, key focus points to correct errors; *distance between bases*—adapted as needed; *motivational strategies*—rewards for successes, choice of rewards; *partner*—some practice partners meet needs better than others; *technology*—use of ball pitching machine. Can you add to the list of variables? The larger the number of relevant variables, the more fluent the teacher. Fluency is also seen in the number of different games, drills, and movement education challenges that you can devise for practicing a particular skill, and in the many different ways you can word a question, give instructions, and explain a problem. The more synonyms known, the more fluent you are. Persons who know sign language are more fluent than those who rely entirely on verbal communication. The essence of fluency is *find another way.*

Flexibility

Flexibility is making change with ease, especially about different categories and kinds of ideas. It is adaptability to changing situations and stimuli, freedom from inertia or blockage of thought, and spontaneous shifting of mind-set. Flexibility in teaching Bob can be illustrated by the ability to shift categories during assessment and brainstorming processes. In getting acquainted with Bob, the teacher can switch from the category of interests (does Bob want to learn to catch?) to relevance (do Bob's friends play catch?) to sport socialization (what kind of lessons has Bob already had in catching?). The teacher also shifts easily among the following categories of variables in discovering the kinds of balls Bob could catch: (a) size, (b) weight, (c) color, (d) direction, (e) path, (f) postures, and (g) lighting.

Flexible persons do not usually list all possibilities in one category and then move in orderly fashion to another category; instead, they move back and forth among categories with ease. This helps them to plan and teach in a **holistic** manner (i.e., see the whole, synthesize parts from many categories, combine them to make a new whole).

Originality

Originality pertains to unusual, new, and clever ideas, such as different kinds of balls and gloves during the individualized skill assessment or goal/objective-setting phase. The teacher wants to motivate the student and/or maintain his or her interest. The balls and gloves might have velcro strips on them to make catching easier, or they might have bells embedded in them and painted faces to enhance interest and motivation. Balls might smell and taste good, like an orange or marshmallow, and be offered as a reward for effort and/or success.

Unique starting and stopping signals, lighting conditions, and background music also can enhance interest. Putting game elements together in new and different ways to create adapted sports and new recreational play activities is also originality. Consider, for instance, how an egg-tossing game might be devised to reinforce and motivate catching skills. Originality

Table 3.6   Behaviors in the creative process.

Behavior	Meaning
Cognitive	
1. Fluent thinking: To think of the *most*	Generation of a quantity, flow of thought, number of relevant responses
2. Flexible thinking: To take *different* approaches	A variety of kinds of ideas, ability to shift categories, detours in direction of thought
3. Original thinking: To think in *novel* or unique ways	Unusual responses, clever ideas, production away from the obvious
4. Elaborate thinking: To *add on* to	Embellishing upon an idea, embroidering upon a simple idea or response to make it more elegant, stretching or expanding upon things or ideas
Affective	
1. Acceptance: To reach out and embrace	To feel a sense of identity and empathy with others, accept self and others in spite of weaknesses, generally feel good about life and human beings, perceive differences among people as inevitable and normal
2. Imagination: To have power to envision	To see each human being as unique, different from all others; visualize what this person can become, dream about things that have never happened; feel intuitively that this person can grow, develop, and succeed; have a mind that reaches beyond barriers and boundaries
3. Curiosity: To have a problem-solving mind	To be inquisitive and wonder, toy with ideas, be open to alternatives; seek new and different ways; ponder the mystery of things
4. Caring: To be driven to action	To become involved; find the inner resources to endure and persist until solutions are found; have faith in ability to bring order out of chaos, find missing pieces, derive solutions
5. Courage: To be willing to take risks	To devise and try new strategies; expose oneself to failure and criticism; support and defend persons, ideas, or things that are different or unpopular

might playfully be thought of as the crazy things a teacher does to keep from going crazy when skill mastery requires lots of repetition.

Elaboration

Elaboration refers to the richness of interesting details or extras supplied. Think about the last lecture you attended. Did the speaker just state facts, or did he or she supplement points with anecdotes, illustrations, examples, poems, or problem-solving exercises? During catching practice, for example, elaboration might be evidenced by the use of imagery and metaphors: "Run to meet the ball . . . play like it's a bolt of lightning . . . if you don't stop it, the forest will catch on fire"; "Reach out for the ball . . . think of it as a puppy or child falling out of a window . . . don't wait for it to come to you . . . go after it, gently, gently, now draw it in toward your chest."

The idea of catching might be embellished by coordinating skill practice with a story, music, drama, costumes, or puppets (see Figure 3.11). After each successful catch, various reinforcers might make the experience more elegant. Catching practice with a wind machine or electric fan on at one station and flickering lights at another station are embellishments, particularly when interwoven with a story.

Affective Creative Behaviors

The five affective domain creative behaviors are acceptance, imagination, curiosity, caring, and courage (see Table 3.6). These behaviors stem from feelings and emotions, rather than ideas and thoughts, and highlight sensitivity to human needs and situational problems. Sensitivity varies among individuals, but good self-concept and confidence in your abilities are related to creative behaviors. Teachers have to believe in themselves and expect success.

Acceptance

Acceptance is favorable reception. Teacher acceptance can be defined as behaviors showing that a student is perceived and treated as capable, worthy, agreeable, and welcome. Acceptance is often measured in terms of approach and avoidance behaviors. Certainly, you must approach, and be relatively close to, a student to assess her or his abilities and plan how to adapt instruction. You can be close to a student in many ways: (a) physically (hug, touch), (b) visually (smile, eye contact), (c) auditorily (warm, pleasant voice), and (d) mentally (an affinity for each other's ideas, thoughts, beliefs; a similar learning or problem-solving style, and so on).

Figure 3.11   A child who is fearful or doesn't want to play needs a teacher with creative behaviors. Here, the puppet says, "Please let me play with you . . . I want to roll you a pretty ball."

List the things that teachers say and do that help you to feel capable, worthy, agreeable, and welcome and prioritize them in terms of importance. How does your ranking of items compare with those of classmates? The specific behaviors of acceptance probably have different meanings for different individuals.

The state of acceptance between two persons provides the environmental readiness for other creative behaviors. Some teachers, however, find it easy to accept persons (and things) that are different in appearance, sound, smell, and touch, whereas others find it hard. Which are you? This pertains partly to flexibility, the ability to shift back and forth between categories of similarity and dissimilarity in people, foods, cars, beds, and the like. Some persons prefer sameness, whereas others like to liven up their existence with new and different things, people, and experiences. Which are you?

Acceptance is also closely related to empathy, an innate quality that varies from person to person and is not well understood. **Empathy** is identification with or vicarious experiencing of the feelings, thoughts, and attitudes of another. Empathy is often explained as the ability to walk in another's shoes, to see and feel the world as another does. Thus, it encompasses both sensitivity and responsivity. "Awareness Days" to enhance understanding of individual differences often include challenges to able-bodied (AB) persons to spend a day in a wheelchair or to play a game while blindfolded or wearing earplugs. Such simulated activities promote empathy and, thus, acceptance.

Imagination

Imagination is the power to envision things and people as different from what they are. Within the adapted physical activity context, imagination is the ability to visualize all that a person can become. Although imagination can dwell on the negative, the emphasis in teaching is on positive thinking. Are you an optimist or a pessimist?

Consider the effect of teacher expectations. If a teacher imagines that a student can do something, does this make it easier? What behaviors convey that the teacher imagines the student to be a leader, an athlete, or a scholar in the future? For instruction to be adapted, the process must be imagined. You must intuitively feel good about the capacity of students to change and have a clear view of the direction to lead.

Curiosity

Curious behaviors are inquisitive and searching. Some persons seem to be fascinated by the unknown; they spend a lot of time analyzing how and why things work. Others can solve problems, if challenged to do so, but typically are not curious enough to ask questions. Which are you? Some persons are interested in how the human mind works and spend a lot of time thinking about behaviors. Others are more fascinated by machines or laboratory apparatus. Which is more like you? Within the adapted physical activity context, curiosity is spontaneous involvement in problem-solving behaviors in order to answer self-generated questions.

Caring

Caring has many definitions, each of which connotes the ability to feel deeply and intensely. For our purposes, **caring** is operationally defined as having feelings and beliefs so strong that you get involved in positive action directed toward making things better for an individual or group. As used in this model of creative behaviors, caring is a complex emotion. It is intertwined with faith in your ability to create, in the probability that people and things will change in the desired direction, and in the meaning of life. Caring also is linked with the inner resources to endure and persist until solutions are found (i.e., caring enough usually evokes the stamina to keep going).

Courage

Courage is the quality that enables you to try something new, to delve into the unknown, and to expose self to failure or criticisms. Because the essence of creativity is finding new, different, and original ways to assure success for people with problems, the probability is high that at least several of the attempts will fail or receive criticism. Courage enables you to work alone, if need be, in the generation of new ideas and solutions.

Courage is needed also in adapted physical activity specialists who act as advocates for persons with disabilities and who fight for removal of attitudinal, aspirational, and architectural barriers. Proposals to change the environment, even when changes clearly benefit the lives of persons with disabilities, are often met with criticism because of the expense and inconvenience involved. To create and adapt, you must be able to withstand pressures from those who prefer traditional ways. Likewise, to become a close friend of someone different in appearance and abilities requires the courage to withstand peer pressures and the advice of significant others. To create is to dare to take risks.

 OPTIONAL ACTIVITIES

1. Spend 5–10 hr with a selected family that has one or more persons (any age) with a disability. Invite yourself, and offer to help with a recreational activity or family outing. Maybe you'll get a free meal! Be a participant-observer, and jot down reflections in your journal after you come home. Do not take notes in the family's presence. You may wish to choose families with different cultural backgrounds from your own.

2. Visit direct and related service personnel mentioned in this chapter; interview or observe as needed to expand your level of knowledge on service delivery.

3. Visit nursing homes or assisted care facilities to generalize the information in this chapter to the oldest and most fragile of our citizens. If possible, visit a particular person and engage in some physical activities with him or her.

4. Watch for newspaper articles, movies, videos, and so on that expand your knowledge related to this chapter. When possible, invite someone with a disability (any age) to share these with you and discuss them later. Or share these and discuss them with family members to get different perspectives of individuals independently seeing the same thing.

C H A P T E R

4

Adaptation, Advocacy, and Law

Figure 4.1   A top-down instructional (or intervention) model based on adaptation theory and showing person-environment interactions.

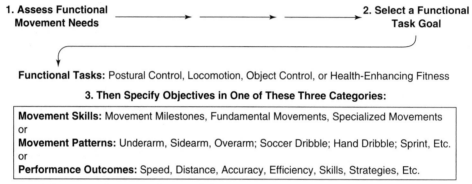

1. **Assess Functional Movement Needs** → → → 2. **Select a Functional Task Goal**

Functional Tasks: Postural Control, Locomotion, Object Control, or Health-Enhancing Fitness

3. **Then Specify Objectives in One of These Three Categories:**

Movement Skills: Movement Milestones, Fundamental Movements, Specialized Movements
or
Movement Patterns: Underarm, Sidearm, Overarm; Soccer Dribble; Hand Dribble; Sprint, Etc.
or
Performance Outcomes: Speed, Distance, Accuracy, Efficiency, Skills, Strategies, Etc.

4. **Instruct or Intervene: Assess, Select Priorities, and Manage Variables so as to MINIMIZE LIMITATIONS AND MAXIMIZE ENABLERS**

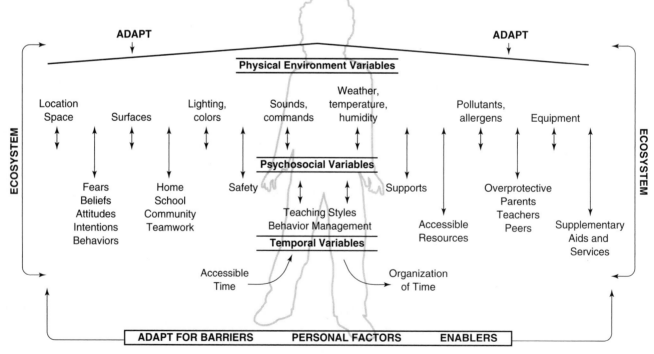

ADAPT   ADAPT

ECOSYSTEM

Physical Environment Variables

Location Space   Surfaces   Lighting, colors   Sounds, commands   Weather, temperature, humidity   Pollutants, allergens   Equipment

Psychosocial Variables

Fears Beliefs Attitudes Intentions Behaviors   Home School Community Teamwork   Safety   Teaching Styles Behavior Management   Supports   Overprotective Parents Teachers Peers   Supplementary Aids and Services

Temporal Variables

Accessible Resources

Accessible Time   Organization of Time

ECOSYSTEM

ADAPT FOR BARRIERS   PERSONAL FACTORS   ENABLERS

5. **Evaluate the Lesson or Program and Plan Change**

1. Reflect on adaptation in your life. How much do you adapt in your own activities of daily living? Give concrete examples. What makes you adapt? What are your feelings about adaptation? Why? Do you adapt more or less than most persons? Why?

2. Apply the instructional model in Figure 4.1 in your critical thinking about adapting physical education to overcome environmental barriers and personal weaknesses and to maximize environmental enablers and personal strengths. Describe specific persons with disabilities and relate your thinking to each one.

3. Relate barriers, personal factors, and enablers to achievement of the National Association of Sport and Physical Education (NASPE) standards. Describe persons, real or imaginary, with disabilities and consider the programming they need to meet NASPE standards.

4. Reflect on the link between adaptation and advocacy. What kinds of experience have you had with advocacy? Make and implement plans to broaden your advocacy experience. Be involved in at least one advocacy activity for your profession.

5. Apply the 5L advocacy model to planning your personal résumé and portfolio for the end of this course and for the completion of your degree and search for employment. How does involvement in advocacy better prepare you for employment? What advocacy activities will you be able to list?

6. Critically think about the laws that underlie adapted physical education service delivery. Why are such laws needed? What parts of specific laws do you like and dislike? Why? Link laws with historical events.

This chapter is about adaptation, advocacy, and the law. Adaptation is presented first because it is the metatheory on which the adapted physical education profession is founded. Advocacy and the law are unique to the professions of adapted physical education and special education in that no other area of the curriculum requires teachers to learn to defend the rights of their students. In a sense, however, law as covered in this chapter is a presentation of promising educational practices. In the best of all worlds, ethical, bright, and creative teachers would discover these practices on their own and use them because they are effective, right, and good, not because they are required by law.

Adaptation

Adapted physical activity takes its name from the process of adapting. It seems fitting, therefore, to call this body of knowledge *adaptation theory.* Ernst Kiphard of Germany was the first to suggest that a theory of motor adaptation should be evolved to describe the work of adapted physical educators. Kiphard (1983) stressed individual and environmental interactions as a means of maintaining homeostasis (a state of dynamic equilibrium). Persons not only adapt to the environment but alter and change the environment each time they respond to it (i.e., adaptation is a reciprocal process).

Adapted physical activity, as a profession and emerging discipline, potentially has many theories, but adaptation seems an appropriate central theme to guide **theorizing,** the process of critically thinking about relationships among concepts (variables) and systematically constructing theories. Experts define theories in many ways (Fawcett & Downs, 1992). A simple definition follows: A **theory** is a cluster of interrelated concepts that enhances understanding of a phenomenon. Theories may be used to describe, explain, or predict. A **metatheory** is a grand, unifying theory that encompasses and helps to synthesize many other theories.

At its most global level, adaptation is an umbrella process that encompasses related services, and such supports as accommodations (small changes), modifications (large changes), and supplementary resources or aids. According to

IDEA, these four terms have separate definitions and should not be used as synonyms. *Related services* refers to supportive services that are required to assist a child with a disability to benefit from special education. The other three supports are provided mainly to enable children with disabilities to be educated with their peers to the maximum extent possible.

At the curricular or intervention level, adaptation is a purposeful change process (guided by a qualified professional) to promote physical education goal achievement of students with environmental barriers and personal limitations that affect performance. *More specifically adaptation is the art and science of assessing, prioritizing, and managing variables to facilitate the changes needed to achieve desired physical activity or movement outcomes.*

An Adapted Physical Education Model

Figure 4.1 presents a top-down instructional model for teaching motor skills and patterns that is based on adaptation theory. Variables that might need adaptation are superimposed on a figure of a child's body to emphasize a holistic, age-appropriate, person-centered approach. Adaptation theory asserts that certain environmental variables create barriers and risks when they interact with personal variables in a goal-oriented physical education setting. Other person-environment variables serve as enablers, and it is the teacher's role to help the student find or create the best situational match of all interacting variables. The model begins at the top of the page with the instruction to assess functional movement needs. Depending on the level of disability severity, these may be activities of daily living (ADL) needs or physical education/leisure needs.

Selecting a Functional Goal

After completion of assessment, goals are agreed on. **Goals** are statements, written in measurable terms, that meet the following criteria: describe what a student can reasonably be expected to accomplish within a 12-month period in each school subject, relate to state standards, enable a student to be involved in and progress in the general curriculum, and are analyzable into short-term objectives or benchmarks. Lessons on writing goals and objectives will be included in Chapter 5, but it is important at this point to have a clear vision of the top-down organizing center (frame of reference). Following a top-down model means that you start with the chronological age of the student and focus on acquisition, generalization, and maintenance of movement skills and patterns that will enrich the quality of family, school, and neighborhood activities. Goals for young children may be functional competence in postural, locomotor, or object control needed to perform ADL or activities of physical education and leisure (PEL). **Functional competence** means being able to use the movement skills and patterns in meaningful, age-appropriate drills and games and to be able to perform under varied conditions (e.g., to catch a ball coming at ankle height, knee height, and chest height at slow, medium, and fast speeds; to run on varied surfaces like concrete, sand, and grass of different heights over level, uphill, and downhill slopes). Goals for older children and adolescents will probably be functional competence in one or more forms of sport, dance, and aquatics.

Assessing, Prioritizing, and Managing Variables

Simultaneously with the selection of the functional goals for the year, the physical educator, student, and parents identify the environmental variables that must be changed. Figure 4.1 lists these variables under physical environment, psychosocial environment, and temporal variables. *The specific location of each variable on Figure 4.1 is unimportant; the variables can be placed in any order.* Engaging in adaptation decisions leads to awareness of *barriers* to be overcome, *personal limitations* that may or may not be modifiable, and *enablers* to facilitate desired change.

For example, Tim, age 8, who has asthma that is not yet totally managed by medication might be assigned the **functional task goal:** *to engage in moderate to vigorous exercise five times a week, at least 20 min each session, without having an asthma attack during the last month of the school year.* The minutes do not have to be consecutive. Looking at Figure 4.1, the **environmental barriers** to be overcome might be (a) weather, temperature, humidity; (b) pollutants, allergies; (c) location of activity; and (d) overprotective parents, teachers, and peers. **Personal limitations** that may or may not be modifiable are (a) unmanaged asthma condition; (b) Tim's fear of an attack; (c) Tim's inconsistency in using inhaler correctly and at prescribed times; and (d) Tim's inexperience in judging how hard and how long he can play without an attack. **Enablers** might be (a) attitudes and behaviors of school personnel and parents (i.e., flexibility in changing the location of activity because physical environmental barriers cannot be altered); (b) accessible resources and supports to provide individual attention; and (c) home, school, community teamwork.

Teacher behaviors might include (a) arranging for Tim's physical education to be indoors, (b) using the resources of the American Lung Association (local branch in all big cities) and the school nurse to help parents and Tim understand correct inhaler techniques and the relationship between asthma and properly selected and conducted exercise, (c) having a responsible adult remind Tim of when it is time to use the inhaler, (d) negotiating with Tim and his parents to sign up for water exercise and swimming lessons at the Y, and (e) assigning a cross-age peer tutor (an older boy) with asthma to serve as a model and counselor for Tim.

Further, because Tim tends to have attacks during endurance activities but does well with sprints and short all-out effort in sports, the teacher examines the temporal variables of class work, and arranges for Tim to rotate in and out of running games every 3 or 4 min (i.e., play as hard as he can 4 min, do slow restful activities like shooting baskets 4 min). The peer tutor explains this to Tim and says it works well for him. The peer tutor also goes to Tim's home to work with him on physical education homework (i.e., a schedule for increasing the number of minutes of moderate to vigorous exercise [MVE] week by week) both on land and in the swimming environment.

Agreeing on Short-Term Objectives and Using Them to Guide Instruction

Once the plan for assessing, prioritizing, and managing variables has been formulated, objectives must be written and implemented. Tim, his parents, and school personnel ideally collaborate in setting objectives for the 6-week grading periods and put the objectives in the form of a written contract that everyone signs. This contract hangs on the wall at home, is in a file or on a personal clipboard that Tim can access in the physical education office, and is on the teacher's and/or paraprofessional's personal digital assistant (PDA) or palm computer.

Engaging in Continuous Assessment

Before and after class periods, students are asked to answer what things helped you do well today and what things kept you from doing well today? What could we change to make class more pleasant or more successful for you? What can you change for yourself? What do you need help in changing? Given the size and demands of most general education classes, these questions are better answered at a computer station in the gymnasium or locker room, than in person and only take a minute or two for a student. The alternative is to click on a tape recorder and talk into it or fill out a short survey form. The underlying principle is to engage the student in critical thinking and make him or her feel responsible for making environmental conditions the best they can be.

Students also need to record the number of minutes they worked on a task, the extent of their effort, and their scores if the activity can be made quantifiable. This can be done in journals and portfolios and presented to the teacher as requested.

Evaluating the Overall Program and Planning Change

Periodically, like at the end of each grading period, all aspects of the program are evaluated by as many participants as possible. Decisions are made about whether barriers have been overcome, personal limitations accepted or changed, and enablers maximized to enhance goal achievement. Changes are planned as needed, and the cycle of instruction or intervention is begun anew. In summary, the top-down model based on adaptation theory has four steps. The model is applicable in general education (GE) or in specially designed settings for students not able to function in the GE program.

With partners, apply the adaptation instructional model to children with various kinds of disabilities. First, describe a particular student and select one or more functional goal tasks. Then show how the four steps might be implemented. Also try implementing the four steps in a real teaching or service delivery setting.

Adaptation of Teacher Communication

Starting, stopping, and quiet signals are important variables to alter in terms of class needs. The teacher's hand extended high in the air is almost universally used as a quiet signal with students raising their hands into the air, in unison, to silently spread the instruction. Occasionally, however, there may be a wheelchair student with severe cerebral palsy in class who has a *symmetric tonic neck reflex.* When this student looks upward to see the hand signal, the reflex causes his or her lower body to straighten and stiffen so that the body slides out of the chair or, at best, becomes unbalanced. In such cases, the signal clearly needs to be changed to a different kind of arm signal, a light flash, or a gentle sound. Loud sounds, like whistles, cause the *startle reflex* in many persons with brain damage, meaning they jump as with surprise.

When teaching children with attention deficit hyperactivity or certain kinds of cognitive problems, it is often best to have students sit when you need to explain a rule or a strategy rather than just stop and stand because standing quietly is a challenge to most children, hyperactive or not, in the middle of an exciting game. A count signal is often helpful: "Stop, sit, and freeze 1-2-3-4-5."

Applications of the Adaptation Model

Persons with hearing impairments, deafness, or blindness need everyone around them to care enough to adapt by talking loudly and clearly, keeping pathways clear of clutter, and remaining aware of when persons hear versus when they do not. As noted on Figure 4.1, the variables associated with beliefs, attitudes, intentions, and behaviors are the key to adaptation. If persons are motivated to make something work, they are likely to do so. Following are some examples.

Adaptations for Hearing Impairment and Deafness

Simple observation reveals that a 13-year-old (Kay) has a mild hearing loss and does not understand much of the speech of teacher or classmates outside of a 5-ft radius (see Chapter 26). If there is any background noise (e.g., ball bouncing, air conditioning and heating sounds, whispering of classmates), hearing is even more of a challenge.

Kay's parents have decided not to buy hearing aids until the condition worsens; their hearing specialist has told them that Kay's condition is borderline. Kay pretends that she hears more than she does because she does not want to be singled out for attention, especially when certain special boys are around. After assessing the conditions in which Kay can and cannot hear (i.e., the person-environment interactions), the teacher will encourage Kay to set some rules for herself like (a) whenever

Figure 4.2   Example of a behavior contract signed by both parties.

Behavior Contract
I will show self-direction in trying harder to hear and understand by
1. Moving so I am always looking a speaker in the face.
2. Trying to read speech and gestures and facial expressions.
3. Placing myself within 5ft of a speaker.
4. Asking persons to "Please repeat."
5. Using a buddy for hearing help when the gym is really noisy.

Kay Snyder
September 1, 2004

I agree that I will facilitate Kay in her self-direction and encourage all students to use gestures or signs when talking and to care that everyone can hear.

Ms. Sharon Bowers
September 1, 2004

someone is speaking whom I want to hear, I will change my location as needed to place my self within 5 ft of the speaker; (b) I will move as needed to be able to see the face of the person speaking; (c) I will try to **read speech** *(this skill used to be called lip reading, but now it is accepted that one reads another's whole body in order to communicate);* (d) when I still cannot hear, I will watch my classmates closely and follow their actions; (e) I will work to overcome my embarrassment when I need to ask persons to repeat or to reduce background noise that they have instigated; and (f) I will consider telling some of my best friends that I do not hear well and need their help. *All of these self-rules are adaptations.*

This example shows that it is better to facilitate a student in creating self-help adaptations than for the teacher to assume full responsibility. This process can be similar to a contract between student and teacher, with each party trying hard to improve on communication (see Figure 4.2). There must also be agreement about the way that success of the adaptations will be monitored.

The adaptations in the same gymnasium for a deaf 13-year-old (Juan), who mostly communicates by gesture and sign language, are similar but typically require the school to employ an **interpreter** (Best, Lieberman, & Arndt, 2002). Parents or others may request this interpreter at the IEP meeting. A good adaptation also is the use of peer tutors as partners. *Deafness, as opposed to hearing impairments, describes a person unable to understand speech via the ears, with or without hearing aids.* Juan is entirely dependent on what he sees for communication. Because sight is so important, ordinary indoor lighting must be increased to optimal lighting, equipment must be ordered in the colors that make seeing easiest for Juan, and background colors must contrast with equipment.

Adaptations for Visual Impairment

Jim is legally blind, meaning that his eyes see at 1 ft what average eyes see from 10 ft, providing the lighting conditions are good (see Chapter 27). Jim has particular trouble with outdoor lighting because of the variables of weather (cloudy), pollution (usually makes the sky hazy by noon in big cities), and time of day (near sunset). Jim likes track and field. In good lighting, he can run around the track independently. However, darkened conditions make running activities unsafe for persons who are likely to bump into obstacles or stumble on uneven surfaces. Not much can be done about these barriers except to play sports inside or to use guide runners as buddies. Frequently, all persons with vision impairments are called blind (as by the United States Association for Blind Athletes), but blindness can encompass many different degrees of visual acuity. The same thing is true of other disabilities. Never take a definition for granted! Remember, adaptation must be personalized, based on assessment.

Adaptations for Mental Retardation

Mental retardation implies that there are limitations in attention, memory, thinking, applying, generalizing, evaluating, and other aspects of cognition. Let's consider three examples. Let's say that Sue, age 10, in Mrs. Garza's GE physical education class frequently seems confused about the station where she should be working and the activities she should be doing. One task goal selected for Sue by the IEP team is *When the class is given instructions about where to move in the gymnasium and which activity to practice, Sue will take 10 seconds to assimilate the instruction and, when requested (Sue, tell me what I told you to do!) will repeat what the teacher said as she does the requested act.* Achievement of this goal will be at the 80% success rate during the last month of the school year.

Applying the adaptation model, Mrs. Garza decided that the major barrier was temporal variables (i.e., Sue needed more time than peers to process and act on instructions and psychosocial variables (i.e., Sue needed a buddy or special friend). Personal factors that needed to be accepted or changed were (a) slowness in processing and acting on information, (b) confusion when persons talked fast and used long sentences, (c) reluctance to change workstations expressed by slowness in compliance, (d) preference for sitting and watching rather than for practicing the skill, and (e) no special friend to make the class meaningful. Enablers were beliefs, attitudes, intentions, and behaviors of the GE physical educator; the availability of an adapted physical education specialist for consultation; and Sue's willingness to please, when given special attention.

The adapted specialist videotaped some of Mrs. Garza's lessons, and collaboratively they decided that she talked too fast and expected compliance in an unreasonable amount of time. **Time delay intervention theory** recommends that persons with cognitive limitations be given 10 or more seconds to answer or to act before an instruction is repeated (Zhang, Horvat, & Gast, 1994). Mrs. Garza increased the time interval between the instruction and the expected response and further clarified the assigned station for the day by hanging a large photo of Sue on the sign post next to the station. She also increased the number of times she said Sue's name followed by

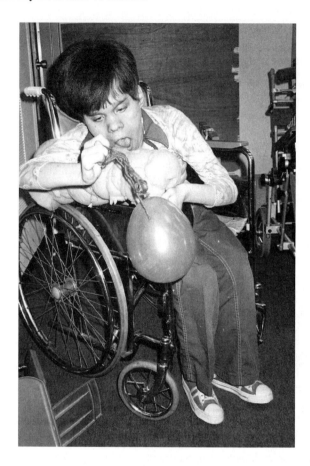

Figure 4.3 In a task analysis, the manipulation of light balls (like balloons) comes before heavy balls. This teenager has so little arm and shoulder strength that shaking a balloon on a string is the first ball-handling activity he is able to master.

positive feedback during class sessions. These adaptations allowed Sue to meet her functional task goal for the year.

Adaptations for Fitness Needs

Equipment, facilities, body position, time and space requirements, and other variables can be easily adapted by creative teachers and students working together to achieve personal bests. Following are some principles to guide adaptations for person-environment problems of strength, endurance, balance, agility, coordination, or accuracy.

Problems of Strength and Endurance

1. Lower the net or basketball goal.
2. Reduce the distance the ball must be thrown or served (a) between bases, (b) between serving line and net, (c) between partners.
3. Reduce the weight and/or the size of the ball or projectile. Balloons are probably lightest, whereas medicine balls are heaviest (Figure 4.3).
4. Reduce the weight of the bat or striking implement. Shorten the length of the striking implement or choke up on the bat.

5. Lower the center of gravity. Games played in a lying or sitting position demand less fitness than those in a standing/running position.

6. Deflate air from the ball or select one that will not get away so fast in case the student misses a catch and has to chase the ball.

7. Decrease activity time. Reduce the number of points needed to win.

8. Increase the number of rest periods during the activity.

9. Utilize frequent rotation in and out of the game or a system for substitution when needed.

10. Reduce the speed of the game. Walk rather than run through movements.

11. Consider ambulation alternatives—for example, one inning on scooterboards, one inning on feet.

Problems of Balance and Agility

1. Lower the center of gravity. On a trampoline, for instance, practice logrolls, creeping, and four-point bounces before trying activities in a standing position. Stress bending the knees (or landing low) when jumping or coming to quick stops.

2. Keep as much of the body as possible in contact with the surface. Flat-footed ambulation is more stable than on tiptoe. Balancing on four or five body parts is more stable than balancing on one.

3. Widen the base of support (distance between the feet).

4. Increase the width of lines, rails, or beams to be walked on. Note that straight lines are easier to walk than curved ones.

5. Extend arms for balance. Holding a fishing pole horizontally in front of the torso while walking the beam facilitates balance.

6. Use carpeted rather than slick surfaces. Modify surfaces to increase friction. Select footwear (rubber soles) to reduce falls.

7. Learn to fall; practice different kinds of falls; make falls into games and creative dramatics.

8. Provide a barre to assist with stability during exercises or have a table or chair to hold on to.

9. Understand the role of visual perception in balance; learn to use eyes optimally.

10. Determine whether balance problems are related to prescribed medications. If there appears to be a relationship, confer with the physician.

Problems of Coordination and Accuracy

1. For catching and striking activities, use larger, lighter, softer balls. Balls thrown to midline are easier to catch and strike than those thrown to the right or left. Decrease the distance the ball is thrown and reduce speed.

2. For throwing activities, use smaller balls (e.g., tennis balls). If grasp and release is a problem, try yarn or Nerf balls and beanbags.

3. Distance throwing is an easier progression than throwing for accuracy.

Figure 4.4 Adapting equipment (like attaching a string to the ball) and using backstops increase easy recovery of ball and maximize time devoted to practicing a skill.

4. In striking and kicking activities, succeed with a stationary ball before trying a moving one. Increase the surface of the striking implement; choke up on the bat for greater control.

5. Reduce frustration when balls are missed by using backdrops, backstops, nets, and rebounder frame sets. Or attach a string to the ball for ease of recovery (Figure 4.4).

6. Increase the size of the target or goal cage to be hit, the circumference of the basket to be made. Give points for nearness (like hitting backboard) to avoid feeling failure until basket is actually made.

7. In bowling-type games, use lighter, less stable pins. Milk cartons are good.

8. Optimize safety by more attention than usual to glasses protectors, shin guards, helmets, and face masks. Do not remove the child's glasses!

Case Study: Jim Learns to Play Goal Ball

Jim is one of several young teenagers with varying degrees of blindness who are choosing to learn goal ball. Jim loves going to camp on weekends and during the summer because it offers opportunities to compete in sports he really likes and in which he can excel. He loves the camaraderie of being on a team and fully contributing as much, or more, as the other kids. Jim has always wanted to be like his big brother, 5 years his senior, and the town's football hero.

Jim is aware that blindness is a low-incidence disability and that no other teenager with vision loss like his is within easy travel distance of his town. It is thus impossible to get a team together without a lot of travel time, money, and volunteers. Jim really appreciates his family's efforts to support his interest in team sport. He has tried track, swimming, horseback riding, judo, and other individual sports especially recommended for athletes with visual impairment, but he doesn't care much for these sports. For many years, Jim didn't know he was blind; he thought blindness was total lack of vision and he knew he could see a lot of things. He could see well enough to get around, and he put himself in the same category as other kids who wore thick glasses. He tried everything that was offered in physical education class, but he was never good enough to feel wanted on a team.

At camp, though, Jim was introduced to sports developed specifically for persons with blindness: goal ball and beep baseball. Everyone called these *blind sports*. Jim was tested by a vision specialist who confirmed that he was a B3 (see Table 4.1). Wow! He was surprised that he had to wear an eyeshade when he played goal ball and beep baseball. The coach explained that the reason for the eyeshade was to create an opportunity for fair competition between two teams. Although some persons with blindness were totally without vision (the B1s), most could see to some degree. Moreover, their vision seemed to change with environmental conditions like intensity of light and the color of the clothes that people wore. Jim quickly learned that persons who qualified for blind sport were B1s, B2s, and B3s (see Table 4.1). The United States Association for Blind Athletes (USABA) that governs most blind sports chose *blindness* as the best descriptor of the visual impairment that made him and the other campers different from their sighted friends whose thick glasses made their vision normal or 20/20.

In goal ball, two teams of three players compete on a volleyball-sized court. The movement skills are specialized: when on defense, blocking a *bell ball* of basketball size from rolling across their goal line and, when on offense, striving to get the ball over the opponents' goal line. The ball is put into play after each goal with an underarm throw (similar to a bowling pattern) from a designated area in front of the goal line. Everyone has to be quiet so the ball can be heard coming. The boundaries of the goal ball playing area are marked by heavy thick tape that can be felt with the fingertips. Sometimes the

Table 4.1   Sport classifications for blindness.

B1	Totally blind
B2	Partially blind, about 40% of normal vision
B3	Legally blind, about 80% of normal vision

condition of the floor surface affects the way the ball rolls or sounds. On hot, humid days everyone's sweat drops on the floor and makes it slippery. Players stop the bell ball from going over the goal line any way they can; sometimes they fling themselves in the ball's path and land heavily on the floor (see Figure 4.5). Elbow and knee pads protect body parts, to some extent. Soles of shoes and fabric of clothing, however, affect how players slide across the floor. Tall, heavy kids with a lot of padding don't feel contacts with the floor quite as much as the skinny kids.

Jim is growing fast (something called the adolescent growth spurt) and expects to be big and tall like his dad and older brother. The coach says Jim has real potential to participate in the USABA national games. The best part of the activity, though, is his new buddies. Having only three on a team makes for a lot of closeness. Because the low incidence of blindness prevents finding an equal number of B1s, B2s, and B3s for each team, which presumably would make for *team balance or fair competition*, the USABA supports the *rule adaptation of eyeshades* for everyone. Jim thinks the eyeshades are weird for someone considered blind, but he loves the rough, tough play. He is pleased that he is skilled enough that his parents and brother come to watch him play. He hopes his parents think that his play is as good as his brother's in football.

Analyze the parts of this case study that illustrate the physical and psychosocial environment variables in Figure 4.1. What person-environment interactions within the sport ecosystem comprise barriers, personal limitations, and enablers? What adaptations have been made and by whom? Critique these adaptations and suggest other adaptations that might be made. How might Jim's functional task goal be written? What is the performance outcome?

Davis (2002), in his excellent book Inclusion Through Sports, *recommends that goal ball be taught in general physical education classes so that it becomes a sport for all at the local level. Numerous physical educators have played this game as an awareness level activity in their university classes, and they attest to the fun and challenge of the skills and strategies. What might be the pros and cons of making goal ball a part of the general physical education curriculum?*

Obtain more information on how to play goal ball and encourage your peers to join you in a game.

Adaptation Strategies and Creativity

Good teachers have always used adaptation strategies to match instruction with the capability of individual students and ensure safe, successful learning. Some creative personalities can adapt

Figure 4.5 Goal ball players, wearing eyeshades and knee and elbow pads, stop the bell ball from passing over the goal line any way that they can. Three persons are on each team.

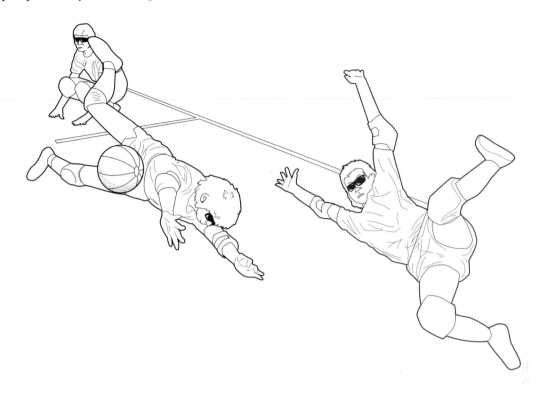

all kinds of things without formal instruction, but most professionals need systematic instruction to become qualified to provide adapted physical education services. *The essence of adaptation is to determine how many variables need to be changed and how many ways they can be altered (fluency), to think of different categories of change (fluency), to find new ways that no one else has tried (originality), and to explore details that may help in achieving desired outcomes (elaboration).*

The psychosocial person-environment variables are affected most by the number of persons present in the instructional context and their beliefs, attitudes, and behaviors in relation to the student with a disability, the activity focus of the day, the teacher, and the aides. The more persons present, the more background noise. Research indicates that females (both teachers and peers) tend to be more accepting and inclusive of children with disabilities in physical education than males. The creativity and adaptation knowledge of everyone present affects accessibility of supplementary aids, services, and supports and tolerance for changes in curriculum and instruction that enhance opportunities for participation for all.

Overactive Perceptions and Subsequent Distractibility

Some individuals are more sensitive to sights, sounds, smells, and touch than others. They cannot seem to block out extraneous human and background variables like those listed in Table 4.2. Variables that children are aware of can be assessed by games like "What do you see? What do you hear? etc." interspersed with bouts of vigorous activity followed by a return to

their floor spots. Teachers need to find out whether extraneous variables distract from learning and adapt accordingly. Persons who wear hearing aids will probably be extremely sensitive to sounds because aids magnify almost everything.

Adapting or Specially Designing Sports for Specific Disabilities?

Numerous sports have been subjected to slight adaptations so that persons with disabilities can play for health, recreation, or competition outcomes (Davis, 2002; Paciorek & Jones, 2001). A cardinal principle in adapting sport or games is to make as few changes as possible so participants, at least those with minor limitations, can feel that they are fulfilling valued sport roles in the same way as their childhood heroes and models (usually persons without disabilities) and current associates. *Sports 'N Spokes,* the voice of wheelchair sport, for instance, has recently published athlete discourse on removing adaptations (changing two bounces in wheelchair tennis to the one bounce in stand-up tennis, changing the number of seconds in the lane in wheelchair basketball from 5 to the standard 3 in stand-up basketball) so players can show their full talents (Thiboutot, 2002). In general, adult athletes with disabilities like to feel that their sports are specially designed, not adapted or special in any way. Adapted physical activity professionals seldom understand this stance in regard to adaptation because they are proud that adaptations provide opportunities for more players. A compromise seems to be calling such sport *disability sport* (Davis, 2002; DePauw & Gavron, 1995; Paciorek & Jones, 2001) or *blind sport* or *CP sport* or *dwarf sport.*

Table 4.2 Perceptions that influence learning.

What Child Sees	What Child Hears	What Child Smells	What Child Feels
Model or demonstration	Verbal instructions	Perfumes	Physical touch
Facial expression	Voice	Soap/water	Close/distant
Gestures	Footsteps	Bad breath	Light/heavy touch
Postures	Breathing	Perspiration	Firm/weak grasp
Clothing/style/color	Gum chewing	Tobacco	Short/long contact
Jewelry	Gestures	Alcohol	Friendly/unfriendly
Makeup	Clothing	Garlic	Hot/cold
Hairstyle	Background	Dust, dirt	Rough/smooth skin
Height/weight	Distracting	Mothballs	Hair
Body proportions	Facilitating		
Eye contact, how much			
Locomotion, how much			

Interacting Variables for Adaptation

Familiarity with variables that can be changed to make a task easier or harder is important. Many teachers use the **Find Your Own Space** game to increase children's awareness of the physical environment. This warm-up activity begins with stretching in every direction, coming close to classmates but not touching them. The area can be *open* with lots of space to stretch in, *cluttered* with many bodies and equipment, or *organized* like an obstacle course. Children are challenged to do all kinds of locomotor activities, including imaginary movements like Spider-man, or a snake, or an elephant, which require them to change their body profiles to agile and athletic, to low and elongated, to big and heavy. Word imagery may be enough to guide this activity, or large pictures may be added as prompts. The variations of Find Your Own Space are as limitless as your imagination. The activity can involve everyone running in a different direction about a huge gymnasium in search of pennies, cardboard stars, or holiday objects; or follow-the-leader challenges can take children along lines on the floor, over mats and rugs, and between cones or chairs (see Figure 4.6). Following are variables that can be altered to increase students' awareness of what makes an activity easier or harder.

1. **Task variables.** These include specific instructions about the task to be learned or practiced. These vary, of course, for locomotor, object propulsion, and object reception tasks. If the task is to throw a ball, the following factors should be considered:

    a. Speed—fast, medium, slow; constant or changing.

    b. Pathway—horizontal, vertical, curved, zigzag.

    c. Direction—constant, changing; to midline, preferred side, or nonpreferred side; forward, backward; to a target or unspecified.

    d. Height—way above head, eye level, chest or waist level, ground level.

    e. Accuracy—no error, some error, lots of error.

    f. Force—hard, medium, soft.

2. **Physical environment variables.** These include

    a. Space—open, closed; blank or structured by lines, ropes, or barriers; large or small.

    b. Support, wall, and ceiling surfaces—their stability and colors; their influence on sound, lighting, and movement. The support surface, for example, can be moving or stationary when the goal is to enhance balance. Or the walls and ceilings can be made to move. Or a floor or wet grass may be slick.

    c. Lighting—bright, dull; direct, indirect; positioning to avoid looking into the sun.

    d. Sound—loud, average, soft; clear, muffled; use of music and various kinds of accompaniment to guide or structure movement.

    e. Temperature and humidity.

    f. Allergens, pollens, molds, dust.

    g. Equipment for play, sport, exercise, mobility, communication. Which equipment is brought by student (e.g., wheelchair, communication device) and which is supplied by teacher.

3. **Object or equipment variables.** Balls, for example, can be described in terms of the following categories:

    a. Size—small, medium, large, or 8-inch, 10-inch, 13-inch.

    b. Weight—light, medium, heavy, or 5 oz, 1 lb, or 6 lb.

    c. Color—blue ball against white background, yellow or orange ball against a black background.

    d. Surface—*smooth* like a balloon or leather ball; *rough* with tiny indentations like a basketball; *cushy* with many soft, rubber, hairlike projections; consistent or changing.

    e. Texture—soft, firm, or hard; consistent or inconsistent.

    f. Sound—silent, beeping loud or soft, jingling with bells, or rattling with noisemakers.

    g. Shape—round, oblong, or irregular.

    h. Movement—stationary or moving.

4. **Psychosocial environmental variables.** This refers to attitudes/feelings about self and others. It encompasses the nature and number of persons sharing the space, how they are perceived by the teacher and the learner, and how they affect learning. Is only one person recognized as the teacher, or are several individuals helping and sometimes

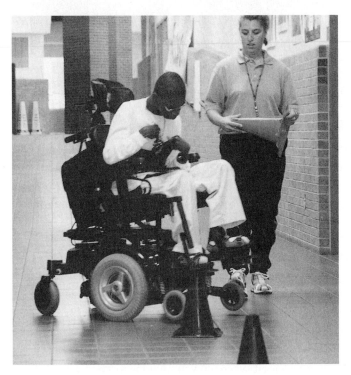

Figure 4.6 This high school student with CP in a motorized chair practices choice making in a Find Your Own Space activity by signaling to the teacher the distance he wants between the cones he will practice weaving around.

giving conflicting directions? Are peers viewed as supportive, indifferent, neutral, or hostile? What are expectations, reactions, and actions? Are partners and peer tutors used?

5. **Learner variables.** These include interest, previous experience, personal meaning of a new skill or activity, modality preferences, learning style, self-concept, strengths and weaknesses, and demographics like age, gender, race, and socioeconomic class. Strengths and weaknesses can be categorized by domains (cognitive, affective, psychomotor) or by specific fitness and movement abilities.

6. **Instructional variables.** These include teaching style, type of feedback, method of presenting new material, level of assistance during practice, structured use of time, and physical distance between learner and teacher.

7. **Temporal environment variables.** These include how you structure use of time and determine appropriate speed of instructions and activities.

   a. Planned time, unplanned time.

   b. Time on task, number of trials within time period.

   c. Duration of time for each set of instructions and other parts of lesson.

   d. Time intervals between cues, performance, correction, reinforcement.

Adaptation theory posits that professionals who are knowledgeable about variables are able to match abilities with content and teaching style to create optimal learning opportunities. **To adapt** means to make suitable, to adjust, or to modify in accordance with individual needs. *Adaptation involves individualization.* For some persons, *adapt* may mean to make a task easier, but for others, the challenge is to make it harder or more interesting. For most, *adapt* simply means to find another way: to experiment, discover, create!

Adaptation and Service Delivery

Adapting is important in all aspects of service delivery. Each of the seven services constituting the PAP-TE-CA model in Chapter 1 (planning, assessment, preparation, teaching/counseling/coaching, evaluation, consulting, and advocacy) are made more viable by appropriate adaptation. Although these services are described in considerable detail later in the text, *an overview of adapting in relation to each is presented here to assist with practicum experiences and other 1:1 initiatives.*

Planning

Most university students have little control over the people they are assigned for practicum work. Planning thus requires getting ready for anything. Visiting ahead of time, getting acquainted with staff and facilities, and acquiring general information about the neighborhood and such variables as ethnic group, socioeconomic status, and leisure-time practices are helpful.

Whenever possible, obtain photograph and videotape clearance for your practicum student. Access to files is also essential. Discussing these needs with supervisory personnel and sharing ideas about responsibilities and benefits creates the structure for an optimal practicum experience.

Planning, after the initial meeting, involves getting acquainted, establishing rapport, and cooperatively agreeing on goals. For example, assume that you are assigned an 8-year-old named Bob who is receiving physical education in an integrated setting. A unit on catching and throwing is under way, and Bob's catching proficiency is far below that of his classmates.

Planning involves gathering information about relevant variables so that time and space can be used wisely. Instructional planning is often enhanced by asking Who? What? Where? When? and How? Let's consider each of these in relation to Bob:

   Who? The *who* is obviously Bob, but this question also involves thinking through yours and Bob's relationship to the other students in the class. Should lessons be confined to interactions only between Bob and you (i.e., a pull-out type of instructional arrangement), or should part of each class period be spent interacting with other students? If the answer is other students, then which ones, how many, and in what roles?

   What? The *what* is primarily the motor skill of catching because a multidisciplinary diagnostic team has already indicated that this is a major goal for the year. Specifics about catching, however, will be determined cooperatively by you and Bob as part of instructional assessment.

   Where? The *where* is the location you select or are assigned for your one-to-one interactions with Bob.

Negotiate for a private space with as few distractors as possible. Make a list of other important variables. What kind of equipment is needed? Do you want the same location for each lesson, or is it desirable to schedule different learning stations?

When? The *when* is the number of minutes allocated to physical education instruction each day. For example, if your time allotment is 30 min, how much of this time each day should be devoted to catching? Your decisions will depend largely on assessment data. The *when* variable can also involve your motivating Bob to spend after-school and weekend time on catching.

How? The *how* (pedagogy) should be related to assessment data and determined cooperatively by you and Bob. Find out what kinds of balls, gloves, backboards, and related equipment are available and the procedures to be used in reserving them. Often, you must create or purchase your own equipment. The practicum experience is a good time to begin your personal suitcase (preferably one with wheels) with homemade balls and other novel objects that enhance goal attainment (see Figure 4.7). *How* also involves planning to ascertain that Bob has balls at home for practice and that parents and significant others are motivated to help him.

In summary, planning is extremely complex because it relates to every aspect of service delivery. There is daily, weekly, and semester planning. Some of this is done by the teacher alone, but much of it is cooperative.

Assessment as Part of Teaching

Assessment involves examination of both the environment and the individual to determine what needs to be changed and what can remain the same. **Environment** is total lifespace (physical, social, and psychological) and can be broken down into hundreds of variables, each of which may affect behavior. Consider, for instance, how light and noise factors influence test results of persons with different disabilities.

In Bob's case, the goal is to learn to catch. Goals must be operationalized by breaking them down into objectives. Prior to establishing objectives, however, explore personal meaning. Does Bob care about learning to catch? Do his friends know how to catch? Does he have opportunities to play catching games? What kind of instruction has he already had? Where? By whom? Has he had previous experiences that cause fear, anxiety, or doubt? Through question-and-answer interactions, teacher and student together cooperatively agree on the goal, verbalize it, and perhaps write it or sign a contract indicating intent to teach and learn.

Assessment is individualized to focus on strengths as well as weaknesses. Students participate in choice making. What kinds of objects can the student catch? What movement variables must be addressed? The best way to find out is usually to ask the student and/or engage in cooperative problem solving. Together, teacher and student identify present level of performance, determine learning style, and work out details concerning pedagogy. This process should be activity oriented,

Figure 4.7 Physical educators need suitcases on wheels to transport their homemade equipment.

fun, and free from anxiety. Encourage the student to discuss what task requirements he or she wants and/or needs. If Bob says, "Hey, I think I can catch that big yellow ball," then you may say, "Good, where do you want me to stand when I throw it?" Then a few tosses may be exchanged before other variables are brainstormed.

The level of task difficulty appropriate for Bob is established by experimenting with balls with varying object dimensions (size, weight, shape, color, texture, sound) and movement dimensions (speed, force, direction, pathway, height at moment of contact). Environmental and instructional variables also are considered. **Environmental variables** include (a) postures while catching (sitting, standing, running), (b) use of glove/nature of glove, (c) lighting, (d) noise control and/or choice of verbal cues, (e) assistive devices to help with balance, and (f) floor or ground surface. **Instructional variables** that relate to task difficulty include amount of assistance needed, nature of assistance, length and wording of verbal instructions, and use of demonstrations. Also important is time lapse between an instruction and required response. Some children require more time to process information than others. Thus, assessment focuses not only on what the student can do but also on environmental and instructional variables to be manipulated.

Preparation, Writing Objectives

Preparation in regard to instruction refers primarily to determining the objectives to be met and the activities needed for learning to occur. Specific objectives are cooperatively set by teacher and student, and amount of practice time and effort are agreed on. An **objective** is a specific statement that includes (a) condition, (b) behavior, and (c) success criterion. The acronym CBS serves as a memory device. For example,

C **Condition:** Given a ball of a certain size, weight, color, texture, and sound, thrown in a certain way from a set distance,

B **Behavior:** Bob will perform a two-hand functional catch

S **Success Criterion:** in 7 out of 10 trials.

To achieve this objective, Bob may sign a contract in which he agrees to do 50 catches, with various balls under a variety of conditions, every class period for 6 weeks. Or he may agree to go to the catching station and practice a certain number of minutes three times a week. An important part of individualization is the student's understanding of both objective and process.

Teaching/Counseling/Coaching

Adaptation in teaching/counseling/coaching requires individualization. This is easy in a one-to-one practicum setting, but individualization does not necessarily mean teaching one-to-one. Learning to individualize in group settings is important, since teachers are often responsible for 20 or more students.

For example, while working with Bob on catching, you could consider pedagogies that might be used in assisting 30 students to meet personalized objectives with regard to catching. One approach is creative utilization of gymnasium space so that many different stations, each offering a progressively more difficult level of challenge, are operative. Another is to encourage students to assume partial responsibility for their learning by using contracts, task cards, and videotape technology. Partner and small-group feedback permits students to help one another.

Movement education is an approach that permits many students to work simultaneously on the same skill but at their own level of difficulty. In movement education, the teacher asks questions that guide students in discovering the ways their bodies can move and how they can use movement elements (time, space, force, and flow) in new and different ways. For example, a movement education session on catching could involve every person having one or more balls and the teacher asking questions about the following:

Time (fast, slow concepts; rhythms). Can you throw your ball into the air somewhere in front of you and then very swiftly run and catch it? Can you do this same thing but change the toss so you can move very slowly and still catch it? Can you do this same thing except toss the ball against a wall and catch the rebound?

Space (concepts of level—high, low). How high can you throw your ball into the air and make a successful catch? Try some different-sized balls. What difference does this make? Find a partner and see how low you can toss the ball to him or her and still have a successful catch. How far away do you need to stand from each other? Can you toss a ball so it arrives at exactly waist height for your partner?

Force (concepts of hard, soft; heavy, light). What makes it hurt when you catch a hard ball? How can you change a toss so that it does not hurt? Can you toss and catch a ball with different body parts? How about just your

wrist and fingers? Now how about a toss and catch that uses shoulders, elbows, wrists, and fingers? Which way results in a soft throw? a hard throw?

Flow (concepts of graceful vs. jerky; free vs. floorbound). Can you follow through in the direction of your toss—let your whole body flow with the movement? Can you relax when you catch and pull the ball in toward you? Try jumping up as you catch a fly ball. Now try catching the same kind of ball but play like your feet are glued to the floor. What is the difference in the feeling?

In movement education, there is no right or wrong answer, *so the teacher does not make corrections or give demonstrations.* The secret is to generate questions that motivate each student to discover all he or she can about catching. Often, novel tasks, such as catching objects thrown into the air with a large cup, are helpful (see Figure 4.8). Such a task promotes hand-eye coordination as well as creativity in thinking up items that can be tossed and caught. Movement exploration involves few discipline problems because there is no set formation and only two rules: (a) stay on task, and (b) respect other persons' space and objects.

Games analysis, or the games design model, updated by Morris and Stiehl (1999), is a systematic approach to changing games so that students can learn functional competence by practicing skills within game settings. In this approach, games are analyzed into six components: (a) purposes, (b) players, (c) movements, (d) objects, (e) organization, and (f) limits/rules. One component is changed at a time to create a new game.

Catching balls pitched by a machine or thrown by a teacher or partner is probably the best way to learn to catch because more trials are afforded than in games. Nevertheless, changing drills into games often enhances interest and the motivation to give best effort for a long time. Following are some ways to apply game analysis strategies to catching.

Circle call ball is a traditional game in which about six students stand in a circle with one person in the center, holding a ball, who starts the play by calling the name of anyone in the circle and then tossing the ball vertically into the air. Upon hearing his name, Bob runs in and catches the ball. If successful, he becomes the new "it" in the center and calls someone else's name. If not successful, he makes a choice to return to his place in the circle or to go to a ball catching station for more one-to-one practice. Sometimes there is a rule that players can leave the group and go to the ball catching station only after they have had 10 misses. In the adapted physical education version of this game, the goal is to adapt the difficulty of the vertical toss to each person's ability so that the team can keep the ball from touching the ground as long as possible. The size of most classes permits several teams to be playing consecutively so there can be competition in regard to which circle keeps the ball in play the longest.

Circle call ball can be altered by using balls of different sizes, textures, or colors or by using different cues to determine who comes to the center of the circle. Objects other than balls can be used. My students particularly liked an adaptation in which a small rubber doll was used instead of a ball, and I

Figure 4.8 A movement education activity that facilitates catching skills is to challenge first-graders to find how many ways they can toss objects in the air and catch them with a cup.

named persons Firefighters #1, 2, 3, 4, 5, and 6 for practice in numbers as well as reinforcing the importance of firefighters. Before the doll was thrown into the air, the child in the center called out: "There's a baby in a burning house. The mother is tossing her out the window. Firefighter #3 to the rescue." The children liked the sameness of the dialogue each time, and this gave each of them practice in talking loudly and clearly. Because the doll was rubber, they could play this adaptation in water as well as on land. They also chose to adapt the distance they stood from the ball tosser and whether they were facing the ball tosser or all standing with their backs to this person. After a while they wanted the person to throw two or three objects up in rapid succession and cue several persons to come into the center.

Catch the cane (or broomstick) is a variation of circle call ball except that the person in the center holds a long stick of some kind upright, calls out a cue for one person to come to the center, and then releases the broomstick. The game purpose is to catch the stick before it hits the ground. It can be adapted in ways similar to circle call ball: a canoe paddle or any long pole.

Games can be invented that involve tossing and catching balls over volleyball-type nets of different heights. Again the emphasis is on helping one another catch and keeping the ball(s) in the air as long as possible, rather than throwing so as to make a person miss. Traditional **four corners volleyball,** for instance, can be played by having students toss and catch rather than use volleyball skills to get the ball(s) into the other team's territory (see Figure 4.9). Start with three or four balls in play and work up to six or eight. The game purpose is to keep tossing balls over the net into any quarter desired so as to keep all balls out of one's own territory. When the whistle blows after about 3 min, students must freeze, sit down immediately, and hold balls in their possession over their heads. The team holding

the most balls loses. The game can be made more difficult by adding a third net to the crisscross configuration, making the balls smaller, and by increasing the number of balls.

These games, thus far, improve only the eye tracking and catching skills needed for balls arriving from a downward direction. What games can you adapt for practice in catching balls of various sizes arriving at chest, waist, or knee height and coming to the left, right, and center? An easy adaptation might be circle call ball with the action cue being, "Mary, a ball's coming to you knee high to the left." The person on Mary's right could be taught to run behind her, catching the ball and "backing her up" if she misses. Using the six games components of Morris and Stiehl (1999), adapt some traditional games to teach catching and other game skills. Participate in a class session in which you lead groups in the games you have adapted or you guide them in making adaptations of their own.

*Tag is a fun game to adapt because different safety positions can be declared for each adaptation. How many safety positions can you think of? My favorite is **turtle tag.** The only way you can be safe is to drop on the floor, on your back, with your four limbs extended into the air, like a turtle flipped over on its shell. Performing the turtle stunt several times during a game enables tag to contribute to achievement of the goals of agility and body control as well as running and dodging. Tag can also be played with "it" carrying an object that is given to the person who is tagged. An adaptation can be throwing the object at a person who has an option of dodging or catching it and becoming "it" if she or he makes a successful catch. Using games analysis methodology, adapt tag and other games to broaden the goals that they can achieve.*

Figure 4.9   Four Corners Volleyball adapted to reinforce catching and throwing skills instead of volleying skills.

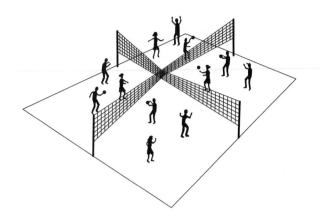

Counseling goes hand in hand with teaching, a recognition that students with movement or fitness problems need someone to talk to. Counseling in adapted physical education uses the knowledge base of sport psychology. Students are helped with relaxing, focusing, imaging, and the like. See Chapter 16 for movement activities to achieve these goals.

Coaching, properly planned and conducted, follows the same principles as teaching and counseling. Adaptation is the key to success as each athlete is helped to achieve a personal best. Coaches are sensitive to individual differences in participation incentives and other psychosocial parameters, as well as improvement in skill and fitness.

Evaluation Applied to Grading and Program Change

Evaluation is individualized because the objectives that guide everyday lessons contain success criteria. Students should be permitted to help decide how these success criteria relate to a letter grade. Various schemes can be agreed upon, with different percentages for effort, improvement, and achievement. Here, as in sport competition, the emphasis should be on achieving one's personal best (PB) rather than comparison with classmates and/or norms.

Given a student like Bob, for example, what percentage of his grade should be based on effort, improvement, and achievement? What other criteria should be used in grading? Evaluation should also be directed toward teachers, the environment, and the service delivery program as a whole. What criteria should be established to evaluate these things? How should evaluation lead to program change?

Consulting and Advocacy

Consulting and advocacy also are individualized in accordance with each student's needs. In regard to catching, for instance, the child may be referred to a vision specialist or optometrist. Parents may be encouraged to set up homework programs and to build innovative equipment. The teacher advocates both for

the student and for high-quality physical education and recreation experiences.

Considerations in Adaptation

The preceding section does not mention Bob's disability because such information often is not relevant to the adaptation process. Adapting should be based on assessment, with no preconceived ideas about what persons can or cannot do. A philosophy of adapting for individual differences and the evolution of successful service delivery practices should be based on principles or guidelines that apply across several areas. The following are ideas to consider.

Barriers and Enablers

Adaptation requires thinking about the strengths and weaknesses of persons in environmental or functional terms. To do this, you must strive to increase your awareness of variables that serve as barriers and enablers to performance and learning. **Barriers** are interactions between persons and environments that serve as limitations or constraints. **Enablers** are interactions that facilitate goal achievement; enablers must be maximized. Each student must be afforded the combination of variables that best facilitates goal attainment. This is achieved through *ecological task analysis.*

Adapting in Different Domains: Holism

When a student is placed in a group setting, the adaptation process may need to be directed toward goals in the affective and cognitive domains instead of, or in addition to, the psychomotor domain. For example, to participate in games, a student must have cognitive skills, such as understanding game formations and such play concepts as chase, flee, safe, you're out. Adapting instruction to teach the mental operations for mastering rules and strategies is much harder than focusing exclusively on skills or fitness. Success in a gymnasium is often perceived as feeling good about oneself. This attribute is related to game performance and to social interactions with peers as well as to perceived efficacy in motor skills. Sometimes, the structure of a class needs to be temporarily changed or adapted to permit work toward goals of social competency and acceptance.

Cooperative, Reciprocal Process

Adapting, regardless of the setting and goals, is a cooperative, reciprocal process shared by teacher and student(s). When students have a role in assessing and planning, they are more likely to support and advance instructional activities. Although collaborative decision making is more time-consuming than authoritarian patterns, the potential outcomes are richer and lead more directly to self-actualizing individuals who care about each other and know how to work together.

Choice-Making and Self-Determination

The essence of adaptation is choice making. The physical educator makes choices as needed but shifts this responsibility to the student as much as possible by asking many questions and waiting for an answer. In most cases, students will need to be systematically taught to make choices that will result in safe, successful, and fun physical activity for everyone. Self-determination is not meant to evolve as selfishness but rather as a feeling of responsibility to the whole (i.e., the chain is as strong as its weakest link), and thus play and game roles of value need to be created for each person. Winning is for the team, the school, or the family, not exclusively for oneself. When someone maintains health-enhancing fitness, this helps everyone in the family, not just oneself.

Some choices that can be infused into instructional activities are as follows:

1. Let students select the music they want while they do warm-up runs around the gym. Or if more structure is needed, offer two choices and ask, "Which one of these two do you want today?" When appropriate, switch to "Which one of these three do you want today?"

2. Let students choose the order in which to do warm-up or practice activities and to give the start and stop signal for self and partner.

3. Organize space so there are two or more learning stations. Let students choose what station they need to work at the most; then let them choose what station they can go to for reward (i.e., fun practice on what they are already good at).

4. Let students choose the individual number of trials of practice they will perform at school, the amount of physical activity homework they will do after school, or the kind of refreshment they will have at break. It is best to create a system for recording choices like a contract or a chalkboard entry, and it is often necessary to discuss, negotiate, and explain pros and cons of choices. Reinforcement for healthy choices should be abundant.

5. Create a practice environment where students can choose color, size, configuration, and texture of balls and targets; where balance beams are different widths; and where nets are different heights.

Valued Role Status and Adapting

This section replaces the section on normalization in the last edition. The concept of normalization has lost favor in that it is no longer acceptable to many of us to separate people into *normal* and *not normal* and to advocate that the *not normal* have the same opportunities as the *normal,* as though *normal* is the criterion that everyone must strive to meet. *The disability rights movement insists that no segment of the population be established as the criterion against which others are compared;* they believe that human beings cannot be compared and that the goal for each person should be a personal best. Normal means statistical average, and it is impossible for all people to reach average.

The American Association for Mental Retardation (AAMR, 2002a, p. 166) substitutes *role status* for normalization. AAMR defines **role status** as "a set of valued activities that are considered normative [appropriate] for a specific age group." Chief among valued roles are one's health status, educational level, employment setting, recreation-leisure patterns, community participation, and living arrangement. Within every setting or context, a person should be helped to acquire a role that is valued by self and by significant others. *Role status evolves as an outcome of participation; the more involved per-*

sons are, the more likely they will come to be needed, expected, an integral part of the whole. The role may be simply a wonderful smile or an occasional hug, but most societies value such contributions. Adapting in physical education means helping each person to find many valued roles (i.e., to become the best they can be!). Adapting applies to persons with and without disabilities because social roles emerge with positive interdependence among people who are capable of caring about each other.

Family Orientation and Physical Activity Homework

Adapting requires family interest and support to be truly effective. The ultimate goal of adapting is to find ways to make physical activity meaningful, safe, and successful at home and in the neighborhood. Parents must admire and respect physical educators and vice versa. In particular, teachers must recognize that parents are the experts on their own children and let parents know that they want to learn from them, that they do appreciate their efforts. They must build rapport as partners and avoid competition as to who has the most power or knowledge. Adapting is using the talents of everyone. This involves choices about who to use for what, when to use different talents, and where.

Use of Social Criteria

Adapting supports the use of social criteria when making decisions about appropriate conditions, apparatus, dress, games, sports, and toys. Care should be taken that students will not be teased or ridiculed because of adaptations. For example, a group of teenagers with severe retardation might enjoy *ring-around-the-rosy* because it is appropriate to their mental ages (2 to 7 years). If such persons, however, go home or to their sheltered work environments and say, "I had a good time at the club meeting last night when we played ring-around-the-rosy," this will likely cause smiles. Appropriate adaptation would be selection of a simple square or social dance activity.

Sport Classification Systems

Adaptation involves using functional classification systems to structure activity so that everyone has an equal opportunity to participate in sports and learn about cooperation and competition. Fairness in team sports depends on the balance of abilities among teams. This balance can be achieved in many ways. One way is to assign points to different ability levels and then require that the combination of players in the game at any given time must not surpass a set sum (e.g., 12 points). Wheelchair basketball is a game governed by this type of classification system. Rules followed in the United States require that every player be classified as a 1, 2, or 3, depending on his or her functional abilities. Players on the floor cannot total more than 12 points (see Figure 4.10). This system allows teams to use their members as they wish, with various combinations of classifications on the floor.

Another approach is to require that one player with low functional ability be in the game at all times. Regardless of approach, the key is to eliminate the practice of having persons sit on the bench or serve as scorekeepers and managers. Classes (as opposed to after-school sport structures) must afford all

Figure 4.10 The U.S. team balance system allows each team to have only 12 points on the floor (e.g., a team may have players worth 3, 3, 3, 2, and 1 point in play). Most amputees and athletes who can walk with a slight limp count as 3 points each; athletes with less functional capability count as 2 points or 1 point, respectively.

caught but not held or carried, (b) the ball is slightly deflated, making it lighter and softer, and (c) the serve may be thrown over the net rather than hit. The second treatment, to make the game still more accessible to unskilled students, included the following changes: (a) court dimensions and net height were reduced to that of badminton to accommodate difficulties due to weaknesses in strength, speed, and endurance; (b) an 18-inch balloon replaced the volleyball to assist hitting success and accurate passes; (c) a rule required that every player touch the ball before it could be passed over the net to facilitate participation of students with less skill; and (d) players could serve the ball from the front line of the court to increase the possibility of a successful serve.

The purpose of this experimental research study was to determine whether the two ways of playing made a significant difference in levels of participation and enjoyment. Participation was measured by (a) active time on task, (b) inactive time on task, (c) off-task time, (d) successful passes, and (e) unsuccessful passes. Enjoyment was measured by a 4-item scale: (a) I enjoyed this volleyball game very much; (b) Playing the volleyball game was fun; (c) I would describe this game as very interesting; and (d) The game held/kept my attention. Interviews were used to supplement the enjoyment survey. Reading this study can stimulate many related research projects, which are much needed to strengthen the adapted physical activity knowledge base.

Read the study by Kalyvas and Reid (2003), select one or two partners, and design a similar research study. Present your project to a class or journal club. If possible, conduct a pilot study to begin to gain skill in collecting data. Look for other studies on adaptation in the physical education and disability sport literature.

The *Journal of Teaching in Physical Education* (*JTPE*) sometimes publishes research on adaptation. Illustrative of this is a study comparing tennis racket lengths (26, 27, and 28 inches) in relation to a beginning player skills test and last 5-day game playing achievement over an 18-day tennis unit (Pellett & Lox, 1997). Findings revealed that beginner-level college students who used the shortest length racket made significantly better scores on the skill test of the forehand drive, but not of the backhand drive. No differences were reported between the three racket length groups on game-play results. Much research of this type is needed to compare the effectiveness of adaptations to equipment and other environmental variables with various age groups and genders.

students an equal opportunity to participate. This demands adaptations. Students must be helped to understand that the purpose of team sports in the instructional setting is different from that in the recreational or competitive setting.

Research on Adaptation

International and national organizations on disability sport are continuously conducting research on how to change sports. Much of the scholarly world remains unaware of this research because the athlete, coach, wheelchair/assistive device expert, and sports medicine personnel who collaborate in changing sport classifications and sport rules seldom share their findings in the scholarly journals used in higher education. Paralympic-level sports leaders seldom think of themselves as researchers. Nevertheless, their validity evidence that an experimental treatment or intervention works (i.e., a change in a rule, a piece of equipment, or the way athletes are classified to ensure team balance) is in the steadily improving performance scores of athletes with disabilities. *Theirs is true action research: the creating and testing of new forms of sport or movement.* Sherrill believes that the leaders in Paralympic sport are among the best researchers she has ever seen, and anyone seeking to do disability sport research should collaborate with athletes and coaches in designing and conducting studies.

At the school-age level, surprisingly little research has been published on adaptation of sport. Kalyvas and Reid (2003) gave us a pioneer study on children, ages 7 to 12, with and without physical disabilities in a reverse integration school setting in Montreal, Canada, where children without disabilities were enrolled in a school originally built for children with disabilities. **Newcomb,** a lead-up game for volleyball, served as the first experimental treatment with three adapted rules: (a) the ball may be

The Link Between Adaptation and Advocacy

Adapted physical education and special education are among the few curricular areas that continuously must advocate for the individuals they serve. Likewise, both curricular areas are frequently called on to justify their existence and to explain their benefits as part of free appropriate public education (FAPE). Physical activity itself, despite its documented importance to health, requires constant advocacy for persons of all ages to give exercise and sport the attention they need. Issues of attitude, prejudice, discrimination, oppression, and power (covered in Chapter 2) are always present.

Adapted Physical Education and Special Education Advocacy Issues

Some experts argue that adapted physical education and special education will not be needed if extensive reforms are achieved in GE. This book argues against this viewpoint, in that individual differences in teachers and administrators (particularly in attitudes, creativity, and ability to adapt) are simply too diverse to meet the enormous diversity of needs of all persons in physical activity and related areas within one vision or under one umbrella.

Just as the two houses of Congress and the Supreme Court create a system of checks and balances that protect rights and maximize our quality of life, a coordinated system of special education and GE ensures the best education possible. The nature of the two systems will change with time, as all things do, but advocates will always be needed to protect the rights of the less powerful, to give them unconditional love and acceptance, to genuinely enjoy teaching and coaching them, and to focus their research on them. Specialized preservice professional education (e.g., separate courses and practica in adapted physical education and disability sport, infusion of disability content into all coursework and service experience), in-service training, and staff development are required as well as easy accessibility to consultants, team teachers, and supports to operationalize the philosophy of inclusion and keep it working. To achieve these goals, university professors with doctoral degrees in adapted physical education are much needed (Zhang, Joseph, & Horvat, 1999).

Fully prepared specialists who want the challenge of teaching persons no one else knows how to manage (or wants to try) will always be needed. Some states and cities have created particularly outstanding adapted physical education programs (e.g., California, Minnesota, Louisiana), while advocates in others still strive to strengthen state and local support. Creation of a prevalence-based formula to project the need for adapted physical educators in public schools revealed that 22,116 additional teachers were needed nationwide (Zhang, Kelly, Berkey, Joseph, & Chen, 2000).

Since the 1970s adapted physical education (as a school-based profession) has had to devote much advocacy effort to convincing one school district at a time throughout the nation to add adapted physical education specialists to their employees. *Generally, parents have collaborated in this effort, especially those who have insisted, at IEP meetings, on adapted physical education services by a qualified expert.* Moreover, employment, transportation, communication, architectural, and other barriers abound in the community that affect the quality of life (including physical activity opportunities) for everyone. Funding and other supports are always needed for disability sport, Paralympic training and travel, and for recreation services for persons with disabilities. These are some of the *causes* for which today's professionals advocate.

Physical Education Advocacy Issues

Physical educators, in some ways, are like the members of stigmatized social minorities discussed in Chapter 2. Historically, physical educators have fought to have physical education valued as an academic subject, equal in value (although, of course, different) to reading, writing, mathematics, and science. Many of us believe that grades in physical education should count in the same way as other subjects and that equal time should be accorded to health, fitness, and leisure instruction and practice as to other life areas. Today, however, some laws and policies consider physical education to be nonacademic. Practices vary widely throughout the world. In the United States, each state makes its own laws about physical education requirements. *Local school districts can provide better services than the state requires, but not worse.* Communities where parents are active in advocacy are able to have outstanding physical education programs.

If good physical education instruction is in jeopardy for GE students, this influences the quality of adapted physical education services. Local school districts are not required to give students with unique needs more instructional time in physical education than their GE peers. The reality that most students with disabilities are kept in general physical education, considered their least restrictive educational environment (LRE), means that their instruction is presumably equal to that of peers: equally good or equally bad. Adapted and general physical educators, who want the best for their communities, must therefore learn as much as possible about advocacy and bond with parents who want the best for their children to promote physical education as a strong, fully accountable instructional system with after-school and weekend opportunities.

Many *preservice* physical educators indicate that they just want to teach; they don't want to be involved in law or committee work; they love children and they want to spend all their time with the children. A person who accepts employment with this attitude will soon be challenged *to adapt to new ways of believing and behaving.* Every job function is infused with the need to advocate for the children and families you serve, for the value of the services you deliver, and for the supports and resources you need. Advocacy pervades all aspects of your life, at work and during leisure, if you are fully committed to the goal of healthy, active lifestyle for all citizens in your community. It is therefore important to learn as much as possible about advocacy.

Advocacy Movement in Physical Education Begins in 1973

Originally advocacy was associated only with the law, and advocates were conceptualized as persons who worked in legal services, usually to plead someone's cause. For physical educators, advocacy began to assume a larger meaning in 1973, when *project directors of federal grants on physical education and recreation for the handicapped* (the appropriate term of the times) met to begin formation of an organization that would advocate for continuation and expansion of physical education and recreation's rightful share of federal funds and for laws and policies to support the highest quality of professional preparation possible. This organization was officially founded in 1975, the year that PL 94-142, the Education for All Handicapped Children Act (the predecessor to IDEA) was enacted, and membership was opened to all interested persons. In 1992, the name changed to the National Consortium for Physical Education and Recreation for Individuals with Disabilities (NCPERID).

Table 4.3 Websites for getting involved in the National Consortium for Physical Education and Recreation for Individuals with Disabilities (NCPERID).

NCPERID does not have a permanent address like most organizations. Although it meets every year (usually summers), most of its advocacy work is done at the committee level. Officers change annually. Following are ways to establish contact.

Newsletter Editor,	
Daniel Webb	dwebb@ncat.edu
APENS Chair, Tim Davis	www.cortland.edu/apens
Legislative Chair, David Auxter	dauxter@bellatlantic.net
Legislative Cochair,	
Robert Arnhold	robertarnhold@sru.edu

The official newsletter of the NCPERID is called *The Advocate,* because the organization advocates for inclusion of physical education and recreation for students with disabilities in federal law and for high-quality implementation of law, including excellence in professional preparation and service delivery, at the state and local levels (see Table 4.3 for contact information). Many persons today mistakenly assume that the federal laws that protect and promote adapted physical education services for students with disabilities are permanent. They do not realize that the NCPERID and other advocacy groups work constantly to maintain these laws and their funding. *Palaestra* includes a feature called "Legislative Update" in every issue, which is written by NCPERID legislative committee cochairs. The active participation of every adapted physical educator is needed in this effort.

Advocacy Movement for Independent Living Also Begins in 1973

At the same time physical educators were first becoming aware of the need for advocacy, persons with severe physical disabilities were struggling for the right to independent living and the opportunity to acquire university degrees that would make employment more accessible. These individuals are legends known and admired by almost everyone familiar with disability history. For persons who wish to establish close rapport with people with disabilities, it is important to appreciate their heroes. Not to know some of these persons is like telling an African American that you have never heard of Martin Luther King.

The founder of the independent living movement, Ed Roberts, in 1973 spent 18 hr a day in an iron lung as a result of quadriplegic postpolio but was able to move about in a motorized chair, to turn pages of a book with a stick clenched between his teeth when out of the iron lung, and to brilliantly defend his cause. Ed's story begins 10 years earlier with the struggle for funding and acceptance into the University of California at Berkeley (UC, Berkeley). At that time, persons with paraplegia were accepted into several universities, but no one with severe quadriplegia was believed capable of university attendance and subsequent employment. This prejudice affected thousands of persons who had survived the many polio epidemics in the first half of the 20th century as well as those with

Figure 4.11 A Center for Independent Living (CIL) provided Linda Johnstone (Class 6 cerebral palsy) with a good job and got her involved in advocacy. Note how the computer keyboard and telephone dialing systems are adapted in accordance with law.

quadriplegia caused by automobile and sport accidents. Roberts eventually finished a doctoral degree at UC, Berkeley and was responsible for recruiting 12 more students with quadriplegia into the university (Shapiro, 1993). Together, these persons fought for disability rights at Berkeley and are credited with obtaining the funding for the first dormitory run exclusively by people with disabilities, the first ramps on city streets, and the renovation of apartments in Berkeley so that they were accessible for independent living.

The independent living movement, begun by these pioneers in 1973, continues to empower persons through the work of employees with disabilities in over 300 locations throughout the United States (Charlton, 1998; Shapiro, 1993). These Centers for Independent Living (CILs) have been the major impetus over the last 30 years for helping persons with severe disabilities to be able to move into accessible apartments in the community, to find employment, and to develop the feelings of empowerment and the philosophy to advocate for legislation that would help them achieve equal opportunity and valued lives (see Figure 4.11).

To continue the story of Ed Roberts, in 1975 he was appointed the director of the California Department of Rehabilitation, the first person with a severe disability to hold such a position. Roberts totally reformed this department while continuing his leadership with CILs and other innovations related to better quality of living for all. *Physical educators and sports personnel who work with persons with severe disabilities will find CILs are extremely helpful* when such persons want to move away from home and find a job, like their peers. Because students relate especially well to the adults who coach after-school sports or run camps, they often rely on these persons for help in all aspects of their lives.

Find out about other disability rights pioneers and leaders by referring to such sources as Shapiro (1993), Hockenberry (1995), and Charlton (1998). The international perspective is reported well by Charlton. Among the persons who you may wish to read about especially are Judy Heumann, Justin Dart, Wade Blank, the Joseph P. Kennedy family, John Hockenberry, and Christopher Reeve. Develop written or oral reports, bulletin boards, or electronic displays. Use these to help persons understand advocacy and disability rights. Explore how persons with disabilities have advocated for sport and dance. Who are these advocates?

The Human Rights Movement and Advocacy

Professionals who care about quality of life for all individuals and who believe that an active, healthy lifestyle is an essential part of quality of life *typically extend their advocacy to many social minorities.* Such professionals are guided by their knowledge of ethics, citizenship, and government and critically think about such declarations as

We hold these truths to be self-evident; that all men [human beings] are created equal, that they are endowed by their Creator with certain unalienable rights, that among these are life, liberty, and the pursuit of happiness. (The *Declaration of Independence,* Congress, July 4, 1776)

What does this mean in a physical education class? In accessibility to water fountains, curb cuts, parking spaces, transportation from home to recreation and sport areas, availability of healthy food, safe neighborhoods, and loving, supportive adults? What does **equal** mean? Does removing students from general physical education or denying them access affect their liberty under law? Why? Does requiring all students to be in general physical education affect the pursuit of happiness of some? These are difficult questions that challenge all thinking persons, and there is seldom complete consensus. Knowledge of laws, court cases, and events regarding human rights help you to arrive at your own reasons as to why you support or do not support human rights of the various social minorities. *History shows that equality of opportunity does not come easily.* The Civil War (1860s) was fought to achieve the right of all males, regardless of race or color, to vote. Approximately 50 years later, in 1920, women won the right to vote. Persons of color, women, individuals with disabilities, and other minorities are all related in the sense that their rights are often violated. One way or another, they are denied citizenship privileges, including equal opportunities for education and physical activity. Why does this happen? What can you, as a professional, do?

Advocacy for equal and/or appropriate physical education is but one link in the chain of events whereby minority groups have fought discrimination. From 1950 to 1980, several groups sequentially achieved access to equal educational op-portunity. Figure 4.12 shows the relationship between the U.S. Constitution and early laws.

Blacks

The human rights movement intensified after World War II, when the battle against school segregation culminated in the 1954 federal Supreme Court case *Brown v. Board of Education of Topeka, Kansas.* This litigation resulted in the ruling that the doctrine of "separate but equal" schooling for Black students was unconstitutional in that it violated the Fourteenth Amendment. According to the Fourteenth Amendment:

No state shall make or enforce any law which shall abridge the privileges or immunities of citizens of the United States, nor shall any State deprive any person of life, liberty, or property, without due process of law; nor deny to any person within its jurisdiction the equal protection of the laws.

In spite of the Supreme Court's ruling that segregated education was unconstitutional, most local school districts did not change their policies and practices. *Thus, the 1960s brought the demonstrations, boycotts, and violence now known as the civil rights movement.* President John F. Kennedy (1960–1963) urged the enactment of federal legislation to end the widespread discontent, and shortly after his assassination, the Civil Rights Act of 1964 (PL 88-352) was passed by the 88th Congress. The struggle for equal education and other rights continues today (Irons, 2002), and is exacerbated by high levels of poverty, disability, and lingering prejudice.

Females

In the 1960s, the groundwork was also laid for legislation to prevent sex discrimination in education. These efforts resulted in Title IX of the Educational Amendments Act of 1972 (PL 92-318). Thus, the doctrine of separate but equal found unconstitutional for Blacks in 1964 was also declared illegal for females. The Fourteenth Amendment was cited as the basis for making school physical education programs coeducational and for justifying resources for providing equal opportunity for females and males. Equality of opportunity, however, still has not been achieved, and advocates must remain active.

Persons With Disabilities

The 1960s were also a time of beginning awareness of mental retardation (MR). President John F. Kennedy was particularly interested in MR because his oldest sister (Rose) had this condition. In 1961, he created the first President's Panel on Mental Retardation. Most persons with MR were served by residential facilities in the 1960s, and this panel worked to upgrade conditions and increase awareness of alternative living arrangements. Acting on the panel's recommendations, President Kennedy encouraged enactment in 1963 of the first major MR legislation, the Mental Retardation Facilities and Community Mental Health Centers Construction Act.

Amendments to this law in 1967 initiated the advocacy movement for physical education and recreation (PE-R) for

Figure 4.12 The human rights movement is rooted in the Constitution and based on two concepts: (a) that federal aid is a necessary intervention, and (b) that separate but equal is not constitutional. (MR-MH = Mental Retardation-Mental Health; ESEA = Elementary and Secondary Education Act.)

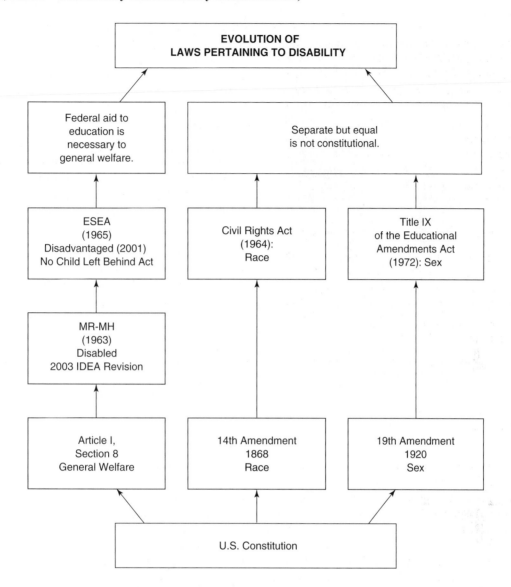

persons with disabilities. *Specifically, the Mental Retardation Amendments of 1967 (PL 90-170) provided funds for university training programs to teach physical educators and recreators how to work with individuals with MR.* In 1970, funding of PE-R training was switched to the new Education of the Handicapped Act (EHA), and authorization of grants for graduate programs and research in PE-R continues today under IDEA. The legislation introduced by Edward Kennedy was periodically reauthorized and is now known as the Developmental Disabilities Act (DDA).

Through the example set by the Kennedy family, professionals began to take an active interest in MR. Many physical educators became involved in **Special Olympics,** the sport movement for persons with MR, founded in 1968 by Eunice Kennedy Shriver, a sister of President Kennedy. Senator Edward Kennedy of Massachusetts has led the battle in Congress

for legislation to protect the rights of persons with disabilities and to improve education (see Figure 4.13).

The Disadvantaged or Poor

The 1960s also brought concern about disparities in education provided by rich and poor school districts. Local and state governments either could not or would not do anything about the welfare of many disadvantaged students. Therefore, the federal government began to intervene, using legislation as a means of enhancing the education and health of disadvantaged and/or minority group children. The Democratic party spearheaded this movement, citing the General Welfare Clause of the U.S. Constitution as its basis for action.

The first federal law to provide substantial aid to education was the Elementary and Secondary Education Act (ESEA) of 1965. This legislation provided funds for *compensatory*

Figure 4.13 Eunice Kennedy Shriver and Edward Kennedy in the 1960s were among the first advocates for physical education and recreation for people with disabilities.

education for disadvantaged students. ESEA is amended periodically, and advocates must work to keep the law the way they want it. The most recent ESEA revision (2001) is called *No Child Left Behind.*

The Sports Movement and Advocacy

Physical educators are generally interested in advocating for high-quality training and competition for students of all ages and for opportunities for elite athletes to participate in professional sports and/or the Olympics. In sports, many inequities exist between the socially dominant group (i.e., male, White, middle class) and the social minorities (Coakley, 2001). A comparison of the Olympic and Paralympic Games history lends insight into areas where advocacy is particularly needed. The modern-day Olympics, initiated in 1896, allowed only men to compete, but women won the right to compete in swimming events in 1912. Subsequently, through much strong advocacy, women have been admitted to almost as many events as men. The year 1936 is remembered for the prejudice against Jews and all nonwhite ethnic groups. From 1960 until 1992, athletes from South Africa were not allowed to participate in the Olympics because of their country's apartheid racial policies. The year 1972 is remembered for the raiding of the Olympic Village by Arab terrorists, which resulted in the deaths of 11 Israeli Olympians and 4 Arab gunmen.

It is noteworthy that Paralympics, the equivalent sports movement for elite athletes with disabilities, was not founded until 1960, and for the first four Olympiads, allowed no one to compete except athletes with spinal paralysis (e.g., spinal cord injuries, postpolio, spina bifida). For Paralympic advocates, it has always made sense for the Paralympics to be held in the same year and in the same city as the Olympics, but this was not the case on a regular basis until 1988, in Korea. When the Paralympics and the Olympics were not held in the same city, history documents prejudice and politics as causes; host Olympic cities simply did not want to make their cities accessible for large numbers of persons with disabilities. There were not enough advocates!

Also of interest is the early exclusion philosophy of the spinally paralyzed sport movement, led by Sir Ludwig Guttmann at the Stoke Mandeville Centre near London. Athletes with other disabilities (amputees and blind) were not allowed to compete in the Paralympics until 1976 (Canada). Elite athletes with cerebral palsy and those with les autres conditions like dwarfism and congenital malformations did not compete in the Paralympics until 1980. Athletes with intellectual disabilities were not permitted into the Paralympic movement until 1992, when their games were held in a different city from the main Paralympics site. This chronology shows the power of advocates working to equalize the value of athletes with different kinds of disabilities and the marketability of their sport events.

From 1984 onward, a strong advocacy movement has existed among the spinally paralyzed elite sport group for wheelchair events to be made full medal events of the Summer Olympics. The advocates were able to get demonstration wheelchair races into the Olympic schedule in 1984 and thereafter, but the philosophy of the Olympics continues to exclude events that require changes of any kind. Wheelchair basketball advocates insist that wheelchair basketball is not an adaptation of stand-up basketball but a unique and exciting separate game in its own right that can meet the stringent Olympics standards for addition of a new sport. Athletes in wheelchairs can compete in the Olympics if no adaptations are needed (e.g., archery).

Although this section has emphasized advocacy in regard to Olympics and Paralympics, *advocacy is needed most of all at the local level to provide knowledge about the benefits of sports for people with disabilities, to recruit spectators to their events, to engage in fundraising, to start and maintain programs, and to support individual athletes.* Special Olympics, which chose not to become involved in the Paralympic movement, has an outstanding advocacy program at the international and national level, but state chapters and local teams always need advocacy, particularly donations or volunteers to conduct fundraising or help with meets.

Find out the names of local sport clubs or organizations that serve persons with disabilities, interview leaders, and assess their respective need for advocacy. Who has the most support? Why? Also find out if your community has any athletes who are past or present Paralympians or international level Special Olympics. Assess their need for help with funding and media coverage. Find some university or community group to help you sponsor a fundraising event for an individual athlete or a group. Or select other ways to advocate like media, bulletin boards, providing transportation for groups to games.

Federal Intervention: General Welfare Concerns

Advocates must know and use both state and federal law. Federal law can be enacted to intervene with state policy and practices only when the courts rule that the general welfare of citizens is inequitable or endangered. **General welfare,** which refers to health and education, has its constitutional basis in Article I, Section 8, of the U.S. Constitution. This is often called the **General Welfare Clause.** Abbreviated, Section 8 states:

> The Congress shall have the power To . . . provide for the common Defense and general Welfare of the United States . . . To make all laws which shall be necessary and proper for carrying into Execution the foregoing Powers.

The General Welfare Clause, interpreted differently by Republicans and Democrats, generates much controversy in regard to issues concerning states' rights and federal control. However, the General Welfare Clause is one basis of legislation that assures students with disabilities free, appropriate education, including, if necessary, physical education services that are specially designed. This legislation, referred to throughout the book, is called the Individuals with Disabilities Education Act (IDEA).

LRE and Inclusion Philosophies

A major issue is the best class placement and services for students with disabilities. Some advocates believe that a wide variety of educational settings (e.g., general, resource, separate) should be made available so that a student's abilities can be matched to a particular learning environment. Other advocates believe that all students should be educated together in the general instructional program. These two belief systems are called **least restrictive environment (LRE)** and **inclusive placement** philosophy, respectively.

LRE placement, which is supported by the law (IDEA), requires that multidisciplinary assessment and the combined judgment of parents and school personnel be used to keep all students in GE instruction with the help of supports, supplementary aids, and services. LRE supports the student's right to be in the general classroom unless assessment data indicate that prescribed goals cannot be met in that setting, **even with support services.** In regard to physical education, a student might be assigned to

1. general physical education with no support services,
2. general physical education with support services,
3. specially designed integrated physical education (e.g., a buddy for every student with a disability; a community recreation setting to learn transition skills),
4. a resource room, separate setting, or one-to-one tutoring.

Central to LRE practice is the school district's compliance with the law that there be available a **continuum of placement options and services** as explained above. This works well in special education, but inadequate advocacy and resources have hindered its operationalization in adapted physical education.

Inclusive placement, in contrast, requires the same placement (general physical education) for everyone, with the assumption that appropriate support services will be made available in the mainstream. Advocates of inclusive placement believe that the Fifth and Fourteenth Amendments are violated when students are removed from the general classroom. However, the courts do not agree that IDEA, when properly implemented, violates constitutional law. Advocates for inclusive placement encourage lawsuits to clarify ambiguous parts of the law and promote critical thinking. For an excellent review of court cases, see Block (1996).

Inclusive placement philosophy is not the same as **inclusion philosophy,** which refers to attitudes and beliefs of acceptance that promote positive, meaningful integration. *Both LRE and inclusive placement belief systems support inclusion philosophy.* The law (IDEA) clearly states that the LRE for most students with disabilities is the GE classroom and that no student can be removed from the general setting unless the IEP process documents a failure to achieve prescribed goals, even with the help of support services.

Essentially, the conflict regarding LRE versus inclusive placement centers on a very small percentage of students with disabilities, less than 5%. These are students with severe and profound disabilities (see Chapter 10) and/or with special mobility, vision, or cognition needs that require specific transition training for community sports involvement.

Due Process and Advocacy

Due process is the constitutional guarantee that fair and impartial treatment procedures will be followed whenever life, liberty, or property rights are challenged or removed. IDEA specifies many due process requirements for removing a student from general education, but many individuals (especially parents) need help in understanding the legal process. An excellent resource for parents and professionals is an annually updated guide by Siegel (2002) available through www.nolo.com. Advocates play an important role in ensuring that due process is followed. Following is basic information that advocates must know.

Due process comes from two constitutional amendments. The **Fifth Amendment,** which applies only to the federal government, states, "No person . . . shall be deprived of life, liberty, or property without due process of law." The **Fourteenth Amendment** extends this concept to state government operations, stating, "nor shall any State deprive any person of life, liberty, or property without due process of law."

Due process, within the educational context, pertains to fair treatment in the removal of students from general education classes and/or subjecting them to assessment or other procedures different from those for their peers. In general, law distinguishes between two types of due process: substantive and procedural. **Substantive due process** pertains to whether the rule that was violated was fair and reasonable (Dougherty, Auxter, Goldberger, & Heinzmann, 1994). For example, is the rule that all students be educated in general classrooms reasonable? Is the rule that all students must have vaccinations before attending school reasonable? Both of these rules pertain to life, liberty, or property rights. **Procedural due process** guarantees a person the right and a meaningful opportunity to be heard and

Table 4.4   Organizations adapted physical educators join to increase leverage.

Adapted Physical Activity Council (APAC), within the American Association for Active Lifestyles and Fitness (AAALF), of AAHPERD

Council for Exceptional Children (CEC)

International Federation of Adapted Physical Activity (IFAPA)

National Consortium for Physical Education and Recreation for Individuals with Disabilities (NCPERID)

North American Federation of Adapted Physical Activity (NAFAPA)—a branch of IFAPA

Disability Sport Organizations of Choice (see Appendix C, Tables C.2 and C.3)

Specialized Disability Organizations of Choice (see Appendix D, Tables D.2 and D.3)

Note. Student membership fees and conference discounts are available for each of these. There is no membership fee for aligning with NAFAPA.

to protest before action can be taken in regard to his or her life, liberty, or property. *Assignment to separate special education is considered action in regard to basic constitutional rights.*

Advocacy Behaviors—the Five Ls

Advocacy can be broken down into several tasks or behaviors known as the five Ls: (a) look at me, (b) leverage, (c) literature, (d) legislation, and (e) litigation.

Look at Me—Individual Action: Modeling

First and foremost, advocacy involves setting a good example, modeling a positive attitude toward both physical activity and persons with disabilities. Each time adapted physical activity professionals are seen in a friendship relationship with persons who are disabled, this is advocacy. Each time professionals support a candidate running for public office and become actively involved in promoting education and human rights as campaign issues, they are demonstrating advocacy.

Leverage—Group Action

Leverage refers to group action as a means of gaining advantage in the fight for human rights. Whereas one individual can make a small difference, a professional organization can create pressures that make elected officials vote in desired ways (see Table 4.4). Websites for these organizations are in the appendix. Adapted physical activity professionals therefore belong to several organizations and expect part of their membership dues to be applied toward advocacy activities. They are also active in organizations run jointly by parents and professionals. Only by joining together with persons who have similar concerns can sufficient leverage be created to make a difference. Most organizations provide website and hard copy alerts to issues of concern and opportunities for organized advocacy.

Leverage also can be wielded by supporting or boycotting businesses and industries. For example, buying products from stores that employ persons with disabilities is an advocacy activity. Knowing the companies that financially support disability events and organizations guides advocates in their choice of what brands to buy.

Literature

Literature refers to assertiveness in using the written word and accompanying photos to change beliefs, attitudes, and actions. E-mail, websites, and all forms of the media can be powerful

Figure 4.14   Dr. David Beaver, editor-owner of *Palaestra,* **and Dr. Dean Zoerink, past president of the National Therapeutic Recreation Society, discuss resources on advocacy and service delivery.**

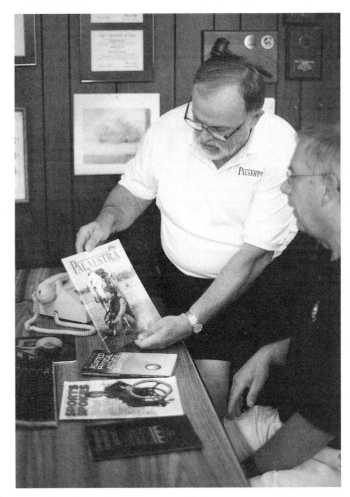

change agents. Letters to the editor of a newspaper and to elected officials are particularly powerful forms of advocacy. Chain letters can be initiated to further a cause. Research concerning the efficacy of physical education and recreation programs and/or attitudes toward persons who are different can lead to the publication of findings that advance specific advocacy goals (see Figure 4.14). Reading and using new information in change strategies is as important as writing (see Table 4.5).

Table 4.5   Magazines and journals for everyone.

Title	Publisher
Adapted Physical Activity Quarterly	Human Kinetics www.humankinetics.com/
Challenge	Disabled Sports USA www.dsusa.org
Exceptional Parent	Exceptional Parent www.eparent.com
JOPERD	AAHPERD joperd@aahperd.org
Palaestra: Forum of Sport, Physical Education & Recreation for Those with Disabilities	Challenge Publications, Ltd. www.palaestra.com
Paraplegic News	Paralyzed Veterans of America www.pn-magazine.com
Quest	NAPEHE, via Human Kinetics www.humankinetics.com/
Spirit (for Contributors only)	Special Olympics www.specialolympics.org
Sports 'N Spokes	Paralyzed Veterans of America www.sportsnspokes.com
Strategies	AAHPERD strategies@aahperd.org
Teaching Exceptional Children	Council for Exceptional Children www.cec.sped.org

Note. Abbreviations are JOPERD = *Journal of Physical Education, Recreation, and Dance;* AAHPERD = American Alliance for Health, Physical Education, Recreation, and Dance

Legislation

Legislation is the preparation and enactment of laws at the local, state, and national levels. Advocates must know the laws at each level of government that pertain to education and human rights and must monitor school and agency administrators to be sure that these laws are enforced (Siegel, 2002). Advocacy also involves acquainting others (especially parents) with laws and encouraging them to become involved in the legislative process. The Council for Exceptional Children (CEC) and AAHPERD offer outstanding legislative services and websites that help members compose letters to legislators.

Advocates must be involved in the politics of taxing and spending. Although raising taxes is unpopular, the money to run schools and social services is largely dependent upon such government revenue. Legislation thus not only encompasses the making of laws about education and human rights but also the enactment of laws that generate money. Advocates need to be assertive in deciding how federal (as well as state and local) money is spent, must monitor appropriations carefully, and must ascertain that education (especially physical education) gets its fair share.

Litigation

Litigation is the use of the judicial process (i.e., due process hearings, lawsuits, court action) to force the creation of new laws or compliance with existing laws. Advocates encourage parents and persons with disabilities to use due process procedures when rights are violated. These procedures, which are described in IDEA and other laws, include a hierarchy of activities that begin with an impartial due process hearing and end with court action in response to a lawsuit filed by an attorney. Usually, problems are resolved in the early stages of formal negotiation, and lawsuits are not necessary. Sometimes, however, governmental agencies, schools, and business and industry do not obey laws unless forced to do so.

Advocacy: A Way of Life

Advocacy is a way of life. It governs the way we teach, influences the friends we select, and affects the products we buy. To be a good advocate, we must believe in ourselves, in the democratic process, and in the power of individuals to create change. We must *care* enough to learn about legislation and litigation and to use these processes to improve quality of life.

Classic Lawsuits and Resources

Two classic lawsuits are particularly important. **The principle of school integration** is derived from the 1954 case of *Brown v. Board of Education of Topeka, Kansas.* In this litigation, the U.S. Supreme Court ruled that the doctrine "separate but equal" in the field of public education was unconstitutional and deprived the segregated group (Blacks) of rights guaranteed by the Fourteenth Amendment.

The principle of zero reject, or free appropriate public education for all children, has its roots in the 1972 class-action suit *Pennsylvania Association for Retarded Citizens (PARC) v. Commonwealth of Pennsylvania.* The court ruling that no child can be excluded from public school programs led directly to enactment of PL 94-142 in 1975. This case continues to serve as the basis for challenging the constitutionality of excluding children with severe disabilities from public school programs.

Other especially important lawsuits are reviewed in a 1986 issue of *Exceptional Children* (vol. 52, no. 4) and in an article by Block (1996). Of particular note is the *Rowley* case that clarified the meaning of *appropriate education* (Turnbull, 1986) and the *Daniel R. R.* case that clarified LRE doctrine (Block, 1996). The *Rowley* case indicated that **appropriate** must be interpreted as adequate or sufficient, not as "the best" available. The *Daniel R. R.* case resulted in standards to determine when separate class placement may be more appropriate than general class placement, with support services.

The 21st century is a time of lawsuits because persons are no longer willing to have their rights violated. Resources for persons considering legal action appear in Table 4.6. Parents or advocacy organizations acting in their behalf are more likely to file lawsuits related to school-based disability services than anyone else. Often the mere threat of a lawsuit will coerce persons into better job performance and more careful compliance with the law. In a perfect world, there would be no laws and no lawsuits because persons would care for each other and

Table 4.6   Resources for persons interested in protecting human rights through litigation (or learning more about lawsuits).

American Bar Association Commission on Mental and Physical Disability Law	www.abanet.org
Center for Law and Education	www.cleweb.org
Disability Rights Education and Defense Fund	www.dredf.org
EDLAW, Inc	www.edlaw.net
LRP Publications	www.lrp.com
Office of Civil Rights	www.ed.gov/offices/OCR
Special Ed Advocate	www.wrightslaw.com

there would be no prejudice or discrimination. Some court cases, like the two classics described earlier, provided the impetus for laws to be enacted. Others, like the *Rowley* case and the *Daniel R. R.* case, focus on interpretation of laws already passed.

Learn more about court cases related to disability. What would schools be like today if no laws pertaining to race, sex, and disability had ever been passed? What would everyday life be like? At what age did you become aware of law? How interested are you in advocacy related to law today? Why?

Basic Concepts in Federal Law Advocacy

Effective legislative advocacy requires an understanding of (a) how laws are numbered, (b) the difference between authorization and appropriation, (c) the procedures by which a bill becomes a law, (d) the protocol followed in determining rules and regulations for implementation of a law, (e) how copies of laws can be obtained, (f) enforcement of laws, (g) ways to find your congresspersons, and (h) the importance of the *Annual Report to Congress*. An understanding of basic concepts pertaining to federal laws will generalize to state-level legislative action since all states but one (Nebraska) are organized like the federal government with a Senate and House of Representatives.

The Numbering of Laws and Bills

How does a law like PL 94-142 derive its number? The first number indicates the Congress that enacted it. The second number states the law's rank or order. For example, PL 94-142 was the 142nd bill passed by the 94th Congress.

A Congress keeps the same number for a 2-year period. *The number changes at the beginning of each odd-numbered year.* The first Congress was 1789–1790, reminding us that George Washington was inaugurated in 1789. We celebrated the U.S. Constitution's 200th birthday in 1987; this was the Bicentennial, and the 100th Congress (1987–1988) was in progress. Can you use this information to determine the number that bills passed during the current 2-year period will have?

The Structure of Congress

Congress changes its number every 2 years because the entire membership of the House of Representatives ($N = 435$) is elected every 2 years. Members of the Senate hold 6-year terms, and one third of the Senate's 100 members are elected every 2 years.

Before enactment, bills have separate Senate and House of Representatives numbers. This is because the two structures of Congress consider and pass bills independently. For example, the influential Americans with Disabilities Act, enacted in 1990, was Senate (S) 933 and House of Representatives (HR) 2273. After both Houses passed the bill and it was signed by the president, the Americans with Disabilities Act became PL 101-336. Knowing HR and S numbers is important in advocacy activities pertaining to getting a law passed. When you write a letter to a congressperson, for example, urging him or her to vote for a law, it is essential to cite the law's number. Advocacy organizations can generally supply these numbers.

Authorization and Appropriation

Almost all laws involve the granting of money to carry out particular programs or initiatives. Two terms are used to designate decision making about money: authorization and appropriation. **Authorization** is the authoring of a mandate that empowers Congress to grant money, up to a specified ceiling level, to carry out the intent of a law. **Appropriation** is decision making about the actual amount to be given each year to particular programs or initiatives. Authorization is like promising an ice-cream cone contingent upon whether or not there is money to pay for it. In contrast, appropriation is like handing someone a dollar and saying, "Buy your ice-cream cone." Authorizations always involve greater sums of money than appropriations.

Authorization comes from specific laws like IDEA and may be **formula-based** (permanent) or **discretionary** (usually established for 3-year periods). In contrast, appropriation is determined year by year in conjunction with the preparation of the overall government budget. Only the president can initiate the annual appropriations bill, but both Houses must agree on expenditures. Once decisions are made, the money appropriated for a particular program is given to the federal agency responsible for overseeing that program. If advocates want federal money to be spent on programs for persons with disabilities, they must be assertive in conveying this wish to their congresspersons.

Enactment of Laws

Except for the annual appropriations bill, which is the president's responsibility, members of Congress are responsible for writing bills and introducing them to the Senate and House of Representatives. Much of this work is done by *legislative aides,* and input from individuals and professional organizations is welcomed. Committees and subcommittees from both branches of Congress study proposed bills, conduct hearings, gather testimony, and make numerous revisions. Over 95% of the 10,000 to 15,000 new bills introduced every 2 years die at the subcommittee level because of lack of support. The other 5% advance to the floor, are voted upon, and (if approved by both the House

Table 4.7 Federal laws influencing adapted physical activity from 1998 on: An extension of Table 1.3, which summarized laws from 1973 to 1998.

IDEA regulations released (*Federal Register,* March 12, 1999) for implementation of Reauthorization of IDEA of 1997, PL 105-17

PL 107-110
No Child Left Behind Act (NCLBA) of 2001: Revision of Elementary and Secondary Education Act (ESEA)
http://www.ed.gov/offices/OESE/esea/progsum/title1b.html
   107th Congress
   Highly qualified teachers in every classroom by end of
     2005–06 school year (On website, see Report to Congress
     from the U.S. Department of Education (USOE),
     "Meeting the Highly Qualified Teachers Challenge"

Physical Education Progress (PEP) Act of 2001 provides funding to local school districts, who in exchange for funding, agree to provide GPE for all district students. *Palaestra Winter 2002* says 28 PEP grants were approved for 2002.

Rehabilitation Act Amendments of 1998 expected to be reauthorized in 2003

IDEA 1997 expected to be reauthorized in 2003. Only Parts C and D will be reauthorized. Part C is infant and toddler program. Part D refers to support programs.

Figure 4.15 Formats used in writing and recording law. Can you describe each source? Do you know where each source can be found?

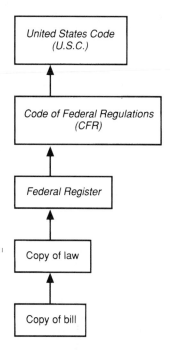

An important advocacy role is presence at public hearings and the submission of both oral and written testimony. Have you ever done this? Learn about hearings for federal and state laws from your Education Service Center and attend a hearing. Write testimony to be submitted.

and the Senate) are signed by the president and become laws. Advocates can monitor how their legislator votes and who speaks for and against bills by reading the *Congressional Record,* a daily periodical found in most university libraries.

Many bills are reauthorizations of earlier legislation. IDEA legislation is typically reauthorized (i.e., updated or amended) every 3 to 5 years. Various advocacy groups monitor the rewording of laws and typically keep educators informed through organizations like AAHPERD and CEC. Occasionally, adapted physical activity professionals are requested to participate in letter-writing campaigns or telephone action. Table 4.7 shows new and reauthorized laws that affect physical activity services.

Regulations

After a bill is signed into law by the president, a period of several months is required for the federal agency responsible for implementation to write the official regulations. Until these are published, a law cannot be enforced. Hearings must be held throughout the nation so that all interested persons can offer suggestions and recommendations for implementing a new law. Written and oral testimony presented at hearings is used in formulating proposed rules. Proposed rules are then published in the *Federal Register,* after which more hearings are held and experts are brought to Washington, DC, to help with decision making. The final regulations are then published in the *Federal Register.*

Obtaining Copies of Laws and Bills

Advocates obtain copies of laws and bills so that they know firsthand what is going on. They share these with parents and others who may be less assertive in obtaining copies. A powerful strategy is carrying a copy of the law or its regulations to meetings where policy and/or compliance are to be discussed.

Figure 4.15 shows the documents in which law is printed at its various stages of development. These documents can be found in most university libraries and on several websites. Books like Siegel (2002) contain most of the CFR text.

The *Code of Federal Regulations (CFR)* and *United States Code (U.S.C.)* **codify** (i.e., systematize and classify) everything on a particular topic into the same bound volume. The *CFR,* which is published annually, codifies the laws from the previous 12 months. EHA and IDEA information is codified in Volume 34 of the *CFR.* The *U.S.C.,* which is published every 6 years, codifies legislation over a longer time period. IDEA information is codified in Volume 20 of the *U.S.C.*

Knowledge of the *CFR* and *U.S.C.* helps in understanding the referencing system used in finding laws and citing particular passages. For example, the definition of physical education in IDEA is referenced as 34 *CFR,* 300.14 or 20 *U.S.C.* 1401 [16].

Enforcement of Laws

Once a law is enacted, many years are required for 100% compliance. Often, if no one points out that rights are being violated, no attempt is made to enforce the law. The parts of IDEA that pertain to physical education are not being enforced in many school districts. One reason is that parents have not forced compliance. Perhaps they do not understand the law, or they may not appreciate the importance of physical education in the health, fitness, and happiness of their children.

Teachers, if they want to keep their jobs, often cannot challenge school administrators directly. A viable approach to improved law enforcement is to work through parents, acquainting them with the success of other parents and getting them involved in sport and recreation activities that heighten their awareness of the values of physical education (Kennedy, French, & Henderson, 1989).

Finding Your Congresspersons

Citizens in every state elect two senators and several representatives who shape the legislation of this country. These persons maintain offices in Washington, DC, and in various cities throughout their state. Everyone is welcome to visit these offices, and advocates use this approach to get acquainted with legislative aides and advance the IDEA cause. *While a face-to-face meeting with congresspersons is preferable, their legislative aides usually represent the first level of access.*

If you know the names of your congresspersons, you can reach them in Washington, DC, by telephoning the Capitol Operator at (202) 224-3121. Or you can contact them by writing to the following addresses: U.S. Senate, Washington, DC 20510, or U.S. House of Representatives, Washington, DC 20515.

To obtain names of congresspersons, as well as information about other government officials, books like the *United States Government Manual* and the *Official Directory of the Congress* can be found in your library or ordered from the Superintendent of Documents, U.S. Government Printing Office, P.O. Box 371954, Pittsburgh, PA 15250-7954. The telephone number for ordering documents by mail is (202) 512-1800.

Using the Annual Report to Congress

The U.S. Department of Education is required each year to publish the *Annual Report to Congress,* which describes (a) progress made in implementation of IDEA legislation, (b) national and state statistics pertaining to service delivery, and (c) needs (met and unmet). This report, published since 1979, typically is about 300 pages long and is the best primary source available for staying abreast of IDEA implementation.

The *Annual Report to Congress* can be obtained at no cost by writing or telephoning the Division of Innovation and Development, Office of Special Education Programs, Switzer Building, Washington, DC 20202, telephone (202) 205-9864. Copies of these reports are also available through websites.

Laws of Special Importance in Adapted Physical Education

Figure 4.16 summarizes tracks of legislation that are important. Each has a different number every 3 to 10 years. Most laws, unlike IDEA, do not identify specific disability categories. Instead, **disability** is conceptualized as an impairment that substantially limits one or more of the major life activities (e.g., walking, breathing, seeing, hearing, learning, working).

Figure 4.16 is a playful attempt to weave advocacy, the major points of several laws, and the adventures of Dorothy and Toto in the *Wizard of Oz* as they sought to find their way home to Kansas after a tornado lifted them into a faraway place. Judy Garland's wonderful song *Follow the Yellow Brick Road* can serve as the imagery for advocacy stepping-stones that take us to the branches of an advocacy tree and *Somewhere Over the Rainbow* (another of Judy Garland's songs) where the intended outcomes of legislation come true. Almost everything a beginner needs to remember about specific laws is in Figure 4.16. *It may be helpful if you write the current number for each law above its initials.* However, the numbers change with the relatively frequent reauthorizations, so many experts now refer to laws by their initials and dates (e.g., IDEA 1997, OASA [Olympic Amateur Sports Association] 1998).

Further, it is important to know that Section 504 and the Americans with Disabilities Act (ADA) are **civil rights laws** overseen by the Office of Civil Rights, whereas IDEA is a **federal funding statute** whose purpose is to provide financial aid to states in their efforts to ensure adequate and appropriate educational services for individuals, ages 0 through 21. IDEA is overseen by the Office of Special Education and Rehabilitative Services (OSERS) within the U.S. Department of Education.

School-age children can be made eligible for adapted physical education services under either IDEA or Section 504. *IDEA eligibility requires that the impairment have an adverse effect on educational performance, whereas Section 504 eligibility requires that the impairment affects at least one **major life activity** (i.e., walking, seeing, hearing, speaking, breathing, learning, working, caring for oneself, and performing manual tasks).* Students under IDEA would be unable to learn in general physical education, even with supports (i.e., obtaining no education benefit), whereas students under Section 504 might be earning an A in physical education, but having to overcome tremendous challenges like breathing difficulties caused by asthma or mobility difficulties caused by cerebral palsy. IDEA provides funding for eligible students, which often is used to help employ adapted physical educators; Section 504 does not.

Placement under IDEA may be any combination of adapted and general physical education, whereas placement under Section 504 is usually in GE classes. In IDEA, **appropriate** education *means services that provide adequate educational benefits* for individuals with disabilities. In Section 504, **appropriate** *means an education comparable to the education of students who are not disabled.* IDEA requires an IEP, whereas Section 504 requires an accommodation plan.

In general, "the major differences between IDEA and Section 504 are in the flexibility of the procedures. For children to be identified as eligible for services under Section 504, there are less specific procedural criteria governing the requirements of school personnel. Schools may offer less assistance and monitoring with Section 504 because there are fewer regulations by the federal government" (deBettencourt, 2002, p. 22). Following are some specifics about each of the laws in Figure 4.16.

Figure 4.16   Follow the yellow brick road to somewhere over the rainbow: A model summarizing laws, outcomes, and advocacy behaviors. (MR-MH = Mental Retardation-Mental Health; EHA = Education of the Handicapped Act; EAHCA = Education for All Handicapped Children Act; IEP = Individualized Education Program; IFSP = Individualized Family Service Plan.)

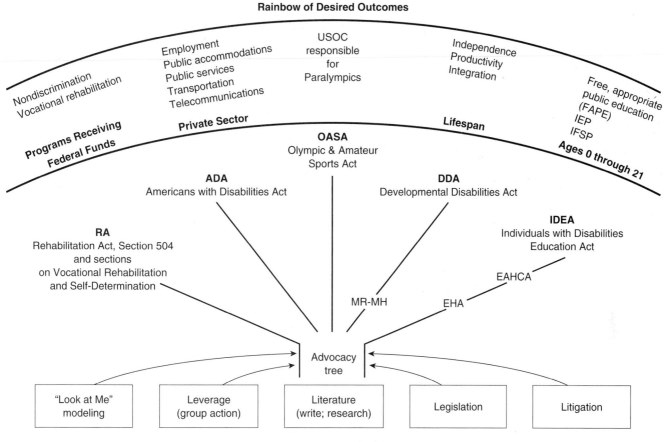

The Yellow Brick Road of Advocacy Stepping-Stones to
the Rainbow of Desired Outcomes

PL 93-112: The Rehabilitation Amendments, Section 504

PL 93-112, enacted in 1973 but not implemented until its rules were printed in the *Federal Register* in 1977, includes many mandates but is best known for Section 504, often called the "Nondiscrimination Clause" (*Federal Register,* May 4, 1977). Section 504 states:

> No otherwise qualified handicapped individual . . . shall, solely by reason of his handicap, be excluded from participation in, be denied the benefits of, or be subjected to discrimination under any program or activity receiving Federal financial assistance.

This means that schools conducting physical education instruction, interscholastic athletics, and extraclass activities must provide qualified students with disabilities an equal opportunity with nondisabled peers for participation. Such opportunities must be given in the least restrictive environment, which is usually the general program. Persons with artificial limbs or one eye or kidney cannot be barred from sport competition. Likewise, athletic events in public places receiving federal funds (almost all do) must be accessible to all spectators, including those in wheelchairs. All facilities do not have to be accessible as long as programs are accessible. Students with disabilities must have access to at least one playing field, gymnasium, and swimming pool if able-bodied (AB) students are provided opportunities for sports, dance, and aquatics programs.

Most institutions that receive federal funds designate one of their staff as a **504 compliance officer** and often have a campus Office for Disability Services. This person or office is contacted regarding problems related to physical, learning, living, and work environments. Institutions also establish 504 committees or councils, which serve as advisory and advocacy bodies. Such committees often conduct awareness programs and assess barriers.

Membership on the 504 committee is a good volunteer activity for students who want to learn advocacy skills. Become a member and/or find ways to work with the 504 officer or office.

The Rehabilitation Act Amendments of 1992, 1998, and 2003/2004

In addition to its well-known Section 504, the Rehabilitation Act also governs the Vocational Rehabilitation Program, "the federal and state cooperative effort that provides employment services nationally for working-age individuals with disabilities" (Wehman, 2001, p. 11). This law has the potential to affect adapted physical activity services in many ways, particularly those for young adults, ages 18 through 21, who must be provided a transition plan as part of their IEP. For example, many adapted physical educators are recognizing the importance of getting involved in transition planning, which begins at age 14, so that individuals can receive community-oriented leisure education as well as vocational education. *A local rehabilitation officer must attend transition planning and implementation meetings so that there is coordination between school and vocational services.* The adapted physical educator will need also to interact with the rehabilitation officer.

Additionally, the benefits of vocational education partly determine the ability of adults with disabilities to work and earn wages that may be spent on healthy, active leisure as well as housing, food, and other necessities. Adults with good wages are better able to join community fitness and sport clubs and to pay for transportation needed to travel to and from fitness and recreation facilities.

IDEA

IDEA began as PL 94-142, the Education for All Handicapped Children Act (EAHCA). The title of this act was changed to Individuals with Disabilities Education Act (IDEA) in 1990. It requires that physical education services, specially designed if necessary, be made available to students declared eligible by the IEP process and that these be free, appropriate, and in the least restrictive environment. IDEA separates **direct services** (i.e., required special education) from **related services** (not required unless proven needed as a *prerequisite* to benefiting from special education). By including physical education as a part of the special education definition, *IDEA specifies physical education as a direct and, therefore, required service.*

In terms of its contributions to special education as a whole, IDEA mandates five rights for children and youth with disabilities:

1. Right to a *free* education
2. Right to an *appropriate* education
3. Right to *nondiscriminatory* testing, evaluation, and placement procedures
4. Right to be educated in the *least restrictive environment*
5. Right to *procedural due process* of the law

It is reauthorized about every 3 years and assigned a new number. Regulations for IDEA 1997 were not printed until 1999. Idea 2003 is expected to be enacted as this text goes to print. Table 4.7 summarizes legislative activity from 1998 on.

Americans with Disabilities Act

The Americans with Disabilities Act (ADA) (PL 101-336), passed in 1990, applies to all discrimination, regardless of funding source. The purpose of this law is to end discrimination against persons with disabilities and to bring them into the economic and social mainstream of American life. The law addresses five areas in which discrimination was rampant in the 1980s: (a) employment in the private sector, (b) public accommodations, (c) public services, (d) transportation, and (e) telecommunications.

Some examples follow. All facilities, whether or not they receive federal funding, must provide equal access and equal services to persons with disabilities. This includes playgrounds, swimming pools, health spas, bowling alleys, golf courses, gymnasiums, and the like. Separate but equal will not be tolerated. Under ADA, persons with disabilities can no longer be denied insurance or be subject to different conditions based on disability alone. The nation's telephone services are being remodeled so that persons with hearing and/or speech impairments have services functionally equivalent to individuals without impairments.

Developmental Disabilities Assistance Act and Bill of Rights Act

The Developmental Disabilities Assistance and Bill of Rights Act (DDA) of 1990 (PL 101-496) and subsequent amendments emphasize three goals (independence, productivity, and integration into the community) and mandate that state-level Developmental Disabilities Councils direct their efforts toward achievement of these goals. DDA activities are regulated and funded by the U.S. Department of Health and Human Services. Goals are achieved through (a) individual and family support, including federal funds for child welfare and older Americans; (b) education; (c) employment; (d) income, including the Supplemental Security Income and the Social Security Disability Insurance programs; (e) housing; and (f) health, including Medicaid programs.

Unlike IDEA, which defines disabilities categorically (e.g., mental retardation, severe emotional disturbance), the DDA uses the following definition:

Developmental disability is a severe, chronic disability which:

(1) is attributable to a mental or physical impairment or combination of mental and physical impairments;
(2) is manifested before the person attains age twenty-two;
(3) is likely to continue indefinitely;
(4) results in substantial functional limitations in three or more of the following areas of major life activity: (a) self-care, (b) receptive and expressive language, (c) learning, (d) mobility, (e) self-direction, (f) capacity for independent living, and (g) economic self-sufficiency; and
(5) reflects the person's need for a combination and sequence of special, interdisciplinary, or generic care, treatment, or other services which are of lifelong or extended duration and are individually planned and coordinated. (Section 102(5) of PL 100-146)

Community programs that can show success in helping persons with developmental disabilities achieve independence, productivity, and integration may apply for grants. Physical activity and recreation programs, if properly conducted, can promote these goals.

Figure 4.17 Athletes with cerebral palsy participate actively in the governance of the National Disability Sport Alliance Association, which is affiliated with the U.S. Olympic Committee (USOC). Pictured from left to right are Dick Hosty, Ken Wells, Wendy Shugal, and Sal Ficara.

Amateur Sports Act (ASA) and Olympic and Amateur Sports Act (OASA)

When the U.S. Olympic Committee (USOC) was reorganized in the 1970s and plans made for better promotion and coordination of amateur athletics, sports for athletes with disabilities were included in the master plan. Specifically, PL 95-606, the Amateur Sports Act (ASA) of 1978, charged the USOC

> to encourage and provide assistance to amateur athletic programs and competition for handicapped individuals, including, where feasible, the expansion of opportunities for meaningful participation by handicapped individuals in programs of athletic competition for able-bodied individuals. (Article II, 13, p. 2)

ASA enabled athletes with disabilities to use the U.S. Olympic Training Center at Colorado Springs (see Figure 4.17), and their sport organizations to be assisted by USOC. A Committee on Sports for the Disabled (COSD) advised the USOC until the late 1990s. The Olympic and Amateur Sports Act (OASA), PL 105-277, replaced ASA in 1998. The OASA authorized the USOC to serve as the National Paralympic Committee. *The disability sport organizations were moved to the USOC community membership category.* This move was considered inclusive in that the Paralympics is now governed more-or-less in the same way and by the same body as the Olympics.

Physical Education Mentions in IDEA

The following mentions of physical education in IDEA form the basis for public school practices. Advocates must be ever vigilant that school personnel are complying with the law. The following direct quotations are taken from Title 34 of the *Code of Federal Regulations* (CFR).

Physical Education Definition

> (2) *Physical education* is defined as follows:
>   (i) The term means the development of:
>   (A) physical and motor fitness;
>   (B) fundamental motor skills and patterns; and
>   (C) skills in aquatics, dance, and individual and group games and sports (including intramural and lifetime sports).
>   (ii) The term includes special physical education, adapted physical education, movement education, and motor development.

This definition differentiates physical education from such related services as occupational and physical therapy. The term *skills,* as used in IDEA, encompasses mental and social (as well as physical) skills needed to learn rules and strategies. Nowhere in IDEA is there a definition specifically for adapted physical education.

Physical Education Requirement

121a.307 Physical Education

(a) *General.* Physical education services, specially designed if necessary, must be made available to every handicapped child receiving a free appropriate public education.

This passage, together with the mention of physical education in the special education definition, comprises the legal basis for adapted physical education service delivery for students with disabilities.

Integration in Regular Physical Education

(b) *Regular physical education.* Each handicapped child must be afforded the opportunity to participate in the regular physical education program available to nonhandicapped children unless:

(1) the child is enrolled full-time in a separate facility; or

(2) the child needs specially designed physical education, as prescribed in the child's individualized education program.

The intent is to place each student in his or her *least restrictive environment* based on individual assessment data and multidisciplinary deliberation. To justify segregation, the IEP process must document that the present level of performance, goals, and objectives are such that needs cannot be met in the general physical education setting, *even with supports and supplementary aids and services.*

Special Physical Education

(c) *Special physical education.* If specially designed physical education is prescribed in a child's individualized education program, the public agency responsible for the education of that child shall provide the service directly, or make arrangements for it to be provided through other public or private programs.

Specially designed physical education, as defined, does not have to be full-time placement in a separate class. It can refer to specific conditions imposed on general class placement, like limited class size, the presence of an assistant for one-to-one instruction, and the availability of wheelchairs and other special or adapted equipment. Just as special education is taught by a certified special education teacher, specially designed physical education should be planned and, when possible, implemented by an adapted physical activity specialist.

IEP Principles and Practices

The IEP and the IEP process are praiseworthy concepts that have shaped and changed practices in the field. Most of the principles that guide school district practices in relation to assessment, evaluation, and placement have their roots in the IEP process and thus come from IDEA-Part B. Among the most important of these principles are the following:

1. A student shall be considered nondisabled until sufficient evidence is presented that he or she meets criteria to be labeled disabled. This principle is similar to that followed in a court of law: All persons are considered innocent until proven guilty. Educational classification is a legal procedure with due process requirements.

2. The general education placement shall be considered the most appropriate placement for each student until evidence is presented, through the IEP process, that special services are required and that these services cannot be provided in the general classroom, even with supports and supplementary aids and services.

3. A student may be declared disabled in one curricular area but not another. The placement decision for each subject matter area must therefore be made separately and independently from all others.

4. Placement decisions shall be based on comprehensive assessment data generated by instruments that are *valid* for the purpose for which they are being used.

5. The assessment procedures used in making placement decisions must meet the specific criteria stated in IDEA.

6. Placement decisions must be based on multidisciplinary data and made by teams of experts rather than one person.

7. School districts should make available a continuum of placements and services so that students in separate education settings can be moved into progressively more inclusive environments.

8. Placement decisions must be reviewed at least once each year to determine whether the student is ready yet for a more inclusive environment and to update goals and objectives.

9. Every student shall be placed in his or her least restrictive environment.

10. Due process procedures to protect the rights of every student shall be clearly delineated.

More extensive coverage of these principles is provided in Chapters 5 to 7 on service delivery.

The Need for State Laws

IDEA forms the legal basis for adapted physical education only for students declared disabled by IEP or IFSP eligibility procedures. Many, many other students have psychomotor problems serious enough to merit adapted physical education intervention. Federal law cannot be passed to improve the GE system for nondisabled students since education is not a power given to the U.S. government by the Constitution.

The only way to ensure high-quality physical education, including adapted physical education when needed, for all students *is through state legislation.* Many states have or are working on legislation that parallels IDEA. Physical educators should work actively with state legislators to ensure that the physical education passages in IDEA are included and expanded to encompass nondisabled students in state law.

OPTIONAL ACTIVITIES

1. Create a hard copy or electronic file on ways to adapt physical education activities for selected persons of different ages and performance levels. Test as many of your adaptations as possible with real people and/or discuss them with classmates (e.g., how many ways can you think of to adapt instruction when teaching throwing, catching, or base running)?

2. Get involved in campaigning during a local, state, or national election. Interview candidates or their aides on issues pertaining to disability and other causes you value. Plan and implement strategies for making candidates' views known.

3. Determine which stores and businesses in your community employ persons with disabilities. Also find out which ones contribute money or services to disability organizations or events. Create ways to advocate for these stores and businesses.

4. Reflect on which content in this chapter was most meaningful and why. Write a paper that includes these reflections as well as ways to make other content more meaningful.

5. Think of all the ways you can to apply information in this chapter, and develop a reasonable time line for trying these out.

6. Especially for graduate students: Reflect on adaptation as the theoretical and practical basis of adapted physical activity service delivery. Engage in theorizing about the relationships between the variables involved in adapting physical activities for persons with disabilities.

C H A P T E R

5

Curriculum Planning and Evaluation Guided by Attitude Change

Figure 5.1 A life situation for consideration (*A*) Bob (on crutches) and Joe (in the wheelchair) are 10-year-olds with average intelligence. Both are average or better students in their fourth-grade classroom but have had little opportunity to learn sports, dance, and aquatics. (*B*) Jim is 5 years old and obviously small for his age; he learns slowly but tries hard to please. (*C*) Dick has a brace on one leg and lots of problems with asthma. How will you and your school district plan for these students? What philosophy will guide your planning?

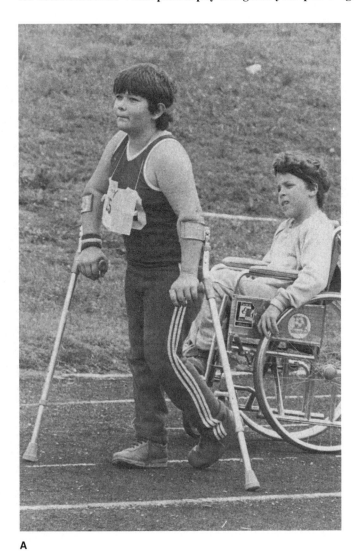

A

B

C

1. Develop goals and objectives for students in Figure 5.1. Create more assessment data as needed.

2. Understand that organizing centers (i.e., frames of references, themes, or emphases) guide planning and curriculum design. Apply this concept to goal areas, top-down and bottom-up approaches, and different kinds of placement. Which four goal areas do you prefer for most elementary school students with disabilities? Why? Contrasting top-down, bottom-up, and interactional approaches, which do you prefer? Why?

3. Contrast least restrictive environment (LRE) and inclusive placement philosophies. Which approach do you prefer? Why? For graduate students, who are the adapted physical education leaders who agree and disagree with your preference? Review some of their published work.

4. Discuss eight variables that should be considered when making decisions about placements and services. Add other variables to the ones in this chapter. Explain the importance of each.

5. Explain four steps in planning instruction for a semester or year: (a) calculating instructional time, (b) planning use of time, (c) developing instructional units, and (d) making decisions about space, equipment, and resources. Describe a student, state goals with objectives based on present level of performance; calculate available instructional time for a school year of 200 days (physical education 3 times a week, 30 minutes each time); and develop a sample semester plan to guide service delivery.

Chapters 5, 6, and 7 pertain to PAP-TE-CA service delivery. This chapter concerns planning, evaluation, and attitude change design, because these are fundamental to decision making in all other parts. Chapter 6 focuses on assessment, and Chapter 7 describes teaching and consulting.

Planning: The First PAP-TE-CA Service

Planning may be a school district, school, classroom, or individual function. However, because many adapted physical activity specialists are employed to plan and implement service delivery for an entire school district, we begin planning at this level. It is important for general physical educators to understand and participate in school district planning because all decisions affect them. The United States has approximately 16,000 school districts, each governed by a local education agency (LEA), which is recognized by and responsible to the state education agency (SEA). A **school district** thus can be defined as a city, community, or other designated local structure that is responsible for the governance and funding of public schools. *In accordance with the philosophy of this text, a school district is conceptualized as a combined home-school-community entity that shares resources.*

School district planning refers to shared decision making about the philosophy, principles, policies, and practices that guide the day-to-day operation of schools and the development and use of resources to meet educational needs. Administrators and consultants often do most of the planning for school districts, but ideally everyone is involved. Much of this chapter is designed to help develop competencies that will enhance planning at the school district, school, and classroom levels. Philosophy developed for a school district usually generalizes to schools and classrooms within the system.

School systems have different visions of what physical education programs can and should accomplish. Visions are typically operationalized by statements of purpose and goals. In

Chapter 1, purpose and goals were introduced. The following section provides detail concerning each and also clarifies the difference between goals and objectives.

Purpose, Goals, and Objectives

In adapted physical activity, the terms *purpose, goal,* and *objectives* are used in specific ways. A **purpose** is the overall aim or intention. The purpose of adapted physical activity is the same as that of general physical education: to change psychomotor behaviors, thereby facilitating self-actualization.

Goals are broad, global statements that are long range in nature, whereas **objectives** are short term and traditionally contain three parts: (a) conditions, (b) behavior to be developed or changed, and (c) success criterion. These definitions come from federal legislation that guides the development of individualized education programs (IEPs). Long range refers to annual, semiannual, or quarterly statements that guide instruction. Table 5.1 presents nine goal areas. Usually, time permits work on only three or four goals. Therefore, teachers must use assessment data to select the measurable goals most appropriate for each individual.

To make a goal measurable, it must be broken down into specific, short-term measurable objectives that require 3 to 5 hours for achievement. Often, lesson plans allocate only 5 or 10 minutes per session to an objective, so work continues over several weeks. For example, consider the goal of developing a good self-concept in the athletic domain. An objective might be: *Given opportunity to engage in a leisure activity like skiing for 30 minutes and to evaluate success after the activity, student will say at least one good thing about physical self* (see Figure 5.2). If the goal were to develop fitness, then the objectives might be: *Given instructions to do as many curl-ups as possible in 30 seconds, student will complete 25;* or *Given the opportunity to ski on slopes for 3 hours, student will be able to engage in ski activities continuously with no more than three refreshment and toilet breaks, not to exceed 15 minutes each.*

A. **Positive Self-Concept** (Chapter 8)
To develop a positive physical self (Fox, 1997) and body image through activity involvement; to increase understanding and appreciation of the body and its capacity for movement; to accept limitations that cannot be changed; to demonstrate self-confidence in physical activity.

B. **Social Competence/Inclusion** (Chapter 9)
To learn social behaviors that promote inclusion (i.e., how to interact with others—sharing, taking turns, following, and leading); to develop beliefs and attitudes about self and others that facilitate equal-status relationships; to reduce social isolation; to learn how to develop and maintain friendships; to demonstrate good sportsmanship and self-discipline in winning and losing; to develop other skills necessary for acceptance by peers in the mainstream.

C. **Sensorimotor Integration** (Chapter 10)
To minimize serious, multiple problems that stem primarily from central nervous system (CNS) dysfunctions (e.g., cerebral palsy, stroke, traumatic brain injury) and interfere with body control, upright postures, and locomotion. Some of these problems are muscle or postural tone abnormalities, pathological reflexes, postural reaction delays, associated movements or overflow, stereotypies, spasticity, ataxia, and tactile-kinesthetic-vestibular-visual (TKVV) disorders that interfere with initiating and sustaining exploratory movement.

D. **Motor Skills and Patterns** (Chapter 11)
To learn fundamental motor skills and patterns; to master the motor skills indigenous to games, sports, dance, and aquatics participation; to improve fine and gross motor coordination for self-care, school, work, and play activities.

E. **Perceptual-Motor Learning** (Chapter 12)
To reduce clumsiness or developmental coordination disorders (DCDs) associated with perceptual-motor, cognitive, attention, and memory problems; to develop and/or reinforce specific underlying movement abilities (e.g., static and dynamic balancing; hand-eye, head and trunk rotatory, and foot-eye coordinations; imitating models; following auditory instructions; motor planning and sequencing; rhythm and reaction time abilities).

F. **Health-Related Fitness and Active Lifestyle** (Chapter 13)
To meet health-related standards for cardiorespiratory endurance, body composition, muscular strength and endurance, and flexibility; and to develop beliefs and attitudes that lead to fitness and a healthy lifestyle.

G. **Postures and Appearance** (Chapter 14)
To remediate posture problems (e.g., round shoulders, kyphosis, scoliosis) and accommodate structural deviations that cannot be changed except by surgery (e.g., hip and knee joint problems); to improve appearance and body mechanics; to decrease muscular imbalance and prevent injury.

H. **Sports Skills for Recreation, Competition, and Transition** (Chapter 15)
To have fun and develop positive beliefs and attitudes that lead to lifespan active, healthy lifestyles; to learn play, game, and sport rules and strategies to enhance leisure time choices and habits; to develop the knowledge and commitment to use community resources and to seek help when needed.

I. **Dance and Tension Release Skills** (Chapter 16)
To learn dance activities that can be used throughout the lifespan to achieve numerous goals; to have fun; to learn physical activity approaches to tension release and relaxation.

J. **Aquatics Skills for Recreation, Competition, and Transition** (Chapter 17)
To learn aquatic activities that can be used throughout the lifespan to achieve numerous skills; to have fun; to develop the knowledge and commitment to use community resources and to seek help when needed.

Objectives have three parts, which can be remembered by the acronym CBS:

C   1. Conditions, referring to the *given statements* used to start the objective (e.g., Given opportunity to engage in vigorous activity of choice for 10 min; Given instructions to throw a ball [tennis-size, soft, blue] at a floor target 10 feet away.)

B   2. Behavior that is denoted by an action verb (e.g., *say, do, perform, demonstrate, show, run*) and is observable and measurable

S   3. Success criterion such as "at least one good thing" *or* "25 curl-ups" *or* "continuously with no more than three breaks of 15 minutes each"

Purpose and goals are integral parts of a philosophy. They determine the kind of assessment administered and thus establish the framework of opportunity. Objectives are not part of a philosophy; they are tools or vehicles for accomplishing goals.

Each of the GOAL AREAS in Table 5.1 contributes to self-actualization in one of three domains (affective, psychomotor, or cognitive).

Try writing objectives for each goal area. Remember that an objective should require only 3 to 5 hours for achievement.

Figure 5.2 Students with severe mental retardation can be taught skiing when skills are task analyzed and objectives are carefully written.

Figure 5.3 Good teachers take students to community facilities for instruction in motor and social skills that carry over into everyday life.

Goal Area Organizing Centers

Organizing centers are frames of reference, themes, or emphases that provide a focus for programming (i.e., instruction, recreation, therapy). Goals serve as organizing centers or themes for school district planning and curriculum design. Goals may also serve as themes for programs offered by community agencies and organizations for all age groups. Each of the goal areas in Table 5.1 contributes to self-actualization in one or more domains (affective, psychomotor, or cognitive). These goals are the basis for the organization of Part II (Chapters 8–17). Each chapter presents specific assessment and pedagogy strategies to accomplish a goal.

An important part of school district planning is to determine whether home-school-community team members value all of these goals and to resolve differences concerning which goals are most important. Often parents see self-concept and social competency for inclusion as the critical needs to be met, whereas physical educators are likely to rank motor skills and fitness highest. Community and therapeutic recreation personnel, in contrast, emphasize the values of fun and training in lifelong leisure skills and lifestyles. These leisure skills may be associated with intense competition (e.g., wheelchair basketball, Paralympics, Special Olympics, Deaf sport) or with recreational activities. Professionals who work with individuals with severe multiple disabilities typically identify with sensorimotor integration, perceptual-motor learning, and adapted dance and aquatics. These goals are particularly effective in meeting needs of individuals who are nonambulatory.

School districts with sufficient resources should seek to make all goals available to professionals who plan assessment, curricula, and after-school programs. The essence of individualization is choice, and the more choices district programming offers teachers, the better they can meet the needs of students and operationalize the concept of reasonable accommodation. When resources are not available within school facilities, planning teams need to consider home and community facilities and determine how transportation can be arranged and financed (see Figure 5.3).

Each of the goals in Table 5.1 can be achieved in general physical education classes, if support services are available. Physical educators must understand how educational trends such as inclusive education and outcome-based instruction influence the implementation of goals at school district and classroom levels.

Most of the goals in Table 5.1 can be matched with commercially available curriculum models like the Special Olympics Sports Skills Program and Body Skills (Werder & Bruininks, 1988) or operationalized in models created by professionals that are based on their original thinking, ideas from the literature, or participation in workshops. These curriculum models are described in Chapters 8 through 17. In some cases, where curriculum models are associated with a specific disability, the models are presented in Chapters 18 through 27.

Functional, Developmental, and Interactive Organizing Centers

Planning involves selecting organizing centers or frames of reference that can help facilitate teamwork and organize efforts. This section highlights three organizing centers: (a) functional, (b) developmental, and (c) interactional. Each represents a different body of knowledge. Although a delivery system could be based on one perspective, good professionals utilize information from each organizing center to individualize and adapt instruction.

Table 5.2   Traditional task analysis of target throw for person with severe mental retardation.

Short, Easy Chain	Longer, Harder Chain		Hardest Chain	
	10.	Praise self; say "Good, I threw the ball."	10.	Same
	9.	Look where ball goes.	9.	Same
	8.	Follow through.	8.	Same
	7.	Release ball.	7.	Same
	6.	Swing throwing arm forward.	6.	Add trunk rotation.
	5.	Swing throwing arm backward.	5.	Add trunk rotation.
4. Look where ball goes.	4.	Assume shoulder-to-target stance.	4.	Same
3. Release ball.	3.	Look at target.	3.	Same
2. Pick up ball.	2.	Pick up ball	2.	Same
1. Look at ball.	1.	Look at ball.	1.	Same

Note. Steps are taught separately and linked together by forward or backward chaining.

Professionals must have a good understanding of both function and development. **Function,** derived from the Latin *functio* (meaning "activity," "performance"), refers to the acts, tasks, or activities that a person can perform. **Development,** derived from the Old French *desveloper* (meaning "to unwrap"), refers to changes that occur throughout the lifespan (i.e., the unwrapping or evolving of the human being).

Functional Frame of Reference (Top Down)

The functional frame of reference focuses on the roles and functions needed for success in a specific activity. Assessment determines whether or not the person can perform these functions. Then instruction is directed toward mastery of task or activity components that comprise the function.

The pedagogy used is typically **behavior management** (i.e., a precisely planned, systematic application of cues and consequences to guide the student through a series of tasks or activities that are ordered from easy to hard). Behavior management begins with analysis of an age-appropriate function. This may be either an ecological task analysis like that discussed in Chapter 4 or a traditional analysis that breaks a task into smaller, teachable steps (see Table 5.2). Next, the teacher determines the cues and consequences to be used. A **cue** is a command or instruction telling the student what to do. A **consequence** is immediate feedback designed to either increase or decrease a behavior.

For example, in teaching a target throw, using the functional approach and behavior management, the teacher models (demonstrates) the task and gives a simple cue like, "Jim, pick up the ball." If the student imitates correctly, the consequence is an immediate **reward** (i.e., verbal praise, "Good, Jim, good!" or a reinforcer known to be especially effective with Jim). If Jim does not make the desired response within 5 seconds, a **correction procedure** is initiated (e.g., "No, watch me pick up the ball. I pick up the ball with my fingers. Jim, pick up the ball."). Learning is primarily by repetition. These same cues and corrective strategies are used until Jim is successful in a set number of trials. Then, the instruction proceeds to the next task in the easy-to-hard sequence (e.g., "Watch how I face the target. Jim, face the target.").

In the functional approach, little or no attention is given to whether the student has progressed through the developmental levels or stages associated with the function to be taught. Underlying the functional frame of reference is the philosophy that tasks, activities, and pedagogy should be age-appropriate.

Developmental Frame of Reference (Bottom Up)

The developmental frame of reference focuses on the abilities that society expects individuals to have at certain chronological ages and on developmental sequences. This approach has its roots in the traditional body of knowledge taught in such courses as developmental psychology, human development, and motor development. In this approach, standardized assessment instruments with norms are used to determine whether or not a person is performing at or near the level of others the same age. The norms begin with infancy and progress upward. Any pedagogy, including behavior management, may be used. The same developmental sequence is followed, however, for all students, with the entry level into the sequence individualized. A **developmental sequence** is a list of tasks or activities in which items are ordered according to the mean chronological age that each is achieved by typical infants and children (see Table 5.3).

Central to developmental theory is the assumption that learning proceeds in a spiral, upward direction, with performance at each level dependent on knowledge and skill acquired at earlier levels. For example, persons are taught a long jump only after they have mastered jumping down from a 1-ft height and demonstrated that they can perform stand-to-squat and squat-to-stand position changes without losing balance. This is because these tasks are developmentally easier than the long jump. Likewise, persons are taught tosses at floor targets before wall targets because downward tosses, aided by gravity, require less strength and thus are developmentally easier than horizontal tosses.

The developmental frame of reference is particularly applicable to infants, toddlers, and young children. A knowledge of the developmental milestones generally achieved at each age enables professionals to plan and deliver appropriate assessment, teaching, and evaluation services.

Table 5.3 Developmental sequence for teaching/testing throwing.

Task	Criterion to Pass	Average Age (in Months)
1. First voluntary grasp	Grasps objects, holds 5 sec	4–5
2. First voluntary release	Releases object on command	10–11
3. Throw (hurl) playground ball	Travels 5 ft forward	24–29
4. Throw (hurl) tennis ball	Travels 7 ft forward	24–29
5. Throw tennis ball	Shows trunk rotation, follow-through; ball travels 10 ft	42–47
6. Use underarm toss to hit wall target from 5 ft	Hits target two of three trials with tennis ball	42–47

Note. Distance objectives (e.g., "Throw hard!") are worked on before accuracy objectives.

Interactional Frame of Reference (Ecological)

The interactional frame of reference is a combination of functional and developmental perspectives based on critical thinking about individuals and their ecosystems. During the school years (i.e., from birth through age 21, according to federal law), development and function are inseparable. This is because general education is organized by grades, with each grade level representing a mixture of chronological age and function. Although some special education students are placed in nongraded, self-contained classrooms that serve several age groups, development remains an important consideration. The goal is to keep as many special education children in inclusive settings as possible. To do this, the teacher must be ever mindful of the school and classroom ecosystem and the many interacting variables that affect goal achievement.

Thus, development and function are two sides of the same coin. *Development is a vertical or longitudinal perspective.* The developmental frame of reference focuses on how far up the age-related continuum of motor skills a person can progress. In contrast, *function is a horizontal perspective.* The functional frame of reference focuses on environmental demands and the functions required to perform at adequate levels. Good teachers move back and forth between these two frames of reference, utilizing both in their daily service delivery. *The combination of these two approaches is an interactional or ecological perspective.*

Placement vs. Services Organizing Centers

Available placements for students is a traditional organizing center that affects curriculum design. Figure 5.4 shows that the planning of adapted physical education depends on whether the school district follows the least restrictive environment (LRE) or the inclusive approach. In inclusive placement, the goal is for *all students* to receive the services and supports that enable them to benefit from instruction. The current trend is to deemphasize placement and to focus on services. Special education and adapted physical education are no longer considered places but rather service delivery systems that can operate in any environment or placement.

Least Restrictive Environment Philosophy

LRE philosophy, as originally developed, was the use of the individualized education program (IEP) process to place students in their LRE for each content area. An environment was considered least restrictive when it (a) matched individual abilities with appropriate services so that students derived educational benefits and (b) preserve as much freedom as possible. *For this philosophy to work, there must be a continuum of available placements for each subject matter area.*

Many school systems never created a continuum of placements for every subject. They placed students either in separate adapted physical education or in general physical education. This practice did not provide enough options for matching individual abilities with appropriate services.

By the 1990s, interpretation of the LRE mandate in federal law changed to state that the LRE for most students with disabilities was general physical education, with supports. Today physical educators must take the initiative in making general physical education the best it can be for all students.

Inclusive Philosophy

The original inclusive philosophy insisted that all students be in the general classroom. Some proponents asserted that any other placement is discriminatory. However, IDEA today takes the stance that removal from the general classroom is justifiable only if instruction with the use of supplementary aids and services is documented as not providing sufficient benefits.

One Adapted Physical Educator in Every School District

Regardless of which philosophy guides a particular community, general physical educators should advocate and negotiate for at least one full-time adapted physical educator in their school district. This is because *support services* are an integral part of all approaches. Ideally, this specialist should be funded from both the special education and GE budgets and should assist all students with special psychomotor needs, not just those declared eligible by the IEP process. This can be done through either consultation or direct services.

Support Services

The term **support services** refers to supplementary aids and services (the definition used in IDEA legislation, 20 *U.S.C.*, 143). This is usually the presence of extra personnel in the general classroom (e.g., adapted physical education specialist, special educator, specially trained adult aides, peer or cross-age

Figure 5.4 Planning, assessment, and IEP decision making depend on whether the school system follows the least restrictive environment (LRE) or inclusive philosophy.

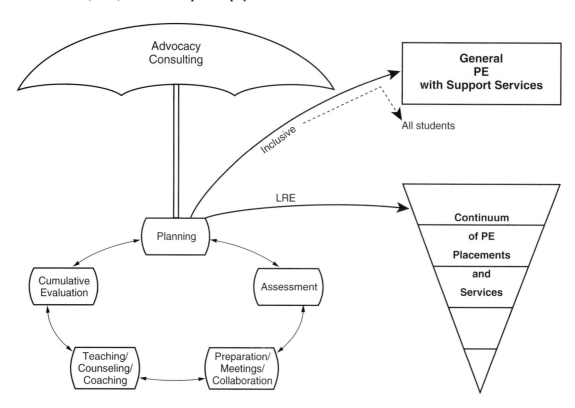

tutors). Extra personnel may also be available in a nearby adapted physical activity resource room, learning center, or counseling office.

Support services include things as well as people. The availability of video cameras and monitors for students to observe and analyze their movement patterns is an aid to instruction. Likewise, the availability of machines that pitch balls provides clumsy students with the thousands of practice trials needed. To individualize instruction, there must be much adapted equipment and sufficient space to set up different stations for varying the time and space attributes that determine degree of difficulty of motor skills. Likewise, computer and electronic technology can be used in many creative ways to reinforce students' effort and ease teacher load.

Support services are often not automatically provided. General physical educators must learn to ask, to negotiate, and to create. Success breeds success. The better a teacher is, the more likely he or she can convince the principal of the need for support services. Remember, support services cost extra money. Your requests will be weighed against others and sometimes be deferred. A positive and persistent attitude, coupled with a strong knowledge base of negotiation techniques, will eventually yield results. Warm, positive relationships with parents are also helpful. Parents often can find the time and energy to raise money, negotiate with the principal, and pose innovative alternatives.

The basic question to be posed to administrators is "Where is our school district adapted physical educator? Can you arrange for him or her to visit and help me?" Once this spe-

cialist is identified, he or she can act as a mediator in obtaining support services. If no specialists are employed by the school district, then general educators can be advocates for the creation of such a position. Another basic question is "What in-service training can you provide for me in order to learn more about adapting instruction?"

Read about supports in Chapter 21, and find out more about the AAMR (2002a) supports paradigm. Consider how selection of a supports paradigm might affect school district and school planning.

A Continuum of Placements and Services

For schools and school systems to plan services, decision makers must be aware of options. Figure 5.5 shows the different placements that might be used. Within the LRE philosophy, each step of this continuum is least restrictive for some students. Home- or hospital-bound instruction might be the only option immediately after surgery and in long-term illnesses. Most terminally ill and medically fragile children, whether at home or in a hospital can benefit from specialist-guided work on physical education goals. Caring school districts make home visits and family involvement possible.

The second step, full-time adapted physical education in a separate class, also depends on the philosophy and creativeness of the school system. Such programs usually follow a

Figure 5.5 A continuum of placements and services for schools that implement the LRE philosophy. The most imagination is needed at the "Part-time in Adapted PE" level.

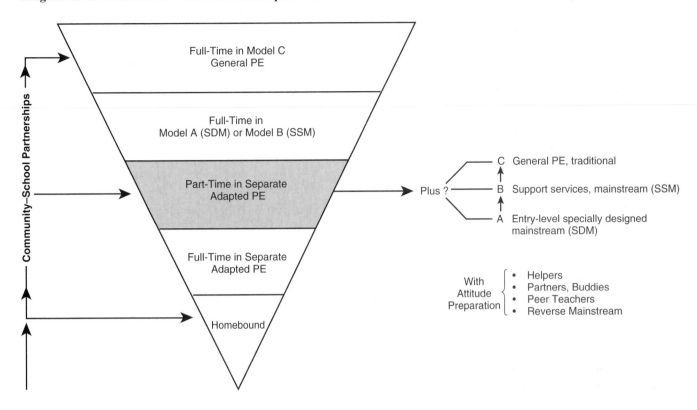

curriculum model like the data-based gymnasium (Dunn, Morehouse, & Fredericks, 1986).

Progressing up the continuum in Figure 5.5, the third step—part-time adapted physical education—is the beginning of the transition from separate to inclusive placement. This critical step is analogous to the resource room concept in special education. Placement at this level demands two decisions: (a) How shall time be distributed between separate and general physical education? and (b) What shall be the nature of the general physical education?

Figure 5.5 suggests that the answer to the second question should be Model A, B, or C. LRE philosophy requires having options, an area in many school systems in which imagination is nonexistent. However, it takes only one person to understand and advocate for a system like that in Figure 5.5.

Model A, an entry-level specially designed mainstream program, is usually implemented by an adapted physical activity specialist. *This is a system specially designed to integrate students with disabilities for the first time.* General education students volunteer to help, receive special training, and are carefully selected for exemplary attitudes and peer teaching abilities. Among the variations of Model A that have been successful are (a) partners or peer tutors (Lieberman et al., 2000); (b) helpers (Slininger, Sherrill, & Jankowski, 2000) and (c) reverse mainstream strategies (Kalyvas & Reid, 2003). In these variations, the ratio of students with and without disabilities is about equal.

Models B and C are conducted by general physical educators. In these, the ratio of students with and without disabil-

ities is about 1:10, the same as in society in general. Model B is a support services mainstream class. Teaching style, content, and orientation are adapted to promote personal goal achievement. This intent is much harder to implement than it sounds and requires training and experience. Model C is a class in which mastery of regulation sports or a designated fitness criterion is the main goal.

Variables Affecting Placement and Services

Planning service delivery begins with evaluation of general physical education. Before making IEP recommendations, you need to know about class size, teaching style, skill performance level of students, and many other environmental variables. Only by systematically examining such variables can you plan intelligently for differently abled students. Evaluation may result in placement in existing programs and/or the creation of new curriculum models and services.

Class Size

When physical education classes contain over 30 students, it is difficult and perhaps impossible for one person to individualize and adapt. This is not only because of pupil-teacher ratio limitations but because space in the average gymnasium does not permit more than about five learning stations. *The optimal size for small-group interaction and skill practice is two to six students at a station.* There must be ample space between stations, particularly when balls are involved, to ensure safety. Individualization implies personalization, and there should be the possibility within every class session of calling every student by name at least once, praising him or her for something, and engaging in personal talk. Class sizes larger than 30 build in defeat, contribute to teacher burnout, and intensify discipline problems.

Class size should be negotiated. For students with attention deficit disorders, hyperactivity, and behavior problems, the maximum class size may be 10 or 12. For students with severe disabilities, the class size specification may also entail provision of a permanently assigned partner or aide. Class size should be matched with assessment data on social competence and learning style. Class size can be manipulated by decreasing the number of students or by increasing the number of teachers.

Teaching Styles: Traditional and Inclusive

Muska Mosston in 1966 introduced the idea of a spectrum of teaching styles in which students are given increasing freedom and responsibility for their own learning. Over the years, 11 teaching styles have evolved (Mosston, 1992; Mosston & Ashworth, 1986, 1990). These styles are loosely combined into two categories: traditional and inclusive.

Traditional Style

Method of judging student success is the major factor that distinguishes between traditional and inclusive styles in Table 5.4. In the traditional style (also called command, practice, reciprocal, or self-check), all students must achieve a uniform standard or minimal competency level. The correct or efficient movement pattern is modeled and explained, and students are expected to approximate this pattern through on-task practice of specific, assigned activities. Feedback is largely corrective to enable students to meet age-appropriate minimum standards. Ultimately, each student passes or fails each task or step.

In the traditional style, all students usually practice the same activity or participate in the same game. Sports and games are played by regulation rules to enhance generalization to able-bodied leisure activities. Minimum health-related fitness standards are identical for everyone. Most traditional classes teach motor skills, fitness activities, and leisure competencies this way. The placement question then is, "Does the differently abled student, given his or her present level of performance, have a chance at achieving the required minimum competency set for each class objective?" If so, what kind of support services will this student need when placed in the general education class?

Inclusive Style

The inclusive teaching style, according to Mosston (1992), accepts multiple performance standards and personal bests. Sports and games are not played by regulation rules; hence, the emphasis is not on mastering traditional sports. Instead, the major goal is getting to know and care about oneself and others through movement. Emphasis is on finding many ways of doing one skill, activity, or game, rather than one correct or efficient way. Feedback is facilitative rather than corrective, with students encouraged to explore their personal best and/or a collaborative best with a partner or small group.

Table 5.4   Two teaching styles used in general physical education.

Command (Traditional)	Inclusive (Adapted)
1. Regulation rules	Flexible rules
2. Do as I say	Find your own way
3. Focus on average	Focus on individual
4. Minimal competency expectancy for all	Individual personal-best expectancy

In the inclusive style, students are given a choice about degree of difficulty. This means that every activity is task-analyzed from easy to difficult. Within the class, students are all performing at different levels. Traditional games are adapted so that there is no elimination and every student is maximally active.

With the inclusive style, differently abled students can be accommodated in general physical education. Many general physical educators, however, have never been taught how to adapt and include all students. Others find it difficult or impossible to apply this style because class size is too large or space is inadequate for parallel group activities of different difficulty levels. Finally, this style is inappropriate when the class goal is to learn regulation sports.

In conclusion, persons who make IEP decisions should check on the teaching styles used in general physical education. Ideally, every school has some classes representative of each style. Then the placement can be general physical education with an inclusive teaching style and support services. See Model B, Figure 5.5. If no such classes exist, then general physical education is probably not an appropriate assignment.

Competence Level of General Education Students

Whether or not students can succeed in a general class taught in a traditional style depends on how close their performance is to the class mean (numerical average) on the skills, knowledges, strategies, and behaviors being taught. Persons who make IEP decisions should have access to general class statistics. These may be for a class, school, school district, or some larger conglomerate like several school districts from different parts of the country.

If running speed, for example, is important to success in the activities to be taught (e.g., low organized games), then a student's speed should be compared with that of an average student. Table 5.5 shows that, in the school system represented, the average 6-year-old boy runs the 50-yd dash in 9.9 sec. The standard deviation (SD) is included in the table to allow determination of whether a score meets the criterion of being no more than 1 standard deviation from the mean. This is a good criterion for deciding whether or not a student needs special help.

Means and norms are essential guides when making placement decisions involving traditional classes governed by regulation teaching styles. A knowledge of the average student's skills, rules, strategies, and behaviors in the traditional class lends insight into the probability of success for students with disabilities.

Ta b l e 5.5   50-yd dash times (in seconds) for grades 1 to 6 (SD = standard deviation).

	Boys						Girls					
Grade	1	2	3	4	5	6	1	2	3	4	5	6
Age	6	7	8	9	10	11	6	7	8	9	10	11
Mean	9.9	9.3	8.8	8.5	8.2	8.1	10.3	9.5	9.2	8.7	8.6	8.3
SD	1.0	.9	.7	.7	.7	.7	1.0	.9	.9	.7	.6	.7
						Percentiles						
95	8.4	8.1	7.8	7.5	7.4	7.1	8.9	8.2	8.0	7.6	7.7	7.2
75	9.2	8.7	8.3	8.1	7.8	7.7	9.5	8.9	8.7	8.3	8.2	7.8
50	9.9	9.2	8.8	8.6	8.2	8.0	10.2	9.3	9.2	8.7	8.6	8.3
30	10.4	9.6	9.0	8.9	8.6	8.4	10.9	9.7	9.5	9.0	9.0	8.7
25	10.6	9.9	9.1	9.0	8.6	8.5	11.0	9.9	9.6	9.1	9.1	8.8
15	11.0	10.2	9.4	9.3	8.9	8.8	11.3	10.4	9.9	9.5	9.4	9.1
5	11.6	11.0	9.9	9.6	9.5	9.3	12.0	11.1	10.8	10.1	9.8	9.5

Note. From Margie Hanson, *Motor Performance Testing of Elementary School Age Children,* p. 265, unpublished doctoral dissertation, University of Washington, Seattle.

The ability to use rules and strategies in a game setting and/or to exhibit appropriate behaviors is difficult to assess by standardized tests that yield norms. In this area, videotapes are recommended. Experts can then view videotapes of the differently abled student in several game settings and determine whether or not he or she can fit into and benefit from instruction in these settings.

Content Orientation: Competition, Cooperation, or Individualistic

Orientation refers to whether the content in a particular class emphasizes competition, cooperation, or individual achievement. Two brothers, David and Roger Johnson (1975; Johnson, Johnson, Holubec, & Roy, 1984), both professors at the University of Minnesota, have spearheaded a comprehensive research movement that shows that classroom orientation significantly affects the differently abled person's social acceptance, performance level, and rate of learning. *Their findings indicate that a cooperative goal structure is more appropriate for differently abled persons than the other two orientations.*

Table 5.6 shows the desired characteristics of the cooperative learning structure. The recommended small-group size is 2 to 6, depending on the students' social skills and the amount of time available to work on a particular task. The shorter the time, the smaller the group should be. *Positive interdependence, the most important characteristic of the cooperative learning structure, is often promoted by joint reward systems, such as partner or group grades or points.* The goal is to create a system whereby everyone helps everyone else, and success (task completion, winning, praise) depends on everyone's contributions. Remember Allport (1954) also said this.

Many physical activities can be taught and practiced using a cooperative group structure. For example, throwing, catching, and volleying practice can be structured around the challenge of which group can keep the ball in the air the longest while giving everyone an equal number of trials. Traditional team games can be changed so that a certain number of people must touch the ball (e.g., three or five passes) before it

Ta b l e 5.6   A comparison of cooperative and traditional learning groups.

Cooperative Learning Groups	Traditional Learning Groups
Positive interdependence	No interdependence
Individual accountability	No individual accountability
Heterogeneous	Homogeneous
Shared leadership	One appointed leader
Shared responsibility for each other	Responsibility only for self
Task and maintenance emphasized	Only task emphasized
Social skills directly taught	Social skills assumed
Teacher observes and intervenes	Teacher ignores group functioning
Groups process their effectiveness	No group processing

Note. From *Circles of Learning: Cooperation in the Classroom* (p. 10) by D. W. Johnson, R. T. Johnson, E. J. Holubec, & P. Roy, 1984, Alexandria, VA: Association for Supervision and Curriculum Development.

goes over the net or is used to make a basket or goal. Team bowling or shooting scores can be highlighted instead of individual ones.

Our society, however, expects most students to learn the rules, strategies, and skills of regulation team and individual sports before graduation. These activities are essentially competitive, even though cooperation with teammates is stressed. If the class goal is to teach mastery of regulation sports, then placement of a differently abled student in the class is inappropriate unless the ability to participate fully and to succeed, with or without supports, can be documented in the assessment process.

Content to Be Taught

Like any other subject matter, the nature of physical education content varies by grade. Elementary school physical education is easier to adapt than secondary because the emphasis is on teaching basic skills, rules, and strategies and on developing minimum fitness. This content can be taught using traditional or inclusive styles within competitive, cooperative, or individualistic orientations. In middle and secondary school, increasingly more time is spent teaching regulation sports that will generalize into lifelong leisure and fitness practices. Curriculum at this level assumes that basic skills, rules, and strategies have been mastered, so accommodation of students without these abilities requires team-teaching and the running of parallel programs.

At the secondary school level, most good physical education programs use a multiactivity curriculum approach that covers several units over the school year. Ideally, some units teach regulation team sports, but others focus on fitness, movement education, dance, gymnastics, swimming, individual sports, and recreational games. The student with a disability may have potential for success in some of these but not others. Therefore, the IEP team should not assign secondary school students to generic general physical education but rather to specific instructional units that are appropriate.

Use of Community Resources and Role Models

When full participation is not possible in regulation sport units, arrangements should be made for students to receive parallel instruction in sports specific to their disability (e.g., wheelchair basketball or handball) or to learn an individual sport not usually taught in general physical education. An excellent approach is for school systems to employ athletes with disabilities to provide such instruction. The student not only benefits from new content but is introduced to role models and community resources. A growing number of athletes with disabilities are earning physical education degrees and qualify superbly for employment. If available athletes have not had teacher training, then special arrangements for in-service and supervision may be needed.

Disability-specific instruction often involves transportation to locations where special sports equipment and facilities are available. Budgeting for this is as important as transportation for the school's football team, but resources often are obtained only through advocacy and negotiation. Some school systems collaborate with community recreation programs, which make available transportation, facilities, and staff. This is an excellent way to facilitate transition from school to community resources, and many experimental mainstream programs can be devised.

Teacher Attitudes and Preparation

The attitudes and preparation of general physical education teachers ultimately determine success for the differently abled student. The availability of support services influences how teachers feel and their assessment of personal competency. Generally, we feel good about things we think we do well. Preservice and in-service preparation in adapted physical education enhances competence and contributes to good attitudes. A personality that is warm, friendly, and open to new people, ideas,

and strategies creates a GE climate that promotes humanistic learning for students with disabilities.

Overall Program Quality: Summary

In summary, the overall quality of the general physical education program affects planning, assessment, and placement. One role of the adapted physical education specialist is to serve as a liaison between general physical education and special education and ascertain that students with disabilities are properly assessed and placed. At IEP meetings, information should be available, not only about the student, but about the GE environment: (a) class sizes; (b) teaching styles; (c) skill level of GE students; (d) competition, cooperation, or individualistic orientation; (e) content; (f) use of community resources; (g) teacher attitudes and preparation; and (h) overall program quality. These factors should be adapted when necessary.

Service Delivery for General Education Students

Many GE students also need adapted physical activity services, but they are not eligible for help under the IEP-based special education model. Many school districts, however, want to serve students who are overweight, unfit, or clumsy, even though IDEA does not apply to them. When a continuum of placements is available, there is no rule that only students with disabilities can have adapted physical activity. Upon the recommendation of the physical educator, principals or school counselors can initiate an assessment-placement process for GE students similar to that used for students with disabilities.

Many GE students need help as much or more than special education students. Families also need help. The 21st century offers opportunities for new, creative models that apply the content of this chapter to all persons, not just those with disabilities recognized by law. *For students with problems not covered by IDEA, it is possible that they may qualify for adapted physical education services under Section 504. The criteria that must be met are (a) has or has had a mental or physical impairment that substantially limits a major life activity and (b) is regarded by others as disabled.*

Selecting Goals and Writing Objectives

A school curriculum guide lists objectives that are age appropriate for certain grades. Table 5.7 presents some illustrative objectives. Each of these objectives should be achievable after 3 to 5 hours of instruction. Remember, however, that instruction pertaining to a specific objective is typically spread out over several weeks. Think of objectives not only as guides to curriculum and lesson plans, but also as statements of tests to be passed at the end of instruction.

Remember that objectives have three parts: (a) condition, (b) behavior, and (c) success criterion (CBS). The objectives in Table 5.7, as in many curriculum guides, do not include conditions. This is because conditions are highly individual, depending on resources and many other factors, and thus are space-prohibitive in a textbook. Teachers must add the conditions when they choose to use a specific objective. Examples for some conditions for objectives in Table 5.7 follow:

Table 5.7 Illustrative measurable objectives for selected goals as they might appear in a curriculum guide or an IEP.

Measurable Goals with Objectives Underneath. The conditions part of the objectives are not given to save space.

A. To Demonstrate Positive Self-Concept in Relation to Fitness, Motor, and Leisure Performance

1. To score at 60th percentile on sport section of a standardized self-concept scale
2. To demonstrate understanding and appreciation of self by stating accurately one's personal best time, distance, or score on selected tasks like mile run, 50-yd dash, overarm throw (Define accurately so demonstration can generate a numerical score)
3. To demonstrate belief in ability to improve through hard work by stating high (but realistic) levels of aspiration on selected tasks and performing within 15% of aspiration (I will be able to; I expect to)
4. To demonstrate pride by stating five concrete physical activity achievements
5. To demonstrate commitment to change by showing chart kept over several weeks and/or journal that describes time spent in exercise, games, sports, and dance and/or a diet plan

B. To Demonstrate Functional Competence in Selected Play and Game Behaviors

1. To participate successfully in five selected games by
   a. Remaining on task for the entire game without verbal prompting from teacher or peers
   b. Following all rules without prompts
   c. Not being tagged, made "it," or sent to prison more often than other players (Yes/No measure used on each)
2. To get into the following formations with nine other students within a count of 10 sec: single circle, file, line, double circle (Yes/No measure on each formation)
3. To demonstrate appropriate use of the following play objects and apparatus by playing for 3 min in response to "Show me how you play with this:" tricycle, wagon, life-size doll, cloth tunnel (Define appropriate by criteria that can be assessed yes/no)
4. To show a journal that records at least 1 hour of participation in at least three different sport activities at community facilities each week

C. To Demonstrate Functional Competence in Selected Motor Skills and Patterns

1. To perform three of four components of a mature run, throw, and jump (Use TGMD-2 as measure; see index)
2. To increase overarm throw distance by 10 ft
3. To decrease 50-m dash speed by 0.5 sec
4. To demonstrate the first five steps or focal points in a task analysis or learning progression (Yes/No measures used on each)

D. To Demonstrate Functional Fitness and a Healthy Lifestyle

1. To demonstrate back and hamstring flexibility to run sprints 5% faster than baseline; or to do 15 jump shots within 5 minutes; or to kick 30 soccer balls within 10 minutes hard enough that they go at least 30 feet
2. To demonstrate sufficient cardiorespiratory endurance to engage in a vigorous team sport for 15 minutes (define vigorous)
3. To demonstrate sufficient arm and shoulder strength to hit the backboard or rim or make a basket at an 80% success rate over 10 trials

Note. "To demonstrate functional competence" means to perform within an average range for one's age and gender.

For Objective A1: Given the Harter Self-Perception Scale in accordance with instructions in the manual

For Objective A4: Given a notebook to use as an activity journal, daily reminders to write in the journal, and a deadline for submitting it

For Objective B3: Given 5 min in a 10-ft-by-10-ft room with five pieces of play apparatus (tricycle, wagon, long rope, life-size rag doll, cloth tunnel) in designated places and three children (A, B, and C) present

For Objective C2: Given a regulation softball, a wall target (60 by 40 inches in size) set at a designated

distance and height, the command, "Throw as hard as you can," and three trials

Now that you can identify the parts of an objective, select some goals for the children in Figure 5.6 and try writing some objectives for them. Use the format in Table 5.7 so that the relationship of objectives to goals is clear. State whether the objectives are for Child A, B, or C. Table 5.8 presents a checklist of criteria to determine whether or not your objectives are correctly written.

Figure 5.6   Three students with distinctly different needs.

 Which goals would you set for each? Write objectives for each of these students and use criteria in Table 5.8 to evaluate your objectives.

Child A is age 6, is partially sighted, has minor learning problms, expresses lots of fear about new experiences, and is an only child of parents who tend to be overprotective.

Child B is age 10, has three brothers and athletic parents, has been adopted as mascot of the local wheelchair basketball team, talks about basketball all the time, but refuses to try other sports and to recreate with able-bodied peers.

Child C is age 9, has severe mental retardation, does not play spontaneously, has a mild congenital heart defect, and lives with a mother and older sister who are not athletic.

Selecting Curricular Models

Packaged curricular models often include goals and objectives, thereby minimizing teacher work in this area. Curricular models for use throughout a school system are often selected by teams of teachers from different schools who serve on curriculum committees. Choices reflect philosophy, prioritization of physical education goals, breadth of knowledge about possible options, and resources.

Curricular models vary widely. Some are developed by individuals or school systems with minimal financial support, whereas others come from well-funded research grants that permit program ideas to be tested over a period of years. Most curricular models include both assessment and instructional components. See Appendix E for addresses of companies that make available curricular models. It is not necessary, however, to purchase ready-made models. Many professionals create their own models by combining ideas from existing models with original ideas from their personal experience. Following are some models that have been popular in adapted physical activity and are still in use. Most of these models are described in more detail in later chapters that focus on either the model's major goal or on the population for which the model was designed.

I CAN and ABC Models

Developed by Janet Wessel of Michigan State University, these two models are applicable to general and adapted physical education. *I CAN* (Wessel, 1977) is an acronym for four principles believed to underlie successful teaching:

I   Individualize instruction

C   Create social leisure competence

A   Associate all learnings

N   Narrow the gap between theory and practice

The Achievement-Based Curriculum (ABC) model is a 1980s refinement of the I CAN model (Wessel & Kelly, 1986). Wessel is now retired, and work concerning these models is guided by Luke Kelly at the University of Virginia. The PAP-TE-CA model followed in this text is an adaptation and expansion of the curriculum components (plan, assess, prescribe, teach, evaluate, and modify) used in the I CAN and ABC models.

In addition to excellent information about curriculum development (Wessel, 1977), I CAN included a criterion-referenced assessment system in which hundreds of motor skills were broken down into observable tasks that could be assessed pass/fail; these tasks were presented developmentally, making

Table 5.8 Checklist for evaluating objectives that you write for specific goals.

Criteria	Objectives 1	2	3	4
1. Describes learner behavior, not teacher behavior				
2. Describes product, not process (i.e., the terminal behavior, not the learning activity)				
3. Includes a verb that specifies one definite, observable behavior				
4. Contains a single learning outcome, not several				
5. Contains three parts: condition, behavior, and success criterion (CBS acronym)				
6. Matches assessment data to specified behavior				
7. Focuses on functions that are usable and relevant in everyday life				
8. Selects behavior that is achievable through 3 to 5 hours of instruction and practice				

the system particularly applicable to individuals with cognitive and motor delays. The system was described as diagnostic-prescriptive, in that numerous learning activities were prescribed to help achieve various motor, fitness, and leisure goals. I CAN was packaged in boxes that held 9- × 12-inch cardboard sheets and is still available through the Pro•Ed Company.

The Data-Based Gymnasium

Developed by John Dunn and associates at Oregon State University in the late 1970s and later refined, the data-based gymnasium (DBG) model is "a prescriptive physical activity program for students whereby decisions are based upon the student performance data" (Dunn et al., 1986, p. 170). This model is marketed as a book (Dunn et al., 1986), which has served as the major primary source for behavior management and task analysis in adapted physical education. Assessment is criterion-referenced, based on lengthy task analyses that break skills into phases and steps. Many forms are provided for recording multiple trials, preferred cues and reinforcers, and information about baseline, review, revision, and maintenance of individual programs. These forms have led to DBG often being called a "clipboard approach."

Originally DBG was developed specifically for individuals with severe disabilities, but now its principles are recognized as appropriate to anyone who can benefit from behavior management. Embedded within DBG is a component called the Game, Exercise, and Leisure Sport Curriculum; this section presents task analyses for many motor skills. **Forward chaining** (adding parts to the task in the order in which they naturally occur) and **backward chaining** (starting with the whole and adding parts in reverse) are emphasized. DBG is available from Pro•Ed.

Body Skills: A Motor Development Curriculum for Children

Developed by Judy Werder and Robert Bruininks (1988) of Minnesota, this curriculum was developed in the 1980s to complement the Bruininks-Oseretsky Test of Motor Proficiency (BOTMP) (Bruininks, 1978), a major diagnostic test used by adapted physical educators. The curriculum is based on data from a criterion-referenced measure called the Motor Skills Inventory (MSI) as well as the BOTMP, a norm-referenced instrument.

Body Skills encompasses 31 motor skills important to children ages 2 to 12 years. Developmental sequences leading to mature skill are presented pictorially. Instructional units are provided on body management, locomotion, body fitness, object movement, and fine motor development. This curriculum is available through the American Guidance Service (see Appendix E).

Special Olympics Sports Skills Program

Developed in the 1980s by the staff at the Special Olympics International (SOI) headquarters, the SOI Sports Skills Program offers separate sports skills guides for numerous summer and winter sports. Although developed for people with mental retardation, this curriculum is applicable to both general and adapted physical education and to all age groups for whom regulation sports training is appropriate.

Each guide includes long-term goals, short-term objectives, criterion-referenced assessment checklists, and detailed task analyses with excellent illustrations. Goals and objectives encompass skills, social behavior, and functional knowledge of rules. These excellent guides are available through state Special Olympics offices, or SOI (see Appendix C).

Moving to Inclusion

The Moving to Inclusion model developed by the Active Living Alliance for Canadians with a Disability (1994) and Fitness Canada, in cooperation with 11 national organizations, provincial education departments, and other expert sources, is available in both English and French. Nine excellent, well-illustrated books, all entitled *Active Living Through Physical Education: Maximizing Opportunities,* are available on these subjects: introduction, multiple disabilities, amputation, skiing, cerebral palsy, visual impairment, Deaf or hard of hearing, intellectual disability, and wheelchair.

Moving to Inclusion is referred to as a national initiative, and readers of the manuals are encouraged to mail in a personal data form and become part of the Moving to Inclusion Network. By their definition, **inclusive physical education**

is a step-by-step process;

includes all students;

has a range of activities and supports; and

is based on the needs and interest of students.

Each book emphasizes and elaborates on four principles:

1. Activities are modified and individualized as necessary.
2. Expectations are realistic yet challenging.
3. Assistance is provided only to the degree required.
4. Dignity of risk and availability of choices are respected and fostered.

Assessment instruments include Transport Skills Checklist, Object Control Skills Checklist, and Basic Movement Skills Observation Profile. The latter, which uses *satisfactory, developing,* or *not observed* responses, includes 15 tasks and assesses the development of manipulative and transport skills, balance ability, and body/space awareness. The impact of Moving to Inclusion is being felt worldwide (see Figure 5.7). This model is available through Moving to Inclusion, 707A-1600 James Naismith Drive, Gloucester, Ontario, Canada K1B 5N4.

You Stay Active

You Stay Active, a model developed jointly by AAHPERD and the Cooper Institute for Aerobics Research (CIAR) in 1995, is a comprehensive recognition program built around the AAHPERD's Physical Best fitness materials and CIAR's FITNESSGRAM (see Chapter 13). It provides teachers with materials to help teach and reinforce the message of lifetime physical activity. The model emphasizes providing recognition

Figure 5.7 Dr. Lisa Silliman-French, adapted PE coordinator of Denton Public Schools, makes sure that special education children are included in general classes.

for regular participation in physical activity rather than awards or bribes for specific physical fitness achievements. This strategy marks a shift from the traditional school practice of focusing primarily on fitness tests and physical best criteria.

The You Stay Active book includes an activity promotion program called *It's Your Move,* Fit for Life Activity Logs for monitoring activities over an 8- to 10-week period, a Get Fit 6-week general conditioning exercise tracking program, and many other materials. It also stresses the inclusion of students with physical disabilities and recommends the recent work of Seaman (1995). The You Stay Active model is available from the Cooper Institute for Aerobics Research, 12330 Preston Road, Dallas, TX 75230.

Check whether your professor or the university library has copies of these curriculum models. Suggest that pairs of students select one model and make a presentation on that model to the class or to a parents' group. Try to find other models that might guide inclusive physical education.

Using, Creating, and Evaluating Curricular Models

Evaluate these models and determine whether to use the whole model or parts. In particular, use these models to stimulate your personal creativity and initiative. For example, several of these models include descriptions of how to involve parents and other

Table 5.9   Calculating available instructional time for the year.

1. *Total number* of instructional weeks available: 180-day school year = 36 instructional weeks 230-day school year = 46 instructional weeks (Christmas, spring, summer vacations already excluded.)	36	weeks
2. Subtract 2 weeks of the total time available to allow for *canceled physical education classes* resulting from conference time, psychological testing, swimming schedule, snow days, field trips, voting days (gym in use), holiday assemblies, beginning and end of school, and others.	−2	weeks
3. Subtract 2 weeks of the total time available to allow for **flextime** (unplanned adjustments that need to be made to allow for additional instructional needs).	−2	weeks
4. Total weeks available (#1 minus #2 and #3) =	32	weeks (16 each semester)
5. Total days available: a. Multiply #4 by the number of physical education classes per week.	× 5 = 160	days gym/week days gym/year
b. Multiply total number of days by the length (minutes) of your physical education class (instructional time—not dressing or set-up time).	× 30 = 4,800	min gym/day min gym/year

volunteers in programming (e.g., Dunn et al., 1986; Wessel, 1977). How can you incorporate this idea into your curriculum planning? In general, models that are collaboratively developed by the people who use them work better than models exported from other sources. Regardless of whether models are adopted or personally created, much planning is needed.

Planning Instruction for the Year

Procedures involved in planning instruction include (a) calculating instructional time, (b) planning use of time, (c) developing instructional units, and (d) making decisions about space, equipment, and resources.

Calculating Instructional Time

Before determining number of objectives, calculate available instructional time for a specific class and/or student. Table 5.9, based on Wessel's (1977) I CAN system and the ABC curriculum (Wessel & Kelly, 1986), shows how the school calendar is used to do this for the academic year. Table 5.9 shows that the average student assigned to physical education 5 days a week (30 min a day) has 4,800 min (80 hr) of instructional time. This is 2,400 min (40 hr) a semester, a phenomenally short amount of time for the changing of behaviors.

Planning Use of Time

The next step is to decide how many objectives can be achieved in 2,400 min. Remember that students who are disabled or clumsy typically learn more slowly than the social majority and that young students learn more slowly than older ones. Approximately 270 min (4.5 hr) are required for a preschool child with developmental delay to master one objective (Wessel & Kelly, 1986). Low-skilled students in elementary school and secondary school require about 210 min (3.5 hr) and 180 min (3 hr), re-

spectively, per objective. To calculate number of objectives per semester, divide time needed to master one objective into total instructional time. For example, for elementary school:

$$\frac{2{,}400 \text{ min per semester}}{210 \text{ min per objective}} = 11.43 \text{ objectives per semester}$$

The next decision involves how many objectives should be selected from each goal area. *Most IEPs include three or four goals, each broken down into three or four objectives.* Time estimates often relate only to teaching motor and fitness skills; much research is needed on amount of time required to teach rules, strategies, and games. Research is also needed on amount of time required to increase cooperative behaviors and peer interactions and to decrease the many negative behaviors that constitute discipline problems.

Developing Semester Plans

The last step in group planning of time usage is to arrange objectives into instructional units and to specify the beginning and ending date of instruction for each unit. The IEP form, remember, requires a projected date for beginning service delivery. Legislation requires that progress on achievement of objectives must be reviewed for students with disabilities every 12 months. Many states require more frequent reviews. This should be considered in determining number of instructional units and duration of each unit. For convenience, assume that the periodic IEP review falls at the same time as the end of a semester (i.e., after about 2,400 min of instructional time).

Table 5.10 presents a sample semester plan for a student who requires approximately 270 min to achieve an objective (i.e., a preschool child who is slow or a student of any age with a severe disability). In 16 weeks, students on this plan are expected to complete four full objectives and make progress toward six others.

Table 5.10   Sample semester plan to guide service delivery.

Instructional Unit		Time in Minutes	Time Spent Each Week, in Minutes	Number of Weeks
1. Running games				
a. Motor skill—running		1,050	105	
b. Self-concept		450	45	
c. Social interactions		Embedded	Embedded	
d. Play and game concepts		Embedded	Embedded	
	Total	1,500	150	10
2. Aquatics				
a. Water entry and locomotion		270	67.5	
b. Breathing		270	67.5	
c. Self-concept and body image		60	15	
	Total	600	150	4
3. Creative movement/dance				
a. Portraying animals		100	50	
b. Moving to accompaniment		100	50	
c. Abdominal strength		100	50	
	Total	300	150	2

Note. a, b, c, and *d* refer to specific objectives. If 540 min are allocated, two objectives can be achieved. If 270 min are allocated, one objective can be achieved. If fewer than 270 min are allocated, there is not time for completion of one objective.

Develop objectives for the units in Table 5.10 for hypothetical students. Then develop some original sample semester plans like that of Table 5.10 and write objectives. Remember that planning should always be done in units of minutes.

The amount of time required for a student to achieve an objective varies widely. The estimates of 270, 210, and 180 min for preschool, elementary, and secondary students are based on averages. Difficult objectives naturally require more time than easy ones. The art of writing objectives is enhanced by keeping in mind the number of minutes. *Flexible time* is needed for review and reinforcement of skills, knowledge, rules, and strategies learned in previous units. The planning of instruction is directed primarily toward new learning.

Other Decision Making

Planning also entails decision making about space, equipment, and resources. Size of class is tremendously important, because every student should have maximum on-task time. This means that, in a ball-handling unit, every student should have a ball and not be standing in line, waiting for a turn. It also means that every student has a chance to learn sports by practicing as a member of a regulation-size team, not by being 1 of 15 players scattered over the softball field. If too many students are assigned to a class in proportion to available space and equipment, selection of objectives and time planning are obviously affected.

Of particular importance is ascertaining that facilities are barrier-free and conform to the ADA. This is not only important for students with disabilities but also for teachers and consultants with disabilities (Figure 5.8). Decisions must also be made about the purchase of (a) books, journals, and videos

that should be available at school for teachers, (b) equipment, and (c) tests and curriculum materials. Resources to help with these tasks are in Appendix E, Tables E.1 through E.4.

The Link Between Planning and Evaluation

Whenever a plan for school district or school physical education is developed, an evaluation protocol should be written at the same time. Evaluation protocols typically entail a method of coming to agreement on the criteria (standards) to be used to evaluate each aspect of the program and subsequently using these criteria.

Evaluation consists of formative and summative processes that enable judgments about the effectiveness, efficiency, and affectiveness of a program. *Formative* and *summative* are terms that indicate *when* evaluation occurs. **Formative evaluation** is continuous examination that provides immediate input to decision makers and enables revision or reformulation on a day-to-day basis. **Summative evaluation** is systematic examination of a program during its final days or at its conclusion; it contributes to decision making about which program variables to keep the same and which to change. As a systems model, PAP-TE-CA includes both formative and summative evaluation (see Figure 5.9).

Effectiveness, efficiency, and affectiveness are criteria to guide evaluation (Idol et al., 1994). **Effectiveness** refers to achievement of objectives. **Efficiency** refers to achievement of objectives in accordance with preestablished timelines, resource utilization, and cost. **Affectiveness** refers to whether service providers, receivers, and significant others enjoyed being involved in the program (this is assessed by self-reports). These criteria are often incorporated into a 5-point Likert scale that permits rating the extent that each criterion is met.

Figure 5.8 Steps rather than ramps still challenge teachers and consultants with disabilities.

Figure 5.9 Services included in the adapted physical activity delivery system with detail on evaluation types.

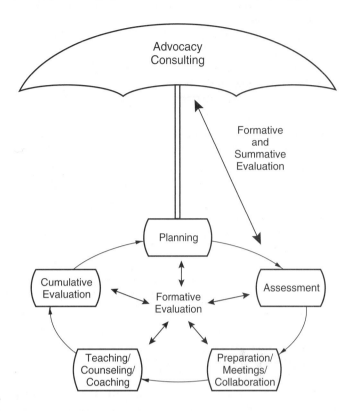

Several models are available to guide program evaluation. See Sherrill and Oakley (1988) for a description of four popular models, and *Empowerment Evaluation* (Fetterman et al., 1996) for futuristic ideas. The most popular model in adapted physical activity is the **discrepancy evaluation model (DEM)** of Provus (1971), and this is recommended for use in PAP-TE-CA service delivery. See Chapter 7 for sample survey. DEM calls for formative and summative evaluation of inputs, processes, and outcomes.

In DEM, evaluation involves

1. Appointing an evaluation committee that includes representatives from all participant groups
2. Agreeing on program standards or criteria
3. Determining whether a discrepancy exists between some aspect of the actual program and its standard(s)
4. Using this discrepancy information to identify and correct weaknesses in the plan that guides the program

The Link Between Planning and Professional Philosophy

Planning is guided by philosophy of individuals and groups, collectively. An indicator of true professionals is possession of a well-developed philosophy that guides actions, including program planning, evaluation, and change. Philosophy, in turn, comes from knowledge and experience. The more breadth and depth one has, the more usable the philosophy will be in a variety of contexts. Some persons develop philosophy through trial and error, but most rely on favorite theories that describe, explain, and predict what will happen when elements of plans are enacted. Following are a few of Sherrill's favorite psychosocial theories. They are time-tested works, mostly posited in the 1960s and 1970s, with changes made each decade to keep the theories current and applicable to present and futuristic decision making.

Self-Actualization Theory of Maslow

Self-actualization is an individual's self-fulfillment of her or his potentialities, the inner drive to become all that one can be. Self-actualization theory evolved out of Maslow's hierarchy of human needs, first formulated as motivation theory in Maslow's text *Motivation and Personality* (1954). This hierarchy of needs looked like a pyramid, with physiological needs like hunger and thirst at the bottom and aesthetic and creative needs at the top (see Figure 5.10). The needs are arranged in a hierarchy to illustrate Maslow's contention that motivation is concentrated primarily on one level at a time. According to Maslow, individuals cannot move to a higher level until at least a minimal degree of satisfaction is derived at the lower level.

Maslow's hierarchy has implications for physical activity service delivery. One is that deficiency needs should be addressed in a particular order. Professionals should ascertain that (a) nutritional and fluid needs are being met, (b) prescribed medications have been taken, and (c) temperature, lighting, and other environmental conditions are conducive to physiological well-being.

Concern about safety needs includes psychological security as well as physical safety. Freedom from fear, anxiety, and

Figure 5.10   Self-actualization theory evolved out of Maslow's hierarchy of human needs.

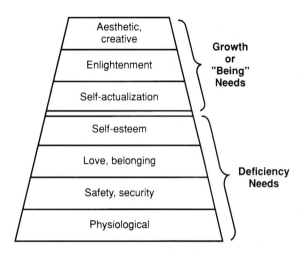

confusion is a prerequisite for attending to and learning subject matter. Students must not be afraid of teachers or of failure. The safety mandate of Maslow's hierarchy thus guides educators to select assessment and learning tasks that build trust, faith, and confidence. Students must be helped to perceive the teacher as a partner in learning and classmates as a support group.

The love and belonging step has been interpreted as emphasizing the social basis of learning. Students need to be loved, appreciated, and accepted for who they are rather than what they can or cannot do. If love is unconditional, then persons can become intrinsically motivated to do their best because they are not worried about pleasing the teacher and being liked. Maslow's writing emphasizes the fragility of the inner being. Self-actualization theory suggests that the whole person (the self) must feel safe, loved, and accepted before the ego can survive objective, corrective feedback directed at specific behaviors. Only when love and belonging needs are met is the student able to benefit from formal motor skill and fitness instruction that enhances competence, mastery, achievement, and other outcomes related to esteem.

According to Maslow (1970, p. 45), "satisfaction of the self-esteem need leads to feelings of self-confidence, worth, strength, capability, and adequacy, of being useful and necessary in the world." Once this need is met, individuals are internally motivated to become all that they can be. Concurrently, they feel responsible for making the world a better place to live. Good teaching, according to Maslow's theory, is not changing the person but rather manipulating the environment so that needs are met.

General education is based on the belief that ordinary students can develop these behaviors and become self-actualizing without concrete, specific help from teachers. This may be the case when development is typical and no illness or disability intensifies deficiency needs. Adapted physical activity, however, is concerned with people who require professional expertise. A different philosophy is needed when the process of becoming entails conquering environmental barriers and personal limitations rather than the self evolving naturally. Maslow's theory thus has been extended and refined by many leaders in the search for ways to help teachers, students, and athletes become self-actualizing.

Self-Concept Theory of Rogers

Carl Rogers, recognized worldwide as the father of humanistic counseling, systematically applied self-actualization theory to teaching, counseling, and rehabilitation. Of his many contributions, the one most relevant to adapted physical activity is the idea of the fully functioning self. Rogers posited that *self-concept is the central concept in psychology and provides the best perspective for understanding an individual's behavior.*

Rogers hypothesized that all of us have an **ideal self** and a **real or actual self.** The more congruent these two selves are, the more fully functioning and self-actualizing we are. According to this theory, teachers must spend time talking to students and helping them clarify the self they really want to be. *Personal goal setting is an important part of this theory.* Teachers must know how to ask the right questions to motivate students to assess themselves, set goals, and follow through.

Rogers posited that people come to know themselves through experiences, including verbal feedback from others. To maintain or enhance congruence between ideal self and real self, people tend to seek out experiences that confirm the self they want to be and avoid experiences that cause discrepancy. The clumsy child who wants to become a good athlete may avoid practice and block out corrective feedback because these experiences are painful. They heighten realization of how separate the ideal and the real selves are. Creating a make-believe world and daydreaming about the self are easier. Knowledge of this phenomenon helps teachers to understand why the behaviors of so many students seem counterproductive to the logical approach to acquiring motor competence.

Defense Mechanisms

When persons cannot cope with discrepancies between experiential feedback (kinesthetic, visual, verbal) and the ideal self, they develop *defense mechanisms* of distortion and denial. **Distortion** alters the meaning of the experience (i.e., the individual begins to perceive self and world as he or she wants to see it rather than how it really is). **Denial** removes or blocks from consciousness things that are hurtful. Illustrative of distortion and denial are findings that self-concept scores of youth with physical disabilities on a physical appearance scale are higher than the norm for able-bodied youth (Sherrill, Hinson, Gench, Kennedy, & Low, 1990).

When disability causes the body to look different and/or limits motor prowess, *distortion and denial may be mechanisms for trying to keep the self integrated and psychologically healthy.* According to Rogers, these mechanisms lead to conceptual rigidity and maladjustment. They are like putting Band-Aids on a wound rather than treating it. Sooner or later, the wound festers. Rogers therefore developed a system of counseling techniques to help persons modify the way they conceptualize themselves. This system, described in his most famous book (Rogers, 1951), was first called *client-centered therapy* and later referred to as *person-centered therapy.* The approach is also called Rogerian counseling or teaching.

Rogers applied his theory directly to teaching in his book *Freedom to Learn* (1969). In it, he described teachers as facilitators and stressed that the warmth, empathy, and genuineness of teachers make students free to learn (see Figure 5.11). He emphasized that students learn to use freedom and to become internally motivated only when they are given freedom. From Rogers come many of the indicators of good teaching that are taught in education courses and also the belief that teaching and counseling should be inseparable.

Principles Underlying Self-Concept Theory

Implications of the fully functioning self theory (also called person-centered theory) for adapted physical activity are many. Threads of this theory run throughout the text. First and fore-

most, however, is *the principle that self-concept should be the central concern in planning and implementing service delivery.* Second is *the principle that physical educators should have the counseling skills to help students resolve problems in the psychomotor domain.* Sport psychology courses are increasingly becoming the source of training in this area. Techniques for enhancing the performance of athletes need to be generalized to persons with disabilities and, perhaps even more important, to clumsy children.

Personal Meaning Theory of Wright

Personal meaning theory, attributed to Beatrice Wright, stresses that it is the personal meaning of a disability that is important rather than the disability itself. This personal meaning is derived from a host of psychosocial factors "that underlie the way *disability as a value loss* is perceived and reacted to by other people, as well as the self" (Wright, 1983, p. 6). Author of *Physical Disability: A Psychological Approach* (1960) and a second edition with a modified title, *Physical Disability: A Psychosocial Approach* (1983), Wright acknowledges that Kurt Lewin and Carl Rogers most influenced her thinking. Wright is considered the major pioneer theorist in contemporary rehabilitation psychology. The implications of personal meaning theory in disability are discussed in Chapter 2, which describes how physical education and sport have different meanings for each individual. The teacher must be especially aware of the social environment in learning.

The application of personal meaning theory to adapted physical education leads to formal and informal assessment of personal meaning in relation to the activities to be taught. Students should be actively involved in planning their instructional program, encouraged to set goals, and taught how to monitor their progress.

Fun is the reason most children give for participation in youth sports and other forms of physical activity. To facilitate the development of an active lifestyle, teachers need to explore with students the personal meaning of fun. For some individuals, this seems to have a social basis, whereas for others it seems to be challenge or mastery oriented.

One approach to assessing personal meaning is the use of instruments that measure the importance of sports and physical appearance (Fox & Corbin, 1989). For example, students may be given pairs of items like those that follow and asked to circle the one of each pair that better describes how important something is to them:

Some teenagers don't think that being athletic is that important.	BUT	Other teenagers think that being athletic is important.
Some teenagers think that how they look is important.	BUT	Other teenagers don't care that much about how they look.

Harter (1988)

Only by caring about personal meaning can you personalize instruction. Know and accept that physical activity and competence are not the central constructs in everyone's lives. For some persons, finding a job, acquiring a close friend or lover, or gaining access to a social group may be foremost. Take the time to listen and to show the link between physical activity and other goals.

Personal meaning is often studied through qualitative research (e.g., Guthrie & Castelnuovo, 2001; Promis et al. 2001; Wheeler et al., 1999). Sport sociology categorizes personal meaning theory under **interactionalist theory,** emphasizing that personal meaning comes mainly through social interactions (Coakley, 2001).

Social Cognitive Theory of Bandura

Social cognitive theory, proposed by Albert Bandura (1977, 1986, 1997), is the conceptual framework for many theories that sometimes are classified as behaviorism and associated with behavior management. Preference for the term *social cognitive* is based on the role that cognition and the total social environment play in response teaching and learning. There is always some kind of cognition between the stimulus (cue or command) and the response (verbal or physical performance). *The one-to-one relationship between the teacher and the student in behavior management makes the context social rather than exclusively instructional. Even individuals with severe mental retardation respond differently to cuegivers they like and those they dislike.*

Self-Efficacy Theory

Bandura (1977) proposed self-efficacy theory as a conceptual framework for changing fearful and avoidant behaviors. As such, it has considerable relevance for low-skilled individuals. According to Bandura (1986), **perceived self-efficacy** is "a judgment of one's capacity to accomplish a certain level of performance" (p. 391). It is concerned, not with skills, but with what we think we can do with these skills. *Self-efficacy is also defined as a situation-specific form of self-confidence.*

Self-efficacy is typically measured with a yes/no response scale in relation to specific questions (e.g., "Can you jump over a 3-ft height?" "Can you run a 12-min mile?" "Can you score 7 out of 10 on a volleyball serve test?"). Another approach is to ask individuals their degree of certainty that they can do something: 0%, 20%, 40%, 60%, 80%, 100%. An **efficacy expectation** is a good predictor of actual performance. If an individual expresses a negative efficacy expectation, the humanistic professional does not force him or her to try the task. Instead, the reasons for the belief are explored, and four antecedent events are used to change the belief (see Figure 5.12). Partner- or team-teaching practices are helpful when implementing self-efficacy theory because they allow giving students with negative expectancies a choice. The students can either go to the resource teacher station for help or stay and watch the successful performances of others. A time limit, however, is placed on the watching option (also called *symbolic modeling* or *vicarious learning* by Bandura).

Figure 5.12 shows the four sources of information posited by Bandura as determinants of an efficacy expectation. *Of these, Bandura believed that personal mastery experiences were the most important. He stressed that success raises expectations of further success and discussed structuring the environment to ensure efficacy.* Students should be taught to visualize themselves and others coping successfully with the phobia or fear. Performance accomplishments thus can be direct or indirect. As a pioneer in social learning theory, Bandura believed strongly in partner follow-the-leader type activities called **participant modeling.** He also supported cognitive training to control anxiety and to cope with stress.

Self-efficacy theory seems similar to the self-concept theories described in Chapter 8, but Bandura (1986) pointed out several differences. Mainly, self-efficacy is more cognitively oriented. It is a *judgment* that one can do something, regardless of whether the consequences are pleasant. A skilled combat soldier might judge himself to be efficacious but derive neither pleasure nor self-esteem from his work. In contrast, according

Figure 5.12   Model showing antecedent events used in Bandura's self-efficacy model to change efficacy expectations.

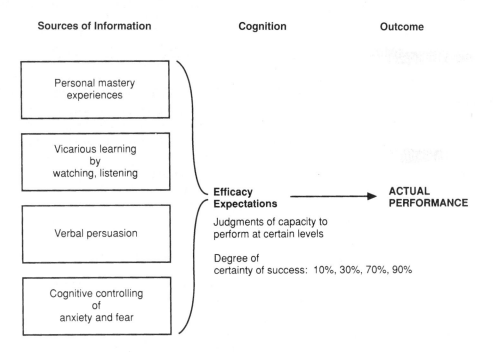

to Bandura, most self-concept theories emphasize feelings. This is not entirely true in that some approaches treat self-concept as an attitude with cognitive, affective, and behavioral dimensions.

Self-Determination Theory (The Exercise of Control)

Self-determination theory posits that a high degree of perceived personal control over life's events contributes to intrinsic motivation, goal achievement, and psychological well-being (Deci & Ryan, 1985; Wehmeyer, Kelchner, & Richards, 1996). In his 1997 book, *Self-Efficacy: The Exercise of Control,* Bandura focuses on how efficacy beliefs "operate in concert with other sociocognitive determinants in governing human adaptation and change" (p. vii). Emphasis on personal efficacy in individual pursuits is expanded to encompass collective efficacy and its role in enablement and empowerment. **Perceived collective efficacy** is "a group's shared belief in its conjoint capabilities to organize and execute the courses of action required to produce given levels of attainments" (p. 477). Applied to our profession, this means that physical educators must have clear beliefs concerning our collective capabilities to change physical activity patterns and enable healthy lives. Physical educators thus need to understand the exercise of control (perceived and actual) and consider ways it can be enhanced. Vallerand and Reid (1990) provide an excellent review of various self-determination theories.

Perceived Control or Locus of Control Theory of Rotter

Perceived control, also called **locus of control** (LOC), is the perception of the connection or lack of connection between one's actions and their consequences. Julian Rotter (1966) posited that persons vary in LOC along an internal to external continuum. Some persons are in the middle, but others tend to be either internally or externally controlled. **Internal LOC** is

belief and/or perception that events in one's life are dependent upon ability and effort. **External LOC** is the feeling that events in life are not based on one's actions but are a result of chance, fate, luck, or controls imposed by others, like task difficulty. **Confused LOC** is lack of understanding or inability to decide what causes events.

Child development theory emphasizes that LOC shifts from external to internal as students mature. The degree of this shift depends, however, on child rearing and classroom teaching practices and on such variables as health and disabilities that may prevent independent thought and action. Some persons remain more externally than internally controlled throughout life. This includes many persons with severe mental retardation or emotional disturbance.

Because of the tendency of parents and society to overprotect persons with disabilities and deny them control of their own lives, physical educators need to stress independence, personal control, and responsibility. Remember expectancy theory. Expect persons to assume control over the situational factors in their lives, and gradually, they will assume that control.

Learned Helplessness of Seligman

Learned helplessness is a particular problem in a person with a disability or chronic illness when nothing the person does seems to help the condition. Likewise, learned helplessness has been associated with demoralization because of repeated failure in motor activities despite best efforts. When, over a period of time, persons come to believe that there is no relationship between effort and outcome, the result is reduced motivation, low self-esteem, and generalized depression (Seligman, 1975). Physical educators must recognize the learned helplessness syndrome and work to prevent it.

Types of Motivation

Motivation refers to all of the forces (internal and external) that focus behaviors, start and stop them, and determine their frequency and duration. Deci and Ryan (1985) distinguish between three types of motivation: (a) intrinsic, (b) extrinsic, and (c) amotivation. **Intrinsic motivation** refers to forces that are 100% self-determined; these come directly from voluntary activity and are experienced as fun, pleasurable, and satisfying. **Extrinsic motivation** may be self- or other-determined, depending on who sets the goals and establishes rewards and sanctions; these forces are focused on either obtaining rewards or avoiding sanctions. **Amotivation** refers to absence of forces because no cognitive link is established between behavior and outcomes. This may occur because mental function is frozen at or below the level of a 7- or 8-month-old infant or because life experiences are so confusing and overpowering that persons no longer try to make sense of cause-effect relationships.

Achievement Goal Theory

Several achievement goal theories emphasize the importance of perceived ability, dispositional tendencies toward goal orientation (ego or task), motivational climate (performance or mastery), situational factors, gender, and cognitive level on goal setting and achievement (e.g., Causgrove Dunn, 2000; Parish & Treasure, 2003; Nicholls, 1989). Persons with **ego orientations** set goals that emphasize the "I" in comparison with others, aiming to win or to be among the best in an activity. These persons achieve best in a **performance climate,** defined as one that emphasizes traditional normal curve expectations and competition for grades, recognition, and praise. In contrast, persons with **task orientations** set goals in relation to overcoming barriers, completing specific tasks, and achieving their personal best. They achieve best in a **mastery climate,** one that "emphasizes self-referenced criteria for success, encourages effortful striving, and minimizes the negative consequences of making errors" (Parish & Treasure, 2003, p. 175).

Achievement goal theory is especially important in adapted physical activity because *mastery motivational climates* for children with movement difficulties result in higher perceived competence (Causgrove Dunn, 2000). Children with higher perceived competence (or ability) exert more effort in completing tasks, whereas those with lower perceived competence tend to drop out (Bouffard et al., 1996). In general, promoting a mastery motivational climate in physical education fosters self-determination and increases involvement in physical activity (Parish & Treasure, 2003).

Other Psychosocial Theories

Additional theories related to self-perception, physical self-concept, motivation, and pedagogy are presented in Chapter 8. Among these are competence motivation theory, personal investment theory, teacher expectancy theory, and attribution theory.

Essential to the application of all of the theories covered so far are the many attitude theories. Following is a brief discussion of general attitude theory, reasoned action theory, planned behavior theory, and contact theory.

Reflect on these theories that Sherrill believes are the psychosocial basis for adaptation. Learn more about them. Which two of these theories do you like best? Why?

Facilitating Attitude Change

In most school districts and schools that support inclusive classroom instruction, considerable planning must be devoted to ways to develop positive attitudes toward teaching students with and without disabilities in the same setting. This section presents basic information about attitude theories and the practices they underlie.

Since the early 1980s attitudes have been recognized as the key to inclusion of students with disabilities in general physical education (Rizzo, 1984; Sherrill, 1986). Attitudes are **social constructions.** This means, among other things that (a) people (usually social majorities) construct the meanings of disability and of inclusion and (b) meanings vary by time, geography, and specific theory. The simplest definitions of **attitude** are *affect* (feeling or emotion) *for or against an object* (Thurstone, 1931) and *favorable or unfavorable evaluation* (cognitive judgment) *of an object* (Ajzen & Fishbein, 1980). **Object** (sometimes called target) may be anything: a set of behaviors, the self, other persons, a disability, a religion, a racial or ethnic group, or an idea. The more specific the object is, the easier it is to plan change.

In this text, we build on the definition of Ajzen and Fishbein (1980) and define **attitudes** *as enduring sets of evaluative beliefs, charged with feelings and emotions, that predispose a person to certain kinds of behaviors.* Whereas Ajzen and Fishbein define attitudes exclusively as *evaluative beliefs,* we include feelings and emotions in our definition to emphasize that beliefs must be strong enough to elicit involvement of the affective domain (i.e., a passion to act for or against an outcome, a mission, a feeling from the heart or soul). We contend that beliefs cannot be totally separated from feelings and emotions.

The Attitude-Behavior Link

Proponents of attitudes as the key to inclusion emphasize that the process of facilitating positive attitudes is complex. Physical educators are just now beginning to address the attitude-behavior link. Some persons have studied attitude simply because they were interested in attitude. However, the main reason to study attitudes is to better understand the link between attitudes and behaviors. If valid measures of attitude can be obtained, they can be used as predictors of teachers' behaviors and can provide information about which school personnel need inservice training and staff development the most. Likewise attitude surveys administered to university students can provide insight into their level of readiness for employment in inclusive physical education settings.

Reasoned Action and Planned Behavior Theories

The attitude theories used most often in adapted physical education are the reasoned action theory of Ajzen and Fishbein (1980) and the planned behavior theory of Ajzen (1991). Both

Figure 5.13 The theory of reasoned action approach to attitude assessment and behavior change. Note that beliefs, attitudes, intentions, and behaviors are separate components. (Based on concepts of Icek Ajzen/Martin Fishbein, *Understanding Attitudes and Predicting Social Behavior,* © 1980.)

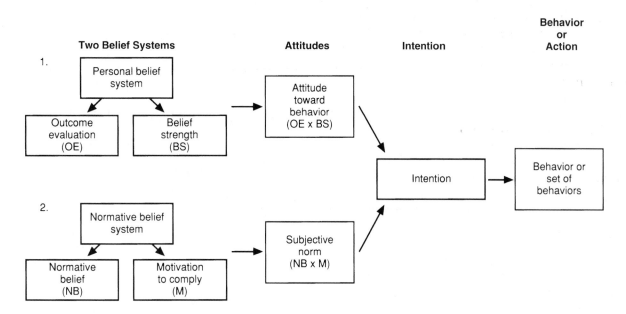

theories use the components depicted in Figure 5.13 to explain the posited link between attitudes and behaviors. The planned behavior theory includes one additional component: **perceived behavioral control,** which is determined by answers to such questions as (a) What factors make it *easier* for you to practice inclusive teaching? and (b) What factors make it *harder* for you to practice inclusive teaching?

Both reasoned action and planned behavior theories are attitude measurement theories rather than attitude pedagogy theories. As such, they guide the development of instruments and the testing of selected components believed essential in the attitude-behavior link. Rizzo (1984) based his popular attitude survey concerning inclusive teaching on the *attitude toward behavior component* of reasoned action theory. Much research subsequently has been published on this portion of theory in the *Adapted Physical Activity Quarterly.* Recently, other physical educators have begun to explore planned behavior theory (e.g., Conaster, Block, & Gansneder, 2002).

Components of the Attitude-Behavior Link

To change a behavior, the professional must address several interacting components (see Figure 5.13). *We therefore start by identifying the specific behaviors to be changed.* The process to be followed is similar to that used in writing goals, objectives, or benchmarks.

Behaviors are single acts or sets of acts that occur under certain conditions, toward a specific target, for a specified time that can be observed and assessed. Let us assume that the behavior to be targeted is *using inclusive strategies in a general physical education class.* According to Ajzen and Fishbein (1980), each inclusive strategy should be broken into four parts. These can be remembered by the acronym ACTT.

A *Action:* broken down into observable, measurable tasks. For example, analyzing the goal of using inclusive strategies with José into such subgoals as say hello, say the name of, smile at, praise efforts of, and find a partner for.

C *Context:* environmental conditions that must be present when the act is demonstrated or practiced (e.g., at school or in neighborhood; whenever the person is within 3 feet of me; or whenever the person is in a specific room).

T *Target:* object toward which the acts are directed. This should be one or two specific persons, not a general target like all persons with disabilities.

T *Time:* period of time over which act(s) must occur or number of times that act(s) must occur.

For example, inclusive strategies directed toward a child with a disability might be

1. Say hello, using the child's name, when he first enters the gym. Time criterion is every class period from 8/30 to 9/30.
2. Smile and say something personal and encouraging whenever the child comes within 3 feet during physical education class. Time criterion is 3–5 times during every class for 10 consecutive classes.

Intervention is a carefully planned and conducted exposure to (or immersion in) specific conditions that are believed to cause a desired behavior or act. For example, in contact theory, *contact with specific conditions present is the intervention.* In fitness theory, *exercise with specific conditions present is the intervention.* In both examples, specific conditions of the intervention must be planned with special attention to **frequency**

Figure 5.14   A model for attitude change based on contact theory.

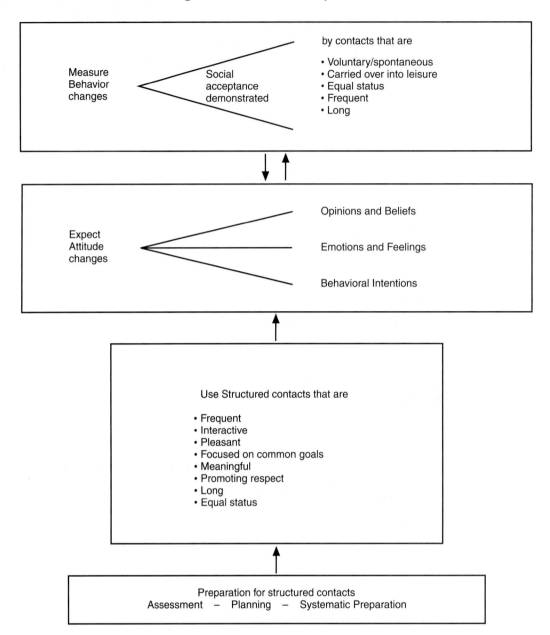

(how many sessions), **intensity** or **intimacy** (how much effort by self and/or others) and **time** (duration in minutes, weeks). Planning of conditions is so universally important that the acronym **FIT** is used as a memory device.

Beliefs (see Figure 5.13) are products of *critical thinking about (a) personal beliefs, (b) significant others' beliefs, (sometimes called normative beliefs and considered social pressures) and (c) perceived control beliefs.* Reasoned action theory uses only personal beliefs and normative beliefs, whereas planned behavior theory uses all three sets of beliefs.

Attitudes, defined earlier, when strong enough, lead to intentions. Attitudes may be inferred from belief statements or assessed directly by asking persons whether a target object is good or bad, attractive or ugly, useful or useless, and the like. Rizzo (1984) used belief statements to infer attitudes.

Intentions are indications of how a person plans to act in relation to a specific target object. Illustrative intentions are I will use partner inclusive strategies for José 10% of each class period over the next 6 weeks and I will devote at least 30 minutes a day for 6 weeks to planning social inclusion strategies for students with disabilities in my class. Intentions are predictors of behavior.

Using Contact Theory to Promote Inclusion

Contact theory is the body of knowledge that guides philosophy and practices for increasing acceptance, appreciation, and inclusion of others perceived as different from oneself. In sociological terms, these are persons who are stigmatized and/or members of disadvantaged cultural subgroups. Contact theory

Table 5.11   A teacher's personal beliefs about adapting instruction for a student with a disability.

My Adapting Instruction for Joe Will Result in These Outcomes/Consequences:	Outcome Evaluation (OE)			Belief Strength (BS) That Outcome Will Occur			Attitude (A) OE × BS = A
	Good		Bad	Certain		Uncertain	
1. Joe will achieve goals.	③	2	1	3	②	1	6
2. Other students will achieve their goals (i.e., Joe's presence will not interfere with learning of nondisabled students).	③	2	1	③	2	1	9
3. Adaptations needed will increase pressures on me so I'm more tired at night, maybe grouchy.	3	2	①	3	②	1	2
4. I'll have to give up some of my recreation to find the extra time needed for planning and individualizing.	3	2	①	3	②	1	2
5. The principal will be pleased and give me a merit raise.	③	2	1	3	2	①	3
Total Attitude Toward Behavior Score							22

Note: Highest possible total attitude score is 45.

is important because it helps to understand friendships, social behaviors, and inclusive and exclusive practices in everyday life. Understanding, in turn, leads to the question, "Will I be a good model for my students?" Contact theory also guides the examination of prejudices, stereotypes, discrimination, and oppression in physical activity settings.

Contact Conditions Associated With Favorable Attitudes Toward Inclusion

According to Allport (1954), four conditions must be present in contact situations for the development of favorable attitudes: (a) parties involved must share equal status; (b) the community (i.e., significant others like administrators and parents) must support and sanction inclusion; (c) individuals must be in pursuit of common objectives (i.e., be actively cooperating in meaningful activities); and (d) the association must be deep, genuine, and intimate (i.e., "of the sort that leads to the perception of common interests and common humanity between members of the two groups" [Allport, 1954, p. 281]).

Since the 1950s, numerous experts have reworded this list, but new wording has not changed the requirements (Amir, 1969; Fishbein, 2002; Oskamp, 2002). A simplified list of contact conditions includes equal status, frequent, of long duration, interactive, pleasant, focused on common goals (i.e., cooperative), meaningful, and promoting respect. Each of these conditions is observable and measurable (characteristics of a good goal). Figure 5.14 presents a model designed for university teacher education, in-service training, and staff development. Starting at the bottom of Figure 5.14, appropriate preparation enables teachers to embed structured contacts into their lesson plans. This in turn should lead to attitude changes in children with and without disabilities. Careful planning is the key. Attitude changes lead to intentions, which it is hoped result in children showing social acceptance of one another. This social

acceptance is assessed by the number and intensity of contacts that meet the criteria in the top box of Figure 5.14.

Case Study of a New Teacher

In a general physical education setting, the teacher has just been assigned a 14-year-old with cerebral palsy. The teenager, named Joe, has average intelligence, good speech, and Class 4 functional motor ability (i.e., no involvement of the upper extremities, but needs a wheelchair for ambulation; see Chapter 25 on cerebral palsy). There are 27 other 14-year-olds in the class, all of whom are able-bodied (AB) and represent the usual wide range of sport skills. The teacher has no assistant. The boy, Joe, arrives on the first day of the spring term, accompanied by an individualized education program (IEP), written by a multidisciplinary team in accordance with federal law and school district policy. This IEP briefly states Joe's annual physical education goals, including short-term instructional objectives. The teacher notes that these are compatible with those of the general education students. For Joe to achieve these goals, however, the teacher will have to adapt instruction. The question is, will he or she do this? How can classroom behavior be predicted?

According to the theory of reasoned action, two inventories should be administered to the teacher: (a) one to determine the teacher's personal beliefs about adapting instruction and (b) one to determine the teacher's normative beliefs (social pressures) about adapting instruction. Each inventory would include 5 to 7 items, each of which would be rated on two 3-point scales. From these scores, an attitude toward behavior and a subjective norm would be derived, which, in turn, could be used to predict strength of intention to adapt instruction and probable actual behavior.

Table 5.11 presents an example of how personal beliefs about adapting instruction might be measured. Each of the five items represents an outcome or consequence of adapting

Table 5.12   A teacher's normative beliefs about adapting instruction for a student with a disability.

My Significant Others Believe I Should Adapt Instruction for Joe:	Normative Belief (NB)			Motivation to Comply (M)			Subjective Norm (N) NB × M = N
	Yes		No	Strong		Weak	
1. My spouse or housemate	3	2	①	3	②	1	2
2. My mother	3	②	1	3	②	1	4
3. My principal	③	2	1	3	②	1	6
4. My best friend	3	2	①	3	②	1	2
5. Other teachers in my school	3	②	1	3	②	1	4
Subjective Norm Score							18

Note: Highest possible score, when there are five significant others, is 45.

instruction. Note that there are separate items in relation to the consequences for (a) Joe, (b) general education students, and (c) the teacher. Note also that both positive and negative consequences are included. In the first response column of the inventory (Outcome Evaluation), the teacher circles the numbers to express her or his overall feeling about each outcome. In the second response column (Belief Strength), numbers are circled to indicate degree of certainty that the outcome will occur. The third column (Attitude) would not appear on the actual inventory. It is included here simply to illustrate how the attitude score is derived.

Table 5.12 presents an example of how normative beliefs about adapting instruction might be measured. Each of the five items represents a significant other. In the first response column (Normative Belief), numbers are circled to indicate the degree of probability that significant others will support the behavior. In the second response column (Motivation to Comply), the teacher circles numbers to indicate degree of motivation. The third column (Subjective Norm) would not appear on the actual inventory but is included to show how this score is derived.

The attitude score of 22 out of 45 (48.9%) from the first inventory and the subjective norm score of 18 out of 45 (40%) from the second inventory are then examined in terms of the relative importance of these two variables. This provides insight into the relationship between attitude, subjective norm, and intention. In this example, the teacher's commitment to adapting instruction, as expressed by intention, ranges somewhere between 40 and 49%. With such a low intention level, the teacher probably will not do much adapting in relation to the boy's special needs. This kind of information is valuable in that it helps (a) teacher trainers assess where more work on belief and attitude change are needed, (b) principals assess which

teachers are likely to do the best job and which teachers need more in-service training, and (c) prospective teachers assess themselves and set personal change goals.

 OPTIONAL ACTIVITIES

1. Pretend you are an adapted physical education specialist and employed in a community with seven elementary schools, two middle schools, and one high school. This is your first year in this community, and you will be the only adapted physical educator. You are the first adapted physical educator the community has ever employed, and they expect you to establish adapted physical education services for kindergarten through transition services for ages 18 through 21. Describe the planning that you will use to establish services and the approximate amount of time various tasks take. What philosophy will guide the services you establish? What resources will you need? What do you expect to be the outcomes of your work at the end of the first year?

2. Study the appendix tables on journals, supplies, and equipment in Appendix E. Order catalogs from various companies, and decide what minimal and maximal purchases would be reasonable to get a service delivery program established.

3. Assume you wish to determine general physical education teachers' degree of comfort in adapting activities for students with disabilities in their mainstream classes. How would you approach this task? Why? How would you follow up with activities to facilitate attitude change?

6

Assessment, the IEP, and the Accommodation Plan

Lisa Silliman-French and Claudine Sherrill

Figure 6.1   **The legislative basis of assessment in adapted physical education services eligibility.**

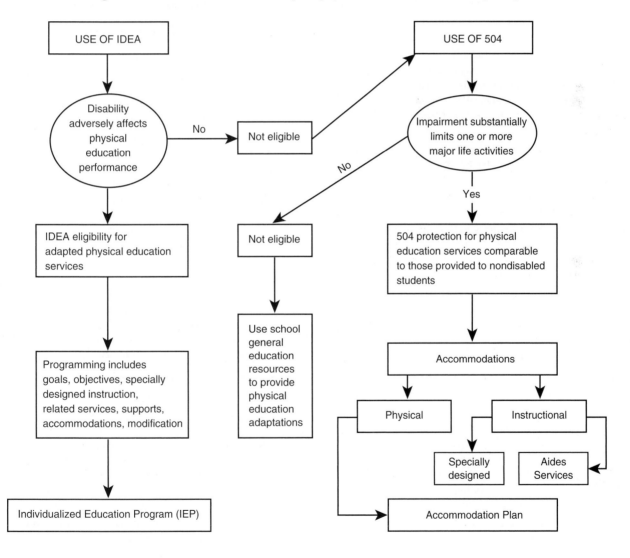

1. Reflect on the six purposes of assessment in adapted physical education service delivery. How are these similar and different compared with the ways general educators use assessment? What is your experience with each purpose? Set personal goals for learning the purposes through observation and practice.

2. Review copies of the instruments described in this Chapter, which can probably be found in your library or in your professor's office. Practice administering some of these instruments and writing reports of your findings. Critique your experiences while administering the instruments.

3. Critically think about who should collect data relating to the different purposes of assessment, what makes them qualified, what they should collect data on and why, what are the best instruments for different age groups and performance strengths and weaknesses, and how you would justify use of instruments if someone challenged your choices.

4. Use data collected by you or given to you to write reports of screening, comprehensive assessment, IEPs, and accommodation plans for selected persons. Reflect on the purpose of these reports and IDEA requirements that you must incorporate into your writing.

Assessment is the foundation of direct service delivery, the key to good teaching, and the determining factor in empowering persons to achieve the quality of life to which they aspire. Assessment plays a major role in every professional's work, because service delivery is based on hundreds of decisions each day, and every decision should be related to the collection and interpretation of data about students and their environment.

General and adapted physical educators are expected to meet basic knowledge standards in the areas of measurement and evaluation (APENS standard 4), assessment (APENS standard 8), and program evaluation (APENS standard 12). Much confusion about these terms exists, partly because the federal government uses the term *evaluation* in IDEA to encompass all forms of data collection, interpretation, and data-based decisions. In contrast, most contemporary textbooks use the term *evaluation* in relation to making judgments about programs or service delivery and *assessment* in relation to making judgments about individuals and the environmental variables that influence their behaviors.

Definitions of Key Terms

Measurement is the collection of data that yields numbers (e.g., weight, height, calories, time on task) or the administration of tests, that when scored, result in numbers. Measurement also encompasses the assignment of numbers to words given as responses or descriptors (e.g., 1 = no; 2 = yes) and the computation of simple statistics like range, mean, and standard deviation that help to interpret averages and individual differences.

Evaluation refers to making judgments about service delivery, teacher performance, programs, classrooms, schools, community facilities, or other large-scale phenomena. Evaluation was covered in Chapter 5, because it is linked with planning.

Assessment refers to data collection (both numerical and word descriptors), interpretation, and decision making about individuals interacting with environments that serve as barriers or enablers. Most professional literature and publications about testing individuals, assigning grades, or determining the need for special services, during the last decade, have carried *assessment* in their titles (e.g., Burton & Miller, 1998; Elliott, Braden, & White, 2001; Kleinert & Kearns, 2001). According to Elliott et al. (2001, p. 2), **educational assessment** is an "information gathering and synthesizing process for the purpose of making decisions about students' learning and instructional needs." We assume that the *information gathering* is about both the individual and the environment.

Legislative Basis of Some Assessment Practices

IDEA and Section 504 of the Rehabilitation Act form the legislative basis for assessment practices that relate to determining the eligibility of students for special educational placements and services, including adapted physical education (study Figure 6.1). IDEA applies only when assessment shows that one of IDEA's disability categories adversely affects physical education performance. When the IEP committee decides that a disability is not severe enough to adversely affect performance, 504 protection can be sought. If the 504 committee determines that the student is not eligible for its protection, then school personnel can initiate supports on a volunteer basis. Whereas extra school funds must be made available for IDEA students, no funding is mandated for 504 students. Additionally, IDEA and 504 address nonbiased assessment, use of an individual's native language or commonly used form of communication (e.g., sign language) in testing, and description of procedures to be followed when parents disagree with assessment results or decisions based on them.

Recent Changes in Assessment

Major ways that assessment has changed over the two decades are (a) substitution of educational for medical terminology and practices (e.g., deletion of words like *diagnosis* and *prescription* and reliance on multidisciplinary decision making rather than the authority of one medical expert); (b) increased interest in ecological assessment, which gathers and synthesizes information about both the individual and the environment rather than assuming the problem or weakness is totally within the individual; (c) broadening the placement concept from a continuum of least restrictive environments (places) to include supports, supplementary aids, and services in general education (GE) settings; (d) implementation of the ongoing standards-based reform; (e) innovation of new practices (e.g., authentic assessment, alternate versus alternative assessment, portfolios, rubrics or standards); and (f) use of Section 504 of the Rehabilitation

Act to declare students eligible for adapted physical education services when they are not eligible under IDEA. Additionally, new and revised tests are available. Illustrative of these in motor and fitness testing are Test of Gross Motor Development-2 (Ulrich, 2000), Brockport Physical Fitness Test (Winnick & Short, 1999), Peabody Developmental Motor Scales-2 (Folio & Fewell, 2000), and the Sports Skills Program Guides periodically revised by Special Olympics International.

The notion of national education standards and the initiation of large-scale state and school district assessments in each subject matter area has its roots in **Goals 2000: Educate America Act of 1994,** PL 103-227 (Kleinert & Kearns, 2001). In the beginning, many students with disabilities were ignored in the implementation of this law. Because the inclusion of students with disabilities in testing resulted in lowered averages, state and local school administrators tended to exclude possible low-scoring students from the GE curriculum, its standards, and its comprehensive testing movement.

IDEA 1997 changed all of this, requiring that by 2000, students with disabilities would be required to participate fully in the general curriculum or have a justification in the IEP for not participating and not taking the same tests as GE peers. IDEA 1997 also required that students attending physical education classes taught by GE physical educators or classroom teachers would not be placed in separate adapted physical education classes until adaptations, accommodations, modifications, and supports were tried and documented as having limited or no success. The terms *accommodation* and *modification* were given new, specific meanings in relation to testing.

Testing accommodations were defined as

Changes in the way a test is administered to or responded to by a student. Testing accommodations are intended to offset distortions in test scores caused by a disability without invalidating or changing what the test measures. Common testing accommodations involve extra time, assistance with directions, assistance with reading, and enlarged print size (Elliott et al., 2001, p. 187).

Modifications were defined as

Changes that alter the level or content of the test. Examples include giving a lower grade level of the test or deleting or changing the content of a test. Modifications are distinct from testing accommodations in that testing accommodations change noncontent aspects of the test (Elliott et al., 2001, p. 184).

Alternate and alternative assessment were also given special meanings. **Alternate assessment** was defined as an assessment "used in place of a regular test because of the nature of the severity of the student's disability and the student's course of study" (Elliott et al., 2001, p. 181). Based on IDEA 1997, alternate assessment is specifically for those students for whom the GE assessment methodology cannot be accommodated. The student's IEP team makes this decision (Kleinert & Kearns, 2001; Losardo & Notari-Syverson, 2001).

Alternative assessment refers to assessment that differs from traditional multiple-choice, essay, and performance tests. The *alternatives* are typically products done over several weeks or months (e.g., portfolios, work samples, group projects, videotaped and photo essays, sport days or festivals, fitness demonstrations, teacher observations, and interviews). New concepts related to alternative assessment include authentic assessment, multiple measures, and performance assessment. An assessment is considered **authentic** when it measures performance in situations and tasks that resemble family and neighborhood settings and real-life tasks. Such settings have long been called *ecologically valid* because they yield meaningful data that relate directly to making lesson plans that address everyday needs. Authentic assessment is often referred to as occurring in a *natural setting.* In physical education, data from observation of a game or drill setting should supplement data collected in a formal test situation.

Purposes of Physical Education/Activity Assessment

Purposes of assessment are (a) screening and referral, (b) making decisions about eligibility and programming in IEP and 504 meetings, (c) making decisions about instructional and environmental adaptations in day-to-day teaching, (d) determining student progress and providing feedback to the performer and concerned parties, (e) determining transition and lifespan needs, and (f) classifying sport participants on functional capacity to facilitate fairness in competition.

Screening and Referral Decisions

Screening is the assessment process used to determine who needs a referral for further testing. General physical educators routinely screen at the beginning of the school year to get acquainted with students' needs, but screening of a particular student can be requested any time by parents, school personnel, or other appropriate persons. Each school district has its own screening form (see Figure 6.2) and own process. Ideally, screening is collaborative with both a general educator and adapted physical educator involved. Increasingly, parents are being involved.

Figure 6.2 presents an illustrative screening form, which is filled in first by a general educator. Once completed, the form is given to the assigned adapted physical educator who then screens the student and collaborates with the professional who referred the student. This information then assists in making one of the four recommendations at the bottom of the form. If further assessment is needed, a request for permission must be sent home to the parents/guardians. In addition, a medical screening form is generally sent home prior to formal/informal assessment to obtain relevant medical information on the student (see Figure 6.3).

Eligibility and Programming Decisions

This purpose is associated with the *comprehensive assessment,* conducted by a qualified professional, that follows a referral and forms the basis for making recommendations about adapted

Figure 6.2 Adapted Physical Education Screening Form. (Note the instructions below are for the General Educator. Later, the adapted physical educator will put checks in the APE column).

General Educator   Educational Diagnostician   Adapted Physical Educator

_____   _____   _____
Initial Date   **Initial** Date   **Initial** Date

Student _____ ID# _____ DOB _____
School _____ Type of class (unit) teacher _____
Evaluation requested by _____ Medical concerns _____
Major concerns about student in physical education _____
_____
School contact for adapted physical education _____
Method of ambulation _____ Form of communication _____

Below are some behaviors that indicate a student's ability to move efficiently and interact effectively with others. Please check the appropriate responses in the General Education (GE) column. If these tasks do not apply, list your concerns on the next page.

PRESENT LEVEL OF PERFORMANCE	YES		SOMETIMES		NO	
	GE	**APE**	**GE**	**APE**	**GE**	**APE**
Motor Movement Skills:						
Demonstrates capability for voluntary movement						
Reacts to noise/activity/touch						
Rolls from front to back						
Sits assisted/unassisted						
Stands assisted/unassisted						
Walks in cross pattern						
Runs in cross pattern						
Ascends/descends stairs						
Jumps with mature pattern						
Hops (1 foot) with mature pattern						
Leaps with mature pattern						
Gallops with mature pattern						
Skips with mature pattern						
Slides with mature pattern						
Walks a straight line/heel-to-toe						
Stands on one foot for 5 seconds						
Catches an 8.5 inch ball with mature pattern						
Bounces and catches a playground ball to self						
Kicks a stationary ball with mature pattern						
Kicks a rolled ball with mature pattern						
Throws a ball with mature pattern						
Turns own jump rope using rhythmic form while jumping						
Cognitive Development:						
Can remember visual and/or auditory information						
Can understand cause and effect						
Exhibits appropriate on-task behavior						
Can follow directions						
Affective Development:						
Indicates a dislike for physical activity						
Prefers to play solo						
Has a low frustration tolerance, cries easily						
Tends to be impulsive						
Shows physical or verbal aggression toward others/self						
Has a short attention span						
Distracts others						
Respects authority, rules, and others						

continues

Figure 6.2 Adapted Physical Education Screening Form—Page 2.

Student _____

ADAPTED PHYSICAL EDUCATION SCREENING FORM – Page 2

Body Mechanics/Posture: (Check all that apply)	YES		SOMETIMES		NO	
	GE	APE	GE	APE	GE	APE
☐ Posture – head/trunk/feet misalignment						
☐ Muscular/Skeletal/Neurological impairment						
☐ Underweight/Overweight						
Mobility Skills (nonambulatory): **(Check all that the student demonstrates)**						
☐ Transfers in and out of wheelchair						
☐ Has acceptable range of motion						
☐ Can open doors						
☐ Can push up ramps						
☐ Can reverse direction						
☐ Can use brake						
☐ Can pivot in wheelchair						
☐ Can perform a wheelie						

Teachers' Comments _____

_____

_____

Thank you. Please return this completed form to Special Education Diagnostician in your school.

••

To be filled out by the Adapted Physical Educator

Date of Classroom Visit(s): _____   _____   _____   _____   _____

Recommendations:

☐ The student is functioning within acceptable limits in general physical education and does not need any further assessment at this time.

☐ The student is able to be included in general physical education class with appropriate support by the general physical educator and/or consultation services by the adapted physical educator.

☐ The student appears to be experiencing difficulty in the area(s) indicated above and will need further assessment by the adapted physical educator for appropriate placement with some type of special services.

☐ The student can benefit from activities provided by the classroom teacher.

_____   _____   _____
Signed   Date   Position

Form used by Denton Independent School District, Texas

F i g u r e 6.3   Student Medical Screening Form for Parent.

This form is used by the physical education teacher to gather medical data to ensure safe and successful participation in physical education.

Please indicate below any medical considerations that may impact your child's physical education participation. **All information will be kept confidential.**

Name of Pupil	Date of Birth	Grade	Classroom Teacher
Name of Parent/Guardian		Telephone Home Work	
Name of Emergency Contact		Telephone Home Work	

Please be specific.   **Diagnosis**

Condition	Permanent	Temporary	Estimated Duration
Neurological/Genetic Disorder (e.g., seizures, hyperactivity, coordination problems)			
Heart or Lung Condition (e.g., heart murmur, asthma)			
Orthopedic Condition (indicate area and extent of the condition, e.g., broken bones, spina bifida)			
Sensory Impairment (e.g., vision, hearing, tactile)			
Behavioral Considerations			
Medication (list all medications being taken and potential side effects; use reverse side if needed)			
Diabetes I or II Insulin? ☐ Yes ☐ No			

Does your child have a shunt?   ☐ Yes ☐ No

If Down syndrome, does your child have atlantoaxial instability?   ☐ Yes   ☐ No
If yes, please provide a copy of x-ray results.

Parent/Guardian Signature	Date

Please use the back of this page to indicate any conditions or concern not listed above.

Note. Adapted from the Texas Woman's University Issues Class (French, Fall 1995).

physical education services to the IEP committee. The results of this assessment are reported in a written document, which IDEA calls the **Full Individual Evaluation (FIE).** Because IDEA defines *physical education* as physical and motor fitness, motor skills and patterns, and skills (broadly interpreted as movement, knowledge, sportsmanship, and behaviors) in sports, dance, games, and aquatics, the comprehensive assessment must address *present level of performance* in these areas. The resulting data allow the IEP team to determine the discrepancy between the student's level of performance in physical education and that of peers with similar age, gender, and background.

The extent of the discrepancy helps the IEP team decide whether the student's disability adversely affects physical education performance and thus qualifies him or her for adapted physical education services. *Note that the trend is now determining eligibility for services, whereas previously the practice was to determine eligibility for placements.* **Programming** refers to the activity of the IEP committee in its multidisciplinary decision making about duration and type of adapted physical education services needed, by whom, where, and how. Additionally, programming includes determining measurable goals for the coming year, short-term objectives related to the goals, and other information required by law.

Most states set time lines concerning the length of time allowed for the eligibility and programming processes. For example, in Texas, once an official referral is made, the professional has only 60 days to complete the FIE. Once the FIE is completed, the IEP committee must meet within 30 calendar days to review the assessment data, write the IEP, and get signatures approving the IEP content from all parties involved (review Chapters 4 and 5 for further detail).

The eligibility and programming protocol associated with Section 504 are slightly different from those described for IDEA (Council of Administrators of Special Education [CASE], 1999). This is because the assessment data must show that the student has an impairment that substantially limits one or more major life activities and needs accommodations for physical education opportunities (including use of community resources) to be comparable to those of nondisabled peers (see Figure 6.1). Section 504 assessment procedures may be needed at any age, whereas the IEP procedures are used only from ages 3 through 21.

Day-to-Day Teaching Decisions

The third purpose of assessment is to inform day-to-day curriculum and instruction decisions and to assist with problem solving about individual adaptations to maximize safety and

---

Figure 6.4   Assessment of dynamic balance is a good way to start the year.

success. General physical educators screen and assess at the beginning of the school year as a means of getting acquainted with students' needs and interests so as to prepare unit and lesson plans that are appropriate for their classes (see Figure 6.4 on p. 149). Much of this assessment is informal, ecological, and fun oriented. Thereafter, teachers assess continuously, both informally and through the formal administration of tests and surveys. Whenever possible, teachers involve students in their own assessment and in record keeping (charts, graphs, journals) that allow them to keep track of their progress.

Assessment to enable good teaching is the same for general and adapted physical education, except that the latter field requires more training and experience in making adaptations. Thus, adapted physical educators are often assigned as consultants or partner teachers to help general physical educators.

Student Progress and Feedback Decisions

Grading procedures and type of feedback to parents and students vary by school district. Professionals agree that grading should relate directly to goals and objectives. This practice is easier to implement when all students of a particular age group have more or less the same physical education goals and objectives. The inclusion of students with disabilities in general education, however, means that goals and objectives are more individualized than ever before; therefore, tracking progress is much more time-consuming. Moreover, laws like *Goals 2000: Educate America Act of 1994* and the *No Child Left Behind Act of 2001* support the use of high standards for all and standardized testing to drive assessment practices.

The trend today, because of federal laws, is use of large-scale standardized assessments in such subjects as reading, language arts, mathematics, science, and social science. For more information on this trend, see the websites in Table 6.1. Large-scale assessment is intended to stimulate top-down alignment of curriculum, instruction, and assessment, thereby promoting achievement of state standards at each grade level, and permitting evaluation of a school's accountability in terms of achieving standards (Elliott et al., 2001). According to the National Center on Educational Outcomes (1999), states should include 98% of all students (including 85% of students with disabilities) in statewide assessments.

It is not known yet whether physical education will follow the trend of academic subjects. However, in this era of accountability, the need for physical education programs to demonstrate accountability is greater than ever. According to Rink and Mitchell (2002, p. 209), "One unintended outcome of the standards, assessment, and accountability movement is that any program not included in the high stakes state level assessment, for all practical purposes, does not count." Based on their experience in helping South Carolina establish a statewide physical education assessment program, Rink and Mitchell (2002) described a process for others to follow in initiating physical education reform. Louisiana has established an adapted physical education assessment system based on statewide standards.

Today's teachers of students with disabilities have many dilemmas. Which students with disabilities should be graded on the same tests and criteria as GE students and which students should be given alternate and alternative assessments and/or receive testing accommodations and modifications? Clearly, such questions must be answered individually for each student. IDEA requires that the IEP team assist in answering such questions and that reasons for modifications be recorded on the IEP.

Little research has been conducted on grading practices for students with disabilities in various LREs. Duchane and French (1998) reported that a comparison of the grading practices for secondary school students with and without disabilities in GE classes revealed significant differences, particularly in the use of written and skills tests. For both types of

Table 6.1   Websites for general and adapted physical educators.

Assessment reform	Information on your state standards	www.achieve.org
	Your state website	www.ccsso.org/seamenu.html
IDEA	Up-to-date information	www.ideapractices.org
Your own state	States' testing guidelines	www.ccsso.org
	States' testing accommodations and alternate assessment practices	www.coled.umn.edu/NCEO
PE Central Log IT	Program offers students, teachers, school, classes, and parents the opportunity to record their physical activity.	www.peclogit.org/logic.asp
PE Central: Adapted Physical Education	A site that provides adapted physical educators a workbook containing separate worksheets for more than 20 of the most commonly used adapted physical education assessment tools.	www.a-ape.com
Online Technology	A website and newsletter listserv that provides software, instructional material, consulting and professional development in the field of physical education.	www.pesoftware.com
PELINKS4U	A website that provides a variety of information with several links in which more information can be obtained on technology in physical education. This site is a nonprofit program from Washington University promoting active and healthy lifestyles.	www.pelinks4u.org

students, goals and objectives pertaining to fitness, movement, and cognitive understanding of movement played only a small part in grades. Criteria used most often were participation, dressing, and effort, a sad commentary on teachers' understanding of the basic principle that grades should be based on content-oriented goals and objectives.

Sport Classification Decisions

Sport classification is a system of ecological assessment designed to group persons with disabilities with others of similar functional capacity so as to facilitate fairness in determining who should compete against a specific other in physical education, recreation, and disability sport settings. How this system works (specifically how it applies to wheelchair basketball and goal ball) has already been discussed in several chapters. Sherrill believes that this system is more appropriate than any other when teaching sports to students with orthopedic impairments, cerebral palsy, traumatic brain injuries, strokes, les autres conditions, amputations, and blindness. Therefore, sport classification is emphasized in the chapters on disabilities in Part III.

In disability sport competitions, classification must be done by certified classifiers; however, in schools, most adapted physical educators can estimate which set of criteria (i.e., profile) best describes a student whom they are observing performing basic sport skills. The classification system advocated by the National Disability Sports Alliance (NDSA, 2002) is most useful in that it provides eight classifications, encompassing the range of students who use motorized chairs (Class 1) through ambulatory students with minimal coordination problems and good balance (Class 8). In conjunction with each classification, NDSA recommends sports that best match that profile of ability. Adapted physical educators can use these curricular recommendations to create ecological, criterion-based assessment for classification. Following are illustrative NDSA classifications:

Class 1. Severe involvement in all four limbs. Limited head and trunk control. Unable to grasp a softball. Poor functional strength in upper extremities, often necessitating the use of a motorized wheelchair for independent mobility.

Class 2. Severe to moderate involvement in all four limbs, but able to handle a manual chair (either by propelling with legs or arms). If arms, the movement is very slow. Poor functional strength and severe control problems in upper extremities.

Class 5. Involvement of lower limbs but able to perform locomotor movements upright with or without assistive devices. This is the only class that may ambulate with crutches, canes, or walkers. Good functional strength and minimal control problems in upper extremities.

Class 7. Moderate to minimal involvement of one side (hemiplegic). Good functional ability in nonaffected side. Walks/runs with noted limp.

Note that sport classification is an example of criterion-referenced assessment. Each profile contains specific criteria that must be met. In time, it is likely that each of these classifications will be expanded to include specific sport tasks a student can be expected to achieve. Some classifications (like those just stated) are general, but many are sport-specific (i.e., swimming, track, field). Adapted physical educators can apply to take classification training and to qualify as a certified classifier by contacting NDSA or other national disability sport associations.

Norm-, Criterion-, and Content-Referenced Tests

Traditionally, tests administered in formal settings have been classified as norm-referenced, criterion-referenced, and content-referenced instruments. When assessment is conducted as part of the IEP process, the protocol must be formal and adhere to legislative requirements. Written parental permission must be obtained. Legal specifications include these: (a) the tests must be validated for the specific purpose for which they are used, (b) the test administrator must be able to document training and skill in the protocol used, and (c) the tests must be administered in the student's native language or in sign if this is the preferred modality. *No one procedure can be used as the sole criterion* for IEP decisions, and decision making must reflect the consensus of a multidisciplinary team, the parents, and, when possible, the student. Chapter 4 provides direct quotes from the law in relation to these requirements.

Formal assessment for IEP purposes requires that test directions be followed precisely. This means that students may fail some items. The teacher must develop skill in helping students to handle such failures and to remain optimally motivated. When testing is for purposes other than IEP decision making, the humanistic teacher adapts the items and the environment to ensure success.

Norm-Referenced Tests

A **norm,** an abbreviated form of the word *normal,* is a statistic that describes group performance and enables comparisons. **Norm-referenced** means that an instrument has been administered to several hundred persons and that statistics are available on the performance of chronological age groups and perhaps genders.

There are many kinds of norms, such as (a) percentiles, (b) standard scores, and (c) age equivalents. Among the best examples of percentiles and standard scores is Table 6.2, adapted from Ulrich's (2000) manual for the Test of Gross Motor Development-2 (TGMD-2). The range of scores on the locomotor subtest is 1 to 48. Percentiles extend from 0 to 100. A score at the 50th percentile means that 50% of those who have taken the test scored higher and 50% scored lower than that score. Any student who consistently scores below the 50th percentile should receive special help. But when is performance low enough to warrant placement in a separate setting? *Some states set the standard at the 30th percentile; others suggest the 15th percentile.* Performance at the 15th percentile means that 85% of the individual's chronological peers score above him or her. Tables of percentile can be found in most test manuals and in assessment textbooks.

Table 6.2 Illustrative percentile ranks, raw scores, and standard scores for the Locomotor Subtest of the Test of Gross Motor Development-2 (TGMD-2) for males, ages 6 through 10.

Percentiles	Ages with Raw Scores						Standard Scores
	6–0 through 6–5	6–6 through 6–11	7–0 through 7–5	7–6 through 7–11	8–0 through 8–11	9–0 through 10–11	
<1	1–12	1–14	1–16	1–19	1–20	1–23	1
<1	13–15	15–17	17–19	20–22	21–23	24–26	2
1	16–18	18–20	20–22	23–25	24–27	27–29	3
2	19–21	21–23	23–25	26–28	28–30	30–32	4
5	22–24	24–26	26–28	29–31	31–33	33–35	5
9	25–28	27–29	29–31	32–34	34–36	36–37	6
16	29–31	30–32	32–34	35–37	37–38	38–39	7
25	32–34	33–35	35–37	38–39	39–40	40–41	8
37	35–37	36–39	38–40	40	41–42	42–43	9
50	38–39	40–41	41–42	41–42	43	44	10
63	40–41	42	43	43	44	45	11
75	42	43	44	44	45	46	12
84	43	44	45	45–47	46–48	47–48	13
91	44	45	46–47	48	•	•	14
95	45	46–47	48	•	•	•	15
98	46–47	48	•	•	•	•	16
99	48	•	•	•	•	•	17
>99	•	•	•	•	•	•	18
>99	•	•	•	•	•	•	19
>99	•	•	•	•	•	•	20

Printed with permission of D. Ulrich (2000) an PRO-ED.

Norm-referenced tests can be classified according to the population on which they are based: (a) GE students or (b) students with disabilities. For IEP decisions, GE norms should be used, even though the student may be mentally retarded, blind, or physically disabled. When a student is placed in a GE class, the assumption is that she or he is not disabled in that particular school subject, regardless of medical condition. This means that performance should be equivalent to that of GE class members.

Ideally, local school districts develop their own tables of percentiles. Any test that yields numerical data can become a norm-referenced instrument if administered to enough persons. A rule of thumb when developing norms is that there must be at least 50 males and 50 females for every age or grade group represented. Once norms are developed and related statistics are computed, a test is considered *standardized*.

Criterion-Referenced Tests

Criterion-referenced tests are designed to measure mastery learning and/or assess achievement of developmental milestones, mature movement patterns, and minimal fitness levels. Usually, the format is a checklist, task analysis, or set of behavioral objectives. Data yielded are pass/fail rather than numbers.

Illustrative of a criterion-referenced approach is the FITNESSGRAM (Cooper Institute for Aerobics Research, 1999b) (see Table 6.3). In this test, one mastery standard is set in each fitness domain for every age group. The mastery standard is presented as a range of scores (low to high) that indicates the healthy fitness zone. These standards are, of course, subject to change.

Ulrich's (2000) TGMD-2 is illustrative of tests in which the standard is well accepted. For example, there is general agreement that four performance criteria must be met for a run to be judged mature. Ulrich incorporated these into his TGMD-2 (see Table 6.4). Other criteria could be added to these, like "Eyes focused straight ahead (not on feet)," but research shows that most observers can assess only three or four things at one time. The key in this kind of criterion-referenced test is to identify the most important criteria. Ulrich's (2000) TGMD-2 includes excellent criteria for six locomotor skills and six object control skills (see Chapter 12).

Criterion-referenced instruments related to motor skills typically emphasize process rather than product. They enable teachers to analyze the components of a skill and write objectives that focus on weakness or immaturity of arm, leg, trunk, or head action. Activities can then be directed toward a particular criterion (e.g., "Demonstrate improving running form by bending elbows" or "Pass Criterion #2 on the run").

Table 6.3 Illustrative criterion-referenced standards: The Prudential FITNESSGRAM standards for lower (L) and upper (U) ends of the healthy fitness zone.

Boys

Age	One Mile (min:sec)		Body Mass Index		Curl-up (# completed)		Push-up (# completed)		Modified Pull-up (# completed)		Pull-up (# completed)		Flexed Arm Hang (seconds)	
			L	U	L	U	L	U	L	U	L	U	L	U
5	Completion of		20	14.7	2	10	3	8	2	7	1	2	2	8
6	distance. Time		20	14.7	2	10	3	8	2	7	1	2	2	8
7	standards not		20	14.9	4	14	4	10	3	9	1	2	3	8
8	recommended.		20	15.1	6	20	5	13	4	11	1	2	3	10
9			20	15.2	9	24	6	15	5	11	1	2	4	10
10	11:30	9:00	21	15.3	12	24	7	20	5	15	1	2	4	10
11	11:00	8:30	21	15.8	15	28	8	20	6	17	1	3	6	13
12	10:30	8:00	22	16.0	18	36	10	20	7	20	1	3	10	15
13	10:00	7:30	23	16.6	21	40	12	25	8	22	1	4	12	17
14	9:30	7:00	24.5	17.5	24	45	14	30	9	25	2	5	15	20
15	9:00	7:00	25	18.1	24	47	16	35	10	27	3	7	15	20
16	8:30	7:00	26.5	18.5	24	47	18	35	12	30	5	8	15	20
17	8:30	7:00	27	18.8	24	47	18	35	14	30	5	8	15	20
17+	8:30	7:00	27.8	19.0	24	47	18	35	14	30	5	8	15	20

Girls

Age	One Mile (min:sec)		Body Mass Index		Curl-up (# completed)		Push-up (# completed)		Modified Pull-up (# completed)		Pull-up (# completed)		Flexed Arm Hang (seconds)	
			L	U	L	U	L	U	L	U	L	U	L	U
5	Completion of		21	16.2	2	10	3	8	2	7	1	2	2	8
6	distance. Time		21	16.2	2	10	3	8	2	7	1	2	2	8
7	standards not		22	16.2	4	14	4	10	3	9	1	2	3	8
8	recommended.		22	16.2	6	20	5	13	4	11	1	2	3	10
9			23	16.2	9	22	6	15	4	11	1	2	4	10
10	12:30	9:30	23.5	16.6	12	26	7	15	4	13	1	2	4	10
11	12:00	9:00	24	16.9	15	29	7	15	4	13	1	2	6	12
12	12:00	9:00	24.5	16.9	18	32	7	15	4	13	1	2	7	12
13	11:30	9:00	24.5	17.5	18	32	7	15	4	13	1	2	8	12
14	11:00	8:30	25	17.5	18	32	7	15	4	13	1	2	8	12
15	10:30	8:00	25	17.5	18	35	7	15	4	13	1	2	8	12
16	10:00	8:00	25	17.5	18	35	7	15	4	13	1	2	8	12
17	10:00	8:00	26	17.5	18	35	7	15	4	13	1	2	8	12
17+	10:00	8:00	27.3	18.0	18	35	7	15	4	13	1	2	8	12

© The Cooper Institute for Aerobics Research, Dallas, Texas.

Note. The trunk lift standards are the same for boys and girls: L = 6 inches, U = 12 inches. The backsaver sit-and-reach for boys is 8 inches at all ages; for girls, varies from 9 to 12 inches.

Criteria can also be written in task analysis format. Systems like I CAN (Wessel, 1976), the Data-Based Gymnasium (Dunn et al., 1986), and the Brigance Diagnostic Inventory (Brigance, 1999) all use lists of progressively more difficult tasks like that shown in Table 6.5. Such lists are particularly helpful in teaching students with severe disabilities. Instructional objectives can be worded like this: "Pass four of six items on the ball-rolling task analysis." If the test includes information on the age at which a student should be able to perform each task or item, the instrument is considered standardized.

Content-Referenced Tests

Content-referenced tests are teacher-made tests that are designed to measure what is being taught. Such tests permit the teacher to assess where a student falls in relation to the continuum of possible scores or behaviors. A content-referenced test becomes criterion-referenced when the teacher designates the scores required to pass or to earn particular letter grades. Content-referenced tests are typically used in **curriculum-embedded instruction.** This is the process of concurrently teaching and testing (i.e., data are continuously collected as an integral part of instruction).

Formal Assessment Instruments Most Commonly Used

Instruments most commonly used for IEP purposes in adapted physical education appear in Table 6.6. Most of the tests used to determine what kind of adapted physical education services are needed are norm- or criterion-referenced.

Table 6.4 **Criterion-referenced test for a run from the Test of Gross Motor Development-2 (TGMD-2).**

Performance Criteria	Trial 1	Trial 2	Score
1. Arms move in opposition to legs, elbows bent	0	1	
2. Brief period where both feet are off the ground	1	1	
3. Narrow foot placement landing on heel to toe (i.e., not flat-footed)	1	1	
4. Nonsupport leg bent approximately 90° (i.e., close to buttocks)	0	0	
		Skill Score	

Note. Under "Trials," 1 denotes pass, 0 denotes fail.

Table 6.5 **Task-analysis test for rolling a ball.**

Task	Standard or Criterion
1. Sit and roll or push a ball	Ball travels 1 ft
2. Sit or stand and roll or push a ball	Ball travels 2 ft
3. Same	Ball travels 5 ft
4. Same except direct the ball toward a specific target 10 ft away	Ball travels 8 ft in direction of target
5. Same	Ball travels 10 ft and touches target
6. Same	Same except ball touches designated area on target

Note. When possible, have child choose the size and color of the ball.

Ecological Assessment

An **ecological approach** *is a way of addressing person-environment-activity (or task) interactions.* In assessment, this means three things: (a) surveying the environment (physical, psychosocial, temporal) for barriers and enablers to task/activity achievement; (b) analyzing the task/activity for degree of difficulty, including rate, sequence, quality, frequency, and duration; and (c) assessing the individual's goodness of fit and success in the environment for learning and the task/activity being learned (Nihira et al., 1994; Overton, 2003; Sax & Thoma, 2002). These processes are similar to those described in Chapter 4 as adaptation, when a content-embedded curriculum with teaching and testing interwoven is being implemented. Overton (2003, p. 14) presents a shorter definition: "method of assessing a student's total environment to determine what factors are contributing to learning or behavioral problems."

Following are the components comprising the framework for an **ecological assessment** of Sax and Thoma (2002, p. 112), adapted for use by physical educators:

1. Target the environment where learning a sport will best occur (school or community facilities, home, neighborhood). Identify environmental conditions (e.g., lighting, layout, accessibility, number of persons sharing space, proximity, noise, dress code, classroom climate).

2. Determine the subenvironments (e.g., transportation system, locker room, gym or bowling alley) where students will be required to perform skills.

3. Identify the activities students will be required to perform (e.g., taking bus, finding bowling alley, greeting and interacting with people, rolling balls, keeping score).

4. List the skills associated with each activity (i.e., do task analysis of each activity).

5. Record student performance in skills and social interactions.

6. Analyze discrepancies between student performance and expected outcomes (as established by goals and objectives).

7. Determine environmental and instructional changes to improve student performance.

Ecological assessment mainly uses surveys (yes, no; 4- or 5-point scales) to collect data directly or indirectly. Everyone in the environment may be asked to answer questions in order to obtain multiple perspectives. Briefly, an **ecological survey** is a checklist or rating-type instrument designed to assess the person-environment-activity match in various settings. An example of an ecological survey appears near the end of this Chapter (see Figure 6.17).

Assessment in Natural Environments

Ecological assessments typically use **natural environments**. The best natural environments for observation of adolescents and adults are the facilities in the home, school, and community settings where they generally engage in physical activity.

For children and youth, a room or outdoor area full of apparatus and play equipment makes an excellent initial assessment environment (see Figure 6.5). There should be ladders and ropes to climb, ramps or slides for moving up and down, bars to hang and swing from, balance beams and interesting surfaces to navigate, tunnels, and a variety of movement challenges like swinging bridges, structures that rock, and walls made of tires or heavy cargo nets. The apparatus should provide access for wheelchairs and be appropriate for all kinds of individual differences.

This kind of setting allows observation of whether or not persons know how to play, like to play, or have the language and motor skills to play. Most persons, given this environment, will demonstrate the full repertoire of their locomotor movement patterns. They will run, jump, leap, hop, climb, swing, roll, slide, and the like. Moreover, you can observe the personal meaning of each movement pattern, determine which movements are favorites and why, and develop a list of movement strengths and weaknesses. To assess object play (including the use of balls, striking implements, targets, and hoops), place additional equipment around the room.

To assess social interactions, introduce two persons to a play or sport environment, then three, then four, and so on.

Table 6.6 Assessment tests most frequently used in 2002, 1993, and 1985 in adapted physical education in the United States.

Year	Measure	Type of Measure
2002	1. Test of Gross Motor Development-2 (Ulrich, 2000)	Norm- and criterion-referenced
	2. Bruininks-Oseretsky Test of Motor Proficiency Short Form (Bruininks, 1978)	Norm-referenced
	3. Adapted Physical Education Assessment Scale (Los Angeles, CA 1989)	Norm-referenced
	4. Brigance Diagnostic Inventory of Early Development (Brigance, 1999)	Norm-referenced
	5 Brockport Physical Fitness Test (Winnick & Short, 1999)	Criterion-referenced
1993	1. Test of Gross Motor Development (Ulrich, 1985)	Norm- and criterion-referenced
	2. Bruininks-Oseretsky Test of Motor Proficiency (Bruininks, 1978)	Norm-referenced
	3. Peabody Developmental Motor Scales (Folio & Fewell, 1983)	Norm-referenced
	4. Motor Skills Inventory (Werder & Bruininks, 1988)	Criterion-referenced
	5. Assessment, Evaluation and Programming System (Bricker, 1993)	Criterion-referenced
1985	1. Bruininks-Oseretsky Test of Motor Proficiency (Bruininks, 1978)	Norm-referenced
	2. Brigance Diagnostic Inventory for Early Development (Brigance, 1978)	Norm-referenced
	3. Hughes Basic Gross Motor Assessment (Hughes, 1979)	Norm-referenced
	4. Purdue Perceptual Motor Survey (Roach & Kephart, 1966)	Norm-referenced
	5. I CAN Curriculum Assessment (Wessel, 1976)	Criterion-referenced

Note. Most frequently used assessments in adapted physical education were reported by Ulrich in 1985 and 1993 (Sherrill, 1998) and by Turney, French, Pyfer, & Kinnison in 2002.

Observe who initiates interactions, listen to what they say to each other, and note the kind of partner and small-group activities that evolve. Take notes, preferably on a Palm Pilot.

When possible, videotape observations. Videotapes provide study aids for beginning teachers and are especially helpful in university classes to focus attention on real persons and environments instead of imagined ones. Videotapes also provide permanent records of locomotor, object control, and social abilities. As such, they can be used to justify IEP recommendations and guide programming.

Assessment of Play and Game Concepts

Children with developmental delays often lag behind GE peers in cognitive development, understanding of game and sport rules (moral development), and social maturation. It is often these developmental delays rather than skill limitations that are barriers to their full inclusion in mainstream physical education. Because this text favors functional assessment (top down, starting at the chronological age of a student and teaching competencies appropriate to that age), it is helpful to understand expectancies for each chronological age level. Piaget's cognitive-developmental theory (1920s through 1980s) remains the best known and most accepted source in this regard (Crain, 1992). Piaget stated that four stages marked the development of cognition. Following is a review of these stages, adapted to teaching play and game concepts, including cooperation and competition.

Sensorimotor Performance (Ages 0 to 2)

Sensorimotor mental operations are the brain's translation of sensory input (e.g., visual, auditory, tactile) into initial meanings that form the basis of later cognitive, affective, and

Figure 6.5 Play apparatus can be used to assess many different kinds of abilities. Here, Dr. Ellen Lubin Curtis-Pierce, an authority in early childhood adapted physical activity, uses the London trestle tree apparatus test environment.

psychomotor function. The input can come from self or others. Infants first act on their environment during these years and begin to acquire **inner language** (meanings that relate to experience rather than words).

In typical development, primitive reflexes are integrated at about 4 months, so that voluntary, purposive movement can occur. Once this barrier is crossed, only about 4 months are required for independent sitting, rolling, crawling, and creeping patterns to emerge. Each additional pattern brings new sensory information for the brain to process and assign meaning.

The first 2 years of life are thus primarily a time of sensorimotor integration, the development of beginning locomotor and object control patterns, and the emergence of thought and social play behaviors. The ability to imitate is acquired during these years, and children learn appropriate responses to yes/no and short commands like "Come here," "Sit down," and "Throw me the ball."

Preoperational Performance (Ages 2 to 7)

Preoperational mental operations involve thought that is tied to perception rather than logic and is limited by language, memory, and attention capabilities. The years from age 2 to 7 are clustered together because they are the time when children first acquire receptive and expressive language. **Receptive language** refers to the understanding of specific words and signs. **Expressive language** refers to talking or using signs.

At age 2 children can use about 300 words, and at age 7 they can use several thousand. Play tends to be parallel until children have sufficient language and mobility skills to interact with each other. **Parallel play** means that children establish play

space near each other, do similar activities, and sometimes even imitate each other but do not directly interact without help.

In many disabilities, delayed or different language development affects progression up the social play channel. **Associative play** is the term given to early interactive activities in which children talk to each other as they explore the environment (locomotor, playground apparatus, wheeled toys) or engage in "make-believe" (doll play, cowboys and Indians, monsters, gangsters). Nonambulatory children, even if they have language, typically cannot initiate associations with others until they are fitted with wheelchairs. Thus, passivity and external locus of control (LOC) are reinforced by life events for these children, while their able-bodied peers are beginning the transition from external to internal LOC and self-determination.

Cooperative play is the term for participation in simple, low-organized games that have only one or two rules, like ring-around-the-rosy, follow-the-leader, and "Run to a pretend home when given a cue indicating make-believe danger like 'The wolf is coming.'" Cooperative play is associated with kindergarten, or age 5, although it is often taught earlier to children attending nursery schools. Cooperation assumes that the mental operations of attending to short game directions, sharing a group activity, and taking turns being "it" are developing. These operations must be carefully taught, because children are naturally **egocentric,** or I-centered, until concrete mental operations emerge at age 7 or 8.

Preoperational performance is essentially perceptual or perceptual-motor, in that, for children at this developmental level, early thought processes center on similarities and differences (i.e., matching, classifying) and ways to please adults or the powerful others in their lives. Rules and concepts are synonymous in early play. Imitation games are matching activities that demand perception of similarity or difference in relation to a leader's movements. Stop-and-start games like musical chairs demand perception of same/opposite or reversal concepts. Retrieval games (fetch the ball; bring me all the blue objects) require here/there concepts. As children begin to acquire an understanding of these and other rules, their need to please adults is so great that they adhere rigidly to rules and tattle on peers who seem to deviate. Prior to age 7 (concrete mental operations), failure to follow a rule usually means that the child lacks the cognition or memory to grasp or apply the rule.

Attention and memory capabilities are limited to two or three chunks until about age 7. Assessment should ascertain the length of sentences and the number of sentences in instructional sequences that an individual can process. Before about age 7, most children learn movement skills primarily by trial and error (kinesthetic input) and visual input. Thereafter, auditory input becomes increasingly useful to most individuals.

Preferred sensory modalities for input and the number of modalities that can be accommodated should be assessed also. Obviously, blindness, deafness, and mobility impairments change the ways in which individuals attend to, comprehend, and remember instructions. Such psychomotor problems also affect self-determination in terms of spontaneous exploration of the social and physical environment. The extent to which children act on the environment without adult or peer prompting should be assessed.

Concrete mental operations are thought processes that involve problem solving, cause-effect linkages, and generalizing to identical situations and things of a tangible nature. Concrete things can be seen, heard, touched, smelled, or tasted. With regard to social play or game skills, this means that children begin to assimilate role reversal and cause-effect rules like "I flee until I am tagged; then I am *it* and I chase"; "I am *in* the center of the circle dodging until the ball hits me; then I am *out* and throw the ball at others"; and "I am at bat until I hit the ball; then I must run to the base on my right."

Careful assessment of each of these game concepts is essential to goal setting and teaching the whole person. These concrete mental operations are closely associated with social competence and inclusion by peers. The horizontal line between ages 7 and 8 in the model is the barrier that must be crossed before persons are mentally, socially, and emotionally ready to function as team members in both cooperative games and competitive sport activities. This is also approximately when children change from being *egocentric* (I-centered) to *empathetic* (able to understand the view or role of another) and when they begin to make social comparisons ("Am I as good as others, better, or worse?"). (See Figure 6.6.) Most persons with moderate mental retardation (IQs of about 35 to 55) never cross this barrier. Persons with mild mental retardation, in contrast, are usually able to participate successfully in team competition but at older ages than most peers.

Moral development is interwoven with cognitive and social development. From age 7 on, children increasingly identify with their peers and begin to test their authority against that of adults by exploring the limits of rules. Cause-effect mental operations enable children to consider relationships like these: "If I break this rule, the adult might punish me, or my peers might get angry with me"; "If I break this rule and no one notices, I or my team might benefit." The ability to perform cause-effect thinking in relation to game rules and strategies should be assessed.

Moral development entails comprehension of standards like personal best, active living, and optimal wellness as well as rules. Standards like these are more abstract than game rules, and abstractions are not easily handled by most children until age 11. Nevertheless, because of the tremendous variability among children, conventional wisdom suggests an assessment of "what if" mental operations regarding personal best, winning and losing, succeeding and failing, and health and sickness. As children realize that rules are not absolute and that personal ability is not identical with effort, they begin to make conscious lifestyle choices that relate to physical education goals. Assessment should encompass examination of these choices and the reasons for these choices.

Assessment should also determine the number of choices or alternatives that the individual's cognitive ability permits: Can the individual intelligently make choices between two things, or three, or four? This is essential to teaching for self-determination and self-actualization.

Memory for sequences increases during the concrete operations years, from about 3 to 7, as does the ability to

Figure 6.6 Ideally, team competition should be introduced at about the third-grade level, when children are socially and cognitively mature enough to handle complex interactions with teammates and opponents.

attend to several things simultaneously and block out irrelevant information.

Seriation, usually called **sequencing** in physical education, is the ability to remember sequences, as in *I'm Going to Grandmother's House*. **I'm Going to Grandmother's House** (GH) is a game in which each child repeats in correct order what other children have said and then adds something new. For example, Child 1 says, "I'm going to Grandmother's house and I'm taking my toothbrush." Child 2 says, "I'm going to Grandmother's house and I'm taking my toothbrush and my dog." Child 3 says, "I'm going to Grandmother's house and I'm taking my toothbrush, my dog, and my pajamas."

The traditional GH game assesses only auditory memory for things. Physical educators often alter the memory assessment to focus on movement. For example, Child 1 takes three hops; Child 2 does three hops and one twirling umbrella step; and Child 3 does three hops, one twirling umbrella step, and five jumping jacks. This approach can be used with or without words, depending on what kinds of memory are to be assessed. Until children acquire the mental operation of sequencing, they cannot remember game rules and act appropriately, as in what to do in softball when a fly ball happens, a batter hits a foul ball, or runners are on first and third bases. Table 6.7 presents an illustrative game checklist for screening cognitive readiness for games. Readiness depends both on cognition (the number of concepts that can be handled at one time) and motor skill (speed, coordination).

Cognition is also affected at every age by body composition, height and weight, motor skills, and fitness. This is because cognition is primarily based on concrete perceptions, and

Table 6.7   Game checklist for screening cognitive readiness for games.

Sensorimotor
Peekaboo-type games
Imitating movements of another
Retrieving objects someone else throws
Coactive moving with another
Rolling a ball back and forth to adult

Preoperational (1 to 2 concepts)
Follow-the-leader
Find the hidden object or person
Musical chairs
Red light, green light; Mother, may I
Action song games
Run-on-cue games, everyone does same thing
T-ball, with no strategy, one rule[a]
Soccer, with no strategy, one rule[a]
Basketball, with no strategy, one rule[a]

Concrete Operations (3 to 7 concepts)
Tag
Relays
Role-reversal running games
Hide-and-seek
I'm Going to Grandmother's House, movement version
Simon Says
Dodgeball
Kickball
Keep the cageball up
Lead-up games to sports
Regulation sports

Formal Operations
Complex sport competition strategy
Creating or choreographing

[a]Many children aged 3 to 7 are wearing uniforms and are believed to be playing T-ball, soccer, basketball, and the like. Observation reveals, however, that typically only one or two rules are being enforced (e.g., get the ball and make a goal; get the ball and run; inbounds and out-of-bounds).

it is difficult to consider abstractions that have never been experienced. Thus, directions to grasp the ball in a certain way, rotate the trunk, or release the ball at a specific angle are perceived differently and produce learning styles that are different from what may be considered average or normal for a certain age. Children with disabilities often have shorter than average heights and limbs and thus experience the world in a different way. The same is true of individuals in wheelchairs, whose eye level is different from that of peers, and of people with coordination problems whose kinesthetic input may be different from that experienced by peers.

Table 6.8 presents an instrument to guide your observations of individuals who are chronologically or mentally at elementary school ages. This instrument is designed for use in natural settings.

Duplicate several copies of this instrument and use them to screen the present level of performance of individuals of different ages with and without disabilities. Find a partner who will assess the same individuals and plan a time to discuss the similarities and differences in your findings. Remember to look for strengths as well as weaknesses.

Formal Mental Operations (Ages 11 and Up)

Formal mental operations involve the use of inductive and deductive logic, the ability to critically and creatively think about abstractions, and skill in simultaneously processing many cause-effect and relationship ideas. Formal mental operations involve the understanding, application, and creation of formal thought structures like theories, models, and strategic game plans. Participation in most sports and games does not require

this level of cognition, but following the complex game strategy of coaches or engaging in group decision making about complex game strategy is a formal mental operation.

The best way to assess formal mental operations is by talking to persons about abstractions or by observing them talking to others. Abstractions often require problem solving about feelings and the variables that affect feelings, your own as well as those of others. Some paper-pencil instruments allow insight into formal mental operations.

Of particular importance to developing a lifespan active healthy lifestyle is **attributions analysis,** the ability to examine cause-effect relationships among ability, effort, fate, luck, and task difficulty in maintaining desired levels of fitness, wellness, and satisfying leisure. Specifically, **attribution** means a cause or a reason for why something happens. Children engage in simple attributions analysis of concrete behaviors and outcomes from about age 7 on, but serious attributions analysis about such abstractions as life, death, and health requires formal mental operations. Assessment of adolescents should focus on their understanding of relationships among inputs, processes, and outcomes. This is the key to setting goals that will promote understanding of the relationship between quality of life and health behaviors like exercising, not smoking, and practicing safe sex.

Sherrill Holistic Assessment Survey

Figure 6.7 presents an assessment form to examine the whole person in relation to physical education competencies (cognitive, moral, social, and motor). The figure is also excellent for reviewing the content presented on the preceding pages. Any form of data collection can be used to guide decision making, but Sherrill recommends observation of informal play as well as structured games and sports in a variety of natural settings.

Table 6.8   Observation form for recess or free play.

OBSERVATION FORM COMPLETED BY _____

1. Name of Person Observed _____
2. Gender _____   3. Chronological age _____
4. Dates of observation, setting, number of children present, available equipment, and other conditions. _____
   _____

5. Circle motor skills and patterns student used. Use + or − after circle to indicate skill level.

Log roll	Walk	Ascend stairs	Strike	Serve
Crawl	Run	Descend stairs	Bat	Catch
Creep	Jump down	Hang from bar	Bounce ball	Kick
Scoot	Jump over	Climb	Dribble, hands	Trap
Rise-to-stand	Leap	Dodge	Pivot	Dribble, feet
Stand-to-lie	Hop	Throw	Volley	Tag

   Others _____

6. In general, compared to peers of same age, how would you rank motor skills and patterns?

Superior	High	Average	Low	Inferior
Top 10%		Middle 50%		Bottom 10%

7. Which hand was preferred in throwing/striking? **R**   **L**   **No preference**
8. Which foot was preferred in kicking?   **R**   **L**   **No preference**
9. Which motor skills and patterns were used most? _____
10. What is major method of ambulation?

Independent	Braces, prostheses	Crutches, canes	Walker	Wheelchair

11. In general, compared to peers of same age, how would you rank activity level?

Hyperactive	High	Average	Low	Hypoactive

12. What problems, interactions, or other variables seemed to be contributing to high or low energy level?
    _____

13. Which stage best describes mental operations?

Sensorimotor	Preoperational	Concrete	Formal

14. What level best describes rules understanding and compliance?

No comprehension	Rigid adherence	Inconsistent	Flexible adherence

15. What best describes language and communication ability compared to peers?

Highly verbal	High average	Average	Low average	Nonverbal

16. What best describes social play level compared to peers?

Solitary	Parallel	Associative	Cooperative	Cooperative/Competitive

17. What best describes readiness level on cooperation-competition continuum?

Egocentric	Cooperation with 2–5 others	Personal best self-testing	Individual or dual competition	Team competition

18. Circle the ONE RUBRIC PHRASE that seems to best describe initiative, understanding of instructions, and mental flexibility.

Initiative	Understanding of instructions	Mental flexibility
A self-starter	Grasps instructions fast, accurately	Leads in generating new ideas
Has considerable initiative	Understands, asks good questions	Gets excited about new ideas
Average, same as most peers	Average, same as most peers	Prefers familiar, dislikes risks
Responds to prodding	Confused, but tries	Resists change, complains
Relies entirely on others	Confused and helpless	Appears unable to change

19. Who did the person interact with the most? One person or several? _____
20. In programming for this person, what three physical education goal areas (see #22) seem to be his or her major strengths? Why? _____
21. What three physical education goal areas (see #22) seem to be his or her major weaknesses? Why?
    _____

22. Rank this student's goal areas that need work from 1 (most important) to 9 (least important)

    _____ 1. Self-concept
    _____ 2. Social competence, inclusion
    _____ 3. Sensorimotor integration
    _____ 4. Perceptual-motor learning
    _____ 5. Motor skills and patterns
    _____ 6. Physical fitness and healthy active lifestyle
    _____ 7. Postures, appearance
    _____ 8. Fun, leisure, relaxation
    _____ 9. Dance, aquatics, and sports competence

Figure 6.7   Sherrill Holistic Assessment Survey.

Average Age	Piaget's Stages of Cognitive Development	Kohlberg's Levels of Moral Development	Levels of Social Play Development	Levels of Motor Development
Adult		Universal ethical principles		Increasingly advanced sport skills
16				
15				
14				
13				
12	Formal mental operations; abstract thought		Individualized leisure preferences	
11				
10		Flexible rule adherence, common sense	Team sports	
9	Attribution analysis Game strategies		Individual/dual sports, relays, and lead-up games	Beginning sport skills, especially ball skills
8	Concrete mental operations; cause-effect linkages; relationships	Sportsmanship		
7				
6			Low organized games and movement education	Skill combinations
5		Rules are regarded as sacred and absolute— rigid adherence	Cooperative play	Skip Strike Catch
4	Preoperational mental operations and perceptual-motor thought; language links	No comprehension of rules but responds to consequences	Associative or interactive play	Hop Throw
3				Jump Kick
2		Responds to "no"	Parallel play	Run
1				Walk
8 months			Peekaboo games	Creep Crawl Roll
6 months			Solitary play	Righting reactions Beginning limb control
4 months				Head, neck control Eye control
Birth	Sensorimotor mental operations	No compliance with verbal instructions	Eyes and mouth responsive to sensory input	Reflexes

Moral development, an often misunderstood term, refers to progressive understanding of rules and standards. Moral development is a part of cognitive development but is presented separately in the figure because of the importance of mastering sport and game rules and assimilating societal standards of sportsmanship, fitness, and wellness.

To use this model, make a copy of Figure 6.7 for each child. When you have completed your observations, circle the descriptor in each column that best represents the child's present level of performance. Be able to cite anecdotes that support your decisions.

Figure 6.7 shows that development is a vertical, bottom-up process. Each age (see the left-hand column of the figure) is associated with specific milestones, tasks, or functions that are societal expectations.

Developmental theory posits that the sequence of milestones/tasks is uniform but that the rate of development varies. For example, adults with severe mental retardation may function at a cognitive level of 2 to 3 years of age. Their progress is very slow and may even appear frozen.

To interpret what this means for programming, find ages 2 to 3 on the assessment and programming model in Figure 6.7 and read horizontally across. The figure shows that persons with a mental age or cognitive level of 2 to 3 years are primarily in the perceptual-motor stage of reasoning, unlikely to understand rules beyond "yes" and "no," seldom able to initiate and sustain meaningful play interactions, and likely to have a repertoire of locomotor motor skills that includes only roll, crawl, creep, walk, and run. There are, of course, many individual differences within this range of abilities and some exceptions. But assessment of function must be grounded in this developmental framework.

Some persons progress faster up some channels than others because of a combination of genetic and environmental factors. Few children in our society actualize their potential, partly because they do not have the internal motivation and partly because teachers and parents do not know how to help. Children with disabilities are more likely than their peers to have **uneven development across channels.** Therefore, assess each channel separately and identify strengths to build on.

The assessment survey in Figure 6.7 is based on the classic theories of Jean Piaget (1936, 1962), Lawrence Kohlberg (1984), and Mildred Parten (1932). Many physical educators have applied and updated these theories. Although parts of these theories have been challenged, the data about average ages at which individuals exhibit abilities remain valid.

Assessment of Responsivity

Another area important to observe is responsivity to stimuli. Four descriptors are used: (a) **hyper** (over, above, too much), (b) **average**, (c) **hypo** (under, too little), and (d) **fluctuating**, inconsistent, or labile. Persons who are hyperactive or hypoactive need special environmental adaptations, and teachers should ask questions about (a) energy levels and similar states of parents and siblings; (b) side effects of drugs, prescribed and nonprescribed; (c) presence of headache or illness; and (d) other variables (personal and environmental) that might affect responsivity.

Inattention, impulsivity, and hyperactivity are considered separate responsivity disorders. They often occur together but may appear independently of each other. Because these often contribute to learning disabilities, they are described in detail in Chapter 20. Age affects each of these, and assessment should determine the amount of time a person can concentrate and remain on task.

Planning Assessment

Each time assessment is planned, you should adhere to the following procedures:

1. Establish the specific purpose of the assessment.
2. Decide on the specific variables to be assessed.
3. Establish criteria for the selection of instruments or data collection protocols.
4. Review all available instruments and protocols that purport to assess the variables you selected.
5. Select the instruments or protocols to be used and state the rationale for selection (i.e., discuss how each meets every criterion).
6. Select the setting for the assessment.
7. Determine environmental factors to be considered and/or adapted.

Establishing Specific Purpose

Remember there are four purposes of assessment: (a) screening and referral, (b) diagnosis and placement, (c) instruction and student progress, and (d) sport classification. Select procedures that achieve your main purpose.

Relating Assessment to Goals and Variables

Assessment should relate to the goals of the school system and/or teacher. If self-concept is an important goal, then dimensions of this variable should be assessed. If social competence or play and game behaviors are expected outcomes of instruction, then these variables should be broken into assessable components. If motor skills and patterns are the goals, then locomotor and object control skills should be examined.

Using Criteria to Select Instruments

The universally accepted criteria are validity, reliability, and objectivity (Burton & Miller, 1998; Yun & Ulrich, 2002). Other criteria may be added, depending on special needs. All criteria are important, but federal law mentions only validity and states that instruments must be validated for the specific purpose for which they are used.

Validity comes from the Latin word for "strong." It means founded on truth or fact and capable of being justified, supported, or defended. In regard to a test, validity refers to the extent to which a test measures what it is supposed to measure. Think of the last exam you took. Did it measure what the teacher taught? If so, it was valid. Sometimes there is a discrepancy between what teacher and students think has been taught.

Broadly generalizing, there are three kinds of validity. **Content validity** is the extent to which test items match the information or skills that were taught. Often, a panel of experts is used to verify a test's content validity. **Criterion validity** is the extent to which an instrument derives the same score/rank as another instrument or protocol believed to assess the same thing. **Construct validity** is the extent to which statistics support three constructs: (a) the instrument discriminates between two groups known to be high and low in the attributes being measured; (b) the test items, when subjected to factor analysis, fall into logical clusters; and (c) the instrument is sensitive enough to show changes caused by instruction.

Reliability is also a statistical concept. There are two types: (a) stability and (b) internal consistency. Test-retest measures indicate stability of performance over several trials, also called **repeated measures reliability.** Alpha coefficients and other special formulae indicate internal consistency for a single administration. High internal consistency is evidenced when all items assessing a particular topic or skill elicit the same or consistent responses. The highest possible reliability coefficient is 1.00; thus, .80 or .90 is considered high.

Objectivity, sometimes called interrater reliability, refers to several scorers or raters each perceiving a performance in the same way and giving the student the same rating or grade. This is especially important in observational assessment.

Reviewing Available Instruments

Every physical education professional should maintain a file of instruments with information about purpose, age range, validity, reliability, and objectivity. Some textbooks include copies of instruments. Most, however, do not because of copyright laws. In such cases, you must write to commercial companies and pay a small charge for sample copies. See Appendix E for addresses.

The classic reference book for use in reviewing and evaluating instruments is the *Mental Measurements Yearbook,* edited by Buros (1938 to 1978 editions), and now in its 15th edition (Plake, Impara, & Spies, 2003). In spite of its title, the book includes reviews of many physical and motor measures and indicates where they can be ordered. It also includes a list of research studies related to each instrument. Zittel (1994), Cowden and Torrey (1995), and Burton and Miller (1998) provide excellent examples of ways to review instruments.

Selecting Instruments

Many instruments measure the same things. Therefore, you must be able to show that your selected tools have higher validity and/or reliability than other possible choices. Moreover, to satisfy federal legislation, written documentation must show that the instrument is valid.

Do not make up assessment instruments by pulling items from several different sources. Doing so changes validity and reliability. Teachers who wish to create a new instrument may do so by enrolling in graduate studies and making this their thesis or dissertation. Properly done, this task requires thousands of hours.

Determining the Setting

Once the purpose of assessment is clarified and instruments are selected, you must decide which setting will elicit the best performance.

1. Should data be gathered in an individual or a group setting?

2. If a group, how large? Does everyone take the instrument at the same time, or do some students watch or assist while others perform?

3. Should the setting be formal or informal? Should the students know they are being assessed?

Setting depends largely on the purpose of the assessment. Because testing in relation to placement is a legal process, it must be done in a formal context. Settings for other purposes should be individualized because students respond to assessment with different degrees of anxiety, frustration, and coping.

An informal setting, whenever possible, seems best. The Yellow Brick Road, a screening instrument to assess perceptual-motor strengths and weaknesses, illustrates a setting that maximizes abilities and minimizes anxiety (Kallstrom, 1975). The setting is based on the movie *The Wizard of Oz.* Four stations are established for doing tricks that Oz characters request. In full costume, the Cowardly Lion gives instructions at one station, the Scarecrow at another, the Tin Man at another, and Munchkins at another. A yellow brick road made of contact paper stepping-stones provides the structure for getting from one station to another. Periodically, music is played from the movie. Each child carries a ticket for admission to the stations on the way to finding the Wizard. Reinforcement is provided by punching the ticket when each task is performed. When the ticket shows four punches, the reward is admission to a play area that is supervised by the Wizard, who is also in costume.

This game-like setting can be varied in as many ways as themes exist. What a wonderful way to be tested! For older students, a carnival or field day often achieves the same purpose.

Determining Environmental Factors

Students cannot be assessed within a vacuum. How they perform is influenced by hundreds of factors: weather, room temperature, allergens, gender and mood of the test administrator, and presence or absence of spectators. Test administrators are likewise influenced by environmental factors, particularly when the assessment is primarily observational. In such cases, test administrators must place themselves where they can see best, where sun is not in their eyes, and where the angle of observation is most favorable.

In general physical education, the tradition has been to keep all environmental factors constant (i.e., all students use the same equipment and follow uniform procedures). For some students, this practice inevitably results in failure. IDEA now specifies that accommodations may be used during IEP-oriented assessment.

Instructional assessment, like learning, should be success oriented. The ecological approach requires that equipment should be altered in accordance with individual needs. In a test of striking, throwing, or catching ability, for instance, the characteristics of the striking implement and/or object are varied along a continuum from easy to difficult (see Figure 6.8). Motor performance over several days or weeks is recorded on a profile sheet that describes assessment conditions. The charts in Figures 6.8B and 6.8C are examples of profile sheets. The date recorded in each box in these profile sheets indicates when there was success in 7 of 10 trials, the criterion established in the instructional objectives and written on the physical education IEP.

Formal Test Administration Procedures

Both common sense and federal law dictate humanistic testing procedures. The following are required:

1. Professionals who administer instruments should be able to document that they have formal training and

Figure 6.8 Test condition variables and profile sheets. Dates in grids are dates of first satisfactory performance. (Adapted from G. S. D. Morris, *How to change the games children play* [Minneapolis: Burgess, 1976], pp. 62–67).

Striking implement	Trajectory of object being struck	Size of object being struck	Object direction in flight	Weight of object being struck	Color of object being struck	Anticipation location	Speed object is traveling
Hand ↓ Paddle ↓ Bat	Horizontal ↓ Vertical ↓ Arc	Large ↓ Small	Right ↓ Left ↓ Center	Light ↓ Heavy	Blue ↓ Yellow ↓ White	How far must the performer move before striking the object	Slow ↓ Fast

A. Test-condition variables that can be altered to attain success-oriented assessment.

Easy ————————→ Difficult

		Color		
	Size	C_1	C_2	C_3
Easy ↓	S_1	3/15		
	S_2		3/21	
	S_3		3/22	
Difficult	S_4		3/29	4/22

Key for object size

S_1 = Largest ball (18" diameter)
S_2 = Large ball (14" diameter)
S_3 = Small ball (12" diameter)
S_4 = Smallest ball (8" diameter)

Key for object color

C_1 = Blue
C_2 = Yellow
C_3 = White

B. Striking profile sheet for individual student.

Easy ————————→ Difficult

		Angle of trajectory		
	Texture	A_1	A_2	A_3
Easy ↓	T_1	3/15		
	T_2		3/21	
	T_3		3/22	
Difficult	T_4			4/22

Key for texture

T_1 = Balloon
T_2 = Nerf ball
T_3 = Rubber ball
T_4 = Softball

Key for angle of trajectory

A_1 = Horizontal plane
A_2 = Vertical plane
A_3 = Ball travels in arc

C. Catching profile sheet for individual student.

competence in the protocols used. This means that most adapted physical activity professionals must complete graduate courses in assessment and remain up-to-date by attending workshops on specific instruments.

2. A team approach should be used to determine underlying abilities that need to be assessed (e.g., vision, hearing, social and emotional status, motor and cognitive abilities, communication status) in order to problem-solve about findings on goal-related testing.

3. Tests should be administered in the student's native language and in the most appropriate communication mode (e.g., sign language, large-print written directions, words enunciated clearly against a quiet background). Professionals are responsible for finding, training, and supervising test administrators with language abilities that meet students' needs.

4. Multidisciplinary assessment teams should include parents or solicit input from parents on what children can and cannot do to ascertain that performance at school is consistent with performance at home and in other settings.

5. No single test should be used as the sole criterion for placement or for determining instructional needs. Several valid tests or protocols that purport to measure the same thing should be administered.

6. When the purpose of testing is IDEA or 504 eligibility for adapted physical education, parental written permission must be obtained, and due process procedures must be followed.

Additional considerations in test administration that are not required by law but are important in increasing the likelihood of personal best performance by students and the overall usefulness of the data include the following:

1. Assessment should be focused on **functional competence** (i.e., proficiency in life functions like locomotion, play, work, and self-care). Functional competence makes tests **ecologically valid** (meaningful) for a particular individual.

2. Assessment should cover motor skills, fitness, game and sport concepts, and social competence in several contexts:

Table 6.9   Test of gross motor development-2 (TGMD-2).

Purpose

To identify children ages 3 to 10 years who are significantly behind their peers in the execution of 12 gross motor skill patterns into 2 subtests (i.e., locomotor and object control).

Description

Two subtests are designed to assess different aspects of gross motor development: locomotion and object control. The examiner is required to judge the presence or absence of 3 or 4 motor behaviors in each of 12 gross motor skills: run, gallop, hop, leap, horizontal jump, skip, slide, two-hand strike, stationary bounce, catch, kick, and overhand throw. Each skill is illustrated in the test manual.

Validity

Content validity was established by having three content experts judge whether the specific gross motor skills selected represented skills that are frequently taught to young children. *Construct validity* was established by testing the hypothesis that gross motor development would improve significantly across age levels. It was also supported by testing the hypothesis that children with MR would score significantly lower than peers of similar age. The test was also validated for instructional sensitivity. The results indicate that the test is sensitive to formal instruction in gross motor development.

Reliability

Test-retest reliability coefficients for the 12 gross motor skills ranged from .84 to .96. Interscorer reliability estimates for the skills ranged from .79 to .98 for 10 raters. Reliability of mastery decisions was reported also for samples using the total test score.

Primary Sources

Ulrich, D. A. (1984). The reliability of classification decisions made with the objectives-based motor skill assessment instrument. *Adapted Physical Activity Quarterly, 1,* 52–60.

Ulrich D. A. (2000). *The Test of Gross Motor Development.* Austin, TX: PRO•ED.

Ulrich, D. A., & Ulrich, B. D. (1984). The objectives-based motor skill assessment instrument: Validation of instructional sensitivity. *Perceptual and Motor Skills, 59,* 175–179.

Ulrich, D. A., & Wise, S. L. (1984). The reliability of scores obtained with the objectives-based motor skill assessment instrument. *Adapted Physical Activity Quarterly, 1,* 230–239.

Address for Ordering

PRO•ED, 8700 Shoal Creek Blvd., Austin, TX 78757. Website: www.proedinc.com/store/9260.html

---

(a) informal play, (b) structured game or sport settings, and (c) formal drills or tests. Check for generalization to different environments and settings.

3. Tests should be administered frequently. Individuals with disabilities show more variability than nondisabled peers.

4. Test performance should be videotaped when possible. Show the videotape to parents, and discuss what different viewers see and why.

5. Records should be kept of information that will help with interpretation, such as whether test behavior was typical, whether compliance or attention span problems were present, and whether the child seemed fearful or anxious.

6. Cultural, gender, and other kinds of bias should be avoided in selecting, administering, and interpreting tests.

7. Before the day of the testing, the student should meet the outside experts brought in specifically to do the testing. Consider ways to promote rapport between the student and the outside experts.

8. Test anxiety should be minimized. Remember that different things cause anxiety in different people, and these things may vary day by day for the same person.

TGMD-2 and BOTMP Philosophies

This chapter has acquainted you with the Sherrill Holistic Assessment Survey, which is recommended for screening and planning instruction. This section introduces two instruments that are widely used for IEP decision making: (a) the Test of Gross Motor Development (TGMD-2) and (b) the Bruininks-

Oseretsky Test of Motor Proficiency (BOTMP). The TGMD-2 and BOTMP represent different philosophical approaches. The TGMD-2 assesses qualitative performance of 12 gross motor skills believed to be fundamental to sport and game success. In contrast, the BOTMP purports to measure underlying abilities that are predictive of motor skills performance and physical education success. These underlying abilities are grouped into eight areas (e.g., running speed and agility, balance, bilateral coordination), each of which is given a score. When selecting a test, be sure that it reflects your philosophy.

Test of Gross Motor Development (TGMD-2)

The TGMD-2, validated for ages 3 through 10, involves the administration of 12 test items (see Table 6.9). Criteria for assessing the quality of performance for each item appear in Chapter 11, so these will not be repeated here. Refer to Table 6.4, however, for a quick reminder of how the criteria are stated. Note that TGMD-2 does not require that times, distances, or accuracy measures be recorded; the emphasis is completely on determining whether the student exhibits mature form on the major components of each skill.

Locomotor Skills

The locomotor skills tested in the TGMD-2 are these:

1. Run 50 feet. (Instruct the student to "run fast" from one line to another.)

2. Gallop back and forth between two lines set 25 feet apart. (The student should go the 25-foot distance three times.)

Table 6.10   Bruininks-Oseretsky Test of Motor Proficiency (BOTMP).

Purpose

To assess motor performance of children from 4.6 to 14.6 years of age. Validated specifically for use in placement of students.

Description

Two forms are available: short and long.

Short Form

Norm-referenced, with 14 items assessing eight factors: (a) running speed and agility, (b) balance, (c) bilateral coordination, (d) strength, (e) upper-limb coordination, (f) response speed, (g) visual-motor control, and (h) upper-limb speed and dexterity.

Long Form of BOTMP

Same as short form, except with 46 items.

Scoring

Total test scores, subtest scores, and gross motor and fine motor composite scores can be derived. (See Figure 6.8.)

Validity

BOTMP is a revision of the well-known Lincoln-Oseretsky Test of Motor Proficiency. Content validity and construct validity are confirmed by similarity between factor analysis studies of BOTMP and works of many scholars.

Reliability

For short form: Test-retest rs ranging from .81 to .89 for 126 children. For long form: Test-retest rs ranging from .80 to .94. For the separate subtests, rs ranging from .15 to .89.

Primary Sources

Beitel, P. A., & Mead, B. (1980). Bruininks-Oseretsky test of motor proficiency: A viable measure for 3–5 year old children. *Perceptual and Motor Skills, 51,* 919–923.

Broadhead, G., & Bruininks, R. (1982). Childhood motor performance traits on the short form Bruininks-Oseretsky Test. *Physical Educator, 39,* 149–155.

Bruininks, R. H. (1978). *Bruininks-Oseretsky Test of Motor Proficiency Manual.* Circle Pines, MN: American Guidance Service.

Bruininks, V., & Bruininks, R. (1977). Motor proficiency of learning disabled and nondisabled students. *Perceptual and Motor Skills, 44,* 1131–1137.

Address for Ordering

American Guidance Service, 4201 Woodland Rd., Circle Pines, MN 55014
Website: www.agsnet.com

Bruininks-Oseretsky Test Items
(*Denotes items on short form)
Factor: Running Speed and Agility Subtests: 1 on both long and short forms
*30-yard shuttle run

Factor: Balance
Subtests: 8 on long form, 2 on short form
1. Standing on preferred leg on floor for 10 seconds
*2. Standing on preferred leg on balance beam for 10 seconds
3. Standing on preferred leg on balance beam—eyes closed—for 10 seconds
4. Walking forward on line on floor, 6 steps
5. Walking forward on balance beam, 6 steps
6. Walking forward heel-to-toe on line on floor, 6 steps
*7. Walking forward heel-to-toe on balance beam, 6 steps
8. Stepping over response speed stick on balance beam

Factor: Bilateral Coordination
Subtests: 8 on long form, 2 on short form
*1. Tapping feet alternately while making circles with fingers, 90 seconds
2. Tapping—foot and index finger on same side synchronized, 90 seconds
3. Tapping—foot and index finger on opposite side synchronized, 90 seconds maximum
4. Jumping in place—leg and arm on same side synchronized, 90 seconds
*5. Jumping in place—leg and arm on opposite sides synchronized, 90 seconds
*6. Jumping up and clapping hands
7. Jumping up and touching heels with hands
8. Drawing lines and crosses simultaneously, 15 seconds

Factor: Strength
Subtests: 3 on long form, 1 on short form
*1. Standing long jump
2. Sit-ups, 20 seconds
3. Knee push-ups, 20 seconds—for all girls and boys under age 8
4. Full push-ups—for boys age 8 and over

Factor: Upper-Limb Coordination
Subtests: 9 on long form, 2 on short form
1. Bouncing a tennis ball 5 times and catching it with both hands
2. Bouncing a tennis ball 5 times and catching it with preferred hand
*3. Catching a tennis ball 5 times with both hands tossed from 10 feet
4. Catching a tennis ball 5 times with preferred hand tossed from 10 feet
*5. Throwing a tennis ball overhand at an eye-height target 5 feet away (1 practice and 5 trials)
6. Touching a swinging ball with preferred hand, 5 trials
7. Touching nose with index fingers—eyes closed, 90 seconds
8. Touching thumb to index fingers—eyes closed, 90 seconds
9. Pivoting thumb and index finger, 90 seconds

Table 6.10 Continued.

Factor: Response Speed
Subtest: 1 on both long and short forms
Stopping a falling stick with preferred thumb. The teacher holds the response speed stick against the wall and then drops it.

Factor: Visual-Motor Control
Subtests: 8 on long form, 3 on short form
  1. Cutting out a circle with preferred hand
  2. Drawing a line through a crooked path with preferred hand
 *3. Drawing a line through a straight path with preferred hand
  4. Drawing a line through a curved path with preferred hand
 *5. Copying a circle with preferred hand

  6. Copying a triangle with preferred hand
  7. Copying a horizontal diamond with preferred hand
 *8. Copying overlapping pencils with preferred hand

Factor: Upper-Limb Speed and Dexterity
Subtests: 8 on long form, 2 on short form
  1. Placing pennies in a box with preferred hand, 15 seconds
  2. Placing pennies in two boxes with both hands
 *3. Sorting shape cards with preferred hand
  4. Stringing beads with preferred hand
  5. Displacing pegs with preferred hand
  6. Drawing vertical lines with preferred hand
 *7. Making dots in circles with preferred hand
  8. Making dots with preferred hand

---

  3. Hop three times, first on one foot and then on the other.
  4. Leap. (Instruct the student to run and leap over a beanbag from one foot to the other.)
  5. Horizontal jump. (Instruct the student to "jump far.")
  6. Slide back and forth between two lines set 25 feet apart, always facing the same direction.

Object Control Skills

The TGMD-2 tests the following object control skills:

1. Two-hand strike a stationary ball with a bat. (Place a 4-inch lightweight ball on a batting tee at waist level; tell the student, "Hit the ball hard.")
2. Stationary dribble of an 8- to 10-inch playground ball (for 3 to 5 yrs) and a basketball (for 6 to 10 yrs) with one hand. (Tell the student, "Bounce the ball 4 times with one hand.")
3. Catch with both hands a 4-inch plastic ball. (Toss the ball underhand from 15 feet away so that it arrives at a height between the student's shoulders and waist; tell the student, "Catch it with your hands.")
4. Kick a stationary 8- to 10-inch playground ball placed on a beanbag by running 10 feet to contact the ball and aiming it at a wall that is 20 feet from where ball rests. (Tell the student, "Kick the ball hard at the wall.")
5. Overhand throw of three tennis balls at a wall that is 25 feet away. (Tell the student, "Throw the ball hard at the wall.")
6. Underhand roll a tennis ball. (Tell the student to roll a tennis ball hard at two cones 4 feet apart.)

Discussion of the TGMD-2

A value of this test is the very clear and short directions given to the student. One practice trial should be followed by two test trials. Each performance criterion is scored as 0 (fail) or 1 (pass), generating a possible total score of 48. The test manual gives information about the average age at which most children pass each criterion. The criteria tell teachers exactly what to look for when analyzing skills and also provide guidance for writing lesson plans that specify work on a particular component of a motor skill. Videotaping performance of these items on a regular basis is ideal in that it creates a permanent record and permits both parents and student to see improvements that occur as a result of school instruction and homework practice of skills.

Bruininks-Oseretsky Test of Motor Proficiency

The Bruininks-Oseretsky Test of Motor Proficiency (BOTMP) is widely used as a placement instrument (see Table 6.10 on p. 165). This instrument purports to measure the specific abilities that underlie success in motor skills. **Motor proficiency** is not a synonym for motor performance; rather, it refers to the specific abilities on which performance is built. *The best definition of motor proficiency is the specific abilities measured by tests of running speed and agility, balance, bilateral coordination, strength, upper-limb coordination, response speed, visual-motor control, and upper-limb speed and dexterity.* This method of defining a constellation of abilities is called an operational definition and is frequently used in research.

A copy of the test manual is needed to administer the BOTMP. The item descriptions in the test manual give an operational definition of each factor—for example, bilateral coordination is what is measured by (a) jumps, (b) rhythmic tapping, and (c) index finger touching of body parts (i.e., a kinesthetic measure).

You need special training to score and convert BOTMP raw data to point scores and subsequently to standard scores. Figure 6.9 shows scoring for the long form. Norms are available for composite scores, but not for the individual factors. For the short form, norms are given in the test manual only for the total battery score. Broadhead and Bruininks (1982) have published means and standard deviations for short-form items.

The major decision with regard to the BOTMP is whether to use the long or short form. The long form requires about 1 hr to administer, whereas the short form takes about 20

Figure 6.9 Bruininks-Oseretsky Test of Motor Proficiency test score summary. (*A*) Example of how BOTMP raw scores are converted to point scores. (*B*) Example of conversion of a student's point scores to norms. (Reproduced with the permission of American Guidance Service, Inc. *Bruininks-Oseretsky Test of Motor Proficiency* by Robert N. Bruininks. Copyright 1978. All rights reserved).

SUBTEST 1: Running Speed and Agility Guide for Converting Raw Scores.

RECORD POINT SCORES FOR COMPLETE BATTERY ▼

RECORD POINT SCORES FOR SHORT FORM ▼

1. Running Speed and Agility SF*

TRIAL 1: 8.7 seconds   TRIAL 2: 7.5 seconds

Raw Score	Above 11.0	10.9-11.0	10.5-10.8	9.9-10.4	9.5-9.8	8.9-9.4	8.5-8.8	7.9-8.4	7.5-7.8	6.9-7.4	6.7-6.8	6.3-6.6	6.1-6.2	5.7-6.0	5.5-5.6	Below 5.5
Point Score	0	1	2	3	4	5	6	7	8	9	10	11	12	13	14	15

POINT SCORE: 8

POINT SCORE SUBTEST 1 (Max: 16)

A

SAMPLE OF TEST SCORE SUMMARY FOR CHILD AGE 5 YEARS, 9 MONTHS

SUBTEST	POINT SCORE Maximum	POINT SCORE Subject's	STANDARD SCORE Test (Table 23)	STANDARD SCORE Composite (Table 24)	PERCENTILE RANK (Table 25)	STANINE (Table 25)	OTHER Age (Equiv.)
GROSS MOTOR SUBTESTS:							
1. Running Speed and Agility	15	8	21				7-8
2. Balance	32	16	13				5-2
3. Bilateral Coordination	20	9	23				7-11
4. Strength	42	5	11				4-11
GROSS MOTOR COMPOSITE			*68 SUM	56	72	6	6-5
5. Upper-Limb Coordination	21	13	*21				6-11
FINE MOTOR SUBTESTS:							
6. Response Speed	17	5	16				6-2
7. Visual-Motor Control	24	18	23				8-5
8. Upper-Limb Speed and Dexterity	72	27	20				6-8
FINE MOTOR COMPOSITE			*59 SUM	64	92	8	6-8
BATTERY COMPOSITE			*148 SUM	63	90	8	6-9

*To obtain Battery Composite: Add Gross Motor Composite, Subtest 5 Standard Score, and Fine Motor Composite. Check result by adding Standard Scores on Subtests 1–8.

Short Form

	POINT SCORE Maximum	POINT SCORE Subject's	STANDARD SCORE (Table 27)	PERCENTILE RANK (Table 27)	STANINE (Table 27)
SHORT FORM	98				

B

Table 6.11   Competency Test for Adapted Physical Education (CTAPE).

Purpose

A content-referenced test with criteria to determine if students in Grades K through 2 meet minimum state standards for general physical education. Performance at 1.5 standard deviations below the mean meets eligibility status for assistance.

Description

Consists of six levels, each addressing the identified grade level minimum standards in competency-based curriculum for general physical education. **Level I and II,** for ages 6 through 8, test content pertaining to locomotor skills, manipulative skills, body/spatial awareness, and balance skills. **Level III,** for ages 9 through 10, test sport and fitness skills in addition to locomotor skills, manipulative skills, and body/spatial awareness. **Levels IV and V,** for ages 11 through 14, test locomotor skills, sport skills, gymnastics skills, and fitness skills. **Level VI,** for ages 15 and older, concentrates on sports skills, gymnastics skills, and fitness skills. Administered individually in small groups in approximately 20 to 30 minutes, ages 6 to 14 years, 11 monthly. Ten percent or below on the test level is considered significantly below average population, and special assistance should be considered.

Validity

Content validity, which is verified by numerous experts and supported by extensive use for placement; especially in Louisiana.

Reliability

No statistics reported, but experts agree CTAPE yields reliable data.

Reference

Adapted Physical Education Task Force, Louisiana Department of Education (2001)

Address for Ordering

Janice Frugé
Division of Special Populations
Louisiana Department of Education
P.O. Box 94064
Baton Rouge, LA 70804
Phone: (225) 342-3674
Email: jfrugé@doe.state.la.us
Website: http://www.doe.state.la.us/

---

min. In general, the short form is recommended as a screening instrument. The long form is used for IEP decision making because it is a better discriminator of students who need help (Verdeber & Payne, 1987).

Widely Used Tests Without Norms

Illustrative of other tests used by adapted physical educators are the Competency Test for Adapted Physical Education (CTAPE), the Brockport Physical Fitness Test (BPFT), and Project MOBILITEE. These tests are described in Tables 6.11 to 6.13. These tests are used for multiple purposes and do not require as much statistics background as TGMD-2 and BOTMP. For example, the Denton Independent School District selects these tests over many others that adapted physical educators use because they yield valid data. CTAPE is one of the few options that includes tests for secondary students. BPFT, which is associated with the widely used FITNESSGRAM (Cooper Institute for Aerobics Research, 1999a), uses standards to indicate healthy fitness zones in place of norms. BPFT seems to have replaced PROJECT UNIQUE, the earlier work by Winnick and Short (1985); Winnick does not mention UNIQUE in the 2000 edition of his textbook. MOBILITEE (Gossett, 1981), although

old, is the only test we know that offers good measures of present level of performance in aquatics, dance, and individual and group games specifically for persons with severe cognitive disabilities, including those in wheelchairs.

Other tests like the outstanding task analyses in the Sport Skills Program Guides (Special Olympics, International, 1995–1999), the ACTIVITYGRAM (Cooper Institute of Aerobics Research, 1999b), and the Milani-Comparetti Test (Meyer Rehabilitation Institute, 1992) that assess reflexes and developmental motor milestones are described in chapters in Part II of this text. Part II links assessment with instruction designed to meet specific goals.

Interpreting Data and Recommending Services

Once data are collected, time must be spent on interpretation and on writing the results. Some school systems employ adapted physical educators and other specialists full-time to collect and interpret data. There is widespread agreement that adapted physical educators should have statistics and computer competencies. Of particular importance in making recommendations for services is an understanding of normal curve theory.

Table 6.12   Brockport Physical Fitness Test (BPFT).

Purpose

A health-related, criterion-referenced physical fitness test appropriate for students ages 10 to 17 years with and without disabilities. Target disability populations are visual impairments, mental retardation, and orthopedic impairments.

Description

The test battery includes 27 different test items from which teachers may choose. Typically, students would be tested on between four and six test items from three components of fitness, body composition, aerobic functioning, and musculoskeletal functioning.

Validity

Concurrent, construct, and content validity data have been determined for each item. Information was based on data from 1,542 youngsters gathered in conjunction with Project Target, which was funded by the U.S. Department of Education. The FITNESSGRAM served as the prototype for the BPFT.

Reliability

Test-retest reliability was reported for individual items.

The reader is referred to the technical manual for detailed information on validity and reliability. Computer software is available also from Human Kinetics.

Reference

Winnick and Short (1999)

Also see Chapters 13 and 23 in Sherrill (2004)

Address for Ordering

Human Kinetics

P.O. Box 5076

Champaign, IL 61820

Phone: 800-747-4457

Website: www.humankinetics.com

Table 6.13   Movement Opportunities for Building Independence and Leisure Interests Through Training Educators and Exceptional Learners (MOBILITEE).

Purpose

A curriculum-referenced test for students with moderate and severe mental retardation in elementary and secondary school. Users of MOBILITEE claim that its items are appropriate also for other disabilities.

Description

This is an informal criterion-referenced test that includes **physical (health-related) fitness** component (muscular strength, muscular endurance, flexibility, and cardiorespiratory endurance); **motor fitness** component (speed, agility, power, balance, and coordination); **fundamental motor skills** component (throwing, catching, running, striking, jumping, hopping, and kicking); and **individual and group games** component. There is also a component related to behavior assessment in the areas of teamwork, leadership, and self-concept. Students in wheelchairs may be given parts of the fundamental motor skills assessment items.

Validity and Reliability

No statistics reported on validity or reliability indicators. However, hundreds of school districts use MOBILITEE, and experts claim that it yields valid data.

Reference

Gossett (1981)

Address for Ordering

Hopewell Special Education Regional Resource Center

Attn: Diane West

5350 West New Market

Hillsboro, OH 45133

Phone: 937-393-1904

Diane.West@mail.scoca.K-12.org

Website: www.hopewellserrc.org

Figure 6.10 This normal curve is the theoretical model that guides test interpretation and educational placement. The percentages inside the curve have been rounded off to facilitate memory. In reality, the 3% is 2.27%, the 13% is 13.59%, and the 34% is 34.13%. In reality, the shapes of the curves for the IQ and sit-up data also would be different. (SD = Standard deviation.)

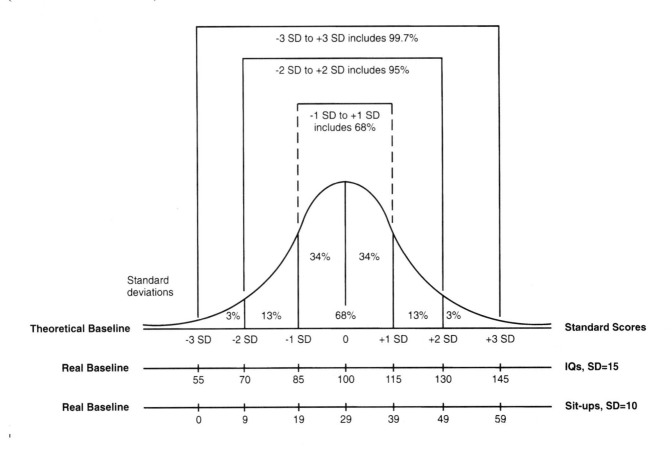

Normal Curve Theory

The **normal curve** is a theoretical model derived by mathematicians that shows statistically how persons will place when tested. The model is based on the laws of chance and shows that scores, when graphed, depict a bell-shaped distribution (see Figure 6.10). This phenomenon occurs because, when large groups are tested, most persons (roughly 68%) score in the middle of the distribution. On Figure 6.10, the markers −1 SD to +1 SD indicate the middle 68% of the distribution, −2 SD to +2 SD indicate the middle 95% of the distribution, and −3 SD to +3 SD indicate the middle 99.7%. It can be seen that 68% of the population have IQs between 85 and 115 and can do between 19 and 39 sit-ups. These persons are considered statistically normal or average.

The laws of chance dictate that an equal number of persons score in the areas above and below the center point designated as 0 on the baseline of the normal curve model. Adapted physical educators are mainly concerned with people who score on the left-hand side of the curve.

Originally, normal curve theory was applied mainly to interpretation of intelligence tests because school placement was made solely on the basis of mental functioning. Persons scoring in the middle 68% of the distribution were placed in regular education. Those scoring in the upper 16% were assigned to advanced or faster-paced classes, whereas those scor-

ing in the lower 16% were assigned to special education. Today, placement is typically based on achievement tests, but the concept is the same. The laws of chance and the resulting normal distribution of data can be applied to many human attributes. Thus, everyone involved in assessment and placement must understand normal curve theory.

Some states, for instance, have set **placement criteria** for assignment to adapted physical education. These are illustrative of such criteria:

1. Score 1 standard deviation below the mean
2. Score 1.5 standard deviations below the mean
3. Score below the 30th percentile

What does all of this mean? Do you agree with these standards? In states where no universal placement criteria have been agreed on, school districts often set their own cutoff points. If asked to do this, how would you respond? Moreover, should placement decisions be based only on normal curve theory, or are there other considerations?

The following sections should help you to develop the knowledge base needed to make and/or understand placement decisions. The information also will enable you to interpret test results and use them to develop instructional objectives and to plan lessons. For every test administered, teachers are especially interested in two things: (a) average performance and (b) individual differences. Normal curve theory relates to both of these.

The normal curve is a model to aid with interpretation of real scores. To achieve this, the baseline (horizontal line) of the normal curve depicts only *standard scores* (-3, -2, -1, 0, $+1$, $+2$, $+3$), also called z scores. A **standard score** is a number that is used in *conversion, transformation,* and *interpretation*. During test interpretation, real scores are substituted for standard scores. For example, when sit-up data are being interpreted, the 0 and 1 might be replaced with 29 (an average sit-up score) and 10 (a measure of individual differences called a standard deviation). On a z-score scale, the mean is always 0, and the standard deviation is always 1.

Mean, Median, and Mode

Normal curve models always have a vertical line in the middle that is labeled 0. This 0 represents the mean, median, and mode. The **mean** is the average score on a test. The **median** is the midpoint of the scores, the point above and below which 50% of the group score. The **mode** is the one score made most frequently. When real data are graphed, the mean, median, and mode may not fall at precisely the same spot. With real data, especially when a test has only a few items, there may be more than one mode.

Thus, the theoretical model may or may not be a good fit for real data. The goodness of fit depends on whether the real data were collected from over 100 persons and are representative of the full range of individual differences in the population. Tests that are marketed for use in making placement decisions are administered to large groups so that the resulting data will fit the normal curve model.

The mean, median, and mode are called **measures of central tendency** because they describe the center, or middle, of the score distribution. Once teachers know the class average, they are interested in whether their students mostly scored close to the mean or were spread out along the baseline. Note how the baselines of the normal curves in Figure 6.10 are divided by markers into equal spaces. Some baselines have 10 equal spaces, while others have 8, 6, 4, or 2. The number of spaces depends on the individual differences (i.e., spread of scores) and the number of persons tested. The normal curve model uses 6 equal spaces, but real data may result in any number.

Standard Deviations

Standard deviation (SD) is the term for a marker on the baseline that indicates the degree that scores deviate from the mean. A standard deviation is a **measure of variability** or individual differences. Standard deviations are written as -1, -2, and -3 to show how far scores deviate to the left and as $+1$, $+2$, and $+3$ to show how far scores deviate to the right. When real data are involved, the standard units (1, 2, 3) are transformed to actual values.

Figure 6.11 shows some real standard deviations and how they are used in calculations. To determine how far a real score deviates from its mean, the standard deviation is multiplied by 1, 2, or 3 and subtracted from or added to the mean.

Overarm throw data in Figure 6.11 illustrate this. The average throw for a Grade 6 boy is 115 ft. The standard deviation is 22. Thus, the calculations are $115 - 22 = 93$ and $115 + 22 = 137$. If the data are normally distributed, then the interpretation is that about 68% of Grade 6 boys throw between 93 and 137 ft. Any Grade 6 boy unable to throw 93 feet is performing below 1 standard deviation. To find out who is throwing below 1.5 standard deviations, subtract 33 ($22 + 11$) from the mean and get 82 ft. To find out who is throwing below 2 standard deviations, subtract 44 (2×22) from the mean and get 71 ft.

Applications

This information is useful in many ways. One application is the structuring of teams and practice groups. To equalize chances of winning, class teams should be balanced in terms of ability. If throwing is an important skill in the game being played, then an equal number of students scoring -1 or -1.5 standard deviations below the mean should be on every team. This is true also of persons scoring $+1$ or $+1.5$ standard deviations above the mean. In the old days, students scoring below 1 standard deviation would have been grouped together and taught separately. Today, the trend is to integrate them in carefully balanced teams or practice groups.

Another application pertains to decision making about special help and/or placement. Standard deviations are sometimes used as cutoff points for deciding when a student needs adapted physical education placement. Figure 6.11 shows what the -1 and -2 standard deviations cutoff points for Grade 6 boys on the overarm throw, 50-yd dash, and long jump would be. Most school systems, however, use standardized test batteries like the BOTMP and the TGMD for making placement decisions.

To aid in placement, the raw scores yielded by these batteries have been converted to **normalized standard scores** or quotients that have the same mean and standard deviation for each age group. To obtain a normalized standard score or quotient, simply use tables in the test manual. No math is involved.

For example, on the BOTMP, there are tables for converting (a) raw scores to point scores, (b) point scores to standard scores, and (c) battery composite standard scores to normalized standard scores. These normalized standard scores range from 20 and below to 80 and above. The mean is 50 and the standard deviation is 10 (Bruininks, 1978, p. 135). Figure 6.11 shows that the 1 standard deviation cutoff mark is 40 (M $-$ 1 SD).

Use of a cutoff for the BOTMP has more meaning if standard deviations are equated with percentile ranks. The 1 standard deviation mark is the 16th percentile. This means that 16% of the test manual standardization sample scored below 40 and 84% scored above. If a cutoff of 1 standard deviation is used for placement, only a few students will receive the benefits of separate placement (i.e., about 16 out of every 100). This is perhaps an acceptable criterion if the regular physical educator who serves the other 84 students is assisted by an adapted physical education consultant and/or specially trained aides and peer tutors.

The TGMD-2 conversions are less complicated than those of BOTMP. First, look up the standard scores for the locomotor and object control subtests and add them together for

Figure 6.11 Transformation of z scores to real data for placement and teaching. The math calculations involve subtracting and adding the standard deviation (SD) to the mean (M), starting in the center of the curve and working outward. Also shown in this figure is the relationship between percentiles and standard deviations. (TGMD = Test of Gross Motor Development; BOTMP = Bruininks-Oseretsky Test of Motor Proficiency.)

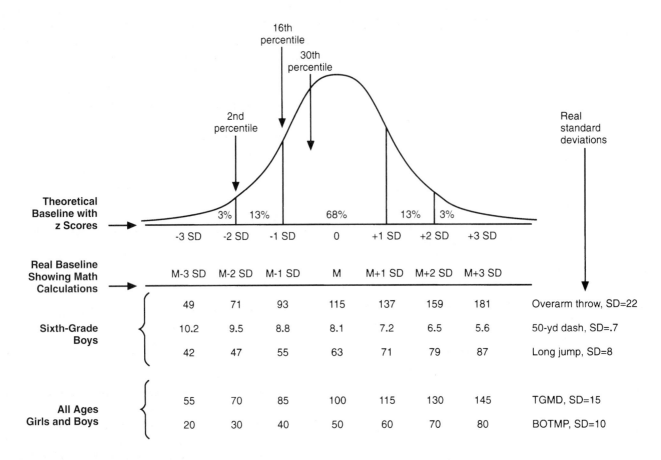

a summed standard score. Then, turn to the test manual page that converts summed standard scores to quotients. These motor quotients range from 46 to 154, similar to the system used in IQ test scoring. The mean is 100, and the standard deviation is 15 (Ulrich, 1985, p. 26). Figure 6.11 shows that the 1 standard deviation cutoff mark is 85, derived by subtracting 15 from 100.

These examples show that adapted physical education specialists who attend IEP meetings and assist with placement decisions need special training, not only in administering tests, but also in using test manuals to interpret data. Separate courses in assessment should be provided to teach about BOTMP, TGMD-2, and similar standardized tests. Criterion- and content-referenced tests are fine for teaching, but norm-referenced standardized tests should be used for placement decisions.

Standard Scores (z and T conversions)

The preceding section introduced the idea of standard scores. These are conversions or transformations of raw scores into equivalent units that permit adding different items or subscales. Whenever composite battery scores are needed, raw scores must be converted to standard scores because adding data yielded in different units, like seconds, feet, and counts of sit-ups or push-ups, is impossible.

There are many kinds of standard scores: z scores, stanines, and T scores, to name a few. Of these, z scores are most common because they are a part of normal curve theory. The $-3, -2, -1, 0, +1, +2, +3$ baseline of the normal curve shows standard scores, also called the standard scale of measurement. This scale always has a mean of 0 and a standard deviation of 1.

To convert raw scores to z scores so that they can be added, the following formula is used:

$$z \text{ score} = \frac{\text{Student's score} - \text{Mean score}}{\text{Standard deviation}}$$

In Figure 6.11, for example, if an 11-year-old boy long-jumped a distance of 48 inches and the mean and standard deviation were 63 and 8, respectively, the calculation would be

$$z = \frac{48 - 63}{8} \text{ or } \frac{-15}{8} = -1.88$$

In Figure 6.11, for a softball throw of 40, the age group mean and standard deviation are 115 and 22, respectively. Thus,

$$z = \frac{40 - 115}{22} \text{ or } \frac{-75}{22} = -3.41$$

For a 50-yd dash time of 9.8, the age group mean and standard deviation are 8.1 and .7, respectively. Thus,

$$z = \frac{9.8 - 8.1}{0.7} \text{ or } \frac{+1.7}{0.7} = 2.43, \text{ reversed to } -2.43$$

Note that in calculations that involve speed, a low score is considered better than a high score. Thus, the sign of the z score is always reversed.

Once the conversions are completed, the z scores can be added:

Long jump	−1.88
Overarm throw	−3.41
50-yd dash	−2.43
Sum	−7.72
Average	−2.57 or −2.6

On the normal curve baseline, this average z score will fall:

```
  −2.6
   |
───┼─────┼─────┼─────┼─────┼─────┼─────┼──
 −3│   −2    −1     0    +1    +2    +3
```

This student's composite score falls about 2.6 standard deviations below the mean, which indicates that the individual definitely qualifies for adapted physical education placement in a separate class with a specialist.

Conversions

After z scores, the second most frequently used type of standard score in adapted physical education assessment is the stanine. **Stanine** is a contraction of the words *standard nine* and refers to a system of standard scores with a range of 1 to 9, a mean of 5, and a standard deviation of 1.96, which is typically rounded to 2. Figure 6.12 shows that the nine stanines equal the plus and minus 2 standard deviations of the mean area in a normal curve. Stanines of 4, 5, and 6 are interpreted as average. Stanines below 4 are low, and stanines above 6 are high. Stanines permit generalizations about which students fall within the middle 20%, 54%, 78%, and 92% of the mean (see stanine percentages line in Figure 6.12). They are more precise than z scores in describing placement but less precise than percentile ranks. Both BOTMP and TGMD-2 provide the option of reporting data in stanines.

T scores are standard scores that range between 20 and 80 with a mean of 50 and a standard deviation of 10. To transform a z score to a T score, this formula is used:

$$T = (10)z + 50$$

Norms

As mentioned earlier in the chapter, the three types of norms are (a) standard scores (e.g., z scores and stanines), (b) percentiles, and (c) age equivalents. Suppose, for example, that on the first subtest of BOTMP—running speed and agility—a child aged 5 years, 9 months made the following scores:

Raw score	Percentile	Stanine	Age equivalent
7.5 sec	72%	6	7.8

The raw score has little meaning until it is converted to one of the norms. A *percentile* of 72 means that the child scored higher than 72% of his or her agemates. The *stanine* of 6 means that the child scored in the high average range. The *age equivalent* of 7.8 indicates that the raw score was the midpoint score for all children 7 years, 8 months old. School records often state only one norm for each raw score. Regardless of whether the percentile, stanine, or age equivalent is reported, teachers are expected to be competent at interpretation.

Like BOTMP, the TGMD-2 manual provides percentiles, stanines, and age equivalents. The TGMD-2 also provides many other statistics, including the ages at which 60% and 80% of the standardization sample achieved the performance criteria for each of its six locomotor and six object control skills.

In summary, most major instruments used for IEP decisions provide several kinds of norms: standard scores like stanines and z scores, percentiles, and age equivalents. Percentiles are the most common.

Assessing Students With Severe Disabilities

Severe disability is defined as an IQ under 35 (i.e., a mental age between 0 and 3 years), serious emotional disturbance or autism, and/or multiple disabilities like Deaf-blindness and cerebral palsy/mental retardation combinations. These persons are often nonverbal, nonambulatory, and dominated by primitive reflexes. Sometimes they are ambulatory but cannot or will not stay in one place and attend to instructions. Obviously, assessment is a challenge. Standardized instruments often are not appropriate.

When assessing such individuals, first establish rapport. Even though they may appear oblivious of you, take the time to get acquainted. Talk to them like you would to anyone else; try to initiate some kind of play, like peekaboo or copycat. If they make a movement, mirror them and see if they notice. **Mirroring** or reflecting another's movement shows acceptance and is especially recommended for persons who are autistic or emotionally disturbed.

Obtain background information from other persons and the files. Often, such students are on behavior management programs and respond to certain signs/words and reinforcers. Remember, no student is too severely disabled to receive physical education services. Assess play and game behaviors as well as motor skill, fitness, perceptual-motor function, and sensory integration.

Questions to guide assessment include these:

1. Does the person attend to what you say or demonstrate? If not, does he or she respond to loud noises, light flashes, or other unusual stimuli (i.e., give evidence of seeing or hearing)? Keep trying until you find something.

2. What words/signs/gestures are understood? Often, these are on the individual's communication boards.

3. Does the person have some kind of expressive language (signs, words, pointing, eye blinks, facial expression)?

4. Can the person imitate? What kind of instructions will he or she follow?

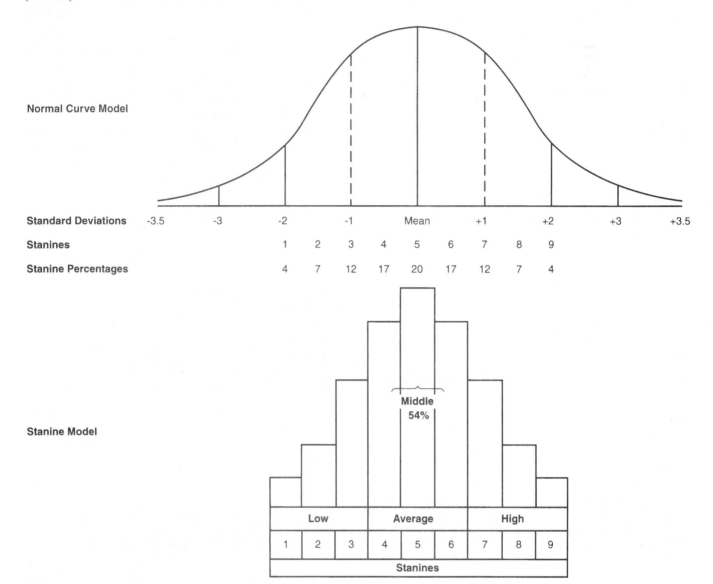

Figure 6.12 Relationships between kinds of norms, the normal curve, and the stanine bar graph with examples from the Bruininks-Oseretsky Test of Motor Proficiency (BOTMP) and Ulrich's Test of Gross Motor Development (TGMD).

Normal Curve Model									
Standard Deviations	-3.5	-3	-2	-1	Mean	+1	+2	+3	+3.5
Stanines			1	2	3	4	5	6	7	8	9
Stanine Percentages			4	7	12	17	20	17	12	7	4

Stanine Model

Middle 54%

Low   Average   High

| 1 | 2 | 3 | 4 | 5 | 6 | 7 | 8 | 9 |

Stanines

5. What reinforcers (food, tokens, verbal praise, hug, touch) obtain the best responses?

6. What is the primary means of ambulation: (a) feet, (b) regular wheelchair, (c) motorized wheelchair? If regular wheelchair, is it propelled by hands or by feet?

7. How can muscle tone be described (normal, fluctuating, hypotonic, hypertonic)?

8. What primitive reflexes dominate or affect movement? Do head movements elicit associated movements? How can these reflexes be minimized or controlled?

9. If in a wheelchair, what is the disability? In most instances, it will be cerebral palsy, spina bifida, or muscular dystrophy.

10. If cerebral palsy, assign sport classification to obtain general idea of movement function. This primarily involves noting the type of ambulation, the hand-grasp function, and the range of motion (i.e., ability to independently move body parts). See Figure 6.13 and Chapter 25 on cerebral palsy.

11. Are there any contractures and/or abnormal postures or pain that need immediate attention?

12. Do the wheelchair and/or braces and assistive devices fit correctly? Is the person correctly positioned for physical education activities? Are body parts properly strapped?

These questions show that assessment competencies for students with severe disabilities are different from those of others. In general, criterion-referenced instruments (particularly the task-analysis types) work better than norm-referenced. Usually, the emphasis is on range of motion and postures, rather than strength and skills.

Instruments especially appropriate for certain kinds of severe conditions are described in Chapter 25 on cerebral palsy,

Class 2 lower athlete with no functional arm movements performing a distance kick with a 13-inch playground ball.

Class 3 athlete performing a club throw for distance.

Class 2 upper athlete almost making a bull's-eye with a 5-oz soft shot.

Chapter 22 on emotional disturbance and autism, and Chapter 21 on mental retardation. For students who appear to be functioning motorically at birth to 5-year level, developmental inventories are useful.

Rubrics

An informal assessment technique that many physical educators now use to assess student progress is **rubrics,** which in the past were referred to as scorecards, checklists, or task analyses.

Rubrics are criteria (i.e., standards) that are used to specify the elements of performance that can be used to determine strengths and weaknesses (Lund, 2000). For example, depending on the nature of the disability, rubrics can help educators determine criteria to evaluate performance. In Figure 6.14, a rubric is presented for a student in a wheelchair for assessing the skill of hitting a ball off a tee. This information can be used as a checklist for screening, for an informal assessment, and for programming. Table 6.8, in Item 18, presented three rubrics

Figure 6.14   Rubrics for a student (age 11) who is a wheelchair user (lower limb involvement with severe arm weakness) in middle school.

Student Name: _____   Adaptations: _____

Please mark the level of performance with a check (√) using different colored checks to signify different evaluation periods.

Goal: Using a softball bat, strike an indoor softball off a batting tee a distance of 20 feet in a game situation 4 out of 5 times at bat.

Rubric	Never	Sometimes	Usually	Always
1. Student uses only one arm to hold bat and strikes ball.	___	___	___	___
2. Student can place hands in position with dominant hand on top of bat and nondominant hand on bottom.	___	___	___	___
3. Student shifts body weight in direction of swing.	___	___	___	
4. Student can hit ball off tee with rotation of body.	___	___	___	___
5. Student can make contact with ball 2 out of 5 times.	___	___	___	___
6. Student can make contact with ball 3 out of 5 times.	___	___	___	___
7. Student can make contact with ball 4 out of 5 times.	___	___	___	___
8. Student can hit ball in fair territory for 5 feet.	___	___	___	___
9. Student can hit ball in fair territory for 10 feet.	___	___	___	___
10. Student can hit ball in fair territory for 15 feet.	___	___	___	___
11. Student can hit ball in fair territory for 20 feet.	___	___	___	___

designed to assess initiative, understanding of instructions, and mental flexibility. Illustrations of rubrics can be found in many sources (e.g., Lieberman & Houston-Wilson, 2002).

Case Study of a School District

To show the diversity of IEP and 504 needs within a school district, this case study describes assessment within one independent school district (ISD) in north Texas. Denton ISD has an enrollment of 14,385 students, ages 3 through 21. Of these, 2,064 have been identified through the IEP process as having a disability in one or more subject areas. Of these 2,064 students, the IEP Committee has found 122 to be disabled in physical education and eligible for services from adapted physical education specialists. The other students, although considered special education, are not deemed to be disabled in physical education or, considering resources, are thought to have their motor needs adequately served by their special education teachers who receive in-service training from physical educators and other supports.

Denton ISD employs a full-time adapted physical education coordinator, with a doctoral degree in adapted physical education, who conducts year-round staff development and in-service training for special educators, general physical educators, and paraeducators; parent training; supervision and mentoring of adapted physical educators; advocacy and liaisoning with administration and community resources; organization of after-school and weekend sport events; consultations; meet-

ings; curriculum development and evaluation; and other administrative responsibilities.

Denton ISD also funds three full-time adapted physical education positions, which are divided among Texas Woman's University graduate students, who are employed for workloads ranging from 10 to 30 hours a week. At present, four of these are certified adapted physical education specialists (CAPES). This staff collectively devotes 120 hours a week to adapted physical education services, half to students directly or through consultation and half to assessments, meetings, paperwork, transportation, and other tasks. The Denton service delivery model allows for flexibility in programming, especially important because of the number of students in general education environments who must receive different services at the same time.

Develop a similar case study of the community in which you live or one that is nearby. Obtain facts through observations, interviews, and documents indicating policies and statistics. Ask to see copies of the forms they use for screening, assessment, and IEP and 504 decisions. If possible, attend one or more of their IEP meetings. Ask for anecdotes about the most interesting or exciting meetings they have attended. Ask about issues they perceive.

Adapted and general physical educators in Denton ISD are invited to IEP meetings that involve students who have been referred because of physical education difficulties. These professionals work closely with parents. As soon as they complete the comprehensive assessment, they share findings with the parents. A Denton ISD policy is to contact the parents a week before the IEP meeting to share and discuss the proposed IEP for their child. At the annual IEP meeting, the adapted physical educator presents informal observations and recommendations for the new IEP. This usually requires 3 to 5 minutes.

If the adapted physical educator cannot attend an IEP meeting, he or she contacts the parents before the meeting and discusses the adapted physical education IEP annual goals, objectives, and services recommendations. This communication facilitates desired changes to the physical education IEP because the parent then advocates for the content of the written reports submitted in absentia. It also develops a professional and positive relationship between the parents and the adapted physical educator.

Denton ISD has developed a continuum of services in which students can receive the most appropriate physical education services. IDEA requires that a continuum of placements (or services) be made available. The **Denton ISD continuum** is as follows:

1. Level 1: general physical education setting with no support
2. Level 2: general physical education with adapted physical education consultation
3. Level 3: general physical education with direct support from the adapted physical educator in general physical education
4. Level 4: general and adapted physical education
5. Level 5: adapted physical education in disability setting with GE students joining in (reverse mainstreaming)
6. Level 6: separate adapted physical education

Four case studies about adapted physical education students in Denton ISD follow. Each involves a different situation. Illustrative forms used in the IEP or the 504 processes are presented in Figures 6.15–6.22. Each of these students is placed in the LRE based on numerous factors.

Case Study of a New Student in the School District

Lucy, age 9, with Asperger syndrome (see index) and a new student in the school district, started fourth-grade physical education instruction with her peers in the mainstream setting. By October, the special education diagnostician had decided that Lucy needed an IEP meeting and had referred her to several specialists for screening and assessment. Among these was Mr. O'Brien, the adapted physical educator. The classroom teacher had already completed the district screening form (see Figure 6.2). Mr. O'Brien used the same screening form as the classroom teacher, and the two collaborated in making the screening decision, which was checked at the bottom of the form. Based on the screening data, Mr. O'Brien decided to observe Lucy informally during her general physical education and to assess her formally with the CTAPE (Louisiana Department of Education, 2001). By law, he needed the parents' consent to follow up the screening process, and the special education diagnostician obtained this permission. Additionally, the medical screening

form was sent home to the parents (see Figure 6.3) to complete so that school personnel would have a more in-depth awareness of any medications, contraindicated activities, and so on.

Based on a comprehensive assessment of Lucy's present level of physical education performance, Mr. O'Brien wrote the FIE (see Figure 6.15). While these procedures were taking place in physical education, teachers in other subject matter areas were also screening and conducting comprehensive assessments. At the IEP meeting, Mr. O'Brien recommended that Lucy continue to participate in general physical education but also receive additional adapted physical education services a minimum of 2 times a month for 30 min each to work on object control skills. The IEP committee agreed that Lucy work on her volleyball, catching, and jump rope skills (see Figure 6.16). Further, it was agreed that Mr. O'Brien consult with the general physical educator in person once a month before each unit to assist with adaptations that Lucy might need during class. Additionally, the general physical educator was invited to e-mail him as needed.

Case Study of Boy in General PE Who Has a 3-Year IEP Review

Nick, a 16-year-old wheelchair user who has moderate to severe lower limb cerebral palsy, but minimal problems in his upper limbs and trunk (i.e., a CP Class 4) had functioned well in general physical education, with occasional input from the adapted physical educator for 3 years. Therefore, he now needed to be assessed for a 3-year IEP review. The adapted physical educator decided to use (a) an ecological survey that focused on community-based individual sports (see Figure 6.17) because Nick's parents were concerned about his continued involvement in sports when he graduates and (b) the BPFT (Winnick & Short, 1999), because physical fitness seemed to be his area of greatest need. A medical screening form was also given to the parents to update, as with all other students who qualify for adapted physical education services (see Figure 6.3).

Before her in-depth assessment, the adapted physical educator, Ms. Trocki-Ables, consulted with Mr. Evans, the physical educator, regarding Nick's performance during his general physical education class. Mr. Evans reported that, with help from the paraeducator, Nick was successful in most activities. Nick enjoyed participating in community-based activities such as basketball and volleyball, although he seemed to have difficulty sometimes because of his overall level of fitness. Further, Mr. Evans stated that he could use some suggestions during other sports units (i.e., football, floor hockey) related to adaptations for Nick so he could participate more appropriately with his peers. He also stated that Nick enjoyed his friends and demonstrated socially appropriate behavior during instruction.

Based on an interest survey, Nick identified the following sports that he would like to participate in with family and friends: bowling, team sports, and swimming. All these activities were readily available within the community and supported by his parents.

Based on two assessments and informal observations, the FIE was developed and presented to the IEP committee (see Figure 6.18). In addition, an IEP (see Figure 6.19) was

Figure 6.15   FIE/Assessment Report for Lucy.

▨ **Initial Assessment**   ☐ **3-Year Assessment**   **IEP Date: 11/04/2003**

Name: Lucy Hanson   **ID:** 123-45-6789   **DOB**: 05-21-94
Examiner: Tim O'Brien   **School**: Wilson Elementary

Sources of Data (Formal and Informal Measures)   **Assessment Dates**
1.   Competency Test for Adapted Physical Education (CTAPE) -Level III (LA, 2001)   10/21/02
2.   Informal Observations during General Physical Education   10/15; 10/17/02

☐   ☐   Based on the assessment, the student demonstrates a need for supplementary adapted
Yes   **No**   physical education in order to make appropriate progress in the general physical
                   education setting.

LEARNING COMPETENCIES: Strengths and Weaknesses

Physical and Motor Fitness:
-able to perform the 50-yd dash in 11 seconds (slightly below average 10.8)
-attempts to perform a standing long jump (score of 6 out of 12; below average)
-attempts to jump rope (score of 1 out of 12; below average)
-able to perform a crab walk (score of 17 out of 17; exceeds expectations)
-attempts to perform a vertical jump (score of 5 out of 10; below average)
-able to perform windmills continuously (score of 9 out of 9; exceeds expectations)
-attempts to perform trunk rotations (score of 1 out of 4; below average)
-attempts to perform jumping jacks (score of 3 out of 11; below average)

Fundamental Motor Skills and Patterns:
-attempts to jump rope (score of 1 out of 12; below average)
-able to hop 3 times on one foot (score of 3 out of 3; average)
-able to gallop backwards (score of 10, average is 9)
-able to overhand throw a tennis ball (score of 5 out of 5; average)
-able to throw a tennis ball overhand at a target (score of 24, average is 15)
-attempts to kick an 8.5" ball with the outside of foot (score of 7 out 15; below average)
-attempts to run and kick an 8.5" ball (score of 2 out of 6; below average)
-able to dribble an 8.5" ball 5 times forward and 5 times backward (score of 18 out of 18; exceeds expectations)
-able to catch a 3.5" softball tossed from 10' away (score 2 out of 3; below average)
-able to field a softball rolled from 20' away (score of 9, average is 8)
-able to strike a softball pitched from 20' away (score of 27, average is 24)
-attempts to overhand pass a self-set 13" beach ball (score of 1 out of 12; below average)
-attempts to punt a soccer ball (score of 8 out of 9; slightly below average)
-attempts to trap a rolled soccer ball (score of 4 out of 12; below average)
-able to dribble a soccer ball (score of 11, average is 9)
-able to walk heel-to-toe on a 2" line (score of 15 out of 15; average)

Informal Observations:
-Lucy is able to execute most skills in the average range for children her age; Participates well with her peers in
general physical education; Lucy is able to participate in activities with verbal prompting from the general
physical educator; and she stays on task during instruction.

Recommendation(s)/Modification(s):
-Check for understanding and model activities. Use verbal prompting when appropriate.

Recommendations for Instructional Setting:
Her overall score on the CTAPE Level III was 48% out of 100%, which indicates a moderate motor deficit.
Placement in general physical education with adapted physical education services a minimum of two times per
month for 30 minutes each. In addition, consultation services with the general physical educator a minimum of
two times a month for 15 minutes for activity modifications.

Tim O'Brien
Signature of Evaluator, Denton ISD

Certified Adapted Physical Educator (CAPE)
Position

Figure 6.16   Individualized Education Program (IEP) for Lucy.

Denton ISD Adapted Physical Education Instructional Services

APE Services: 2 x month 30 min each

Date Draft Completed _____
Date Accepted by IEP Committee _____

Name of Student: Lucy Hanson   School: Wilson Elementary   Grade: 4th

Duration of Services From   11/04/03   **to**:   11/04
                                 Month/Day/Year   Month/Year

Present Level of Performance:

Able to overhead pass a volleyball to a partner a distance 4'. Able to catch a 3.5" softball tossed from 5' away. Able to jump rope 8 times continuously.

Goal(s):

Perform a mature overhead pass a distance of 10' using a 13" beach ball. Catch a 3.5" softball a distance of 10' away. Self-turn a jump rope 20 times consecutively.

Short-Term Objectives — The Student will be able to:	Indicate Level of Mastery Criteria	Assessment Procedure	Assessment Codes (show percentage of progress every six weeks)					
			Date 12/19	Date 2/14	Date 4/11	Date	Date	Date
Overhand pass a 13" beach ball with a mature pattern to a partner a distance of 6', 8', and 10' with the ball going a minimum of 5' in the air.	80%	2, 8	P=6'	M=6'	M=8'			
Using 2 hands, catch a 3.5" softball tossed 15' high from 6', 8', and 10' away.	75%	2, 8	I=6'	M=6'	P=8'			
Self-turn a jump rope and jump 10, 15, and 20 times consecutively.	90%	2, 8	I=10	P=10	M=10			
Engage in one or more adapted games using a beach ball or softball with one or more persons.	85%	2	I=one game one person	P=one game one person	M=one game one person			

Assessment Procedure Codes:

1. Teacher-made tests
2. Observations
3. Weekly tests
4. Unit tests
5. Student conferences
6. Work samples
7. Portfolios
8. Other: CTAPE (Level III)

Assessment Codes:

M = Mastered
A = Almost mastered
P = Progressing at expected rate
I = Improvement needed

Figure 6.17 Ecological Survey: Wheelchair Bowling for Nick.

Goal: Nick (in manual wheelchair) will demonstrate functional competence in one or more bowling games in a community facility with family.

Assessments: Observe the student and determine if he is able to:
    (a) travel to bowling facility
    (b) locate retractable bowling ball, lanes, and scoring system
    (c) bowl independently

Skills Checklist

	Date Completed	
	Yes	No
1. Selects correct retractable ball size		
2. Selects a bowling lane		
3. Aligns wheelchair up in lanes		
4. Rolls retractable ball safely		
5. Scores the number of pins knocked down		
6. Takes turn in correct order		
7. Completes a 10-frame game independently		

Transition Checklist

	Date Completed	
	Yes	No
1. Travels safely to bowling lanes		
2. Crosses parking lot in a safe manner		

3. Enters building through appropriate doors
   -uses w/c accessible ramp
   -enters building safely		

4. Goes to front counter		
5. Tells attendant that he is here to bowl		
6. Pays bowling fee		
7. Obtains a retractable bowling ball		
8. Locates bowling lane		
9. Joins his bowling team with appropriate social interactions		
10. Registers name on electronic scoring system		

recommended and approved. At the IEP meeting, the adapted physical educator recommended that Nick continue to participate in the general physical education class with a paraeducator and receive adapted physical education services 2 times a week for 30 min each to work on his IEP goals of overall fitness and sports skills. To meet the IDEA requirement for a transition plan built into the IEP from age 14 on, Pam Trocki-Ables agreed to supply Nick and his parents information on lifetime community-based sports organizations within his community. Parents also agreed to involve Nick in the community cerebral palsy sports program and in a youth wheelchair basketball pro-

gram conducted by city recreation personnel. In addition, the parents indicated that they wanted Nick to learn to use local transportation with the assistance of the school staff, including the adapted physical educator.

Case Study of a Boy in a Self-Contained Motor Activity Program

Shane, age 7, is in a self-contained, adapted life skills class with six students of similar age and ability on a mainstream school campus. The IEP committee requested that Shane be assessed

Figure 6.18   FIE/Assessment Report for Nick.

☐ **Initial Assessment**   ☐ **3-Year Assessment**   **IEP Date: 11/20/2003**

Name: Nick Thibault   **ID:** 269-94-2878   **DOB**: 3/04/85
Examiner: Pam Trocki-Ables   **School**: Denton High School

Sources of Data (Formal and Informal Measures)	Assessment Dates
1. Brockport Physical Fitness Test (BPFT) [Winnick & Short, 2000]	9/8/03
2. Ecological Survey	9/29/03 – 10/03/03
3. Informal Observations during General Physical Education	9/4/03

☐   ☐   Based on the assessment, the student demonstrates a need for supplementary adapted
Yes   **No**   physical education in order to make appropriate progress in the general physical
education setting.

LEARNING COMPETENCIES: Strengths and Weaknesses

Physical and Motor Fitness:
-able to do a reverse curl with a 1 lb weight 6 times (passing)
-able to perform 23 seated push-ups (35 preferred)
-able to push/walk 40 m in 52 seconds (minimal score of 60 seconds)
-able to reach back and touch with one hand the opposite scapula on the modified Apley test (2 points)
-able to go beyond 8 feet on the wheelchair ramp test (minimal score 15 ft)
-able to bench press 35 lbs 47 times (minimal score 50 times)
-body mass index was 65" tall and 123 lb (scored a 21)

Fundamental Motor Skills and Patterns:
-able to use a retractable bowling ball
-able to push his wheelchair and dribble a basketball 10 feet
-able to pick up a rolling basketball using the wheel of his chair
-attempts to overhand serve a volleyball over a regulation volleyball net from half court
-able to strike a 3.5 inch softball tossed from 10 feet

Informal Observations:
-Nick enjoys participating in basketball and volleyball with his friends. Nick also bowls with his family using a retractable bowling ball. He is able to travel with a family member or friend on the local transportation system with support. He is also beginning to understand the bowling scoring system.

Recommendation(s)/Modification(s):
-Adapted equipment (i.e., retractable bowling ball).
-Extra time to complete task.

Recommendations for Instructional Setting:
Adapted physical education services two times a week for 30 minutes each. Further, participate in general physical education class with a paraeducator.

Pam Trocki-Ables
_____   Certified Adapted Physical Educator (CAPE)
Signature of Evaluator, Denton ISD   Position

Figure 6.19   Individualized Education Program (IEP) for Nick.

Denton ISD Adapted Physical Education Instructional Services

Page _____ of _____

APE Services: 2 x a week for 30 min each

Date Draft Completed _____
Date Accepted by IEP Committee _____

Name of Student: Nick Thibault   School: Denton High School   Grade: 10th

Duration of Services From   11/20/03   **to**:   11/04
                                        Month/Day/Year   Month/Year

Present Level of Performance:

Able to push wheelchair up a ramp a distance of 8 feet. Able to perform 23 seated push-ups. Able to serve a volleyball overhand from 4.5 m. Able to bowl, with a retractable ball, a game of bowling but needs assistance with scoring.

Goal(s):

Push wheelchair a distance of 30 feet up a ramp for 3 times consecutively.   Perform 35 seated push-ups continuously. Overhand serve a volleyball from a distance of 9 m over a regulation volleyball net. Bowl and score 3 games independently.

Short-Term Objectives The Student will be able to:	Indicate Level of Mastery Criteria	Assessment Procedure	**Assessment Codes** (show percentage of progress every six weeks)					
			Date 2/14	Date	Date	Date	Date	Date
Push wheelchair 10, 15, and 30 feet up a wheelchair ramp for 3 times consecutively.	80%	2, 8	P=10					
Perform 25, 30, and 35 seated push-ups continuously.	80%	2, 8	I=25					
Serve a standard volleyball overhand over a regulation net from 5, 7, and 9 meters.	70%	2	P=5					
Bowl with a retractable bowling ball and score 1, 2, and 3 games independently at a local bowling facility.	90%	2, 8	P-1					

Assessment Procedure Codes:

1. Teacher-made tests
2. Observations
3. Weekly tests
4. Unit tests
5. Student conferences
6. Work samples
7. Portfolios
8. Other: BPFT, Ecological Survey

Assessment Codes:

M = Mastered
A = Almost mastered
P = Progressing at expected rate
I = Improvement needed

by Ms. Morales, the adapted physical education teacher, for his 3-year IEP review. Ms. Morales chose to use Project MOBILI-TEE (Gossett, 1981) for this, because it was the most appropriate assessment system for Shane's low cognitive and motor skills. Observations of his motor activity program were used also to write the FIE. At the IEP meeting, Ms. Morales presented her assessment results (see Figure 6.20) and a new, revised IEP (see Figure 6.21) for consideration. The IEP committee approved the recommendations for continued daily physical education instruction by his special education teacher in a self-contained setting. Ms. Morales will provide adapted physical education services once a week (20 minutes each session) and will consult with the classroom teacher on a monthly basis. Adapted equipment and data sheets will be provided to the classroom teacher to help facilitate Shane's progress throughout the academic school year. The special education teacher and paraeducators will also receive several hours of staff development and consultation from the adapted physical education coordinator.

Case Study of a 504 Student

Jake is an 8-year-old with bilateral coordination difficulties (i.e., throwing, kicking) in general physical education. He also has chronic asthma that is not yet well managed, and he is therefore often absent from school or unable to participate fully. The IEP committee did not believe that he qualified as disabled in physical education under IDEA, but the parents continued to ask for Jake to have special help. Jake was referred to the adapted physical educator, Ms. Kim, for a basic gross motor assessment screening to provide suggestions for the requested help. Ms. Kim used the screening form first and then observed Jake during his physical education class. She then obtained permission from the 504 committee and parents to assess Jake using the TGMD-2 (Ulrich, 2000) to determine his basic gross motor skill level for possible 504 eligibility. Based on these two assessments, a written report was prepared for the 504 committee meeting (see Figure 6.22). At this meeting with the 504 members, including the parents, it was agreed that Jake met 504 criteria because his condition substantially limited one or more major life activities (breathing and mobility). Ms. Kim described accommodations to the general physical educator and parents on how to reduce his breathing and mobility difficulties. The 504 committee further recommended that year-round swimming in an indoor pool (at least one lesson a week) be initiated because swimming is the sport of choice for persons with asthma. Further, Ms. Kim agreed to consult with the general physical educator once each semester to follow up on the accommodations suggested and, if needed, to make changes. In addition, the adapted physical education teacher will telephone the parents to address any concerns of Jake's motor skills at least twice a semester.

Parts of the IEP

Chapter 4 introduced the parts of the written IEP and the team process that must be followed in making IEP decisions. These parts are

P—Performance, present level

A—Annual measurable goals, including short-term objectives

S—Services to be provided, also supports, adaptations

T—Transition services, recommended at all ages but a written plan required at age 14 with implementation required at age 16

D—Dates and duration

E—Evaluation (assessment) to determine whether objectives are achieved

The acronym *PAST-DE* was recommended for remembering these parts, based on the idea that the age of ignorance about disability is *past* and/or *dead.* IDEA 97 added some required content for IEPs. The content included a statement of what kinds of assessments were used to make IEP decisions and, if a recommendation is made to remove a student from GE, a full description of all adaptations made that were unsuccessful before this decision was made.

The individualized physical education program (IPEP) is a term used in some schools to distinguish between the physical education document and the legal school document that includes all subjects. The IPEP is submitted to the IEP team members for their consideration. Some school systems include this kind of detail about physical education in their IEPs, but most include only a few sentences.

If a student is placed in general physical education, no information except the assignment "general physical education" is required on the IEP. However, if support services are needed, parents should be taught to insist that these be written into the IEP. Likewise, conditions believed necessary for learning to occur, like limited class size, specific teaching style, and formal adapted physical activity training for teachers and aides, should be written into the IEP. The IEP is a legal document that determines services. Both professionals and parents must sign the IEP for it to meet requirements of the law; this gives parents considerable negotiation power. An important role of the physical educator is to teach parents what to negotiate for.

The IPEP in Figure 6.23 was written by an adapted physical activity specialist with special training in BOTMP, TGMD-2, and other kinds of assessment. Classroom teachers and general physical educators as well as IEP team members should be given copies of the IPEP. The IPEP, although not required by law, is an excellent help in programming for all students with special needs. It is therefore recommended as the document that is used for committee meetings as well as for IEP meetings. General physical educators should ask their administrators to supply consultant help to assess students with problems and to write IPEPs. If class sizes and free time permit, general physical educators may assume responsibility for writing their own IPEPs.

The IPEP in Figure 6.23 is missing some parts required by IDEA 97. What are these? Compare the assessment and programming approach in Figure 6.23 with that used in the Denton ISD. Discuss strengths and weaknesses of each.

Figure 6.20   FIE/Assessment Report for Shane.

☐ **Initial Assessment**   ☐ **3-Year Assessment**   **IEP Date: 12/10/2003**

Name: Shane Griffith   **ID:** 246-80-2468   **DOB:** 8/11/95
Examiner: Michele Morales   **School:** Borman Elementary

Sources of Data (Formal and Informal Measures)   **Assessment Dates**
1. Project MOBILITEE (Gossett, 1981)   10/30/03 & 12/11/03
2. Informal Observations during Motor Activity Program   11/17/03 – 11/27/03

☐   ☐   Based on the assessment, the student demonstrates a need for supplementary adapted
Yes **No**   physical education in order to make appropriate progress in the general physical
    education setting.

LEARNING COMPETENCIES: Strengths and Weaknesses

Physical and Motor Fitness:
-able to run from one point to another; wide base and wide arms (2 out of 4)
-attempts to jump in place; can jump down from step but lands one foot at a time (1 out of 4)

Fundamental Motor Skills and Patterns:
-able to throw small balls (tennis ,whiffle, yarn balls) but uses same side throw with arm and foot (3 out of 4)
-attempts to catch ball with arms stretched, but does not grasp the ball to hold (1 out of 4)
-attempts to strike a ball but uses only one hand with chopping action (1 out of 4)
-attempts to kick stationary ball; approaches ball and kicks it as part of walk/run (1 out of 4)

Informal Observations:
-Shane participates in adapted physical education and attempts many of the activities with physical assistance.
Shane appears to especially enjoy the warm up routine with music. Shane enjoys running and skipping around the
room. Shane also enjoys placing items in order or by colors. Time on task is very limited.

Recommendation(s)/Modification(s):
-Participate in small group instruction.
-Model activities to be performed then possible physical prompting if no response.
-Extra time to complete task.
-Establish eye contact before instruction.

Recommendations for Instructional Setting:
Adapted physical education services one time a week for 20 minutes each. Further, participate in a daily motor
activity program provided by the classroom teacher and staff with consultation services from the adapted physical
education teacher one time monthly.

Michele Morales
Signature of Evaluator, Denton ISD

Certified Adapted Physical Educator (CAPE)
Position

Figure 6.21   Individualized Education Program (IEP) for Shane.

Denton ISD Adapted Physical Education Instructional Services

Page ____ of ____

Date Draft Completed _____
Date Accepted by IEP Committee _____

APE Services: 1 x a week for 20 min each

Name of Student: Shane Griffith   School: Borman Elementary   Grade: Adapted Life Skills

Duration of Services From   12/10/03   to: 12/04
                          Month/Day/Year   **Month/Year**

Present Level of Performance:

Able to throw a beanbag at a target with a mature pattern from a distance of 10 feet; Catch an 8.5" playground ball with 2 hands tossed from a distance of 5 feet; and kick a stationary ball as part of a walking approach to the ball.

Goal(s):

Perform a mature overhead pass a distance of 10' using a 13" beach ball. Catch a 3.5" softball a distance of 10' away. Self-turn a jump rope 20 times consecutively.

Short-Term Objectives The Student will be able to:	Indicate Level of Mastery Criteria	Assessment Procedure	Assessment Codes (show percentage of progress every six weeks)					
			Date 2/14	Date 4/11	Date	Date	Date	Date
Throw a beanbag, yarn ball, and tennis ball at a 4' x 4' target with a mature pattern from a distance of 10 feet.	85%	2, 8	P = Beanbag	M = Beanbag				
Catch an 8.5" playground ball with 2 hands tossed from distances of 6, 8, and 10 feet.	80%	2, 8	I = 6'	A = 6'				
Kick a 8.5" stationary ball in an intended direction for a distance of 6, 8, and 10 feet.	80%	2, 8	M = 6'	P = 8'				

Assessment Procedure Codes:

1. Teacher-made tests
2. Observations
3. Weekly tests
4. Unit tests
5. Student conferences
6. Work samples
7. Portfolios
8. Other: Project MOBILITEE

Assessment Codes:

M = Mastered
A = Almost mastered
P = Progressing at expected rate
I = Improvement needed

Figure 6.22 Written Report for the 504 Committee (Accommodation Plan) for Jake.

TO: Parents/Guardians
FROM: Ms. Heejung Kim
            Adapted Physical Educator
RE: Physical Education Accommodations

During the first and second 6 weeks of the 2002-2003 school year Jake (age 8) was screened with the Denton ISD Adapted Physical Education Screening Form (see Figure 6.2) and assessed with the TGMD–2 (2000) by the adapted physical education teacher. Jake was also observed during his general physical education classes, where his unmanaged asthma was obvious.

- On the Denton ISD Adapted Physical Education Screening Form Jake was able to perform the following with a mature pattern: walking, galloping, sliding, throwing, and able to stand on one foot for 5 seconds. He demonstrated difficulty with the following skills: jumping (not using arms fully and bending legs), hopping, leaping, skipping (able to demonstrate on one side), catching consistently with a mature pattern, bouncing and catching a playground ball to self, kicking a rolled ball with a mature pattern, and jump roping.

- Based on the scores from the TGMD-2, Jake scored an overall Gross Motor Quotient of 88, which indicates his gross motor performance was below average for his chronological age. He demonstrated difficulty with hopping, leaping, horizontal jump, stationary dribble, and catching. Jake performed above average on running, galloping, sliding, striking and kicking a stationary ball, overhand throw, and underhand roll.

- During the general physical education observation period, he had some difficulty with activities that involved moving his body while using different manipulative implements (i.e., balls, hockey sticks). Although, when both the object and he were stationary, he was much more successful.

The adapted physical educator recommended that Jake continue to participate in the general physical education program with accommodations for his breathing and mobility difficulties to be determined collaboratively by the adapted and general physical educators. Further, it was agreed that, when participating in continuous movement sports like basketball and soccer, Jake could opt to rotate out of a game every 3 minutes, rest, and then rotate back in. Jake would also begin weekly swim lessons in an indoor pool. The adapted physical educator agreed to consult with the general physical educator two times a semester to follow up on the accommodations suggested and, if needed, to make appropriate changes.

Illustrative report used by Denton Independent School District, Texas

Figure 6.23   Sample IPEP.

Alief Independent School District—IPEP

Parent Signature of Approval _____   Date _____

Name ___Amy S.___   Date _8-1-04_   School ___Washington Elem.___

D.O.B. _7-3-99_   Age _5_   Grade _Early Childhood_   Classification _OI_

APA Specialist _C. Pope_   Projected Starting Date of Services _9-2004_

Physical Abilities/Disabilities ___Mild Cerebral Palsy — L. side, hemiplegic spastic, ambulatory___

Related Services ___OT, PT___

PRESENT LEVEL OF PSYCHOMOTOR PERFORMANCE
1. On BOTMP Long Form, Amy received overall percentile rank of 6 and stanine placement of 2. Her age equivalent score was below her actual age (5–9) on all 8 BOTMP subcomponents, but greatest weaknesses were in balance and strength components because she has not yet learned to compensate for L side spasticity on jump and land in balance skills.
2. On TGMD, Amy failed to meet criteria for mature performance on all 7 locomotor skills and 2 of 5 object control skills (2-hand strike, catch with both hands). Performed well on items requiring only one hand.
3. On social play skills, Amy is just entering associative play level and appears to have had little experience interacting with other children; plays no group games. She attends well, seems eager to please, but timid.

ANNUAL GOALS
1. Develop functional competence in locomotor and object control skills.
2. Improve social interaction skills to cooperative play level.
3. Play 10 low organized games, with success, with nondisabled peers.
4. Improve static and dynamic balance by learning to adapt to spasticity.

ILLUSTRATIVE SHORT-TERM OBJECTIVES
1. Perform various jumps without falling (pass, fail criterion).
2. Pass TGMD criteria for mature catch with two hands.
3. Interact with 3 or more classmates, when play is videotaped for 30 min.
4. Demonstrate success in 10 games on videotape: Pass specific criteria for success in each game.

SERVICES AND PLACEMENT FOR 12-MONTH PERIOD, BEGINNING SEPTEMBER 1
1. General PE 5 times a week, Model A, specially designed mainstream (SDM), with same age or slightly older buddy assigned fulltime to her.
2. Class size limited to 16, 8 with disabilities and 8 without.
3. General PE teacher with one adult aide, both of whom have documented adapted PE training within the last 3 years.
4. Adapted physical activity specialist-consultant available as needed.
5. School district curriculum guide available that lists appropriate games for age group and includes task analyses.

TRANSITION
1. Parent-guided homework plan agreed on that involves neighborhood children at least 3 times a week, 50 min each time.
2. Contact made with local branch of NDSA, with weekly visits to observe and interact with others with cerebral palsy.

Helping Students Develop IEPs/IPEPs

With the increasing emphasis given to participation of students in IEP meetings, curricular materials are available to help teachers prepare students for this involvement (NICHCY, 1995; Van Reusen & Box, 1994). It is recommended that students be taught to read, study, and recommend changes in their IEPs several weeks before the formal meeting. Work on the IEP should be woven into classes over the entire year using a combination of class discussions, seatwork, one-on-one meetings with various teachers who contribute to their IEP, and homework done either individually or with parents. Some of the benefits students derive are these:

Learning how to speak for themselves

Developing some of the skills necessary for self-determination and independent decision making

Understanding assessment, engaging in self-testing, and performing at their personal best in tests administered by others

Learning more about their strengths and weaknesses and how these relate to goals, objectives, and prescribed activities

 OPTIONAL ACTIVITIES

1. Describe the role of the general physical educator in the assessment process. If possible motor and physical weaknesses are identified, identify three professionals who could provide you assessment information used to evaluate students who demonstrate chronic motor and physical problems in class. Justify your selection of each (e.g., see Shapiro & Sayers, 2003).

2. Based on IEP requirements, select and justify a variety of appropriate assessments for a 12-year-old student who is clumsy and has been referred to the adapted physical education teacher. Use IDEA 97 as part of the justification of each instrument.

3. Develop a script for a simulated IEP meeting and role-play each participant. Participants include administrator, parent, adapted and general physical education teachers, student, and diagnostician. Do the same for a 504 meeting.

4. For graduate students, debate the use of an instrument such as TGMD-2 as a sole instrument for placement and/or instruments such as the Bruininks-Oseretsky as an authentic assessment technique.

CHAPTER

7

Teaching and Consulting

Figure 7.1   Peer teacher demonstrates hitting a piñata for a classmate with Down syndrome.

1. Identify indicators of effective teaching, and discuss how input, process, and outcomes can be used to guide decision making that leads to effective teaching.

2. Identify and discuss at least 10 instructional principles. Cite examples of how you or others have applied these principles in practicum or salaried teaching experiences. Are these the most important instructional principles? Why? What is missing? What other principles can you think of?

3. Differentiate among traditional task analysis, ecological task analysis, and activity analysis and demonstrate competence in each.

4. Analyze four teaching styles, from most to least restrictive, and describe each in relation to (a) learning environment, (b) starting routine, (c) presentation of new activities, and (d) execution. Relate teaching styles to behaviors that

students with various disabilities might exhibit. Share concrete examples with a partner.

5. Discuss behavior management concepts in relation to teaching, and describe some specific techniques. How much experience have you had with behavior management? What behaviors make you most uncomfortable? Why? How do you plan to change?

6. Identify characteristics of a healthy counseling relationship and discuss them in relation to teaching. How much time do you anticipate listening to students and parents when your employment is full-time? Why?

7. Given some case studies of families, schools, and communities, discuss how to obtain and use consultant services in those cases. Or make up some case studies demonstrating your understanding of consultant services.

This chapter pertains to two components of the PAP-TE-CA model: teaching/counseling/coaching and consulting. Although these functions can be treated as independent entities, they are clustered together in this chapter because of their close interrelatedness. Four concepts underlie the decision to group these functions together.

1. All functions are processes of facilitating permanent change (i.e., learning) while building and/or preserving ego strength so as to evoke personal bests in performance (see Figure 7.1).

2. **Counseling,** in this text, is defined as a helping relationship based on good interpersonal communication skills rather than as functions performed by a salaried professional called a counselor. *For students and teachers to become better listeners and helpers, completion of courses in counseling is highly recommended.* Adapted physical activity professionals are often asked to listen and help with individual and family problems. Teaching sometimes cannot progress until these problems are addressed.

3. **Consulting,** in this text, is defined as providing (a) support services to parents, teachers, and other professionals; (b) adult education, which may include various forms of in-service education, parent training, and collaborative teamwork; and (c) expert advice and contract services, such as assessment or evaluation for a school district. All teachers are asked to serve as consultants in their area of expertise at one time or another. In particular, physical educators often serve as consultants for parents and classroom teachers who instruct children in movement skills and game concepts. Adapted physical activity specialists who are employed as consultants are first and foremost teachers.

4. Coaching is a specialized teaching function that requires particular competencies. **Coaching,** in this text, refers to responsibility for after-school sport training and competition in a home, school, or community context.

This chapter therefore focuses on teaching as a generic function that can encompass counseling, coaching, and consulting. The emphasis, however, is on **teaching** as service delivery within the classroom that is directed toward setting and achieving physical education goals. **Pedagogy,** the art and science of teaching, is synonymous with content taught in methods courses. In APENS (NCPERID, 1995), this encompasses standards on unique attributes of learners, curriculum theory and development, and instructional design and planning.

Indicators of Effective Teaching

Curricular models, service agencies, and sport organizations capture the essence of effective teaching in their acronyms and mottos (see Table 7.1). As you read this chapter, relate the ideas in Table 7.1 to principles and processes of good teaching. In Chapter 1, it was emphasized that good teaching is adapting. Adaptation should result in the following indicators of effective teaching, which are based on research (Siedentop, 1983):

1. The development of a warm, positive climate

2. An appropriate matching of content to student abilities (ensuring success-oriented activity)

3. A high percentage of time devoted to lesson objectives

4. High rates of on-task behaviors

5. Shared responsibility for learning and demonstrated self-determinism (choice making) by students

Instructional Model to Guide Thinking

Teaching is a chain of decision making (Mosston & Ashworth, 1986, p. 4). To guide these decisions, Table 7.2 presents an instructional model with three basic parts (input, process, and outcomes). **Input** refers to information about all of the variables that affect teaching and learning. Decision making about planning, assessing, and prescribing determines the quality and quantity of input. **Process** refers to the actual interactions that lead to behavior change. Decision making about these

Table 7.1   Acronyms and mottos associated with good teaching.

1. **I CAN:** Individualize, Create social leisure competence, Associate all learnings, Narrow the gap between theory and practice (Wessel, 1977).
2. **ABC:** Achievement-Based Curriculum (Wessel & Kelly, 1986).
3. **PAP-TE-CA:** Plan, Assess, Prepare, Teach, Evaluate, Consult, Advocate. This is an expansion of the ABC model.
4. **ACTIVE:** All Children Totally Involved in Exercising (Vodola, 1976). This means no waiting in lines, a ball or rope for every student.
5. **Every Child a Winner** (Owens, 1974): Recognition for personal bests, emphasis on a warm, positive classroom climate.
6. **Find Another Way** (Gold, 1980): This motto refers to the teacher's creativity in finding a way each student can succeed on every task.
7. **Catch 'Em Being Good** (O'Leary & Schneider, 1980): This is a behavior management principle that emphasizes giving five praises before each correction.
8. **Moving to Inclusion** (Active Living Alliance for Canadians With a Disability, 1994): This refers to the teacher's creativity in finding ways to include students in the general instructional setting and in obtaining support services.
9. **Data-Based Gymnasium** (Dunn, Morehouse, & Fredericks, 1986): This refers to basing all decisions in the gymnasium on student performance data.
10. **PEOPEL:** Physical Education Opportunity for Exceptional Learners (Long, Irmer, Burkett, Glasenapp, & Odenkirk, 1980). *Opportunity* here refers to every student having a partner to enable learning and success.
11. **Special Olympics motto:** "Let me win. But if I cannot win, let me be brave in the attempt."
12. **National Disability Sports Alliance (NDSA) motto:** "Sports by ability, not disability."
13. **Disability Sports/USA motto:** "If I can do this [sports], I can do anything."
14. **Alcoholics Anonymous motto:** "God, Grant me the *serenity* to accept the things I cannot change; the *courage* to change the things I can; and the *wisdom* to know the difference."

interactions is typically guided by principles. **Outcomes** refers to the desired results; these are usually stated as goals.

Theories Underlying the Model

Systems theory, dynamical systems theory, and ecological theory (Boss, Doherty, LaRossa, Schumm, & Steinmetz, 1993) all contribute to instructional models. The I CAN, ABC, and ACTIVE curricular models are examples of systems theory. PAP-TE-CA illustrates dynamical systems theory and ecological theory.

    Systems theory, which evolved in the 1940s in conjunction with computer technology and information processing, is a linear approach to input, process, and output systems that enhances understanding of the whole. Systems theory starts with input (all the information that comes from planning, assessing, and prescribing), then moves to process (teaching, counseling, coaching, and consulting), and then focuses on outcomes that provide feedback for revising the process and starting the cycle again.

    Dynamical systems theory, which has been popular since the 1990s, is a modification of traditional systems theory, based on a recognition of the increasing complexity, multidimensionality, and interactiveness of the many chaotic systems in life (Smith & Thelen, 1993). For example, variables within the PAP-TE-CA model are conceptualized as continuously interacting in all directions (i.e., the systems are dynamic and sometimes described as chaotic). This is consistent with the trend away from linear thinking and toward interactional or dynamic thinking.

    Ecological theory, also increasingly popular since the 1990s, is an approach to analyzing the interactions and interde-

pendence between humans and all aspects of their environment, both physical and social. The PAP-TE-CA model, like the philosophy of this text, is ecological.

Interactiveness of Model Components

The evolving PAP-TE-CA model, consistent with trends of the 21st century, uses input, process, and outcome instructional components but emphasizes the dynamic, multidirectional, chaotic complexity of what occurs in the classroom. This complexity has long perplexed researchers and serves as one explanation of why so little research has been conducted on effective teaching in physical education. The model in Table 7.2 is based on reviews of research but also presents ideas and principles based on experience. This model is used to guide the organization of content about teaching on the following pages.

Inputs That Influence Teaching

Inputs have traditionally been classified as (a) **presage,** which means human predictor variables like age, gender, and perceived competence, and (b) **context,** which means nonhuman predictor variables like class size, facilities, and equipment (Dunkin & Biddle, 1974; Pivik, McComas, & Laflamme, 2002; Vogler, van der Mars, Cusimano, & Darst, 1992). Context variables like class size are better predictors of student achievement than presage variables are (Hellison & Walsh, 2002; Vogler et al., 1992). Neither experience nor expertise seems to affect teacher time usage in mainstream physical education (Vogler et al., 1992). However, experience does positively influence adapted physical activity planning behaviors (Solomon & Lee, 1991).

Table 7.2   Instructional model to guide thinking.

Inputs	Processes	Outcomes

Assessment of people (presage variables)
   Student
   Teacher
   Peers
   Family
   Significant others
Assessment of environment (context)
   Barriers
   Resources
   Class size
   Facilities
   Equipment
   Space
   Lighting, color
   Sound, distractions
   Etc.
Assessment of time
   PE time
   Recess
   Other class time
   After-school time
Assessment of opportunity
   Philosophy
   Cultural factors
   Economic factors
   Possibility of change
   Probability of change
	1. Maintain a warm, positive climate.
	2. Individualize instruction by making adaptations.
	3. Promote a data-based gymnasium.
	4. Use ecologically valid activities and settings.
	5. Devote a high percentage of time to class objectives.
	6. Maximize time-on-task with success.
	7. Emphasize variability of practice and contextual interference.
	8. Try a wide variety of strategies and techniques.
	9. Adapt teaching styles to individual needs.
	10. Apply behavior management strategies.
	11. Weave counseling into teaching.
		1. Students achieve IEP and other objectives.
		2. Teachers achieve objectives.
		3. Significant others achieve objectives.
		4. Laws and school policy are followed.
		5. Lawsuits are avoided.
		6. Family pride, school pride, and community pride are enhanced.
		7. Collaboration by home, school, and community is increased.

Teacher expectancy about student ability is an important variable in the teaching process (Karper & Martinek, 1985). Attitude research (Rizzo & Kirkendall, 1995; Rizzo & Vispoel, 1992) indicates that academic preparation in adapted physical activity and perceived competence of teachers (as opposed to age, gender, and experience) are significant predictors of attitudes toward teaching children with disabilities. This finding helps school systems justify in-service training for teachers.

Input About People

Concerning people (both students and teachers), some of the variables related to input are age, gender, ethnicity, socioeconomic class, culture or subculture, self-concept, attitudes, knowledge, actual and perceived competence, creativity, interests, concerns, motivations, expectations, perceptions, body build, emotions, personality, fears, health, fitness, teaching styles, preferred sensory modalities, abilities and disabilities, past history of opportunities and barriers, and beliefs, attitudes, and practices of significant others. Many of these variables are **situational or contextual,** meaning that they change with the situation, are positive when the person feels comfortable, and otherwise are negative.

Some personal variables affect physical education learning more directly than others. The use of cooperative or collaborative approaches to planning, assessing, and prescribing increases the likelihood of identifying and addressing the best set of personal variable inputs. In particular, the student variables of interest, motivation, and perceived usefulness of physical activities interact with process to affect goal achievement. These variables are strongly influenced by family and neighborhood leisure practices, facilities, and values; therefore, PAP-TE-CA functions should be based on concern for ecosystems rather than for individuals. Effective teachers make home visits and/or devise sport events that families attend, thereby creating opportunities for getting acquainted.

Input About Environment

Concerning physical environment, some of the variables are class size, facilities (indoor/outdoor), equipment, and school, home, and community resources (Pivik et al., 2002). When students have sensory or mobility impairments, it is especially important to analyze these categories into such components as space and surfaces, lighting and color, sounds, smells, weather and temperature conditions, pollutions and allergens, barriers, distance to bathrooms and water fountains, and optimal location of equipment. Skillful management of these variables and their relationships with people is extremely important in effective teaching.

Table 7.3   Thirty-minute lesson plan for running skills.

I.	**Introductory Activities**	**5 min**
	a. A 1-min or less attendance-taking protocol	
	b. Obstacle or challenge course *or*	
	c. Group aerobics with music	
II.	**Body of Lesson**	**21 min**
	a. Self-testing (state number of trials)	5 min
	b. Two games (8 min each)	16 min
	2 min—instructions	
	1 min—get into formation	
	5 min—actual activity	
III.	**Summary/Evaluation/Cool-Down**	**4 min**
	a. Group or partner discussion *or*	
	b. Individual counseling	
	Total	**30 min**

Input About Time

Careful planning, assessing, and prescribing of physical education time is critical to effective teaching. Of course, lesson plans are important in all kinds of teaching, but their use is essential in structuring goal-specific instruction for students with disabilities.

Developing Lesson Plans

Lesson plans should include three parts: introductory activity, lesson body, and summary. Table 7.3 outlines a 30-min elementary school lesson plan designed to achieve goals in running skills, self-concept, social interactions, and play and game concepts.

The **introductory activity** (about 5 min) is usually an obstacle course, game, or dance activity in which everyone is involved. Physiologically, this is warm-up time, but instruction should be directed toward self-concept and social interactions by stressing that warm-ups are the way we show respect and appreciation for our bodies and prevent injury. Also during this time, we get in touch with our body and establish a mental attitude favorable to learning. The first 5 min are also a time for partner interactions, particularly in class structures guided by social competence and inclusion goals.

The **lesson body** (21 min) is specific to the individual. It is divided between self-testing and game activities for achieving functional competence. Note that a group game usually requires at least 8 min (2 min of teacher talk, 1 min to get into formation, and 5 min of actual activity). Every minute must be carefully used. Waste during transitions from one activity to another can be eliminated by the rule that everyone must be in place within 60 sec. The transition time is structured by counting, a timer that buzzes, or tape-recorded music.

Self-testing is usually done in stations and guided by task cards. These state what skill is to be practiced, under what conditions (e.g., size, weight, and color of ball; distance from target; type of target), and number of trials. Task cards are kept at stations, stored in individual mailboxes or in files containing clipboards. Or they may be made of heavy cardboard with string attached for wearing around the neck.

The **summary** (4 min) can be activity or talk time or both. Physiologically, this is cool-down and relaxation time. In terms of self-concept, this is evaluation and cooperative goal-setting time. Emphasis should be on (a) "How are we going to use what we learned today?" (b) "To whom can we show our new skills?" (c) "How much can we practice this at home?" and (d) "Who can we practice with?" Students need this kind of reinforcement to internalize that they have learned something, met their goals, and so on.

Linking Lessons With Objectives

Each part of the lesson plan should be directly linked to objectives. Some of these require time of their own, whereas others are embedded in activities that teach motor skills and practice. There are not enough minutes of instructional time in a semester to permit free play. When free time is awarded as part of a behavior management approach, the freedom should be to choose from among established activities that reinforce learning of objectives, not the freedom to engage in social dance, card games, and other activities that are unrelated to physical education objectives.

Table 7.4 shows specifically how class activities contribute to four objectives for running games. Motor skills and patterns are broken down into two objectives, and most of class time is spent on these. Skill time, however, is task analyzed into listening, getting into formation, and actual learning or practice. Self-concept is broken down into two objectives and allotted 10 min, the parts of the lesson designated as introduction and summary. Social interactions and play and game behaviors are broken down into two and three objectives, respectively, and allocated no time because their achievement is embedded in other activities.

Using Out-of-School Time

When working toward lifespan active, healthy lifestyle, teachers must involve students and parents in structuring out-of-school time to include physical education and recreation experiences. All should cooperatively agree upon homework that requires students to submit activity logs or journals recording the number of minutes spent in vigorous physical activity each day and time spent in various roles (spectator as well as participant) in community facilities. Family trips should be planned to include disability sport events like wheelchair basketball and tennis, Special Olympics, and Deaf sport. Likewise, families should participate together in mainstream sport events.

Socializing Children Into Sport

These uses of time may be considered transition activities in the IEP, but essentially family and community sport and fitness activities are the primary means for socializing children into sport. The earlier these activities begin, the more likely it is that individuals with disabilities will develop beliefs, attitudes, and practices necessary to achieve active, healthy lifestyles. Families in which neither parent has an interest in or time for sport

Table 7.4   Daily plan showing how objectives direct the use of time.

Goal	Objectives	Minutes per Day

Motor skills and patterns	1. To run 50-m dash in 9.9 sec or less
	Activity—Self-testing: Race against best time
	  a. Listen to instructions
	  b. Get into formations
	  c. Stay on-task
	2. To demonstrate functional competence in 10 running games
	Activity—Running games
	  a. Listen to instructions
	  b. Get into formations
	  c. Stay on-task
		20

Self-concept	1. To feel good about self in running activities
	Activity—Embedded
	Activity—Discussions
	  a. Pregame visual imagery: "I am good at running"
	  b. Prompts and praise
	  c. Postgame evaluation: Tell things you did well
	  d. Ask others what you did well
	2. To respect self and body
	Activity—Embedded
	Activity—Warm-up and cool-down
	  a. Listen to instructions
	  b. Stay on-task
	  c. Discuss why this is good for body
	  d. Praise and prompts
		10

Social interactions	1. To say hello and good-bye to at least 3 relevant persons 2. To praise at least one person during every 5 min of game time Activity—Embedded, but may need prompts	0
Play and game behaviors	1. To listen to 2 min of teacher talk (game instructions) without interruption 2. To stay on-task during a 5-min game 3. To get into designated formations within 60-sec count Activity—Embedded, but may need prompts	0

Note. Social interactions and play and game behaviors are not assigned minutes of their own because their achievement is embedded in other activities.

should be encouraged to employ a "big brother" or "big sister" or find resources for transporting the children to community recreation programs. Adapted physical activity professionals are key people in promoting the wise use of leisure time.

Input About Opportunity

The last input in Table 7.2 to be assessed, planned, and prescribed is opportunity, which can be broken down into family, school, and community positives and negatives in relation to individual students. Opportunity is largely determined by cultural, economic, and moral variables: for instance, how power structures choose to allocate resources, and whether minority groups challenge choices that they perceive as unfair. Assessment should focus on philosophy, the identification of what needs to be changed, and the planning of strategies to promote change. Under philosophy, topics of particular concern include architectural, attitudinal, and aspirational barriers; placement practices

and contexts; criteria used to evaluate teachers and programs; expectations and traditions; required curricular elements or content by outside agencies; and the support of significant and/or powerful others.

The Teaching Process and Outcomes

Effective teaching is defined in many ways. At the beginning of this chapter we said that teaching is effective when certain indicators are present. These indicators can be converted to instructional principles (see the Processes column of Table 7.2), and evaluation can focus on the extent to which these principles are followed. Effective teaching can also be defined in terms of product or outcomes—specifically, whether the process results in optimal goal achievement (see the Outcomes column of Table 7.2).

The next section presents instructional principles. In implementing these principles, teachers must constantly be aware of the four types of inputs (people, physical setting, time, opportunity) and skillfully manage input, process, and outcome interrelationships so as to promote optimal goal achievement.

1. Maintain a Warm, Positive Learning Climate

Warm, positive environments involve personalization; nurturing; high rates of positive interactions; high but realistic expectations; cooperative relationships and activities; mutual respect; availability of many choices; treatment with dignity, fairness, and inclusiveness; seeing every child as a winner; and focusing on abilities, not disabilities. Teachers need to establish criteria for determining whether their classrooms have warm, positive climates. The theory guiding this principle comes primarily from Maslow (1954, 1970) and Rogers (1951, 1969).

One criterion might be the number of times that students are called by their first names and the number of times they receive personal attention, assuming that these episodes are positive in nature. The use of a videotape protocol or a small tape recorder attached to the body enables teachers to check themselves on the number and types of personalizations. For example, when a 9-year-old boy in a wheelchair was integrated into a class of 20, Heikinaro-Johansson et al. (1995) reported that personal attention was given to this student an average of 5 times, each episode varying from 0.5 to 1.8 min in duration, during 45-min sessions.

Others have defined a positive climate as one in which teacher-student interactions are (a) more positive than negative or corrective, (b) more skill than behavior oriented, and (c) more specific than general in nature (Vogler, van der Mars, Darst, & Cusimano, 1990). For example, an analysis of 30 mainstreamed elementary classes indicated 70% positive feedback, 10% negative feedback, and 20% corrective feedback; 72% motor skill feedback and 28% behavior feedback; and 63% general and 37% specific feedback (Vogler, van der Mars, et al., 1990). Thus, 2 out of 3 of the criteria for a positive climate were met. The last criterion, giving specific rather than general feedback, is one that teachers often fail to meet, indicating that more attention should be given to this in teacher training.

Feedback, broadly defined, includes all interactions (verbal and nonverbal). Who initiates these interactions and under what conditions is important, especially when inclusiveness is a criterion for a warm, positive climate. Students must be systematically taught to praise each other and to give other kinds of positive feedback (see Chapters 8 and 9).

2. Individualize Instruction by Making Adaptations

A warm, positive learning climate is also enhanced by teacher flexibility in assessing and implementing adaptations that might help individual students be more successful. This principle was explained fully in Chapters 3 and 4. Equipment, facilities, body position, time and space requirements, and other variables can be easily adapted by creative teachers and students working together to achieve personal bests. The metatheory underlying this principle is adaptation theory (Kiphard, 1983; Sherrill, 1997a, b). This metatheory is supported by the work of many

leaders (e.g., Kalyvas & Reid, 2003; Morris & Stiehl, 1999; Mosston & Ashworth, 1994).

3. Promote a Data-Based Gymnasium

The data-based gymnasium (DBG) concept is usually associated with a behavior management curriculum model (Dunn et al., 1986). In this text, however, the concept refers to **individualization of instruction,** which means basing classroom decisions on student performance data. The use of an IEP or IFSP individualizes goals, objectives, and overall instructional services for a set number of weeks, but *the DBG concept emphasizes minute-by-minute individualization* within a specific lesson. This requires continuous assessment and record keeping in conjunction with instruction. The number of trials is prescribed for practice of each part of a motor skill or game, and a pass or fail is recorded for each trial. Hence, DBG is often called the clipboard system. DBG is supported by the many behavior management theories (e.g., Lavay, French, & Henderson, 1997; Lucyshyn, Duncap, & Albin, 2002).

Part Method Versus Whole Method

DBG was developed originally for students with severe mental retardation, whom research shows to learn better by the part method than by the whole method (Weld & Evans, 1990). The **whole method** (total task presentation through demonstration and/or verbal instructions) is typically used (a) with students who have no cognitive or attention problems and (b) when the task to be learned is relatively easy. When a student has difficulty learning through the whole method, various whole-part-whole combinations are generally introduced. It is important to demonstrate the whole, however, so students can conceptualize where their practice of parts is leading.

Two types of part methods are common. In the **pure part method,** each part is practiced separately many times before all are combined or chained. Beginning swimming illustrates this, in that a float is practiced many, many times before arms, legs, and breathing are added. In the **progressive part method,** parts of a skill are chained together in a particular order, generally in either a forward or a backward order.

Traditional Task Analysis by Parts and Steps

The use of part methods of teaching depends on skill in **task analysis,** the breaking down of a task into its parts and the ordering of these parts from easy to hard. For example, for persons with mild to moderate mental retardation, bowling might be broken down into four parts:

A. Raise the ball chest high and step forward on the right foot.

B. Step forward on the left foot and push the ball forward.

C. Step forward on the right foot and swing the ball backward.

D. Step forward on the left foot, swing the ball forward, and release the ball in the direction of the pins.

Typically, either forward or backward chaining is prescribed as the strategy for practicing a task analysis and encoding a motor skill into short-term memory. **Forward chaining** refers to practicing the first part in the chain until a specific criterion is reached, then learning the second part and combining it with the first, then learning the third part and combining it with the first and second parts, and so on. Using the bowling task analysis, a forward chain might be A; A and B; A, B, and C; A, B, C, and D. **Backward chaining** is the reverse (e.g., D; C and D; B, C, and D; A, B, C, and D). *Backward chaining is particularly effective in movement patterns like bowling, throwing, and kicking,* in which the last step is dramatic and constitutes a reward within itself (e.g., the noise of a ball hitting a target or striking a ball). Research particularly supports backward chaining for teaching bowling (Hsu & Dunn, 1984).

The number and size of parts in a task analysis must be consistent with the student's ability level. For persons with severe mental retardation, Phase 1 of a task analysis might be this:

A. Sit facing the pins and holding an adapted ball by its spring-loaded retractable handle.

B. Swing the arm forward with assistance and release the handle.

Phase 1 would be repeated until a criterion is met, like Knocks down at least one pin in 8 out of 10 trials. Then Phase 2, in which B is altered to include a backward and a forward swing, with assistance, is introduced. In Phase 3 the adaptation might be no assistance. Phase 4 might involve doing the movement from a standing position.

After practice of parts enables a student to perform a motor skill that is fairly functional, the teacher develops checklists of easy to difficult steps to guide further learning of the skill. **Steps** are learning increments or additional breakdowns in task phases that gradually increase task difficulty. Examples of some checklists of steps follow.

A first checklist or learning progression might read:

1. Jump down from an 8-in step.
2. Jump down from a 12-in step.
3. Jump down from an 18-in bench.
4. Jump down from a 24-in bench.
5. Perform a challenge course that requires jumping down from varying heights.

A second learning progression might read:
1. Jump forward 6 in.
2. Jump forward 12 in.
3. Jump forward 18 in.
4. Play a game with others called "Jumping the stream" or "Crossing the brook."

A third learning progression might read:
1. Jump over a rope 3 in high.
2. Jump over a rope 6 in high.
3. Jump over a rope 12 in high.
4. Play a game with others that involves jumping over a rope or bar.

Note that task analysis teaching should end with the ability to perform the task in a game, sport, or fitness setting. This ability is called **functional competence.**

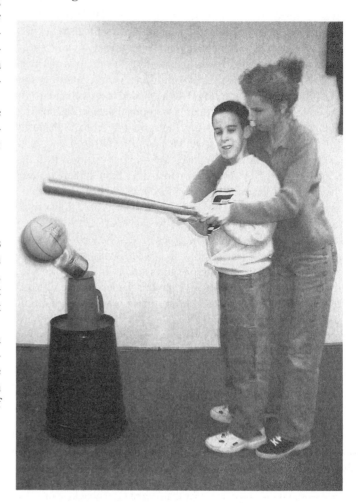

Figure 7.2 Physical and verbal assistance enhance teaching children with severe disabilities to bat. Note that the target is waist high to make the skill easier. A ball on top of a coffee can is an excellent target because noise is reinforcing.

Levels of Assistance

In performing a task or sequence of tasks, students require different levels of assistance: physical, visual, verbal, or a combination of these (Figure 7.2). Evaluation and record keeping entail writing next to the task the type of assistance needed. A student might progress, for instance, through the following levels of assistance:

1. **P**—Performs overarm throw with *physical* and verbal assistance.

2. **D**—Performs overarm throw with visual and verbal assistance (i.e., a *demonstration* accompanied by explanation).

3. **C5**—Performs overarm throw with much verbal assistance (i.e., *cues* throughout the sequence).

4. **C1**—Performs overarm throw with minimal verbal assistance (i.e., one or two *cues* only).

5. **I**—Performs overarm throw with no assistance (i.e., *independently*).

These five levels of assistance can be applied to a single step within a task analysis or to a movement pattern or a sequence of movement patterns (i.e., folk dance). Use of initials to represent levels facilitates ease of record keeping and lesson writing.

Physical assistance should always be accompanied by verbal cues. These cues can be spoken, chanted, or sung. Physical assistance should never be called "physical manipulation" (a medical term often used in therapy and orthopedics). Several learning theorists have created good synonyms for physical assistance. The term **coactive movement,** taken from the Van Dijk (1966) approach from Holland, is now widely used throughout the world in working with individuals who are Deaf-blind (Leuw, 1972). In coactive movement, the bodies of the teacher and student move as one, closely touching, in activities like rolling, seat scooting, creeping, knee walking, and upright walking. As the student gets the feel of the task, the distance between the two bodies is gradually increased. The emphasis is then on **mirroring** (i.e., imitating the teacher's movements).

Behavior Management

The DBG concept also requires record keeping on which kind of instructions (cues) and reinforcements (rewards) are best for each student. This information is often specific to a particular task analysis, so lots of data are maintained on each student, with dates that indicate mastery of phases and steps of the task analysis. DBG obviously requires a very low teacher–student ratio, preferably one to one, so students are totally active during the lesson. This requires the training and supervision of volunteers. Additional information about behavior management is provided later in the chapter because behavior management can be used in conjunction with any instructional principle or program.

4. Devote a High Percentage of Time to Class Objectives

The principle of devoting a high percentage of time to class objectives emphasizes that every class activity should pertain to a particular objective on the student's IEP. The average time allocated to elementary and secondary physical education is 30 and 50 min, respectively. This means that no time can be wasted. There should be no free time. If free time is promised as a behavior management strategy for being good, the free time should be structured as two or three choices of activity, each of which relates to instructional objectives.

Since the early 1980s effective teaching in physical education has been assessed by examining teacher behaviors. Research indicates that teachers spend too much time on managerial tasks (about 25 to 30%) and on instruction (defined as demonstrating and explaining, about 30%), which leaves only 40 to 45% of class time for students to be actively involved in movement related to class or individual objectives (Siedentop, 1983).

Following are categories of teacher behaviors used in analyzing use of time. Videotape yourself or have a friend observe and analyze how you spend your time by putting

tally marks next to each observed behavior. This principle is guided by Siedentop (1983) and many others.

Teacher Behaviors

Teacher behaviors include the following:

1. **Managing:** Taking roll; making general announcements; giving directions about getting into formations, using equipment, or following safety rules; organizing activities and transitions; record keeping; attending to recording equipment, aides, or volunteers

2. **Instructing:** Demonstrating and explaining activities related to instructional objectives; conducting closure episodes related to objectives

3. **Monitoring:** Observing students but giving no feedback

4. **Feedback:** Responding to student words or actions that relate to instructional objectives (i.e., teacher responses to students who are engaged in assigned motor activity). *Specific feedback* (related to the task) is preferred over *general* feedback like global phrases, "Good!" "Great."

5. **Controlling:** Using disciplinary techniques directed toward off-task behaviors of students

Concerns About Teacher Behaviors

Most research shows that teachers talk too much and too long when giving initial instructions and that they spend too much time getting students into game formations, stations, or floor spots. Another common weakness, once students begin to practice or play, is to observe but not offer specific feedback. Effective teaching takes lots of energy because the teacher should be moving constantly from student to student, using their names, and giving specific praise and correctional feedback. Teacher movement around the room, location at specific intervals, and proximity to students are additional variables to assess. A good rule of thumb *is to always be standing within a giant step of one or more students,* close enough that they can hear feedback and establish eye contact. Another guideline is to blow the whistle or interrupt the whole class as little as possible, because such actions cause transitions in student attention and decrease on-task time (Vogler, van der Mars, et al., 1990).

5. Maximize Time-on-Task With Success

Time-on-task is defined as the actual number of minutes that a student is engaged motorically in activities related to his or her individual objectives. This variable is often called **Academic Learning Time–Physical Education (ALT-PE)** because the curriculum and instruction subdiscipline uses this abbreviation (DePaepe, 1985; Temple & Walkley, 1999; Vogler, van der Mars, et al., 1990; Webster, 1987). Success is defined in various ways but usually refers to (a) the student and teacher feeling good about the learning process, (b) mastery or observable improvement, and (c) agreement between the student and the teacher that a personal best is occurring or has been exerted. These criteria must be written so they are measurable (e.g., as Likert scales). Following are categories of student behaviors that can be used in assessing how students use class time.

Student Behaviors

Student behaviors include the following:

1. **Management responses:** Following teacher instructions pertaining to class routines and activities that do not provide practice of motor skills, fitness, games, or other objectives (e.g., listening for roll call, getting out or putting away equipment, moving to stations or getting into formations)

2. **Knowledge assimilation:** Receiving information or instructions pertaining to objectives

3. **Time-on-task:** Engaging in tasks related to objectives (a) with success (implying appropriate), and (b) without success (implying inappropriate)

4. **Waiting:** Unoccupied or inappropriately occupied time between turns or beginning of new activity

5. **Time-off-task:** Time spent not engaged in the activity in which student should be engaged

Concerns About Student Behaviors

Research indicates that time-on-task is low compared with other categories (Vogler, van der Mars, et al., 1990), largely because of teaching behaviors. The principle of maximizing student time-on-task should be given high priority. Support for this principle is the central theme of several curricular models (e.g., ACTIVE, Every Child A Winner, You Stay Active).

Research has documented that several strategies do increase time-on-task; these should be used as much as possible. Individualized instruction within a mainstream setting, for instance, increases time-on-task (Aufderheide, 1983). The use of peer tutors (DePaepe, 1985; Webster, 1987) and of specific feedback and reinforcers (Webster, 1993) also increases time-on-task.

Of particular concern is how integration of students with severe disabilities into general classrooms affects the time-on-task of students with and without disabilities. Physical education research concerning this issue indicates that students with severe disabilities need extensive support services when taught in mainstream settings (DePaepe, 1985; Vogler et al., 1992). For example, Vogler et al. (1992) reported that behaviors of students with severe disabilities were significantly less motor-appropriate and more off-task than those of nondisabled peers and that the experience level and expertise of teachers seemed to make no difference in this finding. Special education research tends to find comparable levels of engaged time for students with and without severe disabilities (e.g., Hollowood, Salisbury, Rainforth, & Palombaro, 1994), but high levels of support services are present in such studies.

Although time-on-task is important, be aware that the underlying assumption that students learn by repetition deserves consideration. The amount of practice and the type of practice (massed versus distributed; blocked versus random) is specific to individual students and tasks. **Massed practice** is continuous (with very little rest, less than 5 sec between trials), until a criterion is reached, and is associated with pure part and progressive part instruction (Weld & Evans, 1990). **Distributed practice** is intermittent or episodic, with breaks for rest or different content.

When whole or whole-part-whole pedagogy is used to teach a new skill to students without disabilities, *distributed practice* is considered better than massed; *short* practices are better than long; and *frequent* practices are better than infrequent. Little is known, however, about how students with disabilities respond to different kinds of practice, although some research has focused on blocked versus random order of tasks and indicates that random order of presentation is better (Painter, Inman, & Vincent, 1994; Porretta & O'Brien, 1991).

6. Use Ecologically Valid Activities and Settings

The instructional principle of using ecologically valid activities and settings emphasizes selecting content that enables the student to function better in her or his ecosystem (i.e., the real world). In the I CAN instructional model, the *A* for "Associate all learnings" refers to strategies that increase ecological validity. *This is variously called the principle of social validity, ecological validity, or functionality.* Each term captures the idea that the activity is practical, useful, meaningful, age appropriate, developmentally appropriate, and generalizable to real-life situations. Because traditional task analyses often do not meet these criteria, ecological task analysis has been proposed as an alternative approach (Balan & Davis, 1993; Davis & Burton, 1991). This principle is supported by leaders in many fields (e.g., Block, 2000; Lucyshyn et al., 2002; Sherrill, 1998).

Ecological Task Analysis (An Adaptation Process)

Ecological task analysis (ETA) is an adaptation process that starts with the selection of a real-life function, focuses on relationships between the learner and the environment, and analyzes variables into factors and levels that relate to real-life conditions. **Function** refers to the ability to perform the tasks of daily living, work, or play. Depending upon its complexity, function can be specified as *tasks* (locomotor, nonlocomotor, and object control), *problem-solving processes* (skills, strategies, rules, interpersonal relations), or *lead-up activities* (games, drills, relays, races, or routines). Figure 7.3 shows the process of (a) specifying a function; (b) selecting a target task; (c) analyzing the task into variables, factors, and levels; and (d) determining the conditions requisite to success.

Ecological task analysis can be applied to planning, assessment, or instruction. These are often interwoven and occur simultaneously rather than sequentially. Whenever possible, the student is involved in each step.

In explaining the theory underlying task analysis, Davis and Burton (1991) emphasized that ETA focuses on relationships between the learner and the ecosystem, not on parts. Thus, ETA creates new relationships as variables, factors, and levels are altered to enhance success.

Table 7.5 shows that, ultimately, many factors and levels compose the conditions requisite to performing self-care,

Figure 7.3　Vocabulary for ecological task analysis. Note that a task is analyzed into *variables*. Variables are analyzed into *factors*. Factors are analyzed into levels that are designated when writing goals.

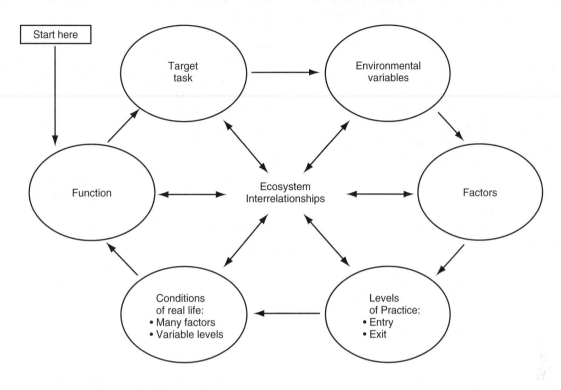

Table 7.5　Illustrative ecological task analysis.

Variables	Factors	Levels
1. Ball	Size	Large, medium, small
	Momentum	None, slow, fast
	Height	Waist, higher, lower
2. Model or demonstration	Type	Live, videotaped
	Age	Same age, older, younger
	Pattern	Forehand, backhand
3. Verbal instructions	Duration	Short, medium, long
	Timing	Concurrent, before
4. Reinforcers	Type	Verbal, smile, touch
	Timing	Immediate, delayed
	Frequency	Every trial, every three trials

play, or work functions. **Condition** is defined as the combination of relationships that students must handle to be successful in real life. For example, to play simple ball games, they must cope with changing speeds and directions of the other players as well as the ball. If outdoors, they must also cope with variable ground, lighting, and sound relationships.

　　Instructional objectives, to be effective, must specify conditions. If the *function* is to play a tennis lead-up game and the *task* is to strike a ball, then the *objective* might be *"Given certain conditions, the student will strike a tennis ball over the net so that it lands inside the boundary lines."* The conditions might be (a) a regulation racket, (b) an outdoor court with good surface, (c) 15 trials not facing the sun and 15 trials facing it, (d) wind factor not more than 10 mph, and (e) balls directed at slow and medium speeds so that they land in front of the student into three areas designated as midline, left, and right. Conditions in a objective should be as close as possible to the typical game setting.

　　Assessment and ecological task analysis are interwoven in the adaptation process of moving the student from entry to exit level. For most beginners in racket sports, for example, the easiest ball-size level is large. The easiest momentum level may be none, so practice consists of running three steps forward and striking a suspended motionless ball. Waist high is the easiest height level for most persons. Teachers involve students in helping to select the easiest levels and then summarize findings into a plan that describes the entry-level condition and specifies the number of practice trials. For some variables, there is general agreement about a complexity continuum from easy to difficult. However, what is easy for one person may not be easy for another. Therefore, assessment encompasses cooperative teacher-student problem solving to determine the order in which tasks are taught.

Generalization or Transfer

Classroom learning is meaningless if generalization does not occur. **Generalization** refers to the transfer of learning from one piece of equipment to another and from one setting to another. In students with intact intelligence, generalization usually occurs without specific training. When teaching students with MR, however, generalization should be built into task sequences. For example, a learning progression might read

1. Roll 10-in rubber ball toward milk cartons.
2. Roll 10-in rubber ball toward bowling pins.
3. Roll bowling ball toward bowling pins.
4. Roll boccia ball toward target ball.
5. Roll 10-in rubber ball toward persons inside a circle (as in dodgeball).

Such tasks should be practiced on different surfaces (grass, dirt, floor) and in different environments (gymnasium, outdoors, bowling alley). Use generalization training to develop creativity in students. Repeatedly ask, "How many things can we make roll? How many places can we go to roll things? At how many targets can we roll things?"

Acquisition, Retention, and Maintenance

These terms, used in behavior management, refer to phases of mastery and generally are assessed objectively by recording the number of correct trials completed. Acquisition or initial mastery occurs when the objective (a set number of correct trials during one session) is met. Retention and maintenance, sometimes used as synonyms, refer to demonstrated ability several days (or months) later than the acquisition date. It is important that all phases be conducted in ecologically valid settings.

Activity Analysis

Activity analysis is the process of breaking down an activity into the behavioral components requisite for success. In physical education and recreation, the activity to be analyzed is usually a game, sport, or exercise. The process can, however, be directed toward activities of daily living, leisure, or work. Whereas special educators and physical educators commonly use the terms *task analysis* and *activity analysis* interchange-

ably, therapeutic recreation specialists and occupational therapists prefer *activity analysis*. This is because they are concerned with the total activity, not just the motor skill and fitness requisites.

Activity analysis typically entails consideration of the three educational domains: cognitive, psychomotor, and affective. Table 7.6 presents an activity analysis for a simple tag game. This type of detailed analysis is needed in teaching games to students with severe disabilities. Note the use of props like a beanbag, squeaky toy, orange, or make-believe tail; a prop is usually necessary with children deficient in pretending skills; otherwise, they simply cannot understand the point of chasing and fleeing.

Prior to being taught the simple tag game described in Table 7.6, children should have learned games involving only one or two concepts: *stop-start,* as in "red light, green light," musical chairs, and follow-the-leader; and *safety–not safety,* as in "Flying Dutchman" and "huntsman" (see Chapter 15). In developmental progressions for teaching games, tag is relatively difficult. Tag involves eight concepts: start–stop, safety–not safety, chasing, tagging, fleeing, dodging, penalty, and changing roles. When mental retardation is severe, each concept must be taught and practiced separately; then, chains of concepts must be practiced. Task and activity analyses are essential processes in the assessment and instruction of students with disabilities.

7. Emphasize Variability of Practice and Contextual Interference

The essence of teaching students who are clumsy or have disabilities is captured in the motto *Try another way* (Gold, 1980). Success-oriented physical education depends on the collaborative creativity of the teacher and students in practicing skills in as many ways as possible and trying alternative pedagogies and adaptations until the best way for a particular individual or group is found (see Figure 7.4).

Research indicates that having students practice at many levels (e.g., large, medium, small balls; short, medium, long distances) and under variable conditions leads to success (Eidson & Stadulis, 1991; Weber & Thorpe, 1989). This is called the **variability of practice principle** and is supported by creativity theory and movement education pedagogy.

Closely associated with the variability of practice principle is **contextual interference,** a motor learning term for testing memory by involving persons in an unrelated activity between skill practice time and retention testing time. The unrelated activity is the contextual interference. An example is when you come to class ready to take a test, but your professor gives a lecture the first half of the period and the test the second half. The lecture, filled with new material, interrupts your concentration on the old facts; it serves as contextual interference.

Blocked Versus Random Trials

To understand the difference between blocked and random trials, suppose you wish to teach beanbag or soft shot throwing at a floor target. When a regulation soft shot and target are used, this task is an official cerebral palsy sport for individuals with severe disabilities (see Chapter 25). You need to specify the

Table 7.6 Behavioral requirements of a simple tag game: An activity analysis showing teaching progression.

Cognitive

1. Responds to name
2. Follows simple directions:
   a. "Sit down."
   b. "Stay."
   c. "Stand up."
   d. "Run."
3. Responds appropriately to cues:
   a. "Stop," "Start"
   b. "Good," "Bad"
4. Attends to teacher long enough to grasp game structure and rules:
   a. Visually
   b. Auditorily
5. Understands fleeing role:
   a. "You (Amy) have a beanbag, squeaky toy, orange, or make-believe tail."
   b. "Someone (Bob) wants it."
   c. "You (Amy) do not want Bob to have object."
   d. "You (Amy) run away from Bob when I give cue."
6. Understands chasing role:
   a. "Bob chases you when I give cue."
   b. "Bob chases you until
      (1) you touch safety base or
      (2) he tags you."
7. Understands concept of safety base
8. Understands concepts of tagging, penalty, and changing roles
   a. "When tagged, the penalty is you must give Bob the object."
   b. "You change roles because you want the object (i.e., you chase Bob or someone else who has object)."

Affective

1. Has fun
   a. Is not frightened by being chased
   b. Is sufficiently involved that attention does not wander
   c. Smiles and/or makes joyous sounds
2. Shows awareness of others
3. Displays competitive spirit
4. Tags other person gently

Psychomotor

1. Performs motor skills
   a. Runs
   b. Dodges/ducks
   c. Tags
2. Demonstrates sufficient fitness
   a. Does not become breathless
   b. Does not develop muscle cramps

types of throws (underarm, overarm, and side or hook), the number of trials, and the order of the trials. A good decision might be 15 trials of each type of throw every day for 6 weeks. In a **blocked condition,** students would perform all trials of one type of throw before practicing the next type of throw. In a **random condition,** students would practice each type of throw in a random order, with no type performed more than two times consecutively. Research indicates that students in a random practice condition tend to develop accuracy in the target toss more quickly than students in a blocked condition do (Painter et al., 1994).

Contextual Interference, Retention, and Transfer

After skill practice each day, a good strategy is to provide a **contextual interference activity** for about 10 min during which

students play a game that does not necessarily use the skills just practiced. Then a **retention test** is given (e.g., two trials of each type of throw at the target) in either random or blocked order. This allows the teacher to check whether the skill level achieved during practice is retained. Usually random order is prescribed in retention tests because most game situations call for random responses. A **transfer test** is also often administered; this is a test that uses the new skill in performing a novel task. In this example, a novel task might require transfer of learning from beanbags and a floor target to the use of balls to knock down a bowling ball.

Ecological Task Analysis, Movement Education, and Creativity Theory

Ecological task analysis (ETA), movement education pedagogy, and creativity theory all offer pedagogy that supports variability of practice. Each of these approaches emphasizes exploring the many different ways a task can be performed and encouraging students to make choices with respect to the use of their body parts, objects, and equipment.

Two traits of creativity—fluency and flexibility—are important in variability of practice.

Conceptualize a movement education session in which you want every student to have a ball or projectile of some kind. They do not all have to have the same kind. How many different kinds can you think of? **Fluency** *is your ability to generate a large number of relevant responses. When you thought of different kinds, did you vary your ideas with respect to size, weight, shape, color, texture, and composition?* **Flexibility** *is your ability to shift categories and think of different kinds. Table 7.7 gives a sampling of the fluent and flexible responses you might have made.*

Having thought of numerous alternatives, the next step is to match balls and projectiles with the students' abilities. A student who has coordination problems needs something big and soft. One with grasp and release problems (cerebral palsy) might do best with a yarn or Nerf (sponge rubber) ball. A student who is blind needs an object with a bell or noisemaker in it, whereas a student who is visually impaired simply needs a bright color like yellow. Someone in a wheelchair can profit from a string attached to the ball to facilitate recovery, whereas a hyperactive or high-energy student can enjoy a "crazy ball" with unpredictable bounces and great distance capacity.

Table 7.7   How creative are you?

Regulation Round Balls That Vary in Size, Weight, Texture	Homemade Projectiles	Projectiles of Varying Shapes
Baseballs	Beanbags: 3 × 3 in small; 5 × 5 in jumbo	Airplanes (paper, cloth)
Basketballs	Clay	Arrows
Boccia balls	Cork	Balloons
Bowling balls	Felt	Beanbags (soft shots)
Cage balls: 18, 24, 30, 36, 48, 60 and 72 in	Foam	Beans
Croquet balls	Leather	Clubs
Golf balls	Nerf ball	Coffee can lids (plastic)
Field hockey balls	Nylon sock, stuffed	Coins
Lacrosse balls	Paper crumpled into ball	Darts
Marbles	Plastic: Ping-Pong balls, scoop balls, whiffle balls	Discs
Medicine balls: 4–5 lb, 6–7 lb, 8–9 lb, 11–12 lb, 14–15 lb	Rubber	Footballs
Playground balls: 5, 6, 7, 8½, 10, 13, and 16 in	Snowballs	Frisbees
Racket balls	Sponge	Hoops
Rhythm balls: 3¼-in	Velcro-covered yarnballs	Horseshoes
Soccer balls		Javelins
Softballs: 9, 10, and 12 in		Lemmi sticks
Table tennis (Ping-Pong)		Paper plate Frisbees
Tennis ball		Peas
Tetherball		Pucks: shuffleboard, ice hockey
Volleyball		Rings (quoits): plastic game rings, embroidery hoops, canning rubbers
Water polo ball		Rocks (pebbles)
		Shots: iron or plastic
		Shuttlecocks
		Yardsticks

Next, pretend that you have a class of 10 students, each with a different disability, but all needing to work on objectives pertaining to throwing. Your assessment records reveal that the students represent all the different stages of throwing ability. Specific objectives to be worked on have been circled on each student's assessment form. In this kind of setting, the more projectiles the students experiment with, the more likely it is that their skills will generalize from one game or sport to another. The important thing is that the students do not get bored, that each has a maximum number of trials to practice, and that each experiences some success.

Developing throwing skills often takes 5 or 10 min of every class period for several weeks. How many different targets can you think of, and how will you organize your space for the different kinds of projectiles and targets? Appropriate degree of difficulty is essential to both success and motivation. How can you change projectiles and/or targets to organize stations for students needing easy, medium, or difficult learning progressions? The number of different kinds of targets you conceptualize is a measure of fluency. If your targets are of different colors, sizes, shapes, heights, widths, and materials, you have demonstrated good flexibility (the ability to think of different categories). If some of your targets make noise or fall down when they are hit, you are more likely to maximize on-task practice time. Have you devised moving as well as stationary targets? Targets that integrate story, television, or movie themes are a measure of originality. If these have a lot of detail, lending themselves to different scoring systems, you have demonstrated elaboration.

So now you have targets! How many different kinds of games can you devise for teaching and practicing throwing? How many different scoring systems can you think of? How many ways can a student experience success? Try applying this process to teaching other motor skills. Will it work in the development of specific play and/or social skills?

Individualization and Variability

Instruction can be individualized through creative teaching and/or adapting pedagogy, content, and environment to specific needs of students. The individualized education program (IEP) required by law is based on the belief that teachers are creative. Individualization does not mean teaching one-to-one, but changing classroom organization and pedagogical approaches to meet the needs of individuals.

Integration of students with disabilities into general physical education tends to make classes more *heterogeneous* (encompassing wide individual differences). Integration does not necessarily increase heterogeneity with regard to psychomotor abilities, however, since students in general classes have always displayed a wide range of motor abilities. Some students with disabilities are better in motor ability than their nondisabled peers. Mental retardation (MR), learning disabilities (LD), and emotional disturbances (ED) primarily affect heterogeneity in cognitive and affective behaviors (i.e., actual game behaviors like rules, strategies, sportsmanship). Sensory impairments primarily affect mode of presentation and enhancement of environmental stimuli.

All in all, integration within the gymnasium setting affects group dynamics and interpersonal relationships more than actual motor teaching and learning. Individual differences generally intensify problems of classroom management, motivation, and discipline. *Teachers of mainstream physical education must be excellent—more competent in every respect than general physical educators with students of the same or similar ability levels.*

No longer is good physical education a teacher standing in front of the entire class and instructing all students simultaneously on the same skill. With the trend away from ability grouping in all educational settings (not just physical education), the role of teaching is changing from information giver to learning facilitator. Most mainstream physical education seems to function best in classes organized as *learning stations* with an adult teacher aide, a peer tutor, or a cross-age tutor responsible for each station (Jenkins & Jenkins, 1981).

The mainstream physical educator then moves from station to station, giving attention and assistance as needed. Much of the mainstream teacher's work must be completed before class: reviewing assessment data; developing *task cards* for individuals, pairs, and triads and *learning plans* for stations; and teaching (in-servicing) aides and student leaders. Unless teachers are allowed planning periods for such management tasks, mainstreaming is apt to function less than smoothly.

8. Try a Wide Variety of Strategies and Techniques

Many strategies and techniques can be used to individualize and personalize instruction to achieve desired outcomes. Among these are learning stations; task cards, videotapes, and computer technology; peer teachers; and teachers who are athletes with disabilities.

Learning Stations

Learning stations may vary according to the number of students assigned, permanency of assignment, nature of learning tasks, and type of teaching style. In an elementary school unit on games, for instance, the largest station may be the playing area for the game itself. Additionally, there should be two or three smaller learning stations (two to six persons in each) with different instructional objectives being implemented at each. A student who experiences a problem pertaining to a skill, rule, strategy, or interpersonal relationship (sportsmanship) during the game goes to the appropriate learning station for help (Figure 7.5). One station may be for motorically gifted students who do

Figure 7.5   A student who exhibits jumping difficulties during a basketball game has rotated out of the game to a *learning station,* where he receives individualized help with vertical jumping. Dr. Joanne Rowe assists.

not need the game for skill practice as do their peers. Such athletes should have the opportunity for *new learning* of alternative skills/sports. Physical education should be primarily a time of *learning for everyone,* with practice (repetition) and competition occurring mainly after school and during weekends.

In an alternative gymnasium/playing field arrangement, the student might elect (or be assigned) to the same station for several days or weeks. A different sport, dance, or movement education activity is taught at each station. Peers and cross-age tutors can serve as teachers at the stations. Occasionally, an adult athlete with a disability from the community can be recruited to teach a unit at a particular station, thereby serving as a model for students and facilitating positive attitude change.

Still another classroom arrangement is rotation of students from station to station for learning different skills during the same period. Not all students have to rotate around all stations. The *direction* of rotation (counterclockwise), however,

Figure 7.6 (A) Adapted physical educator Linda Thibault teaches one of her students to enter personal performance data on a handheld computer. (B) The student later passes this knowledge on to able-bodied peers.

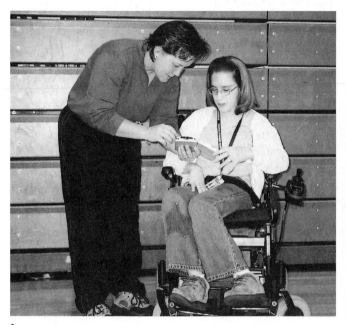

A

B

should be the same for everyone, to avoid confusion. The *time* for changing stations can be the same for everyone (on a set signal) or can vary according to individual differences in learning and completing task cards. For students for whom changing stations may be confusing or impossible without help, *buddies* can volunteer (or be assigned) as partners for the day or the unit.

Task Cards, Videotapes, and Computer Technology

Predeveloped learning materials are necessary for individualized and personalized physical education. These may be task cards that the student picks up as he or she enters class, audiovisuals as individualized learning packages or modules that the student can carry along, or an infinite variety of other materials. Computers are within the price range of most school districts and increasingly will be used to record IEPs, behavioral objectives, and progressive, day-by-day achievements of students. The new rage among teachers and students alike is the handheld computer, also called a personal digital assistant (PDA). Persons who learn handheld computer technology first enjoy the prestige of teaching others (see Figure 7.6). Videotapes can capture trial-by-trial performance and provide immediate, personalized feedback for the student as well as assessment data that can be used later by teachers.

Peer Teachers

Peer teaching may be unidirectional or reciprocal. In the **unidirectional or traditional approach,** the teacher selects and trains students without disabilities to help peers with disabilities. Selection is an honor, and students must meet criteria and

complete intensive training to qualify for the peer teacher role. In models like PEOPEL (Long, 1980) and Challenger Baseball (Castañeda, 1997), every student with a disability has a peer teacher, partner, or buddy. In general physical education, only one or two students typically need peer tutors; these may come from inside or outside the class but should be required to complete training before assuming responsibility. In the **reciprocal or newer equal-status approach,** students take turns in the tutor and tutee roles.

Students who have been peer tutors praise and encourage each other more, express more empathy, provide and ask for more feedback, and show evidence of more meaningful, interactive contacts than do students without such experience. The reciprocal peer teaching approach is based on the belief that students with disabilities should not be denied these benefits. Also, students without disabilities are more likely to perceive peers with disabilities as equal in status if they are exposed to reciprocal sharing of tutor responsibilities.

Special education research indicates that students with disabilities can be successful in reciprocal peer tutor roles in academic settings (Byrd, 1990), but no physical education research on this topic has been reported. Mosston and Ashworth (1986), however, fully describe reciprocal teaching for general physical education and provide many examples of criteria sheets to guide peer interactions. Criteria sheets include the task broken down into sequential parts, specific points to check during performance, illustrations of the task, samples of verbal feedback, and reminders of the peer tutor's responsibilities. Central to the effectiveness of this style is good teacher monitoring and continuous refinement of peer tutors' verbal feedback skills.

Figure 7.7 Dr. Abu Yilla, of the University of Texas at Arlington, challenges a child to take the ball away from him in a modified keep-away game.

Peer teaching is helpful in achieving many physical education goals, but it is especially associated with the goal of social competence and inclusion. See Chapter 9 for additional coverage.

Teachers Who Are Athletes With Disabilities

To be able to conceptualize themselves as self-determined adults, it is important that students with disabilities have opportunities to see individuals with similar disabilities in salaried positions of status. According to Bandura's (1977) self-efficacy theory, self-confidence can be facilitated by direct association with people who serve as models or by videotapes, books, pictures, posters, and other sources that feature models. This textbook emphasizes the employment of athletes with disabilities in as many roles as possible. Such individuals can teach motor skills, fitness, and other content to students with and without disabilities (see Figure 7.7).

9. Adapt Teaching Styles to Individual Needs

Teaching style is important to the learning success of all students (Byra, 2000). Muska Mosston, in 1966, revolutionized physical education pedagogy by describing a spectrum of seven teaching styles and suggesting that teachers master all styles.

APENS (NCPERID, 1995) recommends that competency be achieved in the following teaching styles:

1. Command
2. Reciprocal
3. Task
4. Individualized
5. Guided Discovery
6. Divergent or Exploratory
7. Cooperative Learning

Mosston emphasized that teaching style should match the needs of students and, thus, vary from group to group. The ultimate goal, however, is to progressively increase the student's responsibility for his or her learning by moving from the command and practice styles to learner-initiated and self-teaching styles.

The command teaching style is for students with severe mental retardation, severe learning disabilities, severe emotional disturbance, autism, severe hyperactivity or distractibility, and inner or receptive language deficits. Four basic principles guide the creation of a learning environment for the command teaching style:

1. Use optimal structure.
2. Reduce space.
3. Eliminate irrelevant stimuli.
4. Enhance the stimulus value of specific equipment or materials.

Table 7.8 describes in detail the optimal teaching procedures within four styles, synthesized by Sherrill from the many styles of Mosston. These four styles, based on Sherrill's experience, simplify decision making in adapted physical education. Particular attention is given to the learning environment itself and to starting and stopping protocols. In the mainstream setting, different teaching styles may be in operation at the various learning stations. The same teaching style the child experiences in other subject areas should be used in physical education. Especially for students with severe disabilities, such *consistency* is imperative.

Teaching styles to a large extent determine educational environment (Mosston & Ashworth, 1986, 1990). The IEP should indicate the teaching style for which the student is ready. The guiding principle is to facilitate progress from the teaching style and environment that are most restrictive (command style) to the one that is least restrictive (motor creativity). Some children who need *optimal structure* and lack the ability to cope with freedom (manage their own behaviors) may remain at the command or traditional skills level throughout their schooling. Others, who have no cognitive, perceptual, or behavior problems, may enter the spectrum at the guided discovery level.

Table 7.9 summarizes the characteristics of most and least restrictive teaching styles for ordinary students. Remember that what is most restrictive for most students may be least restrictive for students with severe disabilities.

Behavior management is a pedagogy specific to the command teaching style. Because of its effectiveness in work-

Table 7.8 Four teaching styles, reflecting increasing freedom for learners.

Situation	Least Freedom		Most Freedom	
	Command Style	*Traditional Skills Style*	*Guided Discovery Style*	*Motor Creativity Style*
Learning environment	Small space/Clearly defined boundaries/Floor spots/Circles and lines painted on floor/Equipment always set up in same location/Cubicles available	Normal play space/Clearly defined boundaries/No floor spots/Regulation sport markings painted on floor/Equipment at different stations	Space varies/Boundaries clearly defined, but space changes with each problem/Imaginary floor markings/Equipment moved freely	Determined by student within the limits imposed by school rules about use of space and equipment
Starting routine	Student goes to assigned floor spot or station and sits/Waits for teacher to give *start* cue	Student goes to space of own choice and warms up/Warm-ups may be prescribed as a set routine for each piece of equipment *or* Warm-ups may be created or chosen freely by student	Same as traditional skills approach except that student assumes responsibility for own warm-ups, explores alternative ways of warming up, discovers best warm-ups for self	Determined by student within the limits imposed by school rules about use of time
Presentation of new learning activities	Teacher states objectives/Teacher designates student leaders/Teacher puts students into formation/Teacher gives directions: One task presented at a time, accompanied by demonstrations	Teacher states objectives/Students choose own leaders/Teacher puts students into formation/Teacher gives directions: Several tasks presented at a time, accompanied by demonstrations	Teacher states objectives/Teacher establishes structure in form of questions designed to elicit movement/Teacher offers *no* demonstration; stresses that there is no one correct answer, and reassures pupils that no one can fail	Student states objectives/Student establishes own structure, poses original movement or game questions
Execution	**Student** Practices in formation prescribed by teacher/Starts on signal/Moves in unison with peers to verbal cues, drum, or music/Stops on signal/Rotates or changes activity on signal; in same direction (CCW)	**Student** Chooses own space or formation for practice/Chooses own time to start/Moves in own rhythm/Chooses own time to stop/Rotates or changes activity when chooses; in same direction (CCW)	**Student** Finds own space/Chooses own time to start and stop/Moves in own rhythm/Finds movement responses to teacher's questions/Considers movement alternatives/Discovers movement patterns most efficient for self	**Student** Finds own space/Chooses own time to start and stop/Moves in own rhythm/Finds movement responses to own questions through creative processes
Feedback	**Teacher** Moves about room/Offers individual praise/Identifies and corrects movement errors by verbal *cues* and modeling	**Teacher** Moves about room/Offers individual praise/Identifies and corrects movement errors by *questions* that evoke answers from students	**Teacher** Moves about room/Offers words and phrases of acceptance/Poses additional questions to individuals/Gives students names of their movement discoveries	**Teacher** Moves about room/Offers words and phrases of acceptance/Mostly observes and shows interest/Reinforces initiative

Note. CCW = counterclockwise; teacher may be an adult or a peer.

Table 7.9   Characteristics of teaching styles.

Least Freedom	Most Freedom
Teacher-Dominated Assisted Movement	**Student-Dominated Independent Movement**
Coactive/enactive	Self-initiated
Shaping/chaining	Exploring/creating
Homogeneous Grouping	**Heterogeneous Grouping**
Much structure	Little structure
Assigned floor spots	Free choice
Move on cue	Free choice
Drum or music	Own rhythm
Same role	Different roles
Reduced Space Decreased Stimuli	**Increased Space Increased Stimuli**
One instruction	Several instructions
No equipment	Lots of balls/props
One "it"	Several "its"
One base	Several bases
Indoors	Outdoors
Enhanced Stimulus Intensity	**Weakened Stimulus Intensity**
Bright lights	Normal lighting
Loud signals	Soft, quiet signals
Colorful equipment	Regulation colors
Increased size balls, bases	Regulation size
Memorable texture	Regulation texture
Exaggerated teacher gestures and facial expressions	Typical teacher gestures and facial expressions
External Motivation	**Intrinsic Motivation**
Rewards/awards	No external rewards
Praise	Facilitating/accepting
Consistency of teacher	Flexibility of teacher

ing with students with severe MR and ED conditions, it is presented separately.

10. Apply Behavior Management Strategies (ABA)

Behavior management is a precisely planned, systematic application of cues and consequences to guide students through tasks or activities that are ordered from easy to difficult. It is used primarily in the functional teaching approach and comes from a philosophy and body of knowledge called **behaviorism,** also referred to as **applied behavior analysis** (ABA).

All humanistic teachers are, to some extent, behaviorists or, in more contemporary terminology, *social cognitivists* (Bandura, 1986; 1997). This is because contemporary teacher education stresses such practices as (a) breaking goals down into behavioral objectives, (b) assessing students on observable behaviors, (c) task-analyzing activities to be taught and ordering them into easy-to-hard sequences, (d) matching instruction to

specific assessed needs, and (e) carefully managing the learning environment to maximize desired behavior changes. These practices are important in humanistic teaching.

There are many forms of behaviorism. Followers of B. F. Skinner, who created operant reinforcement theory in the 1940s, today are called *radical behaviorists* (Bandura, 1986). These theorists believe that behavior is cued by the stimuli that precede it and shaped and controlled by the reinforcing stimuli that follow it. Originally, behaviorism did not recognize thought or cognition as a mediating variable. Neither did it consider self-concept or the affective domain. The theory had only three components: (a) a stimulus or situational cue, (b) a reflex-type response or behavior, and (c) a consequence.

In the 1950s, cognitive psychology or cognitivism began to replace stimulus-response psychology. As its name indicates, **cognitivism** centers on the mental processes involved in learning new skills and demonstrating appropriate behavior. The predominant cognitive model since the early 1970s has been *information processing* and the development of strategies to improve attention, memory, perception, and cognition. Most behaviorists today are cognitive behaviorists in that they recognize the role of thought in interpreting a stimulus and deciding on a response.

Whereas cognitivism emphasizes attention, memory, perception, and cognition, **behaviorism** is concerned with the development and application of learning theories to weaken, strengthen, or maintain a specific behavior. In the real world of teaching, there is considerable overlap between use of instructional strategies to improve information processing and the application of behavior management principles to weaken, strengthen, or maintain specific strategies.

General ABA Procedures

General ABA procedures include (a) specify the desired behavior including the waiting time between cue and performance; (b) establish **baseline performance** by graphing the number of times the behavior normally occurs; (c) apply the intervention; (d) select and apply appropriate consequences (i.e., reinforcers and punishers); and (e) continue graphing the number of times the behavior occurs to see if the intervention is effective—that is, the desired behavior increases in frequency.

Figure 7.8 illustrates the kind of graphing procedure used to record changes in play behaviors with toys and social interactions as the result of an **educational intervention.** The intervention in such programs is generally social reinforcement, attention, and praise for showing the desired behavior and no attention otherwise. While such graphing and recording of frequency of behavior is time-consuming, the technique is used in many settings.

In Figure 7.8, one person was observed for 10 sessions to determine baseline interactions with peers and toys. On the IEP, this student's present level of performance, derived from the graph's baseline, was written as follows: (a) "Joe usually has no interactions with peers during play sessions (i.e., he is in the parallel play stage)," and (b) "Joe interacts with toys for about 20 sec out of every 5-min play period; the remainder of the time he stares into space, rocks, or watches others."

Figure 7.8 Frequency of social interactions with peers and appropriate play behaviors with toys for a child over a 6-week period (30 sessions).

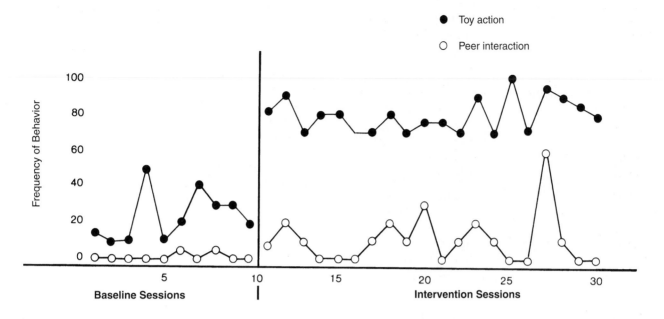

Table 7.10 Illustrative short-term objectives derived from baseline observations.

Condition	Behavior	Criterion Level
While playing in a room with five to seven other children,	Joe will interact positively by initiating conversation, sharing a toy, or coactively using toys in episodes of at least 3 sec duration	for an average of 6 episodes per 5-min observation over 20 sessions.
While playing in a room with tricycle, jungle gym, slide, drums, balls, dolls, and toy cars and trucks,	Joe will interact with toys in appropriate ways for 3-sec episodes	for an average of 80 episodes per 5-min observation session over 20 sessions.

Using this baseline information, the teacher described Joe's desired behaviors in the form of short-term objectives, as depicted in Table 7.10. Then, during 20 sessions of intervention, with appropriate consequences, Joe was given 10-min, specific lessons on how to interact with peers and toys, followed by 5 min of free play. Behaviors tallied and graphed during the free-play period (see Figure 7.8) show that Joe's peer interactions varied from 0 to 50, with an average of 7.75; Joe, therefore, achieved the first objective. With regard to the second objective, Joe's toy interactions improved tremendously, but not quite enough to meet the criterion level. See Chapter 22 for more details on ABA.

Cues and Consequences

Behavior management is based on the concepts of **cues** and **consequences,** the actions used by a teacher to change student behavior. Behavior management, in its strictest and most effective sense, demands a one-to-one relationship so that virtually every response of the student can have an immediate consequence. Nothing the student says or does goes unnoticed.

Cue is the behavior management term for a command or instruction telling a student what to do. Three rules should be followed in giving cues:

1. Make the cue as brief as possible in the beginning (i.e., "Sit" or "Stay" or "Ready, run").
2. Use the same cue each time.
3. Never repeat a cue until the student makes some kind of response. If correct response is made, reinforce. If no response or wrong one is made, use a correction procedure.

The correction procedure is to say, "No, that is not correct; do it this way," and then demonstrate again and/or take the student through the task coactively.

A **consequence** is the immediate feedback to a behavior that increases or decreases its occurrence (see Figure 7.9). For instance, for aggressive behavior (hitting, kicking, biting, and the like), the consequence should be punishment. For noncompliant behavior ("I don't want to"; "I can't"; "I don't have to"), the consequences should be ignoring the student's words

Figure 7.9 A basic principle of behavior management is *Catch 'em being good!* Authorities recommend a 5:1 praise/criticism ratio. When teachers issue a criticism or correct a motor skill, they should offer at least five praises around the class before criticizing anyone again.

or actions and, if appropriate, coactively taking him or her through the activity.

A consequence can be **reinforcement** (causing a behavior to increase), **punishment** (causing a behavior to decrease), or a **time-out** (ignoring inappropriate behavior, removal from a reinforcing environment, or withholding of reinforcers). Rules to be followed in enacting consequences are these:

1. Give immediate feedback to every response the student makes.
2. Accompany nonverbal reinforcement (food, tokens, hugs) with words or, for Deaf students, signs.
3. Reinforce within 2 sec after a student responds correctly.
4. Ignore inappropriate behavior that affects only the student.
5. Punish inappropriate behavior that hurts others.

The use of consequences to teach or manage behavior is also called **contingency management.** A **contingency** is the relationship between a behavior and the events following the behavior. Giving **tokens** (or points) for correct responses or good behavior is a method of contingency management, providing the tokens are meaningful to the students and can be traded in on things or privileges of real value.

To encourage practice of motor skills, tokens are sometimes given for a set number of minutes or practice trials in which an individual, a team, or an entire class exhibits on-task behavior. **Response cost** is another method of contingency management. In it, points, tokens, or privileges are taken away when students fail to show appropriate behaviors.

In summary, behavior management pedagogy is based on four general concepts: **cues, consequences, task analysis,** and a **data-based gymnasium.** Most authorities consider behavior management the best pedagogical approach for instructing students with severe mental retardation, autism, and emotional disturbance. In the continuum of most to least restrictive teaching styles and environments, behavior management is least restrictive for students with severe problems, but, strictly applied in its entirety, is most restrictive for most students.

Time Delay Interventions

These interventions refer to systematically planning the number of seconds the teacher should wait before giving a prompt. The two types of time delays are progressive and constant (Chen, Zhang, Lange, Miko, & Joseph, 2001). For example, in a task analysis procedure, using **progressive time delay,** a teacher might wait 1, 2, 3, 4, and 5 seconds, respectively, between the cue and the expected behavior (Chen et al., 2001). In **constant time delay,** teachers often follow a *10-second wait principle* between asking a question and expecting the answer.

Specific Behavior Management Techniques

Although few physical educators have the student-teacher ratio necessary for using behavior management in its entirety, all good teachers use some behavior management techniques. Teaching a complex motor skill to GE students, for instance, requires the techniques of shaping, chaining, and fading. Reinforcement and punishment are integral parts of the structure of every classroom. Table 7.11 presents specific behavior management techniques commonly used in physical education.

11. Weave Counseling Into Teaching

Counseling is any teacher communication about a student's personal problem that is helpful rather than neutral or hurtful. Most counseling is based on cognitive psychology and incorporates tenets of attitude, self-concept, and motivation theory. This section is short because counseling techniques are woven throughout this text.

Characteristics of a healthy counseling relationship are active listening, understanding the other's point of view, acceptance, willingness to become committed and involved, and genuineness. There is a difference between hearing what is being said and understanding what is being felt. You need both skills. Taking the time to **actively listen** is a challenge that many busy teachers find difficult, but persons with disabilities need to be able to talk through problems related to movement and fitness,

Table 7.11 Specific behavior management techniques.

Technique	Description
Shaping	Reinforcing small steps or approximations of a desired behavior; an analogy might be the praise "You're getting warmer" in the old game of finding a hidden object. Inappropriate or undesired behaviors are ignored.
Chaining	Leading a person through a sequence of responses, as is done in a task-analyzed progression of skills from easy to hard. The sequential mastery of a folk dance with many parts might also be considered chaining.
Backward chaining	Starting with the last step in the chain. For instance, in an overarm throw, the backward chain would begin with the release of the ball; then the forward swing of arm and release are practiced; and then the backswing, the foreswing, and the release are practiced. Usually, manual guidance is used in backward chaining.
Prompting	The cue or stimulus that makes a behavior occur. It can be physical, verbal, visual, or some combination of sensory stimuli. In physical education, prompting is often the behavior management term for physical guidance of the body or limb through a skill.
Fading	The gradual removal of the physical guidance as the person gains the ability to perform the skill unassisted. It can be gradual reduction in any reinforcement that is designed to help the student become increasingly independent.
Modeling	The behavior management term for demonstrating.
Positive reinforcement	An increase in the frequency of a behavior when followed by an event or stimulus the student finds pleasurable. This term should not be confused with *reward*. Although a reward is pleasurable, it does not necessarily increase behavior.
Negative reinforcement	An increase in the frequency of a behavior as a result of removing or terminating something the student perceives as unpleasant, such as being ignored, scolded, or punished by teachers or peers or hearing a loud buzz every time a postural slouch occurs. *Negative reinforcement* is when students exhibit good behavior because they are intimidated or frightened by the consequence. In contrast, *positive reinforcement* is when students exhibit good behavior because they look forward to the consequence.
Punishment	The opposite of both positive and negative reinforcement. Punishment is anything that decreases the frequency of a behavior. A spanking, in the behavioral management context, is not punishment unless it decreases undesired behavior.
Extinction	Failure to reinforce (i.e., ignoring a response or behavior). It is a method of decreasing the frequency of a behavior. It can occur unintentionally, as when teachers are too busy or too insensitive to reinforce, or it may be done purposely to eliminate a previously reinforced response to make way for the teaching of a new behavior.
Premack technique	A method of reinforcement that involves pairing something a student likes with something the teacher wants him or her to learn or do. The promise of free play when work is done (i.e., a choice between activities that promote personal goal achievement) illustrates this technique.
Contract teaching	A method of ensuring understanding and agreement between student and teacher concerning what is to be learned. A contract is a written document signed by all parties concerned. It lists what is to be learned and the possible consequences of learning and not learning.
Time-out	Withholding of reinforcers, ignoring inappropriate behaviors, or removal from a reinforcing environment. When a game or activity becomes so stimulating to a student that he or she cannot control negative behaviors, there should be a quiet place to go. Time-out can be either required by a teacher or opted by a student.
Good behavior game	Use of a group contingency approach in which all students are affected by the behaviors of each individual. Rules governing good behavior are in writing. The goal of the game is to accumulate points that can be used in buying a pleasant consequence (like free time or a field trip) agreed on by majority vote. Points are gained by adhering to rules and are subtracted for breaking rules.

use of leisure time, and barriers that limit self-actualization through sport.

Techniques associated with active listening are (a) establishing and maintaining eye contact, (b) squarely facing the person who is talking, (c) maintaining an open posture (i.e., not crossing the arms or legs because these gestures suggest disagreement or closing out the speaker), (d) leaning slightly forward to show interest and involvement, and (e) appearing relaxed and comfortable. In counseling, the person being helped (the helpee) does most of the talking.

The following are three roles associated with active listening:

1. **Encourager.** During pauses, the listener says "Uh-huh," "Go on," "Yes," and "Then what happened?" This enables the student who is upset to calm down and gain perspective as he or she hears self and considers reasons and alternatives.

2. **Interpreter.** In this role, the teacher attempts to clarify and objectify the student's feelings by restating the student's words in a different way, more clearly and objectively. For example:

   Student: I know that everyone is always laughing at me because I am so clumsy and awkward. No one wants me on the team. I don't have many friends.

   Teacher: You resent the fact that your classmates seem to judge you on the basis of your athletic ability and not for who you are.

3. **Reflector.** The teacher responds with reflective statements that convey an understanding and acceptance. The role moves beyond paraphrasing into reflecting the feelings of the student and indicating that it is OK or normal to have such feelings. The teacher asks questions to help guide the student into positive thinking and problem solving. For example:

   Student: I hate being fat. I hate myself because I can't take control and do something about it.

   Teacher: Yes, lots of people feel that way. Have you considered asking a friend to help you? Who are some people who might tackle this problem with you?

During a counseling session, the teacher's attitude and responses should make it easier for a student to listen to himself or herself. When the student perceives that the teacher thinks that she or he is worth listening to, the student's self-respect is heightened. When another self (the teacher) can look upon the student's obesity, awkwardness, or lack of fitness without shame or emotion, the student's capacity to look at himself or herself grows. Realization that whatever attitude the student expresses is understood and accepted leads to a feeling of safety and the subsequent courage to test new ideas and try different methods of improving self.

Conferences with students should be held in a quiet setting where the teacher is free from interruption. Students should be assured that information will be kept in confidence. Two feelings are most important for optimal growth and positive change: (a) "I exist; therefore, I am lovable" and (b) "I am competent." Early conferences may be devoted to getting acquainted, finding common interests and values, and sharing ideas. An invitation to go fishing, take a walk, or eat out may contribute to the establishment of rapport more readily than formal interviews or conferences. Only when the student feels lovable and competent is he or she ready for preplanned regular counseling sessions.

Every word spoken by a teacher carries some meaning to the student. Likewise, shifts in postures, hand gestures, slight changes in tone, pauses, and silences convey acceptance or nonacceptance. *Over 50% of the teacher's responses in a counseling session should fall into the reflection category.* The teacher sets the limits on how long a session may last, but the student determines how short it can be. In other words, a student should feel free to terminate a session whenever he or she wishes.

Successes and failures in the gymnasium are accepted with equanimity. Neither praise nor blame is offered. The teacher uses words primarily to reflect what the student is feeling in a manner similar to that employed in the counseling session. On some occasions, the teacher may imitate the movement of the student, using this technique to reflect how the student looks to another and to reinforce the belief that others can accept the student and his or her movement as the best of which he or she is capable at the moment. Imitation of movements, performed without words, shows willingness to suffer what the student is suffering, to feel as he or she feels, to perform through his or her body, and to walk in his or her shoes.

Success in counseling depends on the skill of the teacher in the following functions: (a) seeing the student as a coworker on a common problem, (b) treating the student as an equal, (c) understanding the student's feelings, (d) following the student's line of thought, (e) commenting in line with what the student is trying to convey, and (f) participating completely in the student's communication. The teacher's tone of voice is extremely important in conveying willingness and ability to share a student's feelings.

As counseling proceeds, the student should grow in self-acceptance. The following criteria may serve as one basis for evaluation: (a) the student perceives self as a person of worth, worthy of respect rather than criticism; (b) the student perceives his or her abilities with more objectivity and greater comfort; (c) the student perceives self as more independent and more able to cope with problems; (d) the student perceives self as more able to be spontaneous and genuine; and (e) the student perceives self as more integrated, less divided.

Counseling techniques are also used in instructional models like the personal-social responsibility model of Hellison (1995). Such models emphasize awareness, talking, and listening by peers as well as, reflection time, respect, and helping by the teacher (Hellison & Walsh, 2002).

Leisure counseling is particularly important in helping persons with disabilities generalize skills learned at school to the community setting (Schleien, Meyer, Heyne, & Brandt, 1995; Taylor, 1987). This involves asking persons what they want to do during free time and helping them overcome environmental and personal constraints. Often, it is necessary to provide information about opportunities and resources; this can be done through field trips written into the IEP under transitional services and conducted as part of school physical education.

Counseling is very time-consuming. Teachers need to know when and how to refer students for additional help. **Support or empowerment groups** are often as facilitative as one-to-one counseling (Chesler & Chesney, 1988).

Summary of Sherrill's Model

For the instructional model that guides this chapter, broad standards to be used for evaluation purposes might be as follows:

1. **Inputs**
   a. People, environment, time, and opportunity inputs were considered in planning, assessing, and IEP decision making.
   b. Team approaches were used in the input process, and law and school policy were followed.
   c. Professionals involved in input decisions met high standards of professional preparation and performance.

2. **Processes**
   a. Teachers, students, and significant others collaborated in the implementation of major instructional principles.
   b. Resources and support services were sufficient for instruction to meet the criteria of effectiveness, efficiency, and affectiveness.

3. **Outcomes**
   a. Desired outcomes were achieved.
   b. Team approaches were used in evaluation.

A checklist for evaluating school district adapted physical education practice appears on the McGraw-Hill website at www.mhe.com/hhp.

Consulting

Adapted physical activity (APA) consulting is a specialist role incorporating such multiple functions as (a) support services and team teaching to enable goal achievement; (b) adult education, including various forms of in-service education, parent training, and collaborative teamwork; (c) expert advice and specific administrative responsibilities, such as assessment or evaluation for a school district; and (d) identifying and coordinating resources for home-school-community and interdisciplinary cooperation.

Creating the Consultant Position

With the current trend toward interpreting the least restrictive environment (LRE) in physical education as the general classroom, every school district needs one or more APA consultants to assist general physical education teachers. This is especially urgent at the elementary school level, where most instruction is conducted by classroom teachers rather than physical education specialists. Because APA is a relatively new profession, *strong advocacy is needed to increase the awareness of administrators,* *school board members, and parents of the benefits of building an APA consultant-administrator into their budget.* Following are three approaches to achieving this goal.

The 5L Model

Remember the 5L model of advocacy described in Chapter 4:

1. *Look At Me*—Providing examples and models
2. *Leverage*—Group action, such as recommendations from the parent-teachers association (PTA) and/or various teacher organizations or unions
3. *Literature*—Letters to the newspaper, articles in journals that administrators and parents read, awareness flyers, and so on
4. *Legislation*—Involvement in bills and policies regarding taxation and how taxes and other resources are used
5. *Litigation*—Registering formal complaints and initiating due process hearings when students with disabilities are found sitting on the sidelines instead of receiving physical education instruction comparable to what their peers receive

The 5L advocacy model, properly implemented, is a team or partnership between parents and teachers to convince the power structure to allocate resources for the employment of an APA consultant-administrator as well as direct service delivery APA personnel. The strongest of the 5Ls is litigation, an action that only parents can initiate. Typically parent complaints and requests for hearings are resolved in the parents' favor without initiation of a lawsuit, but parents need knowledge about their children's rights, the characteristics of good physical education instruction, and the due process procedures to be used when these rights are violated (Siegal, 2002).

Cowden Administrator In-Service Model

Another approach to convincing administrators to employ an APA consultant-administrator is to design action research directed toward changing attitudes and practices. Illustrative of this is a doctoral dissertation by Jo Cowden (1980), now a professor at the University of New Orleans, based on involvement of 25 administrators in the Fort Bend Independent School District (ISD) of Texas in 9 hours of in-service training (three half-day workshops) spaced over 3 weeks. Some pretest-posttest significant differences occurred in the 36-item administrator opinion survey (Cowden & Megginson, 1988), but the more important outcome was the decision by school district administrators to employ its first full-time APA specialist.

Collaborative University/Public School Model

Another approach is for school districts in cities with universities to employ a full-time APA consultant-administrator to initiate and sustain collaborative planning on how resources of the public school and university can best be used to provide excellent school-based instruction for students with disabilities while concurrently meeting the need for high-quality, supervised, structured practicum experiences for university students (see Chapter 6 for a case study of this model). Denton ISD, in con-

Figure 7.10 Graduate students preparing for IEP meetings under the mentorship of Dr. Lisa Silliman-French (center) in her collaborative school-university professional preparation program.

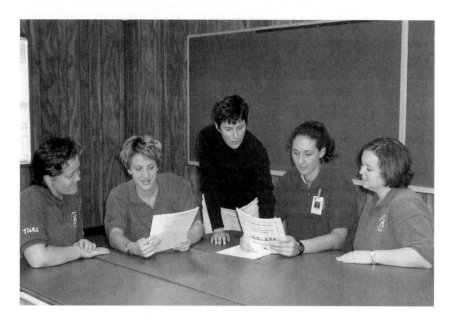

junction with Texas Woman's University, is pioneering in the development of this model, which is implemented by Ron French and Lisa Silliman-French, both of whom have doctorates in adapted physical education. This model is an outstanding example of the Look At Me strategy of the 5L advocacy model. Graduate students acquire valuable IEP and teaching experience as they take coursework (see Figure 7.10).

Performing Consultant Work

Consultants, of course, may be employed either part-time or full-time. Job descriptions vary considerably. Chapter 1 lists competencies that school districts should expect specialists to have. Figure 7.11 presents a consultant model, designed specifically to facilitate integration, that has been validated by research (Heikinaro-Johansson et al., 1995).

School district work typically begins with some kind of **needs assessment,** a special type of program evaluation based on ratings of program or school district conditions that exist and should exist (i.e., a discrepancy evaluation model). Following the collection of these "exist and should exist" data from teachers, paraprofessionals, students, parents, therapists, and others, a team of experts performs a discrepancy analysis, decides on the conditions that most need attention, and sets school district goals for change (Cowden, 1980; Heikinaro-Johanssen & Sherrill, 1994; Sherrill & Megginson, 1984).

An instrument called the Survey of Adapted Physical Education Needs (SAPEN), which was validated by five national experts and has alpha reliability coefficients of .73 to .91 on its various scales (Sherrill & Megginson, 1984), is used for school district needs assessment related to adapted physical education. Table 7.12 shows a sample item from SAPEN.

The SAPEN needs-assessment approach, which has been used in both the United States and Finland, is helpful in several ways. First, the discrepancy analysis data often convince

school district administrators to employ additional APA personnel. Second, if an APA consultant-administrator is already part of the school district team, the data provide direction for making needed changes and initiating some kind of intensive or limited assistance to physical educators (see pp. 132-133).

In the **intensive assistance program** specified in Figure 7.11, every Monday a consultant delivered to a general classroom teacher lesson plans that guided the integration of a 9-year-old boy in a wheelchair into general physical education. On Tuesday, when the lesson plan was taught by the classroom teacher, the consultant observed her and the paraprofessional, collected videotape data to document the effectiveness of the lesson, and provided feedback to the teacher for improvement. On Thursday, the teacher and the paraprofessional taught the lesson a second time so that they had an opportunity to use the feedback. This procedure was followed for 2 months before the general classroom teacher felt secure enough to agree to only monthly visits from the consultant.

In the **limited assistance program,** the consultant visited the general classroom teacher only once a month. Lesson plans were supplied as in the intensive assistance plan, and the classroom teacher assumed responsibility for videotaping lessons for the consultant to see and evaluate. Frequent telephone contact was substituted for direct contact, but this approach was not nearly as effective as the intensive assistance plan.

Little research has been published on the use of consultants in physical education, although the literature is full of recommendations concerning the need for such specialists. Each consultant must experiment with approaches that fit her or his school district's resources. Continuous evaluation will supply feedback for refining service delivery. Lytle and Collier (2002) have published some outstanding research on consultant perspectives and responsibilities.

Figure 7.11 Illustrative school district consultant model. (From P. Heikinaro-Johansson, C. Sherrill, R. French, & H. Huuhka (1995). Adapted physical education consultant model to facilitate integration. *Adapted Physical Activity Quarterly, 12*(1), 12–33.)

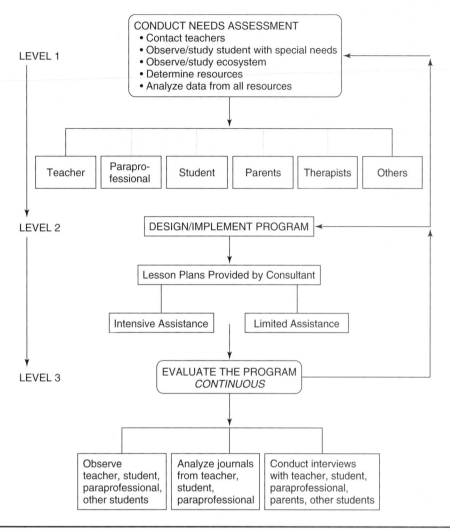

Table 7.12 Format of a needs assessment instrument.

Survey of Adapted Physical Education Needs (SAPEN)

Give Your Opinion Now Exist							Give Your Opinion Should Exist					
6-Completely Agree	5-Mostly Agree	4-Slightly Agree	3-Slightly Disagree	2-Mostly Disagree	1-Completely Disagree	Please circle in the left-hand column the number that you feel best represents the services that *now exist* in your school district. Circle in the right-hand column the number that best represents your opinion about what *should exist*. IT IS CRITICAL THAT YOU CIRCLE A NUMBER FOR EACH ITEM IN EACH COLUMN. When done, double check to see if you have responded to every item using both columns.	6-Completely Agree	5-Mostly Agree	4-Slightly Agree	3-Slightly Disagree	2-Mostly Disagree	1-Completely Disagree
6 5 4 3 2 1						1. A curriculum manual describing physical education instruction/ services for students with disabilities is available.	6 5 4 3 2 1					
6 5 4 3 2 1						2. Elementary school students with disabilities receive at least 150 minutes of physical education instruction each week.	6 5 4 3 2 1					
6 5 4 3 2 1						3. Administrative personnel understand that adapted physical education services are separate and different from those provided by a physical, occupational, or recreational therapist.	6 5 4 3 2 1					

OPTIONAL ACTIVITIES

1. Check the library for scholarly resources on consulting. Learn all you can about this type of employment. If possible, go to work with a consultant and shadow him or her throughout the day. What did you learn of most value? Why?

2. How does the input, process, output teaching model in this chapter capture the essence of what is most important in teaching students with disabilities in different settings? What are the strengths and weaknesses of this model? Why? If you were asked to create a one-page model that synthesized the most important points about teaching, what would you produce? Work with a partner, and develop a model that is uniquely yours.

3. Take turns observing each other teaching in a practicum or employment-type setting. Assess strengths and weaknesses in terms of the principles in this chapter, and put your findings in written format. Feel free to add additional principles to the list.

4. Which three of the principles are *most* meaningful in your teaching? Why? Which three of the principles are *least* meaningful to you? Why?

5. Prepare and conduct a debate on what makes a good teacher of children with disabilities. Do research on the assessment of teacher performance. What do experts think is a good teacher?

PART

II

Assessment and Pedagogy for Specific Goals

CHAPTER

8

Self-Concept, Motivation, and Well-Being
Claudine Sherrill and April Tripp

Figure 8.1 People with disabilities must be helped to view themselves with high efficacy and self-concept. This is important to total well-being. (A) Valuable team members in games. (B) The challenge of outdoor education activities. (C) Athletic competition.

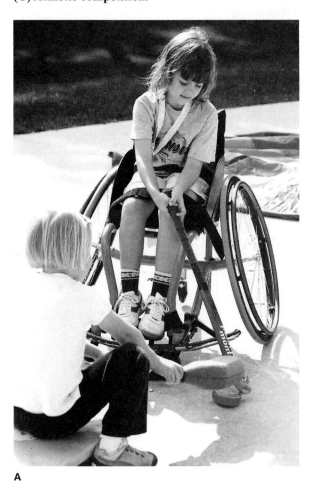

A

B

C

1. Explain how self-concept can be included as a goal in physical education.

2. Explore all the areas of your own self-concept in relation to the different terminology.

3. Practice writing measurable objectives for self-concept to be used in lesson plans and IEPs; get ideas from assessment instruments.

4. Administer sample instruments in this chapter and discuss findings and implications for physical education with a colleague.

5. Think of a traditional game or activity you enjoy in physical education and make adaptations so it includes a self-concept component.

The development of positive physical self-concept is an important goal in adapted physical activity service delivery (see Figure 8.1). Physical self-perceptions are linked to mental well-being, motivational states, and goal achievement in exercise and sport (Fox, 1997). Students with low motor coordination and fitness levels need program goals directly related to improving self-concept. This goal area was identified in Chapter 5:

> **Positive physical self-concept:** To develop positive feelings about the physical self; to increase understanding and appreciation of the body and its capacity for movement; to accept limitations that cannot be changed; to develop motivation to achieve personal bests; to adapt tasks and the environment to make the most of strengths (i.e., to work toward self-actualization).

The purpose of this chapter is to increase awareness of the self-concept variables important to lifelong physical activity success and participation; to develop competencies in assessment and writing goals and objectives; and to introduce principles, practices, and models that contribute to self-concept.

Self-Concept Theory

Self-concept is a dynamic, multidimensional, interactive, and nonlinear system; this is depicted in Figure 8.2. Self-concept (also called self-perception) is a multidimensional construct in that it includes the cognitive, affective, and behavioral domains. These three domains constantly interact with each other, creating change that is often nonlinear in the ways that it influences self-perception. Self-perception influences beliefs, attitudes, and feelings; this in turn affects motivation and actions. The whole system works in reverse as well. For example, perceived physical competence (affective) will influence exercise participation (behavioral). In the reverse, exercise participation will influence one's perceived physical competence.

Carl Rogers is the father of self-concept theory. He captured its essence by stating that self-concept is the central construct in teaching and provides the best foundation for helping persons understand and change their behaviors (see Chapter 5). People with movement difficulties are more likely to experience failure in physical activities; therefore it is important for teachers and coaches to understand that these people will avoid participation in order to protect their self-concept. By choosing appropriate activities, making adaptations, and organizing the environment for success, teachers can influence in meaningful ways the self-perception of individuals who have movement difficulties. This can contribute to a more positive self-concept (Sonstroem, 1997).

Terminology and Assessment Approaches

Definitions of terms related to self-concept goal as part of a self-system have changed considerably since the 1980s. New assessment approaches emphasize that global self-concept is actually made up of smaller more specific components such as the physical self, social self, and scholastic self. Each of these components can be further broken down into cognitive, affective, and behavioral domains as indicated in Figure 8.2. *Cognitive* refers to beliefs about self. *Affective* refers to attitudes, feelings, and emotions that are associated with evaluation by self or others. *Behavioral* refers to thought and action that reflect intention.

Today self-concept terminology is driven by multidimensional models. Be sure your terminology matches that used in the instruments you are administering. Older instruments tend to use the terms *self-concept, self-esteem,* and *self-worth* interchangeably, but newer instruments make sharp distinctions between these terms.

Self-concept has two meanings, both of which are included in Figure 8.2. Traditionally, *self-concept* has been an umbrella term for all of the beliefs, feelings, and intentions that a person holds in regard to the self. The newer meaning of **self-concept** is observable or measurable knowledge that a person holds about the self. This includes awareness of many identities, roles, and competencies that contribute to personal uniqueness. This newer meaning encompasses everything in the cognitive domain, but particular attention has been given to identity, level of aspiration, self-efficacy, and movement competence.

Identity

Identity is self-knowledge about who one is, what one can do, and selves or roles most central in one's life. For example, a woman might view herself as a professional, a spouse or partner, a daughter, a mother, a Catholic, a Democrat, a soccer player, a physically attractive person, a healthy individual, and able-bodied (AB) with average vision and hearing. Each of these selves implies different competencies and responsibilities. These many selves shift in importance, depending on specific situations, demands, and expectations. Identity theory is based on the works of Erik Erikson (1950, 1968).

Figure 8.2 Two definitions of self-concept: *(A) Self-concept* as an umbrella term that encompasses the cognitive, affective, and behavioral domains. *(B) Self-concept* delimited to mean only the cognitive or knowledge aspects of self.

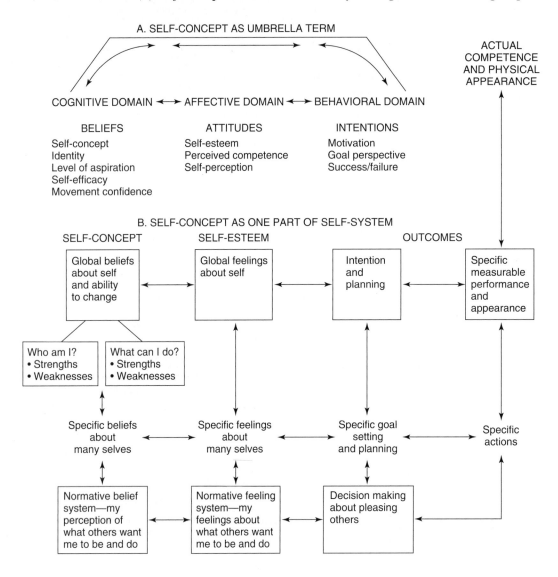

List all the identities that apply to you. Look at the list at the bottom of page 219 and consider:

1. *Which of these identities are the ones you choose?*

2. *Which of these identities describe an unchangeable characteristic?*

3. *Which of these identities have had positive connections or experiences associated with them?*

4. *Which of these identities have had negative connections or experience associated with them?*

5. *Would you want to be defined by any one identity? Why or why not?*

6. *Do you see the connections between identities and labeling people?*

Unless people are taught to value physical activity as essential in their lives, they may give little attention to this di-

mension of their identity. A major goal of physical education is to teach specific behaviors for managing the challenges and barriers that threaten to diminish one's value of physical activity. Especially important is providing opportunities for people to participate in physical activity on a regular basis so it becomes part of a daily routine.

Individuals with disabilities have more complex identities than their AB peers because of the numerous ways disability interacts with other dimensions of the self, experience, and society (D. Reeve, 2002; Sherrill, 1997c; Watson, 2002). Identity in the early years evolves largely in response to social feedback from family, caregivers, and teachers. The attitudes and behaviors of these persons determine whether children think of themselves in predominantly categorical ways (e.g., as disabled or nondisabled) or as multidimensional selves with many strengths and weaknesses. Ideally, as individuals progress through different life stages, their identity becomes increasingly integrated. This means that they become more confident in their knowledge of self, who they are, who they want to be, and how to reduce discrepancies between actual and ideal selves.

In identity theory, there are two approaches to the creation of a self-identity. The first model is based on the assumption that there is an essential, natural, or intrinsic meaning to any identity. This identity is based on a shared social experience, origin, or structure (Hall, 1996). In this view of identity, people choose self-identity as they act through their bodies upon the world, and people experience and comprehend the world through their bodies. The second model posits that identities only exist as opposites, are multiple and temporal, and designed to propagate difference, such as male and female or disabled and nondisabled, serving only to strengthen essentialist arguments (Corker, 1999).

Physical education and sport is most concerned with identity as a physically active and healthy person. Assessment of identity as an active person with a healthy lifestyle should answer questions like these:

1. Do you see yourself as a couch potato, a recreational athlete, or an elite athlete? Why?

2. Do you see yourself as a daily exerciser, a 1-day-a-week exerciser, or as someone too inconsistent to have a clear exercise identity? Why?

3. Do you see yourself as a friend of people who exercise and engage in sports, or is your social identity primarily linked with nonactive people?

4. Do you have social supports for constructing an active, healthy lifestyle? Give examples.

Identity and notions of the self in people with disabilities has aroused much interest in social science. Do people with disabilities know who they are because of the fact that they have impairment, because they face discrimination as a group, or because of whom they believe themselves to be? These are the fundamental questions in any analysis of identity and disability. In a qualitative analysis of adults with disabilities, only 3 of the 28 participants incorporated disability within their identity (Watson, 2002). For most of the participants, impairment was not seen as important to their sense of identity or self. One example is Archie (a pseudonym) who reports that his self-identity rests in what he is able to do and not how he does it, and if it can't be done it is because of societal and environmental barriers, rather than a result of an impairment. Archie, who does not want to be identified on the basis of impairment, demands a different way of defining *normal* and *other.* Importantly, there is no denial of impairment. For Archie, self is a product of self-determination, autonomy, and choice.

For most people, having a disability becomes part of the everyday experience; it is normal and just a fact of life. It has become part of their being, their existence, and their identities are self-constructed in such a way as to negate disability as an identifier. Awareness of the self is predicated on what they feel themselves to be, not what others suggest they should be.

Level of Aspiration

Level of aspiration is a self-stated, specific goal (like 8 out of 10 free throws or 30 sit-ups in 30 sec) that is set after a first per-

formance of a task. This is sometimes called *goal setting* and can be used just like a daily objective set by the student. Asking individuals to state their level of aspiration to a partner or to write it down typically improves performance. *Individuals with cognitive limitations and/or movement difficulties, however, tend to overestimate or underestimate their abilities.* Level of aspiration should therefore be considered a measure of both self-understanding and self-confidence. Students should be taught to understand and correct discrepancies between their level of aspiration and actual performance scores.

Level of aspiration can also be assessed by asking an individual to show you where he or she wants to stand when performing a throwing, striking, or kicking task using a target or asking the student to indicate what size target or ball she or he wants to use. This should be done in a one-to-one setting so the student cannot be influenced by the choices of others. The "show me" approach is particularly useful with young children and individuals with limited verbal ability. Level of aspiration, like other kinds of goal setting, is a cognitive ability, and outcomes are often used to make inferences about the self.

Self-Efficacy

Self-efficacy is "a judgment of one's capability to accomplish a certain level of performance" (Bandura, 1986, p. 391) or a situation-specific expression of self-confidence. This judgment is made after a level of aspiration has been stated. Once the student states a level of aspiration on a task, the teacher asks for the student's estimate of certainty of success on that task. Responses may be percentages (e.g., 30%, 70%, 90%) or categories (e.g., very sure, sort of sure, not very sure) depending on the student's developmental level. For example, before a test, the teacher asks, "How sure are you that you can run a mile today in less than 12 minutes?"

The self-efficacy theory of Bandura (1986, 1997) was discussed in Chapter 5. Efficacy and feelings of confidence can be increased by providing role models who have overcome similar problems and barriers, by designing activities to ensure mastery, by verbal persuasion, and by teaching students how to control anxiety and fear. Efficacy assessment should examine which of these approaches seems to work best for a particular person. Research indicates that self-efficacy will influence what students choose to do, how much effort they invest in the activity, how long they persevere in the face of disappointing results, and whether the tasks are approached with anxiety or confidence (Biddle, 1997). In Figure 8.3 you see a little girl putting forth a lot of effort to be successful.

Affective Dimensions of Self

Affective dimensions of the self include self-esteem, perceived competence, and self-perceptions (see Figure 8.2). Self-esteem is a global entity, whereas other terms are associated with instruments that yield separate scores for physical, social, scholastic, and other selves.

Self-Esteem

Self-esteem is positive self-regard, self-worth, or overall good feelings about the self. Self-esteem is seen by many as the best

Figure 8.3   This young girl approaches the task with confidence.

indicator of the well-being of the self-system; it is often used as a measure of mental health as it includes properties of emotional adjustment, general coping with life, and life satisfaction and well-being. Self-esteem is often regarded as an overall measure of success of the self-system. Some theorists distinguish between the terms **global self** (measured by a scale specifically designed to examine overall feelings) and **total self** (determined by adding together scores of all the specific self-perception subscales of an instrument).

Self-esteem is influenced by exercise and increased fitness as demonstrated by the psychological model of physical activity participation (Sonstroem, 1978). In this model, participation in physical activity leads to increased physical ability or fitness, which produces psychological benefits that can be measured as self-esteem enhancement. That is, increases in physical activity lead to increases in perceived physical competence that concurrently lead to increases in self-esteem. Creating a challenging instructional environment in physical education where all students can meet with success is important to the development of self-esteem because people tend to engage in behaviors that increase or maintain positive self-esteem; this is labeled the self-development or self-enhancement hypothesis (Sonstroem, 1997).

Perceived Competence

Perceived competence is domain-specific self-esteem that relates to ability or skill to perform specific tasks. This term was popularized by Susan Harter (1985), who demonstrated that perceived competence can be measured and profiled in many different domains (e.g., scholastic, athletic, job, close friendships, social acceptance, romantic appeal, physical appearance, and behavioral conduct). Harter's first instrument, called the Perceived Competence Scale for Children, in 1985 was renamed the Self-Perception Profile for Children. Subsequently all of her other instruments, with the exception of a pictorial scale for ages 3 to 7, bear the term *self-perception* in the title rather than *perceived competence*.

The essence of Harter's theory is that perceptions of competence in domains of importance and perceptions of social support impact one's level of self-worth. Within Harter's developmental model, global self-worth changes over the early childhood (4 to 7 years) as self-representation first becomes differentiated. By middle childhood (8 to 13 years), there is a shift from the confusion of actual with ideal self to the use of social comparison to evaluate the self. In middle childhood, self-perceptions become more differentiated. These domains change and differentiate through adulthood. Negative self-perceptions begin to develop when individuals attempt to define themselves in certain ways but do not possess the required abilities to actually perform in these ways. *Self-perception ratings are the best predictors of global self-worth (GSW).* Perceptions of physical appearance, social acceptance, and behavioral conduct contribute significantly to prediction of GSW (Rose & Larkin, 2002). This has important implications for people who want to meet the cultural demands of play, games, and sport but lack the motor resources. Students with motor difficulties who struggle in physical education and on the playground are likely to experience humiliation before their peers, teachers, and parents; this will affect their perceptions of competence.

The Self-Perception Profile for Learning Disabled Students (SPPLD) of Renick and Harter (1988) yields valid data for children ages 8 to 19 years with and without learning disabilities. Using the SPPLD, Shapiro and Ulrich (2002) provide evidence that students with learning disabilities maintain good feelings about themselves in physical education and sport. In general, however, research has indicated that students with learning disabilities do not feel equally competent in all areas of their lives; it is important to understand the contribution of physical competence and positive experiences in physical education and sport to the sense of personal worth.

Current research in perceived competence (Causgrove Dunn, 2000) suggests that physical education classes emphasizing a mastery motivational climate may result in higher perceived competence in children with movement difficulties. A **mastery motivational climate** is one that measures success by such criteria as trying hard and personal improvement rather than winning and outperforming others. A mastery motivational climate may benefit the self-perceptions of children with movement difficulties in the short term and also contribute to long-term changes in the way individuals approach lifetime physical activity.

Self-Perception

Self-perception denotes all kinds of attributes, from global to situation-specific. Whereas Harter developed one physical-domain self-perception scale (for athletic competence), Kenneth Fox in England and colleague Chuck Corbin in America (1989) developed the Physical Self-Perception Profile (PSPP) (see Figure 8.4) for the measurement of the multidimensionality

Figure 8.4 The hierarchical physical self-esteem model that guided the development of the Physical Self-Perception Profile of Fox and Corbin.

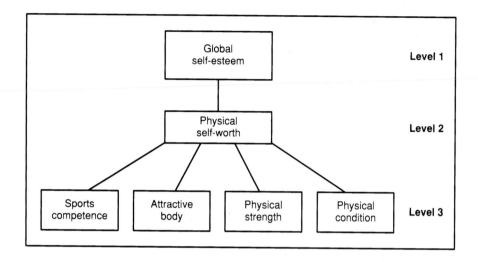

of the physical self (physical self-worth, sports competence, physical attractiveness, physical strength, and physical condition). The PSPP has been modified for use with British adolescents (Biddle et al., 1993) and for American adolescents (Whitehead, 1995).

How important is your physical appearance to you? Think about the influences of society and especially the media. On a continuum of:

very little __ __ __ __ __ __ a lot

Which space best represents your perspective? Why? What things influence you most? Least?

Fox (1997) increasingly is recognized as the father of contemporary physical self theory, which is undoubtedly a powerful element of the self-system. Self-perception has considerable practical relevance as teachers and coaches design effective interventions in exercise, sport, and the increasing problem of weight loss and management. Research over the last 20 years demonstrates that self-perceptions of physical competence, particularly perceptions of sport competence in males and evaluations of physical condition in females, are related to favorable life adjustment (Sonstroem, 1997).

Behavioral Domain and Achievement

A discussion of self-concept terminology would not be complete without a definition of the behavioral domain, because all theories seek to link cognitive and affective aspects of self to motivation and/or achievement behaviors (see Figure 8.2). **Behavioral domain** is the broad term for the cluster of behaviors that relate to initiating and sustaining skill practice and fitness activity. These behaviors can be assessed directly by observation or inferred from various scales. When using observation, the teacher records incidents that document that participants try harder, concentrate more, persist longer, pay more attention, perform better, and choose to practice longer.

Achievement Goal Perspectives

Goal perspectives are personality orientations that motivate individuals to demonstrate competence and effort in specific contexts. Most individuals fall into one of two goal perspectives: task orientation or ego orientation. These goal perspectives interact with self-concept dimensions in the lifelong construction of the self.

Task orientation means defining success in terms of achieving a personal best. Individuals with task orientation do not compare themselves with others. Their attention is completely focused on trying hard, practicing as much as possible, and achieving personal improvement goals.

Ego orientation means defining success by verifying that one is as good as or better than others. Persons with ego orientation measure success by competing with others and comparing outcomes. They might strive for a personal best, but feelings of task mastery are not enough to make them feel good about themselves. Feeling good is linked with being like others or achieving recognition as being better than others.

Goal perspective differences have been reported in athletes with disabilities (Skordilis et al., 2001). In general, female athletes with disabilities are more likely than males to approach sport participation with a task orientation, while, regardless of gender, wheelchair marathoners are more ego oriented than wheelchair basketball players.

Are your goal perspectives task oriented or ego oriented? Maybe you feel you are a little of both. On a piece of paper make two columns and label one Goal and the other Task. List your preferences in the appropriate columns. Do you see any patterns?

Success and Failure

People interpret outcomes of success or failure in relation to effort, personal investment, and enjoyment. Success is closely

Table 8.1   The subscales comprising several inventories.

Self-Perception Profile: What Am I Like of Harter	Self-Description Questionnaire (SDQ) of Marsh	Multidimensional Self-Concept Scale (MSCS) of Bracken
1. Behavioral conduct	Academic	1. Competence
2. Scholastic	Math	2. Academic
3. Physical appearance	Reading	3. Physical
4. Athletic competence	General-school	4. Family
5. Social acceptance	Nonacademic	5. Social
6. Close friendship	Physical abilities	6. Affect
7. Romantic appeal	Physical appearance	
8. Job competence	Peer relations	
9. Global self-worth	Parent relations	
	Global	
	Total academic	
	Total nonacademic	
	Total self	
	General self	

associated with feeling good about oneself, one's team, one's supports, or specific products and processes. **Products** can be task or ego oriented (I met my performance goal; I achieved a personal best; I came in second in the race; I won the free-throw contest). **Processes** can center on feeling good about mastering a task (task orientation) or demonstrating that one is as good as or better than one's peers (ego orientation).

To create an instructional environment that enhances self-esteem, teachers and coaches must identify each student's definitions of success and failure relative to her or his own goal perspective. Always ask students to explain their understanding of success and failure.

Assessment Issues

Many standardized instruments yield self-concept and self-esteem data. Most of these instruments have been normed, however, for use with individuals without a disability. A tremendous need exists for examination of the validity and reliability of instruments in relation to specific disabilities, age groups, and genders in the affective domain as well as the skill and fitness areas. Teachers should use their common sense in determining the validity of instruments and should cross-check data yielded by the instruments with other kinds of observations, including interviews and diaries or journals. To assess reliability, teachers should administer instruments frequently and chart individual scores. For more information on validity and reliability issues related to physical self-concept, see Marsh (1997).

Authorities disagree on the age when self-concept can be measured. It is believed that *an accurate estimate of feelings about concrete aspects of the self can be obtained at about age 4 or 5 years.* Pictorial inventories in which the child chooses between two drawings ("Which one is more like you?") are typically used until about age 8 (i.e., the emergence of third-grade thinking and evaluation capacity). Thereafter, standardized written inventories are typically used unless disability makes pictorial measures preferable.

Another self-concept issue is determining the major domains of self-concept. Table 8.1 lists the subscales included in three well-known inventories. It shows that there is general agreement about most (but not all) of the components. Physical educators must study both scales and items to decide which instruments are most appropriate for their needs. Most libraries have copies of the major self-concept manuals. Otherwise, they can be ordered from publishing companies (see Appendix E).

Assessment Protocol

Self-concept assessment early in the school year can provide the teacher with students' estimates of their physical appearance, athletic competence, and social acceptance. These measures can be helpful in identifying students who need help.

Multimedia and Journals

Self-concept information should be used in individual goal setting. Periodically, ask students to make audio- or videotapes or to develop journals or portfolios about who they are and what they can do at present, what they want for the future, and the work they need to do in physical education to become the self they want to be. This serves as the basis for setting goals, breaking goals into objectives, deciding on activities, and agreeing on the evaluation process and standards.

Another approach is to ask students to identify problems that physical education can help resolve and then check to see if the problems match self-concept data. Problems that students often list include these: (a) "My asthma [or other condition] makes me miss a lot of school and I feel left out," (b) "I don't have the energy to do what everyone wants me to do," (c) "I feel depressed or blah a lot of the time," (d) "I have a lot of friends but no really close friend—I want someone to like me better than anyone else," and (e) "I feel scared (high-strung, nervous) so much of the time." Many students need help in making the connection between physical activity and mental health, tension release, friendships, and energy.

Asking students to keep physical activity journals or diaries is a good technique. Such self-reports should include feelings associated with the activity, as well as the duration and intensity of activity, the goals the activity was directed toward (e.g., fitness, social, fun, relaxation, losing weight), and whether the goals were achieved.

Confidentiality

Self-concept measures are called scales, inventories, or questionnaires. Students must understand that these are not tests, and that there are no right and wrong answers, only individual differences. Students also need to know that their responses will be held in confidence. If you feel that a student needs the services of a professional counselor, then the goal is to convince the student to go to a counselor and share. Never do the sharing for the student, unless you believe the student could harm him- or herself or someone else.

Descriptions of Major Instruments

Familiarity with several instruments allows wise choices to be made in planning the physical education assessment model. Descriptions of several instruments that have good validity and reliability follow.

Harter Self-Perception Instruments

Susan Harter and colleagues at the University of Denver have developed several instruments for different age groups (see Table 8.2). Additionally, there is an inventory that can be used for students with and without learning disabilities ages 8 to 13 (Renick & Harter, 1988). The items for athletic competence on this and the Self-Perception Profile for Children (Harter, 1985) are the same except for simplification of wording on one item and deletion of one item.

Harter's instruments are all characterized by a **structured alternative-response format** (see Table 8.3). Only one box is checked. Students first indicate which of the two descriptions they are most like. Then, within this category, they check "Really True for Me" or "Sort of True for Me." This format reduces the chance that persons will give what they think are desirable responses rather than the truth.

Harter's instruments are different from most others in another way. From age 8 and up, one scale is designed to measure global self-worth. The global self-worth score is derived only from the five items in Table 8.3, and this score is considered separate from the domain-specific self-perception scores. Items on Harter's inventories are never added together to make a total self-concept score.

The number of domains measured increases for each age group. The pictorial scale for young children yields four scores: cognitive competence, physical competence, peer acceptance, and maternal acceptance. The childhood scale yields a global self-worth score and five domain scores: scholastic competence, social acceptance, athletic competence, physical appearance, and behavioral conduct. The adolescent scale measures the same things as the childhood scale, plus close friendship, romantic appeal, and job competence. The college and adult scales measure all of these areas plus more.

Table 8.2   Harter self-perception instruments.

Age Group	Self-Perception Instrument
4–7	Pictorial Scale for Perceived Competence and Social Acceptance for Young Children (Harter & Pike, 1984)—There are two versions of this instrument: (a) preschool/kindergarten and (b) first-/second-graders. For each, there are separate booklets for boys and girls.
8–13	Self-Perception Profile for Children (Harter, 1985)—This is a revision of the Perceived Competence Scale for Children, published in 1979.
Adolescents	Self-Perception Profile for Adolescents (Harter, 1988)
College students	Self-Perception Profile for College Students (Neemann & Harter, 1986)
Adults	Self-Perception Profile for Adults (Messer & Harter, 1986)
Ages 9–19 with learning disabilities (LD)	Self-Perception Profile for LD Students (Renick & Harter, 1988)—This is an adaptation of Harter (1985).

Harter uses the five items in Table 8.4 to measure perceived competence in sports and games. The numerical value of each box is included in these examples to help you understand how items are scored. On the forms administered to students, however, the boxes do not have numbers in them.

For young children and/or those who have difficulty reading, the pictorial format can be used to determine feelings about physical competence and to set goals. Harter uses six pairs of pictures for this purpose.

Harter's self-perception instruments, as well as other inventories related to her theory of competence motivation, can be obtained from Dr. Susan Harter, Psychology Department, University of Denver, 2040 S. York St., Denver, CO 80208.

Multidimensional Self-Concept Scale (MSCS)

Bruce A. Bracken, a professor at The College of William & Mary in Williamsburg, Virginia, developed the Multidimensional Self-Concept Scale (MSCS) in 1992. The MSCS is a standardized instrument for children and youth ages 10 to 18 years. It assesses global self-concept and six context-dependent self-concept domains: social, competence, affect, academic, family, and physical. Bracken's scale is designed using a three-facet taxonomic model that also includes an evaluative perspective (personal or other) and performance standards (absolute, ipsative, comparative, and ideal standards). The MSCS uses 150 Likert-type items with six subscales of 25 items each, therefore,

Table 8.3 Items that measure global self-worth from the Harter (1988) Self-Perception Profile for Adolescents.

Really True for Me	Sort of True for Me	Items			Sort of True for Me	Really True for Me
1	2	9. Some teenagers are often disappointed with themselves	BUT	other teenagers are pretty pleased with themselves.	3	4
1	2	18. Some teenagers don't like the way they are leading their life	BUT	other teenagers do like the way they are leading their life.	3	4
4	3	27. Some teenagers are happy with themselves most of the time	BUT	other teenagers are often not happy with themselves.	2	1
4	3	36. Some teenagers like the kind of person they are	BUT	other teenagers often wish they were someone else.	2	1
4	3	45. Some teenagers are very happy being the way they are	BUT	other teenagers wish they were different.	2	1

Note: Numbers show scoring system and should not be used on inventory given to students.

Table 8.4 Items that measure athletic competence from the Harter (1988) Self-Perception Profile for Adolescents.

Really True for Me	Sort of True for Me	Items			Sort of True for Me	Really True for Me
4	3	3. Some teenagers do very well at all kinds of sports	BUT	other teenagers don't feel that they are very good when it comes to sports.	2	1
4	3	12. Some teenagers think they could do well at just about any new athletic activity	BUT	other teenagers are afraid they might not do well at a new athletic activity.	2	1
4	3	21. Some teenagers feel that they are better than others their age at sports	BUT	other teenagers don't feel they can play as well.	2	1
1	2	30. Some teenagers don't do well at new outdoor games	BUT	other teenagers are good at games right away.	3	4
1	2	39. Some teenagers do not feel that they are very athletic	BUT	other teenagers feel that they are very athletic.	3	4

Note: Numbers show scoring system and should not be used on inventory given to students.

contributing equally to the total scale score. Each MSCS subscale evidences high reliability (coefficient alpha >.90), and the total scale score reliability exceeds .97 for the total sample. The MSCS can be administered to either individuals or groups in approximately 20 minutes. The MSCS can be obtained from Pro-Ed (Appendix E). The MSCS appears to have utility for both research and practice (Bracken, 1996).

Physical Self-Description Questionnaire (PSDQ)

Herbert Marsh of Australia, with colleagues, has developed the Physical Self-Description Questionnaire (PSDQ) for individuals ages 12 and over.

The PSDQ measures 11 components: strength, body fat, physical activity, endurance/fitness, sport competence, coordination, health, appearance, flexibility, general physical self-concept, and self-esteem (Marsh, Richards, Johnson, Roche, & Tremayne, 1994). Of the 70 items, these are illustrative:

3. Several times a week I exercise or play hard enough to breathe hard (to huff and puff).

4. I am too fat.

5. Other people think I am good at sports.

6. I am satisfied with the kind of person I am physically.

7. I am attractive for my age.

Table 8.5 Items that measure attractive body from the Physical Self-Perception Profile of Fox (1990).

Really True for Me	Sort of True for Me	Items			Sort of True for Me	Really True for Me
4	3	3. Some people feel that, compared to most, they have an attractive body	BUT	others feels that, compared to most, their body is not quite so attractive.	2	1
1	2	8. Some people feel that they have difficulty maintaining an attractive body	BUT	others feel that they are easily able to keep their body looking attractive.	3	4
1	2	13. Some people feel embarrassed by their bodies when it comes to wearing few clothes	BUT	others do not feel embarrassed by their bodies when it comes to wearing few clothes.	3	4
4	3	18. Some people feel that they are often admired because their physique or figure is considered attractive	BUT	others rarely feel that they receive admiration for the way their body looks.	2	1
1	2	23. Some people feel that, compared to most, their bodies do not look in the best of shape	BUT	others feel that, compared to most, their bodies always look in excellent physical shape.	3	4
4	3	28. Some people are extremely confident about the appearance of their body	BUT	others are a little self-conscious about the appearance of their body.	2	1

Note. Numbers show scoring system and should not be used on inventory given to students.

The PSDQ instrument uses a 6-point **Likert response format** varying from 1 (false) to 6 (true). Possible responses are these: false, mostly false, more false than true, more true than false, mostly true, and true. Marsh has probably published more research on self-measurements than anyone else, and his instruments are widely used around the world.

The PSDQ manual and instruments are available from Dr. Herbert Marsh, University of Western Sydney, Macarthur, P.O. Box 555, Campbelltown, NSW 2560, Australia, fax (046) 28 5353. Marsh includes all the questionnaire items in many of his published articles (e.g., Marsh et al., 1994), but manuals are needed to know which items measure which components and to learn how to score.

Physical Self-Perception Profile (PSPP)

The PSPP, developed by Kenneth Fox and Chuck Corbin in 1989, is widely used in North America and England. The theoretical model underlying this instrument appeared in Figure 8.4, showing that four domains (sports competence, attractive body, strength, and physical condition/stamina) contribute to global physical self-worth (PSW), which in turn contributes to global self-esteem.

The PSPP consists of 30 items, 6 each for its four subscales and one global PSW scale. A slightly revised format called the Children and Youth version of the Physical Self-Perception Profile (CY-PSPP) is recommended for Grades 7 and 8, and the actual profile items are included in the article by Whitehead (1995).

Scoring is by four-choice, structured, alternative-response scales, which are believed to reduce the **social desirability effect,** a term given the test-taking behavior of individuals who give answers they think the teacher wants rather than what they really believe about themselves. Table 8.5 provides a reminder of what the structured, alternative response format looks like as well as insight into how to measure the attractive body domain. The attractive body domain was chosen for illustration because it is *the PSPP scale that best predicts, and thus contributes most to, global feelings of physical self-worth.* Physical educators can use this scale early in the year and assist students to understand the relationship between physical activity and development of an attractive body.

The PSPP can be ordered from the Office for Health Promotion, Northern Illinois University, DeKalb, IL 60115, or from Dr. Kenneth Fox, Exercise and Health Sciences, University of Bristol, Tyndall Avenue, Bristol, UK BS8 1TP. A book edited by Fox (1997) and entitled *The Physical Self: From Motivation to Well-Being* is the most comprehensive source of information available on physical self-perception; this book includes a chapter on disability.

Develop your own questionnaire for assessing self-concept in physical education. Why did you choose each question? Are they connected to experiences you have had? What influenced your choice of questions?

Disability, Self-Concept, and Self-Esteem

Findings about self-perceptions vary considerably depending on type of disability, age at onset of disability, severity of disability, number of years since onset of disability, gender, support systems, social status, peer acceptance, attitudes, and expectations of significant others (see Figure 8.5). Factors exerting the most influence seem to be age at onset and severity of disability. *In general, boys have higher perceptions of physical competence than girls.* With increasing age, children's perceptions of physical competence more closely correlate with their actual motor competence. Last, individuals who have high perceptions of competence in a given domain are more intrinsically motivated in that domain, exert more effort, persist longer, have higher levels of achievement, and experience positive affect (McKiddie & Maynard, 1997).

Congenital Disabilities

In general, research indicates that individuals with learning disabilities, cerebral palsy, or mental retardation have lower self-esteem than nondisabled peers. It is noteworthy that all of these conditions are congenital, and researchers comparing congenital and acquired types of disability consistently report lower self-concepts when the disability is congenital. However, this finding of lower self-esteem, especially in children with learning disabilities (LD), needs to be viewed with caution. When examining similarities and differences in self-perceptions and values among children with and without disabilities, *one way that children with LD maintain high self-perceptions is to discount domains in which they experience difficulty* (Shapiro & Ulrich, 2002). When examining ratings of importance of physical competence across children with and without disabilities, children without disabilities rated success in the physical domain to be more important than did children with LD. Gender differences were also evident, in that girls had lower perceptions of physical competence than boys. These findings suggest that, despite differences in their self-evaluations and their competence judgments, students with and without disabilities share common perceptions with regard to the value of success within the physical domain. Physical educators need to highlight, particularly for girls and children with LD, the usefulness and importance of motor skills. This can be done through creating personal meaning for the students by connecting the content taught in physical education to real experiences in the children's lives.

The birth of a visibly different child affects all aspects of parenting and family relations. The more severe the disability is perceived to be, the more it tends to lower expectancies and to reduce the likelihood that the child will be treated like other children. Parents of such children tend to be overprotective, ambivalent in attitudes and child-rearing practices, and uncertain about how to access support systems related to physical education, recreation, and sport. From age 4 years onward, un-less planned intervention promotes their acceptance, children who are different begin to experience social rejection and avoidance by peers. Patterns of sport socialization tend to be different from those for AB peers. These and many other factors affect self-concept and help to explain why individuals with congenital disabilities need special help with self-esteem.

Acquired Disabilities

Age of onset of disability is an important variable affecting physical self-perceptions and self-concept. Disabilities that are acquired early in life may affect psychosocial and motor development. Most physical disabilities are acquired later in life through vehicular and other accidents, violence, disease, famine, and/or poor health and fitness practices. Because spinal cord injury typically occurs after age 16 years, most research on physical disability focuses on young adults. A person who experiences a spinal cord injury requires about 4 years for psychological adjustment. Comparisons of individuals who have had injuries for 4 or more years with AB peers indicate no significant difference in self-perception. In a review of physical activity for individuals with sensory impairments and psychosocial problems, Sorensen (1999) illustrates the difference of being born Deaf and losing hearing later in life.

In some research, persons with disabilities have higher self-perceptions than their AB peers do. This has been explained by the **growth through adversity phenomenon.** Successful coping empowers the development of an exceptionally strong, integrated sense of identity and competence. Coping is discussed later in this chapter because of its obvious importance in self-esteem.

Variability in self-esteem among persons with physical disabilities parallels that of AB peers. The life experiences of persons before disability shape their self-perceptions, so no generalizations can be made about all or most people. Hutzler, Fliess, Chacham, and Van den Auweele (2002) revealed that curricular inclusion of children ages 9 to 15 years does not affect empowerment, which has been linked to self-esteem. Acquired disability, by itself, does not permanently change global self-worth. Little is known, however, about physical self-perceptions of individuals of different ages with physical disabilities. When the onset of disability is during adolescence or other stressful times in life, help with self-esteem is an essential need.

Athletes with Disabilities

Almost all research on adult athletes with disabilities reports self-measures equal to or higher than those of individuals without disabilities. Research also indicates that athletes with disabilities have higher self-concepts than nonathletes with disabilities (Adnan, McKenzie, & Miyahara, 2001). Thus, the relationship between sport participation and self-esteem is clear, although statistics do not indicate whether sport caused the self-esteem or whether it existed already and was the prime motivator for becoming involved in sports. According to the dynamical systems or interactionist perspective, the relationship between sport participation and self-esteem is supported both by gains that occur during participation and by the motivation that prompts participation.

Figure 8.5 Support systems and others' attitudes and expectations are essential to good self-concept.

In one of the most extensive reviews of general self-concept and self-esteem research, Hutzler and Bar-Eli (1993) concluded:

> In general, the studies reviewed reveal significant positive changes varying in intensity and duration in the self-concept of disabled populations after sports participation sessions. In addition, significantly higher values of self-concept were observed among disabled people regularly participating in sports compared with sedentary, inactive individuals (p. 221).

In Sherrill's (1997c) extensive review of research on self-esteem development in athletes with disabilities, sport seems to offer positive enhancement opportunities. The sport environment could provide an excellent setting for exploring the processes that constitute the social construction of disability identity. Important mediators of empowerment through sport are (a) *at the individual level,* achievement goals, identity, and self-efficacy; (b) *at the group level,* motivational climate, group identity, and collective efficacy; and finally, (c) *at the societal level,* the cultural context and political efficacy (Pensgaard & Sorensen, 2002).

Research supports the idea that general self-esteem probably consists of two or more components, including self-efficacy and self-respect. **Self-efficacy** means confidence in your ability to think and in the processes you use to judge, choose, and decide. It is knowing and understanding your interests and needs. It incorporates self-trust and self-reliance. The experience of self-efficacy generates the sense of control over your life, the sense of being at the center of your existence as contrasted with being a passive spectator and victim of events. **Self-respect** means assurance of your values. It's an affirmative attitude toward the right to live and to be happy, toward freedom to assert your thoughts, wants, needs, and joys. Self-efficacy

and self-respect are dual pillars of healthy self-esteem. As a physical educator, in order to nurture the self-esteem of students, one must begin with acknowledging every student in the class as important by paying attention to her or his needs and planning lessons that provide meaningful instruction for everyone regardless of ability level.

Case Study of Physical Education Counseling

Typically the sixth-graders entering Herndon Middle School think they know everything about motor skills and they are now ready to play the sport by the sanctioned rules as seen on television and everywhere else in the media. Judy, a new sixth-grader this year, is slightly obese and uses a wheelchair because she has spina bifida. Judy wants to keep up with her peers as she has done all through elementary school and she wants to play the sport, too. The first month of the soccer unit is a disaster for Judy. Not only is it difficult to manipulate her chair on the grass outside, but even with an adapted "hooking device" to gather up a soccer ball with her chair her participation is limited. Judy is also feeling the pressure to have a "thinner" body and one that is more beautiful by society's standards. Judy begins to withdraw, and her physical education teacher, Ms. Castel, notices her behavioral change. The first thing Ms. Castel does is schedule some one-to-one time with Judy to begin the process of personal goal setting for the next unit, which will be basketball. Ms. Castel will work to help Judy to begin to measure her success by her own standards and not by those of her peers or the media. Judy selects her own goals to work toward in basketball, with Ms. Castel's help. Together they create a plan that specifically states what Judy will do in class. Since one of Judy's goals is to lose weight, Ms. Castel helps her design a plan that includes basketball type activities that are aerobic. This is a good example of creating a motivational climate, providing student counseling, and contributing to long-term positive change for a student.

Individuals with Movement Difficulties

Many individuals have movement difficulties severe enough to affect their self-perceptions, social interactions, and involvement in physical activity. Their conditions are often called motor awkwardness, clumsiness, or developmental coordination disorder (DCD).

Research concerning children and adolescents with movement difficulties indicates the following:

1. Children ages 6 to 9 years are more introverted than children without movement difficulties, are significantly more anxious, and have lower perceived physical competence and social acceptance than peers.

2. Children ages 6 to 9 years with movement difficulties spend less time in positive social interactions, are vigorously active less often, and play less often on large playground equipment.

3. Females have lower physical self-perceptions than males. Children who think physical competence is important tend to perceive themselves as good in this area. Severity of awkwardness leads to more self-perception problems in Grade 3 than in other grades, presumably because older children tend to discount evaluative input that is damaging to their self-esteem (Causgrove Dunn & Watkinson, 1994).

4. Almost 50% of children diagnosed as motor delayed at age 5 remain clumsy in adolescence.

These findings indicate that individuals with movement difficulties need adapted physical education services that specifically address their self-esteem as well as their motor difficulties. What is unknown is how decisions about program design should be made and what kinds of intervention work (Henderson & Henderson, 2002).

Development of Self-Concept

Initially, self-concept is formed at home and includes only factors relating to home and family. By the second grade, however, the school and other interactions outside the home have begun to exert a major influence on self-concept formation. By this age, children with visible disabilities realize that their appearance is different from that of their peers; this naturally affects their self-concept. Thus, with increasing age and experience, the ego identity of individuals expands to include more and more domains or dimensions.

The concept of the self also becomes more stable and resistant to change as persons grow older. With young children, day-to-day (and sometimes moment-to-moment) variability is a problem in self-concept measurement. It is easy to change the young child's mind about self or almost anything. Every experience causes fluctuations because the self is not yet integrated by a formal system of thought. *Understanding of these facts guides teachers to assess self-concept several times rather than once.* Then an average is recorded as the estimate of real self.

The issue of stability must also be considered in evaluating self-concept change. Before age 8 (or the equivalent mental functioning), significant change scores may be obtained as a result of special programs of short duration. To ascertain that such self-concept changes are permanent, it is necessary to assess again about 1 month later. After age 8, self-concept becomes increasingly difficult to change. Long-term, intensive programs in which family and school work together are most effective in causing change.

Progress from one life stage to another affects self-concept, because persons must meet new societal expectations and adjust to changes in body (e.g., puberty, old age) and abilities. The transition into adolescence, with its challenge to succeed in romantic and job realms, may cause fluctuations in self-concept. Likewise, changing one's comparison group, as in the shift from high school to college or from one job to another, affects self-concept.

The longitudinal development of self-concept in persons with disabilities and/or health problems has received little study. Much depends on coping skills, social support, and the intensity and duration of stress. The comparison group that a person uses in evaluating self also makes a big difference. A clumsy child in a class of good athletes may have lower physical self-esteem than a clumsy child in a class with peers of similar ability. On the other hand, placement outside the mainstream may cause feelings of inferiority.

In your opinion right now, how important is it to include strategies to improve self-concept in your physical education daily lessons for all age groups? Think about your answer. What has influenced your opinion—your own experience, knowledge, feelings? Is your answer true for some age groups and not others or in some settings/environments (e.g., athletics, classroom, adventure education)?

General Principles of Self-Concept Enhancement

Five principles serve as guides to enhancing self-concept. Which of the following principles would you rely on the most as you teach differently abled students?

1. **Principle of Reflected Appraisals.** This principle emphasizes that children grow up seeing themselves as they *think* others see them. This has been called the **looking-glass or mirror phenomenon.** Every facial expression, gesture, and word of another is interpreted as having meaning for oneself. The more perceived significance of the other, the more influential the reflected appraisal. Because many persons do not interpret the feelings and actions of others accurately, you must work to ensure that your gestures and words communicate your true intentions.

   You must be aware of individual differences in sensitivity related to reflective appraisal. Clarification is important: "I like you but I do not like this particular behavior." "You are a good person, but this behavior is not acceptable." Equally important is the principle "Catch 'em being good." The more frequently you praise students with specific positive feedback when you see them doing

Figure 8.6   Social comparison theory states that self-concept is formed through the lifetime process of comparing self to others. This is an ego orientation.

something well or behaving in a thoughtful, caring, responsible way, the more often the reflected appraisal (both conscious and subconscious) will be positive.

2. **Principle of Self-Attribution.** This principle, derived from behavioral theory, states that past behavior (i.e., through feelings of efficacy or competency) affects the formation of self-concept. We make attributions about ourselves on the basis of our observations of a particular behavior. After eating a large meal, for instance, we think, "I'm a real pig." After achieving a success, we infer, "Hey, I'm pretty good." Self-concept is thus based on past behaviors and one's explanation of the cause of those behaviors. Implications for teaching are reminding students of past successes, encouraging reflection on reasons for success, and structuring situations so that the same conditions are present as when the remembered success occurred.

3. **Principle of Mastery Challenge or Perceived Competence.** This principle, derived from humanistic psychology, is future oriented, whereas the self-attribution principle is past oriented. *Mastery challenge* is the principle of making students feel safe, loved, and appropriately challenged so that they see themselves as competent before trying the task. If Maslow's hierarchy of needs is met by creating a physically and emotionally safe and success-oriented environment, then persons are intrinsically motivated to work toward more difficult goals. Positive self-concept develops when persons set

goals (consciously or unconsciously), expect to be successful, and then validate their expectancies.

Shaping the environment so that the vital ingredients in Maslow's hierarchy are present in the environment is a shared responsibility of everyone in the ecosystem. Teachers must also respect the freedom of a student to say, "I'm not ready yet. I want to do it but I can't by myself." This opens the way for teacher-student and peer partnerships based on the idea: "Trust me. I'll lead you through it. Together we can be successful. Then, when you are ready, you can try it alone."

4. **Principle of Social Comparison.** This principle, based on the social comparison theory of Leon Festinger (1954), states that self-concept is formed through the lifelong process of comparing oneself to others (see Figure 8.6). Between the ages of 5 and 7, children begin to make peer comparisons ("I'm better, the same, or worse than others"). *This information source becomes increasingly important, peaking at about ages 10 to 11.* Thereafter, persons tend to develop predominantly either a task or an ego orientation. *Task-oriented* persons judge themselves in terms of effort ("I did the best I could"), whereas *ego-oriented* persons judge their self-worth by means of social comparison.

Humanistic teaching tries to de-emphasize social comparison and help persons feel good about their own ability and effort. Students are taught to set personal goals and record learning progress by charting scores and behaviors. Using a student portfolio or journal is a good way for students to track changes and can also serve as an individualized assessment tool for the teacher at the end of a unit. Questions emphasized are "Did you achieve your goal?," Did you make a personal best?," "What behaviors caused set-backs?," and "How did you learn to manage lack of progress?" Record keeping or journaling should include more than outcomes; it should also include attributions (reasons) like effort, ability, and chance.

5. **Principle of Personal Meaning.** This principle emphasizes that self-concept is a structure with many dimensions that have unequal salience (prominence).

There is a hierarchy of what is personally meaningful for each person. Teachers must provide the kind of instruction and content that meets the unique personal goals and needs of the students they serve. Teachers can help students find personal meaning by assisting students to explore the answers to the following questions:

- Who am I in physical education?
- What would I like to do with the skills I learn in physical education?
- What am I doing when I am most happy?
- What is my purpose for working hard in physical education?
- Is the process of physical education just as important as the product (outcome)?

Writing Goals and Objectives for the IEP

When assessment indicates that a student has low self-concept, this problem should be addressed in writing on the IEP. The goal might read *"To demonstrate improved self-concept in the physical education or sport setting."* For observation and measurement purposes, 10 indicators of average or better self-concept follow. They can be written as specific objectives for the IEP or for class lessons.

1. Voluntary, enthusiastic participation (without prompts) in class activity 80% of class time.
2. Body language (smiles, noises, gestures, body postures) that reflects general well-being and enjoyment of class activities 90% of class time.
3. Movement confidence (i.e., absence of crying, whining, complaining, hiding, and other fear or anxiety indicators) when participating in small-group activities 90% of class time.
4. A high level of energy or effort directed toward goal achievement 80% of time.
5. Problem-solving behaviors by adapting tasks or the environment to cope with challenges; trying many different ways 4 of 5 times when presented with a difficult task.
6. Asking for help when it is needed 90% of the time.
7. Cheerful, attentive responsiveness to corrective and praise feedback 4 of 5 times after feedback is given.
8. Persistence in sustaining practice and obtaining help 80% of observed time.

9. Accuracy and realism in judging when a task is mastered as recorded in a self-kept journal 100% of the time.
10. Independence in judgments about success/nonsuccess; using feedback from one's own body rather than comparing oneself to others or waiting for external feedback as recorded in journal 80% of the time.

The assessment process for the IEP document as well as teacher or parent feedback related to the effectiveness of instruction could include videotapes, observation checklists, personal charting, student journals, or portfolios. A baseline ability level for the student's objectives is stated on the IEP so progress can be reported on a regular basis.

A Self-Perception Model to Guide Pedagogy

Perceived success and perceived failure are linked with different self-concept profiles. Figure 8.7 presents a model that shows differences between people who fail and those who succeed in the physical education setting. This model helps professionals write objectives and plan pedagogy that addresses problems that arise in conjunction with failure. To read Figure 8.7, start with the box that says *Mastery Attempts and/or Social Acceptance and Inclusion in Games.* A quality physical education program strives to provide as many attempts as possible to master movement tasks and to promote social acceptance and inclusion. Move up the right side of the page and note that perceived failure has an effect on many variables. The end result, at the top of the table, is the influence of failure and lowered physical self-perceptions on classroom motivation. Move up the left side of the page and note the reverse.

Following is a discussion of variables that need special teacher attention when a student perceives his or her attempts to master a task or achieve a sense of belonging to the group are mostly met with failure. Much research is needed on each of these variables in relation to people with disabilities and movement difficulties.

Enjoyment

Enjoyment is a positive emotional response that is indicated by observable expressions of fun, pleasure, and liking. Enjoyment is typically assessed by ratings of self or others in response to questions like these:

1. Do you *enjoy* playing in Little League this season?
2. Are you *happy* playing in Little League this season?
3. Do you have *fun* playing in Little League this season?
4. Do you *like* playing in Little League this season?

Self-ratings of enjoyment using such questions with a 5-point scale (*not at all, a little, sort of, pretty much, very much*) is the strongest predictor of **sport commitment,** which is defined as the psychological state representing intention to continue sport participation. Self-ratings of enjoyment of specific activities in a class setting likewise offer insight into commitment and feelings about the self.

With low-skilled students, enjoyment must come from sources other than kinesthetic feedback and the good feeling that comes from mastering a task. Enjoyment is needed to keep

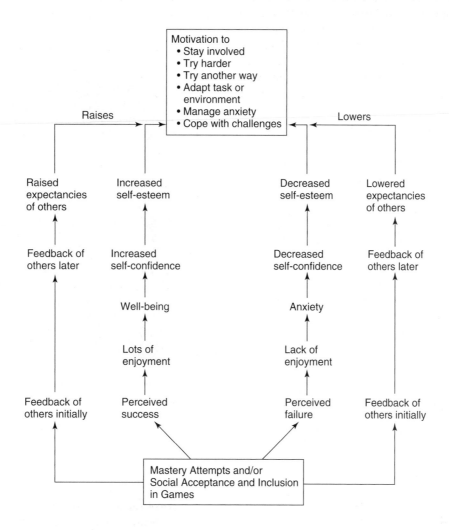

low-skilled students persevering in practice. Teachers should carefully structure the physical education environment to achieve a warm, positive social climate so students with movement difficulties can experience enjoyment through feelings of acceptance and inclusion in class.

Personal Investment

Personal investment refers to focusing energy and other resources on the achievement of physical activity goals. Most individuals respond to failure by investing a little less of themselves in the next effort. This seems to be a protective defense mechanism, in that failing does not hurt as much when the effort to succeed is not an all-out personal best. Often people convince themselves that the task is not really important and use this line of reasoning to support their decreased investment. In self-concept terminology, this behavior is called **discounting.**

High personal investment is closely associated *with internal locus of control (LOC)* and voluntary behaviors that would enhance the possibility of task mastery. A decrease in success performing a task leads to teacher feedback that is different from the feedback successful students receive. Teachers typically offer more prompts and encouragement immediately

after a failure. If the feedback seems to have little effect on student improvement, teachers tend to give up, gradually lessen feedback, and lower their expectations. Students recognize this change and internalize the message that their skills are not that important.

Anxiety

Anxiety is a heightened level of *psychological* arousal that produces feelings of discomfort, both psychologically and physically. As such, anxiety is linked with self-esteem, motivation, and performance outcomes. Individuals often feel anxious because of fear of being rejected or repressed anger. There are also medical or biochemical associations to anxiety. Two types of anxiety must be addressed. **Trait anxiety** is a predisposition to worry. Persons high in trait anxiety tend to worry about almost everything and to perceive many situations as threatening. **State anxiety** is situational. It is an emotional or mood state specific to a threat, challenge, or desire to do well in a situation deemed important, like a test or a sport competition. State anxiety is high in situations where the individual expects to fail.

Some instruments purport to measure general trait and state anxiety, but the trend since the 1970s has been to assess *sport-specific anxiety.* Illustrative instruments are the Sport Competition Anxiety Test (SCAT) of Martens (1977), a measure of trait anxiety, and the Competitive State Anxiety Inventory-II (CSAI-II) of Martens, Burton, Vealey, Bump, and Smith (1990). These instruments are all available through Human Kinetics Publishers (see Appendix E).

The CSAI-II is based on multidimensional anxiety theory that posits that two types of state anxiety and situational self-confidence interact to affect sports performance. The two types of state anxiety are cognitive and somatic. *Cognitive* refers to mental worries, and *somatic* refers to body tensions like rapid heartbeat, dry throat, and excessive sweating.

Instruments have been developed that measure worry about social approval in exercise settings. Illustrative of these is the Social Physique Anxiety Scale (SPAS) of Hart, Leary, and Rejeski (1989). This instrument is particularly useful in determining the amount of discomfort that persons who are overweight or have physical disabilities experience in mainstream exercise classes. Physical appearance is a particularly important psychological construct associated with social acceptance. People with disabilities may be prone to high social physique anxiety because of fear that their physical appearance will result in negative peer appraisal (Martin, 1999).

Self-Confidence and Self-Esteem

The combination of perceived failure, lack of enjoyment, diminished personal investment, and anxiety contributes to lowered self-confidence and poor self-esteem. As shown in Figure 8.7, these influence motivation and external feedback. It is especially important during physical activity to give specific praise and feedback, as well as offer incentives for such observable behaviors as staying involved in the activity, trying hard, testing alternative ways, seeking help, managing anxiety, and coping with challenges. The physical activity experiences of students with movement difficulties need to be carefully planned, monitored, and individualized to meet their unique needs.

Pedagogy in Relation to Low Self-Concept

Teaching practices that enhance self-concept generally also contribute to improvement of attitude toward movement and/or physical education. The practices that follow can be used with all students. Large class sizes and various other factors, however, often make the practices impractical for general physical education, which is why they are described here as critical to effective teaching in adapted physical education.

1. **Conceptualize individual and small-group counseling as an integral part of physical education instruction.** Remember, the characteristics of a healthy counseling relationship are active listening, empathy, acceptance, willingness to become involved in another person's problems, and commitment to helping a person change in the way he or she chooses, which may or may not be the way you would choose. In Figure 8.8 Dr. April Tripp of the University of Illinois works one-on-one with a student to help build her confidence. Listening to a student, asking questions to draw him or her out, and taking the initiative in following up when the student seems to

Figure 8.8 Dr. April Tripp counsels a young girl during a moment of one-on-one time.

withdraw are ways of showing that you genuinely care. Movement-based resources on counseling that work well in a physical activity setting include *Life Cycle* by Lagorio (1993) and *Islands of Healing* by Schoel, Prouty, and Radcliffe (1988). Both of these books have lots of activity ideas.

2. **Teach students to care about each other and to show that they care.** This is sometimes called *social reciprocity* and begins with the facilitation of one-to-one relationships, followed by increasingly complex social structures. *Reciprocity* is an interaction in which persons positively reinforce each other at an equitable rate, thereby increasing the probability of continuing interactions. Reinforcement can be facial and gestural expressions, verbal praise, or cheering for one another. Students typically model the teacher's behavior toward people who are different or disabled. Therefore, you must model encouragement, positive expectation, faith that the student really is exerting his or her best effort, and day-by-day acceptance of motor and social outcomes. Resources to develop caring in movement settings include *Tribes: A New Way of Learning and Being Together* by Gibbs (2001) and *Character Education Connections* by Stirling (2000).

3. **Emphasize cooperation and social interaction rather than individual performance.** When necessary, assign partners who will bring out the best in one another rather than allowing chance to determine class twosomes. Match students with the same care used by computerized dating services. Remember, the creation of a friendship is often more valuable than any other factor in enhancing self-

concept. Show awareness of emerging friendships and praise students for behaviors that help and support each other. A wonderful resource that stresses game modifications to meet individual needs and create cooperation at the same time is *Inclusive Games: Movement Fun for Everyone* by Kasser (1995).

4. **Stress the importance of genuineness and honesty in praise.** Accept, but do not praise, motor attempts that are obviously unsuccessful. Students work hard for teacher approval; criticism can cause anxiety and nervousness. Provide such input as: "Hey, this isn't like you. Tomorrow will be better." or "What's wrong? Let's try another way of throwing the ball!" or "I can tell you are upset by your performance today. You seem to be trying very hard and still not reaching your goal. How can I help?" Apply the same kind of sports psychology strategies to students with disabilities as you do to the able-bodied. In the real world of sport and competition, it is not effort that counts, but success. Therefore, structure lessons so as to build in success.

5. **Build in success through the use of task and activity analysis.** Also important is identifying the student's unique learning style. Does she or he learn best through visual or auditory input, or a combination of the two? Or must the student learn kinesthetically through trial and error? Motor planning and subsequent performance is enhanced in most students if the students talk aloud as they perform, giving themselves step-by-step directions. Use very specific cue words and be consistent. Often visual imagery or thinking in pictures helps. In many clumsy students, the mind grasps what is to be done motorically, but the body simply does not do what the mind wills. Do not repeatedly tell students what they are doing wrong. Instead, find different ways to practice the task. Ask questions and let them tell you what works best. When possible, videotape or film and provide opportunities for students to watch and analyze their motor performance. Allow students to set their own goals while helping them to identify the steps they will need to take to reach their goal. Periodically sit down with students and discuss how progress toward their goal is coming and encourage modifications if necessary.

6. **Increase perceived competence in relation to motor skill and fitness.** There is no substitute for success. Perceived competence enhances intrinsic motivation to persevere. However, competence is typically perceived in terms of a reference group. In adolescence, especially, students are influenced by the media and peers. Help students feel that they are competent by focusing on the things they do well while providing plenty of support when they take risks. Feeling physically competent plays a big role in physical activity, and the influence of the media and the "body beautiful" syndrome is everywhere you look. Students with disabilities need to be able to discharge their feelings related to their body. It is only then that they can assess their thought process. As a teacher you can help by providing a safe environment to

do this while at the same time helping them appreciate all the positive things about their body by exploring their senses of touch, taste, smell, and hearing. Use dance and noncompetitive sports to focus less on winning and more on competence.

7. **Convey that you like and respect students as human beings, for themselves as whole persons, not just for their motor skills and fitness.** The bottom line is that many clumsy students will remain clumsy in spite of best efforts of self, teacher, and peers. This is the rationale for separate instructional settings and sport organizations like the National Disability Sports Alliance and Special Olympics. Students need realistic **reference groups** for forming opinions about themselves and for setting physical activity goals. Clumsiness and low skill do not have to be reasons for disliking and avoiding movement. Too often, physical educators have equated skill with fun. The emphasis, instead, should be on teaching all individuals to enjoy health-related physical activity and to be able as well as motivated to continue being active after leaving the public school setting. Movement is intrinsically fun and satisfying when one does not feel different from everyone else and embarrassed by that difference.

8. **Stress movement education and motor creativity rather than sports competition in the early stages of learning.** Many clumsy students can excel in fluency, flexibility, originality, and elaboration, largely because *try another way* is an intrinsic part of their lifestyles. Such students can find much satisfaction in choreographing original aerobic exercise, dance, gymnastics, and synchronized swimming routines. Likewise, clumsy students may be adept at creating new games and/or changing rules, strategies, and skills in existing ones. The teacher who truly values individual differences conveys this to students who, in turn, learn to value themselves as the "different drummers in the physical education world." In this regard, the words of Henry David Thoreau remain timely:

> If a man does not keep pace with his companions, perhaps it is because he hears a different drummer. Let him step to the music which he hears, however measured or far away.

9. **Enhance self-concept by leisure counseling directed toward achieving desired leisure lifestyle.** Help students to see the relationship between physical education instruction and present, as well as future, use of leisure time. Activities to be learned and practiced during class time ideally should be selected by the student rather than the teacher. Because many adults with disabilities are unable to find full-time employment, it is especially important that they learn early that leisure can be meaningful and active. Wholesome attitudes toward choosing active leisure-time pursuits contribute to good self-concept in persons who have an abundance of leisure time.

10. **Help students to feel that they are in control of many aspects of their lives.** People can change many of the

things they do not like, providing they are willing to put forth enough effort. Other things we must accept and learn to manage. Teach coping strategies, assertiveness, and initiative. Help students sense control by developing autonomy. Allow students to select their own goals, decide what activities have meaning, and those that do not. Assist students to practice self-direction and to learn from consequences rather than self-blame. Expect students to take responsibility for their choices and actions.

Games to Enhance Self-Concept

Here are examples of games designed to focus on constructs related to self-concept that are appropriate for use in a movement setting. Individuals of all ages enjoy these activities; they are fun and nonthreatening to most people. Both of these activities work well as "icebreakers" or opening activities. Invite your participants to play these kinds of games, but do not force anyone to go beyond his or her comfort zone. There can be value in the act of reflective observing. Ask nonparticipants to spend their time watching and to reflect on what they saw happening and how it made them feel. Like motor skills, self-concept is a developmental process.

Mirroring

Ask students to choose a partner and designate who is A and who is B. Tell them that, in the first round, As will be leaders and Bs followers. A and B stand directly facing each other. A is to move in any way he or she wants to—the more bizarre and ridiculous the better. The movement should include facial expressions as well as body movement. B is to act like a mirror and imitate every movement that A makes. A should feel like he/she is looking into a mirror. After about 3 to 5 minutes, reverse roles so that B is the leader and A the mirror. This activity allows people to be "in charge" and to have someone else pay close attention to what they are doing. After the exercise is over, ask them if they enjoyed it. Then ask the class to talk about which role was easier for them—leading or following? What is difficult about leading (fear of being judged, feeling the pressure to be creative or funny, feeling awkward, etc.) and about following (giving my authority to another, feeling inferior to my partner's leading, not getting to do what I want to do, making mistakes in following my partner's movements)?

Snowballs

Give individuals a piece of paper and ask them to write the following (or you can choose other questions pertinent to your purposes):

> In the upper right-hand corner, write something you love to play.
>
> In the bottom right-hand corner, write something you like to do with your free time.
>
> In the upper left-hand corner, write something in physical education you are very good at.
>
> In the bottom left-hand corner, write a wish you have for the future.

After each person has completed this task (people can get assistance or can dictate if this is necessary), each person wads up his or her paper and turns it into a snowball. Then everyone has a snowball-throwing blizzard in which they toss the snowballs at each other, retrieve them from the floor, and throw them again and again. After several minutes, the action is stopped and everyone must retrieve one snowball, searching until they are all found and each person has one. Each person opens up his or her snowball and must search by asking questions to find the person whose snowball they have. After participants have found the person they are looking for, they are instructed to form a circle in which they place the person they found on their right (which can take a while because it is a cooperative challenge all by itself). Participants are then asked to introduce the students they found and tell something they learned about them.

Motivation Theories and Pedagogy

Motivation refers to either the forces that cause behaviors or the internal state that focuses behaviors toward goal achievement. Of particular importance for motivation is the belief that one can actually perform the task or behavior. Therefore, motivation to take part in a behavior will not occur in the absence of self-efficacy. Theories used in adapted physical activity are discussed in the following sections.

Competence Motivation Theory

Competence motivation is the desire to engage in achievement-oriented activities in which one's competence can be demonstrated. Competence motivation theory posits that persons engage in activity because they feel intrinsically oriented in that area and see themselves as having control. The more competent persons feel, the more they will sustain interest and persist in the activity. This, in turn, leads to high physical achievement, positive emotion, and low anxiety.

Of the several competence motivation theories, the one best known in physical education is by Susan Harter (Weiss, 1987). This is perhaps because she not only has developed theory but also has validated instruments for testing the theory. The competence motivation process can be explained mainly by four variables: (a) perceived competence, (b) perceived control, (c) motivation orientations, and (d) actual physical performance (see Figure 8.9).

Harter's theory predicts that those high in perceived physical competence will be more likely than others to participate in physical activity and sport. Perceived competence (high or low physical self-esteem) is interrelated with perceived control (internal, external, or unknown). These factors both influence motivation orientations and actual physical achievement. Harter recommends measurement of five motivation orientations (see Figure 8.9). *Preliminary research shows that the score on the challenge scale is most predictive of actual physical achievement, but this may vary with task and ability levels.*

Individuals act in ways that are consistent with their (a) perceived competence, (b) perceived control, and (c) motivation orientations. Therefore, plan strategies that make students feel that they are competent and that they have at least partial control over task variables and outcomes. **Ecological task analysis,** when student and teacher jointly analyze variables and set goals, is a way of enhancing perceived internal control. With regard to the five motivation orientations, find

Figure 8.9 Competence motivation theory based on work of Harter.

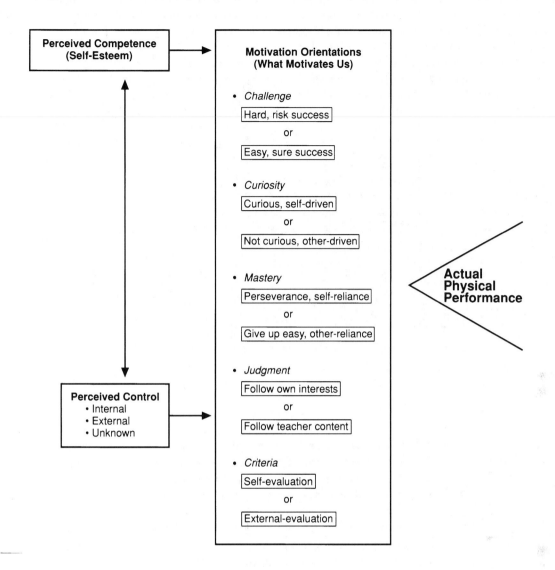

ways to reinforce orientations that keep students intrinsically motivated and actively involved. Competence motivation theory essentially is a rationale for giving self-esteem equal attention with motor skill instruction.

Teacher Expectancy Theory

Expectancy theory embodies two basic assumptions: (a) Persons will perform as they think others expect them to perform and (b) persons will expect of themselves what others expect of them. This theory, also called Pygmalion theory, takes its name from George Bernard Shaw's play *Pygmalion,* which was made into a famous Broadway play and later became the movie *My Fair Lady.* In *Pygmalion,* an English professor boasts that he can change an ignorant, unkempt young woman from the London slums into a beautiful, polished lady with perfect manners and flawless speech. Professor Higgins succeeds in achieving this with Eliza Doolittle, changing her from a person who makes a living by selling flowers on the street to a much-sought-after woman of high society. He does not, however, change the way he perceives and treats her, as indicated in Eliza's comments to one of her suitors:

You see, really and truly, apart from the things anyone can pick up (the dressing and the proper way of speaking, and so on), the difference between a lady and a flower girl is not how she behaves, but how she's treated. I shall always be a flower girl to Professor Higgins, because he always treats me as a flower girl, and always will; but I know I can be a lady to you, because you always treat me as a lady, and always will.

—George Bernard Shaw, *Pygmalion*

This passage clearly illustrates the importance of positive thinking, believing, and acting. Just as coaches convey to their athletes the expectation that they will win, so must physical educators demonstrate belief in persons with disabilities. How the perception of oneself influences motivation and success is called the **self-fulfilling prophecy;** persons unconsciously fulfill expectancies held by themselves and others.

Rosenthal and followers (Rosenthal & Jacobsen, 1968) have conducted so much research on Pygmalion theory that it is also called *Rosenthal theory.* The **Rosenthal effect** (i.e., the outcome of expectancy theory) is said to be operative in classes in which teachers communicate positive expectations to students. In physical education, Thomas Martinek, professor at the University of North Carolina at Greensboro, has spearheaded most of the relevant work in physical education on the effects of teacher expectation on self-concept.

Physical attractiveness, as well as mental, physical, and social performance, has been shown to affect teacher and, later, employer expectations. Persons whose physical disability makes their appearance visibly different from that of peers often are exposed to low expectations and special treatment that sets them still further apart.

Think back to your physical education teachers in elementary, middle, and high school. What was your sense of their expectations for your performance? How did this influence your choices and participation? Think back to a more recent situation, maybe at work or in a family situation or a relationship with someone significant to you. How do the expectations they have for you influence your behavior?

Attribution Theory and Training

Attributions are causal inferences or perceptions of why things happen. Attribution theory focuses on the relationships between event outcomes (success vs. failure; winning vs. losing), beliefs about causes, and subsequent emotions and behaviors. Attribution theory, as begun by Bernard Weiner (1972, 1992), is an umbrella motivation theory subscribed to by most cognitive psychologists. It posits that the need to understand self, others, and the world in general is a major phenomenon in personal fulfillment and self-actualization.

Weiner identified four major causes that persons use to explain success and failure outcomes: (a) ability, (b) effort, (c) task difficulty, and (d) luck. Attribution theory is so complex that it is helpful to define each term by giving examples. Figure 8.10 presents the items used by Gail Dummer and associates (1987) to study the attributions of athletes with cerebral palsy. This model shows only the stability and locus of causality aspects of attribution. Immediately after their events, athletes used a 9-point response scale to rate each of the attributions in Figure 8.10. Additionally, they rated one item on affect ("I enjoy competition"), which was not in Weiner's model.

Persons with severe disability and/or low skills use different attributions than able-bodied peers and thus need different motivational approaches. Persons with severe disabilities tend to explain their successes and failures more by luck and task difficulty than by ability and effort. This is an indication of external locus of causality or control. Task difficulty is closely related to feelings about the person who required the task or determined its difficulty (e.g., "The teacher doesn't like me. Otherwise, he [or she] wouldn't make the task so hard." or "The teacher doesn't give me the help I need.").

Low-skilled children often attribute poor performance to a lack of innate ability (e.g., "I'm just not good enough"). This may be because of feelings of inferiority or the inability to differentiate between ability and effort. Children progress through several developmental levels in the acquisition of attributional skills. *Until age 5 or 6, children believe that effort and ability are the same; they evaluate themselves in terms of simple task mastery* (e.g., "I did it" or "I didn't do it"). Between ages 7 and 9, children begin to understand effort. This leads to the misconception that effort is the sole determinant of outcome (e.g., if persons put forth the same effort, they will achieve

---

Figure 8.10   Illustrative attributes organized according to Weiner's model (Dummer et al., 1987).

Stability Factor

	Stable	Unstable
Internal	**Ability** I perform well because of my ability. I have special skills for this task.	**Effort** I tried hard. I was physically ready. I was mentally ready. I perform well in these situations. I used the right strategy.
External	**Task Difficulty** I spent a lot of time working on my skills.	**Luck** I was lucky. I was able to meet the challenge.

Locus of Causality Factor

equal outcomes). Around age 9, children can finally handle abstract thought and thus begin to accurately distinguish between effort and ability. At about age 12, this understanding matures, and children can analyze relationships between event outcomes and multiple causative factors.

Among students with cognitive disabilities, the ability to understand and use attributions to improve their performance may be delayed or limited. Special educators recommend the use of attributional training or retraining to meet this challenge. Procedures include (a) discussion of beliefs regarding the causes of failure and success; (b) instruction on the meaning of ability, effort, chance, and task difficulty; and (c) use of self-talk as a metacognitive and control strategy when doing tasks. Self-talk might resemble this:

> Why did I goof or make a mistake last time? Maybe it was chance, but probably not. Maybe it was because the task was too hard. Probably not, because the teacher thinks I can do it. Maybe I just don't have the ability. This is silly. I have control over my ability. I can improve my ability. I can do this by effort. OK, now I am going to do this task again and try harder.

Attributional training requires that students talk through tasks with passages like this one. It also provides stories, poems, and mottos about effort and self-control and encourages visualization of the self expending effort and succeeding.

Judgments that teachers and significant others make about attributions are as important as self-judgments because they influence the way students are subsequently treated. Attribution does not take place in a vacuum, but rather occurs within a social setting such as a gymnasium full of peers. Hareli and Weiner (2002) propose that identical attributional information often leads to different emotions in the performer versus those observing the performance, thereby shifting the current focus of attribution research from the individual to include the social setting. For example, a teacher who believes that a student has low ability will reduce the level of difficulty for that student. On the other hand, a teacher who believes that the student is not trying hard enough will enact various motivational strategies. Obviously, all classroom interactions are dependent upon attributional analysis, and perceptions may be accurate or inaccurate, emotional or personal.

Stress and Coping Theory

Stress, which is closely akin to anxiety, has many meanings but usually is associated with major life events or a chronic environmental situation that complicates or interferes with effective functioning. Illustrative of such events are the onset of a disability, the loss of a close friend or a family member, chronic illness, and a change of jobs, schools, or communities. **Stress** refers to negative responses to harm, threat, or challenge that occur when perceived demands exceed perceived resources. However, sometimes events and situations that are usually considered pleasant, happy, rewarding, or successful can be stressful. Stress responses can be physical (like hives, listlessness, and weight gain or loss) or emotional (like temper outbursts, bouts of crying, and generalized numbness or irritability).

There is much in our culture that conspires, from an early age, against the appropriate acknowledgment, acceptance,

and discussion of persons with disabilities. Disability and chronic illness complicate life in myriad ways, causing everyone's roles to change and heightening stress. A person might be unable to attend school or work, enjoy sex, or meet interpersonal demands for long periods of time. Often there is **role ambiguity,** conflict, and confusion because persons do not know what to expect of each other and/or do not like the new roles forced on them by their own or a significant other's disability or illness. Students are subject to stress-inducing environmental events just like adults. Teachers are in an excellent position to help students learn how to manage stress by virtue of their daily contact with them. Adapted physical activity service delivery must include close contact with parents and a partnership approach to learning coping strategies.

Campbell and Jones (2002a, 2002b) have extended the knowledge base on sources of stress and cognitive appraisal of stress sources to wheelchair basketball. Elite male players experience sources of stress relating to the overall competitive process, organizational aspects of a tournament, communicating or relating to important others, demands/costs of playing, and lack of disability awareness.

Coping is the cognitive appraisal of demands and resources, decision making about needed changes, and assertiveness in making these changes. The **transactional stress model,** on the basis of which many coping strategies have been developed, is presented by Lazarus and Folkman (1984). Of particular importance is the mental flexibility to think of and try many different ways to solve problems. Mental flexibility, a component of creativity, can be taught through ecological task analysis (ETA), movement education, and other specially designed gymnasium activities (see Chapters 7 and 9). This is an important part of the self-concept goal area (i.e., learning to understand and appreciate the self, to accept what cannot be changed, and to change what can be changed). Meeting challenges through coping strategies contributes to good self-esteem and positive affect (Crocker, 1993).

 OPTIONAL ACTIVITIES

Observe a physical education class and note the following during your observation by providing evidence as to what you saw to verify your answer:

- Do students willingly share their strengths and gifts?

- Do students volunteer information about themselves, their experiences, and their concerns?

- How do other students respond when people share? Are they supportive or scornful when large discrepancies of skill or talents are apparent?

- Do students "know" things about each other? Would they know who collects trains and who has a dog? Are they aware of differences in culture, family, and skills?

- Do students share what is hard for them? Do they tell people when they are struggling with the skill, confused, hurt, angry?

CHAPTER

9

Inclusion, Social Competence, and Attitude Change
April Tripp and Claudine Sherrill

Figure 9.1 Inclusion has many meanings, depending on age, context, and physical activity goals. (A) and (B): Both are examples of equal-status relationships in an inclusive environment.

A

B

1. Some experts believe in inclusion and others do not. What do you believe? Why?

2. What will you do regarding social inclusion competence (intention) when you visualize yourself as a physical activity professional?

3. How can you help students accept each other on the basis of individual worth? What are the risks of not teaching respect of individual worth?

4. When and how do children learn who is "in" or "cool" and who is "not"?

5. Interview one male and one female physical education teacher and ask the teachers about their feelings and approaches to teaching students with disabilities.

Inclusion has many meanings, but typically it is linked to quality of life in the least restrictive environment (LRE) and social competence. This in turn is linked with attitudes of individuals with and without disabilities. Inclusion is guided by the fundamental principle of valuing diversity. Belonging, acceptance, and a sense of being supported are essentials of an inclusive environment. The most prevalent barriers to including students with disabilities are related to teacher preparation and teacher attitudes as well as perceived and actual barriers to instruction that can include equipment, programming, and time (Folsom-Meek et al., 1999; Lieberman et al., 2002; Pivik et al., 2002).

Two of the most important personal powers associated with individuals with disabilities and successful inclusion are high self-efficacy and high goal perspective (task and ego) (Hutzler et al., 2002). These constructs are discussed in Chapter 8. Individuals with high self-efficacy and goal perspective would most likely insist on being included, modify the task to meet personal needs and goals, and suggest ways the teacher or coach could help. Above all it is important for teachers and coaches to remember that not all individuals with disabilities approach situations and interactions in the inclusion environment in the same ways.

Inclusion is mediated by many factors: internal and external, controlled and uncontrolled, and active and passive. People of all ages, types of disabilities, and experiences demonstrate individual differences in the ways they respond when experiencing very similar situations in movement settings. Creating physical activity *environments that respect diversity and encourage individual improvement are the best approaches* to the design of successful inclusion, a safe place to practice social skills, and explore attitudes. Remember that inclusion means everyone belongs; it is made up of reciprocal relationships, somewhat like a community, that require preparation, training, support, and courage.

Social Inclusion Competence

As you read the following definition of the social inclusion competence goal area, think of how it applies to individuals of all ages, with and without disabilities, and the meaning of each component in a physical activity setting.

The **social inclusion competence goal area** encompasses the following: to learn social behaviors that promote inclusion (i.e., how to interact with others—sharing, taking turns, following, and leading); to develop beliefs and attitudes about self and others that facilitate equal-status social relationships; to reduce social isolation; to learn how to initiate and maintain friendships; and to develop other skills necessary for acceptance by peers with and without disabilities in exercise and sport settings.

Figure 9.1 shows two types of inclusion: in a general physical education class and on a wheelchair basketball team. Yilla (1994, p. 18) stresses the importance of both kinds of inclusion in the following statement:

> One primary function of education is to equip students with lifetime skills. It is logical to extend this to adapted physical education and to ask the question, "What do fully ENabled, disABLED adults do for their physical activity? and then equip students with disabilities to emulate their adult peers. I, like a number of ENabled, disABLED adults, employ a continuum of LRE placements in my life. I work and study in a fully integrated environment. When I compete I am in the realistically segregated environment of wheelchair basketball. When I recreate, I can be at almost any point in the LRE continuum.

The purpose of this chapter is to increase awareness that social inclusion competence is an ecosystem problem; to develop beliefs, attitudes, and behaviors that promote acceptance and inclusion; to develop competencies in assessment and writing goals and objectives; and to encourage critical thinking about principles, practices, and models. Physical educators often are reluctant to establish social competence as one of their two or three major instructional goals, but research emphasizes the importance of social competence in lifespan physical activity involvement. The ability to develop friends who support and encourage physical activity is essential in exercise adherence, sport self-efficacy, and inclusion.

Creating an Inclusive Environment

An inclusive environment is one that offers all individuals tasks that are equally interesting, equally important, and equally engaging. This is no easy task in our diverse society. An inclusive environment is made up of the physical space and equipment, the social-emotional atmosphere, and the teaching strategies that are used. The **physical space** should be barrier free and include a variety of equipment related to the lesson/activity (i.e., vary size, height, weight, texture, color, etc). Setup of the activity area and equipment should invite all individuals to participate, with something meaningful available for everyone. The **social-emotional atmosphere** should be free of stress, emphasizing cooperation rather than survival of the fittest, fastest, or strongest. Furthermore, students should have structure and rules. Attention should be given to use of inclusive and bias-free language, as well as interaction patterns. **Teaching strategies** should incorporate techniques that promote collaboration between instructor and learners, respond to different learning styles, promote self-responsibility, provide opportunities for independent learning, and use a variety of informal assessment tools to guide instruction. Finally, **flexibility** is the hallmark of an inclusive environment.

The very first step in creating an inclusive environment is for teachers and coaches to identify their own beliefs or stereotypes about others who are different. Our own expectations of others can become self-fulfilling prophecies through the way we design our learning environment.

 Ask yourself the following questions to examine your personal awareness.

"Do I know what it is like not to be able to make a good throw?" Describe feelings as you understand they might be.

"Do I know what it must be like to participate from a wheelchair?" Close your eyes and visualize this along with how it would feel.

"Do I know what it is like to participate from a constant state of confusion?" Remember back to a time you got involved in something way too complicated; what would it be like if you felt like that constantly?

It is much easier to teach when the teacher and student are similar; it becomes progressively more difficult to teach individuals who are markedly different. Keep in mind that many physical educators and coaches are gifted athletes; this experience will frame the way they teach. However, this dilemma can be overcome through examining personal beliefs (such as in the exercise described previously), using a reflective approach to teaching, and practicing new teaching styles.

It is not enough to integrate individuals with disabilities into physical activity settings and assume that by exposure or contact people will develop skills and learn to appreciate each other's differences. Actually, this practice can make the situation worse if there is not sensitive and careful consideration of the physical activity environment. Physical activity professionals must create an environment where all individuals feel safe, physically and emotionally, to explore and develop their abilities, as well as have the respect of their peers and instructor while doing so. The values associated with an inclusive environment include:

- Uniqueness—everyone has special qualities
- Empowerment—believing in self
- Belonging—feeling a part of the whole
- Security—knowing rules are enforced fairly
- Purpose—setting realistic goals and feeling challenged

Types of Inclusion

Physical inclusion, or the assignment of all students to general physical education, is a standard practice in the United States. Exceptions to this practice occur primarily with the 3 to 5% of the population with disabilities who have severe to profound retardation and/or multiple disabilities that make success in the general classroom unlikely. Exceptions also occur when parents request adapted physical education services part- or full-time in separate settings that afford opportunity for instruction individualized to meet special needs.

Instructional Inclusion

Instructional inclusion refers to involvement in learning activities in the general class. This will depend on the extent to which the instructional objectives of a student with a disability are similar to those of peers and the extent to which resources are available to support inclusion. If the severity of the condition makes objectives different, then the student can engage in activities with a paraprofessional or a peer tutor in the same physical setting, but probably with few interactions with classmates who do not have a disability. Teachers can plan warm-up exercises or closure activities that everyone does together, but these will not necessarily lead to social interactions.

Social Inclusion

Social inclusion refers to positive personal interactions with classmates that contribute to feelings of accepting and liking each other. Of particular importance is whether these interactions are **unidirectional,** with nondisabled persons taking most of the initiative and seeing themselves as helpers, or **equal status,** with both parties reaching out to include each other. Equal-status relationships lead to shared initiative in social inclusion (see Figure 9.2).

Whereas physical inclusion is achieved easily by administrative mandate, instructional and social inclusion are challenges that require considerable commitment and hard work. Case study data from actual physical education programs reveal two themes: segregated inclusion and social isolation. Findings from Place and Hodge (2001) indicate that, *in inclu-*

Figure 9.2 **Although you can mandate inclusion, you cannot mandate friendship.**

sive physical education classes, students with and without disabilities infrequently engage in social interactions. The average percentage of time that classmates gave to students with disabilities was 2% social talk and less than 1% in each category for praise, use of first name, feedback, and physical contact.

Characteristics of an Inclusive Environment

If you were to ask students with disabilities what makes a "good" day in an inclusive physical education class and what makes a "bad" day, this is what they would tell you (Goodwin & Watkinson, 2000):

> *Good days* are filled with a sense of belonging, skillful participation, and sharing in the benefits. *Bad days* are overshadowed by negative feelings of social isolation, questioned competence, and restricted participation (p. 144)

It takes substantial effort on the part of a physical activity professional to provide a sound instructional setting for students with disabilities included in a general physical education class. Good teachers indicate that they struggle constantly to find methods of organization and instruction in order to achieve learning gains with students with disabilities (LaMaster et al., 1998). In addition, teachers surveyed by LaMaster et al., (1998) believed that they were inadequately prepared to cope with the challenges of inclusion. On the other hand, Block and Zeman (1996) argued that, with proper support services, students with severe disabilities can be included in general physical education without negatively affecting the program for students without disabilities. Most of the concerns that physical education teachers have about including students with disabilities into general physical education focus on management (Lienert, Sherrill, & Myers, 2001). One teacher stated, "I can't possibly give these students the attention they need with all these other kids in here, I need to see them in a smaller group. It's just not fair to the other kids when these kids need so much extra help; even with an aide in here, it just isn't enough" (synthesized from quotes of many teachers, pp. 7–13).

The task is a daunting one; however, all physical activity professionals must forgo bandwagons and adopt a strong philosophical stance that guides our best efforts toward the reconceptualization of inclusion as both an attitude and a process based on social justice (DePauw & Doll-Tepper, 2000). Characteristics of a good inclusive instructional program include:

- Employs higher-level decision-making skills
- Develops skills for social interaction
- Eliminates stereotyping
- Provides instruction that has personal meaning to individuals of diverse ability and experience
- Teaches conflict resolution skills
- Responds to different learning styles
- Uses evaluation techniques that allow different ways for individuals to demonstrate achievement
- Uses techniques to improve self-esteem
- Uses local and community resources
- Incorporates cooperative and collaborative learning experiences to balance competition experiences

- Balances the needs of the individual and standards of learning

Physical Education Placement and the Law

Social competence is important because federal law states that separate class placement is justifiable only when "the nature or severity of the disability is such that education in general classes *with the use of supplementary aids and services* cannot be achieved satisfactorily." This means that teachers and students must have the social competence to accept and include students with disabilities in general classes. It also means that individuals with disabilities and their families must want inclusion and have the social competence to help change the attitudes and behaviors of others.

Illustrative court cases challenging educational placements indicate that school systems must apply three standards in removing students from regular classrooms (Block, 1996):

1. The school system must document that supplementary aids and supports were tried for a reasonable amount of time and that these steps did not enable satisfactory education.
2. The school system must document that the student did not benefit from mainstream placement (i.e., did not make reasonable progress toward IEP goals).
3. The school system must document that the presence of the student with a disability, even with supplementary aids and supports present, was so disruptive to the class that the safety and/or learning of other students was seriously impaired.

School systems that have been placing students with mild and moderate disabilities in separate physical education classes need to be rethinking their procedures. Professionals must be prepared for school system shifts in philosophy and practices and must know the kinds of supplementary aids and supports to request in order to maximize the likelihood that students will benefit from general physical education instruction.

Curriculum Models That Support Inclusion

Numerous physical education models have been created to help students with special needs gain the social competence and other skills to function independently in general physical education. Curriculum models that support inclusion have some common characteristics. First, they focus on essentials; the instructor clearly states what each learner will come away with as a result of the activity. Second, individual success is the measure of achievement. Teachers work to balance individual needs and stated standards. Finally, curriculum models that allow for flexibility of content, product, and process provide many options for meeting the individual needs of each learner.

Reverse Mainstreaming

Reverse mainstreaming refers to the integration of nondisabled students into the facilities for students with disabilities (i.e., a separate school or class). The ratio of disabled to nondisabled should be approximately 1 to 3, and the teacher-pupil ratio approximately 1 to 8. This type of program should be conducted by experienced adapted physical educators and works well with a station approach. Keep in mind that students in separate facilities will typically have more severe disabilities. Make sure the nondisabled students are prepared for this by conducting prior training and awareness activities.

Peer and Cross-Age Tutors

One of the oldest models of peer teaching is the PEOPEL (Physical Education Opportunity Program for Exceptional Learners) Project, which originated in Arizona and was disseminated through the National Diffusion Network and the Office of Special Education (Long et al., 1980). In the PEOPEL model, nondisabled high school students complete a one-semester physical education careers class that trains them to work with peers who have disabilities. They are then assigned to PEOPEL classes, where they serve as peer tutors to provide individualized instruction based on task-analyzed objectives. Generally, PEOPEL classes are comprised of 12 students with disabilities and 12 peer tutors under the supervision of an adult instructor.

Trained peer tutors are effective at assisting participants to improve their motor performance in integrated physical education classes (Houston-Wilson et al., 1997). Many high schools today have similar programs in place for service learning or leadership that can be used to recruit peers to assist in physical education. Check with the school counseling office, as they usually organize these kinds of programs. Peer tutoring facilitates mainstreaming and encourages students with special promise and leadership potential to choose physical education as their university major.

Many helping interactions, including peer tutoring, are used extensively without adequate sensitivity to the recipients' responses to being helped. The way help is given, the behavior of the person giving the help, and the context in which the help is given all interact and give meaning to the helping act. An act of help can be self-threatening or self-supporting. Situational conditions of help that imply inferiority can lead to negative self-perceptions. However, situational conditions that communicate caring and concern can facilitate favorable self-perceptions (Goodwin, 2001).

Cross-age tutor programs are effective in many communities (see Figure 9.3). Older students, designated as members of the "Honor PE Corps," are released from their classes one or two periods a day to work in elementary schools as physical education teacher aides. Such students generally are required to meet certain criteria and to complete after-school or weekend training programs. The honors corps often functions as a club (sometimes a subdivision of Future Teachers of America) and meets periodically for in-service training. Service learning programs that are required for graduation can also serve as a source for cross-age tutors.

Reciprocal Peer Tutoring and Teaching

Special education literature reports that children with learning disabilities, mild mental retardation, autism, and behavior disorders can function effectively as peer tutors and should be given opportunities to learn through reciprocal tutoring and teaching with nondisabled partners. So much of the time we think of students with disabilities as the recipients of help, not

Figure 9.3 Research shows that children can often teach other children more effectively than adults can. In mainstream physical education, well-skilled children are often given special training to qualify as *peer teachers.*

the givers. With the right support students with disabilities are quite capable of acting as peer tutors. Being in a "leadership-type" role is very empowering.

Children with and without disabilities who have been peer tutors praise and encourage each other more, express more empathy, provide and ask for more feedback, and show evidence of more meaningful, interactive contact time than children in control groups.

A good place to begin when setting up a reciprocal peer tutoring program is the reciprocal teaching style described by Mosston and Ashworth (1994), who note that even third-grade children are capable of observing and correcting one another's movement errors. Research shows that children *learn* through teaching. *Students with disabilities need the opportunity to teach.* Success in reciprocal teaching depends largely on preclass organization—the development of task cards or tangible instructions for pairs to follow with regard to learning objectives, principles of good performance, and a good peer training program (Houston-Wilson et al., 1997).

Instructional Content That Supports Inclusion

Instructional models that are centered on the individual, with an emphasis on participation, and allow for a variety of ways to be successful can make the process of inclusion easier. Inclusive instruction teaches people how to succeed, how to accept the

Table 9.1   Inclusion models.

1. **Specially Created Instructional Groups**
   Reverse mainstreaming
   Peer and cross-age tutors
   Reciprocal peer tutoring and teaching
   Unified Sports
   Challenger baseball
   Structured cooperative goal groups
2. **Specially Selected Instructional Content**
   Games design model
   Cooperative or new games
   Adventure education
   Movement education
3. **Supplemental Human Supports**
   Paraprofessional designated for student
   Paraprofessional assigned to teacher
   Consultant assigned to teacher
   Adult athlete with disability volunteer
   Dual and team teacher collaborations
   Video and data collection personnel
4. **Written Plans Specifically for Inclusion**
   Goals and objectives
   Behavior management plans
   Curriculum plans
   Social skills intervention and direct instruction
5. **Facility, Equipment, and Transportation**
   Accessible
   Close proximity
   Success-oriented

strengths and limitations of everyone involved, and how to strive for improvement. Table 9.1 provides a summary of alternatives and reminds us that other types of support may also be needed.

Games Design Model

The games design model is a systematic approach to changing established games and developing new games that (a) are inclusive in nature, (b) meet individual needs, and (c) promote cooperative problem solving and creativity among students and teacher. G. S. Don Morris of California State Polytechnic University in Pomona first described games design pedagogy in 1976; his classic book (Morris & Stiehl, 1999) has undergone several revisions and it is recommended as a supplementary text for adapted physical education courses.

Although many elementary school physical education textbooks discuss ways of changing games, Morris was the first to suggest a model. According to his model, three steps are required in designing games:

1. Understanding the basic structure underlying all games

2. Modifying the basic game structure

3. Managing the game's degree of difficulty

If a game is to be changed, the first procedure is to identify the game's components and develop a chart like that in Table 9.2. All games can be broken down into six components: (a) the number and function of players, (b) equipment and space requirements, (c) movements (what, who, when, where, how), (d) organization (game formation), (e) limitations or rules, and (f) purpose(s). Teachers can then manipulate or change components of games as they plan a lesson in order to meet the needs of all students.

Teachers can also teach the students to use games design to create new games. When working with students who are beginners at games design, select one category in which to make a change. In kickball and softball, for example, two bases might be used instead of four. Under limitations, the out-of-bounds rule might be eliminated so there are no foul balls—the batter runs on everything. Or the method of putting the ball in play might be changed, with each batter choosing her or his own way. Much of the value in the games design model when students do the creating is practice in problem solving and creative thinking.

As students become increasingly adept at implementing change, several components can be altered simultaneously. An important role of the teacher is to provide guidance without passing judgment. Provide the students with criteria for changes. For example, tell students that they can change anything as long as (a) all students get to play all the time (i.e., there is no elimination) and (b) all students have an equal opportunity of success.

Table 9.2   An analysis of a traditional game (softball) into six components.

Players	Equipment	Movements	Organization Pattern	Limitations (Rules)	Purpose
9 per team	Ball Bats Four bases Gloves Backstop	Throw Catch Field Pitch Bat Tag Run Slide	Offense at bat, defense in field, each covering designated areas	Diamond, run bases counterclockwise, defense pitches ball, three strikes equals out, three outs per team each inning, seven innings, out-of-bounds rules, fly ball rule, etc.	Win, or practice skills, or have fun! Which is priority?

The games design model is an excellent way to enhance students' understanding of the many components that make up a game and how any game can be changed so everyone has an opportunity for meaningful participation. A common criticism of many games like softball and kickball is that half the students are sitting and watching all the time. Students offer great solutions when posed a problem like this using the games design model.

One variation that my students devised was *Everyone-in-Action Softball.* Each time the ball was put into play (batted, thrown, kicked), everyone on the batting team had to do one of the three things (sit-ups, rope jump, stair stepping) until the batter rounded all the bases. The defensive team had to run to whoever fielded the ball, form a file behind that player, and pass the ball backward and then forward so everyone touched the ball two times before the original fielder could yell "Fisheye!" This call permitted the batter to cease running and the batting team members to quit their respective fitness activities. The score was the number of bases run. The students changed this game hundreds of ways and never seemed to tire of it.

Cooperative Learning and New Games

Cooperative learning is an accepted instructional strategy to promote learning achievement and social interactions across the curriculum. Furthermore, cooperative learning positively affects the social acceptance of students with disabilities by their AB peers. When individuals work cooperatively they develop unanimity of purpose and of need to promote group learning (Ashman, 2000).

The cooperative or new games model has been explained and promoted by Terry Orlick of Canada and colleagues since 1978. Orlick points out that games are played cooperatively in many cultures (e.g., Eskimos, Chinese, New Guineans) but that, in North America, few games are designed specifically so that everyone works toward one common, mutually desirable goal. Alternatives to the competitive games and sports that currently dominate physical education are needed. Cooperation, according to Orlick (1978),

> is directly related to communication, cohesiveness, trust, and the development of positive social-interaction skills. Through cooperative ventures, children learn to share, to empathize with others, to be concerned with others' feelings, and to work to get along better. (pp. 6–7)

Four criteria must be met for an activity to be considered cooperative: (a) All players help each other to achieve a common goal, (b) everyone's efforts are accepted, (c) everyone is involved, and (d) everyone has fun. To bring a diverse group of individuals together is not always easy: One reason to play games is for "fun." LeFevre's (2002) book, *Best New Games,* is a great resource for cooperative, interactive, and trust activities.

Illustrative of a cooperative game is devising as many ways as possible for a small group (three to six people) to keep a beach ball in the air (see Figure 9.4). One way, of course, is volleying, but another way is to permit the use of any body parts. Try everyone assuming a sitting or shoulder-lying position and the rule that only feet or legs can touch the ball. Or try a blanket, parachute, or tablecloth series of tosses with everyone holding on. Each group tries to better its best time in the air. Groups never compete with one another to see who can keep the ball in the air the longest.

Numerous partner activities and stunts can be devised, such as three-legged runs and three-armed target tosses. Sometimes, the variation is one person blindfolded and one sighted. Carrying stunts also are fun: How many ways can three people cooperate to carry another person or some object like a tumbling mat or chair?

When physical education teachers use cooperative learning design and/or small-group learning, in order for learning to be maximized, four ingredients are necessary:

1. Forming teams
2. Positive interdependence
3. Individual accountability
4. Collaborative skills

Physical activity professionals will find lots of good information and resources on cooperative learning in physical education in Steve Grineski's (1996) book.

Do you think inclusive techniques such as peer tutoring, cooperative games, adventure or risk taking activities, and games design should be part of most physical education programs regardless of whether the students have disabilities or not? If you answered yes, why do you feel that way? If you answered no, what are the obstacles?

Unified Sports

Unified Sports is a mainstream model introduced by Special Olympics International (SOI) in the 1980s. Although developed by SOI specifically to promote integration of persons with and without mental retardation, the idea can be applied in many ways. At present, SOI has applied the Unified Sports concept to such sports as aquatics, athletics, basketball, boccia, bowling, cycling, golf, roller skating, sailing, soccer, softball, table tennis, tennis, and volleyball. Castagno (2001) found that athletes with and without mental retardation demonstrated positive changes in self-esteem, basketball skills, and attitude toward mental retardation through participation in an 8-week Unified Sport basketball program.

Two principles guide Unified Sports: (a) age grouping and (b) ability grouping. Team members are matched as closely as possible on chronological age, and teams compete with other teams composed of members of the same age. Within a team, the sport abilities of players with and without mental retardation are matched so that the nonretarded peers do not dominate or assume peer tutor relationships. Persons with disabilities other than mental retardation can be members of Unified Sports teams, but they must be counted as nonretarded. At all times, 50% of the players on the floor or field must be mentally retarded.

Figure 9.4 Cooperative games.

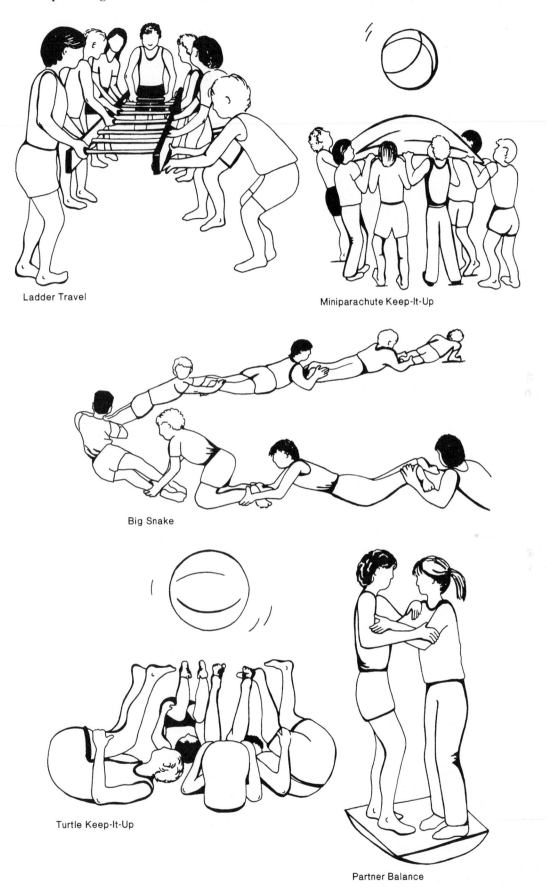

Ladder Travel

Miniparachute Keep-It-Up

Big Snake

Turtle Keep-It-Up

Partner Balance

Figure 9.5   **Adventure activities to overcome fears.**

Jump forward from various distances to grab horizontal bar.

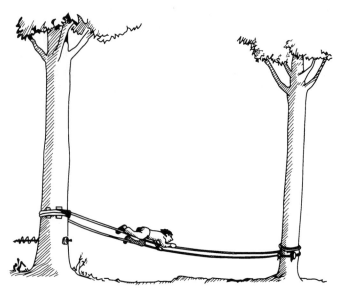

Traverse parallel ropes at various distances from ground.

Move from swing to swing at various distances from ground.

Adventure Education

Adventure activities are challenges that involve ropes courses, jumps, climbs, and swings, with several persons helping one another (see Figure 9.5). Sometimes called outdoor adventure, the idea is to successfully cope with fears and anxieties and/or to develop trust and other social behaviors. The ropes to be traversed can be any distance from the ground. This is true also of various kinds of beams to be walked and jumped from. There are also walls to be climbed, rope ladders to be mastered, and map and compass orienteering activities.

Teachers need special training about safety aspects, and a budget is needed to underwrite ropes courses and other equipment. Recently a number of specialized pieces of equip-

ment have been designed to provide access to individuals with mobility impairments to participate in adventure education activities. The adventure concept and activities have been successful with many types of disabilities, low self-esteem, or relationships problems. Information can be obtained from Project ADVENTURE, P.O. Box 100, Hamilton, MA 01936 or contact by e-mail at www.pa.org.

Movement Education

Movement education was described in Chapter 3 as an approach that permits many students to work simultaneously on the same skill but at their own level of difficulty. In movement education, the teacher does not demonstrate or ask students to do so. Instead, lessons are built around problems that are solved through movement and have no right or wrong answers. Often, a series of questions is used to guide discovery of body, effort, space, and relationships. Mosston and Ashworth (1986) designated this general approach a "guided discovery teaching style."

The idea of movement education was first proposed by Rudolph Laban, a Hungarian who spent most of his adult life in England and greatly influenced the teaching of dance and movement both there and abroad. His two classic books, *Modern Educational Dance* (1975) and *The Mastery of Movement* (1960), are the primary sources for movement education pedagogy.

Both general and adapted physical educators should learn to use the movement education model. This model is described in many elementary school physical education methods texts, often under the headings of educational gymnastics, dance, and games.

Creative dance, educational gymnastics, and developmental movement are other terms used for teaching styles that stress fluency, originality, and imagination (components of motor creativity). This approach not only guides exploration of what the body can do but teaches students how to relate to each other in partner and small-group problem solving and choreography. McCall and Craft (2000) have developed an excellent resource book for preschoolers of all abilities titled *Movement with a Purpose*. This book applies a child-centered approach and is filled with many activities for children with special needs.

Multicultural Strategies

Our world continues to become more and more diverse marked by dramatic demographic changes in culture, ethnicity, sexuality, religion, and disability. Physical educators are being called on to provide a curriculum that is both transdisciplinary and multicultural, in addition to providing adaptations to meet the individual needs of all students. Diversity should be viewed as an asset and a positive challenge in our societal structure. Understanding diversity is a prerequisite to being an effective teacher. The use of multicultural strategies can be an effective tool for teaching in diverse and inclusive physical education programs. Clements and Kinzler (2003) use a multicultural approach to teach responsibility, social skills, and respect for differences through physical education. All physical activity professionals need to be aware of the individual needs that result from a student's diversity as well as disability and to be prepared to address both in an instructional program.

Attitude Change Intervention

No matter what the curriculum model and the instructional design, attitude change intervention to support inclusion and social justice must be embedded in every lesson plan. Some students already have good attitudes (demonstrated by their day-by-day actions or behaviors) and can be used as models, helpers, and tutors. However, most students tend to have neutral (indifferent) or bad attitudes toward social interactions, friendships, and other aspects of inclusion competence. Attitude, the key to behavior change, is so difficult to modify that a separate section on this goal concludes the chapter. First, however, we must address writing goals and objectives.

Writing Goals and Objectives

The IEP should specifically describe the environment, that is, be it a general physical education class or a separate setting, in which instruction in physical education will take place. For inclusion to occur, specific goals and objectives should be written emphasizing inclusion and agreed upon by everyone in the inclusion setting: (a) students with and without disabilities, (b) the teacher in charge, and (c) consultants, paraprofessionals, volunteers, and others brought to the class as supplemental human supports. For example: *Demonstrate ability to interact positively with a same-age partner while working on specific motor skill or fitness objectives for 80% of observed time.* Illustrative specific behaviors to be assessed and timed at the 80% criterion level are these:

a. Maintain eye contact with your partner.
b. Maintain physical proximity to your partner (e.g., within an arm's length).
c. Initiate talk with your partner.
d. Engage in response talk with your partner.
e. Model or demonstrate for your partner.
f. Ask your partner to model or demonstrate for you.
g. Praise your partner for effort.
h. Praise your partner for achievement.
i. Use your partner's first name.
j. Give appropriate corrective feedback (one chunk at a time).
k. Ask for "hands-on" help.
l. Give "hands-on" help.

This list could go on forever! It illustrates, however, specific behaviors that *students with and without disabilities must demonstrate to achieve social competence as partners.* Students must receive constant reminders to work on these objectives and regular feedback concerning how well they are doing. A list of these objectives should be posted at each station, and the teacher should rotate around the stations, pointing to the lists and asking such things as, "Are you remembering Item C?" Self-evaluation and examples of success in class discussions and in journals further reinforce the need to attend to objectives.

Partnership and small-group social inclusion competence should probably be acquired before true inclusion can be expected in any of the specially selected instructional content models, such as games design, new games, or adventure education. Outcomes of instructional programs grounded in social inclusion competence include friendship and support that carries over into other settings.

IEP teams must decide whether student needs supplemental human supports to benefit from instruction or can make do with existing human resources in the class (see Table 9.1). Decisions should also be made about the best way to prepare students with and without disabilities for the inclusion experience.

Social Interactions

Virtually all motor and fitness activities in a gymnasium require social interactions, because space must be shared with others.

Students must be aware of safety as they move through space and/or propel objects. *Listening to class instructions, watching and imitating a motor skill, and getting into game formations are all social skills.* In elementary school, many games involve holding hands in circles or lines, changing places, taking turns, and sharing equipment. As games become more complex and require an understanding of offense and defense, much social competence is needed.

This social competence is typically taken for granted, but consider how the ecosystem changes when a student with visual or hearing impairments is integrated into the class. Consider how a person with cognitive limitations or a different kind of mobility might change ways of communicating or using space. Describe some probable interaction challenges and propose ways to meet them. Give actual dialogue as in writing a play or skit.

Special needs should be acknowledged by an IEP goal, such as the following: *Demonstrate ability to perform necessary social interactions in a class of 25 [specify class size] while working on physical education skills and playing games 80% of observed time.* Specific objectives related to this goal might be these:

1. Demonstrate insight into when help is needed and request help in an appropriate way.
    a. Hold up a hand and ask for help from the teacher.
    b. Call the name of a peer within a 5-foot radius and request help.
    c. Go across the room or the needed distance to ask someone for help.
2. Say thank you and/or give praise to the individual who helps.
3. Give corrective feedback in an appropriate way to the individual who tries to help you but does not know how.
4. Greet three or more individuals upon arrival to class or on the way to an assigned station.
5. Initiate positive social interactions of at least 3-min duration with at least one same-age peer.
6. Sustain social interactions an average of ___ minutes.
7. Do "high fives" with class members at appropriate times.
8. Yell, scream, cheer, or express excitement about the game and show support for your teammates in the same ways that others do.
9. Request a turn or ask to be included, if you have been excluded from an activity.

These objectives should be measurable by specifying the number of times within set time periods, stating the duration of time an interaction should be sustained, or indicating the number of social interactions with different people in a specific class period. Note that each objective is interactive and requires the cooperation of others. Failure to achieve an objective should be analyzed ecologically, with consideration given to all human and environmental factors. When a major goal for the student is

Figure 9.6 Deborah Buswell and Kerrie Berends, adapted physical educators, analyze videotapes to obtain social behavior data.

social competence or inclusion, *support personnel for collecting data as to whether or not the goal is being achieved should be planned and included in the school budget* (see Figure 9.6).

Friendship

Another approach to goal setting is to emphasize the development of friendships that will promote involvement in physical activity and sport. See Martin and Smith (2002) for assessment of friendship quality. The most frequently reported barrier to physical activity involvement is lack of a friend, companion, or advocate with whom to share the experiences. It is important, therefore, to teach social competence for overcoming this barrier. The following are illustrative goals and objectives that might be met at the 80% level (i.e., success in 4 out of 5 trials)

Demonstrate an Understanding of the Factors That Enable People to Initiate Relationships.

1. Identify two potential friends with similar recreational interests.
2. Identify one potential friend who lives close enough to one's home to make after-school visiting realistic (or problem-solve ways to enhance getting together in after-school hours).
3. Identify one student in class who is likely to say yes to an after-school invitation.

Demonstrate an Ability to Initiate and Respond to Invitations for After-School Exercise and Play, and Keep a Journal or Photo Album to Document Evidence of Achieving Each Objective.

1. Keep a journal describing how you invited one or more students to join you to exercise or play during nonschool hours.
2. Keep a journal of invitations you have received from others to play or exercise together.
3. Respond appropriately to an invitation and take initiative in getting to the play or exercise site [this involves many steps, like asking parents' permission, finding transportation, and reading the clock to leave at the right time].
4. Respond appropriately to a rejection of a play invitation (i.e., something like "That's OK, maybe next time!").
5. Ask an adult or a peer for help when you are unsure of how to handle an invitation, rejection, or other social interaction.

Social Inclusion Competence

Social inclusion competence objectives might also address discipline problems or specific behaviors that make students unacceptable to peers and/or other age groups. The following are illustrative goals and objectives for students. Typically the teacher assumes responsibility for recording behaviors to document the student's achievement of these objectives.

Demonstrate Social Behaviors That Are Acceptable to Peers and Teachers in the Physical Activity Setting.

1. Decrease the number of your violations of physical education class rules by 50% of charted time.
2. Increase the duration of time between warnings from the teacher for inappropriate behaviors by 50% of charted time.
3. Decrease the number of your incidents of crying, temper outbursts, etc. (specify one behavior in each objective) during class to less than two in four-week period.

Demonstrate Dress, Grooming, and Postures Similar to Those of Peers.

1. Increase the number of days that you come to school with clean fingernails (hair, body odor, or whatever grooming problem needs to be corrected) as charted 90% of the time.
2. Increase the number of days that you wear clothes, shoes, caps, makeup similar to those of your peers as charted 90% of the time.

Remember, objectives must be measurable. However the measurement is individually determined and can be varied from the examples provided here.

Problems of Social Acceptance

The goals and objectives stated in the preceding section address many reasons why students with disabilities experience problems with social acceptance in mainstream physical education.

Many nondisabled peers have the same problems. In general, social acceptance is related to one's (a) repertoire of social skills, (b) physical attractiveness, and (c) competence in areas deemed important by peers. *For boys, athletic competence is the area most likely to determine acceptance and popularity.*

Many physical educators therefore emphasize increasing physical attractiveness, motor skills, and fitness as a means of improving social acceptance. This approach works with some students but almost always requires supplementary instruction focusing on increasing the student's repertoire of social skills. Many students who need adapted physical activity services, moreover, have underlying ability deficits or health problems that preclude their physical attractiveness, motor skills, and fitness from ever approximating those of their peers. Teachers must find ways for these individuals to be socially accepted despite their differences. Now that we have entered an age of high-tech solutions to many of our dilemmas there seems to be an overreliance on technologic solutions to personal and social problems. Teachers must use caution not to utilize techniques that maintain, if not create, the very problems they were supposed to solve.

Illustrative Social Skills Curriculums

Specially designed curriculums have been developed for students who need systematic instruction in social skills, the most popular being Hellison's 1995 Teaching Personal-Social Responsibility Model (TPSR). Other models include "The Waksman Social Skill Program" (Waksman, Messmer, & Waksman, 1988) and "The ACCEPTS Program" (Walker et al., 1988). These curriculums use various combinations of cognitive training, behavior management, self-esteem, and empowerment techniques. Typically, also, the physical environment is carefully planned, and staff–student ratios permit much individual and small-group instruction and counseling. Following are descriptions of two such curriculums.

ACCEPTS: The Walker Social Skills Curriculum

ACCEPTS is an acronym for A Curriculum for Children's Effective Peer and Teacher Skills. The goal of this curriculum is to teach social competence requisite to successful adjustment in regular classes in Grades K through 6 (Walker et al., 1988). The program can be purchased from Pro·Ed (see Appendix E), or this description can help you create your own original social skills curriculum.

ACCEPTS includes assessment procedures for selecting children who can benefit from this program, teaching guidelines for effective instruction, role-playing scripts and formats for teaching 28 social skills, and behavior management techniques. Table 9.3 lists the 28 social skills. Each of these is taught through this nine-step procedure:

1. **Definition.** The teacher defines a specific behavior, then guides student discussion of examples and applications.
2. **Positive example.** A videotape of correct behavior is shown, and/or the teacher models the right way to behave.
3. **Negative example.** A second videotape is shown, but this one shows the wrong way to behave.

Table 9.3   Content of ACCEPTS curriculum: 28 social skills.

Area I.   Classroom Skills
　　　　1. Listening to the teacher
　　　　2. Responding appropriately when the teacher asks you to do something
　　　　3. Doing your best work
　　　　4. Following classroom rules
Area II.   Basic Interaction Skills
　　　　1. Eye contact
　　　　2. Using the right voice
　　　　3. Starting
　　　　4. Listening
　　　　5. Answering
　　　　6. Making sense
　　　　7. Taking turns talking
　　　　8. Asking a question
　　　　9. Continuing practice of these skills
Area III.   Getting Along Skills
　　　　1. Using polite words
　　　　2. Sharing
　　　　3. Following rules
　　　　4. Assisting others
　　　　5. Touching the right way
Area IV.   Making Friends Skills
　　　　1. Good grooming
　　　　2. Smiling
　　　　3. Complimenting
　　　　4. Making friends
Area V.   Coping Skills
　　　　1. Responding appropriately when someone says "No"
　　　　2. Responding appropriately when you express anger
　　　　3. Responding appropriately when someone teases
　　　　4. Responding appropriately when someone tries to hurt you
　　　　5. Responding appropriately when someone asks you to do something you can't do
　　　　6. Responding appropriately when things don't go right

4. **Review.** The teacher reviews, restates the definition, and guides more student discussion.
5. **Positive example.** A third video scene is shown; this one shows an applied behavioral application.
6. **Role-playing activity.** The teacher models a correct behavior and then involves the students in a role-playing situation to practice the behavior.
7. **Positive example.** A final video scene of correct behavior is shown, and/or the teacher models to give closure to the instruction.

8. **Criterion role-playing.** Students play assigned roles and are evaluated in accordance with criteria or standards. If their performance is successful, they move on to the next step. If not, they must go through the previous steps again.
9. **Informal contracting.** The teacher presents the students with natural situations that will occur outside of class, and the students respond with verbal commitments to behave correctly. These are considered contracts.

Many of the modeling and role-playing activities in ACCEPTS relate to physical education and playground behaviors. The role-playing scripts are very short and involve only the teacher and one child. Many scripts focus on **coping,** a complex behavioral set that requires cognitive appraisal of demands and resources, decision making about needed changes, and assertiveness in making these changes. This program is based on the assumption that some children do not learn proper social skills spontaneously. They misbehave because they do not know how to act or are confused by the complexity of a social situation.

The skills in Table 9.3 look very simple, but many students with severe disabilities who are being assigned to general physical education lack experience in interacting with others. Often these students are accompanied by a personal paraprofessional and interact only with this adult rather than with peers. Involvement in a social skills curriculum should be written into the IEP of these students so that they can benefit socially from the mainstream setting. Benefits often do not occur without special training.

Responsibility in PE: The Hellison Curriculum

The best-known physical education model based on empowerment and responsibility was developed by Hellison (1995) and has had many revisions (Hellison & Walsh, 2002). This model effectively empowers students to take charge of their lives and assume increased responsibility for others and the total ecosystem. The model involves direct instruction regarding five kinds of responsibility that the students need to take on:

Level 1
Respecting the rights and feelings of others
Self-control
The right to peaceful conflict resolution
The right to be included

Level 2
Participation and effort
Exploring effort
Trying new things
A personal definition of success

Level 3
Self-direction
On-task independent
Personal plan
Balancing current and future needs
Striving against external forces

Level 4

Caring about and helping others

Prerequisite interpersonal skills

Compassion

Without rewards

Contributing member of the community and beyond

Level 5

Outside the gym

Although each level is easy to understand on its surface, to effectively teach using Teaching Personal-Social Responsibility (TPSR) one must understand important nuances involved in a more detailed explanation of the components. Four themes provide a framework for effectively shifting responsibility to the students:

1. Empowerment—believing that people can make decisions and sometimes need practice doing it.

2. Integration—Infusion of personal and social responsibility with the subject matter.

3. Transfer—Using the skills learned in values associated with TPSR outside the gym.

4. Relational—The entire TPSR model hinges on building relationships, giving students a voice, and beliefs that every student matters and all students have strengths and do not just need to be fixed.

Kevin Kaardal (2001) has written a book titled *Learning by Choice in Secondary Physical Education* that serves as an excellent companion book to Hellison's work. Kaardal provides many ideas on how students can select their own activities, organize themselves, plan objectives, follow through, and stay on course. Kaardal's work focuses on "facilitating" rather than "teaching" classes and helps develop personal and social responsibility.

Hellison's personal-social responsibility model can be accommodated within many different curriculum designs, but some time must be allocated for individual counseling. When students are independently working at stations or carrying out personal plans, teachers can pull one student at a time for counseling. Most of the time this means checking in to see how they are doing and feeling, sometimes exchanging perspectives or coevaluating the students' level of responsibility. If a student's problem requires specialized skills, a referral to a professional should be made.

When you become a physical activity professional, be it in public or private school, with people who are very young or over 65 years, what recreation and/or sport practices will you use to work toward an inclusive physical activity experience for all? Why did you select these practices? Where did you learn them?

Attitude Change Theory and Practice

Attitudes play a central role in the integration of persons with disabilities into general physical education and sport. They affect how individuals are taught and accepted, as well as what support and services are made available to them. **Attitudes** indicate one's predisposition to either approach or avoid something. Approaching or avoiding behaviors, in turn, evoke new attitudes about self and environment. The attitude-behavior relationship can be conceptualized as a continuous circle with change occurring in both directions. Review basic information on attitude change in Chapter 5. It focuses on changing teacher attitudes, whereas the following content pertains to changing student attitudes. There is little consensus about the structure and origins of attitudes toward persons with disabilities, except that the factors contributing to their formation are multifaceted and complex.

Attitudes may be directed toward many kinds of psychological objects: self, other persons, a racial or ethnic group, religion, a disability, an undesired difference, exercise, physical activity, an idea, a behavior, or a situation. The more global a psychological object is, the more difficult it is to measure attitude toward it and plan change. When we feel uncomfortable about something or dislike it, *we should try to identify what exactly it is about the object or person that we don't like.* Once we determine the specific behaviors causing our attitudes we can then take steps to change these behaviors. An often-used motto in education is "Accept people, change behaviors!"

Physical educators need to understand the major theories that guide attitude change and apply these theories in everyday teaching (Rizzo & Vispoel, 1991; Tripp & Sherrill, 1991). Five approaches to attitude change—(a) contact theory, (b) persuasive communication theory, (c) social cognitive theory, (d) reasoned action theory, and (e) planned behavior—are described in the sections that follow. These theories can be applied to attitude change in relation to any psychological object. The emphasis in this chapter, however, is on attitudes toward persons with disabilities.

Contact Theory

Contact theory posits that contact between individuals with differences produces positive attitudes when the interactions are frequent, pleasant, and meaningful (see Figure 9.7). Gordon Allport (1954) is acknowledged as the pioneer who created the structural framework for contact theory, which serves as the basis of inclusion practices in schools and communities.

Contact does not promote positive attitudes unless specific interaction experiences are planned and the environment is carefully structured. Favorable conditions that tend to promote the development of positive attitudes are (a) equal-status relationships, (b) a climate that requires frequent contacts, (c) cooperative rather than competitive or individual activities, (d) contacts that are pleasant and rewarding, (e) modeling of positive attitudes by teacher and significant others, and (f) scientifically planned and applied persuasion.

Ideally, structured contacts in the instructional setting should result in positive attitude and behavior changes. Social acceptance implies that contacts are voluntary, spontaneous, of equal status, and generalized. For example, social acceptance would be indicated by the person with a disability being included in after-school activities with increasing frequency and duration.

Figure 9.7 Dr. Terry Rizzo talks to children about attitudes and emphasizes the importance of contact between people representing all kinds of individual differences.

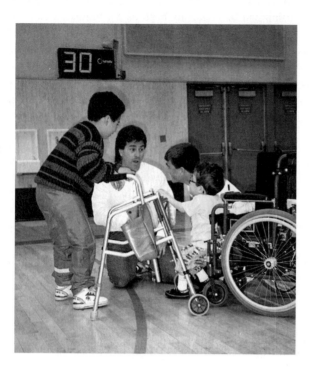

Figure 9.8 This strong and confident woman athlete persuades observers to see her as quite capable.

Persuasive Communication Theory

The use of persuasion to change attitudes is a common approach. Persuasion can be through direct methods (lectures, one-to-one talks, small-group discussions, films, presentations by persons with disabilities) or indirect methods (personal contact, role playing, or simulating activities of persons who are different). When you are exposed to persons with disabilities who are "strong" and "confident" (see Figure 9.8) you are persuaded to view the person more positively. Thus, a body of knowledge has emerged called *persuasive communication theory.* Hovland is acknowledged as the father of this theory, also called the Yale approach, which was first posited in the early 1950s.

Proponents of persuasive communication theory define attitudes as multidimensional. Attitude change is posited to progress through four stages: (a) opinion change, (b) perception change, (c) affect or emotional change, and (d) action change. Information is carefully designed to (a) catch attention, (b) increase comprehension, and (c) promote acceptance.

A good example of persuasive communication theory is presentations or performance of elite athletes with disabilities. In public schools, creating opportunities for students with disabilities to talk about themselves and ways people can help them is a way of combining persuasive communication with contact theory.

Social Cognitive Theories

Research continues to illustrate that "difference" is first and foremost a socially contingent phenomenon. The way we inter-

pret, label, and respond to people, be it at an individual level or more broadly between groups, is for the most part a product of the particular social setting in which we are situated. *Attitudes are formed primarily from total life experiences rather than from the passive cognition* emphasized in persuasive communication theory. Four total life approaches follow.

1. Field or Ecological Theory

Kurt Lewin, whose work is associated with the Massachusetts Institute of Technology and the University of Michigan, is acknowledged as the major pioneer in the early evolution of social cognitive attitude theories. Lewin's field theory evolved from the Gestalt psychology of the 1930s, which posited that behavior is determined, not by stimulus-response methodology or passive cognition, but by the total environmental field or lifespace. This field consists of an organized system of psychosocial stresses or forces, analogous to a gravitational or electromagnetic field, which must be kept in balance.

Behavior can be understood by analyzing the total field, or lifespace, today called the ecosystem. Ecosystem consists of the total psychological world (i.e., everything that is seen, heard, sensed, or inferred). **Field theory,** then, emphasizes analysis of the individual, the environment, and the interactions. Behavior change occurs when teachers manipulate person-by-situation interactions. Lewin's field theory is particularly useful when using Hellison's Personal-Social Responsibility Model in the physical education setting.

2. Group Dynamics Theory

Attitudes are strongly influenced by the norms and goals of groups to which people belong or aspire to belong. This is especially true in adolescence, when the need for group affiliation is very strong. Within most groups, various pressures cause members to behave, think, feel, and dress alike.

Covert and complex reward and punishment systems exist within group structures. Areas particularly dominated by group pressures are friendships and treatment of minorities. Some groups are open, whereas others are closed. Teachers need to understand the group dynamics of their community, school, and classroom and know which leaders and groups are most open to including new members. Open groups are generally the best people to select as partners for students with disabilities when beginning a new program or activity. *When class leaders model social acceptance behaviors, others follow.* Therefore, try to get leaders involved! Values clarification in individual or small groups often helps persons to reflect more deeply in the influences they are exposed to in the class, society, and media. Chapter 3 presents information on focus groups and other ways to help individuals clarify values and change beliefs. Often values clarification is helpful for parent and community groups.

3. Cognitive Dissonance Theory

This theory, developed by Leon Festinger (1957), states that dissonance (discomfort) occurs when an individual holds two cognitions that are inconsistent with each other. For example, all individuals create personal boundaries to distinguish the "same" from "other." Discomfort or anxiety can be created when this boundary is threatened. A decision must be made as to keep personal boundaries in place or allow for change.

To reduce cognitive dissonance, an individual chooses from three alternatives: (a) maintain one's position in the direction of the norm, (b) try to influence the group norm, or (c) reject the group as irrelevant. Individuals will choose to either maintain, influence, or reject the norm based on the power or importance of the unstated norm and the extent that the person viewed as "different" exceeds one's boundaries of comfort. Difference, or in this case disability, threatens order and control; it is the opposite of the norm. The real premise underlying cognitive dissonance theory is that negative behavior toward disability may stem from a fundamental inability to tolerate anxiety.

When professionals adapt the organization, rules, or equipment in games and sport so everyone can participate, they run the risk of experiencing this as a threat; in other words, there is too much discrepancy between inclusion strategies and what they accept as standard or the norm. *The source of difference is founded in the process of identity formation.* In the end there is much support for early experience of inclusion in physical education and sport so children grow up to accept difference in this setting as the norm.

4. Social Learning and Efficacy Theory

Albert Bandura, today's leader in social cognitive theory, first became known for his social learning and self-efficacy theories (see Chapter 5). These theories stressed that behaviors can best be changed through a combination of activities that include (a) vicarious learning by watching and listening to *models,* (b) structured direct experiences that provide cognitive self-confidence, called *self-efficacy,* and (c) cognitive training that teaches analytical, self-reflective, and self-regulatory thought through such techniques as imagery and mental rehearsal.

Bandura's (1986) famous book *Social Foundations of Thought and Action: A Social Cognitive Theory* summarized the ways that behavior, cognition, personal factors, and the environment can be used to achieve specific outcomes.

Bandura's (1997) focus as a social-learning theorist is primarily in the cognitive rather than the affective domain. He does, however, discuss attitude, noting that the assumption that attitudes determine behavior is only partially true. Bandura emphasizes that experiences accompanying changes in behavior also alter attitudes. Bandura's primary contribution to attitude theory is the perspective that helps us dismiss unproductive arguments about which occurs first (attitudes or behaviors). Physical activity professionals using Bandura's theory to guide practice would create environmental conditions in the gymnasium to facilitate acceptance and inclusion of all persons.

There is much variability within disability; some conditions are seen as less favorable or desirable than others. Take a look at the list of disabilities below and rank from 1 to 15 the ones you would most prefer to have if you yourself had to have a disability (1 is the most preferred and 15 is the least). This kind of ranking can sometimes tell us more about ourselves than disability per se. What do you think about your fears, biases, concerns, or comfort levels when you look over your ranking outcome? Ask someone you are comfortable with, a friend or family member, to do the ranking too and share your results.

Rank	Disability	Rank	Disability
_____	*Totally blind*	_____	*Amputee (single limb)*
_____	*Totally deaf*	_____	*Severe stutterer*
_____	*Mentally retarded*	_____	*Epilepsy*
_____	*Wheelchair user because of spinal cord injury*	_____	*Harelip*
		_____	*Asthma*
_____	*Cerebral palsy— uncontrolled body movement*	_____	*Diabetes*
		_____	*AIDS*
_____	*Emotionally disturbed*	_____	*Autism*
		_____	*Brain injury*

Reasoned Action Theory

Reasoned action theory (see Chapter 5) has been popularized in adapted physical education by Dr. Terry Rizzo of California State University at San Bernardino, who developed an attitude inventory for teachers based on this theory. Recently, a children's attitude survey based on reasoned action theory was published (Verderber, Rizzo, & Sherrill, 2003). The term *reasoned action* indicates that behaviors originate in people's belief systems. Thus people can be taught to reason about the right way to act in an inclusive physical education setting.

[symbol] *Remember the NASPE standards for students (see Chapter 1). Which standard is met when teachers apply the theory of reasoned action?*

Planned Behavior Theory

Planned behavior theory is an extension of reasoned action theory. Ajzen (1985, 1991) proposed the theory of planned behavior to correct a weakness in the belief systems aspect of reasoned action theory. This weakness was the assumption that the behavior to be changed was totally under the control of the person doing the reasoning. In actuality, many factors (e.g., health, time, money, skills, cooperation of others, administrative mandates) affect the amount of ability persons have to carry out their intentions.

Planned behavior theory adds a third belief system to the model. This belief system is called **perceived behavioral control** and is defined as beliefs concerning how easy or difficult it will be to perform the desired behavior. Ajzen (1991) stated that the additional belief system is comparable to Bandura's perceived concept of self-efficacy (i.e., judgments about how well one can execute courses of action in specific situations). It supports the idea that situation-specific self-confidence correlates highly with success.

Perceived behavioral control is typically assessed by responses on 7-point scales. The following items are illustrative:

1. If I wanted to, I could lose 10 lbs in the next 3 months.
   Respond: *Likely* 7 6 5 4 3 2 1 *Unlikely*
2. For me to lose 10 lbs in the next 3 months is _____ .
   Respond: *Easy* 7 6 5 4 3 2 1 *Difficult*
3. How much control do you exert over the decision to lose 10 lbs in the next 3 months?
   Respond: *Complete Control* 7 6 5 4 3 2 1 *Very Little Control*
4. I believe I have the resources required to enable myself to lose 10 lbs over in the next 3 months.
   Respond: *True* 7 6 5 4 3 2 1 *False*

Implementation of planned behavior theory entails direct instruction and counseling on how to reason about all of its components plus an additional perceived behavioral control component included in the model. Much of the instruction on reasoning pertaining to control relates to learning how to manage time and resources as well as how to negotiate for more time and resources. These tremendously important skills are often clustered together under the self-determination goal. Attention should also be given to self-concept and role identity in relation to control matters, because these variables influence behavioral intentions.

Using Attitude Theories

Five groups of attitude theories have been described: (a) contact theory, (b) persuasive communication, (c) social cognitive theories, (d) reasoned action, and (e) planned behavior. Use of these theories will help you plan many aspects of service delivery and can be particularly helpful in advocacy activities. It is important for you to feel comfortable with theories and theorizing.

[symbol] *Feel free to criticize these theories, test them, play with them, and propose changes. Consider each theory a building block in our wall of knowledge about individual differences, attitudes, and behaviors. Each generation of teachers and researchers leaves its mark on this wall. Are you ready to begin? Try it; you'll like it! Select one theory, write out your plan for testing it, follow through, and write the results.*

Attitude Assessment

Attitude change begins with an assessment of attitude components and related behaviors. Then objectives can be written and instructional time and activities planned. Attitude instruments are typically called surveys, adjective checklists, opinionnaires, inventories, rating scales, and sociometric measures. Attitude measures are never called *tests,* a term properly used only when there are right and wrong answers and the domain examined is cognitive. Responses to attitude inventories are not considered right or wrong, good or bad, but only a reflection of feelings or beliefs at a given time. This fact is important to convey to respondents before conducting an attitude assessment; otherwise, persons may tend to give socially desirable ("right") answers rather than the truth, a phenomenon called **response bias.**

Following, with the exception of Rizzo's PEATID-III, are *descriptions of attitude instruments developed specifically for children.* Teachers should administer these instruments before involving students in systematically planned contact activities to determine entry-level beliefs and attitudes of each student. Survey data then guide development of specific, individualized, measurable objectives for each student. Later, when planned intervention is completed, the instruments should be administered again to determine the effectiveness of the intervention in causing change.

CAIPE-R

The Children's Attitudes Toward Integrated Physical Education–Revised (CAIPE-R) inventory, by Martin Block (1995b), consists of a description of a student with a disability, then 12 to 14 statements, depending on the sport featured in Part 2 of the inventory (see Table 9.4). Following are two illustrative descriptions of target children. Only *one* description is presented to students, usually with a picture. Then students mark their responses according to the 4-point scale. The example in Table 9.4 assumes that the students have been given a description of "Mike" (Target Child 1).

Target Child 1

Mike is the same age as you are. However, he has mental retardation, so he doesn't learn as quickly as you can. Because of his mental retardation, he also doesn't talk very well, so sometimes it is hard to understand what he is saying. Mike likes playing the same games as you do, but he does not do very well in the games. Even though he can run, he is slower than you and tires easily. He can throw and catch and hit a softball, but not very well. He likes soccer, but he cannot kick a ball very far. He also likes basketball, but he is not very good at shooting or dribbling, and he doesn't really know the rules of the game.

Target Child 2

Bart is the same age as you are. However, he cannot walk, so he uses a wheelchair to get around. Bart likes playing the same games as you do, but he does not do very well in the games. Even though he can push his wheelchair, he is slower than you and tires easily. He can throw a ball, but not very far. He can catch balls that are tossed straight to him, and he can hit a baseball off a tee, but he cannot shoot a basketball high enough to make a basket. Because his legs do not work, he cannot kick a ball.

Table 9.4   Examples from the Children's Attitudes Toward Integrated Physical Education–Revised (Block, 1995b).

Insert here a description of a child who might be coming to class

Part 1

1. It would be OK having Mike in PE class.
   Yes   **Probably Yes**   **Probably No**   **No**
2. Because Mike cannot play sports very well, he would slow the game down for everyone.
   Yes   **Probably Yes**   **Probably No**   **No**
3. If we were playing a team sport such as basketball, it would be OK having Mike on my team.
   Yes   **Probably Yes**   **Probably No**   **No**
4. PE would be fun if Mike were in my PE class.
   Yes   **Probably Yes**   **Probably No**   **No**
5. If Mike were in my PE class, I would talk to him and be his friend.
   Yes   **Probably Yes**   **Probably No**   **No**
6. If Mike were in my PE class, I would like to help him practice and play the games.
   Yes   **Probably Yes**   **Probably No**   **No**
7. During practice, it would be OK to allow Mike to use special equipment such as a lower basket in basketball or a batting tee in softball.
   Yes   **Probably Yes**   **Probably No**   **No**

Part 2

What rule changes during PE do you think would be OK if a kid like Mike were playing?
8. Mike could hit a ball placed on a batting tee.
   Yes   **Probably Yes**   **Probably No**   **No**
9. Someone could tell Mike where to run when he hits the ball.
   Yes   **Probably Yes**   **Probably No**   **No**
10. The distance between home and first base could be shorter for Mike.
    Yes   **Probably Yes**   **Probably No**   **No**
11. Someone could help Mike when he plays in the field.
    Yes   **Probably Yes**   **Probably No**   **No**
12. If the ball were hit to Mike, the batter could only run as far as second base.
    Yes   **Probably Yes**   **Probably No**   **No**

Note: For permission to use this instrument for research, contact Dr. Martin E. Block, Curry School of Education, University of Virginia, Charlottesville, VA 22903.

PEATID-III

The Physical Educators' Attitude Toward Teaching Individuals with Disabilities–III (PEATID-III) by Terry Rizzo 1995 is a revision (terminology only) of the much used PEATH II (Rizzo & Kirkendall, 1995) and PEATH I (Rizzo, 1984), which are based on reasoned action theory. *PEATH* is the acronym for Physical Educators' Attitudes toward Teaching the Handicapped questionnaire, a title now changed to PEATID. Recently Folsom-Meek and Rizzo (2002) determined that the PEATID III yields valid and reliable data for use with future professionals.

PEATID requires that teachers read definitions of disability conditions from the PEATID instruction sheet and then answer 12 statements, based on their understanding of the definitions. A Likert-type 5-point scale is used to score their responses.

VISIPIPE

The Verderber Inventory of Students' Intention to Participate in Inclusive Physical Education (VISIPIPE), based on reasoned action theory, is developed specifically for middle school children (Verderber, Rizzo, & Sherrill, 2003). VISIPIPE consists of five separate subscales: (a) intention; (b) attitude, inferred from behavioral beliefs and outcome evaluations; (c) normative belief; (d) determinant of the normative belief; and (e) attitude toward behavior.

Illustrative items for the first four subscales were

1. I would choose a student like Jimmy or Monica for my partner when doing exercises in PE (measures intention).
2. Everyone will learn to get along better with others and how to play together in games (measures behavioral belief [BB] strength).
3. Learning how to get along better with others and how to play together is good (measures outcome evaluation with respect to BB).
4. My parents think I should work and play with students who have severe disabilities in PE class (measures normative belief).
5. I usually do what my parents say I should do (measures determinant of normative belief, also known as *motivation to comply*).

The fifth subscale (attitude toward behavior, also called belief attitude) has no items. It is calculated as the sum of the products of BB strength and outcome evaluation. Each cluster of survey items (e.g., items 1 to 5) relates to *specific behaviors* that the teacher wishes to facilitate through application of attitude change theories and practices (e.g., contact or persuasive communication). Students thus learn to reason about the concept presented in each item and to make conscious decisions about future behaviors or actions. The VISIPIPE holds much promise.

Sociograms

Sociograms (see Figure 9.9) are visual records of students' responses to questions like these:

Figure 9.9 **Two types of sociograms for examining peer attitudes.**

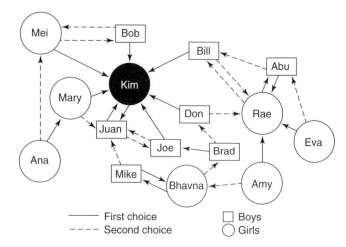

First choice — Boys □
Second choice - - - - Girls ○

A
Arrows show first and second choices of best friends in a class of 16 students.

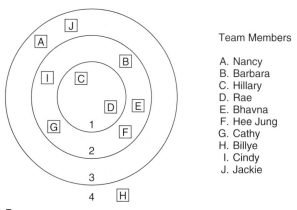

Team Members

A. Nancy
B. Barbara
C. Hillary
D. Rae
E. Bhavna
F. Hee Jung
G. Cathy
H. Billye
I. Cindy
J. Jackie

B
Boxes in center show leaders, whereas succeeding rings show persons considered less relevant to group goals.

1. What two people in this class do you *most* like to play with in PE class and after-school sports?
2. When I assign you to exercise stations (or sport teams), what two persons do you *most* want to be with?

These are excellent measures of attitudes. Questions can also ask whom students would *least* like to be with, because peer acceptance and peer rejection are independent dimensions of interpersonal attractiveness. Sociograms give teachers good information about *stars* (the most popular individuals) and *isolates* (the least popular individuals). Also valuable is information about whether choices are *reciprocal* (if Kim chooses Juan, does Juan choose Kim?). Cliques can also be identified in sociograms.

In Figure 9.9, it is clear that Kim and Rae are stars, or the class leaders. They also are the centers of cliques and seldom interact with each other, although Bill and Don are *peacemakers* who maintain links with both cliques. Most important in adapted physical activity service is the need to help Amy, Ana, and Eva find some close friends. Sociograms can be as simple or complex as teachers wish. Color coding the arrows helps when more than two responses are recorded.

If the goal is simply to identify leaders and isolates, then the archery target sociogram (see Figure 9.9) can be used. Following are directions to give your students: Classify each team member as nearly as possible to how you view her influence on the behavior of the other team members as it relates to the overall team goals. Place the player's name within the numbered circle as you view the strength of her influence on the other team members.

1—Players with great influence (Bull's eye)

2—Players with influence sometimes (Inner rung)

3—Players who never influence others; they are primarily followers (Outer rung)

4—Players who are not even followers; they merely "occupy space" (Completely off target)

Adjective Checklists

The adjective checklist is based on the assumption that adjective choice reveals opinions and feelings. Many such checklists are available for attitude measurement, but the Siperstein (1980) checklist in Table 9.5 was developed specifically for use with schoolchildren and has provided data for several published studies. Either the name of a particular child or a category (e.g., mental retardation) can be placed in the blank to elicit responses. After using this checklist, students should be helped to understand the fallacy of generalizations. For example, a term like *slow* is relative. Does it mean slow in running, slow in learning, or slow in giving affection? Also, because a person is slow on one dimension does not mean that he or she should automatically be judged slow on other dimensions.

Sources of Attitude Instruments for Students

Table 9.6 lists attitude instruments and states sources in journals that have articles about these instruments. Some addresses

Table 9.5   Siperstein adjective checklist for describing classmates.

If you had to describe _____ to your classmates, what kinds of words would you use? Below is a list of words to help you. CIRCLE the words you would use. You can use as many or as few words as you want. Here is the list:

healthy	honest	bored	dishonest
slow	ashamed	helpful	smart
sloppy	neat	dumb	unhappy
clever	lonely	friendly	mean
alert	pretty	sad	ugly
alright	cruel	careful	happy
crazy	proud	glad	kind
greedy	weak	stupid	
cheerful	bright	careless	

are stated. These instruments can be used as worksheet activities as well as for assessment and goal writing.

 OPTIONAL ACTIVITIES

1.   Based on the information and ideas you have read in this chapter, develop your own attitude assessment instrument. Address the influence of the intention to perform a given behavior in a way that is developmentally appropriate for the age group you will use as a sample. Now use your instrument to assess the attitudes of five students in an inclusive physical education class. How do their responses compare with one another? Did the students respond in the way you wanted them to? Why?

2.   Read articles in *APAQ* on how to develop and examine the validity and reliability of attitude surveys (e.g., Block, 1995; Rizzo, 1984; Kudláček, Válková, Sherrill, Myers, & French, 2002; Verderber et al., 2003). Write reviews of these articles and use the content in ways relevant to you.

Table 9.6   Types of children's attitude inventories with references and some addresses.

Social Distance Measures

1. *Cowell Personal Distance Scale*—Uses a 7-point scale to indicate acceptance (e.g., into my family, as a next-door neighbor, into my school).

2. *Siperstein Friendship Activity Scale*—Uses a 4-point Likert scale to measure behavioral intentions in regard to 15 activities.

3. *Bagley and Greene PATHS (Peer Attitudes Toward the Handicapped Scale)*—Uses a 5-point social distance scale (in my home, in another group, in no group, outside of class, at home) to rate descriptions of 30 students.

4. Slininger et al., Contact Intention Scale. Based on Siperstein et al., (1988). Uses a 4-point scale to measure behavioral intentions in relation to 10 activities.

Cowell, C. (1958). Validating an index of social adjustment for high school use. *Research Quarterly, 29,* 7–18. (Appears in Barrow, McGee, & Tritschler, 1989, p. 261.)

Siperstein, G., Bak, J., & O'Keefe, P. (1988). Relationship between children's attitudes toward and their social acceptance of mentally retarded peers. *American Journal of Mental Retardation, 93*(1), 24–27.

Bagley, M., & Green, J. (1981). *Peer attitude toward the handicapped scale.* Austin, TX: PRO•ED.

Slininger et al. (2000). Children's attitudes toward peers with severe disabilities: Revisiting contact theory. *Adapted Physical Activity Quarterly, 17,* 176–196.

Adjective and Phrase Checklists

1. *Siperstein Adjective Checklist for Describing Classmates*—Asks students to circle as many adjectives as they wish to describe a peer. List includes 16 positive and 18 negative adjectives.

2. *Children's Attitudes Toward Handicapped Scale (CAHS)*—Asks students to respond to 20 descriptors of a peer by circling one of three phrases for each (e.g., are lots of fun, are fun, are not any fun).

Same source as Siperstein Friendship Activity Scale. These can be ordered from Dr. Gary Siperstein, Center for the Study of Social Acceptance, University of Massachusetts, Boston, MA 02125.

Rapier, J., Adelson, R., Carey, R., & Croke, K. (1972). Changes in children's attitudes toward the physically handicapped. *Exceptional Children, 39,* 219–223.

Children's Attitude Measures—Likert-Type Scales

1. *Children's Attitudes Toward Integrated Physical Education-Revised (CAIPE-R)*—Uses a 4-point Likert scale (yes, probably yes, probably no, no) to respond to 12–14 feeling and intention statements.

2. Verderber Inventory of Students' Intention to Participate in Inclusive Physical Education (VISIPIPE, 2003).

Block, M. E. (1995). Development and validation of the Children's Attitudes Toward Physical Education-Revised Inventory. *Adapted Physical Activity Quarterly, 12*(1), 60–77.

Contact Dr. Joan Verderber, 2004 Exmoor Place, Glendora, CA 91741-3964. Verderber et al. (2003). Assessing student intention to participate in inclusive physical education. *Adapted Physical Activity Quarterly, 20,* 26–45.

Measures Designed for Children with Disabilities

1. Hutzler Situational Reaction Grid Children use 0 (never happened) to 10 (always happened) to indicate their reactions to seven inclusion situations printed horizontally across the grid. Five possible reactions are listed verbally.

Hutzler et al. (2002). Perspectives of children with physical disabilities on inclusion and empowerment: Supporting and limiting factors. *Adapted Physical Activity Quarterly, 19,* 300–317.

C H A P T E R

10

Sensorimotor Learning and Severe Disability

Figure 10.1   Children with developmental delays, including cerebral palsy, need teachers who understand all of the systems of the body, as well as environmental interactions and constraints. Of particular importance is knowledge of (*A*) postural and balance reactions and (*B*) reflexes that interfere with body control.

A

B

1. Titles for Chapters 10 and 12, respectively, are based on Piaget's levels of mental function: sensorimotor, ages 0 to 2, and perceptual-motor (preoperational), ages 2 to 7. Review the description of these levels in Chapter 6 and reflect on individuals who are much older than these chronological ages levels but whose physical activity goals and objectives are similar. Assess your experiences with such persons, set personal goals and objectives, and plan ways to expand these experiences during this course.

2. This chapter also forms the foundation for understanding motor behavior of persons with severe cerebral palsy who may or may not have impaired mental function. Try to find persons who can benefit from the many activities in this chapter, observe specialists or parents working with them, and volunteer for direct experience. Critique activities and pedagogy used.

3. Individuals with mental age function of 0 to 2 learn primarily through sensory stimulation, assisted and coactive movement, imitation, one- or two-word instructions, facial and body language, and tangible rewards. *Use these as you explore and reflect on the 50+ activities recommended in this chapter.* You can practice activities with typical infants and toddlers, but remember the content of this chapter is designed for school-age persons with severe neurological limitations.

4. Reinforce information about reflexes by practicing on lifesize dolls with movable head, trunk, and limbs. Reflect on how pathological reflexes impact physical education experience.

5. Aim for awareness level of competence. Know that much supervised practice is required to provide persons with severe disability the help they need. A whole course or internship can be built around this chapter.

This chapter begins a three-part series on assessment and pedagogy of motor skills and patterns for individuals who are delayed in age-appropriate learning. This section is a crossdisciplinary adapted physical activity approach to **motor behavior** (i.e., motor development, motor learning, and motor control) and is guided, to some extent, by APENS Standard 2.

Chapter 10 focuses on individuals with severe, multiple disabilities who, regardless of chronological age, benefit from techniques associated with infants and toddlers (ages 0 to 2) or persons who inability to walk has seriously limited the experiences through which they might have enhanced their mental ability. *According to Piaget, early learning is through sensorimotor mental operations.* Many of the individuals whom this chapter targets are *nonambulatory,* mainly because of pathological reflexes and postural reactions, and/or *nonverbal* with little inner and receptive language (i.e., they exhibit little understanding of spoken or signed instructions).

Some students who need help with the reflexes and postures are, however, like 9-year-old Kay (see Figures 10.1 and 10.25). Kay's mental function is partly at Piaget's preoperational (perceptual-motor) level and partly at his concrete operations level. However, many of her motor problems are the same as Ted's and sensorimotor seems to be the best name for the type of physical education programming that may help her most. Chapter 10 specifically addresses muscle and postural tone; tactile, kinesthetic, vestibular, visual, and auditory integration; reflex and postural reaction problems; awareness level functions; fundamentals of neurology necessary to understand severe disability; and theories underlying interventions (see Figure 10.1).

Chapters 11 and 12 focus on ambulatory individuals who, regardless of chronological age, learn the way that young children (ages 2 to 7) learn. *According to Piaget, this is through perceptual-motor (preoperational) mental operations.* Chapter 11 presents task-specific intervention or direct instruction that is used in general physical education with average children or those with small delays. Chapter 12 presents an alternative approach (perceptual-motor learning) for individuals, regardless of chronological age, who need special help to supplement direct instruction. The perceptual-motor approach is also called the **underlying abilities approach** or more recently the **movement skill foundations approach** (Burton & Rodgerson, 2001).

Intrasensory and Intersensory Integration: Ted's IEP Goal

The first level of intervention for students with severe disabilities is help in making sense of the environment. Visualize Ted, age 7 or 8, whose **cerebral palsy** (damage to the motor part of the brain) is so severe that he is nonambulatory, dominated by flexor muscle tone with fisted hands that are relatively useless, and has no speech. Whenever Ted turns his head to look at something, a pathological reflex is activated that causes the arm on his chin side to move whether he wants it to or not. *If Ted had only cerebral palsy, his mental function would be average or better.* However, some of the motor parts of the brain have dual functions. Ted's records indicate that he has damage to the frontal lobe of the brain, which controls cognition, memory, and voluntary movement. He also has damage to the parietal lobe, which is why he has no speech (a motor function) and is delayed in tactile and kinesthetic integration.

The spasticity that keeps Ted's hands fisted means he cannot learn sign language, so he communicates by touching an electronic device with his one usable finger. No one yet has been able to assess his mental potential; at present he seems to be performing mentally at about a 2-year-old level. It is not known whether this reflects mental retardation or severe delay because Ted's physical and speech limitations have drastically reduced the life experiences through which he learns. Ted spends most of his daytime hours strapped into a wheelchair and staring into space unless someone is working with him one-to-one. Most of his classmates have similar conditions, so social interactions are limited.

Ted's tactile, kinesthetic, visual, auditory, and other senses bring in information from the environment that travels up the spinal cord to the brain, but Ted has not yet achieved proficiency in interpreting the sensory information. The tactile receptors on Ted's skin send messages to the brain that enable him to feel warmth, but no one has helped Ted to understand that the warmth comes from the sun that he sees through the window and that he hears persons talking about on this hot July day. Nor does Ted yet understand cause and effect. The sun is in his eyes, but he does not know that, if he moves his head, he can cause the outcome he wants (no sun in his eyes!). It is likely, though, that Ted will learn this soon and that he will begin to learn many things through movement.

Through movement, Ted will improve his **kinesthetic sense,** which tells him where his body parts are in space and how much they must move to achieve certain outcomes. This improved function of his kinesthetic sense is **intrasensory integration** (enhanced function within one sensory system). When Ted begins to make the link between information afforded him by the tactile, kinesthetic, and visual systems, he will be improving his **intersensory integration** (enhanced interacting between two or more sensory systems).

Ted attends public school, is in a special education class with five other children, and supposedly receives the same number of physical education minutes each week as nondisabled peers in his school. Ted's physical education is taught by his classroom teacher with consultant help from an adapted physical education specialist. Twice a week, Ted receives 30 minutes of one-to-one instruction from an adapted physical educator. *The adapted physical education specialist must have a wealth of knowledge about neurologically impaired movement and activity interventions to address muscle tone, reflex, and postural reactions problems.* As important as knowledge is *creativity* in making activities interesting for oneself and the classroom teacher as well as the student. Also essential is a vivacious delivery manner that will make the student want to pay attention and learn.

This chapter presents beginning-level information for working with students like Ted of all ages. Ted is probably more disabled than most of the students with cerebral palsy that the physical educator will see. With help, however, even Ted's mental age may soar, so that he can mentally keep up with some nondisabled peers, but his movement repertoire will probably remain that of an infant who has not yet mastered walking. Nevertheless, Ted can be taught to engage in adult sports like boccia, shuffleboard, and indoor soccer (see Chapter 25 on cerebral palsy). Physical education instruction can also help him learn initiative and skill in interacting with others.

Ted's IEP goal for adapted physical education this year is to **demonstrate improvement of intersensory and intrasensory integration.** Some measurable objectives related to this goal follow:

1. Given the instruction, "Look at me," from someone positioned on his left or right, Ted will turn his head to face the speaker and hold this position for 30 seconds every time he is asked to do this over a 2-week period. Concurrently, Ted will exert conscious effort to control the arm on his chin side and keep it stationary (i.e., will strive to enable his head to move independent of his arm; also referred to as **normalizing a pathological reflex**).

2. Shown an up-and-down balloon striking movement with the cue, "Hit the balloon," Ted will imitate this movement by raising his arm and striking a balloon 6 out of 10 attempts on test day.

3. Given a shuffleboard overlay on a long table and the cue, "Push hard," Ted will use his hand to push an object, making it slide a distance of 3 feet or more, and achieve this distance criterion in 6 out of 10 trials every day for 2 weeks.

All three of these objectives result in both improved intersensory and intrasensory integration. In reality, intersensory and intrasensory integration occur concurrently. The remainder of this chapter breaks intersensory and intrasensory integration into its component parts.

Many factors affect intrasensory and intersensory integration. Among these are normalcy of central nervous system (CNS) development; damage to the CNS by injury, disease, or activity deprivation; normalcy of function of other body systems; environmental enablers and constraints; motivation, and aspects of psychosocial functioning that influence effort and persistence. Table 10.1 presents brief definitions of the major psychomotor problems of concern in sensorimotor integration.

Before studying specific sensory integration problems, it is helpful to think about the nervous system and gain insight into its complexity. Knowledge about nervous system function facilitates teamwork with therapists and rehabilitation personnel and aids in communication with parents. Assess your present knowledge and study as much as needed to pass a quiz on the neurology essentials in this chapter.

The Organization of the Nervous System

The nervous system is organized as a **central nervous system** (brain and spinal cord) and a **peripheral nervous system** (12 pairs of cranial nerves, 12 pairs of spinal nerves, and the autonomic nervous system). The central nervous system (CNS) is of special interest in working with persons who are clumsy or have developmental coordination disorder (DCD). Imagine thousands of neural impulses (some sensory, some motor, some interpretive, some cognitive) traveling at various speeds inside the CNS. The pathways that neural impulses travel are called **dorsal** (back) and **ventral** (front) tracts. Figure 10.2 shows the parts of the CNS that perform major functions.

Parts and Functions of the Spinal Cord

The spinal cord is comprised of **tracts** (pathways) containing nerve fibers that carry impulses to and from the brain. Impulses that originate in sensory receptors in the skin, muscles, tendons, and joints travel up the spinal cord in **dorsal ascending sensory tracts** (see Figure 10.2). The names of these tracts, like *spinocerebellar* and *spinothalamic,* indicate the starting and end points of the tract. For example, the **spinocerebellar tract** starts in the spinal cord and ends in the cerebellum. Each tract carries only one kind of sensory information (e.g., touch, pain, heat,

Table 10.1   Major psychomotor problems related to the nervous system: Definitions.

1. **Muscle or postural tone irregularities.** An abnormal amount of tension within a muscle or muscle group. *Hypertonus* is too much tension, a stiff appearance, and reduced range of motion. *Hypotonus* is too little tension, a flaccid or floppy appearance, weakness, or paralysis. *Fluctuating tonus* is involuntary shifting between hypertonic and hypotonic states.
2. **Sensory input system problems.** Problems of structure or function of sensory organs or nerve fibers that carry impulses to the brain. These are generally manifested as impaired acuity (accurateness of seeing, hearing, touching) or sensitivity (too much, *hypersensitive;* or too little, *hyposensitive*).
3. **Sensory and perceptual central processing problems.** Organizational problems within the brain. Difficulty translating input into desired or appropriate output.
4. **Reflex integration problems.** Reflexes are involuntary, predictable changes in muscle or postural tone in response to sensory input. *Reflexes* are normal in newborn infants, but these reflexes are *pathological* when they persist beyond infancy.
5. **Postural reaction problems.** Reactions are automatic responses to sensory input that keep body parts in alignment, enable control, maintain balance, and prevent falls.
6. **Associated movements or overflow.** The inability to move one body part without associated movements of other parts. Sometimes called *differentiation problems.*
7. **Stereotypies.** Purposeless, rhythmical, patterned movements of body parts (such as leg kicking) that are normal in infants but pathological when they persist as rocking, waving, wriggling, or banging mannerisms.
8. **Ataxia.** Generalized motor clumsiness related to balance and coordination difficulties. Largely related to a lack of movement and position sense (kinesthesis), but influenced by all the movement sensory systems (tactile, kinesthetic, vestibular, visual).
9. **Spasticity.** Multidimensional impairment of voluntary movement that can be of either cerebral or spinal cord origin. **Spasticity caused by cerebral damage** (the most common) is *hypertonus* complicated by overly active reflex activity so that movement is restricted, stiff, and clumsy. **Spasticity caused by spinal cord injury** is the occasional occurrence of spasms or jerks in muscles below the injury level.

---

movement) and has a specific destination. Sensory information is sometimes called **afferent,** meaning "to or toward the brain."

Motor commands that cause movement originate inside the brain and are called **efferent,** meaning "out of the brain." Motor impulses travel down the spinal cord in **ventral descending motor tracts.** Inside the brain, these tracts have special names (*cortical* or *noncortical; pyramidal* and *extrapyramidal*), but outside they are simply called motor tracts. Sensorimotor problems typically occur inside the brain, not in the spinal cord.

Parts and Functions of the Brain

The major parts of the brain toward which sensory integration remediation is directed are the brain stem, midbrain, cerebellum, cerebral cortex, and internal capsule of the cerebrum (see Figure 10.2). Each of these has specific functions in preventing clumsiness and motor pathology.

The Brain Stem

The **brain stem** regulates muscle and postural tone and reflexes (see Table 10.1 for definitions of these). In normal development, reflexes are associated with infants. However, in adapted physical activity, reflexes are associated with clumsiness and/or pathology in individuals of all ages. The brain stem receives sensory information from all of the **sensory modalities,** except vision and smell, and thus performs a lot of organizational activity.

Pathological muscle tone and reflexes are caused when the *brain stem receives sensory information* about touch, pressure, or movement experienced by body parts *and does not permit this sensory input to travel to higher levels of the brain.* Instead the brain stem immediately converts the sensory infor-

mation into reflex motor commands that are sent down the spinal cord to excite muscle fibers to change length. *This results in a shifting of muscle tone or a movement of a body part.*

The brain stem also contains the structures that regulate attention, arousal, wakefulness, and general activity level. These processes involve filtering incoming sensory information and selectively transferring some sensory impulses to higher levels of the brain while inhibiting others. Damage to the brain stem can result in attention and activity excesses in either direction—too much (*hyper-*) or too little (*hypo-*).

The Midbrain

The **midbrain,** located at about ear level deep inside the brain, regulates postural reactions. These include all of the **automatic patterns** that enable stability and mobility in activities of daily living (ADL). The midbrain also receives all of the sensory information from the eyes, which helps to explain why vision is so important to balance.

The Cerebellum

The **cerebellum** has many functions but is particularly important in the automatic performance of skilled movement so that conscious thought is not needed. The cerebellum is also essential to good balance and the timing of fast movements.

The Cerebrum

The **cerebrum** is divided into the cerebral cortex (the six-layer outer covering of the brain) and the internal capsule. The **cerebral cortex** performs all of the higher-level mental functions that enable thought, emotion, perception, memory, language, and voluntary, spontaneous movement (see Figure 10.2).

Figure 10.2 Areas of the cerebral cortex that perform specific functions, noncortical structures (specified at left) that affect these functions, and spinal cord tracts that carry neural impulses to activate functions.

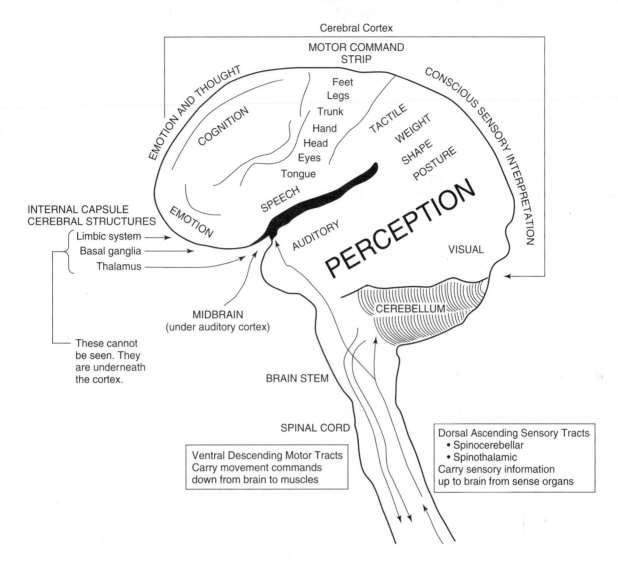

The **internal capsule** contains clusters of cell bodies that perform specific functions. Greatly simplified, these include the **limbic system,** which regulates emotion; the **basal ganglia,** which enable steady postures and movement without tremors; and the **thalamus,** which acts as a major relay station for sensory impulses.

Sensory information is processed, integrated, or organized in the cerebral cortex. Simplified, the **occipital** (rear) lobe governs vision and visual perception. The **temporal** area (above the ears, the temples) governs audition and provides memory for both auditory and visual experiences. The **parietal** (side) area is responsible for the interpretation of skin and muscular sensations and speech. The **frontal** area includes the motor strip, where motor impulses for voluntary movement originate, and the sites of cognitive function and personality. *In reality, there is much overlapping of function.* This information, however, gives insight into the amount of organizational activity that occurs within the cortex.

Almost all of the cerebral cortex is involved in organizational activity that affects voluntary movement. Remember that voluntary movement is functionally inseparable from attention, perception, cognition, and memory. Much of everyday movement, however, is involuntary or automatic and under the control of lower levels of the brain. In severe disability, problems at lower levels of the brain are typically addressed before problems at higher levels. **Involuntary** refers to reflex or brain stem activity, whereas **automatic** refers to postural reactions (midbrain activity) and skilled movement patterns that are performed without conscious thought (cerebellar activity).

*Devise games to play with classmates to learn this content. Consider **circle call ball** where everyone takes the name of a different CNS part and must catch a ball or perform some task when the name is called.*

Cortical and Subcortical Disorders

For assessment and intervention purposes, movement disorders are classified as cortical and subcortical. **Cortical disorders** can be improved by conscious thought, practice, and determination and thus are responsive to ordinary teaching methods. **Subcortical disorders** typically do not respond to ordinary teaching methods and thus constitute a particular challenge. Intervention directed toward cortical disorders is called **perceptual-motor** because perception (interpretation) is a cognitive activity. Intervention directed toward subcortical disorders is called **sensorimotor** because sensation, neurologically defined, occurs without cognition. Many individuals who are clumsy have both cortical and subcortical disorders, so teachers need to decide specifically which problems must be addressed first.

Cortical Functions

Cortical refers to functions of the cerebral cortex (the outer covering of the cerebrum) and the cortical tracts that carry neural impulses. The **cerebral cortex** performs all of the higher-level functions, including the planning and execution of conscious movement, and helps to regulate excitation and inhibition processes that determine muscle and postural tone. The **cortical tracts** carry impulses from one part of the brain to another, thereby enabling the integration and association of different kinds of data.

Subcortical Functions

Subcortical refers to functions of all the CNS structures except the cerebral cortex and cortical tracts. Subcortical functions include (a) skilled movements that no longer require conscious attention and (b) automatic movements like postural reactions and basic movement patterns that enable activities of daily living (ADL). Common problems include early reflexes that have not been integrated, overflow movement, stereotypies, inefficient protective mechanisms like the postural reactions, integration deficits that interfere with smooth, accurate movements performed at the desired force and speed, and arousal/attention deficits.

Clearly, clumsiness pertains to a breakdown between cortical and subcortical functions. Consider persons who bend their elbow or do not keep their eyes on the ball in tennis. These persons generally cognitively understand what to do, but they cannot make their body do what their mind wants. Identifying specific problems for remediation is difficult because all of the neural functions interact in complex ways. Usually something is wrong with **central processing** (the generation, organization, or relaying of neural impulses inside the CNS).

Following are sections on several factors that affect sensorimotor function. The first factor to be assessed and attended to is muscle and postural tone.

Muscle and Postural Tone

Muscle tone refers to contractile tension or firmness within a muscle or group of muscles, whereas **postural tone** refers to the mobility and stability functional capacity of the total body, especially the tone of the postural muscles that hold the body upright against the pull of gravity. The **postural muscles** (also called antigravity muscles) are the extensors of the head, neck, trunk, and lower extremities and the flexors of the upper extremities.

Muscle Families and Actions

Muscle families is a simplified way of referring to prime mover groups on the same surface that perform the same actions. The **extensor families** are on the posterior surface and the **flexor families** are on the anterior surface, with one exception—the muscle groups that work on the knee joint are the opposite of the rest of the body, with the extensors (quadriceps) on the anterior thigh and the flexors (hamstrings) on the posterior thigh. The **adductor families** are on the medial or inside surface and pull body parts toward or across midline. The **abductor families** are on the lateral or outside surface and pull body parts away from midline. The prefixes *ad-* ("to, toward") and *ab-* ("away from") help us remember direction of movement.

Rotator muscle groups are more complex in location. Most inward rotators are on the anteromedial surface, and most outward rotators are on the posterolateral surface. Thus, inward rotators tend to work with adductors, and outward rotators tend to work with extensors. This is particularly evident in spastic gaits of cerebral origin, which are called **scissors gaits,** because the inward rotators, flexors, and adductors of the hip joint are tighter than their antagonistic or opposite muscle groups and therefore cause a pigeon-toed walk. This tightness has nothing to do with strength and is caused by an imbalance in excitation and inhibition impulses that come from the brain.

 Play games like Simon Says to reinforce names of muscle families and actions. Learn this content well.

Reciprocal Innervation or Inhibition

Reciprocal innervation (also called inhibition) is the neural process that regulates muscle and postural tone. Simply explained, reciprocal innervation is the act of muscles on one surface *contracting* (the prime movers or agonists) while muscles on the opposite surface (the antagonists) are *relaxing.* For smooth, graceful, and effective movement to occur, this continuous shifting of muscle tone must be perfectly timed and balanced. This shifting of muscle tone is complex, with upper motor neurons (those in the brain) responsible for generating **excitation** (facilitation) and **inhibition** (suppression) impulses. Excitation increases muscle tone, and inhibition decreases muscle tone.

Muscle Tone Disorders

The muscle tone disorders are **hypotonia** (floppiness), **hypertonia** (stiffness, spasticity), and **fluctuating tone** (mixed cerebral palsy). These are associated with both congenital and acquired conditions that cause severe damage to the motor part of the brain (see Figure 10.3). Illustrative *congenital* conditions are Down syndrome, severe mental retardation, and cerebral palsy. Illustrative *acquired* conditions are stroke, brain disease, and traumatic brain injury.

Some muscle tone disorders can be helped, and some cannot. For example, persons with spastic cerebral palsy tend to have hypertonia problems throughout their lifespan. Their upper extremities are dominated by flexor tone, and their lower extremities are dominated by extensor tone.

Figure 10.3 In severe spastic cerebral palsy, hypertonia is manifested by flexor tone dominance in the upper body, causing the head to be bent. Hands are often fisted and using the stick control on a power chair is hard.

Assessment of Muscle Tone Disorders

Muscle tone is assessed through either observation and palpation (examination by touch) or electromyography (EMG). It is easy to discern muscle tone disorders, and this task is typically conducted as a fast screening procedure. Muscle tone of different body parts varies according to the area of the brain that is damaged. *Each part of the body should therefore be screened separately with a coding system to record observations in different environments.*

> *1 point—Hypotonia:* Floppiness, inability to resist gravity, inability to grasp or hold an object. An abnormally large range of motion, with no control, that results in froglike lying and sitting postures.
>
> *2 points—Normal muscle tone:* Balance between excitation and inhibition and prime mover and antagonist muscle groups; ability to use muscles in groups or to isolate a given muscle if necessary. A distinction is made between normal relaxed tone and innervated, moving tone.
>
> *+1 point—Hypertonia:* Spasticity, a feeling of tightness or resistance to passive stretch, limited range of movement. In severe cases, **joint contractures** (permanent fixations) might be present.

A *special note* should be written for *fluctuating muscle tone.*

Fatigue, anxiety and environmental variables (e.g., temperature, noise, demands) influence muscle tone, so the examiner should note such conditions. Also, several observations over different days should be used.

Hypotonia Intervention

Many infants with severe disability exhibit low tone and consequently are delayed in achieving motor milestones like lifts head, sits, and rolls. These individuals (often throughout their lifespan) initiate little spontaneous, purposeful activity and must therefore be massaged, bounced, rocked, rolled, swung, tilted, or carried by another to obtain sensory input that will help normalize muscle tone (i.e., reduce hypotonia so tone looks like that of others). Motivation devices like mirrors, noisemaking objects, and electronic devices that create music or activate vibration should be used to encourage and reinforce spontaneous movement..

By age 3 or 4 years, individuals with severe hypotonia will probably be fitted with wheelchairs to help with correct positioning and mobility. Special systems of strapping body parts to the chair permit upright postures. Physical education instruction should begin in the mainstream with services provided as needed. A major goal is to develop strength to use body parts in ADL. Many individuals with *hypotonia* (individuals with brain injury and stroke at all ages as well as infants) experience extreme muscle tone shifts after a few months and thereafter have *hypertonia* (spasticity).

Hypertonia (Spasticity) Intervention

Inhibition or relaxation techniques (slow, rhythmic, repetitive actions) are recommended to decrease spasticity. These should be done in warm water (90 to 98 degrees F) and on every possible land surface. A major strategy for decreasing overall spasticity is rotation of the trunk by the teacher, with the student on a large beachball or therapy ball, tiltboard, hammock, or other apparatus that enables rolling and rotation.

Spasticity compromises postural reactions, so activities that address these goals are important. This calls for many kinds of static and dynamic balances on all kinds of surfaces in all kinds of positions (lying, sitting, four-point, standing, etc.).

Stretching exercises are important also, because spasticity limits range of motion and eventually causes joint contractures (permanent fixation) if frequent, appropriate stretching is not done. *Exercises should use patterns opposite the spastic postures.* For example, slow elevation of the extended, outwardly rotated arm over the head inhibits the fixed spastic flexor position of the arm. For more information on stretching, see the chapters on cerebral palsy and relaxation.

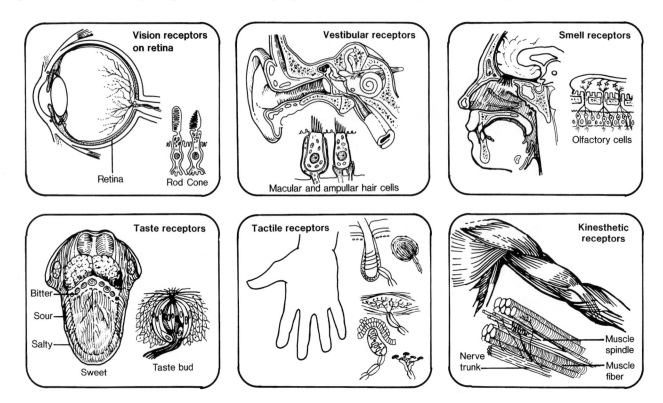

The chapters on dance and aquatics also describe appropriate total body activities. The goal is to independently perform stretches in good alignment. If the individual cannot do so, then stretching should be provided by an outside source.

Sensory Input Systems

Ten modalities provide sensory input that must be organized and processed. These are (a) touch and pressure, (b) kinesthesis, (c) the vestibular system, (d) temperature, (e) pain, (f) smell, (g) taste, (h) vision, (i) audition, and (j) the common chemical sense. With the exception of the last one, these senses are familiar to all of us. The common chemical sense controls the complex reaction to such activities as peeling an onion (eyes burning, nose sneezing) or eating a hot pepper. Each modality has a special type of end organ (sensory receptor) that is sensitive only to certain stimuli, and each has a separate pathway from the sensory receptor up the spinal cord to the brain. Figure 10.4 depicts some of these sensory receptors.

Sensory systems especially important to motor learning are tactile and deep pressure, kinesthetic, vestibular, and visual. When these systems exhibit delayed or abnormal functioning, motor development and/or learning is affected.

Tactile Integration

The tactile system is probably the most fully developed resource at birth, as evidenced by the infant's cries signifying discomfort with wet diapers. Therefore, many authorities recommend targeting this system when working with individuals with severe learning problems who are nonambulatory and compromised in many aspects of movement. The brain organizes tactile system input in many ways and has different locations for processing light touch, deep pressure (massage or weight taken on body parts, such as the soles of the feet), cold, heat, and different kinds of pain that originate in skin receptor organs.

Tactile integration disorders of most interest to physical educators include these:

1. Tactile defensiveness: Touch (one's own and that of others) causes generalized discomfort, irritability, or temper outbursts.
2. Tactile craving or aggressiveness: A greater than average need to touch and be touched.
3. Body image and object awareness problems related to body boundaries, feeling the difference between self and not-self, and processing information that comes from touch.

Assessment of Tactile Integration Problems

Observation in natural settings is probably the best approach. Self-reporting works well with older individuals. Assess yourself and others.

Tactile Defensiveness

Look for the following tactile defensive behaviors:

1. Stiffening when tactile praise like a shoulder touch or pat on the back is given; ducking or moving aside to avoid a hug or tactile praise

2. Complaining more than peers about feeling dirty or sweaty or hot or cold, or showing distaste through gesture and facial expression

3. Avoiding tight clothes, shoes, gloves, automobile seat belts, elevators full of people, and other variables that increase tactile input

4. Disliking certain food textures, unusual sensitivity to these

5. Complaining that peers tag too hard in games or push too much in lines; inability to cope with normal roughhousing among peers

Note that these behaviors might be specific to certain body parts or might occur in response to touch anywhere on the body.

Tactile Craving

Look for the opposite extremes in identifying tactile craving behaviors. Remember, however, that response to touch is cultural and also specific to families. Check whether the individual is responding as other family members do or is showing excessive extremes.

Body Image and Object Awareness

In regard to these problems, check for tactile awareness through informal observation and formal testing. Problems include these:

1. **Stereoagnosia**—inability to identify shapes, textures, and other characteristics of three-dimensional objects by touch alone

2. **Finger or body part agnosia**—inability, when eyes are closed, to recognize which body part has been touched; also called one-point discrimination or localization problems; called **tag agnosia** when individuals do not realize they have been tagged as part of a game

3. **Multiple-point discrimination agnosia**—inability to identify two or more body parts touched simultaneously

4. Affective domain concerns pertaining to body and object touch, feelings, or attitudes that interfere with wellness or learning

Activities for Intervention

Reduce tactile defensiveness by pairing touch activities with reward and gradually increasing the amount of touch that can be tolerated (specify seconds or minutes of tolerance on the objective). For tactile craving, pair reward with not touching. For improved awareness, also give reward. Manipulate different environmental variables for generalization; use both land and water settings.

1. Use massage, either by hand or vibrator, to activate deep pressure receptors. Massage can be by another or by self. Encourage stroking or rubbing of own body parts. The back of the hands and the forearms are the least defensive and thus constitute the first progression activity when severe tactile defensiveness is present.

2. Stroke or brush body parts with fabrics and brushes of different textures. Coarse or rough textures are more easily tolerated than smooth textures, so build the teaching progression from coarse to smooth. Use a washcloth to rub the skin in a tub, spa, or pool.

3. Introduce weights of different textures as part of touch-feel-lift progressions in weight-lifting units. Stuffed animals are good with young children; use hug-and-release movements as well as touch-and-lift.

4. Conduct activities with a reach-in grab bag or box that require guessing the object one is touching without use of sight. Have children run from one station to another where different touch-and-guess activities are done.

5. Conduct "blind person's bluff" type games in which blindfolded persons try to catch and identify others. Do this on land and in water.

 Write IEP objectives for both strengths and weaknesses. Remember to plan rewards specific to each individual's assessed preferences.

Kinesthetic Integration

The kinesthetic or muscle sense system enables organizational activity in both the noncortical and the cortical areas of the brain that contributes to movement awareness (time, space, force, flow) and coordination of body parts. Problems include these:

1. *Time*—inability to feel whether body parts are moving or stationary; if moving, inability to feel the speed of the motion

2. *Space*—inability to feel where body parts are in space, the direction in which they are moving, and whether body parts are bent or straight, aligned or not aligned, upright or inverted

3. *Force*—inability to feel the amount of force being exerted or the amount of weight being pushed, pulled, lifted, or lowered

4. *Flow*—inability to feel the smoothness or jerkiness of movement, especially in transitions from one speed to another, one direction to another, one shape to another, and so on

Receptors in every muscle, tendon, and joint contribute to kinesthesis, and this sensory system matures with movement experience. Kinesthetic integration is specific to muscle groups and thus difficult to assess, because the isolation of muscle groups—so that only one acts at a time—is impossible to achieve in a nonlaboratory setting. Noncortical kinesthetic integration (i.e., without thought) occurs during reflex integration, postural reaction emergence, and achievement of basic motor milestones or body control tasks. As soon as infants (or persons who have had a stroke) become consciously aware of a movement, cortical kinesthetic integration merges with noncortical. Thereafter, the degree of kinesthetic integration determines the ease of learning and automatizing all movement patterns.

Assessment of Kinesthetic Integration Problems

Assessment strategies vary according to whether the individual can understand and use language. *Before language,* observe the following:

1. Reflex integration
2. Postural reaction emergence
3. Motor milestone achievement
4. Unsolicited, spontaneous imitations of movement

After language, observe the following:

1. Ability to imitate body movements on command (assess separately the time, space, force, and flow aspects of movement)
2. Ability to do a movement (independently or assisted), feel it kinesthetically, and then repeat it exactly after increasingly longer periods of time have elapsed

Activities for Intervention

Write IEP goals for both strengths and weaknesses. Plan rewards specific to each individual's assessed preferences. Use the following activities:

1. Movement drills that emphasize exact repetition of a movement.
2. Games that require movement targeted toward a stationary point, like "pin the tail on the donkey," "hit a ball off a tee," or "jump exactly to a designated point."
3. Games that require movement targeted toward a moving object, like intercepting or striking a ball directed toward specific locations on the body (e.g., chest level, waist level).
4. Assisted and coactive movement. In **assisted movement,** the teacher guides body parts of the student through desired movement. In **coactive movement,** the student and teacher are in full-body contact, and the two move in unison.
5. Extension activities. The kinesthetic receptors are activated by changing the tension within muscle, tendon, and joint fibers. Therefore, any movement involving prolonged contraction of extensor muscles against gravity is especially facilitative. *Scooterboard activities done in a prone position with the head up heighten kinesthetic awareness of midline.* Applying pressure to the sites where muscles attach to bones normalizes muscle tone, relaxes muscles, and increases kinesthetic awareness. This practice is based on the same theory that underlies neck and back rubs as a means of reducing tension.
6. Movement exploration approaches.

Note that activities for kinesthetic integration invariably encompass tactile, vestibular, and visual input. Use blindfolds after individuals are 6 or 7 years old or can tolerate occlusion of vision. Minimize other input system actions as much as possible.

Vestibular Integration

The **vestibular system** originates in the inner ear area of the temporal lobe, where hair cell receptors take in information about the position of the head and all of its movements, however subtle (see Figure 10.5). This information, when interpreted and acted upon by other parts of the brain, helps to maintain static and dynamic balance. The vestibular system is the most important structure in the regulation of body postures. It prevents falling, keeps body parts properly aligned, and contributes to graceful, coordinated movement.

Equilibrium and balance, once used as synonyms, are now defined separately. **Equilibrium** is a biomechanical term denoting equal forces acting upon an object. In the human body, the forces exerted by muscles must equal external forces to keep the body upright against the pull of gravity. **Balance** is a more global term, referring to the control processes that maintain body parts in the specific alignments necessary to achieve different kinds of mobility and stability. Most persons with movement problems have difficulty with balance. Four sensory systems (vestibular, kinesthetic, tactile, and visual) interact with environmental variables to enable balance. These, especially the vestibular system, are of considerable interest in adapted physical activity.

The **vestibular apparatus,** the part of the vestibular system that provides sensory information, is named for the hollow, bony *vestibule* (chamber) within the inner ear. This vestibule contains a *labyrinth* (maze) of interconnecting membranous tubes and sacs filled with fluid. The tubes are three **semicircular canals** arranged at right angles to each other. Two are vertical, and one is horizontal (see Figure 10.6). They are named superior, inferior, and horizontal (or anterior, posterior, and lateral). The **sacs** are the utricle and saccule. When the head is upright, the utricle is in a more superior position. The two types of structures (canals and sacs) take in different kinds of sensory information about head movement.

The sensory receptors of the canals and sacs have different names. The hair cells of the canals are called *ampullae, cristae,* or *ampullary cristae* and are located in the bulbous enlargements of the canals at the point where they join the utricle. The hair cells of the sacs are called *maculae* or *otoliths.* To help remember, visualize Big Macs from McDonald's in sacs. Thinking of the sacs in straight lines on the counter correctly associates the maculae with linear movements of the head.

The maintenance of balance involves both sensory input and motor output. Vestibular impulses are carried via the vestibular nerve (eighth cranial) to four vestibular nuclei (clumps of gray matter) in the medulla (brain stem) (see Figure 10.5). Here, many motor impulses are generated to control balance. Some go directly to muscles that activate reflexes and/or reactions, some go to the cerebellum, and some go to midbrain nuclei or cranial nerves that innervate the eye muscles.

This process is very complicated because vestibular impulses are modified, reorganized, and integrated by tactile, kinesthetic, and visual input. Balance in young children is heavily influenced by vision, whereas adults rely more on tactile and kinesthetic input (Shumway-Cook & Woollacott (2001). This explains why children and persons with developmental delays

Figure 10.5 The vestibular system. The *sensory component* consists of the semicircular canals (rotatory input) and sacs (linear input). The *motor component* consists of the four vestibular nuclei and the vestibulo-spinal tract. The vestibular nuclei relay information about the position of the head to many parts of the brain.

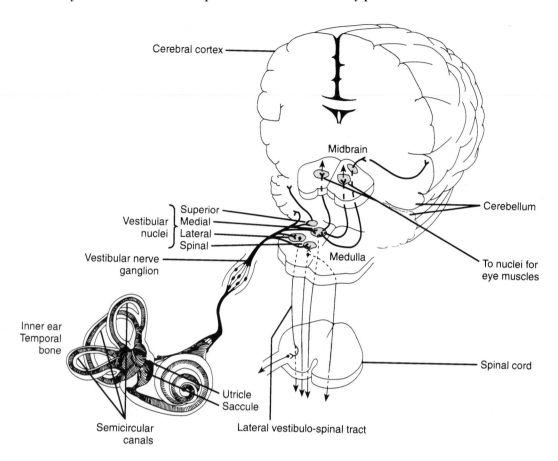

should be encouraged to focus their eyes on a designated point during balance activities. Blindfolds are a good activity for adults who are working on balance.

Assessment of Vestibular Integration

Vestibular function is activated by changes of head position. Assessment thus requires that challenges be made that cause momentary losses of balance (**perturbations**) that change head position. Many of these can be observed in natural playground settings in conjunction with the use of swings, seesaws, merry-go-rounds, and other apparatuses that owe their popularity to children's natural craving for vestibular stimulation. Assessment activities can be divided into natural activities and vestibular spinning.

Natural Activities That Change Head Position

1. For individuals with severe, nonambulatory conditions, use rocking motions in arms, rocking chair, tilt board, or therapy ball.
2. For others, use natural play environments with as many pieces of apparatus as possible (playground equipment, balance beams, swinging bridges, and changing-consistency locomotor surfaces like moon walks, mattresses, water beds, and trampolines).

Note whether head change causes pathological reflexes. If not, record the ease with which body parts adapt to head changes.

Vestibular Spinning Activities and Nystagmus

Vestibular testing is done by specially trained therapists by rapid spinning of individuals sitting on a stool; 20 seconds of spinning normally results in 9 to 11 seconds of **nystagmus** (rapid eye movements), an automatic midbrain response. A longer or shorter duration of nystagmus indicates a lack of vestibular integration. No dizziness or discomfort, or the opposite, including nausea, signal vestibular problems also. Vestibular spinning should be used only by individuals with special training (Ayres, 1972). Spinning is contraindicated when individuals are seizure-prone or have inner-ear or upper-respiratory infections. This test is extremely unpleasant for some and fun for others.

Activities for Intervention

Write IEP objectives based on strengths and weaknesses. Plan rewards specific to each individual's assessed preferences. *Note that vestibular remediation cannot be isolated from kinesthetic integration.* The use of blindfolds can negate effects of visual integration, but typically the goal is TKVV (tactile, kinesthetic, vestibular, visual) integration, not work with a single system.

Figure 10.6   Semicircular canals and sacs (utricle and saccule).

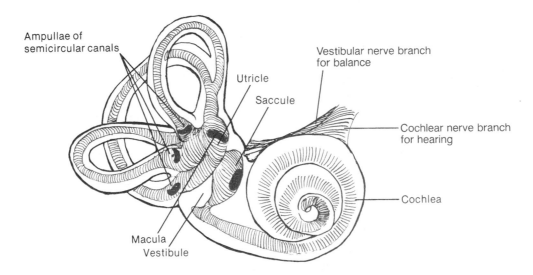

1. Use activities listed in the assessment section.
2. Use movement exploration activities and games that incorporate spinning and rolling.
3. Create numerous static and dynamic balance challenges in all positions. Use vestibular (balance) boards, hammocks, large balls, and equipment that can be used to cause momentary losses of balance (see Figure 10.7).

Visual Integration

The visual system is comprised of many subsystems, some reflexive and some voluntary. All are important in postural control and motor performance. The many subsystems can be organized into two types of vision: (a) refractive and (b) orthoptic.

Refractive Vision (Acuity)

Refractive vision refers to visual acuity, the product of light rays bending and reaching the receptor cells (rods and cones) of the retina. Visual impulses are transmitted via the optic nerve (second cranial) to many parts of the brain for interpretation. Refractive problems include **myopia** (nearsightedness), **hyperopia** (farsightedness), and **astigmatism** (blurring and distortion). Refraction is influenced by the size and shape of the eyeball, which changes with age. At birth, the eyeball is short (about three-fourths of adult length), which explains why young children tend to focus more easily on middle-distance items than on near ones.

Orthoptic Vision (Eye Coordination)

Orthoptic vision refers to activity of the six external muscles of the eyeball, which are innervated by cranial nerves 3, 4, and 6. These muscles move the eyeballs up, down, in, out, and in diagonal directions. Of particular importance is **binocular coordination,** the ability of the two eyes to work in unison. Physiologically, because of their separate locations, each eye receives slightly different sensory stimuli and thus forms a different image. The two eyes must work together to fuse these

Figure 10.7   The use of unstable surfaces is an intervention for vestibular deficits. Note the activity involves reaching for a ball that the teacher moves from place to place.

separate images into one which, when interpreted by the brain, is seen as a solid with height, width, and depth dimensions and interpreted in relation to distance. The closer something is to the eyes, the greater the disparity between the images and the harder it is to fuse them into one. Likewise, the farther away the two eyes are set from one another, the more difficult the fusion (see Figure 10.8).

Figure 10.8 Eye problems affect vision and sensorimotor function. (*A*) Eyes set abnormally far apart interfere with binocular coordination. (*B*) Strabismus in Down syndrome interferes with depth perception.

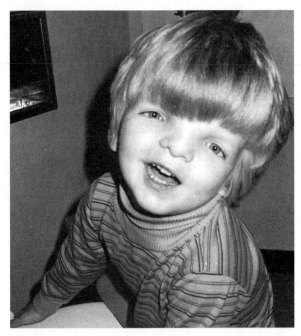

A

B

Binocular coordination is closely linked with balance and postural reactions. We take for granted the subcortical processing of three dimensions of space and the automatic adjustment of body parts to avoid bumping into things, falling, and other inappropriate movements.

Depth perception is often used as a synonym for *binocular coordination,* but this oversimplification is inaccurate. **Depth perception** is the mental process of deriving mean-

ing from visual space-time relationships, as in judging the distance of a balance beam from the ground or the speed/distance of a moving object. It is dependent upon three complex mechanisms, one of which is binocular coordination. *Simplified, depth perception is problem-solving about near/far relationships.* Abilities can be classified as static (near/far judgments about stationary things) and dynamic (near/far judgments about moving things). Developmentally, we refine static perception abilities first. By age 12, depth perception is usually mature.

Eye muscle coordination problems are common among persons with disabilities. These include (a) developmental delays in binocular coordination and depth perception, (b) **strabismus** (squint or crossed eyes), and (c) pathological **nystagmus** (constant, involuntary movement of the eyeballs). Strabismus is associated with cerebral palsy, Down syndrome, and fetal alcohol syndrome (see Figure 10.8). Nystagmus has a high prevalence among visually impaired persons with **albinism** (blond, blue eyes, pale skin).

Assessment of Visual Integration

Most screening tests used by teachers relate to vision for reading rather than for body control. Findings regarding binocular control in near-vision tasks (30 inches or closer) do not generalize to the depth perception demands in dodgeball, catching, and striking activities. Vision problems related to hand-eye and foot-eye coordination should be assessed by observing students performing striking, kicking, dodging, tagging, and catching skills. Note differences when the ball is stationary and when it is moving toward the person at midline, to the right, and to the left.

When vision problems are suspected, an **ophthalmologist** (eye specialist) should be consulted. Refractive problems are treated by prescriptive glasses or surgery. Some orthoptic problems like strabismus can also be treated with surgery.

Ophthalmic problems of individuals with developmental disabilities are usually very complex. The best description of ophthalmic testing in adapted physical activity literature is offered by Mon-Williams, Pascal, and Wann (1994). After testing 500 children, aged 5 to 7 years, these researchers concluded that many children with developmental coordination disorder (DCD) do not have ophthalmic problems. It was suggested, therefore, that assessment should focus on the higher levels of visual processing that relate to cognition.

Activities for Intervention

The best way to enhance vision for body control is to provide lots of practice in many and varied movement tasks. The breakdown in vision typically is not exclusively a problem of the eyes but rather the complex process of integrating inputs from several sensory modalities and translating them into appropriate motor outputs.

1. Use suspended-ball activities in which the height of the ball is periodically changed so the head and eyes must practice accommodations.

2. Do lying and locomotor activities on tables of different heights so the eyes look down and accommodate. When appropriate, switch from tables to wide balance beams.

3. Lift the child into the air and do various airplane activities so the child sees the world from different perspectives.

4. Practice object handling from many positions: midline and looking up, down, and sideways. This includes prone-, supine-, and side-lying on mats as well as on apparatus of different heights and tilts to give looking downward new perspectives.

5. Practice with (a) the body stationary, (b) the body in locomotion, and (c) the body moved by external forces like swings, balance boards, scooterboards, merry-go-rounds, escalators, treadmills, and the like. Only the creativity of the professional limits the ways vision can be practiced and enhanced.

Infant and Pathological Reflexes

Whereas motor development books describe infant reflexes, adapted physical activity texts emphasize pathological reflex-activity that interferes with motor performance. The following section briefly reviews infant reflexes and stereotypies because nonambulatory individuals with severe cerebral palsy and traumatic brain injury exhibit many postures and patterns similar to those of infants. Failure to totally integrate reflexes is a problem in clumsiness or developmental coordination disorder at all ages.

Infant Reflexes and Stereotypies

Infant reflexes are involuntary, predictable muscle and postural tone shifts that are age-specific and important to typical development between birth and 9 months of age. These movement pattern shifts can be spontaneous or elicited by external stimuli. In this text, reflexes that appear to be spontaneous are called *stereotypies*. This is to avoid confusion, *because reflexes traditionally have been linked to specific sensory input (e.g., head turning).*

In infancy, all reflexes are good and serve a definite purpose. Reflexes are the building blocks on which the developing sensorimotor system rests. Each reflex contributes to either the achievement of spontaneous, voluntary movement abilities (e.g., head lifting, unilateral reaching, sitting) or the emergence of lifelong, automatic, postural reactions that serve righting, protection, and equilibrium functions. This is important because infants are born without the capacity to think about a movement and then plan and execute it.

Stereotypies are rhythmical, presumably pleasant, movements of body parts that are performed over and over for no apparent reason. Kicking stereotypies are among the first to appear, usually at about 4 weeks of age. Stereotypies tend to appear just before infants display voluntary control of body parts and seem to provide needed input for maturation of the CNS. Most reflexes are integrated (disappear) by about 9 months, and most stereotypies are integrated by about 12 months.

Age-Appropriate Integration of Reflexes and Stereotypies

When reflexes and stereotypies do not disappear in infancy, they are classified as pathological and targeted for intervention. **Integration** refers to the neural process of layering over, inhibiting, or suppressing reflexes and stereotypies.

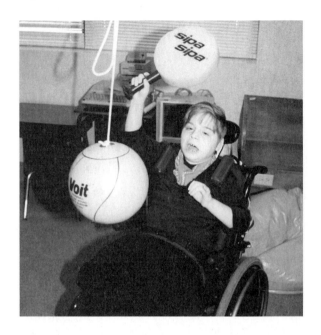

Figure 10.9   **Reflex problems make movements look clumsy.**

Integration, however, occurs in various degrees. Under fatigue and stress conditions, integration sometimes breaks down. This is especially true when trying new motor skills or responding to a surprise motor demand, as when someone tosses you the house keys. Integration is never total or complete. Abnormal reflex activity is recognizable in clumsy movement at all ages. Although new cortically initiated movements continuously layer over reflex patterns, the layering or integration varies greatly from individual to individual.

Pathological Reflexes

Reflexes that are not integrated at the developmentally appropriate times become pathological, in that involuntary shifts of muscle tone, however subtle, interfere with smooth, coordinated movement (see Figure 10.9). Consider what makes a movement look clumsy. Often the underlying causes are imbalances in force, timing, and rhythm and/or tenseness. Individual differences in reflex integration help to explain the many degrees of clumsiness seen in the so-called normal population. Adapted physical activity personnel have only recently begun to think of abnormal reflex activity as a source of clumsiness, but occupational therapists have advanced this idea for years (Ayers, 1972).

Abnormal retention of reflexes contributes to the clumsiness associated with cerebral palsy, the most common orthopedic impairment in the public schools, and many other disabilities. Both general physical educators and APA specialists need to understand the reflexes that interfere with skilled sport, dance, and aquatics performance.

Reflexes Important in Physical Education

Approximately 30 primitive reflexes dominate infants' motor behavior. In extensive observation of clumsy students, Sherrill

Table 10.2   **Reflexes of most importance to physical educators.**

Reflex	Average Age of Dominance	Dominant Muscle Tone	Body Part to Watch	Distribution
1. Tonic labyrinthine–prone	0–4 months	Flexion	Total body	Total
2. Tonic labyrinthine–supine	0–4 months	Extension	Total body	Total
3. Asymmetrical tonic neck	0–4 months	Flexion-extension	Arms	Asymmetrical
4. Symmetrical tonic neck	6–8 months	Flexion-extension	Arms-legs	Symmetrical
5. Moro	0–4 months	Extension	Arms-hands	Symmetrical
6. Hand grasp	0–4 months	Flexion	Hands-arms	Symmetrical
7. Foot grasp	0–9 months	Flexion	Toes, feet	Symmetrical
8. Extensor thrust	0–3 months	Extension	Legs	Symmetrical
9. Crossed extension	0–3 months	Flexion-extension	Legs	Symmetrical
10. Positive supporting-legs	3–8 months	Extension	Legs-trunk	Symmetrical

Note: Content for table was taken from Fiorentino (1981) and the *Milani-Comparetti Motor Development Screening Test Manual* (1987). Age range in which reflex is considered normal varies considerably, with some sources adding 1 to 2 months to those cited above.

has found that only about 10 reflexes affect physical education performance (see Table 10.2). Only these reflexes are covered in this text, and they are presented in a special format so that you can copy the information on each one and paste it on a 5-inch-by-7-inch study card (see Figures 10.10 through 10.19).

Table 10.2 shows the average age range during which each reflex dominates in normal development and indicates that most reflexes are integrated by 4 months of age, and all are integrated by 9 months of age. *Integration, however, is never total or complete.*

Table 10.2 shows the muscle tone that becomes dominant in each pattern, thereby interrupting the balance between opposing muscle groups. When the predominant tone is flexion, more tension is seen on the anterior surface of the body than the posterior. Usually, the affected body parts are bent. When the predominant tone is extension, the opposite is true. The posterior surface shows tenseness, and the body parts are straightened and sometimes stiff. The exception to this generalization is knee joint actions.

Table 10.2 also summarizes the body parts affected by the reflexes and the nature of the muscle tone distribution (total, symmetrical, or asymmetrical). The two reflexes affecting the total body are the most serious. Reflexes affecting the legs interfere with locomotor activities, while those affecting the arms and hands make ball-handling patterns look awkward.

The following explanations of each reflex include three parts: (a) description, (b) contributions during the time the reflex is normal, and (c) problems caused by abnormal retention of the reflexes.

Tonic Labyrinthine Reflex (TLR)—Prone   *Normal at Ages 0–4 Months*

Description
Increased flexor tone in response to any change in the position of head. Figure 10.10A shows an infant in prone; the TLR is responsible for this position. Figure 10.10B shows an older child who is severely delayed.

Contributions
Stimulates flexor tone of total body.

Problems
Results in abnormal distribution of muscle tone and inability of body segments to move independently of one another. Prevents raising head, which, in turn, prevents development of symmetrical tonic neck reflex, righting reactions, and Landau extensor reaction. Shoulder **protraction** (abduction) results in inability to move arms from under body (see Figure 10.10B). Infant or person with severe disabilities dominated by TLR is virtually helpless. Compromises any activity done against gravity from a prone position.

Figure 10.10   Two examples of tonic labyrinthine reflex—prone.

A   Normal infant dominated by flexor tone

B   Child with severe brain damage cannot lift head or pull arms out from under body

Description

Increased extensor tone in response to any change in position of head.

Contributions

Helps create a balance between extensor and flexor muscles.

Problems

Domination by extensor tone, which holds shoulders in retraction (adduction) and prevents or compromises head raising, bringing limbs to midline, and rotation (turning) of body. In persons with severe disability, may contribute to windswept (**opisthotonic**) position (see Figure 10.11A).

Figure 10.10   Two examples of tonic labyrinthine reflex—prone.

A   Normal infant dominated by flexor tone

B   Child with severe brain damage cannot lift head or pull arms out from under body

Figure 10.11   Two examples of tonic labyrinthine reflex–supine.

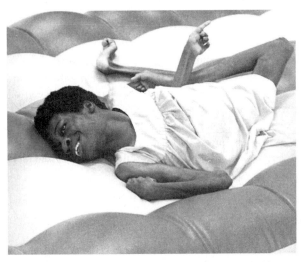

A Older adult showing **opisthotonic** or **windswept** position, spasticity in which head and heels are bent backward

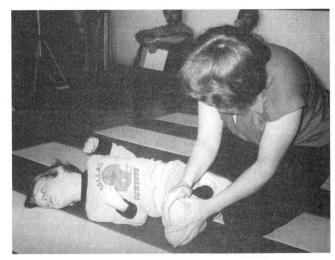

B Six-year-old with severe cerebral palsy cannot roll over, lift head, or bring hands to midline

Description
On-guard, fencing position activated by rotation or lateral flexion (tilt) of head. Increased extensor tonus of limbs on chin side and increased flexor tonus of limbs on head side.

Contributions
Helps break up flexor and extensor pattern dominance so that each side of body can function separately.

Problems
1. Prevents learning to roll from supine to prone and vice versa since extended arm gets in the way.
2. Interferes with limb movement, which, in turn, impairs normal hand-eye coordination development. Associated problem is loss of visual fixation.
3. Prevents independent flexing of limb to bring it toward midline, as in playing with object or feeding self. Helps explain why persons bend their elbow in tennis forehand drive; as head rotates to left to see ball, right elbow flexes.
4. Causes one arm to bend or collapse in the beginning forward roll position if head tilts or rotates even slightly.
5. In sport positions that involve a rotated head, such as softball batting or tennis stance, prevents or compromises the bat or racquet crossing midline and, thus, properly following through.
6. In severe conditions, may contribute to scoliosis, subluxed or dislocated hips, or windswept lying position.

Failure of the reflex to become integrated explains much of the clumsiness physical educators observe, especially in relation to ball

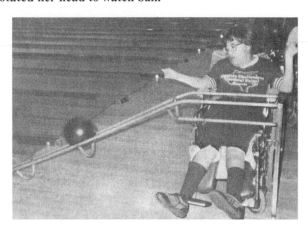

Figure 10.12   Adolescent with cerebral palsy exhibiting asymmetrical tonic neck reflex because she rotated her head to watch ball.

activities (see Figure 10.12). Many of the verbal cues that physical educators give ("Keep your eye on the ball"; "Don't bend your elbow"; "Remember to follow through") are not commands that can be entirely consciously implemented. Thus, bright, but clumsy, students often think and sometimes respond, "I know what I'm doing wrong, but my body won't do what my mind tells it."

Description
Flexion and extension movements of the head influence muscle tone distribution in relation to upper and lower body. Head flexion increases flexor tone of upper body and extensor tone of lower body; head extension does the opposite (see Figure 10.13). Predominant upper-body muscle tone is always that of the head and neck.

Contributions
Contributes to such important motor milestones as lifting and supporting upper body on arms and rising to four-point creeping position.

Figure 10.13   Two symmetrical tonic neck reflexes (STNR).

Flexion STNR: Head flexion causes legs to extend

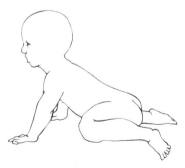

Extension STNR: Head extension causes creeping or bunny-hop position

Problems
1. Flexion STNR compromises sitting position. Head down activates extensor thrust in lower extremities; increases high-guard position of arms. Head up contributes to good sitting posture but increases difficulty of hand and arm activities that entail flexion, like lifting arm for overarm throw.
2. Looking down at ground or balance beam when walking compromises distribution of muscle tone; helps to explain gait of toddler with arms in high guard and abnormally stiff leg action and/or tendency to toe walk.

3. Extension STNR prevents reciprocal flexion and extension movement of legs needed in creeping (i.e., with head up, child is frozen in bunny-hop position).
4. Compromises ability to do certain stunts, exercises, and animal walks with head up. Makes holding legs extended difficult in regulation push-up position, in prone scooterboard activities, and in wheelbarrow races.
5. Compromises ability to do exercises, stunts, gymnastics, and synchronized swimming that require head held down in tucked position with knees simultaneously tucked to chest. Explains why "tuck position" is difficult to maintain as head changes position from flexion to extension (i.e., why persons come out of their tuck too soon).

Description

Flexion of toes (clawing motion) in response to deep pressure stimulation of soles of feet, as in standing or when object is pressed against toes (see Figure 10.14).

Contributions

Tactile stimulation enhances body awareness. The reflex also strengthens foot muscles.

Problems

Interferes with balance in walking and standing. Often seen in conjunction with **positive supporting reflex** (increased extensor tone that results in toe walking, see Figure 10.17).

Figure 10.14   **Foot grasp reflex.**

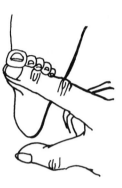

Description

Increased extensor tone throughout the body evoked by stimulus of sudden pressure to soles of feet. Most often observed in conjunction with sitting postures, a common problem in nonambulatory persons with cerebral palsy (see Figure 10.15). In first 2 months, sometimes mistaken for early standing ability.

Contributions

Strengthens extensors, thereby promoting balance between flexor and extensor postural tone.

Problems

Inability to maintain proper sitting position; entire body stiffens so that person slides out of wheelchair unless strapped in. Usually occurs in conjunction with positive supporting reflex of legs and/or tonic labyrinthine supine reflex or symmetrical tonic neck reflex. Often, the abnormal movement produced by one or both of these is called an *extensor thrust pattern* (i.e., the term is not limited to action of the extensor thrust reflex alone).

Figure 10.15   **Extensor thrust reflex or pattern.**

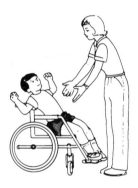

Description

Elicited by flexing or tapping medial surface of one leg. One leg reflexly affects the other (see Figure 10.16A). Evidenced when one leg cannot flex (as in kicking a ball) without associated extension of the other leg. Also evidenced when medial surface of upper legs touches or rubs against one another; this stimulus contributes to scissoring. Correct positioning in wheelchair, with bolster between thighs, prevents this.

Contributions

Helps to break up dominant symmetrical flexion and extension patterns. Facilitates development of extensor tone to stand on one leg while the other leg flexes (i.e., permits reciprocal leg movements needed for creeping and walking).

Problems

1. Prevents coordinated leg movements needed to crawl, creep, and walk.

2. Causes scissoring of legs (see Figure 10.16B).

3. Sometimes serves as substitute for absent positive support reflex in athetosis and ataxia. Child can stand only on stiffly extended legs and raises legs too high in walking.

Problems Combined With Positive Supporting Reflex

1. Affects kicking in a standing position. When leg is lifted to kick ball, a strong extensor spasm affects support leg and causes loss of balance. Child loses balance because he or she pushes reflexly against ground with ball of support foot (positive supporting reflex thereby reinforcing extensor spasm); this is accompanied by knee hyperextension and clawing of toes. To prevent falling backward, reflex activates flexion of trunk at hips and brings kicking leg down and forward, leaving weight-bearing foot, leg, hip, and shoulder behind. This rotary movement prevents straight follow-through in the kick.

2. Affects walking pattern. Results in hyperextended knees, clawing of toes, and hip flexion in support leg to prevent falling. This is typically compensated for by forward flexion of head and lordosis.

Figure 10.16   Two examples of crossed extension reflex.

A   Test position response

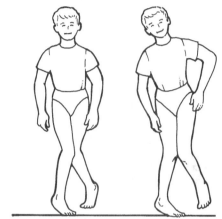

B   Scissors gait response

Description

Increased extensor tone (plantar flexion at ankle joint) caused by soles of feet touching floor or footrests of wheelchair.

Contributions

Strengthens hip and leg extensors needed for straight-back sitting and standing.

Problems

1. When fully present, prevents independent standing and walking; creates difficulty (along with extensor thrust reflex) in wheelchair posture adjustments and/or wheelchair transfers because sensory input from foot plates stimulates soles of feet, which, in turn, increases extensor tone.

2. When partially present, affects walking gait by causing toe walking)prevents placing heel on floor), contributing (with crossed extension reflex) to scissoring, narrowing base of support, and producing backward thrust of trunk with compensator lordosis and arm out to assist with balance (see Figure 10.17).

3. Also interferes with kicking a ball (see crossed extensor reflex).

Figure 10.17   Two examples of positive supporting reflex.

Toes point and feet stiffen on landing in assisted jumping

Toe walk pattern, usually unstable

Description

The body stiffens and arms and legs involuntarily spread and close in repsonse to unstable lying/sitting surface or falling movement (see Figure 10.18). This reflex can occur while lying, sitting, or standing.

Contributions

Contributes to development of extensor and abductor strength of upper extremities, including fingers; serves as precursor to propping and parachute reactions.

Problems

Interferes with learning to sit and using the arms for balance. Prevents using one arm at a time.

Caution

Do not confuse with **startle reflex,** a similar response except that the stimulus is a loud noise.

Figure 10.18   Two phases of the Moro reflex.

Spread phase

Close phase

Description

Flexion of fingers in response to object being drawn across palm or hypertension of wrist (see Figure 10.19).

Contributions

Tactile stimulation by object in hand is the beginning of eye-hand coordination and visual body awareness.

Problems

Interferes with development of voluntary grasp and release mechanism; compromises tactile sensory input.

Figure 10.19   Hand grasp reflex.

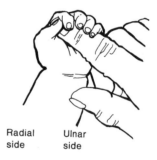

Radial side   Ulnar side

Assessment Criteria for Physical Education Reflexes

The following criteria help determine the presence of pathological reflexes. Use this sheet as a checklist.

Tonic Labyrinthine–Prone

1. Total body dominated by flexor tone.
2. Difficulty in moving one body part independently from others.
3. Head lift from prone difficult.
4. Arm movement to rear limited by shoulder protraction (abduction).
5. Pivot prone, swan, and front rocker stunts difficult.
6. Arm movement upward and outward limited.
7. Slouched walking posture.

Tonic Labyrinthine–Supine

1. Total body (except hips) dominated by extensor tone.
2. Difficulty in moving one body part independently from others.
3. Head lift from supine difficult.
4. Tuck position in supine difficult.
5. Arm movements to midline difficult.
6. Trunk rotation movements difficult.

Asymmetrical Tonic Neck Reflexes

1. Head turn causes limb tension or movement.
2. Extensor dominance on face side of body and flexor dominance on nonface side.
3. Difficulty with logroll; arm gets in the way.

4. If the head turns, the limbs cannot continue midline movement.

5. Head and trunk rotation to right in softball or tennis backswing makes bending right arm difficult.

6. Head and trunk rotation to left for contact and follow-through makes straightening right arm difficult.

Symmetrical Tonic Neck Reflex

A. Head-down position
   1. Stiff leg action in walking.
   2. Tendency to toe walk.
   3. Tucking legs to chest difficult.
   4. Lifting leg difficult in kick follow-through.
   5. Crouch starting position compromised.
   6. Arms and upper body more flexed than desired.

B. Head-up position
   1. Excessive knee and ankle flexion.
   2. Tendency to shuffle or walk flat-footed.
   3. Inability to keep legs straight in wheelbarrow walk stunt.
   4. Legs cannot move reciprocally in animal walks.
   5. Arms and upper body more extended than desired.

Moro Reflex

1. Sitting balance problems.
2. Use of arms in balance impaired.
3. Bilateral movement response to loss of balance.

Hand Grasp Reflex

1. Release activities in ball handling difficult.
2. Letting go of pool edge for swim race difficult.
3. Flat hands in contact with floor difficult.

Foot Grasp Reflex

1. Balance problem.
2. Difficulty doing flat-footed or heel walk.

Extensor Thrust Reflex

1. Slides out of chair unless strapped in.
2. Total body dominated by extensor tone.

Reflex Integration in Teaching

If not integrated, the pathological reflexes discussed in the preceding section affect physical education instruction. First, they explain why some students continue to make movement errors in spite of corrective feedback. Good examples are students who continue bending the elbow in tennis strokes, who fail to follow through across midline in throwing, and who cannot get the total body to work together smoothly in a forward roll or jump. Such students often say, "I know what I'm supposed to do. I can visualize every part. I just can't make my body do what my mind says." In essence, these students are saying that they do not have the cortical control to override reflex patterns. Visual and auditory instructions (their own self-talk or the teacher's input) are not effective when used alone because they

are directed toward the thinking parts of the brain when the problem is at the lower levels.

Four Principles of Reflex Integration

In working with students with reflex problems, remember these four principles:

1. Maximize tactile, kinesthetic, and vestibular (TKV) input.
2. Use total body movement patterns and games that inhibit reflexes (i.e., emphasize opposite patterns).
3. Increase practice time and time-on-task for correctly executed patterns.
4. Intensify individual assistance so that patterns are performed correctly. Pay particular attention to head position.

Strategies That Involve TKV Input

TKV input is maximized mainly by five strategies. *Coactive movement* is the professional term for teacher and student moving together, bodies touching, so that the student receives input from all three modalities (TKV) concurrently. *Passive assistance* refers to the teacher's moving only one body part of the student. *Tactile cueing* refers to tapping or rubbing a body part to reinforce memory. *Balancing activities* (both static and dynamic) give the CNS practice in processing input from TKV modalities as well as vision. Balancing should be interpreted as achieving and maintaining stability in all kinds of positions. *Reward* emphasizes frequent praise and correctional feedback. Use rewards specific to individual preferences.

The Four Most Troublesome Reflexes with Interventions

Of the 10 reflexes, the four initiated by head movements are generally the most troublesome. These are the tonic labyrinthine reflex–prone (TLR–prone), tonic labyrinthine reflex–supine (TLR–supine), asymmetrical tonic neck reflex (ATNR), and symmetrical tonic neck reflex (STNR). In these four reflexes, the student cannot move the head without initiating associated movements or subtle muscle tone tensions of other body parts.

Intervention is thus directed toward practice in moving the head and (a) keeping everything else stationary or (b) simultaneously performing body part movements that are the opposites of what the reflex mechanisms enact. This is essentially the same as repeatedly performing a skill the *right way* as called for in the **principle of specificity** (i.e., practice the specific pattern in which you want skill). Achieving the *right way*, however, is often impossible without special focus on the head. See Figure 10.26.

The **tonic labyrinthine reflexes** help explain coordination and control problems in exercises done from lying positions like, for example, sit-ups from supine, trunk lifts from prone, rolling over, and moving rapidly from lying to standing positions, as in recoveries from falls and dives in such sports as volleyball. The tonic labyrinthine reflexes also help to explain the abnormal standing, walking, and jumping postures seen in many persons with severe disability. When gravity acts to pull the head downward and the total body responds by assuming a flexion posture, the reflex responsible is the TLR–prone. When the head, for any reason, is thrown backward and the total body responds in an extension posture, the reflex responsible is the TLR–supine.

The **ATNR** and **STNR** are operative when only part of the body responds reflexively to head movements. The ATNR explains clumsiness in activities involving head and trunk rotation. Head turning causes obligatory extension patterns of limbs on the face side and simultaneous obligatory flexion patterns on the nonface side. Think how many sport patterns require turning the head to the right and left and how obligatory arm responses or subtle muscle tone shifts make movements look and feel awkward. In contrast, the STNR explains clumsiness in activities that involve the top and bottom parts of the body working together. When the STNR is operative, up and down head movements cause obligatory bilateral arm and leg responses.

Sometimes, several reflexes, rather than one, contribute to lack of coordination and control. This is often the case in the jump. In addition to the STNR, the jump may be affected by the four reflexes that act on the feet and legs: foot grasp, extensor thrust, crossed extension, and positive supporting-legs. Except for the foot grasp, these reflexes all cause extension of the lower extremities and interfere with the flexion needed to land smoothly and comfortably. These four reflexes also affect locomotion. Extreme pigeon-toed walking (hip adduction and inward rotation patterns) called **scissoring** is elicited by crossed extension and positive supporting reflexes.

TLR–Prone Intervention Activities—Emphasize Extension

1. Stunts in prone on mats that involve lifting the head (easiest progression), or head and shoulders, or trunk with arms outstretched forward over the head or sideways. These stunts have many names: *pivot prone, swan, wing lifts, airplane.*

2. Stunts in prone in water while supported or moving independently: various floats, glides, and transitions between tucked and straight positions.

3. Prone lie in full extension or net hammock or blanket that is pulled along the floor by another or suspended in the air and gently rocked or swung.

4. Prone lie in full extension on a therapy ball, slant board, or other surfaces of various textures that can be rocked; practice in controlled transition from full extension to full tuck to full extension.

5. Prone lie in full extension on scooterboard. Holding onto a rope when being pulled by another, or pulling a rope that is attached to wall to move self. Create scooterboard games and challenge tasks.

6. Rise-to-stand games from prone lie and stand-to-prone-lie transitions on mats, trampolines, floors, and surfaces of various consistencies. Start running games and relays from prone lie instead of crouch.

7. Use the fully extended prone lie as a safety position in tag games.

8. Push-ups and other fitness activities from prone.

9. Walking activities at various speeds, while performing novelty tasks like carrying objects on the head. Check that the students do not look at their feet, because this is an indication that the TLR–prone is not integrated.

TLR–Supine Intervention Activities—Emphasize Flexion

1. Stunts in supine on various surfaces that involve tucking the head and making the body into a ball. Often novelty rolls are done in tucked position and given names like *egg roll, human ball.* Avoid forward and backward rolls until this reflex disappears.

2. Stunts in supine in water while supported or moving independently; practice transitions between tuck-and-extend sequences in supine.

3. Partial and bent-knee sit-ups and curl-ups.

4. Supine tuck position games and exercises with unilateral, bilateral, and crosslateral arm or leg movements or timed holds.

5. Use the supine tuck in drills from standing position or as a safety position in tag games; this is called turtle tag—you look like a turtle upside down.

ATNR Intervention Activities—Emphasize Head Turn

1. Rotations of the head to the left (L) or right (R) while keeping other body parts motionless. *Simon Says* games with surprise commands to turn the head and penalty for moving other body parts.

2. Creeping forward or backward, with head turned to one side.

3. Animal walks and stunts with eyes straight forward. Students must respond appropriately when leader calls out surprise commands: "Look to left" and "Look to right." Have the students do the same thing on a balance beam or while performing other locomotor challenges.

4. Head exercises like turn head to side, touch chin to shoulder, and hold (an excellent exercise for forward head posture problem); check that students move only the head; have them view videotapes of their movements to see if they moved other body parts.

5. Sideward rolling that is initiated by the head while other body parts are kept motionless.

6. Racket games that require keeping the side to the net. Check that when students rotate head and trunk, they maintain the elbow in correct position.

7. Corrective postures, like hand on hip or right hand holding right ear, that will tend to prevent a body part from moving in response to head movement.

STNR Intervention Activities—Emphasize Head Up or Down

1. Activities in which the upper and lower body can do the same or opposite things, like bend the head and legs in a supine body tuck and lift the head and neck from a prone lie.

Figure 10.20 Basic exercises that help to integrate reflexes and reinforce tactile-kinesthetic-vestibular function.

Body tuck. Helps normalize tonic labyrinthine reflexes.

Rollover with limbs on one side flexed. Helps normalize asymmetrical tonic neck reflex.

Pivot prone, swan, or wing lift. Helps normalize tonic labyrinthine and symmetrical tonic neck reflexes.

Head lift and hold neck co-contraction. Promotes strength.

Prone-on-elbows or belly crawl. Helps normalize symmetrical tonic neck reflex.

Four-point or creeping. Promotes strength.

Standing. With practice on stand-to-squat, stand-to-sit, stand-to-lie, and vice versa.

Walking. Arm opposition and trunk rotation begin at age 4 to 5 years.

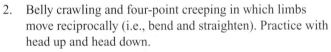

2. Belly crawling and four-point creeping in which limbs move reciprocally (i.e., bend and straighten). Practice with head up and head down.

3. Jumping and diving activities with progressively more difficult coordinations.

4. Partner stunts like walking on hands with the head up while the legs are held extended (wheelbarrow), or dumping sand (the same activity, but with an up-and-down motion instead of a forward walk).

5. Horseback and bicycle riding in which the upper body is straight and the lower limbs straighten and bend.

6. Scooterboard and other wheel apparatuses in which the arms and legs work reciprocally.

7. Rope and tree climbing.

Overflow (Associated Movements)

A common indicator of clumsiness is associated movements, also called overflow. These are undesired reflex responses of body parts that should remain stationary. Examples are (a) facial grimaces when concentrating on a hand-eye or hand-foot motor task, (b) an increase in muscle tone or a mirroring action on the noninvolved side when trying to perform one-arm or one-leg acts, and (c) unnecessary, uncoordinated, or funny-looking movements of the arms during locomotion. Associated movements are caused by poorly integrated reflexes. They are remnants of the mass flexor and extensor patterns present at birth, when body parts cannot move independently of one another. As such, associated movements occur in early childhood, diminish by ages 6 to 8 years, and generally disappear by adolescence.

Simply telling a student to stop an associated movement does not work because reflex mechanisms can be overridden only by many, many repetitions of the correct movement pattern. Programming should therefore include many activities that help the nervous system to organize sensorimotor processes and facilitate subcortical motor planning. Examples of such activities are shown in Figure 10.20. Others are presented in Chapters 12, 16, and 17.

Postural Reactions

Reactions are automatic responses to sensory input that act to keep body parts in alignment, maintain equilibrium, and prevent injury. Some reactions replace reflexes, but others emerge to perform unique functions. In normal development, reactions appear between the ages of 2 and 18 months. With a few exceptions (e.g., the Landau and body derotative), these reactions persist throughout life. Some authorities believe that delays in the appearance of postural reactions are more detrimental to motor success than reflex disorders, especially in severe mental retardation (Molnar, 1978). Many persons, of course, have both reflex and reaction problems.

This text uses the terminology of the Milani-Comparetti Assessment System (see page 287) and such leading authorities as Crutchfield and Barnes (1995) and Levitt (1995). Reactions are primarily important for their role in balance and help to explain why so many clumsy individuals have balance problems.

Assessment of Postural Reactions

There are basically three categories of reactions: (a) righting, (b) parachute, and (c) equilibrium. *Righting reactions* are adjustments of the head or trunk. *Parachute reactions* are protective extension movements of the limbs. *Equilibrium reactions* are total body responses. To assess the presence of these reactions, teachers must hold, tilt, or position the children in specific ways (e.g., see Figure 10.21).

Five Righting Reactions

Righting reactions are the automatic postural responses elicited by sensory input that signals that the head or trunk is not in midline. The first three righting reactions (head-in-space, optical righting, and Landau) are up, down, and sideways compensatory actions, whereas the last two reactions (body derotative and body rotative) are rotational movements. Figure 10.21 illustrates the righting reactions.

Head-in-Space or Labyrinthine

The head-in-space righting reactions emerge at about 2 months of age and persist throughout life. They are elicited by holding the child vertically upright in the air and then slowly tilting him or her forward, backward, and sideward (see Figure 10.21). In each tilt, the head automatically moves in the direction opposite the tilt. Of course, the entire body follows the head, so this mechanism helps a person to return to an upright, midline position. **Midline** is defined as the position in which the nose is vertical and the mouth and eyes are horizontal. The head-in-space righting reactions are elicited by vestibular input. Hence, the head-in-space righting reactions are also called labyrinthine or vestibular patterns.

Optical or Visual

The optical righting reactions are precisely the same as the head-in-space reactions except that the responses are elicited by visual input instead of vestibular input. Optical righting develops soon after the head-in-space reactions appear and remains active throughout the lifespan. The optical righting reactions are dependent upon the integrity of the head-in-space reactions and the integration of the primitive reflexes that act on the head. Persons with abnormal muscle tone distribution, like those with cerebral palsy, can use vision to know the head is not properly aligned. However, this knowledge cannot enable correction of the head alignment problem. In young children and/or those

with severe disability, no attempt should be made to assess or work with head-in-space and optical righting separately. With older individuals, however, a blindfold may be used in head-in-space work to eliminate visual input.

In summary, the vestibular and visual systems work together to always return the head to midline. Body parts follow the head, and balance is preserved. These reactions must be overridden by higher CNS centers in activities requiring purposeful loss of balance (e.g., falls for fun, various activities in dance, gymnastics, and aquatics, and diving).

Landau Reaction or Body-in-Sagittal Plane Righting

The **Landau reaction,** also called body-in-sagittal plane righting, is an extension response of the trunk, hips, knees, and ankles that occurs in prone position when the head is lifted (see Figure 10.21). As the term *sagittal* indicates, the righting is in the up-and-down or flexion-extension plane. The Landau develops shortly after the head-in-space reactions are established. In essence, the Landau is a spreading of the extensor tone of the lifted head down the muscles of the back and legs.

The Landau is assessed from a prone position in the air or water, called *ventral suspension.* The Landau is one of the few reactions that is integrated instead of persisting throughout life. It serves a specific developmental function not needed after about 3 years of age. Specifically, the Landau facilitates the change from the flexion posture of infancy to the fully extended prone position with head up and back arched, called the *pivot prone, swan, wing lift,* or *front rocker.* The Landau overrides the STNR pattern (head extended, arms extended, legs flexed) so that the legs can be fully extended at the same time the head and arms are extended. The ability to maintain a pivot prone position is one of the first milestones in mastering the one-handed reach and grasp from a prone position. Without the Landau, the pivot prone pattern cannot emerge.

Body Derotative (Segmental Rolling)

The body derotative is an automatic segmental rolling response that occurs when the examiner rotates a body part. Until the age of 4 months, the infant does not have this reaction, and the body plops over as a rigid unit, called a **logroll pattern.** From age 4 months until about 5 years, the normally functioning individual responds to external body part rotation by rolling over one segment at a time (head, then shoulders, then trunk, then hips, or vice versa). Abnormal retention of the ATNR delays segmental rolling, because the extended arm is stiff and will not get out of the way.

Body Rotative (Rise to Stand)

The body rotative or rise-to-sit/rise-to-stand reaction is elicited by placing a wide-awake child in a supine lie. The body rotative is the ability to move segment by segment from a supine lie to some other position: a four-point, a sit, or a stand, depending on developmental level. If children have the coordination to rotate up to a more functional position, doing so is a normal response.

Rise-to-stand or **scramble up,** a widely used screening activity for all age groups, is derived from the body rotative reaction. Beginning in a supine lie, the person is challenged to rise to a stand as fast as he or she can. Observation of the efficiency of this action provides insight into overall coordination.

Figure 10.21   Four types of righting reactions. Optical righting reactions constitute the fifth type.

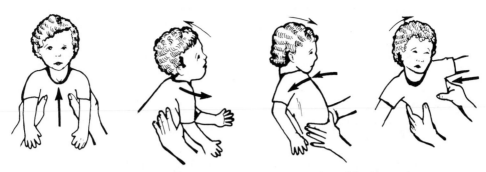

Head-in-space and optical righting reactions when held upright and tilted forward, backward, and sideward. *Bottom arrow* shows movement created by teacher's positioning or testing. *Top arrow* shows head movement that results if child has normal response.

Body righting in sagittal plane (Landau): Head and trunk lift

Body derotative (segmental rolling)

Body rotative (rise to sit or stand)

The speed of rise-to-stand (body rotative) is the righting reaction most often examined in school-age children (see Figure 10.21).

Parachute or Propping Reactions

The parachute or propping reactions are protective extension movements of the limbs used to break or prevent a fall. There are four such reactions, named for the direction in which the body is falling (downward, sideward, forward, and backward) (see Figure 10.22). The **downward parachute,** which refers to being dropped or falling feet first, is the only one that involves the legs. The other three reactions are the natural propping responses of both arms (falling forward or backward) or one arm (falling sideward).

The parachute reactions, like the reflexes that cause arm movements, are elicited by vestibular input, which signals a change in the movement of the head. The arm-propping reactions are generally tested from a sitting position, with the examiner gently pushing the child off balance. Developmentally, the **downward parachute** develops first (about 4 months); in it, the child extends and spreads the legs, thereby automatically preparing for a wide-based and therefore safe landing. The **sideward parachute** develops next, at 6 to 8 months, then the **forward parachute** at 7 to 8 months, and the **backward parachute** at 9 to 10 months. All of the parachute reactions remain throughout the lifespan. These reactions are often delayed or absent in persons with severe disability and thus constitute adapted physical education goals.

Figure 10.22 Four types of parachute or propping reactions (protective extensions). All responses are limb movements.

Downward. Normal response to downward thrust: abduction, wide base, 4 months on.

Sideward. Normal response to sideward thrust, 6 to 8 months.

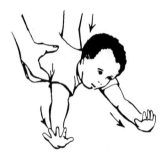

Forward. Normal response to forward thrust, 7 to 8 months.

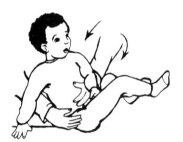

Backward. Normal response to backward thrust, 9 to 10 months.

Equilibrium or Tilting Reactions

The equilibrium (or tilting) reactions are total body responses that, when mature, prevent falls. They appear between the ages of 5 and 18 months and remain the entire life. These reactions, initiated primarily by vestibular input, can be elicited in any position the body assumes, but testing is usually limited to five positions (see Figure 10.23). These are presented in the correct assessment order, from easiest to hardest. Ages in Figure 10.23 indicate the average age at completion or mature response.

To assess these reactions, the teacher must have or be able to create an unstable surface that can be tipped about 15° in any direction. A mat or cushion can be moved from side to side, or a tilt board or large ball can be maneuvered to cause loss of equilibrium. These reactions can also be observed in trampoline work or in locomotor activities on unstable surfaces.

The equilibrium responses are all rotatory and can perhaps best be observed by focusing on the spinal curvature needed to maintain balance. Curves are described as **convex** (rounded like the back of a *C*) or **concave** (hollow like the front of a *C*). In mature equilibrium responses, the concavity of the spinal curve is always uphill. *The face and trunk are rotated toward the uphill side.* In some sources, the uphill side is called the stressed side (Ramm, 1988). In forward-backward tilts, the face and trunk bend or curve toward uphill. In side-to-side tilts, the face and trunk rotate toward the up side.

The position of the limbs also should be noted. Limbs on the uphill side are abducted (raised or held away from midline) and extended. Limbs on the downhill side tend to be adducted (drawn in toward the body) and flexed. Forward-backward tilts elicit bilateral arm movements (i.e., both arms do the same thing). Sideward tilts cause the arms to do opposite things.

In typical development, this rhythmical shifting of the arm and leg positions with the up-and-down movement of the tilting surface is automatic and graceful. Absence or immaturity of these reactions results in balance problems. If the student's balance is disrupted to the extent that the reactions are not effective in recovering an upright posture, the arms will automatically move into the protective extension patterns of the parachute reactions to break the fall.

Standing equilibrium may involve steps as well as shifts in alignment of body parts. **Stepping reactions** (also called hopping, shifting, or staggering reactions) are the steps a person automatically takes to keep his or her balance in a standing posture. Stepping reactions also occur as the last component of a mature kick (see Chapter 11). Stepping reactions often are seen when children try to maintain a one-foot balance.

Postural Reactions Summary

Postural reactions must be present for individuals to adjust to changing environmental conditions during locomotion. Changes

Figure 10.23   Five types of equilibrium reactions when board is tilted 15°. Note the concavity of the spinal curve is always uphill in the mature response. Also, the face and trunk are rotated toward the uphill side.

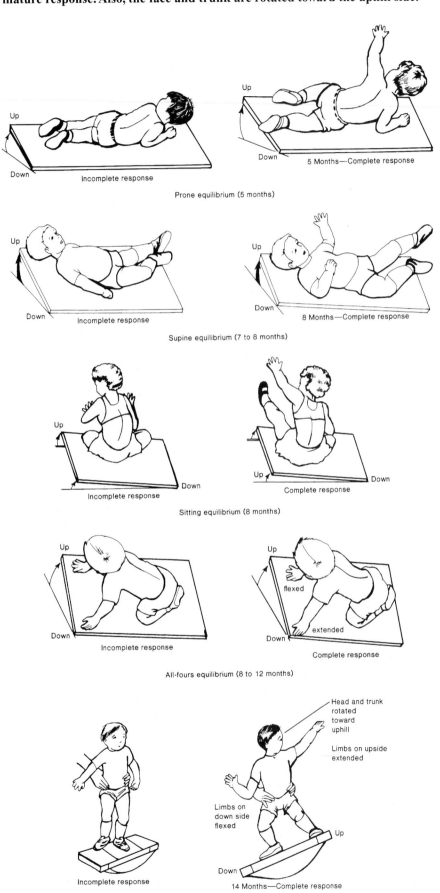

Prone equilibrium (5 months)

Supine equilibrium (7 to 8 months)

Sitting equilibrium (8 months)

All-fours equilibrium (8 to 12 months)

Standing equilibrium (14 to 18 months)

in the slope and texture of a surface, the uneven height of grass, or a hole in the ground are likely to cause clumsy-looking responses or falls when reactions are not mature. Likewise, immature reactions compromise the agility and gracefulness of activities involving the shifting of weight and the moving of body parts against gravity, as in jumping and hopping.

It is noteworthy that all postural reactions are functioning by age 18 months, the time when most children perform their first jumps, using two-foot takeoffs. The distance achieved is 4 inches on a long jump and 2 inches off the floor in a vertical jump. Walking sideward for 10 ft, which also occurs at 18 months, also requires postural reactions. Harder activities, like walking tiptoe and taking three steps on a low balance beam, occur at 24 months, when the postural reactions are more mature. Older children who cannot perform movement skills at the 18-month criterion level typically have postural reaction deficits.

Activities for Intervention

Intervention entails thousands of trials in which the individual performs the same righting, parachute, and equilibrium tasks over and over again. The positions used for testing are the same as those used for intervention. See Figures 10.21, 10.22, and 10.23.

To promote generalization of practice, many different environments and pieces of equipment are used (i.e., indoors/outdoors, noise/no noise; light/dark; soft/hard surfaces; level/slanted surfaces; water/air; windy with air current caused by electric fan/nonwindy). Different clothes and shoes are worn also because these influence postural reactions to the environment. Velcro is used to strap various kinds of weights to body parts, and back- and chestpacks are worn to give the nervous system practice in adapting to change.

Overall Assessment Approach: Milani-Comparetti

Before writing goals for the IEP and determining appropriate pedagogy, it is important to plan an overall assessment approach that is applicable to individuals with either nonambulatory or ambulatory clumsy conditions. Of the many assessment systems, the Milani-Comparetti (MC) protocol is perhaps the easiest and most appropriate for physical educators. This screening system, which requires only about 5 min to administer, was originally developed for ages birth to 2 years (Milani-Comparetti & Gidoni, 1967), but now it is frequently used with individuals of all age groups with severe body control problems. The address for the test manual is in the Optional Activities at the end of this chapter, and a training film can be obtained from the same source.

Figure 10.24 shows that the MC scoring system is divided into two sections: **spontaneous behavior** (motor strengths) and **evoked responses** (reflexes and postural reactions). Months listed horizontally across the top of the chart indicate the ages at which responses are normal, to aid in the estimation of motor delays. Although function on the MC can be scored numerically (Ellison, Browning, Larson, & Denny, 1983), most teachers use letters to note absence (*A*) or presence (*P*) of spontaneous behavior, reflexes, and reactions. Figure 10.24 shows the MC scoring protocol for a 9-year-old girl with severe cerebral palsy.

Spontaneous Behaviors on the MC

Spontaneous behavior encompasses motor tasks in nine broad areas: four head positions, three body postures, and two active movement sequences. Following are brief descriptions of each.

Head Control

Assess head control in four positions. As early as 1 month of age, infants can hold the head upright when they are held vertically in the air or against someone's chest. The angular lines on the MC chart next to "Body held vertical" denote growing control from a few seconds at 1 month of age to several minutes at 4 months of age. In contrast, many adults with cerebral palsy have difficulty with this task.

In "Body lying prone," infants exhibit three distinct developmental stages:

1.5 months Lifts head momentarily

3.0 months Holds head up 45° to 90° with chest up

4.0 months Holds head up; props self up on extended arms

In "Body lying supine," the infant lifts the head at about 5 months (note the location of the word *lifts* on MC chart). This head lifting is observed in conjunction with playing with feet.

In "Body pulled up from supine," the stick figures on the MC chart indicate the amount of head lag normal at each age when the body is pulled upward by the arms.

Body Control

Assess body control in three positions. Stick figures on the MC chart indicate normal performances. Five developmental stages are depicted for "Sitting." These are based on the amount of spinal curve and the ability to fully extend legs. Independent sitting is achieved between 6 and 8 months. The *L3* next to the second figure on the MC chart indicates that the progressive head-to-foot uncurving of the vertebral column has extended downward to the level of the third lumbar segment by the age of 4 months.

"All-fours" refers to three developmental stages. *Forearms/hands* denotes a propping position, with head and chest up and weight taken on the forearms. This propping behavior begins between the ages of 3.5 and 6 months. The *creeping position* is listed as 4-feet kneeling; it begins between the ages of 7 and 9 months. *Plantigrade* refers to a bear-walk position (4-foot walking with straight arms and legs).

"Standing" also develops through several stages, the first of which is controlled subcortically by supporting reflexes. When the infant loses this reflex, *astasia* occurs. This is a condition in which weight is taken momentarily, after which the body collapses. When infants take weight on their feet at about age 5 months, this is a more mature movement under cortical control. Independent standing does not occur until about 10 months.

Active Movement

"Standing up from a supine (lying) position" is evaluated in terms of amount of trunk rotation and arm assistance. Note four

FIGURE 10.24 Milani-Comparetti assessment for Kay, a 9-year-old girl with athetoid cerebral palsy affecting control of head and all four limbs. An *A* on the chart indicates absence of a response, and a *P* indicates presence of a response. Note that absence is interpreted as bad under spontaneous behaviors and under righting, parachute, and tilting reactions, but as good in relation to primitive reflexes. The circled areas indicate the body positions that were attained. To interpret, the "Spontaneous Behavior" section indicates the actions Kay could perform independently. The "Evoked Responses" section indicates that all five reflexes were still present and that all reactions except *body derotative* were absent (i.e., Kay could do mature segmental rolling but otherwise totally lacked head and neck control and body equilibrium).

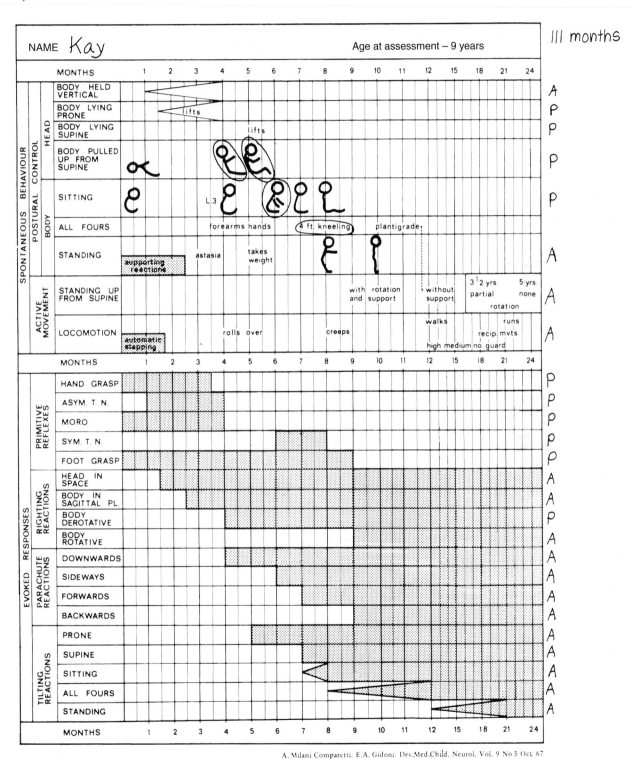

levels on the MC chart, extending from 9 months of age until 5 years. The mature rise-to-stand requires no trunk rotation and no arm assistance. "Locomotion" emphasizes rolling over between 4 and 6 months of age, creeping at around 7 months of age, and walking at about 12 months of age. The terms *high, medium, no guard* refer to the position of the arms.

Evoked Responses

Evoked responses encompass five early reflexes and three types of postural reactions (righting, parachute, and tilting or equilibrium). Reflexes and postural reactions are associated with subcortical function and sensorimotor integration. This section develops awareness and reinforces understanding of the need for both adapted and general physical educators to understand reflexes and reactions.

Application to a 9-Year-Old

Let's now apply our knowledge about motor milestones, reflexes, and reactions to Kay, a 9-year-old born with cerebral palsy (CP) affecting all four limbs (see Figure 10.25). Kay's intelligence quotient is about 90 (i.e., low average). She is in the fourth grade of a public school in which she is included in first-grade spelling and mathematics classes. The rest of the school day, she is in a self-contained class for multidisabled students. Kay receives adapted physical education on a one-to-one basis three times a week, 30 min a day. She also receives physical, occupational, speech, and music therapy in 30-min sessions.

Kay needs special equipment to help her function independently. She lacks the arm strength and control to maneuver a manual wheelchair, so a motorized chair is required. Kay is nonverbal, so a head pointer is essential so that she can point out words on a Bliss symbol board and on electronic aids that facilitate typing and artwork. Figure 10.24 shows that all five early reflexes are present: hand grasp, ATNR, Moro, STNR, and foot grasp. This knowledge guides the physical educator in selecting which throwing, striking, and kicking patterns to teach Kay.

Also present is the **crossed extensor reflex** (not covered by the MC chart). This reflex adversely affects kicking a ball from a standing position and other reciprocal leg movements. When one leg is lifted to kick the ball, a strong extensor spasm affects the support leg and causes loss of balance (see Figure 10.25D). The crossed extensor reflex explains much of the awkwardness in young children learning to kick, as well as problems of students with CP.

Pedagogy in Relation to Reflexes and Reactions

Physical education for young students with abnormal reflexes and balance problems is guided by the **neurophysiological treatment approach of Bobath** (1980), which is supported by Levitt (1995) and others who specialize in cerebral palsy and related disorders. This approach rests on two principles:

1. Inhibition or suppression of abnormal reflex activity
2. Facilitation of righting, parachute, and equilibrium reactions in their proper developmental sequence

The first principle is achieved primarily through correct positioning and the proper selection of activities. With students who are severely disabled, correct positioning is achieved through specially designed wheelchairs and strapping of body parts. Maintaining the head in midline is especially important, since head rotation and flexion/extension elicit the ATNR and STNR, respectively. Velcro ties are often used to prevent undesirable head movement. Targets and/or balls to be hit off tees should be placed at eye level or, in the case of floor targets, far enough away so that the student does not drop the head to look downward. As long as therapists are striving to inhibit or suppress abnormal reflex activity, physical educators should cooperate. Often, however, this goal is reevaluated at age 7 or 8 years, *if it becomes evident that it may not be achievable. In this situation, the emphasis may change to finding ways the student can utilize reflex activity to his or her advantage.* For instance, a side position to the target, with the head rotated to the right, thereby eliciting the ATNR, may make it easier to release objects with the right arm.

The second principle is achieved primarily through exercises, stunts, and games that follow the natural developmental sequence whereby students gain the strength and coordination needed to attain a proper balance between mobility and stability (i.e., voluntary control over purposeful movement as well as maintenance of a set posture against the pull of gravity). Students in GE physical education more often have problems with equilibrium reactions than other types. See Figure 10.26 for additional tilting activities to supplement exercises shown in Figure 10.23. To understand students like Kay, we must know the neurological bases of movement.

Neurological Bases of Motor Performance

Adapted physical activity specialists need to understand the neurological bases of motor performance. General educators also need to understand the neurological basis of clumsiness and some of the theories that guide teaching practices. The sections that follow introduce or review fundamentals.

Nerve Cells and Synapses

The average adult has approximately 100 billion nerve cells, called **neurons.** Each neuron has a cell body, one axon, and several dendrites. Figure 10.27 shows how the appearance of these cells changes from birth until about 15 months. During this time, in typical development, the **dendrites** rapidly form many treelike branches that receive impulses from other neurons. Through this **dendritization,** each neuron becomes interconnected with approximately 10,000 other neurons.

The **axon** conducts impulses away from the cell body (the executive part of the neuron). The speed and efficiency with which neurons transmit impulses determine, to a large extent, motor control. The junction between two neurons is a **synapse.** From the time that sensory input is received until a mental or motor response occurs, hundreds (and sometimes millions) of neurons are involved via synaptic linkups throughout the body.

There are many kinds of neurons. In general, their functions are described as (a) motor, (b) sensory, or (c) associative or internuncial. The location of the cell body and the pathway of its fibers (dendrites and axon) determine function.

Figure 10.25   Kay, a 9-year-old born with cerebral palsy affecting all four limbs. All five pathological reflexes are present.

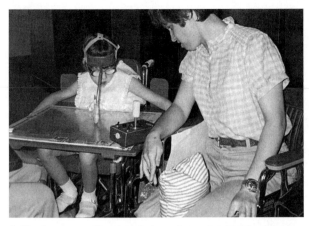

A. Kay has no arm/hand control, so she uses a head pointer to touch symbols on a communication board. This photo also shows absent head control in body held vertical, the first MC item. Kay's teacher, who also has CP, shows poor head control.

C. Under "all four" on the MC chart, Kay can maintain the prone-on-elbows position and can do 4-ft kneeling (the creep position) but cannot hold this position long or creep. She also cannot do *plantigrade* (the all-fours stunt witht straight arms and legs called the *bear walk*) because of pathological reflexes.

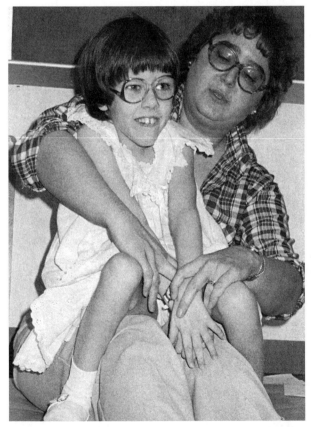

B. Kay passed three of the five sitting postures on the MC. She can sit in good alignment only with help because of the presence of reflexes and the absence of reactions.

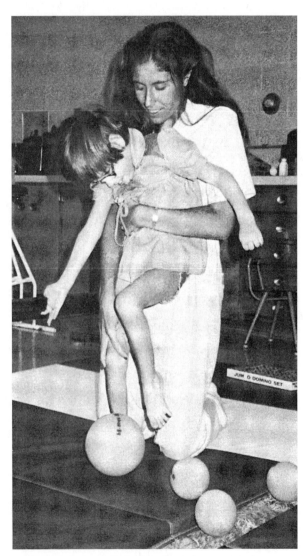

D. Kay should do kicking activities only from a seated position. The crossed extensor reflex interferes with kicking in a standing position.

Figure 10.26 Tilting activities to reinforce equilibrium reactions. Activities like these should be prescribed for Kay and children like her. Also recommended are other balance activities in a sitting position like horseback riding, riding three- or four-wheel cycles, and riding in a wagon or on a scooter board pulled by another.

Backward tilt   Level   Forward tilt

Forward tilt should result in extension/hyperextension of head, neck, and trunk and in abduction of scapulae. *Backward tilt* should result in flexion of head, neck, and trunk and abduction of scapulae.

Backward tilt   Level   Forward tilt

Sideward tilt should result in rotation of the head and trunk toward the uptilting side. There is also flexion and abduction of the limbs on the uptilting side; the opposite characterizes limbs on the downtilting side.

Backward tilt   Level   Forward tilt

Forward tilt on all-fours results in symmetrical extension tonic neck reflex posture.

Figure 10.27 **Growth of nerve cells (neurons) during infancy. Each nerve cell has three parts: cell body, dendrites, and axon. Cell bodies are located in the brain and spinal cord. Dendrites and axons are the nerve fibers that comprise nerves throughout the body and neural pathways (tracts) inside the spinal cord and brain.**

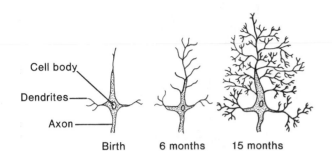

Cell body

Dendrites

Axon

Birth   6 months   15 months

Motor and associative neurons have their cell bodies in the gray matter of the spinal cord or brain (see Figure 10.28). *They receive information via a dendrites-to-cell body pathway.* The cell body then sends an action impulse to another part of the spinal cord or brain or to an effector organ (muscle) via its axon.

Sensory neurons, in contrast, have their cell bodies in the dorsal root ganglia of spinal nerves, close to where these nerves issue from the spinal cord (see Figure 10.28). *Their cell bodies receive sensory information also via a dendrites-to-cell body pathway.* The cell body then directs the axon to carry the sensory message to the dendrites of a motor or associative neuron.

Billions of different kinds of neurons are thus interacting or synapsing all of the time. Think, for instance, about movement when you have been sitting and decide to get up. The impulse to move originates in the thinking part of the brain (cerebral cortex), which generates thousands of action impulses that are transmitted from neuron to neuron down through the various parts of the brain to the spinal cord. Since getting up from a chair requires almost all of the body parts to move, motor neuron axons carrying the command to move must simultaneously exit at each level of the spinal cord via the 31 pairs of spinal nerves. The exit is always via the anterior or ventral root of the spinal nerve.

Thousands of individual nerve fibers are grouped together into bundles to make a nerve (see Figure 10.28). Note how the dorsal and ventral roots join together in the spinal nerve. Thus, inside every spinal nerve are (a) sensory fibers carrying messages from receptor organs in the skin, muscles, tendons, ligaments, and bones back to the spinal cord and (b) motor fibers carrying messages from the brain and spinal cord out to the muscles and other effector organs.

Myelination

Approximately 5 months before birth, **myelination** begins. This is the development of the fatlike protein and lipid substance that forms the covering of axons and influences their ability to conduct impulses. At birth, some parts of the nervous system (optic tract, motor and sensory roots of the 31 pairs of spinal nerves) have a moderate amount of myelination, but others have none.

Myelination continues rapidly from birth until 3 or 4 years of age, when it is mostly complete except for the associa-

Figure 10.28 **The peripheral nervous system. (A) Each of the 31 spinal nerves emerges from the spinal cord by a dorsal (posterior) root and a ventral (anterior) root. The dorsal root transmits sensory messages, whereas the ventral root transmits motor messages. (B) The roots merge after leaving the vertebral area to form a nerve. Nerves are made up of nerve fibers called dendrites and axons.**

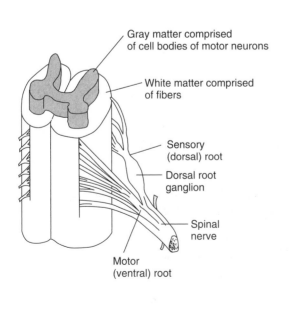

Gray matter comprised of cell bodies of motor neurons

White matter comprised of fibers

Sensory (dorsal) root

Dorsal root ganglion

Spinal nerve

Motor (ventral) root

A

Connective tissue

Bundle of nerve fibers

One nerve

One nerve fiber

Blood vessel

Myelin sheath of fiber

B

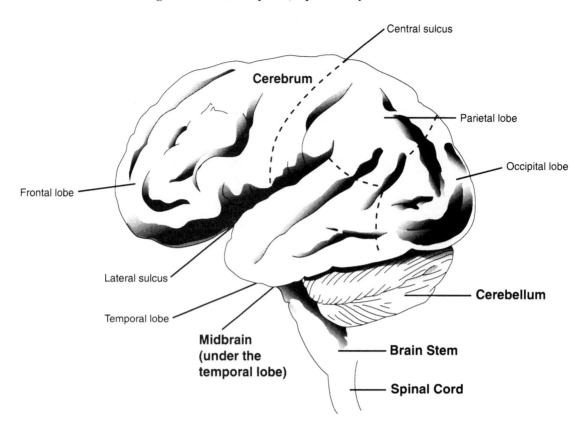

tion areas of the brain—in these areas, myelination is finished between ages 20 and 30 years. Sensorimotor and cognitive function can occur before completion of myelination in related nerves and CNS parts. However, efficiency of movement and thought patterns is believed to relate to degree of myelination. Specifically, myelination is associated with improved speed, precision, steadiness, and strength.

A characteristic of nerve cell injury and disease is **demyelination** (the disintegration of the myelin covering of the nerve's fibers) and subsequent loss of motor coordination. Demyelination is the cause of **multiple sclerosis,** a CNS condition that mainly occurs in adults (see the index).

The Human Brain

The human brain, much simplified, can be thought of as composed of white and gray matter. The **white matter** is comprised of all the nerve fibers. These are grouped together as tracts and given names (e.g., pyramidal and extrapyramidal). In the cerebrum, these tracts collectively are called the **internal capsule.** The **gray matter,** made up of concentrations of cell bodies, is (a) the cortex or outer covering of the cerebrum and cerebellum and (b) nuclei with specific names like thalamus, hypothalamus, and basal ganglia. The cerebral cortex performs all of the higher-level mental functions (voluntary movement, perception, cognition, and memory). The cerebellar cortex is less well understood but plays an important part in regulating both voluntary and involuntary movements, especially during rapid

changes in body position and equilibrium. The nuclei located within the white matter of the cerebrum perform or govern reflex or regulatory functions.

The cerebral cortex, which is smooth before birth, rapidly develops numerous **convolutions** (folds, hills, gyri) and **depressions** (grooves, sulci, fissures). Some of these, like the central sulcus that separates the frontal lobe from the parietal lobe, have names. The cerebral cortex is divided into right and left hemispheres. In right-handed persons, the **right hemisphere** governs spatial, artistic, and creative abilities. The **left hemisphere** governs analytical and verbal skills, like mathematics, reading, and writing.

Figure 10.29 shows that each hemisphere is divided into four lobes: frontal, parietal, occipital, and temporal. Each lobe performs different functions. *Simplified,* the **occipital lobe** governs vision and visual perception. The **temporal lobe** governs audition and provides memory storage for both auditory and visual experiences. The **parietal lobe** is responsible for the interpretation of skin and muscular sensations and for speech. The **frontal lobe** is the site of processes pertaining to cognition, personality, and voluntary movement. In reality, there is much overlapping of function.

Figure 10.29 also shows the brain stem, the cerebellum, and the **midbrain,** a small, distinct area between the brain stem and the cerebrum. Theorists on reflexes and postural reactions posit that the evolution of voluntary movement is related to the structure and function of (a) the *brain stem,* which governs reflexes; (b) the *midbrain,* which governs postural reac-

Figure 10.30   The rapid growth of the body and brain before birth.

Age	Length	Appearance
4 days		
23 days	2 mm	Ectoderm / Mesoderm / Endoderm
28 days	4 mm	
45 days	17 mm	
7 weeks	2.8 cm	
12 weeks	8.8 cm	
28 weeks	38.5 cm	
First postnatal year+		

Embryo at 28 Days
Forebrain — Midbrain — Hindbrain — Neural tube

Embryo at 45 Days
Thalamus/Hypothalamus — Midbrain — Cerebellum — Medulla — Cerebrum — Limb bud

Infant at Birth
Limbic system with thalamus and hypothalamus — Cerebrum — Midbrain — Cerebellum — Medulla — Spinal cord

tions; and (c) the *cortex of the cerebrum and cerebellum,* which governs equilibrium and voluntary movement.

Brain growth follows a specific pattern. The brain stem becomes functional first, then the midbrain, and last the cortical areas controlling voluntary movement. This explains why infants are born with reflexes, righting reactions begin at about 1.5 months of age, and voluntary movement is evident at about 4 months of age. In typical growth and development, this happens so fast we hardly notice. In delayed or abnormal development, teachers must devote much time and energy to reflexes and reactions.

Development of the Central Nervous System

Just as the body progresses through stages of development (embryo to fetus to infant), so also does the CNS. Beginning as cells called the *ectoderm* (see age 23 days in Figure 10.30), the CNS evolves into the neural tube that, 28 days after conception, has subdivided into four distinct parts: forebrain, midbrain, hindbrain, and neural tube (spinal cord). Long before birth, these structures evolve into the parts of the CNS with which we are familiar. The hindbrain separates into medulla and pons (the brain stem); the cerebellum develops later, in the ninth week. The midbrain expands in size, but its name does not change.

The forebrain evolves into a cerebrum with several interdependent structures. The innermost of these are the thalamus, hypothalamus, basal ganglia (clumps of cell bodies), and limbic system. The outermost part is the cerebral cortex.

Parts of the Central Nervous System

Knowing the function of each part of the CNS is essential to understanding individual differences in motor functioning. The following is a simplified explanation of each.

1. **Spinal cord.** A cord composed of numerous tracts (pathways), each of which contains nerve fibers carrying impulses to and from the brain. Each tract has a distinct name and function. The name typically indicates the direction in which impulses are carried and the two parts of the CNS connected by the pathway. Illustrative *ascending pathways* are spinocerebellar and spinothalamic. Illustrative *descending pathways* are corticospinal and vestibulospinal. The speed and efficiency with which impulses are carried up and down these tracts are major determinants of motor coordination and control. Spinal cord damage results in muscle weakness or paralysis and lack of sensation.

2. **Medulla.** The upper part of the spinal cord that regulates such vital functions as respiration, heart rate, and blood pressure. Contains nuclei (cell bodies) from which cranial nerves 9 to 12 emerge. These nerves pertain to swallowing, chewing, salivating, moving the tongue, and speaking.

3. **Pons ("bridge").** Mainly, fibers forming a bridge between the medulla and the cerebellum. Contains nuclei from which cranial nerves 5 to 8 emerge. The *eighth cranial nerve* is the vestibulocochlear nerve. The vestibular branch is important in the reflex control of head, neck, and eyes and helps regulate coordination and posture. The cochlear branch is important in audition.

4. **Brain stem.** The bundle of nerve tissue that extends upward from the spinal cord to the base of the cerebrum. The brain stem regulates reflexes. It contains all of the centers for the 10 sense modalities except vision and smell. Some authorities say that it includes the medulla, pons, and midbrain. Others say that it includes only the medulla and that the pons and midbrain are independent structures. The primary reason for considering these three structures together is the presence in all of them of the *reticular formation,* also called the reticular activating system (see Figure 10.31).

5. **Reticular activating system (RAF).** A complex network of nerve fibers with tiny clumps of cell bodies that connects the brain stem with virtually all other parts of the brain. Its main functions pertain to reciprocal innervation, activation, wakefulness, and arousal; thus, it is important in attention, learning, and behavior deficits involving hyperactivity versus hypoactivity. The RAF filters incoming sensory impulses and prevents sensory bombardment of the cortex by selectively transferring some sensory impulses upward and inhibiting others. This permits the cortex to process significant stimuli, rather than coping with all neural impulses.

6. **Midbrain.** A short portion between the pons and the cerebral hemispheres or upper part of the brain stem. Contains nuclei for nerves pertaining to vision. These are in the red (rubro) nucleus. The midbrain is essentially a **servomechanism** (relay center) for transmitting impulses related to righting and postural reactions. The rubrospinal tract starts here.

7. **Cerebellum ("little brain").** Essentially, a servomechanism (relay center) for transmitting nerve impulses from kinesthetic and vestibular input and for regulating postures and automatic movement. The cerebellum is important in excitation (activation) and inhibition of muscles, a major determinant in smooth versus jerky movements. It is especially important in the control of fast movements. It is also believed to be the structure that, after training and practice of a new motor skill, assumes responsibility for automatic rather than conscious control of motor performance. A major goal of physical education is to motivate students to practice a new skill until it no longer requires motor planning (i.e., conscious thought). At that point, performance

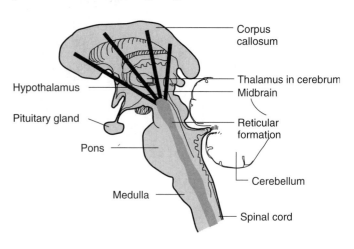

Figure 10.31 **Side view of brain stem, midbrain, and lower cerebrum. This level of the brain governs the primitive reflexes and righting reactions.**

becomes subcortical, or automatic, meaning that it can be executed at the cerebellar level.

8. **Thalamus ("little chamber or anteroom").** A football-shaped cluster of nerve cells deep within the cerebrum, located immediately above the midbrain. One part acts as a servomechanism for relaying sensory impulses, and the other helps to regulate arousal in relation to activity. Except for smell, each of the senses relays its impulses through the thalamus.

9. **Hypothalamus.** A group of small nuclei underneath the thalamus and close to the pituitary gland that integrate autonomic nervous system responses, thereby playing a key role in *homeostasis* (the regulation of balance in internal bodily functions). Among these are regulation of physical growth, heart rate, body temperature, sleep and wakefulness, hunger, dehydration, emotion, and control of stress. This regulation occurs primarily through stimulation of glands that release hormones.

10. **Basal ganglia.** Masses of subcortical gray matter (cell bodies) in the interior of the cerebrum, mainly in the corpus callosum area near the junction of right and left cerebral hemispheres. Some of the basal ganglia have specific names: globus pallidus, putamen, caudate nucleus, subthalamic nucleus, and substantia nigra. In general, the basal ganglia help to regulate posture and movement, particularly slow movement. Damage to basal ganglia results in such conditions as athetosis (involuntary, purposeless, slow, repeated motions), tremors of face and hands, and Huntington's chorea.

11. **Limbic system.** A ring of interconnecting pathways and centers in the cerebrum that includes the hypothalamus, thalamus, basal ganglia, and other subcortical nuclei that are important in control of emotional responses and activity levels (i.e., hyperactivity vs. hypoactivity). *Limbus* is Latin for "rim" or "border"; the limbic system forms the inner rim of structures that comprise the evolutionarily old cortex. It is closely connected to the sense of smell in that

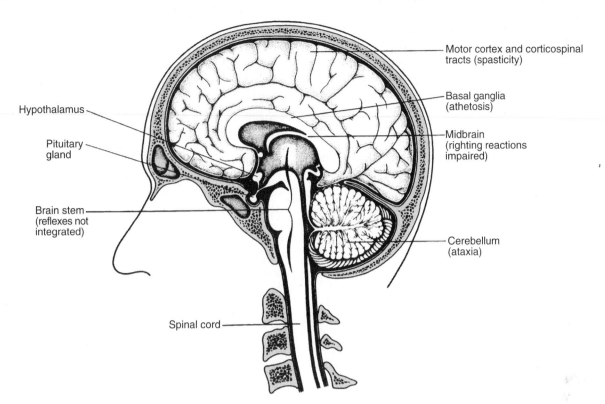

Motor cortex and corticospinal tracts (spasticity)

Basal ganglia (athetosis)

Midbrain (righting reactions impaired)

Cerebellum (ataxia)

Hypothalamus

Pituitary gland

Brain stem (reflexes not integrated)

Spinal cord

the olfactory bulbs and tracts are nearby. Evolutionally, the cerebrum is believed to have begun as a center for smell.

12. **Cerebral cortex ("bark of tree").** Six layers of gray matter (cell bodies) that comprise the outer part of the cerebrum. The cortex performs the higher level functions: voluntary movement, perception, thought, memory, and creativity. Cortical areas are named according to function: sensory, association, and motor. *Sensory areas* interpret impulses from 10 kinds of sensory receptors. *Association areas* link sensory and motor input and create associations essential to verbalization, memory, reasoning, judgment, and creativity. *Motor areas* control voluntary movement; damage to the motor cortex and/or its descending tracts results in spasticity.

13. **Corpus callosum.** A bridge of nerve fibers that connects right and left cerebral hemispheres, thus allowing them to keep in touch with one another. An important function is transfer of learning from one hemisphere to another.

Be able to pass a quiz on these 13 parts of the CNS. How many different ways can you practice learning this information? Share with others.

Pyramidal and Extrapyramidal Systems

Pyramidal and *extrapyramidal* are terms used to describe the higher-level motor control systems of the brain. The systems are named after large, pyramid-shaped cells of the cerebral cortex. The pyramidal system includes motor neurons that form the corticospinal or pyramidal tracts. The extrapyramidal system includes motor neurons not in the pyramidal system (i.e., those that are extra). Names of some of the extrapyramidal tracts are vestibulospinal, rubrospinal, and reticulospinal.

The pyramidal tracts are mostly concerned with the voluntary initiation of controlled movements. The extrapyramidal tracts are mainly responsible for automatic reactions and postural control.

Upper and Lower Motor Neuron Disorders

Figure 10.32 indicates disorders caused by damage to motor neurons in the brain. These conditions are often called upper motor neuron syndromes to distinguish them from motor problems that have their origin in the spinal cord (i.e., lower motor neuron syndromes). Most lower motor neuron problems are the result of spinal cord lesions that cause weakness or paralysis. The main upper motor neuron problems are spasticity and athetosis. **Spasticity,** caused by pyramidal system malfunction, is primarily a problem of overexcitation or too much tightness in muscles. **Athetosis,** caused by extrapyramidal breakdown, is a problem of excessive movement (i.e., inhibition is impaired). **Ataxia,** or general incoordination, may be either an upper motor neuron disorder (cerebellum) or a lower motor neuron problem. In the latter, degeneration of cell bodies in the posterior spinal cord interferes with kinesthesis.

Neurological Bases of Clumsiness

Clumsiness, the inability to perform culturally normative motor activities with acceptable proficiency, is caused by delayed or abnormal CNS development, musculoskeletal limitations, and other constraints. *The severity of the CNS condition(s) typically determines whether the person is called clumsy or cerebral palsied.* Without sophisticated laboratory equipment, determining the CNS site and other contributing factors is difficult. Always, the problem is complex; certainly, sound motor functioning cannot occur without intact sensory and central processing systems.

An approach to explaining clumsiness, used in the therapies and in adapted physical activity, entails examining the criteria met by a mature, intact CNS (see Table 10.3) and directing remediation at specific problems. Instead of concern with specific parts of the brain, **systems or distributed motor control models** recognize that sensorimotor integration is shared by several parts or is broadly distributed (Crutchfield & Barnes, 1995; Thelen & Smith, 1994). *Proponents of these models assert that there is no strict hierarchy of control from one part of the brain to another. Instead, requirements of the task and environmental conditions determine brain function.* Biomechanics is also important in these models, with attention given to musculoskeletal constraints like overall shortness, limb lengths, and postural deviations.

Systems models emphasize that intervention should be directed toward several CNS parts simultaneously, and practice should be variable, utilizing all resources. *Teaching the whole child, not the separate systems, means working simultaneously on reflexes, reactions, voluntary movement, and environmental constraints.*

Theories That Guide Practices

APENS Standard 2 on motor behavior indicates that physical educators should understand neuromaturational/hierarchical models and dynamic systems theory. This recommendation supports only minimal competency in that many other important theories provide background for intervention (see Shumway-Cook & Woollacott (2001). The following are brief descriptions of theories that are pertinent to adapted physical activity.

Maturation or Neuromaturation Theory

Maturation theory posits the orderly, sequential appearance of developmental milestones in accordance with an inborn biological timetable. Environment is important also but not capable of changing essential genetic potential.

Theories Based on Hierarchical Levels of Function

Several developmental theories are based on hierarchical levels of CNS functioning. Among these are the neurophysiological theory of the Bobaths, the reflex-testing theory of Fiorentino, and the sensory integration theory of Jean Ayres. The three levels of reflex/reaction development that form the basis of these theories are presented in Table 10.4.

Neurodevelopmental/Neurophysiological Theory

The origin of neurodevelopmental/neurophysiological theories is generally accredited to Karel Bobath, a physician, and his wife, Berta Bobath, a physical therapist. The Bobaths

Table 10.3   Criteria that a mature, intact central nervous system must meet.

1. **Reflex integration.** Reflexes are involuntary muscle and postural tone shifts that normally are integrated during infancy. Reflexes must be integrated before coordinated, graceful, voluntary movement can occur.
2. **Optimal functioning of reactions.** Reactions are generalized involuntary responses that pertain to static and dynamic balance. Developmentally, reactions replace early reflexes.
3. **Freedom from ataxia.** Ataxia is incoordination characterized primarily by irregularity and lack of precision in voluntary motor acts. Ataxic behaviors include overshooting or undershooting the object when reaching for something or going through an obstacle course; problems include spilling, bumping into things, knocking things over, or stumbling for no apparent reason. In stepping over an object or climbing stairs, persons with ataxia tend to lift their feet too high. An ataxic gait is characterized by irregular steps.
4. **Freedom from athetosis.** Athetosis is involuntary, purposeless, relatively slow, repeated movement that interferes with steadiness, accuracy, and control of one or more body parts.
5. **Freedom from spasticity.** Spasticity is hypertonus (too much muscle tone) that results in reduced range of movement, overly active tonic reflex activity, and stiff, awkward-looking movements. Spasticity occurs only in relation to voluntary movement.
6. **Freedom from associated movements.** The ability to move one body part without associated movements of other parts. This problem is sometimes called *overflow*.
7. **Freedom from sensory input problems.** Visual and auditory problems affect the teaching/learning process in mastering new motor skills and patterns.
8. **Freedom from other constraints.** These constraints might be in the body (e.g., orthopedic, health), in the environment, or in interactions of the body and the environment.

(B. Bobath, 1985; K. Bobath, 1980) posited that (a) delayed or abnormal motor development is the result of interference with normal brain maturation, (b) this interference is manifested as an impairment of the postural reflex mechanism, (c) abnormal reflex activity produces abnormal degree and distribution of postural and muscle tone, and (d) righting and equilibrium reactions should be used to inhibit abnormal movements while simultaneously stimulating and facilitating normal postural responses.

The **normal postural reflex mechanism,** according to the Bobaths, is the product of interactions among three factors: (a) normal postural tone, (b) reciprocal innervation, and (c) the proper emergence of developmental sequences of postural reactions and voluntary movement. Interference with any of these factors requires treatment or therapy. The Bobaths thus stressed

Table 10.4   Normal reflex/reaction development.

Level of Development	Level of CNS Maturation	Motor Behaviors
Primitive reflexes	Spinal cord and/or brain stem	Prone-lying Supine-lying
Righting reactions	Midbrain	Right self, turn over, sit, crawl, creep
Equilibrium reactions	Cortical	Stand, walk

that all movement behavior is postural (we assume thousands of postures each day) and that the integration of reflexes and the emergence of righting and equilibrium reactions form the basis of normal movement.

Mary Fiorentino, an occupational therapist from Connecticut, built upon the ideas of the Bobaths and other developmentalists and synthesized existing knowledge about reflexes and reactions into **reflex testing theory** in the 1960s. Fiorentino (1963) described and illustrated 37 distinct reflexes and reactions, organized according to the scheme presented in Table 10.4. Later Fiorentino (1981) wrote a comprehensive text on the influence of reflexes and reactions on normal and abnormal motor development. This fully illustrated text is an outstanding resource.

Jean Ayres, an occupational therapist with a doctoral degree in neuropsychology, outlined **sensory integration theory** in the 1970s. A professor at the University of Southern California, Ayres focused most of her research on learning disabilities. Her ideas, however, have been widely applied, especially in infant and early childhood programs. Ayres's theory emphasizes that the nervous system must be integrated at the lower levels before cognitive approaches like watching demonstrations and listening to directions can be successful. Development is spiral, with the integrity of each system built on sound functioning of the level immediately below it.

Ayres continued to refine sensory integration theory and practice throughout her lifetime, and colleagues continue this work (e.g., Fisher et al., 1991). Ayres's (1989) final definition of sensory integration, published shortly after her death, was

[s]ensory integration is the neurological process that organizes sensation from one's own body and from the environment and makes it possible to use the body effectively within the environment. The spatial and temporal aspects of inputs from different sensory modalities are interpreted, associated, and unified. Sensory integration is information processing. . . . The brain must select, enhance, inhibit, compare, and associate the sensory information in a flexible, constantly changing pattern; in other words, the brain must integrate it. (p.11)

Ayres believed that movement therapy should be directed at six levels: spinal cord, brain stem with emphasis on reticular formation, cerebellum, basal ganglia, old cortex and/or limbic system, and neocortex. She cautioned, however, that, in reality, several CNS levels function simultaneously in human motor behavior.

Therapy is based on several principles:

1. Because the brain stem is developmentally the lowest level of the brain, it receives the greatest focus of therapeutic attention. The brain stem regulates reflexes. Therefore, reflex inhibition and integration are important parts of therapy.

2. Tactile stimulation contributes to generalized neurological integration and enhances perception of other sensory modalities.

3. One approach to normalization of vestibular mechanisms is swinging and spinning activities. These can be initiated by the child or therapist, but extreme care should be taken to avoid overstimulation (nausea, dizziness).

4. Activities involving extensor muscles should be emphasized. Prone-lying on a scooterboard with head held high is an illustrative extensor muscle activity. Among the many scooterboard tasks recommended are 30 ways to descend a ramp that is elevated at one end about 2 ft.

5. Body control activities should be emphasized. Some of these are (a) moving on all-fours through tunnels or obstacle courses, (b) jumping games, and (c) balancing tasks.

Parts of sensory integration theory have been challenged (Arendt, MacLean, & Baumeister, 1988) and defended (Cermak, 1988; Ottenbacher, 1988). Most of the activities recommended by Ayres, however, have been used in elementary physical education and in therapeutic settings for many years. The activities appear sound, but researchers are still trying to explain neurologically how and why they work.

Information-Processing and Systems Theory

Ayres (1989), in her final work, defined sensory integration as information processing. **Information-processing theory,** popular from the 1950s through the 1980s, posits that the central nervous system works in a linear fashion like a computer. Motor behavior, according to this theory, occurs in a chainlike fashion (sensory input, central processing, motor output) and can be modified by feedback. In contrast to neuromaturational theory, which emphasizes heredity and biology, information-processing theory mainly focuses on environment, stimulus-response mechanisms, and the role of cognition in altering behavior. The reflex-hierarchical theories explained in the previous section contain many elements of information-processing theory.

Crutchfield and Barnes (1995) state that "it is not possible to dispense with the concept of hierarchy in modern theories of motor control" (p. 6). Brain growth is hierarchical, and modern neuroscience confirms that certain parts of the brain perform specific functions. The brain, however, functions holistically so that the total effect of damage to certain parts cannot be predicted. Recognition of the complexity of brain function has altered the traditional belief that retention of specific reflexes directly prevents neural maturation of higher levels of the brain. Today, we know that many systems of the body dynamically interact with each other and the environment and influence neural function. There are many ways to promote reflex integration, and intervention should be ecological as well as hierarchical.

Systems theory, a theoretical framework for explaining and predicting the involvement of *all of the bodily systems,* as well as biomechanical forces like gravity and inertia, is an outgrowth of information-processing theory. Each profession has its own application of systems theory, but motor control specialists see its value mainly in broadening intervention to include consideration of biomechanical factors rather than emphasizing only the central nervous system. To achieve this, professionals would need good preparation in biomechanics.

When answering "Which theory of motor control is best?" Shumway-Cook and Woollacott (2001) posit the systems approach, as they expand its meaning to incorporate "many of the concepts proposed by other theories of motor control" (p. 22). They emphasize that we should see movement as a "dynamic interplay between perception, cognition, and action systems" (p. 22) and should use all of these components in intervention. The outstanding motor control book of Shumway-Cook (physical therapy) and Woollacott (exercise and movement science) clearly incorporates the principles of *dynamic systems theory* into the systems theory perspective.

Dynamic Systems Theory

Dynamic systems theory, which is based on the principles of modern biology and physics, is extremely complex (Kelso, 1996; Kugler, Kelso, & Turvey, 1982; Smith & Thelen, 1993; Thelen & Smith, 1994). Common synonyms for *dynamic systems theory* are *ecological theory* and *action theory.* However, the use of these terms often indicates that only selected aspects (i.e., usually a modified or simple version) of dynamic systems theory is being discussed.

Some of the key principles of dynamic systems theory are the following:

1. Function, rather than an inborn genetic timetable or a generalized motor program (schema) within the brain, drives movement behavior.

2. Multilevel subsystems (e.g., reflexes, genes, joint structure, muscle strength, percent body fat, visual perception) dynamically interact with the supports and constraints (limitations) of the ever-changing environment to produce movement.

3. The central nervous system, like all of the other systems and subsystems, works in a holistic, plastic, and self-organizing fashion.

4. Intervention should be based on a dynamic interplay between perception, cognition, and action systems.

Dynamic systems theory guides research and practice in many scientific fields. Esther Thelen, a developmental psychologist at Indiana University, is acknowledged as the leader in applying this theory to help explain infant motor development. *The first adapted physical activity leader to investigate dynamic systems theory is Dale Ulrich,* professor at the University of Michigan, who has conducted several studies with his wife, Beverly (e.g., Ulrich & Ulrich, 1995; Ulrich, Ulrich, Angulo-

Kinzler, & Yun, 2001). The Ulrichs have studied both rhythmical stereotypies and the emergence of locomotor patterns in infants with Down syndrome.

Eclectic Theory

In this chapter, an attempt has been made to incorporate parts of several theories. This is called *eclecticism.* Given the complex movement behavior of individuals with severe cerebral palsy and other forms of developmental disability, it may be plausible that different theories are needed to explain intra- and interindividual differences (Shumway-Cook & Woollacott, 2001). In particular, individuals with severe brain damage might lack the capacity for the self-organizing behavior that is central to dynamic systems theory.

 OPTIONAL ACTIVITIES

1. Review APENS Standard 2 for insight into what some experts believe general and adapted physical educators should know about motor behavior of persons with disabilities. Remember motor behavior encompasses motor development, motor learning, and motor control. Space is too limited in theis textbook to cover everything, so engage in personal projects to learn content not covered.

2. Assess adapted physical activity and occupational therapy literature for information and research on motor behavior of individuals with disabilities. Write a review or critique of the literature pertaining to a specific disability.

3. Ask faculty specialists in motor behavior to adapt content of their courses to include some content on persons with disabilities; invite them to speak to your adapted physical education class or club. Ask parents to share what they know about these topics.

4. Assess the resources your library provides. View videotapes and films. If videotapes of the Milani-Comparetti test are not available, contact the Meyer Rehabilitation Institute, www. unmc.edu/mrimedia/catalog.html#cc.

5. Read part of all of some of the sources cited in this chapter, and apply or reflect on ways you can apply their content.

6. Write brief case studies (imaginary or real) of persons targeted in this chapter. Debate the most appropriate physical education placement and services for each person. Use passages from IDEA 1997 and 2003, and note that these may be interpreted in different ways. Include the 1972 class action suit *Pennsylvania Association for Retarded Citizens (PARC) v. Commonwealth of Pennsylvania* (see Chapter 4) and other relevant court cases in your debate.

CHAPTER

11

Motor Skills and Patterns

Figure 11.1 Practice of skills in a game setting leads to functional competence.

1. Basic locomotor and object control skills for persons who are ambulatory, who use assistive devices (crutches, canes, and walkers), and who use manual and motorized chairs are all presented in this chapter. Why? How are the basic motor skills alike and different for people with varied forms of ambulation?

2. Assume that you have a student using each of the forms of ambulation mentioned above in GE physical education class. What are some of the adaptations you might make during warm-up runs around the gym, basic sport drills, and practice games?

3. The performance standards emphasized in this chapter are built around Ulrich's Test of Gross Motor Development-2 (TGMD-2). Use these *process standards* (i.e., criteria), after you read about each basic skill, to assess a child between the ages of 3 and 10. Write findings in IEP format, *using Figure 11.3 as your model.* Consider how each set of criteria can be built into lesson plans for teaching motor skills.

4. Use Tables 11.1, 11.3, and 11.7 in as many ways as you can think of (to develop a pass/fail type test, to explain to parents the discrepancy between their child's performance level and standards, etc.). How can these tables help you decide what motor skills to facilitate in children ages 4 months through 6 years? Give concrete examples. Consider how these teaching/testing progressions (TTPs) can help you plan lessons for children who are motorically delayed. Give concrete examples.

5. For motor skills to pass the **criterion of functionality,** they must be usable in activities of daily living (ADL), including physical education games and after-school leisure activities. Consider games that enable practicing each motor skill, teach some of these to children or peers, and jot observations in your journal.

6. Read the TGMD-2 test manual (2000) and find and read research based on the TGMD-2. Plan and conduct some research of your own.

A primary goal of adapted physical education is **functional competence** in motor skills and patterns (see Figure 11.1). This chapter discusses assessment of and instruction in motor performance. Knowledge in these areas must extend beyond that of the general physical educator to include all kinds of individual differences, including motor development delays, abnormal muscle tone (spasticity, athetosis, paralysis, and paresis), structural deviations, and learning problems.

Motor skills and patterns is the term used in the federal definition of physical education. **Skills,** as defined in motor learning literature, are acts or tasks that must be *learned* in order to be correctly executed. **Patterns** is a broader term. It refers to acts or tasks that have a similar appearance. A pattern may be learned, or it may emerge naturally as the result of normal motor development. In this text, the terms *skills* and *patterns* are used interchangeably.

Basic Questions in Assessing and Teaching Motor Skills

Table 11.1 lists basic locomotor and object control skills covered in this chapter. Instruction should begin by assessing **present level of performance** (the term specified by law) and setting goals and objectives that match assessment information. The five basic questions that guide assessment and instruction also appear in Table 11.1. The sections that follow show that assessment and instruction proceed together. Hundreds of trials are required to learn a motor skill. Task sheets that guide instruction should provide space for recording success or failure on each trial.

Performance

Assessment at the first level addresses whether the student can perform a skill (yes or no) in a particular context under designated conditions (see Figure 11.2). Three *contexts* that are very different are (a) informal play, (b) structured games, and (c) formal command-response situations. Students may, for example,

Table 11.1 **Basic locomotor and object control skills and questions that guide assessment.**

Locomotor Skills	Object Control Skills
1. Walk or use wheelchair	Grasp and release
2. Run	Underarm roll
3. Ascend/descend stairs	Throw
4. Jump	Catch
5. Hop	Bounce/dribble
6. Leap	Strike
7. Gallop	Kick
8. Skip	Stop/trap
9. Slide	

Basic Assessment Questions for Each Skill

1. Performance—Does student perform skill?
2. Functional competence—Does student use skill in activities for fun and/or fitness?
3. Performance standards—Does student meet form, distance, accuracy, speed, and function standards for age group?
4. Constraints—Does student have muscle tone, bone, or joint abnormalities that limit success and/or contraindications to be remembered? Do environmental variables enhance or limit performance?
5. Biomechanics or form—Is form immature, mature, or adapted to accommodate pathology? Which TGMD-2 process standard should be addressed first?

---

perform a skill in an informal play setting but be unable to do so in the other settings because of comprehension or motivation problems. Therefore, informal play (preferably in a small group) should be observed first.

If the student does not play spontaneously and/or try to imitate classmates, then one-to-one testing is initiated to deter-

Task _____ Overarm throw _____ Date _____ 9/12 _____

Student name _____ J. Garza _____ Partner/aide name _____ CS _____

Objective _____ To throw 30 ft (i.e., distance required for some aspect of a game) _____

Context: C1 Informal play   (C2 Structured game)   C3 Formal drill or test

DIRECTIONS:

Go to station _____ #2 _____ . Work on objective under the circled task conditions. Record number of trials attempted and succeeded in boxes at bottom.

SIX TASK CONDITIONS (EACH LISTED FROM EASY TO HARD)

Object Size
(O1) Tennis ball
O2 Small softball
O3 Regular softball

Texture/Weight
T1 Nerf or sponge
T2 Rubber
(T3) Regulation tennis ball

Assistance
A1 Maximal
(A2) Many prompts
A3 Three or fewer prompts
A4 No assistance

Instructions (Language comprehension)
(I1) Short, two to three words
I2 Medium, four to seven words
I3 Long, eight or more words

Modeling/Teacher Talk
M1 Coactive movement
M2 Talk, then demonstrate
M3 Demonstrate, then talk
(M4) Concurrent visual-verbal
M5 Talk only

Reinforcers Based on Personal Preference
R1 Maximal: Token, hug/pat, (praise), (smile)
(R2) Two or three of above
R3 Same as most peers
R4 Self-praise
Other _____

Trials (Tr)—Record Performance Here: Use O for attempted and X for succeeded.

	1	2	3	4	5	6	7	8	9	10	11	12	13	14	15
Throw 21 ft	O	O	O	X	X	X	X	X	X	O	X	X	X	X	X
Throw 24 ft															
Throw 27 ft															
Throw 30 ft															

mine the conditions needed for successful performance. The first condition to be considered is language comprehension, including what language (English, Spanish, sign) is being used and how many words are in the instructions (two to three, four to seven, eight or more). Often, the problem is simply communicating what needs to be done and how!

Some students do not comprehend and/or pay attention to words. For them, the next condition is assistance, including how much assistance is needed (maximal, many prompts, three or fewer prompts, no prompts) and what kind of demonstration/teacher talk (physical, verbal, visual, or a combination) should be used. *No assistance* means that the student understands and responds to verbal instructions. If this is not the case, then demonstrations and words are used in various combinations to find the type of demonstration/teacher talk condition that works best (verbal, then visual; visual, then verbal; concurrent visual and verbal). On occasion, physical (kinesthetic) assistance may be needed. This is called **coactive** to emphasize that it is more than physical manipulation. Under this maximal input condition, the teacher uses both verbal and physical prompts. The student says or sings the key words in unison with the teacher. Levels of assistance then range from none to maximal, which means a combination of physical-verbal-visual input.

In addition to these instructional conditions, environmental variables also influence success. Among these are size, weight, and texture of an object, as well as surface, slope, and stability of the movement area. Also important is the number of persons at each station and whether or not the student can work independently or needs a helper. Footprints and floor markings can ensure that every person at a station is in the right place and in his or her own space. The direction a student faces should also be controlled to block out irrelevant stimuli or to systematically teach coping skills in relation to multiple environmental input.

Conditions are important in both testing and practice. Figure 11.2 shows how conditions are designated. A common practice in adapted physical activity skill development is a clipboard for each student containing task sheets like Figure 11.2. During a 30-min class, for example, a student might work on different skills at three stations, each of which provides a rich choice of equipment so that level of difficulty can be matched with instructions on the task card. A separate task sheet for each station is on the clipboard. The order of the sheets on the clipboard indicates the order in which the student should progress from station to station.

The task card provides spaces to indicate performance on 60 trials. After each set of 15 trials, an alternate activity may be used to break monotony and/or provide work on another objective, such as abdominal strength (curl-ups), cardiovascular endurance (bench stepping), or tension release (slow stretches). Sometimes, this alternative activity should be in one of the student's areas of strength so that it can serve as a reward. In general, however, the focus should be on completion of as many trials as possible before the signal to rotate to the next station. The greater the student's time on-task, the better the learning outcome.

Reinforcers are not left to chance. Their inclusion on the task sheet signals their importance. *Other* under "Reinforcers" on Figure 11.2 recognizes what works best for each student. *Self-praise* is included as a reinforcer because students need to learn to tell themselves that they are good and to gradually rely on their own self-reinforcement more than that of an external source. The *same as most peers* reinforcer category implies use of specific correctional feedback. Reinforcement obviously can take many forms. The key is for the teacher or partner to respond in some way, thereby showing interest and support.

The *objective* that guides the task sheet can focus on quantitative or qualitative performance or both. Assessment and instruction should attend to each.

Functional Competence

Functional competence refers to proficiency in performing life functions like locomotion, play, work, and self-care. It is not enough, for example, to run or throw a ball in response to demonstrations and prompts in the instructional setting. Students must be able to spontaneously use runs and throws in a variety of settings to achieve a number of purposes (e.g., safety, joy, fitness).

Functional competence also implies performance similar to that of others within the same chronological age range. For mainstream settings to be truly inclusive, all students must have the skills to participate fully, safely, and successfully. For example, to benefit from third- and fourth-grade lead-up games that teach and reinforce softball skills, students must be able to stop a ball on the ground or in the air and to throw it accurately and quickly to a base or teammate. Functional competence thus involves **chaining** together several motor skills and decision making about where to throw the ball.

Performance Standards

Instruction in motor skills is directed toward meeting **performance standards** with respect to form, distance, speed, accuracy, and function. These performance standards (criteria) are a required part of an objective. These task variables are not equally important for all skills, and time limitations usually force teachers to select two or three rather than all five. When an inclusive setting is the placement goal or the student is already integrated, assessment should focus on the skill levels expected of the grade or chronological age level.

Much of adapted physical education is devoted to initial-level skills teaching. Students with motor delays and/or pathology often do not have time to master all of the motor skills of typical children, ages 2 to 7 years. In this case, the walk, run, jump, throw, strike, and kick are usually emphasized.

To help plan the order in which basic skills should be taught to young children, three **teaching/testing progressions (TTPs)** are included in this chapter: walk and run, jump and hop, and object control skills (see Tables 11.3, 11.7, and 11.8). Each TTP breaks skills into observable, measurable tasks that are ordered from easy to hard. By stating a criterion level and the average age at which children without disabilities pass, the TTPs permit the teacher to determine the number of months of developmental delay. This information is often helpful in making IEP decisions and lesson plans.

Constraints

Constraints, within an assessment context, refer to differences of body structure and function and to environmental variables that limit functional ability. These include short stature, obesity, posture problems, deviant sizes and shapes of body parts, amputations, and abnormalities of muscle tone. Environmental variables include noise distractors, equipment, space, and so on. Little is known about good form, mechanical efficiency, and developmental levels when such constraints are present. Indicating pathology in assessment reports is therefore important.

Describing present level of performance for a person with spasticity, athetosis, or paralysis takes many, many words. Therefore, professionals describe patterns in terms of muscle tone.

Types of muscle tone are these:

1. **Spasticity or hypertonus.** Muscle tone is too tight; may be evidenced by contractures or spasms. Usually associated with cerebral palsy but can be caused by many conditions.

2. **Athetosis or fluctuating muscle tone.** Body parts in constant, purposeless motion. A type of cerebral palsy.

3. **Paralysis or atonus.** Common in spina bifida.

4. **Paresis or hypotonus.** Weakness caused by partial paralysis or muscle deterioration. Common in muscular dystrophy.

Problems like round shoulders, swayback, and pigeon toes (see Chapter 14) should be taken into consideration in assessment and instruction of basic movement patterns. Also important are neurological constraints like deficits of balance, coordination, and motor planning. Identification of constraints forces attention on adaptation, especially in regard to ideas about good form and procedures of qualitative analysis.

Biomechanics and Form (Process)

Biomechanics or qualitative analysis of form sometimes focuses on **developmental level.** Most children progress fairly rapidly from immature to mature patterns. Immature patterns, often broken down into initial and elementary levels, are called developmental in that they are appropriate for a particular chronological age. Children with disabilities and/or clumsiness typically display initial and elementary performance levels far longer than peers. This not only results in inefficient and energy-exhausting movement but often affects social acceptance and self-esteem. The "sissy" throw, seen in both girls and boys of elementary age, is an example of an immature movement. This movement pattern, however, is totally acceptable in early childhood, when it would be called developmental.

Mature movement patterns are mechanically efficient, a quality called **good form.** Assessment of form is a *process approach*. Although there are many individual differences in mature form, certain performance criteria must be met. Ulrich's (1985) Test of Gross Motor Development-2 (TGMD-2) is recommended to assess and to teach form.

To assist teachers in visualizing different developmental levels and planning for progress toward mature form, this chapter includes pictorial and checklist assessment instruments. Use of these instruments simplifies writing the individualized education program (IEP) and other reports that require a description of present level of performance.

Figure 11.3 is a sample IEP format that illustrates how present level of performance on the overarm throw is described and how a goal and objectives are written. This information can guide future instruction (i.e., which TGMD-2 standards are failed and thus need the instructor's attention).

Writing Goals and Objectives

Because of heavy workloads, teachers devise many shortcuts to writing goals and objectives. For students whose assessment data indicate that work is needed on basic motor skills, the goal is almost always this: *To achieve functional competence in locomotor and object control skills.* Typically, particular skills, such as running or jumping, are specified. Functional competence for each age or grade level is explained in school district curriculum guides. These explanations include performance standards that must be met and/or a minimal percentile (e.g., the 30th percentile) to be achieved on district norms. Also in curriculum guides are lists of games and sport activities that a student of a certain age or grade should be able to play in order to be in an inclusive classroom.

Short-term objectives are often computerized or printed in list form in curriculum guides so that the teacher can use numbers or abbreviations when making out IEPs for large numbers of students. Objectives, remember, have three parts: (a) condition, (b) behavior that is observable and measurable, and (c) success criterion level. *Remember the acronym CBS.* The part of the objective that requires the most words is the condition, which typically includes many parts. Consider, for example, an objective pertaining to throwing:

Figure 11.3   Overarm throw section of IEP for 9-year-old boy with motor delay. Peers throw 80 to 90 ft.

Present Level of Performance
Form: See below. Mostly Level 3 (homolateral throw). No muscle tone or reflex pathology.

Distance: Throws softball 70 ft, best of 3 trials (15th percentile).
Accuracy: Scores 3 on target overarm throw at distance of 50 ft, 10 trials (below school district average).
Function: Cannot use throw in game setting.
Long-Term Goal—Functional competence for placement with nondisabled 8- and 9-year-olds.

Short-Term Objectives
    Form: 1. Pass TGMD #2, full trunk rotation.
            2. Pass TGMD #4, opposition of limbs.
Distance: 3. Throw softball 79 ft, best of 3 trials.
Accuracy: 4. Score 5 on accuracy test at 50 ft, 10 trials.
Function: 5. Perform throw-and-run and field ball-and-throw sequences in softball lead-up games.

1. Given these conditions,
   - A specified object (size, weight, texture)
   - A set number of trials
   - In a designated context (informal play, structured game, formal test)
   - With appropriate instructions (short, medium, long)
   - With needed assistance (physical, verbal, visual)
   - With necessary reinforcers (token, hug/pat, praise, smile)
2. the student will throw
3. at a designated criterion level (e.g., form, distance, accuracy, function).

Writing out all of these conditions for every objective takes too much time, so most teachers use an abbreviation system (see Figure 11.2). The objective might therefore look like this:

1. Given these conditions, O2, T2, Tr10, C3, I2, A3, R2
2. the student will throw and
3. meet a success criterion level (state what it is).

Individualizing instruction requires considerable record keeping so that the teacher can remember the task conditions under which a student is most likely to succeed. This is often facilitated by creating a clipboard with printed sheets like that in Figure 11.2 for each student. The clipboard system permits an aide, peer tutor, or partner to understand and work toward a designated objective.

As you progress through this chapter, consider the task conditions that can be altered in teaching and/or testing each skill. In locomotor skills, for instance, the surface slope (even, uphill, downhill, variable), surface texture (floor, short grass, long grass, sand), and surface stability (rigid, yielding, variable) might be altered. Likewise, tasks might be executed under a blindfold or a rhythm condition. Try developing your own sheets to show your understanding of task analysis. Test these sheets with children and jot observations in your journal.

Walking: The Foundation Skill

Average children walk between 9 and 18 months of age. In children with disabilities, this skill may be delayed for a few months or up to 6 or 7 years. The average age of independent walking ranges from 20 to 36 months for children who are blind and from 12 to 65 months for youngsters with Down syndrome. Children with cerebral palsy on one side of the body (hemiplegia) usually walk before age 2, but those with all four limbs involved (quadriplegia) often do not walk until age 6 or 7. Many children have confounding neurological deficits that delay walking by several years or prevent it altogether.

Typically, children who are slow to walk are provided physical therapy until age 7 or 8. If functional locomotion is not achieved by this time, experts agree that mobility goals should switch to wheelchair ambulation and to acquisition of wheelchair sport and dance skills.

Adapted physical education typically focuses on the walk as an activity for improving dynamic balance, enhancing physical attractiveness via good postures, and increasing fitness. Beam walking is an important skill in perceptual-motor training and gymnastics. Walking in time to a drumbeat or music is a way of learning rhythm and relaxation. Walking across the swimming pool provides confidence for trying to float. Many persons with health impairments (e.g., obesity, asthma, heart conditions) walk for exercise, at least in the beginning sessions of a fitness or rehabilitation program. Walking can also be a competitive sport; race walking is a popular event among able-bodied persons and is an official track event for Special Olympians.

Among adults, walking is the most popular leisure-time physical activity. Walking or wheeling (the wheelchair equivalent) is something that everyone can do. Thus, physical educators strive to help persons of all ages to make their walking patterns efficient and fun.

Individual Differences in Gaits

One of the first assessment challenges in getting acquainted with a new student is determining whether the walk is mechanically efficient. Figures 11.4 to 11.6 present three groups of gaits categorized loosely by appearance. For each gait, there are many individual differences depending, in part, on whether the impairment is mild or severe. Persons with these gaits are often in general physical education. How will their gaits affect class participation? How will you adapt?

Study these gaits so you will recognize them when shown films, videos, or real persons. Be able to describe present level of performance for each gait and associate it with the probable underlying disability. Does the gait look mechanically efficient? Is it functional? What criteria do you use in answering such questions?

In studying these figures, *remember that cerebral palsy, spina bifida, and muscular dystrophy are the three most common physical disabilities among school-age persons.* These conditions are covered in Part III of this text, but the first knowledge acquired about each condition should be basic walking pattern.

The **shuffling gait** is associated with developmental delays often seen in adapted physical education. *Abnormal retention of several reflexes—tonic labyrinthine-prone, symmetrical tonic neck, positive support, and toe grasp—contributes to shuffling.* When the tonic labyrinthine-prone reflex is present, flexor tone dominates, explaining why some walkers seem always to be looking at the feet. Flexion of the head is also nature's way of facilitating leg extension via the symmetrical tonic neck reflex. When the positive support and toe grasp reflexes dominate, contact with the floor heightens extensor activity, making it hard to bend the knee and lift the foot. Remediation of the shuffling gait should begin with activities in Chapter 10.

Also helpful are games that require reciprocal lifting of feet, as in stepping over bamboo poles, rungs of a ladder, tires, and other obstacles. Tap-dance games, in which the goal is

Figure 11.4   Gaits associated with spasticity and ataxia.

Scissors gait in **spastic cerebral palsy**. The legs are flexed, inwardly rotated, and adducted at the hip joint, causing them to cross alternately in front of each other. There is excessive knee flexion. Toe walking causes a narrow base. Scissoring and toe walking maybe caused also by the *positive support reflex*.

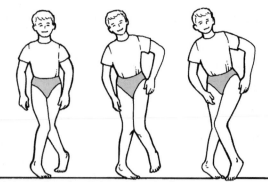

Note tactile stimulation of foot by floor may cause the positive support reflex.

Hemiplegic gait in **cerebral palsy and stroke**. Arm and leg on the same side are involved. Tends to occur with any disorder producing an immobile hip or knee. Individual leans to the affected side, and arm on that side is held in a rigid, semiflexed position.

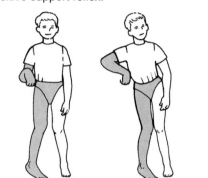

Ataxic or cerebellar gait in **ataxic cerebral palsy and similar conditions**. Individual walks with a wide base, irregular steps, unsteadiness, tendency to reel to one side; has difficulty in judging how high to lift legs when climbing stairs. Too much alcohol and some drugs cause temporary ataxic gaits.

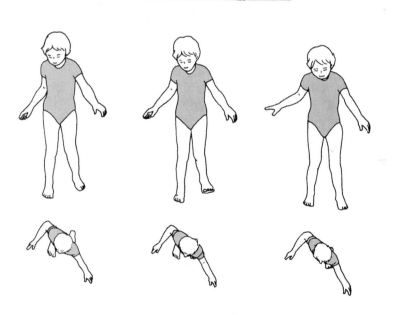

to make noises with different parts of the foot (heel-toe, heel-toe, toe-toe-toe), also help. These can be done in a sitting position or while holding onto a bar for support. Hundreds of walking games, particularly when songs and creative dramatics are woven in, are helpful. Marching, for instance, is fun when children play that they are members of a band or participants in a parade. Walking, combined with carrying loads of different sizes and weights, generalizes to ADL, such as carrying in the groceries, taking out the garbage, and using a backpack for school supplies.

Which of the gaits in Figures 11.4–11.6 have you seen often? Where? How were these gaits affected by environmental variables like evenness of ground and inclination of surface? Did persons with these gaits wear special shoes? How will each gait affect performance of locomotor and object control sport skills? To answer these questions, plan some special practicum experiences for observations and informal questions.

Shuffling or slouch gait.
Associated with central nervous system immaturity (probably retention of tonic labyrinthine reflex-prone and symmetrical tonic neck reflex). Inability of lower body to move independently of upper body. Seen in severe mental retardation. Excessive flexion at hip, knee, and ankle joints, and the trunk is usually inclined forward. Contact with floor is flat-footed. Usually, there is no opposition of arms and legs.

Propulsion or festination gait.
Associated with Parkinson's disease, also called *paralysis agitans.* Individual walks with a forward leaning posture and short, shuffling steps that begin slowly and become progressively more rapid. This gait is seen also in very old persons with low fitness.

Steppage gait. Also called foot-drop gait and is associated with flopping of the foot on the floor. Knee action is higher than normal, but toes still tend to drag on floor. Caused by paralysis or weakness of the ankle dorsiflexors. Results in excessive hip and knee flexor work.

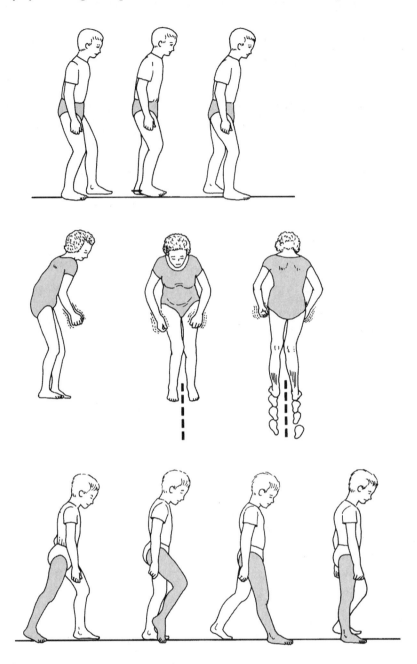

Figure 11.6 Gaits characterized by waddling, lurching, or abnormal lateral movement.

Waddling gait. Main deviation from normal is rolling movement from side to side. This is usually caused by structural problems like bowlegs (genu varum), hip problems and dislocations (coxa vara), knock-knees, or one leg longer than the other.

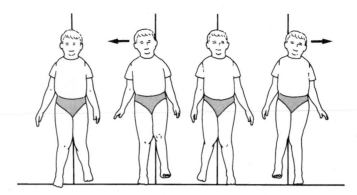

Muscular dystrophy gait. This is an awkward, side-to-side waddle, swayback (lordosis), arms held in backward position, and frequent falling. Shoulder girdle muscles are often badly atrophied. Calf muscles may be hypertrophied but weak because fat has replaced the muscle tissue.

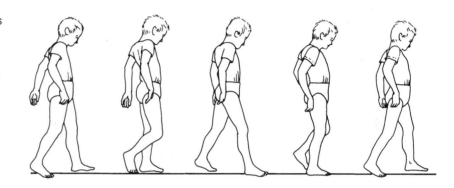

Gluteus maximus lurch. Associated with polio and other spinal paralysis conditions in which the paralyzed limb cannot shift the body weight forward onto the nonimpaired limb. To compensate, the trunk is thrust forward. The gait is thus associated with alternate sticking out of chest (salutation) and pulling back of shoulders.

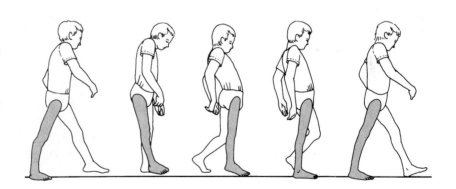

Trendelenburg gait. Limp caused by paralysis or weakness of gluteus medius (the major hip abductor). Pelvis is lower on nonaffected side. In walking, each time the weight is transferred, the body leans slightly in the direction of the weight transfer. Shifting the weight compensates for weak abductors.

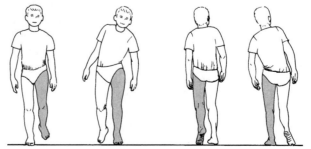
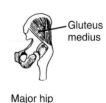

Gluteus medius

Major hip abductor

Figure 11.7   Gaits at different ages. Focus on the shaded leg.

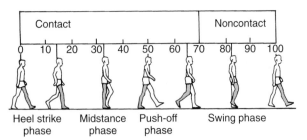

Mature walking gait of children from ages 4 to 5 years and older. A gait cycle begins with the heel strike and ends when the heel of the same leg strikes again. Step and stride length relate to height.

Initial-Toddler

First walking pattern, showing **high guard position** of arms, rigid torso, excessive flexion of hip and knee joints, and flat-footed or toe-walking steps.

Early Childhood

Walking pattern of children until age 4 or 5. There is still no trunk rotation and, hence, no opposition of arm and leg movements. Hip and knee action is still excessive, but heel-toe transfer of weight is beginning to appear.

Developmental Levels in Walking

Walking gait varies with age. Walking matures as the central nervous system (CNS) develops and myelination is completed. If maturation is delayed or frozen or brain damage occurs, a person may exhibit a gait similar to the pattern of a young child. Figure 11.7 depicts gaits of average persons at different ages. Major changes in the transition from immature to mature walking pertain to (a) carriage of arms, (b) trunk rotation, (c) opposition of limbs, (d) hip and knee action, and (e) type of foot plant and pushoff. Especially important in the mature walk is the heel-toe transfer of weight.

Figure 11.8 shows illustrative children with walking problems and strategies that help. The girl with Down syndrome, who is still wobbly because of *hypotonus,* can push a cart filled with weights more easily than walking without something to hang on to. The use of creative dramatics helps to

Figure 11.8   Illustrative walking activities and motivational devices.

Down syndrome with hypotonus

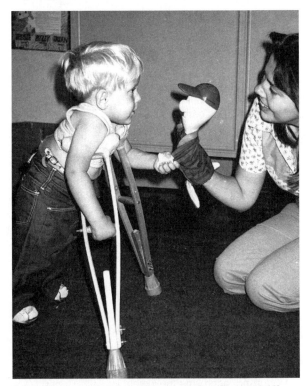

Spina bifida, necessitating swing-to gait (see Figure 11.10)

Figure 11.9 **Crutch gaits used by persons with mild to moderate impairments. The weaker leg is shaded. These persons often compete in track events.**

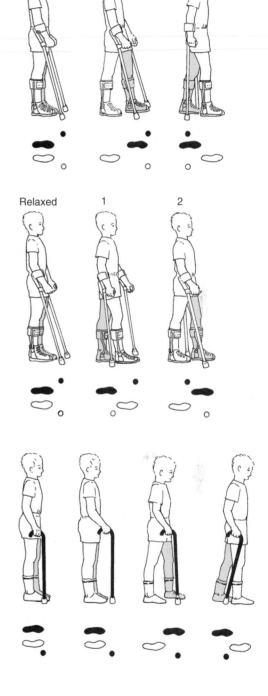

Three-point gait. Both crutches move forward in unison, but the feet move separately. Unlike most gaits, the involved, or weaker, leg takes the first step up to and even with the crutches, so it bears only partial body weight as the good leg then steps out in front of the crutches. The pattern is
1. advance both crutches
2. advance weak leg
3. advance strong leg.

Two-point gait. This gait is most like normal walking and running. It is the fastest of the gaits but requires the most balance because there are only two points of contact with the ground at any time. Whenever a crutch moves, the opposite leg moves in unison. The pattern is
1. advance left crutch and right leg simultaneously
2. advance right crutch and left leg simultaneously.

Hemiplegic gait after a stroke. This gait is similar to the three-point except that one cane is used instead of two crutches. The cane moves first, then the weak leg opposite the cane, then the strong leg. The steps taken with each leg should be equal in length, with emphasis placed on establishing a rhythmic gait.

motivate time on-task. For example, the teacher can make up a story about a little girl taking her doll for a walk and what she sees on the way. The boy with spina bifida needs lots of practice to gain arm and shoulder strength. Puppets are useful motivational devices in keeping a child moving back and forth across the room.

Many students ambulate with crutches or canes. To assess and describe present level of psychomotor performance, crutch gaits must be referred to by name (see Figures 11.9–11.11). Students who use crutches and canes can compete in track-and-field events like able-bodied peers. They are limited only by your ability to teach and coach.

Figure 11.10   Crutch gaits used by persons with severe disabilities.

Step to, swing to, or drag to gait. This is used by persons with little or no control of legs. In public schools, the young child with spina bifida in long leg braces is the best example. In rehabilitation settings, this is the first gait taught to persons with lesions above T10. It is a staccato gait with no follow-through in front of the crutches. All the weight is taken by the arms, while the legs are lifted and swung or dragged forward. The pattern is lift and drop, lift and drop. The crutches shown are **axillary crutches.** Axillary refers to armpit area, and axillary crutches are those that fit under the arms. These should never be used for running because of possible damage to the brachial plexus (a network of nerves under the arm).

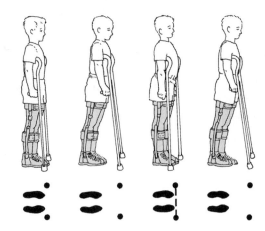

Four-point gait. This gait is used by persons who can move each leg independently. The pattern is
  1. advance left crutch
  2. advance right foot
  3. advance right crutch
  4. advance left foot.
The weaker leg is shaded. The crutches shown are Lofstrand (also called Canadian or forearm) crutches.

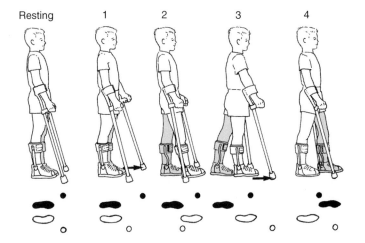

Figure 11.11   Crutch gait used with temporary disabilities or amputation.

Swing-through gait. The person leans into the crutches, lifting the body off the ground by extending the elbows. The body is swung through the crutches so that the good foot lands in *front* of the crutches. Then the crutches are brought forward, and the sequence is repeated.

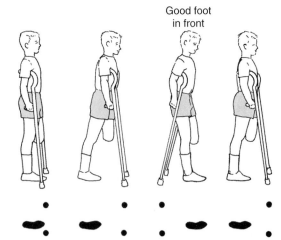

Good foot in front

DO NOT CONFUSE SWING-THROUGH WITH SWING-TO.

    Table 11.2 provides a checklist for evaluating imma-
ture and mature walking. The 11 criteria under the mature pattern can be used as objectives.

♿ *Table 11.3 shows a developmentally sequenced TTP to*
    show walking and running activities. Consider how
these should be done on many surfaces, with different degrees
of incline and stability, with and without blindfolds. How many
ways can you vary each activity? Develop some lesson plans on
walking for children with different needs. Describe current per-
formance for each child.

Table 11.2   Checklist for assessment of walking by persons of different ages.

Directions: Observe the student walking on several different terrains or surfaces (even or uneven), uphill, downhill, and on a level surface. Consider the 11 sets of alternate descriptions and check the one of each set that represents the student's level of performance. Until the child is about age 4 years, most checks will be in the left-hand column. After age 4, the average child exhibits mature walking. Use findings to write specific objectives.

Check One	Developmental or Immature Walking	Check One	Mature Walking

	1. Forward lean
	   a. From ground
	   b. From waist and hips
			1. Good body alignment
			   a. Head up
			   b. Good extension of spine

	2. Wide base of support, with heels 5–8 inches from line of progression		2. Narrower base of support with heels 2–3 inches from line of progression
	3. Toes and knees pointed outward		3. Toes and knees pointed straight ahead
	4. Flat-footed gait		4. Heel-ball-toe transfer of weight
	5. Excessive flexion at knee and hip; no double knee lock		5. Strong pushoff from toes; double knee lock present
	6. Uneven, jerky steps[a]		6. Smooth and rhythmical shift of weight, with minimal up-and-down movement
	7. Little or no pelvic rotation until second or third year. Body sways from side to side.		7. Minimal rotatory action of pelvis (short persons will have more than tall ones)
	8. Rigidity of upper torso		8. Compensatory shoulder rotation inversely related to pelvic rotation
	9. Outstretched arms, also called high guard position		9. Arms swing freely and in opposition with legs
	10. Relatively short stride. In preschool children, the distance from heel to heel is 11–18 inches.		10. Greater length of stride dependent upon length of leg
	11. Rate of walking stabilizes at about 170 steps per minute		11. Rate of walking decreases to about 115 to 145 steps per minute

[a]Jerkiness may be caused by a flat-footed or shuffle gait or by excessive stride length.

Table 11.3   Walk and run skills listed from easy to hard: A developmentally sequenced teaching/testing progression.

Task	Criterion to Pass	Average Age (Months)
1. Walk, Level 1 pattern (see Figure 11.9)	4–5 steps	12–14
2. Walk, Level 2 pattern	10-ft distance	15–17
3. Walk backward	5 steps	15–17
4. Walk sideward	10-ft distance	15–17
5. Run, Level 1 pattern (see Figure 11.11)	10-ft distance	18–23
6. Walk on tiptoes	5 steps, hands on hips	24–29
7. Walk backward	10-ft distance	24–29
8. Walk 4-in beam	3 steps forward	24–29
9. Walk 4-ft circular pattern	Fewer than 5 stepoffs	24–29
10. Walk line on tiptoes	8-ft distance	30–35
11. Walk backward, 4-ft circular pattern	Fewer than 2 stepoffs	42–47
12. Walk 4-in beam	4 steps forward	48–53
13. Heel-toe walk backward, 4-in beam	5 steps, toes touching heels	54–59
14. Walk 4-in beam, hands on hips	8-ft distance	54–59
15. Walk on tiptoes, hands on hips	15-ft distance	60–71
16. Walk 4-in beam, sideward	8-ft distance	60–71
17. Run/walk 1 mile as fast as possible	13 min for boys; 14 min for girls	60–71
18. Run/walk 1 mile as fast as possible	12 min for boys; 13 min for girls	72–83
19. Run 50 yd for speed	9.9 sec for boys; 10.2 for girls	72–83
20. Shuttle run for speed, 12 ft apart, 2 cans	Complete cycle of 2 cans in 12 sec	72–83

Note. Most items come from the Peabody Developmental Motor Scales (Folio & Fewell, 2000).

Assessing and Teaching the Run

Ability to analyze a walk carries over into the teaching of other locomotor skills. Many of the items for evaluation of walking are applicable to running (see Figure 11.12). The run is a locomotor pattern comprised of four phases: foot plant, recovery, pushoff, and flight. Unlike the walk, the run has no period of double support. Children pass through three distinct developmental levels in running (see Figure 11.12). Children without problems demonstrate Levels 1, 2, and 3 at about ages 2, 3, and 5, respectively. All of the components of a mature run, however, are not typically present until age 7 or 8. In adapted physical activity, you will see many developmental delays. Let's consider what to emphasize in teaching the run.

Leg Action

Foot plant, similar to the heel strike in the walk, marks the end of the forward leg swing. The foot plant in the sprint is on the metatarsals; the teacher stresses "Run on the balls of your feet." In the mature run (Level 3), the support foot contacts the floor approximately under the body's center of gravity (CG). In immature runs, the support foot lands in front of the CG. The body lean (line between support foot and CG) in the mature run is at 1 o'clock, whereas it is too far forward or backward in the immature pattern.

Recovery, similar to the midstance in the walk, is the best time to check the presence of a high heel kick. This mechanism readies the knee to spring forward with maximal propulsive thrust in the pushoff phase. In the immature run, the hip and knee may be outwardly rotated and cause a toe-out gait, but this problem heals itself with age. Unless there are muscle imbalances, 6-year-olds can run straight, placing their feet on or near a designated line.

Pushoff, the same term as in the walk, demands excellent balance and coordination inasmuch as the support leg pushes backward and downward while the swing leg lifts forward and upward. *Focal points to be checked are the amount of extension in the pushoff leg and the height of the knee lift of the swing leg.* At the end of the knee lift, the thigh is more or less horizontal to the ground.

Flight is the period of nonsupport, the time when both legs are in the air. As children mature, an increasing proportion of time is spent in flight. In addition, the elevation of the flight decreases, an indication that force is being properly directed forward and not upward.

Arm Movements

The coordination of proper arm movements with the leg actions is the hardest part of the run and the last to appear. Level 3 of Figure 11.12 shows the opposition of limbs and the use of a pumping action of the arms to increase forward momentum. The elbows are kept bent at about 90°. The hand swings as high as the chin in the forward swing; the elbow reaches as high as the shoulder in the backswing. In the less mature runs, the arms' range of motion is very limited.

Assessment Ideas and the TGMD-2

Assessment of the run can be complex or simple, depending on the number of **performance criteria.** Ulrich (2000) in the TGMD-2 indicated that the four most important criteria are as follows:

1. Brief period where both feet are off the ground
2. Arms moving in opposition to legs, elbows bent
3. Narrow foot placement landing on heel or toe (not flat-footed)
4. Nonsupport leg bent approximately 90° (close to buttocks)

Runners should be observed at their fastest speed over a minimum distance of 50 ft in two or more trials. Devise game settings for examining the run (ecological testing). Challenges might be "How fast can you run around the baseball diamond?" "How fast can you run to a designated goal line?" Low organized games, in which students chase and tag one another or run from place to place on cue, also can be used for assessment purposes.

Teach runners start signals ("On your mark, get set, go") that are the same as those used in track meets. Conduct assessment and practice in a class setting in such a way that skills learned can be generalized to Special Olympics or other competitive events. The running task, the finish line, and the concept of personal best should all be clearly understood. When ecological assessment is used, teaching cannot be separated from testing and vice versa.

Pedagogy

Children who lack the concept of running should be introduced to it by walks down hills steep enough to quicken the pace to a run. In early stages of learning, they may hold hands with a runner or be gently pushed into running by doing caboose-type activities (two or three students in a file, with arms around waist of person in front). The student requiring help should do the caboose activities with good runners. Patient teaching is required also to convey the concepts of starting, stopping, and staying in a lane.

Less involved children need special instruction related to running on the balls of the feet, lifting the knees, and swinging the arms. To facilitate running on the balls of the feet, practice can be up steep hills or steps. Jumping and hopping activities also tend to emphasize staying on the balls of the feet. Possible solutions to inadequate knee lift include riding a bicycle, particularly uphill; running up steep hills or steps; and running in place with knee action exaggerated to touch the outstretched palms of hands. Corrections for swinging arms across the body or without vigor include practice in front of a mirror and running with a baton or small weight bar.

Children may need help to understand the concept of speed. Any child with number concepts up to 15 can understand running a 50-yd dash in 9 versus 13 sec. In track meets, emphasis can be placed on personal best by pinning cards with the children's best times on their backs. As they finish a dash, they are told whether or not they beat their own time. Ribbons can be awarded to children who beat their own times rather than (or in addition to) children who beat others. An alternative technique is recording the child's expressed level of aspiration and making awards for meeting or surpassing this estimate.

Use both process and product assessment. When measuring speed, or teaching for speed, plan adaptations for poor

Figure 11.12   Pictorial checklist for assessing running.

Directions: Observe several 50-ft runs. Circle the level that best depicts the pattern you observe and underline the descriptors that can be used on the IEP to indicate present level of performance.

Phases	Foot plant	Recovery	Pushoff	Flight
Main Focal Points	Center of gravity (CG)	Heel kick	Straight-leg push High knee lift	Time

Level 1: Initial
Usually age 18–23 months

CG

Support foot in front of CG

Front leg stiff

Little knee flexion

Limited arm action does not help

Outward rotation at hip and knee joints

Toes point out

Low rear heel kick

Minimal backward-downward thrust

Poor knee lift of swing leg

No flight or short flight

Level 2: Transitional
Usually age 3

Support foot in front of CG

Some knee flexion

Bent elbows begin to work in opposition to legs

Minimal rotation

Toes point straight

Medium rear heel kick

Good backward-downward thrust

Some knee lift of swing leg

Longer flight

Sometimes, too much elevation

Level 3: Mature
Usually age 5

Support foot under CG

Body lean at 1 o'clock

Bent elbows (90° elbow flexion) provide forceful pumping action

Minimal rotation

Toes point straight

High rear heel kick

Back leg straight

Excellent backward-downward thrust

Front thigh horizontal to ground

Very long flight

Little elevation

Force directed forward

Figure 11.13   Adaptation when timing a 50-yd dash for persons with developmental delay.

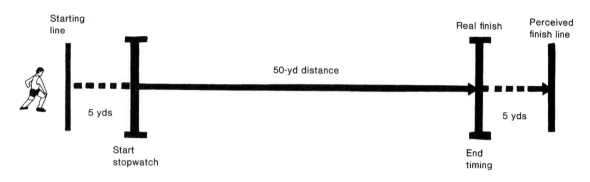

Table 11.4   Comparison of three types of runs.

Phases	Sprint	Middle-Distance Run	Long-Distance Run
Foot plant	Land high on ball of foot; heel does not touch	Land lower on ball of foot than in sprint; heel does not touch	Land low on ball of foot, drop to heel
Knee action	Less rear kick than in other kinds of runs	More rear kick than in sprint	More rear kick than other runs
	Lift knee high and straight forward	Lift knee less high than in sprint	Lift knee slightly as compared to other runs
	Thigh should be more or less horizontal to ground at end of knee lift	Thigh should be less horizontal, about 70° to 80° at end of knee lift	Thigh is less horizontal at end of knee lift than in other runs
Forward body lean	Lean between 25° and 30°—about 1 o'clock	Lean between 15° and 18°—about halfway between 12 and 1 o'clock	Lean about 10°—about one-third of way between 12 and 1 o'clock
Arm action	Pump arms vigorously, with hands reaching chin level or higher	Use slightly less vigorous arm action	Swing arms naturally at about shoulder level

reaction time and the problem of slowing down before reaching the finish line. Typically, both problems are resolved by having the student run further than the timed distance (see Figure 11.13). Regardless of the activity, teach students not to slow down until after they have crossed the finish line.

Types of Runs

The physical educator should be able to assess different kinds of runs: (a) sprinting; (b) middle-distance runs—880 yd and up; and (c) long-distance runs—mile and over for children. The 440-yd dash can be classified as either a sprint or a middle-distance run, depending upon cardiorespiratory endurance. Jogging can be either a middle- or long-distance run. Table 11.4 shows that each type of run varies with respect to foot plant, knee action, forward body lean, and arm action. These four components are generally the ones on which students need the most practice.

The **shuttle run** is traditionally used as a test of running speed and agility and should be practiced frequently. In this type of run, the goal is to shuttle back and forth between two end lines. On a signal, the student runs to a designated line

and picks up an object (wooden block, eraser, sponge); then he or she returns to the starting line and deposits the object on the ground. The distance between lines and the number of objects vary. The popular PACER test uses a 20 m (20 yd, 32 in) shuttle run. The Bruininks-Oseretsky Test of Motor Proficiency (BOTMP) uses a 15-ft distance and one block.

Assessing and Teaching Stair Skills

Functional locomotion in the community requires that children with developmental delays be given instruction and practice in the use of various kinds of stairsteps and ladders. Every school should have playground apparatus that motivates children to want to climb and affords opportunities for seeing the world at different heights (see Figure 11.14).

Ascending is much easier than descending and should be taught first. Slides are particularly good because they eliminate the problem of how to get the child down. Slides do not have to be slick. They can also be carpeted and made with a gentle slope that can be scooted or rolled down. Some apparatus should have only two or three steps, while others should offer more challenge.

Figure 11.14 Play apparatus should be designed so that children practice progressively more difficult kinds of climbing, balancing, and jumping.

Figure 11.15 Thirteen-year-old child with Down syndrome descends stairs in immature fashion, leading with the same foot and marking time on each rung. This pattern is exhibited in the child with no problems at about 23 months of age.

Table 11.5 Average ages (in months) for stair skills.

Developmental Patterns	Ascending	Descending
1. Marking time using handrail	18–23 months	18–23 months
2. Marking time without support	24–29 months	24–34 months
3. Alternate feet using handrail	29–31 months	30–50 months
4. Alternate feet without support	31–41 months	49–55 months

Note: These patterns should be assessed on staircases of variable height (2, 4, 6, 8 inches) and width.

Marking time and *alternate feet* are the terms used to assess performance in ascending and descending. **Marking time** is a pattern in which the same foot always leads. The name is derived from the lead foot marking time while the other foot steps up to create a period of double support on the one step. **Alternate feet** (also called a foot-over-foot pattern) is the mature pattern, in which left and right feet take turns leading, and only one foot is on a step at a time.

Table 11.5 shows four developmental levels of stair skills. Height and width of steps affect success, so assessment and goal setting should be specific to each piece of apparatus. Marking time skills occur at about the same age for ascending and descending, but the balance demands of the alternate feet pattern make descending more difficult. Typically, children cannot use the mature pattern in descending until about 15 months after it has been mastered in ascending. Thus, most children do not exhibit alternate-step ascending and descending until age 4. Persons with disabilities show considerable delay (see Figure 11.15) and thus are often denied the opportunities for motor and social development afforded by playground apparatus.

The mature pattern of stair climbing is an excellent cardiovascular fitness activity. The task can be made more demanding by adding weights (e.g., backpacks, books, stuffed animals).

Jump, Hop, Leap

Teachers must use the terms *jump, hop,* and *leap* correctly to communicate movement challenges to students. Table 11.6 clarifies the meaning of these words. These patterns are similar in that they have three phases: a takeoff, flight, and landing. The jump for distance or height has an additional phase (the preliminary crouch) at the beginning of the sequence.

Table 11.6   Comparison of jump, hop, and leap.

	Jump	Hop	Leap
Takeoff	May be either two-foot or one-foot takeoff	Always a one-foot takeoff	Always a one-foot takeoff
Flight	Weight always transferred to two feet	Weight never transferred	Weight always transferred from one foot to the other
Landing	Always a two-foot landing	Always a one-foot landing on same foot	Always a one-foot landing

Average children learn to jump at about the same time they master the marking-time/ascending-stairs skills. Once a position of height has been attained, it makes sense to want to jump down. The earliest jumps, therefore, are usually step-downs in which one foot leads.

Assessing and Teaching the Jump

Jumping is an extremely difficult skill because of its demand for good balance and bilateral integration. Many persons with severe mental retardation (MR) never learn to jump. Persons with mild MR conditions usually learn to jump, but their movement patterns may be immature compared to those of peers. Likewise, distance jumped sometimes lags 2 to 3 years behind peers.

Jumping is a popular field event, however, in sports days and meets for children. Attending these meets enables prospective teachers to see persons with amputations, blindness, cerebral palsy, and other conditions excelling in jump events. There is widespread agreement that persons can learn to jump if physical educators make this a major goal. Debate this point with classmates after you have observed several children with disabilities jumping or trying to jump.

Once you have assessed present level of performance (see Figure 1.17), the next protocol is assessment to determine how to improve the quality of the jump. For the horizontal jump, Ulrich (2000) suggested the following **performance criteria:**

1. Preparatory movement, including flexion of both knees with arms extended behind the body
2. Arms extended forcefully forward and upward, reaching full extension above head
3. Takeoff and landing on both feet simultaneously
4. Arms are thrust downward during landing

Of these criteria, the arm movements are the most difficult to master. Ulrich (2000, p. 18) reported that 60% of children do not master Criterion 2 until age 9. Arm actions are typically more of a problem than leg actions in children with mild MR.

Because many children with disabilities exhibit delays in jumping, different developmental levels must be recognized (see Figure 11.17). *Persons exhibiting a Level 1 pattern probably have not yet sufficiently integrated the symmetrical tonic neck reflex; they obviously have problems in bilateral coordination (see Chapter 10 for activities).*

Functional Sport Training

The ages at which children master jump, hop, and leap skills are of interest in planning assessment and designing instruction. Table 11.7 presents information about the jump and the hop, and also a teaching progression, with tasks listed from easiest to hardest. In general, children begin to learn jumping skills at about 18 months, hopping at about 30 months, and leaping after they are in kindergarten or first grade.

In the jump, hop, and leap, students must know kinesthetically what the flight phase feels like. Figure 11.16 presents one approach to facilitating a kinesthetic awareness of up and down. The trampoline is another way. Manually lifting the student into the air while saying "*up*" may be necessary. Think of how many ways this can be done, alone and with a partner.

A gymnastics or track-and-field program is recommended to provide practice in jumping. This approach gives older students who still need work on basic skills the self-esteem of having a sport and of training to be an athlete. By using terms like *dismount, vault,* and *mount,* you can lend dignity to basic skill practice.

Jump Down (Dismount)

The gymnastics term **dismount** is a jump from a piece of apparatus down to the floor. Dismounts are used to end routines on the balance beam, the even parallel bars, the uneven parallel bars, the horse, and the buck. Judged for their aesthetic appearance and mechanical efficiency, dismounts may involve difficult movements, such as handsprings and cartwheels, or simple jumps downward using a two-foot takeoff and land.

Children need to know how to get off a piece of gymnastic apparatus or play equipment safely. The first skill that should be taught is the **jump-off dismount** from a *low, wide balance beam.* The dimensions of the balance beam are changed as the child gains confidence. Children who feel secure about their jumping ability will no longer fear falling. Only then should locomotor movements (walks, runs, skips) on the balance beam be introduced.

Jump Over (Vault)

Jumping becomes a sport skill when it is used in track or gymnastics as a means of getting over an outstretched rope or a piece of apparatus. Students can *vault* over many different kinds of apparatus: (a) a low beam about thigh or hip height, (b) a tumbling bench, (c) a vaulting box, (d) a horse, or (e) a buck.

Instead of demonstrating standard vaults and expecting the student to imitate, observe the different movement approaches explored by the student in attempts to get over the apparatus. Which of the following movement patterns offer the student the most success?

Figure 11.17   Pictorial checklist for assessing horizontal long jump.

Directions. Circle the level that best depicts the pattern you observe and underline the descriptors that can be used on the IEP to indicate present level of performance.

Level 1: Initial

Incomplete crouch

Difficulty in using both feet and arms simultaneously

Arms used for balance during flight but not contributing to forward momentum

Feet leading in flight and landing phases rather than arms

Level 2: Transitional

Forward body lean

Arms initiating takeoff

Body not fully straightening out during flight

Insufficient trunk flexion during flight downward

Unsteady landing

Level 3: Mature

Trunk parallel to ground in preliminary crouch

Angle of takeoff about 45°

Body fully extended during upward flight with arms stretched upward

Full trunk flexion during flight downward

Steady landing with arms forward

1. **Squat vault.** Weight taken equally on both arms, knees are pulled upward, tucked to chest, and then continue forward. Body passes over box in a squat position.

2. **Straddle vault.** Weight taken equally on both arms, and legs are abducted in wide-stride semi-sitting position. Hands are on inside and legs on the outside. Body passes over box in this straddle position.

3. **Flank vault.** Initially done with both arms on the box. Standard flank vault is performed with one arm. While arms support weight of body, both legs are lifted simultaneously over the box. The side of the body passes over the box. Sometimes called a *side vault.*

4. **Front vault.** Same as flank vault except that the front of the body passes over the box.

The beginning vault is often a combined side-front vault with both hands on the box and the knees bent as the legs pass over. Most elementary school textbooks recommend that the squat vault be taught first. *The law of individual differences rules that children should not all be introduced to the same progression of vaults nor tested on a single movement pattern selected by the teacher.* When allowed to discover their own ways of getting over, first-grade children can succeed at vaulting. A beatboard or springboard is necessary to attain the height necessary for propulsion of the body over the box.

Jump Up (Mount)

In gymnastics, a **mount** is a jump from a beatboard, springboard, or minitramp onto a piece of apparatus. Mounts are used

Table 11.7 **Jumping and hopping tasks listed from easy to hard: A developmentally sequenced teaching/testing progression.**

Task	Criterion to Pass	Average Age (Months)
1. Step down from 8- to 10-in height	One foot leads	18–23
2. Jump forward, two-foot takeoff	4 in without falling	18–23
3. Jump up, two-foot takeoff	2 in, both feet together	18–23
4. Jump down from 16- to 20-in height	One foot leads	24–29
5. Jump over 2-in high rope	Two-foot takeoff	30–35
6. Jump down from 18- to 24-in height	Two-foot takeoff, land	30–35
7. Jump forward, two-foot takeoff	24 in	30–35
8. Hop in place on one foot	3 times	30–35
9. Jump down from 24- to 30-in height	Two-foot takeoff, land	36–41
10. Hop forward, one foot	5 times on one foot, then 3 times on other	36–41
11. Jump forward, two-foot takeoff	26 to 30 in	36–41
12. Hop for distance	6 in	42–47
13. Hop forward, one foot	8 times on one foot, then 8 times on other	42–47
14. Vertical jump for height	3 in beyond normal reach	48–53
15. Jump down from 32-in height	One foot leads	48–53
16. Hop for distance, preferred foot	16 in	48–53
17. Hop for distance, nonpreferred foot	16 in	48–53
18. Jump and turn 180°	Feet together, hands on hips	54–59
19. Jump sideways back and forth across line	3 times without stopping	54–59
20. Jump forward, two-foot takeoff	36 in	54–59
21. Jump over 10-in-high rope	Two-foot takeoff, land	60–71
22. Hop for speed, 20-ft distance	6 sec	60–71
23. Vertical jump for height	8 in beyond normal reach	72–83

Note. Most items come from the Peabody Developmental Motor Scales (Folio & Fewell, 2000).

Figure 11.16 **Three-year-old improves kinesthetic awareness of up and down as a lead-up to jumping.**

to begin routines on the balance beam, the even parallel bars, the uneven parallel bars, the horse, and the buck.

Children need practice jumping up onto things as well as jumping down. If no apparatus can be improvised, they may jump (two-foot takeoff) *up* the stairs, *up* on automobile tires, *up* on street curbs, *up* on rocks, and so on.

The movement patterns used on the springboard, beatboard, minitramp, and diving board are similar. For better transfer of learning, the child should have experience on all four pieces of apparatus. If the budget allows the purchase of only one, the beatboard is recommended.

Specific tasks that the child can be asked to perform while jumping are these:

1. Clap hands overhead, behind back, in front of body.
2. Land beyond a certain line or marker on the mat.
3. Assume a tuck position in the air.
4. Assume a pike position in the air.
5. Assume a straddle position in the air.
6. Assume a hurdle position in the air.
7. Assume a laterally flexed position in the air.
8. Make a turn in the air.
9. Land with feet together, feet apart, one foot in front of the other.
10. Land with arms in various positions.
11. Land and immediately perform a forward roll.
12. Jump while carrying a rag doll or wearing a backpack.

Movement Exploration on a Trampoline

The trampoline is an excellent vehicle for improving balance. This objective is best achieved if the student is afforded many opportunities for movement exploration while closely supervised by an adult who insists on safe activities.

Emphasis should not be on the learning of such traditional skills as the seat drop during early lessons, but rather upon motor fluency and originality. *The child may attempt rolls, animal walks, rope jumping, turns in the air, and other stunts.* The problems that a child exhibits on the trampoline are the same as those the child has overcome and/or learned to compensate for when on the ground.

Assessing and Teaching the Hop

Taking off and landing on the same foot requires both static and dynamic balance. To determine whether children are ready for hopping instruction, ask them to imitate you in a single-foot standing balance, free leg bent backward, and hands at hips. Given two trials, most children can hold this stance for 3 sec by age 30 to 35 months. If problems occur, have the child practice while one hand holds on to a chair or ballet-type bar. Shortly thereafter, they can hop in place on one foot three times without losing balance (Folio & Fewell, 2000). Or they may hop in place while holding on to a support of some kind. Approximately 6 months later, they can hop forward on the preferred foot five times and the nonpreferred foot three times.

Some insist that hopping forward is an easier developmental progression than hopping in place, but no research seems to have addressed this. Hopscotch and other games using floor patterns require forward locomotion, so this skill may be practiced more.

Little research has been conducted on hopping and disability. Children with mild MR seem to improve significantly in their ability to balance between the ages of 8 and 14 years. When using a test that requires hopping in circular and square patterns, few children with Down syndrome (25%) and moderate MR (5%) are successful. The performance of children with mild MR approaches that of peers, although games like hopscotch are decidedly difficult for about half of them. Students with moderate MR may not exhibit mature hopping patterns until a mean age of 15 years.

Process evaluation of hopping can be guided by the four **performance criteria** that follow (Ulrich, 2000). The student should be asked to hop three times on each foot.

1. Foot of nonsupport leg remains behind body
2. Nonsupport leg swings forward in pendular fashion to produce force
3. Arms bent at elbows and swing forward to produce force
4. Takes off and lands three consecutive times on preferred foot
5. Takes off and lands three consecutive times on nonpreferred foot.

Testing and games of hopping can also involve speed, distance, floor patterns, and rhythmic sequences. Most 5-year-olds can hop 50 ft in about 10 sec. Illustrative rhythmic patterns for older children are as follows:

Hop 1/1. Hop first on the right foot and then on the left foot.

Hop 2/2. Hop twice on the right foot, twice on the left, and so on.

Hop 2/1. Hop twice on the right foot, once on the left, twice on the right, and so on.

Hop 1/2. Hop once on the right foot, twice on the left, and so on.

Performance on such tasks can be assessed with the following 4-point scale:

4—Performs all tasks easily

3—Can alter sides symmetrically

2—Can hop on either foot at will; can alternate, but cannot maintain a rhythm

1—Can perform only symmetrically

Assessing and Teaching the Leap

A **leap** is a special kind of run in which the upward and forward direction of the flight is increased as much as possible. Consequently, the period of nonsupport is greater than the run. Children usually describe the leap as "going way up in the air, stretching out from one leg to the other—like going over a big puddle." The leap is used mostly in crossing-the-brook-type games (leap over an obstacle), gymnastics (stride leap on floor and beam), and creative dance.

When shown a leap across a pretend brook (narrow sheet of paper or cloth), many children as young as 3 years old can follow the leader. However, the leap is usually considered an elementary school skill.

For several leaps in succession, Ulrich (2000) recommended the following **performance criteria:**

1. Takeoff on one foot and land on the opposite foot
2. A period when both feet are off the ground (longer than running)
3. Forward reach with arm opposite the lead foot

These criteria are similar to those used for the run. The main difference is the long flight period. Other criteria, usually emphasized with older children, are full extension of the back leg and pointed toes. The front leg may be fully extended during the entire leap, or bent and held high (deer leap) during the flight and then quickly extended for the landing. In general, the leap in the air is similar to splits on the ground by cheerleaders. Practicing the splits seems to have carryover value in improving leaps.

Assessing and Teaching Rhythmic, Two-Part Motion

The gallop, skip, and slide are rhythmic two-part patterns derived from combinations of the walk, hop, and leap. They are called rhythmic patterns because the major challenge is to capture the long-short rhythm of each two-part combination. Each pattern has a short period when both feet are off the floor, so considerable balance is required for execution. Most children learn the gallop first, then the skip, then the slide.

Gallop

The **gallop** is a walk-and-leap pattern, with the same foot always leading, done in a forward or backward direction in a long-short rhythm. This is the first asymmetrical gait learned by the young child (Clark & Whithall, 1989). The front foot takes a step (walk), which is long in duration, while the back foot tries to catch up with a leap that is short in duration.

Performance criteria for judging the gallop (Ulrich, 2000) are as follows:

1. A step forward with the lead foot followed by a step with the trailing foot to a position adjacent to or behind the lead foot
2. Brief period when both feet are off the ground
3. Arms bent and lifted to waist level
4. Maintains a rhythmic pattern for four consecutive gallops

The rhythmic pattern should be a long-short rhythm. Children may demonstrate a primitive form of the gallop as early as age 3, but the correct rhythmic leg action does not generally appear until about age 5. Between 60 and 71 months, most children can gallop 8 to 10 steps with the same foot leading (Folio & Fewell, 2000).

Rhythmic accompaniment (voice, hand clapping, drum, music) helps in learning to gallop. The idea of moving like a horse or playing cowboys, together with a demonstration, elicits a gallop. You can then cue children to gallop higher and higher and to push with the arms to achieve height.

Skip (Not in TGMD-2)

The **skip** is a walk and a hop, with alternate feet leading, in a long-short rhythm. The pattern is smooth and symmetrical, with each foot taking a long-in-duration walk step followed by a short-in-duration hop.

Performance criteria might be as follows:

1. A long-short rhythm of the step-hop on alternate feet (a step must take twice the time as the hop)
2. Foot of nonsupport leg carried near surface during hop phase
3. Arms alternately moving in opposition to legs at about waist level

The skip is difficult for many children, especially boys, probably because it is seldom used in ADL. To assist with assessment, three levels can be identified:

Level 1—Shuffling or one-foot skipping

Level 2—Jerky and/or inconsistent skipping

Level 3—Mature, smooth, symmetrical, long-short foot action

At Level 1, children alternate a step-hop with a walk; usually, the preferred foot does the step-hop. These children simply lack the bilateral coordination to enable both sides of the body to perform the same way. At Level 2, children can do alternate step-hops, but they are not yet consistent in the long-short rhythm. Level 1 and 2 skipping characterizes most 3- and 4-year-olds. Level 3 emerges at about age 5.

Between 60 and 71 months, most children can skip 8 to 10 steps with mature foot action (Folio & Fewell, 2000). Co-ordination of the arms to move in opposition to the legs often does not appear until ages 8 or 9. Instruction in skipping, like galloping, is facilitated by rhythmic accompaniment. When students seem frozen at the one-footed skip level, skip with them in partner position, holding hands on the problem side.

Slide

The **slide** (a walk and a leap) is identical to the gallop except that it is performed sideward rather than forward and, hence, requires better balance. This is one of the few skills that teach lateral body control and sideward balance.

The following are **performance criteria** for judging the slide (Ulrich, 2000):

1. Body turned sideways so shoulders are aligned with the line on the floor
2. A step sideways with the lead foot, followed by a slide of the trailing foot to a point next to the lead foot
3. A minimum of four continuous step-slide cycles to the right
4. A minimum of four continuous step-slide cycles to the left

In Criterion 2, the foot action must reflect a long-short rhythm. Ability to slide equally well on both sides is seldom seen, and most children perform a mature pattern to their preferred side before their nonpreferred side.

The slide is used in both sport and dance. It is often seen in guarding and blocking in team sports. The slide is used in gymnastics (floor exercise and balance beam). Often, the arms are extended sideward at shoulder height, and children should practice with different arm positions. In dances that use a single circle formation, the slide is one of the easiest and most popular steps. The pattern traditionally used is seven slides to the right with a transfer of weight to the opposite foot on the eighth count, followed by seven slides to the left and a transfer of weight. This sequence should be practiced early.

Assessing and Teaching Object Control Skills

Object control skills may be gross or fine motor. **Gross motor** refers to use of large muscles (i.e., moving the hands, feet, or larger body parts), as in ball handling. **Fine motor** refers to use of small muscles (i.e., fingers) as in paper-pencil-scissors-blocks-shoelace activities. This chapter is delimited to gross motor object control.

Mastery of object control skills is dependent upon development of normal muscle tone, integration of primitive reflexes, maturation of perceptual-motor abilities, CNS organizational and sequencing abilities, and repeated practice. Research shows that perception and action are coordinated from birth (Bard, Fleury, & Hay, 1990); one does not precede the other, as some early theorists posited. *Effective interaction with the environment, however, is not possible until voluntary grasping and holding behaviors appear at about 4 to 5 months of age.*

Most infants thus begin exhibiting pounding, shaking, striking, pushing, and pulling play behaviors during their first year. Many children with disabilities, however, need help in learning these initial object control skills. *The ability to grasp is often absent or weak in persons with cerebral palsy, muscular dystrophy, and conditions that cause hypotonus, paresis, or paralysis.*

Table 11.8   Object control skills listed from easy to hard: A developmentally sequenced teaching/testing progression.

Task	Criterion to Pass	Average Age (Months)
1. First voluntary grasp	Grasps rattle	4–5
2. First voluntary release	Releases cube on command	10–11
3. Roll ball from sitting position	Moves ball 3 ft	12–14
4. Throw (cast) tennis ball	Level 1 pattern (see Figure 11.20)	12–14
5. Kick ball	Steps on or kicks into ball	15–17
6. Throw (hurl) tennis ball	Level 2 pattern (see Figure 11.20)	15–17
7. Throw (hurl) tennis ball	Travels 3 ft forward	18–23
8. Kick ball	Travels 3 ft forward	18–23
9. Throw (hurl) playground ball	Travels 5 ft forward	24–29
10. Throw (hurl) tennis ball	Travels 7 ft forward	24–29
11. Kick ball	Travels 6 ft forward	30–35
12. Catch large ball from 5-ft distance	2 of 3 trials; Level 1 (see Figure 11.21)	30–35
13. Bounce-throw tennis ball against wall 5 ft away	Ball hits floor once before wall contact	36–41
14. Catch large ball from 5-ft distance	1 of 2 trials; Level 2	36–41
15. Throw tennis ball	10 ft with trunk rotation and follow-through	42–47
16. Use underarm toss to hit wall target from 5 ft	Hits target 2 of 3 trials with tennis ball	42–47
17. Catch tennis ball from 5-ft distance	2 of 3 trials; Level 2	42–47
18. Use overarm throw to hit wall target from 5 ft	Hits target 2 of 3 trials with large ball	42–47
19. Throw playground ball	10 ft, 1 of 2 trials	48–53
20. Use overarm throw to hit wall target from 12 ft	Hits target 2 of 3 trials with tennis ball	54–59
21. Bounce and catch tennis ball two times	Two hands, successful 2 of 3 trials	60–71
22. Kick stationary ball into air	Travels 12 ft in air	60–71
23. Run and kick moving ball	Travels 8 ft	72–83
24. Drop-kick ball	Travels 5 ft, 2 of 3 trials	72–83
25. Wall pass and catch at 5-ft distance	Catches large ball on rebound after first bounce	72–83

Note. Large ball is 8 to 10 inches. Wall target is 2-ft-square and 2 ft above floor. A wall pass is like a basketball pass except that you throw at a wall and catch the rebound. Most items come from the Peabody Developmental Motor Scales (Folio & Fewell, 2000).

Adaptations When Grasp Is Absent or Weak

When grasp is impaired, object control focuses on pushing or striking a light object with the hand or a head pointer. Games like wheelchair boccia, bowling, and shuffleboard typically permit use of ramps so that gravity can assist in moving the object. The games can be played on the floor or adapted to a tabletop with sideboards. Balloon tetherball is another game option (see Figure 11.18).

Two-handled paddles and other implements that can be held with two hands offer another alternative. These work well in balloon tetherball and tabletop games like shuffleboard and table tennis. If grasp is too weak, one or both hands can be strapped to the implement or special gloves worn with a Velcro surface that sticks to Velcro strips on the handles.

Use of Velcro or other kinds of straps to attach a paddle, racquet, mallet, or stick to one hand opens opportunities for many types of games for practicing striking skills. Creating oilcloth or plastic tablecloth shuffleboard or target patterns that can be moved easily from floor to tabletop increases game options.

Adaptations When Release Is Difficult

The ability to throw is dependent upon the emergence of voluntary release abilities at about 10 to 11 months. Although the hand grasp reflex is integrated at 3.5 to 4 months, the CNS does not permit voluntary object release until much later. In persons with brain injury that causes hypertonus (namely, cerebral palsy), voluntary grasp and release are impaired throughout the lifespan.

In such cases, the traditional teaching progression may be altered and emphasis placed on striking activities rather than those requiring a release. Striking can be directed at objects in the air, on a table with sideboards, or on a ramp. Either the hand or an implement can be used. Another adaptation for persons with grasp and release problems is use of yarn, sponge, or Nerf balls, a soft discus, or beanbags ("soft puts") when throwing. Floor targets are typically used. *Experiment with wheelchair placement in relation to the target or partner.* Determine which position is best for each student and record this information on the IEP.

Adaptations for Slow Learners

Most children needing adapted PE services are simply delayed in the emergence of grasp and release abilities and follow the developmental sequence of peers, with skills mastered 1 to 3 years later than classmates. Table 11.8 presents the order in which object control skills are learned by most students.

Adaptations for Throws While Seated

Many conditions prevent persons from throwing in a standing position. Roper (1988) is an excellent source for teaching the throw from a wheelchair. Particularly recommended is

Figure 11.18   Object control activities when grasp is weak.

Balloon tetherball

Tabletop activities

Bowling with ramp (chute)

Boccia with chute (height of chute is adjustable)

Two-handed racket for tetherball

Table tennis with double-handle paddle suspended from frame

extensive practice in trunk rotation, with the ball held in a position just behind the head. *The chair should be placed at an oblique angle to the direction of intended throw.* The sides and back of the chair should be as low as possible.

Assessing and Teaching the Underhand Roll

The first ball-handling activity is usually rolling an 8- to 10-inch playground ball toward a person or target while sitting widestride on the floor. For children whose orthopedic impairment prohibits floor sitting, a long table can be used, with partners sitting in chairs at either end. This adaptation allows a pushing rather than rolling pattern.

From rolling in the sitting position, children progress to rolling in the standing position. Ambulatory adolescents and adults needing instruction should probably practice from a standing position because most activities are done standing. They also begin rolling balls toward wall targets, bowling pins, and similar targets. For persons with severe disability, a long cord on the ball facilitates recovery. Through rolling, children have their first visual tracking activities. Stress to the children that they should *watch the ball move.*

The underhand roll from a standing position is used in many sports (e.g., soccer, goal ball). Therefore, it is important to practice this skill for distance and for accuracy. A standard for children ages 3 to 10 is to roll a ball 20 ft through a 4-ft target set off by two cones against a wall. **Performance criteria** on Ulrich's TGMD-2 for assessing the underarm roll are as follows:

1. Preferred hand swings down and back reaching behind the trunk while chest faces cones
2. Strides forward with foot opposite the preferred hand toward the cones
3. Bends knees to lower the body
4. Releases ball close to the floor so ball does not bounce more than 4 in. high

Assessing and Teaching Throwing

Throws should be practiced with objects of many sizes, shapes, textures, and colors. Each lesson should involve hundreds of practice trials, with variety provided at different stations. Use lots of different objects and interesting targets set at varied heights (see Figure 11.19).

In teaching throwing, the first objective is an efficient throwing pattern. The cue used to obtain a good pattern is "Throw hard." The pedagogy is demonstration of the overarm throw and/or manually guiding the student's arm through the correct pattern. No verbal corrective feedback is given, other than "Nice try. Let's do it again. Throw hard." Table 11.8 shows that early throws are assessed in terms of distance achieved. This table (like Tables 11.3 and 11.7) can be used as a pass/fail checklist or a TTP.

Throwing is comprised of several phases: (a) starting position, (b) preparatory or backward swing, (c) forward swing, (d) release, and (e) follow-through. In relation to each of these, specific body parts should be observed: (a) feet, (b) trunk, and (c) arm (shoulder, elbow, wrist, fingers).

Figure 11.20 presents the four developmental levels through which average children, ages 1 to 7, progress. Use of names for each level (casting, hurling, homolateral, crosslateral) saves time when describing performance on the IEP. Many adults with severe/profound MR use the casting pattern. Hurling and the homolateral patterns typically characterize clumsy persons of all ages.

Some persons, however, demonstrate components characteristic of more than one level. The performance descriptors in Figure 11.20 permit the teacher to check the movement components that best describe present performance level. Then, specific components that need work are listed when writing instructional objectives (e.g., Demonstrate Components 3, 4, and 6 of crosslateral pattern).

The overhand throw is assessed by using four **performance criteria** (Ulrich, 2000):

1. Windup initiated with downward movement of hand/arm
2. Rotation of hip and shoulder to a point where the nonthrowing side faces the wall
3. Weight transfer by stepping with the foot opposite the throwing hand
4. Follow-through beyond ball release diagonally across the body toward the nonpreferred side

In addition to task analysis and process assessment, the throw should be examined in terms of **product.** The usual product measures are distance and accuracy. Throws from base to base on a softball diamond permit good assessment of distance and accuracy.

Assessing and Teaching Catching

Catching entails a *reach, bend, pull* movement pattern. It also presupposes integrity of the visual tracking system. It is a more difficult task to master than throwing, and early learning of throwing and catching should probably occur separately at different stations.

The *principle of specificity* should guide the teaching of catching in that large balls demand movement patterns different from small balls. Catching lessons should involve practice with all sizes of balls coming in different flight patterns (horizontal vs. vertical) at different speeds. Little transfer of learning from one kind of catch to another occurs.

Soft and Hard Objects

Figure 11.21 presents levels in catching that can be used in describing present level of performance and writing objectives for the IEP. Remember that catching problems are *visuomotor,* and work with other team members in the development of comprehensive visual programs.

Performance criteria for assessing gently tossed sponge balls follow (Ulrich, 2000):

1. Preparation phase where elbows are flexed and hands are in front of body
2. Arms extended in preparation for ball contact
3. Ball caught and controlled by hands only
4. Elbows bent to absorb force

These criteria are for a 6- to 8-in sponge ball tossed underhand with a slight arc from a 15-ft distance. The ball should arrive at

Figure 11.19   Targets recommended for accuracy throwing and kicking.

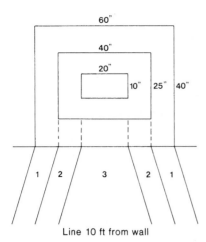

Project ACTIVE target for throwing and kicking assessment.

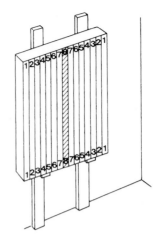

Rarick tennis ball toss target. May be used vertically or horizontally. Parallel divisions are 4.8 inches each.

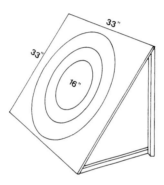

Rarick soccer ball accuracy toss from distances of 9, 12, 15, and 18 ft.

High-toss target for overarm throw.

Precision throw with seven scoring areas.

Figure 11.20   Pictorial checklist for assessing overarm throw.

Directions. Circle the level that best depicts the pattern you observe and underline the descriptors that can be used on the IEP to indicate present level of performance.

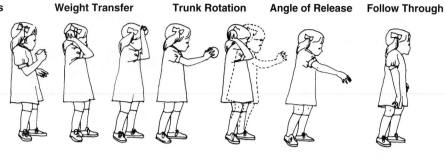

Main Focal Points	**Weight Transfer**	**Trunk Rotation**	**Angle of Release**	**Follow Through**

Level 1: Casting
Usually age
12 to 14 months

Feet stationary; no weight shift	No trunk rotation	Elbow extension supplies force	No follow-through; no involvement of nondominant side

Level 2: Hurling
Usually age
1 to 4 years

Feet stationary; no weight shift	Slight trunk rotation on backswing	Shoulder supplies force	Slight forward rotation; angle of release 80–100°	No follow-through; no involvement of nondominant side

Level 3: Homolateral Throwing
Usually age
3½ to 6 years

Dominant foot steps forward; slight weight shift	Slight trunk rotation on backswing	Dominant side supplies force; angle of release 80–50°	Some follow-through; no involvement of nondominant side

Level 3: Crosslateral Throwing (Mature)

Feet move in opposition to arms; good weight transfer	Full backswing trunk rotation	Total body supplies force; good coordination	Angle of release 45°	Good follow-through; coordinated involvement of nondominant arm

Figure 11.21   Pictorial checklist for assessing catching skills.

Directions. Circle the level that best depicts the pattern you observe and underline the descriptors that can be used on the IEP to indicate present level of performance.

Level 1: Passive Arm Cradle

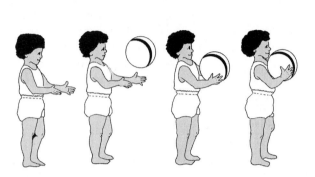

Level 2: Stiff-Arm Clapping

Descriptors: (1) making arm cradle, often with adult help, before ball is tossed; (2) rigid stationary position of feet and body; (3) no response until after ball has landed in cradle; (4) pulling toward chest.

Descriptors: (1) extending arms and spreading fingers, (2) rigid stationary position of feet and body, (3) clapping response when ball touches either hand, (4) gaining control by forearm pull toward chest.

Level 3: Initial Eye-Hand Control

Descriptors: (1) eyes tracking ball from far to near, with most attention given to the source of flight and own motor reponses; (2) body moving to position self in line with trajectory of ball; (3) arms outstretched while running to meet the ball; (4) hands only contacting the ball; (5) ball pulled toward chest.

Level 4: Mature Basketball Catch

Descriptors: (1) eyes tracking ball continuously through entire flight; (2) body moving to position self in line with trajectory of ball; (3) arms, hands, and fingers relaxed until time to catch ball; (4) catch accomplished by simultaneously stepping toward ball, partially extending arms, and spreading fingers; (5) following through by a slight flexion at shoulder and elbow joints.

a point between shoulders and waist, the easiest zone for catching. These criteria are applicable to assessing and teaching catches of different kinds of balls at varied distances.

Visual Acuity and Coordination

Visual acuity, which improves up to age 8 or 9 years, affects catching. Refractive and orthoptive problems (see Chapter 10) may require adaptation in testing and teaching. Check to see that glasses and protective eye gear are appropriate. Many persons with Down syndrome, for instance, are nearsighted (**myopic**). **Astigmatism** causes blurring of the ball. Poor binocular fusion (**integration**) is manifested in double vision (**diplopia**) and functional blindness in one eye (**amblyopia**). Many persons with cerebral palsy and mental retardation have **strabismus** (cross-eyes), which also affects visual acuity and tracking.

Practice in visual tracking of a suspended ball is a good lead-up activity for catching as well as for striking and kicking skills. A tetherball apparatus or a homemade system of balls of different sizes, shapes, and colors suspended at different heights works well. *Simply tracking a moving object is boring, so the activity should entail touching, striking, kicking, or catching the object being tracked.* Developmentally, **horizontal tracking** occurs before vertical tracking, and near-to-far tracking is successful before far-to-near.

Visual tracking should be practiced with (a) *ground balls;* (b) *straight trajectory balls* coming to knee, waist, shoulder, and head; and (c) *fly balls* with curved trajectories. Research shows that, in far-to-near tracking for catching, young children attend to the thrower rather than to the flight of the ball. Developmentally, children next are able to attend both to the source of the flight and to their own motor response. Only with much practice do children achieve the ability to visually monitor the entire flight and make discriminatory judgments with respect to velocity.

Assessing and Teaching Stationary Bounce/Dribble

Ability to dribble is an important factor in basketball success. Beginners can be assessed on this skill by the following **performance criteria** (Ulrich, 2000):

1. Ball contacted with one hand at about belt level
2. Ball pushed with fingertips (not a slap)
3. Ball contacting surface in front of (or to the outside of) foot on the nonpreferred side
4. Ball controlled for four consecutive bounces without having to move the feet to retrieve it

Once children can dribble the ball in place, they add a walk or run. This should be practiced in all directions.

Other bouncing/dribbling skills to be learned are (a) two-hand bounce and catch to self, (b) one-hand bounce and catch to self, and (c) propelling ball by means of a bounce throw or pass. This last activity is typically practiced against a wall and concurrently provides experience with rebounds. When this is the case, the task is called a **wall pass.** It can also be practiced with floor patterns and/or a partner.

Assessing and Teaching Striking

Striking is any arm and hand movement pattern (sidearm, overarm, underarm) used to hit an object. Examples are skills used in tetherball, volleyball, handball, hockey, golf, shuffleboard, croquet, paddle and racket sports, and activities involving batting (T-ball, softball, cricket). In general, these movement patterns are analyzed like the throw. The phases are (a) starting position, (b) preparatory or backward swing, (c) forward swing, (d) contact, and (e) follow-through. In each, judgments are made about action of the (a) feet, (b) trunk, and (c) arm (shoulder, elbow, wrist, and fingers).

Provide opportunities for striking objects of different sizes, weights, and colors with all kinds of implements. Lighting conditions should be optimal, with the student never facing the sun. Carefully regulate the degree of difficulty, keeping in mind the variables in Figure 11.22.

Batting is probably the striking activity most popular in our culture, with children exhibiting skill directly proportional to their parents' interest and willingness to toss them balls. Often, 3-year-olds use implements with large heads (rackets, paddles, special bats) quite successfully. Almost universally, the first striking pattern is a downward, chopping action. As bilateral coordination and strength increase, the swing becomes increasingly horizontal. The following are **performance criteria** for assessing striking a stationary 4-in. lightweight ball on a batting tee at the child's belt level (Ulrich, 2000):

1. Dominant hand gripping bat above nondominant hand
2. Nonpreferred side of body facing the imaginary tosser (feet parallel)
3. Hip and shoulder rotation during swing
4. Weight transfer by stepping with front foot
5. Bat contacts ball

A ball-tossing apparatus that can be regulated for speed is probably more important in adapted physical activity than for the tennis or softball team. If a sharing arrangement cannot be worked out, purchase is of high priority. Homemade systems of pulleys with suspended balls moving horizontally or vertically at different speeds also can be created. Learning to control the direction balls are sent is important. See Chapter 12 for ideas regarding timing and body positioning in relation to the arriving ball.

The principle of leverage (*the shorter the lever, the easier it is to achieve accuracy and control*) should be applied in selecting bats, rackets, and other striking implements. Hitting a balloon or yarn ball with the hand creates a shorter lever for beginners than use of an implement. Thus, balloon volleyball and movement exploration activities comprise an excellent first teaching progression.

Adapted games using field or ice hockey, croquet, and golf concepts, in which a ball or puck on the floor is given impetus, are sometimes easier for clumsy persons to master than

Figure 11.22 Variables to be adapted in teaching striking skills.

Striking Implement	Trajectory of Object Being Struck	Size of Object Being Struck	Object Direction in Flight	Weight of Object Being Struck	Color of Object Being Struck	Anticipation Location	Speed Object Is Traveling
Hand ↓ Paddle ↓ Bat	Horizontal ↓ Vertical ↓ High arc	Large ↓ Small	Right ↓ Left ↓ Center	Light ↓ Heavy	Blue ↓ Yellow ↓ White	How far must the performer move before striking the object?	Slow ↓ Fast

Hand

Paddle

Bat

throwing, catching, and striking games. This is particularly true of persons with grasp and release problems.

Assessing and Teaching Kicking

Kicking is a striking activity using the feet and legs. The popularity of soccer and football gives this skill prime importance. Kicking is analyzed in the same way as striking, using the same phases and body parts to guide observation. Likewise, the variables to be considered in planning teaching progressions are similar.

Table 11.8 indicates that children begin kicking balls between the ages of 15 and 17 months, shortly after they achieve stability in walking. Developmentally, they first kick a stationary ball forward along the ground and later propel it 12 ft in the air (see Figure 11.23). Next, they learn to judge direction and speed and become successful at running and kicking a moving ball.

The following are **performance criteria** for kicking an 8- to 10-in stationary playground, soccer, or plastic ball (Ulrich, 2000):

Figure 11.23 Dr. Dale Ulrich of the University of Michigan administers his Test of Gross Motor Development-2 (TGMD-2) to a student.

1. Rapid, continuous approach to the ball
2. An elongated stride or leap immediately prior to ball contact
3. Nonkicking foot placed even with or slightly in back of the ball
4. Kicks ball with instep of preferred foot (shoelaces) or toe

Verbal instructions are "Run up and kick the ball *hard* toward the wall." The ball is on top of a beanbag about 20 ft from the wall. The child runs 10 ft toward the ball. Many persons who are clumsy in hand-eye coordination activities seem to do well in kicking games. Try experimenting with kicking at various targets. Children also profit from kicking rocks, cans, and other objects as they walk or run. Soccer is the preferred sport in many private schools for students with learning disabilities.

Informational Feedback

Good teaching requires providing informational feedback. *Since most students can attend only to one or two correctional cues at a time, prioritizing which body part should be worked on first is important. Often, head control is selected as the focus, and students are told to keep their eyes on a desig-*nated target. For informational feedback to be helpful, students must be taught a vocabulary of body parts and actions. Movement exploration helps them to match words with feedback from other sources (vestibular, kinesthetic, mirrors, sounds). Taps on shoes and noise-making equivalents in gloves are especially useful in reinforcing correct foot/ankle and hand/wrist positions. For example, children, especially those with mental retardation or learning disabilities, often do not know the meaning of such cues as "Land on the *balls* of your feet."

With average performers, detailed biomechanical analysis is not necessary. Physical educators, however, must become skilled observers to give useful feedback. Most important, they must know how much feedback to give, when, and how. Some students learn best by seeing wholes, others by seeing parts. Learning style determines the nature of both demonstration and verbal input.

 OPTIONAL ACTIVITIES

1. Select one or more children with disabilities, ages 3 through 10; administer tests in this chapter to them, and write an IEP. Follow the format in Figure 11.3 for writing present level of performance, goals, and objectives.

2. For at least one of the children you select for Activity 1, help the child develop a portfolio showing his or her performance on each basic skill. Involve the family if you can, especially in taking photos of the child using these skills in many ways and meeting specific performance criteria. The child should do the printing to explain what each photo shows and to indicate future goals.

3. Use the content in this chapter to develop bulletin boards, Power Point presentations, or products of your choice that will benefit persons and help them better understand the values of physical education for children.

4. Make videotapes of classmates administering test items. Study the skill of the tester as well as that of the child. Also make videos of classmates teaching games that use these skills and of children in free play. Study the various motor patterns. Games can be taught to small groups of children playing in the neighborhood, at malls, fast-food restaurant play areas, or in practicum settings. Get parents' and children's permission before videotaping.

12

Perceptual-Motor Learning

Figure 12.1 **Perceptual-motor model (Ice Cream Cone Version) showing the many movement skill foundations (MSFs) that underlie success in a locomotor or object control skill or pattern. The cone is the foundation.**

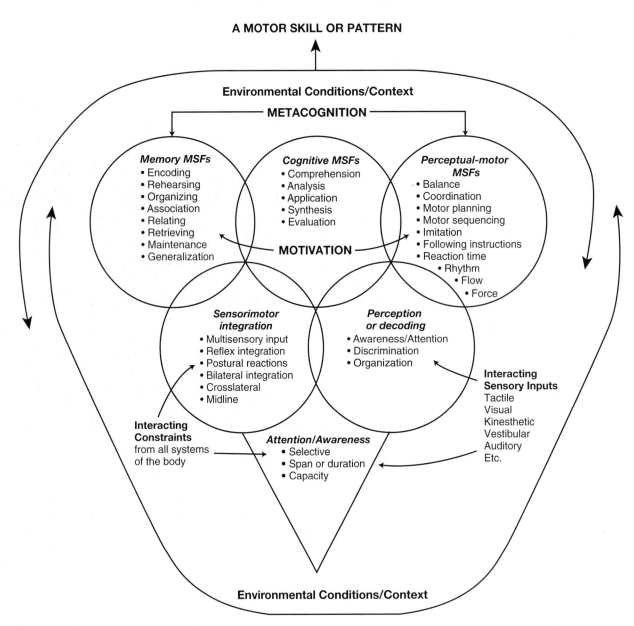

1. Reflect on perceptual-motor learning and its role in physical education. How might perceptual-motor activities contribute to NASPE standards (see Chapter 1)?

2. Study the perceptual-motor model in Figure 12.1. What are its strengths and weaknesses as a guide to this chapter? How might it be used with parents? Consider Figure 12.2 also.

3. How is the content in this chapter similar to and different from that which you have mastered in motor learning courses (Magill, 2001; Schmidt & Wrisberg, 2000)? How does the content in this chapter relate to APENS standard 2 (NCPERID, 1995) on motor learning and motor control?

4. Over 60 activities are presented in this chapter. Experiment with at least one activity for intervening in each perceptual-motor problem. Teach activities to children in either a land or water setting.

5. Discuss breakdowns under (a) sensorimotor integration disorders, (b) perceptual disorders, and (c) perceptual-motor disorders.

6. Explain ataxia, apraxia, and aphasia and read more about them in the library or on websites.

7. Identify and discuss perceptual-motor tests that can be used for comprehensive testing.

8. Explain how practice in basic game and dance formations contributes to perceptual-motor abilities.

Perceptual-motor learning, within the physical education context, is permanent change that occurs in underlying motor abilities and/or movement skill foundations (MSFs) that act (along with environmental variables) as the *determinants of the potential* of large muscle groups to perform sport, leisure, and fitness activities with skill (see Figure 12.1). Some professionals use the terms *perceptual-motor abilities* and *motor abilities* interchangeably as affecting skill (Magill, 2001), but abilities should never be confused with actual skills. **Abilities,** according to Schmidt and Wrisberg (2000, p. 31), are "inherited traits, stable and enduring, few in number, and underlie performance of skills." In contrast, **skills** are "developed with practice, modified with practice, many in number, and depend on different subsets of abilities."

In persons with disabilities, some of the inherited traits have been made less viable by disease, accidents, or genetic errors and may be acting as constraints to movement success; thus skills are harder to achieve through traditional instruction and practice. **Perceptual-motor intervention** is systematic instruction or therapy that uses integrated processes of sensation, perception, and movement to enhance the basic determinants of movement skill potential depicted in Figure 12.1. These determinants will vary with movement goal and level of skill to be acquired; hence, Figure 12.1 can be expanded or altered as the interventionist desires.

Perceptual-motor learning is an appropriate physical education goal for children 2 to 7 years old without disabilities and for individuals capable of cognition at the 2-year-old level or higher who cannot perform culturally normative motor activities with acceptable proficiency. Individuals who meet this latter criterion are often diagnosed as having *clumsy child syndrome, developmental dyspraxia,* or **developmental coordination disorder** (Cermak & Larkin, 2002). Individuals who do not learn well through the direct or task-oriented approach (see Chapter 11) are targeted for help with the specific problems that seem to interfere with movement skill proficiency.

In the perceptual-motor approach, we try to identify the **underlying abilities** that are acting as constraints to movement success. Concurrently, we analyze the environment to determine variables that affect these abilities. Perceptual-motor learning is similar to *motor fitness* in that both are concerned with balance, coordination, and basic abilities. Health-related fitness also relies on a similar underlying abilities approach.

Movement Skill Foundations

Movement skill foundations (MSFs), a term borrowed from Burton and Rodgerson (2001), are the physical, mental, and emotional aspects of a person that facilitate or limit performance of movement skills (Burton & Miller, 1998). Figure 12.1 depicts some of the MSFs that underlie mastery of movement skills. Sherrill has used the term *motor skills and patterns* throughout this text for consistency with the language of IDEA 1977 in the definition of physical education. However, she concurs with Burton that *movement skills and patterns* is a more appropriate term. *Motor* and *movement,* however, are used as synonyms in this text. There is a trend toward using **motor** to indicate neuromuscular or internal processes that are not observable and **movement** to indicate observable outcomes of learning (Burton & Miller, 1998).

In the past, MSFs were referred to as *underlying motor abilities,* but this practice generated confusion because **abilities,** properly defined, are

> general traits or capacities of an individual that underlie the performance of a variety of movement skills. These traits are assumed to not be easily modified by practice or experience and to be relatively stable across an individual's lifetime. The term can also be used to refer to a person's potential movement competencies as opposed to a person's actual movement performances. (Burton & Miller, 1998, p. 366)

Physical education research, for years, has shown that each of the MSFs listed in Figure 12.1 is specific to body position and environmental challenges. For example, there are hundreds of static and dynamic balances; performance of one is not necessarily correlated with performance of another. When physical educators work on balance or the other MSFs, they work on the specific types that relate to the targeted movement skills in the student's goals and objectives. Physical educators know that, properly taught and practiced, balances and the other MSFs improve. Thus, MSFs do not fit the long-accepted motor behavior definition of abilities, which are difficult or impossible to change. Burton's recommendation of the term MSFs is well founded and helps physical educators to become more precise in the use of terms important to their work (a long-accepted characteristic of a profession, the possession of a unique vocabulary).

> *Consider how you and classmates use the word ability. Examine motor behavior textbooks to learn meanings of ability and related words in the professional world. Devise ways to help yourself and others improve your professional vocabulary. Which MSFs do you believe can be changed through good teaching? Why or why not? Sherrill has not included all of the MSFs in Figure 12.1. Which ones are missing? Relate specific examples to children you have known.*

Perceptual-Motor Learning Model

In Figure 12.1 skilled movement is the outcome of a process that is pictured as a five-dip ice-cream cone. The cone or foundation represents attention awareness processes because formal learning cannot occur without them. Each dip of ice cream is analogous to a set of processes requisite to motor learning and performance. Perceptual-motor MSFs, although represented by only one circle, are not viable without the other MSFs. Hence, perceptual-motor training begins with consideration of each set of MSFs and the environmental conditions that influence them.

Figure 12.1 can be conceptualized as **central processing** (what occurs in the central nervous system during learning) or as outputs that physical educators should strive to measure in order to assess changes that are occurring through instruction. The ice cream analogy is used because, like dips of ice cream on a cone, the overlapping areas melt and blend together in motor learning. Everything, of course, is influenced by physical and human environmental conditions. Because learning is so complex, perceptual-motor intervention strives to provide intervention for one or two MSFs at a time.

The components under perception and sensorimotor integration were covered in Chapter 10. We accept the assumption that all systems in the body contribute to learning, not just the neural processes. However, the individuals who need perceptual-motor intervention most often have cerebral palsy and other conditions in which brain dysfunction is primary.

Physical educators often take perception for granted, but formal assessment should be used to determine whether perceptual problems are primarily tactile, visual, kinesthetic, vestibular, auditory, or all modalities combined. Memory, for instance, can be visual, auditory, or combination of sensory input. Cognition is improved best by visual imaging for some persons and by auditory imaging for others. Likewise, some children improve better in perceptual-motor MSFs when provided a visual demonstration while others may need tactile, vestibular, or auditory input.

Processes That Underlie All MSFs

All MSFs are subject to several overlapping processes: perception, attention/awareness, memory, cognition, and intersensory integration. These are explained, with applications to physical education, on the following pages.

Perceptual Processes

Perception, the process of decoding or obtaining meaning from sensory input, is a lead-up activity to problem solving. Consider, for instance, what children learn from such games as *I see something you don't see* or *I hear something you don't hear.* The environment is a room or outside area rich with either visual or auditory stimuli. The leader picks out some object or sound (the degree of obviousness dependent upon players' abilities) and tells players whether they are hot (close) or cold (distant) as they guess the right answer. This game can also be played with a picture that has lots of hidden or embedded objects or a piece of music like "Peter and the Wolf," in which the challenge is to identify different sounds or instruments. Hide-and-seek games and scavenger hunts also call on perceptual abilities; they can involve objects, people, or sounds. *Seeking usually involves moving around a large area so that big muscle exercise is assured as well as practice in perception.* How many games like this do you remember? What did you learn by playing them?

Games like *I See* and *I Hear* provide clues about visual and hearing impairments and whether or not persons are decoding and learning to name things at age-appropriate developmental levels. One measure of perception is the amount of time needed to process a sensation and derive meaning. Another is the amount of sensory information that can be simultaneously converted into meaning. To study problems of duration and capacity, teachers break perception into several subprocesses: (a) awareness, (b) discrimination, and (c) organization.

> *Try games like* I See *and* I Hear *with friends and children. Who appears to find the games easy or hard? Why?*

Awareness, typically the first level of perception assessed, is consciousness at the *there* or *not there* levels. There is light or no light, sound or no sound, smell or no smell, touch sensation or no feeling. Awareness is closely associated with **localization,** knowing where something is. Lack of awareness can be caused by a breakdown at the sensory receptor area (e.g., injury to the eye), during the information transmission process (nerve fibers), at the sensory integration level (noncortical area of brain), or at the perceptual level (cortical areas). Obviously, determining the site of breakdown is important for planning remediation.

Discrimination is multilevel, higher-order awareness or the ability to differentiate between many levels of some variable (e.g., colors, sizes, shapes, identities, similarities, movements, weights, speeds). *For example, children first learn to distinguish between colors (red, blue, green) and then hues or shades of the same color. They first learn to imitate up-and-down movements, as in bye-bye and pounding and shaking* *tasks,* and then learn to discriminate between qualities and can be taught to vary up-and-down movements by making them big and little, fast and slow, straight and curved. Discrimination is dependent on **acuity** (good vision, hearing, or kinesthesis), and sometimes *discrimination* and *acuity* are used as synonyms. Ability to discriminate between two things comes before three things and so on. Discrimination is typically measured by matching, classification, and imitation games and tasks (e.g., *Can you do what I do?* and *Follow-the-leader*).

Organization is the ability to synthesize stimuli into meaningful, conceptual wholes (e.g., trees into a forest, body parts into a person, spaces to be covered into game sense) and to disassemble the parts of a whole (e.g., the separate trees that make up the forest). Organization, for assessment and remediation purposes, is broken down into such subabilities as these:

1. **Whole/part/whole relationships.** "Can you identify this figure even though some parts are missing?" "Can you assemble parts of a puzzle to make a whole?"
2. **Figure/background relationships.** "Can you find hidden or embedded figures?"
3. **Object constancy.** "Can you find all of the balls and bats in this room regardless of color, size, background, and tilt?"
4. **Object position.** "Can you identify which object is rotated or reversed, near or far?"
5. **Sequences.** "Can you put several things in correct sequence or recognize when sequences are faulty?"

Attention/Awareness Processes

Attention and awareness are coupled because, without awareness, there can be no attention. Individual differences in attention affect both performance and learning. There are many kinds of attention, each of which may be specific to a sense modality. Let us consider (a) selective attention, (b) attention span or duration, and (c) limited attention capacity.

Selective attention is the process of blocking nonpertinent information from entering short-term memory. Because what is pertinent varies from second to second, this is an adaptive mechanism that switches attention from one input to another. This process is related to **cue selection** (knowing what cues to attend to).

Professionals often alter the environment to enhance arousal, attention, and awareness. Important variables are

U   Unexpectedness (surprise)

S   Size (large or unusual size)

I   Intensity (loud, bright, heavy)

N   Novelty (new or original)

G   Glorious color (favorite or outlandish)

N   Name (listener's name)

E   Eye contact (a long stare)

T   Touch (hand on shoulder)

These variables, which are known to be successful in capturing attention, can be remembered by the acronym: USING NET.

Attention span or duration refers to the amount of time an individual can attend to the same task. This varies by sense modality, interest level, motivation, meaningfulness of the material, and many other factors.

Attention capacity refers to the number of items or chunks that can be assimilated at one time. *For most adults, this is between five and nine.* An *item* is a letter, musical note, fact, or movement. A *chunk* is a word, phrase, or series of facts or movements. Attention capacity also denotes number of sense modalities that can be attended to simultaneously. Some persons, for example, can read a book and listen to music at the same time. When motor skills are taught by providing a visual demonstration concurrent with a verbal explanation, the teacher assumes that students can attend to simultaneous input from both sense modalities or successfully block out one. When this is not the case, *contextual interference* is said to be occurring.

See Chapter 20 for information on attention deficits and the diagnostic criteria used to identify attention deficit disorder with hyperactivity (ADDH). Chapter 21 also includes information on attention problems and describes specific interventions.

Memory Processes

Motor learning specialists are more likely than therapists to conceptualize disorders as problems of memory rather than perception. This is probably because learning is defined as a permanent change in behavior, and permanency is measured by retention or memory. *In actuality, memory and perception are linked because meaning cannot occur without memory.* Both processes (a) depend upon the integrity of input systems, (b) result in output, and (c) have duration and capacity deficiencies.

There are two kinds of memory: (a) short-term and (b) long-term. The **short-term memory** is a perceptual mechanism in that it is associated with central processing. It is also the source of cognitive, affective, and motor outputs. *Data can be held in the short-term memory store only about 60 sec before decay or loss occurs* (Magill, 2001). Thus, when trying to learn something new, we must immediately use an effective **rehearsal** (practice) **strategy.** We have only about 1 min to get the new information or motor pattern into long-term memory. **Long-term memory** is essentially a storage mechanism; schemas and representations of past actions are organized so that they can be retrieved and linked with new ideas and experiences.

Memory subprocesses have names to help teachers and researchers (see Figure 12.1). Assessment is directed toward determining which processes need specific help. **Encoding** is screening and assimilating new data into short-term memory, a task that requires both attention and memory. Encoding success is evaluated by asking people to immediately imitate a pattern that they have just seen or been coactively moved through. The discrepancy between the model and the imitation reveals the extent of encoding problems. Timing is very important when assessing encoding. Check what a learner can do 15 sec after a demonstration, 30 sec after, and so on. Consider also whether there is **contextual interference** between the time instructions are given and the task is performed. This is the term given to irrelevant stimuli, detractors, or interpolated activity.

Rehearsal refers to practice strategies, whereas **organization** describes planning strategies. Associating, relating, and retrieving can be considered either rehearsal or organization. All of these emphasize the importance of *active learning.* Thus, students are taught (a) self-cueing by talking aloud, (b) repeating aloud cues or labels stated by others, (c) associating or relating with something already known, and (d) imagery. Holding the endpoint of a movement for about 10 sec and concentrating on its feel before beginning another repetition is also emphasized (Hoover & Horgan, 1990; Reid, 1980). **Associating** or **relating** with something already known involves **retrieval,** pulling things from long-term memory and organizing them in new and different ways. **Maintenance** refers to periodically pulling something out of long-term memory and using it so the ability is not lost. **Generalization** refers to ability to apply newly learned tasks to many and varied situations.

Memory does not necessarily imply understanding. Memorizing a list or paragraph is easier than trying to understand it. Dustin Hoffman, in the Oscar winning movie *Rainman,* portrayed a person with phenomenal memory abilities who could not care for himself and live independently. Persons who have impaired mental processes but show genius in recalling dates, performing mathematical calculations, or playing musical instruments by ear are called **savants.**

Memory function (as well as attention, perception, and cognition) is directly related to age. The memory system operates much more slowly in children than adults. *This is probably because children do not yet know efficient rehearsal strategies.* When watching demonstrations and hearing instructions, they do not know what cues to attend to unless carefully taught. *Thus, cue selection is often a breakdown targeted for intervention in perceptual-motor training.* Children also do not use error information unless taught to do so. The younger they are, the more impulsive and less reflective. While still in the preoperative mental stage, children are motivated to have fun simply by doing. They do not try to analyze and improve performance unless systematically taught how to do so. Persons with developmental delays obviously need much help with higher-order cortical functions like analysis.

There appear to be no standardized tests or protocols for assessment of memory functions and processes related to learning large muscle physical education activities. You can, however, identify duration and capability deficiencies by experimenting with the number of words you use in giving instructions. You can also probe periodically by asking students to recall and perform a task that has not been practiced for several days. Later, you should repeatedly ask, "How do you remember? What strategies do you use?"

Cognitive Processes

Perceptual-motor learning cannot occur without cognitive processing. **Cognition,** according to Bloom (1956), includes five measurable processes: comprehension, analysis, application, synthesis, and evaluation. **Comprehension** refers to understanding of instructions. **Analysis** is ability to break a task down into parts and relationships, to consider variables and conditions, and to plan new combinations or orders. Think, for example, of the body parts and time-space-force-flow elements being

assembled and ordered each time a new balance, coordination, or motor-sequencing task is learned. **Application** is analogous to generalization; persons apply new learning when task and environmental demands are varied. **Synthesis** and **evaluation** are higher-order cortical tasks that entail the development of products (movement sequence, choreographed dance or aquatics composition, sport performance demonstrating game strategies) and the ability to judge these products according to standards or criteria. These processes are associated with **metacognition.**

The higher levels of perception, discrimination, and organization are often considered aspects of cognition. After age 7, in typically developing children, perception and cognition are functionally inseparable. Memory and attention limit perception, cognition, and all aspects of perceptual-motor learning. These, in turn, are dependent on language and movement for expression.

Theories that guide contemporary perceptual-motor practices tend therefore to be broad and to emphasize the interrelatedness of sensation, perception, attention, memory, language, cognition, and perceptual-motor abilities. For simplicity, this chapter blends cognition and language together. Each of the other components of learning is addressed.

The theories underlying perceptual-motor learning and training in contemporary adapted physical activity are different from those used by special educators in the 1960s and 1970s. Today's practices are heavily influenced by Jean Piaget (1952), Harriet Williams (2002), Ayres (1972), and proponents of ecological task analysis (Bulger, Townsend, & Carson, 2001; Davis, 1983; Davis & Burton, 1991).

Intersensory Integration

Intersensory integration, the ability to synthesize and use multiple sources of sensory information, is an important factor in perceptual-motor learning. Consider, for instance, the last time that you tried to learn a new motor skill or game strategy. You probably received visual input from a demonstration, auditory input from verbal instructions, and **combined tactile, kinesthetic, and vestibular (TKV)** input from different parts of your body.

Did you use these multiple sources of information equally, or were some sensory inputs more valuable than others? Did you consciously block out some information in order to concentrate on other input? Did extraneous visual, auditory, or other sensory inputs (e.g., temperature, wind, the constraints of clothing) annoy or distract you? The answers to these questions lend insight into your cognitive or perceptual-motor style. Whereas most adults are **mixed-modality learners,** *you might be a visual preference learner, an auditory preference learner, or a TKV preference learner. Are you?*

Personal understanding of one's memory, cognitive, or perceptual-motor learning styles is called **metacognition.** Learning styles often vary with the nature of the motor or cognitive task and environmental variables. Effective integration of multiple sources of sensory information and/or structuring the environment to provide the kinds of sensory input that are most useful are skills that distinguish adults with good motor coordination from those with coordination disorders. One purpose of perceptual-motor learning is to improve metacognition so that individuals can purposively adapt environments and sensory inputs to meet their personal learning needs.

Intersensory integration is age-related (Williams, 1983) and affected by the richness or poverty of the environment. *In most children, visual-TKV integration abilities are relatively mature by age 5, although some aspects continue to improve until ages 11 or 12.* Poorly developed auditory integration abilities explain why most children are not good listeners in early childhood physical education and prefer to find their own best ways of moving through trial and error or imitation rather than follow verbal instructions.

Auditory-visual and auditory-visual-TKV integration abilities are mature enough in most children by age 7 for them to benefit from the predominantly verbal instruction used by many teachers. Auditory-visual integration continues to improve substantially until age 11 or 12 and then plateaus. The slow maturation of auditory-visual integration explains why teachers should carefully plan the number and length of verbal instructions used to introduce physical activities.

In conclusion, most individuals are visual-TKV learners until about age 7, at which time they become mixed-modality learners. Some individuals (about 20% of students with learning disabilities), however, remain predominantly visual learners. Others (about 10% of students with learning disabilities) become predominantly auditory learners. Individuals with visual or auditory learning preferences tend to experience learning difficulties more than mixed-modality peers do. Difficulties typically relate to attention and memory aspects of learning, and often are manifested by behavior problems.

Learning Goals and Objectives

Impairments in perceptual-motor learning are difficult to identify and treat because of the interrelatedness of the many underlying abilities that enable movement. Assessment should result in prioritization of specific abilities and tasks. These should be **ecologically valid,** meaning that they relate to fitness, sport, dance, and aquatic activities that the student wants to master.

Goals can be written broadly, like the following: *to demonstrate functional competence in static and dynamic balances related to basketball skills; to demonstrate functional competence in motor planning and sequencing related to decision-making in age-related games; to correctly follow sets of auditory instructions related to class activities.*

Broad goals, in turn, must be broken down into specific objectives that clearly describe required behaviors and indicate evaluation protocol. Illustrative objectives are the following:

1. To maintain various static and dynamic balances [list them] for a set number of seconds

2. To demonstrate hand-eye, foot-eye, and total body coordinations by performing correctly (pass or fail) selected stunts, tasks, or movement routines [list these]

3. To correctly imitate total body movements or specific body part movements [list these] demonstrated by a model after a 15-, 30-, or 60-sec delay [specify]

4. To perform sequences of seven body positions or locomotor tasks after hearing this sequence one time, given a 60-sec delay between hearing the sequence and the start signal, and given two trials to achieve success

5. To demonstrate efficient motor planning in fielding balls rolled at random to the right, center, and left (12 balls, must touch or stop 9)

6. To respond correctly, within 10 sec, to each of 10 verbal one-word instructions for getting into various game formations [list these]

7. To demonstrate space perception by staying in the correct lane for 10 min of a soccer game

8. To demonstrate dynamic visual perception by kicking or throwing the ball to a teammate who is "open" at least 3 out of 5 times that such openings arise while the student has the ball

9. To rotate correctly from position to position in volleyball, with no errors or obvious confusion, for three consecutive games

10. To run toward the correct base, after hitting a ball, without helper cues, in three consecutive Challenger baseball games.

Revise these objectives so each one follows the CBS three-part system: condition, behavior, success criterion. Write some perceptual-motor objectives of your own.

Writing objectives to guide instruction requires identifying **specific areas of breakdown,** a term used to emphasize the fact that organizational processes within the brain have broken down. A special model has been developed, therefore, to help understand and remediate CNS breakdowns (see Figure 12.2).

The 4A Assessment/Intervention Model

Figure 12.2 synthesizes the information to be presented on the following pages. Although much information is included, the model is named *4A* to emphasize four new terms that are widely used among professionals: *agnosias, ataxias, apraxias,* and *aphasias.*

Inputs and central processing cannot be directly measured, except in laboratories. Teachers therefore focus on **outputs,** the observable behaviors of a student. Specific outputs are called by the same names in the CNS and Output columns, because the processes are inseparable. The 4A model, however, highlights names for general output problems (e.g., agnosias, ataxias).

Agnosias, Ataxias, Apraxias, and Aphasias

Agnosia, ataxia, apraxia, and aphasia are output problems that can be traced to perceptual-motor origins. Each denotes deficits in central processing caused by brain damage. The etiology is often unknown and undifferentiated.

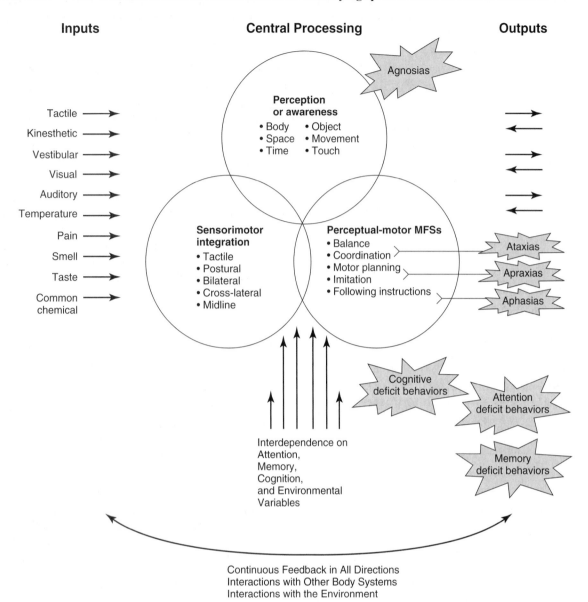

Inputs | Central Processing | Outputs

Perception or awareness
- Body
- Space
- Time
- Object
- Movement
- Touch

Agnosias

Sensorimotor integration
- Tactile
- Postural
- Bilateral
- Cross-lateral
- Midline

Perceptual-motor MFSs
- Balance
- Coordination
- Motor planning
- Imitation
- Following instructions

Ataxias

Apraxias

Aphasias

Tactile
Kinesthetic
Vestibular
Visual
Auditory
Temperature
Pain
Smell
Taste
Common chemical

Interdependence on Attention, Memory, Cognition, and Environmental Variables

Cognitive deficit behaviors

Attention deficit behaviors

Memory deficit behaviors

Continuous Feedback in All Directions
Interactions with Other Body Systems
Interactions with the Environment

Start your study of this model by noting the three columns: Inputs, Central Processing, and Outputs. Consider the complexity of the learning process, and remember dynamic systems theory. All of the systems in the body influence the CNS, and vice versa. The process depicted in the 4A model is not linear; it is multidirectional and chaotic.

Agnosia, a diagnostic term for perceptual disorders, is inability to recognize sensory stimuli when there is no known structural or physiological damage. The word *agnosia* is derived from *a-* ("without") and *gnosis* (meaning "knowledge"). A way to remember agnosia and to distinguish it from all of the conditions beginning with *a* is to associate the pronunciation (ăg-nō′-zē-ă) with *knows* (*noze*), a word that sounds the same while reminding us of its derivation. Agnosias can affect any part of the body or a particular sense (e.g., visual and auditory ag-

nosias). Agnosias for sounds and music are commonly called tone and melody deafness. Agnosias are particularly common after strokes.

Ataxia, from the Greek word meaning "lack of order," is defective muscular coordination, especially in relation to reaching and walking. There are many kinds of ataxia. Different parts of the CNS cause the condition (cerebellar damage in cerebral palsy; degeneration of ascending spinal cord tracts in alcoholism, syphilis, and Friedreich's ataxia). In each of these, the TKV sensations are impaired. Both balance and coordination are affected. Reaching problems are manifested primarily in overshooting or undershooting objects. Walking problems are evidenced by balance deficits and a peculiar reeling or wide-based staggering gait. To help you remember, think about a*tax*ia as very energy-*tax*ing.

Apraxia, essentially the same as dyspraxia, is discussed under motor planning as a thought-organization disorder that is particularly observable in movements that require correct sequencing and timing. Three words (*apraxia, dyspraxia, motor planning*) each include a *p*, the key for keeping apraxia (the *p* word) separate from ataxia (the *t* word) in your mind.

Aphasia, derived from *a-* ("not") and *phasis*, ("speaking"), can be sensory or motor or both. It refers to all kinds of language and communication disorders caused by brain injury, not just speaking problems. The brain injury can be developmental or acquired, as in the case of a stroke or trauma.

Common aphasias are **dyslexia** or **alexia** (reading disorders), **dysgraphia** or **agraphia** (writing disorders), and word-finding problems in speech, like the inability to name an object or action even though we know what it is. Aphasias can encompass any kind of language system, concrete or abstract.

In educational diagnoses, aphasias are often grouped together as **language and learning disorders.** They have no relationship to intelligence and are not caused by sensory deficits. Diagnosis of an aphasia first requires ruling out mental retardation, inability to see and hear, and lack of learning opportunity or motivation. Aphasia relates only to central processing in the association parts of the cerebral cortex. It is possible, of course, to have both aphasias and sensory input deficits, especially in persons with widespread CNS damage who are severely disabled.

Perceptual Disorders

The ability to derive meaning from what we see, hear, and feel is perception, linked, of course, with cognition. MSFs begin to develop shortly after birth, but assessment often is not accurate until language is acquired. Perception builds schema about the body, movement, space, objects, and time. Major breakdown areas of interest to physical educators are visual and auditory perception, body awareness, directional awareness, spatial awareness, and temporal awareness. Breakdowns in these areas (perceptual deficits) are called *agnosias.*

Visual and Auditory Perception

Visual and auditory perception includes the use of vision and audition to make sense of both the external and internal environment. Static and dynamic perception should be assessed separately. **Static perception abilities** can be assessed by (a) guessing games ("What do you see? What do you hear?"), (b) hide-and-seek games ("Can you find a hidden object? Can you locate the hidden source of a sound?"). **Dynamic perception abilities** are harder to assess but more relevant to physical education, where moving balls, as well as moving teammates and opponents, must be perceived and judged. Dynamic visual perception is especially important to sport success. To aid assessment, *children should be taught to talk aloud about what they perceive,* including estimates of speed and landing location, when told to visually track balls of various sizes, shapes, and colors moving at various speeds in different directions and kinds of arcs.

The process of perceiving and making judgments about object interception is called **coincidence-anticipation.** Dynamic visual perception is age related; most children are unable to track and catch balls that travel in an arc until age 8 or 9. Games should be devised that require visual tracking of all kinds of sport objects at distances commonly used in motor skill practice and games. Lots of time should be devoted to passing balls (throwing and kicking) to partners moving at varying speeds.

Body Awareness

Body awareness is the MSF to derive meaning from the body. Illustrative assessment questions are (a) What body parts is the student aware of? (b) What body surfaces is the student aware of? (c) What body positions (upside down vs. erect; leans in various directions; tucked vs. straight) is the student aware of? and (d) What movements is the student aware of? For each of these, determine whether problems are primarily TKV; visual; or auditory.

Body awareness relates to the elements of space and time. These, in turn, are perceived differently under various environmental conditions (light, dark; loud, quiet; soft, hard; stable, unstable; hot, cold) and in various states of motion (externally imposed, self-initiated; fast, slow; airborne; one-, two-, or three-part contact with a surface; linear, rotatory; in balance, out of balance).

Directional Awareness

Directional awareness denotes cognitive and body consciousness of up-down, north-south, in-out, forward-backward, right-left, and other descriptors of location or movement. Directional awareness becomes progressively keener between ages 2 and 8 years, *with up-down typically the first direction learned and right-left the last.* Sometimes, these MSFs are called *discriminations* to indicate a more advanced level than general awareness.

Spatial Awareness

Spatial awareness, which develops after directional awareness, is perception of space and the objects or forms that occupy space. The child understands space first as it relates to her or his own body, then as it relates to other persons and objects. Early awareness focuses on *large* and *small* and on making objects (including the body) fit into spaces. Awareness also expands from stationary to moving objects. In the well-integrated child, spatial awareness is both cognitive and **somatic** (relating to body). In some children, however, there is a split. The mind knows what is happening in space but the body does not, or vice versa.

Temporal Awareness

Temporal or **time awareness** is the MSF to derive meaning in relation to such qualities as fast and slow, now and later, long and short, continuous and intermittent, even and uneven, and set variations in rhythm like 4/4, 3/4, or 6/8. This kind of awareness is needed to succeed in reaction-time tasks and ball-handling activities that require judgments about how fast a ball is moving. Temporal awareness is intersensory, primarily visual-auditory, and very complex. Matching of visual and auditory input, as in judging speeds and distances, usually occurs by chance rather than ability until about age 7. Thereafter, temporal awareness slowly matures, progressing from discrimination to perceptual organization and cognition.

Activities for Perceptual Disorders

Within the physical education context, perception should be combined with big muscle action. Games, movement exploration, and drills in a variety of environments should emphasize *awareness* (there, not there), *discrimination* (different intensities, qualities, and sources), and *organization* (parts/wholes, assembly/disassembly, similarities/differences, correct/incorrect, sequencing).

1. Use follow-the-leader games in moving (visual perception) and in making noises or rhythm patterns (auditory perception).

2. Emphasize follow-the-leader games that entail space and time judgments, like squeezing through narrow openings, climbing over and under barriers, jumping over moving ropes or poles, and navigating surfaces that respond in unpredictable ways.

3. Use blindfolds for locomotor, ball-handling, and object manipulation games. Hitting a piñata or paper sack filled with goodies is fun. *Blindperson's Bluff* is an age-old favorite.

4. Use discover-and-gather games in which cardboard cutouts of different colors, sizes, and shapes are taped to a distant wall or floor. Challenge, "How many times can you run to the wall and bring back something red? Bring back only one thing each time."

5. Scatter parts of broken dolls all over the room and challenge, "Who can find a head, trunk, two arms, and two legs and build a body?" Repeat with other three-dimensional objects.

6. Scatter letters all over the room and challenge children to run about finding the letters to match the word you are showing or to form words and sentences of their own choice. Make sure lots of running is needed!

7. Cut pictures or greeting cards into several pieces and scatter all but one piece of each. Give students the one piece and challenge them to find the others to make a whole.

8. Sound different notes on musical instruments and have students respond with a preestablished stunt for each sound.

9. Bring pets to class and have students imitate animals while learning names for stunts like the dog walk (see Figure 12.3). Animals can also be used to increase awareness of others and how they use time and space.

10. Keep creating. There are hundreds of activities. Be sure that each uses the entire body and thus reinforces motor skills and patterns and builds fitness.

Sensorimotor Integration Disorders and Activities

Major breakdown areas of interest to physical educators are (a) intersensory integration; (b) postural or bilateral integration; (c) laterality, verticality, and directionality; and (d) crossing the midline. Sensorimotor integration disorders coexist with and are often indistinguishable from perceptual-motor problems.

Figure 12.3 Imitating animals while learning names of stunts like the dog walk enhances perception.

When clumsiness or developmental coordination disorder (DCD) of children without other disabilities is analyzed, **sensorimotor integration disorders** refers to generalized breakdown of all or most of the underlying MSFs needed to perform complex basic movement skills such as moving through obstacle courses, jumping, hopping, and game-related ball- and object-handling skills.

Intersensory Integration Related to Movement

Intersensory integration, the ability to synthesize and use multiple sources of sensory information, should be assessed in several environments that afford opportunities to interact with different combinations of sensory input. Obstacle courses in natural environments permit the assessment of many kinds of perceptual judgments. Likewise, use one-sentence movement exploration challenges ("Can you do this?" or "Can you jump?"). The child's motor response provides input into the quality of intersensory integration.

Next, evaluate the child in formal PE learning settings in which the goal is imitation of a model, following instructions with no visual demonstration, or simultaneous processing of a demonstration with verbal instructions. Pay particular attention to the *cues* that the child selects and the *rehearsal strategies* employed. Also try different kinds of *models* to see if this factor affects intersensory integration.

If intersensory integration is a major area of weakness, then check the use of each sense modality individually (i.e., *intra*sensory integration). In particular, *check tactile integration,* because this set of underlying abilities is strongly related to body awareness in various changing environments.

Activities for Intervention

1. Use exercise, stunts, and games in water (see Chapter 17). Stress the feel of *in* and *out* of the water; jump in and climb out again and again.

2. Use lots of rolling activities on different kinds of surfaces. Also use crawling and similar activities that keep most of the body in contact with a surface.

3. Use coactive activities in which two bodies or body parts touch and move in unison.

4. Use rolling activities on unstable surfaces, such as large therapy balls, that elicit protective arm extension.

5. Use barefoot activities on sand, carpet, grass, and interesting textures. Create obstacle courses that require moving across different textures.

6. Use games and relays that require putting on, taking off, and playing in clothes, blankets, or sacks of various textures. Tubular jersey is good for this purpose (see Figure 12.4).

7. Let children body-paint or sponge each other, wrestle in mud, or run in and out of showers from a garden hose. Activities that alternate getting dirty and getting clean are helpful in some kinds of tactile defensiveness.

Postural Integration and Activities

Postural integration refers to the smooth assembly of body parts to perform total body actions. **Bilateral integration** is the smooth working together of both sides of the body or of the top and bottom halves. Also included in this cluster is **unilateral integration,** the ability to move one body part independently without unwanted **overflow** (extraneous movement of other body parts).

Postural or bilateral integration problems are closely related to body awareness, specifically vestibular-kinesthetic awareness of where the body and/or specific body parts are in relation to space. Specifically, movement that shows laterality, verticality, and directionality should be assessed.

Laterality is internal or vestibular-kinesthetic awareness of the two sides of the body, a dimension of body image that evolves through experimenting with the two sides of the body and their relationship to each other. It is measured as side-to-side balance. Laterality is well established by age 3 in most children.

Verticality is internal or vestibular-kinesthetic awareness of up and down that evolves as the infant gains the body control to move from horizontal to upright positions. Some children do not seem aware of forward and backward alignments in postures. Others, when asked to raise or lower limbs a certain distance, do not have the kinesthetic feel to enable success. Problems in rise-to-stand positions and jumping relate to verticality because top and bottom halves of the body must work together.

Directionality is internal or vestibular-kinesthetic awareness of all of the different directions that the body and/or body parts can move. *Directionality* is a broad term that encompasses laterality and verticality. Remember that these MSFs are primarily perceptual-motor; they should be assessed by observing movement, particularly balance, under many environmental conditions that challenge balance.

Game sense, the ability of good athletes to be in the right place at the right time, is an outcome of good postural and bilateral integration. Game sense comes from within, reflecting integration of mind and body and total awareness of the body-in-space phenomenon.

Figure 12.4 Activities inside stretchable, tubular jersey help remediate tactile integration disorders in relation to intersensory integration.

Activities for intervention include the following:

1. Use activities that activate and promote tactile, kinesthetic, vestibular, and visual systems working together—tiltboards and balance boards, barrels, and balls controlled by you—because integration deficits are characterized by inadequate balance for independent control of such apparatus (see Figure 12.5).

2. Use hammock activities (see Chapter 16 on dance therapy).

3. Use traditional playground swings for sitting and standing or specially constructed ones for lying and four-point.

4. Use slides, seesaws, merry-go-rounds, and other playground apparatus that can accommodate nonambulatory children.

5. Use surfaces that respond in unpredictable ways to locomotor movements (rolling, crawling, creeping, walking). These include moon walks, mattresses, trampolines, and changing-consistency balance boards and beams.

6. Lift children into the air and play airplane in various directions.

7. Use wheel toys and vehicles (e.g., scooter boards) to move children across variable surfaces and inclinations.

8. Passively or coactively move children through several trials of up-and-down and side-to-side patterns. (This activity is used when the children cannot move themselves through these patterns.)

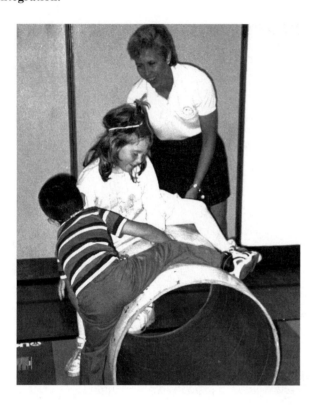

Figure 12.5 The teacher moves the barrel in unexpected ways to help students with bilateral integration.

9. Create reach-and-grasp and reach-and-strike activities that can be done from all positions (prone, supine, sit, four-point, stand) while stationary or moving.

10. With good personal flotation devices (PFDs) and individual monitoring, use water activities. Bilateral arm patterns usually happen spontaneously.

11. Use therapeutic horseback riding conducted by persons certified in this area (Biery & Kauffman, 1989).

Crosslateral and Midline Problems and Activities

Crosslateral integration, the most mature limb pattern, refers to right arm and left leg (contralateral limbs) working in opposition to each other as in a mature locomotor, throwing, or kicking pattern. Age 6 or 7 is when failure to exhibit crosslateral patterns is diagnosed as a problem. Crosslateral integration cannot really be distinguished from crosslateral coordination because crosslateral patterns emerge long after children acquire imitation and modeling abilities.

The MSF to move a limb across the body's midline is a special kind of crosslateral integration. Problems in this area are evidenced in ball-handling activities, such as failure to follow-through in the direction of a throw or a racket swing and difficulty in reaching across the body to field balls coming to the left or right. Standing at a chalkboard and reaching the right hand across the board to the far left to draw a long horizontal line is also a good test. Individuals with problems will walk or take steps as they draw to avoid crossing midline. The mature chalkboard pattern requires keeping the feet stationary. Many midline

problems reflect inadequate integration of the asymmetrical tonic neck reflex (see remediation activities in Chapter 10).

Activities for intervention include the following:

1. Use the previously mentioned activities that reinforce bilateral and unilateral integration. Many authorities believe that these build the foundation on which crosslateral efficiency is built.

2. Use agility locomotor activities that require moving as fast as possible around curves and obstacles.

3. Use exercises and games (supine, four-point, sitting, standing) that require the right hand to touch the left leg or body parts and vice versa. Sit-ups and toe touches with trunk twists are good. Integrate these into Simon Says games.

4. Use games that require crossing midline to pick up stationary and moving objects of all sizes and shapes.

5. Use games that require crossing midline to block or trap objects rolled or tossed. This can be done with hands, broom, hockey stick, or other implement.

6. Use a variety of objects in games that require crossing midline when throwing and striking.

7. Use games that require crossing midline, such as catch the snake (a rope carried by a runner), catch the stick (a broomstick released from vertical), catch the hoop, and catch the soft discus, beanbag, or ball.

8. Use games that require students to leap brooks or barriers.

Perceptual-Motor Disorders and Activities

Perceptual-motor processing varies with respect to amount of time that elapses between perceiving and moving. Task difficulty and novelty obviously affect delays. Much depends on whether the movement impulse or idea occurs within the student (i.e., spontaneous movement exploration) or is externally prompted by a visual demonstration and/or verbal input.

Balance

Balance is to body control what information processing is to cognition. As such, *balance* is the process of integrating sensory input from multiple sources (vestibular, kinesthetic, tactile, and visual) so as to plan and execute static and dynamic postures. Balance is a conscious state and thus capable of some regulation by the cerebral cortex. It is largely determined, however, by various automatic righting and equilibrium reactions. Dynamic balance has a very low correlation with static balance and should be assessed and remediated separately. Balance is extremely task specific, so success on one balancing task cannot be generalized to other tasks, even those of the same type.

Activities for intervention include the following:

1. Use the activities described under sensorimotor integration disorders.

2. Use activities in which the student, rather than the teacher, controls apparatus like tiltboards and balance boards and beams.

3. Challenge students to discover how many ways they can perform static balances. For example, (a) use one, two, or

Figure 12.6 Tiltboards, like the homemade one pictured, are used to improve dynamic balance and thereby enhance vestibular functioning.

three body parts; (b) use different surfaces; (c) alter positions of body parts at different speeds while balancing.

4. Ask students to imitate various static balances. The best known of these is the stork or single-leg stand with sole of nonsupport leg on the inner surface of the support knee; arms are folded across the chest, or hands are placed on hips. Two others are (a) tip-toe balance stand, with heels lifted and hands on hips, and (b) tandem stand on beam (also called heel-to-toe stance).

5. Perform static balances under various visual conditions: eyes open, eyes closed, and eyes focused on targets set at various heights and distances. Try looking at moving targets while balancing.

6. Try static balances while holding different weights in one or both arms or on the head. Use Velcro to attach weights to legs or other body parts.

7. Try holding static balances while raising and lowering the center of gravity.

8. Try dynamic balances under various conditions (see Figure 12.6).

9. Combine creative dramatics with walking a low, wide beam so that students portray characters as a story is read. Have these characters move at different speeds and levels and do lots of turns.

10. Teach gymnastics routines that combine various kinds of balances.

Coordination

Coordination is the CNS processing needed to assemble body parts into a skilled movement. For coordination to occur, there must already be body, object, space, time, and movement schemes stored in long-term memory from past experience. Of particular importance are postural, bilateral, and crosslateral integration and freedom from midline problems. (See Figure 12.7 for arm positions used in intervention.) **Coordination** is thus the cortical activity of short- and long-term memory interacting to refine schema pertaining to the body parts working together.

Coordination, like balance, is specific to the task. Thus, fine motor coordination (use of fingers or toes in manipulative activities) is not much related to gross or large muscle motor coordination (locomotor and object control patterns). This is recognized in standardized motor proficiency tests that have separate batteries or subtests to measure (a) *bilateral coordination* (tapping feet alternately while making circles with fingers, jumping up and clapping hands); (b) *upper limb coordination* (catching a ball tossed from 10 ft, throwing a ball at a target); (c) *visual-motor control* (paper-pencil and scissors activities); and (d) *upper limb speed and dexterity* (sorting shape cards, displacing pegs, making dots in a small circle).

Coordination is often assessed by speed, accuracy, distance, force, and flow measures. Each of these is a task-specific coordination and calls for a different kind of CNS processing. Much research is needed in this area.

Figure 12.7   Arm positions that children should be able to imitate. These positions should be incorporated into follow-the-leader activities with dramatic themes like imitating airplanes or robots. They can be done running, standing, sitting, or lying.

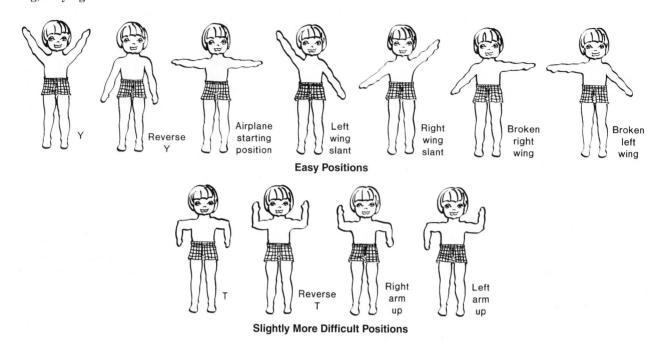

Easy Positions

Slightly More Difficult Positions

Coordination is interwoven with body composition and fitness attributes like body weight, strength, and range of motion. These can act as constraints or enablers. It is also dependent upon static and dynamic balances in the many postures the task demands.

Burton (1990) suggested two basic principles to guide resolving coordination problems. The *first principle is that movement coordination must be developed before movement control.* This principle applies to persons with disabilities who perform a coordination in a stereotypical pattern. For example, they can do the jumping jacks exercise only under certain conditions. If environmental variables are changed, they cannot adapt or generalize. The teacher therefore changes the jumping jacks task in many ways: (a) altering the surface by tilting it or making it soft or slick, (b) changing from land to chest-high water, (c) adding a drumbeat or music to guide the speed or rhythm, and (d) adding weights to limbs or having the person hold streamers.

The *second principle* is that *movement coordination and control should be developed in hierarchial sequences.* This principle emphasizes task-analyzing the body part assembly. The easiest assembly is movement of arms or legs only in a bilateral pattern. Next might be movements of limbs on right side only and left side only (a lateral pattern). Then come combinations: (a) right and left sides together or (b) top and bottom parts together. Swimming is typically taught in hierarchial sequences; other activities should be taught with the same care. Practice at each hierarchial level should include different body positions, speeds, rhythms, ranges of motion, and visual conditions.

Activities for intervention include the following:

1. Teach various coordinations in prone- and supine-lying to eliminate balance constraints of working against gravity.

2. Teach students to say verbal cues aloud as they move (e.g., "in-out" or "apart-together" for jumping jacks). Use words as cues rather than numbers.

3. Teach students to use visual imagery before and during attempting new coordinations.

4. Teach students to hold the endpoint of a coordination 7 to 10 sec and to concentrate on remembering its feel.

5. Alter practice conditions in many ways, including coordinations to music at different speeds.

6. For standing and locomotion coordinations, supply bars or apparatus to hold on to if balance is a constraint.

7. Supply videotaped and other kinds of feedback.

8. Make available time-out environments where students can go to practice in private or with a peer tutor.

9. Reward lots of trials and self-initiated efforts.

Motor Planning (Praxis) and Activities for Intervention

Motor planning and **motor programming** are global terms used in physical education to denote the organizational or executive activity of the neural systems that command coordinated movement patterns. There are many kinds of motor-planning problems. In one kind, persons can see a sequence of body actions and state correctly what they have seen (e.g., "Run to red line, duck under bar, climb up ladder, and then jump down"), *but they cannot execute the sequence.*

The inability to imitate or follow visual and verbal directions in executing a series of actions is **apraxia** (usually acquired) or **dyspraxia** (usually developmental). The ability to sequence develops with age, and inability to sequence should not be considered a dyspraxia until age 6 or 7. **Motor sequencing** is sometimes used as a synonym for *motor planning*

Figure 12.8 Motor planning MSFs are developed by two- and three-part sequences. Here, Dr. Gail Webster challenges a child to find New Mexico and do a forward roll on top of it.

because both abilities denote cortical command systems that activate patterns or chunk responses, rather than initiate single actions such as running, jumping, and throwing.

Of concern in motor planning is whether skills are closed or open. **Closed skills** are repetitive activities in a predictable environment. Examples are bowling, archery, and similar activities in which the target does not change. **Open skills** are those in a multiplayer game setting in which movements of the ball are unpredictable. Obviously, open skills require quick motor planning for success. Planning errors in such cases can be selective or executive. **Selection errors** are mismatches between the expected condition and what really happens. Examples are readiness for a straight ball when a curved one arrives or readiness for a smooth running surface when a hole suddenly appears. **Executive errors** occur when the CNS program is correct but the muscles do not do what they are told because of fatigue or other constraints.

Controversy exists over use of the terms *apraxia* and *dyspraxia* (Henderson & Henderson, 2002). Ayres (1972) popularized the term *developmental dyspraxia* and proposed many remediating physical activities. Apraxia is associated with left hemisphere stroke (Shumway-Cook & Woollacott, 2001). Better terms for IEPs may be *motor planning* or *motor executive* problems.

Activities for intervention include the following:

1. Practice increasingly longer sequences. Start with combining two things and then gradually add more. For example,
   a. *Run* to meet the ball, *catch* or field it
   b. Add to sequence, *"Look* around you"

c. Add to sequence, *throw* ball to proper place

2. Play Travel through the U.S.A. games on large maps made on canvas or painted on the concrete. Teacher or partner gives child two- or three-part sequences to perform (see Figure 12.8).

3. Play I'm Going to Grandmother's House games. The traditional game involves repeating words that others have said and then adding something new. For example,

   Lisa says, "I'm going to Grandmother's House [IGGH] and I'm going to take my pajamas."
   Abu says, "IGGH and I'm going to take my pajamas and my dog."
   Juan says, "IGGH and I'm going to take my pajamas, my dog, and my toothbrush."
   And so on.

   For the physical education setting, this game is changed to movement. The lead-in theme can be changed also. For example,

   Heejung says, "I'm going to a soccer game and I'm going to do three jumps on the way"—(she jumps)
   Bob says, "I'm going to do three jumps (repeating Heejung) and five push-ups"—(he does 3 jumps, 5 push-ups)

   And so on. The movement sequences can be done with or without words.

4. Play **Copy Cat** sequence games in which the teacher or leader challenges the children to remember and imitate, after delays of various lengths, various locomotor or body part stunts or sequences. Delays between the

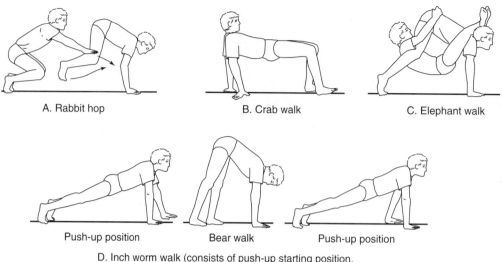

A. Rabbit hop

B. Crab walk

C. Elephant walk

Push-up position

Bear walk

Push-up position

D. Inch worm walk (consists of push-up starting position,
walking on feet up to bear walk position, and then walking
on hands to push-up position)

demonstration and the start signal might be 10, 20, 30 sec and longer, encouraging children to visually rehearse the sequence during the delay.

5. Find out the conditions under which persons best learn sequences: (a) visual demonstration only, (b) verbal instructions only, (c) simultaneous visual demonstration and verbal instructions, (d) visual first followed by verbal, or (e) verbal first followed by visual.

6. Find out if background music helps with motor planning. Experiment with different kinds of music.

7. Provide lots of practice in game settings that require *open skill proficiency.* Vary these settings to match perceptual-motor decision making with greater and lesser demands.

Imitation

Imitation (also called modeling) of a motor act, depending on how many parts are involved, is a complex perceptual-motor ability. Imitation of single hand movements (bye-bye) begins around 10 months of age. As children become aware of other body parts, imitation becomes increasingly sophisticated visual reproduction. Breakdowns in imitation are hard to trace. The origin can be input, sensory integration, one of the perceptual processes (awareness, discrimination, organization), or one of the perceptual-motor processes (balance, coordination, motor planning, and the like). The problem can also be attention or memory. See Figure 12.9 for stunts often used as assess and teach total body imitations.

Following Instructions

Assuming that there is no behavioral disorder, following instructions is a perceptual-motor ability. Breakdown sites for this ability are the same as for imitation except that *audition is the modality used.* The breakdown is often in the complexity of the command. *At age 5 or 6 years, most typical children can follow only three or four commands in sequence.* The more words in a command, the harder to follow. Auditory processing improves rapidly from ages 5 to 8. The ceiling most persons eventually reach for remembering sequences is *seven commands or tasks plus or minus two.* Teach children with problems to stand behind and visually follow peers with good skills.

Comprehensive Perceptual-Motor Testing

When the goal is to teach or improve motor skills and patterns, professionals must decide whether to focus objectives on skills or on the abilities and/or MSFs underlying the skills. The profession is divided about half and half on which approach to take. Chapter 11 described the skill approach. This chapter explains the abilities approach.

Perceptual-Motor Screening

The adapted physical educator must assume initiative in preparing materials to help colleagues identify children who may benefit from perceptual-motor training. The Sherrill Perceptual-Motor Screening Checklist, developed specifically for use by classroom teachers, lists behaviors commonly exhibited by children with learning disabilities and/or mild neurological damage and has proven successful as a screening device for identifying perceptual-motor awkwardness (see Table 12.1). This checklist should be filled out for each child early in the year.

Perceptual-Motor Testing for IEP Planning

Perceptual-motor screening is followed by comprehensive testing to identify areas of breakdown. Table 12.2 presents perceptual-motor MSFs measured by some of the better-known tests. The Bruininks-Oseretsky Test of Motor Proficiency (BOTMP) (Bruininks, 1978) was discussed extensively in

Table 12.1   Sherrill Perceptual-Motor Screening Checklist.

_____ 1. Fails to show opposition of limbs in walking, sitting, throwing.
_____ 2. Sits or stands with poor posture.
_____ 3. Does not transfer weight from one foot to the other when throwing.
_____ 4. Cannot name body parts or move them on command.
_____ 5. Has poor muscle tone (tense or flaccid).
_____ 6. Uses one extremity much more often than the other.
_____ 7. Cannot use arm without "overflow" movements from other body parts.
_____ 8. Cannot jump rope.
_____ 9. Cannot clap out a rhythm with both hands or stamp rhythm with feet.
_____ 10. Has trouble crossing the midline of the body.
_____ 11. Often confuses right and left sides.
_____ 12. Confuses vertical, horizontal, up, down directions.
_____ 13. Cannot hop or maintain balance in squatting.
_____ 14. Has trouble getting in and out of seat.
_____ 15. Approaches new tasks with excessive clumsiness.
_____ 16. Fails to plan movements before initiating task.
_____ 17. Walks or runs with awkward gait.
_____ 18. Cannot tie shoes, use scissors, manipulate small objects.
_____ 19. Cannot identify fingers as they are touched without vision.
_____ 20. Has messy handwriting.
_____ 21. Has difficulty tracing over line or staying between lines.
_____ 22. Cannot discriminate tactually between different coins or fabrics.
_____ 23. Cannot imitate body postures and movements.
_____ 24. Demonstrates poor ocular control; unable to maintain eye contact with moving objects; loses place while reading.
_____ 25. Lacks body awareness; bumps into things; spills and drops objects.
_____ 26. Appears tense and anxious; cries or angers easily.
_____ 27. Responds negatively to physical contact; avoids touch.
_____ 28. Craves to be touched or held.
_____ 29. Overreacts to high-frequency noise, bright lights, odors.
_____ 30. Exhibits difficulty in concentrating.
_____ 31. Shows tendency to fight when standing in line or in crowds.
_____ 32. Avoids group games; spends most of time alone.
_____ 33. Complains of clothes irritating skin; avoids wearing coat.
_____ 34. Does not stay in assigned place; moves about excessively.
_____ 35. Uses either hand in motor activities.
_____ 36. Avoids using the nondominant side of body.
_____ 37. Cannot walk sideways on balance beam.
_____ 38. Holds one shoulder lower than the other.
_____ 39. Cannot hold a paper in place with one hand while writing with the other.
_____ 40. Avoids turning to the nondominant side whenever possible.
_____ 41. Cannot assemble puzzles that offer no difficulty to peers.
_____ 42. Cannot match basic geometric shapes to each other.
_____ 43. Cannot recognize letters and numbers.
_____ 44. Cannot differentiate background from foreground in a picture.
_____ 45. Cannot identify hidden figures in a picture.
_____ 46. Cannot catch balls.

Note. Students with 10 or more items checked should be referred for comprehensive assessment.

Chapter 6 on assessment because it is widely used in making placement decisions. It generates data for writing objectives and selecting remediation activities in six gross motor areas and two fine motor areas. The Ayres tests remain popular with occupational therapists.

Movement ABC

The Movement Assessment Battery for Children (Movement ABC) by Sheila Henderson and Dave Sugden of England (1992) evolved from the popular Test of Motor Impairment

Table 12.2   Perceptual-motor factors that widely used tests purport to measure.

Ayres Southern California Perceptual-Motor Tests (1965–69)	Bruininks-Oseretsky Test of Motor Proficiency (1978) (Ages 4.6–14.6)	Henderson-Sugden Movement ABC (1992) (Ages 4–12)	McCarron Assessment of Neuromotor Development (Ages 3.5–18)
1. Imitation of postures; reproduction of 12 arm and hand movements	1. Running speed and agility—a 30-yd shuttle run	1. Manual dexterity	1. Gross Motor
2. Crossing midline of body; using right or left hand to touch designated ear or eye	2. Balance, static and dynamic	2. Ball skills	Hand strength
3. Bilateral motor coordination; rhythmic tapping, using palms of hands on thighs	3. Bilateral coordination—tapping and jumping tasks	3. Static balance	Finger-nose-finger
4. Right-left discrimination; identification of right and left dimensions of various objects	4. Strength—long jump, sit-ups, push-ups	4. Dynamic balance	Jumping for distance
5. Standing balance, eyes open	5. Upper-limb coordination, mostly ball handling	See Table 12.3 for detail.	Heel-toe-heel walk
6. Standing balance, eyes closed	6. Response speed		Standing on one foot
	7. Visual-motor control—hand-eye activities such as cutting, drawing, and copying		2. Fine motor
	8. Upper-limb speed and dexterity—hand-eye activities such as sorting shape cards and making dots		Beads in box
			Beads on rod
			Finger tapping
			Nut and bolt
			Rod slide

Note: Ayres's most recent test is *Sensory Integration and Praxis Tests* (SIPT). This test measures four factors: (a) form and space perception, (b) somatic and vestibular processing, (c) praxis, and (d) bilateral integration and sequencing (Ayres, 1989).

(TOMI) by Stott, Moyes, and Henderson (1972), later referred to as the TOMI-Henderson revision (Riggen, Ulrich, & Ozmun, 1990). The 1972 edition of TOMI had 45 items, 5 at each of nine age levels, and proved to be impractical for use in the field. In contrast, the Movement ABC has 32 items organized by four age levels so that the general movement competence of a child can be assessed with 8 items (see Table 12.3).

Worldwide, Movement ABC appears to be the most frequently used diagnostic test to identify children who are clumsy. An address for ordering Movement ABC appears in Appendix E. Movement ABC includes the ABC Checklist (48 questions to be answered by teachers or parents, based on observation over 1 to 2 weeks) as well as the ABC Test described in Table 12.3. The Movement ABC manual (Henderson & Sugden, 1992) is an excellent resource that teaches use of the instruments and provides strong coverage on the cognitive-motor approach to intervention.

McCarron Assessment of Neuromuscular Development (MAND)

The MAND (McCarron, 1982), developed and standardized on 2000 U.S. children and youth, ages 3.5 to 18 years, is better known in Australia than in North America. MAND is reported to be a more valid test for identification of motor impairment in Australia, for children ages 5 to 11, than are the BOTMP-S and the Movement ABC (Tan, Parker, & Larkin, 2001). The 10-item MAND includes five gross motor tasks (standing on foot with eyes open, then closed, on one foot, then the other; jumping for distance, forward, then backward; finger-nose-finger with eyes open, then closed; and hand strength, right and left) and five fine motor items. Item scale scores are totaled to yield a neuromuscular developmental index.

Task-Specific Perceptual-Motor Pedagogy

Task-specific intervention is more effective than general training. This principle of specificity applies to underlying MSFs as well as to motor skills and patterns. **Task-specific intervention** means that lesson plans address perceptual-motor weaknesses in specific physical education tasks that are meaningful to the student. The procedures in task-specific intervention are these:

1. Determine a perceptual-motor weakness that compromises physical education performance.

2. Identify a particular game or sport in which the student would like to be more successful.

3. Ask the student to help analyze all the ways that the identified weakness (e.g., dynamic vision tracking, dynamic balance) interferes with success in the selected game or sport.

Table 12.3   Test items for Movement ABC, formerly TOMI-H.

Age Band 1 Ages 4–6	Age Band 2 Ages 7–8	Age Band 3 Ages 9–10	Age Band 4 Ages 11–12
Manual Dexterity			
Put 12 coins in bank. Test each hand. Thread cube-shaped beads onto shoelace.	Place 12 pegs in holes. Test each hand. Thread lace in and out of holes in board. Test preferred hand.	Shift 12 pegs into new rows. Test each hand. Thread three nuts onto bolt. Test preferred hand.	Turn 12 pegs so opposite side is down. Use scissors to cut out elephant.
Stay inside bicycle trail on paper with pen.	Trace flower on paper with pen.	Trace flower on paper with pen.	Trace flower on paper with pen.
Ball Skills			
Catch beanbag thrown from 6 feet with two hands.	Bounce tennis ball on floor and catch with one hand. Test each hand.	Throw tennis ball at wall 6 feet away and catch with two hands.	Throw tennis ball at wall 6 feet away and catch with one hand. Test each hand.
Roll tennis ball into 16-inch goal from 6 feet.	Throw beanbag into box on floor from 6 feet.	Throw beanbag into box on floor from 8 feet.	Throw tennis ball at small circle on wall from 8 feet.
Static Balance			
Stand on one leg for 20 sec. Test each leg.	Do stork stand for 20 sec. Test each leg.	Do one-foot balance on balance board for 20 sec.	Do heel-to-toe balance on broomstick affixed to board for 30 sec.
Dynamic Balance			
Jump over cord set at knee height. Walk line with heels raised, 15 steps.	Jump into 6 squares on floor, 18 × 18 inches. Walk line, heel to toe, 15 steps.	Hop into 6 squares on floor, 18 × 18 inches. Balance tennis ball on board in palm of hand while walking.	Jump and clap while going over cord at knee height. Walk backward heel to toe on line for 15 feet.

Note: Administration requires 20 to 40 minutes.

4. Collaborate with the student in determining specific perceptual-motor tasks that need practice and various activities that will provide practice.

5. Help the student to write a contract in which she or he agrees to practice a specific task a set number of minutes or to do a set number of trials during each class and/or at home as physical education homework.

Usually several weaknesses concurrently compromise movement efficiency, but teachers should focus on one at a time. Individual tutoring or small-group instruction is necessary to remediate perceptual-motor learning problems, because such problems are complex and not easily eliminated. In addition, teachers should realize that participation in games and sports can enhance perceptual-motor learning if instruction and coaching includes references to seeing and hearing, attending to kinesthetic cues, and adaptation to learning styles.

Sport-Related Perceptual-Motor Tasks

The Sherrill Perceptual-Motor Tasks Checklist (SPMTC) was developed to help teachers understand how perceptual-motor training can be integrated with sports instruction (see Table 12.4). The checklist can be used for either testing or teaching,

but Sherrill recommends teaching through repeated testing and challenging, "Can you do this?" The SPMTC includes 10 perceptual-motor areas important to movement success. The tasks in the 10 areas can be reproduced on task cards to guide practice at stations. The tasks in each area are illustrative, and both children and teachers can add to the tasks and cover sports not included in the SPMTC. For example, children need to know the names of body parts to benefit from corrective feedback that refers to correct positioning of parts. Teachers use phrases such as *cock your wrist, run on the balls of your feet,* and *tuck your chin;* children often understand these verbally but lack the mind-body unity to make their body parts comply.

The last task on the SPMTC, lateral dominance, has not been discussed yet in this chapter. **Lateral dominance** (or preference) refers to the ability to use one side of the body more efficiently than the other. In sport this is desirable, but the other side should be capable of coordinated skills also. Usually the concern is with handedness. The relationship between handedness and motor proficiency is not well understood, *but left-handedness is more prevalent among children with learning difficulties than is typical.* Likewise, **mixed dominance** (e.g., being left-handed, right-eyed, and left-footed) is more common. Contemporary theorists do not recommend

Table 12.4   Sherrill Task-Specific Approach to Teaching and Testing.

Checklist for Teaching-Testing Perceptual-Motor Tasks

Name _____ Date _____

I. Major Task: Identification of Body Parts.
Other tasks: Auditory discrimination, memory, and sequencing.

A. Given cues to touch body parts, the student can:
_____ 1. Touch body parts one by one in response to one-word directions:

_____ Mouth	_____ Ankles
_____ Elbow	_____ Head
_____ Eyes	_____ Hips
_____ Feet	_____ Shoulders
_____ Ears	_____ Chin
_____ Wrist	_____ Waist

_____ 2. Touch two body parts simultaneously.
_____ 3. Touch five body parts in the same sequence as they are named by the teacher.
_____ 4. Do all of the above with eyes closed.

II. Major Task: Right-Left Discriminations with Body Parts.
Other tasks: Auditory discrimination, memory, and sequencing.

A. Given cues to touch body parts, the student can:
_____ 1. Use the right hand to touch parts named on right side.
_____ 2. Use the right hand to touch parts named on left side (this involves crossing the midline and is more difficult than item 1).
_____ 3. Use the left hand to touch parts named on the left side.
_____ 4. Use the left hand to touch parts named on the right side.

B. Given opportunities to play Simon Says, the student can follow commands at least 90% of game time.

C. Given cues, the student can:
_____ 1. Use the right hand to touch body parts on the right side of partner.
_____ 2. Use the right hand to touch body parts on the left side of partner.

III. Major Task: Changing Positions in Space.
Other tasks: Auditory discrimination, memory, and sequencing.

A. Given instructions, the student can:
_____ 1. Stand in front of, in back of, to the right of, and to the left of a chair or a softball base.
_____ 2. Run to first base on a softball diamond.
_____ 3. Demonstrate where the right fielder, the left fielder, and the center fielder stand on a softball diamond.
_____ 4. Play a running game with 20 other students for 5 min without bumping into another student.
_____ 5. Climb over a rope or horizontal bar and duck under it in an obstacle course.

B. Given verbal directions in warm-ups *without the benefit of demonstration,* the student can:
_____ 1. Assume the following basic exercise positions: supine lying, hook lying, prone lying, long sitting, hook sitting, cross-legged sitting, kneel, half-kneel, squat, half-squat.
_____ 2. Demonstrate the following different foot positions in response to commands: wide base, narrow base, forward-backward stance, square stance, closed stance, open stance.
_____ 3. Perform a specific exercise seven times, use the eighth count to return to starting position, and stop precisely on the stop signal. For example,
_____ Seven walks and stop
_____ Seven stretches and stop
_____ Seven jumps and stop

IV. Major Task: Crossing Midline for Right Handers.
Other tasks: Auditory discrimination, memory, and sequencing. (Insert appropriate distances)

A. Given verbal instructions with no demonstration, the student can:
_____ 1. Throw a ball diagonally to a target on the far left.
_____ 2. Field a ball on the ground that is approaching the left foot.
_____ 3. Perform a backhand drive in tennis.
_____ 4. Catch a ball that rebounds off the wall to the left.
_____ 5. Toss a tennis ball vertically upward in front of left shoulder.

V. Major Task: Imitation of Movements; Motor Planning.
Other tasks: Visual discrimination, memory, and sequencing.

A. Given opportunities to imitate the teacher in an **Angel-in-the-Snow** sequence, the student can:
1. Imitate **bilateral** movements.
_____ a. Move both arms apart and together while legs remain stationary.
_____ b. Move both legs apart and together while arms remain stationary.
_____ c. Move all four limbs apart and together simultaneously.
_____ d. Move any three limbs apart and together simultaneously while the fourth limb remains stationary.
2. Imitate **unilateral** movements.
_____ a. Move the right arm and right leg apart and together simultaneously while the left limbs remain stationary.
_____ b. Move the left arm and left leg apart and together simultaneously while the right limbs remain stationary.
3. Imitate **crosslateral** movements.
_____ a. Move the right arm and left leg apart and together simultaneously while the other limbs remain stationary.

Table 12.4   Continued.

_____ b. Move the left arm and right leg apart and together simultaneously while the other limbs remain stationary.

B. Given opportunities to imitate the arm movements in Figure 12.7, without verbal instructions, the student can:

_____ 1. Start and stop both arms simultaneously.

_____ 2. Correctly imitate six of nine arm movements.

C. Given opportunities to imitate the arm movements of the teacher who is holding a racket, the student can correctly imitate, while holding a racket, 6 out of 11 arm movements in Figure 12.7.

D. Given instructions to play the **Copy Cat Game,** student will watch teacher perform a sequence of stunts, wait 30 sec, and then perform the sequence in correct order.

    a. Three stunts (tiptoe walk, dog walk, sit-up)

    b. Four stunts

    c. Five stunts

VI. Major Task: Imitation of Sport Movements.

Other tasks: Visual discrimination, memory, and sequencing.

A. Given opportunities to imitate the movements of the teacher, without verbal instructions, the student with a tennis ball can:

_____ 1. Imitate the teacher's movements precisely, using the right arm when the teacher does.

_____ 2. Toss the ball into the air to exactly the same height as the teacher tosses the ball. Stand under a rope to help assess height.

_____ 3. Bounce the ball so it lands on the floor in precisely the same place as does the teacher's (in front of right foot, to the left side of left foot, and so on).

_____ 4. Bounce the ball so that it rises to the same height as the teacher's before it is caught.

_____ 5. Throw the ball so that it touches a wall target in a designated place.

VII. Major Task: Visual Tracking in Sports.

Other tasks: Visual discrimination, memory, and sequencing.

A. Told to track beanbags (easier than flying balls) thrown by teacher or partner, the student can:

_____ 1. Run or move the body so that the beanbag hits some part of him or her as it falls.

_____ 2. Run or move the body so that he or she catches 7 of 10 beanbags before they fall.

_____ 3. Run or move the body so that he or she strikes the beanbag with some kind of a racket, paddle, or bat before it falls.

B. Given opportunities to track 30 ground balls being rolled toward him or her from a 15-ft distance, the student can:

_____ 1. Stop 8 of 10 balls coming to the right.

_____ 2. Stop 8 of 10 balls coming to the midline.

_____ 3. Stop 8 of 10 balls coming to the left.

VIII. Major Task: Static Balances.

Other tasks: Visual or auditory.

A. Given opportunities to explore static balances, the student can:

_____ 1. Balance on one foot with eyes open for 10 sec.

_____ 2. Balance on tiptoes with eyes open for 10 sec.

_____ 3. Balance on a stick, a rock, or a log with one foot.

_____ 4. Perform a knee scale.

_____ 5. Balance while maintaining a squatting position.

_____ 6. Assume a tripod balance or head stand.

_____ 7. Repeat each of the above with eyes closed.

IX. Major Task: Dynamic Balances.

Other tasks: Visual or auditory.

A. Given opportunities to explore dynamic balances, the student can:

_____ 1. Walk a straight line in heel-to-toe fashion for six steps.

_____ 2. Jump backward five times and stop without losing balance.

_____ 3. Walk six steps on a low balance beam while holding a 10-lb weight in one arm.

_____ 4. Alternate walking and squatting on a low balance beam. Use a step-step-step-squat sequence and repeat three times.

_____ 5. Turn completely around three times while walking a low beam.

_____ 6. Play a game that requires fast starts and stops (e.g., _Red Light, Green Light_) for 3 min without falling.

_____ 7. Maintain balance on a tiltboard or stabilometer for 20 sec.

X. Major Tasks: Lateral Dominance in Sports.

Other tasks: Visual or auditory.

A. Given opportunities to explore movement possibilities with beanbags, balls, ropes, bats, pencils, and other implements, the student can:

_____ 1. Demonstrate more skill with the preferred hand than the nonpreferred hand.

    _____ 10 balls tossed from 10 ft

        Record whether caught by R or L hand

    _____ 5 kinds of striking apparatus

        Record whether held by R or L hand

    _____ 10 target throws, beanbags on floor

        Record whether thrown with R or L hand

_____ 2. Exhibit a consistent preference for one hand over the other.

remediation of left-handedness or mixed dominance. They do recommend working with children who seem to have no preference in handedness and children who are especially awkward with the nonpreferred hand.

Teaching Game Formations

Getting students into game formations is a difficult task. This is because persons with disabilities often cannot visually image what they are supposed to do when the teacher says, "Form a circle" or "Everyone stand in two-deep formation on the line." Getting into various game formations is thus important perceptual-motor learning. Likewise, responding correctly to instructions like "Move to the left" and "Go counterclockwise" requires careful teaching.

Design lessons that teach students the names of formations and provide practice for getting into formations with increasingly larger numbers. This practice results not only in perceptual-motor learning but also in improved social awareness and cooperation. Begin with groups of three or four. Give the same verbal cues each time, followed by a count from 1 to 10. Teach students that they must be in the new formation by the count of 10 and that they should help anyone having trouble.

Circles and lines on the floor help beginners, but eventually, form or shape perception should be good enough to enable success without floor cues. Table 12.5 presents the basic game and dance formations that students should learn. The drills or movement exploration column contains the verbal cues that initiate movement.

Children enjoy fast-paced drills to these cues, and various routines can be developed. For example:

Single circle 1–2–3–4–5–6–7–8–9–10

Facing in

Facing out

Facing in, walk forward

Facing out, jump to place

Facing in, clap-clap-clap-clap

Single line 1–2–3–4–5–6–7–8–9–10

Run to the wall

Single circle 1–2–3–4–5–6–7–8–9–10

Easy to Hard Formations

The scattered or random formation is the easiest because it permits persons to stand wherever they wish as long as they do not touch anyone else. This structure avoids discipline problems and teaches respect for each other's space. The verbal cue is "Find your own space. Good, now stretch in all directions to show that you cannot touch anyone. Great, you each have your own space."

To play games, however, structured formations must be learned. Circles and lines are easiest, and most primary school games use these. Files, shuttles, and target-shooting and square dance formations are progressively harder. When girls and boys are partners, the girls traditionally stand on the right.

Two-Deep: Beginning Partner Work

The "two-deep" verbal cue is especially useful and can be used with a circle or line. It comes from the game *Two-Deep*, in which a circle is formed by twosomes, standing one behind the other and facing in. On the outside of the circle is an "It" (person who is chasing) and a target person who is fleeing. To avoid being tagged, the target person can duck inside the circle and stand in front of any twosome. Since there can only be two people in two-deep, the one on the outside becomes the new runner who is chased. The game can also be played as three- or four-deep. It is fun, but the value lies in being able to use the cue "two-deep" whenever you want to structure a partner activity. This also serves as a lead-up to teaching the file or column formation.

Counterclockwise Direction Dominates

Telling children to move right and left often results in bedlam, particularly in activities in which partners are facing. Most experienced teachers therefore use clockwise (CW) and counterclockwise (CCW) terminology. This avoids right-left discrimination problems and also reinforces clock-reading skills.

The counterclockwise direction should be emphasized because this is the traditional direction for running laps around a field, performing partner folk dances, and moving around bases in softball. CCW rotation from station to station helps students to internalize and generalize this. Students typically need lots of practice and structure in moving from one place to another because this skill requires much perceptual-motor processing.

Novel Floor Patterns to Reinforce Academics

Adhesive-paper shapes (circles, triangles, squares) on the floor reinforce form perception and permit lots of games that teach CW, CCW, right-left, and north-south-east-west directions. Maps of states and countries on the floor create similar opportunities. Some gymnasiums have the alphabet in cursive writing on the floor, with all letters 5 to 8 ft high. Various games entail running the letters of the alphabet with the same self-talk used as when learning to write at a desk (e.g., *up, down, up,* and *horizontal* for a cursive *b*).

Teaching Perception Through Volleyball

The lead-up games to volleyball, which are begun at about the third-grade level, can be used to reinforce right-left discriminations and to provide practice in visual pursuit and/or tracking. For most children, these lead-up games represent their initial experience in tracking large objects that move through a predictable low-high-low arc and in catching and/or striking balls that *descend* rather than ascend (like a bouncing ball) or approach horizontally (like a thrown ball).

Newcomb, the best-known lead-up game to volleyball, substitutes throwing and catching various objects over a net for volleying. It is based on the assumption that tracking and catching a descending ball are prerequisites to tracking and striking (volleying). Certainly, catching and throwing are more familiar skills than volleying and serving. *Visual tracking* is an important contribution of volleyball at the elementary grade level.

Table 12.5   Basic game and dance formations.

Formation	Drills or Movement Exploration	Games	Dances
Single circle X X X X X X X X	Facing in Facing out Facing counterclockwise (CCW) Facing clockwise (CW) With "It" in the middle With "It" as part of the circle	Parachute activities Hot Potato Cat and Rat Duck, Duck, Goose Mickey Mouse (Spaceman) With "It" in middle, Circle Call-Ball, Catch the Cane	Farmer in the Dell Hokey-Pokey Loopty Loo Did You Ever See a Lassie? Go In and Out the Windows Captain Jinks Cshebogar
Double circle or two-deep	Both facing in (also called two-deep) Both facing out Facing partner Facing in, side by side Facing out, side by side Facing CCW, side by side Facing CW, side by side Boy rotates CCW, girl remains stationary Girl rotates CCW, boy remains stationary Grand right and left, girl rotates CCW while boy rotates CW	Two-Deep Caboose Dodgeball Run for Your Supper	How D'Ye Do, My Partner Seven Steps Hot Cross Buns Pop Goes the Weasel Skip to My Lou Bleking American Schottische Patticake Polka
Single line or row XXXXX X	Side by side Straight versus crooked Curved Staggered With teacher in front	Mother, May I? Red Light, Green Light Fire Engine (Beef Steak) Midnight	Technique classes in modern dance, ballet, tap dance
Double line or two-deep XXXXX XXXXX	Side by side Two-deep, all facing front Two-deep, all facing back Two-deep, facing partner Two-deep, back to back With net between lines	Brownies and Fairies Crows and Cranes Steal the Bacon Line Dodgeball Volleyball Newcomb	Crested Hen (three students) I See You (any number) Troika (three students)
Single file or column X X X	Each child behind the other Straight versus crooked "It" in front of file Everyone in file facing forward	Follow the leader Huntsman Relays Basketball shooting games	Marching to rhythm
Double file or longways set XX XX XX	Each child and a partner behind lead couple Girl traditionally on the right	Three-legged relay Partner relay Tandem relays	A Hunting We Will Go London Bridge Paw Paw Patch
Shuttle formation drill and relays: XXXXX XXXXX	Two files, facing one another	Throw object and shuttle to end of own file *or* to end of the other file	Good use of space in continuous practice of locomotor skills
Target shooting O X X X X X X	Two files, diagonally facing same goal, like a basket or wall target	Throw and shuttle to end of other file	

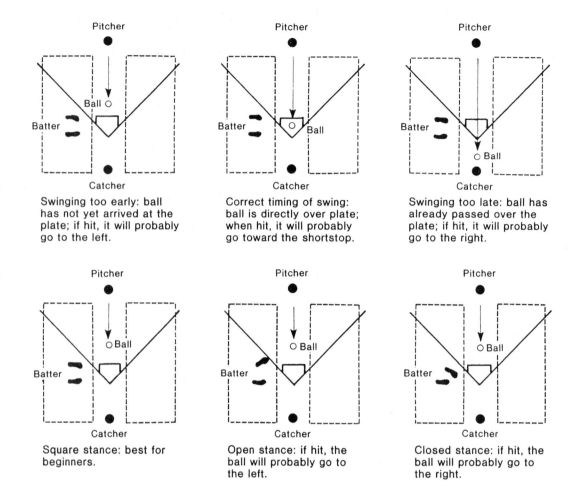

Swinging too early: ball has not yet arrived at the plate; if hit, it will probably go to the left.

Correct timing of swing: ball is directly over plate; when hit, it will probably go toward the shortstop.

Swinging too late: ball has already passed over the plate; if hit, it will probably go to the right.

Square stance: best for beginners.

Open stance: if hit, the ball will probably go to the left.

Closed stance: if hit, the ball will probably go to the right.

Children should not be rushed into mastery of the relatively difficult skills of volleying and serving. Nor should individual differences be ignored and all children forced to use the same skills in a game setting. When a volleyball approaches, each child should have options: to catch the ball and return it across the net with a throw or to volley it across. Likewise, the child whose turn it is to serve may choose to put the ball into play with a throw from behind the baseline or a serve from any place on the right-hand side of the court. Thus, in the early stages of learning the serve, some children may be only three giant steps behind the net, while others may have the coordination and arm and shoulder strength to achieve success from behind the baseline. *Balloons* can be substituted for volleyballs with the very young or very weak.

Team games teach spatial awareness through **position play.** Playing a particular position on the court and rotating from position to position reinforces the concepts of right, center, and left and of front and back. Starting with a small number of children on a team and gradually increasing the number of team members is educationally sound.

Rotation in volleyball depends on the child's ability to make right-left discriminations; ability to walk or move sideward, backward, and forward; and *comprehension of clockwise as a direction.* Teachers who care about transfer of learning and

wish to save children with directional deficits embarrassment on the playground use the concept of rotation in the classroom. They have the child sitting in the *RB* (right back) chair stand, recite, and then allow everyone to rotate in a clockwise position so that a new child is *RB* and preparing to recite.

Teaching Perception Through Softball

A child's success or lack of success in softball, kickball, and baseball may be an excellent indicator of perceptual-motor efficiency, especially with respect to right-left discriminations, crossing the midline, and visual pursuits. No other physical activity offers richer opportunities for perceptual-motor training.

First, the understanding of the diamond and the positions of the players on the field requires the ability to make right-left discriminations. The concept of infield versus outfield offers a new dimension of spatial awareness. The expectation that each player *cover* a particular area of the field and *back up* other players is based upon spatial awareness. Bases are run in a *counterclockwise* direction. Pitches are described as inside, outside, high, low, and curved to the right or left. Decision making by a fielder as to where to throw the ball is based upon visual memory of sequences. Is there a player on third base? On first and third? On all the bases? Where should the ball be thrown first? The batter must make decisions with respect to directions also. If there is a runner on third base, where should the batter hit the ball? If there are runners on first and second base, where should the ball be hit? And so on, *ad infinitum.*

Batting depends not only on visual perception but also on knowledge of timing and stance (see Figure 12.10). A batter who misses the ball is told that she or he swung too early or too late. Batters are taught to purposely swing early or late to control the direction of the ball. Square, open, and closed stances also affect the direction of the ball and thus must be carefully taught. Knowledge gained in games with bats can be generalized to other sports. For instance, when the ball goes to the right instead of over the net in a tennis game, can the child reason why? When the golf ball goes to the left into a sand trap instead of straight down the fairway, does the student know what caused the directional deviation?

 OPTIONAL ACTIVITIES

1. Reflect on whether physical educators should use the term *perceptual-motor learning, motor learning, movement learning,* or something else to encompass the goals, objectives, and activities in this chapter. Engage in debate with others who hold opposite views.

2. Most activities in this chapter are linked with a perceptual-motor problem, but specific objectives are not written. Describe assessment findings from real or imaginary children and develop specific objectives that would call for activities in this chapter. Remember the CBS system for writing objectives (conditions, behavior, success criterion).

3. Adapt activities in this chapter to a water environment and test them with children in a swimming pool. Critique the outcomes. Can some perceptual-motor MSFs be facilitated in water as well as on land? How can some of the MSFs be adapted for young wheelchair users?

4. Read and critique Jean Ayres's (1972) classic book, *Sensory Integration and Learning Disorders,* that is used widely by occupational therapists. Discuss content with some OTs. Pay particular attention to the excellent chapter on developmental dyspraxia.

5. Sherrill obviously respects the works of Allen Burton. Read his assessment textbook (with Miller, 1998) and his *APAQ* article (with Rodgerson, 2001) and reflect on the influence of his work on Sherrill and others. Do you agree or disagree with his pioneering ideas? Why?

6. Read the text on DCD by Cermak and Larkin (2002) and reflect on content that may relate to or enhance content in this chapter. What other information on DCD is available? Check the *Adapted Physical Activity Quarterly* for research.

7. Visit persons who have had strokes that limit their movement, including apraxia and motor planning skills. Such persons are often found in nursing homes and assisted care centers.

C H A P T E R

13

Fitness and Healthy Lifestyle

Claudine Sherrill, James H. Rimmer, and Kenneth H. Pitetti

Figure 13.1   Jim Mastro, internationally known athlete who is blind, serves as role model for university students. Jim can do over 3,000 push-ups in a row.

1. Discuss trends and issues in relation to such concepts as physical fitness, physical activity, rehabilitation, exercise, health, and lifestyle.

2. Identify and discuss efforts to achieve health-enhancing fitness and active lifestyle for yourself and your family or those you live with. What are your greatest risks? Why? What are you doing about these?

3. Use the following websites for up-to-date information:

   Healthy People 2010
   www.health.gov/healthypeople

   Presidential Active Lifestyle Award (PALA)
   www.presidentschallenge.org

   President's Council on Physical Fitness and Sport (NCPFS)
   www.fitness.gov

   FITNESSGRAM/ACTIVITYGRAM
   www.cooperinst.org

   Physical Best
   www.aahperd.org/physicalbest

   National Center on Physical Activity and Disability (NCPAD)
   www.ncpad.org

   American College of Sports Medicine
   www.acsm.org

4. Contrast the current American College of Sports Medicine (ACSM) recommendations for exercise with those of other organizations. Discuss applications and implications for individuals with disabilities.

5. Identify five components of health-related fitness, discuss assessment of each for individuals with average and health-impaired fitness status, and demonstrate ability to administer selected fitness test items.

6. Discuss basic exercise prescription and training concepts such as ratings of perceived exertion (RPE), metabolic equivalents (METS), the Karvonen formula, and proprioceptive neuromuscular facilitation (PNF).

7. Explain adaptations and exercise contraindications that are especially important for (a) severe developmental disabilities, (b) spinal paralysis, (c) other health impairments, (d) limited mental function, and (e) limited sensory function. Relate this to exercise prescription guidelines and fitness components.

Fitness and healthy lifestyle is a major goal in adapted physical activity. This chapter focuses on individuals who lack the knowledge, self-determination, self-confidence, and self-esteem to achieve personal fitness and healthy lifestyle goals. Such individuals need role models, support groups, and excellent teachers and counselors.

Many individuals with disabilities can serve as role models. For instance, Jim Mastro, a Paralympic judo and field athlete who is blind, can perform over 3,000 push-ups in a row (see Figure 13.1). Jean Driscoll, born with spina bifida, and many individuals in wheelchairs because of spinal cord injuries routinely compete in marathons (26.2 miles). Tom Becke and Jaronnie Smith are among the many Paralympians with cerebral palsy (CP) who excel at power lifting as a result of many years of disciplined weight training. Many athletes in both the Paralympics and the Olympics cope with chronic asthma. Similarly, athletes with intellectual disabilities in international competition demonstrate the high levels of fitness associated with disciplined training.

In contrast, many individuals with and without disabilities lack the ability to perform routine daily activity with vigor and have enough energy left over to enjoy leisure and meet emergency demands. Such individuals tend to be overweight and to have sedentary lifestyles. The focus of this chapter is to assist individuals, both with and without disabilities, who lead sedentary lives, to develop a new, active lifestyle in order to improve the quality of their lives.

Recent Changes in the Knowledge Base

The knowledge base related to helping individuals achieve physical activity and fitness goals undergoes constant revision.

New information incorporated into this chapter includes the following:

1. The National Center on Physical Activity and Disability (NCPAD), established in Chicago in 2000, became the first clearinghouse for research and practice information to actively promote healthy lifestyles for persons with disabilities. Funded by the Centers for Disease Control and Prevention, NCPAD is directed by James Rimmer (1994), whose PhD is in the joint areas of adapted physical education and exercise physiology, reflecting the trend that more professionals are combining these two specializations in their graduate work and lifespan research and practice contributions.

   Among its many services, NCPAD provides an electronic newsletter (see www.ncpad.org and cpad@uic.edu), responds to the thousands of questions the office receives, and provides representation for disability rights and opportunities at many government-sponsored policy meetings. Rimmer (1999) was among the first to *advocate health promotion rather than disability or disease prevention.* Rimmer emphasizes that most persons with disabilities are healthy; their needs focus mainly on staying healthy by overcoming exercise, nutrition, and environment barriers; on maintaining motivation to practice healthy, active living; and by developing competence in adapting to life's stresses. Subscription to the NCPAD Newsletter is free.

2. The World Health Organization (WHO, 2001) transformed conceptualization of disability with its new framework for defining, explaining, and classifying the

states of functioning, disability, and health. **Functioning** (neutral or nonproblematic states) and **disability** (problems in functioning manifested as observable, measurable activity limitations) were presented as opposites, both of which are affected by **health state** (feeling of well-being) and context or situation. Much of the current emphasis on barriers and enablers can be attributed to the WHO's influence.

Additionally, WHO launched a worldwide awareness of the health, fitness, and activity needs of older persons by issuing the Heidelberg Guidelines for promoting physical activity needs among older persons (WHO, 1977) and by declaring 1999 the International Year of the Older Person (Sidorenko, 1999). Adapted physical activity personnel, aware that at least 50% of the population acquires disabilities as they grow older, are increasingly embracing the activity needs of aging as a priority.

3. Participation of professionals in international conferences and service projects, along with awareness of cultural variation resulting from immigration, contributed to beliefs that *physical activity should be approached biculturally.* According to Malina (2001, p. 6), "Cultural values vary among ethnic groups and impact physical and mental health. It is important to relate activity habits to ethnicity and immigration history of adults and youth, and to lifestyle differences among groups and between generations." The 21st century brings new awareness of the health needs of all of the persons of the world and the disparity among nations and groups.

4. *Healthy People 2010* (U.S. Department of Health and Human Services, USDHHS, 2000) replaced *Healthy People 2000* as the nation's guide for identifying the most significant preventable threats to health and aggressively working to reduce these threats by 2010. The two major goals of *Healthy People 2010* are to (a) increase quality of life and years of healthy life and (b) eliminate health disparities among different segments of the population. *Healthy People 2010* also designates 28 focus areas, two of which are *physical activity and fitness and disability and secondary conditions.* Ten leading health indicators, each with its own set of objectives, are also specified: physical activity, overweight and obesity, tobacco use, substance abuse, responsible sexual behavior, mental health, injury and violence, environmental quality, immunization, and access to health care. Altogether, 418 observable, measurable objectives are available in *Healthy People 2010* for use in periodically determining progress toward goal achievement. This report provides a strong rationale for much of the work of adapted physical activity professionals.

5. The American Association on Mental Retardation (AAMR, 2002), influenced by WHO (2001), for the first time, included a major section on physical and mental health in its manual on terminology and classification. The *shift to a supports-based paradigm* over the past 10 years has given *physical well-being* more emphasis than ever before. In describing *mental retardation as a multidimensional construct,* AAMR (2002, p. 45)

specified "health (physical health, mental health, and etiological factors)" as one of five major dimensions, all of which are affected positively by individualized supports. Related to health, of course, is physical activity.

6. The American Academy of Kinesiology and Physical Education focused its annual conference in 2000 on *exercise and physical activity adherence* and subsequently published its papers in a special issue of *Quest* (Morgan & Dishman, 2001). These papers emphasize that adherence figures in formal exercise programs have continued to be about 50% over the past three decades. Morgan (2001) thus calls for a paradigm shift that emphasizes the unique nature of the individual rather than principles of behavior derived from the study of groups. The new paradigm would prioritize *preferred exertion over prescribed exertion* and *purposeful physical activity over nonpurposeful types* that are commonly used.

To implement such a paradigm, most professionals will need to increase their competencies in interviewing, in listening, and in analyzing personal meanings of physical activity. Instead of prescribing a criterion-exertion rate to achieve health benefits, as is now done, professionals will need to help persons clarify the exertion rates that seem best for them at particular times and places. The new paradigm will aim to advance self-determination and self-responsibility in physical activity.

7. The internationally known Cooper Institute for Aerobics Research in Dallas, AAHPERD, and the President's Council on Physical Fitness and Sports (PCPFS) began collaborative activities to increase use of the FITNESSGRAM, the ACTIVITYGRAM, and the new Presidential Active Lifestyle Award known as PALA (Cooper Institute for Aerobics Research, 1999a, 1999c; Seaman, 1995). The FITNESSGRAM, which replaced AAHPERD's fitness tests in 1993, thus was joined by two new measures designed to assess *amount of physical activity,* an important health indicator announced by Pate et al. (1995) for the Centers for Disease Control and Prevention and the America College of Sports Medicine and by the *Surgeon General's Report on Physical Activity and Health* for the U.S. Department of Health and Human Services (1996).

The latter report officially confirmed that *enough research has now been accumulated for us to know that physical activity reduces the risk of death in general and in coronary health disease, hypertension, colon cancer, and diabetes in particular.* This fact strengthens the rationale for physical education and adapted physical education instruction and mentoring throughout the lifespan.

8. The American College of Sports Medicine (ACSM, 2000) issued its sixth edition of ACSM's *Guidelines for Exercise Testing and Prescription,* its fourth edition of ACSM's *Resource Manual for Exercise Testing and Prescription* (ACSM, 2001), and its second edition of *Exercise Management for Persons with Chronic Diseases and Disabilities* (ACSM, 2003). Individuals with low fitness often require many weeks to acquire the exercise capacity

to perform at ACSM recommended levels: *exercise 3 to 5 times a week at 60 to 90% of maximal heart rate or 50 to 85% of VO₂max, performing continuous aerobic activity for 20 to 60 min each session.*

9. Authorities have agreed on a minimal physical activity standard for health benefits: *Every adult should accumulate 30 min or more of moderate-intensity physical activity on most, preferably all, days of the week* (Pate et al., 1995). **Moderate intensity** is defined as 3 to 6 METS (work metabolic rate/resting metabolic rate), which is equivalent to the effort expended in walking a mile in 15 to 20 min. For most individuals, meeting this standard calls for walking 2 miles a day at a brisk pace or engaging in equivalent activity. In general, there is agreement that children should also meet this minimal standard.

10. The American Heart Association has issued a minimal physical activity standard that pertains to calories expended during activity: *Activity, for minimal conditioning and health benefits, should consume a minimum total of 700 calories a week spread over three or four sessions a week. For maximal health benefits, activity should consume 2,000 calories a week* (Fletcher et al., 1995). Use of 2,000 calories is the equivalent of walking 20 miles a week.

11. Several books (e.g., Lockette & Keyes, 1994; Miller, 1995; Rimmer, 1994; Seaman, 1995; Winnick & Short, 1999) and research articles (see the *Adapted Physical Activity Quarterly*) for the first time are providing specific, easy-to-understand information about conditioning, training, and testing people with disabilities.

12. The National Consortium for Physical Education and Recreation for Individuals with Disabilities (NCPERID, 1995) has published specific standards to guide the mastery of exercise science knowledge related to adapted physical activity and disability sport. Most of the NCPERID standards are addressed in this chapter and in chapters on specific individual differences in Part III of this book.

Definitions of Fitness, Activity, and Related Terms

Following are definitions that appear in the recent literature. **Physical fitness** is "a set of attributes that people have or achieve that relates to the ability to perform physical activity" (Pate et al., 1995, p. 402). NASPE standards, introduced in Chapter 1, include a **health-enhancing level of physical fitness** (i.e., the ability to pass tests that are believed to be indicators of a physical state that enables persons to perform daily living activities with ease and vigor). The trend is toward conceptualizing physical fitness as a personalized profile that reflects individual beliefs, attitudes, and practices in relation to activity and exercise.

Physical activity is "any bodily activity produced by skeletal muscles that results in energy expenditure" (Pate et al., 1995, p. 402). The amount of energy expenditure, designated in METS or calories, is dependent upon body mass and metabolic

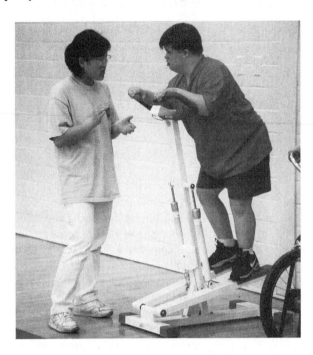

Figure 13.2   Personalized attention should focus equally on self-esteem and fitness goals.

efficiency. There is a trend toward prescribing minutes of general activity rather than specific exercises.

Exercise is "a subset of physical activity defined as planned, structured, and repetitive bodily movement done to improve or maintain one or more components of physical fitness" (Pate et al., 1995, p. 402). The term *exercise* is used more carefully than in the past. Exercise must be planned, whereas activity may be spontaneous and occur in conjunction with either work or play.

Function or capacity typically is a term used to explain limitations. When an individual lacks the functional capacity to sustain activity at a prescribed level of intensity, the goal is generally *to improve exercise capacity tolerance* rather than to improve fitness.

Health, according to the World Health Organization (WHO, 1947), is a state of complete physical, mental, and social well-being and not merely absence of disease or infirmity. WHO (2001) reaffirmed this definition. This definition is **holistic,** meaning that it focuses on the whole person. The trend in the 21st century is toward holistic testing and programming. That is one reason this textbook includes a strong chapter on self-concept, motivation, and well-being (Chapter 8). Self-concept and physical fitness testing and programming should be coordinated (see Figure 13.2).

Wellness is now defined as "a multidimensional state of being describing the existence of positive health in an individual as exemplified by quality of life and a sense of well-being" (PCPFS, 2001). Although AAHPERD has traditionally emphasized fitness more than wellness, there is a trend toward promoting healthy lifestyles as an approach to developing wellness (Corbin, Lindsey, Welk, & Corbin, 2002; Powers & Dodd,

2003). Wellness continues to be conceptualized as *the integration of all parts of health (physical, mental, social, emotional, and spiritual) that results in a healthy lifestyle and feeling good about oneself.*

Rehabilitation Versus Fitness Programming

Rehabilitation is "the restoration and/or maintenance of physical function, which allows an individual to perform activities of daily living (ADL) without incurring high levels of stress or fatigue" (Rimmer, 1994, p. 2). Rehabilitation typically occurs in hospitals and centers that provide services for persons temporarily disabled by surgery, disease, or sedentary lifestyle or permanently disabled by trauma, disease, disuse, or other factors. Therefore, rehabilitation follows a medical model. The cost of rehabilitation is typically reimbursed by insurance.

In contrast, **fitness testing and training** is conducted in many settings and follows many models (e.g., educational, sport, weight loss). Fitness training is associated with goals over and beyond activities of daily living (ADL). These goals are highly personal and might focus on fitness components, time spent in physical activity, or healthy, active lifestyle.

Of particular concern at all ages is prevention of *hypokinetic conditions* like obesity, heart disease, high blood pressure, low back pain, adult-onset diabetes, stress, and bone degeneration (osteoporosis). **Hypokinetic** means insufficient movement or exercise. Although often not manifested until middle age, hypokinetic disease begins in childhood and is aggravated by bed rest and/or activity restrictions imposed by injury, illness, or environmental barriers. The 21st century will be known as a time when physical inactivity began to receive as much attention (or more) as fitness.

Lifestyle Problems of Americans

Lifestyle problems include everything that interferes with wellness (i.e., the positive aspect of health) and negatively affects lifespan. Numerous factors such as diet, stress, smoking, drug abuse, and physical inactivity are risk factors. This chapter, however, focuses on the physical inactivity that characterizes modern life. Recent research indicates that "over half of adults were not regularly active in moderate and vigorous intensity activity at levels sufficient to prevent diseases and disabilities" (Ainsworth, 2003, p. 4). Women, in particular, continue to report "low participation in regular activity with little or no engagement in vigorous activities" (Ainsworth, 2000, p. 37), but researchers are beginning to challenge the accuracy of survey instruments in capturing the types of physical activities that women actually do. In general, activity levels are lower among persons of color, the overweight, the least educated, and the aged.

The School Health Policies and Programs Study (SHPPS) of 2000 indicated that only 9.5% of elementary schools, 15.5% of middle/junior high schools, and 12% of senior high schools provide daily physical education or its equivalent for at least 50% of the school year for students in all grades in the school (Burgeson, Wechsler, Brener, Young, & Spain, 2003). These percentages increase slightly for schools providing at least three days a week of physical education or its equivalent for half of the school year. About 70% of all schools permit students to be exempted from required physical education for one grading period or longer. Common reasons are cognitive disability, permanent physical disability, and religion.

SHPPS 2000 was one of several studies used to obtain the data on which *Healthy People 2010* is based. *Healthy People 2010* thus includes the objective of increasing the percentage of schools that require students to receive daily physical education. Research shows a definite decline in physical activity as children age (McKenzie, 2001). Adolescence is considered a high risk time because girls reduce their physical activity levels by about 7% a year while boys reduce theirs by about 3%. Only about 50% of adolescent boys and 25% of adolescent girls meet standards for exercise more vigorous than 30 minutes a day at a moderate level.

About half of those who set exercise goals fail to follow through (Dishman, 1994). Even in supervised programs established for persons at medical risk, about 50% drop out within 6 months to a year. The best dropout predictors for adults are body weight, percent body fat, and self-motivation. For children and youth, the best predictors are fun, enjoyment, and the desire to please significant others. In general, exercise dropouts tend to be those who need exercise the most. *An important goal of adapted physical activity is to persuade persons with low fitness that regular exercise increases the richness of life and prevents health problems.*

Lifestyle Concerns Pertaining to Disability

Persons with disabilities and health impairments often have to work harder at fitness than able-bodied (AB) peers. Because this process often takes far longer than average and demands considerable perseverance, the benefits of fitness training must be clear.

Fitness is a special concern in adapted physical activity for many reasons:

1. Poor body alignment and inefficient movement patterns increase energy expenditure beyond normal ranges and result in fatigue that reduces job efficiency, leisure-time activities, and overall quality of life (Shephard, 1990).
2. Mechanical efficiency, and thus energy level, is negatively affected by (a) reduced or altered sensory input, as in blindness, deafness, and perceptual deficits (Kobberling, Jankowski, & Leger, 1989); (b) spasticity and abnormal reflex activity (Skrotsky, 1983); (c) use of crutches and prostheses (Fisher & Gullickson, 1978); and (d) loss of functional muscle mass, as in paresis/paralysis (Wells & Hooker, 1990). These and other problems place heavy burdens on the cardiorespiratory and neuromuscular systems.
3. Coping with architectural, attitudinal, and aspirational barriers requires extra energy. Architectural barriers alone increase the energy expenditure of persons with physical disabilities 15-fold over that of able-bodied peers (Miller, Merritt, Merkel, & Westbrook, 1984).
4. Persons with cognitive and/or language disabilities are more likely to be employed in manual labor than desk jobs and thus need high levels of fitness. Fitness training promotes on-the-job success for persons with mental retardation (Beasley, 1982).

Table 13.1 Responses of persons with disabilities concerning active lifestyles.

Reasons for Being Active %		Changes That Would Encourage More Activity %	
To feel better	59	More leisure time	29
To improve flexibility	43	Better or closer facilities	22
To control weight	39	People with whom to participate	22
To relax, reduce stress	38	Common interest of family	19
For pleasure and fun	37	Less expensive facilities	18
Doctor's advice	35	Common interest of friends	15
For companionship	26	Organized fitness classes	11
Fitness leader's advice	21	A fitness test and program	11
To challenge abilities	18	Information on benefits	7
To learn new things	17		

From *Physical Activity Among Activity-Limited and Disabled Adults in Canada* by permission of the Canadian Fitness and Lifestyle Research Institute, Ontario, Canada.
Note: Forty-seven percent responded that nothing would make them increase their activity. Percentages do not add up to 100% because persons could check any number of items.

5. Persons with disabilities need the best possible physiques and exemplary fitness to overcome discrimination and obtain social acceptance. Physical appearance is an important factor in finding employment.

6. Chronic depression and other mental health problems that plague some persons with disabilities can be ameliorated by fitness programs (ACSM, 2000). Persons with disabilities who are active typically rate their emotional well-being and total health higher than do sedentary persons (Canada Fitness Survey, 1986).

7. Many persons with disabilities have never been socialized into sport and/or physically active lifestyles and thus have weight problems and other health concerns associated with sedentary living.

8. Clumsy persons whose body image and self-concept have been negatively affected by balance-coordination-timing problems often find success in walking, jogging, cycling, swimming, and weight lifting. This success can be the springboard for better attitudes toward self.

9. An *activity deficit hypothesis* has been asserted and supported (Bouffard et al., 1996). Children with movement difficulties are vigorously active less often than their peers, engage in fewer social interactions, and play less on playground equipment. Movement difficulties are linked directly with physical inactivity.

10. Obesity is statistically associated with movement problems in children (Marshall & Bouffard, 1994), but problems can be lessened by quality physical education instruction.

Canada has surveyed both its able-bodied and disabled populations (Canada Fitness Survey, 1986), applying a holistic model to determine patterns of physical activity and related beliefs and attitudes (see Table 13.1). Responses of persons with disabilities were similar to those of able-bodied Canadians except that the able-bodied ranked "for pleasure and fun" as the second most important reason. Perhaps persons with disabilities are not socialized early in life to perceive physical activity as fun; often, their first regular exercise is physical therapy. Clearly, more emphasis needs to be placed on enjoyment. Note

in Table 13.1 footnote that 47% indicated that nothing would make them exercise more. Counseling is needed on time management, assertiveness in locating facilities and friends, and ways to increase family support and involvement.

Components of Health-Related Fitness

Fitness, like self-concept, is multidimensional. Individuals can be high in some components of fitness and low in others. According to the American College of Sports Medicine (ACSM, 2000, p. 57), "**Health-related physical fitness** is typically defined as including cardiorespiratory or aerobic endurance, body composition, muscular strength and endurance, and flexibility." This four-component definition guides most fitness testing and programming. *A fifth component, often forgotten, is the composite of beliefs, attitudes, and intentions that give persons the self-determination, self-confidence, and self-esteem to achieve and maintain fitness goals.*

The Cooper Institute for Aerobics Research (CIAR) in Dallas was designated in 1993 as the authority in fitness testing for school-age youth. The CIAR was founded in the 1960s by Dr. Kenneth H. Cooper, a physician and a major in the U.S. Air Force Medical Corps (Cooper, 1968). Cooper popularized **aerobic training,** a progressive physical conditioning program that uses continuous, long-duration, big-muscle exercise to develop cardiorespiratory endurance and related health benefits.

An easy way to define fitness components is by the tests used to measure them and the associated health-related standards, which indicate the levels of performance necessary to achieve health benefits. Because the CIAR-recommended fitness test is the FITNESSGRAM, the items for this test appear in Figure 13.3. More-detailed explanations of the fitness components appear later in this chapter.

The FITNESSGRAM

Directions for administering the FITNESSGRAM tests appear in many sources (e.g., Cooper Institute for Aerobics Research, 1999b; Seaman, 1995). A detailed explanation of the validity and reliability of the tests and other information can be found in

Figure 13.3   FITNESSGRAM tests and healthy fitness zones. (Continued on page 363.) (© Cooper Institute for Aerobics Research.)

FITNESSGRAM Measures of Aerobic Capacity and Body Composition

The Pacer

Alternate Exercise: One Mile-Walk/Run

Age	Girls Good	Girls Better	Boys Good	Boys Better
5				
6				
7		*Participate in run. Lap count standards not recommended.*		
8				
9				
10	7	35	17	55
11	9	37	23	61
12	13	40	29	68
13	15	42	35	74
14	18	44	41	80
15	23	50	46	85
16	28	56	52	90
17	34	61	57	94
17+	34	61	57	94

MEASURES AEROBIC CAPACITY

Skinfold Tests With Calipers

Percent Fat
Sum of triceps and calf skinfolds

Alternate:
Body Mass Index
$$\frac{\text{Body weight (kg)}}{\text{Height}^2 \text{ (m}^2\text{)}}$$

Age	Girls Body Mass Index Good	Girls Body Mass Index Better	Boys Body Mass Index Good	Boys Body Mass Index Better
5	21	16.2	20	14.7
6	21	16.2	20	14.7
7	22	16.2	20	14.9
8	22	16.2	20	15.1
9	23	16.2	20	15.2
10	23.5	16.6	21	15.3
11	24	16.9	21	15.8
12	24.5	16.9	22	16.0
13	24.5	17.5	23	16.6
14	25	17.5	24.5	17.5
15	25	17.5	25	18.1
16	25	17.5	26.5	18.5
17	26	17.5	27	18.8
17+	27.3	18.0	27.8	19.0

MEASURES BODY COMPOSITION

Girls, all ages, 32% to 17% body fat
Boys, all ages, 25% to 10% body fat

the *Technical Reference Manual* (Cooper Institute for Aerobics Research, 1999c). This test is recommended for all school-age individuals with the functional capacity to perform the test items; *this includes most students with disabilities.* To enable individualization, alternative items are specified for students who cannot perform the prescribed six tests. Additionally, a chapter on modification for special populations is included in the test manual.

The FITNESSGRAM is a criterion-referenced test, in that standards, called healthy fitness zones (HFZs), are established to indicate goals that represent good and better protection against health and injury risks in activities of daily living. The lower HFZ level corresponds closely *to the 20th percentile* of the population, and the upper HFZ level is comparable *to the 60th percentile* (Winnick, 1995). These levels might seem low, but research indicates that they are adequate for the average person to be considered healthy.

The FITNESSGRAM, now recommended, and the AAHPERD health-related fitness tests, used from 1980 through 1993, have some similarities. Both tests include the one-mile walk/run, the summed triceps and calf skinfold measures, and the sit-and-reach test. The body position for performing the sit-and-reach test is different, however. The standards are different also, indicating different philosophies about the level of performance necessary for health protection.

The FITNESSGRAM is different from the AAHPERD tests in the following ways: (a) the use of curl-ups instead of bent-knee sit-ups; (b) the addition of push-ups and alternative tests to measure upper body strength; (c) the addition of the trunk lift to measure trunk extensor strength and flexibility; (d) the addition of a PACER test as an alternative to the walk/run; and (e) the emphasis on the use of audiotaped cadences. Following is an explanation of some unique aspects of the FITNESSGRAM.

Figure 13.3   Continued.

Curl-Up Test End Position

Age	Girls		Boys	
---	Good	Better	Good	Better
5	2	10	2	10
6	2	10	2	10
7	4	14	4	14
8	6	20	6	20
9	9	22	9	24
10	12	26	12	24
11	15	29	15	28
12	18	32	18	36
13	18	32	21	40
14	18	32	24	45
15	18	35	24	47
16	18	35	24	47
17	18	35	24	47
17+	18	35	24	47

3 or 4½ inch
measuring strip

MEASURES ABDOMINAL STRENGTH
Complete 75 or as many as
    possible at specified pace.

Start with arms straight, palms down
Knees bent at 140° angle
Feet flat on floor

Curl up until fingers slide to end of
    measuring strip (3 inches for ages
    5–9; 4½ inches for ages 10–17+)
Keep heels in contact with mat

Push-Up

Age	Girls		Boys	
---	Good	Better	Good	Better
5	3	8	3	8
6	3	8	3	8
7	4	10	4	10
8	5	13	5	13
9	6	15	6	15
10	7	15	7	20
11	7	15	8	20
12	7	15	10	20
13	7	15	12	25
14	7	15	14	30
15	7	15	16	35
16	7	15	18	35
17	7	15	18	35
17+	7	15	18	35

Alternate Exercises:
Pull-Up
Flexed Arm Hang
Modified Pull-Up

MEASURES UPPER BODY STRENGTH
Complete as many as possible at
    specified pace.
Start with elbows bent at 90°
    angle, upper arms parallel
    to floor
Push up until arms are straight
Keep legs and back straight

One Trunk Lift (Two trials)

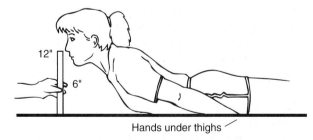

12"
6"
Hands under thighs

MEASURES TRUNK AND BACK STRENGTH AND FLEXIBILITY
No gender differences
Ages 5–9, 6 to 12 inches
Ages 10–17+, 9 to 12 inches

One Back-Saver Sit-and-Reach on Left and Right Sides

Alternate Exercise:
Shoulder Stretch

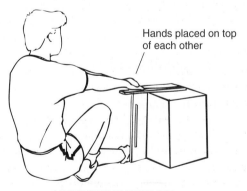

Hands placed on top
of each other

MEASURES FLEXIBILITY
Girls, ages 5–10, 9 inches
        ages 11–14, 10 inches
        ages 15–17+, 12 inches
Boys, all ages, 8 inches

The PACER

The PACER (Progressive Aerobic Cardiovascular Endurance Run), a test that starts easy and gets progressively harder, requires running back and forth across a 20-m distance (20 yd, 32 in) at a pace specified by an audiotape that gets faster each minute, with the pace increasing by one-half second at the end of each minute. Beeps on the audiotape tell the runners when to reverse directions; the goal is to reach the opposite side before the beep sounds. A student who arrives early at a line must wait for the beep to sound before starting to run again. The beginning speeds are very slow (9 sec for 20 m) in order to build in success. If, as the pace gets faster, students cannot reach the line by the time the beep sounds, they are given two more beeps to attempt to regain the pace before being withdrawn from the test. The score is the number of laps completed by the student. The PACER is particularly recommended for Grades 1 to 6 and for individuals with mental retardation.

The Use of Audiotape With Curl-ups and Push-ups

The PACER audiotape, which can be purchased through CIAR, is also used with curl-ups and push-ups. For curl-ups, the cadence is about 20 curl-ups per minute (one curl every 3 sec). Students must continue curls without pausing until they can no longer adhere to the pace or they have completed the test maximum of 75 curl-ups. For push-ups, the correct cadence is 20 push-ups per minute (one every 3 sec). The push-up test is ended if the student cannot maintain the correct cadence, stops to rest, or fails to use correct technique despite corrections; three corrections are allowed.

Alternative Tests for Upper Body Strength

Tests recommended as alternatives to the push-up are the pull-up, the flexed-arm hang, and the modified pull-up. These are all performed with the overarm grasp (palms facing away from the body). The starting position for both the pull-up and the flexed-arm hang is hanging from a bar with arms extended. In the pull-up, the chin must be above the bar on the up position. Most persons with low strength, however, will need to do the modified pull-up test, which starts by lying on the back with the shoulders directly under a bar that is set about 1 or 2 inches above normal reach. An elastic band is placed 7 or 8 inches below and parallel to the bar, and the goal is to pull up until the chin is above this elastic band.

Assessment of Physical Activity

The ACTIVITYGRAM (Cooper Institute for Aerobics Research, 1999a) requires individuals to recall their physical activities over the previous 24 hours in 30-min blocks. This is made easy by the provision of six categories (rest and inactivity, flexibility exercises, muscle fitness activities, active sports, active aerobics, lifestyle activities) from which the recall is made. Individuals also rate the intensity of each activity block (light, moderate, and vigorous). As part of the FITNESSGRAM 6.0 software package, the ACTIVITYGRAM prints a number of findings.

Also used in the assessment of physical activity are heart rate monitors, activity monitors (e.g., pedometers, motion sensors, accelerometers), direct observation, and self-reports. Self-report is accepted as an appropriate means of gathering data.

Brockport Physical Fitness Test

The Brockport Physical Fitness Test (Winnick & Short, 1999) offers a comprehensive assessment program that parallels that of the FITNESSGRAM of the Cooper Institute for Aerobics Research (1999b), which is now recommended by AAHPERD over its older norm-based tests. Like the FITNESSGRAM, the Brockport Physical Fitness Test (BPFT) is a health-related, criterion-referenced test that presents standards to be met by males and females at different ages. *The Brockport Physical Fitness Test Manual* (Winnick & Short, 1999) fully describes *27 test items and presents standards for youth, ages 10 to 17,* in the general population and in five subgroups: mental retardation, cerebral palsy, visual impairments, spinal cord injuries from C6 downward, and congenital anomalies and amputations. A particular strength of BPFT is its recommendation of adaptations and alternatives for personalizing the test for the different disabilities. *Students are tested on four to six items from three fitness components: body composition, aerobic functioning, and musculoskeletal functioning.* Standards for interpreting data are accessed from the BPFT manual. This book is therefore essential to the library of everyone doing adapted physical education assessment.

Following is a description of some of the fitness items adapted for students with disabilities.

1. *Target Aerobic Movement Test (TAMT).* Any aerobic activity may be used as long as it is intense enough to reach a minimal target heart rate and to sustain that heart rate in a **target heart rate zone (THRZ).** Scoring is pass or fail on one trial, which determines if students can stay within or above the THRZ for 15 min. Time is not started until the student reaches the THRZ. The test should be terminated if the maximum values are reached during the warm-up period, which is standardized at 3 min.

   In the BPFT manual (pp. 75–76), a THRZ for moderate intensity exertion is "70 to 85% of a maximal predicted heart rate (operationally defined as 140 to 180)" for persons able to engage in full body exercise. The minimum and maximum 10 sec heart rate values for these persons are 23 and 30, respectively. *For persons with quadriplegia and paraplegia who use arms-only exercise, the standards are different because resting heart rate capacity differs.* When resting heart rate is *less than 65,* the minimum and maximum 10 sec heart rate values are 14 and 17, respectively. When resting heart rate is *over 65,* formulas are used to calculate minimum and maximum 10 sec heart rate values. These are (resting heart rate + 20)/6 and (resting heart rate + 30)/6, respectively. Minimum and maximum 10 sec heart rate for arms-only exercise for persons with paraplegia are 22 and 28, respectively.

2. *Seated push-up.* Student puts hands on the armrests of wheelchair and extends arms to lift and hold the buttocks off of the supporting surface for 20 sec. A 5 sec standard

comes from the necessity for wheelchair users to remove the pressure on their buttocks by changing sitting position every 5 sec. This reduces the risk of developing **decubitus ulcers** (commonly called bedsores), which often take months of prone lying to heal. The 20 sec standard relates to the amount of time a wheelchair user must lift the body via arms to do transfers.

3. *Reverse Curl.* Student picks up a 1-lb object that is resting on the midpoint of the same-side thigh or a table at knee level when the student is seated. The goal is to hold the object with the elbow bent at 45 degrees or greater for 2 sec. and then return it slowly (i.e., controlled against gravity) to the starting position. One trial, with pass or fail scoring, is used.

4. *Wheelchair Ramp Test.* Student in wheelchair pushes a distance of at least 8 ft, but preferably 15 to 20 ft, up a standard size ramp. The American National Standards Institute (ANSI) guidelines specify that a ramp must be at least 36 in (91 cm) wide and constructed with 12 in (30 cm) of run for every inch (2.5 cm) of rise (i.e., if a ramp has an elevation of 14 in, it must be 14 ft long). Low-skilled students should have a spotter behind them.

5. *Modified Apley Test.* To show flexibility, the participant reaches back with one hand to touch the inside border of the opposite scapula, where the tester has placed his or her fingers to indicate the spot to be touched. Each arm is tested. The participant who holds the reach for 1–2 sec is awarded 3 points. For individuals unable to do this, a touch and hold to the top of the head or to the mouth earn 2 or 1 points, respectively.

6. *Modified Thomas Test.* Participant lies supine on a table with the head of the femur level touching a marker tape that is 11 in from the short edge of the table, so that the legs are dangling down. To earn 3 points for the flexibility of the hip flexors, the student pulls one leg toward the chest, as close to the chest as possible, without raising the other leg so that it loses contact with the table surface. The back also must remain in contact with the surface or the score is forfeited. If the stationary leg lifts slightly from the table, the tester reduces the score to 2 or 1, depending on the amount of the bend.

7. *Dumbbell Press.* In a seated position, the student lifts a 15-lb (6.8 kg) dumbbell with the dominant hand by flexing the elbow so that the weight is close in and in front of the shoulder (e.g., like a restaurant worker holds a tray). The weight is then lifted straight up about the shoulder until the elbow is completely straight, then returns the weight to starting position. The test is continued at a steady lifting pace (about 3 to 4 sec per repetition) until a maximum of 50 repetitions is completed or the student cannot continue.

8. *Target Stretch Test (TST).* The tester assesses maximum movement extent at five joints (wrist, elbow, shoulder, forearm, and knee) through use of a modified goniometer. Degrees of movement yielded by the clock face of the goniometer are converted to standards of 2 (better) or 1. Sixteen clock face movement profiles in the manual help testers with interpretation.

The test items just described are designed primarily for wheelchair users or students whose disabilities have resulted in unique movement patterns or reduction in range of motion. *Individuals with blindness or mental retardation generally can perform the same test items as general education classmates.* Everything to administer the test (manual computer software, instructional videotape, skinfold calipers, PACER audio CD/cassette) are available through Human Kinetics (see Appendix E).

Other Fitness Tests

Many other fitness tests are available, of course. Each country has its own test (Government of Canada, 1987), norms, and minimal standards. The President's Council on Physical Fitness and Sports (1987) includes five items: 1-mi run/walk, curl-ups, V-sit reach, shuttle run, and pull-ups. The 30-ft shuttle run is used to evaluate leg strength/endurance/power/ agility, and skinfold measures are not taken. The President's Council supports the use of norms and offers awards to individuals who score at the 85th percentile on all five of its items. The YMCA has its own test battery (one of the few with norms for adults), which is used worldwide (Golding, Myers, & Sinning, 1989). In addition to these batteries, many tests have been validated as measures of a single fitness component. These are fully described in tests and measurements texts. In selecting tests, pay attention to the date that the test was first published and to dates of follow-up validity and reliability research.

School Fitness Testing: History, Issues, Trends

Much controversy has always surrounded the school fitness movement. Each decade, the issue of which tests are best to use has been addressed and temporarily resolved. Likewise, the issue of how high to set fitness standards is argued repeatedly. Other issues are how much time to give fitness testing and training, and whether fitness should be given precedence over sports and motor skills training. A current trend is away from maximum fitness, with everyone urged to make the highest score possible, toward performance within healthy fitness zones (HFZs) believed to provide adequate protection against health and fitness risks. Another trend is to personalize fitness goals and tests, with individuals who aspire to become or remain elite athletes setting higher goals than individuals who prefer recreational activity.

Types of Fitness: Physical and Motor

Two types of fitness historically have been recognized: (a) physical and (b) motor. **Physical fitness** is health-related and includes several components: cardiorespiratory endurance, body composition, muscular strength and endurance, and flexibility. **Motor fitness** is skill-related and includes agility, balance, coordination, speed, power, and reaction time. Since 1980 general physical educators have given little attention to motor fitness. In adapted physical education, however, motor fitness components are helpful in diagnosing problem areas. *In this text, motor fitness is associated with perceptual-motor function* (see Chapters 10 and 12). The Individuals with Disabilities Education Act (IDEA) ncludes the term *physical and motor fitness* in its definition of physical education.

The 1950s: Early Beginnings

Fitness as a physical education goal gained recognition in the 1950s, when Dwight Eisenhower was president and the world was impressed by Russia's shooting of Sputnik into space. The 1950s is the decade of the Kraus-Weber research findings (Kraus & Hirschland, 1954), the founding of the American College of Sports Medicine (ACSM), the establishment of the President's Council on Youth and Fitness (now called the President's Council on Physical Fitness and Sports), and the creation of the first AAHPER Youth Physical Fitness Test.

Kraus-Weber Tests, 1950s

The first fitness test to gain widespread recognition was the six-item Kraus-Weber battery, which included straight- and bent-knee sit-ups, double-leg lift-and-hold from supine and prone, trunk lift from prone, and toe touch from stand. The Kraus-Weber research indicated that American children were less fit than those in several European countries. This finding provided impetus for fitness testing and training in the schools.

First AAHPER Fitness Test, 1950s

The AAHPER fitness test battery originally included seven items, four to measure *motor fitness* (standing broad jump, 50-yd dash, 30-ft shuttle run, and overarm throw for distance) and three to measure *physical fitness* (a distance run, bent-knee sit-ups, and pull-ups or flexed arm hang). The overarm throw was eliminated in the first revision because improper warm-up was causing injuries. The distance run also was subject to much debate. Some authorities accepted the 600-yd walk-run as a measure of cardiorespiratory function, but most supported the 9- or 12-min runs.

Rarick's Contributions on Mental Retardation

G. Lawrence Rarick of the University of California at Berkeley was the first to conduct research on issues related to fitness testing of school-age persons with mental retardation. Rarick's finding that students with MR performed 2 to 4 years behind peers was a major factor in the enactment of federal laws pertaining to physical education and recreation for this population. His work began in the 1950s (Francis & Rarick, 1959) and continued until his retirement in the late 1970s. About 50 test items were administered to hundreds of subjects to determine the factor structure of fitness for educable and trainable MR (Rarick, 1980). *Rarick concluded that persons with MR should be tested with the same items as peers but that separate sets of norms were needed.* His work created the foundation for other researchers.

The 1960s to the 1980s

During the 1960s and 1970s, testing encompassed both physical and motor fitness. In 1980, AAHPERD tests were changed to focus exclusively on health-related fitness. Test batteries and sets of norms for individuals with disabilities were created.

Early Tests for Persons With Mental Retardation

Early tests mirrored the philosophy of the times and contained items similar to, but less demanding than, items for able-bodied peers.

In the 1960s, Frank Hayden of Canada and Julian Stein of AAHPER were pioneers in the adaptation of fitness tests for youth with mental retardation (see Figure 13.4). The AAHPER fitness tests for individuals with mild mental retardation (AAHPER, 1986) and for moderate mental retardation (Johnson & Londeree, 1976) are no longer in print because of the AAHPERD and CIAR philosophy that the minimal standards for health-related fitness are applicable to everyone. Norms for tests published in the 1960s and 1970s are no longer valid.

Tests for Persons With Blindness

Charles Buell (1973), who was legally blind, developed fitness norms and recommendations for youth who were blind or visually impaired. Almost 10 years later, however, Buell (1982) indicated that the regular norms for the AAHPERD health-related fitness tests were applicable to the blind population, with one exception—the distance run. Running requires holding the elbow of a sighted partner, and this slows the speed, leaving the impression that cardiorespiratory endurance is lower than it actually is.

The 1980s Onward: Health-Related Fitness

The 1980 and 1988 revisions of the AAHPERD test included only health-related items. The 1980 battery included (a) a 1- or 1.5-mi run, (b) skin caliper measures of body fat, (c) bent-knee sit-ups, and (d) a sit-and-reach flexibility item. This test was normative, with norms published for each gender by age. The 1988 revision included the same items, except for changes in body fat measurement sites and the addition of pull-ups. The major change in 1988 was philosophical: AAHPERD's 1988 Physical Best Test was recommended for use by all populations, including those with disabilities. *Instead of norms, the criterion level necessary for good health was stated for each item.* AAHPERD philosophy was that the same minimal health standards should apply to everyone and that fitness pedagogy should be individualized, with each student striving for a physical best. This philosophy promoted least restrictive environment and inclusion concepts.

In 1993, as indicated earlier, the AAHPERD Physical Best test was replaced by CIAR's FITNESSGRAM. Several exercise scientists with expertise in adapted physical activity are currently providing leadership in the development of an accurate knowledge base about fitness and individuals with disabilities (see Figure 13.4). See, for instance, the books by Shephard (1990), Rimmer (1994), Seaman (1995), and Winnick and Short (1985, 1999).

The U.S. government has also funded major research grants to investigate the fitness of various populations. Of these, two have been particularly outstanding in the area of severe mental retardation:

1. Data-Based Gymnasium (Dunn et al., 1986) at Oregon State University
2. Project TRANSITION (Jansma, Decker, Ersing, McCubbin, & Combs, 1988) at Ohio State University

Two other projects, directed by Winnick and Short of the State University of New York (SUNY) at Brockport, have contributed to knowledge about various disabilities:

Figure 13.4 Leaders in the fitness movement for individuals with disabilities.

Pioneers in Physical and Motor Fitness

G. Lawrence Rarick

Julian Stein

Frank Hayden

Leaders in Health-Related Fitness

G. Joseph Winnick

Roy Shephard

James Rimmer

Kenneth Pitetti

1. Project UNIQUE (Winnick & Short, 1985), which established norms and test adaptations for adolescents with blindness, deafness, and various orthopedic impairments

2. Project TARGET, published as *The Brockport Physical Fitness Test,* (Winnick & Short, 1999), has established criterion-based health standards for adolescents with blindness, mental retardation, and various orthopedic impairments.

Fitness Classifications Requiring Special Help

Figure 13.5 shows methods of classifying fitness and identifying individuals who require special help. The emphasis in this table is on aerobic capacity, because this is the fitness component that experts believe is most important in preventing heart disease and other hypokinetic conditions.

Adapted physical activity is primarily concerned with individuals classified as having **symptomatic clinical status.** This includes adults unable to walk a mile in 12 minutes, a minimal criterion for relative freedom from health risks, and youth unable to meet FITNESSGRAM minimal standards (a mile in 8.5 to 12.5 minutes, depending on age and sex). Many school-age children who fail to meet this criterion are eligible to be categorized as other health impaired (OHI) and thus receive federal funding for special services. Conditions commonly associated with symptomatic or OHI clinical status are obesity, asthma, high blood pressure, heart disease, and poorly managed diabetes (see Chapter 19).

Individuals with OHI conditions are often referred to specialists who give laboratory exercise tests and write exercise prescriptions. Adapted physical activity personnel should have knowledge about VO₂max and METS in order to collaborate with exercise specialists. Knowledge about these laboratory values is also crucial to understanding principles and theories related to fitness and lifestyle.

VO_2max

VO₂max refers to the maximum amount of oxygen consumed by cells in the final seconds of exercise prior to total exhaustion. VO₂max values are reported in weight-relative units (milliliters of oxygen consumed *times* body weight in kilograms *times* number of minutes exercised, or ml·kg·min). Values typically range from 3.5 ml·kg·min at rest to 56 ml·kg·min during exercise. When best speed is 9 mph or a 6.5-min mile, the amount of oxygen consumed is 56 ml·kg·min.

Age and gender affect VO₂max. Compared with adults, children have high values. VO₂max ranges from 40 to 60 ml·kg·min for boys and 35 to 50 ml·kg·min for girls. VO₂max

Figure 13.5   Methods of classifying fitness (METS = metabolic equivalents).

Functional Class	Clinical Status			VO$_2$max ml • kg • min	METS	Walk/Run Profile	
						Miles per hour	Minutes per mile
Normal and I	Healthy, dependent on age, activity			56.0	16	9	6.5
				52.5	15		
				49.0	14	8	7.5
				45.5	13		
				42.0	12	7	8.5
				38.5	11		
		Sedentary healthy		35.0	10	6	10
				31.5	9		
				28.0	8	5	12
				24.5	7		
II			Limited	21.0	6	4	15
				17.5	5		
III			Symptomatic	14.0	4	3	20
				10.5	3		
				7.0	2	2	30
IV				3.5	1	Bed rest	

(Moderate intensity 3–6 METS — spanning METS 5 through 7)

peaks between ages 17 and 25 and then declines approximately 9% per decade. Average values for males are 10 to 20% higher than for females, probably because men have more muscle mass, higher hemoglobin concentrations, and more active lifestyles. **Hemoglobin concentration** refers to the amount of oxygen that can be carried by the red blood cells. Sex differences in VO$_2$max are not generally significant and meaningful until puberty.

Many factors affect estimates of VO$_2$max of individuals with disabilities, including active muscle mass and understanding of test instructions. Individuals with paralyzed or missing limbs, because of their decreased muscle mass, have lower values than normal. Individuals with mental retardation, if not provided a comprehensive familiarization protocol, may generate low values due to poor motivation and task understanding.

METS

METS refers to metabolic equivalents and represents an alternative way of indicating the amount of aerobic capacity. The range of METS is typically 1 to 16, as indicated on Figure 13.5. Bed rest requires 1 MET, or 3.5·kg·min. Individuals who function within the 1 to 6 METS range have severe fitness problems that interfere with activities of daily living. For example, 5 METs is the criterion level associated with walking up hills and stairs, carrying groceries, and having sexual intercourse. From 3 to 5 MET capacity is needed to take a quick shower, make a bed, scrub the floor, push a power mower, and garden.

Exercise Prescription: Five Components

Exercise prescription is a process of recommending activity for health, fitness, or wellness in an individualized and systematic manner. It is analogous to the individualized education program (IEP) process in that implementation requires (a) assessment, (b) goal setting, (c) decision making about training, (d) establishment of dates and program duration, and (e) evaluation to determine if goals are being achieved.

Components of an exercise prescription are frequency, intensity, time, modality, and rate of progression. These can be remembered by the acronym **FIT-MR.** Guidelines for *aerobic fitness* for able-bodied persons (ACSM, 2000) are as follows:

F   *F*requency—3–5 times a week

I   *I*ntensity—60 to 90% of maximal heart rate

T   *T*ime—20 to 60 min

M   *M*odality—A rhythmic, large muscle activity like walking, jogging, cycling, aerobic dance, swimming

R   *R*ate of progression—Gradual increase in frequency, intensity, and time.

This prescription and most fitness guidelines are based on the assumption that individuals are functioning at the 6 METS level or higher. Table 13.2 shows how exercise prescription guidelines must be adapted for persons with very low fitness. The prescription often reads *whatever is possible,* and the major challenge is to motivate individuals to "better their best," once baseline performance is determined.

Table 13.2 Comparison of exercise prescription guidelines for people with average and health-impaired fitness status.

Fitness Component	Frequency	Intensity	Time
Cardiorespiratory Endurance			
Average	3–5 times a week	60 to 90% of maximal heart rate; or 50–85% of VO_2max	20–60 min
Health-impaired	Several times daily	40 to 70% of maximal heart rate or whatever is possible	3–15 min or whatever is possible
Body Composition			
Average	Usual	Calorie expenditure *equals* calorie intake	Usual
Health-impaired	Daily or several times daily	Calorie expenditure *greater than* calorie intake in low-intensity/low-impact exercise	Long duration
Flexibility			
Average	3 times a week	Slow, static stretch held 10–30 sec	3–5 repetitions
Health-impaired	Daily or several times daily	Slow, static stretch held 5–10 sec	3–5 repetitions
Muscle Strength and Endurance			
Average	2–3 times a week	Maximum weight that can be moved 8–12 times at moderate to slow speed and not interfere with normal breathing	3 sets, 8–12 repetitions per set
Health-impaired	Daily	Exercises or calisthenics like curl-ups and pull-ups at moderate to slow speed; *isometrics*	As many as possible until able to meet FITNESSGRAM standards

Note: Average refers to the typical person wanting to improve or maintain fitness. *Health-impaired* refers to persons who are functioning at the 1 to 6 MET level (i.e., unable to walk a 12-min mile and/or to meet healthy fitness standards for their age).

Frequency refers to the number of exercise sessions per week. The less fit a person is, the more sessions are needed, because individuals can sustain all-out effort for only very short periods.

Intensity (how hard) refers to amount of exertion. For *muscle strength/endurance,* intensity refers to the number of pounds (the weight or resistance) to be lifted, pushed, pulled, or propelled. For *flexibility,* intensity refers to the distance a muscle group is stretched beyond normal length. For *body composition,* intensity refers to caloric expenditure in relation to caloric intake. For *cardiorespiratory fitness,* intensity refers to distance and speed.

Time refers to the number of minutes spent in exercise during each session. Some prescriptions indicate warm-up time, all-out effort time, and cool-down time. Persons who function in the 1 to 6 METS level often become exhausted during time periods that others consider warm-up.

Modality refers to the type of exercise. For *muscle strength/endurance,* modality refers to isotonic, isometric, or isokinetic. For *flexibility,* modality refers to a specific slow, static stretch and whether it is independent (active) or assisted (passive). For *body composition,* modality refers to combinations of diet, aerobic exercise, and counseling. For *cardiorespiratory endurance,* modality refers to type of rhythmic, large muscle activity and whether it is continuous or discontinuous (intermittent).

Rate of progression is analogous to dates and program duration on the IEP. Exercise prescription theory recognizes three stages of progression: (a) initial conditioning (usually 4 to 6 weeks), (b) improvement conditioning (the next 5 or 6 months), and (c) maintenance.

For most persons with poor fitness, progression is slow during the first few weeks. This is the critical time in regard to attitude formation, injury prevention, and weight loss. ACSM (2000) *recommended that exercise intensity during this stage be at a step lower than functional ability.* For example, if a person's best effort is a mile in 18 min, then the targeted goal for the first week might be a 20- to 26-min mile done daily. Table 13.3 presents an illustrative walking program for a person classified as having poor fitness (i.e., unable to perform a

Table 13.3 A 14-week aerobics program illustrating progression.

Week	Distance in Miles	Time Goal in Minutes	Points
1	1	20:00	3
2	1	18:00	5
3	1	16:00	5
4	1	15:00	5
5	1½	27:00	7½
6	1½	26:00	7½
7	1½	25:00	7½
8	1	14:25	10
9	2	33:00	10
10	2	32:00	10
11	1½	21:40	15
12	2	28:50	20
13	2	28:30	20
14	2½	36:00	25

Note: The goal is 30 points a week. This point system is used only for conditioning, not maintenance.

20-min mile). Awarding points is a good incentive, especially when everyone understands that the goal is to work up to the maintenance level of 30 points a week.

Improvement should be targeted mostly for the 5 to 6 months after the initial conditioning stage and will occur only if intensity and time are progressively increased. The rate of this progression depends on the physical and mental state. Whenever there are performance plateaus and/or persons indicate a desire to slow down, the maintenance phase begins. At this point, a decision must be made about the minimum frequency, intensity, and time (FIT) required to maintain the training effect. If regular exercise is stopped or decreased too much, *detraining* occurs. **Detraining** refers to the gradual loss of all that was gained.

Exercise prescription theory constitutes a large body of knowledge. It is not attributed to one person, as are many theories, but is often associated with ACSM, the organization that publishes *Guidelines for Exercise Testing and Prescription* (2000) and offers certification for various levels of fitness expertise. Exercise prescription theory can be broken down into specific theories and/or practices associated with pioneers like Cooper (1968) (aerobic fitness), Lange (1919) and Hellebrandt and Houtz (1956) (the overload principle), DeLorme and Watkins (1948) (progressive resistance exercise), and Hettinger and Müller (1953) (isometric exercise). There is much to be learned. This chapter presents only beginning level essentials.

Personalizing Goals for Various Conditions

The meaning of fitness varies with the nature and severity of disability. Let's consider the needs of some of the populations served and the prioritization of goals to guide training.

Severe Developmental Disabilities

In nonambulatory persons with severe developmental disabilities like cerebral palsy, physical fitness is dependent upon adequacy of the postural reflex mechanism and muscle tone to perform basic movements like lift head, roll over, sit, and crawl/creep. These persons are extremely limited in both mental and physical capacities. They do not play spontaneously and do not initiate movement. Their muscle tone is hypertonic (spastic) or hypotonic (flaccid). A major concern is **contractures,** the permanent shortening and distortion of muscle groups caused by hypertonicity. Problems are not strength and endurance but rather related to basic central nervous system (CNS) function, especially sensorimotor integration.

Major goals for such persons are (a) range of motion (ROM) to prevent contractures and stimulate CNS integration, (b) functional ability to perform movement patterns used in fitness tasks, and (c) exercise capacity tolerance. These goals, strictly speaking, are prerequisites to fitness training (see Figure 13.6). Emphasis is on increasing the time dimension of prescription (i.e., the number of minutes or trials the person will persist or tolerate).

Many individuals with severe disability, however, have limited physical capacities but good intelligence. They are able to use motorized wheelchairs at an early age and to independently exercise. ROM to prevent contractures is their primary fitness goal. *As slow, static stretches increase ROM on one surface, the opposite surface is automatically strengthened.* Thus, ROM and strength are developed concurrently, and muscle imbalances caused by pathology are corrected. Chapter 14 on postures and muscle imbalances is particularly applicable to this group. The breathing exercises described under asthma in Chapter 19 on other health-impaired conditions are also important.

When persons are not at risk for contractures and muscle imbalances, equal attention is given to ROM and strength goals. Free weights, pulleys, and Nautilus- or Universal-type machines are used in ways similar to those in able-bodied programs, but more emphasis is placed on concurrent ROM exercises (Holland & Steadward, 1990; Lockette & Keyes, 1994). Weight control and cardiorespiratory endurance goals depend on mobility options and aspirations to be athletes and/or maintain active, healthy lifestyles.

Spinal Paralysis and Injury Rehabilitation

Strength is a special concern of persons with paralysis, paresis (muscle weakness), or injury that has required surgery. Physical therapy and physical medicine are professions particularly known for work in strength rehabilitation. In paralysis, strength is associated with ROM (i.e., is there enough strength to move the body part?). Residual strength is tested manually (Daniels & Worthingham, 1986) and graded on a 5 (normal) to 0 (complete paralysis) scale as follows:

Grade 5 Normal strength. Full ROM against gravity and full resistance applied by the examiner.

Grade 4 Good strength. Full ROM against gravity with only moderate resistance applied by the examiner.

Grade 3 Fair strength. Full ROM against gravity only.

Grade 2 Poor strength. Full ROM only if the part is positioned so that the force of gravity is negated.

Figure 13.6 Fitness training. (*A*) For individuals with severe developmental disabilities, the emphasis should be on functional ability to perform movement patterns. (*B*) Nonambulatory persons need to develop strength to move their bodies from place to place.

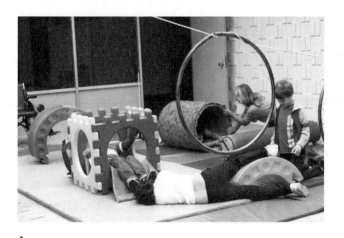

A

B

Grade 1 Trace strength. Muscle contraction can be seen or palpated, but strength is insufficient to produce motion even with gravity eliminated.

Grade 0 Zero strength. Complete paralysis. No visible or palpable contraction.

This system of strength testing is used in sport classification of athletes with spinal cord injury, polio, and related disabilities (see Chapter 23). Volunteer work with a wheelchair team and/or persons in a rehabilitation center is perhaps the best way to learn about strength from a paralysis/paresis perspective.

Strength and flexibility in adapted physical activity are often approached as components of *postural fitness.* Imbalances in strength and flexibility, whether developmental or acquired, cause postural deviations, low mechanical efficiency, and problems of coordination, control, and balance. Chapter 14 on postures presents exercises for developing strength and flexibility in specific muscle groups.

Other Health Impairments

Persons with other health impairments (OHI) are typically more interested in weight loss and aerobic endurance than strength and flexibility. Sedentary lifestyle may have contributed to their disability or vice versa. Often, these persons are coping concurrently with several conditions: heart disease, hypertension, obesity, asthma, diabetes, cancer, and the like. These may have been present since birth or a young age, distorting their perceptions of what feeling good is like. More than likely, however, the onset has been slow and insidious. They do not realize how poor their condition is until challenged to take a fitness test or advised to exercise by their physicians.

Limited Mental Function

Persons with mental retardation (MR) typically have the same fitness needs and capacities as the general population. In the hierarchy of possible goals, weight loss and cardiorespiratory endurance usually rank highest. Of major concern in assessment and programming is the individual's ability to understand speed and distance (i.e., "Run as fast as you can for a mile"). Adaptations like a partner or role model to set the pace are often required (Reid, Seidl, & Montgomery, 1989). Additionally, more care is needed in programming because 20 to 60% of infants born with chromosomal defects like Down syndrome have congenital heart disease. When MR is severe or profound, the autonomic nervous system that regulates heartbeat may be affected. In such cases, the heart rate response to strenuous exercise is not normal, and traditional methods of monitoring exertion are not valid.

A consideration in severe retardation is whether goals like play and game behaviors, social competency/acceptance, and perceptual-motor function should take precedence over fitness. These persons have so many needs that deciding which are most important is difficult. In most cases, however, play and game behaviors are necessary to make fitness training ecologically valid.

Limited Sensory Function

Persons with visual and hearing impairments also have the same fitness needs and capabilities as the general population. Many senior citizens fall into this category and need help with cardiorespiratory fitness.

Aerobic Capacity or Cardiorespiratory Endurance

Aerobic capacity, or cardiorespiratory endurance, is the most important component of health-related fitness. To improve aerobic capacity, individuals must perform vigorous activities that elevate the heart rate over prolonged periods of time. The definition of *prolonged* varies, *but the minimal target time is 3 min.* Individuals who cannot sustain vigorous activity for 3 min may need to begin training with **interval conditioning,** a system in

**Figure 13.7   Work on the bicycle ergometer is one of
the best ways to increase aerobic fitness. Here, Dr. Lane
Goodwin, professor emeritus, University of Wisconsin at
LaCrosse, helps an adolescent with Down syndrome.**

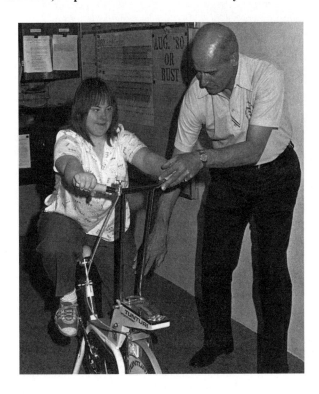

which bouts of 1 min of exercise are interspersed with 1 or 2
min of rest. The goal is to gradually increase the time spent in
vigorous exercise until 20 to 60 min can be sustained with relative ease. Stationary bicycles are often used to achieve this goal
in school and exercise settings, especially when weather is extremely hot or cold (see Figure 13.7).

Assessment of Aerobic Capacity

While laboratory measurement is common in university, hospital, and rehabilitation settings, most adapted physical activity
specialists use **field tests** to estimate aerobic capacity: (a) step
tests, (b) distance runs, and (c) walking tests. Distance runs (12-
min or 1 to 1.5 mi) at the fastest possible speeds are popular, but
fast walking may be maximal effort for many unfit persons.
ACSM recognizes the **Rockport Fitness Walking Test** (Rippe
& Ward, 1989) as a valid aerobic fitness measure. The goal of
this test is to walk 1 mi as fast as possible.

Roy Shephard, a Canadian physician, is a leader in applying fitness concepts to special populations. In an excellent
text Shephard (1990) describes a 12-min wheelchair distance
field test. VO$_2$max on this test ranged from below 12 to above
36, showing that the decreased muscle mass of persons with
paralysis lowers their endurance. Individual differences in
height, weight, usable body parts, and coordination-control parameters make accurate measurement of VO$_2$max a challenge.
Field test results are only estimates of ability.

Common laboratory tests are done on treadmills, bicycle ergometers, wheelchair ergometers, and arm-cranking de-

vices. VO$_2$max values are obtained by protocols in which work
load is progressively increased until exhaustion sets in.

Regardless of whether field or laboratory tests are
used, it is important to be knowledgeable about resting and exercise recovery rates. Watch students for signs of distress, and
know when to stop testing.

Cardiac Resting and Exercise Recovery Rates

Resting heart rate is a good indicator of fitness. The following
ranges are considered normal for each age group (Bates, 1983):

Newborns	110–200
1–24 months	100–200
2–12 years	80–150
13 years and older	60–100

Highly trained adult athletes may have rates as low as 40 beats
a minute. In general, however, resting rates outside these ranges
indicate serious problems. Slow rates are associated with an active lifestyle and fast rates with sedentary habits.

Recovery time after aerobic exercise helps determine
whether exercise demands are appropriate or excessive. Heart
rate should decrease to below 120 after 5 min of rest and to below 100 after 10 min of rest (Cooper, 1982). The faster this recovery, of course, the better. The pulse rates of most persons
decrease to under 100 during the first minute of rest. Generally,
the heart rate decreases during the first 2 to 3 min after exercise
at about the same rate that it increased during activity.

Recovery rates determine the amount of time needed
for cool-down. For healthy young persons, cool-down should
last until the heart rate is about 120. For middle-aged and older
adults, respectively, rates for ending cool-down are 110 and 100.

Respiratory Resting and Exercise Recovery Rates

Recovery breathing rate is also a concern. At rest, normal respiration is 12 to 16 breaths a minute. Recovery to this rate should
require less than 10 min.

Prescribing Aerobic Exercise

Continuous, low-impact exercise is recommended for persons
with low fitness. **Continuous** means that the activity lasts more
than 3 min. This marks the approximate point at which contracting skeletal muscle shifts to aerobic metabolism to produce
energy.

Principles to Guide Work With Low-Fit People

Four principles guide cardiorespiratory or aerobic endurance
work with low-fit people: (a) use low-impact activities;
(b) match frequency, intensity, and time to ability; (c) pay attention to self-concept and motivation; and (d) teach acceptance
that rate of progression will be slower than for average people.
Low- and high-impact activities refer to modality choices. **Low-
impact** includes (a) non-weight-bearing activities like swimming, cycling, and rowing and (b) exercises that put minimal
stress on joints, like walking, cross-country skiing, and slow
stair climbing. **High-impact** includes any activity with a running or jumping component.

Several heart conditions are characterized by lower than normal MHR. Brain stem and autonomic nervous system damage can cause low MHRs. Medications like the beta blockers used to manage high blood pressure and heart conditions suppress both MHR and exercise response. Diabetes can also make MHR an inaccurate value. In cases like this, intensity is generally prescribed by **rating of perceived exertion** (RPE) or METs rather than by heart rate.

Many factors affect heart rate response and must be taken into account. Among these are hot temperatures, high humidity, emotional stress, and medications. Overweight conditions cause hearts to beat faster than average. Infections with fever increase heart rate response so much that elevated body temperature is an exercise contraindication.

Perceived Exertion, Pain, and Dyspnea

Creating a regimen light enough for persons with low fitness requires much experimentation. It is important to provide instruction on intensity and to help exercisers get in touch with their bodies and develop a vocabulary for describing perceived exertion, pain/discomfort, and breathlessness. Table 13.5 presents scales commonly used in exercise assessment, prescription, and communication (ACSM, 2000; Borg, 1998). The rating of perceived exertion (RPE) scale is best known.

For example, using the original RPE scale of 6–20: 9 ("very light"), corresponds to a healthy person walking slowly at a pace he or she can continue for 20–30 min; 13 ("somewhat hard") would be walking at a brisk pace, but it still feels OK to continue walking at this pace for 10–12 min; 17 ("very hard"), the healthy person is really pushing him or herself, it feels very hard and the person is very tired and can only maintain this intensity for 1–2 min; and 19 ("extremely hard"), for most persons, this is the most strenuous exercise they have ever experienced and must stop after 5–15 sec.

Children from age 7 onward give RPEs that correlate highly with heart rate. Overweight persons tend to overestimate RPE (Ward & Bar-Or, 1990) but can be taught accurate perceptions. RPEs eliminate the nuisance of counting pulse rate during aerobic activities. The RPE is also recommended for people whose hearts do not respond properly to exercise. Charts with RPE adjectives in large print are hung on walls to teach about intensity and increase awareness of its importance.

For persons who are unable to sustain large muscle exercise at 55 to 90% of maximal heart rate for 15 min, the goal should be **exercise tolerance** (functional capacity) rather than cardiorespiratory endurance. Tolerance is influenced mainly by (a) cognition/motivation; (b) muscle pain caused by lactic acid accumulation, oxygen deprivation, or tissue swelling; (c) chest pain or stitch in side caused by insufficient oxygen supply; and (d) breathing discomfort, called **dyspnea.**

Everyone experiences some discomfort as intensity of exercise increases, but persons with low fitness often perceive real pain. Asthma and obesity particularly challenge pain threshold. Persons who cannot get enough oxygen into the lower extremities may experience severe hip, leg, or foot pain called **claudication.** The calf is most commonly affected, and the intense pain occurs after only a short distance (half a block to quarter mile) has been covered. Claudication should not be

Table 13.5 Ratings to describe perceptions of exercise intensity and discomfort.

Ratings of Perceived Effort (RPE) Scales

Original Category		Revised Category-Ratio	
6		0	Nothing at all
7	Very, very light	0.5	Very, very weak
8		1	Very weak
9	Very light	2	Weak
10		3	Moderate
11	Fairly light	4	Somewhat strong
12		5	Strong
13	Somewhat hard	6	
14		7	Very strong
15	Hard	8	
16		9	
17	Very hard	10	Very, very strong
18		+	Maximal
19	Very, very hard		
20			

Ratings of Pain and Dyspnea Scales

Pain Scale

1+	Light, barely noticeable
2+	Moderate, bothersome
3+	Severe, very uncomfortable
4+	Most severe pain ever experienced

Dyspnea Scale for Breathing Comfort

1+	Mild, noticeable to exerciser but not observer
2+	Mild, some difficulty, noticeable to observer
3+	Moderate difficulty, but can continue
4+	Severe difficulty, cannot continue

Note: The RPE scales are from *Medicine and Science in Sports and Exercise,* Vol. 14, p. 377–387h, "Rating of Perceived Effort (RPE) Scales." ©The American College of Sports Medicine.

confused with ordinary muscle cramps. It is rare in the general population but relatively common in persons with oxygen deficiency conditions.

The challenge in adapted physical activity is to increase intensity so gradually that discomfort is minimal. Otherwise, persons tend to drop out. *Also, coping with or ignoring discomfort may need to be taught.* Athletes and physical education majors take "No pain, no gain" for granted. In contrast, sedentary persons have no experience in judging exercise-induced discomfort.

Numerical scales are used to objectify ratings of pain and dyspnea (see Table 13.5). An objective for a person with asthma, for example, might be to reduce dyspnea from 3 to 2 during a 1-mi walk for speed. The scales in Table 13.5 should be incorporated into assessment systems that urge all-out effort. Fitness training for health should be adapted (slower, lighter than training for sports) so that activity is associated with pleasure, not pain and dyspnea.

Table 13.6 Relative percentages of components of total body mass.

Component	Average Male (%)	Average Female (%)
Muscle	45	36
Bone	15	12
Fat	15	27
Remainder	25	25

Body Composition

Body composition (also see Chapter 19) refers to the individual components that constitute the total body mass. The relative percentages are shown in Table 13.6. Females have more fat, and males have more muscle tissue. Differences between genders are minimal until puberty, when sex hormones become active and promote development of male and female characteristics. In general, children have less body fat than adults (10 to 15% compared with 15 to 27%). Body composition is largely genetically determined, as evidenced by similarities in fat distribution and body shapes/sizes/builds within families. Genetic predisposition, however, can be tempered by exercise and nutrition. Some disabilities affect body composition. *Spinal cord injuries, for example, increase body fat percentage and decrease lean body mass.* These changes are more pronounced in quadriplegia than paraplegia.

Body fat percentages, rather than body weight, are the major fitness concern. Healthy body fat standards depend on whether or not an individual wants to excel in sports. For nonathletes, desirable percentages of fat are 18 to 30% for women and 10 to 25% for men. For athletes, less fat is desirable: 12 to 22% for women and 5 to 13% for men. Fat reduction goals thus depend on leisure interests.

Assessment of Body Fat

Percentage of body fat can be determined by laboratory protocols and formulae or estimated by skinfold caliper measures. Calipers provide a measure of the amount of fat that can be pinched away from a body part at a particular landmark (see Figures 13.9 and 13.10).

When time is so limited that only one measure can be taken, the triceps skinfold is recommended. To ensure accuracy, measurements are taken three times, and the middle value is recorded. Care must be taken to pinch the skin at precisely the point indicated in test directions. Measurements are usually taken on the right side only.

When possible, several skinfold measures are used. The best combination of skinfold measures is controversial. The FITNESSGRAM recommends a triceps and calf skinfolds combination. The Canadian Standardized Test of Fitness recommends the sum of triceps, biceps, subscapular, and suprailiac skinfolds. Figure 13.10 presents various skinfold measures.

Body Mass Index: Substitute Measure

Body mass index (BMI) refers to weight divided by height or height squared and is accepted as a substitute for body fat measures when skinfold calipers are not available. The BMI (also

Figure 13.9 Triceps skinfold. (*A*) The midpoint of the back upper arm is the standard place to make the measurement. (*B*) Minimum triceps skinfold thickness indicating obesity (in millimeters).

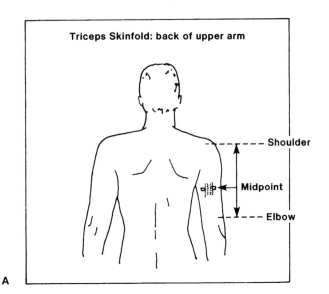

Age (Years)	Males	Females
5	12	14
6	12	15
7	13	16
8	14	17
9	15	18
10	16	20
11	17	21
12	18	22
13	18	23
14	17	23
15	16	24
16	15	25
17	14	26
18	15	27
19	15	27
20	16	28
21	17	28
22	18	28
23	18	28
24	19	28
25	20	29
26	20	29
27	21	29
28	22	29
29	23	29
30	23	30

called the Quetelet index) is the ratio of body weight to the square of body height:

$$BMI = \frac{Body\ weight\ (kg)}{Height^2\ (meters)}$$

Figure 13.10   The triceps skinfold is used with one or more of these skinfolds.

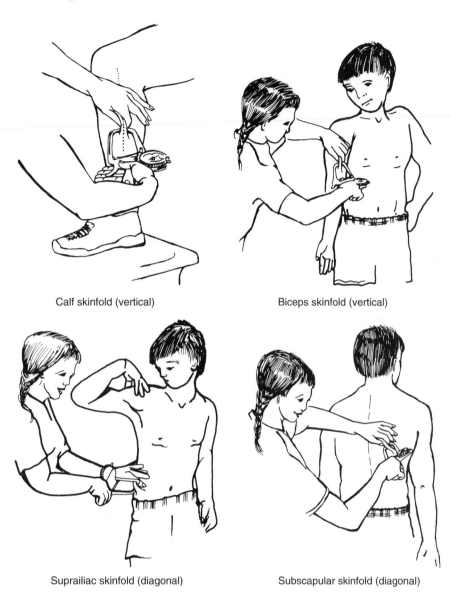

Calf skinfold (vertical)

Biceps skinfold (vertical)

Suprailiac skinfold (diagonal)

Subscapular skinfold (diagonal)

where 1 kg = 2.2 lb and 1 m = 39.37 inches. Health fitness standards for BMI vary with age and gender.

Physical and motor fitness scores should be interpreted in relation to height, weight, and skinfolds. The classic research of Dobbins, Garron, and Rarick (1981) showed that many statistically significant differences between persons with and without MR disappear when adjustments are made for differences in body size.

Height-weight tables heighten motivation for lifestyle changes because they are easily understood. However, the correlation between weight and percent body fat is about .67. Thus, *weight is not a reliable predictor of body fat.* Nevertheless, height and weight are important indicators of normal growth. Most youth reach the final 2% of their height by age 18 (females) and age 20 (males). After about age 45, height begins to decrease, probably because of loss of bone mass and related degeneration of the spinal column. Bone loss **(osteoporosis)** in old age proceeds faster in women than men.

Prescribing Exercise for Fat Loss

Body fat can best be reduced by ensuring that large muscle activity uses more calories than daily intake. This is achieved through change of lifestyle (both exercise and nutrition) and generally requires counseling as well as participation in a support group. Exercise should be aerobic at whatever intensity is possible. Table 13.4 shows the calories expended per hour in various activities for a person weighing 154 lb. *The heavier a person, the more calories are expended.* Tables like this must therefore be adjusted for individual differences. A good formula for this purpose is to increase or decrease the calories by 10% for each 15 lb (7 kg) over or under 154 lb (70 kg).

One pound of fat equals 3,500 calories. No more than 2.2 lb (1 kg) should be lost each week (ACSM, 2000). To achieve this goal, exercise should be increased by at least 300 calories a day. For a 154-lb person whose highest intensity level is 2 mph (one 30-min mi), 2 hr a day must be spent walking to expend 300 calories. Obviously, the more fit a person is, the less time per day is needed to expend calories.

Obesity is addressed in Chapter 19 (other health impairments) because it is a medical problem as serious as asthma, diabetes, and the like. *Obese persons need to be assured that long-duration activity at low intensity is as effective as short-duration/high-intensity activity.* Time management counseling is a high-priority need because most persons have a difficult time finding an extra 1 to 2 hr a day in their schedules to use for exercise. Counseling and support group involvement should continue after weight loss to ensure maintenance of target weight.

Muscle Strength/Endurance

Muscle strength and endurance are developed concurrently in childhood through vigorous activities of daily living. *Strength* is developed every time that muscle exertion is near maximum, as in lifting, pushing, pulling, holding, or carrying a heavy object. Jumping as far as possible, for example, requires a maximal lift of body weight. Pull-ups and rope climbing also demand lifting body weight. *Endurance* is developed whenever a muscular activity continues for several seconds, as in curl-ups, push-ups, running in place, continuous jumps, or short-distance sprints.

Age and gender differences in strength parallel changes in muscle mass. Females tend to show a steady increase in strength until about age 30. Males likewise increase steadily but demonstrate a sudden, rapid increase at puberty (ages 13 to 14), which is associated with testosterone, the sex hormone that stimulates muscle growth. At all ages, the average male is stronger than the average female. After adolescence, muscle bulk (the result of muscle fiber hypertrophy) characterizes males who engage in strength training. *Women in equivalent programs increase in strength but do not develop comparable bulk because of their lack of testosterone.* After age 30, strength plateaus and then begins to gradually decline. The rate of this decline is largely dependent on amount of physical activity.

Assessment of Muscle Strength/Endurance

The **principle of specificity** states that the benefits of exercises done in one position will not transfer when the muscle is used in other positions. There is no such thing as total body strength/endurance, so choices must be made about which muscle groups are the most important to test. Generally, the groups selected are abdominal (curl-ups), upper arm and shoulder (pull-ups, push-ups), hip and thigh (distance jump or sprint), and back (trunk lifts from prone).

Assessment focuses on the number of times an exercise can be done in the prescribed posture or position. Body alignment is very important in both calisthenic-type exercises and weight lifting, because injury can occur when body parts are improperly placed or used. The cadence of exercise is also important, in that *slow* movements indicate control against gravity's force.

When physical disability results in paralysis or paresis, assessment is more comprehensive. In such cases, movement capacity is graded on a 0 to 5 scale (see pages 370–371).

Prescribing Exercise for Muscle Strength/Endurance

Sedentary persons should take all their major muscle groups through both strength and endurance exercises at least 2 days a week (ACSM, 2000). Adapted physical activity for young people uses animal walks, stunts, games, self-testing activities, and movement education to achieve this purpose (see Figure 13.11). For example, *arm and shoulder strength/endurance* can be increased by crab walk, dog walk, lame-dog walk, inchworm, and coffee grinder. Any activity in which the arms support, propel, or lift body weight develops muscles. Hanging, rope or apparatus climbing, and overarm travel on a horizontal ladder are especially good. *Abdominal strength/endurance* is developed by hands and knees creeping and by lifting body parts (trunk or legs) from a supine position. *Back strength* is developed by lifting body parts from a prone position. Swimming is often considered the best all-round muscle developer, and exercises/games can be devised that use arm and leg movements from the various strokes.

Central to the development of muscles is the **principle of overload,** which refers to progressively increasing the demands made on a muscle group. When planning progressions, first increase the number of repetitions, then increase the resistance. Strength/endurance can be developed by three types of activity: (a) isotonic, (b) isometric, and (c) isokinetic (see Figure 13.12).

Isotonic Exercise (Dynamic or Moving)

Isotonic exercise is categorized according to equipment needed: (a) no equipment, as in animal walks, push-ups, and curl-ups; (b) stationary bars for pull-ups; (c) wall, floor, or ceiling pulleys; (d) free weights; and (e) variable resistance machines like the Universal and Nautilus. Free weights are divided into *dumbbells* for one-hand lifts, *barbells* for two-hand lifts, and *cuff weights* that are attached to body parts via Velcro. Machines offer multiple stations for pushing, pulling, and lifting and provide either constant or variable resistance.

Creative teachers devise all kinds of free weights and color-code or mark them to indicate number of pounds. Examples are

1. Stuffed animals filled with 7, 10, and 15 lb of sand
2. Fireplace logs, bricks, or rocks
3. Sacks of potatoes and other grocery store purchases
4. Plastic containers filled with sand or cat sand
5. Backpacks filled with weights
6. Buckets, chairs, and other daily living objects
7. Weights made from tin cans, cement, and broomsticks

Adolescents and adults benefit tremendously from weight training. Prescriptions are stated in terms of sets and the repetition maximum (RM). One set is the number of repetitions done consecutively without resting. RM is the maximal weight that can be lifted in one set. Strength is best developed when the resistance (weight) allows no more than 8–12 repetitions and three sets are performed two or three times a week (ACSM, 2000). This guideline varies, however, with disability and purpose of training. In general, training for muscle endurance

Figure 13.11   Fun activities for developing arm and shoulder strength.

1. Can you do a dog walk? Note that knees are bent.

2. Can you lift one leg and do a lame-dog walk?

3. Can you do a bear walk? Note that legs are straight.

4. Can you do the inchworm walk? Start in push-up position, then inch forward using only your feet to the bear walk position, then inch forward, using only your hands, to the push-up position again.

5. Can you do a seal (walrus) crawl? Only your arms can move.

6. Can you touch your chin to the mat and come back up? This is called *dumping sand*. Can you do the wheelbarrow walk?

7. Can you do the crab walk?

8. Can you hold a bridge?

9. Can you hold a one-arm side stretch?

10. Can you do the coffee grinder?

11. Can you do a rabbit jump? Knees stay bent.

12. Can you do a mule kick? Knees straighten out.

13. Can you do an elephant walk with a partner?

14. Can you do a centipede walk with one or two partners?

Figure 13.12   **Three types of strength training.**

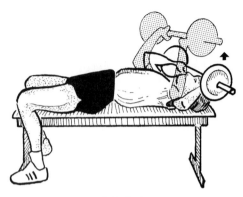

A. Isotonic

B. Isometric

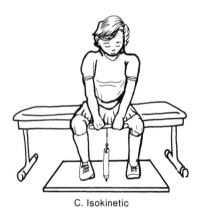

C. Isokinetic

requires use of lighter weights (one half or three fourths of maximum), with greater number of repetitions. In contrast, training for strength uses heavier weights with fewer repetitions.

Progressive resistance exercise (PRE) is a popular rehabilitation technique used to ameliorate weakness and atrophy after surgery. Often called the DeLorme method after one of its founders (DeLorme & Watkins, 1948), PRE is based on maximal resistance that pain tolerance permits to be lifted 10 times (10RM) and a lifting program of 30 repetitions executed several times each week as follows:

1 set of 10 repetitions at one-half 10RM

1 set of 10 repetitions at three-fourths 10RM

1 set of 10 repetitions at full 10RM

Safety is a concern when using free weights. Persons should not lift alone for obvious reasons. Lifts should be slow, smooth, and continuous to avoid injury, and breathing should be natural. Strength training should be coordinated with a good flexibility routine.

Isometric Exercise (Static)

Isometric exercise is a maximum or near-maximum muscle contraction that is held for 6 sec and repeated several times during the day. This exercise is highly specific, strengthening muscles only for work at the same angle as the training. Squeezing a **dynamometer** or tennis ball to develop hand grip strength is an example; *the isometric part of the exercise begins after movement has ceased.* Persons with low back pain use the gluteal pinch and pelvic tilt. Almost everyone occasionally pulls inward on abdominal muscles and holds to improve appearance. Straining during bowel movements is another example of isometric exercise. Arm and leg exercises entail pressing against doorways and walls and pulling against towels, ropes, or tire strips that permit no movement and hence no change in muscle length.

Isometric exercise is the only form of strength training that is not based on the overload principle. Founded by Hettinger and Müller (1953) of Germany, isometrics are especially recommended for persons bedridden or limited in movement for reasons other than cardiorespiratory disease. Because of associated breath holding, isometrics is the worst form of strength training for individuals with heart disease and high blood pressure.

Isokinetic Exercise (Machine-generated)

Isokinetic exercise is associated with constant resistance machines. These keep velocity of a movement constant and match the resistance to the effort of the exerciser. This allows maximal tension to be exerted throughout the range of motion. Illustrative machines of this type are Cybex II, Apollo, Exer-Genie, MERAC, and Hydra-Fitness. Isokinetics is the newest type of weight training and, theoretically, should lead to the greatest improvement.

Valsalva Effect and Contraindications

The **Valsalva effect** is an increase in intraabdominal and intrathoracic pressure that results when breath is held, as in straining to lift a heavy object or to exert maximal force. Increased pressure causes slowing of heart rate, decreased return of blood to the heart, and elevated blood pressure. *Heavy strength training is generally contraindicated in high blood pressure conditions and heart disease.* Breath holding during exercise can also rupture tissues, especially in the abdominal region (**hernias**) and in the eyes when pathology already is present, such as increased internal pressure (**glaucoma**) and torn or detached retina.

Range of Motion and Flexibility

The range of motion and flexibility component refers to ability to move body segments through the actions and planes designated as normal for each joint. For example, movements in three planes are possible at the shoulder and hip joints: (a) sagit-

Figure 13.13   Two types of goniometers with their respective measurement systems. The movable bar indicates the number of degrees a body part can be moved.

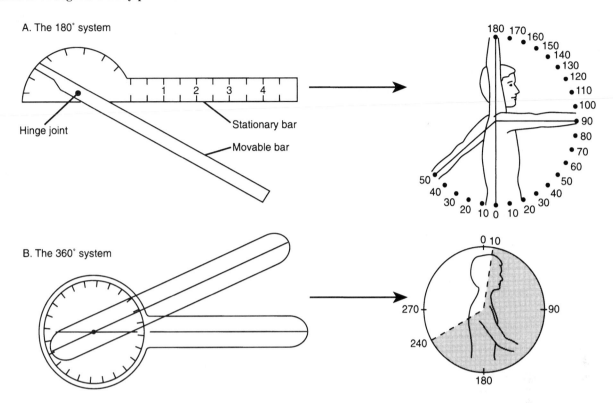

A. The 180° system

Hinge joint

Stationary bar

Movable bar

B. The 360° system

tal plane—flexion and extension; (b) frontal plane—abduction, adduction; and (c) horizontal plane—rotation. In contrast, the elbow and ankle joints permit movement in only one plane.

Range of motion (ROM) is the term used when the movement capacity at a joint is measured in degrees through use of a **goniometer** (a protractor-type device) or a **flexometer** (a 360° dial with pointer that is strapped to the body part). These devices can be purchased through equipment companies (see Appendix E). A knowledge of goniometry is necessary when the goal is increased ROM at designated joints (see Figure 13.13). In pathological conditions that require therapeutic exercise to prevent contractures or to rehabilitate a body part after surgery, ROM is the accepted term. Conditions like cerebral palsy, muscular dystrophy, arthritis, spina bifida, and paralysis require daily ROM exercises. These are typically prescribed by physicians and therapists and carried out by parents, teachers, and aides (Kottke, 1990; Surburg, 1986).

Flexibility is the term used in physical education and sport settings *to specify functional stretching ability* (i.e., ability to stretch well enough to perform activities of daily living and to achieve personal sport and dance goals without injury). *Flexibility tests measure simultaneous function of several joints in performing a function like reaching.* When movement is limited by illness, disability, or sedentary lifestyle, flexibility is the first fitness parameter to suffer. Thus, activity programs for convalescing or sedentary persons often focus on gentle stretching exercises during the first weeks.

Gender, age, occupation, and musculoskeletal differences affect flexibility. At all ages and most joints, females demonstrate more flexibility than males. This difference widens with age. Flexibility seems to improve from childhood through adolescence. Thereafter, it declines steadily. Persons in occupations demanding much physical activity are more flexible than those in sedentary jobs. Flexibility is affected by bony structure or configuration of joints, muscles, tendons, ligaments, and skin. Arthritis, dwarfism, muscular dystrophy, paralysis, cerebral palsy, and burns are examples of conditions that limit flexibility. In contrast, some disabilities like Down syndrome are associated with excessive flexibility.

Assessment of ROM/Flexibility

Flexibility is specific to each muscle group. Since testing all muscle groups is not feasible in large-scale fitness tests, AAH-PERD and its Canadian counterpart *include the sit-and-reach test as a combined estimate of hamstring, hip, and spine flexibility.* These muscle groups, when tight, contribute to injury and/or chronic lower back problems. Tightness is associated with excessive sitting, and the sit-and-reach test is a good predictor of sedentary lifestyle.

Measurement of ROM begins with the body part in anatomical position, which is designated as 0 in the 180° system (see Figure 13.13). The hinge joint of the goniometer is placed over the joint so that both bars point to 0. The movable bar moves with the body part, and its pointer marks the angle of motion achieved. Two or three measures of each movement are taken to ensure reliability. Either the maximum or the average is recorded. Measurements are often taken from a supine position to eliminate balance and gravity problems.

Prescribing Stretching Exercises

The nature of stretching depends on its purpose: (a) to maintain elasticity, (b) to warm up and cool down, or (c) to correct pathological tightness. Chapter 14 on postures and muscle imbalance covers stretches for specific body parts and contraindications. Overall body stretching for maintenance is described in Chapter 16, where yoga and tai chi are emphasized. These are particularly good for older populations.

Regardless of nature, stretches should be only slow and static. **Ballistic movements** (i.e., bobbing and bounces) are no longer considered as stretching exercises and are, in fact, contraindicated when the purpose is flexibility. Modalities used in stretching are (a) active, (b) passive, and (c) combinations. When stretches are directed toward correcting specific tightness, they should slowly move the body part to the extreme of its ROM, where it remains for several seconds. Sport references recommend 10 to 30 sec (ACSM, 2000; Alter, 1996; Curtis, 1981), whereas therapeutic exercise references suggest 5 to 10 sec (Basmajian & Wolf, 1990; Surburg, 1986). Each stretch should be repeated three to five times. *Stretches that take body parts to their movement extremes should be done after warm-ups,* not before. If done incorrectly, stretches can cause injury or worsen disability.

Using Proprioceptive Neuromuscular Facilitation (PNF)

Proprioceptive neuromuscular facilitation (PNF) is a system of stretching that requires the help of an assistant to perform either a contract-relax or a hold-relax exercise sequence that stimulates the **proprioceptors** (sensory receptors in tendons and joints) to enhance functional flexibility. PNF is based on the physiological **principle of reciprocal innervation** (i.e., when an **agonist** (prime mover muscle) contracts, the **antagonist** on the opposite surface relaxes). Relaxation of the antagonist facilitates subsequent stretching of the agonist. In athletic training, PNF is called *superstretching.* In adapted physical activity, PNF is particularly recommended for individuals with cerebral palsy and arthritis.

In the **contract-relax type** of PNF, the individual isotonically contracts a muscle group for 5 to 10 sec while the assistant resists this contraction as strongly as possible; then the individual relaxes the muscle group, after which the assistant moves the body part slowly through its complete ROM to the *limitation point,* where the muscle group cannot safely be stretched further. This three-part sequence is repeated, each time from a new point of greater elongation.

In the **hold-relax type** of PNF, the assistant moves the body part passively through its complete ROM, stopping at the limitation point. At the limitation point, the individual does an isometric or holding type of contraction for 5 to 10 sec, followed by complete relaxation. The assistant supports the body part during the relaxation phase. The hold-relax sequence is repeated several times. The hold-relax type is the method of choice when pain is an issue, as in arthritis.

Beliefs, Attitudes, and Practices

Several theories can be applied to help persons develop fitness and change lifestyle. Statements of goals and objectives should always include targeted beliefs, attitudes, and practices.

Underlying Theories

According to **reasoned action attitude theory** (see Chapters 5 and 9), persons will change their lifestyles to include regular exercise if they are helped to reason out the probable outcomes/consequences and perceive the support of significant others. They are asked to write a personal exercise goal, list the possible good and bad consequences, and then predict the likelihood of these consequences coming true. This becomes their **attitude toward behavior score.** Next, they identify four or five significant others and what these people think they should do. A **subjective norm score** is derived by multiplying this with a rating of personal motivation to comply. Together, attitude toward behavior and subjective norm determine intention to implement the exercise goal and exercise behaviors.

According to **self-efficacy** or **social cognitive theory** (see Chapter 5), one must perceive self as capable of carrying out a desired behavior and expect to succeed. **Efficacy expectations** result when certain antecedents are planned and implemented: (a) reminders of past mastery, (b) role models to provide vicarious learning opportunities, (c) verbal persuasion by self and others, and (d) cognitive control of anxiety, fear, and related negative emotions. These four antecedents represent the most important variables that shape social cognitive behaviors. This comprehensive model works well if the person has been fit in the past and has memories to pull from.

According to **perceived competence theory** (see Chapter 8), three variables affect achievement: (a) perceived competence, (b) perceived control (self, others, unknown), and (c) motivation orientation (challenge, curiosity, mastery, judgment, criteria). Attention to these variables will enhance fitness programming, especially if the person has had little fitness success in the past.

Self-Reports

New assessment approaches include self-reports of motivation, food intake, physical activity, and attitudes about the body and exercise. Illustrative is the Self-Motivation Inventory (Dishman, Ickes, & Morgan, 1980). This 40-item instrument includes items like the following that are rated on a 5-point scale ("very unlike me" to "very much like me"):

1. I get discouraged easily.
2. Sometimes, I push myself harder than I should.
3. I can persevere at stressful tasks, even when they are physically tiring or painful.

Research indicates that the self-motivation score combined with body weight and percent fat is an excellent predictor of exercise adherence. Information yielded by instruments like the Self-Motivation Inventory helps in counseling and individualized teaching.

Diaries or logs of food intake (Block et al., 1986) and physical activity (Baranowski, 1988; CIAR, 1999a) help structure goal setting. They focus attention on goals and provide concrete facts; 24-hr recalls tend to be more accurate than 3- or 7-day recalls. Illustrative of an interview format to assess activity is the following:

Teacher: In order to set goals for after-school and weekend physical activity for the next month, let's think about what you did this past week. Let's start with yesterday, and you list everything you did that was of moderate, hard, or very hard intensity. *Moderate* things are activities that make you feel like you are taking a brisk walk. *Very hard* activities make you feel like you are running. *Hard* activities are those that fall between brisk walking and running. Ready? Let's start.

Client/Student: OK, yesterday was Sunday. I got up about 7 A.M., messed around, took a shower, and went to church.

Teacher: What kind of transportation did you take to church? It is important that you tell me about transportation so that we can determine how much energy you spent. Did you walk, and was the pace slow, medium, or fast? Or did you cycle or take a car?

Client/Student: Dad drove the car, but after church, I went with my friends, and we walked about 12 blocks to Bill's house. We messed around a while and then took the bus to a movie.

Teacher: Then what did you do in the evening?

Client/Student: Shot baskets for about an hour with some friends, watched TV a couple of hours, and studied an hour or so. Went to bed about 11 P.M.

Teacher: So your main exercise for the day was basketball shooting. Can you think of any other activities?

Client/Student: No, it rained most of the day.

Teacher: Then let's go back to Saturday. Tell me about your day. You don't need to tell me everything, just the activities that you consider moderate, hard, or very hard.

The interview continues until the past 7 days are covered.

Weather and Temperature Concerns

Weather and temperature are important in all aspects of fitness testing and training. Persons with disabilities tend to be more vulnerable to extremes of hot and cold than able-bodied peers. This is particularly true in spinal paralysis, cerebral palsy, and the widespread nervous system damage associated with severe MR. The hypothalamus in the brain (temperature regulation center) and the autonomic nervous system must be intact for sweat glands, skeletal muscles, and blood vessels to function properly in temperature regulation. *Nervous system damage above T8 (the eighth thoracic segment of the spinal cord) renders the body incapable of maintaining normal temperature (98.6° F or 37° C).*

Anyone with damage above T8 should be closely watched for **poikilothermy,** a condition in which the body assumes the same temperature as the surrounding environment. Such persons are entirely dependent upon clothing, external heating and cooling systems, and ingestion of warm or cool fluids. Temperature regulation problems do not contraindicate heavy exercise; they simply require appropriate adaptations.

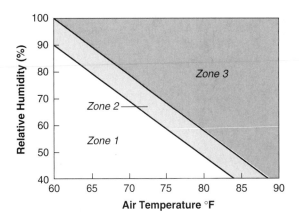

Figure 13.14   **Weather guide for prevention of heat illness. Zone 1 is safe; for Zone 2, use caution; for Zone 3, use extreme caution.**

Regardless of whether temperature regulation problems are present, persons should not be expected to exert all-out effort when temperatures are above 90° or below 50° or when temperature plus humidity exceed 175°. Figure 13.14 presents a simple system for determining when caution and extreme caution are essential. Whereas humidity is the greatest problem in hot weather, wind-chill factor should be considered in cold weather.

Generic terms for body temperature responses are hypothermia (absence of heat) and hyperthermia (excessive heat). **Hypothermia** is associated with frostbite, frozen parts, progressive loss of consciousness, and death. **Hyperthermia** results in heat cramps, heat exhaustion (headache, sweating, dizziness, awkwardness, goose bumps with cold sensation, paleness of face and lips), and **heat stroke** (diminished sweating, loss of consciousness, life threatening when oral temperature reaches 105° F or about 40° C). Obesity and fluid depletion increase the risk of heat-related disorders.

Dehydration, a normal exercise response, is intensified in persons with autonomic nervous system dysfunction. Several prescribed medications also increase thirst. Water and other fluids should be taken at regular intervals during exercise, whether or not the person is thirsty.

Space and Equipment

Schools should have several exercise areas to supplement gymnasium and sport field space. The more equipment available, the more likely people are to use it. Figure 13.15 shows some homemade, inexpensive equipment appropriate for indoor or outdoor use in schools, homes, and community centers. Selection of equipment is typically based on muscle groups weakest in the individuals served. For most children and youth, these are the abdominal and arm and shoulder muscles. Persons in wheelchairs or on crutches also have a special need for strong arm and shoulder muscles. Therefore, equipment for sit-ups, pull-ups, push-ups, and arm hangs/travel is of first priority. Equally important is equipment for aerobic endurance. When space is limited, the equipment of choice is stationary cycles, jump ropes and/or obstacles, stairs for climbing, and benches or

Figure 13.15   Homemade fitness equipment developed by William Price, University of South Florida at Tampa. Each shows ways to adapt for individual differences.

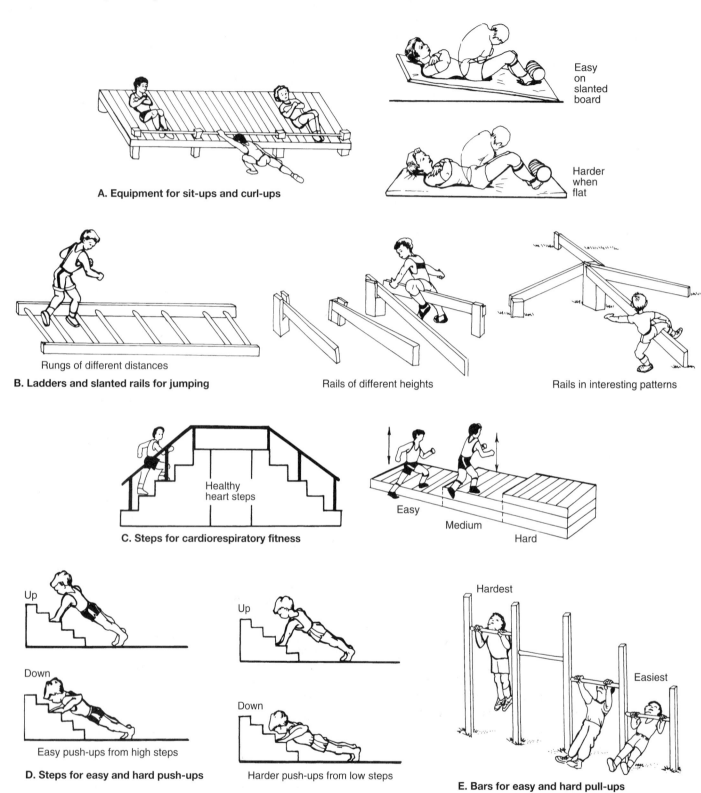

A. Equipment for sit-ups and curl-ups

Easy on slanted board

Harder when flat

Rungs of different distances

B. Ladders and slanted rails for jumping

Rails of different heights

Rails in interesting patterns

Healthy heart steps

C. Steps for cardiorespiratory fitness

Easy   Medium   Hard

Up

Down

Easy push-ups from high steps

D. Steps for easy and hard push-ups

Up

Down

Harder push-ups from low steps

Hardest

Easiest

E. Bars for easy and hard pull-ups

steps for continuous stepping. Tracks and jog/walk/cycle paths with distances clearly marked should be available in schools, parks, and neighborhoods. These require no equipment other than signs.

Lifestyle change requires that schools, homes, and other facilities budget for equipment, plan for space, and provide incentives for use. Equipment should be available in self-contained classrooms, hallways, restrooms, and the like, as well as special exercise stations. Schools should also provide instruction and experience in use of community health and exercise centers to assure carryover when school facilities are not available.

Equipment design should take into account easy, medium, and hard progressions so that individual differences can be met. Inclined boards, for example, can be used to make sit-ups easier or harder. Persons with low abdominal strength should have head higher than feet; many persons in wheelchairs need this adaptation. A bar to tuck feet under provides needed stability and frees partners to do their own exercise. Different heights of pull-up bars, stair steps, ladders, and rails/ropes allow concurrent work by persons of various heights, weights, and abilities.

Organization of the Lesson: Five Parts

Ideally, each fitness session includes five parts: (a) warm-up, (b) aerobic conditioning, (c) flexibility exercises for each major muscle group, (d) muscle strength/endurance exercises, and (e) cool-down. For the average person, sessions last 30 to 45 min because the endurance component requires only 15 to 30 min. For persons with low fitness, however, considerably more time is needed. Often, exercise tolerance is so poor that exercise time must be distributed throughout the day.

Regardless of the fitness components chosen for emphasis, every session should include a 5- to 10-min warm-up and cool-down. During this time, the same muscles and movements should be used as in the regular workout, except at a lower intensity. Typically, 2 or 3 min are spent in walking or slow running, and the remaining time is devoted to slow, static stretches, rhythmical circling of body parts, and gentle calisthenics. Obstacle courses and follow-the-leader activities work well with children. In persons with very low fitness, the warm-up may be all the exercise that can be endured.

Teaching for Fitness: A Review of Principles

A common misconception is that physical activities automatically develop fitness. Two laps around the field or 3 min of calisthenics seldom have the effect desired. The same amount of exercise executed faithfully each day contributes to the maintenance of whatever level fitness already exists, but it *does not improve* fitness.

Fitness lessons should include scientifically planned warm-up, training, and cool-down activities conducted in accordance with the following principles of fitness training:

1. **Individual differences.** Every exercise prescription and/or IEP should be different, based on specific assessment of data, motivation level, and activity preferences. Remember the acronym FIT when making exercise prescriptions:

   F Frequency
   I Intensity or resistance
   T Time or duration

   Let individuals choose their own modality!

2. **Overload/intensity.** Increases in fitness result when the *work load* is greater than usual. Overload is associated with muscle strength/endurance. Intensity relates more to

cardiorespiratory endurance. *Progressive resistance* refers to increasing overload gradually but consistently over time. Overload/intensity can be achieved in the following ways:

   a. Increase the number of pounds being lifted, pushed, or pulled. This results in progressive resistance exercises.
   b. Increase the number of repetitions, sets, or types of exercise performed.
   c. Increase the distance covered.
   d. Increase the speed.
   e. Increase the number of minutes of continuous all-out effort.
   f. Decrease the rest interval between active sessions.
   g. Increase the intensity/type of activity during rest/relaxation phases.
   h. Use any combination of the above.

3. **Frequency.** Training sessions (particularly those of all-out effort) should be scientifically spaced so that there is time for **physiological homeostasis** to occur (i.e., for muscles and lungs to rest). Too frequent practices tend to result in chronic fatigue, muscle stress, and motivation problems.

4. **Specificity/transfer.** Values gained from exercises done in one position or at one speed will not transfer or benefit the person in other positions or speeds. Exercises are highly specific; thus, strength exercises particularly need to be done at many joint angles and many intensities. Warm-ups should use the same movements and positions that will be used later in the game or training exercise.

5. **Active/voluntary movement.** Outcome is most effective when the exercise is *active* (done by the student) rather than passive (done by a therapist or teacher). In the case of persons with severe disability with little or no movement capacity of a particular body part, encourage an all-out effort to initiate the movement, which then can be assisted by the teacher. The student should be actively concentrating and assisting in coactive movement.

6. **Correct breathing.** Breath holding should be avoided because of the Valsalva effect.

7. **Recovery/cool-down.** Persons should not lie or sit down immediately after high-intensity exercise. This tends to subvert the return of blood to the heart and causes dizziness. *Cool-down* should entail continued slow walking or mild activity.

8. **Warm-up.** Warm-ups using movements specific to the game or training to follow should precede high-intensity activity. Warm-up is particularly important for persons with chronic respiratory or cardiorespiratory conditions.

9. **Static stretch.** Slow, static stretches are effective in increasing range of motion and flexibility. Note that ballistic exercises are contraindicated when the goal is to stretch. In spastic cerebral palsy, ballistic exercise elicits an exaggerated stretch reflex.

10. **Contraindication.** If correct postural alignment cannot be maintained during execution of an exercise, it is usually

too difficult a progression and is therefore contraindicated.

11. **Adaptation.** Exercises should be analyzed into easy, medium, and difficult progressions so that each person is doing the adaptation best for him or her. A biomechanical principle often used in adapting exercises is **leverage;** the shorter the lever, the easier the exercise. For instance, straight-leg lifts from a supine position to develop or assess abdominal strength are very difficult since the body (as a lever) is in its longest position. By doing bent-knee leg lifts, the body lever is shortened and the exercise is made easier.

12. **Motivation.** Persons who wish to be physically fit must be willing to pay the price. They must be motivated to tolerate boredom, fatigue, and discomfort. Fitness does not come easily.

13. **Maintenance.** Lifespan fitness requires lifespan activity. Instruction should emphasize maintenance.

14. **Nutrition.** Food and liquid intake should be balanced with activity. Instruction on eating and exercise should be integrated.

15. **Environmental factors.** Activity should be safe and pleasurable. Give particular attention to temperature, humidity, windchill, and pollution.

16. **Ecological or social validity.** Fitness activity should make sense and have carryover value. For example, to persons with severe MR, lifting chairs or sacks of groceries may make more sense than lifting bars and dumbbells.

Exercise Conditioning Methods

This chapter concludes with methods that can be applied to more than one fitness component: (a) interval or intermittent, (b) circuits, (c) continuous, and (d) combinations. For adults, these methods are often built around one modality (weight lifting, running, cycling, swimming). With children, animal walks, stunts, calisthenics, and locomotor activities that are known to develop specific muscle groups are fun. Any large muscle activity done long enough at the right intensity develops cardiorespiratory endurance.

Interval or Intermittent Training

Developed originally to condition long-distance runners and swimmers, interval training can be adapted to any physical activity. It is especially beneficial for persons with asthma, muscular dystrophy, multiple sclerosis, and other neuromuscular conditions. The basic objective is to exercise for short periods of time with rest intervals between.

The interval training prescription (ITP) should be planned for each person individually or for small, homogeneous groups, rather than for the class as a whole (see Table 13.7). After the first 2 weeks, training only twice weekly will result in significant gains in cardiorespiratory endurance.

ITPs require an understanding of the following terms:

1. **Set.** Term that encompasses both the work interval and the rest interval. An ITP may have any number of sets.

2. **Work interval.** Also called a bout. A prescribed number of repetitions of the same activity under identical conditions. Traditionally, the work has been walking, running, or swimming a prescribed number of yards at optimum or near-optimum speed *in an effort to raise the heart rate to a prescribed level.* For variety, work intervals may entail performing an optimum number of squat thrusts, curl-ups, or push-ups within a prescribed number of seconds.

3. **Rest interval.** The number of seconds or minutes between work intervals. During rest, persons should walk rather than sit, lie, or stand. A light activity like walking, arm circles, or toe touches may be psychologically beneficial in that it keeps the mind off exhaustion. The number of seconds comprising the rest interval depends on individual heart recovery rate. *The next repetition should not begin until the heart rate drops to 120 beats per minute or lower, depending on age and fitness status.* If taking the pulse rate is not feasible, the time of the rest interval initially should be approximately twice the amount of time consumed by the work interval.

4. **Repetitions.** The number of times the work is repeated under identical conditions. The amount of effort exerted in each repetition should be more or less constant.

5. **Target time.** The best score that a person can make on the prescribed activity. Target times are generally not set until after the first 2 weeks and are then used as a motivational device to encourage all-out performance.

6. **Level of aspiration.** A statement made by the exerciser indicating expected score or level. This is also a motivational device.

All-out effort is often motivated after the first few weeks by prescribing the speed of the sprint as follows:

One repetition of 660 yd in 2:03

Six repetitions of 220 yd in 0:33

Six repetitions of 110 yd in 0:15

Persons may be guided in developing individualized exercise sessions comprised of sets that reflect their own levels of aspiration. Presumably, this is more motivating than trying to accomplish goals set by others.

In keeping with the overload/intensity principle, the exercise sessions become increasingly more demanding each week. As training progresses, the long, slow runs are gradually replaced with shorter, faster sprints. *For healthy adolescents and adults, a total workout distance of over 1.5 mi must eventually be achieved for maximum benefits.*

Circuit Training

Circuit training is a method that involves moving from station to station. Ideally, the task performed at each station uses different groups of muscles. For adolescents and adults, from 6 to 10 stations are recommended, depending upon available space and equipment. For elementary school children and persons with mental limitations, from 2 to 6 stations may be attempted.

Table 13.7   Sample ITP card for pupils of similar ability.

Day 5	Repetitions (reps)	Activity	Rest Interval	Self-Evaluation		
				Easy	*Medium*	*Hard*
Set 1	4 reps	Sprint 220 yd	Walk for 60 sec between sprints			
Set 2	6 reps	Squat thrusts for 10 sec	Arm circling for 20 sec between bouts			
Set 3	4 reps	Crab walk for 10 sec	Movement of choice for 20 sec between bouts			
Set 4	8 reps	Sprint 100 yd	Walk for 30 sec between sprints			

The amount of time at each station varies, but initially is relatively brief. Thirty seconds at each station, with 10 sec for rotation, is satisfactory. Thus, a four-station circuit can be completed in approximately 2.5 min. As training progresses, the amount of time at each station can be extended or the number of circuits increased. The intensity of the work demanded should be increased gradually in keeping with the overload principle.

Procedures to be followed are these:

1. Ascertain that everyone knows how to perform the fitness tasks.
2. Divide the group into squads of 2 to 6 persons, and assign each squad to a different starting point on the circuit.
3. Practice rotating in a counterclockwise direction from station to station.
4. Develop an individualized circuit-training plan for each student:
    a. Determine the best score on each task during a set time limit like 30 sec. Base future work at each station on *one half to three fourths of the student's best score.*
    b. Determine the best time in completing the circuit and challenge the person to better this time on the next test, which is scheduled after several days of practice.

An alternative or adapted method for young children and persons with mental limitations who cannot work independently is to have a leader at each station who keeps people exercising until the whistle blows. Persons then join hands or form a file and follow the leader to the next station. This procedure works best if someone calls out, "Rotate, 1–2–3–4–5–6–7–8–9–10," and everyone knows that he or she must be at a new station by the count of 10. To implement the overload/intensity principle, time at each station is periodically increased and/or number of circuits is increased. For this adapted method to work, squad members must have similar fitness levels.

Continuous Conditioning

Continuous conditioning refers to exercise that imposes a consistent submaximal energy requirement throughout the training session. Examples are aerobics and rope jumping.

Aerobics

The aerobics exercise program can be divided into three phases: (a) evaluation or cardiorespiratory fitness, (b) a period of progressive conditioning that extends over several weeks, and (c) maintenance of optimal fitness by earning a specific number of points for exercise each week.

Prior to undertaking an aerobics program, individuals are assessed on distance covered in 12 min in the modality of their choice (walking, running, swimming, cycling). They are then assigned to one of six fitness categories based on gender and age. For males under age 50, a good classification hovers around 1.5 mi in 12 min (see Table 13.8). For females, it is slightly less. Aerobic fitness peaks at ages 20 to 29 and then slowly drops.

The fitness classification determines the number of weeks of conditioning required to work up to the maintenance phase of 30 points per week. Use the following guidelines: (a) very poor category—16 weeks, (b) poor category—13 weeks, and (c) fair category—10 weeks. Points are awarded to determine the frequency of walks per week. Persons who score in the "good," "excellent," or "superior" fitness categories do not participate in the program of progressive conditioning. They go directly to the maintenance phase, earning 30 points each week.

The most efficient way to earn 30 points is to jog 1.5 mi in 12 min (for which, 7.5 points are awarded) four times a week. The following activities, each worth 5 points, create a basis for developing an individualized maintenance program:

Bicycling 5 mi in less than 20 min
Running 1 mi in less than 8 min
Swimming 600 yd in less than 15 min
Handball played for a total of 35 min
Stationary running for a total of 12.5 min

For individual sports enthusiasts, one set of singles tennis earns 1.5 points, nine holes of golf earn 1.5 points, waterskiing or snow skiing for 30 min earns 3 points, and ice or roller skating for 15 min earns 1 point. For the bicycle rider who enjoys leisurely pedaling, at least 30 min of cycling is required to earn 1 point.

Aerobic dancing and water exercises, called **hydroaerobics** or **hydrorobics,** are popular applications of aerobic theory.

Table 13.8 **Twelve-minute walking/running test (distance [miles] covered in 12 min).**

Fitness Category	Sex	Age (Years)					
		13–19	*20–29*	*30–39*	*40–49*	*50–59*	*60+*
I. Very poor	M	<1.30	<1.22	<1.18	<1.14	<1.03	<.87
	F	<1.0	<.96	<.94	<.88	<.84	<.78
II. Poor	M	1.30–1.37	1.22–1.31	1.18–1.30	1.14–1.24	1.03–1.16	.87–1.02
	F	1.00–1.18	.96–1.11	.95–1.05	.88–.98	.84–.93	.78–.86
III. Fair	M	1.38–1.56	1.32–1.49	1.31–1.45	1.25–1.39	1.17–1.30	1.03–1.20
	F	1.19–1.29	1.12–1.22	1.06–1.18	.99–1.11	.94–1.05	.87–.98
IV. Good	M	1.57–1.72	1.50–1.64	1.46–1.56	1.40–1.53	1.31–1.44	1.21–1.32
	F	1.30–1.43	1.23–1.34	1.19–1.29	1.12–1.24	1.06–1.18	.99–1.09
V. Excellent	M	1.73–1.86	1.65–1.76	1.57–1.69	1.54–1.65	1.45–1.58	1.33–1.55
	F	1.44–1.51	1.35–1.45	1.30–1.39	1.25–1.34	1.19–1.30	1.10–1.18
VI. Superior	M	>1.87	>1.77	>1.70	>1.66	>1.59	>1.56
	F	>1.52	>1.46	>1.40	>1.35	>1.31	>1.19

From *The Aerobics Program for Total Well-Being* by Kenneth H. Cooper M.D., M.P.H. Copyright ©1982 by Kenneth H. Cooper. Used by permission of Bantam Books, a division of Bantam Doubleday Dell Publishing Group, Inc.

Many persons with lower limb disabilities can walk or run laps in chest-high water even though they cannot walk on land. Continuous calisthenics *produce lower heart rates in water than on land* and are particularly recommended for low fitness, obesity, and heart disease.

Rope Jumping, Continuous

Individual rope jumping and long-rope jumping done to chants or music of different speeds and duration provide excellent exercise, especially for maintenance. The usual cadence of 60 to 80 jumps a minute requires 9 METs, about the equivalent of running an 11-min mile. This high metabolic demand may make rope jumping inappropriate for sedentary persons, especially those who are obese or have heart disease. Rope jumping is a high-impact exercise and particularly stresses joints in obesity, so weight loss is a prerequisite.

Individual rope jumping has been promoted by AAHPERD and the American Heart Association, and an adapted physical education goal may be developing fitness to participate in school "jump for heart" programs. Ropes of different lengths should be available. Ropes should be long enough so that the ends reach the armpits or slightly higher when the jumper stands on the rope's center. Wrists should supply the force to turn the rope so that energy is not wasted with unnecessary arm motions.

Combination Conditioning

Combination methods use both continuous and intermittent activity. Rope jumping, for example, can use the protocol in Table 13.9 until students build up the fitness for aerobic-level jumping. The goal is to be able to jump 60 to 80 times a minute. During the rest, students should walk or do stretches.

Table 13.9 **Illustrative rope-jumping sequences individualized to meet capabilities.**

Easy Sequence	Medium Sequence	Difficult Sequence
1. Rope jump 1 min	1. Rope jump 3 min	1. Rope jump 4 min
2. Rest 60 sec	2. Rest 30 sec	2. Rest 20 sec
3. Rope jump 30 sec	3. Rope jump 1½ min	3. Rope jump 2 min

Astronaut or Football Drills

Astronaut or *football drills* are continuous exercise routines done in response to one-word cues that require changes of body position. The correct response to each cue follows:

1. **Go.** Run in place with vigorous high-knee action. Maintain top speed.
2. **Front.** Drop to prone lying position and assume a ready position to ensure quick response to the next cue.
3. **Back.** Drop to supine position and assume a ready position to ensure quick response to the next cue.

These cues are given in various orders, challenging the student to persist in continuous motion. The principle of overload is applied by progressively increasing the duration of time spent in the "go" position. After students have mastered these cues, others might be added: right side lie, left side lie, squat, long sit, and so on. Astronaut drills teach and reinforce concepts and vocabulary concerning body parts and body positions.

Jogging, Hiking, and Cycling

Long walks are called hikes and can be combined with map reading, nature study, scavenger hunts, and other themes. Hiking, jogging, and cycling are particularly successful when correlated with social studies and/or related to a trip across the state, North America, or another continent. Students can update individual mileage sheets, superimposed upon maps. Merit badges or achievement certificates may be awarded for the completion of every 50-mi distance.

The **scout's pace** can be used in early stages of training as follows: jog 110 yd, walk 55 yd, jog 110 yd, walk 55 yd, ad infinitum. The scout's pace can also be interpreted as meaning run as far as you can, then walk until breath is restored, after which running is resumed. Wheelchair activities are conducted like walks and jogs.

Cycling can be done on two- or three-wheeled vehicles and be stationary or moving. Persons with cerebral palsy or other balance impairments may use special adult-size tricycles available through Sears and similar stores. Cycles must be adjustable to body size. Seat height should permit the knee to be slightly bent when toes are on the lower pedal. Handlebar height should encourage good posture, with slight body lean.

Obstacle or Challenge Courses

Perhaps no activity is as popular with elementary school students as following a leader through an obstacle course. Apparatus for these courses can be purchased commercially or constructed by teachers and parents. Homemade obstacle courses are often built around a theme. Assigning pieces of equipment novel names creates the mood for activity built around space travel, a jungle trek, a western outpost, or an Indian village.

Seldom is a class small enough that all students can move through an obstacle course simultaneously. Congestion and confusion are prevented by assigning not more than 2 students to each piece of apparatus and by having them stand at their assigned apparatus while awaiting the signal "go," rather than all standing in a file behind the leader. Thus, only 14 students can move efficiently through a seven-piece obstacle course at any given time. Flexible teachers post time schedules listing each student's name and stating the time at which he or she is excused from regular class activities to go through the obstacle course.

 OPTIONAL ACTIVITIES

1. Telephone or visit fitness centers in your community, and ask the person in charge if their facilities and programs are accessible to persons with disabilities. Ask them to show you how things are made accessible, the approximate cost, and the potential benefits to persons who train at their center.

2. Do the same activity as #1 for community swimming pools and other physical activity centers. Are the centers accessible to both users and spectators? About how many persons with disabilities use the facilities and programs each day? Why?

3. Read the fitness section in each of the chapters comprising Part III. How is the basic content in this chapter expanded in relation to each disability? What have you learned from additional sources?

4. Administer some of the tests in this chapter to persons with different kinds of disabilities. Write up findings and state goals and objectives based on the findings.

CHAPTER

14

Postures, Appearance, and Muscle Imbalance

Figure 14.1   Mirror work to increase body awareness.

390

1. Many persons with and without disabilities have concerns about their postures and appearance. Consider how professionals can weave assessment and instruction on these topics into the IFSP and IEP processes and GE and adapted physical education instruction. Give some concrete examples.

2. How do postures and appearance relate to each of the NASPE standards for students? How does Chapter 8 on self-concept and Chapter 10, which explains reflexes and postural reactions, relate to this chapter and to specific postural problems.

3. Reflect on your past experience with persons with posture and appearance problems. What postural problems are you already familiar with? Give examples. Which ones do you need to acquire experience with? Observe persons of all ages, and write observations in your journal.

4. Use Figure 14.2 to assess postures on one or more persons, and write a report of present level of appearance with recommendations for change, if needed. Note that formal assessment should be accompanied by observation of persons in ADL. This allows assessment to encompass both static and dynamic postures.

5. Note that many of the exercises in this chapter can be used as class warm-ups or cool-downs for everyone. Create one or more lesson plans that incorporate these exercises in this or other ways. Do not promise that exercises will correct postures; only braces and surgical procedures do this, but exercises help, partly because they increase awareness. Review Chapter 13 on ROM/flexibility.

Improvement of postures and overall physical appearance is an important objective within the fitness/wellness goal domain. Physical attractiveness is strongly related to global self-esteem, efficient movement, sexuality, social, leisure, and work interactions. Many persons are not in tune with their bodies and lack awareness of how they look. Yet we often form lasting first impressions on the basis of appearance.

Persons with disabilities and/or clumsiness particularly need help with postures (see Figure 14.1). Whenever strength and flexibility are targeted as fitness goals, postures must be given special attention.

Many Postures: Plural

Each person possesses not one but many postures. Any position is a posture, and we assume thousands of static and dynamic postures each day—standing, walking, running, sitting, sleeping, stooping, climbing, and on ad infinitum. Josephine Rathbone, a pioneer in postures education and physical disabilities, emphasized that postures is a plural concept (Rathbone & Hunt, 1965). Sherrill was Rathbone's student and believes that much of Rathbone's content, although old, remains important. Head postures cannot be considered without shoulder postures; shoulder postures cannot be taught without back postures; and so on. Reference is thus made to *postures* training; the word is not used in the singular.

Good Postures: Strength and Flexibility

Good postures are mechanically efficient body positions and movement patterns. Mechanical efficiency is possible only when muscles on all the body surfaces are in perfect balance with just the right amount of strength and flexibility. Muscles on the anterior surface (**flexors**) must be in balance with muscles on the posterior surface (**extensors**). Muscles on the lateral surface (**abductors**) must be in balance with muscles on the medial surface (**adductors**). In general the names of muscle groups (flexors, extensors, abductors, adductors, inward and outward rotators) are used when instructing persons about their bodies.

The powerful force of gravity tends to pull body parts downward, thereby tightening and strengthening the flexors. This causes an imbalance between flexors and extensors that underlies the major principle of postures training: *Strengthen the extensors!* The extensors of the neck and back, called the **antigravity muscles,** are the target of most postures training.

 Play games like Simon Says to review this basic information. Be able to pass a quiz on facts presented so far and on the names of bones.

Assessment of Postures

Figure 14.2 presents the assessment form most frequently used in the examination of postures. This form shows the major body parts that should be checked for alignment. Alignment is primarily a matter of muscle balance. Muscles on the right and left sides of the spine, for example, must be of equal strength, or the spine will be pulled out of alignment by the stronger group. Unequal muscle pulls, in time, distort the shape of bones, as well as their position.

Persons with paralysis and spasticity are particularly vulnerable to severe alignment problems. Muscle imbalance is minimized by strapping, bracing, casting, and surgery. Proper positioning when sitting or lying for long periods is obviously important because muscle groups adapt their size and shape to the position in which they spend the most time.

Spinal Column Curves

The development of spinal column curves is mature in most children by ages 7 or 8. Viewed from the side, these are the curves:

1. **Concave.** Cervical spine, composed of 7 vertebrae.
2. **Convex.** Thoracic spine, composed of 12 vertebrae.
3. **Concave.** Lumbar spine, composed of 5 vertebrae.
4. **Convex.** Sacral spine, composed of 5 sacral vertebrae fused in adulthood and called the sacrum.

Figure 14.2 Posture score sheet associated with the New York Posture Test.

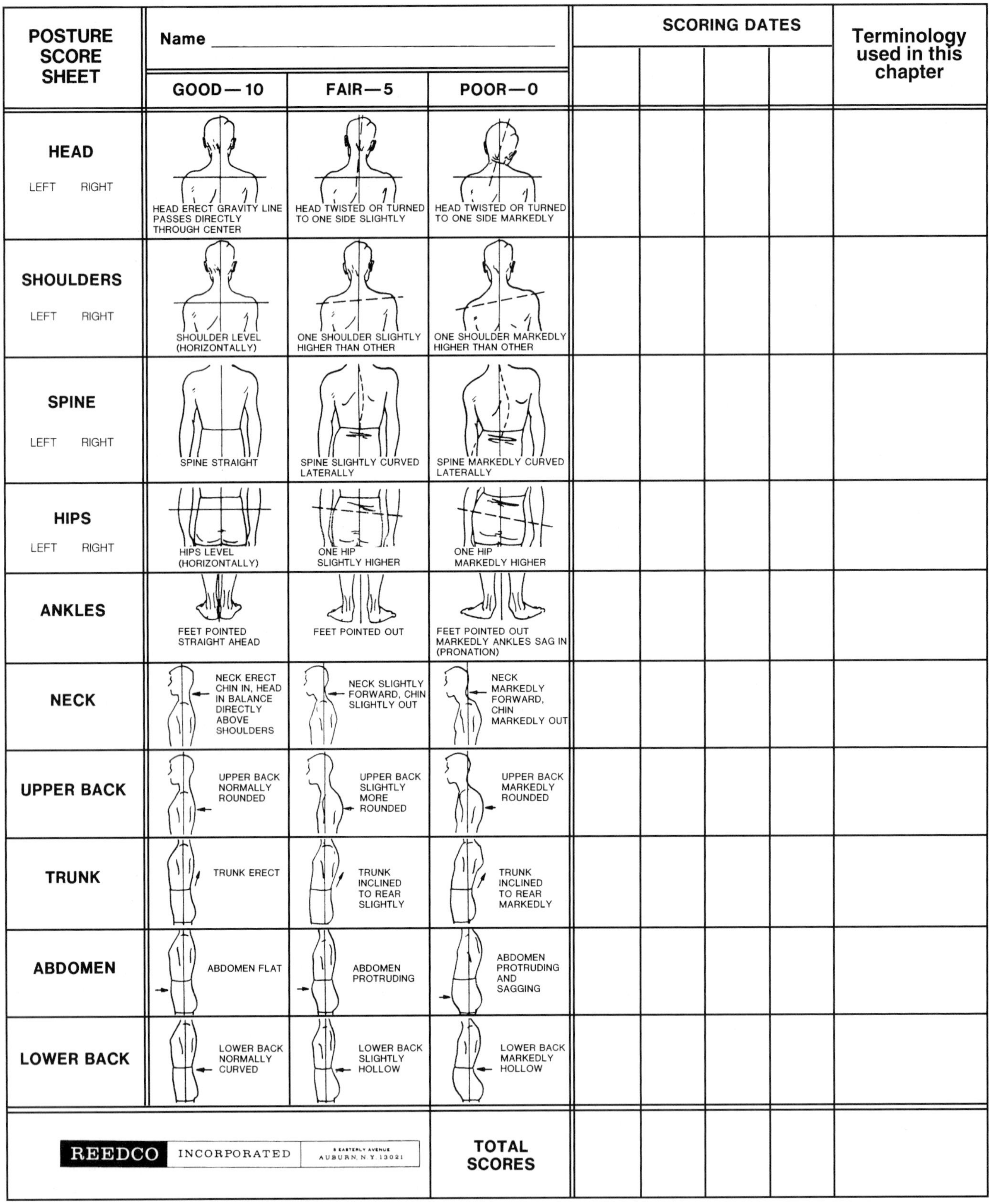

POSTURE SCORE SHEET	Name _____			SCORING DATES					Terminology used in this chapter
	GOOD—10	FAIR—5	POOR—0						
HEAD LEFT RIGHT	HEAD ERECT GRAVITY LINE PASSES DIRECTLY THROUGH CENTER	HEAD TWISTED OR TURNED TO ONE SIDE SLIGHTLY	HEAD TWISTED OR TURNED TO ONE SIDE MARKEDLY						
SHOULDERS LEFT RIGHT	SHOULDER LEVEL (HORIZONTALLY)	ONE SHOULDER SLIGHTLY HIGHER THAN OTHER	ONE SHOULDER MARKEDLY HIGHER THAN OTHER						
SPINE LEFT RIGHT	SPINE STRAIGHT	SPINE SLIGHTLY CURVED LATERALLY	SPINE MARKEDLY CURVED LATERALLY						
HIPS LEFT RIGHT	HIPS LEVEL (HORIZONTALLY)	ONE HIP SLIGHTLY HIGHER	ONE HIP MARKEDLY HIGHER						
ANKLES	FEET POINTED STRAIGHT AHEAD	FEET POINTED OUT	FEET POINTED OUT MARKEDLY ANKLES SAG IN (PRONATION)						
NECK	NECK ERECT CHIN IN, HEAD IN BALANCE DIRECTLY ABOVE SHOULDERS	NECK SLIGHTLY FORWARD, CHIN SLIGHTLY OUT	NECK MARKEDLY FORWARD, CHIN MARKEDLY OUT						
UPPER BACK	UPPER BACK NORMALLY ROUNDED	UPPER BACK SLIGHTLY MORE ROUNDED	UPPER BACK MARKEDLY ROUNDED						
TRUNK	TRUNK ERECT	TRUNK INCLINED TO REAR SLIGHTLY	TRUNK INCLINED TO REAR MARKEDLY						
ABDOMEN	ABDOMEN FLAT	ABDOMEN PROTRUDING	ABDOMEN PROTRUDING AND SAGGING						
LOWER BACK	LOWER BACK NORMALLY CURVED	LOWER BACK SLIGHTLY HOLLOW	LOWER BACK MARKEDLY HOLLOW						
REEDCO INCORPORATED 8 EASTERLY AVENUE AUBURN, N.Y. 13021			**TOTAL SCORES**						

Figure 14.3 Normal postures in *(A)* a two-year-old and *(B)* a preadolescent.

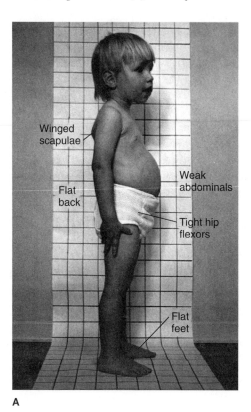

Winged scapulae

Flat back

Weak abdominals

Tight hip flexors

Flat feet

A

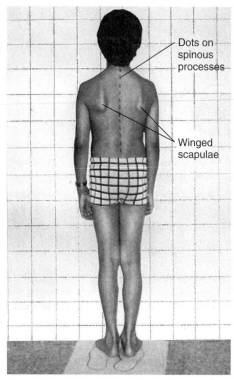

Dots on spinous processes

Winged scapulae

B

Erect, extended carriage results when the thoracic and sacral flexion curves are in balance with the cervical and lumbar hyperextension curves. Whenever one curve increases, the other curves also tend to increase to compensate for the imbalance.

Analysis of Muscle Imbalance

When a posture problem is evident, analyze the imbalance of the muscle groups by considering these questions:

1. Muscles on which surface are too tight—that is, stronger than their antagonists? Which **stretching exercises** are indicated?

2. Muscles on which surface are too loose—that is, weaker than their antagonists? Which **strengthening exercises** are indicated?

3. What role is gravity playing in the muscle imbalance?

Usually, strength exercises are chosen for management of posture problems. Remember the principle of **reciprocal innervation:** When muscles on one surface are being strengthened, muscles on the antagonistic surface are being stretched simultaneously. Regardless of the type of exercise selected, both surfaces are affected (Lowman & Young, 1960).

Normal Postural Development

Infant and toddler postural development depends largely upon vigorous movement. At birth, the entire spinal column of the infant is flexed in a single C curve. Only when the extensor muscles of the neck and back are sufficiently strengthened by random kicking and wiggling do the cervical and lumbar curves

begin to appear. The cervical curve develops at about 4 to 5 months of age, while the lumbar curve begins to develop sometime after the child learns to walk. Children with severe disabilities that prevent walking tend to have **flat back,** a condition denoting the absence of spinal column curves, unless spasticity causes pathological curves. Flat back is normal in all children until age 3 or 4, when they begin to exhibit the opposite condition, **lordosis,** or swayback. This condition is caused by the imbalance in the strength of the abdominal muscles and the hip flexors. The abdominal musculature of the preschool child normally is too weak to maintain the pelvis in a neutral position (see Figure 14.3A). Lordosis, therefore, is typical in a young child and should not be labeled as a postural deviation until adolescence. The degree of lumbar curvature should, however, lessen from year to year.

Winged scapulae, prominence or protrusion of the scapulae, is expected until adolescence (see Figure 14.3B). Winged scapulae is caused by an imbalance in the muscle groups that cause abduction/upward rotation and adduction/downward rotation.

Posture Training Guidelines

Once the present level of postural fitness is assessed and annual goals written to include posture training, short-term objectives are developed. These objectives can be broken down into behaviors. Illustrative target behaviors for improving walking postures are (a) keeps head and trunk erect with eyes generally focused straight ahead; (b) swings arms in opposition with normal range of motion; (c) uses regular, rhythmic, heel-ball-toe transfer of weight; and (d) maintains normal support base—that is, heels, 2 to 3 inches from line of progression.

Figure 14.4   Exercises that are contraindicated when certain problems are present.

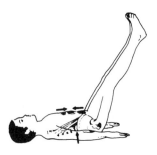

A. Straight leg lift and hold should not be used when persons have weak abdominal muscles and/or lordosis.

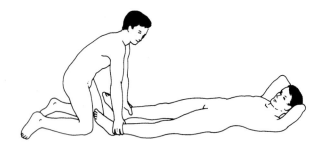

B. Straight leg sit-ups should not be used when persons have weak abdominal muscles or low back problems.

C. Push-ups should not be used when persons have round shoulders.

D. The swan or cobra should not be used when persons have lordosis.

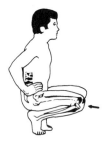

E. Deep knee bends and the duck walk are contraindicated for most students because of the strain put on the knee joints.

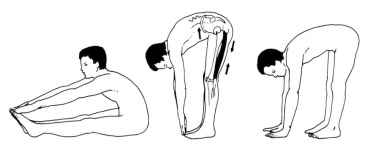

F. Straight leg toe touch and bear walk should not be used when persons have hyperextended knees or low back weakness.

General physical education programming designed to achieve posture training objectives emphasizes use of the kinesthetic, vestibular, and visual sense modalities in such activities as body awareness or proprioceptive training, body image work, static and dynamic balance tasks, and body alignment activities in front of mirrors. Whenever possible, videotape feedback is provided. Sports, dance, and aquatics activities that demand full extension of the trunk, head, neck, and limbs—that is, reaching toward the sky, lifting the chest, stretching upward—are emphasized. Dance, gymnastics (free exercise and balance beam routines), trampolining, and swimming typically reinforce extension, correct body alignment, and good balance. Relaxation training is used to teach and/or reinforce understanding of tightness/tension in muscle groups versus looseness/nontension.

Before using the specific exercises in this chapter, review the content under Range of Motion and Flexibility *in Chapter 13 (pp. 380–382); also use basic anatomy and kinesiology sources to review names of bones, muscles, and prime mover actions that relate to posture and body awareness*

concerns. Try each exercise and strengthen your awareness of each body part's movement extreme. Do exercises slowly and hold the end position 5 to 10 seconds. Repeat each stretch three to five times.

Contraindicated Exercises

Strength and flexibility exercises can cause severe body damage when posture problems are present. Figure 14.4 depicts exercises that are *contraindicated* by certain types of problems. **Contraindicated** is a medical term meaning that there is an indication against (*contra*) prescription of such exercises. The exercises shown may make tight muscles even tighter, as in push-ups and the swan, or they may lead to stretching and tearing of a tight muscle group, as in straight-leg toe touches.

Behavior Management and Postures

Some posture problems can be corrected by behavior management techniques. The types of behavior management apparatus used for correcting postures include these:

1. Response-contingent auditory feedback (music) was used to reward time on-task of postural alignment of individuals with profound mental retardation (Silliman-French, French, Sherrill, & Gench, 1998).

2. A vibrotactile posture harness designed to detect slouching and energize a vibrotactile stimulator on the shoulder whenever slouching occurs. There is no auditory signal, just tactile; the harness is not detectable by others (O'Brien & Azrin, 1970). Eight adults showed a mean 35% reduction in slouching.

3. A foam helmet training device with a mercury switch and buzzer that emits noise whenever the head deviates from the upright position, used in conjunction with a vest containing a buzzer system that makes noise whenever the torso inclines abnormally (Tiller, Stygar, Hess, & Reimer, 1982). Used with one female, age 20 years, in 4 months of training (200 steps each session).

4. Music played during the duration of appropriate posture for a 9-year-old boy with cerebral palsy and mental retardation who needed a physical support of an orthopedic chair and straps for good posture. Johnson, Catherman, and Spiro (1981) reported that response-contingent music is more effective than physical support alone in teaching a child with multiple disabilities good posture.

Forward Head and Neck

Normally, the head is balanced above the cervical vertebrae in such a way that minimal muscle effort is required to resist the pull of gravity. When the earlobe is no longer in alignment with the tip of the shoulder (**acromion**), forward head and neck is diagnosed.

In its *mildest form,* the head tends to droop forward. The cervical spine curve increases so slowly that most persons are unaware that forward head and neck is developing. In the mild stage, the best exercise is mirror work to increase awareness of good head postures.

In more *severe cases,* usually accompanied by round back, the cervical spine hyperextends to compensate for the forward droop of the head and the increasing dorsal convexity of the thoracic spine (Figure 14.5). This results in adaptive shortening and tightening of the cervical extensors, mainly the upper trapezius and splenius capitis and cervicis (Figure 14.6). This tightness is accentuated in the area of the seventh cervical vertebra, where a layer of fat tends to accumulate. The combined prominence of the seventh cervical vertebra and excess adipose tissue is called a **dowager's hump.** The neck flexors tend to stretch, sag, and become functionally worthless. This hyperextension of the neck is sometimes called cervical lordosis.

In mild forward head and neck, the extensors primarily need strengthening exercises. Flexibility is not a problem. As the condition becomes progressively severe, the muscles may feel stiff, tense, and sore. The emphasis in exercise shifts to flexibility, particularly stretching the cervical extensors.

Exercises That Help

1. **Chin-to-shoulder touch stretch.** Attempt to align the head and neck with other segments of the body. Rotate slowly to the left until the chin touches the shoulder. Hold 5 to 10 sec. Repeat to the opposite side.

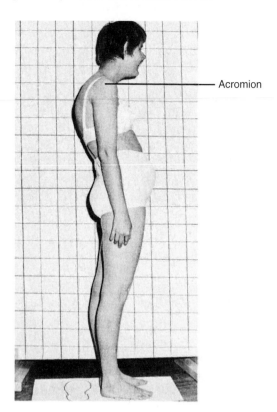

Figure 14.5   Severe degree of forward head and neck causes compensatory dorsal and lumbar curves.

Acromion

2. **Lateral flex stretch with ear touch.** Attempt to align the head and neck with other segments of the body. Laterally flex to the left until the ear touches the shoulder. Hold 5 to 10 sec. Repeat to the opposite side.

3. **Halo push.** Stand or sit with fingers interlaced above the head. Extend the head upward toward the "halo."

4. **Object-on-head walk.** Walk, race, or play games with different objects on the head. Experiment with different head and trunk positions.

Contraindicated Exercises

1. Circling the head

2. Neck hyperextension

3. Activities related to **atlantoaxial instability** (dislocation risk of C1 and C2) when working with individuals with Down syndrome (see Chapter 21 on mental retardation)

Excessive Head Tilt

The top of the head tilting toward the right is called a right tilt (RT). The symbol LT is used for the opposite condition. A head habitually held in a tilted position is often symptomatic of vision or hearing impairments. Almost always, the individual is unaware of the tilt and needs exercises for improving proprioception.

Over a long time, head tilt causes an adaptive shortening and tightening of the neck muscles on the side of the tilt. Tight muscles on the right side may be stretched by lateral flexion exercises to the left, and vice versa. A slow, static stretch and hold is more effective than rhythmic exercises.

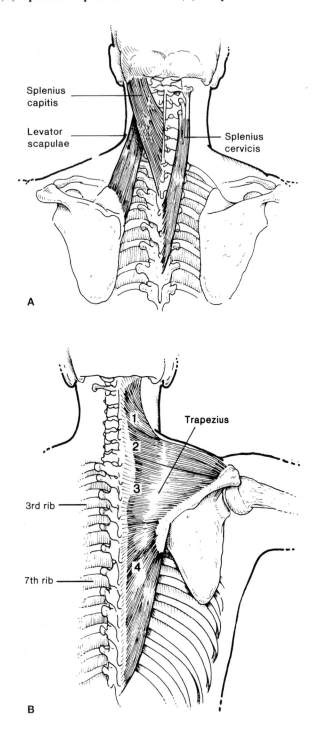

Figure 14.7 The intervertebral disk. *(A)* Flexion of the spine permitted by shift of fluid. *(B)* Compression of the disk occurs when noncompressible fluid of nucleus expands the elastic annulus. *(C)* Normal extended position with annulus fibers held taut; internal pressure is indicated by arrows. *(D)* Section of vertebrae. *(E)* Cross section of intervertebral disk.

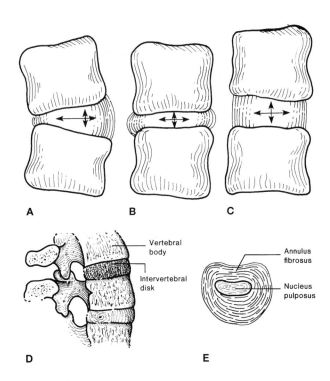

cartilage padding between vertebral bodies (see Figure 14.7). The disk is composed of two parts: the outer annulus fibrosus, known for its strength and elasticity, and the inner nucleus pulposus, which contains fluid that absorbs shock in locomotor movements and maintains the separation of the vertebral bodies. The nucleus pulposus has all the characteristics of a hydraulic system.

Any degenerative disease of the intervertebral disk is characterized by changes in pressure that cause pain. **Scheuermann's disease,** described in Chapter 24 on les autres, is a kyphosis condition affecting adolescents. **Osteoporosis** is a common cause of kyphosis in older adults, especially women. In old age, the fluid content of the nucleus pulposus decreases, and the annulus fibrosus becomes progressively less elastic. These changes limit motion of the back. Any prolonged inactivity seems to contribute to degeneration of the intervertebral disks. Individuals with severe or profound mental retardation whose mobility is limited often exhibit kyphosis at a young age.

Kyphosis

Translated literally, *kyphos* means a sharp angulation. Increasing backward convexity in the thoracic region results in the condition commonly known as humpback, hunchback, Pott's curvature, or round upper back. The condition is rare among normal children in the public school setting.

True kyphosis is associated with degenerative disease of the intervertebral disks. The **intervertebral disk** is the fibro-

Lordosis

Lordosis, also called swayback or hollow back, is an exaggeration of the normal posterior concave curve in the lumbar region. It not only affects the five lumbar vertebrae but also throws the pelvis out of correct alignment (see Figure 14.8).

Lordosis has many possible causes: genetic predisposition; weak abdominal muscles, which allow the pelvis to tilt downward anteriorly; weak gluteal muscles and hamstrings, which cannot counteract this anterior tilt; overly tight lumbar extensors, which contribute to an anterior tilt; overdeveloped hip flexors, which cause anterior tilt; and, on rare occasions, occupations like professional dance.

True lordosis usually has the following characteristics:

1. Anterior tilt of the pelvis.
2. Tight lower back muscles, tight lumbodorsal fascia, tight hip flexors, tight iliofemoral (Y) ligaments, weak abdominals, weak hamstrings, and weak gluteals.
3. Knees may be hyperextended.
4. Compensatory kyphosis may develop to balance the increased concavity; if so, the pectorals and anterior intercostals may be tight also.
5. Upper body tends to shift backward as a compensatory measure.
6. Lower back pain.
7. Faulty functioning of internal organs, including those of digestion, elimination, and reproduction.
8. Predisposition toward dysmenorrhea (menstrual pain).
9. Increased incidence of back strain and back injuries.

Correction of lordosis, at least in the early stages, is largely a matter of increasing proprioceptive awareness so that the student can feel the difference between an anterior and a posterior tilt. Alternate anterior and posterior pelvic tilts should be practiced while lying supine, kneeling, sitting, standing, and performing various locomotor activities. Helpful exercise cues are "Tuck your buttocks in" and "Pinch the gluteals together." Activities like the backbend, which emphasize hyperextension of the lumbar spine, are contraindicated.

Weak abdominals almost universally accompany lordosis. For this reason, strength exercises for the abdominals should be undertaken along with stretching exercises for the tight lumbar extensors. This dual purpose is accomplished to some extent without special effort in accordance with the principle of reciprocal innervation.

Abdominal Weakness

Abdominal weakness is classified as mild, moderate, or severe or as first, second, and third degree. Abdominal protrusion is typical in the young child and usually accompanied by lordosis (see Figure 14.9). This posture defect is almost always present in adolescents and adults who lead sedentary lifestyles, especially if they are overweight. The protruding abdomen also characterizes paralysis or muscle weakness that results from spinal cord injuries.

When a lifestyle changes from active to sedentary, regardless of the reason, abdominal exercises should become a part of the daily routine. In middle and old age, the upper abdominal wall may become slightly rounded, but the musculature below the umbilicus should remain flat and taut.

The *lower part of the abdomen* contracts reflexly whenever the body is in complete extension, as in most locomotor activities. The emphasis upon extension in dance contributes particularly to abdominal strength, as does swimming the front crawl and other strokes executed from an extended

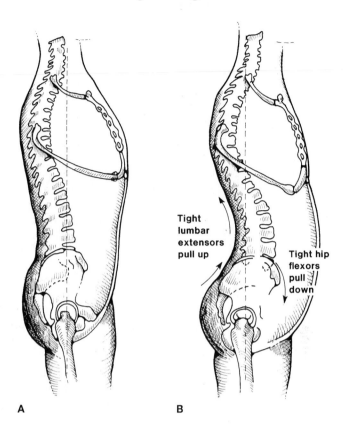

Figure 14.8 Pelvic tilts. *(A)* Normal pelvic tilt (neutral position). The buttocks are tucked in. Anterior and posterior muscles are equal in strength. *(B)* Anterior pelvic tilt causes lordosis and protruding abdomen.

Tight lumbar extensors pull up

Tight hip flexors pull down

A   B

position. The *upper part of the abdomen* works in conjunction with the diaphragm, gaining strength each time breathlessness in endurance-type activities forces the diaphragm to contract vigorously in inhalation.

Visceroptosis is the term used when an abdominal protrusion is severe and the **viscera** (internal organs) drop down into a new position. The stomach, liver, spleen, kidneys, and intestines may all be displaced, resulting in adverse effects upon their various functions. This condition occurs mainly in adults.

Exercise Principles for Abdomen and Lower Back

1. Teach abdominal exercises that will simultaneously stretch the tight lumbar extensors and hip flexors (psoas and iliacus).
2. Use the curl-up bent-knee sit-up position rather than the straight-leg lying position to eliminate the action of the strong hip flexors.
3. Avoid hyperextension of the spine. For most persons, this means avoid the double-leg lift and hold.
4. Avoid prone-lying exercises like the swan and the rocking chair.
5. Eliminate breath holding during exercise by requesting the students to count, sing, whistle, hum, or exhale. Incorrect breathing tends to build up intraabdominal pressure, which may result in a *hernia*. This is called the **Valsalva effect.**

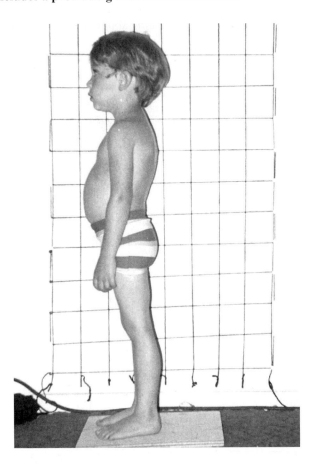

Figure 14.9 Good posture for a normal preschooler includes a protruding abdomen and lordosis.

6. Include lots of twisting movements of the trunk to strengthen oblique abdominal muscles.

7. Gradually build tolerance for endurance-type exercises that cause vigorous breathing, which in turn, strengthens the upper abdominal wall.

8. Use locomotor activities that emphasize extension of the spine. Skipping and swimming are especially good.

9. Take advantage of the extensor reflex elicited in the creeping position.

10. Use the upside-down positions in *yoga* for training the extensor muscles. The neck stand is preferred to the head stand.

11. If there is a history of back problems, avoid sit-ups and exercises using trunk lift from supine.

Exercises in the Creeping Position

For these exercises, always wear kneepads or move across mats. Make these into games. Also use music and create routines.

1. Crosslateral creeping. As the right arm moves forward, the left knee should move forward.

2. Crosslateral creeping combined with blowing a Ping-Pong ball across the floor.

3. Crosslateral creeping combined with pushing an object like a bottle cap or toy automobile with the nose.

4. Angry cat. Alternate (a) humping the back and letting the head hang down with (b) extending the spine with the head held high.

5. In static creeping position, move the hips from side to side. For fun, pin tail on and play wag the tail.

Exercises in Supine or Bent-Knee Sit-Up Position

1. Abdominal pumping (Mosher exercise). Arms in reverse T to prevent arching the back. **Reverse T** means arms outstretched above head. Put book or weight on abdomen. Forcefully push abdomen up and down and feel the weight move.

2. Curl down or reverse trunk curl. Knees and hips are flexed, and knees are drawn toward chest, so curl commences at the lower spinal levels. Obliques are more active in reverse curls than in regular trunk curls. First third of curl is most valuable.

3. Sit-up with trunk twist for maximal activity of oblique abdominals. Feet should not be held down because holding them activates the unwanted hip flexors.

4. Double-knee raise and patty-cake. Keep the knees bent.

5. Alternate ballet legs. From bent-knee position, raise knees to chest and then lift legs alternately, as done in the synchronized swimming stunt by the same name. To make this more difficult, legs can be adducted and abducted in this position.

6. Double knee circling. Keep heels close to thighs, arms in reverse T. Flex the hips until the thighs are vertical. Keeping the shoulders flat, make circles with the knees. *More difficult variation:* Flex knees toward the chest, straighten legs to vertical, and make circles with both feet. Keep the shoulders flat and the heels together.

7. Alternate leg circling. Retract the abdominal wall and flex both knees to chest. Extend one leg and then the other in reciprocal leg circling or bicycle motion. Return the flexed legs to the chest and then lower to the floor.

8. Leg circling games. Vary the difficulty by changing the size of the circles, the number completed before resting, and the speed of the performance. The most difficult is making small circles at slow speed just above the floor. The right foot makes clockwise circles, while the left foot makes counterclockwise circles. Both legs make clockwise circles. Both legs make counterclockwise circles. Describe a figure eight with one foot or both together.

9. Drumming. Feet are used like drumsticks, alternately beating the floor.

10. Alternate knee and elbow touch in opposition. Hands behind neck. Each time, try to reach farther with the elbow and less far with the opposite knee.

11. Supine bent-knee lower trunk twist. Arms in reverse T. Raise both knees until the thighs are vertical. Keep the shoulders flat, and lower the knees toward the mat on one side; return to a vertical position. Repeat to the other side and return. Legs should not be allowed to fall; must be controlled throughout the movement.

Figure 14.10 Right total scoliosis with 80° curve in 16-year-old. The curve was first noticed at age 6.

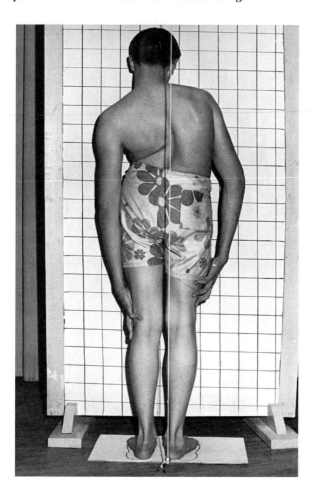

Figure 14.11 In right total scoliosis, the right shoulder is high and carried forward.

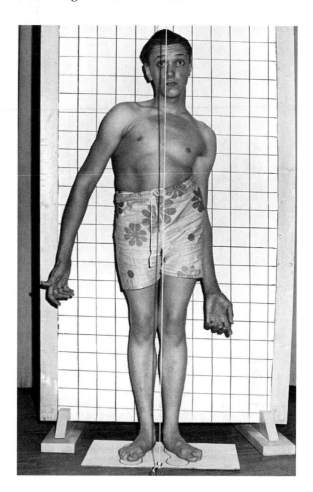

Values of Abdominal Exercises

Abdominal exercises do the following:

1. Relieve congestion in the abdominal or pelvic cavities; this includes expelling gas and improving local circulation.
2. Relieve menstrual pain (dysmenorrhea).
3. Strengthen muscles needed for coughing in asthma and respiratory diseases.
4. Strengthen muscles to improve appearance and function.

Flat Back

Flat back is a decrease or absence of the normal anteroposterior curves. It is the opposite condition from lordosis. The posterior concavity of the lumbar curve is decreased—that is, the normal posterior concavity is gradually changing toward convexity.

Characteristics of flat back include these:

1. The pelvic inclination is less than normal, with the pelvis held in posterior tilt.
2. The back appears too flat, with little or no protrusion of the buttocks.
3. Lower back muscles are weak.
4. Hip flexors, especially the psoas major, are weak and elongated.

5. Hamstrings are abnormally tight.

Flat back is also characteristic of the body build of young toddlers who have not been walking long enough to develop the lumbar curve. No exercises are used with toddlers.

Flat back is associated with the debutante slouch, seen so often in fashion magazines, in which young women pose languidly with hips thrust forward and upper back rounded. Such models are usually flat chested and so thin that the abdomen cannot protrude. It is sad that the fashion world sometimes chooses to present this image to the public, rather than one of good body alignment with average-size busts, hips, and buttocks in gracefully curved balance.

Exercises that help include these:

1. Alternate anterior and posterior pelvic tilts from a hook lying position to increase proprioceptive awareness.
2. Hyperextension of the lumbar spine to strengthen back muscles.
3. Most exercises in supine or bent-knee sit-up position from the previous section.

Scoliosis

Scoliosis is a lateral curvature of the spine (see Figures 14.10–14.13). Although the condition begins with a single

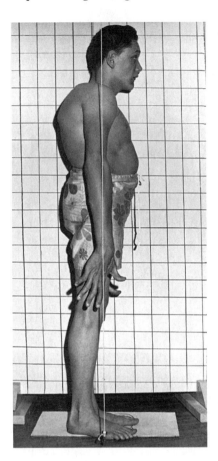

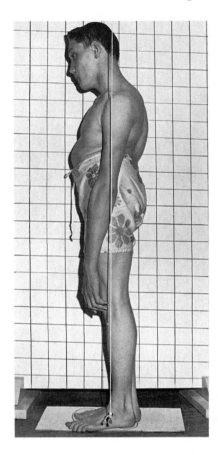

curve, it usually consists of a primary curve and a compensatory curve in the opposite direction.

Characteristics of Left Curve

In the total left lumbar curve to the convex side, the following characteristics may be observed:

1. Spinous processes deviate from midline, rotating toward the concavity of the curve.
2. The left shoulder is higher than the other shoulder and may also be carried forward.
3. The head may be tilted to one side.
4. The trunk is displaced toward the side of convexity. This can limit breathing.
5. Posteriorly, the ribs usually bulge out on the convex side of the curve; the rib cage tends to lose its flexibility.
6. The right hip is usually higher than the other and the right iliac crest more prominent. Said in another way, when there is a lateral pelvic tilt, the convexity of the spine is toward the lower hip.
7. The contour of the waistline is affected, with the notch on the concave side greater than that on the convex.

8. The right leg may be longer than the left. In other words, a long leg will push the hip to a higher level and contribute to curvature on the opposite side.
9. Side bending tends to be freer to the right (concave side) than to the left.
10. Forward flexibility of the spine may be limited as a natural protective mechanism of the body against further deformity.
11. Muscles on the concave side become increasingly tight, while those on the convex side are stretched and weakened.

Keynote Positions

Keynote positions are diagnostic devices or helpful exercises specifically for scoliosis (see Figure 14.14). Among the most common keynote positions are the following:

1. Adam's position—relaxed forward bending held for several seconds from a standing posture. The knees are straight so that the flexion occurs from the hips and spinal column.
2. Hanging with both arms from a horizontal bar.
3. Symmetrical arm raise from a standing position. The individual with a total left curve flexes the right arm at

Figure 14.14
Figure 14.14 Adam's position is assumed to determine whether scoliosis is functional or structural. *(A)* the start and *(B)* the end of Adam's position show a structural condition because the curve does not straighten.

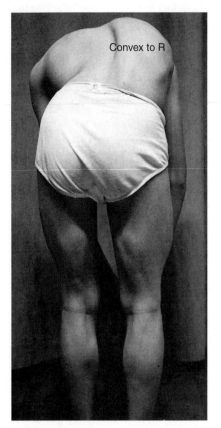

A. Start Position

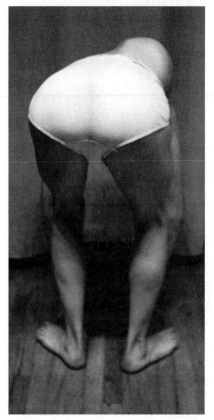

B. End Position

the shoulder joint to whatever height is necessary to straighten the spine. The other arm is maintained in a position of abduction. In some cases, raising both arms and/or raising one leg sideways may help the curve to disappear.

If the lateral curve is not temporarily obliterated by any of these positions, it can be assumed that scoliosis is in a transitional or structural stage. *In such instances, the physical educator should insist that the child be examined by a physician. No exercises should be undertaken without a permission slip from the parents and a medical clearance from the physician.* Ideally, the physician will prescribe specific exercises to be practiced under the supervision of adapted physical education personnel.

Lateral curves are named in terms of the direction of their convexity. Among right-handed persons, the most common type of scoliosis is the *total left curve.*

Exercises That Help

Principles for planning exercises for a child with functional scoliosis include the following:

1. Work on improvement of body alignment in front of a mirror before undertaking specific exercises for scoliosis.

2. Use keynote positions (with exception of Adam's position) as corrective exercises. When a position is

identified in which the curve is temporarily obliterated, spend as many seconds as comfortable in it; rest and repeat.

3. Emphasize swimming and other activities that encourage development of the trunk without placing weight-bearing strain on the spine.

4. Avoid forward flexibility of spine unless prescribed by a physician.

5. Use breathing and chest expansion exercises to maintain flexibility of chest and prevent further distortion of thorax.

6. If you tend to be conservative and wish to avoid controversial practices, *use only symmetrical exercises that develop left and right sides equally.* Exercises for strengthening the back extensors are recommended.

7. If you are willing to use activities that authorities are about equally divided on, try such *asymmetrical* exercises as

   a. Hang facing outward from stall bars and swing legs in.

   b. Hang from stall bars with right hand only (for left total curve). Right side is to the stall bars, and left hand is used whenever needed for balance.

   c. Kneel on right knee, with leg extended to side, right arm curved above head. Laterally flex trunk several times to the left. *The purpose of most asymmetrical*

Figure 14.15 Milwaukee brace fitted to a right thoracic, left lumbar scoliotic curve. It is generally worn 24 hours a day over a long undershirt, and children can run and play in it with few restrictions.

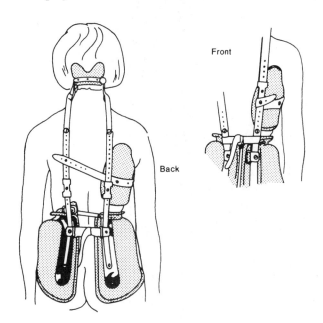

Figure 14.16 Left hip high caused by right dorsal scoliosis with 65° curve. This 18-year-old has worn a Milwaukee brace and had Harrington instrumentation and spinal fusion. Further correction is not feasible.

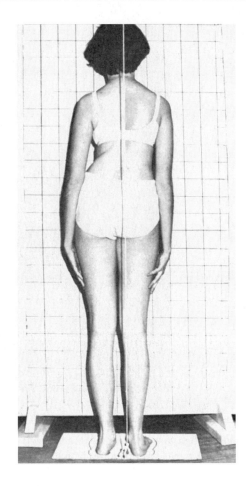

exercises is to stretch muscles on the concave side and/or to strengthen muscles on the convex side. Generally, exercises prescribed by physicians are asymmetrical in nature.

8. Encourage the student with scoliosis to participate in general physical education classes and athletic competition.

Scoliosis is more prevalent in girls and among ectomorphic body types, but it is not confined to either. About 75% of the known cases are **idiopathic** (meaning unknown cause), about 12.5% are congenital anomalies, and the other 12.5% result from paralysis or paresis of muscles on one side of the spinal column. Many persons with spina bifida and poliomyelitis have scoliosis.

Treatment options are bracing and surgery. Bracing is typically used for individuals who are still growing and have a curve of 40° or less. After skeletal maturity is reached and the menstrual cycle becomes regular, scoliotic curves seldom get worse. Curve progression is worse during periods of rapid growth (in adolescents, before and after menarche). Braces are more lightweight than ever before, and most can be worn under clothes so they are not visible. The generic name for most of the braces worn is **thoracic-lumbar-sacral orthosis** (TLSO). Depending on geographical location and who designed the brace, it might be called the Milwaukee, Wilmington, New York, or Miami brace (see Figures 14.15 and 14.16). Most braces are worn 24 hr a day, except for bath time. Some, like the Charleston, are worn only while sleeping. No activity contraindications are specified while wearing a brace.

Many kinds of surgery are available, but all involve straightening the curve with a metal rod attached to the spine by hooks, screws, or wires. After surgery, the person is typically walking within a week, can participate in most activities after 3 or 4 months, and can resume all activities with no restrictions after about a year. Surgery is typically used in children and adolescents only if the curvature is increasing very fast or if there is a lot of pain.

Adult degenerative scoliosis is typically treated by anti-inflammatory drugs, pain medication, and exercise. Surgery is a last resort. Women with osteoporosis are at greater risk for scoliosis than peers.

Web Resources

Of all of the postural conditions, scoliosis is generally the most severe and motivates persons to use websites and all available sources to gain information. Some sources of information are:

www.spine-surgery.com

www.stayhealthy.com

www.srs.org

Scoliosis is the only postural condition that has organizations to supply information, videos, and teachers' guides. Two of these are

The Scoliosis Association Inc., P.O. Box 811705, Boca Raton, FL 33481-1705; Phone 800-800-0669

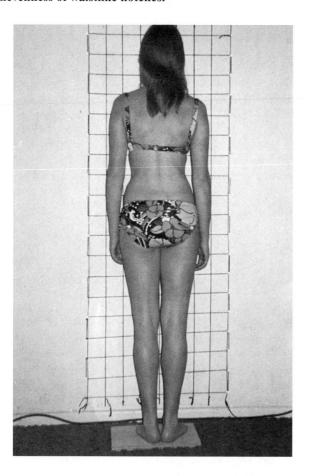

The National Scoliosis Foundation, 5 Cabot Place, Stoughton, MA 02072; Phone 781-341-6333

Uneven Shoulder Height

When the two shoulders are of unequal height, the higher one is recorded as LH (left high) or RH (right high). Shoulder unevenness is best ascertained by using a horizontal line on the wall behind the student. Other techniques include

1. If the head is not tilted, comparing the distance between the shoulders and earlobes on the right and left side.
2. Comparing the level of the inferior angles of the scapulae. The **inferior angles** are at about the level of the seventh thoracic spinous process.
3. Comparing the level of the two clavicles.

Whenever a high shoulder is recorded, a lateral spinal curve convex on the same side should be suspected (see Figures 14.16 and 14.17). If scoliosis is not found, shoulder asymmetries are not a problem. *In normal development, the dominant side of the body has a slightly depressed shoulder and slightly higher hip.* This should not be confused with scoliosis.

Uneven Hip Height

When two hips are of unequal height, the higher one is recorded as LH or RH. Traditionally, the anterior superior iliac spines

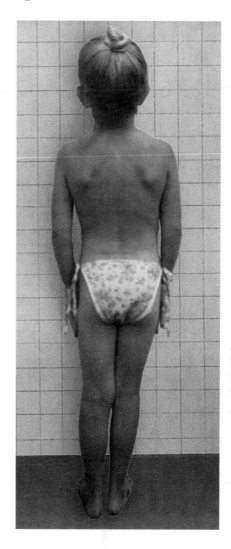

serve as the anatomical landmarks for judging asymmetry. A string may be stretched between these two points.

Differences in hip height may be caused by scoliosis, uneven leg length, or the habit of standing on one leg for long periods of time. To determine leg lengths, the student lies in a supine position. The length of each leg is recorded as the distance from the anterior superior iliac spine to the medial ankle bone.

Winged Scapulae

Also called projected scapulae, **winged scapulae** refers to a prominence of the inferior angles of the scapulae. The scapulae are pulled away from the rib cage, and the vertebral borders are lifted. The serratus anterior, the muscle that normally holds the inferior angle of the scapula close to the rib cage, is believed to be weak when winging occurs.

Winged scapulae are typical in preschool and elementary school children since the serratus is slower in developing than its antagonists (see Figure 14.18). Since the serratus anterior is a prime mover for upward rotation and abduction, it is strengthened by hanging, climbing, and other activities executed above the head. Many girls in our society do not outgrow winged scapulae as do boys. This postural deviation is often a part of the debutante slouch described earlier. Winged scapulae often accompany round shoulders. They are associated also with congenital anomalies and postural conditions in which the ribs protrude.

Round Shoulders

Round shoulders is a forward deviation of the shoulder girdle that brings the acromion processes (shoulder tips) in front of the normal gravitational line. Round shoulders should not be confused with round back (kyphosis). They are distinctly different problems.

Synonyms for round shoulders are abducted scapulae, forward deviation of the shoulder girdle, protraction of scapulae, and separation of scapulae. Round shoulders results when the strength of the shoulder girdle abductors (pectoralis minor and serratus anterior) becomes greater than that of the adductors (rhomboids and trapezius III). To determine the extent of the forward deviation, the distance between the vertebral borders of the scapulae is measured. In the adult, the average spread is 4 to 5 inches, depending on the breadth of the shoulders.

The incidence of round shoulders is high among persons who work at desk jobs and, hence, spend much of their time with shoulders abducted. Athletes often exhibit round shoulders because of overdevelopment of the anterior arm, shoulder, and chest muscles resulting from sports and aquatics activities, which stress forward movements of the arms. This tendency may be counteracted by engaging in an exercise program designed specifically to keep the posterior muscles equal in strength to their antagonists. *Perhaps the easiest way to do this is to swim a few laps of the back crawl each day.* Certainly, the well-rounded athlete who enjoys many different activities is less likely to develop round shoulders than is one who specializes almost exclusively in tennis, basketball, or volleyball.

Changes in Body Alignment from Round Shoulders

The following segmental analysis demonstrates the compensatory changes in alignment of body parts that result from round shoulders:

1. **Head and neck.** Out of alignment and displaced forward.
2. **Thoracic spine.** Increasing convexity that tends to negate the upward pull of the muscles that normally maintain the upper ribs and sternum in a high position. The weak back muscles are elongated by the increased convexity of the spine.
3. **Chest.** Lowered position. The failure of the anterior muscles to exert their usual effect on the sternum and ribs results in a lowered position of the diaphragm, which, in turn, affects breathing.
4. **Shoulder girdle.** Scapulae abducted. Anterior muscles need to be stretched, and posterior muscles need to be strengthened.
5. **Shoulder joint.** Increased inward rotation of the humeral head.

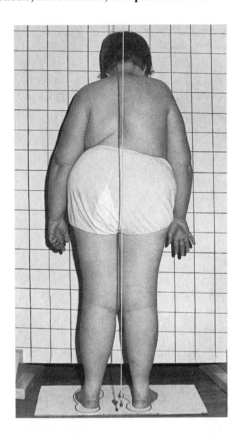

Figure 14.19 Round shoulders can be detected from a rear view by the palms of the hands. This child also has mild scoliosis, knock-knees, and pronated feet.

6. **Arms.** Arms are carried more forward than usual, with palms facing toward the rear, whereas normally, only the little finger of the hand can be seen from the rear (see Figure 14.19). The elbows may be held out close to the body.
7. **Lumbar spine.** Lordosis may develop to compensate for increased convexity of thoracic spine.
8. **Knees.** Knees may hyperextend to compensate for the change in the lumbar curve.

With the alignment of almost all the body segments altered, the entire body slumps, creating the impression of general fatigue. This posture is assumed temporarily in times of extreme mental depression or grief, revealing the unity of mind and body. Persons with mental illness often assume the round-shouldered postures of defeat.

Exercises That Help

Exercises for round shoulders are directed toward the shoulder girdle (scapular) abductors and adductors. *They should simultaneously stretch the tightened anterior muscles and strengthen the trapezius III and the rhomboids.*

1. **Pull resistance.** Sit on a chair facing the wall with pulleys, with the arms extended sideward at shoulder height and the hands grasping the handles. Slowly move the arms backward, keeping them at shoulder height.

2. **Prone lateral raise of weights.** Assume a prone position on a bench. The hands grasp dumbbells on the floor to each side of the body. The weights are lifted toward the ceiling as far as possible, keeping the arms straight. Hold. (Chin should remain on the bench.)

3. **Push against wall.** Sit cross-legged with the head and back flat against the wall. The arms are bent at shoulder height with the palms facing the chest, fingertips touching, and elbows against the wall. Keeping the head and spine against the wall, press the elbows back with as much force as possible.

4. **Head resistance.** Lie on back, arms out to side, palms down, knees flexed, and feet spread. Raise hips and arch back so that shoulders are off mat, supporting weight on feet, hands, and back of head in a modified wrestler's bridge.

Deviations of the Chest

Asthma, other chronic upper respiratory disorders, and rickets may cause changes in the rib cage with resulting limitations in chest flexibility and improper breathing practices. These changes are designated as functional, transitional, and structural, depending on their degree of severity. Congenital anomalies account for many chest deviations.

Hollow Chest

The most common of the chest deviations, **hollow chest** denotes the depression of the anterior thorax that normally accompanies round shoulders and/or kyphosis. Specific characteristics of hollow chest are concave or flattened appearance of anterior thoracic wall, depressed (lowered) ribs, low sternum, tight intercostal and pectoral muscles, limited chest flexibility, and habitually lowered diaphragm that limits breathing.

Hollow chest can be traced to the failure of the neck and pectoral muscles to exert their usual lifting effect on the ribs and sternum. The neck muscles are elongated and weak. The pectoral muscles are excessively tight.

Barrel Chest

Barrel chest occurs in persons with severe, chronic asthma who become permanently hyperventilated because of their inability to exhale properly. Over a period of years, the excess air retained in the lungs tends to expand the anteroposterior dimensions of the thorax so that it takes on a rounded appearance similar to that of full inspiration.

Barrel chest is normal for infants and preschool children. The lateral widening of the thorax from side to side so that it no longer resembles a barrel occurs normally as a result of the vigorous play activities of young children. Individuals with severe disabilities who cannot engage in physical activities often have chests that remain infantile and underdeveloped.

Funnel Chest

The opposite of barrel chest, **funnel chest** is an abnormal increase in the lateral diameter of the chest with a marked depression of the sternum and anterior thorax. The sternum and adjacent costal cartilages appear to have been sucked inward.

Funnel chest, also called *pectus excavatum,* is usually a congenital anomaly. It appears in many persons with severe mental retardation. It also may be caused by rickets or severe nasal obstruction—that is, enlarged adenoids—and characterizes syndromes like **Turner and Noonan,** which are sometimes associated with mental retardation.

Pigeon Chest

Also called chicken breast, or *pectus carinatum,* **pigeon chest** takes its name from the abnormal prominence of the sternum. The anteroposterior diameter of the thorax is increased as a result of the forward displacement of the sternum. The deviation is rare, caused by rickets during the early growth period. It may also be congenital or caused by les autres conditions like **osteogenesis imperfecta** (see index on Chapter 24).

Alignment of Lower Extremities

A quick screening device to judge the overall alignment of the legs is the game known as *Four Coins.* The challenge is, "Can you put a coin between your thighs, your knees, your calves, and your ankles and simultaneously hold all the coins in place?" If the body parts are well proportioned and correctly aligned, this task should present no problem. When the student stands with feet together and parallel, the medial aspects of the knees and ankles should be touching their opposites. Figure 14.20 depicts developmental changes in hip and leg alignment. It is typical for infants and toddlers to have bowlegs and for preschool children to have knock-knees. These conditions generally correct themselves.

Figure 14.20 Mild to moderate bowlegs is normal in infancy and corrects itself, usually by 2 years of age. Children then tend to develop knock-knees, which is most obvious at ages 3 to 4. This condition also corrects itself.

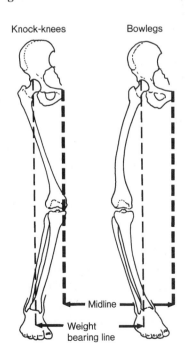

Knock-knees   Bowlegs

Midline

Weight bearing line

Figure 14.21 Anatomy of the hip joint. The acetabulum is a cup-shaped hollow socket that is formed medially by the pubis, above the ilium, and laterally and behind by the ischium.

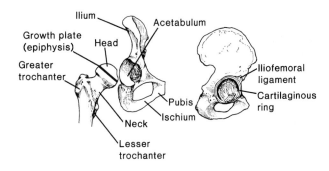

Individual differences in leg alignment and in locomotor patterns are largely dependent upon the hip joint. Students who toe inward or outward in their normal walking gait, for instance, usually have nothing wrong with their feet. *The problem's origin usually can be traced to a strength imbalance in the muscles that rotate the femur at the hip joint.*

Hip Joint Problems

The hip joint is formed by the articulation between the head of the femur and the acetabulum of the pelvis. Figure 14.21 depicts its anatomy. How the head fits into the acetabulum determines function and stability. Important to the understanding of several problems is the angulation of the neck of the femur, depicted in Figure 14.22. Hip joint problems affect leg alignment and gait. Osteoarthritis, usually in old age, causes degeneration that requires hip replacement. Several of these problems are discussed in Chapter 24 on les autres conditions.

Abnormal positioning of the femoral head within the acetabulum is called **coxa vara** (decreased angulation) or **coxa valga** (increased angulation). *Both cause waddling gaits.* Neither condition can be corrected by exercise. Casting, bracing, and surgery are used.

Coxa Vara

The decreased angulation in *coxa vara* may result in the affected leg becoming shorter. Inward rotation and abduction are limited. Bowlegs in early childhood is associated with *coxa vara* (see Figure 14.23). *Coxa vara* also often appears in adolescence. It may be called either **slipped femoral epiphysis** or *adolescent coxa vara* and is more common in males than females. The **epiphysis** (growth center) of the femoral head slips down and backward, making the angulation of the femoral neck more horizontal.

Coxa Valga and Congenital Dislocation of Hip (CDH)

In contrast, *coxa valga* malpositions in childhood are associated with *upward, anterior dislocations of the hip.* The condition is almost always congenital and is often called **congenital dislo-**

Figure 14.22 Angulation of the neck of the femur helps to explain coxa valga and vara. *(A)* Decreased neck-shaft angle shortens leg. *(B)* Normal for adolescents and adults. *(C)* Increased neck-shaft angle lengthens leg. Normal for infants.

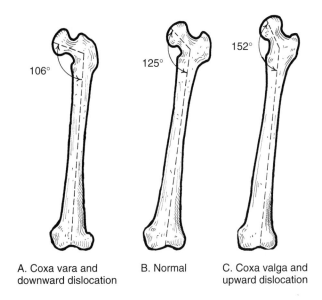

A. Coxa vara and downward dislocation   B. Normal   C. Coxa valga and upward dislocation

cation of the hip (CDH), rather than *coxa valga.* This is the fourth most common orthopedic birth defect. The affected leg is longer, and both inward and outward rotation are limited. Adductors are very tight. Many nonambulatory persons with severe disability develop *coxa valga* between ages 2 and 10; in this condition, the head of the femur is usually displaced upward (like CDH) and posteriorly (unlike CDH).

Knee Joint Problems

Knee joint problems include (a) bowlegs, (b) knock-knees, (c) hyperextended knees, and (d) tibial torsion. These problems may be congenital or acquired through injury. Malalignment increases the risk of **osteoarthritis** and the need for knee replacements in middle and old age. Obesity, over time, injures the knee joint. This is why weight-bearing exercises are often contraindicated for obese persons.

Bowlegs (Genu Varum)

Although the Latin term *genu,* meaning "knee," emphasizes the capacity for knees and ankles to touch simultaneously, bowing can occur in the shaft of the femur as well as the tibia. **Varum** refers to inward bowing. One or both legs may be affected.

The legs of infants often bow during the first few months of walking because of imbalance of strength between the peroneal and tibial muscle groups. By age 2, this problem resolves itself in most children.

Persistent or late-appearing bowlegs may be caused by disorders that affect the epiphyseal plates. Illustrative of these is **Blount's disease,** or **tibia vara,** an outward bowing of the tibia

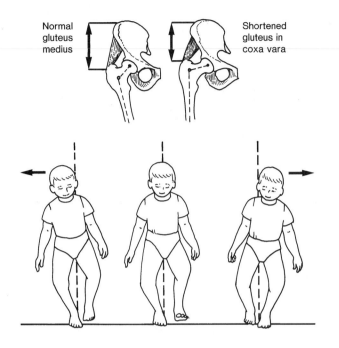

Figure 14.23 Bowlegs in early childhood are almost always accompanied by coxa vara. *(A)* The horizontalization of the femoral neck limits the action of the gluteus medius. *(B)* The result is a waddling gait in which the shoulders incline toward the weight-bearing foot.

Normal gluteus medius

Shortened gluteus in coxa vara

caused by retardation of growth of the medial epiphyseal plate at the top of the tibia. Blount's disease usually occurs between 1 and 3 years of age and is corrected by surgery. Pathological conditions that are often complicated by bowed legs include *arthrogryposis, dwarfism,* and *osteogenesis imperfecta* (check the index at the back of the book for page numbers for more information).

Many individuals with mild to moderate bowing conditions have strong muscles and are not impaired noticeably by this deviation. Bowlegs tends to shift the weight toward the lateral border of the foot and to maintain the foot in a supinated position. Exercises are not recommended.

Knock-Knees (Genu Valga)

The Latin word **valgum** can mean either knock-knees or bowlegs but is used in most adapted physical education references as knock-knees, referring specifically to the *bending outward of the lower legs* so that the knees touch, but the ankles do not.

Knock-knees occurs almost universally in obese persons. In the standing position, the gravitational line passes lateral to the center of the knee rather than directly through the patella, as is normal. This deviation in the weight-bearing line predisposes the knee joint to injury. Knock-knees is usually accompanied by weakness in the longitudinal arch and pronation of the feet (see Figure 14.24).

No treatment or exercises are recommended for knock-knees in children younger than age 7 because, developmentally, this is a normal condition. In severe knock-knees, physicians often prescribe a 1/8-inch heel-raise on the medial border and/or use of a night splint. Severe cases that persist are treated with surgery (**osteotomy**).

Exercises that help include these:

1. Stretch the muscles on the lateral aspect of the leg (peroneal group) by doing supination exercises (inversion and adduction of the foot).
2. Strengthen the tibials by doing supination exercises; this also helps to strengthen longitudinal arch.
3. Strengthen the outward rotators of the hip joint by doing activities that stress outward rotation.

Hyperextended Knees

Also called *back knees* or *genu recurvatum,* hyperextended knees is a deviation in which the knees are pulled backward beyond their normal position. This posture problem can be identified best from a side view (see Figure 14.25). Hyperextension of the knees tends to tilt the pelvis forward and contributes to lordosis, thereby throwing all of the body segments out of alignment.

This condition can be caused by knee extensor weakness, tight calf muscles, Achilles tendon contractures, and bony abnormalities. In cerebral palsy, back knees often result from surgical overcorrection of knee flexion deformities. In spinal cord injuries and polio, the knees are sometimes surgically placed in recurvatum to permit independent walking as an alternative to wheelchair locomotion (see the information on gaits in Chapter 11).

Severe cases of back knees are usually treated by prescription of a knee-ankle brace that holds the foot in slight dorsiflexion and the knee in flexion. Specific exercise should not be done in physical education unless medically prescribed. *Contraindicated activities include touching the toes from a standing position, deep-knee squats, and duck and bear walks.* Standing with knees in hyperextension should always be discouraged by telling people to relax or bend at the knees.

Tibial Torsion

With tibial torsion, the tibia is twisted and the weight-bearing line is shifted to the medial aspect of the foot. The deviation is often more marked in one leg than in the other, with the affected foot toeing inward and pronating. Tibial torsion often accompanies knock-knees, flat feet, and pronated feet (see Figure 14.26). Congenital anomalies of the foot may be accompanied by twisting of the lower end of the tibia. Congenital tibial torsion is usually corrected in infancy by plaster casts, braces, splints, and/or surgery.

Deviations of the Feet

Poor alignment in any part of the body affects the weight-bearing function of the feet. Obesity increases the stress on the joints. Abnormal formation of bones, as in clubfoot (see foot in

Figure 14.24 Knock-knees elongates tendons on the medial side and tightens tendons on the lateral side. Lateral muscles of the lower leg tighten, pulling the outer border of the foot upward and forcing weight onto the inner border.

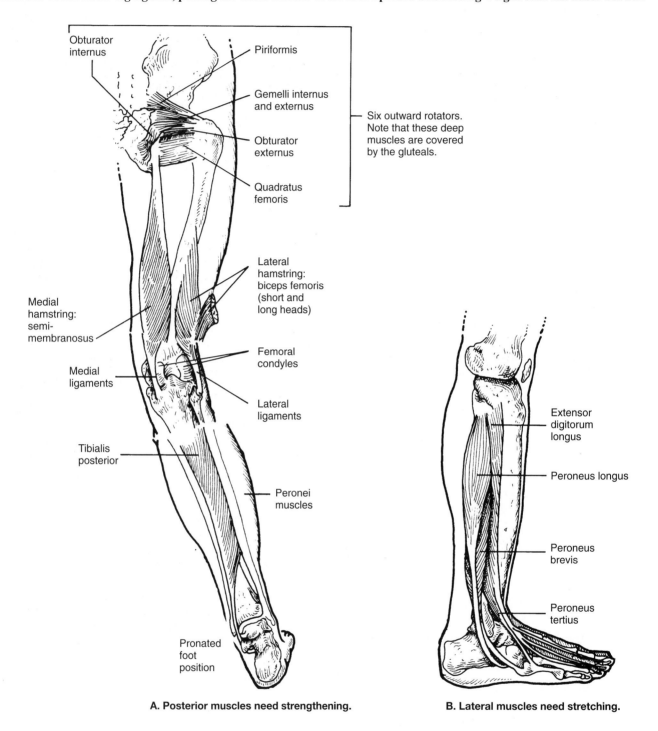

A. Posterior muscles need strengthening.

B. Lateral muscles need stretching.

Figure 14.25 Right knee in hyperextension after knee surgery following an automobile accident. Malalignment of legs contributes to lordosis.

Figure 14.26 Medial torsion of left tibia in a young adolescent with surgically corrected clubfoot.

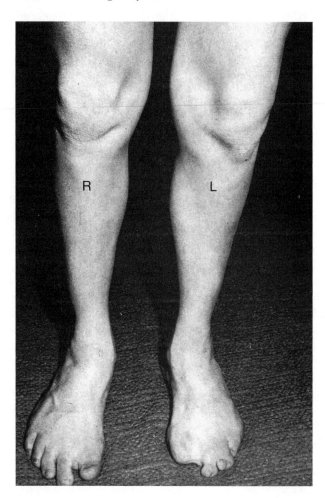

Figure 14.26), also affects alignment, as does weak or paralyzed leg and foot muscles resulting from spinal cord injury or neuromuscular conditions like cerebral palsy.

Toeing Inward

Toeing inward (pigeon toes) is usually caused by a strength imbalance in the hip joint muscles. When the inward rotators—*gluteus minimis* and *gluteus medius*—are stronger than the outward rotators, the student toes inward. This problem is also associated with the scissors gait in cerebral palsy.

Exercises that help include these:

1. Develop proprioceptive awareness of the different foot positions through movement exploration on all kinds of surfaces.
2. Stretch the tight inward rotators by doing activities that emphasize outward rotation. Ballet techniques are especially effective.
3. Strengthen the weak outward rotators by doing activities that emphasize outward rotation.
4. Avoid inward rotation movements.

Toeing Outward

Toeing outward occurs when the posterior group of muscles on the sacrum, called "the six outward rotators," is stronger than the prime movers for inward rotation (see Figure 14.24). Since toeing outward is a way of widening the stance and improving the balance, it may be observed in toddlers just learning to walk, the aged, persons who are blind, and others who are unsure of their footing. *Good exercises are the opposite of those done for toeing inward.*

Supination and Pronation

The two joints of the foot where most of the movements occur—and subsequently, the deviations—are the *talonavicular* and *talocalcaneal* joints (see Figure 14.27). In the former, the talus is transferring the weight of the body to the forward part of the foot, and in the latter, it is transferring the weight to the back part of the foot. How this weight is transferred determines the presence or absence of foot problems.

Normally, the weight of the body in locomotor activities is taken on the outer border of the foot and then transferred via the metatarsal area to the big toe, which provides the

Figure 14.27   Joints are named for the two bones that touch. Thus, the ankle joint is the talotibial joint. The talocalcaneal and talonavicular joints are the sites of *varus* (inward) and *valgus* (outward) foot deformities.

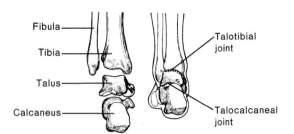

push-off force for forward movement. During this sequence, the foot is maintained in **slight supination,** which is considered the foot's "strong position." All locomotor activities should be performed in this slightly supinated position, which forces the weight of the body to be taken on the foot's outer border.

Pronation, the most common and the most debilitating of foot problems, is defined variously as taking the weight of the body on the inner border of the foot, rolling inward on the ankles, and combined eversion and abduction. *Eversion,* or turning the sole of the foot outward, occurs when the lateral muscles of the lower leg (peroneals) are tighter than the tibials. This deviation occurs mainly in the talonavicular and talocalcaneal joints.

Flat foot is a related disorder. The Feiss line and the Helbing's sign (described under flat foot) are also used for diagnosis of pronation.

Pronation may occur in early childhood as well as other growth periods. In affluent areas, well over 10 to 20% of the children may wear corrective shoes designed to manage pronation (see Figure 14.28). In these shoes, the medial border is built up in such a way as to force the weight of the body to be taken on the foot's outer border. The shoes are prescribed by physicians. Children who wear corrective shoes should not change to tennis shoes for physical education activity; nor should they go barefooted without the permission of their orthopedist.

Exercises that help include these:

1. Begin with non-weight-bearing exercises and do not add weight-bearing exercises until indicated by orthopedist.
2. Emphasize toe-curling exercises to strengthen the flexors of the toes.
3. Emphasize plantar flexion and inversion.
4. Avoid dorsiflexion exercises and maintenance of foot in dorsiflexion for long periods of time.
5. Avoid eversion movements.
6. In picking up marbles and other objects with the toes, stress a position of inversion, as in this sequence:
   a. Pick up marbles with toes.
   b. Deposit into box across the midline, which forces the foot into inversion.
7. In relay activities for correction of pronation, make sure objects held by toes of right foot are passed to the left to ensure inversion.

Figure 14.28   Thomas heel shoes used to correct flat foot and other alignment problems. The medial border of the shoe is extended forward and raised.

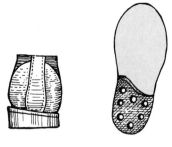

Flat Foot (Pes Planus)

Flat foot may be congenital or postural. If the muscles of the legs and feet are strong and flexible and the body is in good alignment, congenital flat foot is not considered a postural deviation.

Infants are born with varying degrees of flat foot. Strong arches develop as the natural consequence of vigorous kicking and strenuous locomotor activities. Sedentary children do not develop strong arches and tend to be at risk for sprains. Faulty body mechanics, especially pronation, contributes to flat foot. This condition is worsened by obesity.

Two diagnostic tests are used to determine the severity of combined flat foot and pronation disorders (see Figure 14.29). The **Feiss line method,** associated with the front of the leg, requires stretching a string from the kneecap to the big toe and checking how distant the navicular is from the string. The **navicular** (a tarsal bone) should be directly under the string on the top of the foot, where shoelaces are tied. Flat foot is diag-

Figure 14.29   Assessment of severity of flat foot and pronation. (A) Feiss line method, arrows point to location of the navicular. (B) Helbing sign method, arrows show whether Achilles tendon is straight or flared inward.

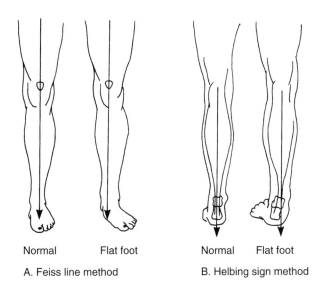

Normal   Flat foot   Normal   Flat foot

A. Feiss line method   B. Helbing sign method

Figure 14.30 Medial view of foot illustrating pain centers and structures that support the longitudinal arch. Pain centers are *(A)* under metatarsophalangeal joints, *(B)* where the plantar ligaments are attached to the calcaneus, *(C)* under navicular, and *(D)* middorsum, where shoelaces tie.

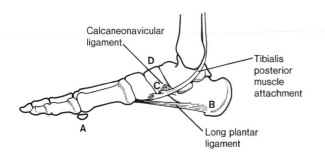

nosed as first, second, or third degree, depending on whether the navicular is 1, 2, or 3 inches from its correct position. The **Helbing sign method,** associated with the rear of the leg, uses a string to determine whether the **Achilles tendon** is straight (correct) or flared inward (flat foot).

Exercises that help include these:

1. Strengthen the tibials by supination exercises like patty-cake, with feet together, apart.
2. Strengthen and tighten other muscles, ligaments, and tendons on the medial aspect of the foot by inversion exercises.
3. Stretch the tight muscles, ligaments, and tendons on the lateral aspect of the foot.

Pain Centers

Examinations of the feet should include questions concerning pain or discomfort in the following five "pain centers" of the foot:

1. sole of the foot under the metatarsophalangeal joints;
2. sole of the foot close to the heel where the plantar ligaments attach to the calcaneus;
3. under the surface of the navicular;
4. middorsum, where shoelaces tie;
5. outer surface of the sole of the foot, where most of the weight is borne (see Figure 14.30).

These areas should be inspected closely for thickness and other abnormalities.

Syndactylism

Extra toes, the absence of toes, or the webbing of toes all affect mechanical efficiency in locomotor activities (see Figure 14.31), but a child with good coordination can learn to compensate well enough to achieve recognition as an outstanding athlete. An example is Tom Dempsey, stellar kicker for the Philadelphia Eagles of the National Football Conference, who had part of his kicking foot missing.

Figure 14.31 Absence of big toe affects balance and locomotor efficiency.

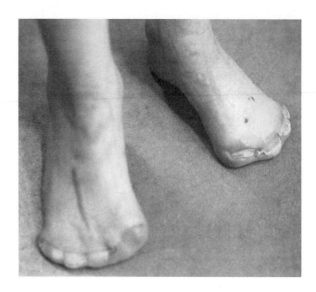

Webbing of toes is usually corrected surgically, and extra toes may be removed to facilitate purchase of shoes. The most debilitating defect is absence of the big toe, which plays a major role in static balance and in the push-off phase of locomotor activities.

Hallux Valgus (Bunion)

Hallux is the Latin word for "big toe" and *valgus* is a descriptive adjective meaning "bent outward." Hence, **hallux valgus** is a marked deviation of the big toe toward the four lesser toes. This adduction at the first metatarsophalangeal joint causes shoes to exert undue pressure against the medial aspect of the head of the first metatarsal, where a bursa (sac of synovial fluid) is present in the joint. This bursa may change as a result of the pressure exerted by the shoe. If the bursa enlarges, it is called a *bunion,* the Greek word for "turnip" (see Figure 14.32). This phenomenon happens so often that the terms **bunion** and

Figure 14.32 Bunion limits flexion of big toe.

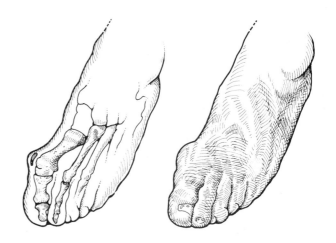

hallux valgus are used as synonyms. If the bursa becomes inflamed, it is called *bursitis.* If the irritation results in a deposit of additional calcium on the first metatarsal head, this new growth is called an *exostosis.*

 OPTIONAL ACTIVITIES

1. Link desired changes in postures with the extension (stretching) activities in dance, aquatics, and movement exploration. Create some lesson plans for different ages that use dance, aquatics, or movement exploration and use these lesson plans for teaching. Write observations in journal.

2. Conduct research on braces, splints, and surgery for specific conditions via books, journals, and the media. Write and/or give the report to class members, or use your new knowledge in ways that will help others.

3. If you can establish rapport with a person with a severe posture condition or someone who has had such a condition corrected, conduct an informal interview to find out about feelings and experiences associated with postures. Often, postures is a sensitive topic, so plan questions ahead of time and proceed gently and empathically. Jot reflections in journal.

4. Postures often deteriorate with old age and/or illness. Why? Study the postures of persons aged 75 and over at assistive care and nursing centers. How does using a walker change postures? Ask persons what kinds of activity they do. How can persons maintain healthy, pleasing postures throughout their lifetimes?

5. Graduate students, read and discuss Chapters 7, 8, 9, 10, and 11 on postural control in the excellent textbook by Shumway-Cook and Woollacott (2001).

CHAPTER

15

Sports Recreation and Competition: Socialization, Instruction, and Transition

Ronald W. Davis and Claudine Sherrill

Figure 15.1 Play and game competence requires attention to social and emotional skills as well as environmental factors and technology.

1. Survey your community and identify the recreational opportunities that exist for persons with disabilities. Try to identify whether these opportunities would be considered recreational, noncompetitive, or competitive. Review old newspaper articles and determine the number of stories printed about sports for persons with disabilities. Establish if pictures accompanied these stories and what section of the newspaper they were printed in (i.e., sports section, entertainment, local news).

2. Make a list of the barriers to active leisure that might exist in your community for persons with disabilities. Take a trip to the local YMCA or YWCA and interview the manager about plans to include persons with disabilities within the programming opportunities.

3. Attend a disability sporting event and make a list of the similarities between the game you are watching and its counterpart from able-bodied (AB) sports (i.e., wheelchair basketball and high school basketball, Special Olympics track and field and high school track and field). After the event, attempt to interview the coach of the disability sport about how he or she prepares athletes (i.e., amount of practice time, skill development, training programs).

4. What steps will you take to include disability sports into your teaching? Give examples. How would you improve the opportunities for families and communities to embrace disability sport in your school or community?

IDEA emphasizes that physical education instruction includes three areas: physical and motor fitness; fundamental motor skills and patterns; and skills in games, sports, dance, and aquatics. The third area is sometimes called *play and game competence, active leisure, or functional competence in sports, dance, aquatics, and other physical activities.* The third area, in particular, addresses the ability to initiate and sustain involvement in physical activities that are fun, meaningful, and satisfying. **Functional competence** is linked with the wise use of leisure time and the development of lifelong active leisure skills. Functional competence is the focus of Chapters 15, 16, and 17, which address sports, dance, and aquatics, respectively.

The philosophy of this text is that sport competence should be developed concurrently with fitness and motor skills. This holistic approach, in turn, leads to active leisure during nonschool hours and adult years (see Figure 15.1). In this chapter, the term *sports* encompasses play and game skills and leisure-time skills.

The Transition Services Mandate in IDEA

The legal basis for school-based instruction in play and game competence is not only in the law's definition of physical education but also in the transition services mandate in IDEA. The term **transition services** means a coordinated set of activities written into the IEP that promotes movement from school to postschool activities, including postsecondary education, vocational training, integrated employment, continuing and adult education, adult services, independent living, and community participation (IDEA, 1997). The law requires a statement of the needed transition services in the IEP for each student from age 14 onward and earlier, if appropriate. This statement is called the **individual transition plan** (ITP). This plan must be implemented by age 16.

How would you use sports or recreational opportunities to address transition for students with disabilities? Where would you include these in the student's programming and how would you guarantee appropriate implementation? Write examples of statements you would use to address this in an ITP.

Independent living and community participation, as specified in the transition services mandate, require skills for leisure as well as for work. To develop leisure skills, students must be provided with functional, community-based, lifetime sport and fitness skills training that is based on individual needs and preferences (Dattilo, 2002; Krebs & Block, 1992). **Functional** means that the activities taught in physical education are age-appropriate and usable in recreation settings with family and friends. **Community-based** means that, whenever possible, instruction and practice occur in the neighborhood settings that students will use after graduation. **Lifetime** means that activities are taught that can be meaningful and satisfying throughout the adult years. Several new books are available that stress lifelong physical activity (i.e., McCracken, 2001).

Leisure, Play, and Sport for All

Active leisure, as a physical education goal, is defined as voluntary engagement in daily large-muscle physical activity that is fun, meaningful, and satisfying during free or discretionary time. Leisure and play are closely associated concepts, which are explained by many diverse theories (K. Henderson et al., 2001; Mannell & Kieber, 1977; Stebbins, 2002). **Leisure** can be a state of mind, free time, or activity engaged in during free time when school and work obligations are fulfilled. What people choose to do in their leisure is a major concern of many professions (i.e., occupational therapy, physical education, and recreation).

Barriers to Active Leisure

The adapted physical activity profession is particularly concerned with barriers to active leisure (see Figure 15.2). Disproportionate numbers of individuals with and without disabilities participate in sport, dance, and aquatics. This has been linked to clumsiness and low self-esteem in the athletic competence (Rose & Larkin, 2002; Smyth & Anderson, 2000). However, the most frequently reported barrier to active leisure is not having a companion, friend, or advocate to share the experience with (Sherrill & Williams, 1996). Other barriers include a lack of money, a lack of transportation, inadequate equipment or facil-

Figure 15.2 Consider the barriers that individuals with disabilities must overcome in order to use community swimming pools.

Figure 15.3 What barriers must be overcome to bring children in wheelchairs together for after-school or weekend club sport? Make a list and share it with classmates.

ities, the desired activity not being available, a lack of time, a lack of specific skills, insufficient support groups, and inappropriate behaviors that diminish peer acceptance in an activity setting (Ferrara, Dattilo, & Dattilo, 1994; Ittenbach, Abery, Larson, Spiegel, & Prouty, 1994). Physical education instruction must extend beyond fitness and motor skills to address each of these barriers as well as barriers that teachers encounter when developing transition plans (Krueger et al., 2000). Chief among these were transportation, social isolation, and budget restrictions.

Identify several sports activities that could be taught to a person using a wheelchair, someone who is blind, or with a visual impairment, and someone who has a hearing impairment. Role-play six persons in the community in a round table discussion about how school-taught skills can be transferred to community facilities.

Abundance of Free Time

Instruction leading to play and game competence and active leisure is particularly important for individuals who have an abundance of free time. Only about one third of the working-age population with disabilities hold full-time jobs, as opposed to about 80% of AB peers (Levine & Edgar, 1994). Overall, the mean earnings of individuals with disabilities continue to be about 35% less than those of AB peers. Problems of employment and salary are far greater for females than for males, warranting particular attention to helping girls and women develop sport skills and active leisure (Altman, 1996).

Sport for All

Internationally, active leisure and play are associated with the "Sport for All" motto and movement (DeKnop & Oja, 1996). This is partly because the Council of Europe (1975) adopted the *European Sport for All Charter* and UNESCO (1978) adopted

the *International Charter of Physical Education and Sport.* These charters and associated funding from the International Olympic Committee and various governments have led to adoption of the Sport for All movement in two thirds of the nations of the world. In many parts of the world, the term *sport* encompasses all kinds of large-muscle physical activity (DePauw & Doll-Tepper, 1989). The Sport for All movement recognizes four types of sport that individuals may choose during nonschool or nonwork hours: (a) top-level or elite sport, (b) organized or club sport, (c) recreational sport, and (d) health or fitness sport. Adapted physical activity aims to get individuals involved in as many of these types of sports as possible (see Figure 15.3).

Sport Socialization

Sport socialization is the process of becoming and staying involved in sport, learning sport roles and values, and acquiring a sporting identity; this process is facilitated by self, others, and environmental interactions. Persons who are socialized into sport think of themselves as athletes with specialized skills and responsibilities (Wheeler, Malone, et al., 1996; Wheeler, Steadward, et al., 1999). The process, of course, is different for people with and without disabilities, as it is for people with congenital conditions and those with acquired conditions (Sherrill, 1997c; Williams, 1994). Children without disabilities are often enrolled in community sport at an early age, thus learning sport roles and acquiring a sporting identity as part of the natural process of growing up and striving to please significant others (Coakley, 2001). When one or both parents are or have been athletes, their children typically are socialized into sport by age 8.

In contrast, the sport socialization of individuals with congenital disabilities is constrained by parents' and teachers' lack of knowledge about sport in relation to disability. There might be considerable debate over whether to involve the child in disability sport (i.e., Special Olympics, Deaf Sport, or Cerebral Palsy Sport), in nondisability sport, or both. Overprotection, fluctuating parental expectations, and a lack of role models

Table 15.1 Questions about interest and involvement in sports from an instrument developed by Susan Greendorfer and John Lewko (1978).

1. How much do you play sports after school and on weekends?

5	4	3	2	1
Very much	A lot	Some	Not much	Not at all

2. How important is it to you that you participate in sports?

1	2	3	4	5
Not important	Not too	In between	Somewhat	Very important

3. How much do you like playing sports?

5	4	3	2	1
Very much	A lot	Some	Not much	Not at all

4. In general, how good are you at sports?

1	2	3	4	5
Not good at all	Not good	In between	Good	Very good

5. How easy is it for you to learn new sports skills?

5	4	3	2	1
Very easy	Somewhat easy	Average	Not very easy	Not easy at all

of athletes with similar conditions delay and complicate serious involvement in sport. As a result, *individuals with congenital disabilities tend to play a more active role in socializing themselves into sport than AB peers do.*

Individuals with acquired disabilities experience **discontinuous sport socialization.** Time of onset of disability is very important; the older the child, the more likely it is that his or her sport socialization will continue along its original path. Injury or disease is an interruption, which calls for reevaluation and consideration of new sport options.

Table 15.1 presents questions that can be used to assess the ongoing sport socialization of children during different sport seasons. The use of these questions as a paper-and-pencil instrument should be supplemented with interviews that explore why the child gives particular responses and how the child defines sport. This instrument can be varied by inserting the child's favorite sport (i.e., basketball, soccer) into each question. Both individual item scores and total scores should be recorded, analyzed, and used to set physical education goals. The questions in Table 15.1 are part of a 40-item inventory called the Sport Interest Inventory (Greendorfer & Lewko, 1978). The other items explore the contributions of father, mother, siblings, teachers, and friends to the sport socialization process.

Physical educators teachers should realize how they can get students with disabilities socialized into sport by including disability sport in their general curriculums. Including sports traditionally played by individuals with disabilities into a general physical education curriculum will impact students with and without disabilities by creating social interactions opportunities for both groups. No longer would the student with a disability have to learn a sport modeled by AB peers, but rather the reverse would be true. By including disability sport, nondisabled students would have the opportunity to learn a sport modeled by a student with a disability. Such an experience would impact social acceptance of the student with a disability and help minimize social barriers (see Davis, 2002).

Assessment of Play and Game Competence

Assessment should involve all members of the family. The leisure expectations, aspirations, and lifestyles of each person should be considered. What does the family do during leisure? What forms of play are valued? Individual and group interviews and casual conversations are the best ways to obtain this information. Leisure surveys (see Table 15.2) or books like that of Paciorek and Jones (2001) and Davis (2002) that show people with disabilities engaging in many activities can be used as props to stimulate talk. Magazines like *Sports 'N Spokes* and *Palaestra* are good also, as are scrapbooks of pictures from various sources. Professionals often must help parents understand that individuals with disabilities can participate in a wide variety of sports and games in numerous settings. During assessment interviews, parents can be helped to understand community resources and to assess their skills in accessing these resources.

Assessment of play and game competence requires an examination of how the child uses her or his free time when alone. It is essential that children have play skills for the hours when they are alone. It is important also to assess the child's play and game competence in the company of others (see Figure 15.4). Play behaviors typically are different when the child is (a) with an adult or older child, (b) with a same-age child, (c) with a child who is younger, and (d) with groups of various sizes. Assessment should address each of these situations. Children who are verbal are generally eager to talk about their favorite playmates, games, and sports. Informal interviews thus serve as an excellent source of data (see Figure 15.5).

Assessment should include making a list of games and sports that the individual can play and another list of the activities that he or she would like to do. Comparing these lists against activities of the same-age peers and family members helps set goals related to inclusion. Barriers to success in these activities should be examined, and action plans should be

Table 15.2   A sport survey to assess active leisure interests and needs.

Directions: Following is a list of sports in which many people with a disability excel! Please circle the number of each sport you have tried three or more times. Then choose the five sports you would most like to be good at and underline them.

1. All-terrain vehicles	28. Power lifting
2. Aquatics	29. Power soccer
3. Archery	30. Quad rugby
4. Basketball	31. Racquetball
5. Beep baseball	32. Road racing
6. Blowdarts	33. Roller skating
7. Boating	34. Rugball
8. Boccia	35. Scuba diving
9. Bowling	36. Shooting
10. Cross-country	37. Showdown
11. Cycling	38. Snow skiing
12. Equestrian	39. Skydiving
13. Fencing	40. Slalom
14. Field events	41. Sledge hockey
15. Fishing	42. Snowmobiling
16. Fitness programs	43. Soccer
17. Floor hockey	44. Softball
18. Flying	45. Table tennis
19. Football	46. Team handball
20. Goal ball	47. Tennis
21. Golf	48. Track
22. Gymnastics	49. Volleyball
23. Hunting	50. Waterskiing
24. Ice skating	51. Weight training
25. Ice sledding	52. Wheelchair dance
26. Lawn bowling	53. Wilderness experiences
27. Martial arts	54. Wrestling

agreed on for overcoming these barriers. Occasionally barriers are too great to be overcome, and assessment must focus on finding alternative activities that are acceptable to everyone involved. Every IEP should include specific games or sports to be mastered.

Assessment of play and game competence also requires a consideration of the skills needed to use community settings (Block, 2000; Schleien et al., 1995; Wehman, 2001). Assessment interviews should make families aware of the rich array of community options for leisure and give them information on how to become involved. After supplying this information and accompanying the parents to examine various facilities, professionals must ask many questions. Suppose the individual with a disability and her or his family decided on a biweekly leisure activity at a particular bowling alley. What issues must be resolved?

1. *Transportation.* Who will supply this? Are lessons needed in using public transportation?

2. *Companionship.* Bowling is more fun when done with someone else. Are family or friends available, or should

Figure 15.4   Multipurpose play apparatus affords an excellent environment for assessing motor creativity.

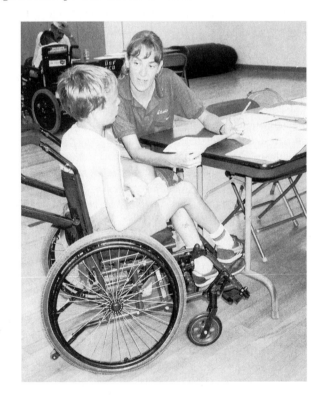

Figure 15.5   Interviews are the best way to determine game and sport interest and needs.

an arrangement be made for a paid or volunteer companion?

3. *Money.* How much is needed? Who will supply it? Are lessons needed in the use of money?

4. *Appropriate clothing and shoes.* Is instruction needed? Does the individual know the shoe size to ask for and have the communication skills to make himself or herself understood?

5. *Selection of ball and lane.* What instruction is needed?

6. *Game and social etiquette.* What instruction is needed?

7. *Scoring*. What kind of scoring is meaningful? What instruction is needed?

8. *Crisis management*. If problems occur, who at the bowling alley can be depended upon for understanding and help? What problems might occur? What are the protocols or plans of action to be followed?

Some communities employ recreation specialists to assist with assessment in the play and game competence area, but these concerns in school-age persons are usually addressed by physical educators. Adapted physical educators especially, in relation to the transition services mandate of the law, should be sure that the assessment protocol affords opportunities to visit many types of sport and recreation settings, to engage in activity at some of them, and to make informed decisions as to which best meets needs. This needs assessment leads to goal setting for the transition part of the IEP.

Another assessment approach is that of functional skill performance. Disability sport requires the execution of specific motor skills. The general physical educator is in a great position to assess these skills since many skills are the same as those taught to students without disabilities. For example, in regulation basketball, the skills of passing, dribbling, shooting, and ball movement are taught. A general physical educator is able to assess and then teach the key components of these skills through a task analysis or skill breakdown approach. By comparison, in wheelchair basketball, the same skills are required; players need to know how to pass, dribble, shoot, and move the ball up and down the court. To teach these skills for wheelchair basketball, the teacher would have to assess performance and teach the student proper skill mechanics once again through task analysis. By including disability sport within the general curriculum, teachers address skill assessment and contribute to sport play. Such an assessment leads the teacher to setting appropriate goals and objectives for the student with a disability (see Davis, 2002).

Perform a task analysis for the skill of passing a basketball as taught in the general physical education class. Identify at least four key teaching points for this skill. Work in small groups to accomplish this activity using role-playing and demonstration techniques. Next, repeat this activity for the sport of wheelchair basketball. Once completed, compare the similarities and differences. If wheelchairs are not available, role-play while sitting in standard desk chairs. Repeat for other sports in which you feel comfortable (i.e., volleyball and sitting volleyball, tennis and wheelchair tennis).

Teaching Play and Game Competence

Teaching begins with agreeing on goals and objectives. This occurs at both the IEP and the classroom levels. The overall goal is usually written as follows: *To demonstrate functional competence in selected play and game behaviors* or, for older students, *to demonstrate functional competence in active leisure behaviors required for participation in community programs.*

Game and Leisure Behaviors for Time Alone

The listing of specific play and game behaviors to be demonstrated should include some activities that can be done alone, because all individuals, especially those reared in small families, have time alone that needs to be filled with meaningful activity. Physical activities that can be done alone (i.e., shooting baskets, jumping rope, riding a bicycle, using backyard or neighborhood park apparatus) depend on available equipment and space in each individual's home. Goal setting and instruction in alone play must therefore be highly individualized. Teachers may need to visit homes to establish lesson plans with content that is realistic and generalizable. This is particularly necessary when working with individuals with severe developmental delays who will not play unless every step of the play process is carefully taught with emphasis on generalization.

Game and Leisure Behaviors for Time with Others

Some instruction, however, should focus on learning the co-operation and competition behaviors essential to partner and group play. Table 15.3 presents a cooperation–competition continuum to guide instruction. Most children, until about age 8, function at the egocentric and small-group game levels. Individuals with severe mental retardation or play delays might be frozen at these levels if their cognitive ability does not permit an understanding of competition. *See Chapter 9 for content specifically on teaching beginning competence in game cooperation.*

Until about the third grade, play and game experiences should be recreational and developmental. The emphasis should be on learning motor creativity and experiencing a wide variety of activities. Every child should be taught to swim and dance at an early age as well as to enjoy the out-of-doors and activities that use natural resources, such as hiking, camping, and boating. Games should be vehicles for having fun, learning basic play and motor skills, and reinforcing self-esteem.

Although parents tend to place children in competitive team sports like T-ball, peewee soccer, and Challenger baseball at very young ages, most professionals believe that *serious competition should not be introduced until about age 8.* Then the best learning progression begins with competition against a single opponent, as in track, swimming, bowling, and the like, then moves to dual or doubles competition, and finally team competition. Children should have opportunities to experience each type of game competition so that they can make informed decisions as to whether they want to become individual or team sport people. In general, however, individual sports are more accessible throughout the lifespan. Thus, individual sports are more important to teach than team sports if time does not permit instruction in all kinds of competition.

Readiness for Serious Competition

The rationale for not engaging children in serious competition until about age 8 lies mainly in human development and self-concept theory. **Serious competition** is defined as understanding score keeping, acknowledgment of winners and losers, and coping with spectator and peer pressures. From a psychological standpoint, competition is *social comparison*, a means of judging whether you are as good as everyone else and developing

Table 15.3   A cooperation–competition continuum to guide instruction.

Levels	Explanation
Egocentric	1. **Individual and group play.** Thinks only of self. Lacks maturity to empathize and cooperate. Wants to be "It" all of the time. Does not share or take turns unless reminded to.
Small-Group Games	2. **Cooperative organized play.** Cooperates with others to achieve a mutual goal, like winning a relay or tagging the most persons.
Individual or Dual Competition	3. **Individual competition.** Competes with one opponent in individual sports like track, swimming, bowling, golf, and tennis. Competes against others also in trying to make the best score in fitness, track, and self-testing activities.
Dual Competition and Cooperation	4. **Dual or doubles competition.** Competes in dual sports like doubles in tennis, badminton, and table tennis. Cooperates with partner in doubles tennis, with team in bowling, and in other situations demanding a limited number of interactions.
Team Competition and Cooperation	5. **Team competition.** Cooperates with team members while concurrently competing with opponents. The smaller the team, the easier the learning progressions in cooperation and competition.

Note. The concept of personal best (self-competition) should be taught and reinforced at all levels.

opinions about your competence in various domains. This, in turn, influences self-concept, mental health, and whether or not an activity is fun.

Before age 5, most children do not understand competition because they are not yet developmentally able to make social comparisons. All sport is therefore recreational. Persons at this level of development (both the very young and the developmentally delayed) engage in sport to please parents and to feel good. Typically, they perform to the best of their ability but have no set goals other than to have fun. They do not understand winning and losing but instead base judgments of self-competence on (a) simple task mastery (either I did it or I did not) and (b) the feedback of significant others, mainly parents. Much of the early Special Olympics philosophy (i.e., the huggers at the finish line in track and swimming) was based on the assumption that most persons with mental retardation function at this level. *Today, Special Olympics philosophy and practices have changed to emphasize assessing athletes individually, determining whether or not they understand concepts of winning, and providing appropriate sport events.*

From ages 5 to 8, children gradually achieve the cognitive capacity to make social comparisons and begin to judge their personal worth by comparing themselves with others. This strengthens the egos of children who are good at sport but weakens the self-esteem of children with motor and play deficits. Until about the age of 8, most children do not have the emotional maturity to handle losing. Exposure to serious competition should not occur until children have developed good self-esteem, are emotionally ready to enjoy the challenge of competition, and fully understand that achieving a personal best is as good as or better than beating an opponent.

The concept of personal best should be introduced in sport around age 7 or 8, with children encouraged to state **level of aspiration** before undertaking self-testing or self-competition tasks. For example, the teacher may ask each child to write his or her anticipated score (level of aspiration) on a daily contract or in a secret place before responding to such

challenges as (a) "How many curl-ups can you do in 30 seconds?" (b) How fast can you run the 50-yard dash?" and (c) "How far can you throw the softball?" By comparing aspirations with actual scores, children are helped to focus newly evolving comparison skills on a personal best rather than on the goal of being better than others.

As individuals mature, most seek both to win and to achieve a personal best. In adapted physical activity, one of the main concerns is children who seldom or never win. Almost no research is available to describe the psychosocial development of children whose social comparisons always tell them that they are performing below average. One approach to this problem is to stress competition against self (i.e., a mastery climate) instead of against others (Causgrove Dunn, 2000). Another way is to emphasize activities that are recreational instead of competitive.

Basic Game and Sport Components

What, besides motor skills and an understanding of cooperation and/or competition, do individuals need to play games? To answer this question, consider the following game components:

1. **Players**—an understanding of roles in individual, dual, and team games. Is everyone playing for individual fun as in early childhood games, or is there an obligation to help a partner or a team?

2. **Equipment**—an understanding of the use and care of play equipment and awareness of safety factors. Given a piece of play equipment, can the child show its appropriate use for a particular game?

3. **Movements**—skill in performing the motor skills in the game context and ability to have fun while performing; the use of strategy in performing motor skills and moving around the play area.

4. **Organizational pattern**—skill in getting into correct formation or going to a particular space to await a turn or play a designated position.

Figure 15.6 This individual with muscular dystrophy has been employed to give after-school lessons in table tennis to a boy with mental retardation.

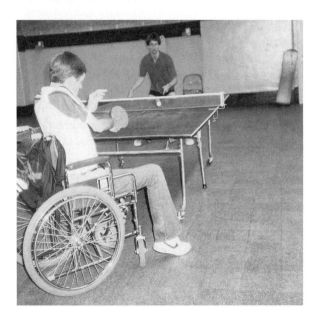

5. **Limitations/rules**—an understanding of adherence to rules within a game context, such as stop and go, time-out, boundaries, safety zones, taking turns, making outs, direction of play, penalties, game cues or jargon, and winning points.

6. **Game purpose**—an understanding of game purposes based on one, two, or more concepts.

Children without disabilities typically learn play and game skills informally from other children in neighborhood play. In contrast, children who require adapted physical activity services often need systematic instruction and practice in each element of every game category (see Figure 15.6). Behavior management techniques (see Chapter 7) are useful in designing instruction and selecting personalized reinforcements.

Empowerment for Transition Into Community Sport

Individuals with disabilities should be involved in after-school and weekend sport at the same age as able-bodied peers in their neighborhood. This requires the teaching of sport skills and game strategies at appropriate ages. Typically the acquisition of adequate motor and social skills for acceptance by peers demands more instruction and practice than the school setting affords. Physical educators must therefore *encourage the establishment of homework or neighborhood tutorial programs.* Initiation of such programs often requires that physical educators supply the names and phone numbers of tutors who can be employed and/or volunteers. It is important that lists of resources include role models and individuals with disabilities similar to those of the child needing services. Contact with such persons can be made through national offices of disability sport organizations like the National Disability Sport Alliance (NDSA).

Involvement in sport first means empowerment of parents to know who to initiate or find programs that meet their children's needs. This is one of the most important jobs of the adapted physical educator who should plan time for frequent visits with parents. Parents need encouragement and support as much as their children do, and there is typically no one else available to assist them in concerns pertaining specifically to sports and games. Physical educators thus should see themselves as instrumental in helping parents make and execute decisions that maximize their children's involvement in appropriate, meaningful sport.

Choices should not be limited to disability or inclusive sports. Parents and children should be introduced to all of the possibilities and, if necessary, supported in creating new possibilities. A library of videotapes showing people with disabilities succeeding in various sport activities should be available for both parents and children to borrow and view. Books and magazines should also be available for loan.

Ultimately, *parents must know how to empower their children to make personal choices to become involved in and stay involved in sport.* This involvement should extend beyond sport participation into leadership and administrative roles in the management of sport events and organizations. They should be acquainted with models who have such roles like Phil Craven, a former wheelchair basketball star, who is president of the International Paralympic Committee (IPC), the highest position available within disability sports. Even at very young ages, children should be encouraged to elect officers for their sport clubs and see themselves as responsible for many aspects of the sport experience.

Use of Community Resources and Transition Outcomes

The use of community resources should begin as field trips that are an integral part of school physical education (see Figure 15.7). These field trips, whenever possible, should include parents or primary caretakers. Field trips should teach the role of spectator at sport events as well as the role of participant or athlete. Field trip events should include both disability and nondisability sport and should be written into the IEP as part of the coordinated set of activities related to transition.

Homework for physical education should require the use of community resources. Proof that homework was done can be in the form of portfolios, journals kept, photographs taken, or signatures by facility managers on forms indicating that the student was present. It is the responsibility of the adapted physical educator to ascertain that community resources meet criteria for attitudinal and architectural accessibility.

The use of community resources is enhanced when students see teachers and their families using these resources. It is also enhanced when students see individuals with the same disabilities as their own using these resources. Community resources can be public (paid for by tax dollars) or private (managed by churches, agencies, or commercial groups). The goal should be for students to be able to independently use as many kinds of sport, recreation, and fitness facilities as possible and to continue this use after graduation from high school. IEP

goals and objectives should list facilities by name and include procedures for maximizing community involvement.

Inclusion of Disability Sport in General Physical Education

General physical educators should realize the value of expanding their curriculum to include sports and games from the content area of disability sport. For teachers to introduce disability sport into their curriculum, they need to consider the following four simple steps modified from Davis (2002):

Step 1—Select the sport you wish to include. Here the teacher should consider sports that are generally taught within a general physical education curriculum (i.e., basketball, soccer, tennis, and track, etc). The assumption is that the teacher has experience teaching these sports and uses a skills analysis approach to teaching.

Step 2—Cross-reference the sport selected to a similar sport within the disability sport context and learn about that sport. For example, basketball and wheelchair basketball, soccer and wheelchair soccer, tennis and wheelchair tennis, track and wheelchair track, or volleyball and sitting volleyball are suggestions for cross-referencing. If general physical educators are not familiar with the skills needed to play each of these disability sports, then they must seek additional resources to learn about them. Modifications from Davis (2002) will be used later in this section to help learn about the disability sports. A skill cross-referencing table can be created to help with this initial step (see Table 15.4).

Step 3—Assess the functional level of performance. All of the disability sports have their own classification criteria, which are used to place individuals with disabilities into appropriate competitions. Without detailing the classification process, participants are

Table 15.4 Skill cross-reference table by Davis (2002).

Sports in General Physical Education Curriculum	Cross-Reference to Disability Sports					
Basketball	**WB**	**IWS**	**S**			
Passing	X	X				
Dribbling	X	X				
Shooting	X	X				
Ball movement	X	X				
Soccer						
Passing	X	X				
Dribbling	X	X				
Throw-in		X				
Block		X				
Track and Field						
Sprints			X			
Relays						
Throw						

WB = Wheelchair Basketball
IWS = Indoor Wheelchair Soccer
S = The Slalom (Track)

assessed using functional or medical guidelines, or both, to determine proper sport participation. For example, participants wishing to play wheelchair basketball or soccer must be assessed, or classified, before entering play to determine their level of performance. The result of the classification process yields a number that is reflective of the athlete's function. *Generally speaking the lower the classification number, the lower the functional level.* Although it is not important for general physical educators to understand each and every class or classification for the disability sport, it is important for them to implement some type of assessment process to determine level of performance. Such a determination helps the teacher select the appropriate skills to be taught and the appropriate goals/objectives to be obtained. Teachers can create basic categories as simple as low, moderate, and high functioning by modifying official sport classification criteria (see Table 15.5).

Step 4—Select the skills and implement the activities/ games. Teachers should consider the game categories (players, equipment, movements, organizational pattern, limitations/rules, and purpose) and the student's level of cooperation–competition as they decide how to implement the games.

General physical educators have the competencies of including students with disabilities by implementing modifications to address motor limitations. For example, teachers know how to shorten base paths or lower targets for students with

Table 15.5   Functional student profiles for wheelchair basketball.

Functional Skill Level	Student Profile
Low	Multiple impairments, unable to manually maneuver a wheelchair, needs assistance positioning in wheelchair, needs assistance holding a ball, might use a power wheelchair.
Moderate	Able to maneuver a manual wheelchair independently for short distances; can hold a ball independently with two hands; has moderate active range of motion and independent sitting posture.
High	Able to maneuver a manual wheelchair independently for longer distances (30–50 ft); can hold a basketball independently with one or two hands; has high active range of motion in upper body, independent sitting posture, and can move continuously for 10 min without stopping.

From Davis (2002), p. 31.

Table 15.6   Wheelchair basketball rules at a glance.

Players	Maximum allowed on court is five players.
Equipment	Regulation basketball for men. Regulation basketball for women and youth. Basketball court 50 ft × 94 ft and no larger than 50 ft × 100 ft. Goal Height—10 ft (8.5 ft for youth). Three point line—19 ft 9 in.
Movements/ Organizational pattern	The game is started with a center jump. Players may use only their hands to move the ball. Players may dribble the ball with one hand. A player may not push or touch the handrims more than two consecutive times without dribbling, passing or shooting the ball. More than two consecutive pushes or touches to the handrim without dribbling is considered **traveling,** which is a turnover. Players may not touch the playing surface while in possession of the ball.
Limitations/rules	Free throws—Position all players on each side of the free throw land, alternating each team member. A member of the opposing team must be allowed first position closest to the basket. All lane players can go in on the release of the shot, but the shooter must wait until the ball touches the rim.
	Blocking Versus Charging—**Blocking** is a legal move and is defined by any player positioning his or her wheelchair to impede another player's movement. The player must have established position first. **Charging** is an illegal move defined as a collision from any angle in which a player fails to gain position first, or make attempt to control his or her own wheelchair at any time. Players are expected to maintain control of their wheelchairs at all times.
	Loss of Possession—The following are awarded loss of possessions to victimized teams: Traveling—more than two consecutive touches to the handrim without a dribble or pass. Anytime any part of the wheelchair, other than the wheels, touches the floor. Offensive player considered charging another player.
	Additional rules— If a player falls out of the wheelchair, play is continued, unless the fall endangers the fallen player or other players. Players may not raise up from the seat to gain an advantage such as attempting to reach for a ball during a rebound. Lifting of the buttocks from the seat to gain an advantage during a game results in a technical foul shot for the opponent. There is no double-dribble rule in wheelchair basketball.

Adapted from Davis (2002).

movement limitations and/or minimal upper body strength. Such modifications only address one domain. What about the remaining two (cognitive and affective)? How are these addressed? One way to address these two domains is to place the student with a disability in a decision-making role within the activity. By doing so, students with disabilities will have more of an equal status in their GE class. Activities suggested later in this chapter are guided by the concept of equal status.

Specifics For Teaching Three Sports

The following sections provide examples of how to implement the four steps (select the sport, cross-reference to a disability sport, assess the student's functional level of performance, and select the skills to be taught during the activities/games) of inclusion modified from Davis (2002). These steps are applicable to numerous settings and age groups. The sports of basketball, indoor wheelchair soccer, and slalom are described.

Wheelchair Basketball

Wheelchair basketball is perhaps the best known of all wheelchair sports. The National Wheelchair Basketball Association (NWBA), founded in 1948, has continued to grow across all levels of competition. The NWBA is organized into three divisions for men (I, II, III) and additional divisions for women,

collegiate, and youth. Wheelchair basketball is also played at the international level as evidenced in the Paralympics and World Championships. A summary of the sport of wheelchair basketball is presented in Table 15.6 using the game categories previously mentioned in this chapter.

Skills to Be Taught in Wheelchair Basketball

The following skills (see Table 15.7) should be taught in wheelchair basketball: passing (Figure 15.8), dribbling (Figure 15.9), shooting (Figure 15.10), and ball movement. Within this next section only the chest pass, continuous dribble, and free throw shooting will be described because these skills can be cross-referenced to regulation basketball (see Table 15.4). Ball movement skills (Figures 15.11 and 15.12) specific to wheelchair basketball include the bounce stop, bounce spin, and ball retrieval.

In Table 15.5 information about student profiles is provided. These student profiles are taken from Davis (2002) and are operationalized from the actual classification system in wheelchair basketball.

Once the student functional profile has been established (Step 3), it is time to implement games/activities to help promote skill development. The games/activities on pp. 393 to 404 are modified from Davis (2002) and should help provide the general physical educator with ideas for teaching.

Figure 15.8   Chest pass used in wheelchair basketball.

A. Preparation for two-handed chest pass: eyes on target; elbows flexed.

B. Execution of two-handed chest pass: elbows extended; thumbs point downward.

Table 15.7   **Wheelchair basketball skills by Davis (2002).**

Skill	Teaching Points
Chest pass	Place hands on each side of the ball; draw ball into chest by flexing elbows; extend elbows forcefully to pass the ball and turn thumbs inward and down upon release.
Continuous dribble	Bounce the ball ahead of the wheelchair closer to the front wheels or casters. Push the ball ahead, and move the hands quickly to the handrims and wheels to push the wheelchair. Continue dribbling the ball forward of the wheelchair while simultaneously pushing the wheelchair down the floor.
Free throw shooting	Make sure the student can successfully shoot a two-handed set shot before attempting a one-handed free throw shot. For a one-handed shot, place the ball in shooting hand with nonshooting hand as support on the opposite side of ball; make sure to select a ball that fits the student's hand. Extend elbow upon release of ball toward the basket and emphasize full extension upon ball release. (Hint: Turn the student slightly in the wheelchair to create an angle by placing the shooting shoulder slightly closer to the basket.)
Bounce stop	Bounce ball to side of wheelchair at the rear axle with a controlled bounce. As the ball bounces up, grab both handrims; the key here is timing the release of ball and reaching for handrims of the wheelchair. Next pull back with both hands to stop the wheelchair and catch the ball as it rebounds from floor. Catch the ball with one hand as the wheelchair stops.
Bounce spin	Complete a successful bounce stop with a one-handed catch by using the hand on the opposite side of ball to stop the wheelchair. As ball hits the floor, the hand on ball side pulls the handrim backward while the opposite hand pushes forward and down (this will spin the wheelchair). This should be executed as "push-pull" movement. As the wheelchair spins 180 degrees, the player's feet will pass under ball at the apex of the bounce so that the opposite arm should be on the ball side ready to make the catch.
Ball retrieval	Approach a rolled ball from the side and not directly from behind or in front, position next to the ball aligning the ball with the mainwheel. Have the player lean over and pin the ball against the mainwheel using the hand; as the wheelchair continues to move forward, the mainwheel will roll the pinned ball up from the floor to allow the player to secure it in his or her lap.

Figure 15.9   **Dribble used in wheelchair basketball.**

A. Stationary one-handed dribble: Bounce near the mainwheel.

B. Stationary one-handed dribble: Fingertip control.

C. Stationary one-handed dribble: Control the wheelchair.

D. Forward dribble: Bounce the ball in front of the main axle using fingertop control.

Figure 15.10   **Free throw shooting in wheelchair basketball.**

A. One-handed shot: Ball is balanced; nonshooting hand supports.

B. One-handed shot: Turn the shooting shoulder closer to the basket.

A. Bounce spin: Bounce the ball near the mainwheel axle. Extend elbow upon ball release.

B. Bounce spin: Control the wheelchair with the opposite hand.

C. Bounce spin: Bounce the ball above the head; pull the ball-side hand back as the ball rises.

D. Bounce spin: Execute the push-pull and spin the wheelchair so that the feet pass under the ball.

E. Bounce spin: Move the wheelchair so that the opposite arm is closer to the ball.

F. Catch the ball with the opposite hand.

Passing Game for Low Student Functional Level

Level of Cooperation–Competition—Small group (see Figure 15.13).

Activity Name—Give and Go.

Player Formation—Two lines facing each other on opposite sides of the free throw lane.

Equipment—Small Nerf ball, deflated playground ball, volley Nerf ball, or junior basketball.

Movements/Organization Pattern—Give one student a ball and on the signal have student move across the lane to his or her partner. Once next to the partner, have student drop the ball on the floor next to teammate.

Limitations/Rules—Once the ball hits the floor, another ball is placed in the partner's possession and he or she must move back across.

Inclusion Suggestion—Student with a disability decides how many times to pass the ball and must indicate decision to the class through his or her own form of communication. Student with a disability can also determine where the ball should start before each exchange.

Shooting Game for Low Student Functional Level

Level of Cooperation–Competition—Small group (see Figure 15.14.)

Activity Name—Pass and Shoot.

Player Formation—(*Same as Give and Go*): Two lines facing each other on opposite sides of the free throw lane.

Equipment—Small Nerf ball, deflated playground ball, volley Nerf ball, or junior basketball, with 2 buckets.

Movements/Organization Pattern—On the signal have student (#1) move across the lane. His or her partner (#2) then *places the ball in the lap* if the student has the functional level to do so.

Limitations/Rules—#1 then continues on to drop the ball into the bucket placed 10 ft beyond partner.

Inclusion Suggestion—Have the student with a disability call out or somehow indicate which bucket his or her partner should shoot at when it is the partner's turn. The student with a disability must make the call prior to shooting.

Figure 15.12   Ball retrieval used in wheelchair basketball.

A. Ball retrieval: Approach the ball from the side and align it with the mainwheel axle.

B. Ball retrieval: Pin the ball against the mainwheel.

Figure 15.13   Give and Go activity.

◆ **Give and Go** (from Davis, 2002, p. 33)

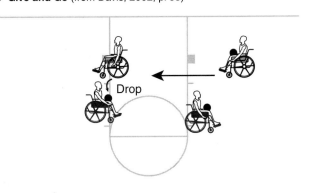

Drop

Figure 15.14   Pass and Shoot activity.

◆ **Pass and Shoot** (from Davis, 2002, p. 35)

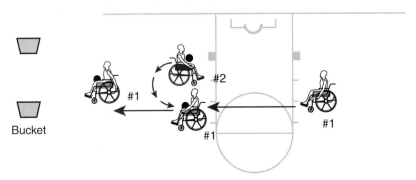

Bucket

#2

#1

#1

#1

Bounce Spin Game for Moderate to High Student Functional Level

Level of Cooperation–Competition—Small group (see Figure 15.15).

Activity Name—Spin City I.

Player Formation—Position students in small circle formations around the gymnasium with one student in the middle.

Equipment—Basketball or 10-in playground ball.

Movements/Organization Pattern—Each circle represents a state within the United States (e.g., Indiana). Each member of the circle represents a city in the state (e.g., Muncie), and the person in the middle represents the capital of the state (e.g., Indianapolis). Place a ball with any city comprising the circle. That person passes the ball to the capital; once the person in the middle catches the ball, he or she must perform a bounce spin and pass the ball to a new city.

Limitations/Rules—As students pass the ball to a new city, they must call the name of city out loud before passing it. As the new city catches the ball he or she must in turn perform a Bounce Spin and pass it back to the capital. The activity continues until all cities have been called. Students without disabilities should perform a crossover dribble or another skill selected by the teacher.

Inclusion Suggestion—Allow the student with a disability to select the new category (i.e., cars, planes, boats, etc).

Ball Retrieval Game for Moderate to High Student Functional Level

Level of Cooperation–Competition—Small group (see Figure 15.16).

Activity Name—Giddy Up.

Player Formation—Students in line formation. Try to alternate a student with a disability with a student without a disability in each line.

Figure 15.15   Spin City activity.

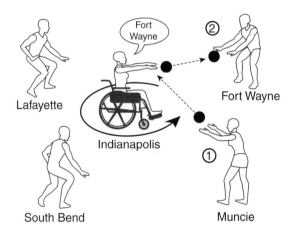

◆ **Spin City I** (from Davis, 2002, p. 53)

① = Start activity
② = Second pass

Figure 15.16   Giddy Up activity.

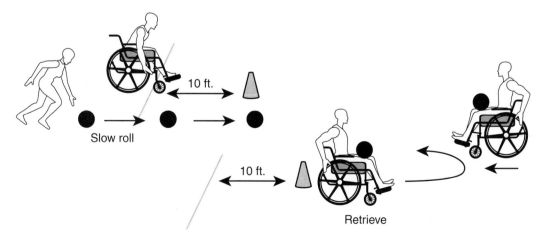

◆ **Giddy Up** (from Davis, 2002, p. 55)

Table 15.8   Indoor Wheelchair Soccer Rules at a Glance.

Players	Basketball court 50 ft × 94 ft and no larger than 50 ft × 100 ft.
	Goal Area—12 ft wide × 8 ft deep.
	Goals—5 ft wide and 5 ft 6 in high (can be made from wood, plastic, or metal).
	Penalty shot line should be marked 19 ft from the basketball endline in front of the goal; this is usually the same as free throw line in basketball.
	Maximum allowed on court is six players.
Equipment	The ball must be a 10-in yellow playground ball inflated to 2 psi.
	All players must play in wheelchair. Motorized scooters are not allowed in an official competition.
	Foot platform heights, at the forward point, cannot be more than 4 3/4 in. from the floor.
	All wheelchairs must have straps extending from one side of the chair to the other, behind the players' legs, 6 in above the platforms.
Movements/ organizational pattern	A legal start is conducted when an offensive player takes the ball inside the center circle and moves it the distance of its own circumference in a direction parallel to or behind the center line. At least one player must touch the ball before a goal can be scored.
	If an offensive player commits a violation prior to the kicker's initial movement, the kickoff is awarded to the opposing team. If the defense commits a violation, the kickoff is rekicked.
Limitations/rules	The ball is in play at all times, (i.e., rebounding off a goalpost, the referee, or until the referee blows the whistle).
	The ball is out of play when it completely crosses over the side line, or end line, or when it makes contact with a building structure above the area of play.
	A two-handed behind-the-head (overhead) throw is used to put the ball in play from a throw in. If a player cannot use both hands, he or she must attempt the overhead throw using one.
	The player has 5 sec to in-bound the ball. If the ball is not in-bounded within 5 sec, a turnover is awarded.
	The ball must travel completely over the line to be considered out of bounds. If a player is struck by a ball while out of bounds, there is no change of possession.
	Defensive players may not interfere with the in-bounding player's reentry to the court.
	In-bounding must be accomplished through the air, if the ball bounces on the line, it will be awarded to other team at the same location.
	Players may use hands, feet, chair or any part of their body to move the ball.
	Players may dribble the ball with one or two hands.
	Players have 3 sec to pass, dribble, or shoot once they have gained possession of the ball.
	Players may not touch the playing surface while in possession of the ball. Only those players who use their feet to propel the wheelchair will be exempt.
	Goalkeepers may leave the goal area with possession of the ball but are then considered as a player on the court and have 3 sec to pass, dribble, or shoot.
	If the ball is in the goal area, other players may try to gain possession. They must avoid:
	a. touching any part of the goal area with their wheelchair or body.
	b. physically interfering with the goalkeeper.
	If an offensive player violates either (a) or (b), the result will be a side out for the other team.
	If a defensive player violates either (a) or (b), the result will be a penalty shot for the other team.
	A goal is scored when the entire ball passes through the plane of the goal line. A goalkeeper can stop a ball halfway through the plane of the goal and hold it stationary for 5 sec, resulting in a throw-in for his or her team.
	Position all players at center court, offensive players on the outside, defensive players on the inside.
	Shooter takes the shot from the free throw line with only the goalkeeper defending.
	No player may move until the ball is considered in play (moves one complete circumference).
	If an offensive player moves before the shot, the ball is awarded to the defense on a side out.
	If the defensive player moves before the shot, the penalty shot is retaken. If the penalty shot is made, no violations are considered.

Table 15.8   Continued.

Limitations/rules (cont.)	Blocking, a legal move, occurs when any player positions his or her wheelchair to impede another player's movement. The player must have established position first. Ramming is an illegal move defined as a collision from any angle in which a player fails to gain position first or make an attempt to control his or her own wheelchair. Players are expected to maintain control of their wheelchairs at all times.
	The following are awarded with throw-ins from the victimized team:

The following are awarded with throw-ins from the victimized team:
   Offensive player enters the goal area to gain an advantage.
   Player touches the floor while in possession of the ball.
   Offensive player considered ramming another player.
   When a player covers the ball with the wheelchair for more than 3 sec.
   When a goalkeeper gains possession of the ball in the play area and carries it back into the goal area.
   Defensive player rams an opponent in a scoring attempt.
   Holding or hooking an opponent's wheelchair or body.
   Defensive player entering the goal area during an attempt to score.
   When an offensive player is pushed into the goal area by a defensive player.

Adapted from Davis (2002), pp. 61–62.

Figure 15.17   Indoor wheelchair soccer court.

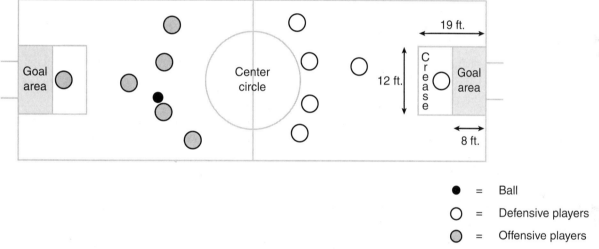

Indoor wheelchair soccer court. (from Davis, 2002, p. 59)

Equipment—Basketball or 10-in playground ball, cones.

Movements/Organization Pattern—Place a basketball with the second person in line and instruct the person to roll the ball forward, *slowly,* given the starting signal. Place a cone about 10 ft in front of each line to serve as a target for the person rolling the ball. The objective of the activity is to have the first person in line retrieve the ball once it has passed the cone.

Limitations/Rules—The retriever cannot move until the ball has passed the cone. Once the ball has been retrieved, that person returns it to his or her team, passing it to the second person in line. Once the second person has the ball, the activity is repeated. Continue until all students have been a roller and a retriever.

Inclusion Suggestion—Allow the student with a disability to determine the order of performance for his or her team.

Indoor Wheelchair Soccer

Indoor wheelchair soccer (IWS) is a sport that is sanctioned by the NDSA. This sport is traditionally played by individuals with cerebral palsy; however, new rules make individuals with spinal cord injuries, amputations, or conditions considered as *les autres* (i.e., muscular dystrophy, multiple sclerosis) eligible to play. A summary of IWS is presented in Table 15.8 using the game categories previously mentioned in this chapter.

Skills to Be Taught in Indoor Wheelchair Soccer

Skills in wheelchair soccer are performed on a court with goal areas at each end (see Figure 15.17). Many of the same skills taught in wheelchair basketball can be used in IWS. Players need to know how to pass, dribble, and shoot the soccer ball. Shooting a goal in IWS is not the same as in wheelchair basketball. To score a goal in IWS, the player might use a throwing motion similar to an overhand throw in baseball. Teachers are directed to follow the suggestions for passing and dribbling, described in

Figure 15.18   Throw-in used in indoor wheelchair soccer.

Figure 15.19   Shot block used in indoor wheelchair soccer.

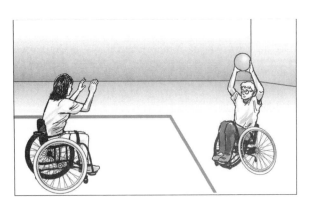

Pull ball forward and overhead. (from Davis, 2002, p. 67)

Goalkeeper Block with arms extended upward. (from Davis, 2002, p. 68)

Table 15.9   Indoor wheelchair soccer skills by Davis (2002).

Skill	Teaching Points
Chest pass	Place hands on each side of the ball; draw ball into chest by flexing elbows; extend elbows forcefully to pass the ball and turn thumbs inward and down upon release.
Continuous dribble	Bounce the ball ahead of the wheelchair closer to the front wheels or casters. Push the ball ahead, and move the hands quickly to the handrims and wheels to push the wheelchair. Continue dribbling the ball forward of the wheelchair while simultaneously pushing the wheelchair down the floor.
Shooting in IWS	Position in wheelchair with trunk stable and balanced, while bringing the ball back and up to a "baseball" throwing position. Raise the ball under control and move up and forward, maintain balance upon release and follow through. Shoot as if using an overhand baseball motion.
Throw-in	The throw-in must be performed with a two-handed overhead motion if possible. Good sitting position and balanced facing the court. Grip ball with two hands similar to the two-handed chest pass. Maintaining balance, raise ball up with both hands over and behind the head. Once ball is completely behind the head, pull both forward to release the ball. Extend elbow upon release of ball toward the court with full range of motion and follow through upon release.
Shot block	The goalie should maintain balanced position, sitting as tall as possible; then as shot is taken, extend arms upward and minimize the space between the arms to help protect the face and head. Goalies should try to block the shot as far in front of the goal as possible.

Table 15.10   Functional student profiles for indoor wheelchair soccer.

Functional Skill Level	Student Profile
Low	Severe disabilities in all four extremities. These students would use a power or motorized wheelchair.
Moderate	Severe to moderate disabilities in three of the four extremities. These students can use a manual wheelchair for short distances. Students with minimal paraplegic (two lower) or hemiplegic (one side) disabilities.
High	Students without neurological or physical disability in the upper extremity or trunk. However, these students will have some severe disability in at least one lower extremity.

From Davis (2002), p. 69.

Figure 15.20   Knock It Off IWS activity.

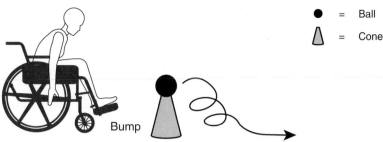

◆ **Knock It Off I** (from Davis, 2002, p. 77)

● = Ball
△ = Cone

Bump

Figure 15.21   Keep It Out IWS activity.

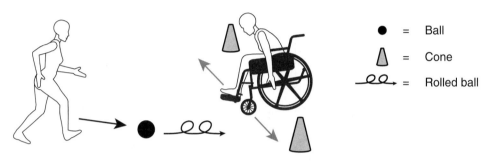

◆ **Keep It Out I** (from Davis, 2002, p. 79)

● = Ball
△ = Cone
🌀➝ = Rolled ball

wheelchair basketball. Only the skills of throw-in (Figure 15.18) and shot block (Figure 15.19) are discussed in this section (see Table 15.9). In Table 15.10 information about student profiles is provided (Davis, 2002). These student profiles are based on the actual classification system used in IWS. The following games/activities are modified from Davis (2002), and complete activity suggestions for IWS can be located in Davis.

Throw-in Game for Low Student Functional Level

Level of Cooperation–Competition—Individual (see Figure 15.20).

Activity Name—Knock It Off I

Player Formation—Place a large ball on top of a tall traffic cone or on top of table.

Equipment—Ten-in or larger playground ball; tall traffic cones, folding table, or bench.

Movements/Organization Pattern—Allow the student with a disability to approach the ball moving forward in his or her wheelchair at a rapid rate.

Limitations/Rules—The student may use any part of the wheelchair or body to knock the ball off the cone or table, making sure to avoid contact with the table. The objective is to put the ball into play.

Inclusion Suggestion—The teacher should have the student practice this activity with wheelchair control in mind and be able to demonstrate to classmates successful completion of this activity. The student should be able to judge the amount of wheelchair

speed needed to knock the ball off the cone and safely put the ball into play.

Shot Blocking Game for Low Student Functional Level

Level of Cooperation–Competition—Individual (see Figure 15.21).

Activity Name—Keep It Out I

Player Formation—Working individually with peer assistant as needed. Place a student with a disability between two traffic cones approximately 15 ft apart.

Equipment—Ten-in or larger playground ball, traffic cones.

Movements/Organization Pattern—Allow an AB student to roll a ball at the student using wheelchair, attempting to roll the ball between the cones.

Limitations/Rules—The objective of the game is to have the student with a disability position the wheelchair to block the ball from passing between the cones.

Inclusion Suggestion—Allow the student with a disability to determine the distance between cones to either increase or decrease the difficulty of the activity.

The Slalom Designed Especially for Motorized Chair Users

The slalom is an event within track and field for athletes with cerebral palsy (CP) and is sanctioned by local and regional chapters of the NDSA. This event is designed for individuals with severe physical limitations who must use a power or motorized wheelchair to move through a series of gates marked on a specific course (see Figure 15.22). The slalom offers an alternative track event for individuals who are unable to sprint race in their wheelchairs using manual propulsion techniques. NDSA also conducts slalom activities for persons with muscular dystrophy, spinal cord injury (quadriplegia), and spina bifida. Any person who cannot manually propel a wheelchair can participate in this event. A summary of the rules for the slalom is presented in Table 15.11.

Skills to Be Taught in the Slalom

There are three basic maneuvers to teach for the slalom: reverse gate (see Figure 15.23), 360° gate (see Figure 15.24), and figure eight gate (see Figure 15.25). The fourth maneuver within the slalom is called the circle gate (not pictured), which requires the same wheelchair movement as the 360° gate, only with a tighter turning radius. Each of these maneuvers motivates students toward a personal best (measured in time) in motorized chair control. See Table 15.11 for points added to overall slalom time when control is momentarily lost.

Figure 15.22 **The slalom course for users of motorized chairs (There should be 13 ft (3m) between each two obstacles).**

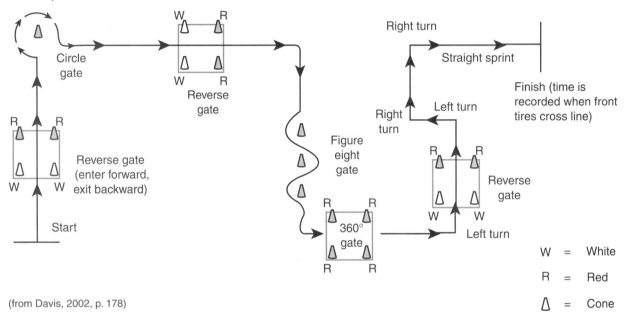

(from Davis, 2002, p. 178)

W	=	White
R	=	Red
△	=	Cone

Table 15.11 **Slalom rules at a glance.**

Players	Official competition is conducted for individuals who have CP or other conditions that require the use of a power wheelchair.
Equipment	Floor tape, PVC pipe cut 16 in tall by 4 in diameter ($n = 26$) or plastic bowling pins, strips of red cloth.
Movements/ organizational pattern	Stationary position at the starting line; front tires behind starting line. Must pass through the course as fast as possible paying attention to direction of travel and type of obstacle (reverse gate, 360° circle gate, figure eight). Avoid body and wheelchair contact with taped lines and markers while passing through the course. All reverse and 360° gates are 1 m square, and the figure eight gate has 3 markers set 1 m apart.
Limitations/rules	The slalom must be conducted on a hard level surface. There are six obstacles within the slalom that the student must complete as fast as possible. Each obstacle presents a challenge for the student to control their wheelchair without accumulating penalty points or seconds. Each time a student makes a mistake at an obstacle it will cost penalty seconds, which are added to the student's total time.
Limitations/rules	1. Skipping an obstacle = if not reentered in the correct order, the student is disqualified. 2. Knocking over a marker = 5 sec added to time. 3. Touching a line with a tire = 3 sec added to time. 4. Touching a marker with the wheelchair or body part = 3 sec added to time.

From Davis (2002), p. 180.

The following games/activities are suggestions to teach the skills of the reverse turn, 360° turn, and figure eight turn used in the slalom (Davis, 2002). These skills can be taught in a general physical education class.

Reverse Turn Game for Low Student Functional Level

Level of Cooperation–Competition—Individual (see Figure 15.26).

Name—Tap and Go.

Player Formation—Working individually with peer assistant as needed.

Equipment—Plastic bowling pins.

Movements/Organization Pattern—Place two sets of three plastic bowling pins on a line facing one another approximately 15 ft apart. Allow 10 ft between each bowling pin per set. Position the student in the middle of two sets facing the first pin of set one. On command, have the student move his or her wheelchair forward, under control, and tap the first bowling pin (if it falls, that's ok). As the tap is made, have the student reverse direction of the wheelchair and spin 180 degrees to face the first pin of the second set. Again under control, have the student move forward with the wheelchair and tap the pin, reverse spin, and move on to the second pin of the first set.

Limitations/Rules—Tap and Go is continued until all pins have been tapped.

Inclusion Suggestion—Student demonstrates to the class the ability to accomplish activity.

Figure 15.24 360-degree turn within all colored markers. Avoid touching lines or markers.

(from Davis, 2002, p. 183)

Figure 15.25 The weave or figure eight gate.

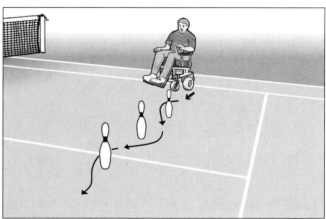

(from Davis, 2002, p. 185)

Figure 15.23 Entering the reverse gate with white markers. Enter forward, 180° turn, exit backward.

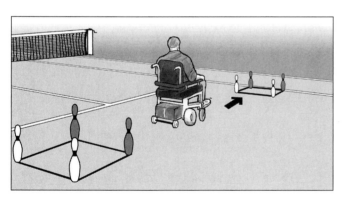

(from Davis, 2002, p. 181)

Table 15.12 The slalom skills.

Skill	Teaching Points
Reverse turn	Enter the reverse gate at the white markers, do 180° turn, and exit backwards by red markers. Then turn wheelchair again to travel forward to next gate.
360° turn	The 360° turn is marked by four red markers at each corner. The student must turn the wheelchair one complete turn and exit the opposite side of the point of entry facing in a forward direction.
Figure eight turn	The student approaches the figure eight gate in a forward direction. Each of the three markers must be woven through before the student can move to the next gate.

Adapted from Davis (2002), p. 181.

Figure 15.26　Tap and Go activity.

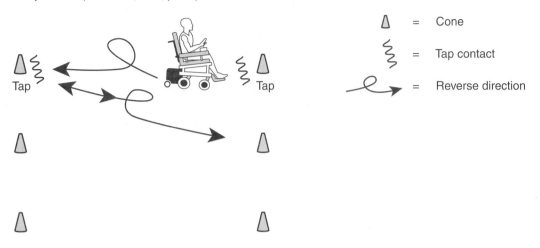

◆ **Tap and Go** (from Davis, 2002, p. 187)

Tap

Tap

△ = Cone

〰 = Tap contact

◯→ = Reverse direction

Figure 15.27　Giant Slalom II activity.

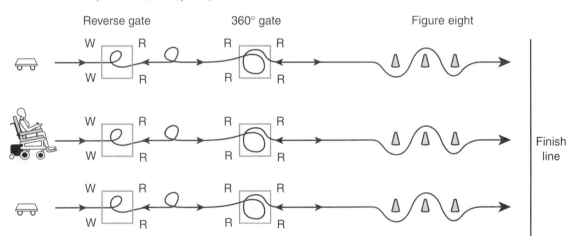

◆ **Giant Slalom II** (from Davis, 2002, p. 195)

Reverse gate　　360° gate　　Figure eight

Finish line

Figure Eight Turn Game for Low Student Functional Level

Level of Cooperation–Competition—Small group (see Figure 15.27).

Name—Giant Slalom II.

Player Formation—Divide the class into three teams in preparation for a relay race.

Equipment—Plastic bowling pins (or equipment to make markers), floor tape, stopwatch.

Movements/Organization Pattern—Using the diagram from the official competition, set up three reverse gates, three 360° gates, and three figure eight gates (one each per team) using red and white markers. Measure each gate 1 m square using floor tape to mark boundaries. Make sure to place each of the three markers 1 m apart for the figure eight gate. Position each gate 4 m apart and allow 10 m for a finishing distance. Line up each team behind their set of gates and *place students without disabilities on scooters.*

Limitations/Rules—On the command to "go" each student travels through the course completing passes through the reverse, 360°, and figure eight gates as fast as possible. You may want to enforce penalty seconds to the total time if a student touches a gate line.

Inclusion Suggestion—Allow the student with a disability to decide what order to complete the course (i.e., reverse gate first, then figure eight, and finish with the 360° gate).

Once AB students have learned the elements of disability sports, they benefit tremendously from seeing the role models that disability sports afford.

Table 15.13   Full medal sports at the 2000 Paralympic Games in Australia.
This list offers empirical research evidence of sports in which people with physical and sensory disabilities can excel.

Sport	Primary Participating Groups
Archery	Amputee and les autres, cerebral palsy, wheelchair[a]
Athletics (Track and Field)	All disabilities
Basketball	Amputee and les autres, cerebral palsy, wheelchair
Boccia[b]	Cerebral palsy
Cycling	Ambulatory and les autres, cerebral palsy, visually impaired
Equestrian	All disabilities
Fencing	Amputee and les autres, cerebral palsy, wheelchair
Goal ball[b]	Visually impaired
Judo	Visually impaired
Power lifting	Amputee and les autres, cerebral palsy, wheelchair
Quad rugby[b]	Wheelchair
Sailing	Amputee and les autres, cerebral palsy, visually impaired, wheelchair
Soccer (Ambulatory)	Cerebral palsy
Shooting	Amputee and les autres, cerebral palsy, wheelchair
Swimming	All disabilities
Table Tennis	Amputee and les autres, cerebral palsy, wheelchair
Tennis	Amputee and les autres, wheelchair
Volleyball	Amputee and les autres, cerebral palsy, wheelchair

[a]The term *wheelchair* in this table refers to conditions under governance of the International Stoke-Mandeville Wheelchair Sports Federation: quadriplegia, paraplegia, spina bifida, postpolio, multiple sclerosis
[b]Non-Olympic sport

Taking Pride in the Paralympic Movement

Individuals with and without disabilities need to understand and feel pride in the Paralympic movement. Helping to develop this pride is an important advocacy role of the adapted physical activity professional. Three facts should be emphasized:

1. The Paralympic Games are the highest-level multisport competition for athletes with disabilities.
2. The Paralympic Games have high eligibility standards that permit only the most elite athletes to participate.
3. The Paralympic Games are governed by criteria similar to those used in the Olympic Games, and Paralympians should be honored in the same ways as Olympians.

Summer Paralympic Sports

Following is a brief description of sports to enable intelligent spectatorism and to guide professionals in prioritizing which sports should be taught to individuals with disabilities. *The Paralympic movement has established proof that these sports, with very few minor adaptations, are suitable for one or more types of disabilities* (see Table 15.13). Although these sports are adapted, athletes with disabilities typically dislike the term *adapted sport.* They prefer that emphasis is placed on the sport (i.e., sport for athletes with disabilities or disability sport), not on the adaptation.

The basic sport skills underlying success are the same as those in AB sports; therefore, individuals with and without disabilities can be taught many of these sports in an integrated instructional setting. An integrated setting is also excellent for recreation, but individuals with disabilities who desire serious competition must generally engage in disability sports that employ classification systems.

Archery

Archery competition distances and rules are the same as for the Olympics except for adaptations in equipment for various disabilities. Competition begins with a qualification round (36 arrows each at 90, 70, 50, and 30 m for men; the same for women except 60 m substituted for 70 m), after which athletes shoot from 70 m only and are eliminated by pairs.

Athletics

In international terminology, **athletics** means track, field, and marathon (26.2 mi). Distances are generally the same as in AB sport. Prior to 1992, only athletes belonging to the same disability category competed against each other. Now a functional classification system is used to try to cluster athletes by abilities. Individuals in wheelchairs thus compete against each other regardless of disability category. Likewise, athletes who are ambulatory compete against each other, regardless of disability category. The exceptions to this trend are events for athletes with blindness and a few events designated specifically for athletes with CP.

Boccia

Boccia originally was for wheelchair athletes with severe CP, but now athletes with other disabilities compete in it. Similar to Italian lawn bowling, the purpose is to throw, kick, roll, push, or

Figure 15.28 Recreational boccia, in which students with and without disabilities keep each other company. The challenge is "Who can roll the balls closest to the small white target ball?"

strike baseball-size leather balls of color toward a white target ball (see Figure 15.28). Any body part or a head-pointing device can be used to give momentum to the ball.

Cycling

Many cycling events are held: tandem biking with sighted guides on a 50/60-m course for athletes with blindness; 5,000-m bicycle and 1,500-m tricycle races for individuals with mild and severe CP, respectively; and road races of various distances (e.g., 65–75 km, 55–65 km, 45–55 km) for athletes with various lower limb capabilities. Road races for tandem bikes are 60/70 km and 110/120 km.

Equestrian

Horseback riding competitions for numerous disabilities conditions are conducted in many countries, but thus far only Cerebral Palsy–International Sports and Recreation Association (CP-ISRA) and International Sports Organization for the Disabled (ISOD) have advanced equestrian competition at the Paralympic level. Events are offered in dressage, handy rider (obstacle course), and equitation in five CP and five non-CP classes. National competitions offer both assisted (use of a side-walker or leader) and unassisted events, *but international competition includes only unassisted events.* In the United States, horseback riding is governed by NDSA.

Fencing

Fencing is a wheelchair sport, organized by type of sword used: foil (flexible blade targeting opponent's torso), epee (stiff blade targeting any part of the body), and saber (heavier, stiff blade, targeting any body part above the waist). Electronic scoring is used.

Goal Ball

Goal ball is a team sport, three players on each team, played by athletes with blindness who wear eyeshades to equalize the amount of sight (i.e., make everyone totally blind). The goal is to throw a basketball-size bell ball across the opponents' court and into a goal cage to score points while the other team defends. The court is 9 × 18 m, and the goal cage is 9 m long and 1.3 m high.

Judo

Judo competition is limited to athletes with blindness; it replaced wrestling at the 1988 Paralympics and has become very popular. After the ritual bow, the two opponents walk toward each other and touch (this is the only rule difference between Paralympic and Olympic judo); then they put their arms at their sides to indicate readiness. After the umpire's signal to start, competitors use approximately 40 basic techniques, plus hold-downs, chokes, and arm bars. Pinning the opponent on his or her back for 30 sec or several other achievements end the match.

Lawn Bowling

Lawn bowling is conducted by International Stoke-Mandeville Wheelchair Sports Federation (ISMWSF) (in wheelchairs) and ISOD (with prostheses, for athletes with amputations). The purpose is to throw wooden balls at a small target ball called a **jack.** Points are awarded after each round. Rules of AB lawn bowls, a popular sport in the British Commonwealth countries, are followed.

Power Lifting

Power lifting includes the bench press, squat, and dead lift for individuals in 10 weight classes. All Paralympic sport organizations offer the bench press, but only the International Blind Sports Association (IBSA) provides competition in the squat and dead lift. Lifters are allowed three trials at each weight. Power lifting is different from weight lifting, which includes the clean and jerk and the snatch. Somewhat confusing is the fact that the bench-press event for athletes with spinal paralysis has traditionally been called wheelchair weight lifting. In the future this event will be called power lifting even though it uses a different style and bench than those used in other Paralympic bench presses.

Shooting

Shooting includes rifle and pistol competition with stationary targets. Four classifications help equalize opportunity:

Class 1—Standing competitors who require no assistance

Class 2—Sitting competitors at paraplegic functional level

Class 3—Sitting competitors at quadriplegic function level

Class 4—Used for rifle only; for standing competitors who cannot support the weight of a rifle and therefore require a shooting stand

Figure 15.29 Swimming competition requires many functional classifications to accommodate individual differences.

Swimming

Swimming competitions use the same distances as AB competition but are complicated organizationally by the need to classify swimmers with physical disabilities into 10 functional classifications in order to match as closely as possible competitors of the same functional abilities (see Figure 15.29). Three stroke categories are used for classification: (a) freestyle, backstroke, and butterfly, (b) breaststroke, and (c) individual medley. IBSA athletes (blind) are not integrated with other swimmers.

Table Tennis

Table tennis competition uses the same rules as AB table tennis but permits a few adaptations, like strapping the paddle to the hand for athletes who lack grip strength. A classification system is used that first divides athletes into wheelchair and ambulatory divisions and then separates athletes into more specific competition classes based on functional ability. All Paralympic disability sport organizations (DSOs) except IBSA promote this sport.

Soccer (Seven-a-Side)

Soccer competition is only for athletes with CP, stroke, and traumatic brain injury who are ambulatory (i.e., Classes 5, 6, 7, 8). In most of the world, soccer is called football. International rules require that at least one Class 5 or 6 athlete (those with lowest functional ability) be on the field at all times: These individuals usually serve as goalies. Class 7 players have hemi-

plegia, whereas Class 8 players have coordination problems but no noticeable limp. The field is 75 × 55 m with goal cages slightly smaller than regulation size. This is because motor dysfunction of cerebral origin makes defending a standard-size goal very difficult. With these exceptions, the rules are mostly the same as regulation soccer.

Volleyball

Volleyball competition is organized into standing and sitting divisions. Standing volleyball is sponsored by ISOD (mainly for athletes with amputations, no rules adaptations). However, a classification system is used to equalize team abilities, especially the number of upper and lower limb disabilities on the court. In the United States, volleyball is an official dwarf sport with only one rule change, a lower net. Sitting volleyball, also sponsored by ISOD, has six players on a team and uses a smaller court (16 × 12 m) and lower net (1.15 m). The major rule adaptations are these: (a) Position on the court is determined by location of buttocks; (b) a player hitting or blocking the ball at the net must maintain contact between floor and buttocks; and (c) a player may block an opponent's serve at the net.

Wheelchair Basketball

Although wheelchair basketball is an ISMWSF sport, since 1982 this competition has been open to anyone with a permanent lower limb disability. Team composition is structured by a sophisticated classification system that assigns each player a certain number of points, based on functional ability and then permits any combination of points on the floor that adds up to 14 points in international competition and 12 points in U.S. competition. Since 1992 international classification has used an eight-class system, in which players are assigned points as follows: 1, 1.5, 2, 2.5, 3, 3.5, 4, 4.5 points. The lower the points, the more severe the disability. In contrast, the United States continues to use a three-class system with players assigned only 1, 2, or 3 points. When women play on men's teams, their classifications are adjusted (e.g., a 3 becomes a 2).

Wheelchair basketball is identical to AB basketball with a few exceptions:

1. The number of seconds allowed in the lane is 5 rather than 3.
2. The player in possession of the ball can take only two wheel thrusts, after which she or he must dribble, shoot, or pass.
3. No double-dribble rule is enforced.
4. Raising the buttocks off of the chair, a physical advantage some players have, is treated as a technical foul.

Wheelchair Tennis

Although wheelchair tennis is an ISOD sport, this competition is open to anyone with a permanent lower limb disability. Instead of a classification system, division play is used to ensure fairness. Men play in five divisions and women in three. Divisions are designated as Open (for the best players), then A, B, C, and D (from high skill to low). Players start in the lowest division and move up by winning regional and then national tournaments. Each knows his or her rank or standing within a division.

Wheelchair tennis is identical to AB tennis with a few exceptions:

1. Two bounces instead of one are permitted.
2. A bounce-drop serve can be used if the overarm serve is not functionally possible. Regardless of type of serve, the back wheels of the chair must remain behind the service line until the ball is contacted.
3. Elastic, tape, or special orthotic devices can be used to bind the racket to the hand to adapt for weak grip strength.

Rugby

Rugby (also called quad rugby or wheelchair rugby) is a team sport in which points are scored by carrying the ball over the opponent's goal line (Yilla & Sherrill, 1994). Played on a regulation basketball court with a four-person team and a volleyball, the sport combines elements of football, basketball, and ice hockey. Ball handlers may take any number of wheel thrusts but must bounce or pass the ball every 10 sec. The ball is passed from player to player by whatever movement patterns individual abilities allow. Rugby was developed specifically for persons who do not have the arm and shoulder strength to participate in wheelchair basketball. A classification system is used that assigns points on the basis of hand, arm, and trunk functions. The combined classification score of the four players on the court may not exceed 8 points.

Yachting

Yachting is a race of sailboats, which is conducted by rules as close as possible to those of AB competition. At the 1996 Paralympics, a 2-square-mile course was used with 23-ft keel boats with open cockpits. Three sailors managed each yacht, and athletes with all disabilities were eligible. Points were accumulated over five days of racing to determine the winning crew.

Winter Paralympic Sports

Following is a brief description of sports performed on snow or ice in the quadrennial Winter Paralympics. Few adaptations are needed for athletes with mental disabilities or deafness. This section therefore emphasizes the adaptations associated with physical disabilities and blindness.

Alpine Skiing

Also called downhill skiing, the alpine skiing competition is similar to AB skiing except that specialized, adapted equipment and classification systems are used. **Outriggers** are special ski crutches attached by hinges to miniskis that enable balance and steering maneuverability in ambulatory skiing. The use of two outriggers and two skis is called **four-track skiing** (see Figure 15.30), an adaptation for individuals with severe balance problems as in CP or with disability of both legs. The use of one outrigger and two skis is called **three-track skiing,** an adaptation

typically used by individuals with single leg amputations or hemiplegia.

Twelve classifications are used to equalize competitive opportunity for individuals with physical disabilities in Alpine skiing:

Class 1—Four-track skiers

Class 2—Three-track skiers

Class 3—Two skis and poles; both legs disabled

Class 4—Two skis and poles; one leg disabled

Class 5/7—Two skis and no poles; both arms or hands disabled

Class 6/9—Two skis and one pole; one arm or hand disabled

Class 10/12—Use of sit ski, pulk, mono-ski, or bi-ski for individuals who are nonambulatory

Poles, **picks** (special short poles for pushing), or short outriggers are used with sitting ski apparatus. Good balance and trunk control are needed for success. The **sit ski,** essentially a sled with a bucket seat affixed, was invented first (1970s) and is still used for learning basic skills and engaging in sports like sledge or ice hockey. The **pulk** is similar to the sit ski except that the pulk has a solid bottom instead of runners. The **mono-ski,** introduced in the 1980s, is a seat (10 to 18 in high) connected to a single ski by means of a complex suspension system that enables speeds approaching 70 mph. **Bi-skis** are similar except that the seat is attached to two skis. For pictures and more information about sit skis, see Chapter 23.

Individuals with blindness also compete in Alpine skiing. Three classifications are used in recognition of different levels of visual acuity (B1–B3). The main adaptation is the use of a buddy or sighted guide to verbally assist individuals down the slope.

Nordic Skiing

Also called cross-country, Nordic skiing includes races, relays, and a biathlon. The **biathlon** is a combination event of shooting and racing. Classifications are similar to those for Alpine skiing. Race distances for athletes with physical disabilities are usually 5, 10, 15, 20, and 30 km. Race distances for athletes with blindness are usually 5, 10, and 25 km.

Sledge or Ice Hockey

For nonambulatory athletes, ice hockey uses **sledges** (like pulks, but with very thin metal runners adapted for hockey), a regulation-size ice rink, a puck, and picks for propulsion and maneuvering the puck. Six players on each team play offense and defense, as in stand-up hockey, except that two picks are substituted for the hockey stick. Gloves and picks can be adapted to accommodate weak hand grips.

Sledge Speed Racing

Sledge speed racing, which is most advanced in the Scandinavian countries, involves racing on sledges that are either self-propelled by picks or drawn by animals (see Figure 15.31).

Figure 15.30 Adaptations for skiing.

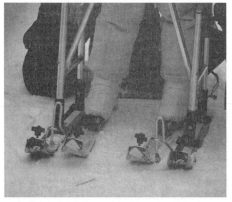

Four-track skiing

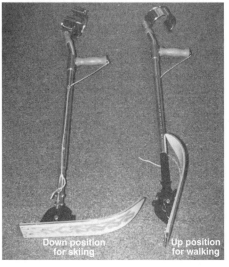

Down position for skiing   Up position for walking

Outriggers

Figure 15.31 Sledge speed racing at Beitostølen, an internationally known center near Oslo, Norway.

Supports for Sport Socialization

Tremendous progress is being made toward sport socialization (both disability and mainstream sport) of youth with disabilities in the 2000s. One value of the Paralympic movement, which trickles down to all levels of sport, is the *employment of a fulltime executive director for U.S. Paralympics* with an office at the U.S. Olympic Center in Colorado Springs (contact charlie.huebner@usoc.org). Huebner, like executive directors of the individual disability organizations (see Chapter 2 and the appendix), is a support for all who establish contact. Commercial sport equipment companies like FlagHouse (FlagHouse.com) are teaming up with adapted physical activity professionals to aggressively encourage disability sport involvement. FlagHouse, for instance, has announced its collaboration with Project ASPIRE specifically for this purpose (See *Palaestra,* Summer 2003).

Magazines like *Palaestra* and *Sports 'N Spokes* increasingly appear in school libraries, physicians' offices, and other public places, where everyone can benefit from reading them. Subscriptions make wonderful birthday and holiday gifts for persons with and without disabilities.

State high school athletic organizations (led by those in Minnesota, Georgia, and Illinois) are steadily enhancing school-based sport participation for all (Matter, Nash, & Frogley, 2002). Under the Illinois High School Association, wheelchair basketball, in 2002, became a fully sanctioned high school sport (Nash, 2002). At the Oregon State Track and Field Championships, wheelchair racers are competing at the same time and place (and sometimes in the same events) as their stand-up counterparts (Hansen & Fuller, 2003). National organizations have evolved specifically to promote sports for children and adolescents with disabilities (e.g., American Association of Adapted Sports Programs (AAASP) and BlazeSports Clubs of America [www.blazesports.com]).

 OPTIONAL ACTIVITIES

1. Perform several sport skills assuming the following positions and/or conditions:

   a. Shoot a free throw from a seated position

   b. Perform jumping jacks with beanbags in the crease of your elbows and between your knees without dropping them to the floor.

   c. Catch a thrown ball with any kind of assistive device using your nondominant hand

2. Visit a health club and assess the usability and accessibility of the facility by reviewing the following areas:

   a. Locker rooms

   b. Shower stalls

   c. Check-in facilities (i.e., desk, and door entries)

   d. Parking access

   e. Free weight and machine access

   f. Accommodations for those with visual impairments

3. Attend a disability sport event (i.e., wheelchair basketball game, swim meet, Special Olympics track and field) and survey spectators' perceptions of athleticism and competition related to the athletes they are observing.

4. Attend a disability sport event (i.e., wheelchair basketball game, swim meet, Special Olympics track and field) and survey the female athletes' perceptions of access to competition, training, and opportunity.

5. Discuss and/or debate the issue of whether individuals without disabilities should be allowed to participate in sports for those with disabilities. (See Brasile 1990, 1992). What other sources can you find?

6. Discuss and/or debate whether individuals with disabilities should compete on AB school-sponsored sport teams. (See Hansen & Fuller, 2003; Nash, 2002). What other sources can you find?

7. Pretend you own a health club facility and you want to purchase equipment that serves persons with and without disabilities. Put a budget together that would meet your needs and those of your patrons by identifying cost, name, and manufacturer of this equipment.

8. Read articles on youth sport in recent issues of *Palaestra* and *Sports 'N Spokes* and consider relevance to your local and state setting. Speak to a parents' group or professional meeting concerning sport opportunies for youth with disabilities and/or write an article for your state journal or a local newspaper.

9. Contact the National Federation of State High School Associations (or your state office) about barriers and opportunities in regard to interscholastic athletic activities and awards for high school students with disabilities.

10. Become familiar with *Disability Sport and Recreation Resources* by Paciarek and Jones (2001) and introduce others to this excellent resource.

CHAPTER

16

Adapted Dance, Dance Therapy, and Relaxation
Claudine Sherrill and Wynelle Delaney

Figure 16.1   Anne Riordan of the University of Utah dances with adolescents with disabilities.

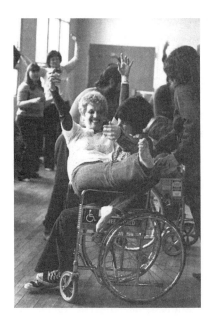

1. Discuss the similarities and differences between adapted dance, dance therapy, and pedagogy for teaching relaxation and stress control.

2. Identify two broad pedagogical approaches and discuss the types of dance associated with each. Assess your experience with each type and develop a personal learning plan for enhancing knowledge and skill.

3. Explain why creative dance is recommended as a first form of movement education for children (see Chapter 4 and index on movement education) and discuss the movement and rhythm elements associated with creative dance.

4. Identify and discuss activities especially recommended for (a) increasing body awareness, (b) improving relationships, and (c) expressing feelings. Relate your ideas to emotional disturbance and other disabilities in which these objectives are important.

5. Explain how dance therapy materials, principles, and tools can be used in adapted physical activity teaching and counseling. Give concrete examples.

6. Observe some children's dance classes taught by different persons; also observe dance lessons or activities for other age groups. Determine and critique dance resources in your community.

It is beautifully apparent that dance and the child are natural companions. If, as Merleau Ponty suggests, our bodies are our way of having a world, the child is busily at home in his own body forming and shaping his own world, its inner and outer hemispheres. He is making himself up as he goes along.

—Nancy W. Smith

Perhaps no part of the physical education curriculum is as important to students with disabilities as creative rhythmic movement boldly and imaginatively taught. It can be enjoyed by the nonambulatory in beds and wheelchairs, by other health impaired persons who need mild range-of-motion exercise, and by the thousands of youngsters who find greater fulfillment in individual and dual activities than in team sports. Whereas much of physical education focuses on cooperation, competition, and leadership-followership, creative dance offers opportunities for self-discovery and self-expression for persons of all ages.

Persons must understand and appreciate their bodies and their capacities for movement before they can cope with the world's external demands. The additional barriers to self-understanding and self-acceptance imposed by a disability intensify the need for carefully guided nonthreatening movement experiences designed to preserve ego strength, increase trust, and encourage positive human relationships. Gesture, pantomime, dance, and dance-drama can substitute for verbal communication when children lack or mistrust words to express their feelings. *Dance programming is particularly important for people with emotional disturbances, behavioral disorders, and learning disabilities.*

Distinction Between Adapted Dance and Dance Therapy

It is important to differentiate between dance as a therapeutic experience, dance therapy as a profession, and adapted dance. Prior to the formation of the American Dance Therapy Association, Inc. (ADTA), in 1966, little distinction between terms was made. Dance conducted with persons with disabilities was typically called dance therapy. Today, the term **dance therapy** is used for dance/movement conducted by persons registered as dance therapists with the ADTA. In this sense, dance therapy is like physical therapy and occupational therapy. Dance specialists

and others who are not registered therapists may use dance with populations who are disabled and/or for therapeutic purposes, but they may not ethically describe their work as dance therapy. So what do we call dance designed to meet the educational and artistic needs of persons with special needs?

Adapted Dance

Adapted dance is a term appropriate to denote rhythmic movement instruction and/or experiences that are modified to meet the needs of persons who have significant learning, behavioral, or psychomotor problems that interfere with successful participation in programs of regular dance in education and art. *Adapt* means to make suitable, to adjust, to accommodate, or to modify in accordance with needs. These needs may be developmental or environmental. Dance specialists may *adapt* curriculum content, instructional pedagogy, assessment and evaluation approaches, and physical environment; the essence of this process of adapting is personal creativity.

Adapted dance focuses on individuals who need assistance in mainstream dance instruction and/or specially designed educational and artistic experiences. The use of adapted dance is not limited to persons with disabilities, but encompasses such special populations as the aged, juvenile delinquents and criminals, substance abusers, pregnant women, and our nation's many obese and/or unfit citizens. It also provides specialized help for clumsy persons, for whom ordinary dance instruction, in the presence of the graceful and the beautiful, is often a nightmare.

Adapted dance is conceptualized especially for persons who are not comfortable and/or successful (for whatever reason) in the general dance setting. Like adapted physical education, adapted dance facilitates self-actualization, particularly as it relates to understanding and appreciation of the body and its capacity for movement. The resulting changes in psychomotor behavior eventually permit full or partial integration in dance as a joyous, fulfilling experience.

Adapted dance can be used to achieve any of the goals of adapted physical activity. A job of the specialist is to determine whether dance, sports, or aquatics is more personally meaningful to an individual at a specific time of need.

Adapted dance can be education, art, or recreation. It can also be therapeutic, but it is not therapy. The foremost pio-

Table 16.1   Websites for Additional Information.

American Dance Therapy Association	www.adta.org
Association for Dance Movement Therapy	www.dmuk.demon.co.uk/index.html
International Institute for Dance Therapy	www.dancetherapy.com
VSA Arts	www.vsarts.org/
National Dance Association	www.aahperd.org/nda/nda-main.html
International Dance Sport Federation	www.idsf.net
International Paralympic Committee Wheelchair Dance	www.paralympic.org/sports/sections/dancing.asp

Note. Many other websites are available via www.adta.org.

neer in adapted dance, particularly in exploring its potential as a performing art, is Anne Riordan (see Figure 16.1), in the Modern Dance Department at the University of Utah (Fitt & Riordan, 1980). In a film titled *A Very Special Dance,* marketed by the National Dance Association, Riordan demonstrates dance as both education and art with persons who have disabilities and are members of the performing group called SUNRISE.

Dance Therapy

The official ADTA (2002) definition of **dance therapy** is "the psychotherapeutic use of movement as a process that furthers the emotional, social, cognitive, and physical integration of the individual" (ADTA website, www.adta.org). Dance/movement is used as nonverbal psychotherapy requiring a therapeutic contract between therapist and client. Thus, dance therapy is a specific treatment modality used in mental illness and emotional and behavioral problems. Dance therapy is not prescribed for other disabilities (like mental retardation and orthopedic impairment) unless the individual has problems that require nonverbal psychotherapy. All dance therapy activities aim to strengthen the body-mind interface.

Similarities of Adapted Dance and Dance Therapy

Both the dance educator and the dance therapist rely heavily on the medium of creative dance to accomplish certain objectives. Dance education can be therapeutic, just as dance therapy can be educational. Certainly, the adapted physical educator who uses creative dance as a means of helping children with disabilities to understand and appreciate their bodies and their movement capabilities is engaged in a therapeutic endeavor (see Table 16.1 for websites that offer more information). But the work should not be considered dance therapy any more than physical therapy or occupational therapy. Since the incorporation of the ADTA in May of 1966, dance therapy has gained increasing recognition as an independent profession that publishes the *American Journal of Dance Therapy,* holds annual conferences, maintains a registry of members who meet rigid standards required for registration, and monitors master's degrees in dance therapy.

Adapted Dance in the Curriculum

Dance is an integral part of physical education. As such, it must be given the same amount of time and emphasis in the curriculum as other program areas. Table 16.2 groups types of dance according to teaching style. Each type teaches a set body of

knowledge and skills that enrich living. Students with disabilities need exposure to dance both as a participant and observer (Boswell, 1989; Jay, 1991; Roswal, Sherrill, & Roswal, 1988; Schmitz, 1989). Aerobic dance is increasingly used for adult fitness (Cluphf, O'Connor, & Vannin, 2001; Stanish, McCubbin, Draheim, & Van der Mars, 2001). Field trips to dance events broaden horizons on use of leisure time and make school-based instruction more meaningful.

The teaching style (guided discovery or explanation-demonstration-drill, Mosston & Ashworth, 1994) determines outcomes. Guided discovery, linked with creative and modern dance, is similar to movement education (Laban, 1960; Sherborne, 1987). **Movement education,** introduced in Chapters 4 and 7, is pedagogy directed specifically toward teaching understanding, appreciation, and acceptance of the body and its capacity for movement through guided discovery (movement exploration) of body parts, movement elements (space, time, force, flow), and creative thinking and moving (fluency, flexibility, originality, elaboration). In dance, movement elements are also used to create compositions depicting ideas, feelings, or themes. Dance often focuses on motor skills and fitness to create and perform. Other goals (self-concept, social competence, etc.) parallel those of adapted physical activity. *Creative dance is recommended as the first form of movement education for children.* It is appropriate for children ages 3 and up who understand language and respond to music, or for Deaf children, underlying beats and vibrations. In middle school and high school, terminology changes from *creative dance to modern dance.*

With exploration-demonstration-drill pedagogy, dance can be a medium for perceptual-motor training, learning about cultural heritage, achieving artistic excellence, developing skills for leisure-time activities and forming friendships. It is particularly valuable in teaching relaxation, ameliorating rhythm and timing problems, and enhancing body image. Folk and square dance, properly conducted, can help slow learners with social studies. Singing games and rhythmic chants also help with academic learning (Bitcon, 1976; Sherrill, 1979).

Note that the references in this section are old, but they are the classics. Talk to dance specialists at your university or in your community to determine if they know of newer published resources. Check lists of theses and dissertations for unpublished sources of information. Reflect on why so little information on adapted dance and dance therapy is available.

Table 16.2   Two pedagogical approaches and types of dance.

Guided Discovery	Explanation-Demonstration-Drill
Creative or modern dance with emphasis on	*Many types of dance, including*
• Space (shape, level, size, path, focus)	Singing games
	Marching/clapping
• Time or rhythm (beat, accent pattern, phrasing)	Tap and clog
	Folk and square
• Force, effort, or weight	Social and ballroom
Heavy → Light	Aerobic
Strong → Weak	Ballet
• Flow	Wheelchair dance
Free → Bound	
Fluent → Inhibited	

Note. Wheelchair dance is a Paralympic event in which countries may compete.

Movement Elements

Creative and modern dance, as well as movement education, focus upon the **movement elements** of space, time, force, and flow. Sally Fitt (Fitt & Riordan, 1980) proposed an excellent model for relating movement elements to dance instruction for students with disabilities. The *element of space* can be broken down into several factors:

1. **Direction and shape.** Right, left, forward, backward, sideward, up, down, in, out, over, under.

2. **Level of movement or of body position.** High, low, medium; lie, sit, squat, kneel, stand.

3. **Dimension or size.** Large, small, wide, narrow, tall, short.

4. **Path of movement.** Direct (straight) or indirect (curved, zigzag, twisted, crooked).

5. **Focus of eyes.** Constant, wandering, near, far, up, down, inward, outward.

The elements of time, force, and flow are explained in Table 16.2. *Excellent videotapes on how to teach the movement elements to children with disabilities are available from Dr. Boni Boswell, Physical Education Department, East Carolina University, Greenville, NC 27834.*

Rhythm Elements

Rhythmic structure in dance has four aspects:

1. **Pulse beat.** The underlying beat of all rhythmic structure. Can be taught as the sounds of walk or run; the ticking of a clock, watch, or metronome; the tapping of a finger; the clapping of hands; or the stamping of feet. The beats can occur in fast, medium, or slow tempos and in constant or changing rates of speed.

2. **Accent.** An emphasis—that is, an extra loud sound or extra hard movement. Syllables of words are accented, and beats of measures are accented.

3. **Rhythmic pattern.** A short series of sounds or movements superimposed on the underlying beat and described as even or uneven. Illustrative of *even* rhythmic patterns are the walk, run, hop, jump, leap, step-hop, schottische, and waltz. Illustrative of *uneven* rhythmic patterns are the gallop, slide, skip, two-step, polka, and bleking. Remember that the polka is a hop, step-close-step and the bleking is a heel, heel (slow), followed by heel-heel-heel-heel (fast). In rhythmic patterns, the duration of time between beats varies. The simplest patterns for children are as follows:

   a. *Uneven* long-short patterns, as in the gallop, skip, and slide in 6/8 tempo:

   b. *Even* twice-as-fast or twice-as-slow walking patterns in 4/4 tempo:

   Walk, ♩ ♩ ♩ ♩ 4 steps to a measure.

   Run, ♫ ♫ ♫ ♩ 8 steps to a measure.

   Slow walk, ⅆ ⅆ 2 steps to a measure.

4. **Musical phrasing.** The natural grouping of measures to give a temporary feeling of completion. A phrase must be at least two measures long and is the expression of a complete thought or idea in music. Phrasing may help to determine the *form* of a modern dance composition, and children should be guided in the recognition of identical phrases within a piece of music. One movement sequence is created for each musical phrase; identical phrases may suggest identical movement sequences.

Rhythm Skills

Many persons with disabilities have difficulty with rhythm. Initial lessons should focus on creative movement with the teacher beating a drum to the tempo established by the student. Make an effort to determine the child's natural rhythm—whether fast, slow, or medium tempo; whether 4/4 or 3/4 phrases; whether there is a rhythmic pattern or underlying beat; whether the child responds to accents; and whether transitions from one tempo to another are made. During this period of observation, encourage the child to make up his or her own accompaniment: with a song, a nursery rhyme, a verse, hand clapping, foot stamping, or a tambourine, drum, or jingle bells. Only after the child has given evidence of moving in time to his or her own accompaniment should you introduce the next stage—conforming to an externally imposed rhythm.

Teaching Dance and Rhythm

Some children require no special help in movement to music. They do not need adapted dance. Others, who have grown up in homes without music or who have central nervous system (CNS) deficits *affecting temporal perception,* must be provided a carefully designed progression of experiences broken down into parts so small that success is ensured. Wearing taps on shoes is a good reinforcer. Likewise, rhythmic instruments, used as part of a dance, promote goal mastery. Music therapists often are available to help. A succession of units might include the following:

1. Creative movement without accompaniment in which an idea, feeling, or mood is expressed.
2. Creative movement, with the child encouraged to add sound effects.
3. Creative movement interspersed with discovery activities in which the child can beat a drum, clash cymbals, or use other rhythmic instruments as part of a dance-making process. No instructions are given on how to use the instruments. They are simply made available, along with the freedom to incorporate sounds as the child wishes.
4. Creative movement accompanied by the teacher or another student using a variety of interesting sounds that fit the child's dance making.
5. Discussions concerning what kind of accompaniment best supports the theme or idea of different movement sequences. Through problem solving, the child tells the teacher what kind of accompaniment he or she wants, the idea is tried, and the child evaluates whether or not it worked.
6. Introduction of the concept that a dance can be repeated over and over again. A dance has some kind of *form*—at least a beginning and an end—and both movements and accompaniment must be remembered so that they can be reproduced.

At this point, students learn the difference between dancing—that is, moving for pleasure—and making a dance. They are helped to see their creation as an art product that may endure like a painting or a musical composition. They take pride in organizing their movement sequences into an integrated whole and comparing their dance-making process and products with those of dance artists on the various films that can be rented. Since children with disabilities typically become adults with an abundance of leisure, spectator appreciation of modern dance and ballet should be developed concurrently with their first attempts at dance making. Perhaps a performing group from a local high school or college can be invited to demonstrate dance compositions. Expecting children to retain excitement about dance making (choreography) is futile unless they are exposed to the art products of others and led to believe that dance is a significant part of the cultural-entertainment world.

Only when dance experiences in which movement is primary and accompaniment is secondary prove successful should you introduce the study of rhythmic skills to children known to be weak in temporal perception. These students typically will be off the beat as often as on it. They are likely to accent the wrong beat of a measure. And they may find the recognition of musical phrases hopelessly frustrating. Dance researchers have not yet designed studies to investigate the learning problems of these students. Some dance educators seem to believe that any child can keep in time with the music if he or she tries hard enough. Such is not the case! Just as reading specialists seek alternative approaches to teaching their subject, dance educators must devise ways in which the child who is rhythmically disabled or mentally retarded can find success. Calling attention to inaccurate response and creating tensions through continuous drill do not solve the problem. Nothing is sadder than a child concentrating so hard on tempo that the joy of movement is lost. The child who does not keep time to the music truly may be hearing a different drumbeat.

Obtain permission to observe dance classes at your university, in the public schools, or at dance studios. Focus on the students who appear to be having trouble and try to determine why. What adaptations might help these persons? Naturally you will find more persons having trouble in required classes than in elective classes.

Wheelchair Dance and Wheelchair Dance Sport

Wheelchair dance takes many forms: modern, ballet, ballroom, folk, square, and fad. (See *Palaestra*, 2003, an article on wheelchair dance in every issue). It may be recreational or high level performance designed to entertain others. A growing number of wheelchair dance professional companies travel from place to place giving outstanding dance performances. When persons lack the ability to push their own chairs, the dance may be primarily the exhilaration felt when being pushed in time to music by ambulatory partners who choreograph original movements or who follow the steps and patterns of well known folk or square dances. When persons can manage motorized or manual chairs, they can be taught almost any form of dance. For those who love dancing and seek to excel in this form of sport, the Paralympics offers competition in ballroom sport called **wheelchair dance sport**, which parallels amateur dance sport, and which may soon be recognized as a medal sport in the Olympic Games.

In wheelchair dance sport, one of each dance couple must have at least a minimal disability that makes walking impossible. The partner may be able-bodied or in a wheelchair. Similar to traditional ballroom dancing, each couple must include a male and a female. Competition is held in such ballroom forms as the waltz, tango, slow foxtrot, quickstep, samba, rumba, pasa doble, and cha-cha-cha. As in able-bodied dance competition, the choreography is original and the winners are selected by a panel of judges.

Activities for All

The pages that follow, written by a registered dance therapist, offer specific ideas that the adapted physical educator can use with children who walk independently or who rely on wheelchairs and other assistive devices. In those parts of the country where dance therapists are available, they may be employed to work cooperatively with the adapted physical educator or to provide consultant services.

Through the therapeutic use of rhythmic and expressive movements, children gain better perspective about themselves, their ideas, and their feelings. They come to know their bodies better. They gain skill and control as they move through space. They find ways to use body action constructively, insight is gained into the meanings implied in their body action, and a more accepting body image develops.

Therapeutic dance encourages and fosters children's faith in their own ideas and in their own ways of expressing these ideas. A sense of personal worth begins to emerge. Children begin to like themselves better as they realize that their ideas do count, are worth listening to and watching, and can be shared. Positive group relationships develop through sharing and experimenting with ideas. Children gain appreciative understanding of other people's ideas and their ways of expressing them.

It is usually characteristic of dance therapy techniques that emotional tensions are worked with indirectly by centering attention on how the muscles can be used—such as hard or fast, or slow or easy ways—rather than by speaking directly to the children's feeling-states. *When children express their tensions in forceful moving-out behavior,* activities are centered around aggressive-moving circle dances or controlled, slow-motion, aggressive pantomime. At other times, fast running, challenging ways of jumping-falling-rolling-pushing-spinning, or tug-of-war can reduce tensions. *When tensions seem high, and forceful moving-out action seems contraindicated* because the children's behaviors are expressed in depressed, turned-in movements, the action moves into gently paced rocking, swaying, swinging, controlled slow rolling, or tension-relaxation muscle isolation movements. *On other occasions, when the children's tension levels are not high,* activities focus on feelings directly at a conscious level. Only then do the children experiment with the different ways that feelings can be expressed through movement.

Objectives and Related Activities

Persons with mental health problems typically need help with three objectives: (a) increasing body awareness, (b) improving relationships and making friends, and (c) expressing feelings.

Activities used in helping people become aware of their bodies and how their muscles work include the following:

1. **Stretches, contractions, relaxations.** Individually, with partners, and in moving circle-dance action.
2. **Opposites movements.** Experimenting with such movements as tall-short, wide-narrow, fast-slow, stiff-floppy, open-closed, heavy-light, high-low.
3. **Feeling the floor different ways with bodies.** By rolling across the floor stretched out full length at varying speeds and levels of muscle tension; rolling around in tight curled-up balls; doing front and back somersaults; crumpling body movements to effect collapsing to the floor; free-falls sideward-forward-backward.
4. **Exploring movement through space.** Making different shapes and patterns; creating geometric patterns, writing imaginary letters and numbers with their bodies stationary and/or traveling.
5. **Using different traveling styles across the floor.** Running, jumping, walking, and creeping; variations within each style; working individually, with partners, and with groups of different sizes.
6. **Muscle isolation.** Using specific parts of the body in movement patterns while the rest of the body remains immobile, or following the action of the specific set of muscles leading a movement pattern; immobilization of body parts by playing *freeze* and *statue* games that stop

movement in midaction; continuing on in movement retaining the *frozen* or *statue* position; having partners arrange each other's bodies into shapes or statues.

7. **Reflection movement patterns of others** (see Figure 16.2). Moving in synchrony with a partner's movements as though looking in a mirror; moving on phrase-pattern behind a partner as though echoing his or her movements; moving in opposite patterns to partner's; reflecting similar or complementary movement patterns, yet different.

Expressing Ideas Through Movement

Encourage individuals' ideas to emerge in a variety of ways. At times, emphasis is on verbalization of abstract ideas, and at other times, the focus is on body movement expression. Many times, verbal and physical expression are combined. The following activities are some of the experiments and experiences that children seem to enjoy:

1. **Single-word or object stimulus.**
   a. "How many different ideas does the word *beach* remind you of?" "What kinds of ideas come to you when you hear the word *beach?*"
   b. "How many different ways can you pretend to use a popsicle stick?"
2. **Imaginary props.** "Without telling us what it is, think of one particular thing or object you could use in three different ways. Show us how you would use it. After you have finished using it three different ways, call on us and we will try to guess what object you were using." Sometimes, after the person has completed his or her turn, and the object has been guessed, the others contribute ideas orally on how the object could also be used. Stress being creatively supportive of each other's ideas.
3. **Word cues.** Words written on slips of paper are drawn in turn; the person translates the word into pantomime or dance movement. As the others think they recognize the word cue, they join in with the movement in their own ways and within their own framework of understanding. When the action is stopped, verbal comparison is made of the meanings given to the movement interpretations. Observations and comments are shared about the different ways used to express the same word-meaning in movement. Movement can then resume with everyone sharing each other's movement styles. The word cues are usually presented in categories:
   a. *Doing*—chopping, hiding, twisting, carrying, hurrying, touching, dropping, sniffing, bouncing, flying, planting, pushing
   b. *People*—old person, mail carrier, maid, nurse, airplane pilot, cook, police officer, doctor, hunted criminal, firefighter, mother, baby
   c. *Muscle isolation dances*—shoulder, head, knee, hip, hand, elbow, foot, leg, back, finger dances
   d. *Feelings*—ashamed, surprised, sad, stuck-up, angry, worried, greedy, jealous, happy, excited, in love, afraid, disgusted

Figure 16.2   Reflecting the movement patterns of others.

e. *Animals*—bee, horse, alligator, lion, snake, spider, elephant, crab, butterfly, worm, monkey, gorilla, mouse

f. *Mime dramas*—underwater adventure, a scary time, at the beach, at a bus stop, going on a picnic, climbing a mountain, a visit to the zoo, on a hike outdoors, an afternoon in the park, a baseball game

g. *A happening story*—a siren blowing, red light flashing, thick fog, whistle blowing, fire burning, animal sounds, gun firing, child crying, dream happening, rushing water

4. **Different ways over and under a rope.** As a rope is gradually raised or lowered, everyone moves over or under it without touching it in as many ways as he or she can.

5. **Idea box.** Everyone puts various objects they find or like—for example, leaves, crayon bits, combs, brushes, tiny statues, clothespins, buttons, pictures, paper clips, rubber discs—into the group's idea box. Periodically, an object is taken from the box to play around with. The different ideas individuals think up about the object can be translated into creative movement, storytelling, or dramatics.

6. **Stories.** Stories are read to the children so that they can make up their own endings and/or think about the possible alternative endings. The stories and the possible endings can be translated into dramatic action, either in part or total.

Expressing Feeling Through Movement

When feelings are focused on directly and at a conscious level, children can experiment with different ways feelings can be expressed through movement. The following activities illustrate some of the ways children can purposefully work with feelings or feeling-tones:

1. **Feeling-tones in music.** As music is played, the children respond in their own movement styles to the *feeling-quality* they *hear* in the music. When the action is finished, the children compare their responses, noting differences in responses to the same music. They also *try on* each other's feeling responses or movement styles as the music is played again.

2. **Descriptive mime or dance movements** to a stimulus word indicating a specific feeling—for example, see item 5, "Idea box," in the preceding list.

3. **Descriptive mime, dance, or story** reflecting the feeling-tone of a spontaneous sound made by the child.

4. **Stories *danced* to the feeling-quality of the music.** Individuals, pairs, or several children take turns as they dance a story they have planned around the feeling-quality in the music. Sometimes, the same music is chosen for all the children; other times, the different groups of children choose different music. When the danced story is finished, the children who watched attempt to relate their observations and interpretations of the story to the dancers. After everyone has had a chance to interpret, the performers describe their own story. When it seems appropriate, children share some of the movement qualities presented in the stories.

5. **Feeling-tones in colors.** Lightweight fabrics of different colors are placed around the floor in order of child's color preference; talk about what a specific color "makes you think about"; list ideas on paper; try on some of the ideas in movement. List ideas about what kinds of feelings might be reflected in a specific color. Experiment and

show through movement how one can move to express the feelings listed, in pairs, groups, or individually. Continue on from one color fabric to another. The single feeling-action can be enlarged into pantomime or dramatizations of a story idea woven around the feeling.

6. **Baseball game (or alternate sport) in different movement styles.** All players work together to reflect a specific feeling in their movement styles as they "play" the game.

   a. *Sad*—The batter waits sadly for the ball to be thrown; the pitcher sadly throws the ball; the batter sadly hits at the ball. If the batter misses, everyone is sad and says so or makes sounds accordingly. The ball is sadly put back into play. If the ball is hit, the batter sadly runs to the base as the pitcher or players sadly go after the ball and try to throw the runner out. Such mood continues throughout the play around the bases until the runner sadly makes a run or is thrown out.

   b. *Happy*—Follows the same format as above. The batter is happy when he or she misses the ball or strikes out. The pitcher is happy when the batter makes a base run or a home run.

   c. *Laughing-angry*—This type of contradictory expressive behavior becomes challenging and hilarious. Different combinations of contradictory feelings/sounds demand special awareness of how one uses expressive action. This also comes close to the reality of the mixed communication many people use in less exaggerated fashion in everyday life.

Adapting Materials and Props

Soft materials are used in all of the areas discussed in the previous section for stimulating a variety of safe activities that are imaginative and self-structuring. Nylon fabrics of different hues in 2.5-yd lengths aid in reducing tension and hyperactivity and in relaxing tight muscles (see Figure 16.3). In response to the floating, smooth quality of the colorful nylon, children move rhythmically—stretching, turning, reaching, and covering themselves in various ways. Their actions seem to reflect a sensuous enjoyment and an aesthetic awareness as the fabrics float and move across their bodies.

Paradoxically, the soft fabrics can become a factor in spatial structuring as well (see Figure 16.4). At times, when children feel extremely tense and seem to have a need for containment, being wrapped completely immobile in the full width of the fabric by either turning when standing or rolling when lying down has a relaxing and quieting effect. Avoid wrapping too tightly and possibly interfering with breathing. Children will sometimes ask for this kind of containment by suggesting familiar activities that have included it in other movement contexts.

Nylon fabrics also provide an intermediary focus for children who find it difficult to relate directly to other persons. Spin-arounds, with partners holding opposite ends of the fabric, aid in keeping distance yet staying together. Wrap-up spinouts allow a moment's closeness with access to quick and immediate freedom from nearness.

Figure 16.3 Soft nylon has a relaxing and quieting effect.

Figure 16.4 Experiencing the spatial structure of soft, floating fabric.

Imaginative play and imagery are stimulated by using the fabric as clothing, costumes, bedding, housing, or light-shields to put a color glow in a darkened room. *Aggressiveness* is accommodated by wrapping a soft yarn ball inside one end of the fabric and throwing it as if it were a comet streaming through space. *Dodge fabric* has aggressive moments of fun and beauty combined when one or several fabrics are loosely wadded into a ball and thrown at a moving human target. The floating open of the fabric(s) while traveling in space sometimes creates unusual beauty. Children also like to lie down and be covered completely with one fabric at a time in layering fashion. As the layers of fabric increase, children typically comment on the constant change of color and the increasing dimness.

Soft, stretchy, tubular-knit fabrics approximately 3 yd long have soothing, protecting properties. The tubular fabrics make excellent *hammocks* on which to lie and be swung (see Figures 16.5 and 16.6). When persons alternate in lifting ends of the fabric, causing the body to roll from side to side, the child feels a special sensation of being moved in space. An interesting sensation of directional change is experienced when running

Figure 16.5 Experiencing the sensation of directional change in a different way.

Figure 16.7 Yarn balls permit safe release of aggressive tensions.

Figure 16.6 Learning trust as the hammock descends.

and bouncing forward into a tautly stretched fabric that *gives* and then bounces the person off backward.

Stretch-tube fabrics also lend themselves well to nondirected dramatic play and fantasy-action. They become roads, rivers, roofs, ghosts, hooded persons, Roman togas, stuffed sausages, pickles, grass, tunnels. Playing inside stretch-tube fabrics is a way for children to shield themselves from direct observation and physical touch contact with other persons, while at the same time being able to look out through the fabric and see other persons. When working inside, the fabrics can become an open-ended tunnel to explore, or a closed and safe haven for being swung, rolled, dragged gently around the floor, or for pretending all alone in fantasy-action. Inside the fabrics can also become a place to experiment with making different shapes and forms by bending and extending body parts against the softly resilient material.

When lying outside on the fabric and being swung gently, spontaneous pantomimes of *dreams* are easily evoked. These dreams come from children's unconscious urges and needs, and the expressive body action accompanying the dream fantasies allows for safe catharsis and emotional release of ten-

sions reflected in the dream content. The fabrics offer opportunity for rocking and swaying when children need comforting and relaxing, without those needs being openly or directly addressed. Games experienced earlier, when the children were simply exploring the use of the fabrics, can be repeated when the need for comforting arises.

Yarn balls about 6 inches in diameter permit many varieties of throwing activities for imaginative play as well as for safe release of aggressive tensions (Figure 16.7). The teacher's imaginative thinking about different ways to throw, jump with, and bat the ball stimulates alternative ways of thinking and also encourages children to risk expressing their own ideas. Warm-up stretches are executed by using different body positions to transfer the ball to the next recipient. One-to-one synchronization of full body action occurs when partners try to support a ball between them with various parts of their bodies while traveling across the room. Yarn balls can be used aggressively for bowling or dodgeball. They also can be vigorously hand-batted back and forth across the floor. More structured and functionally demanding activities are done with rhythmically synchronized toss, catch, and rolling games. *Isolation of body parts* can be experienced by bouncing the ball off different parts of the body or by contacting the ball with a specific body part before releasing and passing it on to another person. In dramatic play and fantasy-action, the balls become various kinds of foods, jewels, rocks, rockets, bombs, and the equipment for pretend games of baseball, kickball, touch football, and bowling.

Dance Therapy Principles

With modification, dance therapy techniques are applicable to persons of most ages and with most disabilities because dance therapy focuses on qualities of nonverbal communication in everyday life. Marian Chace (n.d.), one of the pioneers in the evolution of dance therapy as a profession, was influential in obtaining acceptance of principles that she believed were basic to dance therapy and common to all forms of therapy. These principles relate specifically to patients in a clinical setting but are applicable to students with mental health needs. Chace believed that the dance therapist should keep things simple by leading out from what is happening inside the patient, rather than imposing the action from the outside. The therapist should allow time for things to happen within the ongoing action rather than trying to *do* a lot.

Chace recommended that the dance therapist work toward enriching experiences in a nonjudgmental, neutral way, without moralizing. *This is best accomplished by working with a person rather than on him or her.* The dance therapist must be secure and able to listen to what is going on at the verbal level and yet see subtle, nonverbal cues. The therapist should emanate friendliness, yet remain neutral and resist being caught up in his or her need to be liked by the patient. Patients need to relate to persons who are genuine and truthfully warm. They need relationship space that allows them to give back warmth without feeling threatened by the therapist's needs.

Therapeutic Tools

The *therapeutic tools* used by the dance therapist could be thought of as *rhythm, touch, verbalization, space, and people.* Activities are simply the media for the use of therapeutic tools.

The *movement of the patient,* rather than that of the therapist, is used as a means of establishing the therapeutic relationship. By tuning in and sharing a patient's movements, the therapist can very clearly and quickly relate to the patient. They can *speak* to each other in movement. The therapist then works toward transcribing patients' movements into reality-oriented and functional expressions since patients are unable to do this for themselves. The therapist also tries to influence change in patients' distorted body images through muscular action.

Basically, **rhythm** *is what enables the patient to use body action in safe ways that hurt no one.* Open use of aggressive movements has less therapeutic value than rhythmic action that focuses on body awareness. For optimal results, expressive movement must be under the patient's conscious rather than unconscious control. Rhythmic action also affords an area for relating that is outside both the patient and the dance therapist. It offers the satisfaction of sharing movement and minimizes destructiveness of action. The patient does not feel a need for the movement to be realized in its destructive form. This leaves him or her free to go on to other things, with pathological urges released rhythmically, constructively, and safely, for the moment.

All therapeutic body movement is geared toward getting in **touch** with as much of the skin's surface as possible. Tactile stimulation and muscular contraction allow the patient to regain contact with his or her body surface and to come to understand its boundaries. Direct touch by the therapist reinforces the patient's growing ability to distinguish between himself or herself and others.

Verbalization between the therapist and patient is geared to the meaning of muscular action, rather than the feeling-tone behind the action. The patient comes to realize that his or her movement qualities are reality based and that he or she is capable of purposive movement. Verbalization is not for telling the patient what to do, but for helping him or her to know where he or she is going and why.

Space is an extension and reflection of body image, so the use of space is important. A *patient who is manic and hyperactive* perceives his or her own space zone as wide and scattered and as having tremendous force and power. The dance therapist then uses movements far away from the patient, coming in only tentatively as the patient will allow. The patient already feels that they are *together,* even though they are actually far apart. If *a patient is frozen or constricted in movement,* the space zone is small and constricted. The dance therapist then moves in quite closely, but with care and awareness, because a constricted space is generally a supercharged zone. The dance therapist also uses space to encourage a *coming forward.* Such dance movements can provide safe areas for hostile body action that might have been used out of control. *Going forward* movements can provide safe areas for a withdrawn person to learn that he or she can come out and not be hurt nor hurt anybody else.

The dance therapist's ultimate goal is for patients to work in a group. Group work reduces one-to-one identifications and increases opportunities for patients to assume responsibility for their own growth and not stay dependent on the therapist.

Teaching Relaxation

Techniques of teaching relaxation or stress reduction vary with the age group, the nature of the disability, and the number of minutes available. Coaches and sport psychologists, as well as teachers, use the following activities and others to teach anxiety and stress control (Gorely, Jobling, Lewis, & Bruce, 2002; Screws & Surburg, 1997; Surburg, Porretta, & Sutlive, 1995). Breathing exercises are important in relaxation training (see Chapter 19 under *Asthma*).

Controlling anxiety and stress and relaxing or becoming quiet at will are important goals that everyone needs help in achieving. As you read this section, jot down the goals and objectives that are being addressed and determine measurable ways of determining progress.

Imagery to Facilitate Quiet Time

The *imagery* or ideational approach is appropriate for all ages, but this section focuses on the primary grades (see Figure 16.8). Poems and short stories are excellent to help children become rag dolls flopping, ice cream melting, merry-go-rounds stopping, balloons slowly deflating, icicles melting, faucets dripping, salt pouring from a shaker, bubbles getting smaller, and snowflakes drifting downward. For greater effectiveness, draw the children into discussions of what relaxes them and encourage them to make up their own stories and poems. Asking children to develop lists of their favorite *quiet* things and *slow* activities is also enlightening. Focus on enacting things that start out fast, gradually decrease in speed, and eventually become motionless.

Some ideational approaches used to elicit relaxed movements follow:

You are a soft calico kitten lying in front of the warm fireplace. The fire is warm. You feel so-o-o good.

First, you stretch your right arm—oh, that feels good. Then you stretch your left arm. Then you stretch both legs. Now you are relaxed all over. The fire is so warm and your body feels so relaxed. This must be the best place in the whole world—your own little blanket in front of your own fire. You are so-o-o relaxed that you could fall asleep right now. You are getting sleepy now—maybe you will fall asleep now.

<u>You are becoming a puppet.</u> The change starts in your feet. Slowly, each part of your body becomes lifeless and is completely relaxed, as if it were detached from you. (Speaker should expand as needed.)

<u>Let's make believe we are a bowl full of jello!</u> Someone has left us out of the refrigerator, and we begin to dissolve slowly away. Our arms float down, and our body sinks slowly into the bowl. (Speaker should expanded as needed.)

Figure 16.8 **Imagery as a relaxation technique is often enhanced by giving the children props like scarves, ribbons, or towels.**

Older children and adults, no longer able to assume magically the feeling/tone of an animal or object, continue to find relaxation in the mood of certain poems and stories read aloud. They may lie in comfortable positions in a semidarkened room while listening and attempt to capture the essence of the words through consciously releasing tensions. Instrumental music may be substituted for reading if the group desires. Surburg discusses imagery techniques for special populations in several articles (Screws & Surburg, 1997; Surburg, 1989; Surburg et al., 1995).

Deep Body Awareness

To facilitate deep body awareness, begin the class with everyone in a comfortable supine position (see Figure 16.9). Then direct attention to specific parts of the body, asking persons to analyze and verbalize the sensations they are experiencing. If students seem reluctant to share aloud their feelings, offer such additional guidance as

1. Which parts of your arm are touching the floor? Is the floor warm or cool, smooth or rough, clean or dirty?
2. Can you feel the muscles loosening? If you measure the circumference of your upper arm, how many inches would you get?
3. Can you feel the blood pulsating in veins and arteries?
4. Can you feel the hairs on your arm? The creases in your wrist? Your fingernails? The cuticles? Any scars?
5. What other words come to mind when you think about *arm?*

The underlying premise in deep body awareness is that students must increase kinesthetic sensitivity before they can consciously control it. They must differentiate among parts of a whole and be able to describe these parts accurately. As deep body awareness is developed, each student discovers which thoughts and methods of releasing tension work best for him or her personally.

Deep body awareness should progress from other-directed to self-directed states. The latter is called **autogenesis**

Figure 16.9 **Two girls with Down syndrome participate in a deep body awareness relaxation activity at the close of their physical education class. This constitutes a "cool-down" time to help them make the transition from strenuous motor work to quiet academic learning.**

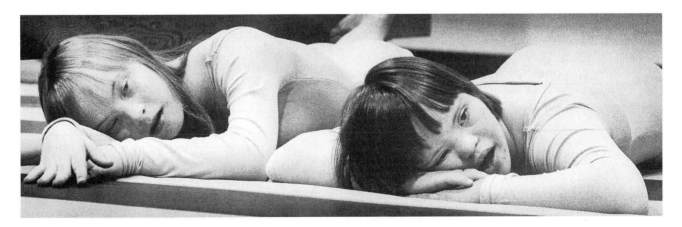

(self-generating). The activities described in this section are often called **autogenic training,** meaning the use of self-suggestion, breathing exercises, and meditation.

Jacobson Techniques

The most widely known of the techniques of neuromuscular relaxation are based on those of Edmund Jacobson, a physician who began his research in tension control at Harvard University in 1918. Jacobson's techniques, known originally as a system of *progressive conscious neuromuscular relaxation,* are referred to as *self-operations control* in his later books (Jacobson, 1970). The progression of activities is essentially the same.

Jacobson's technique mainly emphasized making a selected muscle group as tense as possible, then letting go so that the muscle group completely relaxes. This is extremely difficult for some people. Special training is needed to teach the Jacobson techniques and similar programs.

Yoga

Yoga is a system of physical, mental, and spiritual development that comes from India, where it dates back several centuries before Christ. The word *yoga* is derived from the Sanskrit root *yuji,* which means "to join or bind together." Scholars recognize several branches of yoga, but in the United States, **yoga** generally refers to a system of exercises built on held positions or postures and breath control. More correctly, you should say *Hatha Yoga* rather than yoga when teaching aspects of this system to your students. In the word *Hatha,* the *ha* represents the sun (expression of energy) and the *tha* represents the moon (conservation of energy). In yoga exercises, these two are always interacting.

Hatha Yoga offers exercises particularly effective in teaching relaxation and slowing down children and adults with attention disorders. The emphasis on correct breathing in Hatha Yoga makes it especially valuable for persons with asthma and other respiratory problems. Moreover, the nature of Hatha Yoga is such that it appeals to individuals whose health status prohibits participation in vigorous, strenuous physical activities.

Hatha Yoga, hereafter referred to as yoga, can be subdivided into two types of exercises: *asanas* and *pranayanas.* **Asanas** are held positions or postures like the lotus, the locust, and cobra poses. These positions facilitate stretching. **Pranayanas** are breathing exercises. In actuality, asanas and pranayanas are interrelated since correct breathing is emphasized throughout the assumption of a particular pose. Several of the asanas are identical or similar to stunts taught in elementary school physical education. The yoga *bent bow* is the same as the human rocker (a prone position with hands holding feet). The *cobra* is similar to the swan and/or the trunk lift from a prone position to test back strength. The *plough pose* resembles the paint-the-rainbow stunt (a back-lie with legs stretched up and over the head.

Differences between yoga and physical exercise as it is ordinarily taught are as follows:

1. Exercise sessions traditionally emphasize movement. *Yoga is exercise without movement.*

2. Exercises usually involve several bounces or stretches, with emphasis on how many can be done. Yoga stresses a *single, slow* contraction of certain muscles followed by a general relaxation. Generally, an asana is not repeated. At the very most, it might be attempted two or three times.

3. Exercises usually entail some pain and discomfort since the teaching progression conforms to the overload principle. In yoga, the number of repetitions is not increased. The duration of time for which the asana is held increases in accordance with ease of performance.

4. Exercises ordinarily stress the development of strength, flexibility, and endurance. Yoga stresses relaxation, balance, and self-control.

Tai Chi

Tai chi ch'uan, pronounced *tie jee chwhan* and called tai chi for short, is a slowing-down activity that also promotes balance. (Chen, 2002). In large metropolitan areas, instruction from masters, usually listed in the telephone directory, is available. Tai chi is used by many dance therapists. It also can increase appreciation of Chinese culture.

Tai chi is a series of 108 specific learned patterns of movements called *forms* that provide exercise for every part of the body. The forms have colorful names that tend to captivate children: Grasp Bird's Tail Right, Stork Spreads Wings, Carry Tiger to Mountain, Step Bank and Repulse Monkey, Needle at Sea Bottom, High Pat on Horse, Parting with Wild Horse's Mane Right. The 108 forms are based on 37 basic movements; thus, there is much repetition in the execution of a series of forms.

Tai chi is characterized by extreme slowness, a concentrated awareness of what one is doing, and absolute continuity of movement from one form to another. The same tempo is maintained throughout, but no musical accompaniment is provided. *All movements contain circles,* reinforcing the concepts of uninterrupted flow and quiet continuity. All body parts are gently curved or bent, allowing the body to give in to gravity rather than working against it, as is the usual practice in Western culture. No posture or pose is ever held. As each form is approximately completed, its movement begins to melt and blend into the next form. This has been likened to the cycle of seasons, when summer blends in to autumn and autumn into winter.

Tai chi is simple enough that it can be learned from a pictorial text. Movements can be memorized by repeatedly performing forms 1 to 20 in the same order without interruption. One form should never be practiced in isolation from others. Later, forms 21 to 57 are learned as a unit, as well as forms 58 to 108. *This approach is especially beneficial for children who need practice in visual perception, matching, and sequencing.* Its greatest strength, however, lies in the principle of slowness. Each time the sequence of forms is done, day after day, year after year, the goal is to perform it more slowly than before.

For persons who feel disinclined to memorize and teach preestablished forms, *the essence of tai chi can be captured by restructuring class calisthenics as a follow-the-leader experience in which flowing, circular movements are reproduced as slowly as possible without breaking the continuity of the sequence.* For real relaxation to occur, the same sequence must be repeated daily.

If you have never taken yoga or tai chi, find out where lessons are offered in your community, and take some and/or observe others (all ages) taking classes. Discuss benefits with others.

OPTIONAL ACTIVITIES

1. Although dance is a rich part of the physical education curriculum for children, some universities do not require dance courses of kinesiology majors. If you have never taken dance courses, try some either at the university or at a facility in the community.

2. If your university employs dance specialists or prepares dance majors, confer with these persons about teaching dance to individuals with disabilities, find out if any of them have done this, and if they would like to get involved. Provide them with resources. Do this also with dance teachers in the community.

3. Determine if there are any registered dance therapists living within driving distance (see www.adta.org for lists), confer with them, and observe one or more of their therapy sessions.

4. View films and videotapes on teaching dance and conducting dance therapy; determine which resources your university or departmental library offers. If sparse, see websites for help.

5. Find appropriate music on cassettes or disks, then plan and conduct a session on some kind of dance for a group (any age) that includes at least one person with a disability. See Appendix E.2. Ask a partner to observe and critique you, and then do the same for him or her.

C H A P T E R

17

Adapted Aquatics
Claudine Sherrill and Gail M. Dummer

Figure 17.1 Although this child is orthopedically impaired, he is not disabled in the water. (Photos by Judy Newman.)

1. How does aquatic therapy differ from adapted aquatics?
2. Why are extensive prebeginner skill sequences needed for children with disabilities, and how can these skill sequences be modified for children with different disabilities?
3. Why is it important to have a broad range of aquatic sports and leisure activities available to persons with disabilities?

4. Where can you find information about opportunities for persons with disabilities to participate in aquatic sport and leisure activities? Could you refer them to programs in your community?
5. What skills, knowledge, and resources would you need to conduct or contribute to an adapted aquatics program?

Water can be used for physical and mental rehabilitation, fitness, relaxation, perceptual-motor intervention, self-concept enhancement, fun, and competition (see Figure 17.1). Exercises, stunts, and games traditionally done on land achieve the same goals when executed in the water. Water activity, while beneficial for everyone, may be the program of choice for persons who are nonambulatory, unfit, obese, asthmatic, or arthritic. Because water minimizes the force of gravity, persons can often move with greater ease in a pool than on land. Water also eliminates the risk of joint damage associated with weight-bearing exercise in obesity and certain types of arthritis. Swimming strokes, whether done on land or water, have long been recognized as one of the best systems of exercise.

Aquatic Therapy or Adapted Aquatics?

The history of aquatic programs for persons with disabilities has followed a progression from **hydrotherapy** (now known as aquatic therapy), to adapted aquatics (swimming instruction adapted for persons with disabilities), to inclusive swimming and water exercise programs. Persons with disabilities now participate in the full gamut of aquatic activities, including competitive swimming, open water swimming, diving, synchronized swimming, water polo, triathlon, scuba diving, and boating activities.

    Aquatic therapy refers to water exercise adapted for therapeutic purposes. Goals of aquatic therapy programs typically include improved circulation, muscular strength and endurance, range of motion, balance, and coordination. Services are delivered by physical therapists or specialists who are certified by organizations such as the Aquatic Therapy and Rehabilitation Institute. Hydrotherapy was systematized in the 1930s by Charles Lowman, an orthopedic physician, who today is recognized as the father of hydrotherapy (Lowman, 1937; Lowman & Roen, 1952). Although originally used primarily for persons with physical disabilities, water exercise now is recommended for everyone (Sova, 1999, 2000). Water exercise may be a supplement to land exercise or an alternative. Organizations such as the Aquatic Exercise Association provide curriculum and safety guidelines.

    Adapted aquatics evolved in the 1960s and 1970s as awareness increased that all persons should have opportunities to learn basic swimming skills. The Aquatic Council of AAALF/AAHPERD (1996) defined **adapted aquatics** as a service delivery system providing appropriate aquatic instruction and recreation for participants with disabilities. Services usually are offered by certified swimming instructors who have additional education in disability-related topics. Leaders in this movement were

- *Judy Newman (1976), author of one of the earliest books on adapted aquatics;*
- *Louise Priest, a contributor to the American Red Cross, Council for National Cooperation in Aquatics, and National Safety Council/Jeff Ellis and Associates programs (Priest, 1996);*
- *Grace Reynolds (1973), architect of the YMCA adapted aquatics program; and*
- *Sue Grosse of the Milwaukee, Wisconsin, public schools (Grosse, 1987, 1996; Grosse & Gildersleeve, 1984).*

Useful instructional materials for adapted aquatics include *Swimming and Diving* (American Red Cross, 1992), *Aquatics for Special Populations* (YMCA of the USA, 1987), and *Aquatics: Special Olympics Sports Skills Program* (Special Olympics International, 1992).

    It is a misnomer to think that adapted aquatics services are conducted only in special settings. In fact, the term *adapted* refers to instructional modifications that can be provided in both disability-specific and inclusive programs (Conatser & Block, 2002). Adapted aquatics programs are offered in a wide variety of community, school, and clinical settings (Lepore, Gayle, & Stevens, 1998).

Instructional Models for Beginners

Many persons with disabilities learn swimming through regular Red Cross and YMCA programs. The Halliwick and Sherrill models are for persons who need more help and longer time than general programs provide. These models are similar in that both recommend (a) a one-to-one teaching ratio until swimmers gain confidence for small-group instruction; (b) teachers in the water, stimulating and supporting their swimmers; (c) learning through play and games; (d) emphasis on body awareness, movement exploration, and breathing games; (e) consideration of buoyancy principles, and (f) no use of personal flotation devices (PFDs) except for persons with severe nonambulatory conditions. **PFDs** are inner tubes, arm and head floats, vests, and inflatable swimsuits that aid buoyancy.

Halliwick Water Confidence Model

The *Halliwick water confidence model* is described by Kahrs (1974), by Grosse and Gildersleeve (1984), and by Campion (1985). This model teaches water buoyancy and confidence through various kinds of body rotations, floats, glides, and games. Once persons are comfortable with the buoyancy force of the water, they can learn swimming strokes by traditional methods. The Halliwick model is based on 10 points:

1. **Mental preparation.** Emphasis is on getting to know the instructor, the pool, and the dressing rooms. This is achieved through walking, talking, and showering. The goal is to have fun while learning to feel at ease in the water. Familiar land activities (games, dances, and rhythms) are adapted to water.

2. **Self-sufficiency.** Instruction begins with the teacher and student touching: (a) holding hands during locomotor activities; (b) holding hands, waist, or shoulders in face-to-face and face-to-back movement explorations; and (c) holding hands while being pulled in a horizontal position. *The head is never held because emphasis is on learning to alter body position and regulate balance through independent head movements.* As confidence is achieved, the distance between teacher and student is gradually increased by such devices as a washcloth, floatboard, and towel. Finally, there is no contact, and the teacher moves a little farther away each lesson. PFDs are not sanctioned because they lessen self-sufficiency.

3. **Vertical rotation.** Mastery is achieved by learning to change from vertical to horizontal positions and vice versa. Somersaults are advanced vertical rotations.

4. **Horizontal or lateral rotation.** Mastery is achieved by learning to rotate from back to front and vice versa while in a horizontal position. Logrolls are advanced horizontal rotations.

5. **Combined rotation.** Many games that include both vertical and horizontal rotations are played.

6. **Application of buoyancy.** Games like trying to sit on the pool bottom without floating up are used to develop trust of the water's buoyancy force.

7. **Floating positions.** Movement exploration challenges are used to find different body shapes for floating.

8. **Turbulence floating and gliding.** Students learn to cope with increasing amounts of turbulence. First, confidence is gained in calm water. Then the teacher creates small, medium, and large turbulence conditions by swirling his or her hands in the water near the student's head.

9. **Simple propulsion.** Underwater, symmetrical arm movements (finning, sculling, breaststroke) are added to the back and front glides to promote simple propulsion.

10. **Development of strokes.** Swimming strokes are introduced by traditional methods after Halliwick points 1 to 9 have resulted in complete water confidence.

Sherrill Water Fun and Success Model

The *Sherrill water fun and success model* began as part of a Texas Woman's University practicum program in which university students teach children with developmental disabilities to swim. The three most important goals of the program are (a) to improve self-concept, (b) to increase self-confidence, and (c) to develop courage. Secondary to these goals, the teacher concentrates on dimensions of body image: (a) identification of body parts, (b) improvement of proprioception, and (c) development of such inner language concepts as bent versus straight, vertical versus horizontal, pike versus tuck, back layout versus front layout, and pull phase (application of force) versus recovery phase. As a technique for enhancing self-concept, children are drilled on the *names* of the stunts and skills they learn to perform. As they acquire a vocabulary that enables them to share their successes with others, children seem to demonstrate increased motivation for undertaking new aquatic adventures. Moreover, this emphasis on vocabulary in the swimming setting reinforces words learned in the classroom and the gymnasium, thereby contributing to transfer of learning and reducing development of splinter skills.

Over the years, three prebeginner swimming certificates have evolved. Initially, the levels of competency that the certificates represent were named after fish: minnows, crappies, and dolphins. The children were not as enamored of these appellations as were the adults who created them. First of all, many of them had never seen real fish, alive or dead, and to them, the names were meaningless. Some of the pupils did report firsthand knowledge of fish but remembered the unpleasant odor more than the beauty of movement.

The three certificates subsequently were designated as Explorer, Advanced Explorer, and Floater in accordance with the levels of competency achieved. These certificates were printed on cards of the same size and shape as the standard Red Cross certificates. Originally, they came in different colors, but after the year that a girl with Down syndrome sobbed all through the awards ceremony because her card was not white like her boyfriend's, it was decided to make the cards uniform in color as well as size, shape, and format.

The motor tasks required for passing each certificate are listed in Table 17.1. The major achievement at the Explorer level is to release the teacher's hand and perform basic locomotor movement patterns independently at a distance several feet away from the side of the pool. Putting the face in the water is not necessary to earn Explorer status. Many youngsters initially are so terrified of the water that several lessons are required before they will loosen their deathlike grips on the teachers. Many additional lessons pass before enough courage is developed to let go of the side of the pool and walk independently. Nevertheless, *all* students who earn the Explorer certificate take as much pride in it as their peers do in the Red Cross achievement cards.

The Advanced Explorer certificate represents two major accomplishments: putting the face in the water and willingness to lift the feet from the pool bottom, thereby assuming a horizontal position with the help of the teacher. Also at this level, the child begins experimenting with somersaults, standing on his or her head, walking on hands, and other stunts that are not based on the ability to float.

Earning the third and final prebeginner Floater certificate is dependent upon the ability to relax sufficiently to float for several seconds. At this level, children usually begin to swim. Navigation is more often under the water than on top, and underwater swimming can be used to fulfill the requirement of one-half width. Long before the pupils learn to swim recognizable strokes, they become proficient in many basic stunts of synchronized swimming. They develop creative routines to music that are weird combinations of walks, runs, jumps, hops, stand-

Table 17.1   Beginning competency levels of swimming for the Sherrill model.

Level I, Explorer Movement Exploration in Water	Level II, Advanced Explorer Movement Exploration in Water	Level III, Floater Prebeginning Swimming
1. Enter and leave water alone	1. Put face in water	1. Blow bubbles (10 sec)
2. Walk across pool holding rail	2. Blow bubbles (5 sec)	2. Bracketing on front with kick
3. Walk across pool holding teacher's hand	3. Touch bottom or toes with hands	3. Change of position: stand; front-lying with support; stand
4. Stand alone	4. Retrieve objects from bottom	4. Prone float
5. Walk across pool pushing kickboard	5. Assume horizontal position with teacher's help	5. Change of position: stand; back-lying with support; stand
6. Jump or hop several steps alone	6. Hold onto kickboard pulled by teacher	6. Back float
7. Walk and do breaststroke arm movements	7. Jump into water without help	7. Flutter kick using board
8. Do various locomotor movements across the pool	8. Take rides in back-lying position	8. Jellyfish float
9. Blow bubbles through plastic tube	9. Change of level: squat to stand; stand to squat	9. Perform breaststroke arm movements
10. Blow Ping-Pong ball across pool	10. Play follow-the-leader type water games	10. Swim one-half width any style
	11. Demonstrate bracketing on back with kick (see Figure 17.5)	11. Perform at least one stunt like stand or walk on hands, front somersault, back somersault, tub, surface dive

Note: Tasks within each level may be performed in any order.

ing in place and stroking with arms, and regulation synchronized swimming stunts.

Adapted Aquatics Principles

Some of the differences between an adapted aquatics program and regular swimming instruction are explicit in the following principles for teachers. Many of these adapted aquatics principles also are appropriate for use in preschool programs (Langendorfer & Bruya, 1994).

1. Be in the water with the children rather than on deck (see Figure 17.2). Physical contact between teacher and student is based on the student's needs for security and affection. Although independence in the water is the ultimate goal, do not rush it.

2. Avoid saying "Put your face underwater," a task that students tend to interpret as unpleasant. Instead, introduce gamelike situations that induce the child to attempt the task without conscious realization of what he or she is doing.

3. Use as few words as possible in teaching. Cues like "up," "down," "pull," "recover," and "kick 2-3-4" are substituted for sentences. A well-modulated voice helps to convey the meaning of instructions. Use a *high* voice for *up* movements and a *low* (pitch) voice for *down* movements. Use a loud and forceful voice during the pull phase and a soft and gentle voice during the recovery phase.

4. Move the child's limbs through the desired pattern of movement rather than using the explanation-demonstration technique.

5. Show acceptance of the child through frequent mirroring of his or her movements. Take turns *following the leader* with precise imitation of postures, arm movements, and kicks.

Figure 17.2   A one-to-one relationship in the water facilitates learning.

6. Introduce synchronized swimming, jumping, and diving much earlier than usual in swimming instruction. Emphasize the combination of stunts and locomotor movements—that is, creating sequences (routines) and remembering and executing sequences developed by others.

7. Modify requirements in accordance with individual differences. Plan testing on the basis of the individual's strengths, not preestablished competences that are thought to meet the needs of all beginner swimmers (see research by Gelinas and Reid [2000] in this regard).

Figure 17.3 Comparison of bilateral and crosslateral strokes.

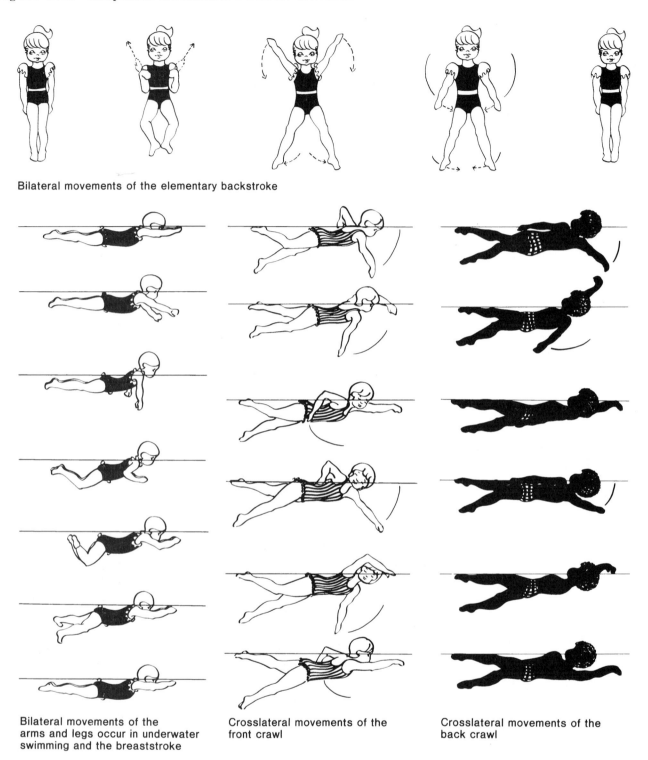

Bilateral movements of the elementary backstroke

Bilateral movements of the
arms and legs occur in underwater
swimming and the breaststroke

Crosslateral movements of the
front crawl

Crosslateral movements of the
back crawl

8. Encourage bilateral, unilateral, and crosslateral movement patterns, in that order. The breaststroke and the elementary backstroke are usually the first real swimming strokes introduced. The bilateral movements of the breaststroke usually appear in underwater swimming without the benefit of instruction. Figure 17.3 compares the simplicity of bilateral strokes with the relative complexity of crosslateral strokes.

Bilateral and Crosslateral Basics

The bilateral movements of the elementary backstroke are similar to those in angels-in-the-snow and jumping jacks. Land drill is used before the children shower or after they dry and dress to ensure transfer of learning. Drill in the water can be facilitated by suspending a hammock from the ceiling, using flotation devices, and lying on a table under the water.

Figure 17.3 shows bilateral movements of the arms and legs in underwater swimming and the breaststroke and in the elementary backstroke, as well as the more difficult cross-lateral swimming strokes. Six kicks of each leg are coordinated with every cycle of arm movements. As the right arm pulls, for instance, the right leg kicks *up,* down, *up.* The emphasis in the flutter kick is on the *up* beat! Arm strokes and leg kicks must be practiced in a horizontal rather than a standing position. Equally important, the teacher should demonstrate new skills in the horizontal position.

No stroke is more difficult to master than the front crawl. Although the rhythm of the flutter kick may come naturally to a few students, it is a nightmare for many others. Land drills to music in 3/4 time with a strong accent on the first beat in every measure may contribute to relaxed, effective kicking in the water; if not, the practice can be justified for its contribution to abdominal strength. Both in land drills and in the water, there is a tendency to collaborate with the force of gravity and accentuate the downbeat; this error must be avoided. Devising some kind of contraption 12 to 18 inches above the floor to be kicked on each upbeat may focus the student's attention on the desired accent.

The flutter kick warm-up exercise should begin in the position depicted in Figure 17.4 rather than with both legs on the floor, since at no time during the crawl stroke are the legs motionless and in the same plane. With poorly coordinated students, it is best to leave the arms motionless in the starting position until the rhythm of the kick is mastered. The verbal cues "right-arm-pull" or "left-arm-pull" can be substituted for "kick-2-3" even though the arms do not move. The first progression for this exercise is lying on the floor; the next progression is lying on a bench with arms and legs hanging over.

When a student demonstrates no progress in the flutter kick over a period of weeks, it can be safely assumed that the desired movement is not *natural* for him or her and that an alternate method of kicking should be substituted. In such instances, the front crawl can be modified into the *trudgeon stroke* by substituting the scissors kick for the flutter kick.

The American Red Cross teaches many basic strokes. The student's ability to perform one or two of these strokes really well is the criterion for success in a program for persons with disabilities. Which stroke(s) the child chooses is not important as long as he or she feels safe in the water and enjoys swimming. One of the purposes of movement exploration is to guide the student toward personal discovery of this stroke.

Activities for the Explorer

Washcloth Games

Give each child a washcloth, and compare the swimming pool with the bathtub at home. Your relaxed flow of questions usually elicits the desired water exploration:

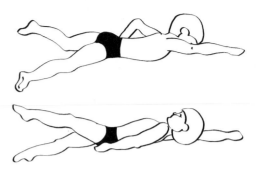

Figure 17.4 Ready position for flutter kick warm-up.

1. "What do you do with a washcloth? Don't tell me; show me!"
2. "What part do you wash first? Did you wring the cloth out before you started to wash? Don't you wring it out first at home?"
3. "Did you wash behind your ears? The back of your neck? Your elbows? Your knees? Your ankles? What about the soles of your feet? Are they clean?"
4. "Do you like to have someone wash your back? If you do, find a partner and take turns washing each other's back."
5. "Can you play throw and catch with your partner by using the washcloth as a ball?"
6. "What happens if you miss the catch? Can you pick the washcloth off the bottom of the pool with your toes? With some other part of your body?"

Sponge Games

Give each child a sponge.

1. "Do you see something at the bottom of the pool? That's correct! There are plates, saucers, bowls, glasses, and cups. Guess what your job is? That's correct! Recover the dishes any way you wish, wash them with your sponge, and set the table on the deck. Whoever finishes the most place settings wins."
2. "Have you ever scrubbed down walls? Each of you find your very own space on the wall and let's see you scrub! Have you ever washed a car? Let's pretend the wall is a car! What else can we pretend the wall is? Does anyone know how to scrub the floor? Let's see!"
3. "See this big inner tube? Let's use it to shoot baskets with our sponges. Can you make your sponge land inside the inner tube?"
4. "What other target games can we invent with the sponges?"
5. *Dodge or Catch.* This game is played like dodgeball except that the child has the option of dodging or catching. Occasionally, someone may get hit full in the face with a wet sponge. Although a sponge cannot hurt, some children feel threatened by this activity; hence, the participants should be volunteers.

The children put their sponges in the water.

1. "Who can get his or her bucket filled with water first? The only way to get water in the bucket is by squeezing out sponges."
   a. *Individual game.* "Who can recover the most sponges, squeeze them out, and toss them back in the water?"
   b. *Partner game.* One student remains in the water recovering sponges and handing them to his or her partner on deck, who squeezes the sponges and tosses them back into the water.

2. Sponges of different colors are floating in the water. Children all have one hand on the pool railing. On the signal "Go," they respond to the question, "Who can recover a blue sponge and put it on the deck first? A yellow sponge? A pink sponge?"

3. Sponges of different shapes or sizes are floating in the water. (Same instructions as before.)

4. "Who can recover two sponges and put one under each of his or her feet? How many of you are standing on sponges? Can you walk across the pool on the sponges?"

Parachute Games

In the water, a large sheet of clear plastic makes the best parachute; round tablecloths and sheets can also be used. All of the parachute activities played on land can be adapted to the water. "Who can run under the parachute?" invariably gets the face in the water. "Who can climb over the parachute?" leads to taking turns riding on the magic carpet that is pulled through the water by classmates.

Blowing Games

Blowing games can be played either in or out of the water; they are important lead-up activities to rhythmic breathing.

1. Give each child a clear plastic tube 12 to 18 in. long. Plastic tubing can be purchased in any hardware store. "Who can walk along with the plastic tube in a *vertical* position and blow bubbles in the water? Who can walk along with the plastic tube in a *horizontal* position and blow bubbles in the water?"

2. "Who can blow a Ping-Pong ball across the water? A toy sailboat? A small sponge?"

3. "On the side of the pool are many balloons that need blowing up. The object is to blow up a balloon while you walk or run across the pool. Who can make the most trips back and forth and thus blow up the most balloons? You may take only one balloon each trip."

4. Inflatable air mattresses and rafts provide ample practice in blowing for several children. Teams of three or four children may cooperate in blowing up a mattress with the promise that they may play on it in the water after it has been sufficiently inflated.

5. Give each child a yarn ball or Ping-Pong ball suspended from a string. "Who can keep the ball in motion the longest by blowing?"

Self-Testing Activities for the Explorer

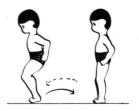

Horizontal or long jump

1. "Who can jump forward across the pool? Who can jump backward? Sideward? How many different ways can you jump? Can you carry something heavy as you jump?"

Vertical jump and reach

2. "How high can you jump?" A pole with flags of various colors provides incentive for progressively increasing the height of the jump. "Which flag did you touch when you jumped?"

Cable jump

3. "Can you jump over a stick, a scarf, or a rope? In which nursery rhyme does someone jump over a candlestick?"

Greet the toe

4. "Can you greet your toe? Can you hop while holding one foot?"

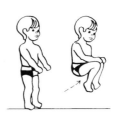

Jump and tuck

5. "Can you jump up and touch your knees? Can you jump up and touch your toes?"

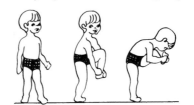

Airplane or single-foot balance

6. "How many different ways can you balance on one foot? Can you do an arabesque? A pirouette?"

Aquatic sprint

7. "How many seconds does it take you to run across the pool? How many widths of the pool can you run in 3 minutes?"

Bracketing with back lean

8. "Can you hang on the pool railing (gutter) and arch your back? Can you do this with the soles of your feet on the wall instead of the floor? Can you do this with only one arm?"

Matching locomotor movements to lines and forms

9. "Can you walk a straight line drawn on the floor of the pool? A circular line? A zigzag line? Can you march on the line? Can you hop on it? Can you do these movements backward? Sideward?"

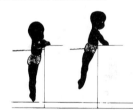

Straight arm support lean

10. "Stand in the water facing the side of the pool with both hands on deck. How many times can you lift your body up almost out of the water with your arms alone? This is like a push-up on land. Can you lift your body upward and maintain a straight-arm support?"

Activities for the Advanced Explorer

Advanced explorers are learning to put their heads underwater and to change level from up to down and vice versa. They are also experimenting with all of the possible ways to enter the water. They are not yet secure about a horizontal position in the water but will assume it when your hand is in contact with some part of their bodies.

Towel Games

1. **Taking rides.** A child who trusts you enough to hold his or her hands and allow the feet to rise from the bottom,

thereby assuming a horizontal position in the water, can be taken on *rides.* These rides can be as dramatic as the child's (or your) imagination, with sound effects for a train, rocket ship, or whatever. Talk to the child, continuously maintaining eye contact and pulling him or her along while walking backward. The next step in the development of trust is to convince the child to hang onto a towel or kickboard while you pull on the other end. Thus, the rides across the pool continue, but the child is progressively farther away from you.

2. **Individual tug-of-war.** Every two children share one towel, each holding onto one end. A line on the bottom of the pool separates the two children, and the object is to see who can pull the other over the line first. As balance and body control in the water improve, teammates can be added until group tug-of-war is played. Only one teammate should be added to each side at a time.

3. **Catch the snake.** A rope about 6 ft long has a towel tied onto the end. You or an agile child pulls the rope around the pool. The object is to see who can *catch the snake* first. The winner then becomes the runner who pulls the snake around the pool.

4. **Beater goes round.** Children stand in a single circle, facing inward. The *beater* stands on the outside of the circle, facing counterclockwise and holding a small hand towel (one not big enough to hurt when a child is hit with it). A second child is running counterclockwise in front of the *beater,* trying to avoid being hit by the towel. He or she can be safe by ducking in front of any player in the circle after he or she has run around at least one-half of the circle. The player whom he or she ducked in front of must now run to avoid being beaten.

5. **Tag.** Towels on the pool bottom are safety rests.

6. **Over and under relay.** Use towels instead of a ball.

Body Shapes Used in Aquatics

The terms *tuck, pike,* and *layout* are used in synchronized swimming, diving, and gymnastics. The Advanced Explorer learns to assume these shapes on land, in shallow water, and in the air. Movement exploration on the trampoline and the springboard in the gymnasium reinforce learning in the pool area. This aspect of aquatics training is designed specifically to improve proprioceptive awareness. The following questions elicit desired responses:

Tuck positions

1. "In how many different ways can you assume a tuck position on land? In the water? In the air?"

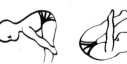

Pike positions

2. "In how many different ways can you assume a pike position on land? In the water? In the air?"

Layout positions

3. "How many ways can you assume a layout position on land? In the water? In the air? Can you do back layouts? Front layouts? Side layouts?"

Curved positions

4. "In how many ways can you make your body curved on land? In the water? In the air? Can you combine a front layout with a curve? A back layout with a curve? A side layout with a curve?"

Early attempts at assuming tuck, pike, and layout positions in the water often result in sinking to the bottom. Many children accidentally discover floating while concentrating on body shapes. Those who do not discover floating gain valuable practice in breath control and balance.

Ways to Enter the Water

Many children prefer a session of jumping and/or diving to swimming. In the beginning, they may wish to have you hold one or both hands and jump with them. Others prefer you to be standing or treading water and awaiting their descent with outstretched arms. Participation in some kind of creative dramatics that demands a jump into the water often subtly evokes the desired response in children who have previously demonstrated fear and reluctance. Themes that have been particularly successful in motivating children to enter the water are (a) playing firefighter and sliding down the fire pole, (b) carrying lighted candles through a dark cave or perhaps the ancient Roman catacombs, (c) going on an African safari, (d) imitating Mary Poppins by opening an umbrella in flight, and, of course, (e) emulating space travelers through various trials and tribulations.

In response to "How many different ways can you enter the water feetfirst?" children may demonstrate the following:

1. Climb down the ladder. Most efficient method is facing ladder with back to water.
2. Sitting on edge of pool, scoot off into water: (a) freestyle (any way you wish), (b) in tuck position, (c) in pike position, and (d) with one leg straight, one bent.
3. Kneeling or half-kneeling, facing water.
4. Kneeling or half-kneeling, back to the water.
5. Squatting, facing water.
6. Squatting, back to water.
7. Standing, facing water using (a) stepoff, (b) jump and kneel in air before contacting water, (c) jump

and tuck in air, (d) jump and clap hands, (e) jump and turn, (f) jump and touch toes, (g) hop, (h) leap, (i) arabesque, and (j) pike drop forward (camel walk position).

Stages in learning to dive

8. Standing, back to water, using (a) stepoff, (b) jump, (c) hop, and (d) pike drop backward.

In response to "How many different ways can you enter the water headfirst?" children discover the various stages in learning to dive. They may also lie on the side and do a logroll into the water or accidently perform a front somersault.

Self-Testing Activities for the Advanced Explorer

Frog jump

1. "Can you jump like a frog under the water?"

Jack-in-the-box

2. "Can you squat in water over your head and then jump up and yell 'boo' like a jack-in-the-box?"

Dog walk when four limbs touch pool bottom; lame-dog walk when three limbs touch bottom.

3. "Can you do a dog walk with your head under the water? A lame-dog walk?"

Mule kick

4. "Can you do a mule kick in the water?"

Seal walk

5. "Can you do a seal walk under the water?"

Camel walk

6. "Can you do a camel walk under the water? This is also called a wicket walk."

Egg sit followed by V sit

7. "Can you do an egg sit at the bottom of the pool? Can you do an egg sit near the surface and sink downward?"

Human ball bounce

8. "Can you do five bent-knee bounces at the bottom of the pool? Pretend that you are a ball being dribbled."

Coffee grinder

9. "Can you do the coffee grinder stunt at the bottom of the pool?"

Knee scale

10. "Can you do a balancing stunt under the water with one knee and both hands touching the bottom? Can you lift your arms and do a single-knee balance?"

Bracketing

Bracketing is the term for holding onto the gutter (rail) of the pool with one or both hands and allowing the feet to rise from the bottom of the pool so that the body is in a horizontal position (see Figure 17.5).

Retrieving Objects From the Bottom of the Pool

Advanced Explorers learn about spatial relationships within a new context as they open their eyes underwater and see objects *through* the water. In the earliest stages of underwater exploration, they may hold both of your hands and submerge with you. Underwater, you and the student may establish eye contact, shake hands, and mirror each other's hand and arm movements. Later, you can challenge the student to retrieve all sorts of things from the bottom. Practice in form, size, weight, and color discrimination can be integrated with the instructions for retrieval of objects.

Activities for the Floater

The Floater is comfortable in the water and can do almost anything but swim a coordinated stroke for 20 yd to qualify for the

Figure 17.5 Bracketing on the front and back.

Red Cross Beginner card. The Floater is probably more competent in underwater swimming than in performing strokes near the surface. This is the period during which the following tasks are mastered: (a) horizontal to vertical positioning, (b) floating, (c) bobbing, (d) front-to-back positioning and vice versa, and (e) simple stunts in synchronized swimming.

Horizontal to Vertical Positioning

Floaters demonstrate ease in moving from a horizontal position to a vertical one. The degree of difficulty of this task varies with amount of buoyancy, specific gravity, and absence or paralysis of limbs. Simple sequencing is introduced, as depicted in Figure 17.6.

Floating

To teach floating to persons with varying body builds and/or amputations of one type or another, you must have some understanding of the following terms: *buoyancy, specific gravity,* and *center of buoyance.*

Buoyancy is the quality of being able to float. The buoyancy of a human being depends on the amount of water that each body part is able to displace and the weight of the body part itself. The larger the surface of the body part, the more water it will displace. For instance, the typical woman with wide pelvis and well-rounded buttocks displaces more water than the average man with his narrow hips and flat buttocks. The lighter the weight of the body part, the less upward force is required to buoy it up. Thus, if a cork and a marble of the same surface area are dropped into water, the cork will float and the marble will sink. Adipose tissue (fat) weighs less than muscle and bone tissue. Thus, if two persons of equal surface areas try to float and one individual is fat while the other is heavily muscled, the fat person will be buoyed upward more easily than the person with well-developed musculature. Buoyancy is explained by *Archimedes' principle,* which states: A body submerged in a liquid is buoyed up by a force equal to the weight of the displaced liquid.

The **specific gravity** of a human being is her or his weight compared to the weight of an equal amount of water, as shown in this formula:

Figure 17.6 Simple sequencing.

Two-part sequence to be practiced in learning change from horizontal to vertical position.

Two-part sequence to be practiced in learning to change position from a back layout to a tuck.

Back float to tight tub to back float is three-part sequence in learning to change positions.

A five-part sequence in changing position.

$$\text{Specific gravity} = \frac{\text{Weight of body}}{\text{Weight of equal amount of water}}$$

After full inspiration, the specific gravity of most adult human beings is slightly less than 1. This means that most adults can float with their head above the surface of the water when their lungs are filled with air. After exhalation, the specific gravity of most adults is approximately 1.02. Only when the specific gravity is above 1.02 do individuals experience difficulty in floating.

The **center of buoyance** (CB) of a human being in water is similar in function to the center of gravity (CG) when the body is not immersed in fluid. Both are areas where weight is concentrated; both serve as fulcrums about which the body rotates.

The CB, for most persons, is located in the thoracic cavity. The more obese an individual is, the lower his or her CB is. The CB is defined as the center of gravity of the volume of the displaced water before its displacement. If an object were of uniform density, its CB and CG would coincide; this is not the case with living creatures, human or fish.

In the water, the body can be likened to a first-class lever, which, like a seesaw, totters back and forth around its fulcrum (CB) until balance is achieved. Only when the CB and the CG are in the same vertical line can a person float without motion.

Figure 17.7 shows that there is no one correct way to float. Each person must experiment until he or she discovers the position in which CB and CG are aligned vertically. The hints that follow may help students cope with problems of buoyancy.

Figure 17.7 Effects of buoyancy on floating explain why there are many correct ways. (CB = Center of buoyancy; CG = Center of gravity.)

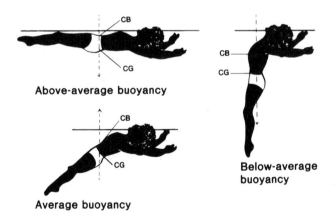

Above-average buoyancy

Average buoyancy

Below-average buoyancy

Below-Average Buoyancy

Men, as a whole, have less buoyancy than women. Black students have less buoyancy than white students. Buoyancy can be increased by raising the CG and hence the CB. This can be done by extending the arms overhead, by bending the knees so that heels almost touch the buttocks, or by assuming a tuck or jellyfish floating position. Hyperventilating—keeping the lungs filled with air and exhaling as seldom as possible—also helps.

Students should not attempt to lift the feet and legs and attain a horizontal position since the feet and legs will only drop downward again, building up enough momentum as they do so to pull the entire body under. Many persons who believe themselves to be *sinkers* could float if they started in the vertical rather than the horizontal position.

Above-Average Buoyancy

The obese person experiences many balance problems in the water for which he or she must learn to compensate. The alternate-arm stroke on the back crawl, for instance, must be performed twice as fast as normal to prevent the body from rolling over. The hips, legs, and feet are often above water level so that no kick is possible.

The most anxiety-ridden experience, however, for the obese beginning swimmer is changing from a horizontal position to a vertical stand. Try as he or she may, it is not easy to make the legs drop and the shoulders and trunk come forward so that the CG and CB are aligned over the feet.

Amputations

Amputations affect the location of the CG and the CB, which, in turn, affects buoyancy and balance. The loss of a limb causes displacement of the CG and CB to the opposite side. Thus, a student who has lost a right leg or arm has a tendency to roll to the left, where the weight of the body is centered. Most persons with amputations, whether congenital or acquired, can become excellent swimmers.

Extensive movement exploration is recommended to enable each person to discover the floating position and swimming strokes that best serve his or her needs. Most students with severe orthopedic disabilities seem to prefer swimming on the back. Specifically, the following strokes are suggested:

1. Loss of both legs—Back crawl or breaststroke.
2. Loss of one leg—Back crawl, elementary backstroke, or sidestroke.
3. Loss of both arms—Any kick that can be done on the back. This person has exceptional difficulty in changing from horizontal layout position to a stand.
4. Loss of one arm—Sidestroke or swimming on back with legs providing most of the power and the one arm finning.
5. Loss of one leg and one arm—Sidestroke with leg on the bottom; arm will create its own effective finning action.

Spasticity and Asymmetric Strength

Persons with spasticity or paralytic asymmetries tend to spin or rotate in the horizontal water position. To stabilize a float, swimmers should turn the head in the opposite direction of the body rotation. Backstrokes should be taught before front strokes, and symmetric strokes should be mastered before asymmetric strokes.

Bobbing

Bobbing is similar to several vertical jumps in place except that all the power comes from the arms. It can be done in either shallow or deep water, but traditionally is associated with water over the head.

Down phase in bobbing   Up phase in bobbing

Bobbing consists of two phases. In the *down phase,* both arms are raised simultaneously upward, causing the body to descend. The breath is exhaled. When the feet touch the bottom of the pool, the arm movement ends. The *up phase* is then initiated by both arms pressing simultaneously downward. This action pushes the body upward. The arm movements in bobbing are different from all others the child has encountered. The concept of displacing water—that is, pushing in the direction opposite from that which you wish to go—should be explained.

Bobbing accomplishes several goals: (a) improves rhythmic breathing, (b) increases vital breathing capacity—that is, tends to hyperventilate the swimmer, (c) heightens proprioceptive awareness, and (d) serves as a warm-up activity. Bobbing is recommended especially for children with asthma. Variations of bobbing are

1. **Progressive bobbing.** The down phase is identical to that of bobbing in place. The up phase, however, is modified by using the legs to push the body off the pool bottom at approximately a 65° angle. The arm movement is basically the same. Progressive bobbing is a survival skill in that it can be used as a means of locomotion from the deep end of the pool to the shallow.
2. **Bobbing on one leg.**
3. **Bobbing in a tuck position.** Down phase: Arms pull upward, legs extend so that feet touch the bottom. Up phase: Arms press downward, tuck knees to chest so that full tuck is achieved at height of up phase.
4. **Seesaw bobbing with a partner.** To begin, partners face each other and hold hands. Then a rhythm is established in which one person is up while the other is down, as in partner-jumping on a trampoline.

Finning and Sculling

After students master a float, several sessions in movement exploration should focus on the arms and hands. Such problems as the following can be posed for the back layout, front layout, tuck, and pike positions:

1. "In the back layout position, how many different ways can you place your arms?"
2. "Which positions of the arms make floating easier? More difficult?"
3. "How many different kinds of movements can you perform with your arms in each position?"

4. "Which of these movements seem to make you sink? If you do sink, which of these movements can help your body rise to the surface of the water?"

5. "Which arm movements propel the body through the water headfirst?"

6. "Which arm movements enable you to execute the following position changes: (a) prone float to stand, (b) prone float to back float, (c) back float to stand, and (d) back float to prone float?"

7. "If you move only one arm, what happens? Can you propel the body directly to the right by using one arm only? Directly to the left?"

8. "In what other ways can you propel the body directly to the left? Directly to the right?"

9. "In how many different ways can you push the water away from you? *Pull* the water toward you?"

Ideally, creative dramatics should be combined with movement exploration so that the child can tell you and/or peers which emotions are being expressed by particular arm and hand movements: Variations of charades can be played in the water, and/or students may *act out* the feeling that a particular musical composition conveys.

Given sufficient time and encouragement, students eventually discover *finning* and *sculling* for themselves. Introduce the names of these movements and explain their usefulness in changing positions in the water. Movement exploration can then focus on how many different ways students can fin or scull.

Finning

Finning is a series of short pushes with the palms of the hands against the water in the direction *opposite* to the one in which the student wishes to move. Each push is followed by a quick, bent-arm recovery under the surface of the water.

Sculling

Many different types of *sculling* are recognized. In the standard scull, the hands are at the hips, close to the body. Movement at the shoulder joints is limited to inward and outward rotation of the arms that seems to be initiated by the hands in their execution of tiny figure-eight motions close to the water surface.

The motion of the hands and wrists consists of an inward and outward phase, each of which is performed with equal force. The palms move toward midline during the inward phase and away from midline during the outward phase so that the water is alternately scooped toward the hips and then pushed away. The thumbs are up during the inward phase and down during the outward phase. If students do not discover sculling for themselves, the movement should be introduced in the classroom and mastered before it is attempted in water. Sculling, for many swimmers, is a difficult pattern to learn through imitation.

Synchronized Swimming Stunts

The regulation stunts usually taught in units on synchronized swimming are similar to those performed in tumbling and gymnastics. Executing stunts in the water improves proprioception, enhances body awareness, and provides practice in movement imitation. The stunts described on the following pages can be mastered early in beginning swimming. The primary prerequisites are a feeling of ease in the water, the ability to scull while floating, and a keen sense of where the body is in space. Many slow learners can be taught to execute simple synchronized swimming stunts long before they achieve skill and endurance in regulation strokes. All stunts are begun from either the front layout position or the back layout position, as depicted below and in Figures 17.8 and 17.9.

Front layout

Back layout

Whereas skilled performers are concerned with the aesthetic appearance of a stunt, the adapted physical educator does not worry about *good form. The stunts are introduced in a manner similar to other tasks in movement exploration.* Very few verbal directions are posed; on some occasions, a casual demonstration motivates the student to attempt new positions in the water. The stunts that follow are listed in order of difficulty under their respective starting positions. *Stunts in which the body is carried in a tuck position are easier than those executed in the pike or layout positions.*

Stunts That Begin in a Back Layout Position

1. **Tub.** "Can you change from a back layout position to a tuck position with the thighs perpendicular to the surface of the water? In this position, can you use sculling to revolve the body around in a circle?"

2. **Log rolling.** "Can you roll the extended body over and over while keeping the legs motionless? This is identical to the stunt by the same name on land."

3. **Back tuck somersault.** "Can you perform a backward roll in a tuck position?"

4. **Oyster, clam, or pike up.** "Can you drop your hips as you simultaneously hyperextend and inwardly rotate the arms at the shoulder joints? When you are touching your toes in a pike position, can you sink to the bottom?"

5. **Back pike somersault.** "Can you assume a pike position with trunk under the water but parallel to the surface? Can you perform a backward roll in this pike position? Which part of this stunt is like the oyster?"

6. **Torpedo.** "Can you scull with your hands overhead so that your body is propelled in the direction of your feet? Submergence of the head and shoulders is optional."

7. **Back dolphin.** "Can you maintain a back layout position as your head leads your body around in a circle under the surface of the water? Can you perform this same stunt with one knee bent?"

8. **Single ballet leg.** "Can you scull across the pool with one leg perpendicular to the surface of the water and the other leg extended on the surface of the water?"

Figure 17.8   Stunts that begin in a back layout position.

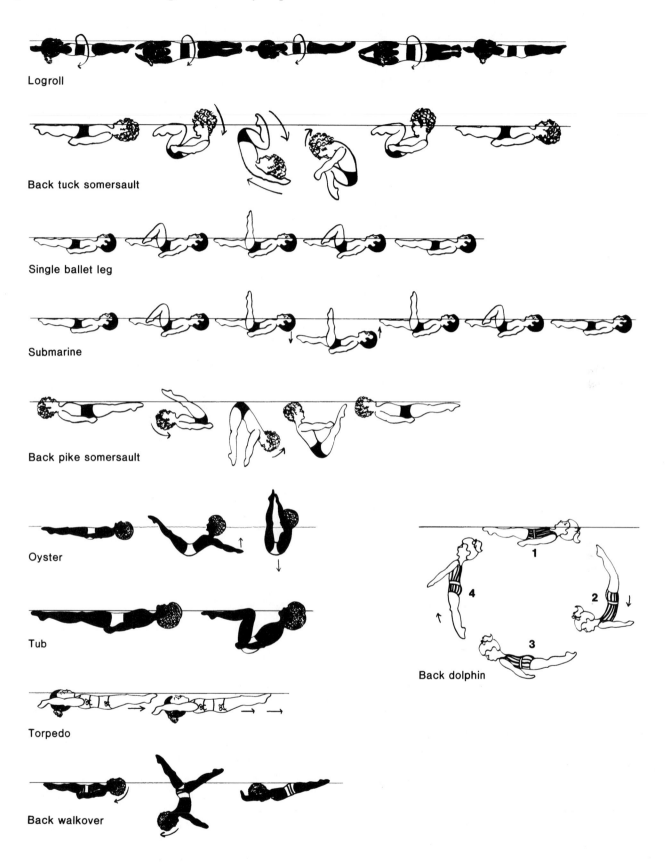

Logroll

Back tuck somersault

Single ballet leg

Submarine

Back pike somersault

Oyster

Tub

Torpedo

Back walkover

Back dolphin

Figure 17.9 Stunts that begin in a front layout position.

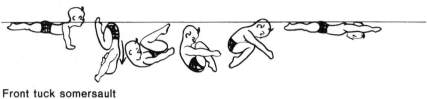

Front tuck somersault

Flying porpoise

Porpoise

Front pike somersault

Front walkover

9. **Submarine.** "While performing a single ballet leg, can you submerge the entire body up to the ankle of the perpendicular leg and then rise to the surface?"

10. **Back walkover.** "Can you start a back dolphin but do *the splits* with the legs while they are above the surface of the water? This stunt ends in a front layout."

Stunts That Begin in a Front Layout Position

1. **Front tuck somersault.** "Can you perform a forward roll in a tuck position?"

2. **Flying porpoise.** "Can you stand on the bottom, push off, and do a surface dive that looks like a flying porpoise?"

3. **Porpoise.** "Can you bend at the waist so that the trunk is almost perpendicular to the bottom, while the thighs remain parallel to the water? From this position, can you raise both legs until the entire body is vertical and then submerge?"

4. **Front pike somersault.** "Can you assume a pike position identical to the beginning of a porpoise? From this position, can you do a forward roll?"

5. **Front walkover.** "Can you assume a pike position identical to the beginning of a porpoise? As the legs come out of the water, they do *the splits* so that you finish in a back layout position.

Rolling in the Water

Methods of rolling from back to front and vice versa in the water each have names within synchronized swimming circles. Use these terms to teach children names for the stunts that they can perform, thereby improving their communication skills.

1. **Half logroll.** "Can you change from back to front float or from front to back float?"
2. **Logroll.** "Beginning from a back layout position with arms overhead, can you execute the logroll by reaching your arm across your body, by crossing one arm over the other, or by crossing one leg over the other?"
3. **Corkscrew.** "Can you logroll from a sidestroke position to prone float or to same side on which you started? If the sidestroke is on the left, a complete roll to the left is executed."
4. **Reverse corkscrew.** "If the sidestroke is on the left, can you execute a complete roll to the *right*?"
5. **Marlin.** "Can you (a) start in a *back layout* position, arms in T position, palms down; (b) roll onto right side, moving right arm to a sidestroke position and left arm to side for a *side layout* position; (c) continue roll onto a front layout position, with both arms in T position; (d) roll onto left side, moving left arm to a sidestroke position and right arm to side for a *side layout* position; and (e) finish in a *back layout* position with arms in T position?"

Stroke Technique for Swimmers With Disabilities

After mastering the beginner skills described in the previous section of this chapter, the swimmer is ready to learn specific strokes such as front crawl, back crawl, elementary backstroke, breaststroke, sidestroke, and butterfly. Optimal stroke techniques have been described and illustrated in various textbooks including Colwin (2002), Hannula and Thornton (2001), and Maglischo (2003), as well as in the instructional materials used in the learn-to-swim courses offered by organizations such as the American Red Cross, YMCA, Swim America, National Safety Council/Ellis and Associates Learn to Swim Program, and Sears I Can Swim.

Swimmers with disabilities sometimes have difficulty achieving the prescribed stroke techniques because of variations in body shapes, range of motion, and muscle function. For example, swimmers with spinal cord injuries and spina bifida often have difficulty maintaining the hips and legs in a horizontal floating position, swimmers with cerebral palsy and stroke may not be able to achieve symmetry in stroke technique across the right and left sides of the body, and swimmers who are blind may have trouble regulating head position while swimming. Teachers and coaches should focus on *principles of reducing resistance and increasing propulsion* (Costill, Maglischo, & Richardson, 1992) when modifying stroke technique to accommodate the unique abilities of persons with disabilities.

Reducing Resistance

Resistance refers to water forces that cause the swimmer to slow down. **Drag** is another word for resistance. Swimmers have some control over two factors that contribute to drag, namely cross-sectional area and velocity. **Cross-sectional area** refers to any body surface that is facing forward (even a little bit) while the individual is swimming. Swimmers can minimize cross-sectional area by using streamlined body shapes. Control of cross-sectional area is especially important at faster swimming speeds because drag increases as a function of velocity.

Reducing Form Drag

Form drag is the resistance caused by the swimmer's body shape as she or he moves through the water. A long, tapered, rounded body shape with a small cross-sectional area is best for swimming because the water flows smoothly around the body.

- **Long** *refers to the length of the body from fingertips to toes. Although swimmers have no control over the height of the body, they can stretch and extend the trunk, arms, and legs to achieve the longest body shape possible.*
- **Tapered** *means smaller and narrower at the ends than in the middle. A swimmer's body shape can be tapered by stretching the arms overhead with the hands together and by stretching the legs behind the body with the feet together. It is very important to taper the shape of the lower body when swimming by using good stroke technique such as a small, fast kick on front crawl or back crawl.*
- **Rounded** *refers to curved body shapes that allow smooth water flow around the body. For example, swimmers can create a more rounded (less angular) body shape by scrunching the shoulders toward the ears during pushoffs or by minimizing hip flexion during leg recovery when swimming breaststroke.*
- **Cross-sectional area** *refers to body width and depth. Some cross-sectional area is associated with overall body size (bigger bodies usually have more cross-sectional area), and some with stroke technique (the depth and width of the arms, legs, and trunk while swimming). A smaller cross-sectional area is better because the body disturbs fewer water molecules and causes less turbulence.*

Both cross-sectional area and form drag can be reduced in several ways, namely good streamlining, horizontal alignment, lateral alignment, shoulder/hip roll, and stroke technique. A **streamlined** body shape is long, rounded, and tapered at the ends with minimal cross-sectional area. To achieve effective streamlining, swimmers might be advised to mimic the shape of a pencil that has been sharpened at both ends. It is easy to understand the importance of streamlining during dives or pushoffs when the body is fully extended and the arms and legs are not moving; however, streamlining is equally important while actively swimming. For example, a streamlined body shape helps to reduce form drag during the glide phase of breaststroke and sidestroke. Form drag can be minimized when swimming front crawl and back crawl by assuming a streamlined position of the opposite arm and leg at the point of hand entry into the water.

A swimmer has a good **horizontal alignment** when the head, shoulders, hips, knees, and feet are all parallel to the surface of the water. In other words, the head, shoulders, hips, knees, and feet should be about the same depth under the water.

Most of the time the body should be at the water surface when swimming; however, after dives and turns, the swimmer should maintain good horizontal alignment while submerged well below the surface. To achieve good horizontal alignment, swimmers should maintain a head position that is in line with the body while swimming, minimize head movements when breathing, breathe quickly so as to minimize the amount of time the head is out of alignment, and return the head to a neutral in-line position as soon as possible after breathing. In addition, the swimmer should avoid excessive front-to-back rocking of the trunk in the short-axis strokes of breaststroke and butterfly.

A swimmer has good **lateral alignment** when she or he moves straight through the water with little or no sideways movement of the body. Likely reasons for lateral alignment problems include inefficient stroke techniques such as a wide, low arm recovery in front crawl or crossing the midline of the body with the hands at water entry. In addition, some swimmers with physical disabilities experience balance and lateral alignment problems because of limitations to range of motion, loss of muscle function, or amputation. The best antidote to problems with lateral alignment is a collaborative problem-solving approach by the swimmer and teacher.

Shoulder/hip roll helps to reduce drag when swimming the long-axis strokes of front crawl and back crawl (see Figure 17.10). Good shoulder/hip roll has several beneficial effects: (a) There will be less cross-sectional area near the surface of the water; (b) it is easier to center propulsive forces directly under the center of gravity; (c) it is easier to center arm recovery directly over the center of gravity; and (d) the large muscles of the chest and upper back will be in a better position to develop propulsive forces. Although arm and leg movements do contribute to shoulder/hip roll, good core body strength is needed to initiate a shoulder/hip roll and to achieve the lateral balance needed to roll equally to the right and left sides. Thus, swimmers should participate in "dry land" exercises to improve and maintain trunk strength. Core strength is especially important for swimmers with physical disabilities who may not have full use of arms and legs.

Form drag increases whenever the arms and legs move away from a streamlined body position. Thus, form drag is a natural consequence of swimming any of the strokes. The swimmer's task is to minimize form drag as much as possible by using the principles of streamlining, horizontal alignment, lateral alignment, and shoulder/hip roll to achieve good stroke technique. Stroke technique errors such as swimming without shoulder/hip roll, dropped hips and legs, a "short" hand entry too close to the swimmer's shoulder, hands crossing over the midline on entry, and low head position should be avoided because these errors increase resistance to forward movement.

Develop a better understanding of form drag. Use a stretch cord to pull the swimmer toward the end of the pool. The swimmer should be instructed to hold onto the end of the stretch cord with his or her hands and to streamline the body as much as possible. Repeat this experiment using different body positions, such as streamlined in a front-floating position, streamlined in a side-floating position, streamlined at the water surface, streamlined in a submerged position, and so on. Also experiment with different head positions, such as in-line

Figure 17.10 Jarrett Perry, an elite swimmer with an above-knee amputation of the left leg, demonstrates the good shoulder and hip roll that contributes to good stroke technique.

with the body, chin tilted up, or chin tilted down. Which body and head positions result in the least drag? The answers may vary somewhat across swimmers, especially for those who have physical disabilities.

Reducing Wave Drag

Wave drag is caused by turbulence at the water surface. It is more difficult to swim in "choppy" water because the waves on top and under the water push the swimmer around. One source of waves is the swimmer's movements. Poor stroke technique causes greater turbulence in the water around the swimmer's body, and in turn, more resistance to forward movement. However, with good stroke technique, the teacher or coach can observe a smooth two-wave or three-wave pattern next to the swimmer's body. These desirable wave patterns can be achieved through effective streamlining, a long body position, and good timing and coordination of arm and leg movements.

Other sources of waves include the movements of other swimmers, swimming pool or beach variables (especially the depth of the water), and weather conditions. Swimmers can avoid "choppy" turbulent water by (a) swimming in an unoccupied area of the pool to avoid the waves created by other swimmers, (b) swimming in pools with lane lines and effective gutter systems that help to dissipate waves, (c) swimming in deep water so that waves from the bottom of the pool or swimming area don't bounce back toward the swimmer, and (d) avoiding open water swimming areas on windy days when waves are most troublesome.

Reducing Friction Drag

Friction drag occurs whenever there is contact between two surfaces, such as the swimmer's body and the water, or between water and air. Friction drag refers to the force needed for water to slip past the body. The friction between the swimmer's body and the water can be reduced by wearing a swimming cap, wearing a tight-fitting swimming suit that doesn't absorb much water, and shaving parts of the body that are not covered by a swimming suit (this technique is used by competitive swimmers). It is difficult to minimize the friction between water and air because most swimming occurs at or near the water surface. Friction drag is considerably less when swimming underwater.

Increasing Propulsion

Propulsion refers to forces created by the swimmer that make the body move forward in the water. Research has shown that swimmers generate more propulsive forces when they move their hands and feet through the water at precise "angles of attack" using optimal hand and foot shapes, and when the "direction of movement" of the arms and legs conforms to optimal stroke technique patterns.

Hand Shape and Foot Shape

Swimmers generate the most propulsion when they shape or cup their hands like shallow spoons. The best **hand shape** is slightly curved with fingers together. The ideal **foot shape** depends on the stroke. Toes should be pointed, the ankles should be plantar-flexed, and the feet should be inverted when swimming front crawl, back crawl, and butterfly. In the breaststroke kick, the feet and ankles should be relaxed during recovery movements, dorsi-flexed and everted at the beginning of the propulsive phase of the kick, and gradually plantar-flexed as the legs move through the propulsive phase of the kick. A combination of these foot shapes are used in the sidestroke kick.

Angle of Attack

Angle of attack, or **hand pitch,** refers to the angle of the swimmer's hand in comparison to the direction of movement. The ideal hand pitch for propulsion is 40°, the angle of attack used in sculling motions. Efficient swimmers use effective sculling actions as part of their arm pulls, regardless of which stroke is being performed. For example, in breaststroke, the hands scull outward and then inward. When performing the front crawl, most swimmers enter the water with the hand and arm stretched out in front of the same-side shoulder, then scull them backward, inward, and upward toward the midline of the body and the hips, and then backward and outward past the hips (an "S" shaped pulling pattern). Swimmers who have mastered the 40° hand pitch and who can apply that skill when swimming the various strokes have a "feel for the water" that enables them to propel their bodies efficiently through the water.

Try this test of ability to maintain a 40° hand pitch in comparison to the surface of the water. Assume a vertical "treading water" position in the water. Using hands and arms only (no kicking), the swimmer should scull rapidly in front of and slightly lower than the shoulders. While sculling, check for a slightly curved hand shape with the fingers together. Also observe the hand pitch. The little finger should be high during the outward scull, and the thumb should be high during the inward scull. The swimmer should "turn the corner" when switching direction from the outward to inward scull (or the inward to outward scull) as quickly as possible without losing pressure against the water. If the swimmer is successful in maintaining the desired hand pitch and in generating sufficient force for propulsion, small whirlpools or eddies will form on the surface of the water above each hand. Small objects placed in the vicinity of these whirlpools will be sucked underwater. Experiment by varying the depth of the hands, the position of the hands in front of or to the side of the body, or by using one hand at a time. Efficient swimmers consistently produce strong whirlpools at the water surface regardless of these variations in arm position.

Direction of Movement

Direction of movement refers to the arm and leg positions that are used when swimming the various strokes such as front crawl, back crawl, elementary backstroke, breaststroke, sidestroke, and butterfly. For example, in the back crawl, the swimmer recovers the arm in a vertical plane directly over the body, the hand enters the water little finger first above the shoulders, the hand reaches under the water surface for the catch, and then the swimmer sculls downward, upward, and downward to complete the pull (an "S" shaped pulling pattern). Although the direction of movements is different for each of the swimming strokes, the same principles of propulsion apply.

Regardless which stroke is being performed, swimmers need to exert pressure against the water opposite the desired direction of movement. It is much easier and effective to apply pressure to still or slow-moving water in comparison to fast-moving water. By using sculling motions with changes of hand and arm direction during a single pull, the swimmer's hand can find the still or slow-moving water that is easier to pull or push. At different times during a single arm pull, the swimmer's hand may be pressing downward, upward, outward, or inward. These changes in direction help the swimmer to create more propulsive force by sculling the hands for a longer period of time across a longer distance, resulting in greater distance per stroke. Swimmers should give special attention to elbow position during the pull. When the elbow is higher in the water than the hand, the hand is in a better position to exert pressure in the proper direction. In addition, the forearm is positioned to serve as an extension of the hand in exerting pressure against the water. *Propulsion is maximized when drag is minimized.* Therefore the swimmer should do everything possible to maintain a streamlined body position, good horizontal and lateral alignment, and effective shoulder/hip roll (in the long-axis strokes).

Additional considerations for the alternating-pull, long-axis strokes of front crawl and back crawl include pulling under the center of gravity so that propulsive forces are delivered close to the body mass that must be moved, and recovering the arms over the center of gravity to minimize the effort that must be exerted during recovery and to achieve balance between the pulling and recovering arms. Rolling the shoulders/hips into a side-floating position will enable the swimmer to use both chest and back muscles to good advantage during the pull. A fast kick with rapid alternating leg movements contributes to propulsion, but the swimmer must take care to regulate the depth of the kick to avoid excessive drag.

Symmetry of arm and leg movements is an important consideration when performing the short-axis strokes of elementary backstroke, breaststroke, and butterfly. Asymmetrical movements lead to problems with lateral alignment, hence greater resistance to forward movement. When swimming the elementary backstroke or breaststroke, special attention should be given to the degree of hip and knee flexion relative to the amount of drag created. In elementary backstroke, the hips should remain in a neutral position and the knees should remain near the water surface, with only the calves and feet underwater contributing to drag. In breaststroke, hip flexion should be minimized in an effort to regulate the depth of the kick and the amount of cross-sectional area that contributes to drag.

Teaching Stroke Technique to Swimmers With Disabilities

Swimming instruction should start with an assessment of the individual's capabilities and reasons for wanting to learn swimming skills. Which swimming skills has the person already mastered? Can the swimmer assume a streamlined body shaped? Which muscle groups are functional? Does the swimmer have sufficient range of motion to perform the various swimming strokes? Does the person have any limitations to body segment lengths such as amputations or dwarfism that might affect ability to generate propulsion? Is the swimmer motivated by a desire to have fun, learn new skills, improve physical fitness, compete, socialize with friends, and so on?

Assessment results should be used to determine instructional objectives. The learn-to-swim courses offered by the American Red Cross, YMCA, Swim America, and other aquatic organizations can serve as the basis for instruction; however, *the selection and sequence of skills to be taught may require adaptation* (Gelinas & Reid, 2000). For example, some persons with hip contractures or asymmetric tonic neck reflexes that affect breathing skills may find it easier to learn back crawl before learning front crawl. Some swimmers with coordination difficulties may find it easier to learn strokes that involve symmetrical rather than alternating arm and leg movements. If the swimmer has a better hip and leg position and less drag while floating than when kicking, it may be advantageous not to kick. Similarly, it is more efficient for some swimmers with hemiplegia to swim with one arm than with both arms. Swimmers who wish to compete may be more concerned with conforming to ideal stroke technique than swimmers whose goal is to improve physical fitness.

Many persons with disabilities benefit from the use of equipment while learning the swimming strokes. Pull buoys, leg floats, kickboards, and other flotation devices allow the swimmer to isolate and practice arm and leg movements. Hand paddles and fins create extra resistance to propulsive movements and therefore help the swimmer to develop greater muscular strength and endurance. Paddles and fins have an added benefit for swimmers with neurological conditions such as cerebral palsy, stroke, and head injury by helping the swimmer to develop a better feel for the correct movements. Stretch cords can be used to provide extra resistance when swimming away from the instructor, or to facilitate increased speed and faster neuromuscular responses when the swimmer is being pulled toward the instructor. Swimmers with disabilities can also benefit from the use of stretch cords or swim bench apparatus to simulate the swimming strokes in dry land practice on the pool deck or in the weight room. This

Figure 17.11 Rudy Garcia-Tolson was the recipient of the 2002 Casey Martin Award based on advocacy and courage to pursue his sport despite his physical challenges. At age 14, he is an accomplished swimmer, runner, and triathlete.

dry land practice can be used as a warm-up activity for swimmers who do not tolerate long sessions in cool water.

Stroke techniques should be modified as needed for swimmers with a disability, using the principles of reducing resistance and increasing propulsion that were discussed earlier in this section. The observations and suggestions in Table 17.2 are based on biomechanical research involving elite swimmers with disabilities (e.g., Daly, Malone, Smith, Vanlandewijck, & Steadward, 2001; Dummer & Bare, 2001; Dummer and Heusner, 1996; Green, 1992).

These guidelines for modifying stroke technique are not sufficient. Instructors and coaches must also apply personal expertise, creativity, and common sense when teaching swimming skills to persons with disabilities. Truly effective teaching and coaching requires a focus on the individual swimmer rather than the disability, and a willingness to imagine possibilities rather than underestimate ability.

Aquatic Sports and Leisure Activities

Persons with disabilities participate in the full spectrum of aquatic activities (see Figure 17.11). Their motives are the same as reasons given by other participants in aquatic sports and leisure activities. The most important reason is fun. Other reasons

Table 17.2   Adaptations of stroke techniques for swimmers with disabilities.

Swimmers with spinal cord injury, spina bifida, polio, and other lower limb impairments

Common Problems	Possible Solutions
Limited muscle function in the hands results in difficulty maintaining an optimal hand shape and hand pitch.	If possible, strengthen the muscles of the forearm, wrist, and hand. Emphasize high-elbow arm positions that allow the forearm to act as an extension of the hand during pulling movements.
Compromised arm and trunk strength and mobility contribute to inadequate shoulder/hip roll, a truncated arm pull characterized by a short deep catch and a short weak finish, a wide straight pulling pattern often with dropped elbows, a wide arm recovery, and early breathing.	If possible, strengthen the core trunk muscles that are used to develop shoulder/hip roll. When teaching the arm strokes, emphasize sculling movements across the longest distance possible with hands moving under the center of gravity. Encourage the swimmer to breathe as late as possible, preferably at the end of the underwater pull.
Limited leg function results in little or no propulsive force from kicking movements and form drag related to low hip and leg positions. Many swimmers with low hips and legs also breathe too early in the stroke, causing further problems with horizontal alignment.	If possible, strengthen the core abdominal and lower back muscles that help to hold the hips and legs in a horizontal position at the water surface. Encourage kicking if the swimmer has usable muscle function in the legs. Experiment with a deeper head position. Use a pull buoy or leg floats (not allowed in competition). Note that hip contractures can help the swimmer to hold the hips and legs at the surface when swimming on the back.
Contractures and other limitations to range of motion may prevent an effective streamlined position and therefore contribute to increased form drag.	Use range of motion exercises, relaxation exercises, and physical therapy interventions to minimize contractures. Anecdotal evidence from swimmers with disabilities suggests that imagery can be used effectively to help minimize contractures.

Swimmers with cerebral palsy, stroke, and head injury

Common Problems	Possible Solutions
Unwanted movements such as persistent postural reflexes (Chapter 10), spastic muscle tone, or ataxic movements contribute to poor stroke technique. Typical problems include limited shoulder/hip roll, asymmetries in arm and leg movements, a truncated arm pull with a short entry and short finish, and difficult breathing in the front crawl stroke.	Use resistance training such as hand paddles, stretch cords, and fins to help the swimmer develop a better feel for desired movements. Extensive repetition of desired movements with resistance can help the swimmer to develop neuromuscular control.
Spasticity in the arms and hands causes difficulty maintaining an optimal hand shape, achieving a 40° hand pitch, and performing sculling movements.	Use relaxation exercises and imagery to help minimize unwanted muscle flexion. Emphasize high-elbow arm positions that allow the forearm to act as an extension of the hand during pulling movements.
Contractures and other limitations to range of motion may prevent an effective streamlined body position and therefore contribute to increased form drag.	Use range of motion exercises, relaxation and imagery exercises, and physical therapy interventions to minimize contractures.
Swimmers with hemiplegia are likely to have asymmetries in stroke technique that affect horizontal and lateral alignment, as well as propulsion.	When the swimmer's movements cause more drag than propulsion, it might be preferable to swim with one arm or kick with one leg. The unused limb should be maintained in as streamlined a position as possible.

Table 17.2 Continued.

Swimmers with cerebral palsy, stroke, and head injury

Common Problems	Possible Solutions
Swimmers with diplegia have limited use of the legs, resulting in little or no propulsive force from kicking movements and form drag related to low hip and leg positions. Many swimmers with low hips and legs also breathe too early in the stroke, causing further problems with horizontal alignment.	If possible, strengthen the core abdominal and lower back muscles that help to hold the hips and legs in a horizontal position at the water surface. Encourage kicking if the swimmer has usable muscle function in the legs. Experiment with a deeper head position. Use a pull buoy or leg floats (not allowed in competition). When leg function is severely compromised, experiment to determine whether it is better to swim without kicking.

Swimmers with amputations

Common Problems	Possible Solutions
Arm and leg amputations can contribute to problems with balance and shoulder/hip roll, causing increased drag as well as difficulty generating uninterrupted propulsion.	Strengthen the core trunk muscles that are used to develop shoulder/hip roll. Swim against stretch cords to identify gaps in propulsion and use principles of biomechanics to determine solutions.
Single-leg amputations can affect the swimmer's ability to achieve a tapered body position while swimming.	The kick should be centered behind the body rather than the same-side hip. When swimming front crawl or back crawl, the swimmer should experiment with a 4-beat kick, kicking twice to the right side and then twice to the left side.
Double-leg amputations frequently lead to poor horizontal alignment, with a low hip position.	Experiment with a deeper head position.

Swimmers with dwarfism

Common Problems	Possible Solutions
The swimmer experiences greater form drag in part because of short stature (increased ratio of cross-sectional area to height), and in part because of short arm length (inability to achieve a tapered, streamlined shape with the upper body).	With the exception of children who still are growing, usually height cannot be modified. If the swimmer's arms are long enough, reduce cross-sectional area by stretching the arms overhead with the hands together.
Ability to develop propulsive forces is negatively affected by short arms and legs. As a result, the swimmer has poor distance per stroke.	Continue to encourage maximum distance per stroke by working on the swimmer's stroke technique, but also increase stroke rate (most dwarf competitive swimmers use considerably faster stroke rates than other swimmers).
Because of short arm length, dwarf swimmers typically need greater shoulder/hip roll than other swimmers in order to achieve a pull under the center of gravity. Without adequate shoulder/hip roll, stroke technique often is characterized by a short catch, wide pulling pattern, short finish, and wide straight arm recovery, as well as problems with lateral alignment.	Strengthen the core trunk muscles that are used to develop shoulder/hip roll. When teaching the arm strokes, emphasize sculling movements across the longest distance possible with hands moving under the center of gravity.
Some swimmers with dwarfism have limited range of motion in the elbow joint, which contributes to limited propulsion from the arms, as well as mild contractures of the hip joint that affect the ability to achieve a streamlined body position.	Deficiencies in elbow range of motion usually are caused by anatomical differences in the skeletal system; hence, exercises will be ineffective to remediate the problem. However, efforts to stretch and strengthen the muscles of the hip girdle can help to minimize contractures at that joint.

Table 17.2   Continued.

Swimmers with les autres conditions

Common Problems	Possible Solutions
Contractures and other limitations to range of motion may prevent an effective streamlined body position, and therefore contribute to increased form drag.	Use range of motion exercises, relaxation and imagery exercises, and physical therapy interventions to minimize contractures.
Compromised muscle function leads to less ability to generate propulsive forces with the arms and legs.	Emphasize correct stroke technique that makes use of the largest muscle groups. Use principles of biomechanics to determine arm and leg positions that offer the best mechanical advantage for the swimmer.

Swimmers with vision loss

Common Problems	Possible Solutions
Inability to use visual references to determine proper head position when swimming can lead to problems with horizontal and vertical alignment. Swimmers who are blind frequently swim with the head too high or too low, or they fail to return the head to a neutral position after breathing.	Use orientation and mobility techniques to communicate and teach proper head position. Move the swimmer's head through the desired movements when teaching stroke techniques.
Lack of ability to see demonstrations, videotapes, etc., leads to inefficient stroke technique.	Use rich verbal descriptions during demonstrations and videotapes. Move the swimmer's body through the desired movements when teaching stroke techniques.
Some swimmers are reluctant to move the hands and arms away from the torso of the body, leading to problems with stroke technique, especially limited propulsion.	Use resistance training such as hand paddles, stretch cords, and fins to help the swimmer experiment with the strength and propulsion that can be generated using different hand and arm positions. Teach arm strokes on a swim bench where the instructor can manipulate arm position.
Stroke technique often deteriorates as the swimmer approaches the end of the pool because of fear of hitting the wall with the body.	Teach the swimmer to use stroke counts to estimate the length of the pool. Use tappers, sprinklers hanging from the backstroke flags near the end of the pool, or other methods of notifying the swimmer that the end of the pool is near.

Swimmers with hearing loss

Common Problems	Possible Solutions
Stroke technique problems typically are associated with communication differences rather than the person's physical capabilities.	Use written instructions, gestures, and sign language in addition to verbal directions. Use frequent demonstrations and ask the swimmer to repeat the desired motions to ensure understanding of correct techniques.

Swimmers with cognitive disabilities

Common Problems	Possible Solutions
Stroke technique problems typically are related to poor cognitive skills rather than the person's physical capabilities.	Give extra attention to principles of motor learning, especially when introducing new skills. Use simple one-part and two-part directions, introduce new skills gradually, and review instructions frequently.

Figure 17.12 Family members often provide swimming instruction to their children with disabilities. Here, father and daughter have dwarfism.

Table 17.3 Aquatic Sports and Leisure Activities.

Participation Motive	Aquatic Sports and Leisure Activities
Fun	Any aquatic sport or leisure activity
Skill development	Learn-to-swim lessons, water safety courses, aquatic therapy
Fitness and health	Fitness/lap swimming, water aerobics, competitive swimming, open water swimming, triathlon
Competition, excitement, and challenge	Competitive swimming, open water swimming, triathlon, diving, scuba diving, synchronized swimming, water polo, sailing, rowing, canoeing, kayaking
Socialization	Any aquatic sport or leisure activity

identified by researchers include skill development, fitness and health, competition, and socialization (Gould, Feltz, & Weiss, 1985; Seefeldt, Ewing, & Walk, 1992). Table 17.3 suggests aquatic sports and leisure activities that address common participation motives.

Skill Development

Learning swimming skills can be fun, and the mastery of swimming techniques enables participation in other enjoyable aquatic activities. Some persons with disabilities learn to swim in programs offered by community recreation agencies, schools, or health clubs; others are taught by family members or friends (see Figure 17.12); and some are self-taught. In addition to basic swimming skills, persons with disabilities seek instruction in

safety courses such as lifeguarding and water safety instruction. Some become instructors, coaches, and swimming officials. Opportunities should be provided for persons with disabilities to advance as far in the sport as their capabilities allow.

Aquatic therapy offers an opportunity for a different type of skill development. In aquatic physical therapy, emphasis is placed on improved circulation, muscular strength and endurance, range of motion, balance, and coordination, rather than swimming techniques. Muscle relaxation is facilitated by conducting sessions in warm water. Because the body is supported by water, there is less stress on the weight-bearing joints; therefore, aquatic physical therapy often is preferred to typical clinical-based therapy. Many individuals who do not require physical therapy benefit from water exercise programs that are based on aquatic therapy principles (Sova, 1999, 2000).

Competitive Swimming

Many options are available to persons with disabilities who wish to become involved in competitive swimming. Some variables to consider are inclusive versus disability-specific programs (see Figure 17.13), the continuum of recreational to elite programs, and swimming pool and open water settings.

Swimmers who choose inclusive programs typically enjoy easy access to coaches with expert knowledge of the sport, good facilities, frequent nearby competitions, and support and friendship from teammates (Dummer, 2001; Dummer & Bare, 2001). Inclusive competitive swimming programs are conducted by USA Swimming, U.S. Masters Swimming, YMCA, community recreation agencies, public school systems, universities, and the counterpart organizations and educational agencies in other nations. Some of these programs are designed for children, adolescents, and young adults (e.g., USA Swimming, Swim

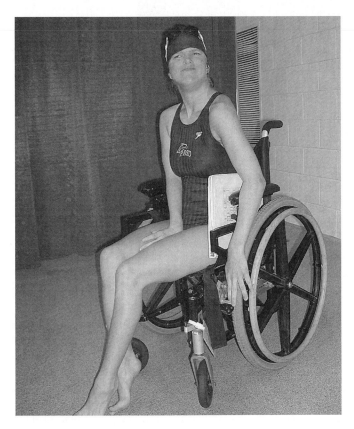

Figure 17.13 Jennifer Johnson competes in "regular" USA Swimming meets and in functional class S1 events in Paralympic international level competitions. She received the 2002 Disabled Athlete of the Year Award from USA Swimming. Jennifer has severe athetoid cerebral palsy.

Canada), but opportunities also are available for adults aged 19 through 100+ years (e.g., U.S. Masters Swimming, Masters Swimming Canada). Of course, interscholastic and intercollegiate programs are available only to students in those institutions. In most inclusive programs, swimmers with disabilities practice and compete together with able-bodied teammates; however, some of these organizations also offer disability-specific events such as the annual USA Swimming Disability Championship and the National Championships for Swimmers with a Disability in Canada.

Swimmers who opt for disability-specific programs generally benefit from coaches with good knowledge of disability, accessible facilities, and teammates who share the disability culture (Dummer, 2001). Swimming programs for recreational through elite athletes are conducted by organizations such as Disabled Sports USA, Dwarf Athlete Association of America, National Disability Sports Alliance, Special Olympics International, USA Deaf Sports Federation, U.S. Association of Blind Athletes, Wheelchair Sports USA, and the counterpart organizations in other nations. At the international level, disability swimming is governed by the International Paralympic Committee (IPC) (swimmers with physical, vision, and cognitive dis-

abilities) and the Comité Internationale des Sports des Sourds (CISS) (Deaf swimmers). The IPC conducts the quadrennial Paralympic Games, as well as the IPC World Swimming Championships, while CISS conducts the Deaflympics and the World Swimming Championships for the Deaf. Swimmers in IPC-sanctioned events are classified for competition according to their abilities in the sport (Dummer, 1999).

In many communities, opportunities exist for both recreational and elite competitive swimmers. Recreational or summer league programs frequently are offered by community recreation departments. In addition, USA Swimming, the YMCA, and the disability sport organizations typically offer entry-level programs for novice swimmers. Elite swimmers who are training for international competitions such as the Paralympic Games, Deaflympics, and Olympic Games usually affiliate with USA Swimming programs.

Swimmers who prefer practicing and competing in open water can also choose open water or triathlon events conducted in lakes, rivers, and oceans. Participation by athletes with disabilities in triathlon events has become so popular that the International Triathlon Union has instituted categories for athletes with a disability in their world championship program. The fact that the IPC is considering the addition of triathlon as a Paralympic Games event provides further evidence of the popularity of this sport. In **disability triathlon events,** wheelchair users compete in swimming, hand-cycling, and wheelchair road racing; amputees compete in swimming, cycling, and running, using prostheses for cycling and running stages; and persons who are blind compete in swimming, tandem cycling, and running with assistance from a handler. Popular established events in the United States include the Atlantic City Ocean Swim and the San Diego Triathlon Challenge.

Other Aquatic Activities

Mastery of swimming skills enables participation in other aquatic sports such as synchronized swimming, diving, water polo, and scuba diving (Green & Miles, 1987; Jankowski, 1995; Robinson, 1986), as well as boating opportunities such as sailing, rowing, and canoe/kayak. Currently water polo is an official sport of the Deaflympics and sailing is an official sport of the Paralympic Games. However, participation by persons with disabilities is increasing in all of these aquatic sports and leisure activities.

Safety

Responsible swimming teachers and coaches are safety conscious. They maintain current certification, knowledge, and skills in first aid, CPR, AED (automatic external defibrillator), and water safety. They are familiar with the facility emergency action plan, and they routinely practice evacuation procedures for swimmers, staff, and spectators, including persons with disabilities. They conduct regular safety inspections of the facility for hazards such as pool chemical imbalances, slippery or rough surfaces, and broken equipment. They check the availability of adequate first aid supplies. They provide adequate supervision of swimmers in both pool and locker room settings. They teach safety skills (such as the ability to assume a back float position

Figure 17.14 Flotation devices can help children to acquire swimming skills but should never be used as a substitute for close supervision.

and yell for help) and safety rules (such as walking on the pool deck and the role of the lifeguard) commensurate with the swimmer's ability to comprehend. They make sure that participants have mastered prerequisite skills before attempting more difficult skills. All of these safety practices pertain equally to persons with and without disabilities.

Teachers and coaches have an additional responsibility with respect to preventing injury to swimmers with disabilities, namely to exercise proper precautions related to disability-related health concerns (American Red Cross, 1996, 1997). For example:

• *Diving should be prohibited for swimmers with atlantoaxial instability (some persons with Down syndrome and some persons with dwarfism), brittle bones, shunts, or hemophilia.*
• *Fitness activities should be adapted for swimmers who have lower-than-normal maximum heart rates or who have trouble regulating body temperature. Fitness activities should also be adapted for persons who use mobility equipment such as wheelchairs, crutches, and walkers because overuse injuries are likely to have a negative impact on all activities of daily living.*
• *Swimmers who lack sensation in the lower extremities should be encouraged to wear pool shoes to prevent injury to the feet.*
• *Wheelchair transfers should be conducted carefully to avoid injury to the swimmer, as well as to the lifters.*
• *Persons who are susceptible to respiratory infections, such as children with Down syndrome, should be taught to dry the hair and skin carefully after swimming.*

The easiest way to learn about such health-related concerns is to ask the swimmer or parents/guardians. Chapter 10 and Chapters 18 through 28 in this textbook also provide useful information for swimming teachers and coaches.

One safety concern that has received considerable attention is the use of **personal flotation devices** (PFDs) such as water wings, foam noodles, life vests, inflatable swim suits, inner tubes, and head/body floats (see Figure 17.14). Many experts recommend the use of PFDs to allow swimmers with disabilities to stay afloat while learning to perform arm, leg, and breathing movements, but only when the swimmer is carefully supervised (Grosse, 1987). PFDs should never take the place of a one-to-one or small teaching ratio for nonswimmers and beginning swimmers.

Finally, teachers and coaches must be concerned about their own personal safety and liability. Situations in which teachers and coaches have inadequate physical strength, swimming skills, or knowledge to handle a swimmer are unsafe, in part because of risk to the teacher or coach, and in part because of inability to protect the safety of the swimmer. Teacher/student ratios should be manageable given the instructor's qualifications and facility characteristics, and certified lifeguards should be employed where necessary or required by state or local laws.

Disability Accommodations

The Americans with Disabilities Act (ADA) requires places of exercise to provide commonsense, reasonable accommodations for persons with disabilities that enable participation and promote full and equal enjoyment of activities. Table 17.4 provides websites for exploring possible accommodations. Both facility

Table 17.4   Websites.

Learn-to-Swim	
American Red Cross	www.redcross.org/services/hss/aquatics
YMCA	www.ymcaswimminganddiving.org
Swim America	www.swimamerica.org/default.asp
National Safety Council/Jeff Ellis and Associates	www.jellis.com
I Can Swim	www.searsicanswim.com/
Aquatic Therapy	
Aquatic Therapy and Rehabilitation Institute	www.atri.org
Water Aerobics	
Aquatic Exercise Association	www.aeawave.com
Competitive Swimming and Open Water Swimming	
International Paralympic Committee (swimming)	www.paralympic.org
La Federation Internationale de Natation	www.fina.org
USA Swimming	www.usa-swimming.org
U.S. Masters Swimming	www.usms.org
Swimming Natation Canada	www.swimming.ca
Triathlons	
International Triathlon Union	www.triathlon.org
USA Triathlon	www.usatriathlon.org
Triathlon Canada	www.triathloncanada.org
Other Aquatic Sports	
U.S. Diving	www.usdiving.org
USA Synchronized Swimming	www.synchro.org
USA Water Polo	www.usawaterpolo.com
Boating Sports	
International Paralympic Committee (sailing)	www.paralympic.org
International Federation of Disabled Sailing	www.ifds.org
USA Rowing	www.usrowing.org
USA Canoe & Kayak	www.usacanoekayak.org

and programming accommodations are needed to achieve this goal (American Red Cross, 1992; Dummer & Bare, 2001).

Facility Accommodations

Safety. Many facility directors fear that safety is a bigger concern for persons with a disability than for other participants; however, this is rarely the case. With a few commonsense precautions, most safety risks can be minimized or eliminated. One of the most important safety practices is an **emergency action plan** that includes adequate emergency signals and evacuation plans for swimmers, staff, and spectators who have disabilities. Visual emergency signals are needed by persons with hearing loss, and auditory signals are needed by persons with vision loss. Evacuation plans should specify assistance for persons with vision, cognitive, and physical disabilities. Wheelchair users may need alternate exit routes or help in negotiating stairs.

A safe pool for persons with disabilities (and other swimmers) has a nonskid, uncluttered deck. A slippery pool deck is especially hazardous for swimmers who use mobility equipment such as crutches, canes, and walkers. Many slips and falls can be prevented by keeping the pool deck as clean and dry as possible and by allowing the use of personal assistants. A cluttered pool deck impairs travel for swimmers who are blind and for those who use wheelchairs and other mobility equipment. The pool staff should keep traffic areas clear of obstacles to prevent accidents. Personal equipment such as wheelchairs, prostheses, or other mobility equipment can pose a hazard to people on the pool deck and should be moved to a safe location while the swimmer is in the water. Swimming pool and instructional equipment should be properly stored when not in use.

Sharp or rough surfaces should be avoided. *A mat at the edge of the pool helps prevent injuries to wheelchair users and other swimmers with physical disabilities when they transfer in and out of the pool.* Towels on rough-surfaced starting blocks help prevent skin injuries for swimmers who dive from kneeling or sitting positions. Sharp-edged lane lines may be an unavoidable problem for swimmers who are blind, causing cuts, scrapes, and bruises. Broken tile and equipment should be replaced or repaired.

The pool depth should be clearly marked for all users. Examples of effective safety practices include the use of a painted or tiled line on the bottom of the pool to mark the transition from standing-depth to deep water, a line of floating buoys to mark the boundary between shallow and deep water, and depth markings on the sides of the pool. Another possibility is a horizontal line on the wall that is the same height as the depth of the water, allowing swimmers to judge the pool depth by comparing their heights with the line on the wall. Swimmers who are blind may benefit from Braille depth markings and the use of a sound source such as a radio or metronome at the shallow end of the pool.

Access. Reasonable accommodations also facilitate access to the swimming pool. Wheelchair users and other swimmers with physical disabilities benefit from wide easy-to-open doors, hydraulic or battery-operated lifts from the pool deck to the water (see Figure 17.15), and steps or ramps into the water; however, most can manage with help from another person and a mat on the pool deck to facilitate transfers. Swimmers who are blind may require an orientation to the facility as well as Braille markings indicating the facility layout.

Water temperature. Desirable water temperature depends on the activity. Swimmers engaged in vigorous activity typically prefer water temperatures ranging from 78°F to 82°F (26°C to 28°C). Warmer temperatures ranging from 82°F to 90°F (28°C to 32°C) are preferred for beginning swimmers, less active swimmers, and participants in aquatic therapy programs. Warmer water temperatures help to maintain body heat and promote relaxation, whereas colder water tends to produce hypertonus and to heighten the spasticity of swimmers with cerebral palsy.

Locker rooms. Locker rooms should be designed or retrofitted to provide a changing area for wheelchair users, including a changing bench and wheelchair-level locker access. Grab bars should be provided in at least one toilet stall and at least one shower stall for use by persons with disabilities (and elderly persons) who may experience balance difficulties. *Covered waste receptacles should be provided in toilet stalls for used catheter supplies, and a hook should be placed on the stall wall or door from which to hang catheter apparatus.* The maximum temperature for showers and sinks should be set to prevent inadvertent scalding. Shower chairs or benches are useful for many persons with physical disabilities. Handheld shower heads or low-level shower controls permit operation by wheelchair users and dwarf swimmers (and children). Sturdy step stools help dwarf swimmers reach high-level shower controls and other appliances in the locker room. When new locker rooms are constructed, consideration should be given to family or companion changing rooms that provide greater privacy for persons with physical disabilities and that permit persons of the opposite gender to assist with personal care tasks.

Programming Accommodations

Eligible to participate. According to the ADA, places of exercise must accommodate **qualified individuals** with **reasonable**

Figure 17.15 **State-of-the-art pool lifts are easy to use. Amanda is lowering her sister Samantha into the water using a battery-operated lift.**

accommodations. A qualified individual is a person who satisfies stated criteria for participation in the program. Examples of such criteria include age limits for infant-toddler lessons or ability to swim 500 yards continuously as a prerequisite for an advanced swimming class. The criteria must be the same for all participants, with no discrimination against persons with disabilities. Though it certainly is permissible to conduct disability-specific programs, persons with disabilities cannot be restricted to those programs, nor can they be systematically excluded from activities designed for the general population.

Nevertheless, some criteria may contraindicate swimming for some individuals. These include infectious diseases with an elevated temperature, uncontrolled epilepsy, uncontrolled incontinence, chronic ear infections (and the months during which tubes are in the ears), chronic sinusitis, allergies to chlorine or water, skin conditions such as eczema and ringworm, and open wounds or sores. Persons who fail health screenings such as the PAR-Q inventory (Howley & Franks, 1997) are denied participation in some programs. Alternatively, they might be directed to an aquatic therapy program pending advice from their personal physicians.

Decisions are often more difficult to achieve when swimmers present health conditions such as seizures, lack of sensitivity to touch or pain, brittle bones, lower maximum heart

rate, or temperature regulation problems that place them at increased risk for accidents or injuries while participating in swimming programs. A meeting should be held to discuss the demands of the activity, safety risks, and methods of minimizing the risks so that the swimmer and family members can make an informed decision about enrolling in the program and so that the teacher or coach is aware of commonsense accommodations that promote safety.

Curriculum. In some cases it may be necessary to adapt the goals, objectives, and activities of a swimming program to accommodate a person with a disability. For example, a wheelchair user in an intermediate swimming class might be expected to perform the arm strokes correctly, but not the kicking movements. Similarly, target heart rates might be modified for a person with Down syndrome in a fitness swimming course. Such modifications should be made in consultation with the swimmer after observing or assessing swimming skills. *As a rule of thumb, the fewer modifications the better.* Inclusion is facilitated when the objectives for persons with a disability match the objectives for other swimmers as much as possible. In addition, it is important to the personal independence and self-concept of the person with a disability to perform swimming skills in the same manner as other swimmers.

Instruction and Communication. Instructors should use effective communication methods for swimmers with a disability. Commonsense adaptations include facing a Deaf swimmer when giving instructions to facilitate lip-reading, using rich verbal descriptions and "hands-on" demonstrations to communicate stroke technique to blind swimmers, and using simple vocabulary and demonstrations when teaching persons with cognitive disabilities. Additional suggestions are offered in

Chapters 18 through 28 of this text. Of course, instructors should provide adequate supervision of swimmers at all times, make appropriate use of instructional equipment, and consider the use of teaching assistants.

Fun. Persons with disabilities are guaranteed opportunities for **full and equal enjoyment** under the ADA (see Figure 17.16). In other words, swimmers with disabilities should have access to the same opportunities as the general population, including various levels of swimming instruction, fitness swimming, competitive swimming, open water swimming, and boating sports. Their full and equal enjoyment—namely fun!—in these activities is dependent upon a safe environment, mastery of swimming skills, and participation with friends and family members.

OPTIONAL ACTIVITIES

1. Interview participants with disabilities in adapted aquatics programs. Ask about the enablers of participation, as well as barriers to participation. Inquire about benefits and outcomes.

2. Observe instruction in adapted aquatics or delivery of aquatic therapy services. Write a short reaction paper on ways in which skills and instruction can be adapted to the needs of participants with disabilities.

3. Attend a swimming meet where athletes with disabilities are competing or precompetition practices. Videotape, if possible. Using photocopies of good stroke technique that you have obtained from swimming textbooks, sketch problems that you observe among swimmers with disabilities. Consider their ability to maintain good streamlining, horizontal alignment, lateral alignment, and shoulder/hip roll, as well as their abilities to achieve correct hand and foot shapes, angles of attack, and directions of movement. What stroke technique advice do you have for the swimmers with disabilities whom you observed?

4. Use the World Wide Web to find news reports about the accomplishments of persons with disabilities in swimming, triathlon, or other sports competitions. Compare their performances to elite athletes who do not have disabilities. Also consider the trends in performance improvements over the past decade.

5. Develop a portfolio of equipment and facility adaptations that can enhance adapted aquatics programs. Take photographs of existing facilities. Also consult sports equipment catalogs and textbooks. Annotate the photographs, photocopies, and illustrations that you collect with remarks about features that contribute to the safety of participants with disabilities.

PART

III

Individual Differences, With Emphasis on Sport

CHAPTER

18

Infants, Toddlers, and Young Children

Figure 18.1 The individualized family service plan (IFSP) goal of crawling to a desired toy is implemented for a motorically delayed 2-year-old infant with Down syndrome. The cold, slick mirror provides tactile stimulation to the bare skin, as well as visual input. The infant's primary locomotor pattern will continue to be belly crawling and/or a bunny-hop movement until he loses the symmetrical tonic neck reflex. Then the IFSP goal will be changed to creeping.

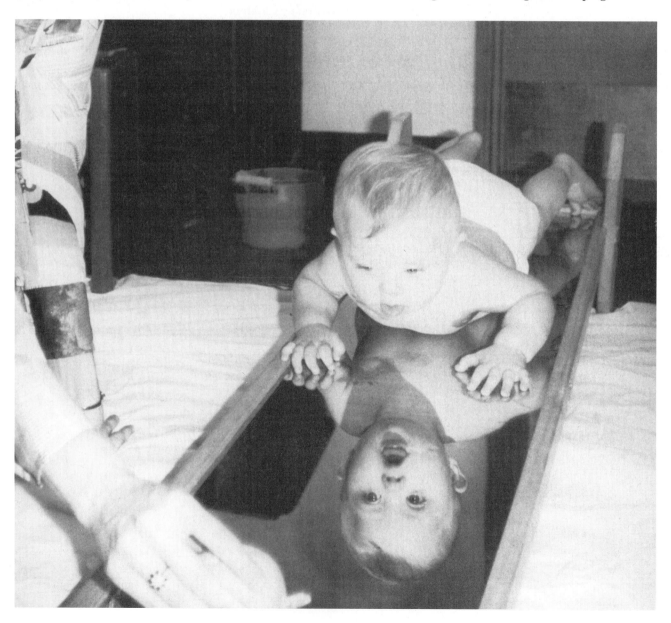

1. Think about infants, toddlers, and young children (ages 3 through 8 years) you have known who seemed delayed or disabled in movement and game skills. Write brief case studies to share with classmates. Case studies should provoke discussion about possible interventions.

2. What are similarities and differences between the IFSP and the IEP? Why are some parts different?

3. Discuss assessment and programming, and describe ways to involve family members. What components in the psychomotor domain should be assessed? Why?

4. List developmental milestones in the accomplishment of various movement tasks and describe some specific activities for different chronological and mental ages. Be sure to include music and chanting in your critical thinking (see Figure 18.1).

5. Identify principles of infant motor development, and give examples of how these principles can be used in explaining behavior and guiding practices.

Early intervention is so important to the future of people with disabilities that federal law makes available educational services from birth onward. This fact was emphasized in Chapter 3 with case studies of home-school-community teamwork. This chapter targets two groups as defined in IDEA: (a) **infants and toddlers,** defined as individuals from birth through age 2, and (b) **early childhood,** defined as individuals aged 3 through 8.

Three Diagnostic Approaches

Eligibility for services is determined by an *individualized family service plan* (IFSP) for infants and toddlers and by an *individualized education program* (IEP) for young children. However, IDEA 1997 mandated that, with special permission, young children could continue services under the IFSP. Approaches vary, depending on the philosophy of IFSP and IEP teams.

Disabled is the term used to describe children who fit into established diagnostic categories (e.g., speech and language impaired, learning disabled, mentally retarded). About 75% of young children with diagnosed disabilities fall into the speech and language impaired category. IDEA 1997 stated that children did not have to be assigned disability categories until age 9. Many school districts are embracing the option of identifying children as having *developmental delays* until age 9.

With developmental delays (not the same as *developmentally delayed* in DD legislation of 2000 (see Glossary) is an approach that permits states to establish their own criteria as to what constitutes performance significantly below average. IDEA indicates that developmental delays can occur in five areas: (a) cognitive, (b) physical, (c) language and speech, (d) psychosocial or emotional, and (e) self-help skills. Statistical criteria are usually established for diagnosis—for example, (a) functions at 75% or less of his or her chronological age in two or more areas, (b) scores at least 1.5 standard deviations below the mean, or (c) scores below the 30th percentile. Two or more tests, with good validity and reliability, are used to make a diagnosis. Other diagnostic procedures include documented, systematic observation by a qualified professional, parental reports, developmental checklists, and criterion-referenced instruments.

At risk for developmental delays refers to infants and toddlers who have been exposed to adverse prenatal, perinatal, or postnatal factors that are likely to cause clearly identifiable delays before age 3. Among the many factors contributing to risk are disadvantaged socioeconomic environments, prematurity and low birth weight, difficult or traumatic delivery, maternal age of under 15 or over 40, a family history of genetic disorders and/or problem pregnancies, and mothers with substance abuse or chronic health problems (Cratty, 1990; Hamilton et al., 1999; Tarr & Pyfer, 1996).

Many of these factors lead to multiple disabilities. Alcohol, for example, now recognized as the leading cause of birth defects in the United States, results in a condition called fetal alcohol syndrome (FAS), which is a combination of mental retardation, ADHD, motor incoordination, and other problems. Crack or cocaine babies manifest a similar profile, although Leitschuh and Dunn (2001) reported that motor coordination problems may not persist beyond age 3. These and several other conditions are discussed in Chapter 21 on mental retardation. The term *developmental delays* is, however, a more accurate descriptor of multiple disability conditions than any one category. Figure 18.2 depicts illustrative children with developmental delays.

The Individualized Family Service Plan (IFSP)

The individualized family service plan (IFSP) is used with infants and toddlers in place of an individualized education program (IEP). IDEA 1997 states that parents and educators can extend the IFSP, by mutual agreement, beyond age 3. The IFSP includes eight parts:

1. The child's present level of performance in the five functional areas of development

2. A statement of the family's resources, priorities, and concerns relating to enhancing the child's development

3. A statement of the major outcomes to be achieved and the criteria, procedures, and time lines used to determine the degree to which progress is being made and whether modifications or revisions are necessary

4. A statement of specific early intervention services necessary to meet the unique needs of the child and his or her family, including frequency, intensity, and method of delivery

Figure 18.2 How would you assess the needs of each of these children?

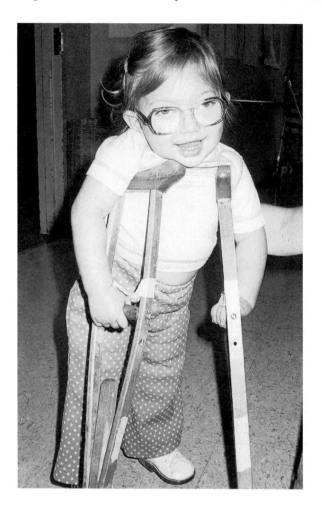

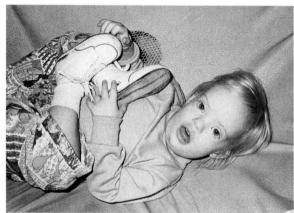

5. A statement of the natural environments in which early intervention services shall be provided, including a justification of the extent, if any, to which the services will *not* be provided in a natural environment (i.e., the child's home or day care)

6. The projected dates for initiation of services and the anticipated duration of the services

7. The identification of the service coordinator from the profession most immediately relevant to the child's or the family's needs who will be responsible for the implementation of the plan and coordination with other agencies and persons

8. The steps to be taken to support the transition of the toddler with a disability to preschool or other appropriate services (IDEA, 1997).

This written plan is based on family/professional collaboration. Services can be delivered anywhere, including the home. Service delivery personnel work with families as well as infants and toddlers. This has implications for increased emphasis on home-based programs of adapted physical activity that are developed and monitored by professionals (Sayers et al., 2002).

The Individualized Education Program (IEP)

The IEP, for children aged 3 or older, contains six components that can be remembered by the acronym *PAST-DE*.

P Performance, present level

A Annual goals, including short-term objectives

S Services to be provided, including special education, related services, and supplementary aids and services

T Transition services

D Dates and duration

E Evaluation to determine whether objectives are achieved

In addition to these components, IDEA now requires that

1. the statement of present level of performance include the ways in which the disability affects child's involvement and progression in the GE curriculum (or for preschool, in activities that would be appropriate);

2. annual goals be measurable;

3. goals and objectives help the student to be involved in and progress in the GE curriculum, as well as meet other educational needs that result from the disability;

4. services shall include program modifications that allow students to be involved in and progress in the GE curriculum and to participate in extracurricular and other nonacademic activities; and

5. a description be included of any modifications in state- or districtwide assessments of student achievement that are needed for the student to participate. If the team determines that the student will not participate in such an assessment (or part of an assessment), a statement must be included of why that assessment is not appropriate for the student and how the student will be assessed (Council for Exceptional Children, 1999).

Family involvement is important in all aspects of writing and implementing the IEP. New assessment approaches involve family members (Losardo & Notari-Syverson, 2001), and specification of services in both the IEP and the IFSP usually includes a home component and parent training.

Obtain a free catalog via www.brookespublishing.com and see the many assessment instruments that involve parents. Especially check the Infant-Toddler and Family Instrument (Apfel & Provence, 2001); the Ages and Stages Questionnaires (ASQ) revised by Bricker and associates (1999); and Bricker's (2002) Assessment, Evaluation, and Programming System (AEPS), which includes separate volumes for ages 0–3 and 3–6, and the AEPS family report (64 pages).

Assessment Concerns

Assessment in the psychomotor domain is influenced by parents' concerns. These often pertain to developmental milestones and an estimation of the number of months of delay (see Figure 18.3). Many standardized instruments are available (Cowden & Torrey, 1995; Zittel, 1994), but Sherrill recommends the use of checklists and videotapes in a play-oriented, natural setting (see Chapter 6 on assessment). Three checklists in Chapter 11 present developmentally sequenced teaching/testing progressions that are particularly helpful:

Table 11.3—Walk and run skills

Table 11.7—Jumping and hopping tasks

Table 11.8—Object control skills

These checklists, however, should not be used in a formal manner with the child asked to do a particular skill and then evaluated. *Instead, observe informal play in many settings* (both land and water), both alone and with other children of various ages. Give priority to skills that are needed for everyday success. This includes social play skills, self-concept, and self-confidence as well as motor skills. Encourage parents to help with assessment procedures.

Figure 18.3 Developmental milestones in achieving normal walking gait. Note correct terminology for *crawl* (on belly) versus *creep* (on hands and knees). Ages given are *average* time of appearance.

Use of the Test of Gross Motor Development-2 (TGMD-2, Ulrich, 2000), described fully in Chapter 11, allows teachers to identify specific skill components that need work (Zittel & McCubbin, 1996). One approach to improving skills in decision making about assessment is to study protocols used in research. The July 1996 issue of *Adapted Physical Activity Quarterly,* edited by Lauriece Zittel, is devoted to delays of infants, toddlers, and young children.

If the infant, toddler, or child cannot perform age-appropriate motor milestones, then the professional must ask why. Typically there are multiple reasons, and *the ecological approach to testing demands that three factors be analyzed: the task demands, the individual's functional ability, and the environment.* The task demands and the environment should be systematically altered until success is achieved. For example, locomotion should be attempted on many different surfaces and inclines, with different kinds of models, motivation, and reinforcers.

Figure 18.4 At about 6 months of age, an infant is no longer dominated by flexor tone. Note ability to reach with one arm, while the other arm remains motionless. Arms and legs can fully extend.

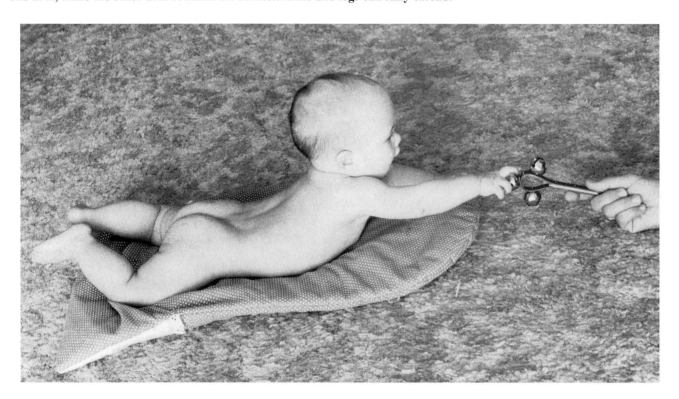

Reflexes and Postural Reactions

Cerebral palsy is a factor in so many developmental delay conditions that teachers should understand reflexes and postural reactions. **Reflexes** are involuntary changes in muscle tone elicited by certain stimuli or conditions. These changes range from barely noticeable, subtle shifts in muscle tension to undesired movements of body parts (see Chapter 10 on sensorimotor integration directed specifically toward management of reflexes). **Reactions** are automatic movement patterns that replace reflexes in accordance with an inborn timetable and environmental opportunities. Most reactions are lifelong and act to protect the body and/or help it maintain equilibrium.

Newborn infants have no motor control because every position change elicits reflexes. When in prone position, they are in a flexed fetal posture referred to as *flexor tone dominance* because the anterior surface muscles contract in response to the tactile stimuli from the surface. Movement to a supine position causes the extensor muscles on the posterior surface to automatically contract. This is called *extensor tone dominance.* Any movement of the head likewise causes associated movements of other body parts. Until infants are 3 or 4 months of age, they seldom initiate voluntary, purposeful movement (see Figure 18.4).

As the central nervous system (CNS) matures, with or without intervention, automatic reactions and voluntary spontaneous movement patterns emerge to override reflex control of muscle tone. This process is analogous to layering; it is continuous and lifelong. The more a specific voluntary act is practiced, the more the reflex activity that could have interfered is layered over or suppressed.

When the CNS is damaged (as in cerebral palsy, stroke, and traumatic brain damage), delays often occur in the integration of reflexes and the emergence of postural reactions and voluntary movement. In such cases, goals and objectives may focus on sensorimotor training.

Hypotonia

Hypotonia is insufficient muscle tone, a manifestation of muscle weakness that is present in many infants, toddlers, and young children with disabilities. In particular, hypotonia is associated with Down syndrome and may be the major reason that these children are delayed in acquiring locomotor skills. Infant activity programs that utilize treadmills (Ulrich et al., 2001) and ankle weights (Sayers, Cowden, Newton, Warren, & Eason, 1996) have been effective in helping to overcome hypotonia and related problems.

Activity-Deficit Problems

Amount of activity and opportunities for activity should be assessed through interviews with family members and other caretakers. Most individuals with severe disabilities spend more time lying or sitting than peers do, and this inactivity causes many problems. *Attention to proper positioning and providing a stimulating environment may increase self-initiated movement, so assessment should include questions about where and how the individual is placed during waking hours, how many stimuli are present, and whether positioning enhances movement.* For example, rolling, crawling, and creeping are easier on a hard surface than on a soft surface like a mattress. Large mirrors provide feedback. The presence of other children and/or family pets provides models and increases incentive to move.

Body Image Concerns

Body image should be assessed also. **Body image** is all of the feelings, attitudes, beliefs, and knowledge that a person has about his or her body and its capacity for movement. These include psychomotor, affective, and cognitive understandings that begin in infancy. Development of body image is fundamental to shaping a good self-concept, especially in early childhood, when most feelings about the global self stem from movement and language experiences.

Body image development in early childhood is synonymous with sensorimotor development. Table 18.1 shows that different terms are applied to body image constructs at different ages. Body image objectives are (a) to develop body awareness, (b) to develop pride in the body and self-confidence in using it, and (c) to develop self-initiative in moving in new and different ways. Nondisabled children often achieve these objectives without help, but in adapted physical education, these objectives are major challenges. Progress toward these objectives should be assessed.

Body schema is the diagram of the body that evolves in the brain in response to sensorimotor input. The body schema enables the infant to feel body boundaries, identify body parts, plan and execute movements, and know where the body is in space. Figure 18.5 depicts an adult brain, showing developed potential. The motor projection areas of the brain are topographically organized, with each part controlling specific muscles that, in turn, control body movement. At birth, this capacity to control movement is not yet developed. Remember the motor development principle of general-to-specific activity (i.e., generalized mass activity is replaced by specific responses of individual body parts). Each movement of the body or its parts by the infant or another provides sensorimotor input (kinesthetic, vestibular) to the brain, which causes the body schema to evolve.

Sensory input from the skin, muscles, and joints (touch, pressure, temperature, pain) also contributes to the early development of body schema. Figure 18.6 shows that the body schema develops in a *cephalocaudal (head-to-tail) direction,* with the infant first becoming aware of eating/drinking and then of seeing. Later, the infant gains control of the head/neck muscles (turning the head from side to side, lifting the head), then the shoulder and arm muscles for reaching, then the hand/finger muscles (grasping, holding toys), and finally the muscles of the lower extremities. Figure 18.6 shows also that a disproportionately large cortical area is devoted to muscle groups responsible for fine muscle control, such as that required for lips and fingers.

Body schema continues to develop and change throughout the lifespan. As the child matures, cognitive and affective dimensions are added to the psychomotor parameters. If problems occur, the body schema is affected, motor planning is damaged, and faulty movements occur. Figures 18.6 and 18.7 show body image milestones to be assessed from ages 4 weeks to 36

Table 18.1 Terms used in different stages of body image development.

Developmental Stage	Body Image Construct
Sensorimotor (0 to 2 years)	Body schema
Preoperational (2 to 7 years)	Body awareness
	Self-awareness
Concrete operational (7 to 11 years)	Body image
	Self-concept

Figure 18.5 Areas of the brain related to bodily movement.

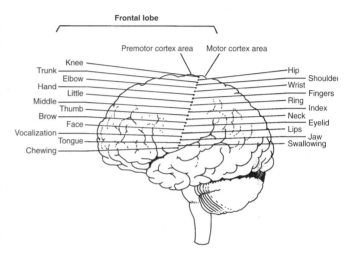

Lateral view of the adult brain, showing premotor and motor cortex strips on the frontal lobe.

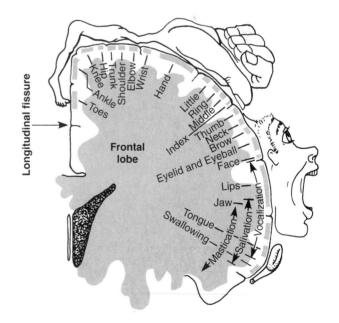

Specialized areas of the brain that evolve in response to sensorimotor input. Voluntary movements are controlled in the same area of the motor strip in all human beings.

months. Many of these milestones can be considered play and game skills.

During the sensorimotor period (ages 0 to 2), children learn to imitate facial expressions, limb movements, and body positions. Visual input is the most important sense modality in imitation, since seeing others motivates the child to locomotion. Needing or wanting an object (food/toy) within the visual field is another reinforcer of imitation. These facts help explain why sensorimotor development is delayed in children who are congenitally blind.

Motor planning (praxis) also emerges during the sensorimotor period as cognition develops and the child wants to manipulate objects/toys and to move from place to place. Early voluntary movement can leave the child feeling competent and loved or clumsy, scorned, and pitied. Thus, body image components in the affective domain begin to interweave with those in the psychomotor domain.

Figure 18.6 **First milestones in the development of body image. Average ages are given.**

4 weeks
or
1 month

Sensorimotor input from movement by another.
Lifting head is first voluntary movement.

16 weeks
or
4 months

First awareness of hands. Can voluntarily bring hands to midline.
Rolls over, providing sensorimotor input regarding total body in space.

28 weeks
or
7 months

First interest in mirror play and awareness of face.
First awareness of feet.

40 weeks
or
10 months

Laterality is reinforced when balance is maintained in sitting, creeping.
Imitation of movements begins, usually with bye-bye and shaking head yes and no.

Figure 18.7 **Later milestones in development of body image. Average ages are given.**

1 year
or
12 months

Sensorimotor input from walking and changing positions from up to down.
Competence feeling from casting balls/objects that others must retrieve.
Feelings about body as good/bad from toilet training.

1½ years
or
18 months

Understands and can say "Up," "Down" (first movement concepts).
Is learning names of body parts.
Increased competence from hurling balls/objects.
Retrieves balls for self.

2 years
or
24 months

Has about 300 words in vocabulary.
Can name body parts of doll.
Understands on-off concepts, then in-out, turn around.
Beginning imitative play with dolls, projects feeling about self into doll play.

3 years
or
36 months

Understands over-under, front-back, big-little, short-tall/long, high-low.
Copies circles, crosses on paper, but cannot yet draw a person.
Balances on one foot.
Rides tricycle.

Table 18.2   Principles of motor development that apply to most children.

1. **Dynamic systems.** Movement is the product of many systems and subsystems that are constantly interacting and changing. When one system is delayed or injured, other systems are affected.
2. **Reflex integration and reaction emergence.** An inborn timetable is followed, whereby reflexes are suppressed and righting, protective extension, and equilibrium reactions emerge. These developments, in conjunction with environmental opportunities, enable voluntary movement patterns to unfold and coordination and control to be acquired.
3. **General-to-specific activity.** Generalized mass activity is replaced by specific responses of individual body parts. The child learns to assemble the parts of a general pattern before altering the parts to meet specific environmental demands.
4. **Cephalocaudal direction.** Gross motor development begins with head control (strength in neck muscles) and proceeds downward.
5. **Proximodistal coordination.** Muscle groups near (*proximo-*) midline become functional before those farther away (distal) from midline do. For example, a child learns to catch with shoulders, upper arms, and forearms before catching with fingers. Movements performed at midline (in front of body) are easier than those that entail crossing midline (to left or right of body—i.e., more distant from midline).
6. **Bilateral-to-crosslateral motor coordination.** *Bilateral* movement patterns (both limbs moving simultaneously, as in arm movements of the breaststroke or reaching for an object at midline) are the first to occur in the human infant, followed by *unilateral* movement patterns (right arm and right leg moving simultaneously or vice versa), followed by *crosslateral* patterns (right arm and left leg moving simultaneously).
7. **Mastery or effectance motivation.** The drive to explore, master, and control the environment is *innate;* thus motor development is affected by challenges in the environment and individual capabilities in meeting challenges.

Note. Any principle may need to be adapted when congenital or acquired movement limitations alter capacity or ability.

Language Development

Language development affects learning to move and concurrent development of body image and self-concept. Assessment should cover words related to the body and movement.

From birth until 2 years of age, children normally acquire a speaking vocabulary of about 300 words. Among these are names of common body parts, like hands, feet, face, tummy, nose, eyes, ears, and mouth. Self-awareness develops in a definite order: hands, feet, face, and trunk. The emergence of language for body parts and movements reinforces the growing understanding and appreciation of the body.

In the preoperational stage, speech develops rapidly (from 300 words at age 2 to several thousand words at age 7) and gradually takes precedence over movement as a means of expression. During this time span, children also begin to perceive themselves as competent and lovable, or the opposite. The way they look and move has much to do with such perceptions (see Figure 18.7).

Self-Concept

Pictorial instruments for assessment of various aspects of self-concept are recommended for ages 4 through 7 (see Chapter 8). Interviews are useful also in determining how children feel about their competence in locomotor and object control skills and their ability to play games with specific others. The richness of interview data is enhanced by showing children photographs and videotapes of themselves in game play with others.

Principles of Motor Development

Principles of motor development help explain function in young children and thus serve as guides to assessment and programming (see Table 18.2). Disabilities and delays, of course, affect function, and professionals should pay particular attention to movement that seems to violate basic principles.

The principle of *dynamic systems* is a relatively new principle, adopted from dynamic systems theory (Smith & Thelen, 1993; Ulrich & Ulrich, 1995). *This principle is included as acknowledgment that all systems (e.g., skeletal, muscular, nervous, metabolic) affect motor development, are interactive, and tend to promote self-initiating and self-organizing movement behaviors.*

The principle of *reflex integration and reaction emergence* emphasizes *that reflexes and reactions are the foundation of early movement coordination and control.* One reason for balance problems is failure of the equilibrium reactions to fully function. Problems with coordination and control stem partly from inability to move a specific body part without undesired associated shifts of muscle tone in other parts; this occurs because reflexes have not been sufficiently integrated. Likewise, smooth, reciprocal contraction and relaxation of muscles is determined by reflex mechanisms.

The principle of *general-to-specific activity,* also called *differentiation,* explains reflex integration and motor control. The newborn responds to stimuli with generalized mass activity. With CNS maturation, with or without intervention, children are progressively able to move specific body parts without associated overflow movement. This principle explains why early childhood physical education stresses movement exploration and imitation of total body actions (e.g., animal walks, rolls, jumps) rather than activities that require specific body parts to be used in accordance with visual and auditory input. This supports *whole-part-whole pedagogy.* General or whole body challenges are the focus until reasonable control of body parts is achieved.

The principle of *cephalocaudal direction* explains why emphasis is placed on head control in intervention. The infant achieves control of head (*cephalus*) before control of the lower spine (generalized to *caudo,* meaning "tail"). This principle is violated by persons dominated by reflexes who learn to sit, crawl, and creep but cannot hold the head erect and motionless.

The principle of *proximodistal coordination* explains the emphasis on midline activities. The nervous system matures from the midline (spinal column) outward. Thus, muscles closer (*proximo-*) to the midline have mature innervation before those farther (distal) from midline. Muscles moving the head, neck, scapula, and trunk become coordinated to permit sitting, crawling, creeping, and standing before muscles of the arms and legs become coordinated enough for throwing, catching, and kicking. Likewise, large muscles of the shoulders and hips become coordinated before the small muscles of the hands and feet that move the digits.

The principle of *bilateral-to-crosslateral motor coordination* provides insight into developmentally appropriate exercises and games for infants and toddlers with vision. **Bilateral movements** are arms or legs simultaneously reaching, spreading, or closing. At about 4 months of age, when voluntary movement control begins, infants bring both hands to midline and begin looking intently at them. This seems to be the beginning of awareness of body parts and cognition that parts can do something. Shortly thereafter, infants in supine or propped sitting positions reach and grasp with both hands. They also learn to hold the bottle with both hands.

By age 6 or 7 months, infants can succeed in purposeful **unilateral movements,** usually the reaching of one arm to grasp a toy. Some children with disabilities, however, cannot perform unilateral movements without undesired overflow activity in the opposite limb. Games like waving bye-bye are often used to assess early unilateral development. Imitations of single arm or leg movements are used as remediation for children who appear to be frozen at the bilateral level.

From 7 or 8 months of age onward, infants should be able to use either unilateral or bilateral movements, depending on task demands. Toddlers and young children should not be corrected when they throw with the right arm while the right foot steps forward or while the feet remain stationary. This immature movement pattern typically fades as motivation to *throw hard* increases.

Crosslateral movements are those in which the limbs work in opposition (e.g., the left leg moves forward with the right arm). These evolve naturally in walking patterns but are typically not exhibited in throwing and kicking patterns until age 5 or 6. Many adults who are clumsy still do not consistently use opposition. Crosslateral coordination is essential to good balance, and the emphasis on balancing activities in early childhood is partly to support neural maturation that will lead naturally to opposition (see Figure 18.8).

The principle of *mastery or effectance motivation,* first espoused by White (1959), recognizes the innate urge to move, play, and explore the environment. Infants, toddlers, and children typically are active in shaping and changing their environment. Thus, *motor development is not a passive phenomenon but instead reflects complex, continuous interactions among the indi-*

Figure 18.8   This heavily braced child is using the Pedalo, an apparatus from Sporttime that facilitates development of dynamic balance that will lead to crosslateral patterns.

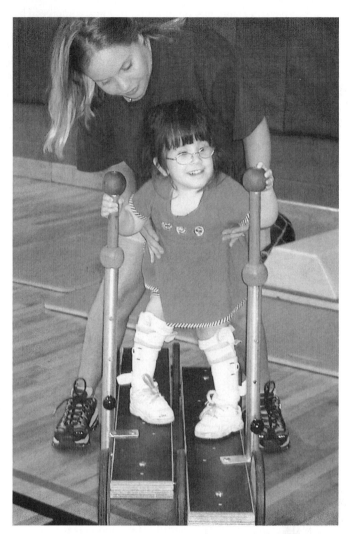

vidual, the environment, and the task demands. Naturally, disability affects innate urges, changing the resources available for moving, exploring, and problem solving. Concurrently, adults tend to overprotect children with disabilities and to limit their opportunities for self-initiated learning. The principle of mastery or effectance motivation reminds adults to maximize opportunities for movement exploration and to encourage self-initiated activity.

Uniform sequence, often referred to as *orderly progression,* is no longer recognized as a principle in this textbook. *Deviance from uniform sequence has been reported in too much research (e.g., deJong 1990; Ulrich et al., 2001) for uniform genetically-determined sequence to be accepted as a fundamental truth that guides adapted physical activity practice.* Numerous intervention studies show that instruction and other person-environmental interactions can instill behaviors without progression through traditional developmental progressions. Developmental progressions, however, are still included in assessment instruments and offer insight into which tasks are easier than others for most persons.

Services and Programming

The trend is toward home-based services for infants and toddlers with delays/disabilities in inclusive classrooms and play settings (Guralnick, 2001). When children cannot safely or successfully participate in an inclusive environment without assistance, several options are possible. Typically, an aide is provided to assist the general educator in meeting the child's special needs, and/or a consultant or resource teacher helps with environmental and instructional adaptations. Sometimes, a pull-out arrangement is used in which the child leaves the general classroom for a few hours each week for special tutoring and/or therapy. Every attempt is made to keep children in inclusive settings so that they can be afforded the same socializing and learning experiences as nondisabled peers.

Instruction and Intervention Approaches

Several sources on methods and materials for teaching motor and play skills to young children with disabilities appeared in the late 1970s and early 1980s (e.g., Sherrill, 1979; Watkinson & Wall, 1982) and remain sound. Janet Wessel, with Lauriece Zittel, updated and expanded her work with a book called *Smart Start: Preschool Movement Curriculum Designed for Children of All Abilities* (Wessel & Zittel, 1995). The PREP play program (Watkinson & Wall, 1982), used widely in Canada, is described in Chapter 21. These early works all emphasized holistic, integrated approaches, play, creativity, and concurrent attention to language development. Following are descriptions of approaches developed specifically for early childhood.

Language-Arts-Movement Programming (LAMP)

The language-arts-movement programming (LAMP) model evolved from several years of federal funding in the creative arts area to Texas Woman's University and the National Committee on Arts for the Handicapped in Washington, DC (now VSA). Ideas were tested in several schools and results were published as qualitative research (Eddy, 1982; Sherrill & McBride, 1984). Additionally, a book described many instructional techniques (Sherrill, 1979).

The acronym *LAMP* is intended to conjure up the vision of Aladdin's lamp and the magic of wishes that can come true (i.e., all children can learn when teachers believe in themselves and creatively use all of their resources). In this model, arts (creative drama and dance, music, storytelling, puppets, painting, drawing, and constructing) are the medium for unifying movement and language, and vice versa (see Figure 18.9).

Language, in this model, is operationally defined as speaking, singing, chanting, or signing. It may come from the teacher only, the teacher and child in unison, or the child only. Language is used to express the intent to move and/or to plan and rehearse a desired movement sequence, to describe movement as it occurs, and to praise once the action is completed. The combining of language and movement to teach concepts and develop schemas is powerful because the whole child is involved in active learning. The use of **self-talk** (verbal rehearsal) is a sound pedagogical device. Learning words/labels for what they are doing enhances recall. Self-talk also facilitates time-on-task because it keeps attention focused on the movement goal.

Figure 18.9 Pounding movements are the first object control skills developed. They are easily integrated into running and language activities.

A useful strategy is to create action songs or chants to familiar tunes like "Mulberry Bush," "Farmer in the Dell," and "Looby Loo" or nursery rhyme rhythms. The words must teach the name of the movement, associated body parts, or concepts about space, time, and effort (i.e., be relevant to the action). For example, beam walking on a low, wide beam might inspire a "Row, Row, Row Your Boat" chant like this:

Walk, walk, walk your feet
Gently down the beam
Merrily, merrily, merrily, merrily
It is fun to walk a beam!

Or a simple repetitive chant like this:

I am walking, I am walking
You walk, too, You walk, too
Walk, Walk, Walk; Walk, Walk, Walk
And Stop, Freeze . . . Quiet, shh . . .

Young children with disabilities/delays need more repetition than peers without disabilities. For repetition to provide the needed reinforcement, however, the child must be paying attention and receiving the kind of teacher input (eye contact, smiles, praise, pats) that makes him or her feel competent and good about self. Question and answer chants in unison with movement help to achieve this goal:

Teacher: "Can you kick? Can you kick?"
Child: "I can kick. I can kick."
Teacher: "What did you kick? What did you kick?"
Child: "A ball. I kicked a ball."
Teacher: "Good, now go get the ball. Bring it here."

The same words are used over and over so that children develop vocabulary and improve memory for sequences. Rhythmically synchronous background music can also help young children remember movement sequences (Staum, 1988).

LAMP begins with much structure in that the goal is to simultaneously teach motor skills, language, and play concepts so that the child, in turn, develops the capacity for solitary play. When he or she begins interacting spontaneously with the environment (objects, playground apparatus, or people) in appropriate ways, this initiative is praised and reinforced. Emphasis then is on helping the child progress from solitary to parallel to interactive/cooperative play. Young children need language (both receptive and expressive) to engage in cooperative play and to benefit from small-group movement and game instruction. The LAMP model promotes integrated motor-language-cognitive development.

Activity-Based Intervention (ABI)

Activity-based intervention (ABI) is an approach for children from birth to age 5 that emphasizes that IFSP and IEP goals should be implemented as part of activities of daily living rather than taught as isolated school subjects (Bricker & Woods-Cripe, 1998). ABI, first published in 1992, was one of the first early childhood curriculums to promote naturalistic learning. Block and Davis (1996) apply ABI to adapted physical education instruction. Among the points emphasized are the following:

1. Analyze the child's activities of daily living (ADL) and select movement and social play skills needed for success in ADL. Such skills are *functional* and *generalizable.*

2. Establish activity centers in home and school environments with a wide variety of toys, equipment, and apparatuses that will motivate the child to engage in activities that facilitate achievement of specific goals (i.e., create environments in which IFSP/IEP goals are *embedded in activities* that children choose).

3. Emphasize child-initiated activities. Let the child choose the order of rotation from one activity center to another, and support her or his choice of specific activities. Participate in activities with individual children by imitating, mirroring, or paralleling their movements and sounds. Let the child lead!

4. Systematically use logically occurring antecedents and consequences to guide the child toward targeted goals. **Antecedents** include smiles, body language, questions, comments, imitations, and other actions that serve as prompts. **Consequences** include reinforcers that make the child feel good about movement exploration.

♿ *Watch the 14-minute VHS videocassette on ABI for practical examples of how ABI can turn everyday events into opportunities to promote learning. The video is available through Brookes (see Appendix E.4).*

Transdisciplinary Play-Based Intervention (TPBI)

Transdisciplinary play-based assessment (TPBA) and transdisciplinary play-based intervention (TPBI), designed for children between infancy and 6 years of age and tested in the Denver public schools, are explained in books (Linder, 1993a, 1993b) and videotapes. Four areas of development are targeted: (a) cognitive, (b) social-emotional, (c) communication and language, and (d) sensorimotor. The material on sensorimotor development was written by occupational therapists and encompasses

much of the content presented in Chapter 10 of this book (e.g., normalizing muscle tone, facilitating reactivity to sensory input, encouraging the emergence of equilibrium reactions and voluntary movement).

The major value of TPBA and TPBI lies in their philosophy of transdisciplinary cooperation among professionals, their involvement of family members, and their highlighting of play as the major medium for early childhood learning. According to Linder (1993b, p. 27), "Through play, the child acquires, practices, and adapts skills in all developmental areas."

Assessment

The TPBA is conducted in a creative play environment that includes materials and equipment that will facilitate demonstration of the full range of the child's behaviors. Although the entire team is involved in observation and subsequent data analysis, only one team member (called the play facilitator) interacts with the child. As in ABI, the child is allowed to lead the play and the facilitator imitates, models, and expands on the child's actions. After 20 to 25 minutes of this unstructured facilitation, the role of the facilitator changes slightly to entice the child to try new toys, materials, and activities.

Child–child interaction and parent/caretaker–child interaction are assessed also in both unstructured and structured facilitation. The child can be a familiar peer but should be of the same sex and have slightly higher functioning ability than the child being assessed.

The TPBA ends with 10 to 20 minutes of motor play and a snack, both of which yield additional data for full information about the child's abilities. Altogether, a total of 60 to 90 minutes are required for the TPBA.

Intervention

The philosophy of TPBI is "child-centered, family-focused, peer-oriented, culturally and developmentally relevant, and based on pleasurable play interactions" (Linder, 1993b, p. 13). TPBI is similar to ABI, in that play centers are used and children are allowed to select activities. Parents and teachers follow the child's lead and encourage self-initiated activity (see Figure 18.10). Gradually the child is helped to understand the concept of taking turns leading. The emphasis is on adults' creating environments and supplying materials that motivate children to explore and problem-solve. This approach is very similar to that used in movement exploration, creative dance, and dance therapy.

♿ *Obtain the two videotapes on TPBI assessment from your library or Brookes Publishing (see Appendix E.4). Try some of the ideas in the book and videotapes, share with others, and critique.*

Sensorimotor Integration

Chapter 10 fully discusses sensorimotor integration. New approaches, designed specifically for infants and toddlers, include progressive interactive facilitation and dynamical systems treadmill intervention (see Figure 18.11).

Figure 18.10 Dr. Lauriece Zittel, coauthor of Smart Start, encourages a child-initiated activity.

Progressive Interactive Facilitation

The progressive interactive facilitation approach, proposed by Cowden et al. (1998), encompasses content presented in Chapter 10 of this text and many occupational therapy textbooks (e.g., tactile-kinesthetic-vestibular stimulation, normalization of muscle tone, correct positioning, and supervised practice of activities to enhance stability and mobility). Cowden, however, refines and extends this content and adds a pediatric strength component that utilizes ankle weights and individualized resistance training. The use of this approach with infants with Down syndrome, aged 18 to 38 months, contributes to the acquisition and refinement of independent upright locomotion (Sayers et al., 1996; Sayers et al., 2002).

Dynamical Systems Treadmill Intervention

Dale and Beverly Ulrich (Ulrich et al., 2001) have completed considerable research showing that infants with Down syndrome, when supported on a motorized treadmill, can perform alternate-foot stepping patterns. Their findings indicate that muscle strength and postural stability training contribute to independent locomotion. Many factors other than neurological maturation contribute to improved motor function. These findings can be used to challenge several motor development principles.

Motor Skills and Patterns

Most, but not all, children with delays/disabilities have motor skill problems. Typically, patterns like sitting, crawling, creeping, standing, and walking emerge later than is average.

Chapter 11 on motor performance presents easy-to-hard sequences for teaching locomotor and ball-handling skills to children ages 1 to 8. The pedagogy described in Chapter 11 applies to toddlers and early childhood.

Figure 18.11 *(A)* Dr. Jo Cowden applies pediatric strength intervention. *(B)* Dr. Dale Ulrich works with an infant on a treadmill.

A.

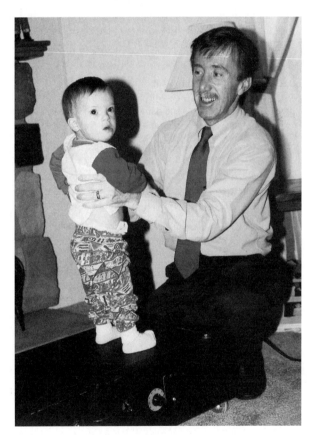

B.

Object control and toy play is an important learning objective. Children with developmental delays need instruction and practice with many kinds of objects before ball-handling skills are introduced.

Table 18.3 depicts levels in learning to manipulate play objects. Toy play is largely dependent on evolution of voluntary grip (about 5 months) and voluntary release (about 12 months); these abilities are often impaired in children with CP and others slow to integrate reflexes. Toy play is also dependent on visual integrity. Children who are blind are usually delayed in developing

Table 18.3   Developmental levels in toy or object play.

Level	Activity	Level	Activity
1	**Repetitive manual manipulation.** Usually an up-and-down shaking movement of rattles and other noisemakers. May be an autistic behavior. All repetitive movements of this nature are described as *stereotypic behaviors.*	7	**Personalized toy play.** Occurs first as imitation, usually in conjunction with toy dishes, dolls, and stuffed animals. Pretending to feed a toy or rocking it to sleep are early play behaviors. Riding a broomstick horse or using wheel-toys to get from place to place is another example. Child can respond, with gesture, to question, "What is this toy for?" These activities usually begin **between ages 1 and 2 years.**
2	**Oral contacts.** Mouthing of objects. Also considered stereotypic behaviors.	8	**Manipulation of movable toy parts.** This includes all the commercial toys (dolls and trucks, for example) with parts that can be turned, pushed, or pulled without coming apart. This manipulation is purposeful, often combined with dramatic play. Also includes doorknobs, zippers, Velcro fasteners, horns, and bells. These skills appear **between ages 1.5 and 2.5 years.**
3	**Pounding.** Developmentally, the first purposeful play movement to appear. It cannot occur until voluntary, one-handed grasp appears, usually at about **5 months of age,** and child can sit upright with support so that at least one hand is free.	9	**Separation of toy parts.** This includes putting puzzles (large parts) together and taking them apart, dressing and undressing dolls, connecting and disconnecting cars of a train, building towers with blocks, and pinning tail on donkey and body parts on drawing of a person. These skills emerge **between ages 2 and 3 years.**
4	**Striking, raking a stationary object.** Most children enjoy raking food pellets or other objects off of a table surface at **about 7 months of age.** An *ulnar* (toward ulna and little finger) *raking* movement generally occurs before the more mature *radial* (toward radius and thumb) *movement.* With older students who are severely disabled (especially those with cerebral palsy), striking is easier than throwing.	10	**Combinational uses of toys.** This refers to dramatic play like tea parties, doctor/nurse, cowboys in which toys, costumes, and props are used in various combinations. **Well developed by ages 3 to 4 years,** at which time fine motor activities (drawing, printing, coloring, cutting) begin to interest many children.
5	**Pulling or pushing.** This includes pulling toys by strings and pushing toys on wheels. In most children, it occurs **at about 10 months of age** after evolution of pincer grasp (i.e., use of thumb and index finger). In older students with severe disabilities, pushing skills include box hockey and shuffleboard-type games in which a stick is used to push the object. Rolling balls back and forth to a partner is classified as a pushing activity.	11	**Cards and table games.** These activities involve fine motor coordinations (i.e., moving checkers from place to place, handling dice, holding cards). These skills become functional **at about age 5.**
6	**Throwing.** The first two levels are called casting and hurling (see Chapter 11). *Casting* and *hurling* are often done from a sitting position. This skill cannot evolve until the child can voluntarily *release* objects—a motor milestone that occurs **at about 12 months of age.**	12	**Active ball play.** Children are typically socialized into various kinds of ball games by **age 7 or 8 years.**

object manipulation skills. Throwing a ball is not as motivational for children who cannot see as for those reinforced by visual input.

Table 18.3 is recommended as a checklist for assessing what infants, toddlers, and young children do with objects. It can help determine amount of delay and guide program planning. Assessment should be conducted in both free-play and imitation settings. Often, children with disabilities learn to imitate before they show initiative in free play.

If a child shows no interest and/or ability in manipulating objects, the developmental sequence in Table 18.3 may be useful in writing lesson plans. Starting with up-and-down movements, like shaking a balloon tied to the wrist or a rhythm instrument (try sewing tiny bells into gloves), may be easiest. Pounding movements, as in using a drum or hammer, come early in the developmental sequence. Children should be taught to tap the bat on home base, release the bat, and run before batting is

introduced. Remember: *All children can learn if professionals use appropriate task analyses based on an awareness of which activities are the easiest to learn.*

Perceptual-Motor Learning

Chapter 12 offers ideas for teaching children who need special help in mastering motor skills and patterns. The perceptual-motor approach is more play oriented than skill oriented. Many different environments are used for increasing the child's understanding of her or his body and what it can do (see Figure 18.12).

Self-Concept

The early years are a critical period in the formation of self-concept (Wright, 1983). By ages 4 to 5 years, feelings about the self can be measured in four domains—cognitive competence, physical competence, peer acceptance, and maternal acceptance

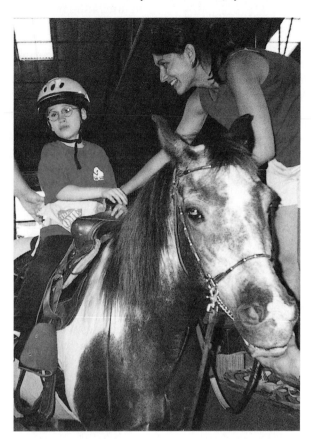

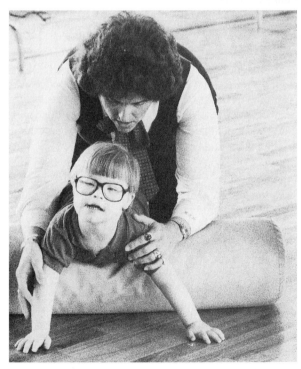

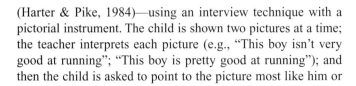

(Harter & Pike, 1984)—using an interview technique with a pictorial instrument. The child is shown two pictures at a time; the teacher interprets each picture (e.g., "This boy isn't very good at running"; "This boy is pretty good at running"); and then the child is asked to point to the picture most like him or

her. This and other assessment approaches show that preschoolers have begun to form definite concepts about both their acceptance and competence.

Children with orthopedic disabilities become gradually aware that they are different and/or have a disability between the ages of 3 and 7 (Dunn, McCartan, & Fuqua, 1988; Wright, 1983). However, even when aware that arms or legs are different, they tend to deny difficulty in running or problems in doing things that others do (Teplin, Howard, & O'Connor, 1981). Most children do not begin to compare themselves with others until ages 7 or 8. Self-evaluation of physical appearance and abilities thus is strongly rooted in what persons tell them. *Much research is needed on how young children with disabilities perceive themselves, what shapes their beliefs, and what influences their behaviors.*

Growing awareness of self as a person with differences, disabilities, or limitations should not be left to chance, which is often both traumatic and cruel. *Parents should begin providing general information to young children about their disability at age 3 or 4* (Dunn et al., 1988; Wright, 1983). Typically, children ask questions that initiate discussions or become involved in interactions with siblings or peers that require mediation. Responses should be matter-of-fact and stress assets rather than comparisons.

Wright (1983, p. 240) offers examples of good and bad answers to the question: "Do you think I'll ever be able to walk like everyone else?"

> *Good:* "Probably not, but you are learning to walk better, and that is good. And do you know that there are lots of other things you can do? Let's name some of them."
>
> *Bad:* "Probably not. But even if you can't walk as well as some people, there are other things that you can do better than some people."

Young children thus should be helped to understand their limitations in a friendly and caring atmosphere. As younger and younger children receive special education services, caretakers outside the family circle may have to answer first questions about being different and cope with interpersonal situations in which peers point out shortcomings.

Most children with severe disabilities/delays are inevitably exposed to discrimination and prejudice (Wright, 1983). They should therefore be prepared for difficult social encounters. Storytelling, role-playing, and discussion help with learning appropriate responses to others' thoughtless and inconsiderate behavior. A number of books are now available that feature children coping with disabilities. Among these is the "Kids on the Block" book series (with or without puppets) available from Twenty-First Century Books, 38 South Market Street, Frederick, Maryland 21701. Each "Kids on the Block" book describes a child with a different disability (e.g., cerebral palsy, asthma, diabetes, AIDS) who copes in appropriate ways, feels good about self, and interacts with nondisabled children.

Social Competence and Inclusion

Social rejection and avoidance of children who are different begins at about age 4, unless there is intervention to promote interaction and acceptance (Siller, 1984). Research suggests that nondisabled children do not automatically include slow and/or different children in their activities (Jenkins, Speltz, & Odom, 1985). Early childhood educators must therefore devise

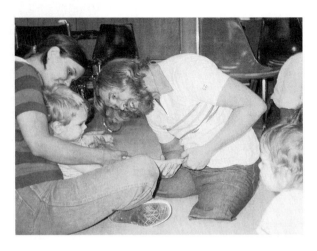

Figure 18.13 Young children need to see persons with disabilities in leadership roles. The teacher shown here is Don Drewry.

curriculums that systematically involve preschoolers in cooperative activities and promote caring, nurturing attitudes.

Experts favor open discussion of disabilities/differences in front of children and recommend inclusion of units covering individual differences in preschool curricula (Dunn et al., 1988). Emphasis should be on each human being's uniqueness and the importance of supporting and helping one another. Children should be helped to see that being different is not bad but simply a chance occurrence. Discussion can center on differences in eye, hair, and skin color; height and weight; the ways people walk, talk, and think; and expressions of individuality in work, play, hobbies, and leisure pursuits. *Movement education and creativity training in which emphasis is on "Find another way" or "Show me all the different ways you can do something" are excellent approaches* to understanding and appreciating individual differences. Likewise, good teachers stress not being afraid of people, places, foods, and other things that are different, but approaching them, assessing them, and getting acquainted.

Stories like the princess who kissed the frog and turned him into a prince can teach sensitivity. Emphasizing that appearances can be deceiving is also important. Too often, Halloween witches and storybook monsters are characterized as physically ugly or disfigured; small wonder that young children without special training begin equating being different with being bad. To counteract these influences, movement activities should feature creatures who look different but are kind, loving, and lovable.

Preschoolers, both with and without disabilities, need exposure to older persons with disabilities (see Figure 18.13). When speakers with disabilities are invited to the early childhood setting, they should explain how they are similar to and different from other people and encourage questions.

Play and Game Behaviors

Children with severe delays/disabilities do not play spontaneously. Neither do they laugh and show evidence of having fun. Thus, a major goal of early childhood adapted physical activity is learning the concept of fun and responding appropriately to social and/or sensory stimulation. Infants without severe disabilities smile and laugh spontaneously in response to pleasurable sights and sounds between 1 and 4 months of age. They begin reaching for objects at about 3 to 5 months and, as soon as they develop coordination, spend considerable energy working for a toy out of reach and exploring what body parts can do.

Social Play

Peekaboo, typically learned between 5 and 10 months of age, is the beginning of social game behaviors. Thereafter, infants seem to know instinctively how to imitate and respond to play activities initiated by significant others. Moreover, when left alone, they move about, explore the environment, and engage in solitary play. Gradually, without much help, they develop body control, object control, and basic movement patterns. Placed in an environment with play apparatus and equipment, most children are self-motivated to run, jump, climb, hang, slide, and balance. Movement is obviously fun, intrinsically rewarding, and inseparable from play.

In children with severe delays/disabilities, this spontaneity is often diminished or absent. Compared with nondisabled peers, they engage in fewer activities and spend much of their time sitting and lying (Linder, 1993a). Assessment of such children should begin with observations of their spontaneous interactions with the environment. Do they initiate contact with people and objects, and is their contact appropriate? How long do they sustain contact? Do they demonstrate preferences for some objects and people? If so, these preferences can guide the selection of reinforcement strategies in shaping behavior management plans.

Table 18.4 presents an inventory developed to assess play and game behaviors and guide programming. No child is too severely disabled to benefit from physical education instruction. The goals, objectives, and pedagogy, however, differ from those used with nondisabled children. The major emphasis should be on the development of play and game behaviors that are movement oriented and result in good feelings about the self.

Toy and Apparatus Play

Because learning to play with toys is closely related to the development of social and motor skills, several researchers have focused on toy play, including early use of wheeled vehicles. Loovis (1985), who studied 3- to 5-year-olds with orthopedic impairments, reported that the tricycle and slide were the most preferred of 20 toys. In general, children spent considerable time using toys in inappropriate ways. Loovis noted that structured play instruction guided by an adult or older child was needed to systematically teach the proper use of toys.

Sport Socialization

Children with disabilities should have the same opportunities for sport socialization as peers. This means that they must see persons with conditions similar to their own in athletic roles both in integrated and nonintegrated sport settings. For attitude development, nondisabled preschoolers should also be exposed to athletes with disabilities. *All young children* should thus be spectators at sport events like Special Olympics, wheelchair basketball and tennis, indoor wheelchair soccer, and boccia. Real-life experiences of this kind should be supplemented with films and videotapes and magazines like *Sports 'N Spokes* and *Palaestra* that feature athletes with disabilities. Several sport organizations that serve people with disabilities are establishing "Futures Teams" by providing recreational activities for children ages 3 and up in the same setting and at the same time that older athletes practice.

Language Development: A Concomitant Goal

Language development is so important that it is integrated into all learning activities (Murata, 2003). Authorities generally identify three areas of language development: (a) inner, (b) receptive, and (c) expressive. Physical education can contribute to each.

Inner Language

Inner language refers to thought, the ability to transform experience into meaning. Consider the infant who cries and receives attention or the toddler who touches something hot and is burned. In both cases, there may be no words, but the average infant and toddler makes a cause-and-effect linkage. Likewise, good and bad feelings derived through movement are translated into approach and avoidance thoughts.

Receptive Language

Receptive language is comprehension of gestures, postures, facial expressions, and spoken words. It is also understanding of the symbols or signs used to represent words. Receptive language presupposes integrity of memory, including the ability to remember sequences. Memory may be primarily auditory, visual, or proprioceptive, or a blending of all three.

Receptive language skills are dependent upon inner language, and vice versa. The following passage describes the interrelationship between the development of receptive language and inner language skills in Helen Keller at age 7, who was both deaf and blind:

> My teacher placed my hand under the spout. As the
> cool stream gushed over one hand, she spelled into
> the other the word water, first slowly, then rapidly.
> I stood still, my whole attention fixed upon the
> motions of her fingers. Suddenly, I felt a misty
> consciousness, as of something forgotten—a thrill of
> returning thought; and knew somehow the mystery of
> language was revealed to me. I knew then that
> "w-a-t-e-r" meant the wonderful cool something that
> was flowing over my hand. That living word
> awakened my soul, gave it light, hope, joy, set it free!
> There were barriers still, it is true, but barriers that
> could in time be swept away.
>
> I left the well-house eager to learn. Everything
> had a name, and each name gave birth to a new
> thought. (Keller, 1965, p. 14)

Table 18.4   Sherrill Social Play Behaviors Inventory.

	Mary	Jim	Juan
Autistic/Unoccupied			
Shows no spontaneous play.			
Makes no response to stimuli.			
Shows no object or person preference.			
Makes stereotyped/repetitive movements.			
Pounds/shakes/mouths objects without purpose.			
Self-stimulates.			
Wanders about aimlessly.			
Self-mutilates.			
Solitary/Exploratory			
Reacts to stimuli (approach/avoid).			
Reacts to persons/objects.			
Understands object permanence (peekaboo, hide-and-seek).			
Explores body parts.			
Explores objects/toys.			
Shows object preference.			
Shows person preference.			
Parallel			
Establishes play space near others.			
Shows awareness of others but doesn't interact.			
Plays independently with own things.			
Plays on same playground apparatus as others.			
Follows leader in imitation games and obstacle course.			
Associative/Interactive			
Initiates contact/play with others.			
Talks, signs, or gestures to others.			
Imitates others.			
Rolls/hands toy or ball to another without being asked.			
Retrieves objects for another without being asked.			
Offers to share objects/toys.			
Engages in make-believe play with others.			
Takes turns talking/listening.			
Cooperative			
Participates in small-group games.			
Sustains play in group of three or more for 5 min.			
Follows simple game rules.			
Understands stop/go.			
Understands safety zone, boundary line, base.			
Understands "It"/not "It."			
Understands game formations (circle, line, file, scattered).			
Plays games demanding one role (fleeing).			
Switches roles to achieve game goals: hide/seek, chase/flee, tag/dodge.			

Table 18.5 Words representing language concepts that can be acquired through movement lessons.

Self	Space	Time	Force*	Flow
Body parts	**Directions**	**Speed**	**Force**	**Qualities**
Fingers	Forward	Fast	Strong	Hyperactive
Elbow	Backward	Medium	Medium	Uncontrolled
Shoulders	Sideward	Slow	Weak	Free
Knee	Inside	Accelerating	Heavy	Abandoned
Body surfaces	Outside	Decelerating	Light	Exaggerated
Front	Up	**Quantity**	**Qualities**	Fluent
Back	Down	A lot (long)	Sudden, explosive	Inhibited
Top	Left	A little (short)	Sustained, smooth	Restrained
Bottom	Right	Variable	**Creating force**	Bound
Inside	**Levels**	**Rhythm**	Quick starts	Repressed
Outside	High	Pulse beats	Sustained, powerful	Tied up
Body movements	Medium	Accents	movements	Overcautious
Bend/flex/curl	Low	Rhythmic patterns	Static balances	**Movement**
Straighten/extend	**Size/dimensions**	Even	**Absorbing force**	Smooth, graceful
Spread/abduct	Large	Uneven	Sudden stops on balance	Rough, awkward
Close/adduct	Medium	Phrases	Gradual absorption,	Continuous
Turn/rotate	Small	Numbers	"give" as in catching	Staccato
Circle	Wide	Concepts	**Imparting force**	
	Narrow	Sequences	Rolling	
	Pathways (floor or air)	Processes	Bouncing	
	Slanted		Throwing	
	Straight		Kicking	
	Curved		Striking	
	Zigzag			

*Some persons prefer the term effort or weight.

Until age 7, Helen Keller had neither inner language nor receptive language in the ordinary sense. The following passage, however, does show that inner language can develop without vision and audition if the child possesses sufficient intelligence to capitalize upon proprioceptive cues:

> I cannot recall what happened during the first months after my illness. I only know that I sat in my mother's lap or clung to her dress as she went about her household duties. My hands felt every object and observed every motion, and in this way, I learned to know many things. Soon, I felt the need of some communication with others and began to make crude signs. A shake of the head meant "No" and a nod, "Yes," a pull meant "Come" and a push, "Go." Was it bread that I wanted? Then I would imitate the acts of cutting the slices and buttering them. If I wanted my mother to make ice cream for dinner, I made the sign for working the freezer and shivered, indicating cold. (Keller, 1965, p. 14)

Children vary widely with respect to receptive language skills. The emphasis placed on *learning to follow directions* reveals that many teachers are not satisfied with the receptive language of their pupils. Physical educators should cooperate with classroom teachers in designing movement experiences that reinforce the meanings of words (see Table 18.5). Children should be taught the names of the things they can do, the pieces of apparatus and equipment used, and the games played.

Augmentative and Alternative Communication

Augmentative and alternative communication (AAC) should be started as early as possible for toddlers and young children who have difficulty speaking and hearing. **AAC** is "any approach designed to support, enhance, or supplement the communication of individuals who are not independent verbal communicators" (NCPERID, 1995, p. 139). This includes many children with severe autism or cerebral palsy. Under AAC are sign, gesture, and body language systems and such assistive devices as manual communication boards, simple switch boards for saying "yes" and "no," and all kinds of computer technology that permits communication by touching a switch or key or moving the eyes to activate a communication system (i.e., known as *touch talkers* and *light talkers*). Physical educators should be proficient in using whatever kind of communication system that special educators and speech therapists are teaching (Standard 9, Instructional Design and Planning, APENS (NCPERID, 1995).

Table 18.6   Websites Pertaining to Infants, Toddlers, and Young Children.

National Association for the Education of Young Children	www.naeyc.org
Council for Exceptional Children	www.cec.sped.org
Family Voices	www.familyvoices.org
Ideas That Work	www.ideapractices.org
Kid Speech	www.kidspeech.com/signs.html
PE Central	www.pe.central.vt.ed
Zero to Three	www.zerotothree.org

Note. Look up websites related to the American Speech-Language-Hearing Association (ASHA) and get acquainted with the ASHA journal.

Expressive Language

Expressive language can be verbal or nonverbal. It presupposes integrity of both receptive and inner language. The way a child speaks and writes reveals his or her memory of words, sequences, and syntactic structures. It also lends insight into the child's ability to discriminate between words and letters that sound and look alike. *Nonverbal language includes sign, gesture, and facial expression.* Young children with a disability often rely on nonverbal language. See Chapter 16 on adapted dance and dance therapy for more information on expressive language. Also see descriptions of movement programs designed to develop language (Connor-Kuntz & Dummer, 1996; Murata, 2003; Wessel & Zittel, 1995).

Speech Augmentation

All child-adult movement lessons should be augmented by constant talking, chanting, or singing that link words to movements (Sherrill, 1979). Murata (2003) explains responses to children's first attempts at speech. For example, if the child says "Go," the professional should augment with, "Yes, we *go* to the gym now." If the child says "Ball," the professional should augment with "Yes, we *throw* the ball" or "Yes, we *play* with the ball."

 OPTIONAL ACTIVITIES

1. Review the Chapter 4 content on IFSP and weave it into the content in this chapter. Based on your life experience or recent observations, develop some case studies of children ages 0 to 3 who might benefit from an IFSP. Share with classmates and discuss each other's work.

2. Read some of the cases in *Lives in Progress: Case Studies in Early Intervention* by Williams (2000) and discuss content with classmates. How much was physical activity and motor performance covered? Why?

3. Use Table 18.6 to look up additional information on websites and share with someone who will benefit. Find other websites that are helpful and share.

4. Attend some IFSP meetings and jot down reflections in your journal. Critique the roles and contributions of team members.

5. Accompany some professionals on home visits and reflect on their roles and contributions. Ask them the kinds of preparation they have had on how to communicate with parents and how you might go about getting such preparation.

6. Have conversations with parents of infants, toddlers, and young children as often as possible. Listen to their perspectives on physical activity and motor development and, if needed, serve as an advocate for these areas.

Figure 19.1 Students classified as *other health-impaired* (OHI) typically do not look disabled but have chronic or acute health problems that adversely affect their educational performance.

1. Discuss the role of exercise, diet, and lifestyle in managing each condition in Table 19.1. Relate what you have read to real-life experience with conditions and to persons you have seen on media or read about.

2. Given any condition in Table 19.1, be able to write a physical education IEP or accommodation plan. State age, gender, and other relevant information. Include environmental variables to be altered.

3. Discuss the role of medication in managing OHI conditions and identify major drugs related to each. State side effects that affect exercise programming.

4. Explain contraindicated practices, activities, and environmental variables associated with OHI conditions.

5. Demonstrate skill in using websites at end of chapter to answer specific questions you or others may have.

Other health impairments (OHI) is an official U.S. Department of Education diagnostic category for limited strength, vitality, or alertness caused by chronic or acute health problems that adversely affect educational performance. In the lifespan approach to adapted physical activity, this definition is expanded to also include health problems that interfere with work productivity, leisure activities, and life satisfaction. **Chronic** refers to long duration, whereas **acute** means rapid onset, severe symptoms, and a short course. Asthma, for example, is a chronic condition that is managed by medication and healthy lifestyle. Occasionally, however, an **acute episode** (i.e., an asthma attack) may occur.

This chapter is an extension of Chapter 13, "Fitness and Healthy Lifestyle." Much of physical education is aimed toward either preventing or coping with OHI problems, especially those that pertain to weight and cardiorespiratory function. When physical education fails to instill the habits needed for healthy lifestyle, adapted physical activity expertise may be needed. People with disabilities are at particular risk for OHI problems because of inactive lifestyles and stress related to societal barriers.

Common OHI Conditions

OHI conditions covered in this chapter are listed in Table 19.1. The incidence of these and other conditions is presented in Appendix B. Many persons cope with multiple OHI problems. Much of the time they simply do not feel good. This state of "not feeling good" affects initiative and morale. Aerobic fitness is a particular challenge, and many persons give up, exacerbating their conditions by developing negative feelings about themselves and physical activity, becoming increasingly sedentary, and gaining weight. Adapted physical activity services in school and community settings are needed to create support groups for working toward common goals (e.g., weight loss, improved breathing, a 12-min mile) and to teach ways that exercise can develop self-confidence and manage stress (see Figure 19.1). *These services should supplement rather than replace general activity programs.*

Medication and Use of the PDR

Most serious OHI conditions are managed by drugs. Adherence to prescribed doses is essential to wellness, and physical educators must be able to discuss side effects and exercise indications and contraindications. The *Physician's Desk Reference (PDR)*, which is revised annually, is the primary source of choice, but many reference books and websites are available. Medications can be identified by *family names* (e.g., diuretics or thiazides), *generic names* (chlorothiazide), and *trade or brand names* (Diuril). Generally, generic names are needed to find drugs in reference books. For ease of reading, this and subsequent chapters primarily use family names. Following is a brief discussion of commonly used medications that affect exercise response. Several of these drugs also alter heart and blood vessel responses to heat stress, increase the risk of dehydration, and interfere with the body's ability to dissipate heat during exercise (ACSM, 2000).

Diuretics

Diuretics are used to manage obesity, heart disease, high blood pressure, and several other conditions. **Diuretics** are water pills that stimulate urination in order to rid the body of excess fluids and to reduce **edema** (swelling caused by a fluid accumulation). When exercisers take diuretics, professionals must allow frequent bathroom breaks and check periodically for dehydration. Diuretics, when combined with vigorous exercise and hot weather conditions, can cause adverse side effects like **hypovolemia** (diminished blood volume caused by fluid loss) and **hypokalemia** (diminished blood volume caused by serious depletion of potassium), both of which are life-threatening conditions. Early danger signs are dizziness, weakness, and muscle cramps. These side effects can be prevented by drinking water and eating foods high in potassium (e.g., fresh fruits and vegetables). Persons taking diuretics should maintain regular fluid-intake levels.

Blood Pressure Drugs

The most common medications prescribed for high blood pressure are alpha- and beta-blocker drugs, calcium channel blockers, and angiotensin-converting enzyme (ACE) inhibitors. Diuretics are often included in these tablets. These drugs all lower blood pressure but have side effects that must be prevented or managed. Some speed up heartbeat and some slow it down. *Alpha- and beta-blockers are contraindicated in asthma and diabetes* because of side effects (i.e., blockers depress functions needed to keep bronchial tubes open and to signal blood sugar changes associated with diabetes crises). ACE inhibitors and calcium channel blockers seem to have fewer side effects and reduce the tension within blood vessel walls, dilating them and allowing the blood to move more freely.

Beta-blockers work directly on the sympathetic nervous system, blocking or depressing nerve impulses underlying cardiovascular function, and are probably prescribed more often than the other drugs. Beta-blockers are extremely effective but mask exercise effects, preventing the heart rate from increasing as it should with vigorous exercise, and *thereby making the pulse an invalid indicator of effort.* It is not possible to determine maximum heart rate (MHR) response in ordinary ways and to plan exercise programs based on MHR. Persons taking beta-blockers have early exercise fatigue and lowered maximum oxygen uptake. Some newer beta-blockers have built-in sympathomimetic agents to lessen side effects. Clearly, special training is needed to conduct exercise when beta-blockers are involved.

A common side effect of most blood pressure medications is **hypotension** (dizziness or lightheadedness when changing from sitting to standing positions). Hypotension frequently causes falls and injuries in persons who are medically fragile. To minimize hypotension, teach slow pacing of position changes.

Heart Medications

Common medications are classified as nitrates, digitalis preparations, and heart rhythm regulators. Additionally, diuretics are often prescribed. Because obesity, high blood pressure, and diabetes often occur with heart conditions, medications for these conditions are taken concurrently. **Nitrates** (e.g., nitroglycerin) are used for heart attacks and angina symptoms; nitrates relax and dilate smooth muscles, thereby increasing heart rate and oxygen supply and decreasing blood pressure.

Digitalis preparations (e.g., dioxin) are associated with aging, when congestive heart failure and conduction abnormalities are most likely to occur. Digitalis preparations lower heart rate but do not affect blood pressure.

Heart rhythm regulators are the same beta-blockers and calcium channel blockers that lower blood pressure. They can be used to manage speed of heartbeat. Alpha-blockers are *not* rhythm regulators because they do not affect heart rate.

Corticosteroids for Severe Inflammation

The adrenocorticosteroids (usually called **corticosteroids** or **steroids**) mimic the hormones (glucocorticoids and mineralocorticoids) secreted by the cortex (outer covering) of the adrenal gland located above each kidney. These hormones are **systemic,** meaning that they influence the biochemistry of all body systems. Corticosteroids are typically used as a last resort, when other medications are not effective. Many persons with severe, chronic conditions that cause swelling, pain, and respiratory distress (e.g., arthritis and asthma) take corticosteroids. Cancer may also be treated by corticosteroids.

Even when taken only for short periods, steroids cause many side effects, like edema (excessive fluid retention), hyperactivity, increased appetite, insatiable hunger for sweets, fungus infections, and mood swings. Withdrawal results in depression, even when daily dosages are progressively decreased. Long-term prescription of the corticosteroids has such side effects as weight gain, growth retardation, diabetes, high blood pressure, and osteoporosis. Steroids are used when no other medication is effective, so persons must learn to accept and manage side effects.

Asthma Drugs

Most asthma drugs **dilate** (widen) the bronchial tubes in the lungs. An adverse side effect of these beta-2-adrenergic agonists is *increased heart rate.* Asthma drugs may be tablets or aerosols; many cause mild generalized irritability. The Advair diskus, used only twice a day as a long-acting preventative, is an inhaler for powder forms of beta-adrenergic bronchodilator and corticosteroid combinations.

Seizure Drugs

Drugs used in controlling seizures have side effects like poor reaction time, incoordination, attention problems, and drowsiness. Approximately 25 to 50% of people with cerebral palsy (CP) and 35% of people with severe mental retardation take seizure medication at some time during their lives. Side effects put people with these conditions at a considerable disadvantage, but many are able nonetheless to become excellent athletes.

Medication Guidelines

Most persons with chronic OHI must take medication every day at approximately the same time. Physicians prescribe medication because benefits outweigh adverse side effects. Physical activity professionals should follow these guidelines:

1. Ask for a written statement listing all medications individuals are taking and their side effects. Read about these medications, and then interview the individuals to determine their understanding of the drugs they take.

2. Ask individuals about exercise adaptations they may need, and seek to increase their awareness of drug/exercise interactions.

3. Remember that every person responds to medications differently, and responses vary from day to day. Discipline problems, mood swings, and undesirable activity levels often can be traced to medication.

Lifestyle and Risk Factors

Medication is not enough to effectively manage OHI problems. Lifestyle becomes more important when health is compromised. Physical activity professionals must emphasize good eating, sleeping, and exercise habits and promote environments and models that encourage maintenance of a healthy lifestyle. This includes zero tolerance of street drugs, tobacco, and unsafe sex practices. Today's health risks are so grave that adults must talk openly about previously taboo subjects and must set clear standards for ethical conduct. Coaches and exercise counselors often come to know all aspects of individuals' personal lives and thus have tremendous influence.

OHI problems, like other kinds of disabilities, must be treated as family concerns. Families can be those of origin or of choice, but significant others should be identified and involved in all aspects of adapted physical activity.

This chapter begins with weight/obesity problems because they must be addressed first when persons make a commitment to fitness. Almost all of the other conditions listed in Table 19.1 are commonly complicated by overweight. The principles guiding exercise selection for people who are overweight are applicable to most OHI conditions.

Overweight/Obesity Syndrome

Definition of the overweight/obesity syndrome depends on assessment approach (see Chapter 13). Criteria for obesity, based on the use of skinfold calipers to determine percent body fat, are a percentage of body fat greater than 25% for males and greater than 30% for females. With height-weight tables, the traditional criterion for **overweight** is 10 to 20% above ideal weight for sex and age. The criterion for **obesity** is 20% above ideal weight. Persons over 50% of their ideal weight are considered **super obese.**

Ideal weight depends on sex, age, body type, ethnic or cultural expectations, athletic goals, and work demands. Governments issue guidelines for healthy weight, based on averages within the population (see Table 19.2). Some persons over age

Table 19.2   Guidelines for healthy weight.

In reading the weight range on the chart, higher weights generally apply to men, who have more muscle and bone; lower weights apply to women.

Height Without Shoes	Weight Without Clothes	
	19–34 Years	**35 Years and Over**
5′	97–128	108–138
5′1″	101–132	111–143
5′2″	104–137	115–148
5′3″	107–141	119–152
5′4″	111–146	122–157
5′5″	114–150	126–162
5′6″	118–155	130–167
5′7″	121–160	134–172
5′8″	125–164	138–178
5′9″	129–169	142–183
5′10″	132–174	146–188
5′11″	136–179	151–194
6′	140–184	155–199
6′1″	144–189	159–205
6′2″	148–195	164–210
6′3″	152–200	168–216
6′4″	156–205	173–222
6′5″	160–211	177–228
6′6″	164–216	182–234

From a 1992 news release from the U.S. Departments of Agriculture and Health and Human Services.

40 can grow a little heavier without added health risks. The main concern is with fat distribution.

Importance of Fat Distribution

Fat distribution varies by age and sex. Infants and young children have a continuous layer of adipose tissue beneath the skin, often called baby fat. The amount is fairly small, 10 to 15%. As children age, the subcutaneous fat becomes thicker in some areas than others (e.g., triceps, abdomen, calf). These are the sites used in skinfold fat measurement. Hormones associated with the adolescent growth spurt cause thickening of fat deposits in different areas for females than males. In general, females have larger fat cells in the buttocks and hips, whereas the fat of males centers around the upper body, especially the abdomen. These fat distributions are popularly referred to, respectively, as pear and apple shapes. *The apple shape, common in both sexes with obesity, carries more health risk.* In general, hormones and genes influence fat distribution more than diet and exercise.

Incidence and Prevalence

Obesity affects 5 to 25% of school-age children and youth, depending on criteria used, and an even higher percentage of adults. Overweight and obesity affect 55% of the United States adult population (i.e., 97 million) (Brunner, 2001).

Causes of Obesity

Causes of obesity are endocrine, medication-induced, or non-endocrine. Typically, the physician rules out endocrine and medication-induced etiologies before delving into other possible causes.

Endocrine obesity is caused by malfunction of glands that secrete hormones. The fat is typically concentrated about the breasts, hips, and abdomen, and the face is moon-shaped and ruddy. **Cushing's syndrome,** or cushingoid obesity, is the most common form. Overall, less than 10% of obesity is caused by endocrine disorders.

Medication-induced obesity is caused by the corticosteroids and has the same appearance as Cushing's syndrome. The most common of these corticosteroids—prednisone and cortisone—are used to reduce inflammation and manage such severe chronic conditions as arthritis, asthma, cancer, leukemia, and kidney disease.

Nonendocrine obesity, the most common condition, is caused by interacting hereditary and environmental factors that result in an imbalance between caloric intake and output. Studies show that, when parents are within average weight zones, only 8 to 9% of the children are obese. When one parent is obese, 40% of the children are likewise. When both parents are obese, this percentage doubles. Eating and activity patterns learned early in childhood and passed down from generation to generation seem to be as much a factor as genetic predisposition.

Long-Term Management of Obesity

Long-term management of obesity has been likened to that of alcoholism and drug abuse. The problem can be solved temporarily, but never cured. *Of the many persons who diet, only 10% achieve lifetime weight control.* Clearly, new strategies must be tried, with physical educators playing a leading role in cooperative home-school-community programming. Lifestyle prescriptions must focus jointly on food intake and exercise output, and self-responsibility for monitoring behaviors and seeking help must be taught.

ACSM Guidelines

Three guidelines structure program planning (ACSM, 2000):

1. Maintain a *minimum* intake of about 1,200 calories a day.
2. Engage in a daily exercise program that expends 300 or more calories a day. For weight-loss goals, exercise of long duration/moderate intensity is generally best.
3. Lose no more than 2.2 lb (1 kg) a week. Gradual weight loss prevents metabolic imbalances.

Formula for Estimating Calories

The number of calories to be targeted each day depends on sex, age, height, weight, and exercise. New formulae allow more-accurate prediction of individual needs.

For Females: 655.1 (a constant) + (9.6 × your weight in kilograms) + (1.8 × your height in centimeters) − (4.7 × your age in years) × (your exercise code)

For Males: 66.5 (a constant) + (13.8 × your weight in kilograms) + (5 × your height in centimeters) − (6.8 × your age in years) × (your exercise code)

The exercise codes to be entered into the formula are as follows:

1.2—confined to bed
1.3—sedentary active
1.4—moderately active, exercises 3 to 4 times a week
1.6—very active, exercises more than 4 times a week
1.7—extremely active, exercises more than 6 times a week for more than 1 hr duration

Following is a sample calculation for a female, age 62, 144 lb, 5 ft tall, with a 1.4 exercise code:

Weight = 144 lb ÷ 2.2 = 65.45 kg
Height = 60 in × 2.5 = 150 cm
Formula: 655.1 + (9.6 × 65.45) + (1.8 × 150) − (4.7 × 62) = 1262 × 1.4 = 1767

To lose weight, this woman must consume fewer than 1,767 calories a day.

Lifestyle Prescription and Caloric Balance

The *FIT* acronym introduced in Chapter 13 on fitness can be modified to include both exercise and eating:

F Frequency (Three to five small meals a day at set times and places with no snacking in between; daily exercise)

I Intensity (At least 1,200 cal distributed properly among the six food groups; exercise intensity great enough to expend at least 300 cal a day)

T Time (Each meal of long duration, with food eaten slowly, chewed well, and supplemented with pleasant conversation; exercise duration long enough to expend at least 300 cal a day)

The **principle of caloric balance** is extremely important in lifestyle prescription. This principle specifies that, for weight loss to occur, *exercise expenditure calories must exceed food intake calories.*

Food Groups and Exchange Lists

A **food guide pyramid** issued by the U.S. Department of Agriculture (USDA) and the U.S. Department of Health and Human Services almost universally guides nutrition education. Recommended daily amounts of six food groups are indicated by the part of the pyramid on which they lie. The least servings should come from the top of the pyramid (Level 1) and the most from the base of the pyramid, Level 4. The six food groups are

1. bread, cereal, rice, and pasta group (6 to 11 servings);
2. vegetable group (3 to 5 servings);
3. fruit group (2 to 4 servings);
4. milk, yogurt, and cheese group (2 to 3 servings);
5. meat, poultry, fish, dry beans, eggs, and nuts group (2 to 3 servings); and
6. fats, oils, and sweets (use sparingly).

Recently the USDA has published a pyramid for young children, and the American Diabetic Association (ADA) has revised the pyramid to meet the needs of persons with diabetic conditions. Inasmuch as most persons with diabetes II are overweight or obese, the following ADA changes are applicable to these conditions:

1. Cheese was moved to the meat group.

2. Dry beans were moved to the bread group.

3. Alcohol was added to the fats group. One drink counts as two servings of fat (about 90 calories).

Exchange lists recommended by the ADA should be considered by persons who are overweight and have tendencies toward any of the diabetic conditions. These exchange lists include the same six food groups as the pyramid and are included in most books pertaining to diabetes (e.g., Caron & Henry, 2002; Hiser, 1999; Labat & Maggi, 1997). Exchange lists indicate the specific amount of carbohydrates, proteins, and fats in each food group and thus help when persons decide to diet by counting carbohydrate or fat grams. The food guide pyramid and the ADA exchange list are often criticized for not dividing the bread (etc.) group into the separate categories of refined (processed, usually white) and nonrefined, natural, or complex. For losing weight, the **nonrefined carbohydrates** are better choices than the refined.

Principles Guiding Food Selection

The easiest way to control caloric intake is to use a system of food servings or exchanges. Several principles guide food selection:

1. **Six Foods Principle.** Eating right requires a knowledge of the six food groups and the amounts that constitute servings. To lose weight, reduce the size or number of portions but keep all meals approximately the same size. Inclusion of these food groups in every meal ensures that the six nutrients necessary for wellness are ingested. *These nutrients are carbohydrates, proteins, fats, minerals, vitamins, and water.* Only the first three generate calories.

2. **The 2:1 Food Group Principle.** This principle states that the number of servings in the bread/cereal/grain group and the fruit and vegetable group should be twice that of the milk/dairy product group and the meat or protein equivalent group. This ratio ensures that the correct proportions of nutrients are eaten. The recommended daily dietary intake is 55% or more carbohydrates, 30% or less fats, and 15% or less proteins.

3. **Dietary Fat Reduction Principle.** Reducing dietary fat is especially important for weight loss. This is because 1 gram of fat is 9 cal whereas 1 gram of carbohydrates or protein is only 4.5 cal. Major sources of fat are mayonnaise, salad dressing, cooking oils, meat fats, butter, and cheese. Reducing fats also helps to control blood pressure and cholesterol problems.

Principles Guiding Exercise Selection

1. **Non-Weight-Bearing Activities Principle.** Non-weight-bearing activities minimize stress on joints and feet. Exercise modalities of choice for most obese persons are water-based exercises, cycling, and mat activities in lying and sitting positions. Water-based exercises include swimming, treading water, locomotor and stationary activities in waist-deep water, and pedaling a cycle ergometer placed in the water so that only the head and shoulders are out. Obese persons can typically perform for longer durations at higher intensities in water than on land. Heart response to exercise in water is different from that on land. Therefore, *if exercise prescription is based on heart rate, assess target intensity range in the water.*

2. **Walking for Long Duration Principle.** When walking is the preferred exercise, it should be done only on a level surface to minimize joint stresses. A temperature-controlled environment is recommended to keep perspiration under control. Long-duration, low-intensity walking causes weight loss more effectively than traditional aerobic exercise. *Research shows that most obese persons do not lose weight until walking time is at least 30 min a day. Two hours daily is recommended.* Remember that heavy persons spend more energy per minute than light persons. An exercise leader of average weight should perhaps wear waist or ankle weights or carry a backpack to get the feel of exertion and learn to empathize.

3. **Exercise for Enjoyment Principle.** Alternate exercise modalities and use stimulating music to reduce boredom and enhance enjoyment. Use Table 13.4 on page 373 in the fitness chapter to determine amount of exercise needed to burn 300 cal. Adapt this table to individual weights as explained in the footnote. Regardless of modality chosen, remember that the emphasis is on attitude change and on developing the habit of daily exercise.

4. **Partner and Support Group Principle.** One day of not exercising for an obese person is like falling off the wagon for an alcoholic. Teach persons how to ask for help with motivation. A buddy system generally helps. If this is not possible, create a telephone help-line that persons can call for assistance. Emphasize praising and reinforcing each other.

5. **Time Management Counseling Principle.** Help persons who are obese with time management. Weight loss is not typically achieved in a physical education or exercise class because obese persons lack the fitness to exercise at high intensity. Additional time must be committed. Teach and reinforce realistic expectations. If time cannot be found, the individual will have to settle for losing fewer pounds each week.

6. **Teach Exercise Fallacies Principle.** Teach that spot reduction is an exercise fallacy. Fat distribution depends on genetic code. Exercise may decrease the circumference

of a body part by firming up the muscle, but the number of fat cells remains constant. The size of fat cells is reduced only when overall energy expenditure is greater than food intake. Fat-cell size reduction seems to follow a pattern from top to bottom. Most persons notice weight loss in the face and neck first.

Implications for Physical Education

The most successful weight reduction programs are cooperative school/community endeavors that involve the entire family. Programs should be engaged in voluntarily and supported by counseling. The approach must be nonthreatening and nonchastising.

Persons must be reassured that they are loved and accepted. The self, however, is not easily separated from the body. Criticism of excessive body weight thus is often internalized as criticism of self. Many obese persons have built up elaborate defense mechanisms to preserve ego strength. Do not assume that they will be receptive to offers to help with weight loss or that they will admit openly to dissatisfaction with their bodies.

See the videotape of What's Eating Gilbert Grape *(1993) or an alternative that features a person with obesity in a major role. Discuss contents with others and relate them to your life experiences.*

The well-proportioned physical educator often does not realize how unpleasant vigorous exercise can be for obese persons. Realistic program planning results from a consideration of the physical characteristics of obesity:

1. **Distended abdomen.** This results in anatomical differences in the position of the stomach and in the length of the intestinal tract, thereby affecting vital processes. It also creates excessive pressure on the diaphragm, which leads to difficulty in breathing and the consequent accumulation of carbon dioxide, which helps to explain patterns of drowsiness. The distended abdomen makes forward bending exercises difficult or impossible.

2. **Mobility of rolls of fat.** The bobbing up and down of breasts, abdomen, and other areas where excessive fat is deposited is uncomfortable during exercise.

3. **Excessive perspiration.** Layers of fat serve as insulation, and the obese person more quickly becomes hot and sweaty than the nonobese.

4. **Galling between the thighs and other skin areas that rub together.** After perspiration begins, continued locomotion causes painful galling or chafing somewhat similar to an abrasion. Such areas heal slowly because of continuous irritation and sometimes become inflamed.

5. **Postural faults.** Obesity makes individuals vulnerable to knock-knees, pronation, flat-foot, sagging abdomen, drooped shoulders, and round back. These postural deviations all affect mechanical efficiency in even simple locomotor activities.

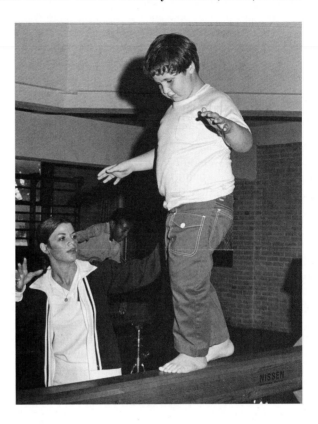

Figure 19.2 Obesity, when classified as either an *other health-impaired* condition or an *orthopedic impairment,* is eligible for special education or 504 funding. Such children often need adapted physical activity more than students who are mentally retarded, blind, or deaf.

6. **Skeletal immaturity.** The growth centers in the long bones of obese adolescents are particularly susceptible to injury, either from cumulative daily gravitational stress or sudden traumas from such strenuous or heavy activities as contact sports, weight lifting, and pyramid building.

7. **Edema.** Obesity seems to promote fluid retention. Ankles, breasts, and wrists swell, particularly during the menstrual period. Diuretics are often prescribed.

8. **Broad base in locomotor activities.** The combination of knock-knees, tendency toward galling between thighs, and pronation results in a slow, awkward gait with feet often shoulder-width apart.

9. **Fear of falling.** Added weight makes falling from heights both painful and dangerous (see Figure 19.2).

10. **Excessive buoyancy in water.** The inability to keep most of the body submerged makes the mastery of standard swimming strokes difficult.

Allow persons with weight problems privacy in dressing and showering if requested. Standard gymnasium clothes may be impossible to find, and long pants may be more appropriate than shorts. The heavier a person is, the more important it is that certain activities be avoided. These activities include tasks that involve lifting his or her own weight, such as chinning and rope climbing, and those that entail lifting external weights, such as weight training, serving as the base of a pyramid, and partner tumbling stunts.

The use of successive contracts, specifying specific goals and rewards after the loss of each 5 or 10 lb, is an effective motivational technique in weight reduction. The student is free at all times to revise the contract to allow more food and less exercise, but few take advantage of this option. Group contracts, in which several persons pledge weight losses, are particularly effective.

Blood Fats Associated With Obesity and Heart Disease

The two blood fats most strongly associated with obesity, heart disease, stroke, and diabetes II are triglycerides and cholesterol. Regular exercise can help keep blood fats at desired levels. **Triglyceride levels** should be below 160 milligrams per deciliter (mg/dl). **Total blood cholesterol levels** should be below 180 mg/dl.

High cholesterol is caused by (a) genetic factors, causing the liver to produce excessive amounts, (b) eating too many animal fats, or (c) a combination. Foods containing the most cholesterol (egg yolk, liver, brain, whole milk, butter, cheese, red meats) should be avoided. Dietary cholesterol intake should be less than 300 mg a day for the average person and reduced further, as needed, by persons with cholesterol problems.

Blood testing provides separate measures for three components of cholesterol: (a) low-density-lipoprotein cholesterol (LDL-C), (b) very-low-density-lipoprotein cholesterol (VLDL-C), and (c) high-density-lipoprotein cholesterol (HDL-C). The first two of these are bad, and the third is good. The term *lipoprotein* reminds us that fats are insoluble in water and must combine with proteins or some other substance to travel through body fluids.

LDL-C and VLDL-C are the bad components of cholesterol. LDL-C is the worst because the excess amounts attach themselves to artery walls, build up plaque, and clog passageways. LDL-C levels above 130 are borderline or risk. VLDL-C is the substance used by the liver to manufacture and transport LDL-C, so its bad effects are indirect. To remember whether LDL-C or HDL-C is bad, it helps to think: L*ousy*, L*ethargic*, L*azy* L*iving is* L*inked with* LDL-C *that* L*ikes to attach to artery walls.* LDL-C can be lowered in most persons by weight loss. However, 75% of the body's cholesterol is manufactured by the liver, and only 25% comes from food. Genes and cholesterol problems appear to be strongly linked.

HDL-C, the good cholesterol, draws fats away from artery walls, serving to counterbalance LDL-C activity. The higher the HDL-C, the better. *Aerobic exercise raises HDL-C activity.* The ratio between total cholesterol (TC) and HDL-C should be about 3.5. Most blood tests give this information.

Medication can lower cholesterol when caloric balance, weight loss, and exercise are not effective. Common medications are colestipol (Colestid), gembibrozil (Lopid), lovastatin (Melacor), and niacin (also called vitamin B_3 or nicotinic acid). Each has minor side effects that do not affect exercising. Illustrative side effects are constipation, increases in blood sugar, reduced absorption of vitamins, and interference with fat absorption.

The Diabetes Continuum

The diabetes continuum begins with glucose intolerance, progresses to insulin resistance, then to Syndrome X, and finally to diabetes (usually Type II). Formerly this was considered an adult-onset continuum, but today components of the diabetes continuum are diagnosed in many children, *especially those who are overweight or obese* (Challem, Berkson, & Smith, 2000). Treatment for all of these conditions focuses on exercise, nutrition, and medication.

1. **Glucose intolerance.** The inability of the body to cope with the **glucose** (sugar) rush that is caused by ingesting large amounts of **refined carbohydrates** (e.g., white sugar, white flour, white rice, white pastas). Refined carbohydrates are absorbed in the bloodstream more quickly than other nutrients, causing a rapid rise in blood glucose. The intolerance of this rapid rise is expressed by a rapid fall in blood glucose precipitated by the pancreas's secretion of insulin (the hormone that regulates the amount of glucose in the blood).

   A prediabetic form of glucose intolerance is **hypoglycemia,** frequent bouts of low blood sugar, in which body cells (especially brain cells) feel starved for energy, causing a person to crave sweets and to feel tired, shaky, nervous, unsteady, or confused (Challem et al., 2000). *This hypoglycemic condition, which is different from that experienced by persons with diabetes, can be prevented by minimizing the intake of sweets and refined carbohydrates.* Eating of natural foods, including whole grain breads and pasta, and adhering to the food guide pyramid recommendations (especially the protein part) is recommended.

2. **Insulin resistance.** A diet-caused condition in which body cells have become insensitive (resistant or nonreceptive) to insulin and *thus the glucose level rises and stays high.* **Insulin** is the hormone that promotes blood glucose uptake by body cells, which in turn convert the glucose into energy. Insulin resistance causes the pancreas to create more and more insulin to compensate for the cells' sluggish uptake.

3. **Syndrome X.** Presence of insulin resistance and one or more of the following: glucose intolerance, upper-body obesity, hypertension, and high blood fats (cholesterol or triglycerides).

4. **Diabetes.** A chronic disorder of carbohydrate, protein, and fat metabolism that occurs when glucose is not assimilated into body cells and thus remains higher than normal between meals and in a fasting state. Diabetes is generally confirmed by an *oral glucose tolerance test;* it should not be self-diagnosed. Causes of diabetes are (a) the pancreas does not produce enough insulin (Type I) and (b) the body cells become resistant to insulin (Type II). In both Type I and II, glucose cannot get into body cells where it is converted into energy. Diabetes, which

literally means "passing through," was named for its most common symptom, frequent urination. *Diabetes is not caused by eating too much sugar; it is caused by a metabolism failure that involves processing of all kinds of foods.* This failure is largely genetic but is exacerbated by eating habits.

Prevalence of Prediabetic Conditions and Diabetes

The prediabetic conditions of glucose intolerance and insulin resistance, separate or combined, affect more than 50% of the North American population (Challem et al., 2000). Several comorbid conditions contribute to the diabetes continuum; approximately 155 million of the North American population are overweight, 50 million have hypertension, and 50 million have elevated cholesterols and triglycerides. These conditions are associated with Syndrome X and place persons at high risk for diabetes II.

Approximately 17 million persons worldwide have diabetes; 3.7 million of them take daily insulin shots (Kaplan-Mayer, 2003). Of these, a growing number are using pump therapy. Diabetes is a high-incidence condition that affects about 6% of the population. Infants have a 1 in 5 chance of becoming diabetic. At least 1 of every 600 school-age children has diabetes. According to the American Diabetes Association, for every 10,000 persons, there will be 1 with diabetes under age 20, 10 between ages 20 and 50, 100 between ages 50 and 60, and 1,000 over age 60. *Diabetes ranks sixth in causes of death for all age groups.*

Diabetes increases the risk of blindness, coronary heart disease, amputations, and kidney and urinary conditions. Within 10 years of onset, 50% have pathological changes in the retina of the eye, called **diabetic retinopathy.** Between the ages of 20 and 65, diabetes is the leading cause of blindness. Diabetes is a contributing factor in 50% of all heart attacks and 75% of all strokes. Persons with diabetes are cautioned to maintain their blood pressure at 120/90 or lower.

Two Types of Diabetes

Type I diabetes is insulin-dependent diabetes mellitus (IDDM) or juvenile-onset diabetes (JOD). This condition has the same incidence for males and females. Its onset is usually before age 25, and the condition is serious because the pancreatic beta cells are capable of producing little or no insulin.

Only about 10% of diabetes is Type I. Rapid weight loss, frequent urination, drowsiness, and fatigue are the classic symptoms. Type I is managed by daily insulin injections or pump therapy, careful monitoring of glucose, and disciplined balancing of food intake and exercise. Type I cannot be cured; it is a lifelong condition. However, individuals with Type I often have fitness and motor profiles similar to those of their nondiabetic peers.

Type II diabetes, which occurs mainly in overweight persons of all ages, is called non-insulin-dependent diabetes mellitus (NIDDM). More females have Type II diabetes than males. Diagnostic symptoms are the same as Type I except there is no rapid weight loss. Type II may be treated with insulin, but usually the emphasis is on diet and exercise. Often, when weight is lost and regular physical activity becomes a part of leisure, diabetic symptoms disappear. When Type II cannot be managed by diet and exercise, **sulfonylurea therapy** (oral tablets) is often used.

Glucose Monitoring

Glucose is a simple sugar that, through carbohydrate metabolism, is converted either to (a) cellular energy, (b) glycogen, or (c) fat. Desired concentration of glucose in the blood is 80–120 mg/dl (milligrams per deciliter). *The glucose level rises slightly after meals and falls as the stomach becomes empty. The level also falls during aerobic exercise,* which enhances cellular glucose intake (see Figure 19.3).

Glucose levels should be checked several times each day. Target blood glucose levels are 60–130 mg/dl before meals, 140–180 mg/dl 1 hr after meals, 120–150 mg/dl 2 hr after meals, and 80–120 mg/dl at other times. If glucose is below target level, a carbohydrate snack is eaten. If it is above, additional insulin or sulfonylurea is taken. *Values above 240 mg/dl contraindicate aerobic exercise, and values above 300 mg/dl contraindicate all kinds of exercise.*

Glucose levels are determined by either blood or urine tests. Today, most persons use a pen-size, battery-operated device called a **glucometer.** A drop of capillary blood is obtained by pricking the side of a fingertip. The blood is placed on a paper strip that is inserted into the glucometer, which gives a precise electronic readout. This is far more accurate than the urine test, in which specially treated paper is dipped in urine and then evaluated for color change.

Ketosis, Usually in Type I

Ketosis and **hyperglycemia** are imbalances between the body's acids and alkalites caused by excess **ketone bodies** (waste products from fat metabolism). **Ketosis,** which results from high-fat diets as well as diabetes, affects the body in many ways: (a) muscle cramps during exercise, (b) decreased ability to fight infections, and (c) increased loss of electrolytes (sodium, potassium, calcium, and magnesium) through excess urination. As the resulting electrolyte imbalance becomes more pronounced, **hyperglycemia** ensues. Hyperglycemia (also called ketoacidosis) progresses from lethargy to drowsiness to diabetic coma (see Table 19.3 for signs). Immediate medical attention is required. Any condition that raises ketone levels increases the risk of hyperglycemia. Among these are (a) infection or illness; (b) diarrhea, vomiting, and stomach upsets; (c) overeating or excessive alcoholic intake; (d) emotional stress; and (e) failure to take enough insulin to offset exercise demands.

Whenever blood glucose tests show that glucose has risen to 300 mg/dl, urine should be checked for ketone bodies. Most physicians want to be contacted immediately when ketones are found in the urine.

Hypoglycemic Reaction, Usually in Type I

The opposite condition of hyperglycemia is hypoglycemia (see Table 19.3). Of the two conditions, hypoglycemia is the more common. It is the reaction that persons with Type I continuously work to avoid as they carefully monitor blood glucose and

Figure 19.3 Two pancreatic hormones (insulin and glucagon) work together to maintain relatively stable blood glucose.

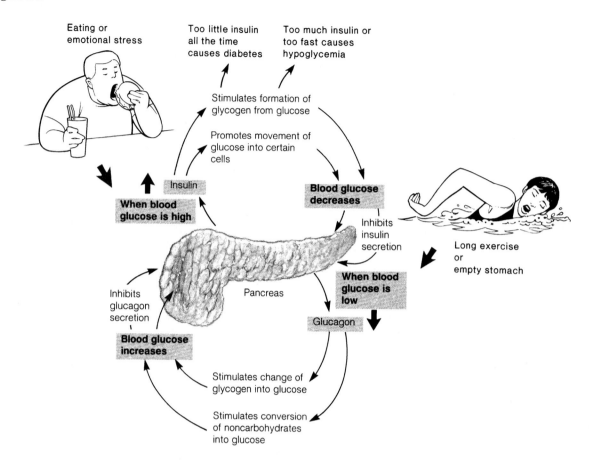

balance food intake with exercise. The movie *Steel Magnolias* showed a hypoglycemic attack.

Hypoglycemic reactions are most likely to occur before meals and during strenuous exercise. Many of the behaviors, symptoms, and signs are normal outcomes of exercise (excitement, perspiration, rapid heartbeat). Physical educators and coaches must monitor these especially carefully during the hour before lunch and dinner. Despite good management, everyone with diabetes I has an occasional hypoglycemic episode.

Management of Diabetes

Good diabetic control is based on proper diet, exercise, and insulin. A change in any one of these necessitates adjustment in the others. All persons with Type I take daily insulin and must acquire knowledge about insulin use and reactions that may occur if insulin dosage is miscalculated. Type II management focuses mainly on lifestyle changes in eating and exercising.

Multiple Daily Insulin Shots for Type I

Insulin shots are **subcutaneous**—that is, under the skin but above muscle tissue. Children are taught to administer their own shots at an early age. Common injection sites are buttocks, upper arms, outer sides of thighs, and lower part of the abdomen. The injection site should be changed frequently to minimize tissue breakdown. Adjusting the injection site according to antici-

pated activity is also important. When the exercise is primarily lower limb, as in track, insulin should be injected into the arm. When both upper and lower extremities are involved, the preferred injection site is the abdomen.

Types of insulin vary with respect to time elapse before peak effect (2–20 hr) and duration of effect (6–36 hr). Rapid-acting insulins begin to work in about 1/2 hr, although peak effect is at 2 hr. Most persons take several injections daily that are mixtures of rapid- and intermediate-acting types and provide overlapping protection.

Insulin is injected before meals, with the largest dose taken before breakfast. It may not be needed before all meals. Persons learn to adjust dosages when corrective measures are needed because of unplanned changes in eating and exercising. The major principle followed for both meals and exercise, however, is consistency in time of day, duration, and amount.

Illness, infection, and emotional stress may make diabetes worse and require extra insulin injections. Medications taken for other conditions also affect insulin dosage. Among those that increase blood glucose are diuretics (water pills that promote loss of fluids), prednisone (anti-inflammatory corticosteroid medication), beta-blockers (used to manage heart and blood pressure conditions), and decongestants (for colds and sinus infections). Birth control pills inhibit insulin action and thus indirectly raise blood glucose.

Table 19.3   Information about diabetic reactions that can become crisis situations.

Focal Points	Hyperglycemia and Ketoacidosis	Hypoglycemia: An Insulin Reaction
Situation	*Unmanaged Diabetes* *Crisis Response to Stress, Infection*	*Reaction to Delayed Food,* *Insufficient Food*
Imbalance	Low insulin, high glucose	High insulin, low glucose
Onset	Within hours	Within minutes
Behavior	Lethargic to drowsy	Nervous, restless, excited, argumentative
	Sitting, lying	Moving about
	Weak, tired all day	Sudden weakness, fainting
Symptoms, signs	Excessive urination	Normal urination
	Excessive thirst, hunger	Thirst, hunger varies
	Abdominal pain	Headache
	Dry skin	Lots of perspiration
	Weak pulse	Rapid heartbeat, palpitations
	Deep, labored breathing	Normal to shallow, rapid breathing
Treatment	Insulin shot	Glucose tabs, candy, juice
	If severe, hospitalization	Glucagon shot
If no treatment	Coma, death	Coma, death

Diet for Types I and II

Persons with diabetes typically know a lot about diet but may need support and companionship in eating correctly. The following guidelines should be emphasized:

1. Follow the consistency principle: Eat meals at the same time every day and exercise likewise.
2. Eat several small meals (about five) instead of three big ones.
3. Keep caloric intake about the same from meal to meal and day to day.
4. Identify foods that cause rapid glucose rise (have high glycemic index) and avoid them. These foods are mainly the white, processed carbohydrates.
5. Emphasize fibers and starches (complex carbohydrates).
6. Avoid food and liquid intake when feeling nervous or anxious.
7. Balance food intake with exercise.
8. Keep glucose tablets, hard candy, or fruit juice available in case low glucose precipitates a hypoglycemic reaction.
9. Eat a nonrefined or natural carbohydrate snack about every 30 min during heavy, prolonged exercise.
10. Coordinate time and amount of food intake with exercise.

Exercise for Types I and II

Regular exercise is extremely important in diabetes management and may be prescribed just like medication. The prescription is typically what is good for everyone: aerobic exercise at least three times a week on alternate days, with each session lasting 45–60 min. The intensity and duration depend on initial level of fitness. Nonexercisers begin with progressive distance and speed walking programs to start attitude and habit changes. Leisure counseling helps persons to discover what is fun for them and to learn new sports (see Figure 19.4).

Figure 19.4   Dr. Bruce Ogilvie, the father of sport psychology, confers with an athlete who is blind. Many persons who are blind also have diabetes and need lifelong leisure and fitness counseling.

Blood glucose is not affected the same way by all types of exercise. *Aerobic exercise lowers blood glucose and is the activity of choice if the glucose level is under 240 mg/dl.* When blood glucose goes above this safety criterion, the opposite is true, and aerobics are contraindicated. Anaerobic exercises like push-ups and weight lifting do not lower glucose and should be used in moderation. They are important for strength development, but a person with diabetes should not select weight lifting as a major sport.

Persons with diabetes typically utilize protein and fat for energy during exercise more extensively than nondiabetics. Extra protein and nonrefined carbohydrates should be eaten 15 to 30 min before exercise when planned intensity exceeds 300 cal an hour. During exercise of this intensity or greater, nonrefined carbohydrate snacks are recommended every 30 min. Persons with diabetes often lose weight by exercise more quickly than nondiabetic peers.

If blood sugar is above 300 mg/dl or ketone bodies are in the urine, exercise is contraindicated. Other conditions that indicate exercise should be stopped or not initiated include (a) infection anywhere in the body, (b) high resting blood pressure, (c) severe pain in calf muscles, and (d) signs of hypoglycemia. These are all temporary problems. As soon as they are resolved, exercise programs should be resumed.

On the day after strenuous exercise, persons with diabetes may need to decrease insulin and eat more because of a tendency toward low blood glucose. This is because muscle and liver glycogen have been depleted, and several hours are required to build up normal storage levels.

Insulin Pump Therapy for Type I

An insulin pump is "a battery-powered, computerized device approximately the size of a pager that delivers insulin through tubing that is connected to a needle or catheter placed under the skin" (Kaplan-Mayer, 2003, p. 180). Insulin pumps, a relatively new treatment approach, are used by only about 12% of persons with diabetes I, possibly because pumps cost about $5,000. The number is increasing as persons understand the advantages of pump use and learn that most insurance companies will cover all or part of this cost as well as money for monthly supplies like blood sugar test strips. For more information, see the following websites:

www.insulin-pumpers.org
www.insulin-pumpers-r-us

Websites of manufacturers include the following:

Animas   www.animas.com
DANA   www.sooil.com
Disetronic   www.disetronic-usa.com

In insulin pump therapy, the pump is worn 24 hr a day, and small amounts of insulin are delivered continuously, as programmed. The wearer must learn how to program the computer in the pump and must monitor blood sugar frequently (maybe 8 to 10 times a day) to program correctly. The insulin pump relies on fast-acting insulin, so the wearer must program ahead of time for the correct amount of insulin to cover all carbohydrates to be eaten. Wearers carry extra insulin cartridges and new batteries with them as do users of other electronic devices. Insulin insertion sites must be changed from time to time; many persons use the abdominal area so the device can be hooked over a waist band or belt, but any area can be used.

Strenuous exercise can be performed while wearing the pump, but wearers must be sure that perspiration does not cause the insertion site to come loose. Whether to wear the pump while competing in contact sports is controversial.

Implications for Physical Education

Emphasis should be on students with diabetes developing healthy attitudes toward exercise and body care. Students need models who have been excellent athletes despite diabetes.

Recommendations for teaching follow:

1. Ask the school nurse or appropriate person for the names of all students with diabetes and keep information readily accessible on emergency protocol, type of diabetes and medication, and special diet and snack needs. This is especially important for after-school practices and trips.

2. Meet with the school counselor or appropriate person and arrange to have students with diabetes *scheduled for physical education after breakfast or lunch.* Explain the importance of not exercising when blood glucose is low.

3. Create a prearranged signal that students with diabetes can use to call for a substitute or to be excused from class to respond to warning signs (i.e., to eat something or to monitor glucose because of feeling funny).

4. Provide breaks for fluid every 15 min during strenuous activity and give special attention to dehydration in hot weather.

5. Insist that students with diabetes protect themselves against sunburn, falls, blows, and the like that damage skin. This includes avoiding contact sports like boxing and football.

6. Pay extra attention to clean, dry socks and proper shoes. Athlete's foot, blisters, and corns can become major problems for students with diabetes.

7. Treat students with diabetes with dignity and expect them to have glucose tablets, candy, or juice on hand at all times, in case of reactions. Keep a backup supply in case a student forgets. Remember that diet soda does not include enough glucose to work.

8. Do not give untrained persons with diabetes physical fitness tests that are concentrated in short time periods. Evaluate fitness over several sessions in which duration and intensity are gradually increased.

9. Teach students with diabetes to exercise with partners who understand diabetes. Pairing persons with diabetes with those who want to lose weight is a good idea because of common interest in food and exercise.

10. Be understanding of mood swings, good and bad days, and behaviors associated with hypoglycemic reaction. Let students talk out embarrassment, frustrations, and concerns.

Cardiovascular Problems

The two causes of cardiovascular disease are acquired and congenital. *Acquired conditions,* the number one cause of death in persons aged 25 and over, primarily affect the arteries that sup-

Table 19.4 Risk factors in cardiovascular disease.

Factors That Can Be Altered

Hypertension (high blood pressure)
Elevated low-density-lipoprotein cholesterol (LDL-C) and
 triglycerides
Tobacco
Diet
Physical inactivity
Body fatness
Diabetes
Emotional stress

Factors That Cannot Be Altered

Heredity
Age
Sex
Race

ply oxygen to the heart and brain. In contrast, *congenital conditions* are typically defects in the structure of the heart walls and valves.

Over 20% of the world's population has acquired cardiovascular disease (Brunner, 2001). This is typically diagnosed after age 50 or 60, but pathology begins in youth (see risk factors in Table 19.4). By age 60, one out of every five American males has coronary artery disease (CAD), the most common disorder (see Figure 19.5 and Chapter 28 on aging). Women also have CAD, but the prevalence is about six times greater in males than females. Blacks have significantly higher death rates than Whites.

With respect to congenital heart disease, about 1% of all newborns have a heart disorder, but 20 to 60% of infants born with chromosomal defects are affected. Alcohol, tobacco, drugs, and viruses like HIV and rubella are also associated with congenital heart disease.

Atherosclerosis and Coronary Heart Disease

Atherosclerosis is a degenerative process that leads to heart attacks, strokes, and circulatory problems. *Athero* is the Greek word for "gruel" (porridge or cereal) and refers to the accumulation of fatty substances resembling gruel inside the arteries. This is a lifespan process, beginning as early as age 3. *Sclerosis* means hardening of the arteries.

With a partner, close your eyes and use visual imagery (cereal inside arteries) to remember atherosclerosis. Develop a list of other terms that can be remembered through visual imagery.

Atherosclerosis begins in childhood as fat streak deposits (see Figure 19.6). These are found in the aorta as early as age 3. Fat deposits subsequently appear in the coronary and peripheral (outside the heart) arteries in late childhood and adolescence. The exact age depends on many factors. The

Figure 19.5 The coronary arteries branch downward from the aorta and encircle the heart like a crown encircles the head. Disease of these arteries is the number one cause of death in persons age 25 and over.

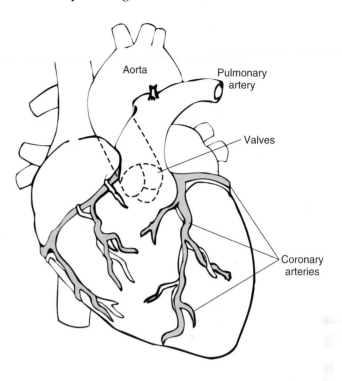

coronary arteries are the heart's only source of oxygen. They branch downward from the aorta and encircle the heart like a crown encircles the head. Coronary is derived from the word *corona,* meaning "crown." Consider how the coronary arteries are as important to the heart as a crown is to royalty. Coronary artery disease (CAD), caused by atherosclerosis, *is the leading cause of death for both men and women in the United States.*

By early adulthood, enough fatty substances have accumulated to be called *plaque* (see Figure 19.6). This atherosclerotic process can be happening anywhere in the body but is most dangerous in the heart and brain. Unlike soft, fatty streaks, plaque is hard with rough edges. *The slow progressive buildup of plaque during the adult years not only narrows passageways but also damages surrounding cells,* causing hemorrhage, ulceration, and **blood clots** known as thrombi (singular: *thrombus*) and emboli (singular: *embolus*). A **thrombus** is a blood clot that remains at its point of origin. An **embolus** is a traveling obstruction; it may be a blood clot or a bubble of gas.

The ages between 40 and 60 represent the clinical horizon for most persons when symptoms of atherosclerosis begin to be noticed (see Figure 19.6). Among the most common indicators are (a) high blood pressure, (b) discomfort or pain during strenuous exercise, and (c) blood analysis that shows high levels of triglycerides, low-density-lipoprotein cholesterol (LDL-C), and very-low-density-lipoprotein cholesterol (VLDL-C). Most persons at risk try to change their lifestyles during these years, and adapted physical activity becomes high priority. At this point or soon, **coronary heart disease (CHD)** is typically diagnosed.

Figure 19.6 Atherosclerosis is a lifespan degenerative process that is related to known risk factors. Note how the arteries change from decade to decade when risk factors are ignored.

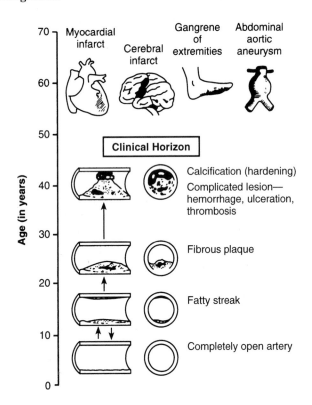

If lifestyle change is ineffective or genetic predisposition to cardiovascular disease is overpowering, pathology is manifested in the form of heart attacks, strokes, circulatory dysfunctions, and aneurysms (see Figure 19.6). The heart, brain, and extremities are primarily damaged by **ischemia,** meaning inadequate oxygen to cells. The resulting cell death is called **infarcts** or **infarction** in the heart and brain and **gangrene** in the extremities. Thus, atherosclerosis is an **ischemic disease.**

Aneurysms are deformities of blood vessels, usually the arteries, caused by structural anomalies, disease, and progressive, long-term weakening of the walls by atherosclerosis and/or high blood pressure. The most common site is the aorta in the abdominal region, but aneurysms can occur anywhere. The most serious aneurysms, of course, are those in the heart and brain.

At particular risk for aneurysms are persons with **Marfan syndrome,** an inherited connective tissue disease associated with tall, thin body types in basketball, volleyball, and other sports requiring height. Undetected aneurysms may rupture during vigorous exercise and cause death (ACSM, 2001).

The atherosclerotic process results in about 1 million deaths in the United States each year. About 60% of these come from heart attacks associated with coronary artery disease (CAD), 20% from strokes, and 20% from overall system failure related to heart muscle degeneration and high blood pressure. Heart attack and stroke usually are not fatal on first occurrence. They are, however, costly in terms of time, money, and mental health.

Heart Attack

Heart attack, called **myocardial infarction** (MI) because cells are dying, is a life-threatening crisis that occurs when the oxygen demand of the heart muscle cells is greater than the coronary arteries can supply. Inadequate oxygen is signaled by chest pain (**angina**) in the area behind the breast bone. This pain may radiate to the jaw, neck, shoulder, or arms. The pain is felt as a continuous, heavy, squeezing pressure lasting 2 or more minutes, rather than sharp or stabbing twinges. Sweating, shortness of breath, general weakness, nausea, and vomiting may also be present.

Persons of all ages have heart attacks, but most often, infarction strikes males ages 50 and above with high-risk profiles. *The first 48 to 72 hr after a heart attack are critical because death of heart muscle cells and their replacement with scar tissue disrupt the rhythm of the heartbeat.* This dysrhythmia often brings on a second attack. The section "Cardiac Rehabilitation for Adults," later in this chapter, discusses adapted physical activity.

Stroke

Stroke, also called cerebrovascular accident (CVA) or apoplexy, is a sudden loss of function (awareness, motor, speech, perception, memory, cognition) caused by ischemia or hemorrhage affecting brain cells. Consciousness is sometimes but not always lost. Recovery of function depends on the site and extent of brain cell death. Strokes can be massive, causing much damage, or small episodes, called **transient ischemic attacks** (TIAs), that are hardly noticed. In a TIA, something causes inadequate oxygen to the brain. TIAs result in muscle weakness, mental confusion, speech difficulty, or other mild problems that last only a few hours. Persons suspecting they are having a TIA should immediately go to their physician or to the nearest emergency center. These are warnings of cerebral atherosclerosis and impending major strokes.

Strokes are more common in males until about age 75, after which the incidence is equal for both sexes. Strokes can occur at any age but are most frequent after age 60. African Americans and Asian Americans are more prone to strokes than European Americans are. *Cerebral thrombosis related to atherosclerotic degeneration is the most common cause.* Visualize the four main arteries and many small branches that supply oxygen to the brain. A blood clot (thrombus) kills brain cells by denying them oxygen, whereas hemorrhage destroys cells by issuing blood into the wrong places. Approximately one-third of stroke victims die. Others recover slowly. Additional information about stroke appears in Chapter 25 on cerebral palsy and traumatic brain injury. Stroke results in disabilities similar to these conditions.

Problems of the Extremities

Atherosclerosis can also affect arteries of the arms and legs, reducing the supply of oxygen to muscles, skin, and nails. This is one reason why the fingernails and toenails of many elderly people become abnormally thick and hard to cut. It also explains why older persons often have cold feet and hands and more frequent bruising and skin breakdown. The best interven-

Table 19.5   Review of parts of the heart and the direction of blood flow.

Function	Pumping Chamber	Upward-Flow Valves	Artery	Circulation Capillary Exchange	Venous Return	Collecting Chamber	Downward-Flow Valves
Left heart systemic circulation	Left ventricle	Aortic	Aortic	Total body	Superior and inferior vena cava	Right atrium	Tricuspid
Right heart pulmonary circulation	Right ventricle	Pulmonary	Pulmonary	Lungs	Pulmonary veins	Left atrium	Mitral or bicuspid

Note. All blood goes through both a systemic and pulmonary circuit. To trace blood flow, read from left to right.

tion is to minimize time spent lying, and to engage in low-intensity exercise.

Legs and feet are more commonly affected by atherosclerosis than upper extremities. The first indication of an inadequate supply of oxygen to muscle is pain, aching, and cramping in the calf caused by walking short distances (e.g., half a block to a quarter mile). This pain is **claudication,** named after Emperor Claudius of ancient Rome, who walked with a limp. As atherosclerosis becomes progressively worse, pain is felt even during inactivity, especially during bed rest. This is because a horizontal position prevents gravity from assisting the blood to flow down to the legs.

In advanced stages of arterial insufficiency, the extremities become increasingly susceptible to injury, disease, and temperature extremes. Open sores do not heal properly, infection sets in, and tissue death may be so great that gangrene requires amputation of affected body parts. This pathology is associated with old age; however, *persons with diabetes are at high risk at all ages.*

Congestive Heart Disease, Usually in Old Age

A weak heart muscle can result from (a) cell death (ischemia) caused by heart attack, (b) work overload caused by structural defects, and/or (c) a sedentary lifestyle. Like other muscles, the heart must be used vigorously a few minutes each day to stay strong. Progressive weakness of the heart is characterized by accumulation of fluid in body parts. This is called *congestion* or *edema.*

A brief review of the parts of the heart and the direction of normal blood circulation enhances understanding of what is happening during congestive heart disease (Table 19.5 and Figure 19.7). **Systemic circulation,** initiated by contraction of the left ventricle, carries oxygenated blood to all systems of the body and returns waste-laden, oxygen-depleted blood. Weakness of the left ventricle is manifested by an inability to pump hard enough to empty the chamber; fluids begin to back up in the left atrium and lungs. **Pulmonary circulation,** initiated by contraction of the right ventricle, carries the deoxygenated blood to the lungs, where wastes are exchanged for oxygen. Insufficiency of right ventricle function causes blood to back up in the right atrium and the veins of body parts.

The left and right sides of the heart react differently to congestion. **Left heart congestion,** the most common, is char-

acterized by fluid in the lungs, shortness of breath, wheezing, and coughing. This condition makes persons particularly susceptible to death by **pneumonia** (lung inflammation caused by bacteria, viruses, and chemical irritants). **Right heart congestion** causes fluid retention in the liver, legs, and feet. Edema anywhere in the body is an indication of dysfunction that is increasing blood volume and making the heart muscle work harder than normal.

Congestive heart disease may progress slowly, with no discomfort felt for years. The weak ventricular muscle, unable to squeeze strongly, simply wears out, and the blood flows too slowly to meet oxygen needs. Persons become less and less fit, eventually dying in their sleep. *This problem is particularly acute among nonambulatory persons with severe mental retardation, brain damage, or physical disabilities, who are dependent upon others to get them out of bed and provide exercise.* The primary cause of death for this population is pneumonia/heart congestion, whereas the primary cause of death for all other adult populations is coronary artery disease. Persons in nursing homes (especially the ill elderly) are at particular risk because the staff is often not able to meet their exercise needs. Congestive heart disease can be ameliorated simply by sitting upright a few hours each day so that fluids can drain, but some persons are too weak to manage this without help. Breathing exercises and games (described later in the chapter discussion of asthma) are recommended also, along with gentle exercise (passive, if necessary) of all body parts.

Conduction Abnormalities and Heart Rate

Electrical impulses are what makes the heart beat. Abnormalities in the heart's electrical conduction system result in various kinds of **dysrhythmias** (fast, slow, or irregular heartbeats) and **blocks** (interruptions or delays in conduction). Many of these require special training to conduct endurance testing and exercise prescription (see ACSM certifications).

The structure within the heart that normally initiates the electrical impulses is the *sinus* or *sinoatrial (SA) node.* Anything that alters these impulses affects heart function. Sometimes, cardiac tissue other than the sinus node produces electrical impulses. When this happens, the heartbeats are called **ectopic,** meaning that they are displaced or in an abnormal position. *Repetitive or frequent ventricular ectopic activity is an exercise contraindication.*

Figure 19.7 **Figure 19.7** **The four chambers of the normal heart and the physiology of pulmonary and systemic circulation. Systemic circulation is shaded. The sinus node is the heart's natural pacemaker.**

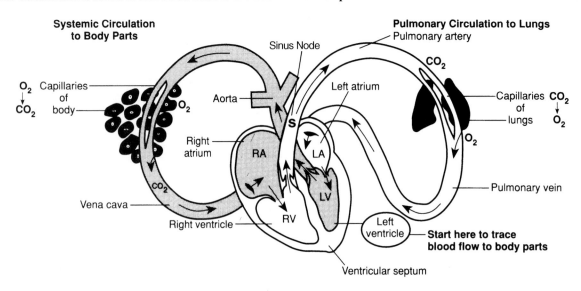

Chronotropic Incompetence

Chronotropic dysfunction or incompetence is a conduction abnormality that causes a chronically slow heart and a sluggish response to aerobic activity. Persons with quadriplegia and high-level paraplegia have chronotropic dysfunction (see Chapter 23). This condition is also relatively common in severe developmental disabilities and postoperative congenital heart defects. *Aerobic fitness testing must be adapted and conducted with caution. Endurance activities may be contraindicated or need to be adapted to a lower-than-normal target heart rate range.*

Sick sinus syndrome (SSS) is a generic term for dysrhythmias that stem from problems of the sinus node (inside the heart, also called the sinoatrial node), autonomic nervous system, and hypothalamus. This term, sometimes a synonym for **chronotropic incompetence,** is applied to persons with widespread, though not necessarily serious, abnormalities of rhythm (e.g., too fast or slow, or alternating fast and slow). Chronic fastness or slowness might not be noticed because the condition develops slowly or is congenital. Some sources say that SSS is most common among the elderly, but the condition has been documented in exercise literature pertaining to disabilities (Rimmer, 1994; Shephard, 1990). Fatigue, dizziness, and **syncope** (temporary unconsciousness) are exercise responses associated with SSS.

Fibrillations and Flutters

Fibrillations (rapid quivers) are incomplete contractions of heart fibers caused by conduction disturbances. **Flutters** are similar but less severe disturbances. While in fibrillation, the heart is unable to pump blood.

Ventricular fibrillation is *the cause of most cardiac arrests and deaths in adults* and is commonly associated with coronary heart attack, electrical shock, and excess amounts of digitalis or chloroform. Electrical devices called **defibrillators** counteract fibrillation and save lives.

Atrial fibrillation also requires immediate treatment because it compromises ventricular filling. Among children and adolescents, the most common cause of atrial fibrillation is **Wolff-Parkinson-White (WPW) syndrome,** a condition precipitated by congenital anomalies of some of the conduction pathways. This is one of the ACSM exercise testing contraindications.

Tachycardias

Tachycardia is diagnosed when the resting heart rate in adolescents and adults is faster than 100 beats per minute. In infants and children, the criterion is much higher. Fast rhythms originating in the sinus node, typically between 100 and 150 beats per minute, are called **sinus tachycardias.** Alcohol, caffeine, and nicotine can trigger sinus tachycardia in healthy persons. Other causes include infection and/or disease with fever, dehydration, anemia, blood loss, hyperthyroidism, anoxia, and certain drugs used to manage asthma (theophylline) and hyperactivity (epinephrine). A fast sinus rhythm may be benign, with no exercise restrictions, or it may signal medical problems. *Fast rhythms (resting rates above 150) caused by problems arising outside the sinus node (i.e., ectopic) typically contraindicate aerobic exercise and endurance testing.*

Bradycardias

Slow heartbeat can indicate either cardiovascular wellness or pathology. Chronic, slow heartbeat (**sinus bradycardia**) in athletes is an indication of excellent cardiorespiratory fitness. Pathology-related causes of bradycardia are the sick sinus syndrome, heart attack, hypothermia (prolonged coldness or freezing), hypothyroidism, complete heart blocks, anorexia nervosa, congenital heart defects not corrected by surgery, and medications like digitalis and beta-blockers designed specifically to slow heartbeats. Slow heartbeat, as long as there is energy to complete desired tasks, is not a problem because persons generally self-select only activities that are comfort-

Figure 19.8   Four valves open and close to regulate blood entering and leaving chambers.

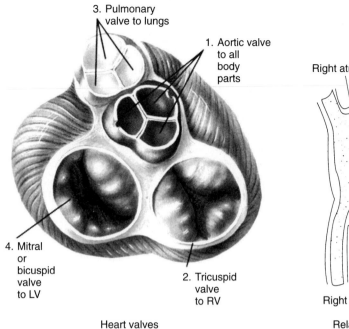

3. Pulmonary valve to lungs

1. Aortic valve to all body parts

4. Mitral or bicuspid valve to LV

2. Tricuspid valve to RV

Heart valves

Right atrium

Pulmonary artery

Left atrium

Left ventricle

Right ventricle

Relationship of heart valves (1, 2, 3, 4) to other parts of the heart

able. *Aerobic activities are contraindicated unless prescribed by a physician.*

For adults, a heart rate less than 40 beats per minute, unless the person is a trained athlete, is an indication for medication and/or an artificial pacemaker. Less than 60 beats per minute is the diagnostic criterion for prepubertal persons.

Heart Block

Heart block is a pathologic interruption or delay in electrical impulse conduction that alters the rhythm of the heartbeat. Blocks may be congenital or acquired through disease or injury. There are many kinds, *but only two are ACSM exercise contraindications:* complete atrioventricular (AV) block and left bundle branch block. If someone has these conditions, get expert help before permitting exercise.

Cardiovascular Medications

Cardiovascular drugs are discussed at the beginning of this chapter. Persons taking cardiovascular drugs can and should exercise. Graded exercise and cardiac rehabilitation programs are discussed later in this chapter. Weight loss is often the first exercise priority.

Inflammation of the Heart Wall

The **pericardium** (the fibrous sac that surrounds the heart and great vessels) contains three layers that comprise the heart wall. Inflammation of these structures results in conditions called *pericarditis, myocarditis,* and *endocarditis.* Inflammation is caused by a variety of viral, bacterial, and unknown agents. Often these

are introduced into the bloodstream during corrective surgery. *Anything inserted into the body (e.g., tubes, shunts, or catheters) can carry a virus or bacteria,* so persons with hydrocephalus, cancer, and diabetes (as well as users of illegal drugs) are particularly at high risk. Inflammation is treated by several families of anti-infective drugs (e.g., antibiotics, antimicrobials) and by corticosteroids. *Exercise is contraindicated until inflammation is under control.*

Valve Defects and Heart Murmurs

Valves are the membranous structures that rhythmically open and close to force the blood within the heart to flow in the right direction (see Figure 19.8). For simplicity, the mitral and tricuspid valves are called the **atrioventricular** (AV) valves because they open at the same instant to permit blood to flow downward from atria to ventricles. The closing of the AV valves is what makes the "lubb" sound in the "lubb-dupp" of the heartbeat and is the mechanism that starts constriction. Shortly thereafter, the aortic and pulmonary valves (called the **semilunar valves** for brevity) open to permit blood to be squeezed upward into the aorta and pulmonary artery. The closing of the semilunar valves marks the beginning of the rest period during which all four valves are closed.

Valvular defects typically cause **heart murmurs** (noises heard with a stethoscope). The cause is typically unknown, unless symptoms can be traced back to an infection. Most valvular defects are mild, and some even heal themselves. About 80% of young children have a heart murmur. Most of these disappear during adolescence.

Most persons with valvular disease have few or no exercise restrictions. Ordinary physical activity does not cause shortness of breath, undue fatigue, palpitation, or chest pain. *Ability to excel in vigorous activity like aerobic fitness tests and lengthy competitive games may be limited, depending on the nature and severity of the defect.*

Valvular defects are of three types: (a) regurgitation, (b) stenosis, and (c) prolapse. **Regurgitation** is the backward leakage that occurs when damaged valves are unable to close tightly. **Stenosis,** or narrowing of the valves, compromises the valves' ability to open widely and permit blood to flow freely. **Prolapse** is the slipping or falling out of place of an organ.

The most common is **mitral valve prolapse** (MVP), in which the valve leaflets flop backward into the left atrium during the heart's squeezing action (systole). The main symptoms are arrhythmias and chest pain. MVP occurs mostly in adults and more often in Down syndrome (14% prevalence) than in the nondisabled population. *MVP is also common in connective tissue disorders like osteogenesis imperfecta, Marfan syndrome, and Ehlers-Danlos syndrome* (see Chapter 24 on les autres conditions).

Rheumatic Fever

Rheumatic fever is the most common cause of acquired heart disease in children and adolescents. In the United States, this disease is rare, but in Third World countries, rheumatic fever continues to be a major cause of illness and death. Some developing countries report an almost equal incidence of congenital and rheumatic heart disease. In sharp contrast, rheumatic fever accounts for only 1 to 3% of children's heart disease in the United States.

Rheumatic fever is an autoimmune disease in which antibodies attack tissues and cause various kinds of inflammation. The disease typically follows inadequately treated childhood **streptococcal infections** (e.g., strep throat or scarlet fever). Fever and sore, swollen joints (polyarthritis) are the most common symptoms. Shortness of breath, chest pains, and exercise intolerance are indications of inflammation of the heart (carditis), a common manifestation. **Carditis** is the term used when two or more of the heart wall layers are affected. **Chorea** or *St. Vitus Dance* (an involuntary twitching of muscles) is an indication of central nervous system involvement. Chorea, which occurs in only 8 to 10% of patients, appears much later than other symptoms, often 2 to 6 months after the strep infection.

Initial treatment is usually hospitalization and medications. Inflammatory treatment is used from a few days to 3 or 4 months, depending on the tissues involved. Bed rest is recommended until symptoms disappear because inflammation anywhere in the body places extra stress on the heart. Children without carditis may return to school in 2 or 3 weeks with no restrictions other than common sense in gradually increasing exercise duration and intensity. Children with carditis recover slowly over many months.

The heart is permanently damaged in about 60% of the children who have rheumatic fever. The mitral and aortic valves are the parts of the heart most frequently affected (see Figure 19.8).

Congenital Heart Defects

The heart problems of children are mostly congenital. The incidence of congenital heart defects is 6 to 10 per 1,000 live births. Surgery is often performed during the first few weeks of life. Ideally, this surgery is undertaken before age 6 so that the child can start school with a normal or near-normal heart and few exercise restrictions. Physical educators should be familiar with the most prevalent congenital heart defects (see Figure 19.9).

Once a congenital defect has been surgically corrected, the chances are good that the child will have no exercise restriction. Many participate in strenuous, high-level, competitive sports. The student should be allowed the freedom to decide how hard to play, since sensations are usually a reliable guide to exercise tolerance. The psychological problems stemming from parental overprotection and preoperative anxieties and fears are generally greater than residual physiological limitations.

Definitions of Terms

A review of the basic terms used in heart disease helps to make sense of the congenital disorders:

Septal—Refers to the septum, a dividing wall between two chambers. In the heart, there is an atrial septum and a ventricular septum.

Patent—From the Latin word *patens,* meaning "wide open" or "accessible."

Ductus arteriosus—A tubelike passageway in the fetus between the aorta and the main pulmonary artery.

Tetralogy—A group or series of four.

Great vessels—The aorta and pulmonary artery.

Stenosis—Constriction or narrowing of a passageway.

Coarctation—Tightening or shriveling of the walls of a vessel; compression.

Atresia—Pathological closure of a normal anatomical opening or congenital absence of the opening.

Shunt—A hole in the septum between the atria or the ventricles that permits blood from the systemic circulation to mix with that of the pulmonary circulation or vice versa.

Cyanosis—Blueness resulting from oxygen deficiency in the blood.

Three Categories of Congenital Heart Defects

Figure 19.9 shows that congenital heart defects fall into three categories: (a) left-to-right shunts, (b) obstructive lesions, and (c) right-to-left shunts. The **left-to-right shunts** are the most common, the easiest to understand, and generally the least serious. Two are holes in the heart structure, and one is a duct that fails to close. In each, oxygenated blood from the arteries seeps through a hole in the heart wall (septum) into the waste-filled blood in the right chambers. This causes a volume overload on the right ventricle and raises blood pressure, but these effects are minimal when holes are small.

Obstructive lesions narrow (a) the valves that govern upward flow of blood or (b) the aorta itself. The most serious is

Figure 19.9 Common congenital heart defects grouped according to impairment. (From *American Heart Association Heartbook.* New York: E. P. Dutton, pp. 243–246. Reproduced with permission. © *American Heart Association Heartbook,* 1980. Copyright American Heart Association.)

Left to Right Shunts (Holes That Raise Blood Pressure)

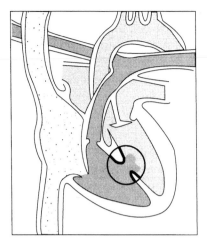

Ventricular septal defect (VSD)

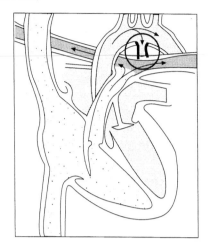

Atrial septal defect (ASD)

Patent ductus arteriosus (PDA)

Obstructive Lesions (Impaired Blood Flow)

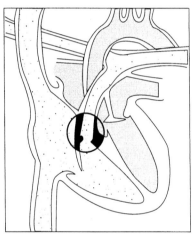

Pulmonic stenosis, valvular (PSV)

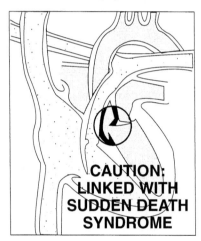

CAUTION: LINKED WITH SUDDEN DEATH SYNDROME

Aortic stenosis, valvular (ASV)

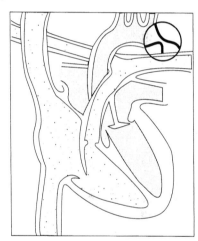

Coarctation of the aorta (COA)

Right to Left Shunts (Cyanotic Lesions)

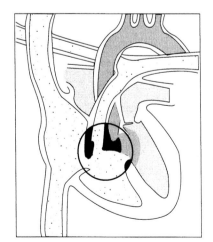

Tetralogy of Fallot (TOF)

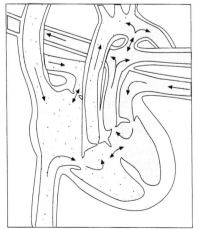

Transposition of the great vessels (TGV)

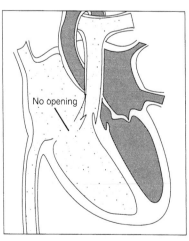

No opening

Tricuspid valve atresia (TVA)

aortic stenosis valvular (ASV), which leads to left heart congestion and has been linked with sudden death syndrome. Strenuous exertion is contraindicated. The effects of **coarctation of the aorta** depend on the location of the narrowing, but high blood pressure is the greatest problem. **Pulmonary stenosis valvular** (PSV) leads to right heart congestion.

The **right-to-left shunts** are caused by complicated conditions, as indicated by their names. In each of these, poorly oxygenated venous blood somehow gets into the aorta, thereby reducing the oxygen being carried to all body parts. The low oxygen content causes skin, lips, and nail beds to take on a bluish tint, a characteristic known as **cyanosis.** Obviously, low oxygen limits energy and endurance. The volume overload on the left ventricle also raises blood pressure.

The Four Most Common Congenital Defects

A brief discussion of the four most common conditions follows. Other defects can best be remembered by visualization and grouping them by type (see Figure 19.9).

Ventricular Septal Defect

The severity of **ventricular septal defect** (VSD) depends on whether the hole in the ventricular septum is small or large. Small holes often close spontaneously in early childhood. Many small- and medium-sized openings that do not close are harmless. Large holes must be surgically repaired. VSD is the most common congenital heart defect. Before surgery, respiratory infections and slow physical growth are particular problems.

In the older literature (e.g., Maurer, 1983), VSD is reported in about 40% of infants with Down syndrome (DS). Now the atrioventricular canal defect is considered the most common lesion in DS (Marino & Pueschel, 1996). The term **atrioventricular canal defect** indicates that the shunt (hole) in the ventricular wall is large enough to be called a canal, particularly when it occurs with shunting in the atrial wall in the area that normally separates the mitral and tricuspid valves. The resulting left-to-right canal causes breathing difficulty, fatigue, feeding problems, and slow growth. In most cases, surgery is performed before age 1.

Patent Ductus Arteriosus

Before birth, there is no need for blood to circulate through the lungs because the placenta takes care of oxygen needs. Therefore, the fetus has a tubelike passageway (the ductus arteriosus) between the aorta and the pulmonary artery that enables the blood to bypass the lungs. At birth, when breathing starts, reflex muscle contractions in the wall of the ductus arteriosus causes this bypass to close within a few days. When this fails to take place, normal circulation cannot be established. Part of the oxygenated blood in the aorta that should be flowing to other body parts leaks into the pulmonary artery via the open duct.

When this seepage is large, the symptoms and treatment are the same as for severe VSD. PDA occurs in about 20% of premature infants and 5% of full-term infants, making it the second most common congenital heart defect.

Tetralogy of Fallot (Most Serious of Four Defects)

Tetralogy (meaning "four symptoms") is characterized by (a) VSD, (b) PSV, (c) an enlarged right ventricle, and (d) a malpositioned aorta that receives blood from both ventricles. This combination of abnormalities was discovered by a man named Fallot and thus is known as Tetralogy of Fallot. The resulting shunt is unoxygenated blood from the right ventricle leaking into the left ventricle, which pumps it throughout the body. The unoxygenated blood, bluish in color, causes the condition known as *blue baby* or cyanosis.

TOF is usually severe, requiring surgery in infancy. Without surgery, spells of breathlessness, increased cyanosis, and loss of consciousness may occur. Breathing can be made easier by holding the child upright against an adult's shoulder, with the knees tucked up to the chest. After surgery, throughout life, maximal aerobic capacity tends to be low.

Pulmonic Stenosis Valvular

PSV, although relatively common, is usually mild. If blood pressure remains more or less normal, surgery is typically not required. In such cases, aerobic capacity is slightly reduced. The less common ASV is the valvular defect that contraindicates vigorous exercise.

Exercise and Congenital Heart Defects

For almost all moderate to severe heart conditions, corrective surgery is performed in early childhood. A healthy, active lifestyle is emphasized thereafter, with walking recommended within 3 days of surgery. Children return to school within 2 to 3 weeks of surgery and soon begin a graded exercise program of walking, swimming, or cycling. Within 4 months of surgery, most children can participate in general physical education with no restrictions.

Table 19.6 is an example of the type of graded exercise program begun 3 days after surgery. See the table note for a description of proper warm-up and cool-down. While parents are encouraged to perform this program with their children (Strong & Alpert, 1982), school or agency personnel often are relegated responsibility. The ultimate goal is ability to exercise 30 min at least three times a week within the upper limit of the target heart rate zone recommended by the physician. See Chapter 13 (pages 344–345 and Figure 13.8) for target heart rate zones.

The target heart rate zone after surgery depends on whether correction was total or partial. *In many postoperative persons, the maximal heart rate is and always will be slightly lower than normal* (see the sections "Chronotropic Incompetence" and "Sick Sinus Syndrome" earlier in this chapter). Persons with postoperative conditions have a lifelong tendency to fatigue more quickly than peers. The general consensus is that teachers and coaches should allow these individuals to impose their own exercise restrictions during vigorous activity. Aerobic exercising and testing should *not* be required unless the teacher has ACSM or equivalent training.

Most physicians recommend participation in sports. After completion of their graded exercise program, most postoperative persons have *no restrictions except for a caution against primarily isometric activities.* Isometrics increase blood pressure because blood vessels reflexly contract during static muscle contraction.

Surgery and Restrictions

Often, no surgery is recommended for mild heart conditions because activity, including sport involvement, is not seriously limited. Children with mild heart conditions typically can engage

Table 19.6   Graded exercise program.

Week	Graded Exercise
1	Walk 10 min, try not to stop
2	Walk 5 min, jog 1 min
3	Walk 5 min, jog 3 min
4	Walk 4 min, jog 5 min
	Walk 4 min, jog 4 min
5	Walk 4 min, jog 5 min
6	Walk 4 min, jog 6 min
7	Walk 4 min, jog 7 min
8	Walk 4 min, jog 8 min
9	Walk 4 min, jog 9 min
10	Walk 4 min, jog 13 min
11	Walk 4 min, jog 17 min
12	Walk 4 min, jog 17 min
13	Walk 2 min, jog slowly 2 min, jog 17 min
14	Walk 1 min, jog slowly 3 min, jog 17 min
15	Jog slowly 3 min, jog 17 min

From W. B. Strong and B. S. Alpert (1982).

Note. Warm-up should consist of stretching and limbering exercises for 5 min, while cool-down should involve 3 min of walking slowly and 2 min of stretching. Check your pulse periodically to see if you are exercising within your target zone. As you become more fit, try exercising within the upper range of your target zone.

in strenuous sports in an instructional or recreational setting, *but high-intensity, competitive sports may be restricted.* In moderate to severe defects, surgery is sometimes delayed until overall health status is improved or a certain age is reached. In the case of delayed surgery, physicians are likely to restrict children to moderately strenuous or nonstrenuous sports.

Implications for Physical Education

Many students from low socioeconomic backgrounds have mild heart defects that go undetected. Follow the ABCDEF plan in making physician referrals when symptoms are observed during vigorous activity:

A Angina, severe chest pain

B Breathing difficulty

C Color changed, bluish or pale

D Dizziness

E Edema, fluid retention and swelling of extremities

F Fatigue

Persons with disabilities, especially the various syndromes caused by chromosomal and inborn metabolic disorders, are more prone to cardiac disorders than others. The prevalence rate of heart disease for various syndromes ranges from 20 to 60%. Many of these conditions are mild and go undetected unless a teacher or coach urges vigorous activity. Particular care therefore should be taken in fitness testing and programming.

Use graded exercise programs like that in Table 19.6 before fitness testing, rather than the pretest-posttest models favored in research. Emphasize activities described in Chapters 13 and 16 on fitness and relaxation. Programming is similar to that for other OHI conditions in that exercise progressions are

slower, and better motivation is needed because discomfort is greater and/or the persons do not yet understand their bodies and the meaning of true exertion. Guidelines for working with obese/overweight and asthmatic conditions are particularly applicable because of shared cardiorespiratory fitness problems.

Cardiac Rehabilitation for Adults

The aerobic exercise phase of cardiac rehabilitation begins about 8 to 12 weeks after a heart attack or coronary bypass surgery. Stress testing is repeated periodically and the exercise prescription revised accordingly. *Persons in cardiac rehabilitation programs demonstrate achievement at the 6 MET capacity before transferring from a medically supervised, individualized program involving continuous heart monitoring to a group program conducted by exercise scientists.* Refer to Chapter 13 on fitness for further information on METs and other activities appropriate in cardiac rehabilitation.

Hypertension

Hypertension, or high blood pressure, is a cardiovascular problem in which the blood exerts a greater than normal force against the inner walls of the blood vessels. This excess force, in time, permanently damages organs, most often the heart, brain, kidneys, and eyes. Hypertension can be caused by atherosclerosis; certainly, anything that obstructs blood flow increases pressure. However, there are many other causes, and hypertension can exist separate from atherosclerosis.

For the population as a whole, hypertension is the leading reason for taking prescription drugs. Approximately 58 million persons in the United States (or about 25% of the general population) have hypertension. Of these, about 5 million are under age 17. The prevalence is greater for males than females and for Blacks than other races. Prevalence increases decade by decade until about age 65 and then levels off. At age 65, approximately 50% of Whites and 60% of Blacks have high blood pressure.

Hypertension places persons at high risk for organ damage until the golden 70s and 80s. *After ages 75 and 85 for men and women, respectively, death rate tends to be lower when blood pressure is higher.* Across the lifespan, however, hypertension is a major risk factor for death by heart attack or stroke.

One reason hypertension is dangerous is that rises in blood pressure typically cause no pain or discomfort. Persons who do not have routine medical checkups are unaware of blood pressure abnormalities. When hypertension progresses to a severe stage, strenuous exercise and other forms of stress may cause headache, visual disturbances, vomiting, and/or convulsions. On the other hand, the condition may continue to be asymptomatic. There are many individual differences.

Blood Pressure Measurement

A *sphygmomanometer* is used to measure blood pressure (see Figure 19.10). Normal blood pressure for adults is 120/90 millimeters of mercury (mm Hg) or less. A value like 120/90 indicates the pressure inside the aorta and pulmonary arteries when the ventricles of the heart contract and relax. The upper number

Figure 19.10 Blood pressure. Study the diagrams for systole and diastole. Can you find the valves that open and close to permit heart action?

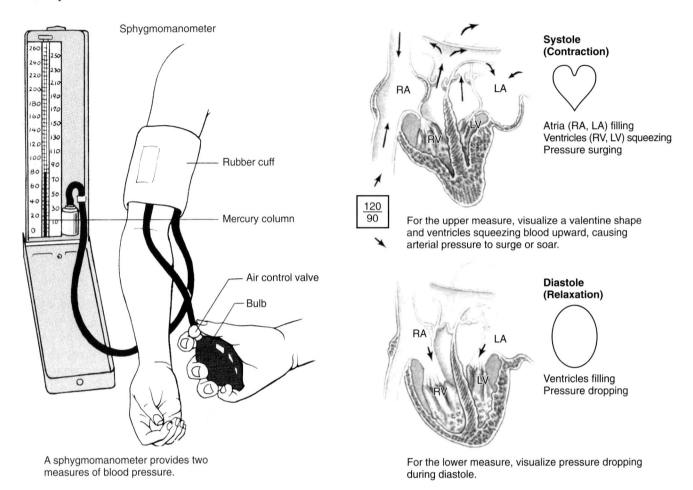

Sphygmomanometer

Rubber cuff

Mercury column

Air control valve

Bulb

A sphygmomanometer provides two measures of blood pressure.

Systole (Contraction)

Atria (RA, LA) filling
Ventricles (RV, LV) squeezing
Pressure surging

$\frac{120}{90}$

For the upper measure, visualize a valentine shape and ventricles squeezing blood upward, causing arterial pressure to surge or soar.

Diastole (Relaxation)

Ventricles filling
Pressure dropping

For the lower measure, visualize pressure dropping during diastole.

indicates **systolic** or contraction pressure. The lower number indicates **diastolic** or relaxation pressure.

Systolic and diastolic pressure are equal in importance. Elevation of either one is cause for concern, but high blood pressure is not diagnosed until after several readings on different days. In research and clinical settings, systolic pressure can be monitored reliably during exercise on a treadmill or bicycle ergometer, but diastolic pressure cannot.

Systolic and Diastolic Pressures

The heart looks like a valentine during systole, the time of greatest pressure, when the ventricles are squeezing all of their blood upward into the arteries and *the atria are bulging* because the atrioventricular (AV) valves have closed (see Figure 19.10). **Systole** (the contraction phase) is the beginning of the heartbeat, the loud "lubb" sound in the "lubb-dupp" heard by a stethoscope. To remember, **V**isualize **V**alentine's Day and **V**entricles (**the 3 Vs**) with **S**queezing the blood upward during **S**ystole, causing the arterial pressure to **S**urge (**the 3 Ss**).

Diastole (the relaxation phase) is easy to remember because the overall heart shape is a relaxed oval. Word derivation helps us to visualize *di-* (two chambers), *-a-* (without), *systole* (contraction). The pressure is at its lowest point when the

ventricles are relaxed, the AV valves are open, and blood is filling the lower chambers. Duration of this low blood pressure phase depends on rate of heartbeat. The slower the rate, the more relaxation and filling time.

Causes of Hypertension

For simplicity, causes of hypertension are classified in two ways: (a) primary or essential (cause unknown) and (b) secondary (cause can be linked with specific disorders or pregnancy). Among adults, 90% of all hypertension is primary.

Pregnancy is a time of particular risk. Blood volume increases to about 30% above normal during pregnancy, and many compensatory mechanisms must operate to keep blood pressure normal. This problem is especially intensified in women with spinal cord injuries (Krotoski, Nosek, & Turk, 1996). *Preeclampsia,* a toxemia of pregnancy condition characterized by hypertension and edema, occurs in 5 to 7% of pregnancies of able-bodied women.

Most severe **childhood hypertension** is associated with kidney disease, obesity, or coarctation of the aorta (a congenital heart defect that narrows the aorta). Unlike adults, the classification is seldom primary. This may be partly because hypertension is asymptomatic and many cases go undiagnosed. Early identification of children at risk for cardiovascular disease is essential. Therefore, physicians now diagnose primary hypertension in children whose blood pressure readings over time exceed the 95th percentile for their age and sex. Those with weight that exceeds the 95th percentile and a family history of hypertension are at greatest risk. Regardless of classification, the single best correlate of hypertension is large body mass (Kaplan, 1990). The best treatment for primary hypertension in children is loss of excess weight.

Classification by Severity

Adult hypertension is classified in four categories: borderline to mild (140/90), mild to moderate (150/95), moderate to severe (160/100), and uncontrolled (170/110). *Medically supervised exercise testing is contraindicated when resting values exceed 200/120.* Nonsupervised physical activity, even of low intensity, should be discontinued whenever resting rates evidence a change from normal pattern. This usually means that medication is no longer effective and that a physician needs to reassess management of the disease.

Table 19.7 shows that different criteria are used in diagnosing and classifying hypertension in children. Blood pressure in healthy persons gradually increases from infancy through adulthood. *This change results from size rather than age differences.* The largest increase occurs in conjunction with the adolescent growth spurt. Because blood pressure is correlated strongly with body mass, height and weight are considered in making a diagnosis.

Typically, when systolic blood pressure is elevated, the diastolic is also, and vice versa. The exception is old age, when **isolated systolic hypertension** (ISH) often occurs because atherosclerosis has decreased the elasticity of major arteries. Cardiac output shows no associated change. The diseased aorta simply cannot distend to accommodate the amount of blood ejected with each ventricular contraction.

Blood Pressure Responses to Exercise

In healthy adults, systolic blood pressure rises by 30 to 60 mm Hg during strenuous isotonic exercise. Diastolic pressure rises little or not at all (see Figure 19.11). In aerobically trained persons, diastolic pressure may even fall. In hypertension, blood pressure response to exercise is exaggerated. Monitoring values before and after exercise is a good practice. In laboratories, where pressure readings during exercise are possible, the criterion for stopping exercise is a value exceeding 250/120. In field settings, exercise pressures of 225/90 are considered high risk.

Isometric exercise and activities involving a Valsalva maneuver like weight lifting are controversial because they increase both systolic and diastolic blood pressures to high rates. ACSM (2000) *says that isometric exercise is not strictly contraindicated in hypertension but should be used with extreme caution.* High repetitions and low resistances are recommended for weight training.

Management of Hypertension

Mild hypertension is managed by accepting responsibility for healthy diet and exercise practices and acting on environmental factors that cause emotional stress. Excess weight must be lost and proper weight maintained. Salt intake, for many persons,

Table 19.7   Classification of hypertension by age group.

Age (in Years)	Mild/Moderate	Moderate/Severe
Infants (<2)	112/74	118/82
Children (3–5)	116/76	124/84
Children (6–9)	122/78	130/86
Children (10–12)	126/82	134/90
Adolescents (13–15)	136/86	144/92
Adolescents (16–18)	142/92	150/98
Adults	150/95	160/100

Modified from Kaplan (1990) and the Task Force on Blood Pressure Control in Children (1987).

Figure 19.11   **Blood-pressure changes in response to vigorous big-muscle exercises in a healthy adult.**

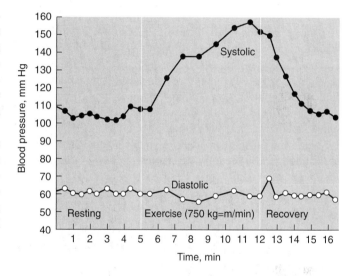

must be reduced. This means use of fresh or frozen foods rather than canned goods, which are high in sodium, and avoidance of high-salt items like bacon, cheese, and pickles. The recommended sodium intake is 1,100 to 3,300 mg daily.

Regular aerobic exercise is beneficial because it reduces blood pressure. This occurs over time, like weight loss. Training effects, however, do not last more than 3 to 6 weeks if exercise is discontinued.

Moderate to severe hypertension requires medication in addition to healthy lifestyle. Physical activity specialists need to understand these medications because of exercise side effects. Among the major classes of antihypertensive drugs are diuretics, vasodilators, and the blocking agents.

Antihypertension drugs affect the validity of heart rate monitoring during exercise. There is no way to separate the heart's natural response to exercise from drug-induced slowness or fastness. Therefore, *collect data on medications and discuss side effects before helping persons to start exercise programs.*

Respiratory Problems

Most of us take breathing for granted. We squeeze air out of our lungs 20,000 times a day and seldom think about the process of respiration. Yet respiratory diseases are the fastest rising causes of death in the United States. This section is about persons who struggle to breathe. They may have *asthma, chronic obstructive pulmonary diseases,* or *cystic fibrosis.* The symptoms are similar in all conditions, and exercise is vital for the maintenance of respiratory fitness. *Almost half of the chronic diseases that affect children under age 17 are respiratory in nature. Asthma, hay fever, and other allergies account for approximately 33% of all chronic disease in this age group.* Bronchitis, sinusitis, and related conditions cause about 15%. Cystic fibrosis, although rare, results in death from chronic lung disorders. The physical activities for these children are the same as those for children with asthma.

Emphysema is primarily a disease of middle and old age, but its origins can often be traced to asthma and chronic bronchitis in earlier years. Over a million Americans lead restricted lives because of emphysema. The fastest-growing cause of total disability in the United States, it is surpassed only by heart disease.

Asthma

Asthma is a chronic lung disease characterized by airway obstruction, airway inflammation, and airway hyperreactivity (Cypcar & Lemanske, 1995). **Airway** refers to the many bronchial tubes that fill the lungs (see Figure 19.12). Asthma is a cellular disorder, always present but only occasionally manifested as acute episodes of coughing, wheezing, and breathing difficulty. Asthma is linked with insufficient levels of theophylline in the blood and various person-environment factors that trigger attacks (e.g., viral infections, weather conditions, exercise, allergens, and irritants like cigarette smoke).

Persons with asthma tend to be multiply disabled in that they frequently have hay fever, allergies, sinus trouble, and upper respiratory infections. In childhood, they tend to be underweight and fragile. In adulthood, most are prone to weight problems and other side effects of an inactive lifestyle.

Prevalence

Estimates of the prevalence of asthma in the United States range from 10 to 35 million, depending on diagnostic criteria. Approximately half of all cases begin in childhood, with more males affected than females. Despite improved treatment modalities, the overall incidence is rising; this trend is particularly evident among minority children of low socioeconomic status. Asthma is the leading cause of chronic illness in children under 17 and is a special challenge for physical education teachers, because 60 to 90% of individuals with asthma have conditions that are triggered by aerobic exercise. This type of asthma is called **exercise-induced asthma** (EIA). Symptoms sometimes develop during exercise but more often appear 5 to 10 min after exercise ends. Some persons experience a recurrence of symptoms 4 to 8 hr after exercise. EIA usually remits within 10 to 20 min, but it can be stopped immediately by puffs from an inhaler.

Asthma Attacks

Asthma is chronic and always present, but *attacks* occur only occasionally. Asthma attacks progress through three stages: (a) coughing, (b) dyspnea, and (c) severe bronchial obstruction.

Coughing warns of an impending attack. In this stage, the bronchial tubes are secreting mucus, which accumulates and

---

Figure 19.12   The lungs are filled with large and small bronchial tubes, called *bronchi* and *bronchioles*, respectively, that are lined with mucous membrane. Also shown is an alveolus, or air cell.

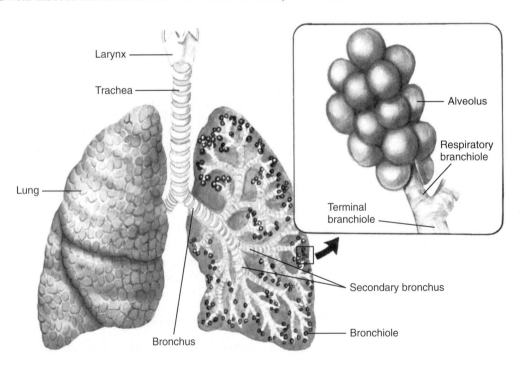

obstructs the passage of air. Coughing is caused by the reflex action of the smooth, involuntary muscles of the bronchioles in an attempt to remove the accumulating mucus. This action is often called a *bronchospasm.*

Dyspnea, meaning breathing difficulty, occurs when the linings of the bronchioles swell, thus narrowing the air passages and diminishing the flow of air. Breathing difficulty is primarily with *exhalation,* and total emptying of air before the next inspiration is impossible.

Severe bronchial obstruction occurs as the airways continue to narrow and become clogged with mucus. Wheezing is caused by the movement of air in and out of the constricted bronchial tubes and through the accumulated mucus. If medication is not used or is ineffective, this stage progresses to **status asthmaticus,** a condition in which breathing is so labored that treatment in a hospital emergency room is needed.

A status asthmaticus condition leaves fluid in the lungs that may cause days of occasional coughing spasms. Physicians emphasize that this fluid must be coughed up and not swallowed. Part of hospital treatment is respiratory therapy to aid weak or exhausted muscles in coughing up mucus.

Persons with chronic asthma have good and bad days. Often, these are related to weather changes, high pollen counts, environmental pollutants, or an infection. A common cold, for example, usually causes the lungs to fill with fluid with a resultant mild status asthmaticus condition. On days when the lungs feel bad and breathing is harder than usual, persons with asthma must decide between slowing down and trying to keep going. Those who make the latter decision often overuse the inhaler, each time thinking that, somehow, another puff will help. It typically does not.

Causes and Medications

Pathology at the cellular level is extremely complex. Simplified, the abnormality is in the *beta-adrenergic receptors of lung cells* that normally maintain balance between nerve fibers that release epinephrine (adrenalin) and those that liberate acetylcholine. Alterations of this balance, whatever the causal factors, cause obstruction, inflammation, and hyperreactivity of the airways.

Most of the medications used to treat asthma are therefore **bronchodilators** or anti-inflammatory agents. These are available in tablet, powder, liquid, or aerosol form, but the aerosol inhalator is the preferred modality (see Figure 19.13). By age 6, most children can be taught to use inhalators. Some individuals take one or two puffs of aerosol only when needed; others follow prescriptions of regular use twice or more daily. Children under age 6 typically must have breathing treatments under adult supervision (see Figure 19.14).

The *beta-adrenergic agonists,* named for the cell receptors they work on, are the most potent bronchodilators. The airways open almost immediately after one or two puffs. There are few side effects (mainly rapid heartbeat) for most people, unless the inhalator is overused. Beta-adrenergic agonists therefore can be used as a preventive or as direct treatment of a beginning asthma attack. Most individuals who are conscientious about adhering to beta-adrenergic agonist treatment have no airway problems.

Many persons with severe chronic asthma also take *theophylline* daily in liquid, tablet, or capsule form. Among its many brand names are Slophyllin, Slobid, Primatene, and Quibron. This medication is needed when the theophylline level in the blood is low, a common deficiency in persons with

Figure 19.13 By age 6, most children can be taught to use an inhaler, but exhalation and inhalation mechanics should be checked occasionally by adults.

Figure 19.14 Young child, with newly diagnosed asthma, taking her morning breathing treatment. This must be set up and supervised by an adult.

asthma that requires periodic blood tests and considerable experimentation to find the right drug dosage. Side effects are insomnia, nervousness, diarrhea, and stomach cramps, but these discomforts disappear over time.

The medication of last resort, used only when the others fail and/or the body is fighting an infection, is the *corticosteroids*. These drugs have many side effects, but they reduce bronchial tube swelling when nothing else will. They are typically taken for only a few days, but chronic asthma is now treated by twice-daily preventatives like the advair diskus that combines corticosteroids with bronchodilators.

The drugs described in this section are prescription medications. All of the drugs mentioned, except for the aerosol bronchodilators, are banned by the International Olympic Committee (IOC). Athletes taking prescribed drugs should report these to their coaches.

Overuse of Aerosol Bronchodilators

Most inhalers carry warnings about the maximum number of puffs to take every 24 hr. Overuse causes nervousness, increased heart rate, high blood pressure, and other symptoms. These side effects are often ignored because they do not seem bad compared with the oxygen deficit that is causing panic. Nevertheless, excessive use of inhalers and other asthma medications can cause death.

Exercise-Induced Asthma

Students who experience breathing problems in physical education are not yet properly managing their asthma and need to be referred to a specialist for further study. Often, considerable time is required to determine the best medication; likewise, time is needed to learn to manage both the environment and stresses related to feeling different from peers. Should the student with asthma want to give up and resume a sedentary lifestyle, the physical educator must inspire the faith and courage to keep trying alternatives. *No student should be excused from physical education because of asthma.*

Role models are particularly helpful. Among the many Olympic athletes who have managed asthma with medication are track star Jackie Joyner-Kersee and swimmers Tom Dolan and Amy Van Dyken.

Persons with asthma can do low-intensity exercise for long periods without an attack. This type of exercise is good for losing weight but does not improve aerobic fitness. Once weight is lost and aerobic fitness is targeted, six basic principles should be followed to prevent attacks:

1. *Use preexercise puffs of aerosol.*
2. *Use long warm-ups of mild intensity.* A 15- to 30-min warm-up is typically needed rather than the 5 to 10 min recommended by ACSM. **Wind sprints** are also good. For example, seven 30-sec sprints, each 2.5 min apart, have a beneficial effect on a distance run performed 30 min later.
3. *Induce a refractory state 45 to 60 min prior to anticipated EIA.* A **refractory state** is a period of protection against further asthma attacks that can be induced by sustaining a

mild EIA episode before a major exercise event (Cypcar & Lemanske, 1995). The mild EIA episode provides protection for approximately 2 hr. This practice is generally used in conjunction with the inhalator, but only 40 to 50% of individuals with asthma experience refractory states, which are not well understood. *A series of six 50- to 100-yd sprints used as part of warm-ups is generally sufficient to induce the refractory state.*

4. *Use intermittent or interval training.* When applied to EIA, this means no more than 5 min of vigorous exercise followed by 5 min or less of rest. This sequence can be repeated over and over. The **5-min criterion** is based on the average amount of time that the nonmedicated person with EIA can engage in continuous vigorous exercise at target heart rate before the onset of an attack.

5. *Select appropriate climatic conditions.* Warm and humid climatic conditions are recommended. This is why swimming is an excellent sport for people with asthma. When outdoor conditions are cold and dry, opt for indoor exercise. Wear a scarf or mask over the face in cold weather to warm the air before inspiration.

6. *Specialize in sports that demand relatively short bursts of energy or adapt time spent in play.* Baseball, softball, volleyball, doubles tennis, weight training, and wrestling are particularly recommended. Arrange intermittent play with 5 min in the game followed by 5 min of rest. Continuous-duration sports of high intensity, such as basketball, soccer, cross-country skiing, and marathons, are contraindicated for most, but not all.

Diaphragmatic Breathing

Most persons with asthma breathe incorrectly all or most of the time, overworking the upper chest and intercostal muscles and underworking the diaphragm. A goal, therefore, is to teach them the two kinds of breathing and for them to feel the difference. The two kinds are (a) shallow or costal (meaning rib cage) and (b) deep or diaphragmatic. To teach this, the physiology of respiration must be explained and practice given in diaphragmatic breathing (see Figure 19.15). The ability to breathe deeply is dependent on the strength of the diaphragm during inhalation and its ability to relax during exhalation.

The **diaphragm** is the dome-shaped muscle that separates the thoracic and abdominal muscles. In inhalation, the diaphragm contracts, descends 1 to 7 cm, and creates space for the lungs to fill with air. Exhalation begins when fullness of the lungs triggers relaxation and upward recoil of the diaphragm. This squeezes the air up and out. No muscle action other than this recoiling is needed in exhalation except during vigorous exercise.

Persons with asthma have more difficulty with exhalation than inhalation. This is because the phrenic nerve that innervates the diaphragm is sensitive to anything that alters the breathing pattern (wheezing, coughing, tightness, exercise, nervous tension). All of these things interfere with relaxation of the diaphragm which, in turn, decreases the amount of air pushed out. During an attack, exhalations progressively let out less and less air. The chest distends and begins to feel heavy and ache.

Figure 19.15   Phenomena of normal breathing.

Inhalation	Exhalation
Bronchial tubes widen.	Bronchial tubes narrow.
Diaphragm contracts and descends.	Diaphragm ascends as a result of its elastic recoil action when it relaxes.
Abdominal muscles relax (return to normal length).	Abdominal muscles shorten, particularly in forced exhalation.
Upper ribs are elevated.	Ribs are depressed.
Thoracic spine extends.	Thoracic spine tends to flex.

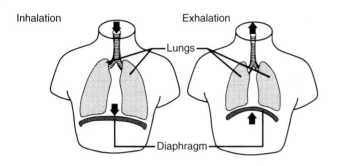

Learning correct breathing therefore is closely related to learning to relax.

Persons who take only shallow breaths allow the diaphragm to weaken. This may not be a problem in a sedentary lifestyle unless a cold, lung infection, or asthma creates mucus or phlegm that must be coughed up. Then the reflex respiratory mechanism is inadequate, and abdominal muscle action must supplement the recoil force of the diaphragm. This explains why the abdominal muscles, especially if they are weak, are so sore after heavy coughing.

Exercise, all kinds, is easier when breathing is diaphragmatic rather than costal. Intensity of the exercise, together with fitness of the diaphragm, determine the extent that abdominal muscles must assist with exhalation. In sedentary persons with asthma, even light exercise may require abdominal activity to expel air from the lungs, whereas in fit persons, the abdominals work only during heavy exercise.

Diaphragmatic breathing is often called abdominal because persons best understand deep breathing by watching and feeling the abdomen protruding in inhalation and flattening in exhalation. Slow abdominal pumping in a supine position reinforces new understandings. Various weights (books, sandbags, etc.) can be placed on the abdomen with a challenge to watch or feel the weight go up and down. Persons may need to be reminded that normal breathing ranges from 12 to 14 breaths a minute at rest and from 40 to 50 during vigorous exercise.

Also of concern is making sure that persons with asthma breathe through the nose rather than the mouth. Many do not because of nasal congestion, but new prescription sprays eliminate this problem. Nasal breathing warms and moistens the air before it gets to the lungs, helping to maintain homeostasis. Mouth breathing does the opposite.

Figure 19.16   Child exhales into spirometer as test of pulmonary efficiency.

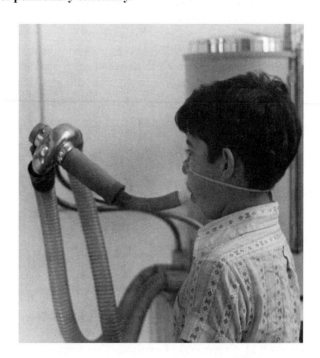

Changing overall pattern of breathing is as hard as permanently losing weight. Nevertheless, diaphragmatic breathing is an important goal. Activities like yoga (see Chapter 16 on relaxation) are a good way to improve breathing patterns. During routine vigorous exercise, persons with asthma must be repeatedly reminded to breathe deeply and slowly.

Spirometers and Peak-Flow Meters

A spirometer test is periodically administered to determine status or improvement in pulmonary efficiency (see Figure 19.16). The test used most often is the FEV_1 (forced expiratory volume for 1 sec). To obtain a computer printout, the person inhales deeply and then blows air out of the mouth into the tube as hard and fast as possible.

The FEV_1 is the number of cubic centimeters of air forcefully exhaled in the first second after a deep inspiration. Normal FEV_1 values range from 500 to 4,500 cc (cubic centimeters) for boys and from 350 to 3,400 cc for girls. Any condition that causes bronchial obstruction and resistance in the airways reduces FEV_1.

The peak-flow meter is similar but less expensive, so persons can keep one at home and periodically test themselves. A scale indicating the velocity of air expelled in liters per second is on the gadget, so no computer is needed. A drop of more than 10% from one's normal reading indicates significant airflow resistance and signals the need to reevaluate one's management protocol with a physician.

Games to Improve Expiration

Breathing exercises are no longer considered a viable approach to the management of asthma. They may be used in chronic obstructive lung disease, cystic fibrosis, muscular dystrophy, and other very severe conditions that cannot be managed by medication and environmental controls. In such instances, they are commonly associated with hospitalization and inability to exercise in normal ways. Research, with one or two exceptions, has repeatedly indicated no significant values accruing from breathing exercises. Games are more effective in improving expiration and also help to clear mucus from passageways. Since the abdominal muscles participate vigorously in laughing, blowing, and singing, games based on these activities can be developed.

Games Using Abdominal Muscles

1. **Laugh-In.** Circle formation with "It" in center. "It" tosses a handkerchief high into the air. Everyone laughs as loudly as possible as it floats downward, but no laughter must be heard after the handkerchief contacts the floor. Anyone breaking this rule becomes the new "It." For variation, students can cough instead of laugh.

2. **Laugh Marathon.** Each student has a tape recorder. The object is to see who can make the longest-playing tape of continuous laughing.

3. **Guess Who's Laughing.** All students are blindfolded. One, who is designated as "It," laughs continuously until classmates guess who is laughing.

4. **Red Light, Green Light Laughing.** This game is played according to traditional rules except that laughing accompanies the running or is substituted for it.

   All games designed to improve exhalation should be played in erect standing or running postures since the spine and pelvis must be stabilized by the lumbar extensors in order for the abdominal muscles to contract maximally.

Blowing Activities

Blowing activities are especially valuable in reducing residual air in the lungs. Learning to play wind instruments is recommended strongly. Swimming offers a recreational setting for stressing correct exhalation. Games found to be especially popular follow:

1. **Snowflakes.** *Equipment:* A 1-in square of tissue paper for each child. *Procedure:* Two teams with each child having one piece of paper. Each participant attempts to keep the paper above the floor after the whistle is blown. When the paper touches the floor, the participant is disqualified. The winner is the team in which a player keeps the tissue in the air for the longest time.

2. **Ping-Pong Relay for Water or Land.** *Equipment:* One Ping-Pong ball for each team and kneepads for each player, if done on land. *Procedure:* Several teams with one-half of the players of each team in shuttle formation. A player blows the Ping-Pong ball across the floor to his or her team member, who blows the ball back to the starting line. The relay continues until each player has blown the ball. The team that finishes first is the winner. Use small teams so waiting for turn is minimal.

3. **Under the Bridge.** *Equipment:* One Ping-Pong ball for each team. *Procedure:* Teams with players standing in single file (about one body length between) with legs spread. The last player in the file blows the ball forward between the legs of his or her team members, with additional blowing provided by the other players to move the ball quickly to the front. If the ball rolls outside the legs of the players, the last player must retrieve the ball and blow it again. When the ball reaches the front, the first player in the file picks up the ball, runs to the end of the file, and blows the ball forward again. The team finishing first is the winner.

4. **Balloon Relay.** *Equipment:* One balloon for each player. One chair for each team placed on a line 95 ft from the starting line. *Procedure:* Children on the teams line up in single file behind the starting line. Upon the signal to start, the first player of each team runs to the opposite line, blows up his or her balloon, places it on the chair, and sits on the balloon until it breaks. He or she then returns to the starting line and tags the next player, who proceeds in the same manner.

5. **Blow Out the Candle.** *Equipment:* A candle is placed on the floor between every two children. *Procedure:* Opponents lie on the floor on opposite sides 8 ft from the candle. Players attempt to blow out the candle from the greatest distance possible. The child who blows out the candle at the greatest distance is the winner.

6. **Ping-Pong Croquet.** *Equipment:* Ping-Pong balls and hoops made of milk cartons taped to the floor. *Procedure:* Each player blows the Ping-Pong ball through the series of hoops, positioned on the floor in the same manner as in a game of croquet. The ball must be moved and controlled entirely by blowing. The hands may not touch the ball at any time. The players who finish first are the winners.

7. **Self-Competition in Candle Blowing.** *Equipment:* Movable candle behind a yardstick placed opposite the mouth (see Figure 19.17A). *Procedure:* Child attempts to blow out lighted candle set at gradually lengthened distances on the yardstick.

8. **Self-Competition in Bottle Blowing.** *Equipment:* Two half-gallon bottles, half filled with water and connected with two rubber hoses and three glass pipes (see Figure 19.17B). *Procedure:* Child attempts to blow water from one bottle to another, first from sitting position and then standing position.

Pursed-Lip Breathing Contests

This can be competition against self or others. Emphasize a short inspiration through the nose and long expiration through gently pursed lips, making a whistling or hissing noise. This is called **pursed-lip breathing.** Try timing the expiration phase with a stopwatch or metronome. Expiration should be at least twice as long as inspiration.

The Physical Activity Environment

Since so many persons with asthma are sensitive to pollens and dust, physical activity should be indoors at least during the seasons of peak incidence of attacks. Ideally, the room should be air-conditioned and dust-free.

Figure 19.17   Blowing exercises.

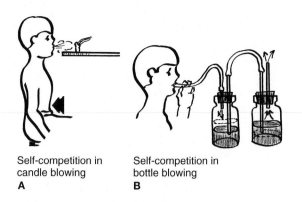

Self-competition in candle blowing
A

Self-competition in bottle blowing
B

Changes in weather, particularly cold, dry air, predispose persons to attacks. Alterations in body temperature—specifically, becoming overheated—seem to cause wheezing. A cold, wet towel on the forehead and/or the back of the neck between activities helps to maintain uniform body temperature.

When the chalkboard is in use, students with asthma should be stationed as far away from it as possible. Nylon-covered, allergen-free mats containing foam rubber as filler are recommended.

Most persons with asthma are extremely sensitive to tobacco smoke. Even if a cigarette is not burning, residual fumes can trigger an attack.

Whereas all children become thirsty during vigorous physical activity, they are generally encouraged to wait until the end of the period to get a drink of water. *In contrast, forcing fluids is an essential part of the total exercise program for students with asthma.* As tissues become drier during exercise, the mucus thickens and is more difficult to cough up. Coughing itself dries out the mucous membranes. The only means of thinning this mucus is through fluids taken by mouth or intravenously. Four or five quarts of water a day are recommended. Cold drinks are contraindicated since they may cause spasms of the bronchial tubes; hence, fluids at room temperature are recommended.

Antihistamines are not desirable for persons with asthma because they tend to dry out the mucus in the airway. If, because of hay fever or other allergies, a person is taking antihistamines, it is even more important that fluid intake be increased.

Psychological Coping

In the past, some persons believed that psychological problems caused asthma. This etiology is not valid. Asthma is a chronic lung disease that, like all illnesses and disabilities, complicates life. Different persons cope with illnesses in different ways, and some handle stress better than others.

The psychological phenomenon known as a *reaction formation* is common among persons with asthma. To prove their worth to others, they tend to establish unrealistically high levels of aspiration and then totally exhaust themselves in all-out effort to accomplish such goals. When it appears that they cannot live up to their own or the perceived expectations of others, an asthmatic attack often occurs, thereby adding more stress. "I could have made the deadline if I hadn't gotten sick!" "I would

have won the match if I hadn't started wheezing." The physical educator will find many children eager to play, despite parental restrictions, and unwilling to withdraw from a game even when they evidence asthmatic symptoms. Many do not impose limitations on themselves, refusing to accept the inevitability of an attack. Like all children, they want to be *normal.*

Chronic Obstructive Pulmonary Diseases

Chronic obstructive pulmonary diseases (COPD), including chronic bronchitis and emphysema, now constitute the fastest-growing chronic disease problem in America. The death rate has doubled every 5 years over the past 20 years.

Chronic bronchitis is a recurrent cough characterized by excessive mucus secretion in the bronchi. The three stages are (a) *simple,* in which the chief characteristic is frequent, deep, labored coughing; (b) *mucopurulent,* in which the mucus is intermittently or continuously filled with pus because of active infection; and (c) *obstruction,* in which a narrowing of the airways makes coughing worse. This is the stage at which the complications of emphysema and/or heart failure occur. The three stages may merge one into the other and span a period of 20 or more years.

Emphysema is a destruction of the walls of the alveoli of the lungs. This destruction results in over-distention of the air sacs and loss of lung elasticity. *Emphysema* is a Greek word that means, literally, "to inflate or puff up." Persons with emphysema have difficulty expelling air. Whereas the normal person breathes 14 times a minute, the person with emphysema may breathe 20 to 30 times a minute and still not get enough oxygen into the bloodstream. The characteristic high carbon dioxide level in the blood causes sluggishness and irritability. The heart tries to compensate for lack of oxygen by pumping harder, and possible heart failure becomes an additional hazard.

Emphysema is more common among men than women. Over 10% of the middle-aged and elderly population in America have emphysema. The specific etiology is still under study, but smoking and air pollution are causal factors.

Persons with COPD tend to restrict their activities more and more because of their fear of wheezing and dyspnea. This inactivity results in muscle deterioration, increased shortness of breath, and increasing inactivity—a vicious cycle! Permanent chest deformities (e.g., kyphosis, barrel chest, pigeon chest) may occur after many years of COPD. The activities recommended for persons with asthma are suitable also for individuals with bronchitis and emphysema.

Cystic Fibrosis

Cystic fibrosis is a genetic disorder of the secretion ability of membranes that line body organs, tubes, and passages. All organs are affected, most importantly the lungs, pancreas, intestinal mucous glands, and sweat glands. Normally, membranes secrete thin, freely moving mucus. In cystic fibrosis, the mucus is thick and sticky, creating two major problems. First, it clogs the bronchial tubes, interfering with breathing, and it lodges in the branches of the windpipe, acting as an obstruction. The resulting symptoms resemble those in asthma, bronchitis, and emphysema. Second, it plugs up the pancreatic ducts, preventing

Figure 19.18 Hospital treatment for persons with asthma, cystic fibrosis, and similar conditions consists largely of special medications via a bronchodilator, chest physiotherapy done by a respiratory therapist, and postural drainage. The major purpose is to facilitate coughing to clear mucus from the clogged bronchial tubes.

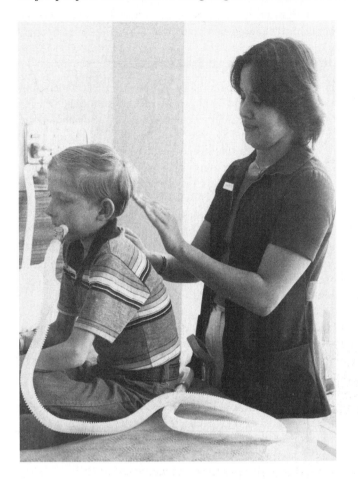 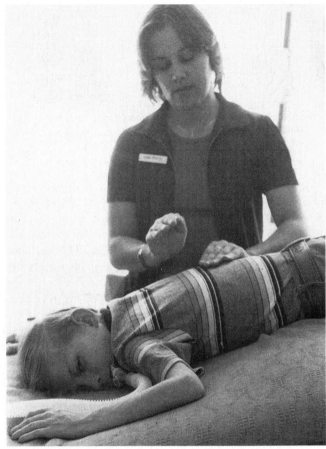

digestive enzymes from reaching the small intestine and thereby causing malnutrition.

Prevalence and Lifespan

Of all of the genetic diseases in the White population, cystic fibrosis is the most common life-shortening condition. In the United States, approximately 30,000 persons have cystic fibrosis and 10 million are asymptomatic carriers. The incidence is 1 in every 2,500 live births in White Americans and 1 in every 17,000 Black Americans. The condition is nonexistent in Asian Americans.

The median lifespan for persons with cystic fibrosis is now about 30 years. This is remarkable, considering that when the condition was first identified in the early 1960s, almost all children with cystic fibrosis died before reaching school age. Currently, about 35% of individuals with cystic fibrosis are age 18 or older.

Medications

Cystic fibrosis is managed by combined pulmonary, gastrointestinal, and psychological therapy. Pulmonary therapy includes daily chest physical therapy (see Figure 19.18), use of the same types of aerosols as for asthma, and relatively frequent use of corticosteroids and antibiotics to treat lung inflammation. Gastrointestinal therapy focuses on good nutrition, with emphasis on pancreatic enzyme replacement. Psychological therapy is family oriented and targets stress management.

Exercise Implications

No sports are contraindicated except scuba diving. Research indicates that people with cystic fibrosis tolerate exercise well. The same principles apply as in programming for individuals with asthma. Depending on the severity of cystic fibrosis, the possible adverse effects of exercise are increased loss of salt and fluid through sweat, decreased tolerance for hot-weather exercise, shortness of breath, increased coughing, and lowered blood oxygen levels. Encouraging and monitoring fluid intake before, during, and after exercise is crucial. Salt tablets are not recommended, but individuals should be allowed to choose salty foods.

Exercise testing to determine the intensity of exercise needed for a personalized fitness program should be conducted by credentialed experts. The maximum heart rate used in prescribing exercise should be a measured actual maximal heart rate, not a predicted one. Lung-related factors limit exercise before the heart can achieve its maximal rate. **Desaturation,** which occurs in severe lung disease, refers to the lowering of blood oxygen (i.e., the hemoglobin count) during exercise. Testing should determine the heart rate at which this occurs, and care should be taken not to exceed this heart rate. Supplemental oxygen is used with exercise if desaturation occurs at very low heart rates. All possible accommodations are made to keep the person exercising as much as possible as the disease progresses.

Treatments for Severe Respiratory Conditions

Persons with severe asthma, chronic obstructive lung disease, and cystic fibrosis generally spend some time each year in the hospital or at home convalescing from attacks that were complicated by colds, flu, or other respiratory illness. Special treatment in hospitals includes postural drainage, thumping by a respiratory therapist, and nebulizer breathing therapy.

Postural Drainage

Postural drainage entails lying in various positions that enable gravity to help the cough drain the bronchial tree of accumulated mucus. The bronchodilator is used before the person assumes 10 different positions. The teacher, therapist, or parent taps the upper torso with his or her fingers, as depicted in Figure 19.18. Each of the positions is designed to drain a specific area of the bronchial tree; hence, the benefit derived from the position depends on the amount of congestion present. Not all positions are required each session.

Nebulizer Breathing Therapy

Although nebulizer machines can be purchased for home use, nebulizers in hospitals are more powerful and enable individuals to inhale monitored amounts of bronchodilators. Machines are used several times daily to loosen thick mucus that accumulates in the chest. Patients are taught they *must* cough up and spit out all mucus.

Hemophilia

The term **hemophilia** encompasses at least eight different bleeding disorders caused by the lack of clotting factors in the blood. The prevalence is 1 in 10,000 persons in the United States. The physical educator who has one child with hemophilia is likely to have several since it is an inherited disorder. Historically, hemophilia has been said to appear only in males and to be transmitted through females. Recently, however, a type of hemophilia in women has been identified.

Contrary to popular belief, outward bleeding from a wound is not the major problem; rather, internal bleeding is. A stubbed toe, a bumped elbow, a violent sneeze, or a gentle tag game can be fatal. Each may cause internal bleeding that is manifested by discoloration, swelling, and other characteristics of a hematoma. The person with hemophilia tends to have many black and blue spots, swollen joints, and considerable limitation of movement. *Minor internal bleeding may be present much of the time.* When internal bleeding appears extensive, blood transfusions are administered.

Over a period of years, repeated hemorrhages into joints, if untreated, result in hemophilic arthritis. To minimize

joint bleeding, the afflicted body part is frequently splinted. Pain is severe, and persons may avoid complete extension. This tendency, of course, results in such orthopedic complications as contractures.

Persons with hemophilia should be encouraged to establish their own limitations in general activity settings. Sports for individuals with hemophilia have been categorized from most to least safe (Beardsley, 1995). The most safe sports are swimming, walking, and table tennis. The least safe (contraindicated) sports are boxing, rugby, football, karate, weight lifting with free weights, wrestling, motorcycling, judo, hockey, and skateboarding. Additionally, adaptations are recommended for several sports, such as avoiding base sliding in baseball, heading in soccer, and jumping dismounts in gymnastics. Joint supports and pads, especially for knees and elbows, are recommended for most sports.

Sickle-Cell Disease (Anemia)

Although discovered by physician James Herrick in 1910, *sickle-cell disease* did not receive widespread attention until the early 1970s. At that time, 1 of every 400 Black Americans was believed to have the disorder.

Sickle-cell disease is an inherited blood disorder that takes its name from the sickle shape the red blood cells assume when the blood's oxygen content is low. Persons with the disease are anemic, suffer crises of severe pain, are prone to infection, and often have slow-healing ulcers of the skin, especially around the ankles. Many do not live to adulthood.

Regular exercise should not be curtailed, *but tests and activities of cardiorespiratory endurance are contraindicated.* Under intense exercise stress, particularly in extreme cold or at altitudes above 10,000 ft, where the air's oxygen content is decreased, persons with sickle-cell anemia may collapse. They should also avoid becoming overheated since the normal evaporation of perspiration cools the skin and may precipitate an attack. Activities involving holding the breath, like underwater swimming, are contraindicated.

The disease develops at the time of conception, but symptoms do not usually appear until the child is 6 months or older. The first symptoms are pallor, poor appetite, early fatigue, and complaints of pain in the back, abdomen, and extremities. The child may not evidence sickle-cell anemia until he or she catches a cold or has an attack of tonsillitis; then he or she reacts worse than peers without anemia.

The course of the disease is marked by a sequence of physiological crises and complications that can be recognized, predicted, and treated, but not prevented. *The crisis results from spasms in key blood vessels.* Agonizing pain is felt in certain muscles and joints, particularly those of the rib cage. A high fever may be present. Some crises are severe enough to require hospitalization. With age, children learn limitations and thus can better control frequency of attacks.

Anemia

Anemia is a condition of reduced oxygen-carrying capacity of the blood caused by deficiency in either red blood cells or hemoglobin, the oxygen-carrying pigment within the red blood cells. Mild anemia is not easily recognizable, but more severe conditions are characterized by loss of color in cheeks, lips, and gums; lowered activity level because of limited amount of oxygen available to burn calories; and increased heart and breathing rates.

There are many kinds of anemia. **Iron-deficiency anemia** is particularly common in females, from adolescence on, and in individuals who are dieting. Athletes at particular risk are long-distance runners and swimmers, who might become iron-deficient as a season of intensive training and competition progresses. Individuals with disabilities at particular risk are those with cerebral palsy and conditions that affect chewing or swallowing and general nutritional status. **Hereditary anemia** is designated by many names, but exercise indications are similar. **Secondary or concomitant anemia** involves conditions that are side effects of other health impairments and/or medications. In particular, cancer, kidney disease, bleeding ulcers, and lead poisoning are typically complicated by anemia.

Anemia, depending on severity and type, is treated by iron-enriched diets, iron medications, and blood transfusions. Vitamin C supplements are also used because they improve iron absorption. Conditions are monitored by frequent blood tests to check hemoglobin and serum ferritin values. Excess iron values in the body can be dangerous, so overdosage should be avoided.

Individuals with mild to moderate anemia *have no physical education restrictions except underwater swimming,* but their performance levels in aerobic testing and training will generally be lower than those of peers. *Anemia is similar to asthma, in that sports that demand intermittent energy spurts are better than highly aerobic team sports like soccer, basketball, and football.* Because of lowered blood oxygen levels and the tendency to fatigue quickly, aerobic conditioning will require strong internal motivation and emotional support.

Individuals with severe anemia are medically fragile, and the amount and type of exercise that can be tolerated should be individually determined. The liver, spleen, or bone marrow can be affected in severe anemia. *Enlargement of the liver or spleen contraindicates all but very mild exercise.*

Menstrual Problems

Three types of menstrual problems complicate exercise involvement. **Dysmenorrhea** (painful menstruation) generally occurs early in the menstrual cycle, usually before the blood begins to flow freely. This pain is often partly caused by an accumulation of gas (flatus) or by constipation. Exercises that relieve flatus, such as the bent-knee creeping position/movement, and several yoga techniques also ameliorate menstrual pain (see Figure 19.19). Severe or continued pain that cannot be relieved by aspirin and exercise signals the need to see a physician. **Menorrhagia** (excessive flow) is not normal and contraindicates exercise. The student should lie in a supine position with legs propped up and should see a physician as soon as possible. **Amenorrhea** is absence of menstruation. This condition occurs frequently in females who diet and/or exercise strenuously.

Premenstrual syndrome (PMS) is a combination of symptoms that occur 2 to 3 days before menstruation starts. Not all females have PMS, but some experience depression, edema (retention of fluids), sore and swollen breasts, lower back pain, and unexplained fatigue. These symptoms affect motivation to exercise.

Figure 19.19   Exercises for dysmenorrhea.

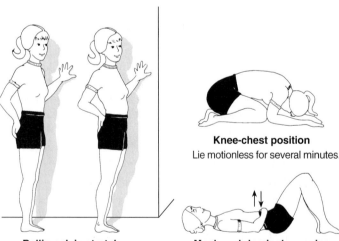

Bellig pelvic stretch
Use hand to push pelvis toward opposite side while strongly contracting gluteal and abdominal muscles.

Knee-chest position
Lie motionless for several minutes.

Mosher abdominal pumping
Pump abdomen up and down slowly.

Golub stretch and bend
Two parts: *On stretch,* lift leg and arm on same side as high as possible, then relax momentarily with arm extended at shoulder height. *On bend,* bring feet together and touch outside ankle with opposite hand. Repeat both parts to opposite side.

Cancer

Cancer, a condition of unknown etiology in which body cells multiply in an abnormal manner and cause tumors, is second only to accidents as a cause of death in children ages 1 to 15 years. Most children who develop cancer, however, do not die; they continue to attend school while undergoing treatment. Each year, about 9,000 new cases are diagnosed in children under age 15. Table 19.8 indicates the incidence of the various types of childhood cancer. Most deaths are caused by leukemia. However, the overall cure rate for all cancers exceeds 70% (Dollinger, Rosenbaum, Tempro, & Mulvihill, 2002).

For the population as a whole, it is estimated that one in every four persons will have cancer. Cancer, the second greatest cause of death in adults, affects more persons in middle and old age than in youth. Over half of cancer fatalities are over 65. Research shows that sport activity is a factor in preventing cancer (Grossarth-Maticek et al., 1990).

Cancer may be treated by one or several of the following: surgical removal of the tumor and affected lymph nodes, chemotherapy, and radiation therapy. About 50 anticancer drugs are available for chemotherapy and may be taken individually or in combinations. Drugs are generally delivered to the bloodstream orally in capsule, liquid, or pill form; injected via a needle into a vein, artery, muscle, the spinal fluid, abdominal cavity, or an organ; or administered intravenously through an IV drip device or a small pump to ensure a constant flow.

Intravenous access catheters or **ports** are frequently implanted to facilitate intravenous infusions of chemotherapy and other substances (e.g., nutrients, antibiotics, blood transfusions, antinausea drugs, pain-killing narcotics) and to facilitate blood drawing. These devices remain implanted for several weeks or months and avoid the discomfort of needles. **Catheters** are temporary plastic tubes implanted under the skin that extend into large veins; the end is left outside the skin and covered by a rubber cap into which a needle is inserted. Catheters need occasional cleaning and an injection of **heparin,** a drug that prevents blood clotting inside the catheter. In contrast, **ports** are entirely under the skin. All that can be seen is a small buttonlike cover that can be punctured thousands of times. Ports need no cleaning or dressing and less frequent heparin injections.

Blood count is monitored regularly during chemotherapy, and therapy is temporarily discontinued when white blood cells (which fight infection) or platelets (which stop bleeding) fall below safe limits. Chemotherapy suppresses the immune system and makes it difficult to fight off infections. When red blood cell count indicates anemia (tiredness, lack of energy), special medications are given to treat this condition so that blood transfusions will not be needed. During periods of anemia and susceptibility to hemorrhaging, physical activity may need to be restricted (Selsky & Pearson, 1995).

Side effects of chemotherapy are sometimes more difficult to manage than the chemotherapy. Side effects include partial or total hair loss, nausea, vomiting, weight loss, decreased exercise tolerance, easy fatigability, and increased susceptibility to infections. Some drugs cause heightened susceptibility to sunburn, which can be managed by liberal use of sunscreen, wearing a wide-brimmed hat, and other commonsense measures. Despite side effects, physicians recommend that most children participate in physical education as well as summer camp activities (Selsky & Pearson, 1995).

Radiation therapy, which is painless, may be external or internal. External therapy may be delivered by X rays, gamma rays, or electrons. Internal therapy consists of radioactive substances given intravenously or implanted directly into the tumor and surrounding areas. Most side effects are the same as for chemotherapy, except hair loss is only in the area receiving radiation. The major side effect unique to radiation is a skin reaction similar to sunburn that progresses through stages of redness, tanning, and peeling.

The psychological effects of physical exercise and the importance of continued involvement in peer activities form the major rationale for keeping students with cancer in physical education, adapting instruction as needed. Exercise adaptations vary with the body part affected by cancer. Except for a few days following chemotherapy or radiation, when the person may feel very sick, mild to moderate exercise is recommended. For information on cancer and aging, see Chapter 28.

 For insight into life with severe ovarian cancer in a middle-aged woman, see the videotape Wit *or the play, if it is available in a local theater. Discuss. How might you interact if expected to work with the main character?*

Kidney and Urinary Tract Disorders

Approximately 3% of American schoolchildren have some history of a kidney or urinary tract disorder. Moreover, urinary-genital malformations account for 300,000 of the common birth defects in the United States, sharing second place in prevalence with congenital blindness and congenital deafness. Only mental retardation affects more newborn infants. *Vigorous exercise is contraindicated when kidney infection is present,* and the physician who has not been oriented to the possibilities of an adapted program often excuses the child from physical education.

Table 19.8 **Incidence of various types of cancer in childhood.**

Type	Relative Incidence (%)
Leukemias	33.8
Lymphomas, including Hodgkin's disease	10.6
Central nervous system tumors	19.2
Adrenal glands and sympathetic nervous system	7.7
Muscle, tendon, fat cancers	6.7
Kidney cancer (Wilms' tumor)	6.0
Bone cancer (sarcomas)	4.5
Eye cancer	2.7
Other	1–2.0

Note. In contrast, cancers of the lung, breast, colon, and skin are most common in adults.

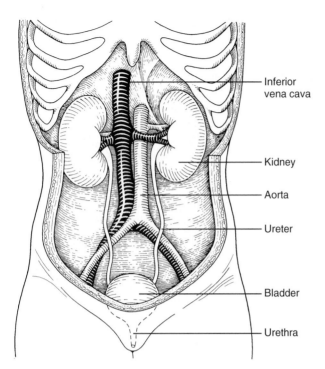

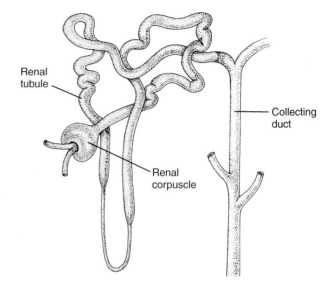

Renal tubule

Renal corpuscle

Collecting duct

One of the million nephrons inside the kidneys

B

The urinary tract consists of the ureter (the tube connecting kidneys with the bladder), the bladder, and the urethra. The kidneys and urinary tract together often are called the *renal tract* or *renal system*.

A

Inferior vena cava

Kidney

Aorta

Ureter

Bladder

Urethra

Biochemical Explanation

Normal functioning of the kidneys is required to excrete urine and to help regulate the water, electrolyte, and acid base content of the blood (i.e., to maintain homeostasis within the body). Problems of fluid retention (edema) and fluid depletion (dehydration) relate largely to the ability of the kidneys to alter the acidity of urine. Urination gets rid of body wastes like urea (an end product of protein metabolism). Renal failure often results in death by uremic poisoning.

Kidney and urinary disorders are many and varied. When both the kidneys and the urinary tract are involved (see Figure 19.20A), problems are often referred to as **renal disorders.** Federal law lists *nephritis* as one of its 11 examples of other health impairments. **Nephritis** (also called Bright's disease) is inflammation of the kidneys. The name is derived from *nephron,* the functional unit within the kidneys (see Figure 19.20B). Each kidney is comprised of about 1 million nephrons, each of which helps to filtrate substances from the blood and, subsequently, changes some of the resulting filtrate into urine and reabsorbs the remainder. This process results in about 45 gal (180 liters) of filtrate every 24 hr; only about 3 liters of this is voided as urine. The ability of the renal system to reabsorb the rest and maintain the balance between all its contents is obviously vital to life. The many possible disorders are too numerous to name and discuss. Approximately 55,000 deaths are kidney related each year.

Kidney diseases often involve reduced blood flow to the kidneys. This problem, in turn, elevates blood pressure. The mechanism causing this is release of an enzyme called *renin* that stimulates production of the hormone *aldosterone* (a mineralosteroid). This hormone causes the kidneys to retain salts and water, increasing blood volume, which, in time, may overload the arterial walls and heart because of increased peripheral pressure causing elevated blood pressure.

Management of Renal Disorders

As last-resort treatments, dialysis and kidney transplants are increasingly successful and affordable. Many congenital disorders are corrected through surgery, as are kidney stones and urinary tract obstructions. Routine management of less severe conditions includes antibiotics to treat infections, drugs to control hypertension, low-salt and other modified diets, and iron supplementation to control anemia.

Persons with spina bifida, spinal cord injuries, and amputations are particularly susceptible to renal disorders. Further detail on management of urinary problems appears in Chapters 23 and 24, which cover these disabilities.

Implications for Physical Education

Students with nephritis are in and out of the hospital many times. Each time they return to school, the fitness level is low. Most physicians concur that persons with kidney and urinary

Figure 19.21 Muscle contractions during seizures are tonic or clonic. They can affect all parts of the body.

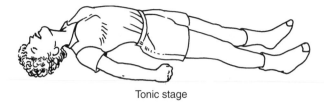

Tonic stage

Clonic stage

Figure 19.22 Neurons within the cerebral cortex have synaptic knobs that release neurotransmitters that cause an increase in membrane permeability to sodium and thus trigger nerve impulses. Problems in synaptic transmission sometimes result in seizures.

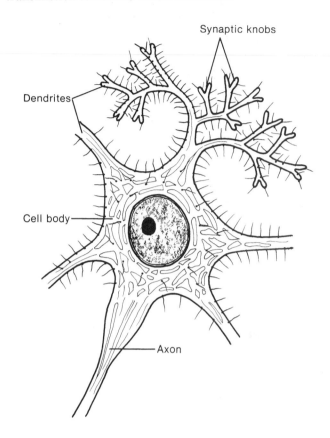

tract disease need moderate exercise. They are adamant, however, that such persons should not be subjected to physical fitness tests nor to actual physical stress of any kind.

Epilepsy

The terms *epilepsy, seizure disorders,* and *convulsive disorders* are used interchangeably to denote a chronic condition of the central nervous system that is characterized by recurrent seizures. This condition is not a disease, but rather an upset in the electrical activity of neurons within the cerebral cortex.

Seizures may or may not be accompanied by **convulsions** (fits), defined as sudden, uncontrolled, and unpredictable muscle contractions and relaxations. Muscle activity in convulsions may be **clonic** (jerky or intermittent), **tonic** (continuous, stiff, or rigid), or both (tonic-clonic) (see Figure 19.21).

Most persons with epilepsy take daily medication that is 100% effective in preventing seizures. They live ordinary lives, and friends seldom know about their condition. A few, however, have periods of short- or long-term uncontrolled seizure activity that require restrictions on driving and exercise.

Biochemical Explanation

Seizures are caused by abnormalities in cell membrane stability. Normally, the cell membrane maintains equilibrium between sodium outside the cell and potassium inside the cell (see Figure 19.22). The balance controls **depolarization,** the cellular process that permits electrical current to be transmitted down the nerve fiber and carry messages to other nerve fibers. Epileptic cells are unable to maintain the normal balance; therefore, depolarization occurs too easily and too frequently. The resulting abnormal discharge of electrical activity spreads to the healthy neurons, causing them to discharge also so that, soon, an entire area of the brain is involved.

Seizures are designated as *focal* or *generalized,* depending on how much of the brain is involved. **Focal** seizures are focused, or localized, in one specific area of the brain, such as, for instance, the motor strip of the right frontal lobe. The synonym for focal is *partial.* **Generalized seizures** involve the entire cerebral cortex (both hemispheres).

Prevalence

Prevalence of epilepsy varies from 3 to 7 per 1,000 in the nondisabled population. Among persons with brain injury, either congenital or acquired, the incidence is much greater. From 25 to 50% of the population with cerebral palsy has seizures. About one third of everyone with severe mental retardation has seizures. Seizures are also relatively frequent in extreme old age.

Age at Time of First Seizure

The age of onset of the first seizure helps to explain why so many physical educators must cope with this problem (see Figure 19.23). Twenty percent of all persons with epilepsy have their first seizure before age 10 (see Figure 19.23). These are usually children with known or suspected neurological damage. Thirty percent of persons with epilepsy have their first seizure in the second decade, while 20% convulse initially in the third decade. The final 30% have their first seizure after age 40.

Figure 19.23 **Ages at which various types of seizures most often occur.**

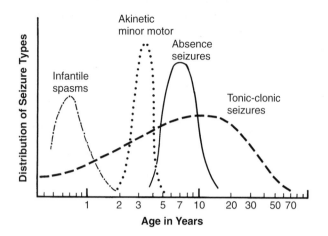

Table 19.9 **International classification system in epilepsy.**

I. Partial seizures
   A. Without impairment of consciousness
   B. With impairment of consciousness
II. Generalized seizures
   A. Absence (petit mal)
   B. Tonic-clonic (grand mal)
   C. Tonic only
   D. Clonic only
   E. Myoclonic
   F. Atonic
   G. Akinetic
   H. Infantile spasms
III. Unilateral seizures
IV. Unclassified seizures

Types of Seizures

Table 19.9 presents types of seizures. Different types of seizures have their first incidence at certain ages (see Figure 19.23).

Partial Seizures

Of the many kinds of partial seizures, the **Jacksonian** is most common. Clonic (jerky) contractions begin in one part of the body, usually a hand or foot, and from that point spread up the limb until all of the muscles are involved. This is sometimes called *march epilepsy* because the contractions march up the limb. The individual usually does not lose consciousness, although speech and other responses may be impaired.

Partial seizures with impairment of consciousness (sometimes called **psychomotor**) are characterized by unexplainable short-term changes in behavior that later are not remembered. One person may have temper tantrums, suddenly exploding for no reason, hitting another, provoking a fight, or throwing things. Another may have spells involving incoherent chatter, repetition of meaningless phrases, and inability to answer simple questions. Still another has episodes of sleepwalking or wakes the family at night with hysterical, unexplainable sobbing.

Generalized Seizures

Absence seizures (previously called petit mal) account for about 8% of all epilepsy. Their symptoms are so subtle that the inexperienced observer seldom notices the seizure. There is an impairment of consciousness, never more than 30 sec, in which the individual seems dazed. The eyes may roll upward. If the person is talking at the time, there is a momentary silence and then continuation, with no loss of unity in thought. These seizures are rare before age 3 and often disappear after puberty. They are more common in females than males.

Tonic-clonic seizures (previously called grand mal) are the most dramatic and easily recognized. They have three or four phases.

1. **Aura.** This is a warning or premonition of the attack that is always the same for a particular person. An aura may be a certain smell, flashing of lights, vague feeling of apprehension, sinking feeling in the abdomen, or feeling of extraordinary rapture. Only about 50% of persons have auras.

2. **Tonic phase.** *Tonic* means constant, referring to the continuous contraction of muscles. The person straightens out, becomes stiff, utters a cry, and loses consciousness. If there is a tonic contraction of respiratory muscles, the person becomes cyanotic. This phase seldom lasts more than 30 sec.

3. **Clonic phase.** *Clonic* refers to intermittent contraction and relaxation of muscles. The clonic phase persists from a few seconds up to 2 or 3 min. The tongue may be bitten as the jaws work up and down. The sphincters around the rectum and urinary tracts relax, causing the person to urinate or defecate.

4. **Sleep or coma phase.** After a period of brief consciousness or semiconsciousness, during which the person complains of being very tired, he or she lapses into a sleep that may last several hours. Upon awakening, the person is either very clear or is dazed and confused. Usually, there is no memory of the seizure.

Occasionally, seizures occur that are entirely clonic or tonic.

Myoclonic seizures are brief, sudden, violent contractions of muscles in some part or the entire body. Often, these are manifested by a sudden head jerk, followed by jerking of arms and legs, and the trunk bending in upon itself. The individual may lose consciousness, but the duration of a myoclonic seizure is much briefer than that of tonic-clonic or tonic- or clonic-only types.

Atonic seizures are similar to absence seizures except that postural tone is momentarily diminished. The individual tends to sag or collapse.

Akinetic seizures (also called sudden drop attacks) cause the individual to suddenly lose muscle tone and plummet to the ground, momentarily unconscious. These seizures may be sometimes purposely aborted. Sudden falling asleep (narcolepsy) may be a form of akinetic seizure.

Infantile spasms (also called jackknife seizures) are usually characterized by a "doubling up" motion of the entire body, although they may be manifested only by head dropping and arms flexing. Infantile spasms typically occur between 3 and 9 months of age, after which other types of seizures may replace them. This problem is associated with severe mental retardation. Infantile spasms should not be confused with the generalized seizures that many infants and children (5 to 10%) have in conjunction with illness and high fever; these are called *febrile seizures* and typically are a once-in-a-lifetime happening.

Unilateral seizures involve only one side of the brain and, therefore, only one side of the body. These may be of any type.

Unclassified seizures are those that do not meet the criteria for any one type or those that are mixed types. About 35 to 40% of epilepsy is a combination of absence and tonic-clonic seizures.

Etiology

The etiology of epilepsy falls within two broad classifications: (a) idiopathic (genetic or endogenous) and (b) acquired (symptomatic or exogenous). **Idiopathic** means that the cause is unknown, and 80% of all epilepsy remains unexplainable. There appears to be a genetic predisposition toward epilepsy, but this is controversial. In general, the parent with epilepsy has 1 chance in 40 of giving birth to a child with epilepsy. The incidence is increased if both parents have epilepsy. **Acquired** epilepsy can be traced directly to birth injuries, brain tumors, oxygen deprivation, lead poisoning, cerebral abscesses, and penetrating injuries to the brain.

Factors That Aggravate Seizures

1. Increases in alkalinity of the blood (see Figure 19.24). These changes are very subtle and minute. *High alkalosis favors seizures.* High acidity inhibits seizures. Diet therapy is used frequently. Acid-producing diets, high in fat content—such as cream, butter, eggs, and meat—have successfully produced a quieting effect. This kind of diet is called a **ketogenic diet** (high in fat). The accumulation of acid products in the blood as a result of exercise is also believed to help prevent seizures.

2. Hyperventilation (overbreathing) that leads to respiratory alkalosis, especially when the exercise causing hyperventilation is suddenly interrupted (Linschoten, Backx, Mulder, & Meinardi, 1990). Holding the breath as long as possible, as in distance underwater swimming, is a common form of hyperventilation that is contraindicated. Breath-holding lowers the carbon dioxide content of the blood, which increases alkalosis. Sports that commonly induce hyperventilation are scuba diving and high-altitude climbing. Taking a deep breath and jumping into water sometimes triggers hyperventilation.

3. Hyperhydration (ingestion of too much water). This can occur during swimming, especially in beginners.

4. Hyperthermia (too much body heat) as sometimes occurs in marathons and triathlons in high temperatures under humid conditions.

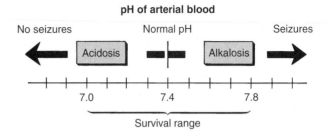

Figure 19.24 Most factors that aggravate seizures relate to electrolyte balance in the cellular fluids, especially the balance between acidosis and alkalosis in the pH of arterial blood. pH, an abbreviation for potential of hydrogen, is a measure used to express relative degree of acidity and alkalosis.

5. Hypoglycemia in diabetes or in persons exercising vigorously over a long duration with no food or liquid.

6. Fatigue, especially sleep deprivation and disturbances of nocturnal rhythms.

7. Sudden emotional stress or excitement like bad news, fright, or anger.

8. Excessive alcohol and caffeine.

9. In women, menstrual periods. Many girls and women have seizures only around their periods. Edema aggravates the onset of seizures.

Seizures, Exercise, and Social Problems

Seizures seldom, if ever, occur during vigorous physical activity. Convulsions are most likely during the cool-down after exercise and during late-night hours.

There is no evidence that intense sport competition increases the likelihood of seizures (Bennett, 1995). Seizure-prone persons must, however, be conscientious in taking their medication, eating properly, and getting enough sleep. Obviously, they must minimize the factors that aggravate seizures. Within the disability sport movement, many athletes take medication to control epilepsy. Occasionally, a seizure occurs, necessitating rest for a few hours. Thereafter, training and competition are resumed. The overall philosophy is that an isolated seizure is no big deal.

The social problems in epilepsy are greater than the medical ones. The person regaining consciousness after a first seizure does not remember anything that happened. He or she is self-conscious and embarrassed. Who wouldn't be? First seizures in adolescence are a particular concern. Individual responses are as variable as human beings themselves, but many persons are reluctant to continue dating or even socializing with a person who has seizures. Driver's licenses, if issued, have restrictions. Employment opportunities are reduced, and insurability under workmen's compensation may be a problem.

Medication

Phenobarbital (Luminal), phenytoin (Dilantin), and Carbamazepine are the drugs used most often in controlling *tonic-clonic seizures.* Teachers who work with children from low-income families see many seizures, almost always caused because a prescription is not filled on time. Epilepsy medications have a number of adverse side effects. Among these are reduced coordination and concentration, poor reaction time, drowsiness, blurred vision, and irritability. Dilantin, in particular, causes gum and teeth problems.

Management of a Seizure

Should a seizure occur, clear the area around the individual. Do not attempt to hold the body down or restrain limbs. Ascertain that the mouth and nose are clear and permit breathing. *Lying in a prone or side position is best.* The seizure should be allowed to run its normal course, with everyone remaining calm.

Implications for Physical Education

Students with epilepsy should participate fully in school physical education and athletics. Collision (football, ice hockey, lacrosse) sports and contact (basketball, soccer, wrestling) sports can be played by the medically balanced student. Boxing should be avoided. Activities like heading the ball in soccer, which involve repeated insults to the head, are controversial.

Activities that might result in a fall (cycling, horseback riding, rope- or tree-climbing, parallel bars, trampoline, balance beam, mountain climbing) should always be done with a partner or group. Likewise, individuals with epilepsy should not swim or engage in other water sports alone. In some students, a specific activity, for unknown reasons, may precipitate seizures. If this occurs *repeatedly,* then that one activity should be restricted.

Students whose seizures are under good control (1–3 seizures in the past year) are no different from their peers. They need good supervision when enrolled in beginning swimming, but so do all children! Likewise, they need a gymnastics teacher who is competent in spotting techniques. Again, this does not make them different from their peers, who also need a good spotter when undertaking activities on the high balance beam, parallel bars, and trampoline. Most important, persons with epilepsy need the acceptance and belonging that team membership ensures.

Physical activities contraindicated for persons who have had more than 10 seizures in the past year are diving, scuba diving, boxing, rodeo, auto racing, motorcycling, mountaineering, and bobsledding (Bennett, 1995).

Environmental Disorders

The three most common environmental hazards to children's health are metal pollution (lead, mercury, zinc), air pollution (including cigarette smoke), and low-level radiation. Of these, the most research has been done on lead (Pueschel, Linakis, & Anderson, 1996).

Lead poisoning is a leading cause of health impairments in children ages 1 to 6 years. Elevations in blood/lead concentration are associated with cognitive and behavioral difficulties. Approximately 5 to 8% of preschool children have elevated blood lead levels. This includes 1 in 20 White children and 1 in 5 Black children.

Approximately 600,000 tons of lead are released by the smelting industry into the environment annually, much of which is carried by winds and deposited in soil where children play. This lead fallout is now the leading cause of lead poisoning. In earlier decades, the main routes of exposure were leaded gasoline, ingestion of paint or paint dust, milk formulas from improperly soldered cans, and tainted drinking water. Houses built before 1960 with peeling or chipping paint continue to be a high-risk factor. The federal Lead Poisoning Prevention Act of 1971 permits large-scale screening of preschool children to identify those at risk, but little else has been done (except in individual communities) to cope with this problem.

Physical educators working in blighted urban areas can expect as many as 40% of their students to carry significant lead burdens, which cause subtle health and behavior problems. Indicators of mild lead poisoning are listlessness, lethargy, irritability, clumsiness, and anemia, all of which contribute to developmental delay. Severe lead poisoning is associated with kidney disease and anemia, both of which lower exercise capabilities. Severe or persistent lead poisoning, without treatment, results in seizures, coma, and eventual death. *Even with treatment, mental retardation and epilepsy often occur.* Lead poisoning is treated by such drugs as edetate calcium disodium and D-penicillamine, which can be taken either orally or by intramuscular injection. The overall treatment is called **chelation therapy.** Most important, however, is removal of students from lead-tainted environments.

Tuberculosis

Tuberculosis, although no longer a common cause of death, still ranks within the top 10 reportable diseases. The incidence of reported tuberculosis is about the same as that of infectious hepatitis and measles. Among causes of death, tuberculosis ranks 19th. A vaccine is about 80% effective in disease prevention. This vaccine, however, often is not used in poverty areas, especially those devastated by drug use and human immunodeficiency virus (HIV). Tuberculosis often occurs as a complication of HIV infection.

Tuberculosis, although usually conceptualized as a lung disease, can affect any tissue in the body. **Tuberculosis** is an infectious disease caused by bacteria (i.e., the tubercle bacillus) and characterized by the formation of **tubercles** (little swellings). In this country, bone and joint tuberculosis is more likely than the other types to come to the attention of physical educators. Of the skeletal sites of tuberculosis, the most common is the spine, followed by hip and knee.

Pott's disease, or tuberculosis of the spine, is a disorder that often results in kyphosis (round upper back). This inflammation of the vertebral bodies occurs most often in children and young adults. Pott's disease is characterized by the formation of little tubercles on the vertebral bodies. Destruction and compression of the vertebral bodies affects the spinal cord and adjacent nerves to the extent that movement becomes extremely painful. The characteristic kyphotic curvature is called a *gibbus,* meaning "hump." The condition of having a humpback is **gibbosity.** A medical synonym for Pott's disease is *tuberculous spondylitis.*

Tuberculosis remains a common cause of **meningitis** (infection of the covering of the brain) during early childhood. The consequences of this disease, even with the best treatment, are severe, with some degree of intellectual deficit occurring in about 20% of children, as well as hearing and vestibular defects. Seizures, hydrocephalus, spasticity, ataxia, and incoordination are common outcomes also.

HIV/AIDS Conditions

Human immunodeficiency virus (HIV) and acquired immune deficiency syndrome (AIDS) conditions affect approximately 36.1 million persons worldwide (Wright, 2001). The epidemic continues to be most critical in Africa and South and Southeast Asia. About 1 in every 300 Americans carries the HIV virus, which causes AIDS. The incidence is much higher among individuals who engage in injection drug use and heterosexual or homosexual vaginal or anal sex without condoms.

The first cases of AIDS were reported in 1981, but the virus that caused AIDS was not identified until 1984. Over the last few years, many changes in terminology, prognosis, acceptance, and high-risk populations have occurred (see Figure 19.25). There is still, however, no cure or immunization.

Stages of HIV/AIDS Progression

HIV/AIDS is a global term for immune system infection, disease, and disintegration that is caused by the HIV virus group, which infects several kinds of cells but mainly targets CD4 lymphocytes. HIV/AIDS can be acquired or congenital. Acquired conditions occur through contact with the blood, semen, vaginal secretions, breast milk, and amniotic fluid of carriers. Congenital conditions occur because infected antibodies are passed on to fetuses by their HIV-infected mothers. The manifestation of symptoms is slightly different in acquired and congenital pathology.

Acquired HIV/AIDS

Acquired HIV/AIDS progresses through three distinct stages, and persons in each stage are carriers (Olenik & Sherrill, 1994; Seltzer, 1993).

Stage 1. HIV infection refers to a symptom-free condition lasting several years that is diagnosed by a positive antibody test that indicates HIV in the blood serum. Most persons in this latency stage do not know they are infected and thus constitute considerable risk to others if they do not practice safe sex and safe needle injection. The average latency period between infection and onset of systems is 8 to 12 years (D'Angelo, 1995).

Stage 2. HIV disease refers to all manifestations of infection prior to the onset of acute, terminal illness. Symptoms are severe weight loss, chronic diarrhea, nonproductive cough with shortness of breath, swollen lymph nodes (neck, armpit, groin), fevers of unknown origin, chronic fatigue, skin rashes, and increased susceptibility to infections.

Stage 3. AIDS, the terminal illness stage, refers to the final months of acute medical crises, many of which require hospitalization and/or complete bed rest. Disintegration of the immune system makes treatment of opportunistic infections and

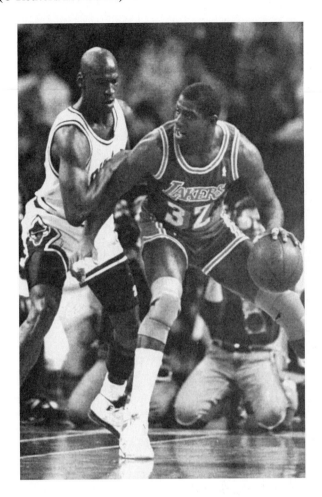

Figure 19.25 Magic Johnson's announcement that he has HIV increased awareness that all people are at risk. (© Reuters/Bettmann.)

cancers ineffective. Pneumonia, Kaposi's sarcoma (cancer), and dementia caused by brain damage are associated with this stage.

Congenital HIV/AIDS

Congenital HIV/AIDS seems to follow three patterns. **Pattern 1,** which includes about 50% of infants born with HIV, is a symptom-free status. These infants test positive until about 2 years old because of antibodies passed on by their mothers. Thereafter, blood tests give no indication of infection, and these children are healthy. **Pattern 2,** the static form of congenital HIV, includes infants who appear healthy until age 6 to 9 months, then exhibit disease symptoms for a short period, and thereafter have a relatively long period of freedom from illness before the AIDS stage begins. Current estimates are that over 60% of these children will survive beyond age 5. **Pattern 3,** the progressive form of congenital HIV, is similar to Pattern 2 except that, once illness begins, health rapidly deteriorates; the mean survival time is 8 months.

Congenital HIV/AIDS attacks different systems in infants than in adults. Congenital etiology results in many infants having central nervous system involvement. The most common manifestations in children are mental retardation, cerebral palsy, developmental delays, and motor abnormalities.

Figure 19.26 Jonathan, a first-grader, tells classmates how he contracted HIV from a blood transfusion during infancy. The machine in front of Jonathan is a portable oxygen tank, an adaptation used for a few months to make breathing easier but later abandoned. (Courtesy of Sharon Schilling, author of *My Name Is Jonathan (and I Have AIDS)*.)

Medication and Exercise

Multidrug therapy, which attacks the virus in various biochemical ways, is showing tremendous promise. The prognosis is best when treatment begins immediately after diagnosis, long before symptoms begin to appear.

HIV/AIDS medications cause such side effects as severe diarrhea, abdominal cramps, anemia, nausea, chronic fatigue, headache, and numbness. The incidence of side effects is greater, of course, in multidrug treatment than when a single drug like AZT (zidovudine or Retrovir), the best-known medication, is used. Side effects of medications decrease the desire and ability to exercise (D'Angelo, 1995), and a major role of professionals is to provide encouragement and support to overcome barriers caused by medication side effects.

Individuals in Stages 1 and 2 of HIV/AIDS can derive physical and mental benefits from exercise. Physicians recommend avoidance of collision sports such as boxing, wrestling, football, and rugby, to protect others, because these sports are more likely to cause blood spills.

Implications for Physical Education

As HIV-infected children increase in number, more will be attending public schools. More teachers and coworkers will also have the syndrome. These persons have the same education and employment rights as everyone else. HIV-infected students fall under the other health impairments category of federal legislation, and their physical education should be conducted accordingly.

Physical education adaptations are similar to those of other OHI children with weight loss, easy fatigue, respiratory problems, and increased susceptibility to infections. They miss more school, which creates social and learning problems. As the condition becomes more severe, children may need to carry portable oxygen tanks with them (see Figure 19.26). Books and videos that present models are essential (e.g., Schilling, 1990; White & Cunningham, 1991). The best-known child model is Ryan White, who was infected through a blood transfusion for hemophilia; he was diagnosed in 1984 and lived 6 years, during which time his battle against discrimination in an Indiana school district became national news.

Ignorance, fear, hysteria, and discrimination are probably the greatest problems to be resolved in physical education as well as in other school subjects. The American Coaching Effectiveness Program emphasizes that AIDS is *not* transmitted by the following (Landry, 1989, p. 22):

1. Competing in sports
2. Coming in contact with sweat

Table 19.10   Websites for OHI conditions covered in this chapter.

Condition/Website

1. Overweight/obesity syndrome
    - North American Association for the Study of Obesity: www.naaso.org
    - Overweight an Obesity: www.cdc.gov/nccdphp/dnpa/obesity
    - American Obesity Association: www.obesity.org
2. Cholesterol problems
    - Cholesterol, Genetics, and Heart Disease Institute: www.heartdisease.org
    - National Cholesterol Education Program: http://rover.nhlbi.nih.gov/chd
    - Good News in Cholesterol Web Site: www.goodnewscholesterol.com
    - Cholesterol Information: www.forcholesterol.com
3. Diabetes continuum
    - American Diabetes Association: www.diabetes.org
    - Children with Diabetes On-line Community: www.childrenwithdiabetes.com
    - IDF—International Diabetes Federation: www.idf.org
4. Cardiovascular problems
    - American Heart Association: www.americanheart.org
    - Congenital Heart Information Network: www.tchin.org
    - Living Well—Cardio Health: www.nutritionalifestyles.com
    - The Stroke Network, online stroke support and information: www.strokenetwork.org
5. Hypertension
    - Hypertension: High Blood Pressure: www.healthsquare.com
    - MEDLINEplus: High Blood Pressure: www.nlh.nih.gov/medlineplus/highbloodpressure
    - Hypertension (High Blood Pressure): www.kidshealth.org/teen/diseases_conditions/heart/hypertension
    - What Is Hypertension (High Blood Pressure)?: www.healthatoz.com/atoz/HeartCare/hypertension
6. Asthma
    - Asthma and Allergy Foundation of America: www.aafa.org
    - American Lung Association: www.lungusa.org
    - American Academy of Allergy Asthma and Immunology: www.aaaai.org
    - Asthma Resource Page: www.lung.ca/asthma
7. Chronic obstructive pulmonary diseases
    - American Lung Association: www.lungusa.org
    - Living with Chronic Lung Disease: www.lung.ca
    - The Chronic Lung Disease Forum: www.cheshire-med.com/program/pulrehab/forum/cldforum
8. Bronchitis and emphysema
    - Bronchitis: www.yourhealth.com
    - HealthWorld Online—Medical Self-Care—Childhood Bronchitis: www.healthy.net/library/books/healthyself/children/bronchitis
    - Emphysema Center: www.chestsurg.org/emphysema
    - NCHS—FASTATS—Emphysema: www.cdc.gov/nchs/fastats/emphysema
9. Cystic fibrosis
    - Cystic Foundation: www.cff.org
    - Cystic Fibrosis.Com: www.cysticfibrosis.com
    - Cystic Fibrosis Web: www.cf-web.mit.edu
10. Hemophilia
    - Welcome to Hemophilia Galaxy: www.hemophiliagalaxy.com
    - Hemophilia Federation of America: www.hemophiliafed.org
    - Hemophilia Association: www.hemophiliaz.org
11. Sickle-cell disease (anemia)
    - Sickle Cell Information Center Home Page: www.SCInfo.org
    - The American Sickle Cell Anemia Association: www.ascaa.org
    - Sickle Cell Anemia—Blood Diseases and Disorders: www.umm.edu/blood/sickle
12. Anemia
    - Anemia Lifeline: www.anemia.com
    - MEDLINEplus Anemia: www.nlm.nih.gov/medlineplus/anemia
    - Anemia: www.kidshealth.org/parent/medical/heart/anemia

Table 19.10   Continued.

3. Having casual contact, such as handshaking or hugging

4. Living with someone who has AIDS and sharing eating utensils, towels, and toilets

5. Kissing

6. Swimming in a pool with someone who has AIDS

Risks and Safe Practices

HIV is often transmitted through sex without condoms and/or with multiple partners. Risk is high under these conditions, whether the relationship is heterosexual or homosexual. Condoms are not 100% safe. The best practice is obviously having sex with one mutually faithful, uninfected partner. Children who are victims of sex abuse and/or who learn about sex from the streets or television are special risk groups. Persons with mental retardation and other disabilities who are not provided prevention education are also at risk.

Another safe practice is to use only sterile needles or syringes. Never share a needle with another, regardless of the fluid being injected. Intravenous drug abusers are a high-risk group because so many have neither the money nor the inclination to purchase sterile needles.

First-aid and emergency care that involves blood should be rendered with rubber gloves. Even when gloves are used, hands should be washed with soap and water. If nosebleeds or injuries result in blood on the floor or equipment, wash the surface clean with a household bleach solution of 1 part bleach to 10 parts water. Towels and clothing with blood contamination are safe after hot-water/detergent washing but should be stored in tied plastic bags until laundered or trashed. These first-aid guidelines come from the U.S. Public Health Service, Centers for Disease Control (CDC).

Wounds that might seep blood should be kept covered during sport activity. Bandages not only protect the injured site but minimize the chance of blood contact by others. Caregivers and teachers should maximize their own skin care and realize that they are at most risk for accidental infection when there is a skin breakdown.

Blood-Borne Hepatitis

Hepatitis B, which is transmitted by exposure to infected blood or other bodily fluids, is often grouped with HIV/AIDS conditions because of the similarity in transmission and in protocols for handling blood spills. **Hepatitis** is inflammation of the liver, the largest organ in the body, located on the right side, immediately below the diaphragm. Hepatitis B can occur with or without symptoms. Individuals with symptoms manifest these from 30 to 120 days after exposure to the hepatitis virus. Early symptoms are fever, headache, malaise, and loss of appetite. Later, **jaundice** (a yellowing of skin and body fluids) occurs along with abdominal pain or discomfort. Approximately 10 to 20% of individuals additionally experience painful joint swelling, rash, and arthritis-type symptoms. An acute disease episode usually spans 3 to 6 weeks, during which mild to moderate exercise may be beneficial.

Hepatitis B, more easily transmitted than the HIV virus, has reached epidemic status. Approximately 10% of individuals with acute hepatitis become carriers. The fatality rate is low, but convalescence is often prolonged. Many persons have relapses of chronic illness. No specific treatment is beneficial during acute hepatitis. A hepatitis B vaccine is highly recommended for professionals who work with high-risk individuals.

 OPTIONAL ACTIVITIES

1. Using real or imagined children and adolescents, write short case studies of persons who might have the other health impairments that affect ages 3 through 21, and whose *conditions adversely affect educational performance,* the criterion for eligibility for IDEA services. Imagine that an IEP committee says each student is not eligible for IDEA services. Develop your cases to make an argument for how and why OHI may affect physical education performance as well as academic performance. Include specific examples.

2. If you cannot make a good case for IDEA eligibility, consider how you can make a case for Section 504 eligibility. Give details. Conduct short debates in class justifying either IDEA or 504 eligibility.

3. Explore ACSM (2000) certifications and study recommended ACSM knowledge, skill, and abilities underlying ACSM certifications. How might these help you provide direct and/or consultant services for students with OHI?

4. Assertively hunt for live examples and models of persons with OHI conditions that you can use with students and parents. For example, Nicole Johnson, who has diabetes I, was Miss America 1999. Creatively use the materials you find to help improve lives of families that are coping with OHI.

5. Use websites on Table 19.10 to obtain extra information that can be shared with families. Develop some home-school-community materials to extend the content obtained from the Web to include more physical activity and sport.

CHAPTER

20

Learning Disabilities, Attention Deficit Hyperactivity Disorder, and Developmental Coordination Disorder

Figure 20.1 An alternative to beam walking is a Cratty floor grid on which every letter of the alphabet and every number can be found. Here a boy with learning disabilities leads his teacher in walking out the number 8.

1. Consider the relationships between learning disability (LD), developmental coordination disorder (DCD), and attention deficit hyperactivity disorder (ADHD). How might each condition affect physical education success? Assess your knowledge and firsthand experience of these conditions and set personal goals for increasing each.

2. Many persons with one or more of these conditions attend university. Determine if any of your classmates has one of these conditions and offer to help as needed (i.e., class notes, tape recording, etc.).

3. Reflect on the many problems associated with LD, DCD, and ADHD. How might these manifest themselves at various ages? Think of specific examples you have seen.

4. Critique the instructional strategies suggested for various conditions in this chapter. Generate ideas for additional strategies. See Shaywitz (2003) on dyslexia.

5. As you assimilate information from this chapter, use it to write IEPs for children with various combinations of LD, DCD, and ADHD behaviors.

6. Find and read the excellent review of literature on ADHD by Harvey and Reid (2003). Look up entries in their reference list and critique physical education research in this area.

7. See such *primary sources* as Ayres (1972) for occupational therapy and Sherrill (1972) for physical education and compare their perspectives with recent sources. Which teaching strategies still work? Why?

Internationally, the term *learning disabilities (LD)* has many meanings. In the United States, LD is a separate condition from mental retardation (MR). In many other countries, and in sports governed by the International Paralympic Committee (IPC), *learning disabilities* is used interchangeably with terms like *mental handicap, learning difficulties,* and *intellectual disabilities.* This chapter presents the American viewpoint that LD is not MR. The official term used in federal legislation is *specific learning disabilities (SLD),* but this is almost universally shortened to *LD.*

This chapter also includes information on attention deficit hyperactivity disorder (ADHD) and developmental coordination disorder (DCD), conditions that are often associated with LD and were previously considered a part of LD. ADHD and DCD were recognized as independent disorders by the American Psychiatric Association in its *DSM* in 1980 and 1988, respectively. Assessment must determine whether an individual has only one condition (LD) or is multiply disabled by the presence of ADHD and DCD, both of which have many clinical variations (Cermak & Larkin, 2002; Harvey & Reid, 2003).

Learning Disabilities

Specific learning disabilities (SLD) is defined by federal legislation as follows:

> a disorder in one or more of the basic psychological processes involved in understanding or in using language, spoken or written, which disorder may manifest itself in an imperfect ability to listen, think, speak, read, write, spell, or do mathematical calculations. (IDEA, 1997, Section 1401)

This part of the federal definition is typically operationalized by two criteria: (a) an IQ of 70 or higher and (b) a severe discrepancy between intellectual ability and academic achievement in one or more areas. A score that is 1.5 or more standard deviations below average on a standardized academic achievement test is generally accepted as proof of a severe discrepancy. The profiles of individuals with LD thus vary widely, ranging from below-average performance in all subjects to gifted performance in all subjects but one, which is seriously below average. This tremendous diversity necessitates careful description of both strengths and weaknesses when referring to an individual diagnosed as having LD.

Historically, so many names have been used to denote LD that the federal definition includes the following statements about what can and cannot be considered LD:

> Such disorders include such conditions as perceptual disabilities, brain injury, minimal brain dysfunction, dyslexia, and developmental aphasia. Such term does not include children who have learning problems which are primarily the result of visual, hearing, or motor disabilities, of mental retardation, of emotional disturbance, or of environmental, cultural, or economic disadvantage. (IDEA, 1997, Section 1401)

This definition assumes that readers are familiar with such terms as **dyslexia** (a severe reading disorder presumed to be of neurological origin) and **aphasia** (impairment of ability to communicate presumed to be of neurological origin). Other types of aphasias are **dysgraphia** (writing disorder), **dyscalculia** (math disorder), and **amnesia** (memory disorder). The most common disorders are reading and spelling (i.e., dyslexia), but any combination of aphasias may result in SLD.

Although U.S. law does not recognize motor disabilities, by themselves, as sufficient for a diagnosis of LD, many authorities believe that a higher than average percentage of individuals with LD have perceptual-motor, motor coordination, and other movement-related problems that require intensive work (see Figure 20.1). In the 21st century, *developmental coordination disorder (DCD) is considered a concomitant condition that should be diagnosed and treated separately.* It is possible to have LD with DCD or LD without DCD.

Developmental Coordination Disorder (DCD)

DCD was officially recognized by the American Psychiatric Association (APA) and the World Health Organization in the late 1980s but continues to be ignored by IDEA. Recognition by the APA makes treatment for conditions eligible for health insurance reimbursement consideration. In the most recent edition of the *Diagnostic and Statistical Manual of Mental Disorders*

(DSM-IV-TR), published by the APA (2000), the diagnostic criteria for DCD are as follows:

> Performance in daily activities that require motor coordination is substantially below that expected given the person's chronological age and measured intelligence. This may be manifested by marked delays in achieving motor milestones (e.g., walking, crawling, sitting), dropping things, "clumsiness," poor performance in sports, or poor handwriting. (p. 54)

This diagnosis is made only if

1. the condition significantly interferes with academic achievement or activities of daily living, and

2. the condition is not caused by a general medical disorder (e.g., cerebral palsy, muscular dystrophy) or pervasive developmental disorder.

3. If mental retardation is present, the motor difficulties are in excess of those usually associated with it (p. 53).

DCD was featured in the April 1994 issue of the *Adapted Physical Activity Quarterly*, which was edited by Sheila Henderson of England, one of the developers of the Movement Assessment Battery for Children (Movement ABC), which was described in Chapter 12. This battery was one of three recommended for diagnosis of DCD. Many of the motor problems described in this chapter are evidence of DCD. However, it is important to note that most children with LD do not "grow out" of motor problems. DCD, for most persons, is a lifetime problem rather than a developmental disorder (Cantell, Smyth, & Ahonen, 1994; Henderson & Henderson, 2002).

Attention Deficit Hyperactivity Disorder (ADHD), an "Other Health Impairment"

ADHD is "a persistent pattern of inattention and/or hyperactivity-impulsivity that is more frequently displayed and more severe than is typically observed in individuals at a comparable level of development . . . some hyperactive-impulsive or inattentive symptoms that cause impairment must have been present before 7 years . . . " (APA, 2000, p. 85). IDEA 1997 regulations added attention deficit disorder (ADD) and attention deficit hyperactivity disorder (ADHD) as an eligible condition for services *under the other health-impaired category.* ADHD and related disorders are discussed later in this chapter.

Comorbidity

A recent discovery is the frequency that ADHD coexists with one or more of the following disorders: anxiety, bipolar mental illness, conduct disorders, depression, developmental coordination disorders, learning disabilities, and oppositional defiant disorders (Papolos & Papolos, 2002; Pliszka, 2000). **Comorbidity** (frequency of overlap or coexistence) is a new term to be added to vocabularies. *The diagnosis of ADHD should be made only after ruling out a mood disorder, because ADHD indicators are seen in mood disorders at all times* (see Chapter 22). Some experts believe that ADHD for some children may be an early stage that culminates in full-blown bipolar disorder

(Papolos & Papolos, 2002). About 12 to 24% of persons with dyslexia also have ADHD (Shaywitz, 2003).

Prevalence of Learning Disabilities

Approximately 2.5 million students in the United States are classified as LD and receive special education services. This represents about 50% of all students in special education and about 5% of the total school-age population. Dyslexia comprises about 80% of all learning disabilities (Shaywitz, 2003). Moreover, it is underdiagnosed. Thus, criteria for identification of LD may be changed in next IDEA revision. From 50 to 80% of persons with LD also have ADHD. Over 40% of students with disabilities who attend university have LD.

Educators are reluctant to assign labels to young children. Therefore, infants, toddlers, and children served under IDEA are often identified as *with developmental disabilities* or *at risk for developmental disabilities.* Many of these children later are classified as LD or ADHD.

Three times as many boys as girls receive special education services for LD. This phenomenon appears to be sociocultural, because research indicates that the number of males and females with dyslexia is equal (Shaywitz, 2003). Many students with other disabilities also have LD. Chief among these are individuals with cerebral palsy or severe hearing impairments.

Etiology of LD

The etiology of LD is biological rather than environmental, although individual ecosystems influence opportunity and ability to learn. The central nervous system is so complex that the reasons for malfunctions of specific parts are little understood. The major *motor problems* seem to have a cerebellar-vestibular basis.

Subtypes of LD

Movement subtypes of LD have been identified since 1976, when Rarick, Dobbins, and Broadhead published *The Motor Domain and Its Correlates in Educationally Handicapped Children.* More recently, subtypes have been described by Lazarus (1990) and Miyahara (1994).

Lazarus (1990) noted two distinct subtypes:

1. Language impaired with subtle motor difficulties, mainly in information processing. This subtype tends to prefer visual learning.

2. Visual-spatial-motor impaired with obvious perceptual-motor problems and clumsiness. This subtype mainly has problems with math, although language can be impaired also, especially in pronunciation and comprehension. Auditory input tends to be the preferred learning modality.

The identification of subtypes depends, of course, on the nature of the tests administered. From the 1900s onward, little research was published on LD in physical education literature. This was because no generalizations about the motor behavior of persons with LD can be made. *Experts agreed that research would have to be linked with movement subtypes or specify LD with DCD or LD with ADHD.*

Historical Perspectives

LD intervention practices in special education and physical education have changed tremendously over the years, particularly the use of gross motor perceptual motor activities (Kephart, 1971) and large muscle games designed specifically to enhance academic learning (Cratty, 1971, 1972). In the 21st century, the pendulum is swinging back toward the use of physical activity to improve mental function and to support classroom goals. Thus spelling and reading are reinforced by target games, arithmetic processes are reinforced by games that use numbers, and writing is reinforced by relays and obstacle courses in which runners stop and write a word or sentence at a designated point. Occupational therapy has steadfastly continued to stress sensory integration activities (Ayres, 1972) over the years.

Special Education

Historically, LD has been linked with reading and speaking difficulties caused by brain dysfunction, but specific pedagogy was not proposed until the landmark publication of *Psychopathology and Education of the Brain-Injured Child* in 1947 by Alfred Strauss and Laura Lehtinen. This book described problems of learning, attention, and hyperactivity that subsequently became known as the **Strauss syndrome.** Four principles for managing the learning environment were stressed that remain important today: *(a) use optimal structure, (b) reduce space, (c) eliminate irrelevant stimuli, and (d) enhance the stimulus value of equipment or instructional material.*

In addition, perceptual-motor training (largely conceptualized differently by special educators and physical educators) was widely accepted as appropriate pedagogy for remediating language and learning problems (Hallahan & Cruickshank, 1973). Much of this training was directed toward fine motor coordination and the perceptual abilities needed in reading and writing activities. *By the 1980s, however, it was clearly evident that fine-motor perceptual-motor training was not effective in remediating academic problems (Kavale & Mattson, 1983).* Several ACLD groups issued formal statements opposing perceptual-motor training in the 1980s, and special educators began to focus exclusively on information processing and knowledge-acquisition.

Involvement of Physical Educators

Physical educators became aware of LD in the 1970s. Sherrill (1972) was the first to write a chapter on LD for an adapted physical education text; it appeared in Hollis Fait's *Special Physical Education.* Sherrill, mentored by ACLD parents and professionals, relied heavily on the works of followers of Strauss: William Cruickshank's *The Brain-Injured Child in Home, School, and Community* (1967) and Newell Kephart's *The Slow Learner in the Classroom* (1971). From Cruickshank, she learned Strauss's principles for managing the learning environment and applied them to the gymnasium setting. From Kephart, she stressed balance activities, midline tasks, and imitation of movement games to remediate clumsiness (see Sherrill Perceptual-Motor Teaching/Testing Checklist in Chapter 12). From association with parents and children, Sherrill formed the self-concept beliefs underlying

Figure 20.2 Teaching balancing, throwing, and spelling concurrently supports the Cratty emphasis that movement enhances academic abilities best when academics are taught directly as part of the activity.

her adapted physical education pedagogy. Today these are being expanded by Shapiro and Ulrich (2002).

Bryant J. Cratty, at the University of California at Los Angeles, also contributed substantially to perceptual-motor pedagogy (Cratty, 1971, 1972). Cratty rejected the special education theories that movement attributes are the basis of perceptual and intellectual development. Instead, he stressed the use of highly structured movement experiences to remediate clumsiness and improve self-control and self-concept. *Cratty believed that academic abilities would be enhanced by movement only if games were developed to teach specific academic skills (see Figure 20.2). He recommended that games be used to supplement classroom instruction, not to substitute for it.*

For several years, the idea that physical activity (perceptual motor or other) would enhance intellectual functioning lay dormant. Then, in the 1990s, with improved technology for researching brain processes, neurophysiologists began to report data-based findings that physical activity does improve mental functions (Hannaford, 1995; Jensen, 1998). Today's physical educators thus are advocating physical activity for LD and DCD for two distinct purposes: (a) to improve general mental function, especially alertness and memory and (b) to resolve assessed problems associated with clumsiness.

Indicative of the importance of DCD to adapted physical activity specialists today is the fact that Sheila Henderson was the invited Rarick Lecturer at the 13th biennial symposium

(2001) of the International Federation of Adapted Physical Activity. The title of the lecture was "Toward an Understanding of Developmental Coordination Disorder"; the published lecture (Henderson & Henderson, 2002) provided an outstanding overview of DCD and stated that research supported task-oriented intervention as more effective than process-oriented intervention only.

Dawne Larkin, at the University of Western Australia, collaborated with an occupational therapist at Boston University, Sharon Cermak, to provide the first textbook entitled *Developmental Coordination Disorder* (2002).

In this textbook, task-specific approaches are covered in Chapter 11, and process (underlying abilities) approaches are presented in Chapter 12. Both are widely used with children with LD and DCD.

Assessment for Identifying DCD

APA (2000) estimates that the prevalence of DCD is 6% in the age range from 5 to 11 years. However, much work is needed on assessment. The criteria for identifying children with DCD require use of valid techniques and agreement about the cutoff point standard that indicates that "motor coordination is substantially below that expected given the person's chronological age and measured intelligence" (APA, 2000, p. 54). The three tests most often used to determine a general ability score that indicates motor impairment are described in Chapter 12. Cutoff point standards have ranged from the 5th percentile recommended for the Movement ABC (Henderson & Henderson, 2002) to the 15th, 40th, and 50th percentiles used with BOTMP (Tan et al., 2001).

The second criterion for identification of DCD (the condition significantly interferes with academic achievement or activities of daily living) has been addressed only by Watkinson et al. (2001). These scholars believe that *activities of daily living of interest to physical educators* can be assessed by the number of activities that children engage in on the playground, and they have developed a valid pictorial instrument to assess this. The instrument is called the Activities of Daily Living in Physical Play (ADL-PP).

All research, until the last decade, was weak on assessment in relation to this area. The following description, however, shows that parents and professionals need to share perspectives and expectations.

Excerpts from a Biography

Louise Clarke, the mother of a boy with LD, devoted several passages to this difficulty in her excellent book:

> There was a new area of incompetence too. Mike's school was very big on athletics. All the men teachers directed at least one sport, and starting in the second grade, there was a great deal of talk about who made what team.
>
> Mike did not make any.
>
> Mr. Klein, the athletic director, was openly contemptuous, and the best Mike got from any of the male staff was amused tolerance. He wanted very much to make a team, and during vacations he and his father threw balls back and forth, or his father

would throw them for him to bat. It was an endless exercise. . . .

> Mike never did get the knack of it. He would miss catches by fractions of inches, but near-misses do not count in games. His batting was so erratic that his father . . . could not field them half the time. (Clarke, 1973, p. 20)

Mike, like many other children with LD, seemed to have trouble primarily in hand-eye coordination and balance. He was an excellent swimmer, winning many ribbons in competitive events from grade school on. Moreover, his strength, cardiorespiratory endurance, and running speed enabled him to perform well on fitness tests. Having completed a PhD in science at Harvard University in his 20s, Mike recalled his physical education experiences and stated,

> My hand-eye coordination was never very good, and it still isn't. But I wouldn't tell dyslexics to stay away from sports, just the competitive sports that put a premium on hand-eye coordination, like baseball or handball. Anything where the margin of error is small. Tennis and squash allow for a margin of error. They demand coordination, but you can get away with it; you don't have to hit the ball every time at dead center of the racquet. (Clarke, 1973, p. 132)

Specific Problems Applicable to LD and DCD

Many persons with LD with and without DCD have difficulty decoding or making sense out of their bodies and space (see Figure 20.3). Following is a description of common problems and instructional strategies to address them.

Immature Body Image and Agnosias

As children mature, they become conscious of their bodies, internalize their perceptions, and acquire a *body image.* Children with LD, however, manifest many problems: (a) finger agnosia,

---

Figure 20.3 **A movement lesson designed to improve hopping and jumping enhances perception of space and time.**

(b) inability to identify body parts and surfaces, (c) inability to translate knowledge of right and left into following movement instructions, and (d) difficulty in making judgments about body size, shape, and proportions. These deficits are thought to stem from brain damage.

Table 20.1 lists screening tests used by many professions to determine if motor problems are mainly of neurological origin. Many of the tests are physical education activities (e.g., heel walking, stork stand).

Improving body image through physical education involves the use of action songs, dances, games, and exercises that refer to body parts (see Figure 20.4). Provide opportunities for children to see themselves in the mirror, on videotape, and on film. Perceptual-motor, relaxation, dance, and aquatic activities can be used specifically to improve body image. Obstacle courses that require problem solving about body size and shape in order to squeeze under or through are especially excellent.

Poor Spatial Orientation

Closely allied to body image deficits are disturbances in spatial orientation. Children with LD are described as *lost in space.* They typically lose their way en route to a destination and show confusion when given north-south-east-west and right-left directions. Moreover, they experience difficulty in estimating distance, height, width, and the other coordinates of space. As a result, they are forever bumping into things and misjudging the space requirements in such tasks as stepping through geometric forms, ducking under a low rope, and squeezing through a narrow opening.

Recommended games must involve obstacle courses, mazes, and maps. Orienteering and treasure hunts are good. Risk recreation and adventure activities in an outdoor setting give meaning to this type of programming. *Instruction in cue detection is important, as well as self-talk and rehearsal, both visual and verbal.*

Overflow Movements

Children with LD display greater levels of overflow than peers. **Overflow** is the inability to keep opposite limbs motionless when performing one-arm or one-leg tasks. This phenomenon, which contributes to clumsiness, is one dimension of **disinhibition,** a generalized disorder of inhibitory control. Disinhibition is linked with impulsivity later in this chapter.

Dissociation and Figure-Background

Dissociation refers to problems in perceiving and organizing parts into wholes. This ability is age-related, with young children able to make sense only of wholes. Awareness that parts make up wholes develops at about age 7 (onset of concrete mental operations), but many children do not fully grasp relationships between parts and wholes until about age 9. The ability to shift back and forth between wholes and parts is prerequisite to success in tasks that require copying or imitating a model. Dissociation causes frustrations in integrating and coordinating movements in response to a demonstration.

We often say that persons *do not see whole* or that they *can't see the forest for the trees.* This ability is also related to game sense, intuitively knowing where to be and what to do. The ability to process and act on several bits of information at one time is dependent on whole-part perceptions.

Dissociation is a consideration in selecting teaching methods. *Problems with whole-part synthesizing and integrating generally indicate the need for whole teaching methods rather than whole-part-whole or part.* **Whole methodology** refers to demonstration of the total pattern with no verbalization other than "Watch me." The child who is learning to run and jump must get the *feel* of the whole before he or she cares much about using the arms properly. Beginning instruction in throwing and striking activities should focus on the target to be hit, not on the stance, grip, backswing, release, and follow-through.

During warm-up, locomotor activities that demand the integrated working together of the whole body tend to be better than calisthenics that emphasize the movement of parts. Thus, runs, hops, jumps, animal walks, logrolls, and tumbling activities are preferable to arm flinging, side bending, toe touching, and body part circling.

When students experience success with whole methodology, instructional strategies that teach and reinforce whole-part-whole learning can be introduced. Demonstrations can include one wrong part that students are helped to identify. Emphasis can be placed also on creative movement: "Show me everything you can do with a ball; now show me one thing you like to do best; now show me three things." Another approach is, "Show me something you can do with your whole body; now show me something you can do with one body part."

Practice in getting into different game and dance formations teaches students to see themselves as parts of a whole. Creative dance, swimming, and gymnastics in which individuals or partners devise an original stunt or movement sequence and then combine it with those of others reinforce understandings of parts versus wholes. Even a pyramid formation can be taught as a whole comprised of parts.

Figure-background and depth-perception problems are part of dissociation. **Figure-background constancy** is the ability to pick one object or figure out of a complex background. For some children, however, balls and classmates blend together

Figure 20.4   Body image work with a real skeleton is exciting. Here, the child and the skeleton are taking turns leading a *Simon Says* type game (e.g., the skeleton says, "Lean to the right!").

Table 20.1   Examples of tests used to verify neurological dysfunction.

Sign	Description	Assessment Questions
Romberg	Student stands erect with both feet together, with eyes open and then closed.	Does student sway or lose balance? In unilateral cerebellar damage, falls are toward side of lesion.
Choreiform movements	Student stands in Romberg position, but with arms held straight out in front, eyes closed, and tongue stuck out as far as possible.	Are there rotary or twitching movements of the fingers, tongue, or head?
Motor impersistence	Same as for choreiform movements.	Can student maintain this position for at least 30 sec?
Tandem stand, walk (also called Mann test sign)	Student stands in heel-toe posture, with eyes open, then closed. Also walks heel-to-toe at least six steps.	What is performance discrepancy between eyes open and eyes closed? Eyes open compensates for ataxia caused by CNS damage.
Heel walking	Student walks on heels at least six steps.	Are anterior foot and toes off the floor and the body in good control?
Stork or one-foot stand (also called one-foot Romberg) Shallow one-leg squat and rise	Student stands on one foot, with eyes open and then closed. If successful, student is asked to squat and rise (one time only), bearing the entire weight on one leg.	Can student stand on preferred leg at least 10 sec and do squat and rise with good control?
Associated movements (synkinesia—*syn* [without] and *kinesia* [movement])	Student touches thumb to index finger of same hand as rapidly as possible, at a rate of about 3 per second.	Can student keep the other hand motionless, or does it mirror the moving hand?
Dysdiadochokinesia (dis-di-ad-o-ko-ki-ne-se-a) from *dys* (bad) + *diadochos* (succeeding) + *kinesis* (movement) (also called alternating motion rate [AMR])	Student alternates pronation and supination movements of one hand as rapidly as possible, with arm bent at 90° angle.	Can student maintain a 90° angle with arms close to body while doing this, or do arms begin to flail wildly?
	If successful, student is asked to do same movement with both hands, beginning with one palm up and one palm down. This is usually done in sitting position, with hands resting on knees.	Can student maintain rapid alternating movements with hands moving in opposite directions?
Finger dexterity: Touching thumb to fingertips (also tests alternating motion rate [AMR])	Student uses thumb to rapidly touch each finger in succession, moving from little finger to index finger and then from index finger to little finger. Eyes open, then closed.	Can student perform this task in 90 sec? Alternative tests are buttoning and unbuttoning, using safety pins, and other finger patterns like pivoting thumb and index finger.
Dyssynergia or dyskinesthesia: Touching nose with index finger or touching two index fingers	From erect stand, arms extended sideward, student touches tip of index finger to tip of nose; also can bend elbows and touch tips of index fingers in front of chest.	Can the student touch precisely the place desired with eyes open, then closed? Are the movements smooth, with no tremor?
Finger agnosia: Perceptual deficit decreasing awareness of external stimuli applied to fingers	With eyes closed or hands hidden from sight, student can identify which finger or part of the finger is being touched. Sometimes, touches are simultaneously to two or three fingers or to parts of the same finger.	Can student recognize and label touches? Can student state what part of a finger has been touched?
Right-left discriminations	Student, on command, touches right and left parts of body as well as external objects.	Can student perform both unilateral (right hand to right ear) and crosslateral (right hand to left ear) tasks?

Figure 20.5 Masking tape figures on wall help children with figure-background problems.

Figure 20.6 Children with rhythm problems need to gain success in moving to their own rhythm before trying to follow an externally imposed one.

or float in and out of focus. Confusions pertaining to near-far, front-back, and high-low are common.

To minimize such problems, follow the principle of stimulus enhancement. Make equipment and apparatus brightly colored to contrast with the background. Balance beams and mats should be a different color from the floor. Masking tape figures on walls and floors should utilize reds and blues, colors that have been shown to be children's favorites (see Figure 20.5). Basketball backdrops and goal cages should stand out boldly against less relevant stimuli.

Visual and auditory games that stress the locations of objects and sounds may be directed toward remediation of figure-background problems. Illustrative of these are such guessing games as *I Bet You Can't See What I See, Who's Got My Bone?, Huckleberry Beanstalk,* and *Hot and Cold.* Scavenger hunts also demand the ability to isolate relevant stimuli from the background.

Motor Planning and Sequencing

Motor planning and sequencing are executive functions that include thought and action in relation to (a) initiating movement, (b) terminating movement, and (c) putting parts in correct order. Problems typically occur when attempting to imitate something that has been seen or heard. Intervention involves games, dance, water play, and gymnastic routines in which an increasing number of movements must be remembered and chained together into sequences. Movement games like *I'm Going to Grandmother's House, Copy Cat,* and *Who Can Remember How Ted Got to the Moon?* simultaneously provide practice in movement and memory.

Temporal Organization, Rhythm, and Force

Some individuals can organize parts into wholes and get them in the right order but cannot cope with rhythm. It is difficult to know whether the underlying problem is perception, organiza-

tion, or a combination. To look right, virtually all body movements must be timed correctly. This is especially true when accuracy, speed, and force are involved.

Another manifestation of this cluster of disorders is the inability to move or dance in time with music or externally imposed rhythms. When other adolescents are developing social and romantic relationships through dance, many youth with LD miss these experiences because rhythm does not come naturally to them, and they have received no compensatory instruction.

Bilateral coordination items in the Bruininks-Oseretsky Test of Motor Proficiency (BOTMP) measure timing. This is done by synchronized, rhythmical tapping of two body parts and imitations of hands-to-thighs rhythmical patterns. This is one of the three areas in which students with LD are weakest.

Pedagogy to remediate these problems includes early instruction in music, rhythm, and dance with teachers especially trained to understand problems (see Figure 20.6). Many students with LD profit from the use of background music or a strong percussive beat (drum or metronome) as accompaniment. The music, of course, should be carefully selected to reinforce the natural rhythm of the skill and the desired performance speed. Videotaping pairs of students (one strong, one weak) doing movement to music enables the student with

LD to make visual comparisons and to develop compensatory strategies since the auditory-kinesthetic feedback circuits obviously are not working properly. Many students with LD, when dancing, do not know they are out of rhythm.

Other Executive Functions

Labeling, rehearsal, elaboration, association, organization, and chunking are among the information-processing strategies that affect academic learning, but little is known about the comparable functions in motor performance and learning (Kowalski & Sherrill, 1992; Reid, 1986, 1987). Many persons with LD say that their problem is not perception: They see, hear, and know what to do but cannot make the body perform as the mind wills.

Adults with LD, when asked to discuss motor executive functions, describe different patterns. Many say that they do not learn effectively from either demonstration or listening to instructions. Instead, they learn new motor skills best by trial and error, helped occasionally by specific, individual, corrective feedback. These people say that being labeled as impulsive or described as having attention deficits is unfair because it is natural to want the teacher to stop explaining when the words and demonstration have little meaning. The only way such individuals can achieve skill is to dig in and find out what, kinesthetically, feels right or works. Other adults with LD indicate that they think they are grasping the explanation, but something seems to happen in short-term memory. The visual and auditory input do not get encoded. Many adults with LD describe extreme difficulty with visualization of motor skills. Others insist that they learn best when one modality (visual or auditory) is used, and only one or two points are made at a time.

Activity Deficit Phenomenon

The **activity deficit phenomenon** (Bouffard et al., 1996), is a sedentary lifestyle that results from avoidance strategies that people with movement difficulties use to preserve self-esteem and manage emotional hurts related to clumsiness. Children as young as 7 begin to manifest avoidance and withdrawal behaviors that put skill development and social-emotional growth at risk. Clumsiness is intensified as years go by and these children engage in less and less physically active play. Often, children with movement difficulties become passive learners in physical education as they use every opportunity to sit out and observe rather than participate.

Early intervention is needed before activity deficit behaviors become a permanent lifestyle. Ways must be devised to permit children with movement difficulties to have fun in physical activity despite their clumsiness. Fun is a highly individualistic feeling, with many meanings. Many individuals find fun in social relationships and will engage in an activity just to be with people they like. *Teachers must find the specific reinforcers* that are most effective in keeping each child intrinsically motivated to stay optimally involved in physical activity.

Instructional Strategies

Whereas adults with LD have generally given much thought to their clumsiness, children become frustrated and often give up.

Spontaneous instructional strategies are not typically applied until about age 7 or 8. Children with LD show delays or absence of these strategies. Instruction must focus on how to become active learners (Bulgren & Carta, 1992; Bouffard & Wall, 1990; Vallerand & Reid, 1990).

Metacognitive Strategy Instruction

Metacognition is personal knowledge about the ways we think, move, and learn. Metacognitive strategy instruction is effective in improving academic skills of persons with LD (Harris & Pressley, 1991) and offers promise in motor learning. Students with LD have little insight into visualization, self-talk, spontaneous rehearsal, and the like. Metacognitive strategy instruction can make students aware of these processes and enhance problem solving about personal learning.

Use of new strategies may be tiring and fraught with uncertainty and anxiety. Thus, class instruction should offer a *balance between traditional explicit learning* (imitation and following verbal instruction) *and movement exploration.* Originality in responding to movement challenges may be a strength of children with LD. Movement education, creative dance, and games that utilize original ideas and dramatic themes are especially recommended (i.e., sometimes, it is good to teach toward strengths instead of weaknesses). Instruction in relaxation is also important.

Modality-Based Instruction

Modality-based instruction is an approach for students who learn better when information is presented through one modality (visual or auditory) rather than both, as is the tradition in physical education. Research shows that most persons are mixed-modality learners by age 7 or 8. About 20 to 25% of children with LD, however, are visual preference learners, and about 10% are auditory preference learners. For these children, presenting information in the preferred modality may be better. Clinicians typically support preferred modality teaching (Dunn, 1990) whereas researchers question it (Kavale & Forness, 1999). Sherrill supports modality-based instruction.

Cognitive Style Matching

Cognitive style refers to the individual's approach to analyzing and responding to stimuli. When the student's style matches that of the teacher, there are few problems. If styles are widely divergent, however, both persons must learn tolerance. Cognitive styles are designated by bipolar adjectives: (a) field dependent, field independent, (b) global, analytical, and (c) impulsive, reflective. **Field-dependent** (FD) people are strongly influenced by the visual field. They see wholes and have trouble finding embedded figures and coping with details. Moreover, they tend to have a fast conceptual tempo, spend little time planning, and need external structure. In contrast, **field-independent** (FI) people exhibit the opposite behaviors.

Either extreme is associated with learning disabilities. The younger persons are, the more likely they are to be field dependent. This helps to explain why children typically are not much interested in details. Persons with LD are more likely to be FD than FI (Lazarus, 1990). Awareness of cognitive styles helps teachers to match instructional demands to strengths. Then, gradually, they can remediate weaknesses.

Self-Talk and Verbal Rehearsal

A self-talk and verbal rehearsal strategy is successful in helping children to learn motor sequences, improve game performance, and control impulsivity (Kowalski & Sherrill, 1992). **Self-talk** usually refers to talking oneself through an activity or sequence. It is simultaneous talking and moving. When the student does jumping jacks, for instance, he or she says *out* as the limbs spread and *in* as they return to midline. When a locomotor pattern is performed, the child says aloud *jump, jump, step, step, step, hop-2-3-4*.

Verbal rehearsal is saying aloud the parts of a planned movement before execution. This is often in response to the teacher's request, "Tell me the three things you are going to do." With guidance, students learn to ask and answer their own questions.

Motivation and Self-Concept Enhancement

Students with LD and DCD typically have lower self-concepts and more external locus of control than nondisabled peers (Cantell & Kooistra, 2002; Causgrove, Dunn & Watkinson, 1994). The reason for this seems to be the accumulation of failure after failure and the inability of parents and teachers to help students build areas of competence that offset acknowledged weaknesses and deficits. External locus of control is manifested by low motivation and passivity. Such responses are easily understood if one considers how it must feel to visualize failure before starting each day.

Not all students with LD manifest these problems. Scores on self-concept inventories depend on **reference groups** (i.e., the significant others to whom individuals compare themselves). When students with LD attend private schools and/or use peers with LD for their social, academic, and motor comparisons, the self-concept seems to be higher than most research indicates. Only about 1% of all students with LD attend private schools, however.

Teams and partners in the integrated gymnasium should be assigned with great care, rather than left to chance. These become the new reference groups and significant others for persons with LD. Games and sports should be adapted to emphasize cooperation rather than competition. For example, volleyball can be changed to a "How long can you keep the ball in the air?" theme. Basketball can be changed to give points for number of passes completed before shooting.

Enhancement of self-concept through success-oriented movement experiences and concomitant individual and small-group counseling is the most important physical education goal for students with LD. Closely related to this goal is helping students with LD gain peer acceptance and make one or two really close friendships that carry over into leisure-time activities. Curriculum models with particular promise are cooperative games (Mender, Kerr, & Orlick, 1982), motor creativity (Sherrill, 1986), games design (Morris & Stiehl, 1999), and social-personal development (Hellison, 1995). See Chapters 8, 9, and 15 for a review of these models and techniques for enhancing self-concept and social competence.

Fitness and Leisure Concerns

Students with LD must be helped to find one or two lifetime physical activities that they can do well enough to feel the satisfaction needed to maintain an active, healthy lifestyle. Although research indicates that individuals with LD are inferior to nondisabled peers on fitness tasks (Harvey & Reid, 2003), such findings probably *reflect differences in experience and motivation rather than capacity deficits.* Students with LD in private schools that employ physical education specialists and provide daily physical education instruction score average or better on standardized fitness tests. There is no neurological reason why individuals with LD cannot excel in strength, cardiorespiratory endurance, and flexibility.

Teachers in LD private schools report that many of their students do well in soccer. There appear to be fewer coordination problems in foot-eye than in hand-eye ball activities. Students with LD need exposure to competitive sport that emphasizes cooperative teamwork and sportsmanship. Remember that children with LD are often delayed in social competence. Private schools in the Dallas-Fort Worth area have developed a soccer league for students with LD so that initial competitive sport experience is against peers with similar skills in a carefully monitored, success-oriented environment.

The play and leisure activities of individuals with LD tend to be different from those of nondisabled peers. Children with LD engage in significantly more solitary play and hold inferior sociometric status compared with others (Causgrove, Dunn & Watkinson, 1994; Gottlieb, Gottlieb, Berkell, & Levy, 1986). Their leisure activities tend to be passive and accompanied by feelings of loneliness (Margalit, 1984). Many demonstrate a kind of learned helplessness in regard to initiating activities with others and depend on their parents and siblings for recreational activities.

Although research on the play and leisure of students with LD is sparse, there is strong indication that leisure education and counseling should be integrated into physical education instruction. School-community partnerships should utilize the expertise of therapeutic recreation specialists and foster generalization of school learning to use of community resources.

Attention Deficit Hyperactivity Disorder (ADHD)

ADHD is a combination of inattention and/or hyperactive-impulsive symptoms that are present in at least two settings and interfere with academic, social, and occupational functioning (American Psychiatric Association, 2000). Some symptoms of ADHD must have been present before age 7 (see Table 20.2). Many individuals with LD have ADHD, but ADHD has been recognized as a separate medical diagnosis since 1980 and an IDEA disability subcategory under *other health-impairments* since 1997.

Three ADHD subtypes are recognized by the American Psychiatric Association (2000): ADHD, combined type; ADHD, predominantly inattentive type; and ADHD, predominantly hyperactivity-impulsivity type. Intervention should be directed toward the specific indicators in Table 20.2, and physical

Table 20.2   Diagnostic criteria for ADHD related to maladaptive behaviors that have persisted over 6 or more months.

A. **Inattention.** At least six of the following:
   1. Often fails to give close attention to details, or makes careless mistakes in schoolwork, work, or other activities.
   2. Often has difficulty sustaining attention in tasks or play activities.
   3. Often does not seem to listen when spoken to directly.
   4. Often does not follow through on instructions and fails to finish schoolwork, chores, or duties in the workplace (not due to oppositional behavior or failure to understand instructions).
   5. Often has difficulty organizing tasks and activities.
   6. Often avoids, dislikes, or is reluctant to engage in tasks that require sustained mental effort (such as schoolwork or homework).
   7. Often loses things necessary for tasks or activities (e.g., toys, school assignments, pencils, books, or tools).
   8. Often is easily distracted by extraneous stimuli.
   9. Often is forgetful in daily activities.
B. **Hyperactivity-Impulsivity.** At least six of the following:
   Hyperactivity
   1. Often fidgets with hands or feet or squirms in seat.
   2. Often leaves seat in classroom or in other situations in which remaining seated is expected.
   3. Often runs about or climbs excessively in situations in which it is inappropriate (in adolescents or adults, may be limited to subjective feelings of restlessness).
   4. Often has difficulty playing or engaging in leisure activities quietly.
   5. Often *on the go* or often acts if *driven by a motor.*
   6. Often talks excessively.
   Impulsivity
   7. Often blurts out answers before questions have been completed.
   8. Often has difficulty awaiting turn.
   9. Often interrupts or intrudes on others (e.g., butts into conversations or games).

Adapted from American Psychiatric Association (2000).

educators should work closely with parents and school personnel in implementing behavior management programs and strategies.

Etiology and Prevalence

The etiology of ADHD is unclear and controversial (Harvey & Reid, 2003). Causative factors are interactive genetic, neurological, and psychosocial factors (Barkley, 1998; Tannock, 1998). Much research is needed to document specific etiologies, which will probably eventually be linked to subtypes of ADHD.

The prevalence of ADHD is approximately 3 to 7% in the school-age population. ADHD is more frequent in males than in females; the ratio ranges from 4:1 to 9:1, depending on the setting. ADHD is also a frequent comorbid condition (see p. 548).

Inattention

Inattention encompasses many separate processes. Among these are **selective attention** (the ability to pick up and attend to the central or desired stimulus), **concentration** (the ability to sustain attention, presumably in an environment conducive to learning), **narrow focusing** (the ability to narrow attention to a particular task in spite of distractions), and **broad focusing** (the ability to effectively attend to many stimuli at one time). Time-on-task is often the way attention is measured.

Attention is affected by many variables. Among these are age (the younger the child, the less able to block out irrelevant detail), degree of difficulty (the harder the task, the shorter the duration of concentration), the number and intensity of distractors in the environment, the novelty and/or interest and fun features of the activity, changes in weather and humidity, and the like. Moreover, definite attentional styles appear to be related to external and internal locus of control, motivation, and incentive (Nideffer, 1977). Some persons attend well to external stimuli, whereas others concentrate better on ideas and tasks that come from within.

Stimuli overload seems to be a particular factor in ADHD. Students cannot block out irrelevant stimuli and thus seem driven to react to everything. Admonishing such pupils to *pay attention* is useless. They would if they could. Inattention consists mainly of errors of omission rather than commission. The main problem is failure to finish tasks.

Impulsivity or Disinhibition

In contrast, impulsivity results from errors of commission. **Impulsivity** is the tendency to move without carefully considering alternatives. It is the opposite of reflectivity. Impulsive individuals finish tasks quickly, often with lots of errors. They are typically the first ones done, demanding "What do we do next?"

Because they do not consider alternatives, they are sometimes perceived as conceptually rigid.

Impulsivity is also associated with **field dependence,** a perceptual-cognitive-behavioral style descriptive of persons who are dependent upon the environment (i.e., the field) rather than their own ideas and internal motivation (Lazarus, 1990). Field dependence is a lack of inhibitory control, a **forced responsiveness** to the field that leads persons to try to please significant others. Impulsivity, or field dependence, is characteristic of young children. As youth mature, they become increasingly reflective or field independent.

Impulsive children may display **catastrophic reactions** to unexpected stimuli like a sharp noise, a scary incident in a movie, or a playful jab from a teammate. They tend to fall apart, to sob uncontrollably, to scream, or to display sudden outbursts of anger or physical aggression.

Hyperactivity

Hyperactivity occurs when children manifest disorders of listening, thinking, reading, writing, spelling, or arithmetic primarily because they cannot sit still long enough to complete a task. Such children are forever wiggling, shuffling their feet, swinging their legs, doodling, pinching, chewing gum, gritting their teeth, and talking to themselves or others. They seem never to tire and require unbelievably little sleep. Hyperactivity may be worse on some days than others. Classroom teachers have been known to send the child to the playground on such days: "You take him . . . I can't teach him a thing in the classroom."

Hyperactivity should not be confused with individual differences in energy, impulse control, and enthusiasm. The older the child is, the more easily he or she can slow down the pace and consciously determine the tempo. Impulse control may be related to hyperactive behavior, but it is not the same thing.

Other Behavioral Problems

Other behavioral problems are social perception inadequacies, perseveration, and misunderstandings that stem from deficits in listening, thinking, and speaking skills. These problems are often confounded by family members with ADHD.

Social Perception Inadequacies

Inadequacies of social perception—namely, the inability to recognize the meaning and significance of the behavior of others—contribute to poor social adjustment. Problems in this area occur concomitantly with both LD and ADHD.

Children with LD often have difficulty in making and keeping friends of their own age (see Figure 20.7). Attention deficits, impulsivity, and hyperactivity are complicated further by their inability to deal with abstractions and double meanings. They become the butt of jokes when they cannot share the multiple meanings of such words as *screw, ball, grass, pot,* and *head.* Moreover, much of the humor in our society is abstract and entirely lost on them. Because they fail to comprehend the subtleties of facial expression, tone of voice, and body language, they do not realize that they are angering, antagonizing,

Figure 20.7 Activities in warm water reduce hyperactivity. Water play should be structured and involve partner interactions. These girls are responding to the question "How many different shapes can you create with one partner, two noodles, and a small hoop?"

or boring others until some kind of explosion erupts. They retreat with hurt feelings, wondering why the others *blew up all of a sudden* or told them *to get out and leave them alone.*

With severely involved children, play should seldom, if ever, be left unstructured. It is far better to delimit the activity with "You may play cowboys with John and Chris in Room 121 for 20 minutes" than to allow the group interaction to continue indefinitely, ultimately ending with a fight of some kind. In schools that have daily recess, the teacher should specify ahead of time names of persons who have permission to play together, the space on the playground they may occupy, and the equipment they may use. Children with social imperception are given freedom only in small degrees, as they demonstrate increasing ability to cope in social situations.

Perseveration

Often interpreted as stubbornness, **perseveration** is the inability to shift easily from one idea or activity to another. Perseveration is present when someone

1. continues to grind on and on long after a pencil is sharpened.
2. continues to bounce the ball after the signal for stopping has been given.
3. continues to laugh or giggle after everyone else stops.
4. repeats the same phrase over and over or gets hung up on one topic of conversation.

Perseveration is the opposite of distractibility. It contributes to a behavioral rigidity, which is evidenced in games when the student refuses to adapt rules or to test a new strategy. One intervention approach is creativity training with emphasis on fluency and flexibility.

Another approach is to plan activities that are distinctly different from each other in formation, starting position, basic skills, rules, and strategies. A circle game, for instance, might be followed by a relay in files. In circuit training, a station stressing arm and shoulder strength might be followed by one emphasizing jumping activities. Games based upon stop-and-go concepts reinforce the ability to make transitions from one activity to another. Illustrative of these are *Red Light, Green Light, Musical Chairs, Cakewalks, Statues,* and *Squirrels in the Trees.*

Principles for Managing Environment

The concepts of Cruickshank (1967) and Strauss and Lehtinen (1947) continue to underlie behavior management. A good teaching environment is based on four principles:

1. Establishment of a highly structured program
2. Reduction of environmental space
3. Elimination of irrelevant auditory and visual stimuli
4. Enhancement of the stimulus value of the instructional materials

Structure

The **principle of structure,** as applied to the physical education setting, requires the establishment of a routine that is repeated day after day and leaves nothing to chance. For instance, the pattern of activities should follow the same sequence each period: sitting on prescribed floor spots while waiting for class to begin, warm-ups always done in the same area and facing the same direction, introduction and practice of new skills, participation in games or dances, return to floor spots, and sitting during *cooldown* period of relaxation and discussion.

If instructional stations are used, a certain piece of apparatus should always be located in the same space and the students should always mount it from the same direction. Rotation from station to station should always be in the same direction, traditionally counterclockwise. Characteristically, after warm-ups, each student goes to his or her assigned station to start instruction, and rotation always proceeds from the same spot. Identical start, stop, and rotation signals also contribute to structure since the child knows precisely which response is appropriate for each signal.

Moreover, the composition of each squad or team should be structured in much the same fashion as are groups for play therapy or psychotherapy. *A balance is maintained between the number of hyperactive and sluggish children so that one behavioral extreme tends to neutralize the other.* The proportion of aggressors and nonaggressors is weighted, as are natural leaders and followers.

Structure also denotes a carefully planned system of behavior management in operation. Cues and consequences are consistent. See Chapter 7 for a review of behavior management.

Space Reduction

The **principle of space reduction** suggests the use of lane markers and partitions to delimit the vast expanse of play area considered desirable for normal children. Special emphasis must be given to boundaries and the penalties incumbent upon stepping out-of-bounds. The major value of low organized games may be learning about boundaries, baselines, and space utilization.

Figure 20.8 Mirrors are extremely important in learning disabilities because visual input enhances kinesthetic and vestibular feedback.

Space reduction necessarily limits the size of the squads, which rotate from station to station. Most elementary school children function well in groups of six to eight; children with LD often require smaller groups.

Extraneous Stimuli Control

The **principle of extraneous stimuli control** demands the maintenance of a neat, clean, well-ordered play area. No balls or equipment are in sight unless they are required for the game in progress. When several squads are each practicing different motor tasks, often on different pieces of apparatus, the student's attention may be diverted by persons at other stations. Partitions to eliminate the extraneous visual stimuli from other stations prevent problems. Similar distractions are present when physical education is held outdoors: Cars in the nearby street, neighborhood animals, leaves rustling on the trees, birds flying overhead, weeds among the grass where the ball is rolling, even the wind and sun command the child's attention. The student with severe hyperactivity should be scheduled only for indoor physical education, where environmental variables can be more easily controlled.

Instructional Stimulus Enhancement

The **principle of instructional stimulus enhancement,** as applied to the physical education setting, implies the extensive and concentrated use of color to focus and hold the student's attention on a particular piece of apparatus, a target, or a ball. Sound may be used similarly. Wall-to-wall mirrors in which students can see and learn to evaluate their motor performance also seem to increase concentration (see Figure 20.8).

Table 20.3 Websites for additional information.

CEC, Division of Learning Disabilities	www.teachingLD.org
Learning Disabilities Association of America	www.ldanatl.org
Children with Attention Deficit Disorders	www.chadd.org
The Bipolar Child (author website)	www.bipolarchild.com
Child and Adolescent Bipolar Foundation	www.bpkids.org
Family Voices	www.familyvoices.org
Davis Dyslexia Association International	www.dyslexia.com

The principles of structure, space reduction, stimuli control, and instructional stimulus enhancement form the basis of a sound physical education program for students with LD. Freedom is increased gradually in accordance with the student's ability to cope.

Modifying Physical Education Content

Students with ADHD obviously need a different kind of physical education content than that which exists in most physical education settings. Adaptations might focus on learning relaxation techniques (see Chapter 16), impulse control, and sport, dance, and aquatic activities that encourage reflectivity and attention to detail. Additionally, strengths should be utilized; Davis with Braun (2003) offer some fascinating ideas in this regard. Individual and small-group counseling helps students to set personal goals for managing their behavior in school and community facilities where fitness and leisure skills are pursued.

The goal, of course, is to learn self-control and self-responsibility requisite to social acceptance in after-school and weekend youth sport. This can be achieved when teachers systematically apply the content in this chapter and related literature.

Medication

ADHD is a medical problem. Most physicians use medication only as a last resort. Nevertheless, a large number of youngsters with ADHD are so uncontrollable that drugs are prescribed: *ritalin* (methyiphenidate), *dexedrine, benzedrine, methedrine,* and *cylert,* all of which are stimulants. These stimulants slow down the child, increase the attention span, and help with concentration. Use of stimulants in hyperactivity is analogous to prescription of insulin for diabetes. Both conditions involve deficits in body chemistry for which drugs compensate. Medication, however, is not always effective (Wilens & Spencer, 2000).

Children do not become addicted to the drugs used in ADHD, and there are no withdrawal problems. The main side effects are depressed appetite and sleeplessness, according to medical sources. Physical educators note, however, that these medications sometimes affect balance and coordination.

 OPTIONAL ACTIVITIES

1. Use Table 20.3 to look up further information, and use this information to help persons (e.g., bulletin boards, presentations, advocacy letters). Record efforts in journal or portfolio.

2. Volunteer to work a certain number of hours each week with difficult children in a setting of your choice. Reflect on experience; critically evaluate your strategies.

3. Recent research indicates that ADHD is not just a childhood and adolescent disorder. Observe adults around you and note whether any of them are displaying ADHD symptoms. If classmates feel like open sharing, discuss conditions in this chapter with them. Encourage persons who have experienced conditions firsthand (themselves or family members) to share insights.

4. Follow up on citations, and read more. Write formal papers for class or publication.

5. Help with assessment and development of physical education goals and objectives for children with LD, ADHD, and DCD. Are dance and aquatics activities especially helpful? Why?

6. Reflect on how many of the ideas and activities in Chapter 22 apply to persons in this chapter.

7. Try writing children's stories about LD, ADHD, and DCD. If possible, let a child or group of children help you write.

8. Learn more about free audio-recording by contacting Recording for the Blind and Dyslexic (RFB&D), 20 Roszel Rd., Princeton, NJ 08540 (1-866-RFBD-585) and help others access this resource.

CHAPTER

21

Mental Retardation, Special Olympics, and the INAS-FID

Figure 21.1 Special Olympics has demonstrated the potential of persons with mental retardation to the world. *(A)* Eunice Kennedy Shriver, the founder of Special Olympics, provides encouragement. *(B)* Action from the Little Stanley Cup game, a feature event of the International Special Olympics floor hockey tournament in Toronto, Ontario.

A

B

1. Reflect on the different names and definitions for mental retardation (MR). Relate these to persons you have known; observe or work with people with MR at various ages and in different roles. Which definition do they like best? Which definition do you like best? Why?

2. Demonstrate your understanding of the AAMR (2002a) supports paradigm and its application in physical education assessment and planning.

3. Discuss frequently occurring medical problems that affect physical education programming as well as motor and cognitive abilities of persons with MR. What are some implications for assessment and programming?

4. Explain how programming differs according to intensity of supports needed, and give examples of models appropriate to guide programming. Discuss classification trends away from IQ and adaptive behaviors toward the four support intensities. How do you feel about this trend? Why?

5. Develop some task analyses and state cues, feedback, and reinforcement for each step.

6. Describe Special Olympics programming and discuss how you would organize and implement a year-round program. What local and state groups will you contact? Why?

7. Given profiles of persons with MR, write physical education IEPs and lesson plans.

Mental retardation (MR) is perhaps the best known of all disabilities because Special Olympics has given it so much visibility (see Figure 21.1). Definitions of MR, however, vary throughout the world. In the United States, mental retardation is distinguished from learning disabilities by federal law that specifies different diagnostic and funding categories. In contrast, Great Britain uses the terms *learning difficulty* and *special educational needs* instead of *mental retardation.*

INAS-FID and Special Olympics Perspectives

The International Federation of Sports for Persons with Intellectual Disability (INAS-FID), which is part of the Paralympic movement, provides opportunities for competition for elite athletes who, in the United States, would be considered mildly retarded. The INAS-FID was founded in Europe in 1986, and its terminology shows that much of the world prefers other terms over *mental retardation* (MR). Beginning with the World Games in Berlin in 1995, the INAS-FID has entered its athletes into Paralympic competition, which previously was held only for athletes with physical or sensory disabilities.

Special Olympics International (SOI), founded in Chicago in 1968, primarily uses the term *mental retardation* (MR). It conducts its own quadrennial summer and winter games exclusively for people with MR, provides comprehensive year-round sports training, and promotes Unified Sports, a program that combines approximately equal numbers of athletes with and without disabilities on teams that compete against each other. Local Special Olympics training activities are available to anyone with MR who is age 6 or older, but rules do not permit competition until age 8.

SOI has chosen to remain separate from the Paralympics for many reasons. One is that the SOI sport movement is so large and meets so many worldwide needs that it does not see its mission as compatible with that of the Paralympics. At most of their Summer World Games, held every 4 years (in the year *before* the Paralympics), over 7,000 athletes from more than 140 countries compete. *Not everyone is a winner, contrary to popular opinion, because SOI philosophy has changed over its 30-plus years of pioneer leadership.* Traditional medals are awarded to athletes who win first, second, and third places. Participation ribbons are given to other athletes in recognition of

their effort and accomplishments. Many levels of competition are supported, and some athletes are elite in the same sense that Olympians and Paralympians are elite. See Appendix F for most recent developments.

Adapted physical activity personnel throughout the world work with Special Olympics at many levels, local through international. The success of individual training and competition programs, typically staffed by volunteers, often largely depends on the leadership of adapted physical activity professionals. Many school systems, therefore, expect their adapted physical educators to work with Special Olympics. Tremendous breadth of knowledge is needed, because Special Olympics is usually a community-based program that serves all age groups.

Individuals eligible to become Special Olympics athletes are persons who

1. have been identified by an agency or professional as having mental retardation; OR

2. have a cognitive delay as determined by standardized measures like intelligence tests; OR

3. have a closely related developmental disability, defined as functional limitations in both general learning and in adaptive skills . . . however, persons whose functional limitations are based solely on a physical, behavioral, or emotional disability or a specific learning or sensory disability are not eligible (Special Olympics International, 2002, p. 8).

The Name Dilemma

The acceptable name for MR has varied tremendously over the years. In the early 1900s, persons with mild/moderate conditions were called **imbeciles** while those with severe conditions were called **idiots.** Thereafter **mental deficiency** became the preferred term, followed by **mental retardation.** Some professionals hope that the name will soon change to **intellectual disabilities** for consistency with terminology used in most of the rest of the world. The Board of Directors of the American Association on Mental Retardation (AAMR) agreed on this name change, but the AAMR membership voted it down in early 2003. The AAMR, founded in 1876, is the oldest and most powerful organization on MR in this country. It provides many services, among which is the publication of an official manual on definitions, classifications, and supports approximately every 10 years and two scholarly journals, *Mental Retardation* and *American Journal on Mental Retardation.*

The Definition Dilemma

Controversy has always surrounded definitions of MR. There are many reasons for this. One reason is that definitions determine eligibility for special education and other support services. For example, a major issue today is whether the upper limit of an intelligence test quotient for diagnosing a person as mentally retarded should be 70 or 75. Parents with children who have IQs between 70 and 75 might want an upper limit of 75, while taxpayers who are conscious of the money that special services cost might want a cutoff of 70. Experts note that in a normal curve distribution there are more than twice as many cases with IQs below 75 (4.7%) as there are cases with IQs below 70 (2.3%) (MacMillan, Gresham, & Siperstein, 1995).

Since the 1950s all definitions of MR have included the concept of **adaptive functioning** (i.e., adaptive behaviors or skills such as dressing oneself, telling time, and conveying one's needs to others). This is because many experts question the validity, reliability, and cultural fairness of IQ tests in determining an individual's performance on various tasks.

Philosophy about MR, eligibility criteria, classification, and support systems is continually changing. The AAMR has pioneered these changes.

Current Definitions of MR

Key concepts in each definition of MR are intellectual functioning, adaptive behavior, and age of onset. IDEA uses the same definition of MR as did PL 94-142:

Significantly subaverage general intellectual functioning existing concurrently with deficits in adaptive behavior and manifested during the developmental period that adversely affects a child's educational performance.

In contrast, AAMR has changed the definition slightly every 10 years. In 1992, the AAMR set forth the following four-part definition.

1. Refers to substantial limitations in certain personal capabilities.
2. Is manifested as significantly subaverage intellectual functioning.
3. Exists concurrently with related disabilities in two or more of 10 adaptive skill areas (e.g., work, self-care, and self-direction).
4. Begins before age 18.

In 2002, AAMR revised the 1992 definition, emphasizing three general adaptive skill categories rather than 10 specific ones and the person-environment interactions that contribute to person-referenced outcomes. AAMR (2002a, p. 13) defined MR as "a disability characterized by significant limitations both in intellectual functioning and in adaptive behavior as expressed in conceptual, social, and practical skills. This disability originates before age 18."

Intellectual functioning was defined as general mental capacity as measured by standardized tests which assess "reasoning, planning, solving problems, thinking abstractly, comprehending complex ideas, learning quickly, and learning from experience" (AAMD, 2002a, p. 40). Many standardized tests are used to assess IQ. The oldest is the Stanford-Binet Intelligence Scale (also known as the Terman-Merrill Scale), which has a mean of 100 and a standard deviation of 16. Figure 21.2 shows markers of 84, 68, 52, and so on when 16 is subtracted from 100 and each subsequent marker. Newer tests like the Wechsler Intelligence Scale for Children-Revised (WISC-R), the Kaufman Assessment Battery for Children, and the Slosson Intelligence Test all have a mean of 100 and a standard deviation of 15. Subtracting this standard deviation from 100 and subsequent markers yields 85, 70, 55, and so on. A 70 on the Wechsler is thus equivalent to a 68 on the Stanford-Binet; both IQs fall two standard deviations below the mean and indicate that general intellectual function is lower than that of 97% of the population.

Adaptive behavior was defined as "a collection of conceptual, social, and practical skills that have been learned by people in order to function in their everyday lives" (p. 14). AAMR (2002) did not list adaptive skill areas as did AAMR (1992) but instead used three general categories (conceptual, social, and practical) that can be measured by valid instruments. *Only one of the three had to be found to be subaverage for the diagnosis to be made, or an overall score for the three categories that was subaverage might be used.* The criterion for eligibility for both intellectual function and adaptive behavior was two standard deviations below the mean. Among the several standardized tests available to measure adaptive behaviors are the Comprehensive Test of Adaptive Behavior-Revised (Adams, 1999) and the AAMR Adaptive Behavior Scales (Lambert, Nihira, & Leland, 1993).

Specific examples of each adaptive skill category were given in AAMR (2002a). **Conceptual** included self-direction, money concepts, reading and writing, and receptive and expressive language. **Social** included interpersonal relationships, responsibility, self-esteem, gullibility (likelihood of being tricked or manipulated), naïveté, following rules, obeying laws, and avoiding victimization. **Practical** included maintaining a safe environment, activities of daily living, and occupational skills (the item that could encompass leisure skills). This list provides insight into the behaviors that AAMR most values and thus would be most likely to support as goals to guide instruction.

AAMR (2002a) emphasized that limitations in adaptive behaviors should be considered in light of four other dimensions: (a) intellectual abilities; (b) participation, interactions, and social roles; (c) health; and (d) context. **Health** was defined as including fine and gross motor skills and ambulating. In summary, AAMR (2002a, p. 49) stated:

Thus a comprehensive and correct understanding of the condition of mental retardation requires a multidimensional and ecological approach that reflects the interaction of the individual and his or her environment, and the person-referenced outcomes of that interaction related to independence, relationships, contributions, school and community participation and personal well-being.

Figure 21.2 Theoretical distribution of IQ scores, based on normal curve with 10 standard deviations, to show mentally retarded, normal, and gifted classifications assigned on the basis of Wechsler and Stanford-Binet test scores.

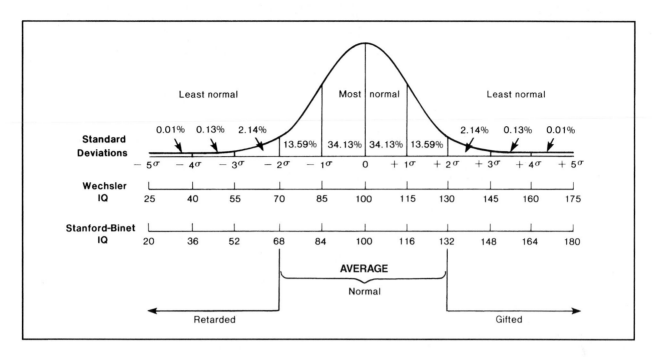

With a partner, try to create an adaptive behaviors scale specifically for physical activity in a home, school, or community context for a selected age group. List items under the adaptive behavior categories of conceptual, social, and practical. Be sure each item is measurable. If possible, test your proposed scale on individuals with MR.

The Supports Paradigm

The 2002 AAMD manual expanded and clarified the supports paradigm introduced in the 1992 AAMD manual. **Supports** was defined as

> Resources and strategies that aim to promote the development, education, interests, and personal well-being of a person and that enhance individual well-being. *Services* are one type of support provided by professionals and agencies. *Individual functioning* results from the interaction of supports with the dimensions of Intellectual Disabilities; Adaptive Behavior; Participation, Interactions, and Social Roles; Health; and Context. (AAMD, 2002a, p. 145)

The new part of this definition and the paradigm it underlies is *the assertion that appropriate application of supports can improve the functional abilities of persons with MR.* Concepts like *inclusive education, supported living,* and *supported employment* exemplify this belief as well as IDEA 1997 and subsequent revisions, which repeatedly call for supports as a means of keeping persons with disabilities in general education.

Figure 21.3 presents the supports paradigm recommended by AAMR (2002a). How can physical education contribute to the **support areas and functions** listed in Figure 21.3?

Note how these support functions relate to the adaptive skill areas in the definition. *In writing goals and objectives, physical educators should consider using the terminology in the AAMR definition and model.* Remember that motor skills falls under health and safety in this paradigm.

Support intensities vary in different life stages and situations. Recommended adjectives for use in assessing intensity of support need follow:

Intermittent refers to short-term support that is made available as needed (e.g., availability of a paraprofessional or resource room).

Limited refers to designated, prearranged support for short periods of time (e.g., use of an athlete role model to teach wheelchair sport skills or an after-school tutor during an instructional unit that will likely be particularly difficult).

Extensive refers to daily support in some, but not all, environments. A personal assistant (PA), for instance, might be needed when a student with multiple disabilities is enrolled in a general physical education class. Adapted equipment might be needed in physical education but not in other classes.

Pervasive refers to constant, high-intensity, possibly life-sustaining supports. This typically involves a full-time PA and provision of such devices as ventilators, catheters, and adapted eating utensils.

Desired outcomes vary, of course, with individual needs and subject matter. The trend, however, is clearly toward instruction that will lead to increased self-direction, independent functioning in the community, and leisure and fitness skills that will enhance health and social inclusion.

Figure 21.3   Supports paradigm for people with mental retardation (AAMR, 2002a).

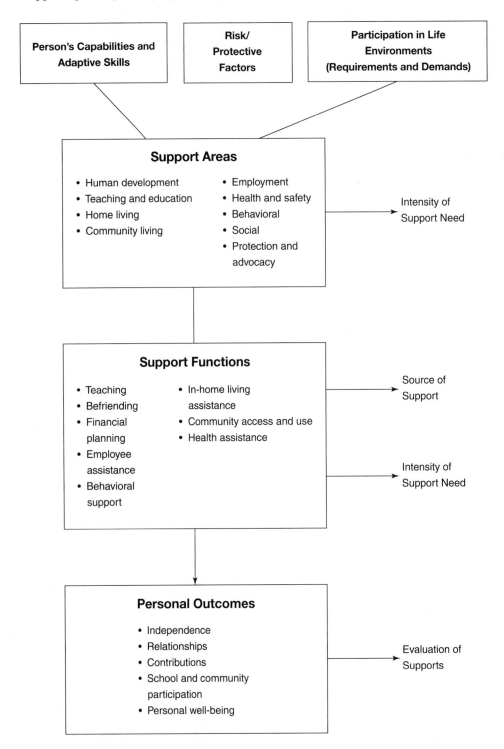

Five Steps in Using the Supports Paradigm

1. Look at Figure 21.3 and identify the relevant support areas for physical education to address for the targeted student. *Most physical educators believe that their greatest contributions can be in the support areas of community access and use* (i.e., recreation/leisure

involvement) *and health and safety* (i.e., health-related fitness and motor skills). Professionals should use the language of the supports paradigm in the IEP process and in determining goals and objectives.

2. Identify relevant support activities for each support area. These should be driven by (a) the individual's preferences

and interests, (b) activities in which the individual does or most likely will participate, and (c) settings in which the individual does or most likely will participate through his or her lifespan. Questions about these support activities need to be integrated into physical education assessment and asked of both students and parents.

3. Assess the level or intensity of support needs. This assessment should include details of frequency, daily support times, and specific types of support when doing physical education at school or physical activity at home or in the community.

4. Write an **Individual Supports Plan (ISP)** to be woven into the IEP or the IFSP. This involves using assessment to determine which support functions are most needed in physical activity (apply your critical thinking to Figure 21.3), which sources of support are available, and which intensity of support need applies to each. For traditional physical education goals, **health assistance** would be the support function addressed. The basic question might be how can physical educators support health assistance? For transition-oriented physical education, **community access and use** would be the targeted support function. The ISP must include a plan to monitor the provision of supports and their outcomes.

5. Provide the supports, conducting both formative (daily) and summative evaluation in accordance with the plan developed in Step 4 to monitor provision of supports and their outcomes.

The approach uses a lot of new terms and concepts but is really what this text and others have been emphasizing for the last 10 years. AAMR is the first organization to fully explain what supports might mean and to provide detail in planning and providing supports. For this reason, Sherrill recommends that every adapted physical education specialist study the entire AAMR (2002a) manual. Its content is outstanding in its challenge to use our critical thinking to change the nature of delivery services and especially the way we conceptualize providing services for persons with severe disabilities in the mainstream.

 Describe a student with mental retardation, real or imagined in a GE physical education class. Use the AAMR terminology to describe the assessment you would use and the goals and objectives you would write in preparation for the IEP meeting. Share your products with partners and revise as needed.

 Sometimes new ideas take a long time to be implemented in the real world. Find out how these ideas about supports are being used in schools near your campus or in your hometown. Ask about both special education and adapted physical education. If not used, try to determine why. If used, try to determine whether school personnel like or dislike the new ideas.

 Is the AAMR paradigm applicable to other disabilities? How? Why?

Level of Severity vs. Needed Supports

IQs are generally specified for four levels of MR function: (a) mild, 52–70; (b) moderate, 36–51; (c) severe, 20–35; and (d) profound, 19 and lower. About 90% of persons with MR fall into the mild classification, 5% into the moderate, and 3.5% and 1.5%, respectively, into the severe and profound. **Severe** refers to persons with good levels of awareness and adequate resources to respond, learn, and function in integrated community settings when extensive support is provided. In contrast, **profound** denotes persons with very limited awareness and response repertoires.

The 1992 AAMD policy revision recognized only two classifications of MR: (a) mild and (b) severe. De-emphasizing the old tradition of using levels of severity for generalizing about each person's needs, AAMD introduced the supports paradigm as a substitute. The 2002 AAMD manual continued its strong commitment to a supports-based classification system to guide assessment and IEP-determination of services rather than the traditional levels of severity that base labels on IQ and adaptive skills. To be on the "cutting edge of new knowledge and practice," adapted physical activity specialists must apply the supports paradigm in everyday work with each individual. The supports paradigm is conceptualized to "fix" the environment and/or society rather than the person with a disability.

Placement and Prevalence

Persons with MR constitute the third largest disability group receiving special education in the United States. Almost 600,000 students in the age range from 6 to 21 years receive services. Most of these students spend some part of every day in general education.

In striking contrast to the past, few persons with MR live in large residential facilities today. Among the 6- to 21-year-old group, only 1.5% are in residential facilities. These are usually children with multiple disabilities, with IQs of less than 35, and from dysfunctional or nonexistent families. Adults with MR who used to live in institutions now mostly reside in the community in small-group homes accommodating six or fewer persons. They still receive mental health/mental retardation (MH/MR) services from a central agency, but living and learning arrangements are as close to those of nondisabled persons as possible.

Prevalence of MR is generally estimated as 3% of the total population, a figure based partly on normal curve theory. This theory posits that 2.28% of the population has low intelligence and that an equal percentage is gifted. To understand how the estimated 2.28% is derived, look at Figure 21.2 and note the percentage of the population that falls into the third, fourth, and fifth standard deviation areas (2.14 + .13 + .01 = 2.28). To arrive at the 3% estimate, authorities add 0.72%, the percentage of the general population with known biomedical conditions that result in MR.

The United States has approximately 7.5 million citizens with MR who live in communities (AAMR, 2002a). About 125,000 infants are born with MR each year. There are about 156 million individuals with MR in the world. Severe MR (when defined as IQ under 50) has an incidence of about 3 to 5 per 1,000 in developed countries.

Etiology of Mental Retardation

Most MR is caused by multiple factors, some biological and some environmental. No clear etiology can be determined for approximately 30 to 40% of individuals with MR, despite extensive laboratory testing. For example, the best known Special Olympian, Loretta Claiborne, has MR of unknown etiology. She and the 30 or 40% of persons with MR of unknown etiology look like ordinary people (see videos of Special Olympics and the SOI magazine *Spirit*). A talented runner, Loretta has excelled in Special Olympoics and in runs primarily for AB persons like the Boston Marathon. When the etiology of MR is known, the predisposing factors are as follows:

Heredity, including normal and abnormal gene mechanisms—5%

Early alterations of embryonic development, including Down syndrome, fetal alcohol syndrome, infections—30%

Pregnancy and perinatal problems—10%

Postnatal infections, traumas, and toxins—5%

Postnatal environmental deprivation conditions and other mental disorders like autism—15–20%

The most common conditions within the combined heredity and early alterations of embryonic development categories are fetal alcohol syndrome, Down syndrome, and fragile X syndrome.

Approaches to the study of etiology are much different than in the past, when specific causes of conditions were sought. Today causes are examined primarily to aid in prevention of MR. Table 21.1 summarizes prenatal, perinatal, and postnatal causes as presented by Luckasson et al. (1992). These causes do not always result in MR; causes are included in Table 21.1 if MR can sometimes be traced to them.

Following is a brief summary of some of the more common categories of causes. Incidences of various syndromes (chromosomal and other) are given in Appendix B.

Chromosomal Abnormalities

Chromosomal abnormalities affect about 7 in every 1,000 births. These disorders usually result from chance errors in cell division shortly after an egg and a sperm unite. With each cell division, 23 pairs of chromosomes should be passed on, each carrying the full DNA and genes to mastermind further development. Of the 23 pairs in each cell, 22 are **autosomes** (important for specific genetic markers), and one is the **sex chromosome pair,** designated as XX (female) or XY (male), which determines gender.

Abnormalities can occur in either autosomes or sex chromosomes. The most common autosomal chromosome disorder is **Down syndrome** (a short-stature MR condition, with distinguishing facial and other features). A common sex-linked chromosome disorder is **Turner syndrome,** caused by a division failure that results in only one X instead of the XX or XY pair in normal cells. Turner is also called XO syndrome. Some chromosomal disorders result in mental retardation (e.g., Down syndrome), but others may not (e.g., Turner syndrome). Turner syndrome, which occurs only in females, results in short stature (less than 5 ft), appearance of a short neck because of low poste-

rior hairline and/or cervical webbing, a broad chest with widely spaced nipples, and failure to menstruate and mature sexually. A comparable condition in males is called **Noonan syndrome.**

Sex chromosome disorders occur more frequently than autosome disorders and cause less severe conditions. Most sex chromosome disorders are primarily characterized by height abnormalities (extra short or tall) and underdeveloped or overdeveloped genitalia. Any syndrome that has X or O in its name is a sex chromosome disorder. There are multiple X female (XXX, XXXX) and multiple X male (XXXY, XXXXY) syndromes; these cause short heights. Two syndromes that occur in males only (XYY and XXY) cause abnormal tallness. XXY is also called **Klinefelter syndrome.**

Fragile X Syndrome

Of particular interest is **fragile X syndrome,** a condition that is inherited rather than occurring by chance. Discovered in 1969, it could not be accurately and consistently diagnosed until the 1980s. *Fragile* refers to a gap or break in the long arm of the X chromosome. This occurs in 1 of 1,000 males and 1 of 2,000 females, but frequently goes undiagnosed. Mental function varies from severe MR to normal, with MR more common in males than in females. Behaviors are often autistic, hyperactive, and impulsive (Dykens, Hodapp, & Leckman, 1994). Physical indicators are large, narrow face, prominent ears, and large testicles.

Other Syndrome Disorders

Faces and other features of children with MR vary widely (see Figure 21.4). Some faces, however, indicate specific syndromes.

Syndromes are named for persons who first discovered them (e.g., Apert) or for distinguishing features (e.g., tuberous sclerosis) or for the causative agent (e.g., fetal alcohol). Most are rare but can easily be remembered by cranial features. **Apert syndrome** is indicated by a flat head appearance, microcephalus, defective formation of facial bones, bulging eyes, and malformed hands and feet (see Figure 21.4E). Although MR is not always present, the malformed hands and feet require physical education adaptations (Weber, 1994).

Cornelia de Lange syndrome is characterized by bushy eyebrows, long and curly eyelashes, lots of body hair, and small stature (see Figure 21.4F). *Amount of MR cannot be estimated by appearance. Occasionally a person with these syndromes has normal intelligence.* **Neurofibromatosis** (von Recklinghausen's disease) can best be remembered by the book, play, and movie about the elephant man (Montagu, 1971). It is the most common of the group of inherited disorders that affect both brain and skin. Indicators are (a) multiple *fibromas* (fibrous tumors that look like nodules) on the skin and in the central nervous system (CNS), (b) scoliosis, and (c) brown spots that look like coffee with cream (cafe au lait) stains. Neurofibromatosis usually does not become a problem until adolescence or adulthood.

In contrast, the less common **tuberous sclerosis** and **Sturge-Weber disease** are primarily neurologic disorders of infancy and childhood. To visualize tuberous sclerosis, remember that *tuber* means swelling and *sclerosis* means a hardening; the condition is characterized by hard little bumps on the nose and

Table 21.1   Disorders in which mental retardation often occurs.

I. **Prenatal causes**
   A. Chromosomal disorders
      1. Autosomes (23 pairs in each cell)
         a. Trisomy 21 (Down syndrome)
         b. Translocation 21 (Down syndrome)
      2. Sex chromosome (1 pair in each cell)
         a. Fragile X syndrome
         b. Short-stature syndromes
            1. Turner (XO)—females only
            2. Noonan—males only
         c. Tall-stature syndromes
            1. Klinefelter (XXY)—males only
            2. XYY—males only
   B. Other syndrome disorders
      Examples are Apert, Cornelia de Lange, Prader-Willi
   C. Inborn errors of metabolism
      1. Amino acid disorder—phenylketonuria (PKU)
      2. Carbohydrate disorder—galactosemia
      3. Nucleic acid disorder—Lesch-Nyhan syndrome
      4. Numerous others
   D. Brain formation disorders
      1. Neural tube closure disorders—spina bifida, anencephaly (absence of brain, sometimes spinal cord)
      2. Hydrocephalus
      3. Microcephalus
   E. Environmental influences, including premature births (i.e., several weeks early)
      1. Fetal alcohol syndrome
      2. Cocaine and/or other drugs
      3. Intrauterine malnutrition
      4. Maternal diseases and accidents; maternal medications that hurt embryo

II. **Perinatal causes (from 28th week of pregnancy through 28 days following birth)**
   A. Intrauterine and/or abnormal labor and delivery
   B. Neonatal
      1. Head trauma at birth
      2. Intracranial hemorrhage
      3. Infections
      4. Nutritional and late-onset metabolic disorders

III. **Postnatal causes (any time before age 18)**
   A. Head injuries
   B. Infections
      1. Encephalitis
      2. Meningitis
      3. Fungal, parasitic, or viral
   C. Degenerative disorders
      1. Rett syndrome
      2. Friedreich's ataxia
      3. Tay-Sachs
   D. Seizure disorders
   E. Toxic-metabolic disorders
      1. Lead, mercury
      2. Late-onset metabolic disorders
   F. Malnutrition
   G. Environmental deprivation
      1. Psychosocial disadvantage
      2. Child abuse and neglect

Figure 21.4 Faces of mental retardation. All of the children shown here have severe MR except child with Apert syndrome. Make up a psychomotor profile for each.

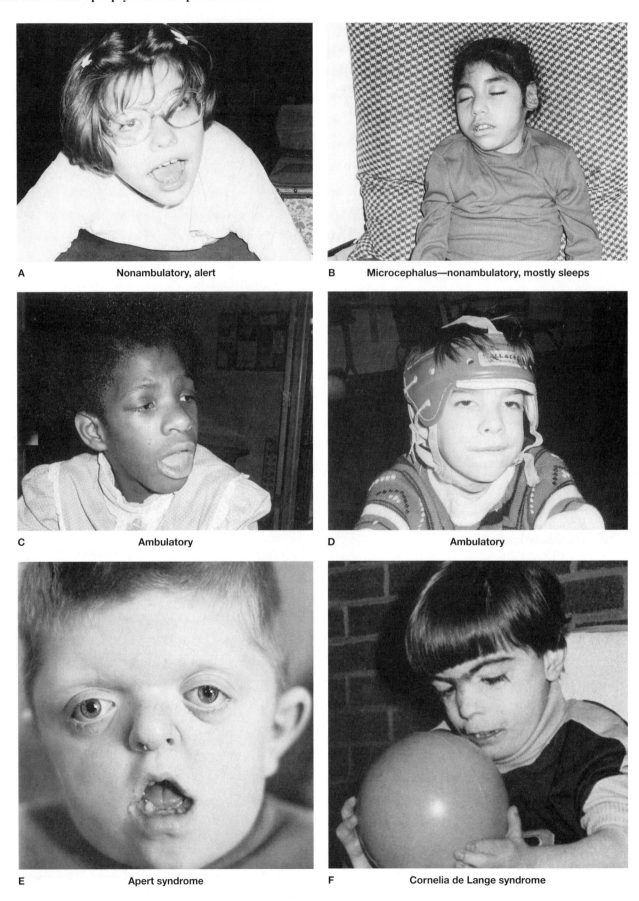

A   Nonambulatory, alert

B   Microcephalus—nonambulatory, mostly sleeps

C   Ambulatory

D   Ambulatory

E   Apert syndrome

F   Cornelia de Lange syndrome

Figure 21.5   Unknown prenatal influences cause *(A)* abnormally small head (microcephalus) and *(B)* accumulation of fluid in the skull (hydrocephalus). Microcephalus is the more severe condition.

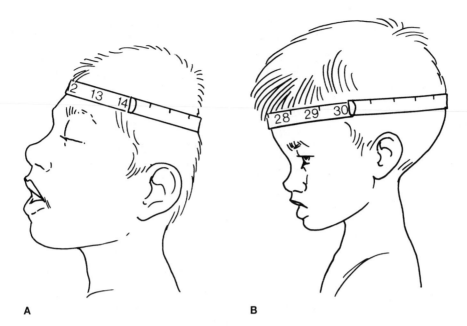

A   B

cheeks that resemble acne. These bumps are also scattered through the brain, heart, and other organs. Sturge-Weber disease is characterized by a large port-wine stain on parts of the face. Both conditions can cause seizures and muscle weakness (hemiparesis), and MR is common.

Prader-Willi syndrome, first identified in 1956, is diagnosed by obesity, short stature, poor development of the genital organs, small hands and feet, and an insatiable appetite. Individuals with this syndrome often have mild MR, postural defects, and motor problems, all of which require special attention from physical educators (Weber, 1993). This syndrome is also linked with diminished metabolic rates that affect activity level and weight management.

Metabolism and Brain Formation Disorders

The metabolism or nutrition category mostly includes inborn errors that cause enzyme deficiencies that interfere with food metabolism. Infants look normal at birth, but within several months evidence changes in appearance and function. Fair-skinned, fair-haired, and blue-eyed infants who begin persistent vomiting can be treated by diet therapy to manage **phenylketonuria** (PKU). If untreated, brain damage is severe. Illustrative other inborn errors of metabolism include galactosemia, Hurler's syndrome, and Tay-Sachs disease. Each is rare.

Unknown prenatal influences cause some infants to look abnormal at birth because of size and shape anomalies of the head (see Figure 21.5). Among these anomalies are **anencephaly** (partial or complete absence of the brain), **microcephalus** (abnormally small brain), **hydrocephalus** (large head caused by a cerebrospinal fluid problem), and **craniostenosis** (narrowed or flat cranium). Generally, microcephalus is associated with severe MR; it is also an indicator of specific conditions like fetal alcohol syndrome.

Hydrocephalus is described in detail in Chapter 23 because it often accompanies spina bifida. Usually, **shunting** procedures return head size to normal, but shunting does not always work. Hydrocephalus does not cause MR immediately. When treatment is ineffective, retardation develops slowly, as increased pressure within the cranium damages the brain.

Fetal Alcohol Syndrome

Fetal alcohol syndrome (FAS) is the most common condition within the infection, toxin, and trauma etiologies. Among pregnant women who drink heavily, the incidence of FAS is about 35%. FAS is also associated with male alcoholism. From 10 to 20% of mild MR in developed countries can be traced directly to parents' drinking. *The Broken Cord* by Dorris (1989), available as a book or videotape, chronicles growth of a child with FAS and provides an excellent bibliography.

Indicators of FAS are (a) significant growth retardation before and after birth, (b) mild to moderate microcephalus (smaller than normal head), (c) altered facial features, (d) other physical and behavioral problems, and (e) diagnosis of MR, usually in the mild range. Altered facial features include almond-shaped, slanted eyes; short **palpebral fissures** (i.e., the opening between the eyelids); low or sunken nasal bridge; short nose; **maxillary hypoplasia** (small, flattened midface); thin, smooth upper lip; and indistinct **philtrum** (the groove between nose and upper lip). Often, there is also **ptosis** (dropping) of the eyelid. Most common physical and behavioral problems are fine motor incoordination, hyperactivity, stubbornness, seizures, ventricular septal defects, and mild cerebral palsy.

Study Figure 21.4. What faces most likely indicate children with FAS? Go through all the photos in this chapter and see if you can recognize syndromes. Select one or more

Conditions Caused by Other Toxins, Infections, and Traumas

Maternal use of crack or cocaine results in smaller than average infants who require immediate treatment for addiction. These "crack babies" exhibit combined MR–cerebral palsy patterns as they grow. Over 10% of infants born in the United States test positive for cocaine or alcohol the first time their blood is drawn (Dorris, 1989).

Use of other drugs like cocaine, marijuana, heroin, methadone, and tobacco also affects the developing embryo and fetus (Leitschuh & Dunn, 2001). Drugs are commonly linked with premature births, small head circumference, low weight, delayed motor development, and failure to thrive.

Sexually transmitted diseases, including HIV/AIDS, are the main maternal infections that cause risk today, whereas *rubella* (measles) was a major factor before immunizations were developed. Childhood infection of the brain (*encephalitis, meningitis*) can result from common diseases like mumps, measles, and scarlet fever.

Traumas include all physical injuries and accidents that injure the brain directly or through oxygen deprivation (*anoxia, hypoxia, asphyxia*). The risk of traumas is heightened when caretakers use drugs and alcohol.

Down Syndrome

Down syndrome (DS) is so different from other MR conditions that it warrants separate, extensive coverage. Many of the differences associated with DS affect physical education programming.

DS is an autosomal chromosomal condition that results in short stature, distinct facial features, and physical and cognitive differences that separate it from other manifestations of MR (see Figure 21.6). Intellectual function varies widely. Function in DS, like that in other kinds of MR, is largely related to infant and early childhood intervention and richness of opportunity to learn in home, school, and community partnership programs. Health and freedom from severe organ defects are also important factors.

Types of Down Syndrome

Chromosomal anomalies, because they occur near the time of conception, affect growth and development of all organs. There are three types of DS: (a) trisomy 21, (b) translocation, and (c) mosaicism.

Trisomy 21 explains about 95% of DS. It is caused by **nondisjunction,** failure of chromosome pair 21 to separate properly *before or during fertilization.* The result is three chromosomes instead of two like all the others and cells that have 47 chromosomes instead of the normal 46 (see Figure 21.6B). The overall incidence is about 1 in 800 live births, but this varies with maternal age. For instance, at age 25, the risk is 1 in 1,000; over age 35, the risk is 1 in 400; over age 45, the risk is 1 in 35. Fathers are also genetically linked to occurrence of DS, but the actual cause of chromosomal nondisjunctions remains uncertain.

Translocation DS occurs when a portion of the 21st chromosome is transferred to and fused with another chromosome (usually number 14, 15, or 22). This condition has a normal chromosome count, but the extra material causes problems. About 4% of DS is of this type.

Mosaicism is very rare, accounting for less than 2% of DS. It results from a chance error in nondisjunction *after fertil-*

Figure 21.6 **(A) The chromosomal abnormality most common is Down syndrome, in which every cell has 47 chromosomes instead of 46. (B) The karyotype was made by photographing a cell nucleus under an electron microscope. Then, the chromosomes were cut out of the photograph, matched up in pairs, and numbered. Although there are several kinds of Down syndrome, the usual problem is in chromosome 21. This affects all aspects of development and function.**

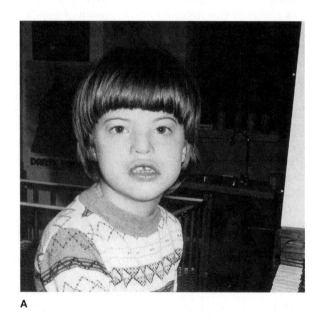

A

B

ization. This causes the infant to have both normal and trisomic cells. The proportion of normal to trisomic cells varies, causing physical appearance and cognitive function to range from almost normal to classic DS (Fishler & Koch, 1991).

Physical Appearance

Persons with DS look like family members but also have many unique clinical features, including these:

- *Short stature, seldom taller than 5 ft as adults.*
- *Short limbs, with short, broad hands and feet.*
- *Almond-shaped slanting eyes, often strabismic (crossed) and myopic (nearsighted).*
- *Flattened facial features, including bridge of nose.*
- *Flattened back of skull, short neck, with excess skin at nape of neck.*
- *Small oral cavity that contributes to mouth breathing and tongue protrusion.*
- *Hypotonic muscle tone in infancy that can be normalized in childhood through regular exercise.*
- *Joint looseness manifested by abnormal range of motion; this is caused by hypotonicity and lax ligaments. This looseness can be an advantage in gymnastics and activities requiring flexibility if muscles are strong enough to provide stability and prevent dislocation.*

Sources indicate over 100 differences in physical features between people with and without DS (Sugden & Keogh, 1990). However, there is wide variation in clinical features from person to person.

Strengths and Weaknesses

Several excellent reviews of the literature summarize research on DS that relates to motor development, learning, and control (Block, 1991; Henderson, 1986; Sugden & Keogh, 1990). *In general, persons with DS tend to function motorically lower than most other persons with MR.* They do benefit, however, from infant and early childhood sensorimotor programming and intensive training in sports. Special Olympics events provide strong empirical evidence that some persons with DS can perform sports like gymnastics and swimming at high levels of proficiency. In contrast, their short heights and limbs deter success in sports like basketball and volleyball.

An area in which persons with DS seem to function higher than others with MR is rhythm (Stratford & Ching, 1983). Music and other forms of rhythmic accompaniment, imaginatively used, seem to facilitate motor learning and practice. Most persons with DS can excel in dance and rhythmic movement. Aerobic dance thus is an excellent strategy for improving fitness because it builds on this strength.

Hypotonia and Skeletal Concerns

Newborn infants with DS, like most severely neurologically involved babies, exhibit an extreme degree of *muscular hypotonia.* This fact has led to the term *floppy babies.* The muscular flabbiness decreases with age, if large-muscle exercise is stressed. The abdomen of the adolescent and the adult generally protrudes like that of a small child. Almost 90% have *umbilical hernias* in early childhood, but the condition often corrects itself. This finding suggests that abdominal exercises be selected and administered with extreme care. Other postural and/or orthopedic problems commonly associated with DS are lordosis, kyphosis, dislocated hips, funnel-shaped or pigeon-breasted chest, and clubfoot.

The lax ligaments and apparent looseness of the joints lead some authors to describe persons with DS as "double-jointed." The structural weakness of ligaments perhaps affects the function of the foot most. Many children with DS have badly pronated and/or flat feet and walk with a shuffling gait. Chapter 11 describes strategies for correcting a shuffling gait.

Motor Development Delays and Differences

Children with DS demonstrate substantial delays in emergence of postural reactions and motor milestones. *Moreover, the developmental sequence is somewhat different, probably because of hypotonic muscle tone.* Research on 229 children with DS in three countries showed that the rank order in which motor milestones are passed differs from that of normal babies (Dyer, Gunn, Rauh, & Berry, 1990). Items passed later than expected involved balance and strength (e.g., standing, walking, throwing a ball). Interventions for improving balance and walking are described in Chapter 18.

The mean age for walking of children with DS is 4.2 years. This, of course, affects exploratory and social play, the major vehicle through which most children learn about themselves and the environment. Ulrich et al. (2001) have shown that intervention enables walking at earlier ages.

In children with DS, the development of manual control (reaching, grasping, and manipulation) is also different than in non-DS peers, possibly because of their short arms and relatively smaller hands and fingers. Other factors that can contribute to hand-eye coordination problems, including difficulty with precision grips, are vision problems, lack of motivation and practice, and neural deficits.

Balance Deficits

Balance is one of the abilities in which persons with DS are most deficient. In this area, they tend to perform 1 to 3 years behind other persons with the same level of retardation. Many persons with DS cannot balance on one foot for more than a few seconds, and most cannot maintain balance at all with eyes closed. In general, basic movements are awkward. Deficits in balance and coordination can be explained not only by physical constraints (e.g., shortness of stature, limbs, and feet; low strength) but also by CNS dysfunction.

Balance deficits act as rate limiters in learning fundamental motor skills and patterns (see Figure 21.7). This, in turn, affects involvement in games, sports, and dance and subsequent motor skill and social learning. As children with DS age, the gap between their motor performance and physical activity involvement and that of non-DS peers widens. Instruction and practice in activities that enhance balance are particularly important. Lifetime sports like cycling, water and snow skiing, skating, and balancing games on floats in the swimming pool

Figure 21.7 This young child with Down syndrome is limited in learning motor skills and patterns. Dr. Katie Staunton at the University of Indiana at Indianapolis is facilitating sensorimotor awareness and integration.

are recommended. Locomotor activities on uneven terrains promote extra attention to balance.

Left-Handedness and Asymmetrical Strength

A higher percentage of individuals with DS than of non-DS peers are left-handed. *This fact should be remembered by persons who demonstrate activities for students to imitate.* Cognitive difficulties limit the ability to transpose and copy activities of right-handed performers. In large-class instruction, left-handers should be grouped together with their own role model.

Asymmetry of strength is also common, with limbs on the left side stronger than limbs on the right (Cioni et al., 1994). This might be an expression of impairment of the left cerebral hemisphere, which is responsible for right-side movement. Asymmetry can cause problems like difficulty in swimming a straight line or awkwardness in assembling body parts to deliver the desired speed or force to a ball. Strength training should be based on assessment that examines problems of symmetry.

Visual and Hearing Concerns

Visual and visual-motor problems are rate limiters to the development of hand-eye and foot-eye coordination; this, in turn, affects success in sports that require ball handling. In general, soccer is easier to learn than catching and striking activities. The most common disorders are **myopia** (nearsightedness or poor distance vision) and **strabismus** (cross eyes or squint). **Nystagmus** (constant movement of the eyeballs) is present more often in persons with DS than in non-DS peers. In adolescents and adults, **cataracts** (cloudiness of lens) occur relatively frequently.

Motor problems are, of course, intensified by the presence of visual disorders, so it is important that children with DS have eye exams as early as possible. Most visual problems can be corrected with glasses, but physical educators should routinely check that glasses are clean and properly aligned. Lens should be shatterproof, and protective goggles and sunglasses should be fitted over regular glasses as needed.

Approximately 50 to 60% of individuals with DS have significant hearing problems. Mild to moderate conductive losses in the high-frequency range are most common (see Chapter 25), causing difficulty in learning to speak, following instructions, and making and keeping friends. Often hearing losses are congenital, caused by abnormally small ear canals and/or other structural anomalies. Acquired hearing losses, which tend to occur in early childhood, are associated with the high prevalence of middle ear and respiratory infections. See Chapter 25 for adaptations that relate to hearing impairments.

Heart and Lung Problems

Approximately 40 to 60% of infants with DS have significant congenital heart disease. The atrioventricular canal defect as the most common lesion (Marino & Pueschel, 1996). The **atrioventricular canal defect** is an opening in the ventricular and atrial walls that normally separate the mitral and tricuspid valves. This opening causes a huge left-to-right shunt at the atrial and/or ventricular level that results in severe respiratory distress until corrected by surgery (see Figure 21.8).

In most cases, infants with atrioventricular canal defect undergo surgery before age 1. Thereafter, capacity for participation in vigorous physical activity is generally normal, except for early onset of fatigue, which compromises the ability to attain a high level of aerobic fitness. Aerobic fitness testing should be approached with care and undertaken only with a physician's approval.

Adults with DS have a 14 to 57% prevalence rate of **mitral valve prolapse** and an 11 to 14% prevalence rate of **aortic regurgitation,** both of which are attributed to the ligamentous laxity (connective tissue disorder) associated with DS (Marino & Pueschel, 1996). These heart conditions are generally asymptomatic and do not contraindicate participation in vigorous sports. However, annual cardiac checkups and careful monitoring of exercise stress testing is recommended because lab tests reveal that there is often an autonomic nervous system imbalance (i.e., reduced heart rates, parasympathetic abnormalities, chronotropic incompetence) irrespective of whether physical signs are evident during exercise. See Chapter 19 for an explanation of these conditions, and consider their implications when planning activity.

Much research is needed on the heart rate responses of persons with DS to different kinds of exercise. This research should clearly indicate whether participants have undergone surgery for congenital heart disease or presently have conditions like mitral valve prolapse that are asymptomatic. Existing research indicates that peak heart rates during treadmill protocols are low compared with those of non-DS peers. Mean peak heart rates during 300-yd sprints, however, are 191, SD = 9 (Varela & Pitetti, 1995).

Figure 21.8 **Atrioventricular canal defect in DS requires early surgery.** *(A)* **Heart valves affected and area where defect occurs.** *(B)* **Surgery to close the opening between the mitral and tricuspid valves.**

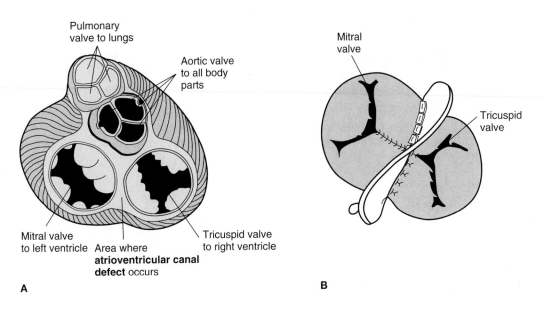

A

B

Breathing during strenuous exercise, swimming lessons, and exposure to high-altitude conditions may be affected by structural abnormalities of the lungs, nasal passages, airways, and chest wall. Lungs of many individuals with DS are **hypoplastic** (underdeveloped) with a smaller than normal number of alveoli (air sacs) (Cooney & Thurlbeck, 1982). An abnormally short nasal passage, narrowed pharynx and bronchial tubes, and/or funnel or pigeon chest postural conditions result in chronic upper airway obstruction and diminished oxygen in all parts of the body (Marino & Pueschel, 1996). These anatomic features, coupled with hypotonia of chest and trunk muscles, make breathing particularly difficult during respiratory infections, which often develop into pneumonia. Asthma also is more stressful than in non-DS persons.

Particular care should be taken in physical education to avoid exposure to weather conditions and other factors that might cause respiratory infections. Death from respiratory infection is 124 times greater in persons with DS than in the general population (Marino & Pueschel, 1996). In addition to skeletal and muscular abnormalities, persons with DS have a higher prevalence of immunodeficiency defects that predispose them to respiratory infections.

Fitness and Obesity Concerns

Obesity is reported in 29.5 to 50.5% of persons with MR (AAMR, 2002a). Fitness of children and youth with DS has been studied extensively in Illinois, where a team of researchers led by Carl Eichstaedt collected data on over 1,000 persons with DS. Comparisons with same- or larger-sized samples of students with mild and moderate MR revealed that subjects with DS performed the poorest on all motor and physical fitness tests except the sit-and-reach test for flexibility (Eichstaedt, Wang, Polacek, & Dohrmann, 1991). Students with DS also weighed more, in spite of shorter heights, and had larger triceps and sub-

scapular skinfolds. Girls with DS also had larger calf skinfolds. These and other normative data appear in the appendix of Eichstaedt and Lavay (1992).

The reason that individuals with DS perform more poorly on aerobic and strength tests than others with mental retardation relates to chromosomal differences that affect all of the body systems. In addition to heart and lung limitations previously described, research now suggests dysfunction of the neuromuscular system, both at the CNS level and at the joints level, that affects strength development (Cioni et al., 1994).

DS is associated with obesity and high blood cholesterol (Chad, Jobling, & Frail, 1990). This physical profile complicates health and impacts on all aspects of motor function. Sedentary lifestyle, poor eating habits, and lack of family nutritional awareness no doubt contribute to weight problems, but *research also indicates that resting metabolism rate of individuals with DS is depressed* (Chad et al., 1990). Implications are that combined exercise-nutrition programs should receive high priority in school and community programming.

Health and Temperament Concerns

The average lifespan of individuals with DS has changed from 9 years old in 1929 to over 50 in the 21st century. Most closely correlated with early death are major mobility and eating problems (severe cerebral palsy). About 75% of nonambulatory persons with DS die of pneumonia. All persons with DS seem highly susceptible to upper respiratory infections. They must be protected against exposure to viruses and temperature extremes.

Self-care and cognitive abilities of adults with DS decline with age to a much greater extent than those of other people. This is linked with early-onset **Alzheimer-type neuropathology,** which is present from about age 40 on (see Chapter 28). Only 15 to 40% of older DS adults show Alzheimer behaviors. However, IQ and general motor skills of children and adolescents with DS plateau in a puzzling manner (Henderson, 1986). Children placed in general education typically need more and more resource help as they grow older.

In general, people with DS are friendly, cheerful, mannerly, and responsible. Although usually cooperative, on occasion they exhibit extreme stubbornness. When they say, "No," professionals experience a real challenge! This occasional stubbornness appears to be a CNS deficit similar to the conceptual rigidity and perseveration associated with brain damage. Persons with DS tend to like routine; professionals need to plan strategy carefully before changing routine. On the other hand, routine can be the key to regular inclusion and practice of needed motor and game skills.

Atlantoaxial Instability

Atlantoaxial instability is an orthopedic problem present in approximately 17% of persons with DS. **Atlantoaxial** refers to the joint between the first two cervical vertebrae, the atlas and axis. Instability indicates that the ligaments and muscles surrounding this joint are lax and that the vertebrae can slip out of alignment easily. Forceful forward or backward bending of the neck, which occurs in gymnastics, swimming, and other sport events, may dislocate the atlas, causing damage to the spinal cord (Figure 21.9).

Since 1983 Special Olympics has required a physician's statement that indicates absence of this condition in persons with DS as a prerequisite for unrestricted participation in Special Olympics. This statement must be based on X rays, the cost of which is typically covered by health insurance or Medicaid. Enforcement of this requirement by school administrators would be prudent also, since contemporary physical education practice favors vigorous activity for children with DS. If this medical clearance is not on file, physical educators should restrict students from participation in gymnastics, diving, butterfly stroke and diving start in swimming, high jump, pentathlon, soccer, and any warm-up exercise placing pressure on the head and neck muscles. This restriction should be temporary, with a time limit set for obtaining the X rays. If students with DS are diagnosed as having atlantoaxial syndrome, they are permanently restricted from these activities; there are, however, many other physical education activities in which they can safely engage.

MR Without DS

Individuals with MR who do not have DS vary so widely that no generalizations can be drawn. Assessment is the only way to determine strengths and weaknesses. There are no characteristics; however, each individual meets the diagnostic criteria of impaired intellectual and adaptive behaviors.

Most individuals with MR pass as "normal" once they have left school. They hold full-time jobs, marry, rear children, and experience the same joys and sadnesses as other people. These individuals tend to have blue-collar (physical labor) jobs that require considerable fitness but make few intellectual demands. By adulthood, persons with mild MR typically function academically somewhere between the third and the sixth grades. *Cognitively, their greatest deficits are in the areas of abstract thinking, concept formation, problem solving, and evaluative activity.*

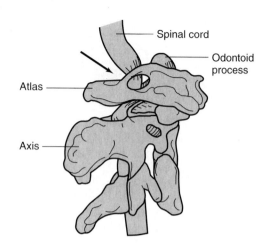

Figure 21.9 Atlantoaxial instability can contribute to a dislocation of the atlas, which can injure the spinal cord. It can be caused by forceful bending of the head either forward or backward.

Approximately 90% of individuals with MR have mild impairments, look like everyone else, and need few adaptations and supports in physical education and sport. If their parents are athletic, they probably will be also. If not, they will have the full range of individual differences in motor function and fitness exhibited by the general population. Some will participate in Special Olympics and INAS-FID events, but most will be involved in community-based recreation and competition. Those who really love sports will probably take advantage of all opportunities in both general and special sport programs.

Like individuals without MR, people with mild intellectual and adaptive behavior skill deficits sometimes need intermittent or limited supports and various kinds of adaptations to succeed in the physical education setting and to develop active, healthy lifestyles. They might be slow in processing instructions and learning new activities. Depending on how parents and teachers handle this slowness, individuals with MR might be teased more than non-MR peers or considered different or odd. This, in turn, can result in motivational problems and insufficient practice to keep up with classmates as skills and strategies become more advanced. Often teachers must address self-concept and social acceptance problems.

MR With Associated Medical Conditions

The more severe a disability is, the more likely it is that there are associated (comorbid) conditions that affect motor behavior. This is particularly true when the primary etiology is chromosomal disorder or brain damage. Physical activity personnel should request access to files that describe medical history, including surgeries, and list medications. Use Chapter 19 to review side effects of medications, or consult the *Physician's Desk Reference (PDR)*.

Seizures (Epilepsy)

One of the most frequent medical problems in people with MR is seizures. About 20% of individuals with mild MR have seizures. In contrast, over 50% of individuals in the lowest ranges of MR (previously designated as profound, IQs under 20) have seizures. Overall, 8.8 to 32% have seizure disorders (AAMR, 2002a).

> See Chapter 19 on seizure disorders, and be sure you know how to handle seizures. A common problem in physical education is that individuals with severe seizure disorders are often so heavily dosed with medication that they are lethargic. Medication affects attention span, balance, and other factors. How will you handle this?

Pain Insensitivity and Indifference

Approximately 25% of individuals with developmental disabilities display signs of pain insensitivity or indifference that place them at serious medical risk (Biersdorff, 1994). Case studies describe individuals who seriously burn their hands as they take dishes, without potholders, from hot ovens; individuals who walk on broken legs and insist they feel no pain; and individuals who have died from appendicitis and bowel obstruction conditions that went undiagnosed because of no indications of pain or discomfort. *Many individuals with self-injurious behaviors display no evidence of pain.* Implications for physical education and sport are obvious. Teachers must carefully check body parts for injuries when accidents occur and not rely on the responses of individuals suspected to have pain insensitivity.

Dual Diagnosis

The term *dual diagnosis* can have many meanings, but in MR literature **dual diagnosis** refers to the co-occurrence of MR with psychiatric disorders. A much larger percentage of people with severe MR have serious emotional disturbances than in the general population (AAMR, 2002a). These individuals might be taking psychotropic drugs (e.g., antipsychotics, tranquilizers) to treat **stereotypic behaviors** (i.e., repetitive, seemingly purposive behavior such as hand flapping and rocking), self-injurious behavior, aggression toward others, property destruction, social withdrawal, and many other problems. Common side effects that affect physical activity involvement are lethargy, hypersensitivity to sunlight, and balance problems.

Behavior problems at all ages have multiple causes. Most are not serious enough to warrant a dual diagnosis, but teachers should be skilled in behavior management techniques (see Chapter 7). Assessment and programming should include examination and modification of environmental factors (both social and physical) that can contribute to behavior problems. The inclusion of students with behavior problems in general physical education requires smaller class sizes and an increased number of adult aides.

Cerebral Palsy (CP)

Many individuals with MR are nonambulatory and/or have speech difficulties because they have CP (see Chapter 25). Those with mild MR can learn to use wheelchairs and experience success in various wheelchair sports. Those with severe conditions, however, might need assistants to push their wheel-

chairs and assist them in getting in and out of wheelchairs. These individuals often need physical education that stresses sensory integration (see Chapter 10). Special Olympics has wheelchair events because of the large number of people with MR who also have CP or other orthopedic impairments.

Pervasive Developmental Disorders

Pervasive developmental disorders like autistic disorder (autism), Rett's disorder, and childhood degenerative disorder are associated with MR but considered separately in diagnostic manuals used by physicians (American Psychiatric Association, 2000). These disorders are described in Chapter 22 because their major clinical features are behavioral and social rather than intellectual slowness. Approximately 75% of individuals with autism function at a retarded level.

Communication and Self-Direction

The more severe the MR, the lower the communication level. *Teachers must present instructions slowly and clearly and be sure that students understand.* Systematic experimentation with sentences of different lengths and structures should determine the best ways to communicate.

Teachers must also take time to let students respond, must provide many opportunities for choice-making, and must facilitate self-direction, another of the adaptive behaviors. **Choice-making** should begin with two choices (would you rather play this or that? would you rather run in this direction or that? do you want a red ball or green? do you want juice or water?) and then progress to multiple choices. In mainstream classes, special emphasis must be given to helping nondisabled peers learn ways to communicate with peers who have disabilities and facilitate their self-direction.

Augmentative or Alternative Communication (AAC)

Some individuals with severe MR who cannot communicate verbally learn to use manual sign or communication board/devices. This requires that teachers and at least some peers learn these communication modes. A recent trend is increased use of augmentative and alternative communication (AAC). AAC devices range from low-tech alternatives like picture boards and notebooks to high-tech devices that use synthetic or digitized speech. AAC devices, especially computers, encourage reciprocal communication, choice-making, and self-direction.

Time Delay Interventions

Time delay interventions is the term used to describe attention to the amount of time an individual needs to answer a question or perform a requested act. The recommended practice is to maintain eye contact with an individual with MR without prompting for up to 10 seconds. This allows individuals who are especially slow in thinking and moving the time needed to react.

Cognitive Ability Related to Motor Learning

Historically, MR has been explained by two theories: (a) the structural difference or deficit theory and (b) the production deficiency or inappropriate strategy theory. The first theory posits structural differences and supports intervention directed toward etiological concerns (Dykens et al., 1994). The second theory drives efforts to find strategies that will help persons with MR learn more efficiently (Bouffard & Wall, 1990; Hoover & Horgan, 1990; Reid, 1986).

Attention

Many persons with MR exhibit problems of overexclusive or overinclusive attention. **Overexclusive,** normal until about age 6, is focusing on one aspect of a task with restricted visual scanning and incidental learning. **Overinclusive,** normal from about age 6 to 12 years, is responsiveness to everything, rather than attending only to relevant cues. Either way, the attentional resources are inefficiently allocated.

Behavior management addresses this problem by shaping the environment so that there are no irrelevant cues (see Figure 21.10). The teacher then uses one particular cue to elicit the desired response (e.g., "Watch me. I roll the ball. Now you roll the ball"). The same cue is used every time, and appropriate behavior is reinforced. This approach is effective in one-to-one teaching but not in ordinary settings, where many environmental stimuli compete for attention. *Eventually, the student taught in this way must be given practice under conditions with progressively more irrelevant stimuli until such time that the instructional setting is normalized.* For example, whenever other students share a room, their presence creates stimuli that must be blocked out.

For most students, therefore, the emphasis is dually on recognizing relevant cues and blocking out irrelevant ones. Teachers begin by highlighting one cue and gradually adding two or three more. Level of cognition determines the number of cues that can be attended to simultaneously. Professionals typically teach *wholes* rather than parts by starting a lesson with a demonstration. As instruction progresses, however, corrective feedback necessarily focuses on parts, and specific cues and strategies are used as attention-getters. **Attention-getters** that help persons focus are

U	Unexpectedness (surprise)
S	Size
I	Intensity (loud, bright, heavy)
N	Novelty (new or original)
G	Glorious color
N	Name (call person by name)
E	Eye contact (a long stare)
T	Touch

Remember these attention-getters by the acronym "USING NET to capture attention." Some applications are (a) having a student wear a colorful elbow band to remember to keep the elbow straight in racket sports; (b) shouting a key word in the middle of a quietly stated sentence; (c) showing a large flash card with the body part or action to be remembered. The "Surprise Symphony" of Haydn reminds us of how effective an unexpected change can be. Consider how the eight attention-getters can be applied to sights and sounds associated with observing and imitating a new motor skill or sequence.

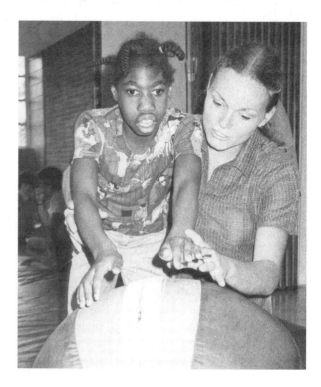

Figure 21.10 The one-to-one task analysis condition works best for persons with severe mental retardation.

Memory or Retention

Persons with MR have long-term memory equal to that of peers (Hoover & Horgan, 1990). However, they have many problems with **short-term memory** (i.e., the encoding of new information into the long-term memory store). Research indicates that we have only 30 to 60 sec to make this happen. Whereas nonretarded persons use spontaneous rehearsal strategies, persons with MR are unlikely to do so. Research shows that they can use rehearsal strategies when carefully taught, but even then, they lag behind peers in spontaneity of application and generalization. Memory strategies from trial to trial tend to vary considerably.

Implications are that teachers should focus on rehearsal strategies and provide many, many trials. *Modeling, verbal rehearsal, self-talk, and imagery are strategies commonly used.* **Modeling** refers to observational learning that requires imitation of a model. The imitation should occur within 30 sec of the observation with no intervening stimuli between visual input and imitation. Teachers should determine whether a student does better with a silent or talking model. With talking models, much attention should be given to how much talk and when.

Verbal instruction should focus on actions or body parts rather than numbers. For example, it is better to say, "Jumping jacks, out-in, out-in, out-in, out-in, walk-walk-walk-walk" than "Jumping jacks, 1-2-3-4, walk, 1-2-3-4." When models do self-talk as they perform, students are likely to imitate this strategy and incorporate it into their unique learning style.

Verbal rehearsal and *self-talk* sometimes refer to the same thing, but a distinction is often made. **Verbal rehearsal** is talking through what we plan to do. **Self-talk** is the strategy of talking while moving. **Imagery,** also called mental practice, involves visualization before beginning an activity.

After several trials of imitating a model, students may profit from questioning that focuses attention on problem areas. For example, the teacher may ask, "What was I thinking when I moved? What was I saying? Where was I looking? Were my feet far apart or close together?" Students working as partners should also learn to ask such questions. Ultimately, students learn to ask these questions of themselves and thus begin to provide self-feedback.

Feedback

Persons with MR do not use feedback as fully as peers. Also, teachers often give lots of praise or motivational feedback but not enough **informational feedback.** *Feedback should include questioning about process as well as product.* Illustrative questions on **process** are "Did the movement *feel* good?" "Did you *tuck your head* when you did the forward roll?" "Did you *watch* the ball?" "Was your *elbow* straight?" Illustrative questions on **product** are "Did you hit the target?" "How far did you throw?" "What was your score?" Questioning is the type of feedback that involves the learner most actively, but feedback can also be passive, with the teacher telling and directing. Regardless of approach, more feedback (providing it is meaningful) leads to more success. This is the rationale for small class sizes, use of peer teachers, and availability of videotaped feedback technology.

Feedback, like input, is dependent on short-term memory. To be effective, it must be received immediately before new stimuli divert the mind from the task just completed. *A general rule is within 5 sec of task completion.* When feedback is delayed, students often need help in linking it with the antecedent. Too often, teachers move around the room saying, "Good!" without taking the time to ascertain that students understand what they are good at and why.

Task Analysis, Repetition, and Generalization

Persons with MR need more trials than peers and instruction in smaller chunks. This is the rationale underlying task analysis. The use of more trials than peers is called **overlearning** or **extended practice.** Little is known about number of successes that should be required before stopping a practice and moving on to something else.

Persons with MR have more difficulty in chaining parts into sequences than peers. Therefore, much attention should be given to practicing progressively longer sequences. Games like *Copy Cat* and *I'm Going to Grandmother's House* (see Chapter 12) can make learning chains of gross motor activities fun (e.g., three walks, two jumps, one bend-and-reach, and sit).

Persons with MR need explicit directions. Whereas nondisabled peers learn incidentally and spontaneously, persons with MR learn best when instruction is direct, specific, and brief. The teacher should frequently ask, "What are we learning? What are we practicing? When are we going to use this?"

Once a movement is learned, periodic practice ensures that it is remembered. This practice should be in variable environments to teach and reinforce generalization. Persons with MR have more difficulty in generalizing than peers.

Crucial to generalization are field trips to parks and recreation centers where leisure skills can be practiced. Instruction must include use of public transportation, how to pay fees, and how to communicate with others who are using the facility.

Motor Performance

Traditionally, professionals have believed that children with mild MR are 2 to 4 years behind non-MR peers on measures of motor performance. This belief is based on the pioneer research of Lawrence (Larry) Rarick (1911–1995), who published extensively in the area of MR and motor behaviors. See Rarick (1980) for a review of this work. Specifically, the belief about the 2- to 4-year delay comes from data gathered in the 1950s (Francis & Rarick, 1959), before the law mandated that students with MR must receive physical education instruction like everyone else.

This belief deserves reevaluation because today the lives of children with MR are very different from in the 1950s. Except for children with chromosomal abnormalities or brain damage, the range of motor performance is probably similar to that of the non-MR population. However, there is probably a slightly larger percentage of children with MR who exhibit **developmental coordination disorder** (DCD) and below-average performance in games and sports. As rules, strategies, and motor skill demands of sports become more complex in late childhood and adolescence, the slow learner becomes increasingly disadvantaged.

The only way to know about the motor performance of an individual is careful assessment. Remember that motor performance is multidimensional. A person might be strong in some areas and weak in others. Most individuals who process knowledge slowly do better with closed skills than with open skills. **Closed skills** are those done in a predictable environment that requires no quick body adjustments. **Open skills** are those done in unpredictable, changing environments that require rapid adjustments. Not only must motor skills be assessed under closed and open conditions, but the total ecology should be examined to determine why motor performance is as it is.

Consider the factors that affect motor performance (e.g., heredity, early instruction and practice, opportunities for continued learning and practice, cognition, motivation, self-concept, health status, medication, body composition, fitness). To learn about these factors, interview as many family members as possible. Observe the individual in as many settings as possible, including community recreation facilities and the home.

Motor Development and Delays

Unless cerebral palsy or other kinds of brain damage cause reflex problems, delays are typically manifested by slowness in the use of the righting, propping, and equilibrium postural reactions and in processing classroom instruction (see Chapter 10). Many activities can enhance postural reactions and mastery of basic motor skills.

Influence of Physical Constraints

Some differences in motor performance between persons with and without MR can be explained by height and body composition. Figure 21.11 shows, for example, that boys with mental retardation perform from 0.50 to about 1.50 standard deviations below the norm (see unadjusted means). When a statistical procedure is used to equate boys with and without MR on height and body composition measures, these differences become much less (see adjusted means). In fact, the boys with MR are no longer significantly different from peers on 5 of the 12 tests (sit-ups, knee extension, knee flexion, 150-yd dash, and 35-yd dash).

The research reporting these findings indicated that boys with and without MR differ significantly on height, width of hips, and skinfold measures. Boys with MR are shorter and have wider hips and more body fat (Dobbins et al., 1981). The implications are that reducing body fat will improve motor performance.

Obesity and Overweight Problems

Persons with MR tend to be overweight or obese, and this condition affects both motor performance and predisposition to physical activity. Obesity varies with gender, severity of MR, and living arrangements (Rimmer, Braddock, & Fujiura, 1993). Females are more likely than males to be overweight. Approximately 59% of women and 28% of men with MR are obese (Rimmer et al., 1993). Individuals with mild/moderate MR have higher rates of obesity than individuals with severe MR. The more restrictive the living arrangement (e.g., large institution, controlled group home), the less likely individuals are to have weight problems. This might be because the few persons who remain in institutions have severe MR complicated by medical conditions like cerebral palsy that affect eating. Another reason might be that state-supported facilities employ dieticians and give high priority to nutrition, whereas individuals living with families or on their own in other housing arrangements often have little knowledge about counting calories and fat grams.

Kelly-Rimmer Equation for Computing Percent Body Fat

Professionals should understand that formulae for computing percent body weight for individuals with MR can differ from those appropriate for the general population (Kelly & Rimmer, 1987). The National Consortium for Physical Education and Recreation for Individuals with Disabilities (NCPERID, 1995), for instance, recommends knowledge of the Kelly-Rimmer equation. This equation is as follows:

% Fat = 13.545 + .48691649 (waist circum.) − .52662145 (forearm circum.) − .15504013 (height cm) + .077079958 (weight kg)

NCPERID also recommends that professionals know how to develop weight programs that emphasize nutrition, exercise, and behavioral intervention (see Chapter 19).

Physical Fitness and Active Lifestyle

Even when persons are actively involved in sport programs, fitness is lower than that of peers without MR (Pitetti, Jackson, Stubbs, Campbell, & Battar, 1989). In general, most attention centers on cardiovascular or aerobic fitness. The lower the IQ and adaptive behaviors, the less able persons are to understand the purpose of a distance run, concepts of speed, and discomfort like breathlessness associated with cardiovascular testing. In general, valid measures can be obtained from persons with mild MR. The *Pacer shuttle run* is especially recommended for cardiovascular testing (NCPERID, 1995; Winnick & Short, 1999).

The Brockport Physical Fitness Test (BPFT, Winnick & Short, 1999) is widely used to measure health-related fitness of persons with MR. The test manual illustrates 27 items, stating modifications for each. From these 27 items, the tester personalizes testing by administering only 4 to 6 items selected specifically to meet an individual's needs and interests. Programming is personalized, based on personal bests on the test items.

Chapters 13 and 19 on fitness and OHI (other health impairments) present several concerns about attempts to apply traditional test protocols to *persons with severe MR*. One is the increased likelihood that the heart will not respond normally to exercise because of autonomic nervous system damage; this condition is called *chronotropic incompetence* or *sick sinus syndrome* and is characterized by a slower-than-expected heartbeat. Another concern is that 20 to 60% of infants born with chromosomal defects have congenital heart disease. Others also may have undetected cardiac defects that require sophisticated technology for identification.

For persons with MR who are overweight, this problem should be addressed before work on endurance activities are begun. Chapter 19 emphasizes that *low-intensity, long-duration activities achieve this goal*. Walking, dance, and water activities are best. The goal in severe MR should be **increased exercise tolerance** instead of cardiorespiratory endurance. Most persons with severe MR do not have the cognition and coordination to use regulation cycling apparatus. Apparatus can be adapted, however, so that they can pedal from a supine stationary position or a 3-wheeled bike. For persons with weight problems, parents should be involved and asked to complete the ACTIVITYGRAM (see Chapter 13) for family members who cannot do this independently.

Consideration also should be given to whether persons with MR will ever need the capacity to sustain a 1- or 1.5-mi run. If family members and significant others regularly run, then this may be an ecologically valid goal. Otherwise, it is probably not. Targeted cardiovascular levels should be matched to game and leisure skills. If persons have few or no physical activity leisure competencies, then developing these competencies should, perhaps, be the primary goal. The desired outcome should be a physically active lifestyle (at least 30 min a day of moderate physical activity) for the entire family. Fun for all should be emphasized, with special praise given to the family member who initiates the activity each day.

Programming Requiring Few Supports

Programming for persons who require few supports is typically directed toward enhancing inclusion. These persons are generally in general physical education or a resource setting de-

Figure 21.11   An example of how deviation from average performance varies when scores of boys with mental retardation (boys ages 6 to 10, with mean IQ of 67) are statistically adjusted for height, hip width, and body fat.

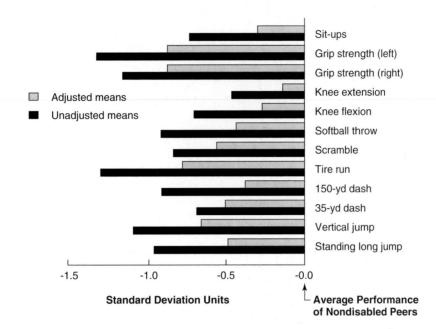

signed to prepare them for the mainstream. Strategies described in the preceding section are used to help them keep up with classmates, develop some physical activity strengths, work on weaknesses, and accept limitations. Several models described in Chapter 9 are helpful in promoting integration and inclusion.

> *The following are additional models that have been developed specifically for persons with mild cognitive delays or slowness. These are presented to stimulate creative thinking and to motivate development of your own models. Select one model and develop an original model that parallels the one described here.*

The Knowledge-Based Model

The knowledge-based model, which focuses on movement problem solving, was developed by Marcel Bouffard, University of Alberta; Ted Wall, McGill University; and colleagues (Bouffard, 1990; Wall, Bouffard, McClements, Findlay, & Taylor, 1985). It is based on observations that movement skill lag in persons with mild MR is related to five major sources: (a) deficiencies in the knowledge base or lack of access to it, (b) failure to use spontaneous strategies, (c) inadequate metacognitive knowledge and understanding, (d) executive control and motor planning weaknesses, and (e) low motivation and inadequate practice.

To improve sport, dance, and aquatics performance, instruction is directed toward three components (see Figure 21.12). **Procedural knowledge** refers to understandings about process; it is information about how to do things. **Declarative knowledge** refers to factual information; it is knowledge about the body, environmental variables, mechanical laws, and getting along with others. **Affective knowledge** refers to feelings about

the self and ecosystem that evolve through use of procedural and declarative knowledge.

Metacognition is knowledge about what we know and do not know. For example, metacognition tells us when to stop studying or practicing. Metacognition also allows us to analyze emotion and determine what we are afraid of or angry about. Persons with MR and/or low motor skills have less metacognition than peers. They do not accurately assess abilities and therefore practice either too little or too much.

Use of the knowledge-based model to guide instruction implies careful teaching of facts and processes, with emphasis on problem solving *so learners are actively involved,* not just listening to someone else. Persons with MR can be successful in problem solving but require more trial-and-error opportunities than peers do. Ecological task analysis is one approach to teaching problem solving; movement education is another. Any question-and-answer teaching style will increase knowledge. Answers can be verbal, gestural, or movement related.

Steps in problem solving that should be explicitly taught and practiced are these:

1. Identify the game or movement function—state what, who, where, why, and how.

2. Assess self and environmental variables. Make changes necessary for safety, comfort, and ease of motion. For instance, if facing the sun, then change position. If too hot, take off jacket. If there is an obstacle in pathway, move it.

3. Engage in motor planning. Use visual imagery, verbal rehearsal, and other strategies.

4. Use feedback from all sensory modalities as well as external sources. Use self-checking routines to regulate

Figure 21.12   Types of knowledge targeted in the knowledge-based model.

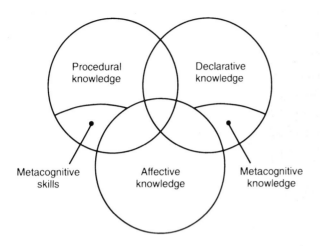

and oversee learning and to determine when practice should be terminated (see Figure 21.13).

5. Evaluate process, product, and feeling and redefine task at set intervals like every 10 trials.

Look for the review of research on the knowledge-based model, with ideas for the future, which will be published by Wall in a 2004 APAQ. Note how models must be studied through pedagogical research that generates evidence of success. Plan and conduct some research of this kind as part of your teaching or volunteer practice.

Special Olympics Sports Skills Program

Developed in the 1980s by staff at Special Olympics International (SOI) headquarters, the Special Olympics Sports Skills Program is based on an illustrated guide for each sport, mandatory training for instructors, and the rule that individuals must complete at least 8 weeks of training in a particular sport before entering competition. Each guide presents a detailed 8-week training program (3 days a week), long-term goal and short-term objectives, a criterion-referenced skills test for pretraining and posttraining assessment, and a task analysis to direct the teaching of each skill. Most guides have been revised in the last 5 years.

Although Special Olympics is usually associated with competition, *the Sports Skills program is purely instructional.* As such, it is appropriate for use in schools, homes, and after-school programs. The task analyses are as helpful in teaching general as adapted physical education. The quality of the instruction depends, of course, on the knowledge, skills, and integrity of the teachers. Although Special Olympics attracts millions of volunteers, there are still too few professionals involved.

A basic tenet of the instructional program is that skill development is not an end in itself but rather a vehicle to an active lifestyle and access to the same sport opportunities as able-bodied peers. This is the rationale for holding local and state competitions. These are designed to enable persons to generalize

skills to real-life situations and to receive intensive positive feedback for effort as well as success. Competitions are also a way of involving family members and neighbors, thereby achieving some hidden agendas relative to awareness and attitude.

Sport skills guides are available for 12 summer sports and 5 winter sports.

Summer	**Winter**
Aquatics	Alpine skiing
Athletics (track and field)	Cross-country skiing
Basketball	Figure skating
Bowling	Floor Hockey
Cycling	Speed skating
Equestrian sports	
Football (soccer)	
Golf	
Gymnastics	
Power lifting	
Roller skating	
Softball	
Table tennis	
Tennis	
Volleyball	

Figure 21.14 presents the long-term goal and short-term objectives for the track-and-field sports training program, an example of criterion-referenced assessment, and an illustrative task analysis. Under assessment, note that the *relays* test item is broken down into seven tasks. The guide provides a separate task analysis for each of these.

The goal and objectives encompass three aspects of sports: skills, social behavior, and functional knowledge of rules. **Social behavior** is operationally defined as good sportsmanship and is taught via task analysis for (a) exhibiting competitive effort and (b) exhibiting fair play at all times. The Special Olympics oath reinforces the concept of competitive effort:

> Let me win
> But if I cannot win
> Let me be brave in the attempt.

Special Olympics Sports Skills Program guides are available from Special Olympics International, 1325 G Street, NW, Suite 500, Washington, DC 20005. They represent only part of a broad-based technical assistance program available through SOI.

Special Olympics Competition and Unified Sports

Special Olympics competition was begun in 1968 by Eunice Kennedy Shriver as a vehicle for awareness, attitude change, and equal opportunity. There have been many changes in policies and practices, but the underlying philosophy has remained the same:

> The mission of Special Olympics is to provide year-round sports training and athletic competition in a variety of Olympic-type sports for people eight years and older with mental retardation, giving them

continuing opportunities to develop physical fitness, demonstrate courage, experience joy, and participate in a sharing of gifts, skills, and friendship with their families, other Special Olympics athletes, and the community. (SOI, 2002, p. 1)

Special Olympics is increasingly community based, with coaches encouraged to use community facilities and to attract volunteers of all ages. Many programs use a reverse mainstreaming approach, with peer tutors interacting with Special Olympics athletes. The official rules book specifically states that athletes may participate in other organized sport programs while participating in Special Olympics. Rules that govern SOI sports are the same as those for regular sports, with only a few adaptations, so generalization from one setting to another is facilitated. All that is needed is a general education teacher or coach who is open and receptive.

To further encourage integration, SOI created the **unified sports model** in 1989. This model, which requires an equal number of persons with and without MR on the floor or field at all times, is explained in Chapter 9. Research by Castagno (2001) further extends knowledge.

SOI has been a major force in creating a body of knowledge about curriculum planning for persons with MR. It

has provided evidence that they can succeed in both team and individual sports (see issues of *Palaestra* that feature Special Olympics). In addition to official sports, SOI sponsors **nationally popular sports.** These are badminton, boccia, sailing, and team handball.

SOI also has a list of prohibited sports that authorities believe are not appropriate for competition (2002, p. 14). These sports are

1. Boxing
2. Fencing
3. Shooting
4. Karate

SOI believes that competitive experiences are not appropriate until age 8. From this age on, all persons with MR are welcome to engage in competition. SOI recommends, however, that sport training begin at age 5. There is a Masters' Division for ages 30 and over, and occasionally, persons in their 60s and 70s participate. *Competition can be serious or recreational.* The important objective is active lifestyle for everyone.

Special Olympics does not use medical or functional classification to equalize abilities of persons competing against each other. Instead, it uses a system called **divisioning,** in which athletes are categorized according to their age, sex, and ability. Divisions must have at least three but no more than eight competitors or teams. The **15% rule** is followed in ability grouping. This rule states that, within any division, the top and bottom scores may not exceed each other by more than 15%. Before individuals are placed in heats or events, they must submit their best times or distances to be used in the divisioning procedure.

In team sports, divisioning is achieved by administering a battery of four or five sport-specific skills to every team member. These scores are added to create a team score that is used in divisioning.

The Stepping Out for Fitness Model

The Stepping Out for Fitness model was developed for adolescents and adults with mild to moderate MR who need programming specifically for fitness. It is described in a book (1990) by three Canadians: Greg Reid and David Montgomery of McGill University and Christine Seidl of Summit School. This book includes 48 lessons, each 40 min long, with graded intensity designed to enable persons to reach targeted heart rates. Sessions are to be conducted two to three times a week.

A unique feature of the model is its use of music in all lessons. Several exercise sequences are presented for popular works like Michael Jackson's "Bad" and George Michael's "Faith." Lessons are built around six themes: (a) calisthenics to music, (b) exercise break package, (c) ball activities, (d) hoop and rope activities, (e) circuit training, and (f) 20-km club. The latter is a challenge *for groups of eight to collectively run 20 km within the time span of six lessons.* During these lessons, two 10-min periods are allocated for running laps.

The instructional model includes five components: (a) assessment, (b) objectives, (c) task analysis, (d) implementation, and (e) postevaluation. Effectiveness of the model is based on a 4-month experimental study conducted by Montgomery,

Figure 21.14   Baton pass in the relay.

Long-Term Goal for Track and Field
The athlete will acquire basic track-and-field skills, appropriate social behavior, and functional knowledge of the rules necessary to participate successfully in athletics competitions.

Short-Term Objectives for Track and Field
1.0 Given demonstration and practice, the athlete will warm up properly before a track-and-field practice or meet.
2.0 Given demonstration and practice, the athlete will successfully perform track skills.
3.0 Given demonstration and practice, the athlete will successfully perform field skills.
4.0 Given verbal and written instruction, the athlete will comply with official athletics competition rules while participating in athletics competition.
5.0 Given an athletics practice or meet, the athlete will exhibit sportsmanship with teammates and opponents at all times.

Illustrative Assessment Checklist for Relay Race

Pre Score	Post Score	Test Item #3 Relays
☐	☐	Attempts to participate in a relay race.
☐	☐	Assumes a receiving position for a visual pass.
☐	☐	Receives the baton in a visual pass.
☐	☐	Performs an underhand baton pass.
☐	☐	Performs baton pass in exchange zone.
☐	☐	Runs designated leg of relay race in proper manner.
☐	☐	Participates in relay race competition.
☐	☐	1–2 Beginner
☐	☐	3–5 Intermediate
☐	☐	6–7 Advanced

_____ Approximate training time (hours)

Illustrative Task Analysis: Receive the Baton in a Visual Pass

Task Analysis

a. Assume proper receive position in front part of exchange zone.
b. Look back over inside shoulder for teammate (incoming runner).
c. Begin running forward when incoming runner reaches a point 4 to 5 m from exchange zone.
d. Keep left hand back with fingers pointing to the left, thumb pointing down and palm down.
e. Watch the incoming runner pass the baton underhanded into your left hand.
f. Turn to look forward, switch the baton immediately to the right hand, and continue relay.

Reid, and Seidl (1988) with 53 subjects. The assessment used is the Canadian Standardized Test of Fitness, although any comparable test is appropriate. The model is dually based on exercise physiology principles and behavior management theory.

Each lesson includes warm-up, conditioning, and cooldown, with activities specifically for flexibility, cardiovascular improvement, and muscular endurance. Behavioral management is applied primarily in the specification of teaching cues (prompts) on lesson plans. The code for understanding cues is

D	Demonstrate
MP	Manipulative prompt
VC	Verbal cue
MG	Minimal guidance
M	Manipulate

The book *Stepping Out for Fitness* is published by CAHPER/ACSEPL, Place R. Tait McKenzie, 1600 James Naismith Dr., Gloucester, Ontario K1B 5N4. It is appropriate for adapted or general settings and can be followed exactly or used as an example for creating a similar program.

Programming for Young Children With MR

Children with or at risk for MR are eligible for public school intervention programs from birth on. Because children learn through play, physical educators should use play to full advantage. Many models are available for teaching motor skills. The PREP program, however, is highlighted here because it focuses on functional competence for play.

PREP Play Model

The PREP play program, used widely in Canada, was developed to guide the physical education of children with mental disabilities, ages 3 to 12 (Watkinson & Wall, 1982). This diagnostic-prescriptive model is applicable, however, to any child who needs individualized instruction in (a) locomotion, (b) large play equipment, (c) small play equipment, and (d) play vehicles. These four areas are divided into 40 specific gross motor play skills (see Figure 21.15).

A task analysis with recommended physical prompts is provided for each skill, as well as group activities for practicing and reinforcing the skills. For example, jumping down is analyzed into four steps:

1. Step down from shin height, one foot to the other foot.
2. Jump down from shin height, with a two-foot takeoff and landing.
3. Jump down from knee height, using the same pattern.
4. Jump down from hip height, using the same pattern.

Figure 21.15 also presents a sample from an instructional episode in which the teacher uses verbal and physical prompts to teach the jump-down skill (see Figure 21.16). Execution is followed by both reinforcement and information feedback. A central feature of PREP is that instruction is carried out while children are at play.

Teachers interact with one child at a time for a 1- to 5-min intervention, so that everyone receives individual attention.

Brief group-teaching episodes provide practice of new skills in a group context. The length of the group session is 3 to 5 min early in the year and progresses to 15 min.

Assessment is structured through use of a free-play inventory (checklist), an individual student profile, and a daily record-monitoring form. The profile permits recording of which step in the task sequence has been completed and the type of prompt (physical, visual, verbal, none) needed.

The PREP manual includes many activities for using locomotor skills in relation to play equipment. In conjunction with each of these, children work on their knowledge base by learning names of body parts and body actions. Prior to playing a jumping game, for example, children sit on a mat and identify body parts to be used. Then they stand and review body actions, like *bend knees* and *swing arms.*

Other Models for Young Children

I CAN: Preprimary emphasizes six skill areas: (a) locomotion, (b) body control, (c) object control, (d) play equipment, (e) play participation, and (f) health-fitness (Wessel, 1980). The *I CAN* acronym, created by Janet Wessel, refers to teacher competencies:

I	Individualize instruction
C	Create social leisure competence
A	Associate all learning
N	Narrow the gap between teaching and practice

Like PREP, I CAN is a diagnostic-prescriptive model that recognizes play as a vehicle for learning. Children are helped to associate preacademic skills (colors, numbers, action words) with games and activities of daily living; this narrows the gap between school and home. A **home activities** program is an integral part of I CAN, and professionals teach parents how to implement specific learning objectives.

Chapter 18 described the **Language-Arts-Movement Programming (LAMP) model,** which is highly recommended for young children with MR because it concurrently teaches language and movement through play activities based in the arts (e.g., dance, music, drama). From infancy on, rhythm and music are strong aids in motor learning.

Programming Requiring Extensive Supports

Approximately 10% of people with MR fall into the severe category, which encompasses the moderate, severe, and profound levels of the old AAMR classification system. Typically, persons with severe MR have multiple disabilities. Their mental function may be frozen somewhere between infancy and 7 years old, or it may improve slowly up to a ceiling of about age 7. Often, when unattended, they do nothing; this lack of self-direction is addressed by extensive supports.

There are persons, defined by the 2002 AAMR system as needing extensive or pervasive supports. Generally, a **personal assistant** (PA) accompanies them most or all of the time. During school hours, this is a teacher aide who needs special inservice training for work expected in physical activity settings.

One job function of adapted physical educators is to create, train, and supervise a helper corps of peer tutors, teacher

Figure 21.15 Examples from the PREP play program.

Skills for Locomotion	Skills for Large Play Equipment	Skills for Small Play Equipment	Skills for Play Vehicles
Running	Ascending an inclined bench on stomach	Throwing	Riding a scooter (sitting)
Ascending stairs	Ascending an inclined bench on hands and knees	Kicking	Riding a scooter down an incline (sitting)
Descending stairs	Walking up an inclined bench	Catching	Tummy riding on a scooter
Jumping down	Jumping on a trampoline	Bouncing	Tummy riding down an incline on a scooter
Jumping over	Seat drop on a trampoline	Hitting with a baseball bat	Pulling a wagon
Hopping on one foot	Swivel hips on a trampoline	Striking with a hockey stick	Riding a wagon
Forward roll	Sliding down a slide	Stopping a puck with a hockey stick	Riding a tricycle
Backward roll	Climbing on a box	Passing a puck with a hockey stick	Riding the back of a tricycle
	Swinging on a rope	Jumping a rope turned by two people	
	Swinging on a bar		
	Swinging on a swing		
	Hanging from knees on a horizontal ladder		
	Rolling around a bar		
	Ascending a ladder		
	Descending a ladder		

Sample Instructional Episode

Teacher behavior	Child behavior	Teacher behavior
1. Teacher says, "Look at me." (PROMPT)	Child looks at teacher. (ATTENTION)	Teacher smiles. (REINFORCEMENT)
2. Teacher says, "Jump down," and holds child's hands. (VERBAL AND PHYSICAL PROMPTS)	Child jumps down onto two feet. (CORRECT EXECUTION)	Teacher says, "Good, let's try again." (REINFORCEMENT)
3. Teacher says, "Jump down like this," and jumps, landing on two feet. (VERBAL AND VISUAL PROMPTS)	Child steps down onto one foot, then other. (INCOMPLETE EXECUTION)	Teacher says, "Land on both feet," and touches both feet. (INFORMATION FEEDBACK)
4. Teacher says, "Try again. Jump," and holds one hand of child. (VERBAL AND PHYSICAL PROMPTS)	Child jumps down onto two feet. (CORRECT EXECUTION)	Teacher says, "Good jump. You landed on two feet." (REINFORCEMENT AND INFORMATION FEEDBACK)

aides, and community volunteers for home, school, and community physical activity settings. Novel approaches to this are use of older students with a higher level of MR who are training for jobs in child care and involvement of senior citizens who enjoy a foster grandparent role.

Excellent resources to help with programming are the journal and newsletter of TASH: The Association of Persons With Severe Handicaps, 29 West Susquehanna Ave., Suite 210, Baltimore, MD 21204. TASH also holds an annual conference. The *Journal of the Association for Persons With Severe Handicaps* includes many articles on leisure skill training.

Persons with severe MR mature slowly motorically as well as cognitively. Most do not learn to walk before age 3. Many learn ambulation between ages 3 and 9. Some need wheelchairs throughout their lives. Physical education in the early years thus focuses on nonambulatory locomotor activities and object control (see Chapters 10, 11, and 12). Hundreds of activities can be invented on land and in the water that use lying, sitting, and four-point positions.

Social skills and communication are major goals because they are prerequisite to game play (see Chapters 9 and 15). Persons with severe MR will typically remain in the solitary or

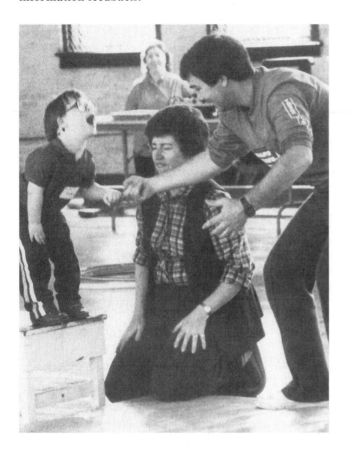 

parallel play stage unless taught to play. With good teaching, they should move into the **associative and cooperative play stages** between ages 9 and 12 and be able to learn simple games (see Chapter 6 on cognition needed for different play stages).

Flying Dutchman, Musical Chairs, and *Catch My Tail* are examples of beginning-level games. In *Flying Dutchman,* a line of students holding hands is walked in any direction. When the verbal cue "Flying Dutchman" is called out by the teacher, the students drop hands and run back to a mat that has been established as home base. *Musical Chairs* can be played without modification, but the students may need help in finding their chairs. In *Catch My Tail,* one corner of a scarf is tucked into the back of the belt of one student, who runs about the room, with the others trying to grab the scarf.

Examples of games not usually successful are *Chicken, Come Home; Cat and Rat;* dodgeball; and relays. In *Chicken, Come Home* and similar activities, the students cannot remember which role they are playing or which direction to run. Only a few seem to understand the concepts of tagging, dodging, and catching. In *Cat and Rat,* there seems to be no idea about who is chasing whom, that one should get away, or that the circle should either help or hinder the players. In dodgeball, they fail to grasp the idea of the game and wander away from the circle. These students can be forced through the motions of a relay but have no idea of its purpose, of winning and losing, or of belonging to a team.

By adolescence, many persons with severe MR are interested in the opposite sex and activities that support romantic interests. Although mental age is delayed, social and recreational interests tend to parallel those they see on television and in the world around them. Many learn individual sports, although they seldom can handle the rules and strategies of unmodified team sports.

Criteria to guide programming include (a) valid and reliable assessment procedures, (b) clearly identified goals and objectives, and (c) activities that are specialized, practical, age-appropriate, developmental, and functional. Underlying these criteria are the principles of valued role status and ecological or social validity. Block (2000) favors the term *life-skills curriculum* to emphasize that age-appropriate, functional activities should be taught in natural environments and based on students' preferences. The following are curriculum models recommended for persons with severe MR. Goals and objectives vary widely, but pedagogy almost always incorporates behavior management with careful analysis, consistent cues and reinforcements, good correction protocols, and variable practice to aid generalization.

Sensorimotor Models

Among the earliest sensorimotor models developed specifically for persons with severe MR is the one by Ruth Webb and

Table 21.2 **Techniques of sensorimotor training for persons with severe mental retardation.**

Goal	Action	Materials Required
To increase body awareness	1. Toweling, brushing, icing, stroking, tapping, contact with textures 2. Applying restraints for short periods, promoting body awareness by cuddling and holding tightly 3. Following flashlight, hanging ball, colored toys, camera flashes 4. Calling name of child; naming objects used, nearby persons, and actions; shaking ball, rattle; presenting music and commands 5. Exposing child to extreme tastes 6. Exposing child to extreme odors 7. Exposing child to extreme temperatures 8. Mirror play 9. Wind movements 10. Vibration	1. Towels, brushes (light), ice bags, textured fabrics 2. Sandbags; splint jackets; strong, gentle arms 3. Flashlight, ball hanging from ceiling, blocks, balls, dolls, camera with flash 4. Wrist and ankle bells; noisemakers; tape recorders; nursery rhymes and records with varying loudness, pitch, and tempo 5. Sweet, sour, bitter, salty substances (honey, lemon, alum, salt) 6. Pungent substances (coffee, cinnamon, vinegar), scented candles, incense, aerosol sprays 7. Two basins with warm and cold water, ice bags, heating pads 8. Full mirror, small mirrors that can be moved horizontally 9. Fans to create wind tunnels, blowing air, fanning 10. Hand vibrators, mattress vibrators
To improve prelocomotion movement skills	1. Rolling 2. Rocking 3. Bouncing 4. Swinging 5. Coactive movements	1. Mats with rough, smooth, hard, soft surfaces 2. Rocking chairs and horses, large beach balls 3. Air mattress, trampoline, jump-up seat 4. Hammocks, suspended seats 5. Physical guidance of body or limbs (Chapter 10)
To improve object manipulation skills	1. Reaching 2. Grasping 3. Holding 4. Releasing 5. Throwing 6. Responding to social cues 7. Developing relationship to one person	1. Toys with various textures, colors, and sounds; water play; sticky clay; sand; finger paint; punching balls 2. Same as 1, yarn balls, Nerf balls 3. Same as 1 and 2 4. Small balls 5. Balls, praise, food treats, affection 6. Same as 5 7. Individual teacher
To develop posture and locomotion skills and patterns	1. Lifting head while prone 2. Sitting 3. Crawling and creeping 4. Standing 5. Riding tricycle 6. Walking 7. Stair climbing	1. Chest support 2. Rubber tube 3. Crawler, scooterboard, creep up padded stairs, inclined mats 4. Standing tables, human support 5. Tricycle with or without seat support and feet straps 6. Parallel bars, human support, pushing weighted cart, coactive movement 7. Practice stairs

associates at Glenwood State Hospital-School in Iowa (Webb & Koller, 1979). Table 21.2 summarizes this model, which focuses on four goals. This model is still excellent. The actions can be easily stated as objectives (e.g., *Show awareness of tactile stimulation by smile and/or approach-type body move-*ments that last 3 or more sec; reach for an attractive object and sustain reaching behavior for at least 5 sec).

The first two goal areas in Table 21.2 are directed toward persons who are nonambulatory, have no language, and seem to be unaware of their environment. They represent the lowest level of function. Only a small percentage of persons with MR fit this description, but under law, they must receive some kind of physical education. The last two goal areas are applicable to many persons with severe MR.

♿ *Given a 30-min class period three times a week and five nonambulatory students, ages 5 to 10, use the activities in Table 21.2 to guide development of some lesson plans. Visualize the students arriving in wheelchairs; some can talk and some cannot. All need as much gross motor activity as possible. Before developing lesson plans, remember to describe present level of psychomotor performance and write goals and objectives. Chapters 10, 11, and 12 will help.*

Data-Based Gymnasium Model

The data-based gymnasium model is the application of special education technology developed by a group called Teaching Research in Monmouth, Oregon, to physical education. The model is fully described in a book by John Dunn, physical education professor, and colleagues (Dunn et al., 1986). Behavior management techniques emphasized are cueing, consequating (reinforcers, punishers, time-out), shaping, fading, and chaining. The teaching approach is **task analysis** with skills broken down into phases and steps.

A unique aspect of this model is the development of a **clipboard of programming management** for each student. Seven pages on every clipboard enable anyone trained in the data-based pedagogy to work with and keep a student on task. For every additional skill sequence targeted, there are 4 additional pages (i.e., motor task sequence sheet, program cover sheet, data sheet, and maintenance file). Thus, some persons' clipboards have 15 or 20 pages.

Another unique feature of the data-based model is its systematic plan for training and using volunteers and parents. The same protocol is used at home as at school, and the data sheet is passed back and forth daily to keep everyone informed of progress.

The data-based model offers task analyses in four areas: (a) movement concepts, (b) motor skills, (c) physical fitness, and (d) leisure skills. It is designed for one-to-one teaching and testing and is appropriate for all age groups. Task analyses focus on ambulatory persons. To use this model, formal training must be completed. Its value, however, is great in stimulating professionals to apply data-based protocol when creating their own models.

Special Olympics Motor Activities Training Program

The Special Olympics Motor Activities Training Program (MATP) *Guide* focuses on four types of activities, so there is something for everyone, regardless of severity of condition (see Table 21.3). Information is provided so that the MATP fits into the IEP model. The long-range goal is:

The participant will demonstrate motor and sensory-motor skills, appropriate behavior, and an understanding of the skills and rules of the MATP that will enable him/her to successfully take part in

Table 21.3   Activities included in the Special Olympics Motor Activities Training program for persons with severe mental retardation.

1.0	**Warm-Up Activities**
1.1	Breathing
1.2	Tactile stimulation
1.3	Relaxation activities
1.4	Range of motion
2.0	**Strength and Conditioning Activities**
2.1	Exercise bands
2.2	Continuous walking
2.3	Toe touches
2.4	Sit-ups
2.5	Aerobic dance
3.0	**Sensory-Motor Awareness Activities**
3.1	Visual stimulation
3.2	Auditory stimulation
3.3	Tactile stimulation
4.0	**Motor Activities**
4.1	Mobility leading to gymnastics
4.2	Dexterity leading to athletics
4.3	Striking leading to softball
4.4	Kicking leading to soccer
4.5	Manual wheelchair leading to athletics
4.6	Motorized wheelchair leading to athletics
4.7	Aquatics

Training Day activities and official Special Olympics sports. (SOI, 1989, p. 6)

Twelve illustrative short-term objectives are stated with the recommendation that volunteers select two to four of the objectives to guide an 8- to 16-week training program. The MATP is designed to supplement (not replace) existing programs and curricula used by parents, teachers, and therapists.

The MATP philosophy encompasses seven points:

1. Training should be fun and teach participants to ultimately self-initiate and choose these activities during their leisure time.

2. Activities should be age-appropriate.

3. Training, not competition, is the emphasis. This training may lead to competition, but 8 to 16 weeks of training should come first.

4. After completion of MATP, every person should have the opportunity to show new skills to significant others in a Training Day program.

5. The **principle of functionality** should guide activity selection. Criteria to be used are (a) high probability of opportunity to use skills in home, school, and community environments and (b) skills will increase self-sufficiency and acceptance. This relates to ecological validity.

6. The **principle of partial participation** shall be followed. This means that persons with severe MR who lack capability for independent function are given whatever assistance and adapted equipment are needed (i.e., their

Table 21.4 **Special Olympics Sports Skills competitive events for persons with severe mental retardation.**

Aquatics
10-m assisted swim
15-m walk
15-m flotation race
15-m unassisted swim
Athletics (Track and Field)
10-m assisted walk
25-m walk
10-m wheelchair event
25-m wheelchair race
30-m motorized wheelchair slalom
25-m motorized wheelchair obstacle race
Ball throw for distance (tennis ball)
Basketball
10-m basketball dribble
Speed dribble
Target pass
Spot shot
Team skills basketball
Bowling
Section B, rules of competition (see use of ramps)
Target bowl
Frame bowl
Gymnastics
Level A wide beam
Level A floor exercise
Level A tumbling
Level A all-around

Soccer (called football in many countries)
Kick and score
Dribble, turn, and shoot
Team skills soccer
Softball
Bat for distance
Base race
Team skills softball
Volleyball
Volleyball pass
Team Handball
Spot shot
Team skills handball
Weight Lifting
Bench press
Modified push-ups
Sit-ups
Exercycle
One-arm curl
Chin-ups

partial participation is supplemented to permit their personal best). This principle obviously relates to using a supports paradigm. See Block (1992) and Krebs and Block (1992) for further explanation.

7. Volunteers should be creative in providing community-based sports and recreational opportunities. They should think integration first, rather than isolation.

The MATP begins with assessment of present level of performance. A task analysis assessment sheet is provided for each of the seven motor activities, with directions to chart the amount of assistance needed for 15 weeks. Codes used are *P,* for physical; *G,* for gestural; *V,* for verbal or visual; and *I,* for independent.

Training techniques emphasize setting objectives that match assessment data, utilizing behavior management techniques like shaping and reinforcing, and charting performance. Several **task analyses** are presented to guide teaching of each motor activity. For example, kicking is broken down into three subtasks:

1. Participant will touch ball with foot.
2. Participant will push ball forward with foot.
3. Participant will kick ball forward.

A separate task analysis is provided for each subtask, as well as general teaching suggestions that emphasize variability of practice conditions and application of skills in lead-up games.

SOI believes that competition, properly conducted and individualized, should be available to everyone who can meet three criteria:

1. Cognitively demonstrate awareness of competing against other athletes
2. Physically demonstrate the ability to perform the movements required by a particular event
3. Adhere to the rules and regulations of the particular sport

This belief is based largely on the **principle of equal opportunity** (i.e., that persons with MR should have available the same opportunities as peers). Competition, when every participant is made to feel like a winner, provides conditions conducive to building good self-concepts. The number of persons who watch, applaud, and praise are important aspects of the self-concept effect. Also important is the emphasis on personal best rather than social comparison.

Table 21.4 lists official Special Olympics events designed specifically for persons with severe MR and multiple disabilities. These are conducted as **individual skill tests** and should be practiced many times in the school setting before being administered in the competitive milieu. Often, Special Olympics meets are the only time that the general public sees persons with severe MR. Philosophy supports the right of these persons to be seen and heard. This is a first step toward societal acceptance and toward inclusion of sport events for persons with severe MR in regular school and community track meets.

OPTIONAL ACTIVITIES

1. Contrast INAS-FID, Special Olympics, and other sports opportunities for persons with MR of all ages. What opportunities are available in the community where you live? How do you go about getting this information? Of the people with MR whom you know, how many have taken advantage of each kind of sport opportunity, including those in an inclusive setting? Why? What are the barriers and enablers?

2. Collaborate with classmates in developing a photo essay or portfolio composed of your own photos. Strive to photograph persons of all ages who are examples of the various syndromes and types of MR in this chapter. Emphasize these persons doing physical activity (i.e., in socially valorized roles). Remember to have photo permissions signed.

3. Give a presentation or develop a bulletin board or other product on the AAMD 2002 supports paradigm. Try using this with parents and get their reactions.

4. Broaden your experience by obtaining more experience in physical activity with persons with MR of many ages and levels of severity. Keep track of the number of hours of direct service and record it in your portfolio.

5. Plan some video nights with friends and see some of the best-known films/videos that focus on MR. These are available at most rental facilities. Examples are *A Child Is Waiting,* 1963; *Being There,* 1979; *The Other Sister,* 1998; *Forrest Gump,* 1994; *Sling Blade,* 1996; *What's Eating Gilbert Grape?,* 1993; *The Loretta Claiborne Story,* 2000; *I Am Sam,* 2001; *Pumpkin,* 2002.

6. Obtain national, state, and local videos of Special Olympics from organization offices, parents, and coaches. Show these to diverse groups and compare reactions and comments. Also find and share newspaper and magazine articles on Special Olympics.

CHAPTER

22

Serious Emotional Disturbance and Autism

Ron French, Lisa Silliman-French, and Claudine Sherrill

Figure 22.1 The child with serious emotional disturbance must be taught how to channel aggression. Behavior disorders are a common problem in public schools.

1. What are my assumptions about why students with behavior problems behave in the way they do? Why do I believe as I do?

2. What are the causes of inappropriate behavior that I can control to a significant degree? How? Why?

3. Compare definitions of emotional disturbance used by the federal government, the Council for Exceptional Children (CEC), and the American Psychiatric Association (APA). Why are definitions different?

4. Explain FBA, BIP, and manifested determination in relation to physical education.

5. Reflect on ways to assess specific behaviors in the physical education setting and write some goals and objectives to guide intervention in reducing undesirable behaviors.

6. Critically think about specific instructional strategies that will help students achieve physical education goals and objectives. Develop descriptions of children with behavioral problems you have known and relate your strategies to them.

The need to manage student behavior is clearly identified in the 2001 No Child Left Behind Act. Students and school personnel need secure and safe environments free from the dangers and distractions of violence, drug use, and ineffective discipline in order to achieve to their full capacity. Teachers and others who serve individuals with disabilities should learn as much as possible about various helping techniques to enable this to occur. In particular, they need to learn how to work with families, because children's behavior is generally rooted in social problems. Consider the following statistics that place many individuals *at risk* for serious emotional disturbance:

• *Approximately 3 million acts of violence and theft take place in public schools (about 16,000 per day), over 100,000 weapons are brought to school each day, and over 40 students are wounded or killed by weapons.*

• *One out of five high school students regularly carry firearms, clubs, knives, or other weapons.*

• *Almost half of the nation's Caucasian children and over four fifths of all African American and Hispanic children live in poverty.*

• *Over 5 million latchkey children live in the United States today.*

• *Half of all high school students are regular drinkers and a third of them drink heavily at least once a week.*

• *Every 59 seconds an infant is born to a teenage mother.*

• *Every 2 minutes a baby is born to a mother who had late or no prenatal care.*

• *Every 2 hours a child is murdered.*

• *From 20 to 60% of children live in one-parent households.*

• *From 35 to 50% of adults report illicit drug use at some time in their lives; an estimated 4.5 million women of childbearing age are current users of illicit drugs.*

• *Over 3 million children each year witness domestic violence, ranging from hitting and punching to fatal assaults.*

• *Violence also is prevalent in television, movies, and newspapers. Most families permit toys that allow children to model behaviors seen on television. Almost all children today need to be taught appropriate ways to express emotions (see Figure 22.1).*

• *Two thirds of students with emotional or behavioral disorders cannot pass competency exams for their grade level and have the highest absenteeism rate of any group of students.*

Statistics vary, of course, by socioeconomic level, ethnic group, cultural background, family structure, and neighborhood. Family pressures are intensified by the birth and rearing of a child with a disability, as they are by disability or illness of any family member at any time. The aging and gradual debilitation of grandparents, many of whom live to be 90 or older, can also add stress. Mental illness also is sometimes present in families, adding to the uniqueness of the complex set of everyday variables that affect behaviors.

A key concept of this chapter is that behavior is caused by a multitude of factors—some environmental, some genetic, and some biological. Team approaches (multidisciplinary, interdisciplinary, crossdisciplinary), with family involvement, should be used to analyze the causes of inappropriate behaviors and to determine interventions. Physical activity personnel are an important part of the team, because individuals often behave differently in activity settings than in academic or workplace sites. This different behavior can be more positive or more negative.

Prevalence of Serious Emotional Disorders

Prevalence statistics for serious emotional disorders vary widely because of differing definitions and diagnostic criteria. The diagnosis of mental disorders is difficult, and most psychiatrists prefer not to attach a label. The prevalence of behavior disorders in the school population ranges from 2 to 22%, depending on the criterion of behavior disorders used. The ratio of boys to girls with mental disorders is approximately 4 to 1. The U.S. Department of Education estimates very conservatively that approximately 7 to 8% of the school-age population is so seriously emotionally disturbed that special education provisions are required.

Suicide increasingly is a problem of childhood and adolescence, ranking as the third leading cause of death in the 15-to-24 age bracket. Statistics for all age groups combined reveal over 25,000 suicides each year. Approximately 2 million Americans have made one or more attempts at suicide.

Delinquency, a legal term reserved for youngsters whose behavior results in arrest and court action, is another manifestation of emotional problems. The crime rate among young persons has increased steadily during the past decade. Long before their initial arrest, many delinquents are described by teachers as defiant, impertinent, uncooperative, irritable, bullying, attention seeking, negative, and restless. Other delinquents are seen as shy, lacking in self-confidence, hypersensitive, fearful, and excessively anxious. A greater than average incidence of delinquency occurs among students who rank lowest in school performance and social standing. This includes many individuals with mental retardation and/or attention deficit disorders.

Many individuals with developmental disabilities have mental illness or severe behavioral disorders. Some estimates suggest that up to 60% of individuals with developmental disabilities also manifest mental illness or a severe behavioral disorder (Shoham-Vardi et al., 1996). **Dual diagnosis,** the co-occurrence of mental retardation and psychiatric disorders, is made with increasing frequency so as to obtain needed resources and support services (Baker, Blacher, Crnic, & Edelbrock, 2002).

Individuals with disabilities are also at greater risk than the nondisabled population for experiencing violence and abuse (Sobsey, 1994). In particular, people with developmental disabilities are at an increased risk for **sexual assault** and **sexual abuse.** Most do not receive adequate training to enable them to say no to sex, drugs, and partner or gang involvement in crime. The trend toward community placement and inclusive settings has intensified these problems, because individuals with mental retardation now daily come into contact with more people, some of whom tease, hurt, and exploit them. Professionals must be increasingly aware of risks and problems and know how to handle them.

Definitions of Serious Emotional Disturbance

Definitions of serious emotional disturbance come from several sources. The three most frequently used are those of federal law, the Council for Exceptional Children (CEC), and the American Psychiatric Association (APA).

Federal Law Terminology

The federal term used in determining eligibility for special education services is **seriously emotionally disturbed** (SED, often shortened to ED). This term means

> a condition exhibiting one or more of the following characteristics over a long period of time and to a marked degree, which adversely affects educational performance:
>
> (A) An inability to learn which cannot be explained by intellectual, sensory, or health factors;
>
> (B) An inability to build or maintain satisfactory interpersonal relationships with peers and teachers;
>
> (C) Inappropriate types of behavior or feelings under normal circumstances;
>
> (D) A general pervasive mood of unhappiness or depression; or
>
> (E) A tendency to develop physical symptoms or fears associated with personal or school problems. (IDEA, 1997, [34 C.F.R. § 300.7(c)(4)])

Originally, this definition included **autism.** In 1981, however, students with autism were included instead in the official definition of *other health impaired.* Finally, in 1990, autism was recognized as an independent diagnostic category. Autism is discussed at the end of this chapter.

CEC Terminology

Many special educators use the term *behavior disorders* rather than *emotional or mental illness.* In 1962, the Council for Exceptional Children (CEC) formed the Council for Children with Behavioral Disorders (CCBD). This organization publishes a quarterly journal called *Behavioral Disorders* and influences special education practices.

APA Terminology

The American Psychiatric Association (APA) is the professional organization that assumes responsibility for publishing the reference book on mental disorders that is used by all of the disciplines that follow the medical model, by courts of law, and by insurance companies. This book, entitled *The Diagnostic and Statistical Manual of Mental Disorders (DSM),* is the definitive source of knowledge about mental disorders, terminology, diagnostic features, prevalence, and course. The content of *DSM* is consistent with *International Classification of Diseases (ICD)* published by the World Health Organization (2001). ICD-10 is scheduled for implementation in the United States in 2004.

Behavior disorders and social maladjustment are not defined in IDEA and do not appear in the *DSM-IV-TR.* Terms such as Oppositional Defiant Disorders (ODD) and Conduct Disorders (CD) do appear in the *DSM-IV-TR* but are not an eligibility category for IDEA services. When determining IDEA eligibility for a student who is being disciplined, school officials should proceed with caution and ask the following questions:

1. Does the student exhibit any of the behaviors listed in IDEA's definition of ED?
2. If yes, has the behavior been exhibited over a long period of time and to a marked degree?
3. If yes, has the behavior adversely affected the child's educational performance and in what ways?
4. If yes, is specialized instruction needed?

Classic *DSM* Mental Disorders

The most common of the 16 *DSM-IV-TR* (2000) diagnostic categories are described in this section. Children and youth, as well as adults, may be diagnosed as having these disorders. The behaviors are essentially the same, regardless of age. *DSM* mental disorders can be diagnosed only by physicians with specialization in psychiatry.

Substance-Related Disorders

When substance use results in behavioral changes that negatively affect work and leisure productivity, social functioning, or the happiness and welfare of family or friends, substance use is labeled a mental disorder. **Substance-related disorders** can be manifested as either *abuse* or *dependence.* Substances can be either *legal* (coffee, tobacco) or *illegal* (marijuana, cocaine, amphetamines). Likewise, they may be medically prescribed to control a chronic health problem or available on the open market. Toxic substances may also include lead or aluminum, rat poison, antifreeze, fuel, and paint. The nature of the substance is not relevant; the diagnostic criteria include inability to reduce or stop use and episodes of overuse.

Schizophrenia and Other Psychotic Disorders

Schizophrenia is the most mysterious and misused psychological word in existence. Half of all mental patients are schizophrenic. Moreover, 1 of every 100 persons in the world has schizophrenia at some time or another. It is a psychotic disturbance that lasts for at least 6 months and includes at least 1 month of two or more of the following: **delusions** (interpreting ideas and events in unrealistic, inappropriate ways), **hallucinations** (perceiving things that do not exist), disorganized speech, grossly disorganized or catatonic behavior, and negative symptoms. **Catatonic** refers to motor extremes, either purposeless hyperactivity or stuporlike hypoactivity. **Negative symptoms** include **affective flattening** (immobile and unresponsive face, poor eye contact, and reduced body language), **alogia** (poverty of speech, as in brief, empty replies), and **avolition** (inability to initiate and persist in goal-directed activities).

Although the word *schizophrenia* is derived from *schizein* (to split) and *phren* (mind), schizophrenic disorders are no longer described as split personality.

DSM-IV-TR states that the onset of schizophrenia is usually in adolescence or adulthood. Nevertheless, estimates of the number of cases of childhood schizophrenia in the United States range from 100,000 to 500,000. There are approximately 4,000 children with psychotic disorders in state hospitals, close to 2,500 in residential treatment and day-care centers, and at least 3,000 children with schizophrenia in day-care clinics.

Psychotic disorders is a broad term that refers to manifestation of delusions, hallucinations, or other serious symptoms that grossly interfere with the capacity to meet the ordinary demands of life but that do not meet the diagnostic criteria for schizophrenia or other mental disorders. The term **psychotic** is used in many ways, but its most common use is to denote *the onset of the active phase of serious mental illness* (e.g., an acute psychotic episode), which typically requires hospitalization. During this active phase, individuals can be dangerous to themselves or others.

Schizophrenia and psychotic disorders are usually managed by daily medication. Failure to take this medication results in **acute psychotic episodes** or active-phase illness. Individuals with schizophrenia typically have motor abnormalities related to the side effects from treatment with antipsychotic medications (APA, 2000). The most common motor abnormality is **tardive dyskinesia,** the presence of involuntary movements of the tongue, jaw, trunk, or extremities (e.g., tongue thrusting, clicking, grunting). These involuntary movements may occur in any of the following patterns: **choreiform** (rapid, jerky, nonrepetitive), **athetoid** (slow, continual), or **rhythmic** (various stereotypies). Tardive dyskinesia is usually mild and is considered a small price to pay for management of serious illness.

Mood Disorders

Mood disorders can be **bipolar** (mood shifts from mania to depression and vice versa) or **unipolar** (usually episodes of extreme depression). **Manic episodes** are defined as the presence (for at least 1 week) of such behaviors as hyperactivity and restlessness; decreased need for sleep; unusual talkativeness; distractibility manifested as abrupt, rapid changes in activity or topics of speech; inflated self-esteem; and excessive involvement in such high-risk activity as reckless driving, buying sprees, sexual indiscretions, and quick business investments. **Depressive episodes** include loss of interest or pleasure in all or almost all usual activities; too much sleep or insomnia; poor appetite and significant weight loss; low self-esteem; chronic fatigue; diminished ability to think, concentrate, and make decisions; and recurrent thoughts of death and suicide.

Until the late 1990s, bipolar mood disorders were considered to be primarily an adult condition. *Now there is evidence that bipolar disorder often occurs in childhood along with attention deficit hyperactivity disorder (ADHD).* Papolos and Papolos (2002) emphasize that bipolar disorder should be ruled out before ADHD medications are prescribed. When the conditions coexist, only bipolar medications should be given. Children with depression, including bipolar depression, tend to withdraw and must be coaxed into activity (see Figure 22.2).

Individuals with bipolar conditions can have rapid cycling (four or more mood episodes during the previous 12 months) or slower transitions with relatively long periods of normalcy between episodes. Individuals with mania usually do

Figure 22.2 **Depression is associated with withdrawal. Here, a teacher guides a rhythmic activity and encourages involvement.**

not want to take medication and typically deny problems because they like the feeling of being high. There are all degrees of mania, with symptoms peaking and then smoothing out. Some individuals, such as musicians, writers, and artists, channel their mania into intense periods of productivity (Jamison, 1993, 1995). Others get their families deeply in debt or alienate close associates with behaviors that are chaotic, embarrassing, or hurtful. The depressive episodes that follow are intensified by acknowledgment of all the problems caused by mania. However, during depression there is no physical or mental energy to cope with anything; this is a time of total fatigue.

Bipolar and major depressive disorders are relatively common. About 1 person in 100 has severe manic-depressive illness, and an equal number have milder variants. *DSM-IV-TR* (2000) states that average age of onset is 18, and both sexes are affected equally. For recent statistics and information about differences between childhood and adult bipolar conditions, refer to the Papolos and Papolos (2002) book or website (www. bipolarchild.com).

In contrast, major depressive illness is twice as likely to affect women. The average age of onset of serious unipolar depression is 27. About 1 person in 20 experiences a major depressive illness at least once during his or her lifetime. Medications are highly effective in treating both conditions. Lithium is the drug of choice in manic-depressive illness, and a wide variety of antidepressants are used for depression. Psychotherapy is typically needed along with medication to help individuals understand the importance of staying on medication.

Anxiety Disorders

Anxiety disorders is the broad diagnostic category that includes panic attacks, panic disorders, phobias, obsessive-compulsive disorders, and other conditions of excessive worry and unease. Each of these is relatively common, with a prevalence of 1 in 100 or greater. Treatment consists of medication in conjunction with outpatient counseling and psychotherapy.

Panic attacks, which occur in several anxiety disorders, are periods of intense fear or discomfort accompanied by a sense of imminent danger or impending doom and an urge to escape. Symptoms vary but can include a pounding heart, sweating, trembling or shaking, shortness of breath, a feeling of choking, chest pain or discomfort, nausea or abdominal distress, chills or hot flashes, and the like. **Panic disorder** is the recurrence of unexpected panic attacks.

Phobias are intense, persistent, and unreasonable fears in relation to specific objects or situations that cause avoidance behaviors. **Agoraphobia** is extreme anxiety about being in places or situations from which escape might be difficult or embarrassing; individuals with severe agoraphobia typically refuse to leave home. Phobias should not be confused with **situational fears,** which many individuals feel when confronted with new and unfamiliar situations or demands like learning to swim or using gymnastic apparatus.

Obsessive-compulsive disorders are conditions in which anxiety is expressed through **obsessions** (recurrent and persistent thoughts, images, or impulses that cause worry or distress) and **compulsions** (repetitive behaviors or mental acts that a person feels driven to perform in response to an obsession).

Usually the compulsions are performed to prevent some dreaded event or situation that in reality is not likely to occur.

Dementia

Dementia is a broad diagnostic term for multiple cognitive deficits, including impairment in memory, that are a significant change from a previous level of functioning and can be attributed to a medical condition, aging, and/or a substance. The most common dementias are those caused by old age, **Alzheimer's disease** (degeneration of the brain associated primarily with old age), head trauma, Parkinson's disease, human immunodeficiency virus (HIV) disease, and long-term substance abuse. Dementia in old age can be diagnosed with or without Alzheimer's disease.

Eating Disorders

The eating disorders category includes gross disturbances in eating behaviors. Most common are anorexia nervosa and bulimia. Although these can occur at any age, their first manifestation is usually in adolescence.

Anorexia nervosa is a condition characterized by significant weight loss, refusal to maintain normal body weight, disturbance of body image, and intense fear of becoming obese. In females, it is accompanied by **amenorrhea** (cessation of menstrual periods). The disorder occurs primarily (95%) in females. The prevalence rate for females in the 12- to 18-year-old age range is about 1 of every 250. This condition leads to death by starvation in about 15 to 21% of the treated cases. Hospitalization is generally required to prevent starvation. The major diagnostic criterion is permanent weight loss of at least 25% of original body weight.

Bulimia is characterized by recurrent episodes of binge eating (the consumption of huge quantities in 2 hr or less), awareness that the eating pattern is abnormal, fear of being unable to stop eating voluntarily, and depressed mood following eating binges. The disorder is more common in females than males and typically begins in adolescence or early adulthood. Persons with bulimia are usually within a normal weight range, but they exhibit frequent weight fluctuations because of alternating binges and fasts. They try to control weight by dieting, self-induced vomiting, or the use of laxatives and medicines. Bulimia is seldom totally incapacitating, although it may affect social, leisure, and vocational functioning. Unlike anorexia nervosa, it does not result in death when untreated. It is, in fact, very much like alcohol and substance abuse.

Impact of Adult Mental Disorders on Children

The disorders described thus far are primarily adult disorders but occur occasionally in children and adolescents. The presence of any of these conditions in family members, especially parents, has a profound effect on children and adolescents. These conditions can alter child-rearing patterns and practices, change the emotional climate of the home, and cause much anxiety to children, who lack full understanding of why events or behaviors are happening. Moreover, considerable prejudice against mental illness still exists in our society, and families often attempt to keep such conditions secret. Children are therefore cautioned not to talk about the illness outside the home and thus can be denied needed emotional support. Children also are often fearful of inheriting these conditions. This anxiety is not totally unfounded, because a genetic predisposition exists for many types of mental illness.

♿ *Make a list of persons with mental illness whom you have known personally through direct experience or through reading or media sources. How are their life experiences alike or different from persons in this text? Advocate for social acceptance of mental illness and for open sharing so persons can support one another. Sherrill emphasizes this because her mother has bipolar mood disorder.*

DSM Disorders in Children and Adolescents

DSM-IV-TR lists 10 conditions that are usually first diagnosed in infancy, childhood, or adolescence (see Table 22.1). Several of these conditions are discussed elsewhere in this book: (a) mental retardation in Chapters 18 and 21, and (b) learning disorders, developmental coordination disorder, and attention deficit hyperactivity disorder (ADHD) in Chapter 20. *DSM* conditions in children and adolescents not caused by ADHD are now described.

Conduct Disorder

Conduct disorder is a pattern of persistent and repetitive behaviors that violate the basic rights of others and/or major age-appropriate societal norms or rules. According to the APA (2000), these behaviors fall into four main groups: (a) aggressive conduct that causes or threatens physical harm to other people or animals; (b) destruction of property; (c) deceitfulness, lying, or theft; and (d) serious violations of major rules (e.g., truancy from school, running away from home, ignoring curfews).

Conduct disorder is one of the most frequently diagnosed conditions in late childhood and adolescence. The prevalence rates for males range from 6 to 16%; those for females range from 2 to 9%. Individuals with conduct disorder are considered at risk for several adult disorders, including substance-related abuse, mood disorders, and anxiety disorders. Moreover, conduct disorder occurs most frequently in children who have parents with mental illness. Without effective interventions, many individuals with conduct disorder become juvenile delinquents.

Oppositional Defiant Disorder

Oppositional defiant disorder is a recurrent pattern of hostile and disobedient behavior toward authority figures that is manifested by at least four of the following behaviors: losing one's temper, arguing with adults, actively defying the requests or rules of adults, deliberately annoying others, blaming others for one's own misbehavior or mistakes, being touchy or easily annoyed by others, being angry and resentful, and being spiteful and vindictive. *In general, the disruptive behaviors associated with oppositional disorder are less serious than those exhibited in conduct disorder.* Before puberty, oppositional defiant disorder occurs

---

Table 22.1 **Disorders usually first diagnosed in infancy, childhood, or adolescence.**

1. Mental retardation
2. Learning disorders
3. Developmental coordination disorder (DCD)
4. Communication disorders
5. Pervasive developmental disorders
   a. Autistic disorder
   b. Rett's disorder
   c. Asperger's disorder
   d. Others
6. Attention deficit and disruptive behavior disorders
   a. Attention deficit hyperactivity disorder
   b. Conduct disorder
   c. Oppositional defiant disorder
7. Feeding and eating disorders
   a. Pica—eating unusual substances
   b. Rumination—regurgitating
8. Tic disorders
   a. Tourette's disorder
   b. Others
9. Elimination disorders
   a. Encopresis, pertaining to feces
   b. Enuresis, pertaining to urine
10. Other disorders
    a. Separation anxiety disorder
    b. Stereotypic movement disorders
    c. Others

Note. Many psychiatrists now add bipolar conditions to this list.

---

more frequently in males than in females; thereafter it affects the sexes equally. The overall prevalence rate ranges from 2 to 16%.

Tic Disorders and Tourette's Disorder

DSM-IV-TR defines a **tic** as a "sudden, rapid, recurrent, nonrhythmic, stereotyped motor movement or vocalization" (APA, 2000, p. 108) and identifies tic disorders as one of the 10 mental disorders usually first diagnosed in childhood. Tics are involuntary, occur frequently during daytime hours, and are diminished or absent during sleep. Illustrative tics are eye blinking, neck jerking, arm flinging, facial grimacing, throat clearing, grunting, barking, jumping, squatting, touching, sniffing, repeating words or phrases, and using obscenities. The latter, called **coprolalia,** is present in only about 10% of individuals with tic disorders.

Tourette's disorder, the best known of the tic disorders, occurs in 5 to 30 children per 10,000 and affects three to four times as many males as females. Age of onset is between 2 and 18 years, but over 60% of affected children exhibit their first tics between ages 5 to 8. Vulnerability to this nervous system disorder is transmitted genetically and expressed in many ways. Some individuals show no symptoms, others have forms of obsessive-compulsive or attention deficit hyperactivity disorder (ADHD), and still others manifest tic patterns that vary in severity. Associated mental disorders, especially obsessions, compulsions, and ADHD, are relatively common. Medications (e.g., Ritalin, haloperidol, Prozac) are often prescribed, and teachers should be aware of side effects.

Individuals with Tourette's disorder are often drawn to athletics, partly because they have good speed, accuracy, and reaction time (Sacks, 1995). By definition, tics are very fast, and children learn early to accommodate their visual-motor coordination and body movements to the tics so that they interfere minimally with other activity. Often during rhythmic activities like swimming, running, and singing such children are free of tics. Adults with severe tic disorders drive cars, fly planes, and succeed in many professions, including surgery (Sacks, 1995). Occasionally, there are tic-free periods, but never for more than 3 consecutive months. Type of tic, severity, and frequency vary from month to month, and severity of the condition often diminishes in adolescence and adulthood. Most individuals with tic disorders have average or better intelligence.

Stereotypic Movement Disorders

DSM-IV-TR places stereotypies in a different diagnostic category from tics. **Stereotypic movement disorders** (often called *self-stimulatory behaviors*) are repetitive, seemingly driven, nonfunctional motor behaviors that markedly interfere with normal activities or result in self-inflicted bodily injury (APA, 2000). These can be independent disorders, but typically they coexist with such conditions as severe mental retardation, autism, deafblindness, or blindness. They are treated by medication, restraints, behavior management, and protective measures.

Self-injurious behaviors (SIBs) occur most frequently in medical conditions associated with severe mental retardation (e.g., Lesch-Nyham syndrome, fragile X syndrome, and Cornelia de Lange syndrome). In **Lesch-Nyham** syndrome, for example, severe self-biting often leads to loss of fingers. In other syndromes, head banging or hitting can result in anemia from loss of blood, infections, retinal detachment, and blindness. Pinching and scratching can lead to chronic skin irritations, bruises, and calluses. The prevalence of SIBs is 2 to 3% in individuals in community housing and 25% in individuals in institutions. Restraints, protective devices (helmets, gloves, splints), medication, and behavior management are used to manage SIBs. A new direction is rewarding self-restraints (Oliver, Murphy, Hall, Arron, & Leggett, 2003).

Less severe stereotypies are rhythmic (e.g., body rocking, head thrusting, hand waving or flicking). The major problem associated with these is social acceptance. Behavior management programs are applied to minimize time spent in stereotypic movement, but some experts believe that ignoring the stereotypy and accepting the person in spite of it is a viable alternative.

Treatment of Serious Emotional Disturbance

Treatment of serious emotional disturbance typically requires medication, psychotherapy and/or counseling, and cooperative home-school-community intervention programs. Lasting improvement seldom occurs unless all three of these programs are skillfully conducted and coordinated. The ecosystem must be changed as well as the individual. Serious emotional distur-

bance has acute phases and periods of remission. During the **acute phase,** individuals typically do not go to school or work. Instead, most are referred to mental health hospitals or outpatient clinics for diagnostic services or crisis management. Today's prescription medications are so effective that hospital stays seldom last more than a few days. Individuals who refuse medication or are careless in taking daily dosages tend to develop dysfunctional lifestyles that interfere with schooling and gradually alienate them from family and friends.

Medication (Drug Therapy or Pharmacotherapy)

Table 22.2 presents four categories of drugs commonly used in managing ADHD and serious emotional disturbance. These drugs enable most persons to lead relatively ordinary lives. The main difficulty in drug therapy is determining the best drug and the appropriate dosage to manage the condition. This usually requires considerable trial and error and a willingness to cope with various side effects. *Most side effects are greatest during the first few weeks,* while the body is adjusting to the drug, and eventually disappear. Occasionally the side effect is violent illness similar to food poisoning or severe flu.

Professionals need to understand side effects and offer support to individuals involved in drug therapy. For *stimulants,* the common side effects are insomnia, loss of appetite, and weight loss. For *antianxiety drugs,* the common side effects are diminished mental alertness and motor coordination, drowsiness, withdrawal, feelings of fatigue, dry mouth, nausea, loss of appetite, forgetfulness, and headaches. For most *antidepressant drugs,* the common side effects are dry mouth, drowsiness, insomnia, rapid heartbeat, dizziness, constipation, and weight gain.

For bipolar drugs, the risk of serious side effects is higher than for other drugs. Blood tests must be taken routinely to check if any organs are being damaged by the medication. Side effects include almost all of those of other drug categories plus diarrhea, unsteadiness, hand tremor, skin rashes, and generalized itching.

Drug therapy, in summary, often results in side effects that alter appearance and movement and are uncomfortable or embarrassing. The classic source of information on medications and side effects is the *Physician's Desk Reference* (published annually), referred to by its abbreviation, the *PDR*. Good physicians monitor dosage carefully to minimize side effects. *Physical activity personnel should assist with this monitoring, because effects of medication are sometimes altered by exercise.* Most individuals with schizophrenia and major mood disorders require daily drug therapy for long periods, often for life. Less is known about the drug requirements of individuals with mental retardation and severe behavior problems. Concern has been expressed that drugs are overprescribed and undermonitored in residential facilities.

Know how to use the Physician's Desk Reference (PDR) *and similar reference books to learn about medications and their side effects. Bring to class evidence that you have looked up at least one medication in the* PDR *or a comparable website.*

Table 22.2 Illustrative medications used in managing hyperactivity and serious emotional disorders (trade names).

Hyperactivity and ADHD management drugs
Ritalin
Dexedrine
Cylert
Antianxiety drugs (minor tranquilizers)
Valium
Librium
Xanax
Prozac
Antidepressant drugs
Prozac
Lithium, Lithobid
Elavil
Effexor
Tofranil
Antipsychotic drugs (neuroleptic, also known as major tranquilizers)
Thorazine
Haldol
Lithium, Lithobid

Note. Lithium and Lithobid are the best-known drugs for bipolar conditions.

Figure 22.3 Counseling often occurs in informal settings when staff know how to actively listen and are willing to get involved.

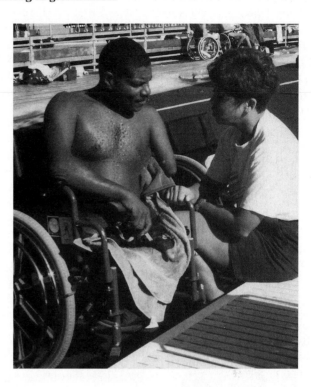

Psychotherapy and Counseling

Psychotherapy is the combined use of drugs and other helping techniques that are prescribed and monitored by a physician who specializes in psychiatry. Psychotherapy is generally carried out by psychologists or counselors in a medical setting. Most psychotherapy follows one of the cognitive psychology systems and relies primarily on verbal strategies. However, **dance therapy** (explained in Chapter 16) is a form of psychotherapy that uses movement as a change agent.

Counseling has many meanings. In this text, **counseling** is *psychological help through interactive verbal communication that is guided by mental health specialists certified in counseling and by teachers and peer counselors who have completed counseling courses and workshops.* Techniques of counseling were covered in Chapters 7 and 8, because the philosophy underlying this textbook is that good teaching is interwoven with counseling. A prerequisite to counseling is establishing trust so that the individual with problems is willing to share problems and learn to assume initiative and self-responsibility. Strategies for establishing trust vary widely, but counselor behaviors should include active listening, empathy, acceptance, willingness to get involved, and knowledge of when and how to make referrals (see Figure 22.3).

A growing number of schools have **peer counseling programs** because of the tendency for many children and adolescents to trust individuals of their own age more than adults. A certified adult counselor is typically responsible for carefully selecting, training, and mentoring peer counselors who work one-on-one or in small groups. Peer counseling is often interwoven with challenging physical activity programs like ropes courses and wilderness camping that help develop trust, cooperation, and positive interdependence (see Figure 22.4). Peer counseling may also involve cooperative care of animals, horseback riding, or Frisbee activities with a dog, because some individuals initially relate better to animals than to people.

Involvement in small-group sharing sessions and support networks with others who have similar problems is another counseling technique. A good example of this approach is the Alcoholics Anonymous program, which has been adapted to many kinds of dependency and special needs. Strategies of particular value are helping persons to understand and share their problems (e.g., to stand in front of peers, admit a problem, and ask for help) and providing mentors who give one-on-one help and support.

Cooperative Home-School-Community Programs

For optimal progress in managing problems, all of the human beings in an individual's life must work as a team. Turnbull and Ruef (1996) state six major challenges in providing support for individuals with severe emotional disturbance:

1. **Assessing problem behaviors.** Family members and school personnel should work together to cooperatively identify specific problem behaviors and decide on strategies for coping and change that will work at home and at school. Often school personnel must provide parents with formal training in behavior management if strategies are to succeed (see Chapter 7). Of particular importance is **consistency** in preventing and handling specific problem behaviors. It is also important to refrain

Figure 22.4 Adult certified in rope course work demonstrates teaching strategies to a peer counselor preparing to work with others. Note instructor's hand holding rope.

from blaming individuals and/or families (i.e., remember that many factors interact to cause behaviors).

2. **Incorporating structure in routines. Structure** is a behavior management strategy that emphasizes sameness in (a) sequence of daily activities, (b) social and physical environment, (c) teaching or parenting style, (d) rules, and (e) consequences of behavior. Structure is discussed in Chapters 7 and 20. The principle of structure, which is associated with the **command teaching style,** is implemented when an individual has extreme difficulty in coping with change or handling personal freedom. Such individuals often display **catastrophic reactions** (temper tantrums, uncontrollable sobbing, aggressive acts) in response to new or unexpected stimuli, such as a different food at mealtime or a chance happening that alters the day's schedule. Inappropriate behaviors are minimized when routines, menus, and the like are written out or indicated by pictures on a bulletin board; everyone knows what to expect, and necessary deviations are carefully explained well ahead of time. **Contracts** that everyone signs can help clarify the roles of various individuals (including the child) in creating and maintaining structure. (See Table 22.3.)

3. **Enhancing communication.** This challenge involves teaching everyone ways to improve verbal and nonverbal communication. Especially important is the use of gesture and body language in expressing positive emotion (see Chapters 8, 9, 15, and 16). Dance therapy often focuses on this concern.

4. **Expanding relationships.** Most individuals with severe problems have few emotionally connected, reciprocal relationships with others outside the family. School and community personnel should help families find trained individuals who will assume friend or companion roles on a volunteer or paid basis. Ideally, inclusion strategies at school lead to the development of genuine friendships, but much work is needed for these to generalize to home and community activities (see Chapters 8, 9, and 15).

5. **Increasing choice-making.** Significant others need to create increased opportunities for individuals with serious emotional disturbance to learn to make choices, to recognize good and bad alternatives, and to face the consequences of their choices (see Chapters 4 and 9). First offer individuals a choice between only two alternatives, then between three alternatives, and later more. Carefully structure the way choice-making is handled.

6. **Reducing stress.** Individuals with problem behaviors and associates who are affected by these behaviors all need to learn stress management and relaxation techniques (see Chapter 16). There should also be voluntary time-out places, where individuals can go to be alone and draw upon inner resources. Likewise, crisis telephone service and special counselors should be easily accessible.

Exercise and Serious Emotional Disturbance

Exercise is an effective means of reducing depression, anger, disruptive behaviors, and stereotypies (ACSM, 2000; Cheatum & Hammond, 2000; Elliott, Dobbin, Rose, & Soper, 1994). Jogging and other forms of aerobic exercise tend to yield better results than less vigorous activity, although as little as 5 minutes of walking can elevate mood. In general, exercise as an intervention for emotional disturbance should be

1. perceived as pleasant and enjoyable;

2. aerobic or as close to aerobic as the individual can tolerate with ease;

3. noncompetitive;

4. nonthreatening (i.e., a closed motor activity that is predictable, repetitive, and routine);

5. of moderate intensity for at least 20 to 30 minutes; and

6. used two or three times a day or as often daily as an individual feels the exercise is beneficial.

The criterion of exercising two, three, or more times a day is based on the assumptions that persons want to exercise and that exercise can serve as a voluntary time-out or a time of reflection and relaxation. Individuals should not be required to exercise as part of treatment or therapy; instead, many options (e.g., swimming, cycling, walking, horseback riding, skating) should be available. *The criterion of wanting to exercise is probably the most important, in that an activity must feel good to have mental health benefits.*

Table 22.3 Sample Behavior Contract

Contract for Isabelle

Isabelle will use appropriate language in her fifth-grade physical education class for 3 weeks. If Isabelle behaves 3 out of the 5 classes for Week 1, 4 out of 5 classes Week 2, and all 5 classes Week 3 she can lead class warm-up activities the next class period.

Agreed _____ _____ _____
                  Student   Teacher   Date

Met Daily Behavioral Standard

Week 1		Week 2		Week 3	
Class	Yes/No	Class	Yes/No	Class	Yes/No
1		1		1	
2		2		2	
3		3		3	
4		4		4	
5	_____	5	_____	5	_____

Number of Days
Student Met Standard   /5   /5   /5

_____ _____ _____ _____
   Student Name   Parent Name   Physical Educator   Date

When possible, exercise should be accompanied by **music** of the individual's choice. This principle requires the availability of headphones. Individuals with manic, aggressive, or hyperactive conditions should be permitted to choose from several selections of slow, quiet music, whereas individuals with depression should be encouraged to choose from fast, energizing music.

Adapting the Public School Program

Students whose behavior problems are so severe that they meet federal law eligibility requirements for special services are often assigned to separate, adapted physical education instruction because their behaviors pose a safety threat to others or severely disrupt regular class activities. A class size not larger than 12 students is strongly recommended because behaviors of such children are extremely hard to manage. Additionally, paraprofessionals should be assigned to individual students, as needed, and supports like portable phones to call for help in case of emergency should be provided.

Increasingly, children with serious emotional disturbance are integrated into general physical education; in such cases, class size should be reduced and peer counselors or partners should be assigned. The physical educator should negotiate for whatever supports are needed to assure everyone's safety.

General Guidelines for Conducting Class

General guidelines for conducting a class of students with serious emotional disturbance are as follows:

1. Display appropriate authority. Let students know you are competent to handle any situation that might arise, but that you expect and will reward good behavior.

2. Explain the class goals on the first day, and describe the routine to be followed during class periods. Provide the amount of structure needed to minimize discipline problems.

3. Meet individually as often as necessary with each student, discuss goals, and cooperatively develop a **contract** that states what each of you must do for the student to achieve each goal. When appropriate, include the student's peer counselor or paraprofessional in these meetings. Help the student see how her or his goals fit with the group goals.

4. Keep class rules simple, and set as few concrete rules as possible. An illustrative set of rules follows:

   Follow directions.

   Keep hands, feet, and objects to yourself.

   Do NOT leave the room without permission.

   Do NOT swear or tease.

   Do NOT yell or scream.

5. Clearly explain the consequences of following and breaking rules. The consequences of following rules are typically individual or group rewards. The consequences of breaking rules typically depend on whether the misbehavior was **aggressive** (e.g., hitting, biting, verbal

Table 22.4   Website Information related to Individuals with Emotional Disturbances

www.sheboygan.k12.us/sisrv/specialed/ed.html	Provides information related to program goals for individuals who are emotionally disturbed.
www.taconic.net/seminars/emot.html	Provides information related to individuals who are severely emotionally disturbed.
www.parentpals.com/gossamer/pages/Emotionally_Disturbed/	Provides articles, news, and special education support for parents and professionals who have or work with students with emotional disturbances.
www.dickinson.k12.ned.us/westdakota/Resource	Provides understanding and teaching of children who are emotionally disturbed.
www.ccbd.net/pdfs/BeyondBehavior	Provides in-depth journal related to students who are emotionally disturbed.
www.nami.org	National Alliance for the Mentally Ill
www.nmha.org	National Mental Health Association
www.bpkid.org	Child and Adolescent Bipolar Foundation

threat) or **noncompliant** (e.g., failure to stay on task or give personal best).

6. Involve the students in setting the consequences, posting these on the wall, and helping to enforce them. Agreement on consequences should occur early in the semester, when a contract is signed by students and teacher, indicating that everyone understands the system. Usually the consequence for **aggressive behavior** is some kind of punishment, whereas the consequence for **noncompliant behavior** depends on its underlying cause. If noncompliance is a form of acting out and trying to get attention, it is ignored. If noncompliance is an indicator of anxiety or confusion, the teacher should ask, "Do you need help?" and then respond accordingly.

7. Demonstrate consistency in enforcing rules and providing positive feedback. Aim for a 5:1 praise/criticism ratio.

8. Use visual cues to reflect daily routines and instruction.

9. Constantly check to see if the individual can verbalize what was said.

     For more information on teaching and managing persons with emotional disturbance, see Table 22.4.

Juveniles Who are Incarcerated

Students with ED are 13 times more likely to be arrested during their school career, and 20% of these students are arrested at least once before graduating (Doren, Bullis, & Benz, 1996). When incarcerated, students with ED receive few if any special education services. Sport is one valued medium that can be used for socializing and transitioning incarcerated juveniles back into society. Because of this, many facilities have excellent recreational offerings and good facilities. Others need to improve physical activity programming, especially for females (Hilgenbrinck, 2001). In general, sports most often selected by young inmates are basketball, softball, volleyball, and weight lifting. The foundation to developing quality physical activity programs for incarcerated youth is a state curriculum guide that legitimizes these programs (Hilgenbrinck, 2001).

Applied Behavior Analysis (ABA) Principles

According to the National Consortium for Physical Education and Recreation for Individuals with Disabilities (NCPERID, 1995) standards, physical educators should apply applied behavior analysis (ABA) principles when teaching students with ED. These principles include the following:

1. Target specific behaviors that need to be changed and carefully define all components of these behaviors.

2. Observe, chart, and analyze the behaviors to be changed.

3. Select and apply specific strategies to achieve behavior changes. Consider the following when selecting strategies:

   • Signals for getting attention, starting, and stopping activities
   • Routines for making transition from one activity to another
   • Techniques for organizing small groups and game formations
   • Strategies for coping with disruptive behaviors
   • Methods of teaching individual goal setting
   • Pedagogy for enhancing self-management and maintenance

4. Select and apply appropriate consequences (i.e., reinforcers and punishers). Assess first to determine which ones are preferred or work best.

5. Periodically evaluate progress toward changing an individual's behaviors and revise her or his behavior change plan.

     More detail about ABA and behavior management appears in Chapter 7. Also see the section on principles for managing environment in Chapter 20. Pedagogy concerning individual goal setting, self-management, and maintenance appears in Chapters 8 and 9, which focus on assessment and pedagogy in relation to self-concept and social inclusion competence.

Transitions From Activity to Activity in the Gym

Transitions from one activity to another are particularly difficult for many children with serious ED. In classes where all students have serious ED, *the use of teaching stations might be contraindicated* until children can handle such change. A progression should be used when introducing children to the routine of rotating from station to station. At first only two stations should be used, then three, and then more when students are ready. Rotation from station to station should always be in the same direction, traditionally counterclockwise. A time limitation (usually 10 seconds) should be given for rotation from station to station. This can be enacted by the cue, "Ready, change stations, 1-2-3-4-5-6-7-8-9-10." By the time the teacher counts aloud to 10, all students should be at their next station. When a student with serious ED is integrated into general physical education, a partner is often needed to get her or him from station to station.

Lesson plans in physical education usually have three distinct parts: introductory activities (roll call, warm-up), lesson body, and summary (cool-down and closing remarks). The lesson body often has several subparts (e.g., different games or practice of different motor skills). Transitions from one part of the lesson to another should be carefully structured. Whereas children without ED thrive on change and the goal is to teach them as many games or drills as possible, children with ED need more time on each activity. They also need specific instruction on getting into game formations and changing game formations (see Chapter 12, pages 352–353). Assessment and, subsequently, individual learning objectives should include such activities as "Given a setting with 11 classmates and teacher's instructions and signal, move from a circle formation to a line formation in 10 seconds in 90% of such class transitions every day."

Behavior Management Techniques

Behavior management, also called **contingency management,** is the major pedagogy used in most physical education classes (LaVay, French, & Henderson, 1997). When a class contains several students with serious ED, much creativity is needed to find effective rewards and punishments. These techniques are covered in Chapter 7.

Ecological Pedagogy and Specific SED Conditions

Serious behavior problems can be reduced by **changing the content of curricular activities** to better meet student interests and needs (Ferro, Foster-Johnson, & Dunlap, 1996). Illustrative changes include modifying the difficulty of an activity, offering students choices of activities and modifiers, and taking students on field trips to reinforce their understanding that activities being learned in class are transferable to community programs.

In summary, physical education instruction of students with serious ED is extremely demanding and requires **small class sizes** and the availability of **many supports.** These requirements should be written into IEPs. Time must be made available for home visits and involvement in cooperative home-school-community intervention programs if teaching is to be effective and result in achievement of transition goals and lifespan healthy lifestyle. Following are brief discussions of how physical educators can cope with or manage specific serious ED conditions.

Strategies for Schizophrenia

Students with schizophrenia generally do not respond well to firm discipline, particularly if they have paranoid tendencies or fear authority figures. The presence of schizophrenic behaviors depends largely on whether medication is working properly. Environmental factors sometimes affect the way prescription drugs work, resulting in good and bad days from a behavioral perspective. High-stress situations, such as competitive sport and challenges to learn new motor tasks that the individual perceives as hard, dangerous, or threatening, should be avoided. Instructional objectives related to the content in Chapter 8 (self-concept), Chapter 9 (social competence), and Chapter 15 (play and recreation) should guide class activities.

Students often seem out of contact with reality or sometimes talk about hallucinations. The best teacher responses to such behaviors are "You know that is not true" or "That doesn't make sense." The teacher should not *play along* with hallucinations or ask questions pertaining to them, thereby appearing to be interested.

In students with schizophrenia, even small bits of criticism can elicit destructive behavior. The physical educator should understand that hostility is basically a **protective reaction.** *Some students feel endangered by criticism or even by helpful suggestions.* Yet such students must be given firm limits. They must also learn that there are adults who do not get angry when they misbehave. The physical educator must combine friendliness and warmth with consistent enforcement of limits. Should a temper tantrum occur, it is better not to try to talk over the noise. A student driven by panic or rage is out of contact with reality, and reasoning will not help. Sometimes, the only alternative for stopping aggressive behavior is physical restraint.

The following suggestions may help:

1. Prevent conflict that might cause temper tantrums. Overlook minor transgressions. Each temper tantrum is a step backward.

2. If the student becomes aggressive, try to distract him or her. Introduce some new toy or game. Use humor.

3. Should a student strike or bite you, do not become ruffled or angry. In a cool, calculated manner, say something like, "Ouch, that hurt! What did I do to cause you to bite me?"

4. Do not show fear or confusion about a behavior. Students with schizophrenia tend to be extrasensitive to the feelings of teachers and might use such information to manipulate the adult. Never say, for instance, "I just don't understand you" or "I don't know what to do with you."

5. Do not use threats of physical violence or abandonment. Avoid all forms of physical punishment, because such punishment reinforces paranoid beliefs.

6. Reward good behavior and structure the situation to avoid inappropriate behavior.

Figure 22.5 Tug-of-war activities with a partner facilitate relating socially to others.

7. Create situations for learning to relate socially to others (see Figure 22.5), before pushing the student into the complex human relationships of team sport strategy.

8. Structure play groups and/or class squads very carefully, maintaining a balance between the number of aggressive and the number of passive persons. The school psychologist may help with this endeavor.

Strategies for Anger and Aggression

Most of the guidelines for working with schizophrenia apply to working with anger and aggression. The major difference is that traditional behavior management strategies (see Chapter 7) are more successful when schizophrenia or other biochemical conditions are not present. Adult and peer counseling should help children identify sources of anger and learn to avoid or minimize contact with the persons or situations that make them angry. The **talking-bench strategy** is used when two persons get into an argument. The individuals go to a designated area, remain seated until differences are resolved, and then report the outcome to the teacher. Time missed from physical activity is made up.

Physical education should include activities that permit students to express hostility in socially acceptable ways: punching a bag, jumping, leaping, throwing, pushing, and pulling. Offensive skills like the smash and volleyball spike can be practiced when tension is especially great. It sometimes helps to paint faces on the balls and punching bags. The teacher can join in stomping empty paper cups turned upside down, and balloons. The making of noise itself relieves tension.

Students must learn that it is acceptable to take out aggressions on things but never on persons or animals. Thus, boxing or wrestling is contraindicated for some students with serious ED. Aggressive persons often can be developed into good squad leaders. Always, they demand special attention—a personal "Hello, John" at the *first* of the period and the frequent use of their names throughout class instruction.

School-based anger management programs for adolescents with serious ED teach the physiology, triggers, and consequences of anger as well as coping strategies for managing anger (Kellner & Tutin, 1995). Students are taught to keep a **hassle log.** This self-monitoring device allows them to record (a) incidents that trigger anger, (b) ways they handled each incident, (c) self-appraisal of the degree of anger experienced, and (d) self-appraisal of skill in handling the incident. Considerable emphasis is placed on helping students identify the signs of anger in their own and others' bodies (e.g., red and twisted face, quickly beating heart, sweaty palms, raised voice). Physical education incidents that cause anger are role-played, with students making up scripts for right and wrong ways to manage anger.

The underlying assumption is that students want to control their anger but lack coping skills. A part of each lesson is therefore spent in teaching and practicing specific skills such as relaxation, assertion, self-instruction, thinking ahead, self-evaluation, and problem solving (see Chapters 9 and 15). An occasional display of uncontrolled anger is not punished but considered as a relapse. Small group size permits everyone to be involved in discussing the incident and suggesting ways they can work together to prevent further relapses.

Strategies for Depression and Withdrawal

More than anything else, persons who are depressed need to be kept active. Yet, they often refuse to participate in physical activity. They have no desire to learn new skills since life is not worth living, they are too tired, or they intend to kill themselves anyway. Some persons will sit for days, crying and thinking of methods of suicide. Whereas most of us are inclined to sympathize with anyone who cries, displaying a rough, noncommittal exterior to individuals who are depressed is best. For instance, the person may be asked, "Do you play golf?" The typical response is a self-deprecating, "I'm not any good" or "I'm not good enough to play with so-and-so." Instead of trying to build up the person's ego, as a teacher might do with a well person, it is best to agree and make a statement like "That's probably true!" In other words, the teacher should **mirror** or restate the person's thoughts rather than contradict him or her. Psychologists concur that praise and compliments only make persons who are depressed feel more unworthy. They feel guilty when others say good things about them and/or are nice to them.

Severe depression is treated with antidepressant medications. Persons who are depressed generally follow instructions but will not engage in activities voluntarily. They often must be taken gently by the arm, pulled to an upright position, and accompanied to the activity site.

Strategies for Anxiety, Fear, and Withdrawal

Most authorities concur that students should not be forced to participate in activities that they fear or intensely dislike. Swimming, tumbling, and apparatus seem to evoke withdrawal reactions more often than do other physical education activities. In most persons, these fears gradually subside when it becomes obvious that the peer group is having fun. Coaxing, cajoling, and reasoning accomplish little. In the case of actual behavior disorders, psychotherapy and other specialized techniques are generally needed.

Desensitization, for example, is a behavior management strategy that uses a carefully planned progression of activities to gradually reduce fear reactions to a stimulus. The underlying assumption is that a stimulus like a snake, climbing apparatus, or entering a swimming pool becomes less frightening when exposure to it occurs in small chunks with continuous reassurance about safety. The following desensitization steps might be used with a child who fears heights and refuses to try activities on a climbing apparatus. The child

1. looks at pictures of other children playing on the climbing apparatus and tells the teacher what she or he sees.

2. plays with dolls on a miniature replica of the apparatus and observes other children playing on the apparatus.

3. walks in a circle around the apparatus while holding the teacher's hand.

4. takes walks with the teacher that each time come closer to the apparatus, until child is willing to reach out and touch the apparatus with various body parts.

5. sits or stands on low rungs of the apparatus while the teacher supports the child's body; duration of time in contact with apparatus is increased gradually.

6. makes transitions from one part of the apparatus to another while the teacher supports the child.

7. agrees to allow the teacher to reduce or eliminate physical support for increasingly longer durations of time.

Other techniques for helping individuals to manage anxiety and fear are embedded in Bandura's (1977; 1997) **self-efficacy theory,** which was originally posited as a framework for changing fearful or avoidant behaviors. Bandura recommended reduction of fear by improving **situation-specific self-confidence** through one of the following four strategies:

1. Enable individuals to feel safe by task-analyzing and structuring activities to ensure personal mastery.

2. Promote vicarious feelings of mastery by watching and listening to models who look successful and appear to be having fun. See Weiss, McCullagh, Smith, & Berlant, (1998).

3. Use personal persuasion by significant others.

4. Provide counseling or psychotherapy that teaches cognitive control of anxiety and fear.

Aquatics and Individuals With SED

Aquatics benefits all persons (see Chapter 17) but is especially recommended for those who demonstrate overanxious, aggressive, and hyperactive behaviors (Jansma & French, 1994). The aquatic program is generally conducted with water temperature at 90° to 93° Fahrenheit when used as a therapy to provide a relaxing effect.

Figure 22.6 Structured aquatic activities like splashing can release aggressive feelings.

Other general benefits can range from an increase in self-image and self-confidence to opportunities to learn social skills and make friends. Some teaching techniques are as follows:

1. Some individuals may be tactile defensive; personal space needs to be respected.

2. Some individuals may demonstrate a high degree of fear. With the assistance of a school psychologist, the instructor can develop and implement a behavior management strategy that incorporates desensitization. Peer models are also effective in the aquatics environment (Weiss et al., 1998).

3. Some individuals may first relate more to inanimate objects such as toys or a flotation device than the instructor. Eventually the object is phased out and replaced with the instructor.

4. Some individuals should have structured aquatic activities (e.g., splashing, kicking) to release aggressive behaviors (see Figure 22.6).

5. Some individuals may have attention span difficulties, restlessness, and disorientation.

   a. Structured lesson should be no more than 5 to 30 minutes based on individual's attention span.

   b. Limit class size and directions (i.e., noise, visual stimuli) to increase time on task.

   c. When possible, use a one-on-one student teacher ratio.

d. Place individual toward the pool wall or face the individual away from seeing the total swimming pool to block out distractors.

6. Some individuals may be unable to self-monitor.

   a. Use student portfolios and worksheets.

   b. Facilitate question and answer periods to help individuals to self-monitor.

7. Some individuals may become easily frustrated and lack patience.

   a. Use systematic and logical skill program instruction.

   b. Build in success to each lesson. The success rate should be 8 successful tasks out of 10.

   c. Use rubrics to make sure each task is analyzed into a sequence of easy to hard parts to provide opportunities for success.

   d. Apply rules; these must be clearly understood to reduce frustration.

   e. Provide time out from instruction as needed (e.g., 5 min of free play).

   f. Redirect individuals who exhibit inappropriate attention seeking behavior such as splashing others. Have the individual catch a ball or use a kick board and kick in a prone float position.

   g. Provide task variation that builds in choices to help decrease restlessness.

   h. Collaborate with the individual's teacher, caregiver, and/or psychologist.

Behavior and Disciplinary Placement Change

More and more, students are displaying inappropriate behaviors such as aggression, noncompliance, and disruption in our schools. IDEA 1997 imposed special requirements for students with disabilities (ED or other conditions recognized by law). Specifically, the law states that members of the IEP team must collaborate in assessing behaviors and developing a behavioral intervention plan (BIP) for any student with a disability who may be at risk for a placement change because of inappropriate school behaviors. Table 22.5 presents a sample BIP. A copy of the functional behavioral assessment (FBA) that provides data for the BIP can be accessed through McGraw-Hill textbook website, www.mhhe.com/hhp.

Functional behavioral assessment (FBA), a process made popular by IDEA 1997, is "a set of strategies for assessing the interaction between a behavior and the environment to form an educated guess about the function of that behavior" (Ryan, Halsey, & Matthews, 2003, p. 9). Functions of behavior, as conceptualized in FBA, are twofold: (a) to obtain or maintain something desirable (i.e., positive reinforcement) and (b) to escape from or avoid something undesirable (i.e., negative reinforcement). Although FBA was not required prior to IDEA 1997, physical educators who use ecological or ecobehavioral assessment to determine a person's preferred reinforcement or reward have been applying FBA (e.g., Silliman-French et al., 1998).

Manifestation determination is the term given to the procedure that must be implemented before a child with a dis-

ability can undergo a disciplinary change of educational placement such as long-term exclusion. The change in placement can be mandated only when documentation indicates that there is no relationship between the student's disability and his or her behavior. In other words, it must be determined that the inappropriate behavior was *not* caused by (a manifestation of) the student's disability. In many cases, of course, inappropriate behaviors are linked to serious ED, and the student remains in his or her placement. The IEP team then must review the student's IEP and develop a BIP to structure attention on eliminating the inappropriate behavior. If the inappropriate behavior is determined by the IEP team *not to be a manifestation* of the disability, the change of placement and/or disciplinary measures applicable for students without disabilities are applied.

Pervasive Developmental Disorders or Autism Spectrum Disorder

Pervasive developmental disorders (PDD) is a broad diagnostic category for severe impairment in reciprocal social interaction or communication skills and/or the presence of stereotyped behavior, interests, and activities. This category includes such conditions as autism (called autistic disorders in *DSM-IV-TR*), Asperger's disorder, and Rett's disorder. Recently, many persons are using the term **autism spectrum disorder** instead of PDD (Reid & Collier, 2002; 2003).

Types of Pervasive Developmental Disorders

In each of the PDDs, infants demonstrate typical development for several months, after which delays or abnormal function become **pervasive,** affecting every aspect of life and seriously limiting the children's ability to learn in the same ways as their peers. Often, specific diagnosis is difficult. Some experts consider all or most forms of PDD to be a part of an autism continuum or spectrum because the basic treatment principles are the same for all types (Wing, 1997). However, professionals should be able to define and discuss each disorder as a separate condition.

Autistic disorder is a severe, lifelong developmental disability that is diagnosed by impaired functioning, with onset before age 3 years, in (a) social interaction, (b) language as used in social communication, (c) imaginative or social imitative play, and (d) repetitive, stereotyped patterns of behavior. This disorder tends to impair motivation to learn, the way sensory stimuli are received, and the ability to attend and subsequently assimilate, retain, retrieve, and utilize various stimuli. Degree of autism varies from child to child; descriptors indicate level of functioning (e.g., high, low). Synonyms include *Kanner's autism, classic autism, childhood autism,* and *early infantile autism.*

The term *autism* comes from the Greek word *autos,* meaning "self," and refers specifically to self-absorption and withdrawal (i.e., lack of responsiveness to other people). Leo Kanner (1943) was the first to describe autism as a syndrome.

Autism is also associated with mental retardation, fragile X syndrome, epilepsy, and other disorders that affect brain function. About 20% of people with autism have IQs above 70; 20% have IQs between 50 and 70; and 60% have IQs below 50. Determining intellectual function is difficult because people with autism tend to score low on tasks demanding verbal

Student: Hayden Speckhardt   DOB: 02-03-1987   Grade: 09   School: Denton High School

Note. Goals are measured annually based on the accomplishment of their objectives for the year unless otherwise noted in the goal's Comments/Mastery Criteria field.

Goal: Increase positive behaviors and/or decrease negative behaviors.

Objectives:

1. The student will respond appropriately within 6, 4, and 2 seconds to teacher and adult directives 80% of the time.

2. The student will complete 3, 4, and 5 physical and/or motor activities during each general physical education class 95% of the time.

3. The student will attend all classes 70, 80, and 90% each week.

Intervention:

If the behavior occurs again, the following consequences will be applied: _____

If the behavior does not recur, the following reinforcement procedures will be applied: _____

If behavior is due to a skill deficit, what behavior(s) or skill(s) needs to be taught to enable student to change behavior?

Person(s) responsible for teaching: Classroom teacher, resource teacher, physical education teacher, music teacher, art teacher, and school psychologist.

Review:

Date:	**Modifications to Plan:**
Date:	**Modifications to Plan:**

---

skills and abstract reasoning but high on tasks requiring memory and visual-spatial or manipulative skills. From 20 to 40% of children with autism have seizures before age 10. Of these, 75% have *psychomotor seizures* (see Chapter 19).

Asperger's disorder is a severe and sustained impairment in social interaction, coupled with repetitive, stereotyped patterns of behavior, that seriously impacts function. Unlike autistic disorder, there are no clinically significant delays in language, cognitive function, self-help skills, adaptive behaviors (except for social interaction), or curiosity about the environment. The major *DSM-IV-TR* criterion for delay in language is inability to use single words by age 2 and to speak in phrases by age 3. Clumsiness is a clinical feature but not an essential criterion for diagnosis (Jones & Prior, 1985).

Hans Asperger (1944), of Vienna, was the first to identify this disorder, but his work did not impact PDD diagnosis and treatment in English-speaking countries until its translation several decades later. Today, Asperger's disorder is often called *high-functioning autism.* Some individuals diagnosed as having Asperger's disorder as adults had classic autism in early childhood but responded well to early intervention.

Rett's disorder, which affects only females, is a severe degenerative condition diagnosed by deceleration of head growth between ages 5 and 48 months, loss of previously acquired hand skills between 5 and 30 months, loss of interest in the social environment, appearance of stereotyped hand-wringing movements and gait and coordination problems, and subsequent development of severe impairment in language and psychomotor function. Rett's disorder also increases risk for **osteopenia** (decreased bone density).

Incidence of Pervasive Developmental Disorders

Incidence statistics vary according to the specific diagnostic criteria used. The incidence of autism is about 15 in 10,000 births; this is about the same as the incidence of Down syndrome (see Appendix B). Autism is about four times more common in males than in females. The incidence of Asperger's disorder is about 3 in 10,000 births. The incidence of Rett's syndrome is about 1 in 10,000 female births. When all of the autism spectrum disorders are combined, the incidence is 19 to 22 per 10,000 (Reid & Collier, 2002).

Autism and the Federal Law

Autism was considered a form of emotional disturbance until 1981, when federal law reclassified it under *other health impairments.* In 1990, the Individuals with Disabilities Education Act (IDEA) recognized autism as a separate diagnostic category. In school settings, however, students with autism are often believed to need behavior management more than anything else.

IDEA defined *autism* as follows:

a developmental disability significantly affecting verbal and nonverbal communication and social interaction, generally evident before age 3, that adversely affects a child's educational performance. Other behaviors often associated with autism are engagement in repetitive activities and stereotyped movements, resistance to environmental change or change in daily routines, and unusual responses to sensory experiences. The term does not apply if a child's educational performance is adversely affected primarily because the child has a serious emotional disturbance. [34 C. F. R. 5300.7(1)]

The law does not yet distinguish between autistic disorder and other forms of PDD. Autism is considered the broad diagnostic category that encompasses all forms of PDD that adversely affect educational performance.

Causes of Autism

The causes of autism are **neurobiological** and **genetic,** not environmental as first posited by Kanner (1943). A specific gene for autism has not yet been identified; however, autism often affects siblings. Autism occurs more frequently than chance would dictate in families with a history of mood disorders, attention deficit disorder, Tourette's disorder, and obsessive-compulsive disorder (*DSM-IV-TR*, 2000). Autism also sometimes appears to be **acquired** and is linked to childhood diseases (e.g., rubella, encephalitis), metabolic problems, and brain injury. However, the specific nature of the link is not well understood.

Savantism and Autism

Savantism is the ability to spontaneously perform musical, artistic, computational, athletic, or other kinds of skills at exceptional levels without benefit of instruction or practice. **Savant talents** usually appear at a very young age. Oliver Sacks, a neurologist, provides good coverage of savants (prodigies) in his book of case studies *An Anthropologist on Mars* (1995). The 1988 movie *Rain Man,* now available on video, provides an excellent portrayal of savantism combined with autism. Dustin Hoffman, as the savant, Raymond, demonstrated genius-level calculational and memory skills but was unable to relate meaningfully to his brother or other human beings.

The incidence of savantism in autism (about 10%) is about 200 times its incidence in the population with mental retardation and thousands of times its incidence in the population at large (Sacks, 1995). J. Langdon Down, one of the first observers of the memory powers of savants, coined the term *idiot savant* in 1887, but today we call such persons *savants with autism* or *savants with mental retardation.* Although savants perform remarkable feats, they typically lack an understanding of what they are doing. For example, some are able to read and memorize hundreds of pages but have no clue as to the meaning of the content.

See Rain Man *and discuss it with peers. Evaluate whether it did a good or bad job in portraying autism. If you were to write a movie script centering about autism, what outline of content would you use? Why?*

Illustrative People with Autism and Intervention Programs

About one third of persons with autism are able to live and work fairly independently by adulthood. The other two thirds remain severely disabled. Traditionally, autism has been considered a lifelong condition, but an increasing number of books by parents describe partial or total recovery from classic autism as a result of intensive, structured early childhood intervention programs (e.g., Kaufman, 1994; Maurice, 1993).

Undoubtedly, the best-known person with autism who lives and works independently is Temple Grandin, who has a doctoral degree and works as an assistant professor in the Animal Sciences Department at Colorado State University. Grandin has published numerous books, including her autobiography *Emergence: Labeled Autistic* (1986), observations about her life entitled *Thinking in Pictures* (1995), and more than 100 professional papers divided between her two major interests, autism and animal behavior. Sacks (1995) has written an extensive case study of Grandin. It is entitled "An Anthropologist on Mars" because this is the phrase she uses to describe her inability to understand and relate to human beings and her intense study of human behavior in an effort to make sense of the world. Grandin (1995) states that today she would be diagnosed as having Asperger's disorder, but as a 2-year-old she demonstrated signs of classic Kanner's autism.

A well-known individual who has recovered from autism is Raun Kaufman, who graduated from Brown University, in Rhode Island. As a young child, Raun was featured in a book and a television movie, both entitled *Son-Rise* (Kaufman, 1994), which are well worth reviewing. Raun's parents established a private institute in Sheffield, Massachusetts, in the early 1980s that continues to be a popular training center for parents of children with autism. This center is noteworthy in that it does not subscribe to classic behavior management, which aims to extinguish autistic behaviors, but instead emphasizes a psychotherapy approach (i.e., acceptance and imitation [**mirroring**] of the child's autistic behaviors until she or he is ready to give them up or replace them with other more age-appropriate activities). Central to this approach is the presence of an adult in a one-to-one therapeutic relationship almost every hour of the day. Much of the intervention used is dance or movement therapy.

In contrast, Catherine Maurice (1993), a parent using a pseudonym, writes about the gradual recovery of her two children with autism and others who are following the behavior management curriculum of Ivar Lovaas at UCLA. Maurice recommends that parents and teachers read *The Me Book* (Lovaas, 1981) and other materials by Lovaas available through Pro•Ed (see Appendix E). The Lovaas program is used in many public schools and follows classic behavior management principles (see Chapter 7).

Whereas the Lovaas program emphasizes direct compliance, the North Carolina TEACCH program uses a cognitive approach that manages behavior by addressing it as indirectly as possible. **TEACCH** is the acronym for Treatment and Education of Autistic and related Communication-Handicapped Children (Landrus & Mesibov, 1985).

TEACCH is a *visual approach* that involves both assessment and instruction in strategies based on the skills, inter-

Figure 22.7 Therapeutic riding enhances sensory processes, acceptance of change, and awareness of the environment.

ests, and needs of individuals with autism. This program involves an organized physical environment, structured daily educational activity schedules, clear and explicit expectations, and the use of visual materials that provide visual cues about how and when to respond. The key areas of instruction are functional skills, communication, and social and leisure skills that will enhance community integration (Bartlett, Weisenstein, & Etscheidt, 2002).

Therapeutic riding is another approach that may be effective when working with individuals with autism. One riding program that grew out of TEACCH was Riding Education of Autistic and Communication-Handicapped Children (REACCH). After individuals with autism leave school, they follow the same schedule at the stable as was used in the classroom. Based on reports of parents and teachers, children with autism also improved in most areas of sensory processing and their reactions to the environment around them after riding (see Figure 22.7).

The Daily Life Therapy (also called Higashi) method of instruction is designed to provide individuals with autism a systematic education through meaningful and real-life experiences within a controlled environment (Larkin & Gurry, 1998; Quill, 1989). The goal is to develop these individuals' abilities to be as close to peers as possible physically, emotionally, socially, and intellectually to achieve social independence and dignity. Physical education is the cornerstone of Daily Life Therapy. Physical education is developmental with a focus on agility, balance, coordination, endurance, and flexibility.

The tenets of Daily Life Therapy were developed by the late Dr. Kiyo Kitahara of Japan, who first tested the program at the Musashino Higashi Gakuen School in Japan and published three volumes detailing pedagogy (Kitahara, 1984). The Boston Higashi School, which serves individuals with autism, aged 3–22, is an exemplary program in the United States.

Parent Involvement Programs

Children with severe autism perhaps present a greater challenge to public school personnel than children with any other disability. Progress, which tends to be slow and inconsistent, requires comprehensive, structured programming across all of the student's environments all 52 weeks of the year. State education agencies (SEAs) are therefore implementing plans for in-home training, parent training, and extended, school day, year-round services (EYS). These services are now written into the IEP or IFSP and monitored carefully.

In-home training is service delivery to the child in the home, community, or other natural environments to assist the child in generalizing skills learned at school to other environments. The designated in-home providers conduct a specific number of sessions and hours each week as determined by the IEP or IFSP committee. Training is guided by specific goals and objectives that promote maximum independent performance of skills in all environments. For example:

> **Goal:** Tony will develop, generalize, and maintain appropriate behaviors that are socially acceptable in all environments.
>
> **Objective:** Tony will demonstrate appropriate behaviors when riding a bicycle with his brother 100% of the time.
>
> **Objective:** Tony will use a bicycle in all kinds of settings, 100% of the time, in ways that are safe to himself and others.

Parent training is similar to in-home training except that it focuses on changing the behaviors of parents and other family members so that they can more effectively generalize behavior management and other instructional programs conducted at school to home and community environments. The specific number of sessions and hours each week are written into the IEP or IFSP. Parent training is conducted in the home.

Extended, school day, year-round services (EYS) are addressed in IEPs and IFSPs because research shows that most children with autism substantially regress if their structured programming lapses for even brief periods of time. One hearing officer in Texas required that the daily written schedule for a student with autism cover 24 hours a day, 7 days a week, including holidays (*Andrew T.K. v. Houston ISD*, reported by Martin, 1996). Time increments in daily schedules should be based on assessed attention spans in performing specific activities. Schedules should be designed so that there is minimal "down time" for engaging in self-stimulating stereotypical movements, commonly called *stimming.* Furthermore, schedules should not include unstructured play or leisure time unless specific objectives require children to learn to use unstructured time. In such cases, the unstructured time is carefully supervised to ensure that progress is being made toward achievement of the objective.

Motor Clumsiness and Generalization Problems in Autism

Students with autism typically evidence motor clumsiness (Berkeley, Zittel, Pitney, & Nichols, 2001; Reid & Collier, 2002). *DSM-IV-TR* specifically notes that motor clumsiness is often observed in individuals with Asperger's disorder (APA, 2000), but motor incoordination is widespread at all levels of autism. Approximately 50% of children with Asperger's disorder and 67% of children with high-functioning autism (IQs in the average or near-average range) demonstrate a clinically significant level of motor impairment (Manjiviona & Prior, 1995). Formal assessment data, however, may be misleading, in that students with autism often will not respond to test directions and can actually perform better than scores indicate. It is important therefore to observe, and document with videotapes, their motor and fitness performance in informal, natural settings.

Goals and objectives should focus on functional motor competence that permits physical activity for fun and fitness in many settings, not just the acquisition of isolated skills. For example:

Goal: Jim will develop, generalize, and maintain appropriate behaviors for participation in Challenger baseball practices and games.

Objective: Jim will drop the bat and run at full speed from home plate to first base 100% of the time on five different playing fields in different locations.

Objective: On signal, Jim will run to his assigned position on the baseball diamond, assume an alert stance, and focus his eyes on the batter and then on the batted ball.

Objective: On the field, in his assigned place, Jim will run to meet an oncoming batted ground ball in the area he is supposed to cover, stoop to field the ball, and then stand and wait for directions on where to throw the ball.

These illustrative objectives indicate three different contexts for practicing running fast. Running should always be linked to a sport situation or an activity of daily living (ADL) in which running is appropriate. Physical and motor activities are not only important to improve the healthy lifestyle of individuals with autism, they can concurrently be used as an effective approach to improve behavior (Elliott et al., 1994). Numerous activities have been suggested by Cheatum and Hammond (2000) to improve motor development problems of individuals with emotional problems and PDD, including autism. Over 100 accompanying activities related to postural reactions, balance, body awareness, ocular control locomotion, fine motor, endurance, and excessive movement are provided.

Autistic Behaviors and Pedagogy

Every individual with autism has a different constellation of autistic behaviors, and this constellation changes with age and environment. *Functional behavioral assessment* of autistic behaviors should therefore be conducted in each of the environments in which the student is expected to function. Furthermore, because autistic behaviors occur on a continuum from mild to severe, the degree of each behavior should be quantified by using a 5-point rating scale.

Physical activity settings are so different from other learning environments that special care is needed in assessment, instructional design, and pedagogy. Following are behaviors that some individuals with autism display and recommendations for intervention. In most instances, the recommendations are for a behavior in the **severe range** of the continuum.

Social Interaction and Social Learning Impairments

Most individuals with autism need intense behavior management programs to learn appropriate nonverbal social behaviors (e.g., eye contact, facial expressions, body postures, gestures). Without these social skills, it is difficult for them to relate to family members, teachers, and peers. Likewise, their lack of interest in the social world means that these children seldom learn through the normal processes of imitation and listening to instructions or advice. Many children with autism appear to be **functionally deaf,** in that they do not seem to hear noises or speech. The only way to get their attention is through firmly taking hold of one or both shoulders. **Firm pressure** is better than light touch because many children are tactile defensive to light touch stimuli.

Most behavior management programs require that the teacher insist on eye contact during one-to-one interactions. This usually means physically holding the child's head in a position opposite one's own head (usually with one hand under her or his chin), giving a specific prompt, "Look at me," and providing a reinforcer for the correct response. Often, in the early stages of learning, the reinforcer must be held up at eye level.

Impairment in social interaction is also manifested by a lack of awareness of appropriate behavior in a gymnasium. Instead of listening to instructions or watching others for cues about what to do and where to go, the child with autism often wanders aimlessly from space to space until taught a particular **floor spot,** which serves as her or his personal space at the beginning of each class and at designated times during class when the teacher calls out, "Floor Spots." Some physical educators have even used automobile tires to provide more physical feedback on a home spot. Because the child's social learning skills are weak, the teacher must provide specific rules that encourage cognition about what to do in different situations. These rules need to be posted in both pictorial and written word formats. Some teachers have incorporated the rules into a rhyme that is said during warm-up activities.

Traditional punishments like time-outs are seldom effective because the child with autism prefers to be alone. Options would be overcorrection or response cost. The emphasis therefore must be on reinforcers that are personally meaningful enough to motivate compliance with the teacher's requests. Food is used more often as a reinforcer with children with

Figure 22.8 Partners must be carefully trained before they are assigned to work with a child with autism. Emphasis must be on helping, not competing.

autism than with other children because social reinforcers tend not to be effective.

After children develop beginning social interaction skills, the content in Chapter 9 should be used to guide physical education instruction. Partners or buddies are extremely important, but such individuals need careful training to understand their partner's social interaction impairments (see Figure 22.8).

Language and Speech Impairments

About 50% of children with autism do not talk. Many were using words before the onset of autism. Loss of language and failure to learn to speak are major features of autism that are addressed immediately upon diagnosis by regular, intensive speech therapy. With help, about 50% of children with autism slowly learn to talk and use language more or less appropriately. Many, however, use stereotyped and repetitive phrases. Problems of echolalia and pronoun reversal are common. **Echolalia** (echoing) is involuntary repetition of words spoken by others. **Pronominal reversal** is generally avoidance of "I" by saying "you." For example, the teacher might say, "Do you want to jump on the trampoline?" The person with pronoun reversal would answer, "You want to jump," meaning "I want to jump." The avoidance of "I" is either a denial of selfhood or an absence of awareness of self, while the substitution of "you" shows some awareness of others. In the gymnasium setting, teachers should follow the child's behavior management plan for re-

sponding to inappropriate language. Many different approaches are used. Some ignore inappropriate speech, some repeat the phrase correctly, and some use specific extinction procedures. For some, the most effective means to communicate will be signing or a communication board. Physical educators must work closely with classroom teachers to ensure the most effective communication system is used.

Among higher-functioning people with autism, communication idiosyncrasies like the "Who's on first?" scenario in *Rain Man* are common. Speech is often used essentially to talk to oneself, not to others. Individuals with Asperger's disorder have no language problems per se, but their social interaction impairment affects their ability to initiate and sustain meaningful conversations with others. Videotapes that depict physical education or sport incidents with appropriate verbal exchanges give these children models to study and follow. Role-playing is also recommended (see Chapter 9).

Difficulty Thinking in Words and Responding Appropriately

Many individuals with autism have difficulty processing auditory input. They are visual thinkers. Grandin (1995), for instance, states that pictures are her first language and words are her second language. Grandin translates both spoken and written words into full-color movies, complete with sound, that run like a videotape in her head. Words representing concrete concepts are easier to translate than words representing abstract concepts. Physical educators should teach to a person's preferred modality (see Chapter 20) and use visualization skills like Grandin's as strengths to help master content. For a visual thinker, demonstrations are more helpful than verbal directions.

Motor Planning and Executive Control Problems

Research indicates that motor planning, sequencing, and other aspects of executive control (i.e., central processing) are weak in individuals with autism (Hughes, 1996; Pennington & Ozonoff, 1996). In particular, **verbal working memory** seems limited. This means that teachers should match length and duration of verbal instructions to individual capabilities. Temple Grandin points out that she can remember only three steps at a time. She has difficulty remembering phone numbers and other things that she cannot translate into mental pictures.

Pedagogy for executive control problems depends, of course, on the severity of autism. In physical education, **memory games** should be used that involve imitating the teacher's movement and receiving reinforcement. Instruction should begin with imitating single movements and progress to imitating increasingly longer sequences of movement. Early childhood singing games (e.g., *Hokey-Pokey, Mulberry Bush*) provide good structure for memory games; some children with autism seem to respond better when words and sentences are sung to them (Grandin, 1995). Chants that teachers make up to teach a particular concept are helpful also, when used over and over. The chants should be simple, and the child should be encouraged to join the teacher in saying the chant. In small-group instruction, this practice is implemented through choral responding (Kamps, Dugan, Leonard, & Daoust, 1994). Imitation

Figure 22.9 A climbing apparatus is often used to teach memory of sequences (e.g., crawl through hoop, then arm-walk across ladder, then go to X-point and stand, then climb to top). Some children can practice two-part sequences while others practice three- or four-part sequences.

and choral responding activities help to remediate social interaction problems.

Self-talk, verbal rehearsal, and visualization activities are also recommended for remediation of executive control problems. **Self-talk,** out loud or silent, is a means of cueing oneself through a sequence of tasks or movements. Self-talk occurs during the movement. In contrast, **verbal rehearsal** is saying aloud the parts of a planned movement before execution. **Visualization** is making the mind see pictures of a planned movement before execution. The teacher should routinely cue children to remember to use these strategies. Figure 22.9 shows children performing a sequence on a climbing apparatus.

Unusual Responses to Sensory Input, Including Stimming

Individuals with autism respond in unusual or bizarre ways to input from one or more sense modalities: sight, hearing, touch, smell, taste, pain, kinesthetic, vestibular. Sometimes the children appear unaware of stimuli (e.g., functionally deaf or blind), but more often their responses are exaggerated. High-pitched, shrill noises that are mildly unpleasant for ordinary people are extremely painful to some children with autism and thus result in anxiety, fear, and anger reactions, such as screaming, crying, or rocking with their hands over their ears. Even the soft buzz of fluorescent lights can cause problems. In some instances, activities are conducted on carpeted floors to decrease irritating

noise. Teachers can remove many distractions by closing doors and replacing lights that flicker or hum. Sounds that should be minimized in physical education settings are school bells, whistles, PA systems, buzzers on scoreboards, chairs or objects scraping on the floor, and echos. Mainstream physical education with large classes and noisy activities are contraindicated for children with catastrophic responses to certain sounds.

Children with extreme sound sensitivity respond better to individuals who talk in quiet tones or whispers. Whereas increasing the loudness of one's voice to impose discipline or emphasize a point is effective with ordinary children, teachers should decrease the loudness of their speech to a whisper when exerting control over a child with sound sensitivity problems.

Visual stimuli like bright colors and moving objects seem to excessively stimulate some children with autism. The stimulations sometimes are serious distractions that prevent attending to the lesson; more often they cause stereotyped behaviors (stimming) like extended gazing or twirling, spinning, or tapping stimming behaviors. The extreme pleasure derived from certain visual stimuli and concurrent body response to stimming is similar to what many people feel during sexual orgasm, except that the pleasure seems to continue for hours or until the child is stopped from stimming. Stopping a child from stimming usually results in screaming, so behavior management protocols for each type of stimming should be written into the

IEP and IFSP and followed. Sometimes self-stimulation behaviors are targeted for elimination, and other times they are modified into acceptable behaviors. A child who stands and rocks, for instance, can be taught to use a rocking chair.

Vigorous aerobic exercise on a motorized treadmill is sometimes effective in preventing stereotypic and hyperactive behaviors (Elliott et al., 1994; Grandin, 1995). More research is needed on the prevention of stereotypic behaviors and the duration of time that such behaviors can be prevented by various forms of aerobic exercise.

Help with organizing and synthesizing excessive visual input is also effective in minimizing undesirable behaviors. Some ideas for this are (a) use charts with pictures and/or color coding to clarify the physical education class routine, including direction of movement from station to station and proper use of equipment; (b) post lists of things to do and things to take home; (c) provide personal reminder lists that can attach by velcro on specially made shirts or pinnies; and (d) use colored tape on floors and walls to designate personal space, targets, and floor patterns like circles and lines.

Many children with autism dislike being hugged. Grandin (1995, p. 62) describes her dislike of hugging as follows: "I wanted to experience the good feeling of being hugged, but it was just too overwhelming. It was like an all-engulfing tidal wave of stimulation. . . . I was overloaded and would have to escape, often by jerking away suddenly." Children who react negatively to hugging and other forms of physical contact are not expressing dislike for the persons who are trying to show affection. Research indicates that children with autism do develop attachment behaviors, but they demonstrate these differently than other children do (Dissanayake & Crossley, 1996). **Sensorimotor integration** techniques (see Chapter 10) are recommended for children who are **tactile defensive.**

Pathological Resistance to Change

Pathological resistance to change is another manifestation of bizarre responses. Emotional outbursts are common when sameness of environment is threatened. Persons with autism want to do the same things every day in precisely the same way. To start a student on a new activity or to make a transition from one activity to another, a hierarchy of prompts is often needed in combination with reinforcements. Achievement of objectives is recorded by writing the number indicating the type of prompt needed (see Table 22.6).

Physically guiding a person with autism through a new movement pattern has traditionally been the pedagogy of choice, but comparison of verbal/visual and verbal/physical teaching models shows equivalent results (Reid, Collier, & Cauchon, 1991). Many persons with autism are **tactile defensive** and thus respond better to verbal/visual input than to verbal/physical.

Making transitions from one activity station to another is particularly difficult and is contraindicated for some students.

Adherence to the *principle of structure,* reviewed earlier in this chapter, makes classes run smoothly. The goal of this high level of structure when teaching is errorless learning. However, structure should be gradually and systematically reduced as an instructional strategy for eliminating pathologi-

Table 22.6 **A hierarchy of extrastimulus prompts and independent functions with numbers for recording student's performance level.**

1. Full physical prompt met with resistance
2. Full physical prompt
3. Partial physical prompt
4. Light touch reminder
5. Pointing prompt
6. Direct verbal prompt (e.g., "Throw the ball")—this can be words or signs
7. Indirect verbal prompt (e.g., "What do you need to do now?" or "Try again")
8. Independent function when in same setting with same teacher and same materials
9. Independent function when in same setting with different teacher and similar materials
10. Independent function when in a variety of similar settings with a variety of people and materials

cal resistance to change. **Fading,** the gradual removal of guidance through the use of a hierarchy of prompts, also serves as intervention.

Stimulus Overselectivity and Attention Problems

Abnormally limited attentional scope, often called **stimulus overselectivity** or overselective attention, is the basis of much bizarre behavior. Inability to select relevant cues and to see whole naturally results in learning problems. An example of stimulus overselectivity is discriminating between two people solely on the basis of shoe color or a piece of jewelry. Teachers should adapt for stimulus overselectivity by (a) wearing plain, simple clothing (preferably all the same color), (b) avoiding whistles hanging from lanyards and jewelry, and (c) removing all distractors from the teaching environment.

Cues (often called **prompts** in autism literature) must be matched to a student's specific assessed needs. Assessment should determine, for a particular task and setting, whether the student needs extrastimulus prompts, within-stimulus prompts, or both. **Extrastimulus prompts,** a hierarchy extending from a full physical prompt to no prompt needed across a variety of settings, are illustrated in Table 22.6. The term **within-stimulus prompts** (called "instructional stimulus enhancement" in Chapter 20) refers to increasing the stimulus appeal of instructional materials, as in creating special lighting and auditory effects or altering the size or color so that the object requiring attention stands out. Physical education research is limited but thus far supports extrastimulus prompting (Collier & Reid, 1987), whereas research on academic teaching supports within-stimulus prompts.

Summary of Teaching Suggestions

Specific teaching suggestions recommended by Connor (1990) and O'Connor, French, and Henderson (2000) include (a) teach to the preferred modality and learning styles, (b) minimize unnecessary external stimuli, (c) limit the amount of relevant stimuli

Table 22.7   Website information related to individuals with PDD

ASPEN of America	www.asperger.org/
Autism Society of America	www.autism-society.org
Center for the Study of Autism	www.autism.org/
Cure Autism Now	www.canfoundation.org/
[a]Daily Life Therapy (Higashi)	www.bostonhigashi.org
Division TEACCH	www.teacch.com
[b]Kaufman, related to Son-Rise	www.son-rise.org
International Rett Syndrome Association	www.rettsyndrome.org/
Lovaas Institute for Early Intervention	www.lovaas.org
National Autistic Society, London	www.nas.org.uk
Nat Institutes of Mental Health	www.nimh.nih.gov
N. American Riding for the Handicapped Assoc.	www.narha.org
Online Asperger Syndrome Information & Support	www.udel.edu/bkirby/asperger/

[a]Also referred to as *International Program for Individuals with Autism.*
[b]Also found under *Autism Center of America.*

presented at one time, (d) limit the use of prompts, (e) teach in a community-based gamelike environment to facilitate generalization, (f) avoid change in routines, and (g) provide a variety of activities that focus on the same goal (i.e., ensure task variation). Research by Collier and Reid (1987) does not support limiting prompts. *Reinforcement, task analysis, and physical prompting are the three keys* to motor skill improvement for most persons with autism according to Reid et al. (1991). Sensory stimulation like that provided by music, dance, and water activities is especially successful in broadening attentional scope and providing substitutes and alternatives for self-stimulations. Children with autism proceed through the same aquatic skill levels of water orientation as nondisabled peers (Killian, Joyce-Petrovich, Menna, & Arena, 1984).

Special Olympics and Community Sports

Most persons with autism are eligible for Special Olympics training and competition (see Chapter 21 on mental retardation). The estimated 80% of people with autism who have IQs under 70 can profit from the same kinds of programming as people with mental retardation. Preoccupation with sameness is a strength in fitness and sport training, and persons with autism often become models of schedule adherence and hard work.

An increasing number of Special Olympics programs are community-based and serve all ages. Involvement in these programs should be supplemented with other activities that support transition to independent use of community sport and fitness facilities.

Website Information

Table 22.7 provides website information about organizations and programs concerning autism. In particular, try the websites on programs of Kaufman, Loovas, the North Carolina TEACCH, and Higashi Daily Life Therapy.

 OPTIONAL ACTIVITIES

1. This chapter contains numerous terms to remember. In groups of four to five students, develop a crossword puzzle that includes at least 50 terms. Exchange completed puzzles with another group and complete their puzzle.

2. Below is a vignette. Write a behavior intervention plan (BIP) using the form provided in Table 22.5.

    > Jerry, a sixth-grade student who is emotionally disturbed and has an IEP, does most of the physical education class activities but he is chronically disruptive. He teases the girls; if he is mistakenly bumped during class, he will start a fight with that student; and he continually interrupts class instruction with inappropriate comments.

    Share your completed BIP in small groups. Write other vignettes and, with a partner, develop BIPs.

3. Observe an inclusive physical education class with a student who is emotionally disturbed or autistic and note the social and physical environment (i.e., formations, bulletin board, routines) that support effective performance and learning. How would you modify the environment?

4. Identify a student you are currently teaching or who you taught in the past who demonstrated chronic behavior problems. This student may or may not have an IEP that indicates a diagnosis of SED or autism. Now determine possible (a) causes, (b) prevention techniques, (c) intervention techniques with prevention techniques that may be effective, and (d) possible resources.

5. In small groups, discuss (a) problems associated with fostering learning in an inclusionary physical education environment that includes a student who has been identified as having SED or autism (consider different types of behavioral disturbances) in group-based activities and give feedback about learning and behavior in this group environment. Develop some possible workable strategies for enhancing behavior and learning. Considering the type of interventions presented in Chapter 7; are there any that you distinctly prefer? Do you reject any? Discuss your reasons for liking or disliking particular approaches.

6. How is programming alike and different for the many forms of SED and PDD. Why?

7. Find and read books like *Embracing the Monster* by V. Crawford (2002) published by Brookes. Crawford

describes her life, which is challenged by comorbidity: the co-occurrence of bipolar disorder, ADHD, and LD. Insights of a psychiatrist are woven into each chapter. Read the old, classic, still valuable *I Never Promised You a Rose Garden* by J. Greenberg; it was also produced as a videotape (1977). What insights can autobiography and biography give you? How much content is devoted to physical activity? Why? After reading a book, reflect on how physical activity programming throughout the lifespan of the person might have helped. Visualize the best kinds of activity.

8. Find films, videos, journals, and newspaper articles that focus on mental illness. These form the basis for what the general public knows and feels about mental illness. Critically think about the content of each, its accuracy, and its impact. Some recommended films are *Benny and Joon* (1993), *Mr. Jones* (1993), *As Good As It Gets* (1997), and *A Beautiful Mind* (2002).

CHAPTER

23

Wheelchair Sports and Orthopedic Impairments

Figure 23.1 Children are introduced to wheelchair sports by BlazeClubs of America in collaboration with local park and recreation agencies. (A) Child is guided by a wheelchair athlete in her first experience in a racing chair. (B) It takes the whole family to become socialized into a lifetime of wheelchair sports. (C) BlazeSports Days, which began in Georgia, is now being carried to children across America.

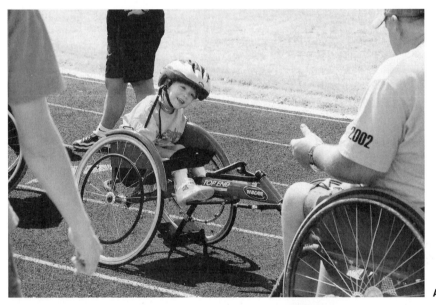

A

C

B

1. This chapter is the first of a series (23, 24, 25) that covers orthopedic impairments (OI) as defined by IDEA and encompassed by the Paralympic sport movement. Scan all three chapters and consider why the content is organized as it is. What other ways might these chapters be organized? List pros and cons for this chapter organization and engage in informal and formal debate. If you wish, send your reflections to the author (csherrill1@earthlink.net).

2. Discuss how organizations can be used as resources for instructing, coaching, and empowering children and youth. Which organizations govern which disabilities and why? Access major disability sport websites; *use your information in ways that benefit others* (e.g., bulletin boards, presentations, lesson plans, etc.). Also find and access websites of athletes who can be used as models for your students.

3. Almost all OI conditions span a continuum including (a) locomotor difficulty, (b) use of crutches, canes, or walkers, (c) use of manual wheelchairs, and (d) use of motorized (or power) chairs. Describe persons in each of these mobility categories whom you have known personally or through media and printed materials. Reflect on what these persons would be like at various ages (e.g., 6, 10, 14, 18, 30, 50, 70) and what kind of physical activity assessment and programming would enrich their lives at the selected ages.

4. Create and implement a plan for getting to know more persons with the conditions in this chapter, becoming better acquainted with different types of wheelchairs, and acquiring the habit of reading *Sports 'N Spokes*.

5. Given age, gender, lesion level, and condition, be able to write a physical education IEP and illustrative lesson plans. Include all parts of a physical education IEP.

Orthopedic impairments are so diverse that separate sport organizations have evolved to meet different needs. Because a major goal of physical education is to develop lifetime leisure sport skills, the next three chapters are organized around the clusters of disability served by major U.S. sport organizations.

The following definition of **orthopedically impaired** (OI) appears in federal legislation:

> **Orthopedically impaired** means a severe orthopedic impairment that adversely affects a child's educational performance. The term includes impairments caused by congenital anomaly (e.g., clubfoot, absence of some member, etc.), impairments caused by disease (e.g., poliomyelitis, bone tuberculosis, etc.), and impairments from other causes (e.g., cerebral palsy, amputations, and fractures or burns that cause contractures). (20 U.S.C. 1401(3) (A) and (B))

Most orthopedic impairments do not adversely affect academic classroom performance. They do, however, require adaptations for safe and successful integrated physical education. Moreover, to learn wheelchair sports, students need some instruction each year built around their specific needs (see Figure 23.1). Wheelchair sport instruction, practice, and competition should be written into the individualized education programs (IEPs) of individuals eligible to play in wheelchairs. The IEP should also address transition and integrated community recreation (Wehman, 2001).

This chapter focuses on **spinal paralysis** (spina bifida, spinal cord injuries, and poliomyelitis/postpolio syndrome). These impairments historically have been grouped together and are served respectively by two multisport organizations: Wheelchair Sports, USA (WS, USA) and Disabled Sports/USA (DS/USA).

Orthopedic impairments are so diverse that Chapters 24 and 25 also address content concerning appropriate adaptations and the specialized sport organizations that physical educators can contact for assistance. Chapter 24 focuses on people served by Disabled Sports/USA (DS/USA) and the National Disability Sports Alliance (NDSA). DS/USA is mainly associated with amputations but also governs winter sports for all disabilities. In the Paralympics, it represents a category called **les autres** (a French word meaning "the others"), interpreted as *all athletes who compete standing up or in manual wheelchairs except those with spinal paralysis, cerebral palsy (CP), and CP-related conditions.* The U.S. Les Autres Sports Association, explained in earlier editions, dissolved in 2001. Chapter 25 focuses on *athletes with CP, CP-related conditions (stroke, traumatic brain injury), and all les autres conditions that require use of a motorized chair.* The National Disability Sport Alliance (NDSA) is featured in Chapter 25.

Disability Sport Organizations and the USOC

Sport organizations are the best source of help for professionals responsible for teaching and coaching sports for persons with orthopedic disabilities. Today's laws make both general and adapted physical educators responsible. Table 23.1 summarizes the disabilities served by the main multisport disability sport organizations (DSOs) in the United States. Each of these DSOs is a member of the U.S. Olympic Committee (USOC), categorized under *Community-Based Multisport Organizations (CBOs)*, along with such predominantly AB organizations as YMCA, YWCA, Amateur Athletic Union, Girls and Boys Clubs of America, and Boy Scouts.

This reorganization in the early 2000s means that the USOC is now officially striving toward inclusion rather than dividing its services into separate AB and disability components. The ultimate goal is integration of young athletes with disabilities into CBOs and, for those athletes who become elite adult performers, inclusion in the sports programs and events conducted by the predominantly AB national governing bodies (NGBs). The goal for many elite athletes has become inclusion in the Olympics, rather than in the separate Paralympics.

Table 23.1   Orthopedic impairments served by major multisport organizations and websites.

Wheelchair Sports, USA (WS, USA) www.wsusa.org/
Spinal cord injuries
Spina bifida
Poliomyelitis and postpolio syndrome

Disabled Sports/USA (DS/USA) www.dsusa.org/
Winter sports for everyone
Summer sports for amputee and les autres
Paralympic competition for les autres

National Disability Sport Alliance (NDSA) www.ndsa.org/
Cerebral palsy
Stroke
Traumatic brain injury
Any condition that necessitates motorized chairs
   Muscular dystrophies
   Arthritis
   Multiple sclerosis
   Arthrogryposis
   Osteogenesis imperfecta
   Muscle weakness conditions
   Burns
   Nonparalytic skeletal disorders
      Congenital disorders (e.g., clubfoot)
      Acquired disorders (e.g., hip degeneration)

Dwarf Athletic Association of America www.daaa.org/
Achondroplasia
Other short stature syndromes

Note 1. Prior to 1991, sports for persons with amputations were governed by the U.S. Amputee Athletic Association. This organization dissolved in 1990.
Note 2. Prior to 2001, persons now served by NDSA were served by the U.S. Cerebral Palsy Athletic Association and the U.S. Les Autres Sports Association.

However, inclusion is a difficult challenge and mostly conceptualized as a long range goal in the sports world.

The USOC employs a full-time executive director of U.S. Paralympics, Charlie Huebner, to help DSOs to (a) achieve both their short- and long-term goals and (b) send a strong, unified USA team to summer and winter Paralympics and related world-level competitions. *Palaestra* honors Huebner as one of its departmental editors (see USP Forum) and provides DSO news, including a comprehensive calendar of events. To contact Huebner, use charlie.huebner@usoc.org. To receive a complimentary subscription to *Olympic Coach E-Magazine,* go to coaching.usolympicteam.com/coaching/ksub.nsf.

DSOs and the Paralympics

As explained in Chapter 2, each DSO is linked with an international organization that is a member of the International Paralympic Committee (IPC), serves more-or-less the same target population as in its home country, and helps to govern the summer and winter Paralympic Games. These games are held at the same site and in the same month as the Olympic Games. *Paralympics participation is for adults only, but Paralympics awareness and spectatorship are important for all age groups.* The Paralympics are inspirational, just as the Olympics are, and provide numerous role models for persons not yet old enough or skilled enough to be Paralympians. Paralympics, like the Olympics, encourage researchers to study elite performance. A *Paralympic Scientific Congress* to share research findings is usually held a few weeks before the Games. This, like other aspects of the Paralympics (e.g., opening and closing ceremonies) is modeled after the Olympics. The Paralympics are important also because most of the game rules and sport classifications that DSOs follow are established by the IPC.

As in any power structure, politics are the medium through which members show support for existing policies and sport rules or strive to create change. IPC is governed by delegates representing specific disability categories and by delegates representing countries. It is important for professionals to learn policies and acquire background concerning how the policies evolved. International policies trickle down to affect national, state, and local policies.

Competition for Children and Adolescents

Opportunities for competitive experience equal to that of AB peers are increasingly available for children ages 5 to 15. Athletes, age 16 and above, usually compete as adults. Skills are learned at sport camps and at seasonal practices and games sponsored by many groups (e.g., DSOs, municipal parks and recreation departments, and service organizations like the Kiwanis and Lions). New children's organizations like BlazeSports Clubs of America (see www.blazesports.com), made possible by the U.S. Disabled Athletes Fund (USDAF), are making tremendous impact.

The National Federation of State High Schools (NFHS) is receiving considerable encouragement to begin including students with disabilities in state meets with AB peers and to ensure that both groups receive comparable recognition and awards for their sport experiences (Hansen & Fuller, 2003). Some states like Minnesota, Georgia, and Illinois have begun statewide adapted athletics and adapted sports clubs to promote school-based sports programs similar to those of AB peers. Georgia's American Association of Adapted Sports (AAASP), developed in conjunction with the 1996 Paralympic Games, is receiving support to become a national model (Nash, 2002).

Mental Function and Wheelchair Sports

The term **wheelchair sports** should be preceded by WS, USA, NDSA, or DS/USA to denote the population served. These organizations limit their sports to persons with average or better intellectual functioning. Special Olympics offers wheelchair activities for persons with cognitive disabilities. The widespread association of the word *special* with mental retardation makes this word unacceptable to most persons with other disabilities. Terminology like *Special Physical Education* or *Special Events Day* should therefore be avoided.

Anatomy of Spinal Paralysis

Spinal paralysis is a broad term for conditions caused by injury or disease to the spinal cord and/or spinal nerves. Paralysis can be **complete** (total) or **incomplete** (partial). **Paresis** is muscle weakness in incomplete paralysis.

Spinal paralysis involves both the central and autonomic nervous systems. The **central nervous system** (spinal cord and nerves) governs movement and sensation. The **autonomic nervous system** governs vital functions like heart rate, blood pressure, temperature control, and bladder, bowel, and sexual activity.

Figure 23.2 shows how 31 pairs of spinal nerves issue from segments of the spinal cord and exit from the spinal column. The nerves are named, not for the segment of the cord they come from, but for their associated vertebrae. The exception is the eighth cervical nerve (C8); there are only seven cervical vertebrae.

Nerves are specified by stating region first (cervical, thoracic, lumbar, sacral) and number second. Thus, Figure 23.2 shows that the diaphragm (muscle that enables breathing) is innervated by C3 to C5, the upper arm is innervated by C5 to C8, and so on. Persons with spinal paralysis typically know their lesion level(s)—for example, C5/6 or T12/L1.

Physical activity personnel should be familiar with the body parts innervated by various nerve groups. In general, cervical nerve dysfunction affects arm and hand movements and breathing. Thoracic nerve dysfunction affects ability to (a) maintain balance in a sitting position and (b) breathe forcefully in aerobic endurance activities that cause respiratory distress. Lumbar nerve dysfunction affects leg and foot movements. Sacral nerve dysfunction affects bladder, bowel, and sexual function.

Severity of Condition

Severity of spinal paralysis depends on (a) the level of the lesion and (b) whether it is complete or incomplete. The higher the lesion, the more loss of function. *Quadriplegia* and *paraplegia* are terms used in many medical conditions to indicate level of severity.

Quadriplegia (also called tetraplegia) means involvement of all four limbs and the trunk. About half of the persons with quadriplegia have **incomplete lesions,** meaning that they are able to walk. The disability caused by incomplete lesions is difficult to predict. Schack (1991) presents an excellent case study of a college-age male with an incomplete C1/2 lesion who is ambulatory and jogs. **High-level quads** are those with complete C1 to C4 lesions. These persons are dependent upon motorized chairs for ambulation and sport. C1 to C4 quads and some C5 quads are encouraged to affiliate with the NDSA. Persons with complete lesions at C3 and above cannot breathe independently and must carry portable oxygen tanks. **Low-level quads** are those with complete C5 to C8 lesions. They use manual chairs and participate in many wheelchair sports (e.g., tennis, basketball, and quad rugby).

Paraplegia means involvement of the legs but often includes trunk balance as well. *Para-* comes from the Latin *par,* meaning "equal" or "a pair." For sport programming, **trunk balance** is the most useful criterion in determining level of severity. Persons with complete T1 to T6 lesions have no useful sitting balance and must be strapped in their chairs. A complete T7 to L1 lesion allows some useful sitting balance, whereas from L2 on there is normal trunk control. Persons with low-

Figure 23.2 Thirty-one pairs of spinal nerves issue from the spinal cord and innervate groups of muscles as shown. (C = Cervical; T = Thoracic; L = Lumbar; Coc. 1 = Coccyx 1.)

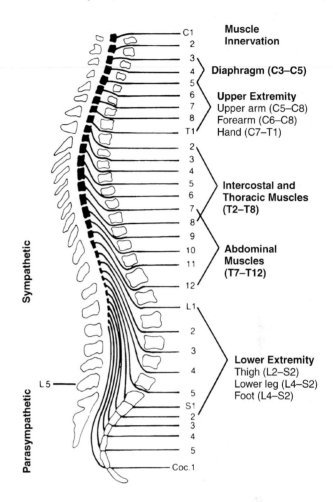

level lesions can walk without assistance (except for braces) but are still classified as paraplegics.

Walking Potential

Many persons judge severity of disability in terms of walking potential. Four classifications, *based on complete lesions,* are used:

T2 and above—Nonambulators

T3 to T11—Walking used only as therapy

T12 to L1—Household ambulators

L2 and below—Community ambulators

A **community ambulator** is defined as someone who can walk 1,000 yd nonstop, ascend and descend stairs, and function independently, with or without braces, in activities of daily living (ADL).

Except for persons with very low lesions, walking requires braces. T3 to T11 ambulators primarily use parallel bars for walking exercise; they wear long leg braces, and persons with the lower lesions can take a few steps with crutches. Most household ambulators wear long leg braces and use crutches. In contrast, community ambulators usually have knee joint control (the quadriceps work) and wear only short leg braces. Persons with ankle joint control (the tibialis anterior and posterior work) may or may not use short leg braces.

Regardless of ambulation classification, people with spinal paralysis are not able to engage in integrated competitive sports safely and successfully from a standing position. This is why the WS, USA promotes only wheelchair sports. Community ambulators may be able to perform some of the skills and exercises in an integrated class (i.e., upper extremity activities) but require adaptations and support services for full integration.

Functional Electrical Stimulation

Technological advances offer the promise of more people walking in the future, but electrically stimulated walking ability is not likely to affect sport potential. **Functional electrical stimulation** (FES) is the computerized application of electrical current to paralyzed muscles to enhance functions like walking, stationary cycling, and hand control. FES machines can be used in physical therapy settings or purchased for home use. This rehabilitation modality, however, continues to be quite expensive. FES is heralded as rebuilding paralyzed muscles, providing neuromuscular reeducation, and helping regain functions like bladder control, hand use, and walking (Petrofsky, Brown, & Cerrel-Bazo, 1992).

Transfers and Rotator Cuff Injuries

Transfers is the generic term for how persons in wheelchairs or on crutches move from one position to another. Ability to transfer back and forth between chair, bed, toilet, automobile, swimming pool, and the like obviously influences capacity for independent living. Transfers are largely dependent on arm and shoulder strength and trunk control. They are categorized broadly as independent and assisted. *Persons with complete lesions above C6 typically need assistance.* **C6 function** (having almost all shoulder movement, elbow flexion, and wrist extension) makes many independent transfers possible.

Efficient transfers are facilitated by weight management and disciplined development of residual muscle ability. Persons who need assistance with transfers are vulnerable to injury when unskilled persons try to help. Particularly at risk are the **four rotator cuff muscles** that stabilize the shoulder joint. These are known by the acronym SITS, referring to the first letter of each muscle (supraspinatus, infraspinatus, teres minor, and subscapularis). The SITS muscles are often injured when persons are lifted by their arms, as in downward transfers to a mat or swimming pool. Learning correct ways to assist is usually a part of orientation or on-the-job in-service. The best approach is always to ask people if they want help. If they say yes, then ask for a description of how to provide it.

Congenital and Acquired Paralysis

Time of onset, of course, is an important factor in physical activity programming. Two types of spinal paralysis—congenital and acquired—have vastly different impacts on development. The child born with paralysis has life events very different from those that surround disability by accident, disease, or war in later life.

The hurt and disappointment of parents coping with a birth defect are often passed onto the child, influencing self-concept and personality development. Overprotection tends to lower self-expectation and achievement motivation. Children with congenital paralysis generally are not socialized into sport unless parents are athletes or adapted physical activity is provided early in life.

Acquired paralysis is associated more with sport success than congenital paralysis. This is because many persons with acquired disabilities have already been socialized into sport. **Age of onset** in acquired disability is extremely important in this regard. Research shows that acquired disability does not change personality and self-concept in adults (Sherrill, 1990b). Less is known about children and adolescents.

In general, physical education and recreation programming is the same for congenital and acquired conditions. *Problems to be resolved and pedagogy depend mainly on age, level of lesion, and complete or incomplete paralysis.* The sections that follow describe the three most common spinal paralysis conditions. Thereafter, the content of the chapter is applicable to each.

Spina Bifida

Spina bifida is a congenital defect of the spinal column caused by failure of the neural arch of a vertebra to properly develop and enclose the spinal cord (see Figure 23.3). This developmental anomaly occurs between the fourth and sixth week of pregnancy, when the embryo is less than an inch long. **Bifida** comes from the Latin word *bifid,* meaning "cleft" or "split into two parts." As yet, there is no understanding of why this anomaly occurs.

Gender, race, geographical location, and socioeconomic status all relate significantly to spina bifida. More girls than boys are affected. Whites have higher rates of spina bifida than other races. In Great Britain and Ireland, about 4 of every 1,000 newborns have spina bifida. In the United States, the incidence is 1 to 2 per 1,000 (about 11,000 newborns each year). Poverty is associated with many of these births, but not all. Families with one child with spina bifida have a 1 in 20 (5%) risk of reoccurrence in subsequent births.

Next to cerebral palsy, spina bifida is the cause of more orthopedic defects in school-age children than any other condition. The survival rate of spina bifida is now about 90% with aggressive treatment. Corrective surgery is generally undertaken within 24 hr of birth, although some physicians prefer to wait 9 or 10 days.

Types of Spina Bifida

From most to least severe, the types of spina bifida are (a) meningomyelocele, (b) meningocele, and (c) occulta (see Figure 23.4). **Meningomyelocele** (often shortened to MM) is by far the most common, and incidence rates (1 to 2 in 1,000) typically refer to it. The derivation of this word is *meningo-* (referring to membrane or covering of spinal cord), *myelo* (denoting involvement of the cord), and *cele* (meaning "tumor"). Figure 23.4 shows how the spinal cord and nerve roots exit through a vertebral cleft and fill a tumorous sac in MM. In **meningocele,** only the spinal cord covering (meninges) pooches out into the sac; the cord and nerves are not displaced. In both conditions, the spinal cord fluid leaks into the sac. Both must be corrected by surgery.

Occulta is so named because the condition is concealed under the skin. The occult, as in magic, astrology, and the supernatural, is hidden or secret. The occulta condition does not cause paralysis or muscle weakness, although it is associated with adult back problems. On some people, a tuft of hair, birthmark, or dimple mark the occulta, but most are not diagnosed unless X rays are taken for other problems.

Nonprogressive Condition

Spina bifida is nonprogressive—that is, it remains the same, never becoming worse. As explained in the section "Anatomy of Spinal Paralysis," the higher the location of MM on the spinal column, the more nerves are affected. Most MM occurs from T12 downward.

As with other types of paralysis, there is no cure. After surgery, MM is managed by passive range-of-motion (ROM) exercises done twice daily by family until the child learns to creep/crawl and engages in enough activity that ROM therapy is not needed. Also important in infancy and early childhood is lots of handling and activity in the prone, side, and upright positions. The emphasis is on establishing **equilibrium reactions** and normalizing, as much as possible, visual and other kinds of input. This is to counteract the tendency of caregivers to leave babies in supine.

Figure 23.3 (*A*) Parts of a single vertebra viewed from the top. (*B*) Spina bifida in a newborn infant.

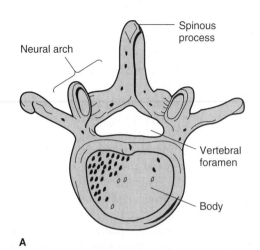

A

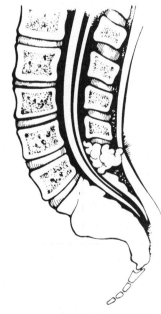

B

Figure 23.4 Three types of spina bifida.

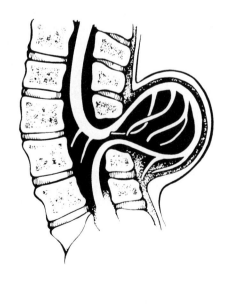

Meningomyelocele

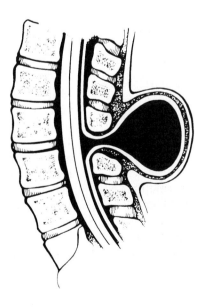

Meningocele

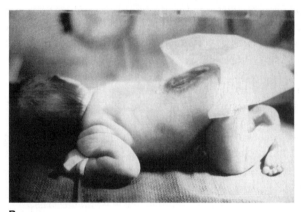

Spina bifida occulta

Developmental Activities

Development of head, trunk, shoulder, arm, and hand control is obviously important for persons with spina bifida. Pushing, pulling, and lifting with the arms are major goals because upper extremity strength must compensate for leg paralysis. Push-and-pull toys, scooterboards, parachute and towel activities, apparatus climbing and hanging, and weight lifting are high priority (see Figure 23.5).

Orthotics (splinting and bracing) is begun in infancy to facilitate upright positioning as close to that of peers as possible. Brief periods of supported standing from infancy onward aid blood circulation and other functions. Many preambulation devices help children learn to stand and walk at about the same age as peers. Crutches are introduced as early as age 2 or 3. See Chapter 11 for different kinds of crutchwalking and gaits. Whereas physical therapists focus on walking, physical educators teach play and game skills, creative expression, and fitness.

Assessment of nonlocomotor movement capabilities lends insight into program planning. The following are questions to guide movement exploration and can be used in general physical education for all children. They can lead to games on land and in the water.

1. What body parts can you bend and straighten? What *combination* of body parts can you bend and straighten? What body parts can you swing?

2. What body parts can you stretch? In which directions can you stretch?

3. What body parts can you twist? What *combination* of body parts can you twist? Can you twist at different rates of speed? Can you combine twists with other basic movements?

4. What body parts can you circle? What *combination* of body parts can you circle?

5. Can you rock forward in the wheelchair and bend over to recover an object on the floor? If lying or curled up on a mat, can you rock backward and forward? Can this rocking movement provide impetus for changing positions? For instance, when sitting on a mat, can you rock over to a four-point creeping position?

6. Do you have enough arm strength to lift and replace the body in the wheelchair in a bouncing action? Can you relax and bounce on a mattress, a trampoline, or a moon walk?

7. What body parts can you shake? What combination of body parts? Can you shake rhythm instruments?

8. Can you sway from side to side? Can you sway back and forth while hanging onto a rope or maintaining contact with a piece of apparatus?

9. Can you push objects away from the body? Do you play games based on pushing skills, like box hockey and shuffleboard? Can you maneuver a scooterboard? A tricycle? A wagon? Can you walk while holding onto or pushing a wheelchair? Can you push off from the side of the swimming pool? Can some part of your body push off from a mat?

Figure 23.5 Scooterboard activities offer young children with spina bifida easy mobility while building arm and shoulder strength.

10. Can you pull objects toward yourself? In which directions can you pull? Can you use a hand-over-hand motion to pull yourself along a rope, bar, or ladder? Can you manipulate weighted pulleys?

11. Can you change levels? For instance, can you move from a lying position to a sitting, squatting, or kneeling position or vice versa? How do you get from a bed, sofa, chair, or toilet to the wheelchair and vice versa?

12. Can you demonstrate safe techniques for falling? When you lose balance, in which direction do you usually fall?

Table 23.2 reviews ambulation goals for persons with spina bifida. Most children with high-level lesions are fitted with wheelchairs before age 5 because long leg braces are too cumbersome for easy walking. Thus, physical education emphasizes wheelchair games and sports and activities performed in sitting or lying positions. Most of these can be done in an integrated setting. Swimming is particularly good, although some persons are hesitant about exposing withered limbs.

Latex Sensitivity

Many individuals with spina bifida have allergic reaction to latex rubber and to powder, food, and other objects that have been in contact with latex (Porter, Haynie, Bierle, Caldwell, & Palfrey, 1997). In severe cases, this may result in life-threatening **anaphylactic shock** (total system shutdown, mainly inability to breathe followed by unconsciousness); otherwise symptoms are the same as for any allergy (e.g., hives, watery eyes, wheezing, rash, swelling). Professionals must therefore avoid using latex items and caution parents and others against latex (e.g., balloons, rubber balls, or equipment like the Koosh ball, Therabands, adhesive tape, Band-Aids). Moreover, wheelchairs, catheters, condoms, and many other ADL objects of latex-sensitive persons must be adapted, with vinyl, silicone, or plastic substituted for rubber. The Spina Bifida Association of America provides updated lists of latex products and alternatives each year (see www.sbaa.org).

Table 23.2   Relationship among location of spina bifida, loss of muscle control, and type of ambulation.

Approximate Location of Vertebral Defect	Point Below Which Control is Lost	Prognosis for Ambulation	Equipment Used for Ambulation	WS, USA Classification
12th thoracic	Trunk	Nonambulatory	Wheelchair, standing brace	Probable Class IV
1st lumbar	Pelvis	Exercise ambulation	Wheelchair, long leg braces, and crutches	
3rd lumbar	Hip	Household ambulation	Long leg braces and crutches	Probable Class V
5th lumbar	Knee	Community ambulation	Short leg braces and crutches	

Note. Table supplied by Dennis Brunt, who has his doctoral degree in adapted physical education and is certified also in physical therapy. (WS, USA = Wheelchair Sports, USA.)

Hydrocephalus

Approximately 90% of infants with MM have **hydrocephalus** (increased cerebrospinal fluid in ventricles of brain). About 25% are born with this condition, and the rest develop it shortly after surgery for spina bifida. Closure of the spinal lesion means that there is no longer an outlet for excessive fluid, which subsequently backs up in the ventricles and causes intracranial pressure and increased head circumference.

Hydrocephalus is surgically relieved by a shunting procedure (see Figure 23.6). **Shunts** (also called tubes or catheters) sometimes become clogged or malfunction and must be replaced. Common symptoms of shunt problems are frequent headaches, vomiting, seizures, lethargy, irritability, swelling, redness along the shunt tract, and changes in personality or school performance. Persons with shunts typically have no activity restrictions except avoidance of trauma to the head (e.g., soccer heading, boxing, headstands, forward rolls). Diving is controversial. The only visible evidence of a shunt is a small scar behind the ear.

Hydrocephalus in spina bifida is associated with the **Arnold-Chiari malformation,** also called Chiari II. This is a congenital defect of the hindbrain in which the posterior cerebellum herniates downward, displacing the medulla into the cervical spinal canal and obstructing the normal flow of cerebral spinal fluid. Chiari II varies in severity and is managed by shunting. There are many causes of hydrocephalus, but in MM, the Chiari II is the most common. See www.pressenter.com/~wacma/ for additional information.

Cognitive Function and Strabismus

The IQs of most persons with spina bifida are average. However, a large percentage have perceptual-motor deficits, specific learning disabilities, and attention deficits. Content presented in Chapter 20 on learning disabilities therefore applies. **Strabismus** (cross-eyes) is relatively common and may partially explain visual perception problems. The restricted mobility lifestyle in early childhood no doubt limits spontaneous learning about space and figure-ground relationships, so sensorimotor deprivation is another explanation.

Cognitive function may be damaged before birth or before shunting is undertaken. In the past, complications arising from shunt-related infections caused subtle brain damage, but improved medical technology is reducing this problem.

Posture and Orthopedic Concerns

Paralysis causes an imbalance between muscle groups that further complicates the orthopedic problems of growing children. Incorrect positioning and/or inadequate splinting and bracing create additional defects. For example, **plantar flexion deformities** often occur because, without movement, the ankle joint freezes in the toes-pointed-downward position. This makes fitting shoes and braces difficult. In high lumbar paralysis, the hip flexors and abductors are normal, but the extensors and abductors are weak or paralyzed. This imbalance often leads to **hip dislocation.** For children who can crutchwalk, hip-muscle imbalance causes **toeing inward** (pigeon toes).

Posture problems vary with lesion level. Persons with T12 to L3 involvement often develop **scoliosis.** Also, the lower extremities of these persons fail to grow properly, so legs are small and frail. In contrast, children with L4 to L5 paralysis tend to develop **hyperlordosis** as they learn to walk. Without crutches, their gait is a side-to-side **gluteus medius lurch** (see walking gaits in Chapter 11). Persons with sacral-level paralysis walk unassisted but may develop a hip-and-knee flexion **crouched gait** because of weak ankle plantar flexors.

The activities presented in Chapter 14 on postures are helpful for these conditions. In most cases, however, problems are aggressively treated by splinting, bracing, casting, and surgery. These modalities remove children from normal movement and play for weeks at a time and further explain skill, fitness, and perceptual-motor limitations associated with spina bifida. Adapted physical activity programming must be aggressive also in teaching these children to appreciate and use their motor strengths and to maintain body parts in good alignment.

Other Concerns

Persons with spina bifida have many concerns common to all forms of spinal paralysis. These include bladder and bowel function, sexuality concerns, skin lesions, and obesity, all of which are discussed later in the chapter. Problems are greater for children—especially young ones who lack cause-and-effect

Figure 23.6 Sometimes, hydrocephalus can be corrected through a surgical procedure called *shunting.* The ventriculo-peritoneal (VP) shunt involves inserting a tube into the ventricles. This tube has a one-way valve that lets fluid flow out of the brain and into another tube that is threaded just under the skin down to the abdomen, where it is reabsorbed by the blood vessels in the membranes surrounding internal organs. A less-often used procedure is to thread the tube into the heart instead of the abdomen. Children with shunts typically have no activity restrictions except avoidance of blows to the head.

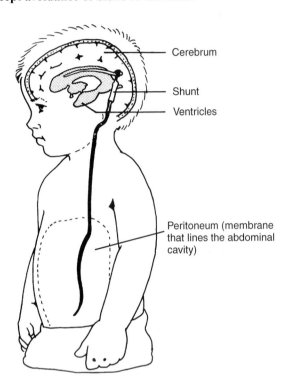

- Cerebrum
- Shunt
- Ventricles
- Peritoneum (membrane that lines the abdominal cavity)

understandings—than adults. Children, for example, often play with abandon, disregarding bruises and blows. Without sensation in the lower limbs, children with MM might not notice and report skin breakdown until serious infection sets in. Children also are more likely to be wearing splints and braces than adults, and many skin problems result from poorly fitted orthoses.

Sport and Active Lifestyle Socialization

Persons with spina bifida have the potential to become fine wheelchair athletes. They are not likely to be able to compete safely and successfully in ambulatory sports without adaptations. *Integrated physical education should be supplemented with intensive training in wheelchair sports so that lifetime leisure options are available.* A growing body of literature is available on physical education needs (Connor-Kuntz, Dummer, & Paciorek, 1995).

Models are especially important because children who frequent medical clinics and have a history of surgery and orthotics often perceive themselves as sickly and unathletic. Jean Driscoll, who won the Boston Marathon eight times, is illustrative of athletes with spina bifida who can inspire children (see

Figure 23.7). Her story and others can be found in *Palaestra* (Huber, 1996), in *Sports 'N Spokes,* and in autobiographies (e.g., Driscoll, 2000).

Spinal Cord Injuries

Spinal cord injuries (SCI) are quadriplegia and paraplegia acquired through some kind of trauma. Estimated causes of SCI are 48% motor vehicles, 21% falls, 14% violence (including war), 14% sport injuries, and 3% other. Diving causes 10 times more SCI than any other sport. Next highest in risk are football and snow skiing.

Industrialized countries report an incidence of 13 to 50 per million. Approximately 10,000 persons in the United States sustain SCI each year. About 80% are males, and most range in age between 16 and 30 years. Age of onset for about half of all SCI persons is under 25.

With improved roadside emergency service and medical technology, *incomplete lesions are increasingly the trend.* Of the estimated 200,000 to 500,000 Americans with SCI, the division between complete and incomplete lesions is about equal. Incomplete lesions, of course, are more conducive to sport success than complete lesions. This is particularly true in quadriplegia. In the sport world, these athletes are called *walking quads. The first question to be asked when programming for SCI is whether the lesion is complete or incomplete.* If incomplete, the potential is unpredictable and can be learned only by trial and error.

Most Common Injuries

The most common injury is quadriplegia—specifically, the middle lesions (C5 to C6). The individual with a C5/6 injury has little or no hand control without adaptive devices, little or no control of the triceps (elbow extensors), and almost no trunk control and mobility. Without good triceps, a person cannot effectively push a manual wheelchair. Therefore, this person is likely to use a motorized chair in ADL and in physical education and sport.

For persons with C6/7 and C7/8 lesions, a properly fitted high-back manual wheelchair permits competition in many activities, especially if the lesion is complete. Success in quad rugby is more realistic than in wheelchair basketball, where teams prefer quads with the most functional ability. Achievement depends largely on a properly designed chair and motivation. Some persons with quadriplegia have completed marathons (26.2 mi). Many play tennis (Moore & Snow, 1994). In relearning how to swim, they may initially need flotation devices but have the ability to swim independently.

The second most common site of injury is the thoracolumbar junction (T12/L1). Persons with this injury can learn all gaits and typically use Lofstrand (forearm) crutches for ADL. They can learn almost any wheelchair sport and, with special apparatus, can stand while snow skiing.

Learning About SCI

The best way to learn about SCI is to attend a wheelchair tennis or basketball game or watch wheelchair track and field and other sports (see Figure 23.8). Almost all marathons include

Figure 23.7 Jean Driscoll celebrating one of her many Boston marathon wins. Driscoll is a model for all women, but especially those with spina bifida.

some racers in wheelchairs. Films also increase awareness, particularly in regard to rehabilitation and emotional growth. Films about war veterans usually depict paraplegia, as in *Coming Home* and *Born on the Fourth of July,* both of which illustrate T11 to L2 injuries. Quadriplegia is shown in *Whose Life Is It Anyway?* (depicting an architect with a C4/5-level injury caused by an automobile accident) and *The Other Side of the Mountain* (depicting an athlete with a C5/6-level injury caused by a skiing accident). The books and plays on which these films are based, as well as many excellent autobiographies, also may be read. Especially recommended are those of Brooklyn Dodger Roy Campanella (1959) and marathoner Rick Hansen (Hansen & Taylor, 1987).

Adapted Physical Activity for Individuals With SCI

Physical activity for individuals with SCI generally centers on strengthening and using the upper extremities and on developing sport skills. Concurrently, the person must learn to use and care for a wheelchair. The best approach with a school-age person is to introduce him or her to models who are wheelchair athletes and to affiliate the individual with a team. These persons also should be instructed in upper extremity activities that can be done in an integrated setting.

Students with SCI should be *asked* what they can do and encouraged to help plan their own physical education and recreation activities. Most important is motivation, optimal involvement with peers, and group problem solving about architectural barriers and transportation. Their problems are similar to those of other wheelchair users: a tendency for the hip, knee, and ankle flexors to become too tight, with resulting **contractures** (abnormal shortening of muscles) from extended

sitting; **ulcers or pressure sores** from remaining in one position too long; bruises and friction burns from rubbing body parts that lack sensation and give no pain warnings; and tendency toward obesity because of low energy expenditure.

Poliomyelitis and Postpolio Syndrome

Poliomyelitis (polio) is a viral infection that causes quadriplegia or paraplegia. The name is derived from the part of the spine attacked by the virus. *Polio* means "gray," referring to the color of the nerve cell bodies it attacks. *Myelitis* indicates infection of the protective covering around the nerve fibers. Specifically, the polio virus destroys only motor nerve cells, which are found in the anterior part of the spinal cord and in the brain. Polio is similar to SCI and spina bifida in that muscles are paralyzed. It is different in that sensation is intact because the virus does not attack sensory nerve fibers. For this reason, athletes with polio are often perceived to have an advantage when playing wheelchair sports.

Polio epidemics from 1915 through the 1950s left thousands paralyzed. Degree of disability varied according to whether the medulla or upper or lower spinal cord was affected. There are three types of polio virus: bulbar, spinal, and bulbarspinal. The bulbar types affected the breathing centers in the medulla, leaving survivors dependent upon iron lungs (now technically improved and called **ventilators**) for respiration. Today, in industrial countries, polio is almost entirely eradicated. In Third World countries, however, it continues to cause paralysis. Worldwide, about 5 million new cases appear each year.

In the United States, there are approximately 300,000 polio survivors with some degree of disability. In the 1980s, about 25% of these persons began to experience new joint and

Figure 23.8 Attending wheelchair tennis tournaments is a good way to learn about spinal cord injury and other orthopedic impairments.

muscle pain, muscle weakness at old and new sites, severe fatigue, profound sensitivity to cold, and new respiratory problems. This combination of symptoms was named the **postpolio syndrome.** Its cause is not yet understood. The postpolio weakness progresses very slowly over many years, requiring gradual lifestyle adjustments.

Franklin D. Roosevelt, U.S. president from 1932 to 1945, is the most famous person to have had polio. Paralyzed early in his political career, Roosevelt could stand and walk only with long leg braces and crutches. Many persons with disabilities visit Roosevelt's statue in Washington DC (see Figure 23.9). Until the 1950s, polio was the leading cause of orthopedic impairments in the United States.

Activity adaptations for polio are similar to those of other types of spinal paralysis. However, paralysis is often incomplete, and judging level of lesion is difficult. Because people with polio have sensation, pain is a concern. Muscle and joint pain are particularly aggravated by cold temperature and excessive exercise. **Overuse syndrome** is pain and muscle weakness associated with diminished function after strenuous use.

Ten Common Concerns in Paralysis

Concerns common to all types of spinal paralysis include (a) sensation and skin breakdown, (b) temperature control, (c) contractures and injury prevention, (d) spasms, (e) atrophy of limbs, (f) urination and defecation, (g) sexuality, (h) heart and circulatory function, (i) blood pressure and autonomic dysreflexia, and (j) weight management and osteoporosis. The exception to this generalization is polio, which affects only motor nerve fibers and leaves sensation intact. In polio, *paralysis is usually incomplete,* and no assumptions should be made. Polio does not impair genitourinary function, so all body elimination processes and sexual activity are unaffected. Each of these concerns has implications for physical activity programming.

Sensation and Skin Breakdown

Feelings of touch, pressure, heat, cold, and pain are impaired by spinal cord lesions. In complete lesions, all sensation below the injury is lost. In incomplete lesions, there is no rhyme nor reason to the pattern. **Spinal nerve dermatomes** are used to enable persons to point to areas of lost sensation or pain (see Figure 23.10). Whereas movement is innervated by impulses that travel the anterior part of the spinal cord, sensation is innervated by impulses that travel the posterior part of the spinal cord.

A person can have motor paralysis and no loss of sensation or vice versa. Usually, however, both are present. The exception is polio. Figure 23.10 shows which nerves innervate sensation of different body segments. Touch, pressure (light and deep), heat, cold, and pain each have different sensory receptors and their own specific tracts in the spinal cord. It is therefore possible to lose some sensations but not others.

Inability to feel sensation makes persons particularly vulnerable to injury and skin breakdown. Wrinkles in socks and poorly fitted shoes or braces cause blisters that become infected. Scooting across the floor on buttocks (ambulation often used in informal settings) and crawling/creeping may cause scuff burns and bruises that go undetected. Lack of cleanliness in relation to urination, defecation, and menstruation causes itching in able-bodied (AB) persons but, when itching cannot be felt, rashes and infection result.

Persons with spinal paralysis should be taught to inspect their body parts regularly to see that all sores, however minor, are cared for. Skin should be kept dry also, with care given to remove perspiration after heavy exercise and to towel properly after swimming and bathing. Circulation problems related to paralysis increase the danger of infection and make healing slow. Infection can cause severe problems (see the section on autonomic dysreflexia later in the chapter).

Of particular concern are pressure sores caused by sitting or lying in one position for a long time. **Pressure sores** (also called *decubitus ulcers* or *ischemic ulcers*) often result in hospitalization. They heal very slowly. To prevent pressure sores, seat cushions are used and persons are taught to frequently change positions.

Sunburn is a special problem because persons with spinal paralysis cannot feel discomfort caused by sun on skin when there is no sensation. Clothes with long sleeves and pants are recommended.

Temperature Control

Spinal paralysis above T8 renders the body incapable of adapting to temperature changes. **Poikilothermy** is the name for the condition in which the body assumes the same temperature as the environment. To prevent poikilothermy, special attention must be given to appropriate clothing, heating, and air-conditioning. Whereas AB persons often do vigorous movements of cold body parts to warm them, paralyzed individuals cannot. Teachers must be sensitive to signs of overexposure, especially in swimming pools and during weather extremes.

Fluid intake is closely related to temperature regulation. Hot and cold drinks are recommended aids. Additionally, persons engaging in activity and/or sitting in the sun should be encouraged to drink water about every 30 min.

Contractures and Stretching

A **contracture** is a permanent shortening and tightening of a muscle or muscle group caused by spasticity, paralysis, or disuse that impairs normal range of motion (ROM). Contractures should be prevented by ROM exercises twice daily. Once a contracture occurs, the treatment is typically splinting, casting, or surgery. Among persons who spend most of their time in wheelchairs, hip, knee, and ankle flexors tend to become too tight. This is true also of AB people who sit a lot.

Stretches should slowly move the body part to the extreme of its ROM, where it is held 10 to 30 sec (Curtis, 1981). These can be done by self, family, or friends. A physical therapist usually teaches technique, after which others assume responsibility. Gentle warm-up exercises should be done before ROM stretches. Stretching is also important prior to sport and dance activity to prevent injury. The same stretches are used as in AB sports.

Spasms of Spinal Origin

Paralyzed muscles in people with lesions above L1 often jerk involuntarily. This is caused by excessive reflex activity below the lesion level. Ordinarily, reflex activity is coordinated by the brain, but in spinal paralysis, impulse transmission is impaired. The stimuli causing spasms vary by person but include sensory input (touch, hot, cold), pathology (bladder infections, skin breakdown), and menstrual period.

Spasms are frustrating and sometimes embarrassing because they draw attention and interfere with activities of daily living. Occasional spasms are good for circulation and help with retention of muscle shape. When spasms are too severe, several treatment options are available: (a) physical therapy, mainly stretching; (b) drug therapy (baclofen, dantrolene, valium, diazepine), (c) nerve blocks, and (d) surgery.

Athletes who use medication should report this to coaches. Use of drugs banned by the International Olympic Committee results in disqualification and loss of medals.

Atrophy of Limbs

Over time, paralyzed limbs decrease in size and lose the attractive shapes associated with good muscle tone. This withering is called **atrophy.** Many persons with lower limb paralysis are self-conscious about this and do not like to wear shorts and swimsuits around AB peers. Trousers should be accepted as sport and dance attire until these individuals are able to accept and appreciate the body as it is.

Persons do tend to stare at atrophied limbs unless sensitized. Prospective teachers should visit rehabilitation and sport settings to see limbs of all sizes and shapes. **Contact theory** posits that repeated contact, combined with attitudinal guidance, decreases discomfort.

Figure 23.10 Spinal nerve dermatomes, showing innervation of sensation.

CUTANEOUS DISTRIBUTION OF SPINAL NERVES

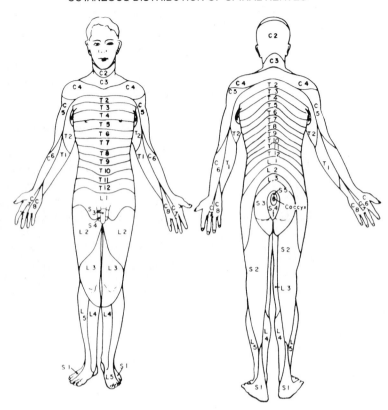

Urination, Defecation, and Latex Concerns

All persons with spinal paralysis above S2 (except those with polio) have some kind of bladder dysfunction, requiring that they urinate in a different way. The most common alternative is **intermittent catheterization,** a procedure of inserting a tube into the urethra for a few seconds and draining urine into a small, disposable plastic bag (see Figure 23.11). Intermittent catheterization is performed several times a day on a rigid schedule to keep the bladder empty and prevent accidents. Persons with incomplete lesions may feel sensation and use catheterization only in response to need. Many of these persons have hyperactive bladders and urinate more frequently than AB peers. *Holding urine is contraindicated.* Architecturally accessible restrooms should be located near activity areas and time planned for use.

In early childhood, catheterization must be done by the teacher or an aide, but later, persons learn to perform this simple, nonsterile procedure for themselves (Porter et al., 2001). Alternatives to catheterization are the **Crede maneuver** (exerting manual pressure on the lower abdomen to initiate urination), the wearing of urinary leg bags, and the use of an indwelling internal catheter (Foley) that remains inside the urethra.

Whatever the procedure, frequent emptying of the bladder is important. Retention of urine leads to **urinary and kidney infections,** a major cause of illness and death among persons with spinal paralysis. Should signs of infection (flushed face, elevated temperature) be noted, no exercise should be allowed without physician clearance. Any changes in urination frequency or in other practices related to urination should be noted.

Defecation is managed by scheduling time and amount of eating as well as by regulating time of bowel movements. If defecation becomes too great a problem, surgical procedures (**ileostomy** or **colostomy**) create an opening (**stoma**) in the abdomen. A tube inserted in this opening connects the intestine with a bag that fills up with fecal matter and must be emptied and cleaned periodically. These bags are not worn during swimming; the stoma is covered with a watertight bandage.

Latex allergies, described under spina bifida, occur occasionally in all forms of spinal paralysis. This dictates adaptation in kinds of catheters, tubes, bags, and bandage materials.

Sexuality

Sexual function is innervated by the same nerves as urinary function (S2 to S4). Lesions above the sacral region (except in polio) may make it necessary to alter roles, methods, and positions for lovemaking, depending on whether the lesions are complete or incomplete. Capacity for erection, ejaculation, and orgasm must be evaluated individually because both parasympathetic stimulation and reflex patterns are involved. Women with spinal paralysis can bear children (Krotoski et al., 1996). Menstruation is not affected.

Figure 23.11 Catheterization as a means of withdrawing urine from the bladder is used by persons with spina bifida, spinal cord injuries, and other conditions that cause urinary incontinence. The catheter is lubricated and then inserted into the penis about 6 inches or into the female opening about 3 inches. Parents can generally instruct teachers in the correct procedure.

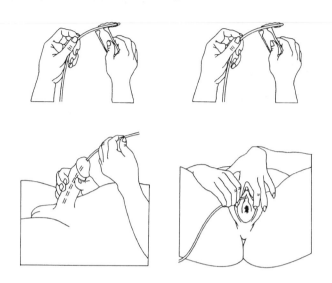

Heart and Circulatory Concerns

Persons with quadriplegia and high-level paraplegia have abnormally low resting heart rates (Shephard, 1990). This condition is called **chronotropic incompetence** or sick sinus syndrome. Likewise, their heart rate response to aerobic exercise is sluggish because of sympathetic nervous system impairment. Lesions at or above T5 affect heart rate response to arm exercise, whereas lesions at or below T10 affect cardiac responses to leg exercises.

Obviously, maximum heart rates and target zones used in aerobic exercise programs for AB persons are not appropriate in high-level spinal paralysis. Instead, baseline data are collected and individual goals set. See the Target Aerobic Movement Test of Winnick and Short (1999) explained later in this chapter.

A major circulatory problem is the pooling of blood in the veins of paralyzed body parts. This is called **venous pooling** or *venous insufficiency* and is caused mainly by sympathetic nervous system dysfunction. Specifically, the **vasoconstrictor function** is impaired, meaning that the vessels cannot constrict and force the blood through the venous valves and back to the heart. Two problems result. First, the sluggish return of blood to the heart lowers stroke volume which, in turn, limits the amount of blood available to carry oxygen to working body parts. Inadequate oxygen (also called **arterial insufficiency**) results in early fatigue and/or limited aerobic endurance. Second, venous pooling increases the cross-sectional area of the veins, creating stress on the vascular walls that is relieved by some of the fluid in the blood leaking into the surrounding tissue. This results in **edema** (swelling).

AB persons have similar problems in jobs that require motionless standing and during pregnancy. We all know the importance of shifting from foot to foot when standing for long periods. People in wheelchairs must use their arms to move paralyzed legs and/or must prop the legs up from time to time. Also recommended is the wearing of **jobst pressure garments** (sometimes called *jobsts*). Recently, many wheelchair racing clothes have been made of tight-fitting elastic fabric that presumably serves to reduce venous pooling. Excessive constriction about the abdomen and upper thighs should be avoided, however, because this is associated with the development of blood clots in the extremities.

Blood Pressure, Autonomic Dysreflexia, and Boosting

The baseline blood pressure of persons with lesions above T6 is typically low. Whereas normal blood pressure for adults is 120/90 mm Hg (millimeters of mercury), the baseline in quadriplegia may be as low as 90/60 mm Hg. Blood pressure responses to exercise (see Chapter 13) must be interpreted in light of this fact.

Autonomic dysreflexia (AD), also called *hyperreflexia,* is a life-threatening pathology that sometimes occurs in lesions above T6. The pathology is characterized by sudden-onset high blood pressure, slowed heartbeat, sweating, severe headache, and goose bumps. AD is triggered by a stimulus within the body below the lesion level, usually by a distended bladder or colon because urination or defecation needs have been ignored.

In AB persons, the need to empty an organ is relayed up the spinal cord, but in individuals with spinal paralysis, the nerve impulses are blocked. This sets off a sympathetic nervous system reflex action that causes blood vessels below the lesion level to constrict, thereby raising blood pressure. Eventually and indirectly, the brain picks up signals and activates the parasympathetic system to bring the sympathetic system under control. It does this by dilating the blood vessels and slowing the heart rate but lacks capacity to act on the high blood pressure.

This physiology is important to understand because many elite wheelchair athletes purposely induce AD states to maximize blood circulation during track and swimming events. This practice, called **boosting,** is obviously very dangerous and should be discouraged (Shephard, 2003). AD states are induced by drinking huge quantities of water before a race or by sitting on a sharp object like a tack.

Anytime a person with a lesion above T6 vomits, loses consciousness, or appears sick during or after an athletic event, AD should be suspected. Usually, the cause is simply forgetfulness or carelessness about urine needs. AD may, however, be caused by infections or irritations like pressure sores, ingrown toenails, or burns below lesion level. *First aid is essential.* First, raise the head to a 90° angle or put the person in a sitting position; this helps lower the blood pressure. Next, drain the bladder or evacuate the fecal matter. If neither bladder nor colon are full, check for other causes. Obviously, there should be no physical activity until blood pressure is normalized. Typically, a physician is consulted.

Weight Management and Osteoporosis

Sedentary lifestyles usually lead to weight problems. Nonathletic persons in wheelchairs are at particular risk. Obesity is a health threat to all of us but is more dangerous to persons whose lean muscle mass is reduced by paralysis. Consider the size difference in leg and arm muscles. AB persons use the big muscles of the lower extremities to move their fat around, whereas persons in wheelchairs and on crutches are dependent on the strength of arm and shoulder muscles. These individuals also have less oxygen available to working muscles because of venous insufficiency. For many reasons, the hearts of persons with spinal paralysis are more stressed by obesity than those of AB peers.

Sedentary lifestyles also lead to **osteoporosis,** the gradual loss of calcium in bone tissue. This makes bones more vulnerable to fracture. Obesity makes transfers more difficult and also heightens risk of fractures.

Sport Classification

Sport classification is an assessment system that (a) guides programming and (b) equalizes opportunity in competition (see Figure 23.12). Each sport has its own classification system, and there is much controversy about fairness (Curtis, 1991; Sherrill, 1999; Tweedy, 2002; Wu & Williams, 1999).

The **medical classification system,** which developed in the 1940s when competitive sports were begun in England for people with spinal paralysis, dominated worldwide until the early 1990s. The medical classification is still used in basketball by the United States (i.e., by NWBA).

A **sport-specific functional system** was adopted in the early 1990s to guide international competition. In a functional system, certified, highly trained **classifiers** observe what persons can and cannot do in a particular sport. Assignment to classes is based on a functional profile. Figure 23.12 shows classifications for the three sports most popular among people in wheelchairs. The number of functional profiles varies for each sport. For example, there are four for track, seven for field, three for basketball in the USA, and eight for international basketball. Each profile is matched with expected function when there is a *complete lesion* at a designated neurological level. Incomplete lesions naturally permit better-than-expected function.

The basketball classification systems also involve assignment of a point value to each player to equalize competing teams. The points of the five players cannot exceed 12 in NWBA play and 14 in IWBF play.

Figure 23.12 **Medical and functional classifications for wheelchair sports. NWBA refers to National Wheelchair Basketball Association. ISMWSF refers to International Stoke Mandeville Wheelchair Sports Foundation. IWBF refers to International Wheelchair Basketball Foundation.**

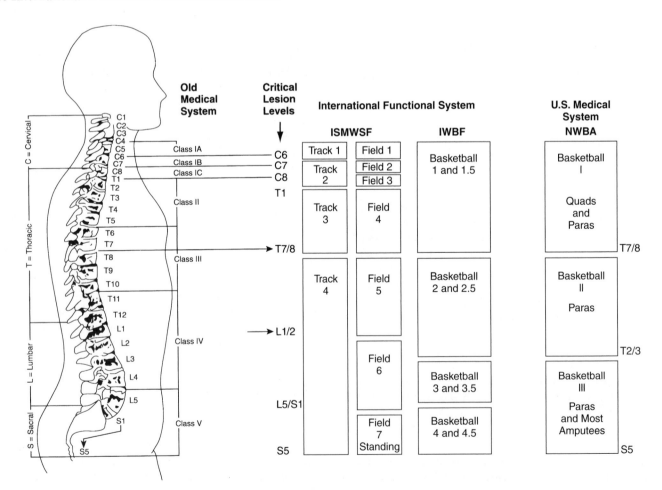

Critical Lesion Levels for Sports

Of the 31 possible lesion levels, only 8 are deemed critical for learning about sport potential. Simplified, each is associated with one or two performance criteria that describe highest function. *Progressive use of arm, hand, and finger muscles is what distinguishes between quadriplegic classes.* The critical lesion levels are

C6—Have elbow flexion and wrist extension

C7—Have triceps (i.e., elbow extension)

C8—Have some finger control

T1—Have all arm, hand, and finger movement

Progressive trunk control and balance are what distinguish between the first three paraplegic classes. The critical lesion levels are

T7/8—Have trunk rotation and fair-to-good sitting balance

L1/2—Have trunk extension from a bent-over position

L3—Have sideward bend and return capacity; trunk moves freely in all planes

L5/S1—Can throw while standing

Programming for Quadriplegia

The major difference in sport function between quadriplegia and paraplegia is sitting stability and ability to rotate the trunk to throw, catch, and dribble balls. *Individuals with complete quadriplegic lesions* seldom are given much playing time on wheelchair basketball teams because of their inability to maintain balance while rotating their trunk and difficulty in raising their arms above the head. Therefore, most athletes with quadriplegia prefer quad rugby, a team sport developed specifically to meet their needs.

Quad Rugby

Quad rugby (also called murderball and wheelchair rugby) is the team game that most persons with lesions from C6 through T1 enjoy. Played on a regulation basketball court with a four-person team and a volleyball, the game combines elements of basketball, football, and ice hockey. The object is to score points by carrying the ball over the opponents' goal line. The ball is passed from player to player and advanced down the floor by whatever movement patterns that individual abilities allow. There must be one bounce every 10 sec (Yilla & Sherrill, 1994; 1998). Quad rugby became a Paralympic sport in 2000.

Figure 23.13 shows the difficulty that people with quadriplegia have in fully extending their arms. Note also that the players use waist bands to strap themselves into their chairs and often hold on to the chair with one hand while controlling the ball or reaching with the other. Arm splints and specially designed gloves compensate for forearm and hand weakness. A classification system ensures an equitable balance between teams of players with C6, C7, and C8 lesions. See the website www.quadrugby.com.

Sports for C6, C7, and C8 Lesions

Individuals with C6 through C8 lesions can engage in all kinds of sport activities. This is because there is (a) sufficient elbow flexion to propel a manual chair and (b) enough wrist extension to enable a crude grasp. Propelling a chair with only elbow flexion is slow and awkward, but it works. The hands remain in contact with or close to the handrim. They are placed either (a) with the back of the wrist behind the handrim or (b) with the palm pushing down on top of the handrim in a forward position. Obviously, gloves are worn. Some athletes have completed marathons, but realistic distances to be conquered in a physical education class appear in Table 23.3, on page 632. The **club** is the **easiest field event** for C6 function, although some persons like the challenge of a discus.

A C7 lesion means that the triceps are intact, allowing elbow extension, a mechanically efficient way to push a chair and give impetus to field implements. Grasp and release is still a problem because there is little finger use.

C8 represents the breakthrough for throwing and striking activities. A **good fist** can be made, and the fingers can be spread. Hand and finger power is not normal but sufficient for fairly good distance with the shot, discus, and javelin. Many persons with C8 lesions enjoy wheelchair tennis.

Remember that many individuals with quadriplegia have incomplete lesions and might therefore perform above expectations. Some can walk and are called *walking quads.* Never place limits on a person.

Sports for C5 and Above Lesions

Individuals with C5 and above complete lesions lack the arm and shoulder strength to use a manual chair in sport events, so activities must be devised that can be done from a motorized chair. The National Disability Sports Alliance (NDSA) promotes sports for persons in motorized chairs. Some of the sports that NDSA makes available to such persons are boccia, indoor wheelchair soccer, track, slalom, and swimming (see Chapter 24). The **slalom,** a race against time in which persons follow an obstacle course, encourages mastery of the hand or mouth device used to guide the chair (see Chapter 15). **Personal floatation devices** (PFDs) make swimming an achievable goal; see Appendix E for companies that sell PFDs. For individuals who cannot move their limbs independently, assistants must provide therapeutic exercises that take body parts through their full range of motion one or more times a day.

Individuals with C1 to C5 lesions exhibit many individual differences. Those with complete lesions above C4 have no appreciable movement of body parts other than eyes, ears, and mouth; they can, however, play computer games with eye movements and move their motorized chairs via mouth devices. Persons with lesions at the C4 level can do head movements, and those with lesions at the C5 level can perform shoulder joint actions and weak elbow flexion. Striking games that use balloons and other lightweight objects are possible, especially when forearm braces are worn.

Breathing Concerns

Christopher Reeve, the movie star who gained fame as Superman, is the best-known person to survive a C1-C2 injury. Watching him in TV appearances lends insight into the abilities

Figure 23.13 Quad rugby, played by four-person teams with a volleyball, is an exciting contact sport in which players crash into each other's chairs and make the most of residual arm and hand function. (Photo courtesy of Mary Carol Peterson, TOP END by Action.)

Figure 23.13 Quad rugby, played by four-person teams with a volleyball, is an exciting contact sport in which players crash into each other's chairs and make the most of residual arm and hand function. (Photo courtesy of Mary Carol Peterson, TOP END by Action.)

of individuals at this level. In medical lingo, Reeve is known as a **vent-quad,** meaning he is dependent on a ventilator (also called a respirator) to breathe. The amount of air the lungs can take in with each breath influences speech. Reeve uses a **sip-and-puff tube** to control his motorized chair. Little independent movement is possible below head level, so round-the-clock medical personnel help him exercise. Reeve (2002) continues to act in and direct movies.

Assessment of Basketball Function and Skill

Beginning teachers and coaches can become familiar with sport function by administering the *Strohkendl Basketball Function Tests.* This assessment system was created in the early 1980s by Dr. Horst Strohkendl (1986) of the University of Cologne in Germany. This system led directly to functional assessment.

Test 1: Trunk Rotation and Sitting Stability

Give the following directions: "Rotate your trunk as far to the right as possible; then bounce and catch the ball. Repeat to the left." Individuals who complete this test with no balance prob-

lems are assigned to Basketball Class II (see Figures 23.12 and 23.14). Individuals with sitting stability problems are assigned to Class I.

Test 2: Chair Sit-Up, Using Abdominal Muscles Only

Give the following directions: "Clasp your hands behind your neck, and lean forward until your trunk touches your thighs. From this position, do a slow, controlled sit-up back to erect sitting position. Use only your abdominal muscles to do this sit-up." Individuals who complete this test are assigned to Basketball Class III (see Figures 23.12 and 23.13).

Test 3: Sideward Bend and Lift Ball Over Head

Give the following directions: "Place the ball to the side of your chair. Then do a sideward bend, pick up the ball with both hands, raise the ball overhead, and then place it on the floor on the opposite side of your chair." Individuals who complete this test are assigned to Basketball Class IV in the international system or are considered an advanced Class III in the USA system (see Figures 23.12 and 23.14).

Figure 23.14   The Strohkendl Basketball Function Tests for assigning player classifications.

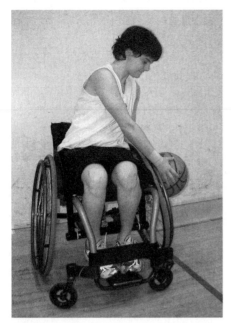

Test 1. Trunk rotation and good sitting stability

Test 2. Chair sit-ups, using abdominal muscles

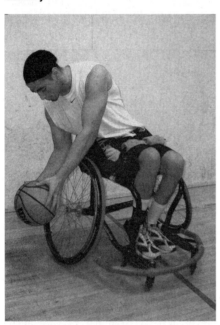

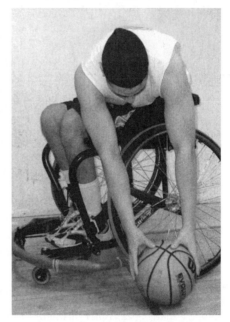

Test 3. Sideward bend; lift ball over head, and place ball on floor on opposite side

♿ *Learn as much as you can about Christopher Reeve as a way of better understanding students with high-level quadriplegia whom you may teach in the future. Watch some of his videotapes before the injury in 1995 and after. Read his autobiographies,* Still Me *and* Nothing Is Impossible, *and consider how disability has changed his relationship to others and to the physical environment and vice versa. Check out the Christopher Reeve Paralysis Foundation website at* www.christopherreeve.org. *Reeve believes that researchers will find a way to restore his spinal function enough for him to walk. Have a small-group or class debate on: Will people like Reeve ever be able to walk? How? Why?*

♿ *People with quadriplegia often need tracheostomy collars, tracheal suctioning, mechanical ventilators, feeding through gastrostomy (G) tubes or jejunostomy (J) tubes, urination through use of clean intermittent catherization (CIC),*

Table 23.3 Goals for persons with complete quadriplegic lesions.

Spinal Cord Level	OT Goals *Self-Care and* *ADL Skills*	PT Goals *Wheelchair and* *Ambulation Skills*	PE and R Goals *Sports, Dance, and* *Aquatics Skills*
Incomplete C5	Type, feed self Use assistive devices	Push manual chair on flat surface; manipulate brakes Stand at tilt table	Power chair sports, dance Boccia; slalom Swimming with flotation devices
C6	Drink Wash, shave Brush hair Dress upper half Sit up/lie down in bed Write, draw Crafts, hobbies	Push wheelchair on sloping surface Turn wheelchair Remove armrests/foot plates Transfer chair to bed, chair to car Stand between parallel bars	Manual chair sports, dance 60-, 100-, 200-, 400-, 800-m track events Club throw, 2-k shot put, discus Weight lifting 25-m front and back freestyle, breast, and butterfly 100-m freestyle swim Archery, air weapons, table tennis Sit-skiing (snow events)
C7	Turn in bed Dress lower half Skin care Bladder and bowel control Crafts, hobbies	Wheel over uneven surface Bounce over small elevations Pick up objects from floor Negotiate curbs Perform almost all transfers Swing-to on parallel bars Drive car with manual controls	1500-m track events Shot put, discus, javelin (no club) Swimming same, except 100-m individual medley (4 × 25), with butterfly as fourth stroke
C8	Same as C7, except more finger control	Same as C7, except more finger control	Same as C7, except 200-m distance freestyle

Note 1. OT = Occupational therapy; ADL = Activities of daily living; PT = Physical therapy; PE and R = Physical education and recreation.
Note 2. For additional PE and R goals, see *Sports 'N Spokes* and books by Davis (2002) and Paciorek and Jones (2001).

and defecation through use of a stoma (hole) in the skin that drains fecal material into a pouch or tube that must be periodically emptied. Most students with these assistive devices are cleared for participating in physical education (Porter et al., 2001), so physical educators wanting to know the whole person will want to learn about these procedures. Arrange to learn from a parent or nurse or by studying references like Porter et al., 2001.

Individuals with lesions at C5 and above have partially or fully paralyzed diaphragms, the muscle responsible for forceful breathing. Current estimates indicate that between 700 and 2,000 school-age children require **ventilator assistance** either full or part-time. Many attend school, and physical educators must devise meaningful physical education experiences to supplement their physical therapy. Not all of these individuals are spinal cord injured; many are in advanced stages of muscular dystrophy, but their programming needs are similar. Games that use residual respiratory abilities are recommended; see

Chapter 19 on asthma. How many games can you devise that utilize blowing skills (e.g., blowing bubbles, darts, table tennis balls)?

Table 23.3 summarizes goals of occupational therapists, physical therapists, and sports and recreation personnel in collaborative service delivery to persons with complete quadriplegic lesions. Note that recommended distances in the PE and R column may change; check with WS, VSA and NDSA.

Programming for Paraplegia

Programming depends on sport classifications, which provide general guidance about what people can and cannot do (see Figure 23.12 and Table 23.4), assuming the lesions are complete. If lesions are incomplete, only trial and error can determine sport capabilities. Almost every sport can be played in a wheelchair (Paciorek & Jones, 2001). Professionals should begin by introducing individuals to *Sports 'N Spokes* and *Palaestra* so that they can see what is possible. Likewise the stories of models in these magazines and/or the opportunity to see models live or on television is of prime importance.

Table 23.4   Goals for persons with complete paraplegic lesions.

Spinal Cord Level	OT Goals *Self-Care and ADL Skills*	PT Goals *Wheelchair and Ambulation Skills*	PE and R Goals *Sports, Dance, and Aquatics Skills*

T1 to T6	Trunk, leg, foot
	Vocational rehabilitation
		Do wheelies
		Transfer chair to floor
		Walk in bars or with walker
			Same as C8 (see Table 23.3),
			   except: 3-k shot put
			50-m front and back freestyle,
			   breast
			Class 2 wheelchair basketball

T7/8 to L1	Same as above	Swing-to on crutches Transfer chair to crutches Use stairs	Same as T1 to T5, except: 400- and 1600-m track relay 50-m butterfly 400-m distance freestyle Snow skiing (upright with special apparatus)
L1/2 to L5/S1	————	All gaits on crutches All transfers	Class 2 wheelchair basketball Same as T6 to T10, except: 200-m individual medley 500-m distance freestyle

L2/3 and below	————	Functional walking without
		   crutches—may use cane,
		   braces
			Class 3 wheelchair basketball
			Standing events

Note 1. OT = Occupational therapy; ADL = Activities of daily living; PT = Physical therapy; PE and R = Physical education and recreation.
Note 2. For additional PE and R goals, see *Sports 'N Spokes* and books by Davis (2002) and Paciorek and Jones (2001).

Models

Among the best-known athletes with paraplegia are

David Kiley, stellar basketball player, who was also commissioner of the National Wheelchair Basketball Association (NWBA)

Sharon Rahn Hedrick, outstanding University of Illinois basketball player, the first woman to complete the Boston Marathon in a wheelchair (in 1977), and the first woman to win a gold in the 800-m wheelchair exhibition events for the Olympics (in 1984)

George Murray, the first wheelchair athlete to break the 4-min mile, and one of the first to wheel across the United States (McBee & Ballinger, 1984)

Bob Hall, the first sanctioned wheelchair entrant in the Boston Marathon (in 1975), who finished with a time of 2:58, who now runs a wheelchair design company called Hall's Wheels (Huber, 1996)

Candace Cable-Brookes, who has won the Boston Marathon six times

Jean Driscoll, who has won the Boston Marathon eight times from 1990 through the present

Peter Axelson, who excels in winter and various recreational sports and is owner-manager of Beneficial Designs, a company that specializes in the design of recreational systems and devices for persons with disabilities (Axelson, 1986)

Mark Wellman, mountain climber and forest ranger, who used his powerful arms to climb up a high rope and light the Paralympic flame at Opening Ceremonies of the 1996 Paralympics in Atlanta (Wellman & Flinn, 1995)

Track and Racing Events for Paraplegia

Only two sport classifications are needed to guide instruction, recreation, and competition in track and racing events. Individuals with T1 to T7/8 lesions (Track Class 3) are significantly different from those with lower lesions (Track Class 4). This difference is primarily in sitting stability, trunk rotation, and the ability to assume the **flexed trunk position** that minimizes aerodynamic drag in racing (see Figure 23.15).

    Individuals with lesions above T6 are at risk for autonomic dysreflexia (AD), sluggish heart rate response to exercise, and venous pooling. Those with lesions above T8 have problems regulating body temperature. These limitations are not constraints to sport participation but are reminders to watch carefully for signs of physiological distress. *In contrast, individuals with lesions below T7/8 are relatively free of medical risk.*

Track and racing chairs, customized to the individual's body build and capabilities, are major factors in success. Professionals should help parents and others realize the importance of buying the right chair for each sporting event and of replacing chairs as technological advances occur. Wheelchair athletes can serve as consultants in helping to make decisions with regard to chairs.

All-Terrain Vehicles and Cycling

The development of all-terrain vehicles (ATVs) has contributed to sport, as well as to trail riding and other off-road adventures. ATVs typically have three or four wheels, low-set seats, and increased distance between front and back wheels.

On-the-road hand cycling has also become popular. Some individuals report that they regularly ride with members of an AB club. The rides are usually 35 to 55 mi of hilly terrain, averaging 15 mi an hour. *Sports 'N Spokes* is the best source of articles on these sports.

Field Events for Paraplegia

Four sport classifications are needed to meet the needs of varying functional capacities within paraplegia. Consider how each of the following influences the way you would teach object propulsion (ball, frisbee, discus, shot put, javelin).

Field Class 4 (T1 to T7/8) includes persons who must hold on to the chair while throwing because of their impaired sitting balance and inability to rotate the trunk.

Field Class 5 (T7/8 to L1/2) includes persons who can rotate their trunks but do not have full backward, forward, and sideward trunk mobility and power in generating force.

Field Class 6 (L1/2 to L5/S1) includes persons who have the functional capacity to lift their thighs off of the chair, thereby imparting more force to the throw. Some individuals also have leg function, such as pressing the knees together, straightening the knees, and bending the knees, that enhances object propulsion.

Field Class 7 (S1 and below) includes persons who have the functional capacity to stand while throwing.

Wheelchair Basketball

Wheelchair basketball, the world's most popular team sport for persons with disabilities, was developed by war veterans in the late 1940s (see Strohkendl, [1996] for a comprehensive history with wonderful photos). Anyone with a permanent locomotor limitation can play, including many persons who never use wheelchairs except during play. In the United States, the NWBA sponsors divisions for everyone. Each division plays by slightly different rules, which means that professionals who are supporting school-to-community transition must acquire the basic information to know which division a student may qualify for. *Junior divisions* (three, as of 2003) serve children under 16, use a junior-size ball, and set net heights at 8.5 feet. *Three adult men's divisions* attract hundreds of competitors, with the most highly skilled in Division I, which plays by NWBA and ISMWSF rules. Division II, for the intermediate-skilled, plays by more modified rules, and Division III is for developmental play with all competition at the local level except for one national tournament. *One adult women's division,* at present, accommodates the 10 women's teams, which conduct women's tournaments separate from those of men. Although this divisional structure offers opportunities by skill level for almost everyone, top-level players do much traveling by plane to compete with players of like-skill.

Women frequently practice and sometimes play with men's teams. Reasons for this are (a) not enough women within driving distance to field an all-female team and (b) not enough highly skilled women available to provide the skill development that playing with men's teams affords. Women's teams generally welcome AB women basketball players who are willing to learn wheelchair skills to practice with them. Many such ABs realize that knee and hip problems will eventually make them eligible to play on wheelchair teams; they become eligible as soon as orthopedic problems limit their contributions to an AB team.

Only a few of NWBA's rules are different from those of AB basketball:

1. Five, rather than 3 sec, are allowed in the lane.
2. When dribbling or holding the ball in the lap, the player can only make two thrusts of the wheels, after which he or she must dribble, pass, or shoot.
3. There is no double-dribble rule in wheelchair basketball.
4. A player raising his or her buttocks off the chair is a physical advantage foul. This counts as a technical foul.

Books available on coaching wheelchair basketball are all old (Hedrick, Byrnes, & Shaver, 1989; Owen, 1982; Shaver, 1981), but websites provide most needed information. See www.nwba.org and http://www.iwb.org/. Obviously, good performance is dependent on learning wheelchair- and ball-handling skills. Quad rugby, although designed for persons with quadriplegia, can serve as a lead-up game to wheelchair basketball. Many of the same skills are used.

International sport classifications to balance team function and promote equity are governed by the International Wheelchair Basketball Federation (IWBF). Since 1992 IWBF has used eight classifications to equalize team abilities. Each classification is assigned points (1, 1.5, 2, 2.5, 3, 3.5, 4, 4.5), and equity is achieved by requiring that the classifications of the players on the floor cannot exceed 14 points. Players in Classes 1 and 1.5 cannot pass any of Strohkendl's Basketball Function Tests and generally have T1 to T7/8 lesion levels or disabilities with comparable ability levels. In contrast, players in Classes 4 and 4.5 can pass all tests, have very minor lower limb disabilities, and generally do not use wheelchairs except for basketball.

Strapping and bracing affect classifications. A player with ankle braces may be a Class III; without the braces he is a Class II. Most players with amputations are in Classes 4 and 4.5 because they can pass all of Strohkendl's tests.

In national competition, countries can choose to use their own classification systems rather than that of IWBF. The United States uses three classifications (see Figure 23.12), with a numerical value of 1, 2, or 3 assigned to players. Players on the floor, according to U.S. rules, cannot total more than 12 points. The two combinations used most often in game play are five players with the following classifications:

3	3
3	3
3	2
2	2
1	2
──	──
12	12

When women play on men's teams, their classification is adapted to a lower level (a III becomes a II; a II becomes a I). This may be an advantage in that a woman counting only 1 point has better function than a man counting 1 point.

Wheelchair Tennis

With the exception of track, field, and swimming, wheelchair tennis is the most popular individual sport. Individuals with quadriplegia, paraplegia, and other orthopedic disabilities can play (Moore & Snow, 1994; Parks, 1997). Wheelchair tennis has few modifications. The main rule change is two bounces instead of one. Persons with limited grip strength can use elastic, tape, or special orthotic devices to bind the racket to the hand. If an overarm serve is not possible, the player uses a bounce-drop serve. The back wheels of the chair must remain behind the service line until contact with the ball is made.

Instead of a classification system, **division play** is used to ensure fairness. In 2003, the five divisions for men and three for women are designated as Open (for the best players), A, B, C, and D. Players move from division to division by winning in regional and then national tournaments; each knows his or her rank or standing within a division. Individuals with quadriplegia compete in a separate division.

Mixed play between wheelchair and stand-up players is encouraged in both singles and doubles. In mixed play, the rules of wheelchair tennis and able-bodied tennis apply, respectively, to the wheelchair and the stand-up competitors. Rules can be obtained from websites www.itftennis.com and www.usta.com/usatennis/wheelchair/index.html.

Wheelchair tennis began in the mid-1970s. Brad Parks, wheelchair user, is recognized as the father of this sport, which began in California and spread rapidly. The National Foundation of Wheelchair Tennis (NFWT), founded in 1980, merged with the United States Tennis Association (USTA) in 1988, giving them responsibility for management and authority (Rafter & Crase, 1998). The USTA is now the association to contact for books, videos, tournament schedules, and other resources. The NFWT no longer exists. The merger has increased financial stability and popularity of wheelchair tennis and has encouraged the development of mixed play. *Sports 'N Spokes* provides excellent coverage of national and international tennis.

♿ *Use websites or* Sports 'N Spokes *to determine dates and locations of wheelchair basketball and tennis tournaments, attend one or more of these, and chat with as many players and family members as possible. Try to arrange for demonstration games on your campus, and (if allowed) participate in the games. Especially try mixed tennis. Write reflections in your journal.*

Sport Wheelchairs

The many types of sport wheelchairs were first introduced in this textbook in Chapter 2 (see Figure 2.15) because an understanding of chairs is essential to becoming a good spectator and advocate of disability sport. Teachers and coaches should strive for a high level of knowledge in this area, because success in sports depends largely on appropriateness and fit of chair. An excellent resource in this regard is the annual review of wheelchairs published by *Sports 'N Spokes.*

People with the disabilities covered in this chapter (spina bifida, spinal cord injury, and polio) are more likely to be using everyday, sport, or racing chairs than the medical model chair, which better meets the needs of individuals with severe, multidisabling conditions. Sport chairs traditionally have had four wheels (two large, two small), but three-wheeled chairs are popular for tennis and basketball. The T-frame design, with one wheel (a caster) in front, minimizes drag, thereby allowing for easier, faster turning. Use of the T-frame design, however, requires relatively good balance.

Figure 23.16 shows the parts of a traditional basketball chair and how the camber tube, chair frame, and foot plate are adjusted in the manufacture of the T-frame chair. In order to communicate with people who use chairs, professionals should know the following facts.

The **height of the chair back** is usually an indication of the severity of the disability. Usually, the higher the chair back, the greater the disability.

Camber tubes or bars, near the center of the large wheels, permit adjustment of the angle of the wheels from 0° (no camber) to 15° (maximum camber). **Camber** is the degree to which the tops of the wheels slant inward (i.e., the bottoms are farther apart than the tops). Camber makes pushing more efficient, lessens the chance that the arm will bump against the wheel, and permits a natural, relaxed position for the elbows.

The small front wheels are called **casters,** and the large wheels are called **main wheels.** The main wheel tires are air-filled (pneumatic), similar to those on bicycles, which requires knowing how to fix flat tires. There are two types of pneumatic tire: (a) the clincher, which has a separate tire and inner tube, and (b) the tubular, in which the tire is sewn around the inner tube.

Handrims or **pushrims,** the part of the chair stroked by the hands, are comparable to gearshifts on bicycles. Relatively large handrims, similar to low gears, are used on sport

chairs, enabling them to start and stop quickly. In contrast, racing chairs have small handrims that enable top speeds on the road but are slow in initial acceleration.

Adjustable seat inclinations and heights are made possible by **axle tubes or plates** in the center of the large or main wheels. Relatively flat seats (no inclination) are used by people with low-level lesions, but people with high-level lesions who need help with balance adjust their seats to slope backward. This keeps their knees relatively high and their buttocks low, and therefore more stable, in the chair. Axle mechanisms allow basketball players to sit as high as rules allow, with the main wheels adjusted backward for greater stability. In contrast, tennis players sit as low as possible, with the main wheels adjusted forward so that the chair can spin around faster and be more maneuverable.

A **bearing** is the outermost part of an axle (see Figure 23.16). Bearings affect the rolling resistance of a wheel (i.e., tightening the axle toward the frame makes wheel revolution more difficult; loosening too much causes wheels to wobble). Bearings may be sealed or not sealed. Teachers should know how to adjust and/or lubricate bearings.

Quad rugby chairs, while similar to basketball chairs, have a heavier, reinforced front framework to permit the chairs to crash into each other. They also have an additional structure at foot level called the offensive or defensive front end to help absorb the shock of purposeful crashes. The footrest is recessed to give more leg and foot protection.

Track and Racing Chairs

Track and racing chairs differ from sport and everyday models primarily in number of wheels, size of wheels (larger) and handrims (smaller), lowered seat position, longer wheelbase (distance from front to back), and much camber (vertical angle of the main wheels). Figure 23.15 depicted these characteristics.

There are many kinds of racing chairs, each personalized to individual needs. Special cage designs allow athletes to lean forward by kneeling with their legs behind them or to tie their legs in a forward position, with knees high, and chest touching thighs. The cages of most racing chairs are very narrow and uncomfortable, so athletes use these chairs only for racing. Travel with athletes requires careful planning for carrying extra chairs.

Wheelchair Sport Techniques

Technique varies according to sport, degree of disability, and type of wheelchair (Cooper, 1998; Yilla, 2000). The following are important points.

1. **Arm Propulsion.** The arm movement is different in track and marathon racing from that in most sports and ADL. Figure 23.17 shows these differences. In athletes with good trunk control, the trunk alternately inclines forward and back during the thrust and recovery phases of the arm in all sports but track.

2. **High Knee Position.** Most athletes race with the knees as high as possible and the center of gravity as low as possible. This position permits optimal forward lean of the

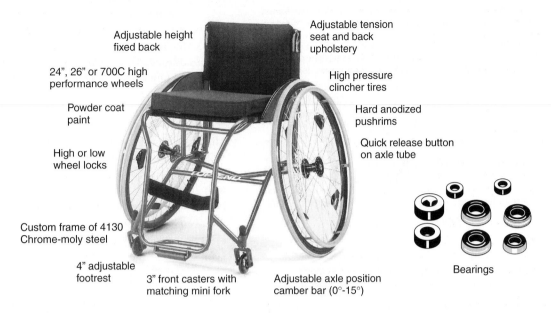

Adjustable height fixed back

24", 26" or 700C high performance wheels

Powder coat paint

High or low wheel locks

Custom frame of 4130 Chrome-moly steel

4" adjustable footrest

3" front casters with matching mini fork

Adjustable tension seat and back upholstery

High pressure clincher tires

Hard anodized pushrims

Quick release button on axle tube

Adjustable axle position camber bar (0°-15°)

Bearings

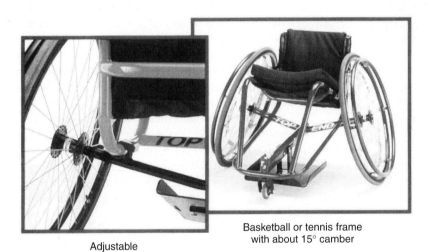

Adjustable axle tube

Basketball or tennis frame with about 15° camber

Adjustable foot plate

trunk, which, in turn, offers (a) lowered wind resistance, (b) better driving position for arms, and (c) increased trunk stability.

3. **Flexed Trunk Position.** Most athletes race with the trunk flexed and as close to the legs as possible. This position minimizes aerodynamic drag. Whereas in early racing history, persons with high-level lesions could not lean over because of trunk instability, new wheelchair technology enables them to assume desired positions. Increasing the sag in the seat and seat back is one way this is achieved.

Wheelchairs in General Physical Education

All schools with an enrollment of 300 or more should have at least two sport wheelchairs as part of their permanent physical education equipment. These chairs should be used in general and separate physical education settings by students with and without disabilities. Experts are now recommending wheelchair sports instructional units for *all* students in general physical education (Davis, 2002). Another alternative is to assign one chair to each team; who is in the chair is relatively unimportant, since all students can benefit from exposure to wheelchair sports. The student with a physical disability, however, has no opportunity to develop locomotor sport skills generalizable to adulthood unless wheelchairs are provided. Wheelchairs can be integrated into all physical education instruction: dance, individual sport relays, challenge courses, and adventure activities. This aspect of instruction should therefore be written into the IEP.

The alternative to providing wheelchair instruction is to limit the physical education curriculum to upper extremity activities done from a stationary position (archery, riflery, table

Figure 23.17 **Wheelchair arm techniques.**

Short propulsion thrusts in ADL activities, basketball, tennis, and most sports except racing. In this technique, the athlete pushes forward and downward (i.e., applies force from A to B) while simultaneously inclining the trunk forward. The handrims are released at point B, the trunk returns to its upright position, and the arms are lifted and repositioned for the next downward and forward push.

| Forward, downward thrust | Beginning of recovery | End of recovery |

Long-duration, circular-propulsion thrust in track and marathon racing. In this technique, which requires small-diameter handrims and correct positioning of the wheelchair seat and back, the athlete maintains hands in contact with the handrims through approximately three-fourths of a circle, applying force the entire time. The grip on the handrim is never released, only loosened to allow repositioning. Shoulder joint extension is especially important in providing final propulsive thrust. The lower the seat, the more important the ability of the arms to lift backward.

| Forward, downward thrust | Force continues | Beginning of recovery |

tennis, horseshoes, bowling), swimming, and horseback riding. No student should be forced to sit on the sidelines or serve as scorekeeper or official because an activity in which he or she cannot participate fully is being taught. If wheelchair integration is not possible, students with orthopedic problems should have access to alternate, physical activity opportunities.

Winter Sports

Persons in wheelchairs enjoy winter sports like everyone else. For mobility on the snow, special apparatus called sit-skis and mono-skis have been invented. The **sit-ski,** similar to a sled with a bucket seat affixed, was invented first and is still used for learning basic skills and playing games like ice and sledge hockey. The sit-ski is propelled by poles or **picks** (special short sticks for pushing). To learn downhill skiing, the beginner practices direction and control while the sit-ski is tethered to an AB skier who stays behind, pulling on the **tether** to assist with control.

In the 1980s, mono-skis were invented for use in downhill skiing, especially racing. Whereas the sit-ski is close to the snow, the **mono-ski** is essentially a trunk-seat-leg orthosis suspended via a linkage system about 10 to 18 inches above

a single ski (see Figure 23.18). Hand-held **outriggers** (forearm crutches with short ski tips attached to the ends) are used for control, including braking.

Sledge and pulk sports for persons with disabilities can be traced to Norway in the 1960s. **Sledge** means fishermen's sleigh, and the first racing was cross-country with dog teams and sledge toboggans. Shortly thereafter, special sledges with very thin metal runners were created. **Pulks** (originally, reindeer-drawn sleighs in Lapland) are similar to sit-skis; they have solid bottoms. Sledge and pulk events can be animal- or self-propelled, using poles or picks. Independent ambulation is often called *pulk poling* or *ice picking.*

Sledge or **ice hockey** is played on a regulation-size ice rink with a puck or small playground ball. Six players on each team play offense and defense similar to stand-up hockey, using picks that double as hockey sticks. Regulation padding, helmets, and gloves are important. A mask is optional. Persons with weak grips use Velcro strips on the gloves and picks (Paciorek & Jones, 2001).

Other popular winter sports that can be adapted for persons in wheelchairs are ice fishing, ice tubing, snowmobiling, snow camping, and cross-country sit-skiing. Just moving from place to place on snow- or ice-covered surfaces, like going out to get the mail, can be a challenge. Use of poles, called **wheelchair poling,** can be an ADL or an organized race for time and distance.

A major consideration in winter sports is appropriate warm clothing because of the temperature regulation problems in spinal paralysis above T6. Layered clothing and waterproof gloves are very important.

Winter sports are governed by Disabled Sports/USA in affiliation with the U.S. Ski Association (USSA) and the International Ski Federation (ISF). Clinics are regularly held for learning to ski and for instructor training and certification. Internationally, the famous Beitostølen Health Sports Center in Norway is best known. Addresses to write for further information follow:

Inge Morisbak
Beitostølen
Helsesportsenter
2953 Beitostølen
Norway

Disabled Sports/USA
451 Hungerford Drive
Suite 100
Rockville, MD 20850
(301) 217-0960
www.dsusa.org

Winter Park
National Sports Center
  for the Disabled
Box 1290
Winter Park, CO 80482
(970) 726-1540
info@nscd.org
www.nscd.org/

U.S. Ski and Snowboard
  Association
Box 100
1500 Kearns Blvd
Park City, UT 84060
(435) 649-9090
www.usskiteam.com

Fitness Assessment and Programming

Little research is available on fitness of children and youth with the conditions in this chapter (Longmuir & Bar-Or, 2000; Rimmer, Connor-Kuntz, Winnick, & Short, 1997; Winnick & Short,

Figure 23.18
Winter sports. (*A*) Sit-ski or pulk used in downhill skiing in the 1970s and 1980s. Peter Axelson is shown in sled he designed. (*B*) Mono-ski for downhill skiing today. (*C*) Sledge hockey players jousting for the puck.

A. Sit-ski or pulk used in 1970s and 1980s

B. Mono-ski with outriggers showing champion Sarah Will

C. Sledge hockey players jousting for the puck

1984, 1999). Longmuir and Bar-Or (p. 47) reported that individuals with physical disabilities, ages 6 to 20, "have significantly lower levels of habitual physical activity, consider themselves less fit relative to their peers, and report more limitations for physical activity participants." Of particular concern was the finding that no significant differences existed between age and gender groups. Rimmer et al. (1997) examined the target aerobic movement test for youth wheelchair users with spina bifida (see description later). All youth met standards, and one-third of the youth finished the test with a mean heart rate above the standard for the arm-exercise only persons. This supports the widespread belief that most youth with spina bifida perform above the level of others with spinal paralysis, presumably because of the outstanding camp and activity programs offered by Spina Bifida Association of America.

Winnick and Short (1984, 1999) have conducted fitness research for youth with disabilities for two decades. Their first big work, PROJECT UNIQUE, generated norms and revealed that youth with spinoneuromuscular conditions, ages 10 to 17, scored significantly lower than general education peers on all fitness tests and that expected improvements from age to age were not occurring. These findings revealed the need for some specially designed or adapted items and for embracing the trend toward standards-based testing rather than normative testing. *The recommended pedagogy today is to teach persons to compare themselves against standards, not against peers.*

The Brockport Physical Fitness Test (BPFT) by Winnick and Short (1999) of Brockport State University in New York is the only field test available with good validity and reliability for assessing the fitness of school-age youth with the conditions in this chapter (see full description of BPFT in Chapter 15).

Following is a description of some of the fitness items adapted for students with physical disabilities.

1. *Target Aerobic Movement Test (TAMT).* Any aerobic activity may be used as long as it is intense enough to reach a minimal target heart rate and to sustain that heart rate in a **target heart rate zone** (THRZ). Scoring is pass or fail on one trial that determines if students can stay within or above the THRZ for 15 min. Time is not started until the student reaches the THRZ. The test should be terminated if the maximum values are reached during the warm-up period, which is standardized at 3 min.

   In the BPFT manual (pp. 75–76), a THRZ for moderate intensity exertion is "70 to 85% of a maximal predicted heart rate (operationally defined as 140 to 180)" for persons able to engage in full body exercise. The minimum and maximum 10-sec heart rate values for these persons are 23 and 30, respectively. *For persons with quadriplegia and paraplegia who use arms-only exercise, the standards are different because resting heart rate capacity differs.* When resting heart rate is *less than 65,* the minimum and maximum 10-sec heart rate values are 14 and 17, respectively. When resting heart rate is *over 65,* formulas are used to calculate minimum and maximum 10-sec heart rate values. These are (resting heart rate + 20)/6 and (resting heart rate + 30)/6, respectively.

Minimum and maximum 10-sec heart rates for arms-only exercise for persons with paraplegia are 22 and 28, respectively.

2. *Seated push-up.* Student puts hands on the armrests of wheelchair and extends arms to lift and hold the buttocks off of the supporting surface for 20 sec. A 5-sec standard comes from the necessity for wheelchair users to remove the pressure on their buttocks by changing sitting position every 5 sec. This reduces the risk of developing **decubitus ulcers** (commonly called bed sores), which often take months of prone lying to heal. The 20-sec standard relates to the amount of time a wheelchair user must lift the body via arms to do transfers.

3. *Reverse Curl.* Student picks up a 1-lb object that is resting on the midpoint of the same-side thigh or a table at knee level when the student is seated. The goal is to hold the object with the elbow bent at 45 degrees or greater for 2 sec and then return it slowly (i.e., controlled against gravity) to the starting position. One trial, with pass or fail scoring, is used.

4. *Wheelchair Ramp Test.* Student in wheelchair pushes a distance of at least 8 ft, but preferably 15 to 30 ft, up a standard-size ramp. The American National Standards Institute (ANSI) guidelines specify that a ramp must be at least 36 in (91 cm) wide and constructed with 12 in. (30 cm) of run for every inch (2.5 cm) of rise (i.e., if a ramp has an elevation of 14 in, it must be 14 ft long. *Low-skilled students should be spotted from behind.*

5. *Modified Apley Test.* To show shoulder flexibility, the participant reaches back with one hand to touch the inside border of the opposite scapula, where the tester has placed his or her fingers to indicate the spot to be touched. Each arm is tested. The participant who holds the reach for 1–2 sec is awarded 3 points. For individuals unable to do this, a touch and hold to the top of the head or to the mouth earn 2 or 1 points, respectively.

6. *Modified Thomas Test.* Participant lies supine on a table with the hip joints touching a mark that is 11 in from the short edge of the table. Both legs are dangling down. The student uses the hands to pull one knee to the chest. If the hip flexors of the stationary leg are not tight, it will remain in contact with the table; this earns 3 points. *Shortened hip flexors* cause the knee of the stationary leg to bend, resulting in a score reduction to 2 or 1. Failure to keep the back in contact with the table results in a 0. Repeat the test, so you have a score for the flexibility of both right and left hip flexors. Remember when you raise the right leg, you are testing the tightness of the left hip flexors. Tight hip flexors contribute to abdominal weakness and lordosis; they also make good, fully extended postures difficult.

7. *Dumbbell Press.* In a seated position, the student lifts a 15-lb (6.8 kg) dumbbell with the dominant hand by flexing the elbow so that the weight is close in and in front of the shoulder (e.g., like a restaurant worker holds a tray). The weight is then lifted straight up above the shoulder until the elbow is completely straight, then returns the weight to starting position. The test is

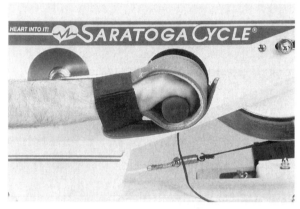

Figure 23.19   Hand-cranking apparatus must be available to develop cardiorespiratory endurance. (Photos courtesy of Saratoga Access & Fitness, Inc.)

continued at a steady lifting pace (about 3 or 4 sec per repetition) until a maximum of 50 repetitions is completed or the student cannot continue.

8. *Target Stretch Test (TST).* The tester assesses maximum movement extent at five joints (wrist, elbow, shoulder, forearm, and knee) through use of a modified goniometer. Degrees of movement yielded by the clock face of the goniometer are converted to standards of 2 (better) or 1. Sixteen clock face movement profiles in the manual help testers with interpretation.

The test items just described are designed primarily for wheelchair users or students whose disabilities have resulted in unique movement patterns or reduction in range of motion. Everything to administer the test (manual computer software, instructional videotape, skinfold calipers, PACER audio CD/cassette) is available through Human Kinetics (see Appendix E).

Research on adults with spinal paralysis also indicates the need for increased fitness. Excellent reviews of literature and training programs appear periodically, usually in proceedings of conferences conducted by IPC or IFAPA (e.g., Bhambhani, 2001) but occasionally in journals (e.g., Canadian Society for Exercise Physiology, 1998; Shephard, 2003). Athletically active persons in wheelchairs have fewer kidney infections, skin break-downs, and other medical complications than sedentary persons

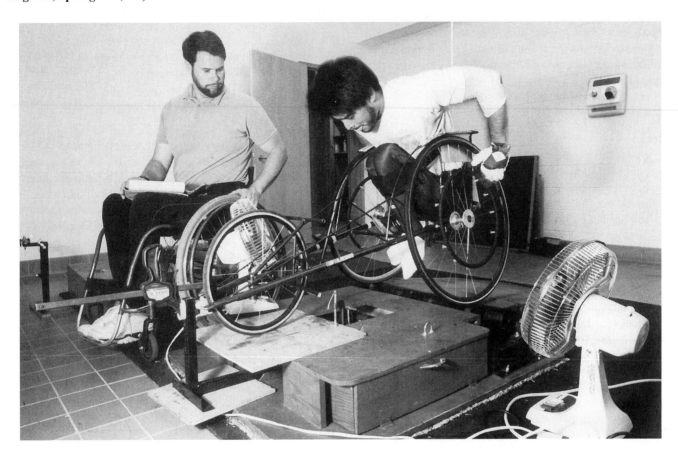

(Stotts, 1986). Athletes tend also to make high self-actualization scores (Sherrill, 1990b, 1997c). In general, it is not disability that affects wellness but, rather, poor attitudes toward exercise and lack of discipline.

Activity specialists should focus on making exercise fun, changing lifestyles, and promoting social support networks. One approach is to develop community-based programs in which wheelchair users can exercise with family, spouse, and friends. Another is to plan attractive risk recreation and/or strenuous outdoor ventures that motivate persons to develop the fitness levels needed for participation. For example, wanting to ride a horse is motivation for developing the arm and shoulder strength to mount and dismount. Likewise, sailboat racing, kayaking, canoeing, rock climbing, and the like require a commitment to strength and endurance training.

Disability tends to isolate people. Children and youth, in particular, do not need further isolation at hand-cranking and arm-cycling machines. Partners can be assigned to face each other and talk while doing distinctly different fitness activities. Unless some kind of positive contact/sharing is assigned and reinforced, it may not happen.

Arm Cranking and Wheelchair Ergometry

Facilities that serve people with physical disabilities (integrated and other) need specialized equipment for assessment and training. Among these are various kinds of arm exercise machines and hand cycles (see *Sports 'N Spokes*). Different kinds of

handgrip designs must be available to help people with quadriplegia (see Figure 23.19).

Heart and circulatory limitations discussed earlier affect training protocol and outcomes. Additionally, the smaller muscle mass of the arms cannot produce the training effects associated with leg work. In individuals with high lesions, arm cranking often cannot raise the heart rate above 120 beats a minute. Goals should be individualized and comparisons with others avoided. Arm exercise done in an upright, sitting position may be so limited by blood pooling in the leg veins that apparatus must be adapted to allow hand-cranking from a supine position (Glaser, 1989).

When the purpose of fitness training is to prepare for athletic excellence, the *principle of specificity* is important. **Wheelchair ergometry** (the use of rollers) is preferred over arm cranking by most coaches. Rollers are to wheelchair users what treadmills are to ambulatory runners (see Figure 23.20). Hedrick and Morse (1991), coaches at the University of Illinois, describe roller training and the importance of a fan for ventilation and periodic fluid intake to prevent dehydration. *Wheelchair ergometry results in a higher maximum heart rate than arm cranking and thus contributes more to fitness.*

Shoulder Joint Injury

Reliance on upper extremities for fitness training makes wheelchair users especially vulnerable to shoulder joint injury. Pushing activities tend to overdevelop anterior arm and shoulder muscles and cause an imbalance in strength between anterior and posterior musculature. Clinical signs are round shoulders, decreased flexibility, discomfort in the muscles between the shoulder blades, and increased risk of straining the rotator-cuff muscle group and/or dislocating the joint. Prevention focuses on stretching the anterior muscles and strengthening the posterior ones. For further information, see Chapters 13 and 14 on fitness and postures.

 ## OPTIONAL ACTIVITIES

1. Check the resources in your university library that focus on disability sport and the Paralympics. Make a list of the books, journals, and videotapes you wish your university would purchase and discuss these with the persons responsible for library orders. Do the same for public libraries in your community.

2. Find resources on past Paralympics and future ones: Athens in 2004 and Beijing in 2008. Wonderful books, full of outstanding photographs, are often published in conjunction with the Paralympics. Probably most accessible in America is *The Triumph of the Human Spirit: The Atlanta Paralympic Experience* available through the Disability Today Publishing Group at 800-725-7136. A good book *Raising the Bar* (2001) can be ordered through www.umbragebooks.com. Use these resources to acquaint students, parents, and others with models, opportunities, and possibilities. Make bulletin board displays at your university and in the community, power point presentations, and so on.

3. Commit a set number of hours to sport and companionship with persons in motorized chairs and manual chairs. Let them teach you everything they know, and share some of your sports expertise with them. Learn how to charge motorized chairs and how to fix tires on both types of chairs. Spend time with different age groups, including those at retirement centers and nursing homes.

4. Find contact information on all of the companies that build wheelchairs in the annual survey of what's available in chairs in *Sports 'N Spokes,* www.sportsnspokes.com. Contact companies for more information; share with others. Visit stores that rent or sell wheelchairs in your city and compare their offerings to those described in *Sports 'N Spokes.*

5. The Australian Sports Alliance has produced an outstanding series of books on coaching athletes with disabilities. See if your library has *Coaching Wheelchair Athletes* (1996) by Goodman, Lee, and Heidt and use it as a resource. If not, contact Peter Downs: peter.downs@ausport.gov.au

6. Review some of the sport videos described in the December 2000 *Sports 'N Spokes.* Find out about more recent videos and review them also. Encourage your friends and family to view and discuss videos with you.

24

Les Autres Conditions and Amputations

Patricia Paulsen Hughes and Claudine Sherrill

Figure 24.1 *Les autres,* meaning "the others," is a sport team referring to all persons with locomotor disabilities who are not diagnosed with spinal paralysis, cerebral palsy, stroke, or traumatic brain injury. A, B, and C show diversity within the les autres category.

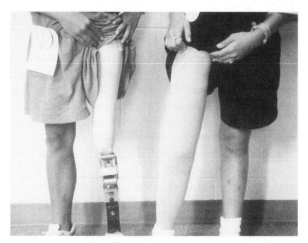

A. Two types of prostheses

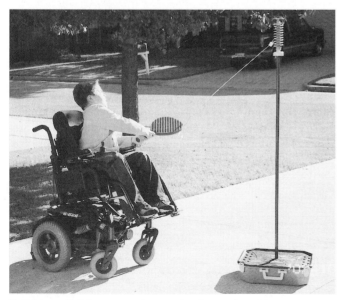

B. Persons in late stages of muscular dystrophy use motorized chairs.

C. Persons wearing prosthesis can enjoy wind surfing.

1. In what ways is programming for les autres conditions similar? In what ways must programming differ?

2. Which les autres conditions get progressively worse? Which conditions get progressively better? Which conditions can have fluctuating levels of involvement? What challenges would be presented in writing an IEP for an individual with a fluctuating ability level?

3. What is the value of sports competition for substantially impaired people in battery-powered chairs? Is competition in that mode equitable or not equitable? Why or why not?

4. Based on your understanding of assessment, what type of instruments would you use for evaluating students with dwarfism, with late stage muscular dystrophy, with osteogenesis imperfecta and other conditions of your choice in this chapter?

5. Go through Table 24.1 and reflect on the conditions that you have had experience with (a) firsthand, (b) through a movie or video, (c) through a website or newspaper, and (d) through biographies and autobiographies. Consider how often sport is highlighted and why. Make plans to enhance your experience.

Les autres conditions and amputations are grouped together in this chapter because, historically, they have been governed by the International Sports Organization for the Disabled (ISOD). *Les autres,* the French term for "the others," is used in sport to denote the *other locomotor disabilities,* namely those not eligible to compete as one with a spinal cord injury or cerebral palsy (see Figure 24.1). Les autres conditions covered in this chapter are listed in Table 24.1.

Individuals with les autres conditions differ enormously. Some require activities in motorized chairs, some can compete in wheelchair sports described in Chapter 23, and some can participate in ambulatory activities adapted to particular needs. This chapter begins with **conditions of progressive muscle weakness.** Some of these, like the muscular dystrophies, have an unknown cause. Others can be classified as neuromuscular in that they are caused by degeneration of motor and/or sensory nerves. The chapter continues with **thermal injuries** (burns), a high incidence condition, that often results in contractures or amputations. Burns limit range of motion (ROM) and can be linked with both the muscular and skeletal systems.

The second half of the chapter presents **conditions that affect bones and joints.** First, conditions that can involve any body part or the entire body are described. These include arthritis, osteomyelitis, arthrogryposis, dwarfism, and osteogenesis imperfecta. Next, congenital and growth disorders that affect only one body part are described. The chapter concludes with a discussion of limb deficiencies and amputations. For most conditions in this chapter, children will be classified as *Orthopedically Impaired (OI)* or *Other Health Impaired (OHI).*

Physical Activity Programming

Most students with conditions in this chapter participate fully in general physical education classes. Sometimes supports and adaptations are needed, particularly for those who are not mobile without assistive devices or wheelchairs. *Swimming is probably the best activity for all conditions.* Beyond this generalization, selection of activities depends on condition. In high school, when the physical education emphasis focuses on competitive sports, students typically are at a slight to moderate disadvantage. Some coaches support their becoming integrated in interscholastic competitions as full or special team members,

while others do not. Regardless of this, secondary school students should be encouraged to try activities sponsored by disability sport organizations. Athletes with amputations who have had good general physical education instruction and practice with able-bodied teams often meet eligibility requirements for Paralympics.

Sport Governing Bodies

Three disability sport organizations (DSOs) in the United States govern competitive sports for persons with the conditions in this chapter. The **National Disability Sports Alliance** (NDSA), in addition to CP sports, conducts activities for individuals whose disability requires use of a motorized chair, crutches, or canes (see Chapter 25). The **Dwarf Athletic Association of America** (DAAA) conducts activities for children and adults with dwarfism and recently has facilitated the formation of an international dwarf sport association. An extremely large and powerful organization named **Disability Sports/USA** (formerly National Handicapped Sports) governs winter sports for all disabilities and all sports for athletes with amputations and with ambulatory les autres conditions. *Physical educators should contact these organizations no later than the 14th birthday of their students to obtain their help in transition from school to community-based physical activity.*

For winter sports in the United States, elite athletes with and without disabilities have been integrated in training and in some competitive events since 1986 when the **United States Disabled Ski Team** (USDST) became part of the **United States Ski Team** (USST). This union promotes collaboration between the disability and nondisability communities in promoting learn-to-ski and racing programs for all ages. These programs then become "feeders" for potential USDST athletes in the Paralympics. Athletes with amputations have always excelled in standing ski events, and many adaptations are available. Centers that provide disability ski opportunities often call their programs **adaptive skiing.**

Read about and/or review videotapes of the 2001 Paralympic Winter Games in Salt Lake City or of the 2005 comparable event in Torino, Italy. Good sources are these magazines: Challenge, Sports 'N Spokes, *and* Palaestra. Do *the same for the 2000 Paralympic Summer Games in Sydney, the 2004 Paralympics in Athens, and the 2008 Paralympics in Beijing. This is a great way to get acquainted with the movement patterns and potentials of persons with les autres conditions and amputations.*

Spend time on the websites of the organizations mentioned in this section. Jot notes down in your journal and be ready to discuss in class.

Individuals with skeletal disorders (amputations, dwarfism) are more likely to become involved in competitive sport than are individuals with muscular weakness conditions. Success depends largely on selecting appropriate sports for one's height, body build, and functional capabilities. Creating an equitable sport classification system is difficult, but the trend within the Paralympic movement is toward sport-specific, functional classifications that include individuals with different medical conditions who appear to have comparable performance capabilities. The sport classifications for track and field

described in Chapter 23 are therefore applied to athletes with les autres conditions who use manual wheelchairs. Experts in each Paralympic sport are endeavoring to create fair, functional classification systems specific to their sports.

Muscular Dystrophies

The **muscular dystrophies** are a group of genetically determined conditions in which **progressive muscular weakness** is attributed to changes that occur in the muscle fibers. The causes of these changes remain unknown. The muscular dystrophies are common in school-age children and rank with cerebral palsy and spina bifida as conditions that physical educators often see. The Jerry Lewis TV fund raising project each Labor Day provides opportunities to learn about muscular dystrophy.

Several different types have been identified since 1850, many of which are rare. The three muscular dystrophies having the highest incidence are Duchenne, facio-scapular-humeral, and limb girdle types. Approximately 250,000 persons in the United States have muscular dystrophy. Of this number, 50,000 use a wheelchair. Specifically, 1 of every 500 U.S. children will get or has muscular dystrophy. Boys are affected five or six times more often than girls.

Muscular dystrophy in itself is not fatal, but the secondary complications of limited mobility heighten the effects of respiratory disorders and heart disease. With the weakening of respiratory muscles and the reduction in vital capacity, the child may succumb to a simple respiratory infection. Changes in cardiac muscle increase susceptibility to heart disease. The dilemma confronting the physical educator is how to increase and/or maintain cardiovascular fitness when muscle weakness makes running and other endurance-type activities increasingly difficult.

Duchenne Muscular Dystrophy

The *Duchenne type* of muscular dystrophy is the most common and most severe. Its onset is usually before age 3, but symptoms may appear as late as age 10 or 11. Males are affected more frequently than females. The condition is caused by a sex-linked trait that is transmitted through females to males. The sister of an affected male has a 50% chance of being a carrier and will pass the defective gene on to 50% of her sons. Persons with muscular dystrophy seldom live to adulthood. Indicators of Duchenne muscular dystrophy include the following:

1. Awkward side-to-side waddling gait.
2. Difficulty in running, tricycling, climbing stairs, and rising from chairs.
3. Tendency to fall frequently.
4. Peculiar way of rising from a fall. From a supine position, children turn onto their face, put hands and feet on the floor, and then climb up their legs with their hands. This means of rising is called the **Gower's sign** (see Figure 24.2).
5. Lordosis.
6. Hypertrophy of calf muscles and, occasionally, of deltoid, infraspinatus, and lateral quadriceps.

The **hypertrophy** (sometimes called **pseudohypertrophy**) occurs when fat and connective tissue replace degenerating muscle fibers, which progressively become smaller, fragment, and then disappear. The hypertrophy gives the mistaken impression of extremely well-developed healthy musculature. In actuality, the muscles are quite weak.

The initial areas of muscular weakness, however, are the **gluteals, abdominals, erector spinae** of the back, and **anterior tibials.** The first three of these explain lordosis and difficulty in rising, while the tibials explain the frequent falls. Weakness of the anterior tibials results in a **foot drop** (pes equinovarus), which causes children to trip over their own feet. See Chapter 11 for illustrations of the muscular dystrophy and steppage (foot drop) gaits.

Within 7 to 10 years after the initial onset of symptoms, contractures begin to form at the ankle, knee, and hip joints. **Contractures** of the Achilles tendons force children to walk on their toes and increase still further the risk of falling. Stretching exercises are very important in preventing and minimizing contractures. Between ages 10 and 15, most children with dystrophy lose the capacity to walk, progressively spending more and more time in the wheelchair and/or bed. This enforced inactivity leads to severe distortions of the chest wall, kyphoscoliosis, and respiratory problems.

Facio-Scapular-Humeral Type

The *facio-scapular-humeral type* is the most common form of muscular dystrophy in adults. It affects both genders equally. Symptoms generally do not appear until adolescence and often are not recognized until adulthood. The prognosis is good, compared with that of the other dystrophies, and life span is average. The condition may arrest itself at any stage. Indicators include

1. Progressive weakness of the shoulder and arm muscles, beginning with the trapezius and pectoralis major and sequentially involving the biceps, triceps, deltoid, and erector spinae.
2. Progressive weakness of the face muscles, causing drooping cheeks, pouting lips, and inability to close the eyes completely. The face takes on an immobile quality, since muscles lack the strength to express emotion.
3. Hip and thigh muscles are affected less often. When involvement does occur, it is manifested by a waddling side-to-side gait and the tendency to fall easily.

Limb Girdle Type

The *limb girdle type* of muscular dystrophy can occur at any time from age 10 or after. The onset, however, is usually the second decade. Both genders are affected equally. The earliest symptom is usually difficulty in raising the arms above shoulder level or awkwardness in climbing stairs. Weakness manifests itself initially in either the shoulder girdle muscles or the hip and thigh muscles, but eventually, both the upper and lower extremities are involved. Muscle degeneration progresses slowly.

Progressive Muscle Weakness

Daily exercise slows the incapacitating aspects of muscular dystrophy. As long as the child is helped to stand upright a few minutes each day and to walk short distances, contractures do not appear. Once the individual becomes a wheelchair user, however, functional ability tends to deteriorate rapidly. Stretching exercises become imperative at this point, as do breathing games and exercises. The recommended intensity of exercise is still controversial (Sayers, 2000).

Eight stages of disability are delineated by the Muscular Dystrophy Associations of America:

1. Ambulate with mild waddling gait and lordosis. Elevation activities adequate (climb stairs and curbs without assistance).

2. Ambulate with moderate waddling gait and lordosis. Elevation activities deficient (need support for curbs and stairs).

3. Ambulate with moderately severe waddling gait and lordosis. Cannot negotiate curbs or stairs but can achieve erect posture from standard-height chair.

4. Ambulate with severe waddling gait and lordosis. Unable to rise from a standard-height chair.

5. Wheelchair independence. Good posture in the chair; can perform all activities of daily living (ADL) from the chair.

6. Wheelchair with dependence. Can roll the chair but need assistance in bed and wheelchair activities.

7. Wheelchair with dependence and back support. Can roll the chair only a short distance but need back support for good chair position.

8. Bed patient. Can do no ADL without maximum assistance.

Even in Stage 8, some time each day is planned for standing upright by use of a tilt table or appropriate braces. Children should attend public school and engage in adapted physical education as long as possible, with emphasis on the social values of individual and small-group games, dance, and aquatics. In the later stages, they may attend school only a small part of each day.

Full participation in games and athletics while the condition is in the early stages may enable the child to form close friends who will stick by as he or she becomes increasingly weak. The child with muscular dystrophy and his or her friends also should receive instruction in recreational activities that will carry over into the wheelchair years. Rifle shooting, dart throwing, archery, bowling, fishing, and other individual sports are recommended. The parents may wish to build a rifle or archery range in their basement or backyard to attract neighborhood children in for a visit as well as to provide recreation for their own child. Swimming is recommended, with emphasis on developing powerful arm strokes to substitute for the increasing loss of leg strength.

Children with dystrophy are learning to adjust to life in a wheelchair just when their peers are experiencing the joys of competitive sports (see Figure 24.3). They are easily forgotten unless helped to develop skills like scorekeeping and umpiring, which keep them valued members of the group. The physical educator should not wait until disability sets in to build such skills, but should begin in the early grades, congratulating them on good visual acuity, knowledge of the rules, decision-making skills, and other competencies requisite to scorekeeping and umpiring. *These integrated activities should not, however, substitute for adapted physical education.*

Muscular dystrophy, along with cerebral palsy and spina bifida, are the most common OI conditions in

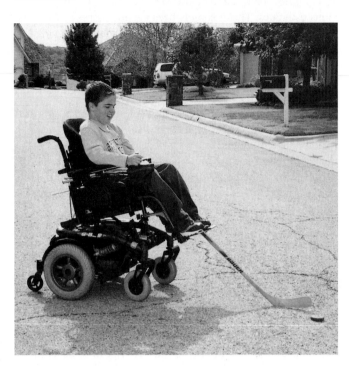

Figure 24.3 **This adolescent with Duchenne muscular dystrophy enjoys playing street hockey with his friends, even though he is now using a motorized wheelchair.**

public schools. With appropriate permissions, conduct a survey of teachers to determine if they have taught any children with these conditions. Conduct interviews with one or two teachers who have had experience and share findings with class.

Multiple Sclerosis

Multiple sclerosis (MS) is an inflammatory disease of the central nervous system (CNS) with variable symptoms and highly unpredictable periods of acute illness (called an attack, exacerbation, bout, or relapse) interspersed with periods of remission. Recently, talk show host Montel Williams announced he had been diagnosed with MS. Some individuals with MS have only one or two attacks in a lifetime, recover well, and never become disabled. About 25% have frequent attacks but recover sufficiently to function like ordinary people. Others become more and more disabled with each attack, and eventually become wheelchair users with highly individual profiles of motor and sensory disturbances, pain, fatigue, and bladder/bowel disorders. Approximately 300,000 persons in the United States have MS.

The cause of MS is unknown, but recent research indicates that 30 to 60% of new clinical attacks occur shortly after a cold, influenza, or other viral illness. Symptoms vary with each individual and with each attack, depending on which part of the CNS is affected. The name *multiple sclerosis* derives from the Greek word *sklerosis,* which means "hardening," and refers to the scar tissue that replaces the disintegrating myelin. **Myelin** is the covering around the axons of most nerves. Axons are nerve branches composed of white matter that carry messages to act from the brain and spinal cord.

The availability of magnetic resonance imaging (MRI) has greatly enhanced diagnostic procedures, and the prevalence of MS is now believed to be two to three times greater than previous estimates. This is largely because mild cases can now be identified. Estimates vary, with 1 out of 600 persons having MS in some communities. MS occurs more frequently in women than men (about a 2:1 ratio) and is most common in Whites, especially those of northern European ancestry. Age of onset is typically between 20 and 40.

MS symptoms are diverse. Each set of symptoms usually lasts 4 to 12 weeks and then gradually disappears, leaving various degrees of disability. During periods of exacerbation, **nerve impulse conduction** through affected areas is abnormal, being either slow or blocked, producing such symptoms as weakness, numbness and tingling, dimness of vision, double vision, slurred speech, fatigue, pain, and urinary incontinence or urgency. In the progressive type of MS, spasticity, tremors, and paralysis can occur in the later stages. Symptoms are treated primarily with medications and the prescription of canes, crutches, walkers, and wheelchairs as needed. Appropriate exercises during periods of exacerbation are slow gentle stretching, walking, and water exercise in relatively cool temperatures.

A unique aspect of MS is **heat intolerance.** Exposure to heat and humidity intensifies problems caused by demyelination and results in rapid fatigue. Any activity that substantially raises the body's core temperature is contraindicated. Morning exercise is recommended because the body temperature is typically lowest in the morning and higher in the afternoon.

Case Study

The following description of MS over an 8-year period was written by Sherry Rogers, who developed MS while a junior physical education major in college:

• *Now with the diagnosis starts the story of the most demanding years of my life. The pain I experienced was tremendous. . . . It was mostly on my right side and the lower part of my back, especially the sciatic nerve of my right leg.*

After about a month of medication every day, I could see some improvement. Then the physician started me on cold showers to stimulate my circulation. All of this and my prayers worked for me. Physical therapy, mainly to exercise my legs, was given me also. . . . I continued to progressively get better control of myself.

Then blindness, seeing only a narrow vision of light, appeared, lasting for about three weeks. Seeing double lasted for about another month. Then my vision progressively got better until it seems normal at present except that I now need glasses to read or do any close work. . . .

There are days when I need crutches to walk and other days when I feel fine and can walk without any assistance. The muscle groups affected the most were all of the voluntary muscles of my right side. The most noticeable to me has been my right hand, which feels like it is asleep all of the time. I again was fortunate because I am left-handed. . . . My strength is about one fourth of what it used to be. My posture has been very much affected. I bend forward from my waist some days when I stand. This is more apparent on some days than others, depending upon my strength. I was paralyzed for about a year. Gradually, I improved until now I walk almost normally. . . .

In spite of my disability, I returned to college and received my Bachelor of Science degree in physical education and was presented the most representative woman physical education major award from Delta Psi Kappa. If there is one thing I could tell you, it is that nothing is certain in this life and it is not to be taken for granted. Make certain that you live to the fullest because you never know what the future holds for you. •

Course of MS

In the most advanced stages of MS, loss of bladder or bowel control occurs as well as difficulties of speech and swallowing. Progressively severe **intention tremors** interfere with writing, using eating utensils, and motor tasks. The prognosis for MS varies. Many individuals have long periods of remission, during which their lives are essentially like those of others.

Program Implications

Type of physical activity depends on the extent of demyelination and the presence of pain, spasticity, tremors, muscle weakness, ataxia, impaired sensation, chronic fatigue, and heat intolerance (Lockette & Keyes, 1994). Movements are often slow and seem to require great energy expenditure. Some individuals with MS, however, are active in wheelchair basketball and tennis.

Although the general consensus is that people with MS can benefit from exercise, the optimal amount of exercise needed for health benefits and the long-term effects of exercise are still largely unknown. Blood pressure and resting heart rate vary among people with MS. Some researchers believe that exercise tolerance among people with MS depends on the duration of the condition and the level of impairment. Water exercise in cool temperatures is universally recommended, however. Adults are encouraged to join a fitness or sport club and/or establish a support group that will help them to stay motivated to exercise routinely. For a summary of the research on exercise for people with MS, see Sutherland and Anderson (2001).

Friedreich's Ataxia

Friedreich's ataxia is an inherited condition in which there is progressive degeneration of the sensory nerves of the limbs and trunk, which results in **diminished kinesthetic input** (i.e., the person has difficulty knowing where body parts are). The most common of the spinocerebellar degenerations, Friedreich's ataxia first occurs between ages 2 and 25 years. The primary indicators are **ataxia** (poor balance), clumsiness, and slurred speech. Many associated defects (diminished fine motor control, discoordination and tremor of the upper extremities, vision abnormalities, cardiac involvement, and skeletal deformities) may also develop and affect sport performance. Degeneration may be slow or rapid. Many persons become wheelchair users by their late teens; others manifest only one or two clinical signs and remain minimally affected throughout their life cycle. The incidence of Friedreich's ataxia is about 2 per 100,000. Several persons with this condition compete in Paralympic-level sport.

Guillain-Barré Syndrome

Guillain-Barré syndrome is a transient condition of progressive muscle weakness caused by inflammation of the spinal and cranial nerves (**polyneuritis**). Weakness, sometimes followed by paralysis, first affects the feet and lower legs, then the upper legs and trunk, and eventually the facial muscles. Some individuals die, and some are left with muscle and respiratory weakness. Most, however, make a complete recovery. Rehabilitation may require many months of bracing and therapy. The incidence is 1 or 2 per 100,000. Equal numbers of males and females are affected.

Charcot-Marie-Tooth Syndrome

Also called peroneal muscular atrophy, **Charcot-Marie-Tooth syndrome** is the most common hereditary neurological disorder and it appears between ages 5 and 30 years. It begins as weakness in the **peroneal muscles,** which are on the anterolateral lower leg, and gradually spreads to the posterior leg and small muscles of the hand. Weakness and atrophy of the peroneal muscles causes **foot drop,** which characterizes the **steppage gait** (see Chapter 11). The condition, which is caused by demyelination of spinal nerves and motor neurons in the spinal cord, is progressive but sometimes arrests itself. Persons with Charcot-Marie-Tooth syndrome may be active for years, limited only by impaired gait and hand weakness. There is no cure, but moderate activity is recommended to maintain strength and endurance.

Spinal Muscle Atrophies of Childhood

Several **spinal muscle atrophies** (SMA) have been identified: Werdnig-Hoffman disease (see Figure 24.4). Kugelberg-Welander disease, and Oppenheim's disease, among others. In school settings, however, these are usually called the *floppy baby syndromes* or *congenital hypotonia* since the major indicator is **flaccid muscle tone.** Most of these atrophies are present at birth or occur shortly thereafter. They are caused by progressive degeneration of the spinal cord's motor neurons.

The conditions vary in severity, with some leveling off, arresting themselves, and leaving the child with chronic, nonprogressive muscle weakness. Others are fatal within 2 or 3 years of onset. Typically, in severe cases, there is a loss of muscle strength, followed by tightening of muscles, then contractures, and finally nonuse. Stretching exercises are essential to combat contractures. SMA is sometimes impossible to distinguish from muscular dystrophy. It can be differentiated from cerebral palsy because there is no spasticity, no ataxia, no seizures, and no associated dysfunctions. Sensation remains intact.

Figure 24.4   This 10-year-old boy has spinal muscular atrophy, Werdnig-Hoffman type. He has average intelligence and attends a special school for children with orthopedic disabilities. Note how scoliosis limits breathing.

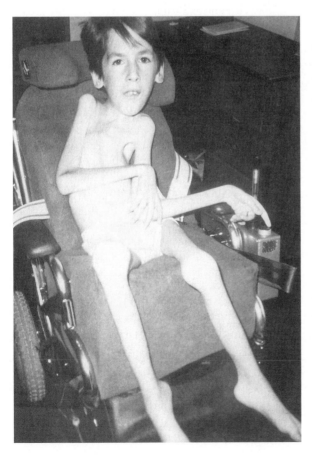
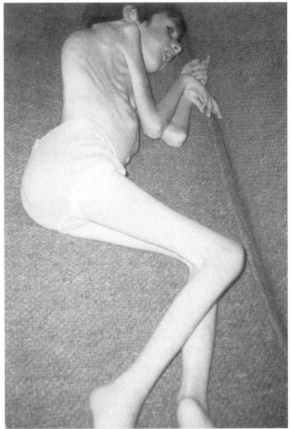

Programming for Muscular Weakness Conditions

Individuals with muscular dystrophy, multiple sclerosis, and the other muscle weakness conditions described here require adaptations that accommodate progressive loss of strength, endurance, and speed. These are often made in general physical education and exercise settings. See Chapters 11, 13 and 14 for specific activities. Principles to guide adaptation include the following:

1. Avoid activities that cause fatigue or pain. Remember that the goal of exercise is to maintain function, not to increase it as long as possible. Ignore the overload principle (Lockette & Keyes, 1994).

2. Increase rest periods during activity. Remember that people with muscle weakness use more energy when exercising than peers do.

3. Use interval training rather than aerobic activities.

4. Create activities that allow personal choice of sport equipment. Make available lightweight bats, rackets, balls, and other sport equipment.

5. Create activities that allow personal selection of distances and speeds in both locomotion and propulsion of activities.

6. Allow choices concerning which time of day seems best for exercise.

7. Arrange for exercise areas where temperature and humidity can be controlled.

8. Be patient. Allow extra time for initiating movement, getting into a comfortable position, and adjusting straps.

9. Introduce wheelchair sports and dance activities before wheelchairs are needed for activities of daily living (ADL). Promote a positive attitude about wheelchair use.

10. Use partner activities. Be sure individuals have partners to talk with during rest periods. Promote the development of friendships.

Thermal Injuries

Approximately 300,000 Americans annually suffer disfiguring injuries from fires. Another 4,500 die each year. The mortality rate is greatest among persons under age 5 and over age 65. No other type of accident permanently affects as many school-age children. Many thermal injuries result in amputations. As more persons are kept alive, physical educators must become increasingly adept at coping with all aspects of thermal injuries. During past decades, persons with more than 60% of their skin destroyed seldom survived. Now, increasing numbers of individuals are returning to society scarred and disfigured.

What kind of physical education should be provided for the young child with extensive scar tissue? How can we help such children find social acceptance? What are the effects of disfiguring thermal injuries upon self-concept? An account of a child with third-degree burns over 90% of his body helps to answer these questions (see Rothenberg & White, 1985). What other accounts can you find and share?

Thermal injury can be caused by fire, chemicals, electricity, or prolonged contact with extreme degrees of hot or cold liquids. Children who have sustained disfiguring thermal injuries, upon entering school, frequently recognize for the first time that they are different from other children. They have been known to describe themselves as monsters. Often, they have no scalp hair and no eyebrows or eyelashes, and scar tissue covers the face.

Scar Tissue

Scar tissue is an inevitable outcome of severe burns. Wound coverage is attained by the growth of scar tissue from the outer edges to the center of the wound. Thick scar tissue forms **contractures** across joints, limits ROM, causes scoliosis of the spine, and shortens underlying muscles. The severity of **hypertrophic scarring** (see Figure 24.5) and scar contracture may be decreased by early splinting, pressure, and therapeutic exercise.

Jobsts, elastic supports made to fit a specified portion of the body, may be prescribed as a means of reducing scar hypertrophy (see Figure 24.6). The purpose of the jobst is to apply constant pressure to the healed areas that are presenting signs of thickening scar tissue. The elastic supports achieve the best results when worn 24 hr daily.

Isoprene splints or *braces* may be applied to areas where the jobsts do not provide adequate pressure to the scar tissue (i.e., the face and hands). Hand splints for abduction of the thumb during daily activities are particularly common. The student wearing such splints should be encouraged to use the hands in physical education activities and should be given no restrictions. The physical educator might need to assist the child in proper cleaning and reapplication of the splint after vigorous exercise.

Program Implications

Several years of rehabilitation and plastic surgery are required for persons with severe burns. They must not be excused from physical education because they are wearing jobsts, braces, or splints. Each student must learn the tolerance of new skin tissue to such elements as direct sunlight and chlorine in freshwater pools. Physical educators may wish to confer with a specialist in thermal injuries.

The young tissue of healed burns is delicate and is metabolically active for about 18 months. Scar tissue has no sweat glands, so the body compensates by sweating more in other areas. As a consequence, individuals with scarring run a higher risk of dehydration and heat stroke. Sunscreen of at least 15 SPF should always be applied for outdoor activities.

Since contractures are a major problem, emphasis should be upon flexibility or ROM exercises. Endurance and strength objectives are also recommended. Dance and aquatic activities are especially beneficial. Many thermal injuries result in amputations, which are discussed later in the chapter.

Arthritis

Over 43 million Americans have some form of arthritis or rheumatic disease. The terms *rheumatism* and *arthritis* are sometimes used synonymously, but technically they are sepa-

Figure 24.5   Hypertrophic scarring of healed burn on lateral aspect of trunk 2 years after burn occurred.

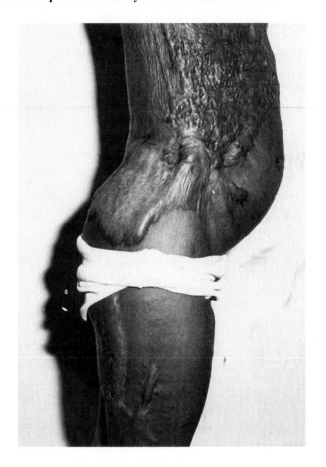

Figure 24.6   Jobsts elastic support jackets applied to arm and hand.

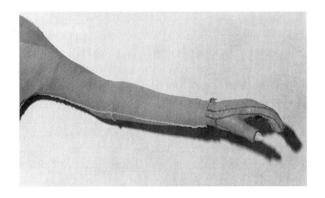

rate entities. **Rheumatism** refers to a whole group of inflammatory disorders affecting muscles and joints and includes all forms of arthritis, myositis, myalgia, bursitis, fibromyosis, and other conditions characterized by soreness, stiffness, and pain in joints and associated structures. *Arthritis* means, literally, "inflammation of the joints." Rheumatoid arthritis is completely different from rheumatic fever, although it can be a side effect of rheumatic fever (see heart conditions in Chapter 19).

Adult Rheumatoid Arthritis and Osteoarthritis

Over 100 causes of joint inflammation have been identified, but most cases fall within two categories: (a) rheumatoid arthritis and (b) osteoarthritis, often called degenerative joint disease. **Rheumatoid arthritis** affects all ages, with the usual onset between 20 and 50 years. It is three times more common in women than men until age 50, when the gender distribution becomes equal. **Osteoarthritis** mainly affects persons age 50 and over and has the same incidence in men and women. Osteoarthritis is the major cause of chronic disability in the older population; advanced cases are aggressively treated with joint replacements that permit full range of motion (ROM) with no pain. One in six older Americans have some form of arthritis.

Joint problems in arthritis are pain, swelling, heat, redness (symptoms of inflammation), decreased ROM, and related muscle weakness. In advanced cases, the affected joint becomes unstable and deformed. Rheumatoid arthritis is most troublesome early in the day, and its characteristic aching and stiffness are relieved by gentle exercise. In contrast, pain in osteoarthritis is associated with use or weight bearing and worsens as the day goes on. Medication is prescribed to reduce inflammation and pain. **Nonsteroidal anti-inflammatory drugs** (NSAIDs) like aspirin and fenoprofere are still used, but recent advances in research have produced Cox-2 Specific Inhibitors that block the inflammation-specific enzyme produced in arthritic joints.

Exercise is strongly recommended, with the **2-hr pain principle** serving as the guide to activity intensity. This principle states that any pain continuing 2 hr after exercise is an indicator that the exercise was too intense or inappropriate (Samples, 1990). Flexibility, ROM, and strength (isometric exercises, if necessary) are primary goals. Low-impact activities that are smooth and repetitive are recommended (e.g., swimming, walking, cycling, ice skating, cross country skiing). Yoga and tai chi are well tolerated. When osteoarthritis affects lower limbs, weight-bearing exercises may be contraindicated; swimming, water exercise, and cycling therefore are often the activities of choice (Barnes, Pujol, & Elder, 2002).

The Arthritis Foundation YMCA Aquatic Program (AFYAP) is the best-known program for persons with arthritis. Recommended water temperature is 83° to 88°F. Information about AFYAP and other programs can be obtained from the Arthritis Foundation, Box 19000, Atlanta, GA 30326 and from YMCAs.

Juvenile Rheumatoid Arthritis

The average age of onset of juvenile rheumatoid arthritis is 6 years, with two peaks of incidence occurring between ages 2 and 4 and between ages 8 and 11. Rheumatoid arthritis affects three to five times as many girls as boys. The specific etiology is unknown. Because young children seldom complain of pain, a slight limp is often the only manifestation of the condition. More than 70,000 U.S. children and youth have juvenile rheumatoid arthritis.

Mode of Onset

The onset of juvenile rheumatoid arthritis is capricious, sometimes affecting only one joint and other times involving several joints. In about 30% of the initial episodes, only one joint, usually the knee, is involved, but within a few weeks or months, many more joints may swell. The onset of arthritis may be sudden, characterized by severe pain, or progressive, with symptoms appearing almost imperceptibly over a long period of time. In the latter situation, joint pain is not a major problem.

Systemic and Peripheral Effects

Rheumatoid arthritis may be *systemic,* (10–20% of cases) affecting the entire body, or *peripheral,* affecting only the joints. When the disease is systemic, the joint inflammation is accompanied by such symptoms as fever, rash, malaise, pallor, enlargement of lymph nodes, enlargement of liver and spleen, and pericarditis. Systemic rheumatoid arthritis in children is sometimes called **Still's disease,** deriving its name from George F. Still, a London physician who first described the condition in 1896.

Knee

The knee is involved more often than other joints, causing a slight limp as the child walks. The characteristic swelling gives the appearance of **knock-knees** (genu valva). Swelling makes knee extension difficult or impossible. Knee flexion deteriorates from its normal range of 120° to 80 or 90°. Flexion contraction usually develops.

Ankle

Involvement of the ankle joint results in a flat-footed gait similar to that of the toddler. Muscles of the lower leg tend to atrophy, and the Achilles tendon becomes excessively tight. Limitation of motion and pain occur most often in dorsiflexion.

Foot

Swelling within the foot joints makes wearing shoes uncomfortable. Characteristic arthritic defects are pronation, flatfoot, *calcaneal valgus* (outward bending), and a cock-up position of the metatarsal phalangeal joints, especially the big toe.

Wrist, Hand, and Arm

Wrist, hand, and arm extension is limited by many factors (see Figure 24.7). A common late manifestation is **ankylosis.** This is an abnormal union of bones whose surfaces come into contact because the interjacent cartilages have been destroyed. Normal grip strength is lessened by the combination of muscular atrophy, contracture, and pain on motion.

Hip

Over one third of the children with juvenile rheumatoid arthritis favor one hip over the other. All ROMs are limited, but the flexion contracture is most troublesome.

Spinal Column

Juvenile rheumatoid arthritis tends to limit motion in the cervical spine (see Figure 24.8). There may be spasms of the upper trapezius muscle and local tenderness along the spine. The thoracic and lumbar spine are seldom involved. In young males, a form of rheumatoid arthritis, classified as **rheumatoid**

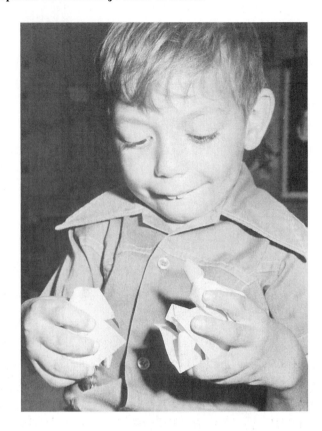

Figure 24.7   **Swollen fingers and hands require special attention in juvenile arthritis.**

spondylitis, causes pain and stiffness in the back. This condition is also called *Marie-Strumpell disease* (see Chapter 14).

Course of the Disease

In spite of enlargement of the liver and spleen, pericarditis, and other side effects, rheumatoid arthritis is rarely fatal. It does cause severe disability in about 25% of the cases and mild to moderate disability in 30%. Complete functional recovery is reported in 30 to 70% of the cases. When the disease affects the entire body, the period of acute illness lasts from 1 week to several months. During this time, children may be confined to home. They require frequent rest periods and daily ROM exercise. When joint swelling is significantly reduced and other symptoms disappear, the disease is said to be in partial or total remission. Unfortunately, periods of remission are interspersed with weeks of acute illness and maximum joint involvement.

Program Implications

The purposes of movement for the child with rheumatoid arthritis are (a) relief of pain and spasm, (b) prevention of flexion contractures and other deformities, (c) maintenance of normal ROMs for each joint, and (d) maintenance of strength, particularly in the extensor muscles. *Daily exercise must begin as soon as the acute inflammation starts to subside.* At this time, even gentle, passive movement may be painful, but every day of inactivity increases joint stiffness and the probability of permanent deformity. Physical activity personnel should work with

Figure 24.8 Limited motion in the cervical spine is shown by a logroll. *(A)* The first half of logroll shows flexion of all body parts when the desired movement requires extension. *(B)* The second half shows the logroll stalled by the extreme flexion.

A

B

Figure 24.9 Cortisone and other drugs used in arthritis tend to inhibit normal growth. This 8-year-old boy is so disabled that he uses a quadricycle in lieu of walking.

parents in establishing a home exercise program. In addition, children should participate in a school physical education program adapted to their needs.

In the early stages of remission, most of the exercises should be performed in water or in a lying position to minimize the pull of gravity. Stretching exercises to minimize contractures are essential. When exercise tolerance is built up sufficiently, activities in a sitting position can be initiated. Riding a bicycle or tricycle affords a means of transportation as well as good exercise. Sitting for long periods of time, however, is contraindicated since it results in stiffness.

Some children, such as the 8-year-old boy depicted in Figure 24.9, are left so disabled that they cannot walk. The gait of the child with severe arthritis is slow and halting. The child has difficulty ascending and descending steps. Any accidental bumping or pushing in the hallway or while standing in lines is especially painful. Older students who change rooms should be released from each class early so that they can get to the next location before the bustle of activity begins. Occasionally, their schedule of courses must be adjusted so that all classrooms are on the same floor and/or in close proximity.

Each body part, even the individual fingers and toes, should be taken through its full range of motion two or three times daily. These stretching exercises may be either active or partner-assisted as in proprioceptive neuromuscular facilitation (PNF). See Chapter 13 on stretching techniques.

Contraindicated Activities

The following activities are contraindicated for individuals with arthritis because of trauma to the joints:

1. All jumping activities, including jump rope and trampoline work
2. Activities in which falls might be frequent, such as roller skating, skiing, and gymnastics
3. Contact sports, particularly football, soccer, and volleyball
4. Hopping, leaping, and movement exploration activities in which the body leaves the floor
5. Diving
6. Horseback riding
7. Sitting for long periods

Recommended Activities

During periods of remission, persons with arthritis who can participate in an activity *without pain* should be encouraged, but

Figure 24.10 Arthrogryposis, overweight, and poor fitness combine to make batting a real chore for this 11-year-old. Arms show the characteristic increase of subcutaneous fat and loss of skin flexion creases, which result in a tubular appearance sometimes described as wooden and doll-like. Despite the awkwardness of joint positions and mechanics, no pain is felt.

Figure 24.11 This lively 7-year-old with arthrogryposis demonstrates his best posture.

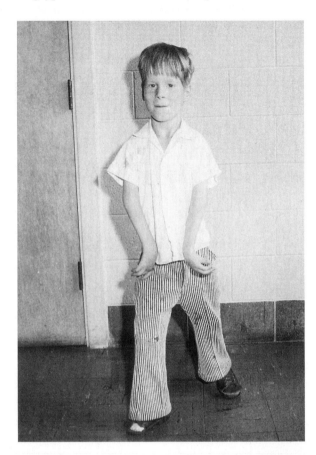

not forced, to do so. Because of the weeks and/or months of enforced rest during acute attacks, circulorespiratory endurance is likely to be subaverage (Takken, Van der Net, & Helders, 2001). Hence, frequent rest periods are needed.

Swimming and dance are among the best activities. The front crawl and other strokes that emphasize extension are especially recommended. Water must be maintained at as warm a temperature as is feasible. Creative dance and yoga also stress extension in their many stretching techniques and afford opportunities for learning to relate to others. Group choreography and performance can provide as many positive experiences as the team sports that are denied. Quiet recreational games include croquet, ring or ball tossing, miniature golf, horseshoes, shuffleboard, and pool. Throwing activities are better than striking and catching activities. See chapters in Part II of this text for specifics.

Medication Side Effects

Cortisone and other steroids are prescribed when NSAIDs like aspirin are not effective. Unfortunately, one of the major side effects of steroids is the inhibition of normal growth, causing children to look several years younger than they really are. Alterations in body growth occur as the direct result of severe rheumatoid arthritis. This stunting of growth, coupled with the overprotection of parents, may contribute to serious problems in peer adjustment. See Chapter 19 for other side effects of steroids.

Arthrogryposis

Approximately 500 infants are born with *arthrogryposis* (pronounced ar-throw-gry-pó-sis) each year in the United States. The incidence is 3 per 10,000 births. **Arthrogryposis** multiplex congenital (AMC) is a nonprogressive **congenital contracture syndrome** usually characterized by internal rotation at the shoulder joints, elbow extension, pronated forearms, radial flexion of wrists, flexion and outward rotation at the hip joint, and abnormal positions of knees and feet. This birth defect varies in severity, with some persons in wheelchairs and others only minimally affected. The contracture syndrome is characterized by dominance of fatty and connective tissue at joints in place of normal muscle tissue. Some or all joints may be involved.

The major disability is restricted ROM. Many persons with AMC have almost no arm and shoulder movement. They can, however, excel in track activities in motorized chairs. Figures 24.10 and 24.11 depict two boys, ages 11 and 7 and from the same school system, who have arthrogryposis. Although both boys have some limb involvement, their greatest problem is the fixed medial rotation of the shoulder joints (see Figure 24.12). Both have normal intelligence, as is almost always the case in arthrogryposis. Until recently, the older boy walked without the use of crutches. His present reliance on them is believed to be somewhat psychosomatic, although articular surfaces do tend to deteriorate with age.

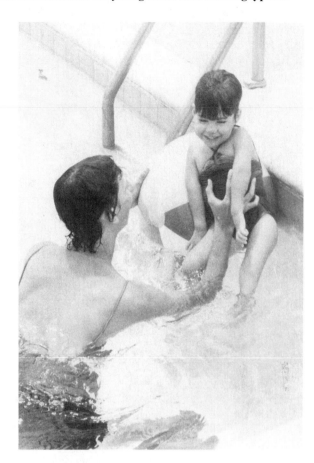

Major physical education goals are to increase ROM (flexibility) and to teach sports, games, and dance for leisure use. Activities discussed under arthritis are appropriate in most cases, as are those in Chapter 25 on cerebral palsy. Programming depends, of course, on sport classification. Swimming is particularly recommended in that it fulfills both goals. It teaches a leisure skill and stretches muscle groups (see Figure 24.13).

Dr. Jo Cowden, at the University of New Orleans, reports movement work with a 4-year-old child with AMC over a 2-year period. Periodic videotapes show that levels of mobility increased tremendously. When the child began the program, she used her chin to pull herself across a mat, rolled from place to place, or used a wheelchair. Now she crawls and creeps through obstacle courses and walks using reciprocal braces with a walker. Like many children with spina bifida, she was taught first to use a standing apparatus and a walker and then progressed to reciprocal braces. Surgery, casting, and bracing have characterized much of her early life. As a potential les autres athlete, this child can swim competitively with flotation devices and engage in slalom, track, and soccer activities in a wheelchair. As important as increasing ROM is developing attitudes and habits favorable to physical recreation.

Dwarfism and Short-Stature Syndromes

Since 1985, the date of the founding of the Dwarf Athletic Association of America (DAAA), persons who meet the sport criteria for short-stature syndrome have preferred to be called dwarfs. Other acceptable terminology is "little people," as indicated by the formation of the Little People of America (LPA), an organization with about 5,000 members that meets annually. The term *midget* is offensive and should never be used.

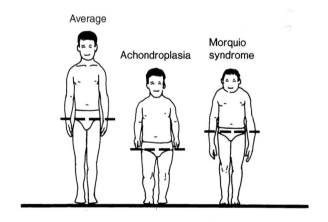

The criteria for dwarfism varies. The height standard for membership of adults in LPA is 4 ft, 10 inches or less, but DAAA uses a 5 ft or less criterion. In general, dwarfs are at least 3 standard deviations below the mean height of the general population and shorter than 98% of their peers (see Figure 24.14). Short stature in dwarfs is caused by a genetic condition or some kind of pathology.

Figure 24.15   Several types of disproportionate dwarfism. Each individual is an excellent athlete.

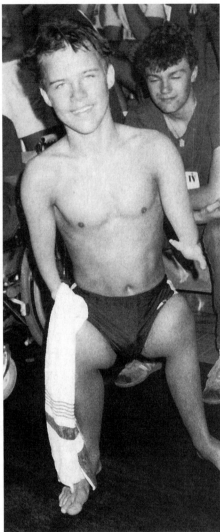

A. Achondroplasia

B. Diastrophic dysplasia with bilateral hip dislocation

C. Spondyloepiphyseal dysplasia (SED)

Disproportionate and Proportionate Dwarfs

Over 250 types of dwarfism affect about 100,000 persons (Ablon, 1988). In general, dwarfs are classified into two categories: disproportionate and proportionate. The disproportionate category is more common.

Disproportionate dwarfs typically have average-sized torsos but unusually short arms and legs. The major cause of disproportionate dwarfism is **skeletal dysplasia** or **chondrodystrophy,** the failure of cartilage (*chondro*) to develop into bone. This is either inherited or caused by spontaneous gene mutations. A controversial treatment is called **limb-lengthening,** in which the long bones are progressively lengthened.

Proportionate dwarfs are persons whose body parts are proportionate but abnormally short. The main cause of this is pituitary gland dysfunction, also known as growth hormone (GH) deficiency, but there are numerous other causes. Many of these conditions can now be treated with growth hormone injections.

Achondroplasia and Hypoachondroplasia

Achondroplasia, the most common form of dwarfism, is a disproportionate body structure with an average-size trunk, short limbs, and, in many cases, a relatively large head (see Figure 24.15A). The name is more easily remembered if we consider the meaning of each of its parts. First of all, remember that skeletal bones begin as cartilage in the embryo. The Latin word for cartilage is *chondro* (pronounced kon-dro). **Chondroplasia** thus refers to normal formation of cartilage because *plasia* means "to mold or form." **Achondroplasia** is simply the prefix *a-* (meaning "without") attached to *chondroplasia*.

Incidence figures for achondroplasia vary from 1 in 10,000 (Ablon, 1988) to 1 in 40,000 births (Scott, 1988). Associated problems are lumbar lordosis, waddling gait caused by abnormally short femoral heads, restricted elbow extension, and bowed legs. Aerobic fitness may be limited by small chest size and narrow nasal passages. In general, however, persons with achondroplasia can be excellent athletes.

Figure 24.16 Track is a favorite sport at the annual competition of the Dwarf Athletic Association of America (DAAA). To prepare for this, school-aged athletes need to train with the school's track team and receive good instruction in general physical education.

Hypoachondroplasia is the term for the tallest dwarfs, individuals who are actively recruited into sport as soon as they are discovered. The prefix *hypo-* indicates less achondroplasia and thus greater height.

Diastrophic Dysplasia

Diastrophic dysplasia is the most disabling of the common forms of dwarfism (see Figure 24.15B). This condition, which often requires crutches or wheelchairs for ambulation, typically involves spinal deformity (usually scoliosis), clubfoot (talipes equinovarus), hand deformities, and frequent hip and knee dislocations. These anomalies are resistant to corrective surgery. Figure 24.15B shows bilateral hip dislocation.

The name *diastrophic dysplasia* is derived from Latin terms for two (*di-, dia-*) problems: failure of nourishment (*trophy* or *trophic*) during prenatal bone growth and *dystrophy*, failure of nerve centers that innervate and/or failure of blood supply that carries nutrients. Occurrence is about 1 per 110,000 live births.

Spondyloepiphyseal Dysplasia (SED)

SED is mainly abnormal development of the growth plates (*epiphyses*) within the vertebrae (*spondylo*) (see Figure 24.15C). This causes a **disproportionately short trunk** with various spinal and limb irregularities. The arms typically look abnormally long. The face and skull in SED are normal, but eye complications are common. Many persons with SED are excellent athletes. The condition occurs about once in 95,000 births.

Program Implications

Profound shortness is obviously a disadvantage in most sports. Moreover, disproportionately short limbs are a limitation in ball handling, racket sports, and track. However, in some sports, such as power lifting and tumbling, average trunk size and short limbs are advantageous (Low, Knudsen, & Sherrill, 1996).

DAAA promotes several sports. Especially popular are basketball, volleyball, power lifting, track, field, swimming, bowling, and boccia. Basketball is played with baskets set at the standard height. The court size is regulation, and the ball size is that used by average-sized women. In volleyball, the net is lowered slightly so dwarfs can spike. Work is underway to create a sport classification system for track, field, and swimming so that competition among persons of different heights and proportions can be more fair (Low, 1992). **Spinal stenosis,** a narrowing of the space around the spinal cord, is particularly common among adults with disproportionate dwarfism. Swimming, bicycling, and other sports that put no pressure on the spine are recommended.

Nonachondroplasia dwarfism is associated with **atlantoaxial instability** (see Chapter 21). Individuals with these forms of dwarfism are required to submit neck X rays prior to sport participation. Contraindicated activities when atlantoaxial instability is suspected are diving, jumping, gymnastics, heading soccer balls, and contact sports.

Several other joint defects limit ROM and contribute to a high incidence of dislocations and trauma. Especially affected are the shoulder, elbow, hip, and knee joints. The inability to completely straighten the elbow causes difficulty with respect to the regulations that govern powerlifting. Thrusting the head forward to gain the advantage when crossing the finish line in track may cause muscle strain if the head is disproportionately large (see Figure 24.16). Strenuous training in track and/or distance running may lead to hip and knee joint trauma. Swimming may be the best lifetime sport to promote because it does not stress joints.

Internationally, dwarfs compete with les autres. The classification system used is considered unfair by many dwarfs, and an international sport organization for dwarfs has been founded so that, in addition to Paralympic sport, dwarfs can compete against one another.

In school settings, adaptations are necessary for dwarfs as well as for nondwarf short people. Class teams, formed to practice basketball and volleyball skills, should be equated on heights or a system whereby the shorter team starts with a set number of points. No one likes to feel that he or she is a disadvantage to the team; the teacher's role is to prevent such feelings by adapting game rules and strategies.

Short Stature and Average or Better Intelligence

Intelligence and mental functioning of dwarfs are the same as in the average-sized population. Several other short stature conditions, in which intelligence is usually average or better, warrant mention. Three conditions are characterized by a disproportionally short neck: (a) **Turner syndrome** (females only), (b) **Noonan syndrome** (males only), and (c) **Morquio syndrome** (both sexes).

Turner and Noonan syndromes are chromosomal, whereas Morquio syndrome is metabolic. Turner and Noonan syndromes have several common features: (a) necks often webbed as well as short, (b) broad chests with widely spaced nipples, (c) low posterior hairline, and (d) various other deviations. Most persons with Turner and Noonan syndromes are not sexually fertile; males have an abnormally small penis, whereas the ovaries in females fail to develop properly. In Morquio syndrome, the trunk and neck are abnormally short, causing the arms to look disproportionally long (see Figure 24.14). Ian Michael Smith, who has Morquio syndrome, portrayed Simon Birch in the movie with the same name. This wonderful movie shows Simon Birch in many sport scenes despite the severe kyphosis, knock-knees, and limited hip and joint flexibility associated with Morquio syndrome.

Short Stature and Mental Retardation

Several mental retardation syndromes are characterized by short stature. These include Down syndrome (1 per 2,000 incidence), Cornelia de Lange syndrome (1 per 10,000 incidence), fetal alcohol syndrome (3 to 6 per 1,000 incidence), Hurler's syndrome (1 per 100,000 incidence), rubella syndrome (1 per 10,000 incidence), and the many infants addicted to drugs before birth. These conditions obviously require physical education adaptations for short stature and short limbs. They are discussed more fully, however, in Chapter 21 on mental retardation since the primary adaptations relate to mental functioning (i.e., task analysis and behavior management).

Osteogenesis Imperfecta

Word derivation is also helpful in visualizing **osteogenesis imperfecta** *(OI)*. *Os* and *osteo* refer to "bone." *Genesis* means "origin." *Imperfecta* clearly indicates that something is wrong with bone formation. The basic defect of OI (pronounced ostee-oh-gen´-e-sis im-per-fect´-ah) is in the **collagen fibers** (a

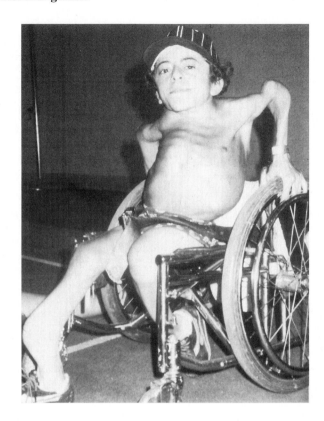

Figure 24.17   A 17-year-old with osteogenesis imperfecta (OI) awaiting his swimming competition at national games.

type of protein) found in **connective tissue** (bone, ligaments, cartilage, and skin). The defect makes bone and cartilage soft and brittle, while causing skin and ligaments to be overly elastic and hyperextensible.

OI is an inherited condition that is present at birth. Bone breaks peak between 2 and 15 years of age, after which the incidence of fractures decreases. Indicators are **short stature** and small limbs that are bowed in various distortions from repetitive fractures. Joints are hyperextensible, with predisposition for dislocation. Most persons with OI are in wheelchairs. Frequent hospitalizations, missed school, and deformed limbs often impact self-concept of individuals with OI (Englebert, Gutmans, Uiterwaal, & Helders, 2001). Undiagnosed cases are often mistaken for child abuse.

Chest defects (barrel and pigeon shapes) limit respiratory capacity and aerobic endurance, and spinal defects are common (see Figure 24.17). These are partly from **osteoporosis** (bone degeneration) caused by lack of exercise. Clearly, adapted physical activity, especially swimming and ROM games, is important. Until the condition arrests itself, usually in adolescence, motorized chairs permit the challenge and thrill of track and slalom events. Use of a 5-oz **soft shot** (beanbag) or discus seldom causes fractures, whereas regulation balls might. Shuffleboard and ramp bowling add variety.

After the condition arrests itself, the person can engage in almost any sport. Wayne Washington, who weighs 112 lb, is a world-class weight lifter with a 290-lb record; he began weight lifting at age 18 (see Figure 24.18). Bill Lehr, a world-

Figure 24.18 **Figure 24.18** **Wayne Washington, who has OI, is an international competitor in weight lifting. Here, he is visiting with a coach before a recreational swim.**

class track and swimming star, also plays wheelchair basketball and has completed the Boston Marathon in 2 hr and 50 min. He has done the 100 m in 18.8, the 400 in 1:16.8, and the 800 in 2:34. About his childhood, Bill says,

> I was born with a broken collarbone, my knees were bent in a way a baby's knees aren't supposed to bend, and in the first 12 years of my life, I must have spent half the time in surgery. . . . When I was growing, I could walk and even run a few yards at a time. Then a bone would break in one of my legs, and they'd have to put a cast on me. I'd be laid up for a few weeks, get out of the cast, but that would only last a week or two before I'd break another bone and have to be put back in a cast again.

Before Bill's condition arrested itself, he had over 40 fractures. From age 7 onward, he was a wheelchair user; he began wheelchair basketball and track at age 12. Telling OI children about world class athletes like Bill Lehr and Wayne Washington and showing them photos and videotapes opens new horizons; this is an important part of the physical educator's job.

The incidence of OI is 1 in 50,000 births for congenital OI and 1 in 25,000 for a later appearing, less serious form called OI tarda. These medical statistics may be inaccurate in that OI students can easily be spotted in every large school system. OI makes persons eligible to compete either with the dwarf or les autres organizations. Promising new treatment for OI involves injections of pamindronate, which inhibits bone reab-

sorption. A 5-year study yielded encouraging results: increase in bone density, bone diameter, and mobility and decrease in number of fractures and perceived pain.

Ehlers-Danlos Syndrome

Several collagen defects are similar to OI but do not cause bones to break. **Ehlers-Danlos syndrome** is an inherited condition characterized by hyperextensibility of joints, with predisposition for dislocation at shoulder girdle, shoulder, elbow, hip, and knee joints. Other features are loose and/or hyperextensible skin, slow wound healing with inadequate scar tissue, and fragility of blood vessel walls. Sports with a high risk of injury are therefore contraindicated. Special emphasis is given to blister prevention (e.g., properly fitted shoes) and hand protection (e.g., gloves). The best activity is probably water exercise. Often splints, braces, or protective devices are beneficial to keep hypermobile joints from dislocating during exercise.

Childhood Growth Disorders

The physical educator working with junior high or middle school youngsters is confronted with a high incidence of **osteochondroses** or growth plate disorders. Such diagnoses as *Perthes' disease, Osgood-Schlatter disease, Kohler's disease, Calve's disease,* and *Scheuermann's disease* all fall within this category and demand adaptations in physical education.

An *osteochondrosis* is an abnormality of an **epiphysis** (growth plate) in which normal growth or ossification is disturbed. Disorders of the growth plate include premature closure, delayed closure, and interruption in the growth process. **Epiphyseal closure** occurs at different ages. Bones of the upper limbs and scapulae become completely ossified at ages 17 to 20 years. Bones of the lower limbs become completely ossified at 18 to 23 years. Bones of the vertebrae, sternum, and clavicle are the last to ossify (ages 23 to 25) and thus are the most vulnerable to growth disorders.

Bone growth and subsequent closure are affected by heredity, diet, hormones, general health status, and trauma. Ill health and malnutrition generally delay overall growth plate closure. Obese children are particularly susceptible to disorders of the growth plate.

Some of the most common sites of growth plate disorders are depicted in Figure 24.19 and listed in Table 24.2. Over 70% of the osteochondroses are found at the first four sites mentioned in Table 24.2. The pathology in all of the osteochondroses is similar. For unknown reasons, cells within the bony center of the epiphysis undergo partial **necrosis** (death), probably from interference with the blood supply. The *necrotic* tissue is removed by special cells called osteoclasts, and the bony center is temporarily softened and liable to **shape deformation,** which may become permanent. In time, the condition arrests itself. New, healthy bone cells replace the dead tissue, and the bones return to normal.

This cycle of changes may take as long as 2 years, during which time the youngster must be kept off the affected limb. Enforcing this rule of no weight bearing on an athletic child is not easy since the child experiences no symptoms of illness and only occasional pain. The primary danger in osteochondroses is not in the present, but rather in the deformity,

Figure 24.19 Common sites of osteochondroses, also called growth plate disorders, because they occur in childhood or adolescence.

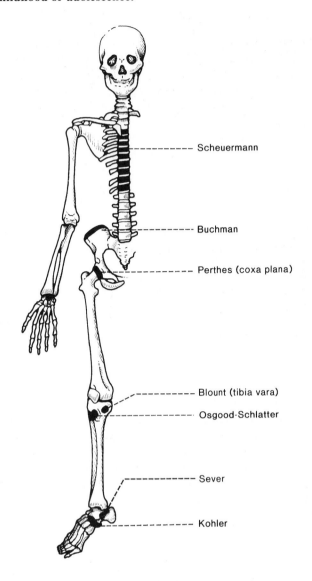

Figure 24.20 Steve Welch, with Perthes' disease, started wheelchair training in childhood and today is a world-renowned tennis and basketball player. Steve uses the wheelchair only for sports.

Table 24.2 Common sites of growth plate disorders, listed in order of incidence.

Bony Part Affected	Name of Disorder
Tibial tuberosity	Osgood-Schlatter
Calcaneus	Sever
Thoracic vertebra	Scheuermann
Head of femur	Perthes (Legg-Calve-Perthes)
Tibia	Blount
Tarsal, navicular	Kohler
Iliac crest	Buchman

limp, and predisposition to arthritis that occur if rules are not followed. Many persons with growth plate disorders qualify as Class 3 wheelchair basketball players. This is because the residual effects of their disorder make it impossible for them to be competitive in stand-up basketball (see Figure 24.20).

Osgood-Schlatter Condition

Osgood-Schlatter disease is a temporary degenerative condition of the **tibial tuberosity** that causes pain and swelling where the patellar tendon inserts on the tibia (see Figure 24.21). It is caused by a partial separation of the growth plate from the tibia, typically brought on by overuse or trauma. Adolescents who are active in strenuous sports involving the knee joint are the most vulnerable. Continuous rope jumping or kicking, for example, places much stress on the knee. Teachers who use contraindicated exercises like repeated squats and the duck walk may contribute to the onset of this condition.

Diagnosis is made by X ray, and treatment varies, depending on severity and the philosophy of the physician. The knee may be immobilized in a brace or cast for several weeks, after which activity is restricted for 3 to 6 months. *In most cases, students are told to avoid explosive knee extension or all knee extension, running, and jumping.* Non-weight-bearing isometric exercises that strengthen the quadriceps and stretch the hamstrings may be prescribed. Swimming and stationary bicycling are also recommended.

Perthes' Condition (Legg-Calve-Perthes)

Perthes' condition, the destruction of the growth center of the hip joint caused by insufficient blood supply occurs most often between the ages of 4 and 8 (see Figure 24.22). Its incidence is 1 per 18,000, and approximately four to five times more boys

Figure 24.21   Site of Osgood-Schlatter disorder.

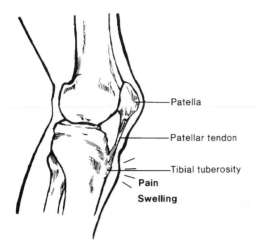

Figure 24.22   Common hip joint growth disorders.

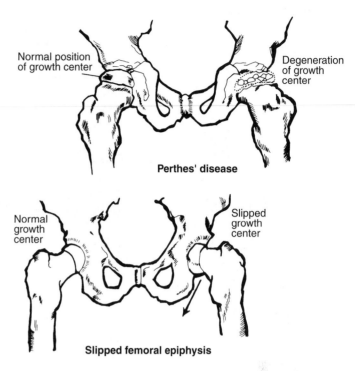

Perthes' disease

Slipped femoral epiphysis

than girls are affected. Typically, the condition lasts 2 to 4 years, during which the child may need adapted physical education—most likely in the mainstream setting. Adapting is needed in choice of activities that can be done while wearing a splint and/or using a wheelchair. Maintaining range of motion is a primary consideration in management. Bracing and surgery are also performed. If the hip joint is not protected (i.e., kept in non-weight-bearing status) during the body's natural repair process, the femoral head becomes flattened and irregular (**coxa plana**), which makes the joint surface incongruent and leads to hip joint degenerate arthritis. Sometimes, despite the best care, permanent damage (usually a slight limp) occurs.

Slipped Femoral Epiphysis (Coxa Vara)

Also called adolescent coxa vara or epiphysiolysis, **slipped femoral epiphysis (SFE)** is a hip joint disorder diagnosed by a waddling gait or a limp that favors one leg. Typically, the head of the femur is outwardly rotated. This is caused by a **downward-backward-medial slippage** of the growth center on the femoral head (see Figure 24.23). Attributed to trauma, stress, or overuse, the condition typically occurs in 11- to 16-year-olds and is associated with obesity. The incidence is 2 to 13 per 100,000. SFE is more common in males (2.2 to 1) than females and in Blacks than Whites. It may also occur in younger children as a result of falls from great heights or abuse and in newborns as a result of difficult deliveries. About 90% of cases are considered "stable," meaning the child can walk, with or without crutches. The other 10% of individuals cannot walk at all and are considered "unstable."

The groin, buttock, and lateral hip are the major pain centers. If the condition is not corrected, the affected leg becomes shorter, and adduction contractures result. These decrease the angulation of the neck of the femur, making it more horizontal and causing an inward inclination (vara position) of the femur. During exercise, persons with SFE show limited hip joint inward rotation and abduction.

Once diagnosed, SFE is usually corrected surgically by pinning the epiphysis in place. More conservative treatment is use of short-leg casts with a crossbar to prevent weight bearing and to hold the femoral head in abduction and inward rotation. *Students are usually restricted from vigorous weight-bearing physical education for about a year.* Activities in which the student is likely to fall are not recommended. Adaptation entails arranging for swimming and/or upper extremity sports and exercises in place of the regular curriculum.

Scheuermann's Disease

Juvenile kyphosis, or *Scheuermann's disease,* is a disturbance in growth of the thoracic vertebrae. It results from *epiphysitis* (inflammation of an epiphysis) and/or *osteochondritis* (inflammation of cartilage), either of which may cause fragmentation of vertebral bodies. One or several vertebrae are involved. The etiology is generally unknown. *During the active phase, forward flexion is contraindicated.* The student should be protected from all flexion movements by a hyperextension brace, which places the weight on the neural arches rather than on the defective vertebral bodies.

Although there is some discomfort, the pain is not great enough to impose limitation of natural movement; sometimes the condition is pain-free. In such instances, convincing the student to refrain from activity may be difficult. Unfortunately, if bracing and nonactivity are not enforced, the resulting kyphotic hump may be both severe and persistent. When X rays reveal the healing of fragmented areas, unrestricted class participation is resumed. Occasionally, the student will continue to wear a back brace, body jacket, or cast for a number of months after the disease is arrested.

Figure 24.23 Hip joint dislocation and slippage.

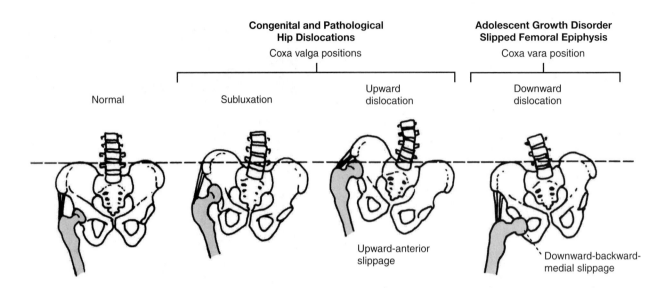

Scoliosis and Chest Deformity

Lateral curvature of the spine is discussed fully in Chapter 14 on postures. Severe conditions are treated by surgery, casting, and braces. As in Scheuermann's disease, vigorous forward flexion of the trunk may be contraindicated. Otherwise, physical activity is seldom restricted unless the condition is caused by concurrent disabilities.

Many of the conditions in this chapter are associated with scoliosis and chest deformities that limit respiration and aerobic fitness. Breathing and ROM exercises and games are important.

Congenital Dislocation of the Hip

Congenital dislocation of the hip (CDH) encompasses various degrees of **dysplasia,** or abnormal development, of the hip socket (acetabulum) and/or head of the femur. This condition is the fourth most common congenital defect. It is more common among girls than boys and usually occurs in one hip rather than both. Its incidence is approximately 1 to 3 per 1,000 births.

Subluxation and *luxation* are synonyms for dislocation, describing the position of the femoral head in relation to a **shallow, dysplasic acetabulum** (see Figure 24.23). In subluxation, the femur is only partially displaced, whereas in luxation, the femoral head is completely dislocated above the acetabulum rim. Nonsurgical treatment involves repositioning, traction, and casting. In the majority of cases in which the child is over age 3, surgical reduction (repositioning) is used. After age 6, more complicated operative procedures, such as **osteotomy** (dividing a bone or cutting out a portion) and **arthroplasty** (reconstructing a joint), are applied.

Reference to congenital hip dislocation on a child's record usually means that he or she has undergone long periods of hospitalization and immobilization in splints or casts extending from waist to toes. Generally, the child has had fewer opportunities to learn social and motor skills through informal play than have peers without disabilities. As in other congenital anomalies, any problems the child manifests are more likely to be psychological than physical.

Pathological Dislocation of the Hip

Dislocation of the hip is a problem commonly associated with persons unable to stand because of severe paralytic or neurological conditions (polio, spina bifida, cerebral palsy). The incidence of dislocation in severely disabled nonambulatory persons is 25%. The average age of dislocation is 7 years, but the range of frequent occurrence varies from 2 to 10 years. Like CDH, the condition is corrected by surgery.

Pathological dislocation may occur at any age. In most cases, the head of the femur becomes **displaced upward and anteriorly.** Pathological dislocation appears mostly in persons with **coxa valga** (increased neck-shaft angle of femur) and hip **adduction contracture.** Coxa valga is present in most normal infants before weight bearing begins; a gradual change in neck-shaft femoral angle accompanies normal motor development. Childhood coxa valga and associated hip dislocation thus sometimes characterize delayed or abnormal motor development.

Clubfoot (Talipes)

Talipes equinovarus, or *congenital clubfoot,* is the most common of all orthopedic defects, with an incidence of 1 out of approximately 1,000 births (see Figure 24.24). **Talipes** comes from two Latin words: *talus,* meaning "ankle" and *pes,* meaning "foot." *Equinovarus* (stemming from *equus,* meaning "horse," and *varus,* meaning "bent in") is an adjective specifying a position in which the entire foot is inverted, the heel is drawn up, and the forefoot is adducted. This forces the child to walk on the outer border of the foot. Manipulation, bracing, and casting are preferred options to correct clubfoot. Surgery is performed as a last resort, followed by casting at 2-week intervals and thermoplastic bracing. Approximately one fourth of all surgeries need to be repeated.

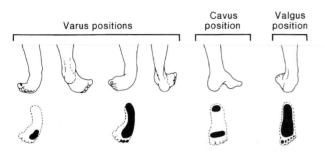

Figure 24.25   Surgically corrected clubfeet of preadolescent boy.

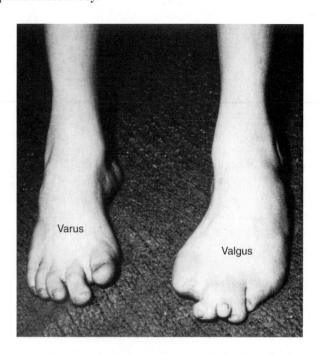

Types of Talipes

Talipes equinovarus varies in degree of severity. Changes in the tendons and ligaments result mostly from contractures. The Achilles and tibial tendons are always shortened, causing a tendency to walk on the toes or forefoot. Bony changes occur chiefly in the talus, calcaneus, navicular, and cuboid. Tibial torsion is usually present.

Several other types of talipes are recognized (see Figure 24.24):

1. **Talipes cavus.** Hollow foot or arch so high as to be disabling.
2. **Talipes calcaneus.** Contracture of foot in dorsiflexed position.
3. **Talipes equinus.** Contracture of foot in plantar-flexed position.
4. **Talipes varus.** Contracture of foot with toes and sole of foot turned inward. Associated with **spastic** hemiplegic cerebral palsy and/or scissors gait.
5. **Talipes valgus.** Contracture of foot with toes and sole of foot turned outward. Associated with **athetoid** cerebral palsy, arthritis, and flat or pronated feet.

Just as *talipes equinovarus,* the most common form, is a combination of two types, so any two types can coexist as calcaneovarus, calcaneovalgus, or equinovalgus.

Program Implications

Figure 24.25 shows the clubfoot of a preadolescent boy who has undergone several operations and spent months in casts and braces. He is an enthusiastic athlete and in the starting lineup of his Little League baseball team. His slight limp is noticeably worse during cold winter days and rainy seasons, when he can hardly walk the first hour or so after awakening. As the day wears on, his gait becomes almost normal, enabling him to run fast enough to hold his own in athletic feats with peers.

Metatarsus varus (in-toeing) is a frequent congenital defect similar to clubfoot except that only the forefoot or metatarsal area is affected. The treatment for talipes and metatarsus varus is similar, beginning preferably within the first 2 weeks of life with casting that may continue for many months.

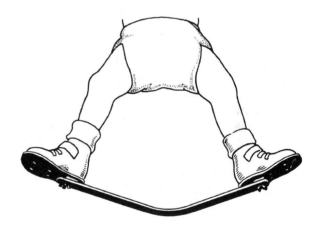

The weight of a cast prevents normal mobility of the infant and may delay the accomplishment of such motor tasks as rolling over, standing alone, and walking.

The Denis-Browne splint is one option for correcting clubfoot and other defects (see Figure 24.26). It may be worn nights only or both day and night. Although it does not permit standing, the splint allows vigorous activities that utilize crawling, creeping, and scooterboards. Current technology also includes thermoplastic braces with Velcro fasteners as a correction option for some.

In spite of correction, the gait of a person with congenital foot problems may continue to be impaired so that persons do not have a fair chance in competitive activities with peers. *Such persons are eligible for wheelchair sports.* Impaired gait is not always present as superstar skater Kristi Yamaguchi and Dallas Cowboys quarterback Troy Aikman can attest to. Both have had clubfeet corrected.

Limb Deficiencies and Amputations

International sport classifications distinguish between *limb deficiencies* (congenital amputations) and *acquired amputations*. Limb deficiencies are considered les autres conditions.

Prevalence of amputations in the United States ranges from 300,000 to over 500,000. This is probably because some estimates include both congenital and acquired amputations, while others include only the acquired. Statistics might be affected also by the fact that many individuals born with limb deficiencies have malformed body parts amputated at an early age so that prostheses can be fitted. Limb deficiencies are much more common than acquired amputations, with a 2:1 ratio usually given. Most sources agree that lower limb amputations are more common than upper limb amputations.

Types of Limb Deficiencies

Many types of limb deficiencies and malformations exist, each with its own name (e.g., thrombocytopenia absent radius, proximal focal femoral deficiency). For simplicity, however, two categories can be used to encompass the many individual differences: **dysmelia** (absence of arms or legs) and **phocomelia** (absence of middle segment of limb, but with intact proximal and distal portions). In the latter, hands or feet are attached directly to shoulders or hips, respectively. In phocomelia (*phoco* means "seal-like" and *melos* means "limb"), the hand or foot is often removed surgically within the first few months after birth. Absence of the fibula, with a congenitally deformed foot, is also a common condition that is corrected surgically.

Joey Lipski, world-class swimmer and track star, is illustrative of a person with dysmelia (see Figure 24.27). Born without arms, he does not wear prostheses in competition. Joey learned to swim at age 8 and at age 15 set world records for his classification in the 100-m freestyle event (2:05.6) and in the 50-m backstroke (57.0). He runs the 100-m dash in 19.5 sec and the 200-m event in 41.42 sec.

Karen Farmer, world-class athlete in discus, javelin, and shot put, was born with a clubfoot and missing fibula. This condition was surgically corrected when she was 18 months old, and a prosthesis was fitted soon afterward. Her shot put and discus records are 10.02 and 32.36 m, respectively. Almost all of Karen's competitive experience has been against AB athletes; she attended Washington State University on an athletic scholarship and says she has never found a sport she could not master.

The cause of limb deficiencies is seldom known. In the 1960s the drug **thalidomide,** used as a sedative and sleeping pill, was identified as having caused hundreds of birth defects and immediately removed from the market. Since then drugs have been tested more carefully before they are placed on the market. Nevertheless, each year many individuals are born with limb deficiencies. Most develop considerable manual dexterity with upper limb body parts and opt not to use artificial limbs (see Figure 24.27). With help, they can find many sports that do not require arms for success (e.g., soccer, track, field, swimming). Individuals with lower limb deficiencies have many

Figure 24.27   Examples of limb deficiencies.

Dysmelia: absence of limbs

Phocomelia: middle limb portions missing with digits extending from upper arms

choices: wheelchair sports, ambulatory sports with prostheses, or activities that can be done without prostheses like swimming and high jumping. For an excellent review of sport opportunities historically for people with limb deficiencies, see Webster, Levy, Bryant, and Prusakowski (2001).

Prostheses

A *prosthesis* (plural: *prostheses*) is a substitute for a missing body part (e.g., limb, eye, breast). A limb **prosthesis** contains several parts: (a) the socket, (b) a connection mechanism (e.g., harness, straps, suspension device, suction apparatus, clamp), and (c) a terminal device, which is either cosmetic or mechanically efficient. Age of prosthetic fitting is obviously very important in subsequent development of motor skills. Upper extremity prostheses are fitted when the child develops good sitting balance, usually between 8 and 10 months of age. Lower extremity prostheses are fitted when the child begins to pull up to a stand, usually between 10 and 15 months. As the child grows, the prostheses must be periodically replaced: every 15 to 18 months for an upper extremity prosthesis and about every 12 months for a lower extremity prosthesis.

Since 1964 immediate postsurgical prosthetic fitting has gradually become the trend. This practice offers several advantages. First, particularly in a person with cancer, a prosthesis and early ambulation contributes to a positive psychological outlook. Second, amputation stumps in children do not usually shrink, and there is no physical reason for delaying fitting. Third, phantom pain is not as prevalent because of early fitting with a prosthesis and weight bearing. Fourth, edema (swelling) is best controlled and wound healing facilitated by an immediate postsurgical socket.

After surgery, individuals go to rehabilitation centers, where they are provided with training in use of the prosthesis by physical therapists and occupational therapists. Ideally, this training includes exposure to playground equipment and recreational activities. If the child does not appear secure in class activities utilizing gymnastic and playground equipment, the adapted physical educator may need to supplement the hospital training.

The usefulness of lower limb prostheses has improved tremendously since 1982, when a **prosthetist** named Van Phillips created the Flex-Foot, a lightweight, energy-efficient prosthesis made of carbon fiber composite, the material used extensively in the aerospace industry for its superior strength and flexibility.

Today, more than 40 models of prosthetic feet are available. People needing high-performance feet, particularly runners, often prefer **energy-storing feet,** which contain a spring. Those who do not perform high-impact activities typically prefer **energy-absorbing feet,** which cushion impact. Popular brands include the Otto Bock Dynamic foot, Seattle Lightfoot, Flex-Foot II, Carbon Copy, and Pathfinder. These and others can be viewed in the excellent magazine, *Challenge,* published by DS/USA.

Case Study: Young Track Star

Tony Volpentest, born with short malformed arms and legs, was the world's fastest leg-amputee for many years. He began track as a high school sophomore, working out and running with the able-bodied team, but initially was able to run the 100 in only

Figure 24.28   Many models of prostheses enable choices to meet specific activity needs.

16.9 seconds, way behind peers. In one season, he bettered his time to 14.3. A year later Tony participated in his first disability sport meet, won all of his races, and learned about Flex-Foot. Today, wearing Flex-Foot, Tony runs the 100 in about 11.26 and the 200 in about 22.67, times that often enable him to beat able-bodied competitors.

Many factors contribute to the success of athletes with amputations. First is hard work. Like most Paralympic athletes, Tony trained 2 to 3 hr a day, splitting his time between track practice and strength training. Technology is also important, and athletes must be helped to find sponsors to cover the cost of prosthetic devices. For example, Tony's prostheses cost about $20,000. If an athlete shows outstanding potential, companies like Flex-Foot Inc. will often donate prostheses. Tony also had the full support of family and coaches, who urged him to get involved in mainstream sport as early as possible. These individuals helped him also with creative solutions to problems like his inability to assume the track starting position because he has abnormally short arms. The solution to this is using two paint cans topped with padding (see Figure 24.29A,B).

Read Challenge *and* Palaestra *to stay abreast of champion athletes who wear prostheses and/or use adapted sports equipment to accommodate amputations. Develop bulletin boards and media presentations concerning role models. Who are the world's fastest amputees today? How fast are they?*

Gaits and Movement Patterns

Individuals with lower limb amputations use many movement patterns. Those with **double-leg amputations** often walk on their stumps when at home or forced to do so by architectural barriers that make wheelchair use impossible. For sports some use wheelchairs, although many prefer the new lightweight prosthetic devices. Those with **single-leg amputations** most often use one of the many models of prosthetic feet available.

Mobility ease varies considerably, depending on whether the amputation is **above the knee** or **below the knee.** Balance is more difficult for someone without a natural knee. Above-the-knee amputees typically wear a prosthesis with a hydraulic device in the knee, similar to a shock absorber, to assist with flexion and extension and enable a normal appearance when walking. Going up stairs, however, necessitates a modified pattern for someone with an above-the-knee amputation, as a prosthetic knee cannot flex or extend to raise the person's weight up to the next step.

Running gaits used by people with prostheses are called hop-skip running and leg-over-leg running. **Hop-skip running** entails the following sequence: (a) stepping forward on the sound leg, (b) hopping on the sound leg while swinging through the prosthetic leg, (c) switching weight to the prosthetic side, and (d) immediately transferring weight to the sound side. The new lightweight prosthetic devices permit **leg-over-leg running** that looks like the able-bodied reciprocal running pattern, except for a slight asymmetry in stride length and time spent on each foot. (See Figure 24.29.)

If a child uses crutches in addition to, or instead of a lower extremity prosthesis, professionals should encourage participation but watch closely for fatigue signs, in that crutch-racing puts much strain on the hip joints. *Racing should be done only with forearm crutches, never axillary crutches.*

Balance

Balance is probably the most troublesome aspect of motor performance for persons with amputations. The natural limb is used for kicking balls while the prosthetic limb maintains the weight of the body. In ascending stairs, the child should be taught to lead with the sound limb; in descending, to lead with the prosthesis in the stable extended position. The bilateral above-knee amputee has more difficulty with steps and often requires a railing and crutch. The weight of a bowling ball or tennis racket in a unilateral upper-limb amputation may cause balance problems. This problem, at least in bowling, can be overcome by developing a scissors step, crossing the leg on the good arm side over the other, and taking the weight of the ball in stride.

Reduced Cooling Surfaces and Perspiration

Amputation or a limb deficiency reduces skin surface area and hence affects the normal heat dissipation process by which the body cools itself. Perspiration is therefore increased in the rest of the body, necessitating special attention to exercise clothing, room temperature, and stump and prosthesis hygiene. Use of a prosthesis increases energy expenditure, which further exacerbates sweating. Perspiration of the stump inside a socket predisposes the skin to bacterial and fungal infections. Adaptations

Figure 24.29 (A) Tony Volpentest, born with deficiencies of both arms and legs, running the 100 m in 11.26 seconds. (B) The adaptation needed at the starting blocks for runners with short arms.

A

B

include monitoring individuals for heat-related illness; encouraging the drinking of extra fluids before, during, and after exercise; and checking that stumps are kept dry.

Skin Breakdown on Stump

Skin irritations and ulcerations on the stump can be prevented by proper socket fit and good personal hygiene if individuals choose to exercise or ambulate without a prosthesis. Socks and gloves covering stumps should be made of porous, absorbent materials. Sunburn should be prevented. Stumps should be washed and dried thoroughly daily or more often, depending on the amount of perspiration.

Muscle Atrophy, Contractures, and Posture Problems

Muscle atrophy and contractures around the stump or limb deficiency should be prevented by daily strength and range-of-motion (ROM) exercises. Hip joint muscles are prone to flexion, abduction, and outward rotation contractures, and knee joint muscles are prone to flexion contractions. These are the muscle groups that should be stretched. Strength exercises should focus on their antagonists.

Unequal leg length and/or use of one side more than the other can contribute to scoliosis and to hip or knee degeneration. **Early-onset arthritis** is a common side effect of mechanical inefficiency. Correct postures should be emphasized. Individuals typically stand with their weight on their good leg rather than distributing their weight equally.

Increased Energy Expenditure

Although high-technology, high-efficiency prostheses featured in this chapter are lightweight, some prostheses (especially those for double amputations) are relatively heavy and increase energy requirements. Loss of muscle mass through an amputation also decreases the number of muscles available to move the body. Obesity further complicates this problem, because the heavier a person is, the heavier the prosthesis must be. The use of crutches with prostheses increases energy expenditure still more. Individuals might therefore fatigue early and require more motivation and support to continue in exercise programs that will increase their strength, flexibility, and aerobic endurance. Some persons choose to use wheelchairs instead of prostheses because most wheelchairs require less energy expenditure than prostheses.

Acquired Amputations

Acquired amputations occur more often in adults than in children. Diabetes and circulatory problems associated with heart disease often necessitate amputations in middle and old age. Injuries, particularly vehicular accidents, are major causes also.

The etiologies of acquired amputations in children in order of incidence are trauma, cancer, infection, and vascular conditions like gangrene. Under trauma, the leading causes of amputations are farm and power tool accidents, vehicular accidents, and gunshot explosions. Most of these occur in the age group from 12 to 21. Children who lose limbs because of malignancy are also primarily within this age group.

Arnie Boldt, the one-legged world champion high jumper, is illustrative of a person with an acquired amputation (see Figure 24.30). Raised on a farm, he lost his lower leg in a farm accident at 3 years of age. Much of his competitive experience has been against AB athletes.

Terry Fox, who died of cancer, is perhaps the best-known individual with an amputation. He devoted the last months of his life to running (with one leg) across Canada to raise money for cancer and increase awareness. His story, available on videotape, is well worth watching.

Case Study: Young Racquetball Star

Fifteen-year-old Chris Coy is much like his peers, with a few exceptions. He was named by *Sports Illustrated* as the 2000 Young Sportsman of the Year. He won the 2000 U.S. National Singles C Level Championship by beating the top-seeded man, who was triple his age. In May 2002, he became the youngest man ever to win the U.S. National Adult Men's A Level Championship. As a result, Chris is now on the USA Paralympic Racquetball Team. Chris's achievements have come in spite of having a prosthetic foot and ankle.

Chris was diagnosed with cancer in his stomach at 5 weeks of age and began chemotherapy immediately, which lasted for 2½ years. His spleen was damaged and removed because of the cancer, which contributed to vascular infection in his leg, necessitating his lower leg being amputated at age 4. Because of the chemotherapy, Chris now has heart deterioration and continues his once-a-year checkups at the Children's Hospital in Dallas. None of the challenges have prevented the teen from becoming an outstanding racquetball player, however. After his parents purchased a health club when Chris was 7, he picked up his first racket. Only one year later, Chris played in his first world championship and earned the sponsorship of Pro Kennex. Chris continues with his 4-hour-a-day practices and also continues to make frequent trips to his prosthetist to replace the prostheses he has broken from diving and sliding on the court. Fortunately, Chris now has the sponsorship of Flex-Foot, the makers of his prosthesis!

Degree of Severity

Persons with acquired amputations often undergo considerable difficulty in adjusting to a missing body part and incorporating disability into their many identities. Additionally, there are often concurrent injuries or health problems that professionals must address. *Nevertheless, in the sporting world, amputations are considered minimal disabilities (except when both legs are lost at the hip).* All of the facts presented under limb deficiencies apply to acquired amputations. In fact, many acquired amputations in children are elective (i.e., acquired) because incomplete or malformed limb parts need to be removed for better fit of prostheses.

PE Adaptations for Persons With Amputations

A main adaptation pertains to dressing and shower rules. Girls and boys should be allowed to wear long pants or the type of clothing in which they feel most comfortable. Shower rules should be waived. The person who is sensitive about changing clothes in the locker room should be given a place of his or her own, and classmates should be encouraged to allow the desired privacy.

The general attitude among physicians is that persons with an amputation can do anything if the prostheses are well fitted. Some children may need no adaptations. Each child should be encouraged to do as much as he or she can.

Sports Programming

Sports programming for children with both limb deficiencies and amputations should be as similar to that of peers in general physical education as possible. From about the age of 14 on, individuals should have opportunities for training and competing with disability sport clubs as well as with their AB peers in interscholastic athletics. The sports advanced by disability sport clubs lend insight into what activities persons with the different sport classifications will excel in; these organizations also provide information about sport prostheses and wheelchairs and sometimes help with equipment costs. Following are brief sections on sport classification and the sports particularly recommended by the Disability Sports/USA. Additionally, *athletes with amputations who use wheelchairs often excel in wheelchair basketball.* In that sport, amputations are considered to be minimal limitations, so athletes' basketball classification is 3 (the highest possible) unless amputation of both legs is so high that no stumps remain.

Figure 24.30   Canadian Arnie Boldt, world champion high jumper.

Table 24.3   Summer sport classifications for persons with amputations to equalize fairness of competition.

Class A1 = Double AK	Class A7 = Double BE
Class A2 = Single AK	Class A8 = Single BE
Class A3 = Double BK	Class A9 = Combined
Class A4 = Single BK	lower plus
Class A5 = Double AE	upper limb
Class A6 = Single AE	amputations

Note. AK = Above or through the knee joint; BK = Below the knee, but through or above the ankle joint; AE = Above or through the elbow joint; BE = Below the elbow, but through or above the wrist joint.

Amputee Sport Classifications

By the time children with amputations reach adolescence, many want opportunities for vigorous competition against others with comparable disabilities. To ensure fair competition, ISOD and Disabled Sport/USA enforce a strict classification system, with nine classifications (see Table 24.3). Some of these are presented in Figures 24.31 and 24.32. Note that the odd numbers (1, 3, 5, 7, 9) denote the greater disability.

Track and Field

Individuals have a choice between ambulatory and wheelchair track. The usual practice is for Classes A1 and A3 to use

Figure 24.31 Amputee sport classifications. Classifications A1 to A4. How would you program for these persons?

Classification A1, double AK

Classification A2, single AK

Classification A3, double BK

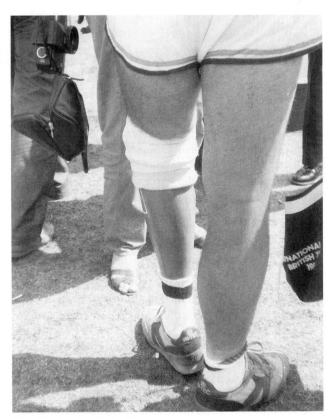

Classification A4, single BK

Figure 24.32 Amputee sport classifications. Classifications A6, A5, and A2. How would you program for these persons?

Classification A6, single AE

Classification A5 (double AE) with girlfriend who has A2 (single AK)

wheelchairs and for Classes A2 and A4 to compete standing, using a prosthesis.

In field events, fewer classifications are used. In field, double arm amputees compete together in one class, whether the amputation is above or below the elbow, and single arm amputees likewise form one class. More severely involved lower extremity amputees use wheelchairs, whereas less involved ones throw from a standing position.

Both long and high jump events are popular. For high jumps, athletes seldom use prostheses. For long jumps, high-performance feet are preferred.

Sitting and Standing Volleyball

Volleyball is governed by the ISOD and, at the Paralympic level, is considered an amputee sport. Trained classifiers evaluate each player, based on level of amputation, muscle strength, joint range of motion, and/or difference in limb length, and determine class for each athlete (A, B, C). There must be at least one Class C player (least physically able) on the floor at all times, and no more than one Class A player (most physically able) on the floor. Six players are on the court at a time, as in regular volleyball. *Sitting volleyball* is similar to *standing volleyball*, ex-

cept that players sit on the floor and the net is lower (Davis, 2002). Specifically, the net is 4 ft high for men and 3 ft 6 in. high for women.

Plan and implement a sitting volleyball game for your classmates or some high school students. Jot your observations into your journal.

Swimming

Persons with limb deficiencies and amputations race against individuals with various other kinds of disabilities in the Paralympic functional swimming classification system (Dummer, 1999) and often win. Prostheses are not permitted in competition. Professionals should know that loss of a body part causes displacement of the center of gravity and center of buoyancy to the opposite side. The intact side tends to sink. Loss of a right arm or leg thus creates a tendency to roll to the left, which can usually be overcome by turning the head toward the affected side. Think about performing a logroll in the water; this is the lateral rotation that persons with missing limbs must learn to control.

Figure 24.33 Therapeutic horseback riding was initiated in England in the 1950s. The first established program in the United States began in 1968, when the Cheff Center in Augusta, Michigan, opened. Don Drewry *(in the photos)* was taught riding by a Cheff Center graduate. Note the specially made saddle.

 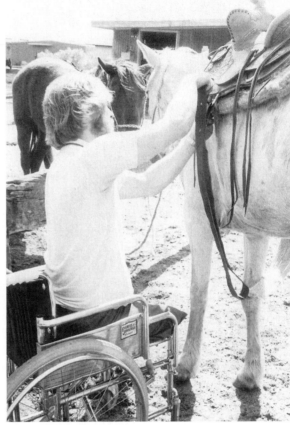

Double-leg amputation increases trunk buoyancy but causes the head to lie low. Stretching the arms out behind the head tends to cause vertical rotation (a back somersault), so considerable movement exploration is needed to decide on a preferred stroke. For instructional and recreational swimming, fins or plexiglass paddles can be attached to stumps. Swimming classification guidelines can be found at usa-swimming.org under "Adapted."

Horseback Riding, Cycles, and Other Vehicles

Recreational and competitive riding is popular. Many individuals propel cycles with one leg. All-terrain vehicles make camping, hunting, and fishing possible. Specially made saddles and other kinds of equipment are often needed in horseback riding (see Figure 24.33).

Other Sports

Use of prostheses and orthoses is regulated. In air pistol, air rifle, sitting volleyball, and swimming, for instance, prostheses and orthoses are not permitted. In archery, the draw may be made with a prosthesis or orthosis, and a releasing aid may be used by Classes A6, A8, and A9. These classes may also receive help with loading arrows into the bow. In lawn bowling, Classes

A5 and A7 may use prostheses or orthoses if they wish. In table tennis, however, these are not allowed. Persons who are unable to perform a regulation serve because of their disability are allowed to bounce the ball on the table and then smash it across the net. Physical educators need a lot of information to help students with amputations prepare for high-level competition.

Winter Sports

Children with and without amputations learn to ski at very young ages; most ski champions with amputations report learning to ski at age 3 or 4. They were born with limb deficiencies or lost limbs in accidents during early childhood or the elementary years (see Figure 24.34). Some learn to ski with a prosthesis, but many prefer their natural state. Competitively, disability skiing is no different from able-bodied skiing. **Alpine races** are run in slalom, grand slalom, super giant slalom, and downhill. **Cross-country** has both classic and freestyle events (Paciorek & Jones, 2001). Within each of these, there are standup events and mono-skier events for athletes with amputations. Special courses in adapted or adaptive skiing techniques are offered to prospective instructors. Information, including access to excellent videotapes, is available through Disabled Sports/USA or the Professional Ski Instructors of America.

Figure 24.34 Instructors with adapted ski certification teach children with amputations basic techniques.

 OPTIONAL ACTIVITIES

1. Watch the movie or video, *Simon Birch* (1998). What strengths and weaknesses did Simon have physically, emotionally, or cognitively? What adaptations for his disability did you note in the movie?

2. Research the story of Terry Fox, see a video, or read the book *Terry Fox* (1983). What does his story teach you about motivation and disability? Also find out about landmines as a major source of amputations in Africa and the Middle East. What adaptations are being made in family life?

3. Watch the movie or video, *I Am Not a Freak* (1991). How does this movie challenge your stereotypical assumptions about people with disabilities? Give examples.

4. Research the history of track and field events for athletes with les autres conditions and amputations at the Paralympic Games. How have time and distance records changed over the years, and in which events? To what factors would these changes be attributable? See *Sports 'N Spokes, Challenge,* and books on the Paralympics; Tweedy (2002); and the Paralympics website: www.paralympic.org.

5. Take a field trip to a center where prostheses are fitted and constructed and/or to a rehabilitation center where persons typically spend their first days after an amputation. Ask about volunteer activities. Inquire of orthopedic surgeons if any older postoperative persons can use your help.

CHAPTER

25

Cerebral Palsy, Stroke, and Traumatic Brain Injury

Figure 25.1 Widespread individual differences exist within cerebral palsy. *(A)* Class 7 and 8 athletes play soccer. *(B)* Class 1 athlete plays indoor wheelchair soccer. *(C)* Class 2 athletes use their feet to propel specially designed chairs.

A

B

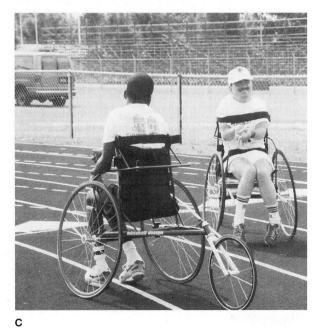

C

1. Why are (a) cerebral palsy (CP), (b) stroke, and (c) traumatic brain injury (TBI) grouped together in this chapter? What are similarities and differences? How do these affect physical activity programming?

2. Contrast associated dysfunctions of the general CP population with athletes with CP. Explain the importance of not making generalizations.

3. Explain four types of motor disorders: (a) spasticity, (b) athetosis, (c) ataxia, and (d) hypotonia. Which chapters in this text offer the most information for each? Which information is most meaningful to you? Why?

4. Describe eight profiles that can be used for physical education-recreation assessment and programming for individuals with CP, stroke, and TBI. Given descriptions of functional ability, be able to correctly assign the profiles, discuss programming, and write IEPs.

5. Identify and discuss person-environment variables that complicate programming for CP, stroke, and TBI.

6. Discuss the National Disability Sports Alliance (NDSA) and other resources in terms of their roles in sport socialization and in lifelong sport interest and activity. Describe sports especially designed for CP.

Cerebral palsy (CP), stroke, and traumatic brain injury (TBI) are grouped together in this chapter because individuals with these conditions have many common needs. CP, by definition, is primarily a motor disorder, whereas stroke and TBI usually (but not always) affect motor function. Often multiple parts of the brain are damaged, and sensory, perceptual, and cognitive disorders of varying degrees of severity coexist with motor problems. Despite multiple disabilities, most individuals with these conditions can participate in a wide range of sport activities (see Figure 25.1).

Cognitive ability is the variable that determines the governing sport organization. When motor impairment occurs *without mental retardation,* individuals are served by the Cerebral Palsy–International Sports and Recreation Association (CP-ISRA) and affiliated national organizations like the Canadian Cerebral Palsy Sports Association and the National Disability Sports Alliance (NDSA), formerly the United States Cerebral Palsy Athletic Association (USCPAA). When a dual diagnosis of mental retardation and motor impairment is made, individuals are served by Special Olympics and the International Sports Federation for Persons with Intellectual Disabilities (INAS-FID).

This chapter focuses on NDSA programming because many individuals who are eligible to benefit from CP sports are not being identified in the public schools and provided with the kind of instruction needed to develop lifespan healthy, active lifestyles. Programming for individuals with CP, stroke, and TBI is challenging because of the many individual differences that occur when the brain is damaged. This requires knowledge of eight sport classifications to guide programming decisions as well as background information on reflexes (see Chapter 10), neurological soft signs and attention deficits (see Chapter 20), and wheelchair technology (see Chapters 2, 23, and 24).

Definitions, Etiologies, and Incidence

Two conditions discussed in this chapter—CP and stroke—are classified by the U.S. federal government as orthopedic impairments. The third condition—TBI—was recognized as a separate diagnostic category by PL 101-476, IDEA, enacted in 1990. Prior to this, TBI in children was associated with CP and learning disabilities.

Cerebral Palsy

Cerebral palsy (CP) is a chronic neurologic disorder of movement and posture caused by damage to the immature brain and accompanied by associated dysfunctions. CP is not hereditary, contagious, or progressive. The disorder varies from mild (generalized clumsiness or a slight limp) to severe (dominated by reflexes, dependence on motorized chair, use of assistive devices for communication, and almost no control of motor function).

About 90% of CP brain damage occurs before or during birth. Common prenatal causes are maternal infections (e.g., AIDS, rubella, herpes), chemical toxins (e.g., alcohol, tobacco, prescribed and nonprescribed drugs), and injuries to the mother that affect fetal development. Maternal age is associated with CP, with the risk increased for mothers under age 20 or over age 34. Prematurity and low birth weight both increase the incidence of CP. Direct damage to the brain can occur during difficult deliveries or under conditions that cause oxygen deprivation (**anoxia, hypoxia, asphyxia**).

About 10% of CP occurs postnatally, with estimates ranging from 6 to 25%. Sources vary with regard to definition of immature brain, with most requiring manifestation of a movement problem before age 2 years but some accepting age 5 as the diagnostic cutoff. Brain infections (encephalitis, meningitis), brain traumas from accidents and child abuse, chemical toxins (airborne or ingested), and oxygen deprivation are the most common causes of acquired CP.

Because diagnostic criteria are controversial, CP incidence and prevalence rates vary. The incidence is approximately 7 per 1,000 live births, and the prevalence is 500 cases in every 100,000 persons. The 2000 census figures for the U.S. population (250 million) are the basis for the estimate that 1,250,000 persons have CP. The condition is more common among males than females and also among firstborn. *CP is the orthopedic impairment most often found in the public schools.*

Stroke

Stroke, also called cerebrovascular accident (CVA) or disease, is the sudden onset of neurological impairment (awareness, motor, speech, perception, memory, cognition) that occurs when the flow of oxygen and nutrients to the brain is disrupted by blood clot blockage (**ischemia**) or bleeding (**hemorrhage**). Strokes can occur at any age, although they are most common after age 60. **Ischemic strokes** are associated with heart disease and high cholesterol levels, whereas **hemorrhagic strokes** are linked with high blood pressure, weak or malformed arteries and veins within the brain, and leukemia. Approximately 80% of strokes are ischemic.

Figure 25.2 shows that strokes affect many functions. **Left-brain strokes** result in weakness or paralysis of the right side; speech/language deficits; a slow, cautious behavioral style; and memory deficits that affect speech. **Right-brain strokes** impair movement on the left side of the body. Recovery of muscle function, including speech, can progress for several months or stop abruptly, leaving the individual permanently disabled. Typically, a paralyzed state gradually progresses from flaccidity (**hypotonus**) to spasticity, to flexor and extensor stereotypic patterns called **synergies,** to return of voluntary movement. The *synergies* look and act like primitive reflexes. Most persons with complete stroke have difficulty with both sitting and standing balance (Shumway-Cook & Wollacott, 2001), and postural reactions must be relearned. During the spasticity stage, contractures must be prevented by daily range of motion (ROM) exercises.

Over 2 million Americans are coping with the residual effects of stroke. This is about 1 of every 125 persons. Strokes are more common in males until about age 75, after which the incidence is equal for both sexes. The incidence of strokes in children is about 2.3 cases per 100,000 population per year, much more common than most people realize. In the past, **early childhood strokes** that resulted in motor impairment were often mistakenly considered CP and called infant hemiplegia. *The major difference is that stroke is followed by gradual improvement, whereas CP is nonprogressive.*

Children show more improvement after strokes than adults with similar-sized lesions, and young children show more recovery than older ones. Nevertheless, the *sequelae* (the conditions following or resulting from brain damage) often include **hemiparesis** (weakness on one side), seizure disorders, learning disabilities, visual perception problems, memory deficits, and speech deficits. These children are prime candidates for adapted physical education and NDSA sports. For more information on strokes, contact www.strokeassociation.org.

Incomplete strokes, also called **transient ischemic attacks (TIAs),** occur in both children and adults. These strokes are characterized by total recovery (Kottke & Lehmann, 1990) but cause several hours of dysfunction in varied areas (e.g., muscle weakness, confusion, speech difficulty, memory and perception problems). Often, TIAs are warnings of severe cerebral pathology and impending major strokes.

Traumatic Brain Injury

Traumatic brain injury (TBI), recognized in 1990 as a separate diagnostic category for IEP-determination of special education services, means

> an acquired injury to the brain caused by an external physical force, resulting in total or partial functional disability or psychosocial impairment, or both, that adversely affects a child's educational performance. The term applies to open or closed head injuries

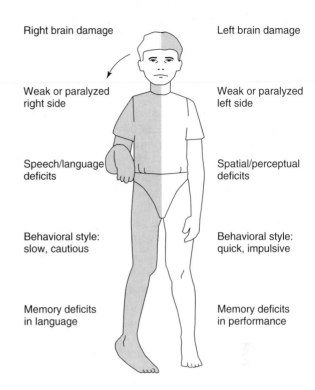

Figure 25.2 Left-brain damage causes disabilities on the right side, as listed. Right-brain damage causes damage on the left side.

Right brain damage

Weak or paralyzed right side

Speech/language deficits

Behavioral style: slow, cautious

Memory deficits in language

Left brain damage

Weak or paralyzed left side

Spatial/perceptual deficits

Behavioral style: quick, impulsive

Memory deficits in performance

resulting in impairments of one or more areas, such as cognition; language; memory; attention; reasoning; abstract thinking; judgment; problem-solving; sensory, perceptual, and motor abilities; psychosocial behaviors; physical functions; information processing; and speech. The term does not apply to brain injuries that are congenital or degenerative, or to brain injuries induced by birth trauma (20 U.S.C. 1401 (3) (A) and (B))

TBI, often called **acquired brain injury (ABI),** to distinguish it from *congenital brain injuries,* most often occur as a result of concussion, contusion, or hemorrhage sustained in vehicular and sport accidents, assaults, and falls. Collectively, these injuries are the leading cause of death and disability for persons under age 35. Each year, over 1 million brain injuries are reported. Some persons with TBI die, but some survive with severe impairments that prevent independent living, and the others learn to live with various **sequelae** that alter sensation, perception, emotion, cognition, and motor function.

Sequelae vary widely, depending on the site and extent of damage. The response of the brain to trauma also varies with age. Some research indicates that children recover more completely than adults, but this is controversial. Generally, recovery spans many years. Often, it appears to be complete, but professionals can detect minor deviations from normal, particularly in behaviors. Residual brain injury is also expressed by neurological *soft signs,* discussed in the next section.

Males sustain twice as many TBIs as females. Presumably, this is because males drive under the influence of alcohol more and are more involved in risk recreation and work activities than females. Over half of TBIs occur in motor vehicular accidents.

The major concern after injury is prediction of amount of recovery. Since 1974 the Glasgow Coma Scale (GCS) has been the major clinical assessment for this purpose. Possible scores on this scale range from 3 to 15 points. Death or a vegetative state is the prognosis of over 50% of persons who score in the 5 to 7 range. The closer the score is to 15, the better the prognosis. The scale is based on three types of response: (a) eye opening, (b) motor, and (c) verbal. Patients who are conscious respond to commands ("Open your eyes"; "Show me two fingers"; "Tell me what day this is") and obviously make the highest scores. The motor responses of unconscious persons to stimuli like pinpricks include withdrawal, abnormal flexion, abnormal extension or rigidity, and no reaction. Medical files almost always include a GCS score.

A GCS score of 8 or less indicates coma. The longer a person is comatose, the worse the prognosis. Children in a coma for more than 24 hr are likely to have IQs less than 85 when tested 6 months after injury. **Posttraumatic amnesia (PTA)** is also a good predictor of future function. Recovery is better when PTA lasts only a few minutes. Often, PTA persists for many months. In fact, permanent memory deficits are common sequelae.

Most school-age students return to general education 3 to 24 months postinjury. This means they are behind their friends in academics and often cannot catch up. Moreover, when left behind academically, they must adapt to new classmates (younger than they are) and cope with losing some or all of their old friends.

School personnel need to use classroom observation checklists (Keyser-Marcus et al., 2002) developed specifically for the ecology of different school settings. Generally these checklists focus on such functional domains as memory, attention and concentration, executive functioning, metacognition, and language (i.e., indicators of aphasia). Teaching strategies in Chapters 20 and 22 are useful in addressing problems in these domains. Give special attention to the principles for managing environment: (a) establish structure, (b) reduce space, (c) eliminate irrelevant stimuli, and (d) enhance stimulus value of the main thing to be learned.

Attention, memory, and visuomotor difficulties are the predominant sequelae in school-age persons. Recovery from motor involvement is better than from cognitive and behavioral sequelae. Typically, however, over one half of children with TBI have some degree of permanent spasticity and/or ataxia. Percentages are somewhat higher for adults. NDSA and Paralympic soccer teams include many players with TBI, particularly those with hemiplegia. The similarity of their motor profiles to those of persons with CP explains why NDSA serves persons with TBI.

Soft Signs and Associated Dysfunctions

Persons described in this chapter have multiple disabilities. **Neurological soft signs** complicate behavioral, perceptual, cognitive, and motor performance and interfere with learning. Soft

Table 25.1   Associated dysfunctions of general CP population as compared to NDSA athletes.

Associated Dysfunctions	General CP Population (%)	NDSA Athletes (%)
Mental retardation	30–70	10–20
Speech problems	35–75	25–35
Learning disabilities	80–90	45–55
Visual problems	55–60	20–30
Hearing problems	6–16	10–20
Perceptual deficits	25–50	60–70
Seizures	25–50	25–35
Reflex problems	80–90	65–75

Note. Estimates for the general population come from published sources. Estimates for NDSA athletes come from the author's research.

signs are indicators of central nervous system (CNS) dysfunction that cannot be substantiated by electroencephalogy (see Chapter 20). Common **behavioral indicators** of brain damage are attention deficits, hyperexcitability, perseveration, conceptual rigidity, emotional lability, and hyperactivity. Interpretation of sensory input is altered by brain damage, resulting in many kinds of perceptual problems (see Chapter 10). Particularly affected is **sensorimotor integration** of tactile, kinesthetic, vestibular, and visual input. Reflex, balance, and muscle-tone disorders are also considered soft signs. Soft signs and other diagnostic criteria indicate many associated dysfunctions in persons with upper motor neuron disorders (see Table 25.1).

In the remainder of this chapter, the abbreviation CP is used to encompass the motor sequelae and associated dysfunctions of stroke and TBI. Physical educators must assess carefully to determine whether students can best be served by a Special Olympics or an NDSA sport-oriented curriculum. The major difference is in intellectual functioning. NDSA specifies average or better intelligence as an eligibility criterion, although some athletes (5 to 15%) are perceived as borderline by coaches.

Table 25.1 describes differences between the general CP population and those served by NDSA. *Textbooks cite prevalence rates for coexisting CP and mental retardation (MR) as between 30 and 70%.* Recognition that speech, language, and motor impairments make valid evaluation difficult is resulting in more learning disability (LD) diagnoses and less classification as MR. When associated dysfunctions make placement and services uncertain, it is better to assume LD and introduce the family to NDSA activities. Many adults with CP describe lifetime academic achievement and self-concept problems that result from incorrect school placement and early exposure to curricula for MR rather than LD.

Electronic communication devices like the Canon communicator and the use of computers to teach language have demonstrated that many persons with CP, previously believed to have MR, have intact intelligence. The speech of many athletes who qualify for international competition cannot be understood without much practice. Interpreters are often used, just

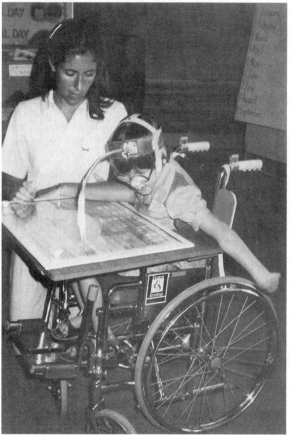

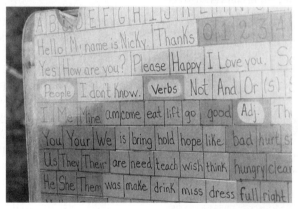

as with individuals who speak in sign or a foreign language. *A person without intelligible speech should never be assumed to be MR.*

Almost all children with CP need speech therapy. Even with intensive training, however, only about 50% improve to the degree that they communicate primarily by talking. Many use communication boards with words or symbols, as depicted in Figure 25.3. Others learn sign language or use computers that convert typed messages into talk (e.g., contact www.communicationaids.com). Efficient typing may demand key guard overlays and other adaptations that make hitting one key at a time easier. Teachers must take the time to listen to persons with CP, stroke, and TBI and to allow them to make many of their own decisions. Despite the effectiveness of computers, the aid of choice in the physical activity setting is often communication boards. These are not affected by drooling, dropping, and exposure to dirt and sweat.

Inadequate communication skills lead to problems in social development. Consider the leisure activities of able-bodied (AB) persons. Almost all require ability to use the hands (cards, board games, arts and crafts, cooking), to converse and/or sing, or to drive a car. About 50% of persons with upper motor neuron disorders do not have these abilities; their leisure and social functioning is therefore very different from that of peers. They can, however, excel in sports designed for their specific ability classification.

Visual defects affect over 50% of people with CP, stroke, and TBI. **Strabismus,** the inability to focus both eyes simultaneously on the same object, is the most common problem—not surprisingly, considering that focus requires six pairs of muscles to move each eyeball. Imbalances in strength cause squinting, poor binocular vision, and inefficiencies in depth perception, pattern discrimination, and figure-background detection. These deficits naturally affect motor learning and success in sports.

Seizures are relatively common occurrences for individuals with upper motor neuron disorders but do not contraindicate sport participation (Adams-Mushett, Wyeth, & Richter, 1995). Over 25% of NDSA athletes regularly take medication to control seizures. Travel and excitement inevitably result in some persons forgetting to take medication. An evening seizure, however, seldom prevents competition on the following day.

Of all the dysfunctions in Table 25.1, reflex problems concern physical educators the most. These prevent maturation of the postural reactions needed for stable sitting and for learning to walk. About half of NDSA athletes are in wheelchairs because of reflex and reaction abnormalities. An additional 20 to 35% have coordination problems related to reflexes, even though the individuals are ambulatory.

In summary, associated dysfunctions explain why NDSA needs a different sport classification system from that of other disabilities. Upper motor neuron disorders typically involve two or more limbs, causing abnormal muscle tone and postures that are worsened by perceptual and reflex problems. For example, few persons with CP are able to excel in wheelchair basketball. To compensate, NDSA recommends alternative sports like **boccia** and **indoor wheelchair soccer,** formerly known as team handball.

Number of Limbs Involved

Number of limbs involved is typically specified on IEPs and other records to help with programming. The terms used, except for *paraplegia,* are the same as those in Chapters 23 and 24.

1. **Diplegia.** Lower extremities are much more involved than upper ones. This term is preferred over *paraplegia.*
2. **Quadriplegia.** All four extremities are involved. In international sports, a synonym is *tetraplegia.*
3. **Hemiplegia.** The entire right side or left side is involved.
4. **Triplegia.** Three extremities, usually both legs and one arm, are involved.

These terms permit description of and programming for functional abilities. Such terms as *mild* and *severe* indicate degree of involvement.

Types of Motor Disorders

Motor disorder in CP, stroke, and TBI is described in terms of abnormal muscle tone and postures (Bobath, 1980; Levitt, 1995; Sugden & Keogh, 1990). The old (1956) neuromuscular classifications of the American Academy for Cerebral Palsy are no longer used. *Instead, three types of CP are recognized: (a) spasticity, (b) athetosis, and (c) ataxia.* Most persons have *mixed types,* and diagnosis indicates which is most prominent. Muscle tone, before the appearance of spasticity, in persons re-

covering from temporary paralysis (e.g., stroke, TBI) is often **hypotonic** (weak, floppy, without tone).

Spasticity of Cerebral Origin

Spasticity, the most common type of motor disorder, is abnormal muscle tightness and stiffness characterized by **hypertonic muscle tone** during voluntary movement. About 65% of people with CP have this as their predominant type. Spasticity is mainly caused by damage to the motor cortex and the cortical tracts that carry motor commands downward through the brain. Damage to the basal ganglia and cerebellum further exacerbates spasticity.

The resulting **hypertonic state** causes muscles to feel and look stiff (see fingers in Figure 25.4). Normally, muscles on one surface relax when those on the opposite surface contract (the reciprocal innervation principle), but hypertonicity results in **cocontraction** or stiffness. This, in turn, makes release of objects difficult or impossible, an obvious problem in learning to throw or in letting go of the pool side when wanting to swim. It also interferes with ability to make precise movements.

Associated with spasticity is the **exaggerated stretch** or **myotatic reflex** that sometimes occurs in muscle groups being stretched. This generic reflex typically serves a protective purpose because it instantaneously withdraws a body part from hurtful stimuli. Damage to the cerebellum, however, results in exaggerated response (recoil, withdrawal, flexion) to stretch receptor input. This exaggerated response ranges in intensity from a subtle timing problem to a violent recoil like a jackknife closing. The latter is strong enough to cause bruising or a bloody nose in a bystander who gets in the way. When sitting next to a person with an exaggerated stretch reflex, be sure to ask which is the dangerous side. All stretches do not activate exaggerated responses, and intensity varies from time to time. In some persons, the stretch reflex is so disruptive that limbs are strapped down (see Figure 25.4).

Among the abnormal postures associated with spasticity are the scissors gait (both legs involved) and the hemiplegic gait (arm and leg on same side involved). The **scissors gait** is a pigeon-toed walk caused by abnormal tightness of the hip joint flexors, adductors, and inward rotators that is associated with retention of the positive support and crossed extension reflexes. Also tight are the knee joint flexors (hamstrings) and ankle joint plantar flexors (calf muscles and Achilles tendon) that keep knees bent and weight on toes (see Figure 25.5). If arms are involved, the tightness follows the same pattern (flexors, adductors, and inward rotators). The spastic arm is bent and pronated, carried close to the body, with a fisted hand. The **hemiplegic gait,** a limp caused by asymmetry in extension (see Figure 25.5), is associated with stroke, TBI, and Class 7 CP.

Abnormal postures are also caused by retention of primitive reflexes in CP, occurrence of synergies in stroke and TBI, and immaturity of postural reactions. Inability to move the head without associated muscle tension in the arms results in many abnormal postures. When such disturbances are severe, persons with spasticity remain nonambulatory.

Athetosis

Athetosis, the second most common type of motor disorder, is constant, unpredictable, and purposeless (CUP) movement

Figure 25.4 Spasticity in some persons may be so great that limbs need to be strapped down during physical activity. Here, Tom Cush, international Class 2 athlete with cerebral palsy, has both arms strapped to chair while he competes in indoor wheelchair soccer. In throwing and striking activities, only one arm is strapped down.

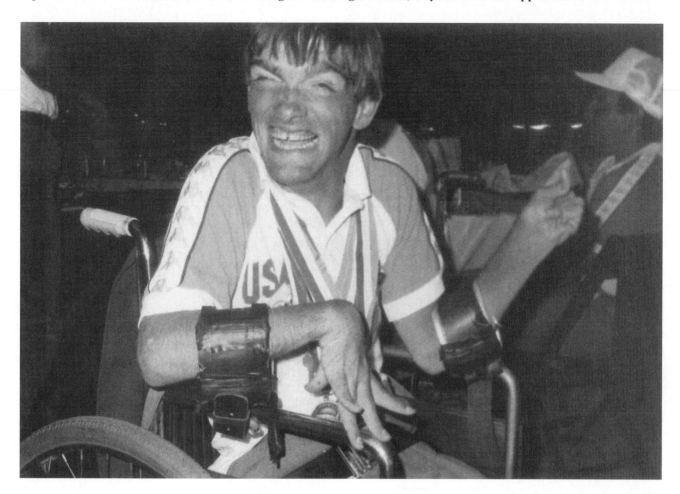

caused by **fluctuating muscle tone** that is sometimes hypertonic and sometimes hypotonic. Damage to the basal ganglia in the cerebral white matter is the primary cause of this involuntary **overflow disorder.** Most persons with athetosis are quadriplegic. About 25% of CP is primarily athetosis.

Constant movement is most troublesome to the head and upper extremities. Facial expression, eating, and speaking are major problems. The head is usually drawn back but may roll unpredictably from side to side; the tongue may protrude and saliva drool down the chin. Lack of head control causes problems of visual pursuit and focus that impair ability to read and perform hand-eye accuracy tasks. Constant movement of the fingers and wrist render handwriting and fine muscle coordinations almost impossible.

Many persons with athetosis use wheelchairs, but some have enough motor control to walk. Their gait is typically unsteady or staggering. They walk with trunk and shoulder girdle leaning backward, reinforcing extensor tonus, to prevent collapsing. Hips and knees tend to be hyperextended, the back in lordosis, and the feet kept dorsiflexed, pronated, and everted (a **valgus** position). Steps are short to help maintain balance. Falls are more often backward than forward. Persons with such gaits compete in track but wear knee and elbow pads and gloves.

There are many types of athetosis: (a) **dystonia,** with fluctuating muscle tone; (b) *mixed with spasticity,* in which muscle tone is mostly hypertonic; (c) *mixed with floppy baby syndrome,* in which muscle tone is primarily hypotonic; and (d) *mixed with ataxia.* Changes from one type to another sometimes occur with age, particularly from floppy baby to dystonic children. Generally, *athetosis* and *dystonia* are synonyms.

Ataxia

Ataxia is a combined disturbance of balance and coordination generally characterized by hypotonia or low postural tone. Ataxia can result from disorders of the spinal cord as well as the brain. In CP, stroke, and TBI, however, the ataxia is of **cerebellar-vestibular origin.** Ataxia is diagnosed only in people who can walk unaided. To compensate for extreme unsteadiness of gait, the arms are typically overactive in balance-saving movements. Falls are frequent.

When persons can maintain balance with eyes open, but not closed, ataxia is usually the diagnosis. Voluntary movements are clumsy and uncoordinated with underreaching and overreaching common. Uneven or unlevel ground, stairs, and stepping over objects are particular problems because of cerebellar-vestibular body awareness deficits.

Figure 25.5 **Abnormal gaits associated with spasticity and ataxia.**

Scissors gait.
The legs are flexed and adducted at the hip joint, causing them to cross alternately in front of each other with the knees scraping together. The knees may be flexed to a greater degree than normal, and the weight of the body may be taken primarily on the toes. The gait is characterized by a narrow walking base. Scissoring may be caused by retention of the positive supporting reflex or the crossed extension reflex. Toe walking may be caused also by the positive supporting reflex.

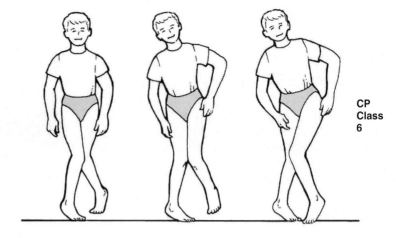

CP
Class
6

Hemiplegic gait.
Both arm and leg on the same side are involved. Tends to occur with any disorder producing an immobile hip or knee. Affected leg is rigid and swung from the hip joint in a semicircle by muscle action of the trunk. Individual leans to the affected side, and arm on that side is held in a rigid, semiflexed position.

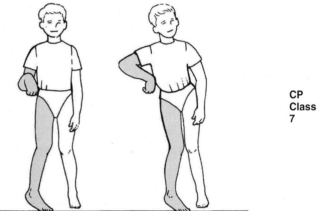

CP
Class
7

Cerebellar gait/kinesthetic defect.
Irregularity of steps, unsteadiness, tendency to reel to one side. Individual seems to experience difficulty in judging how high to lift legs when climbing stairs. Problems are increased when the ground is uneven. Note the similarity between this and the immature walk of early childhood before CNS has matured.

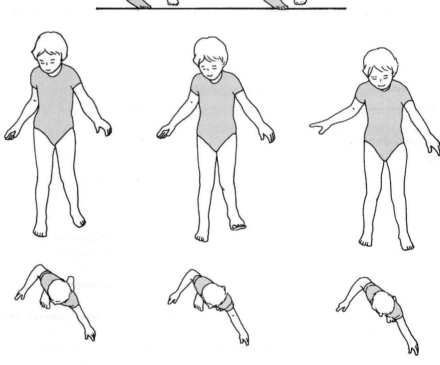

Ataxia varies from mild to severe. A diagnosis of pure ataxia is made in only about 10% of CP. Many persons not diagnosed as disabled probably have ataxia. *Combined disturbances of balance and coordination are common among low-skilled persons.*

Flaccidity/Hypotonia

The terms *flaccidity* and *hypotonia* refer to low muscle tone. Infants and young children are sometimes assigned a diagnosis of flaccidity/hypotonia until type of CP (spasticity, athetosis, ataxia) becomes clear. Adults, however, can have this condition also. Persons in comas are hypotonic. After a severe stroke, the first stage in motor recovery is flaccidity.

Problems in persons with hypotonia are (a) poor head and trunk control, (b) absent postural and protective reactions, (c) shallow breathing, and (d) joint laxity or hypermobility. Hypotonia may be so severe that persons cannot sit or move unaided (i.e., they are in a vegetative state). Hypotonia is associated with damage of nuclei deep in the cerebellum that, in turn, affect motor cortex and brain stem action. In time, the motor cortex may compensate by increasing facilitatory impulses.

Profiles to Guide Assessment and Programming

Sport classifications should be used to write individualized education programs (IEPs) and individualized family service plans (IFSPs). There are eight classes or profiles, four for the nonambulatory and four for the ambulatory. *Classes 1, 2, 3, and 6 designate persons who are the most severely involved.*

Assessment begins with determining whether a person is nonambulatory (Classes 1 to 4) or ambulatory (Classes 5 to 8). This requires careful questioning because many persons who use wheelchairs do not need them. This is particularly true of persons who (a) must navigate hills and other barriers in a school or work environment that demands speed in moving from place to place and (b) are overweight or have low fitness. Persons who cannot ambulate across the room, even with crutches or canes, are assigned to Classes 1 to 4. Those who need crutches or canes (called assistive devices) are placed in Class 5 but can opt to compete as a Class 4. All others are assigned to Classes 6 to 8.

Motor profiles should be sport-specific. Swimming naturally has a different classification system. Following are descriptions of track and field and basic ball handling ability.

Class 1—Motorized Chair

Class 1 includes everyone without the ROM and power to push a manual wheelchair. Such persons have severe involvement in all four limbs and little head and trunk control. They typically are dominated by reflexes, are unable to maintain body parts in good alignment without help, and have limited ROM. When placed in a lying position, they may be unable to initiate a roll, sit-up, or other voluntary movement. Usually, the motor disorder is primarily hypotonic (especially ages 0 to 7) or spastic.

Chapter 10 describes physical education programming for these persons in early childhood. Emphasis is on total body movement activities on mats, in the water, and in apparatus

that can be pushed, pulled, or tilted by the teacher. **Coactive movement** is used to normalize muscle tone and prevent contractures. *If the child is dominated by extensor muscle tone, then flexion activities are stressed as normalizers.* If flexor tone dominates, then extensor activities are emphasized.

If the child has the mental function to learn use of a motorized chair, all kinds of activities are possible. By age 7 or 8, physical education goals should stress track and field. Whether the chair is powered by hand, foot, or mouth switch, speed and control must be learned. Racing for speed can be on straightaways or around obstacles like cones (see Figure 25.6). The child needs to learn how to weave around obstacles, make circles around them, and manage a ramp. The adult competes in slalom events (see Chapter 15).

Appropriate field activities are those using soft implements that can be easily handled, like a soft shot or discus. Throws for distance and height should be practiced, as well as tosses at ground targets like those used in archery. If the hand grasp reflex is still present, release is difficult. It can, however, be overridden by higher cortical levels with much concentration and practice. Games should be devised that give points regardless of the direction the object flies.

Class 1 students can succeed in many game, sport, and aquatic activities if teachers are creative. Because release is so difficult, striking patterns are often emphasized. Inclined boards called *chutes* permit striking to activate a ball in boccia and bowling-type games. Suspended ball and tabletop activities are also good. Lying sideways or prone on mats, persons can use body parts to knock over strategically set bowling pins (Miller & Schaumberg, 1988) and hit or kick objects. In the motorized chair, a game goal may be moving around the room and knocking down pins with the hand. Similar games can be played in the water while lying on floating mats or being coactively moved in a vertical position. A personal flotation device (PFD) should be worn. Many water games should be played before swimming is introduced.

Class 1 persons often require one-on-one assistance. Principals may need to be convinced to supply aides. A record should be kept of each student's time on task (i.e., actual physical activity) or number of trials completed. No child is too disabled to benefit from physical education.

Class 2—Athetosis; 2L or 2U

Class 2 persons can propel a manual chair but have moderate to severe involvement in all four limbs and trunk. Individual differences at this level are so great that Class 2 is subdivided into uppers (U) and lowers (L), with the adjective denoting the limbs with greater functional ability. The 2L propels a chair with feet, with speed and control varying widely (see Figure 25.6). The 2L often is able to do everything with feet (i.e., eating, writing, turning pages) that ordinary people do with hands. Physical education for a 2L emphasizes kicking events and ball handling that is done with the feet. The toes can grasp a soft shot or discus and toss it in various ways. The 2L can learn to tricycle, swim, and do other activities that do not require upper extremities.

In contrast, the 2U relies on arms and learns traditional wheelchair track-and-field activities. Propulsion is weak and slow, however, so that even adult events require short distances

Figure 25.6 Both Class 1 and Class 2 can use personal flotation devices in NDSA swimming but not in international events. In observations, pay particular attention to Class 2 foot-pushing technique.

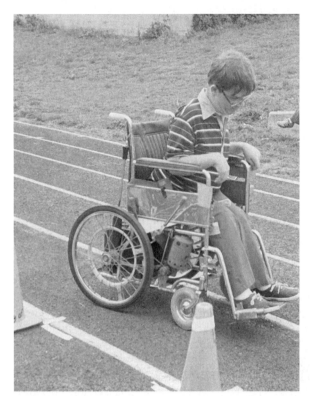

Class 1 in motorized chair

Class 2, propelling with feet

Class 1, all limbs flexed

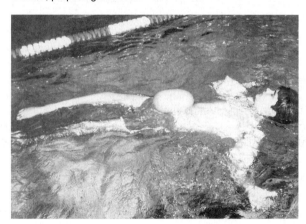

Class 2, some extension possible

(i.e., between 20 and 200 m). Early throwing activities may feature the soft discus and shot, but the 2U, as an adult, must use a regulation (but lightweight) club, shot, and discus. The sooner this equipment is introduced, the better. The legs of a 2U are relatively useless, but the arm stroke can generate enough power for swimming success with and occasionally without a PFD (see Figure 25.6).

Class 2 persons typically have more athetosis than spasticity. Control in accuracy tasks is a challenge, but both 2L and 2U persons engage in bowling, boccia, and other games similar to those played by Class 1 individuals. Bowling balls with retractable handles are available from several equipment companies (see Appendix E). Class 2 individuals also must cope with major reflex and postural reaction problems.

Class 3—Moderate Triplegic or Quadriplegic

Class 3 is similar to a 2U except that involvement is less and motor disorder is usually predominantly spastic. There is moderate involvement in three or four limbs and trunk. Class 3 individuals propel the chair with short, choppy arm pushes but generate fairly good speed. They can take a few steps with assistive devices, but this ambulatory mode is not functional. Some have enough leg control to learn tricycling events.

All wheelchair activities and swim strokes (except butterfly) are possible. Reflex and postural reaction problems affect performance, so wheelchair basketball and tennis are not games of choice because of their speed-distance-accuracy demands. Sports like indoor wheelchair soccer and quad rugby are

Figure 25.7 Class 5 persons may or may not use assistive devices. If they wish, Class 5 persons may compete in Class 4 wheelchair events.

better suited to abilities. In general, physical education should stress sports, dance, and aquatics, with as few adaptations as possible.

Class 4—Diplegic

Class 4 individuals use a wheelchair with the same skill, precision, and speed as people with spinal cord injury and spina bifida. They propel the chair with forceful, continuous pushes, have good strength in trunk and upper extremities, and minimal control problems. Some succeed at wheelchair basketball, but subtle associated dysfunctions like visual perception deficits often interfere with aspirations to be on the starting five. They are not eligible for quad rugby, so indoor wheelchair soccer is the game of choice. They can perform all swim strokes.

Class 4 persons are considered mildly disabled. Unlike others in wheelchairs, their associated dysfunctions are minimal and subtle. They are good candidates for integrated physical education but also need separate instruction in wheelchair sports.

Class 5—With or Without Assistive Devices

Class 5 is the only profile that includes persons who use crutches, canes, and walkers (see Figure 25.7). New rules allow Class 5 persons the choice of using these devices or a wheelchair. If the choice is a wheelchair, the athlete is treated as a Class 4. *Athletes may not compete in some events as a Class 4 and in other events as a Class 5.* The motor disorder is primar-

ily spastic, and involvement is either hemiplegic or diplegic. Spasticity is moderate to severe.

Many activities offer success. Track events include 100- to 400-m distances run on foot. The only contraindication is use of **axillary crutches** (those that touch armpits) because pressure in this area can cause nerve damage. In field events, the major problem is balance. Throws can be from either a standing or seated position. Some persons prefer the tricycle, but others use a bicycle. Class 5 persons are eligible to play indoor wheelchair soccer and need wheelchair skills to make the team. They are also eligible to play NDSA soccer and are groomed particularly for goalkeeper and defensive positions.

Class 5 athletes often do well in wheelchair sports like tennis and handball that are sponsored by other organizations.

Class 6—Athetosis, Ambulatory

Class 6 individuals are primarily affected by athetosis, and associated dysfunctions are severe. They have moderate to severe involvement of three or four limbs, with severe balance and coordination problems. These are less prominent when running and throwing than walking.

In terms of overall severity of condition, Class 6 is often grouped with Classes 1, 2, and 3. Unsteadiness of gait, balance, and reflex problems vary widely. All physical education, however, is ambulatory, with elbow and knee pads recommended because of frequent falls. When mainstreamed, these persons are helped by the presence of a bar or chair to provide support during exercise and other activities that require good balance. In NDSA competition, Class 6 persons have a choice between tricycle and bicycle. Like Class 3 individuals, they can do all swim strokes except the butterfly.

Class 7—Hemiplegic

Class 7 includes only persons with hemiplegia. Spasticity ranges from mild to moderate. Class 7 persons ambulate with a slight limp and are able to pump effectively only with the non-involved arm; the spastic arm is somewhat conspicuous because of its bent, pronated position (see Figure 25.8). The spastic leg is noticeably smaller than the normal one.

Class 7 persons are typically in integrated physical education and able to do everything that peers do, except with more effort. Sue Moucha, an international Class 7 athlete, states:

> I have biked 100 mi in one day, run a marathon, and have successfully completed an able-bodied Outward Bound course, which included rock climbing, rappelling, canoeing, and a mini-marathon. Sports acts as a benchmark. I enjoy physical activities and am eager to do something new. (Moucha, 1991, p. 38)

Class 8—Minimal Involvement

Class 8 persons run and jump freely without a noticeable limp (see Figure 25.9). Their gait is symmetrical in both walking and running. They demonstrate good balance but have noticeable (although minimal) coordination problems. This is usually seen in the hands or in a lack of power or coordination in one limb.

Figure 8.4   Class 7 athletes are hemiplegic and run with a slight limp.

Figure 25.9   Class 8 athletes run freely without a noticeable limp.

Sometimes, associated dysfunctions are more disabling than the motor involvement.

Coping With Special Problems

Among the motor problems that require special attention are (a) delayed development, (b) reflex and postural reaction abnormalities, (c) abnormal muscle tone, (d) contractures, and (e) additional orthopedic defects. Attitudinal barriers constitute a major social problem.

Delayed Motor Development

Children in Classes 7 and 8 often learn to walk by age 2, but others are delayed several years or never learn. All aspects of motor development are typically delayed, which limits the physical, mental, and emotional stimulation that children need. To compensate, early intervention should involve several hours of big muscle activity daily. Chapter 10 presents content to guide programming of nonambulatory children from birth until age 7.

The type of motor performance that a child with CP has at age 7 is predictive of performance as an adult (Bleck & Nagel, 1982). Most children who are going to learn to walk have done so by age 7. Bleck and Nagel (1982, p. 79) emphasize, "Physical therapy to improve the child's walking once he

Figure 25.10   Different manifestations of tonic neck reflexes.

The ATNR causes increased extensor tone in the arm on the face side and increased flexor tone in the arm on the scalp side.

The STNR extends arms and flexes legs.

or she has reached 7 or 8 years is unlikely to be worth the time and effort expended, and other areas of function (like play and sports) should take precedence." These and other physicians agree that emphasis on integration of reflexes should change to instruction in sports, dance, and aquatics at about age 7. *Persons who have not lost reflexes by age 7 will probably have them forever and can be taught to compensate or to use reflexes to enhance performance.* Turning the head to the right, for example, can increase the power of a right-handed movement via the asymmetrical tonic neck reflex. Hyperextending the head can extend arms and flex legs, making the exit from a pool easier via the symmetrical tonic neck reflex (see Figure 25.10).

Postural Reactions

Sports, dance, and aquatics can be used to enhance postural reactions. Emphasis on protective extension of arms during falls (the parachute reactions) and on development of equilibrium should continue. Some sports should be selected for working on weaknesses (e.g., balance beam routines, horseback riding, gymnastics, roller and ice skating, dance, wrestling, and judo), whereas others should build on strengths and the desire to participate in the same activities as peers. Most sport skills, done in correct form, normalize muscle tone. The more difficult principle to implement is avoidance of abnormal postures and stereotyped patterns that may cause injury, contribute to posture deviations, and further social rejection. These are associated with reflexes and muscle tone abnormalities. Hence, work continues in these areas but for different reasons.

Reflexes and Abnormal Postures

Chapter 10 describes the 10 most troublesome reflexes, principles to guide reflex integration, and activities. This section therefore focuses on proper holding, carrying, and positioning.

Holding and Carrying

Class 1 and 2 people, regardless of age, need help in making transfers. Unless body weight prohibits carrying children from place to place, it is both efficient and therapeutic to do so. Figure 25.11 shows several correct ways for carrying on land and in water activities. Many games like airplane and Batman can be played from these positions. Children dominated by **extensor tone** (i.e., stiff all over) should be held close to the body in tucked positions that maintain their head and limbs in flexion. Children dominated by **flexor tone** (i.e., bent or curled) should be held in ways that maintain head and limbs in extension. *Thus, the commonsense principle of keeping body parts in good alignment is followed.*

When apparatus is used, much Velcro, padding, and cushioning is needed to achieve proper alignment. Often, each body part must be strapped in place. Many sources provide ideas for adapting equipment. Such equipment is also available from commercial companies like Sportime (see Appendix E).

Strapping and Positioning

Good alignment in sitting requires that (a) the hips are at 90° flexion and in contact with the back of the chair, (b) thighs are slightly abducted and in contact with the seat, and (c) knees, ankles, and elbows are positioned at 90° flexion. There should be at least 1 inch of space between the knees and the seat to avoid pressure on the tender area behind the knees. The feet should be in contact with a firm, flat surface. The head and neck must be held in midline and kept in extension. Often, strapping is the only way to meet these criteria for a good sitting posture.

Inclusion of wheelchair sports in school physical education requires learning strapping techniques to ensure safety and maximize performance (Burd & Grass, 1987). All-out effort in a wheelchair, without proper strapping, often elicits an **extensor pattern** that tends to pull the body down and out of the chair. This is characterized by spinal, hip, and knee

Figure 25.11   Correct ways to carry children with cerebral palsy.

Inhibiting extensor tone

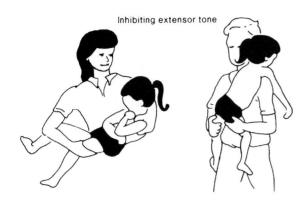

Inhibiting flexor tone

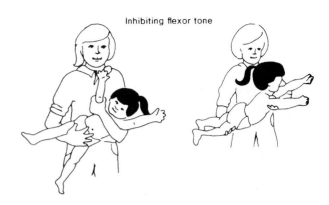

extension and toe pointing (plantar flexion). In conjunction with this, scissoring is a problem.

To control the extensor pattern, a strap should come forward from the rear-underneath portion of the chair, where it is secured to the frame. The strap angle should be about 45°, with the fastening mechanism in front. This type of **lap belt** holds the hips in place much better than a traditional seat belt at waist level. Some persons, however, may need an H strap arrangement that holds both upper back and hips in place.

Knee flexion and the adduction/inward rotation pattern caused by scissoring are controlled by straps placed around each thigh and pulled tight. A single strap across the thighs may be sufficient. Experimentation is important.

The feet and lower legs may need to be strapped in similar fashion. Often, a strap is also placed beneath the feet as a means of elevating the footrests and increasing knee flexion. *Regardless of body part strapped, 2-inch or wider Velcro or webbing should be used to reduce the possibility of circulation and irritation problems.* If swelling or redness occurs or the athlete complains of discomfort, adjust the straps. Extremities should not be strapped for long periods. As soon as competition or the activity ends, straps should be loosened.

Figure 25.12 shows how strapping and positioning inhibit reflexes. A bolster between the thighs inhibits the **crossed extension reflex** that causes scissoring. The extensor pattern can be prevented by positioning self at eye level rather than forcing the student to look upward. Hyperextension of the head can elicit either the extension pattern or the symmetrical tonic neck reflex. In general, both should be avoided. This calls for placement of suspended balls and visual aids at eye level or slightly lower. Figure 25.12 shows a bolster, wedge, and inclined board used to keep the body in extension while in prone position.

During the time that no one is interacting with a severely involved person, positioning is very important. *For the person who cannot initiate voluntary movement, side-lying with the head propped up on a pillow is best.* Foam cushions maintain correct position. The individual should be facing the action. If a person can hold up the head and use arms, a prone position is better. Mirrors on the wall and floor reinforce voluntary movement. Supine lying is avoided because of the helplessness it causes; propped sitting is better.

Severely involved persons spend so much time in wheelchairs that mat work is an important part of physical edu-

cation. *Ideally, the mat area should be an elevated platform about the same height as the wheelchair seat to facilitate transfers.* Bolsters and wedges must be available if students wait turns.

Contraindicated Activities

Activities that elicit or reinforce abnormal movement patterns are contraindicated. **Creeping on all-fours,** for example, may be contraindicated in quadriplegia and diplegia if it increases flexor spasticity. The **frog or W sitting position** (resting on the buttocks between the heels of the feet) should be avoided because it worsens the hip joint adduction-inward rotation-flexion pattern that needs to be eliminated. **Bridging in supine** (pushing down with feet and lifting pelvis from mat), which often occurs in athetosis, should not be allowed because it worsens abnormal neck extension and scapulae retraction. Movement education challenges to walk on tiptoe or to point the toes are contraindicated for persons with tight calf muscles.

Spasticity Problems

Handling techniques require application of three principles. The first is to *maintain symmetry* (i.e., strive to keep body parts in midline). The second is to *use inhibitory actions that are the opposite of the undesired pattern.* The third is to *work from designated key points of central control* (i.e., grasp body parts as close to the joint as possible). **Key points** are (a) the shoulder joint for abnormal arm positions, (b) the hip joint for scissoring, and (c) the head and neck for the arched back extensor spasm.

The fisted hand, a common problem, is worsened by wrist hyperextension. When an activity calls for releasing an object or maintaining an open hand, use both shoulder joint and radioulnar rotation to relax the wrist and fingers. Do not try to pry fingers open.

To correct scissoring in supine, grasp the thighs and gently spread the legs while outwardly rotating and flexing the hip joint. This exercise also decreases plantar flexion at the ankle joint and makes it easier to put on shoes and socks. To correct abnormal arm position, grasp the upper arm and lift it over the head while gently outwardly rotating the arm.

Overall spasticity of the body is decreased by rotation of the trunk. This forms the rationale for **rhythmic rolling activities** on a stationary or moving surface (i.e., large therapy ball) and

Figure 25.12 Methods of inhibiting primitive reflexes. *(A)* Strapping the thighs and lower legs to wheelchair prevents extensor thrust. *(B)* A hard roll or bolster between the thighs maintains the legs in abduction and inhibits scissoring. *(C)* The position of the teacher influences extensor pattern. *(D–F)* Use of bolster, wedge, and inclined board for correct positioning in prone.

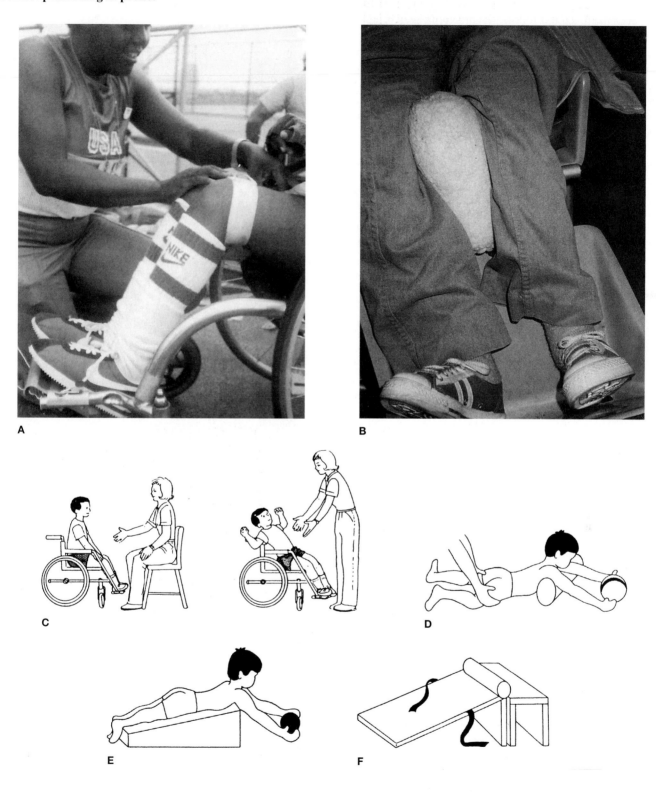

A

B

C

D

E

F

gentle **rocking movements** on lap, ball, or tiltboard. Horseback riding is also helpful, and many therapeutic programs are available. Rotation and rocking activities also create weight-shifting situations that promote development of equilibrium reactions.

Active exercises, for persons able to initiate independent movement, should follow the three principles of correct handling. Rotatory and rocking movements are important for warm-up and relaxation to minimize spasticity. Chapters 16 and 17 on dance and swimming present many good activities. Water play and exercises in a warm pool (about 90°) are excellent. Swim fins are helpful in minimizing the stretch reflex. Sport is strongly recommended for people with spasticity (Richter, Gaebler-Spira, & Adams-Mushett, 1996).

Daily stretching exercises can help prevent contractures. These should be slow, static stretches as described in Chapter 13 on fitness. Participation in sport also prevents contractures.

Botox injections are used to reduce spasticity in CP, stroke, and TBI, but their effectiveness lasts only a few months. In stroke survivors, paralyzed limbs may generate pain, which botox can relieve. It is not yet known how often botox injections should be given at the same site.

Athetosis Problems

Class 2 and 6 persons exhibit more athetosis than spasticity, but both conditions are often present. Although constant, unpredictable, purposeless (CUP) movement would seem a hindrance in aiming activities, persons with athetosis can succeed in bowling, tennis, and golf. NDSA also has accumulated evidence that Class 2 people can excel in aiming activities and recommends bowling and boccia.

NDSA promotes proper warm-up for persons with athetosis. Previous beliefs that athetoid movements provide a natural state of readiness have not been subjected to research and thus have no base for support.

Early childhood positioning and exercise goals are different for athetosis and spasticity. The main goal in athetosis is head and trunk control (proximal stability), which, in turn, tends to decrease undesired limb movement. To promote midline control, infants and toddlers are placed quite early in sitting, kneeling, and standing positions (see Figure 25.13). Upright rather than prone activities are stressed in mat work. Knee walking (wearing pads) is recommended, as well as walking using parallel bars for support. Tricycling and bicycling (both stationary and moving) reinforce midline control, as does horseback riding.

Surgery and Braces

Several surgical procedures correct or relieve problems caused by severe spasticity. A **tenotomy** is surgical sectioning of a tendon. It is primarily used to lengthen the Achilles tendon, thereby reducing toe-walking caused by abnormal tightness. In about 6 weeks, the cutout sections are filled in by new tendon growth. Tenotomy is also used to lengthen the iliopsoas tendon to relieve hip flexion contractures and to lengthen hamstring tendons to relieve knee flexion deformities.

A **myotomy** is a similar procedure except it is applied to muscles, mainly the tight adductor muscles of the hip joint. A **neurectomy** is a cutting (partial or total) of nerves that supply

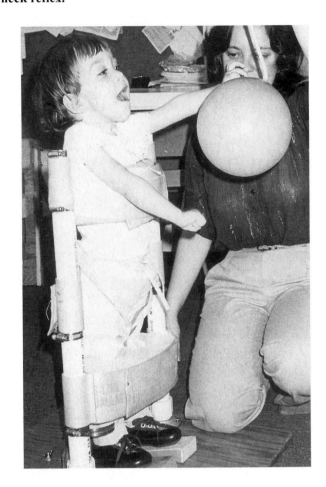

Figure 25.13 Apparatus to help children with cerebral palsy stand is built with straps to keep body parts centered in midline and thus inhibit asymmetrical tonic neck reflex.

spastic muscles. A **tendon transplant** is surgical relocation of the origin of a muscle, also a technique to ameliorate adduction and flexion deformities.

Arthrodesis is the surgical immobilization of a joint; it is sometimes done at the ankle joint to relieve severe **pes valgus** (combined eversion, plantar flexion, and adduction) caused by contractures. **Valgus deformities** occur commonly in ambulatory spastic diplegia. Arthrodesis causes feet to remain in a fixed dorsiflexion position, which gives more stability than pathological plantar flexion.

Braces (orthoses) are also used to control spasticity and to provide needed stability. Figure 25.14 shows some of these, which are typically referred to by their initials: AFOs (ankle-foot orthoses), KAFOs (knee-ankle-foot orthoses), or HKAFOs (hip-knee-ankle-foot orthoses). Orthoses are not considered assistive devices and are allowed in all NDSA events. The **parapodium** and other standing devices are primarily used in early childhood, before independent standing is possible.

Hip Dislocation, Scoliosis, and Foot Deformities

Nonambulatory children with CP are at high risk for hip dislocation. In approximately 25%, the head of the femur becomes displaced in an upward direction. The average age of disloca-

Figure 25.14   Illustrative orthoses.

Hip-knee-ankle-foot orthosis (HKAFO)   Parapodium   Metal KAFO   Metal AFO   Plastic AFO

tion is 7 years. Correction is by surgery. This propensity for hip dislocation explains why learning to properly handle scissored legs is so important.

Abnormal muscle tone, reflex problems, and improper positioning result in a high percentage of scoliosis. Approximately one third have scoliosis and can benefit from the exercises and bracing described in Chapter 14 on postures. Nonambulatory persons are at greatest risk.

Foot deformities are common, presumably because insufficient attention is given to stretching the tight calf muscles and Achilles tendon (heel cord). **Equinovalgus** (abnormal plantar flexion, eversion, and pronation) is associated with ambulatory spastic diplegia, whereas **equinovarus** (abnormal plantar flexion, inversion, and supination) occurs most often in hemiplegia and nonambulatory persons with total involvement. *In both conditions, activities requiring toe pointing are contraindicated.* Dorsiflexion games like walking up (but not down) steep, inclined boards and hills should be devised. In contrast, ambulatory persons with athetosis tend to have a **dorsiflexed valgus foot position.**

Attitudinal Barriers

The multidisabled profiles of persons with CP result in attitudinal barriers that make social acceptance especially difficult. Research shows that persons with CP are ranked last or next to last as friendship choices when several disabilities are compared (Mastro, Burton, Rosendahl, & Sherrill, 1996; Tripp, 1988). This affects success in mainstream activities, self-concept, and motivation. Educational programming must therefore focus on attitudes and seek to ameliorate social delays and associated deficits in play and game knowledges and strategies.

Fitness and CP

Little is known about fitness of individuals with CP because widespread differences in Classes 1 to 8 tend to mask results when research is undertaken. Short and Winnick (1986) compared 309 individuals with CP to 1,192 AB adolescents, ages 10 to 17 years, and reported significant differences on all test items except skinfold measures. Items included sit-ups, leg raises, trunk raises, grip strength, flexed arm hang, pull-ups, standing broad jumps, and sit-and-reach. Interestingly, the subjects with

CP generally did not improve with age, as is the expected developmental trend. Also, expected gender differences were not found on many of the items. Follow-up research, which compared persons with CP/MR dual diagnosis with CP-only diagnosis, indicated no significant difference (Winnick & Short, 1991).

Body build differences may affect fitness measures. Children with CP tend to be short for their age and to have reduced body cell mass and increased body water (Shephard, 1990). Allowance for these differences indicates that the aerobic power of well-trained persons with CP may be essentially normal, even though it is typically reported as 10 to 30% below normal standards.

Spasticity, athetosis, and exaggerated reflex action are associated with **mechanical inefficiency** and tremendous expenditure of energy, even on easy motor tasks. This helps to explain why weight is not typically a problem. Because persons with CP require more time than average to perform activities of daily living (ADL) and to travel to school or work, little time or energy is left at the end of the day for strenuous activities. When asked to prioritize physical education goals, many persons with CP select motor and leisure skills. Once such skills are learned and people are socialized into sport, fitness training becomes more meaningful.

Flexibility has long been the most important fitness goal in CP, but athletes are interested also in strength and aerobic training (Jones, 1988). NDSA sanctions power lifting as one of its competitive sports and encourages weight training, especially free weights, Nautilus, and Universal (Lockette & Keyes, 1994). Research indicates that athletes can engage in a 10-week circuit-training strength program (2 to 3 days a week), supplemented by flexibility training, with no loss of ROM except at wrist and ankle joints, areas not given attention (Holland & Steadward, 1990). Muscle groups of every joint should be stretched daily in conjunction with strength training. This includes muscles not involved in strength training because spasticity is a total body response.

Sports and Aquatics

Sport groups have been testing activities and identifying those in which persons with CP have the most opportunity for success

Figure 25.15 Boccia is a bowling-type game specifically for Class 1 and 2 athletes. A team is composed of three members, one of whom must be Class 1. The object is to give impetus to the ball so that it lands as close as possible to the white target ball. Each player has two balls per round. A team game is six rounds.

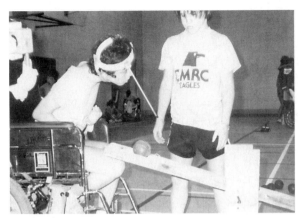

Class 1 athlete with no functional use of arms or legs uses head pointer to give impetus to the ball.

Class 2 athletes either kick or throw the ball into play, depending upon whether they are 2L or 2U.

for over 40 years. In general, persons with CP perform better in individual sports than in team activities.

Team Sports

Only three team sports traditionally have been recommended for people with CP: soccer, indoor wheelchair soccer, and boccia. Classes 6 to 8 are eligible to compete in *ambulatory soccer,* which is played (with only a few exceptions) according to the rules of AB soccer. The game is coed, with seven players on a team; these must include at least one Class 6 and no more than four Class 8 athletes. The game consists of two equal periods of 25 min each.

Indoor wheelchair soccer (IWS) is open to Classes 1 to 8 and to all physical disabilities. IWS uses six-person teams (3 quads and 3 paras), with one motorized chair on the floor at all times. The goal is to get a 10-in. playground ball into the opponents' goal cage, a structure 5 ft in width, 4 ft in depth, and 5 ft, 6 in. in height. The playing area is a regulation basketball court. Basketball skills are used for both offense and defense, except that players with 2L or 6L classifications may kick the ball. The ball must be passed or bounced every 3 sec. IWC is explained in detail in Chapter 15, pp. 428–431.

Boccia, played with leather balls of about baseball size, can be either a team or an individual sport. Balls can be given impetus by throwing, rolling, kicking, or assistive device. Figure 25.15 illustrates this game. Although popular in Europe, boccia is just beginning to be known in the United States. Indoor adapted boccia sets, with game rules, can be ordered through NDSA. All balls except the target ball (which is smaller) weigh 275 g and are 26.5 cm in diameter.

Individual Sports

Individual sports in which persons with CP do well include archery, bowling, bicycling and tricycling, track and field, horseback riding, swimming, rifle shooting, slalom, table ten-

nis, and power lifting (Jones, 1988). Tables 25.2 and 25.3 indicate distances that must be achieved in swimming, slalom, track, and cycling events before persons are eligible for NDSA adult competition. School physical education should use these distances as goals. These tables also summarize events appropriate for the different classes.

Use of PFDs is permitted when teaching persons with CP to swim. Most Class 1 and 2 athletes, because of severe spasticity, need PFDs throughout their lives, regardless of how well they learn to swim. A few internationally ranked swimmers are exceptions to this generalization, but independence from PFDs is not a realistic goal for most Class 1 and 2 athletes. *Speed* is the goal rather than good form, although increasing ROM improves form as well as speed. Flippers are not allowed. Team relays are popular.

Tricycles, bicycles, and horses offer a chance for freedom not possible in wheelchairs. Stationary tricycles and bicycles should be available in adapted physical education resource rooms and for winter use. Three-wheeled adult cycles are available through Sears and other popular chain stores. Like AB students, every child with CP should own his or her cycle and master this means of locomotion. Often, adaptations must be made to tricycles and bicycles; special seats can be used, and feet can be attached to pedals with Velcro straps.

The **slalom**, a wheelchair race against time in which persons follow a clearly marked obstacle course, is a good school activity. Four components of the slalom course are (a) one 360° circle around a cone, (b) one 360° gate and three reverse gates, (c) one figure eight around three cones, and (d) one ramp. These components can be combined in various ways, or NDSA can be contacted for a copy of official slalom courses. Slalom is explained in detail in Chapter 15, pp. 401–404.

Field events are more popular in NDSA than any other activity. These also offer great promise in school physical education. In early childhood, beanbags are typically used. By age 7, terminology changes to **soft shot.** This is because of the social valorization principle; beanbag activities are not appropriate for

Table 25.2   Swimming events for NDSA.

Event	Nonambulatory Classes				Ambulatory Classes			
	1	2	3	4	5	6	7	8
25-m freestyle	×	×						
25-m backstroke	×	×						
50-m freestyle	×	×	×	×	×	×	×	×
50-m backstroke	×	×	×	×	×	×	×	
50-m breaststroke			×	×	×	×	×	
50-m butterfly				×	×			
100-m freestyle			×	×	×	×	×	×
100-m backstroke			×	×	×	×	×	×
100-m breaststroke			×	×	×	×	×	×
100-m butterfly								×
200-m freestyle			×	×	×	×	×	×
200-m backstroke					×			×
400-m freestyle				×	×		×	×
800-m freestyle				×	×	×	×	×
1500-m freestyle				×	×	×	×	×
3 × 50 individual medley			×			×	×	
4 × 50 individual medley				×	×			×

Note. In the United States, Class 1 and 2 can compete with and without personal flotation devices (PFDs). International rules do not allow a PFD.

Table 25.3   Slalom, track, and cycling events for NDSA.

Event	Nonambulatory Classes					Ambulatory Classes			
	1	2L	2U	3	4	5	6	7	8
Slalom	×	×	×	×	×				
60-m weave	×								
20-m			×						
60-m			×						
100-m		×	×	×	×	×	×	×	×
200-m		×	×	×	×	×	×	×	×
400-m		×		×	×	×	×	×	×
800-m		×			×		×	×	×
1,500-m					×			×	×
Cross country									
3,000-m							×	×	×
4 × 100		×	×	×	×		×	×	×
Tricycle									
1,500-m		×		×		×	×		
3,000-m						×	×		
5,000-m						×	×		
Bicycle									
1,500-m						×	×		
3,000-m						×	×		
5,000-m						×	×	×	×
10,000-m								×	×
20,000-m								×	×
Total	2	7	6	6	7	9	12	10	10

Note. All wheelchairs are manual except Class 1.

Figure 25.16 Throwing events for Classes 3–4 are the same as for Classes 5–8 except for the javelin, which is inappropriate for Class 3. Note that Class 3 athletes need waist and leg straps for support and hold onto their chairs during the release. Class 4 athletes do not need straps or arm support.

Class 3 Shotput

Class 3 Club throw

Class 4 Javelin throw

Class 4 Club throw

Figure 25.17 Class 6 athletes have more motor control problems than Classes 4–5. Class 6 ambulates without assistive devices but typically has much athetoid movement, which causes balance and accuracy problems.

Class 6 Discus throw

Class 6 Shot put

older children. Regulation-size soft shots are available through NDSA. For Class 3 and above, instruction should focus on the club, shot put, and discus. The javelin is appropriate for Class 4 and above (see Figures 25.16 and 25.17). *Of the official implements, the club is the easiest to handle.*

Softball throwing and catching are de-emphasized except for Classes 7 and 8 because these are not official field events. Classes 7 and 8, when in integrated physical education instruction, may have limited success in softball games. In general, however, catching is difficult to teach (Rintala, Lytinen, & Dunn, 1990) and takes away time better spent on activities more suited to functional ability. Recreational sports that offer success are adaptations using clubs, sticks, and paddles.

Bowling, like field events, is a sport of choice because it permits many adaptations. The ball can be delivered from a sitting or standing position. Persons with fisted hands can use a ramp (also called a chute), with or without an assistant. The assistant does nothing but follow instructions (voice, gesture, head nod) on how to position the ramp or ball. Many bowlers use balls with retractable handles (see Appendix E).

Tables 25.4 and 25.5 summarize events that require equipment and describe adaptations. Parents should be encouraged to begin taking children to NDSA events at ages 3 to 4 because parents then learn about equipment and begin home

programs. The national headquarters for NDSA is 25 West Independence Way, Kingston, RI 02881.

Paralympics and International Issues

Historically, until the 1990s, athletes with CP participated in international meets only with other athletes with CP. Beginning in 1968, the first meets were conducted by the International Cerebral Palsy Society. In 1978, this society was replaced by Cerebral Palsy-International Sports and Recreation Association (CP-ISRA), which continues to hold meets specifically for athletes with CP. This separatism has been necessitated by the refusal of the Paralympic movement to embrace CP and to offer events to accommodate athletes with the most severe disabilities (i.e., Classes 1–3). The Paralympics does, however, support boccia. CP-ISRA's International Boccia Commission (IBC) also conducts meets independent of the Paralympics.

Although the Paralympics movement began in 1960, athletes with CP were excluded until 1980, when ambulatory athletes were invited to Arnhem, Holland. In 1984, nonambulatory athletes with CP finally gained access to Paralympic competition. Many countries still do not enter athletes with CP into the Paralympics. In particular, they offer no opportunities for athletes in motorized chairs (Classes 1 & 2). As a result nonambulatory athletes are severely underrepresented.

Table 25.4   Boccia, bowling, and field events for NDSA.

Event	Nonambulatory Classes				Ambulatory Classes			
	1	2	3	4	5	6	7	8
Boccia	×	×						
Chute bowling with assistant	×	×						
Chute bowling, no assistant			×			×		
Regulation bowling				×	×		×	×
Soft discus	×							
Precision throw	×							
Distance soft shot	×							
High toss	×							
Distance kick		×						
Thrust kick		×						
Shot put		×	×	×	×	×	×	×
Club throw		×	×	×	×	×		
Discus		×	×	×	×	×	×	×
Javelin			×	×	×	×	×	×
Long jump							×	×

Note. Class 2L do the two kicking events; 2U do the throws.

To combat this problem, more efforts must be directed all over the world to awareness of the potential of people with CP and the contributions that physical education and sport can make to their quality of life. Also, more serious efforts must be directed toward fitness training for persons with CP that generalizes to sport (Pitetti, Fernandez, & Lanciault, 1991). How can you help? In particular, more articles should be published concerning the parents' viewpoints and programs like the MOVE curriculum that work (Whinnery & Barnes, 2002).

 ## OPTIONAL ACTIVITIES

1. Contact the National Disability Sports Alliance (NDSA) by website, phone, or fax and ask for information about sport events they govern that will be located close to you during the next 12 months.

   Website: www.ndsa.org or www.ndsaonline.org
   Phone: 401-792-7130
   Fax: 401-792-7132

2. Identify individuals in your school and community who may have cerebral palsy, stroke, or traumatic brain damage and conduct personal interviews or a survey concerning whether they know about NDSA and use its resources. Find out what kind of sports and physical activities that these persons engage in and why. What are the enablers and barriers?

3. Attend or participate in Special Olympics events and identify athletes with both mental retardation and cerebral palsy. Does Special Olympics serve these persons better than NDSA? Why? Interview athletes and family members to find out how they learned about Special Olympics and if they know about NDSA.

4. Obtain the NDSA sports rules manual and teach a group (your peers or persons eligible for various NDSA activities) an NDSA sport like indoor wheelchair soccer, seven-a-side ambulatory soccer, boccia, and so on.

5. Ask persons with disabilities to teach you about communication devices and describe the conditions under which they are most helpful. Learn to use these devices and to teach others to use them.

6. Visit a senior center (day care or residential) and learn as much as possible about older persons with stroke and related conditions. If possible, observe their recreation and physical activity. Volunteer to extend their physical activity opportunities. Obtain copies of the excellent magazine *Stroke Connection* and share with others: www.strokeconnection@heart.org.

Table 25.5   Official equipment for sports governed by NDSA.

Event	Implement	Weight or Design
Distance, precision, and high throws	Soft shot	5 oz (150 g)
Thrust kick	Medicine ball	6 lb (3 kg)
Distance kick	Playground ball	13 inches
Club throw	Club	1 lb, 14 inches long
Discus	Standard women's discus	2 lb (1 kg), 180 mm diameter
Shot put	Shot put	4, 6, or 8 lb, depending on classification
Javelin	Standard women's javelin except for Class 8 males	
Boccia	Leather-covered boccia ball	275 g, 26.5 cm diameter
Ambulatory soccer	Regulation soccer ball	14 to 16 oz
Wheelchair soccer	Playground ball	10 inches
Weight lifting	Universal weight machine, nonprogressive bench	
Bowling	With or without retractable handle chute (ramp)	Varies; 10 lb for Classes 1 and 2

Note. The soft-shot *precision throw* uses a ground target with eight concentric rings. The athlete has six throws from a distance of 6 ft from the center of the bull's-eye. The bull's-eye counts 16 points. Each ring away from it counts 2 points less than the previous. The soft-shot *high throw* uses high-jump standards, with the bar set at 3 ft and raised 6 inches at a time. The competitor is at least 1 mm from the bar and has three throws per height.

CHAPTER

26

Deaf and Hard-of-Hearing Conditions

Claudine Sherrill and Patricia Paulsen Hughes

Figure 26.1 The Rome School for the Deaf has its own style of sideline conversation. The Deaf community does not use first-person terminology, because Deaf people consider deafness a linguistic difference, not a disability.

1. Currently, Deaf people are entitled to protection under ADA (Americans with Disabilities Act) and eligible for SSI/SSD (social security disability) benefits. If people in the Deaf community believe they are a cultural minority, and not a disability group, should they be protected by law as a disability group? Why or why not?

2. If you were to become the parent of a Deaf child, what type of communication skills would you want your child to acquire? Why? Use several resources.

3. In sports, do Deaf athletes have equal opportunities as compared with hearing athletes? Why? How? What rationale supports separate competition for Deaf athletes? What rationale supports Deaf athletes competing against hearing peers?

4. In which setting could more of the physical education objectives listed toward the end of the chapter be accomplished for a child with deafness—in a residential school or in their neighborhood school? Why?

Deaf and hard-of-hearing (HH) students often excel in physical education. At Gallaudet University in Washington, DC, the only liberal arts college in the world for Deaf persons, student interest in athletics is so high that men and women engage in several intercollegiate sports. This university, founded in 1864, is recognized worldwide for its leadership in sports, education, and sign language (see Figure 26.1). The football huddle was invented at Gallaudet so opponents could not see the game strategies being communicated through sign. Here, too, was the famous revolt of March 1988, when students refused to attend classes until the Board of Regents appointed a Deaf president who could use sign and would advocate for rights (Sacks, 1989). I. King Jordan, the new president, simultaneously signed and spoke his acceptance speech:

> The world has watched the Deaf community come of age. We will no longer accept limits on what we can achieve. . . . We know that Deaf people can do anything hearing people can except hear.

Like Gallaudet, Rochester Institute of Technology (RIT) uses American Sign Language as the major communication mode on campus and emphasizes excellent sports and dance programs (see Table 26.1 for websites that provide information on Gallaudet and RIT, on Deaf sports, and on deaf and HH conditions). Among the websites is one for Gallaudet University Press, the best source of books on deafness and sign for readers from preschool through adulthood.

Some Deaf persons, like Denver Broncos football player Kenny Walker (previously University of Nebraska) and baseball player William "Dummy" Hoy (1862–1961) have gained recognition as outstanding members of hearing teams. Hoy played with both American and National leagues and instigated the development of umpire hand signals. More and more people who are deaf or HH are in mainstream physical education and sports. Some, however, opt to participate in Deaf sport only, where sign language dominates over oral communication.

Deaf Sport and Deaf Community

Deaf sport, a term created by individuals who are Deaf, is explained by David Stewart (1991) in his excellent book *Deaf Sport: The Impact of Sports Within the Deaf Community:*

> Deaf sport is a social institution within which Deaf people exercise their right to self-determination,

competition, and socialization surrounding Deaf sport activities. The magnitude and the complexity of Deaf sport reflects many of the dimensions of being Deaf in a hearing society. In this sense, Deaf sport is a microcosm of the Deaf community (p.2). . . . Deaf sport emphasizes the honor of being Deaf, whereas society tends to focus on the adversity of deafness. (p.1)

Stewart, by birth a Canadian, is a professor at Michigan State University. See Chapter 2 for more information on Stewart.

Deaf sport refers to all of the sport opportunities provided by the **Deaf community,** a term coined by people who are Deaf to describe their cultural and linguistic separateness from the hearing, speaking world. Over the centuries, Deaf persons have tended to cluster together and to take care of one another's needs. They communicate through American Sign Language (ASL). Until recently, few hearing persons knew much about them. *Deaf persons do not advocate person-first terminology. That is why this chapter refers to Deaf people rather than people with deafness.*

The rules, strategies, and skills of Deaf sport are not adapted except for communication modes. Modifications are made only in starting and stopping signals and in the ways officials communicate with players. Deaf sport internationally is governed by the Comite International des Sports des Sourds (CISS), founded in France in 1924. The English translation of this is International Committee on Silent Sports, but the commonly used abbreviation (CISS) is derived from the French name. Summer World Games for the Deaf began in 1924, almost a quarter of a century before international competition was initiated for anyone other than Olympic athletes. The American Athletic Association for the Deaf (AAAD) was founded at the end of World War II (1945), long before organizations for athletes with disabilities were conceived. Every nation has a Deaf community and Deaf sport. In 1999, AAAD changed its name to USA Deaf Sports Federation (USADSF).

Although affiliated for a short time with the Paralympic movement in the early 1990s, Deaf sport has chosen to dissociate itself from disability sport. World Games (now called Deaflympics), like the Olympics, are conducted as quadrennial events. Summer Deaflympics are held on a schedule that runs 2004, 2007, and so on, and Winter Deaflympics are held on a schedule that runs 2003, 2006, and so on. Summer games typically attract around 2,500 athletes from over 30 nations.

To be eligible for participation in Deaf sport, athletes must have a hearing loss of 55 decibels (dB) or greater in the

Table 26.1 Websites for information on Deaf sports, sign-language oriented universities, and general information on Deaf and hard-of-hearing conditions.

Websites on Deaf Sport and Universities

USA Deaf Sports Federation	www.usadsf.org
International Committee of Sports for the Deaf	www.CISS.org
U.S. Deaf Cycling Association	www.home.earthlink.net/~skedsmo/usdca.htm
International Martial Arts Federation of the Deaf	www.IMAFD.org
USA Deaf Track & Field	www.members.tripod.com/~usadtf/
U.S. Association of Deaf Basketball	www.usadb.org
U.S. Deaf Ski and Snowboard Association	www.usdssa.org

Websites for General Information

Convention of American Instructors of the Deaf	www.caid.org
Gallaudet Research Institute	www.gn.gallaudet.edu
Gallaudet University Press	www.gupress.gallaudet.edu
Hard of Hearing Advocates	www.hohadvocates.org
League for the Hard of Hearing	www.lhh.org
National Association of the Deaf	www.nad.org
National Cued Speech Association	www.cuedspeech.org
Registry of Interpreters for the Deaf	www.rid.org
Self-Help for Hard of Hearing People	www.shhh.org

better ear. Deaf athletes are not classified according to severity of hearing loss. Hearing aids are not permitted during competition. Table 26.2 presents sports in which Deaf athletes can compete internationally.

The Deaf community offers an extensive network of sports for all ages and abilities via national sport organizations for every sport, which are affiliated with the USADSF, which in turn is linked with the CISS. Sport is viewed by the Deaf community as a viable means of preserving their language and culture. Intercollegiate, interscholastic, and family-oriented recreational sport competition is valued. Universities and schools for the Deaf compete against each other, but also often compete against mainstream institutions. When the Gallaudet women's basketball team won the Capital Athletic Conference and advanced to the "Sweet Sixteen" round of the NCAA Division III tournament, they published a comprehensive photo essay, *Deaf Girls Rule,* to commemorate the event (Tiefenbacher, 1999).

Illustrative to the many Deaf athletes who compete in both hearing and deaf sport competition is Jamel Bradley, a senior shooting guard on the basketball team at the University of South Carolina. New state-of-the-art omnidirectional hearing aids are permitting him, for the first time, to communicate on and off the court as well as persons with 100% hearing. These hearing aids push the noise of spectators off to the sides so that Jamel can hear the coach and teammates. Despite his loving hearing sport, Jamel is committed to the Deaflympics and the other Deaf sport events he grew up with. No one knows how much technology will change the Deaf world.

Students who wish to compete on their high school teams can do so until age 22 if this practice and competition are written into the IEP. This is because IDEA serves students with disabilities until age 22. Read the excellent story of how Jeffrey Kling, his family, and his IEP committee worked to change the

Table 26.2 Deaf sports organized by the USA Deaf Sports Foundation.

Summer Deaflympic Sports	
Individual	**Team**
Bowling	Soccer
Cycling	Water polo (men)
Wrestling, Greco Roman and freestyle (men)	Handball (men and women)
Swimming	Volleyball (men and women)
Track and field (men and women)	Basketball (men and women
Tennis (men and women)	
Table tennis (men and women)	
Badminton (men and women)	
Shooting (men and women)	

Other Sports (Summer and Winter)	
Golf	Baseball
Ski & snowboard	Flag football
Speed skating	Net sports
	Softball
	Water sports
	Ice hockey

Note. See www.usadsf.org for full contact information for each national sport organization affiliated with usadsf.org. Contact information is available also for eight regional athletic associations.

Ohio High School Athletic Association (OHSAA) rules for interscholastic competition (Stewart, 2001). Physical educators and coaches are sometimes called to testify at impartial due process hearings. Be ready!

Definitions and Concepts

What do we call persons with a hearing loss? Many such individuals do not consider themselves disabled and prefer to be thought of as a cultural and linguistic minority (Butterfield, 1991; Stewart, 1991). They are often proficient in both sign and English and wonder why so much of the world can communicate only in one way. In particular, most Deaf world-class athletes take this stance. In contrast, adults adjusting to a hearing impairment may mourn their loss in ways similar to persons with physical disabilities (Myers, 2000). Obviously, there are many individual differences.

The Deaf community prefers the terms *Deaf* and *hard of hearing,* but IDEA uses the terms *deaf* and *hearing impaired.* Deaf persons believe that *impaired* is too general to have meaning. They associate *deafness* with being unable to hear with the ears, with or without amplification, and *hardness-of-hearing (HH)* as ability to hear with the ears, with or without amplification, even though hearing is hard. Deaf people see these as very different conditions, whereas hearing persons tend to link them together into a continuum of hearing acuity.

IDEA defines **deafness** as

> a hearing impairment that is so severe that the child is impaired in processing linguistic information through hearing, with or without amplification, and this adversely affects a child's educational performance.

IDEA defines **hearing impairment** (HI) as

> an impairment in hearing, whether permanent or fluctuating, that adversely affects child's educational performance but that is not included in IDEA's definition of deafness.

Deaf-blindness, recognized by IDEA as a separate category, is addressed in Chapter 27 because the U.S. Association for Blind Athletes offers programming for persons with deaf-blindness whereas the USADSF does not. This is logical because ability to see sign language is prerequisite to Deaf sport.

Deafness is associated more closely with speech impairment and specific learning disability than other special education categories. About 6 to 8% of Deaf and HH children have diagnosed learning disabilities. In general, Deaf persons have average or better intelligence and perform as well on tasks that measure thinking as their hearing peers. Academic achievement depends largely on educational opportunity. *Many Deaf and HH people have problems with reading and writing beyond the fifth-grade level.*

Language and Communication

The terms *language* and *communication* should not be used interchangeably. Language can be (a) inner, (b) receptive, or (c) expressive (see Chapter 18). Communication is typically described as verbal or nonverbal. Verbal methods are (a) oral, (b) written, and (c) sign (i.e., any modality that uses words). Nonverbal methods are facial expressions, postures, body language, or gestures. Nonverbal also refers to silent demonstrations.

Persons who are Deaf or HH communicate in many ways, depending on (a) the age that the loss was sustained, (b) training, (c) ability, and (d) affiliation with Deaf or hearing cul-

Figure 26.2   Dr. Stephen Butterfield, well-known researcher at the University of Maine, signs test instructions to a child.

ture. Deaf persons usually read lips, a skill called *speechreading,* or rely on *sign language,* a manual communication system in which fingers, hands, facial expressions, and body movements are used to convey meaning (see Figure 26.2). There are many forms of signing: American Sign Language (ASL), also called Ameslan; Pidgin Sign English (PSE), also called Siglish; and Manually Coded English (MCE). Of these, ASL is the recognized language of Deaf and HH people who communicate manually. ASL has its own grammar and syntax, so sentences are not constructed in the same way that words are ordered in English.

Fingerspelling is a system in which a particular hand position is used for each letter of the alphabet. Each word is spelled letter by letter; because it is slower than signing, it is rarely used by itself. Fingerspelling may be the communication system of choice with hearing persons who do not know sign or with deaf-blind persons who cannot see sign. With the latter, the hand positions are made in the palm of the recipient's hand.

When hearing loss occurs before age 3, learning to speak English is slow and laborious. In older children, who lose the ability to hear their own speech and monitor pronunciation of new words, speaking may gradually become less easy. Problems occur because many listeners will not take the time to become familiar with a different speech pattern. This is the same kind of discrimination experienced by foreigners who speak English with an accent (or poorly).

Three approaches to teaching communication skills are (a) **manual,** which includes fingerspelling and signing; (b) **oral or speech only;** and (c) **total communication,** which combines the best of manual and oral methods. *Most school systems today use total communication.* In the past, however, Deaf education was characterized by bitter controversy over the better method, oral or manual. This intensified in the late 1800s, with Alexander Graham Bell (the inventor of the telephone) championing the oral method and Edward Gallaudet (founder and director of Gallaudet University) advocating the manual method. Both of these men had Deaf mothers, but different attitudes prevailed in their households. Eventually, the oral method won, and sign was not taught in most classrooms until the 1970s, when total communication became the accepted philosophical approach (Jankowski, 1997).

Although sign was not allowed in the classroom, it continued to be used in everyday life. Many Deaf people have always regarded sign as their major language, and today sign is widely accepted as a language. Several movies and videotapes depict communication and other issues. Among these, *Children of a Lesser God* (originally a play) is perhaps best known because Marlee Matlin, who is Deaf, won an Oscar in 1987 as best actress for her role. Matlin signed her acceptance speech but later used her voice in various public appearances, thereby drawing criticism from some Deaf persons. In contrast, Kitty O'Neal, who holds the world speed records for women in water skiing and various car racing events, defends the oral method in the video presenting her life story.

Speechreading and Cued Speech

Speechreading, formerly called lipreading, is a difficult skill because many sounds look identical. For example, *b, p,* and *m* are produced by bringing the lips together. *L, t,* and *d* are formed with the tongue on the roof of the mouth behind the front teeth. Words like *man, mat, mad, bat, bad, ban, pan, pad,* and *pat* look the same and can be understood only if the general idea or context of the speech is followed.

Several trap sentences illustrate the problem of speechreading: "What's that big loud noise?" looks the same as "What's that pig outdoors?" the title of an excellent autobiography by Deaf journalist Henry Kisor (1990). Try saying "It rate ferry aren't hadn't for that reason high knit donned co" to someone with earplugs. Chances are that he or she will think you said, "It rained very hard and for that reason I didn't go." According to Kisor (1990), much of speechreading is guesswork. About 30 to 40% is understanding words, and the rest is *context guessing* to fill in the gaps.

Cued speech is a system whereby spoken words are supplemented with hand signs near the face to help persons interpret words that look the same, like *son/sun* and *bat/pat.* Eight specific hand shapes presented in four positions near the face provide a multitude of cues. This system was created by Cornett (1967).

Naturally, it is easier to speechread familiar acquaintances than strangers. During initial meetings, 50% or sometimes less is understood. With continued contact, comprehension increases. However, occasionally, there are persons (about 10%) who are impossible to speechread. These are typically people who move their lips very little, speak fast, show little expression and emotion, chew gum, or have a mustache.

Speechreading is particularly difficult in group conversations or discussions in which the speaker is frequently changing. Obviously, the Deaf or HH individual must be able to see the lips of everyone talking but also be fast in determining which new person is talking. Discussions seldom elicit much talk from speechreaders because they tend to be uncertain about when pauses occur for them to jump in and about the exact time a topic or focus changes. To facilitate involvement, restating the topic and asking the speechreader what he or she thinks is helpful.

Speechreading is much more fatiguing than ordinary auditory processing of words. Most persons speak over 120 words a minute. A cough, sneeze, or other distraction disrupts understanding. Success in speechreading demands high concentration. Young children, of course, focus for shorter periods than older ones. Instruction should be adapted to individual differences.

Proper lighting conditions facilitate speechreading. Care should be taken that Deaf persons are not facing into the sun. This is also important in sign language.

 What other environmental adaptations should be made? Make a list.

American Sign Language and Other Forms of Sign

American Sign Language (ASL) is a bona fide language like Spanish and French, with its own grammar and syntax. Much practice is necessary before communication level reaches the sophistication expected of adults. ASL can express abstract as well as concrete thoughts. It is the dominant language of the Deaf community in the United States and Canada and has regional variations and dialects. ASL is the fourth most commonly used language in the United States (Flodin, 1991). Only English, Spanish, and Italian rank ahead of it.

ASL sentence structure is different from that of English. For example, in English, we might say, "Have you been to Texas?" In ASL, this would be TOUCH FINISH TEXAS YOU QUESTION, with *you* and *question* signed simultaneously.

Most hearing people do not take the time to learn ASL syntax and grammar. Instead, they link signs together in the same order they speak words in English. The result is a form of **signed English** or English signing. In contrast, **Pidgin sign** refers to a mixture of English and ASL. When enrolling in sign language classes, it is wise to ask which kind of sign will be taught.

ASL generally is not the language used in total communication classes in public schools. Signed English permits signs to be presented in the same order that English is spoken and thus enhances the improvement of reading and writing. Some Deaf persons are therefore bilingual in sign. They use ASL in the Deaf community and signed English at school. Additionally, they learn to speak, read, and write English and other languages.

In becoming multilingual, Deaf persons experience the frustrations common to learning foreign languages. Proficiency in English may not be as strong as that of persons who are unilingual. This affects academic achievement. Books and videotapes that teach and/or use ASL in exercise can be ordered from Gallaudet University Press.

Learning Some Signs

Signs are useful substitutes for whistles and shouts in noisy physical education environments. An increasing number of teachers are weaving sign into sport and dance instruction. Many students cannot hear over the background noise, and so sign is a viable instructional supplement.

Signs are easily worked into early childhood games, creative dramatics, and action songs. They enrich the perspective of hearing children who, in the next decade, will be learning sign in elementary school, just as they do Spanish and French.

Learning sign often begins with fingerspelling (see Figure 26.3). Persons generally master their name first and then add signs for "Hi, my name is _____." See Figures 26.4, 26.5, and 26.6. Note that the explanation of *name* in Figure 26.4 refers to the *H* finger.

 Learn to fingerspell the alphabet, and be able to do it in class to your peers and instructor.

When instructions say to move clockwise or counterclockwise, *this is from the viewpoint of the signer, not the watcher.* Note that signs in instructional manuals are shown as they are seen by the watcher. The type of sign used by most hearing beginners is **manually coded English** (MCE). Much formal instruction is needed to use systems like ASL and Pidgin Sign English (PSE).

Signing can be viewed on television when church services for Deaf persons are broadcast. It is also used by the National Theatre of the Deaf, which has toured both Europe and the United States since its establishment in 1967. Most of the company's professional actors are alumni of Gallaudet University. The National Theatre of the Deaf is housed in Waterford, Connecticut.

Interpreters

Educational interpreters should be employed by the school district when Deaf or HI students receive instruction in general education classes. If an interpreter is required for a student to learn in academic classes, then an interpreter should be provided for physical education classes also (Best, Lieberman, & Arndt, 2002). These individuals, who generally hold a national certification, transmit information from spoken English to ASL and vice versa. Interpreters typically position themselves next to the teacher (or anyone whose speech needs to be converted to sign) so that the student has both persons in the same visual field. Information about how to obtain interpreters can be obtained from the Registry of Interpreters for the Deaf (RID) at www.rid.org or the National Association of the Deaf (NAD) at www.nad.org. The educational interpreter may be invited to join the IEP team and perform tasks in addition to facilitating communication between Deaf and hearing persons.

Sound and Vibration

Sound waves are really vibrations. They start at a particular point and spread, much like a rock tossed into a pond makes circles of waves. Most people both hear and feel vibrations. Total deafness means vibrations can only be felt. Consider a rock concert, especially the bass tones. Sounds are conducted to the inner ear through both air and bone conduction. Vibrations, however, are felt by the whole body and convey a basic beat or rhythm.

Central to the understanding of hearing loss are the three attributes of sound: intensity, frequency, and timbre or

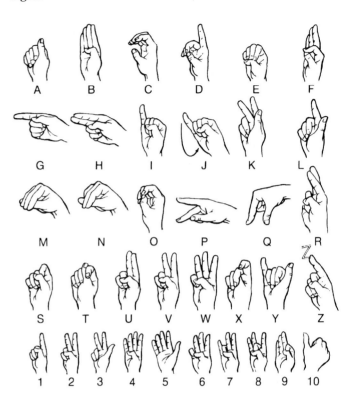

Figure 26.3   Standard fingerspelling and number signs.

tone. Figure 26.7 depicts an audiogram that shows how intensity (the vertical axis) and frequency (the horizontal axis) are used to describe hearing loss. Perfect hearing would be noted by shading the 0 line across all frequencies. The loss depicted is a mild conductive one that can be simulated by placing your fingers in both ears. Figure 26.7 shows that the speech sounds *f, s,* and *th* at high frequencies (pitches) are the first to be lost, along with *p, h, z,* and *v* at lower frequencies. To better understand audiograms and hearing classifications, let's consider the attributes of sound.

Intensity

Intensity refers to the perception of loudness and softness. The unit of measurement that expresses the intensity of a sound is the *decibel* (dB). This term is named for Alexander Graham Bell and literally means one tenth of a bell. A sound at 0 level is barely audible. Speech can be heard from a distance of 10 to 20 ft when the loudness is 35 to 65 dB, depending on the pitch. When the intensity of sound ranges above 100 dB, the sound may become painful.

Frequency

Frequency refers to the perception of high and low pitch. It is measured in terms of hertz (Hz). Most human beings can perceive frequencies from about 20 to 20,000 Hz. The audiogram includes only the frequencies between 125 and 8,000, since these are the most important in daily communication.

Figure 26.4 **Signs to play the *Name Game*. Note eight signs: Four to say, "Hi, my name is _____"; two to say, "What is your name?"; and two to say, "I'm happy to meet you."**

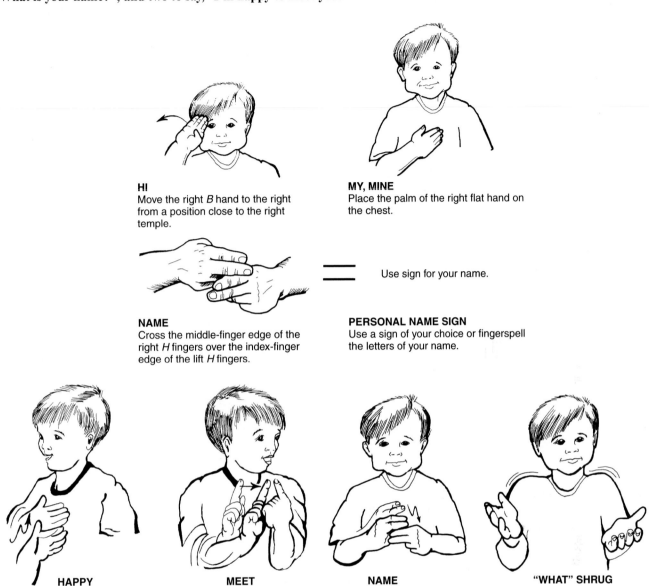

HI
Move the right *B* hand to the right from a position close to the right temple.

MY, MINE
Place the palm of the right flat hand on the chest.

NAME
Cross the middle-finger edge of the right *H* fingers over the index-finger edge of the lift *H* fingers.

Use sign for your name.

PERSONAL NAME SIGN
Use a sign of your choice or fingerspell the letters of your name.

HAPPY   **MEET**

"I'm happy to meet you" in American Sign Language

NAME   **"WHAT" SHRUG**

"What is your name?" in American Sign Language

Three of these frequencies—500, 1,000, and 2,000 Hz—are emphasized in hearing tests. For instance, persons who do not hear frequencies above 2,000 Hz have difficulty in recognizing such high-frequency sounds as the letters *s, z, sh, zh, th* as in *think, th* as in *that, ch* as in *chair, j* as in Joe, *p, b, t, d, f, v,* and *h.*

Check your understanding of pitch on a piano. The lowest note on the keyboard (A) is 30 Hz. Middle C is 256 Hz. The highest C on the keyboard is 4,000 Hz. Check that of your parents or some older persons.

Timbre or Tone

Timbre refers to all of the qualities besides intensity and frequency that enable us to distinguish between sounds, voices,

and musical instruments. It is sometimes conceptualized as the resonance quality of a sound because it depends on the number and character of the vibrating body's overtones. Hearing persons deficient in this area are called *tone deaf.* They can distinguish between some tones but not others. Vowel and vowel combinations (diphthongs) have more easily distinguished tones than consonants.

Testing and Classifying Hearing Loss

Formal hearing tests are conducted by an audiologist or speech and hearing therapist using an instrument called an audiometer. Table 26.3 presents the most widely used system for classifying hearing loss. In general, the first three classes (slight, mild, moderate) are considered HH, and the last two (severe, profound) are considered deaf.

Figure 26.5   Signs to play start-stop games like *Red Light, Green Light.* Note that many games are played with only two signs. These signs are also important for classroom discipline.

START, BEGIN
Hold the left flat hand forward with the palm facing right. Place the tip of the right index finger between the left index and middle finger; then twist the right index in a *clockwise direction once or twice.*

STOP
Bring the little-finger side of the right flat hand down sharply at right angles on the left palm.

Figure 26.6   Signs to reinforce students. These signs should be used frequently in teaching and coaching.

THANKS, THANK YOU, YOU'RE WELCOME
Touch the lips with the fingertips of one or both flat hands; then move the hands forward until the palms are facing up. It is natural to smile and nod the head while making this sign.

GOOD
Place the fingers of the right flat hand at the lips; then move the right hand down into the palm of the left, with both palms facing up.

Hearing loss is so complex that there are many individual differences in how persons with each classification function. Table 26.3 offers generalizations about hearing and speaking limitations. There are, of course, exceptions to the rule. Many persons with a 25- to 40-dB loss can benefit from hearing aids, but 40 dB is the more traditional criterion.

A 3- to 5-ft criterion is useful in making classroom adaptations for slight and mild losses. Students farther away than this may miss as much as 50% of class instruction if they cannot see lips. Consider how this affects learning in various physical education settings.

Put earplugs in your ears for one hour, and try to maintain your typical level of interactions. You can buy earplugs at most drug stores. What happens?

The moderate classification (55 to 69 dB) is of particular interest because 55 dB is the minimum criterion for eligibility to participate in USADSF activities. The 55-dB and greater loss is associated with difficulty in following and contributing to small-group conversations and class discussions. Loud or shouted speech at close range may be heard but not totally understood because of distortions and background noise. Speech training becomes imperative at this level for correct pronunciation.

The 70-dB level is the accepted criterion for distinguishing between HH and deafness. Persons partially hear speech sounds within 1 ft, but they cannot understand most of them, even with amplification. Individuals at both the severe and profound levels may need intensive training in total communication. Interpreters and/or buddy systems are helpful in communicating with hearing people, especially in group settings.

Congenital and Acquired Conditions

Ability to communicate in conventional spoken English is largely dependent upon the age that hearing loss occurs. Therefore, time of onset (congenital or acquired) is important. A syn-

Figure 26.7 Audiogram findings for mild conductive loss superimposed on illustration of various environmental and speech sounds at different frequencies and intensities.

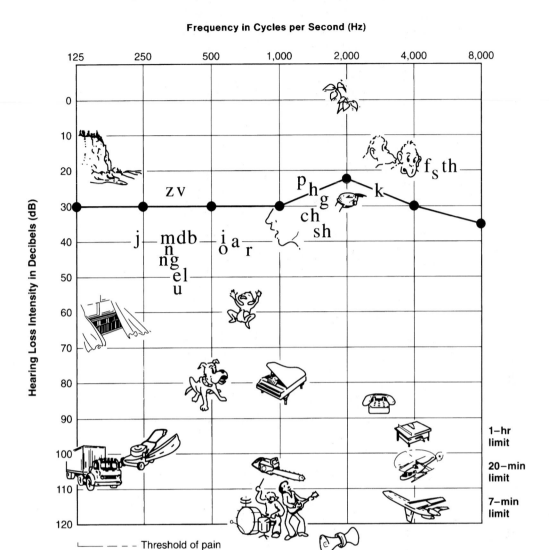

Table 26.3 Classification of hearing loss.

Degree of Loss	Loss in Decibels	Difficulty With
Slight	25–40	Whispered speech
Mild	41–54	Normal speech at distance greater than 3 to 5 ft
Marked or moderate	55–69	Understanding loud or shouted speech at close range; group discussions
Severe	70–89	Understanding speech at close range, even when amplified
Profound	90+	Hearing most sounds, including telephone rings and musical instruments (see Figure 26.7)

Note. 55 dB or worse in one ear is the criterion for sport eligibility in USADSF.

onym for *acquired* is *adventitiously deaf.* The terms *prelingual* and *postlingual* further specify whether loss was sustained before or after the development of language.

With congenital hearing losses, knowing whether parents are hearing or Deaf and what language (sign or spoken English) dominates in the home is critical. This affects all as-

pects of development, especially self-esteem. Deaf children born to Deaf parents typically have significantly higher self-esteem than those born to hearing parents. This is because Deaf children born to Deaf parents are immediately accepted and begin learning language (sign) at a very young age. Only about 10% of Deaf children have Deaf parents.

Acquired hearing losses vary in severity, depending on the degree of loss and age of onset. Among the many persons with acquired hearing losses are Ludwig van Beethoven and Thomas Alva Edison. The last 25 years of Beethoven's life were spent in almost total deafness. His famous Ninth Symphony, the *Missa Solemnis,* and many of his piano sonatas and string quartets were composed after he became totally deaf. At his last appearance at a public concert, in 1824, Beethoven was completely oblivious to the applause of the audience acclaiming his ninth and final symphony.

Types and Causes of Hearing Loss

There are three types of hearing loss: (a) conductive, (b) sensorineural, and (c) mixed. Visualizing the three parts of the ear and the causes of disorders in each part is helpful (see Figure 26.8). The Greek word for ear is *otos,* so inflammation of the ear is **otitis.** The instrument used in an ear examination is an **otoscope.**

Conductive Loss

Conductive loss is diminished sound traveling through the air passages of the external and middle ear. Putting your finger in your ear canal creates about a 25-dB conductive loss. You can still hear, but not as well. A conductive loss results in an HH condition, not deafness.

Disorders of the external ear center around the size and shape of the ear canal. Occasionally, infants are born without a canal (**atresia**) or with one that is abnormally narrow. Usually, however, problems are caused by obstruction (**impacted earwax**), injury, or infection (**external otitis**) and respond well to treatment.

Disorders of the middle ear are more serious, often resulting in permanent damage. The middle ear is the small space between the eardrum (tympanic membrane) and the bony capsule of the inner ear. It includes the **ossicles** (malleus, incus, stapes), the small bones shaped, respectively, like a hammer, anvil, and stirrup that transmit sound waves to the inner ear much like a blacksmith once worked on horseshoes with a hammer. The middle ear also contains the **Eustachian tube,** which connects the nasopharynx passageway with the throat, and is much affected by colds, sinus infections, and allergies.

Inflammation of the middle ear, called **otitis media,** accounts for more conductive disorders than any other condition. Young children are especially at risk, because 76 to 95% have at least one ear infection before age 2. There are several kinds of otitis media. Some are **acute,** characterized by severe pain and swelling. Others are **chronic,** with persons adjusting to

Figure 26.8   Three parts of the ear shown in relation to locations of disorder. Descriptors for air conduction and sensorineural losses are summarized.

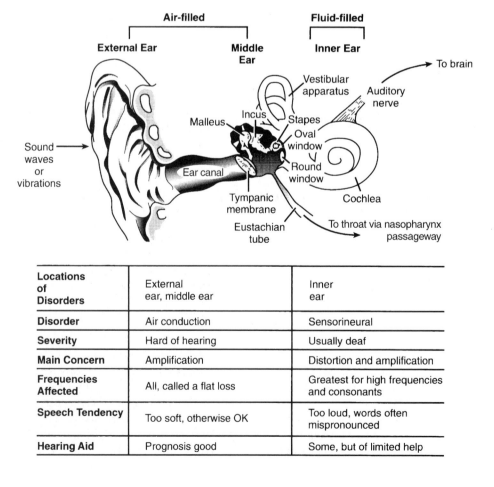

Locations of Disorders	External ear, middle ear	Inner ear
Disorder	Air conduction	Sensorineural
Severity	Hard of hearing	Usually deaf
Main Concern	Amplification	Distortion and amplification
Frequencies Affected	All, called a flat loss	Greatest for high frequencies and consonants
Speech Tendency	Too soft, otherwise OK	Too loud, words often mispronounced
Hearing Aid	Prognosis good	Some, but of limited help

the discomfort and hardly aware of the fluid accumulation behind the eardrum. Many adults with a childhood history of colds, asthma, and respiratory infections do not realize the danger of this fluid until too late (i.e., deafness or HH occurs).

Otitis media (or any condition that causes the tubes to swell or clog) prevents the Eustachian tubes from performing their functions: (a) ventilating and keeping dry the middle ear cavity and (b) equalizing air pressure on the two sides of the eardrum. If corrective measures are not taken, damage occurs. Antibiotics and other medications sometimes require several days to take effect.

When Eustachian tubes are clogged, flying and activities that involve changes in altitude (e.g., mountain climbing, biking) and pressure (swimming, diving, snorkeling) should be avoided. Obviously, colds and infections should be treated promptly to avoid or minimize Eustachian tube clogging.

Middle ear ventilation tubes are used when Eustachian tubes are chronically blocked or infected, a condition most prevalent in young children. These tubes are surgically inserted, under local or general anesthesia, with one end in the middle ear and the other just outside the eardrum. During the months that a tube is in place, swimming is contraindicated.

Sensorineural Loss

Sensorineural loss occurs (a) in the inner ear, where sensory receptors convert sound waves into neural impulses that travel to the brain for translation, or (b) somewhere between the cochlea and the brainstem, particularly the auditory nerve. The hearing apparatus within the inner ear is the **cochlea,** so named because it resembles a snail shell in appearance. The oval and round windows are the passages through which sound waves enter the inner ear and disrupt the fluid and hair cells in the cochlea, the mechanism central to sensory reception. Also housed in the inner ear is the **vestibular apparatus** (semicircular canals) that governs balance. This explains why sensorineural hearing loss and balance deficits sometimes occur together (see Figure 26.9).

Sensorineural loss not only reduces sound but also causes distortions in residual hearing. In young children, this makes learning to speak a real challenge and delays development of language concepts. If loss is total, there is no need for a hearing aid because no amount of amplification will help. If loss is partial, hearing aids will help but not as much as in a conductive loss. Often, hearing aids are used only for auditory and speech training in a structured setting.

Most persons who are born deaf have sensorineural loss. Over 60 types of hereditary hearing loss have been identified, with **autosomal recessive genes** accounting for about 40% of childhood deafness (Kottke & Lehmann, 1990). Often, persons do not know they are carrying these genes. Only about 10% of deaf infants are born to parents who are deaf. Of these, about half have one parent who is hearing.

About 50% of all hearing losses in children have an unknown (idiopathic) etiology. This is largely because hearing losses are often not discovered until language delays are noted. Many of these losses may be genetic.

Among children, **meningitis** (usually a bacterial infection) and various viral infections (e.g., mumps, scarlet fever, encephalitis, measles, HIV) often dramatically wipe out both hearing and balance. Meningitis carries a 1 in 5 risk of hearing loss. An infection of the **meninges** (coverings) surrounding the spinal cord and brain, meningitis is characterized by high fever, vomiting, and stiff neck. From 30 to 50% of its survivors have multiple disabilities.

Maternal illnesses during pregnancy often result in deafness. Many of these, like measles, are controlled by vaccines so widespread epidemics no longer occur. Herpes viruses and **toxoplasmosis** (infection caused by protozoa found in animals and birds) continue to produce serious hearing defects.

Among adolescents and adults, noise is the main cause of new cases of hearing loss (Kottke & Lehmann, 1990). Several million Americans work in occupations with potentially hazardous noise levels (i.e., above 85 dB). Federal laws govern the number of hours that persons can work at high decibel levels and require the wearing of hearing-protection devices, but these laws are not always followed. Additionally, life in big cities is increasingly noisy, especially time spent in travel. Some sports create noise levels that persons mask by wearing **hearing-protection devices** (e.g., shooting, snowmobiling, motorcycles). Rock concerts and personal earphones attached to stereo devices are also sources of hearing damage.

Last, parts of the sensorineural hearing mechanism deteriorate with age, just like other body parts. Reasons for the high prevalence of hearing loss with aging are not clear, but noise is believed to be a major factor. Parts of the conductive system may deteriorate also, but *it is sensorineural loss that causes the problems widely associated with biological aging.*

Figure 26.9   Sensorineural loss is linked to balance or vestibular deficits. Note hearing aid apparatus on chest.

Mixed Loss and Tinnitus

Many persons have mixed (combined) conductive and sensorineural losses. This is particularly true of senior citizens.

Tinnitus is a sound sensation in one or both ears that affects about 6% of the population. Associated with both conductive and sensorineural losses, it is experienced as a whistling, hissing, buzzing, roaring, throbbing, or whining sound. It can be sporadic but is continuous for many people. Medical management is sometimes effective, but most persons simply learn to block out their tinnitus.

Prevalence and Incidence of Hearing Loss

Most sources indicate that 7 to 15% of the population have significant hearing losses. Over 17 million Americans have hearing losses, of whom 2 million (about 1 person in 8) are profoundly deaf (Kottke & Lehmann, 1990). At all ages, hearing loss predominates in males.

Prevalence varies sharply, however, by age group. Profound hearing loss is present in about 1 in 1,000 newborns (Roeser & Downs, 1988). Approximately 3 in every 1,000 children below age 6 have a moderate or greater sensorineural loss in both ears. The rate is increased 15 to 30 times when mild sensorineural loss is included. Conductive losses are more difficult to track because mild conditions often remain undetected; all children who have had middle ear infections are at risk. *Those with Down syndrome, cleft palate, and face/head malformations are at particular risk because of abnormally narrow ear canals.* Numbers increase as disease, injury, and environmental noise take their toll. Among school-age children, about 5 to 7% could benefit from special education services for hearing losses.

The prevalence of hearing loss for the 45- to 64-year-old age group is about 11%, whereas that for the 65- to 74-year-old age group is 30%. *By age 75, approximately 50% of the population has a significant loss.* This is usually for the higher frequencies (i.e., consonants and high-pitched voices and sounds). Background noise (including music) intensifies problems. Speech discrimination is typically more of a problem than loudness; this means that hearing aids may be of limited value.

Presbycusis is the term for degeneration of hearing with age. Although all parts of the auditory apparatus are subject to breakdown, presbycusic changes are primarily sensorineural rather than conductive (see Figure 26.10).

In summary, hearing loss is a high-prevalence condition when older age groups are included. It affects more persons than heart conditions, arthritis, blindness, and any chronic physical disability.

Assistive Listening Devices and Systems

Assistive listening devices and systems (ALDS) include all electronic and electromechanical devices except the personal hearing aid. Over 200 devices are available to amplify sounds, convert them to light or vibration systems, or in some way transmit meaning (e.g., closed-captioned television). Among the sounds relayed are the ring of the telephone, the buzz of an alarm clock, the chime of a doorbell, the warning of a fire alarm or smoke detector, and the cry of an infant.

Figure 26.10 Presbycusis is degeneration of hearing with age. It mostly causes sensorineural losses. (© Thomas Braise/The Stock Market.)

Think about adaptations that might make housing safer, entertainment (television, theatre, sports) more enjoyable, and learning in a large lecture hall or gymnasium more effective!

For the latter, AM and FM radio frequencies can transmit voice sounds when the speaker wears a special device. Decoders are now built into all television sets so that they have the capacity for closed-captioning. New devices are available every day (see Turkington & Sussman, 2000).

Personal Hearing Aids

Who can benefit from a hearing aid? The 40-dB loss is the traditional criterion, but there is a trend toward prescribing them for 25- to 40-dB losses, especially in young children who need help in learning speech and language. Hearing aids amplify sound but do not necessarily make words understandable. Losses over 90 dB typically leave too little residual hearing for amplification to be of help in communication.

Hearing aids work best when the listening environment is quiet and structured and the speaker is relatively close (not more than 4 or 5 ft away) or wearing a special device to transmit sound waves. Hearing aids have the same components as public address systems and amplify in the same way. Their five main parts are (a) input microphone, (b) amplifier, (c) earphone or output receiver, (d) battery, and (e) on/off switch.

Hearing aids are available in four styles, named according to their location: (a) chest or body-worn, (b) behind the ear, (c) eyeglass, and (d) in the ear. The chest style is worn primarily by young children or by persons with multiple disabilities.

Regardless of style, proper maintenance is a daily concern because parts are prone to breakdown. Most malfunctions are caused by dead or weak batteries, corrosion on battery contacts, or improper battery replacement. Other problems include clogged earmolds, frayed cords, cracked tubing, excessive distortion, and poor frequency response. Teachers should not automatically assume that hearing aids are working correctly.

Research shows that 30 to 50% of hearing aids of school-age children are not performing adequately on any given day. Moisture is a particular problem, especially for persons who perspire heavily during activity. Hearing aids can be dried with hair blowers.

Deaf and HH persons have personal preferences about wearing aids in physical activity settings. These should be honored. Hearing aid technology is advancing rapidly. Digital hearing aids allow for different settings that selectively tune out particular frequencies, virtually eliminating ambient noise. Not all students currently wear digital aids, though. A nondigital aid will amplify *all* sound. As a result, persons wearing aids may react negatively to prolonged noise and have frequent tension headaches. What implications does this have for integrated physical education and sport?

Cochlear implants first became available in the mid 1980s, although the basic idea was visualized by Benjamin Franklin more than 200 years ago. Approximately 60,000 people worldwide have received implants at an average cost of $30,000 (most of which is not reimbursed by insurances, according to Garber, Ridgely, Bradley, and Chin, 2002). In brief, the person wears an external device that converts sounds to electrical signals, which are then transmitted to the auditory nerve to reception devices implanted along the nerve, bypassing the inner ear. According to Best et al. (2002), persons wearing implants must remove them before competing in contact sports, swimming, or engaging in balloon activities or other events that might generate static.

Cochlear implants are most effective if an adult becomes severely to profoundly deaf or if the implantation is done shortly after 2 years of age. Research has documented benefits of cochlear implants up until about age 6 in congenitally deaf children, but the benefits decrease significantly the longer the child has gone without the implant (Govaerts et al., 2002).

Implants have generated a lot of controversy within the Deaf community, which maintains that deafness is not a disability, but a cultural minority with its own language, schools, sports organizations, and political structure. A 2002 documentary by Josh Aronson, *Sound and Fury,* is about the struggles two families (one of hearing parents, and the other of Deaf parents) face about whether or not to elect implants for their Deaf children.

 Watch the movie and decide which philosophy you subscribe to. If the movie is not available, use such resources as Jankowski (1997).

Telecommunication Device for the Deaf

A **telecommunication device for the deaf** (TDD) permits telephone communication between two Deaf persons or a Deaf and hearing person. The TDD has three parts: (a) a portable typewriter, (b) a screen that displays one line of text at a time, and (c) two rubber cups into which a telephone handset can fit. The TDD is wired to a regular telephone that makes distinctive beeps when a TDD caller is on the line.

TTY, an abbreviation for teletypewriter, correctly refers to the early models of TDDs, first created in the late 1950s by a Deaf Bell Telephone engineer. Some persons, however, continue to use TDD and TTY interchangeably. The important thing is that government, public, and private offices have available a device that permits communication with Deaf persons. Letterhead stationery, advertisements, and public announcements should include TDD numbers.

Where on your campus and in your community can you make TDD calls?

Educational Placement

Of the special education conditions recognized by legislation, deafness was the first, historically, to receive attention. The first residential schools in the United States, founded in 1817 and 1818, respectively, were for deaf students (see Appendix F). Thomas Gallaudet, father of Edward (who founded Gallaudet University), started the first residential school. By the late 1800s, almost every state had a school for deaf students. Most of these had excellent physical education programs and encouraged sport competition. Historically, Deaf sport has drawn most of its athletes from these schools (Stewart, 1991). This is partly because sport-inclined deaf students in public schools are typically coached by persons who know little or nothing about communicating with deaf persons.

Patterns of educating deaf children have varied, of course, from family to family. Some children have always lived at home while attending public or private schools. With the enactment of federal legislation in 1975 has come a definite trend away from residential school placement. Local communities are required to provide the services that deaf children need in GE public schools. Interpretation of need and compliance with law vary widely, however. Particularly underserved are over 4,000 students in small schools where they are the only persons who are deaf or HH (Butterfield, 1991).

Much debate currently centers on the question of what is the least restrictive educational environment for Deaf and HH students. Where and how can they best learn total communication—in a special school, a special class within a GE school, a resource room pull-out arrangement, or the GE class with a tutor or interpreter? Who will be the leaders in resolving issues?

When a Deaf or HH student attends a GE school, regardless of academic placement, he or she is likely to be assigned to GE physical education. This is because many persons on IEP teams believe that physical education is a good place to work on social interactions. In addition, conventional wisdom suggests that motor performance and fitness are not limited by hearing loss. The exception is the student with inner ear damage that has affected balance. Postural sway due to an impaired vestibular system can negatively affect balance (Butterfield, Lehnhard, Martens, & Moirs, 1998), but some research indicates that balance training can positively affect postural control (Shumway-Cook & Woollacott, 2001).

Some deaf students, like hearing ones, can benefit from adapted physical education services. *Many adapted physical activity personnel take sign classes so that they can use total communication and help others to learn basic sign.*

Assessment of Performance

Federal law states that assessment, for purposes of placement, must be in the student's native language. For many Deaf students, this is American Sign Language (ASL). Others, who rely mainly on speechreading, should have optimal lighting and a speaker they can understand. In some instances, an interpreter may be needed. Deaf students may demonstrate delays or perform below average simply because they do not understand test instructions. Stewart, Dummer, and Haubenstricker (1990) critically reviewed physical education research on Deaf and HH persons and pointed out test administration weaknesses (see Figure 26.11).

Deaf and HH persons rely on a variety of communication modes. In both teaching and research, individual preferences should be honored. Rapport with the tester should be established before assessment, with interpreters used as needed. Motivational cues (e.g., "good," "run faster," "throw harder") should be carefully planned, as should preliminary instructions.

Physical Education Instruction

Instruction, regardless of setting, should be based on assessed needs in the nine physical education goal areas. The following presents research and pedagogy related to each goal for Deaf and HH individuals.

Self-Concept

Feeling good about self in a particular domain determines amount of effort expended and, ultimately, success. If assessment indicates low athletic self-concept in mainstream physical education, possible reasons should be carefully studied. The quality and frequency of communication should be examined and plans for improvement developed cooperatively. In particular, teacher and peers should make sure that praise and encouragement are heard, speechread, and seen (signed) to the same extent as other students.

Other reasons for low athletic self-concept are a school, community, or family that does not value abilities and/or a perception that significant others hold low expectations. Some parents are so concerned with language, speech, and hearing training that they feel there is not time for after-school sports. Other parents may be overprotective. Some schools may stress academics so much that students feel nothing else is really important. In such cases, little energy is put into sports.

Little research has been conducted on athletic self-concept of Deaf and HH persons. Hopper (1988) studied children ages 10 to 14 at Washington State School for the Deaf and reported a relatively low athletic self-concept. Scores were highest in the scholastic domain and lowest in the social acceptance domain. The pattern of self-concepts in different domains may relate specifically to the school attended. Much research is needed in this area.

Social Competence

An important goal of physical education is to help students make friends who will carry over into after-school leisure activities. Meaningful social interaction occurs only when there is planned intervention that requires communication and cooperation. The noise level in most sport settings requires careful planning in this regard. Ideally, when a deaf student is being integrated for the first time, teacher and classmates should learn basic signs. *A partner or buddy ensures that class instructions are understood.*

The IEP team that specifies improved social competence as a goal should ensure that the integrated setting has a class size and a curriculum that enables communication and cooperation. Obviously, the smaller the class, the less noise and the more opportunity for getting to know each other. Maximum class size (about 20) should be written into the IEP. The curriculum most conducive to communication and cooperation includes individual and dual sports, dance, movement education, aquatics, and cooperative games. These are activities that demand partners. The deaf student must be equal to or better than his or her hearing partner in motor skill and fitness to make the relationship one of mutual respect.

Deaf persons with good sport skills can also make lasting friends in team sport settings if the teacher monitors communication and ascertains inclusion. Research shows that members of winning teams like each other better than those on losing teams. The teacher should therefore see that deaf students are assigned to teams that are likely to win.

Some deaf students are shy about talking and may not take the initiative in making friends. They may tend to withdraw and not want to take their turn in leading class exercises. Such individuals need support and incentive systems. A friend who regularly asks, "What do you think?" is helpful. Socialization requires considerable empathy on the part of both hearing and deaf persons.

Fun/Tension Release

A goal of fun/tension release in physical education is especially important because speechreading and sign require tremendous concentration. Background noise creates tension in persons wearing hearing aids as well as in those who speechread with-

---

Figure 26.11 **Three leading researchers from Michigan State University work together in data collection. From left to right: John Haubenstricker, David Stewart, and Gail Dummer.**

out aids. Poor lighting conditions and other environmental barriers also raise frustrations.

Appropriate goals of physical education and sport on some days are (a) to relax and have fun and/or (b) to channel frustrations, tensions, and hostilities into the healthy outlet of physical activity. The former may be accomplished best by cooperative activities, whereas the latter may be best served by competitive sports. Fun is defined in many ways, and teachers should ascertain what is fun for each individual.

Motor Skills and Patterns

Performance in motor skills and patterns is the same as for hearing persons except when inner ear balance deficits exist. Experts widely agree that much of the published research on motor development and performance of Deaf and HH groups is inaccurate (Dummer, Haubenstricker, & Stewart, 1996). Reasons include (a) etiology was not considered, (b) communication of test instructions was not optimal, and (c) learning opportunities were not examined. Reviews of research literature (Goodman & Hopper, 1992; Savelsbergh & Netelenbos, 1992) thus indicate contradictory findings, with most experts concluding that *nonvestibular impaired deaf and hearing persons perform similarly when opportunities are equal.*

Static and dynamic balances of deaf and HH students should be thoroughly tested. When problems are identified, balance should become the targeted area of supplementary instruction. Gymnastics, trampoline, tumbling, dance, and movement exploration are particularly helpful. Physical education programming, however, should be balanced between using strengths and remediating weaknesses.

Leisure-Time Skills

Persons in the Deaf community seem to participate more in Deaf sports than those in integrated settings. This is closely linked to ease of communication and social acceptance.

Many Deaf/HH persons watch lots of television, despite their hearing loss, and receive little encouragement from parents to develop active leisure lifestyles. An important role of physical activity personnel is to acquaint Deaf/HH persons with the many available options and to help them get to know role models. This may entail going with them to various sport events, making introductions, and creating buddy and support systems.

Physical Fitness

The most comprehensive study of the fitness of deaf ($N = 892$) and HH ($N = 153$) students, ages 10 to 17, showed that deaf/HH and hearing peers are similar in body composition, grip strength, sit-and-reach flexibility, 50-yd dash times, and 9- or 12-min endurance runs (Winnick & Short, 1986). Only on abdominal strength (sit-ups) are hearing students superior. This finding has not been explained and needs further research.

Studies with smaller sample sizes present conflicting evidence. Some report that deaf students are less fit than hearing peers (Arunovic & Pantelic, 1997). In general, research on fitness of deaf/HH individuals has the same weaknesses as that on motor performance. Etiology and balance function require

more attention because these factors affect running efficiency in endurance items, sit-ups, and other exercises.

Play and Game Behaviors

Young deaf children particularly need instruction in play and game behaviors because this area is closely associated with language concepts. Hearing peers pick up game rules, strategies, and behaviors in incidental ways and spontaneous neighborhood play. Opportunities for deaf children are limited, not only because of communication and social acceptance, but because speech, hearing, and language training may cut into the hours that others play.

Perceptual-Motor Function and Sensory Integration

Balance is probably the most important component in the area of perceptual-motor function and sensory integration. Research shows a tendency for postural and body awareness activities to improve balance function in deaf and HH individuals. The damaged vestibular system cannot be cured, but compensatory measures are learned.

Body image training is essential for young children who can learn signs for body parts and actions through movement. *Tap dance* teaches sounds the feet can make. The teacher may tap the rhythm lightly on the child's head so that he or she can perceive it via bone conduction while moving the feet. Another possibility is positioning the child so that his or her hand is on the record player, piano, or drum. A system of flashing lights can also be devised to convey rhythmic patterns.

Perceptual-motor activities also can be used to teach language and academics (see Figures 26.12 and 26.13). Training in prepositions (*up, down, toward, away from, in, out*) and other speech forms is made fun by movement. Charades in which partners move like different animals while class members

Figure 26.12 Language concepts are reinforced through movement education challenges given by sign.

Figure 26.13 Games should be invented to reinforce classroom learnings in such subjects as geography and social studies. "How fast and how accurately can you trace the boundaries of the states I call out [sign]?" is the challenge issued by the teacher.

try to guess which animal are fun when signs and words are learned simultaneously.

Creative Expression

Much of deaf education is extremely structured. There is little time for movement exploration and dance unless these are woven into physical education instruction. Several researchers show that creativity, movement skill, and language can be improved when total communication is used in movement exploration on climbing apparatus (Lubin & Sherrill, 1980) and in dance instruction (Reber & Sherrill, 1981).

Balance Problems Related to Infection or Injury

A misconception is that all Deaf and HH persons have balance problems. *Persons with hereditary deafness typically do not have balance problems.* Persons who have had a disease like meningitis or an injury that damaged the *vestibular apparatus in the inner ear* are the ones with balance problems. This is common enough that an organization exists specifically for them: the Vestibular Disorders Association (see www.vestibular.org).

Assessment should focus on identifying the type of balance problems (static or dynamic or both) and the postures and body part movements that seem to interfere the most with ADL and physical education. Then intervention should address specific problems related to ADL and physical education goals. With meaningful intervention and abundant movement opportunities, children learn to compensate for balance deficits. Balance normally improves from childhood through adolescence, when performance plateaus. Then, in old age, when the vestibular mechanism begin to degenerate, balance again becomes a problem.

Balance is also dependent upon good vision. Persons with vestibular deficits particularly need training in using the eyes. *Balance beam walking, for example, is made easier by keeping the eyes focused on a wall spot.* Activities performed with eyes closed or blindfolded obviously complicate balance problems and typically are contraindicated for deaf persons with vestibular deficits.

Individuals, deaf or otherwise, who have balance problems should be given special instruction on the principles of equilibrium. Movement exploration sessions may be developed around the following themes:

1. **Center of gravity.** "What is it? How do your movements affect it? In what movements can you keep the center of gravity centered over its supporting base? Can your hands be used as a supporting base? What happens when your center of gravity moves in front of the supporting base? In back of it? To the side of it? What activities lower your center of gravity? Raise it?"

2. **Broad base.** "How can you adapt different exercises so as to increase your supporting base? In what directions can you enlarge your base—that is, how many stances can you assume? In which direction should you enlarge your base when throwing? Batting? Serving a volleyball? Shooting baskets?"

Persons learn quickly to compensate for poor balance by maintaining the body in mechanically favorable positions. Games and relays on skates, stilts, or using novel apparatus (sack races) teach compensation (see Figure 26.14). Activities should be planned to enhance vision and kinesthesis. All forms of dance and gymnastics increase body awareness. The increasingly popular Asian exercise systems and martial arts—karate, kung fu, and tai chi—also contribute to this objective.

General Guidelines for Deaf and HH Conditions

1. Assign a second-row placement to students who need to speechread. Not only will they be positioned to see lips, but they can also rely on children in front of them for visual cues.

2. Post basic physical education signs around the gym and encourage all students to learn them.

3. Assign a peer buddy to a student with a hearing loss. The buddy can serve as a physical role model, as well as provide one-on-one assistance when the teacher is not available (Liberman et al., 2000).

4. When first meeting a Deaf/HH person, ask if he or she can understand your speech. If not, find someone to help or use paper/pencil communication.

Figure 26.14   Sack races help improve dynamic balance. Note that the starting signal must be visual.

5. Remember that short sentences are easier to speechread than long ones.

6. Speak normally and remember that only 3 to 4 of every 10 words are distinguishable on the lips. Use facial expressions and body language to help convey meaning.

7. When a sentence is not understood, repeat it. If one repetition does not help, then rephrase, using different words or, spell. Remember that some words are harder to speechread than others. Many words look the same. Find alternatives.

8. If you do not understand the other person's speech, do not pretend. Ask for as many repetitions as you need. Suggest, "Tell me again in a different way."

9. Empty your mouth before speaking. This applies to chewing gum, food, tobacco, cigarettes, straws, and anything else that distorts sights and sounds.

10. Keep your lips fully visible. Avoid mustaches, hands in front of face, and Halloween masks. Do not talk while writing on the chalkboard unless your face is visible.

11. Keep lighting conditions optimal.

12. Avoid standing in front of a window or bright light that forces a Deaf/HH person to cope with a glare.

13. When outdoors, position yourself so that you, rather than the Deaf/HH person, face the sun.

14. Minimize background noise and distractions.

15. Do not raise your voice when speaking to a person with a hearing aid.

16. When teaching, use lots of visual aids and demonstrations. Have order of events and class rules posted.

17. When behavior problems occur, consider whether students are seeing and hearing adequately. Note that restlessness often signals fatigue.

18. Encourage students with hearing losses to move freely around the gymnasium in order to be within seeing and hearing ranges.

19. Learn basic signs and weave them into the class structure. Give attention to signs that praise performance and motivate personal bests. *Use these signs concurrently with speech with all students, not just those with hearing losses.*

20. Be aware that head and neck positions that enable persons to see starting signals may affect speed. Communication needs may also affect the way persons want to swim (face out of water) and other activities.

OPTIONAL ACTIVITIES

1. Watch *Mr. Holland's Opus,* paying special attention to hindrances to the father/son relationship because of communication differences. What assumptions did Lee wrongly make about his father? What wrong assumptions did Mr. Holland make about his son?

2. Go to a school setting and observe the following:

   a. A Deaf child in physical education in integrated classes

   b. A physical education class in a school for the Deaf

What similarities in instructional style do you see? What differences? Why is a capital D used in these instructions?

3. Observe a speech pathology language session for a Deaf child and reflect on language acquisition for children who cannot hear. Often, universities offering teacher preparation for teaching Deaf children and those offering speech pathology training have on-campus laboratories.

4. Attend a church service, theater, or other program that provides sign to communicate to Deaf persons in the audience.

5. Contact international, federal, state, and local agencies to find out what services are available for people who are deaf.

6. Assume you are planning a sports day, and some of the participants will be Deaf. Explain the adaptations you will plan for, including a budget to employ interpreters and procedures for locating qualified interpreters.

CHAPTER

27

Blindness and Visual Impairments

Figure 27.1 Charles Buell (1912–1992) gives a child with visual impairment and his sighted opponent a first lesson in wrestling.

1. Differentiate between legal blindness, travel vision, motion perception, light perception, and total blindness. Relate these to the U.S. Association for Blind Athletes (USABA) classifications. Which are easier to use for physical activity programming? Why? Discuss programming for different levels of blindness.

2. Identify some of the concerns and aspirations associated with blindness. Discuss implications for physical activity. Get to know some persons with limited vision in your community and ask for their opinions.

3. Write short case studies of persons of any age, with blindness or deaf-blindness, that show your understanding of the following: (a) haptic perception, (b) spatial awareness, (c) trust and courage, (d) sound usage, (e) physical fitness, (f) orientation and mobility, and (g) adaptations of equipment and facilities.

4. Learn about the USABA and its opportunities for competition; find out if any USABA athletes are in your region and get acquainted.

5. Use websites to find out where games of goal ball and beep baseball are being held and, if possible, attend some, take photos or videos, and jot notes for a report for your portfolio.

6. Discuss existing and needed research concerning vision loss and physical education. Review the contributions of such researchers as Charles Buell, Joseph Winnick, James Mastro, and Lauren Lieberman. What kind of research would you like to do? If you could do research with one of the above, who would you choose? Why?

7. Contact Recording for the Blind and Dyslexic to learn about services and/or to become a volunteer reader. Use www.rfbd.org or 866-732-3585.

Never check the actions of the blind child; follow him, and watch him to prevent any serious accidents, but do not interfere unnecessarily; do not even remove obstacles which he would learn to avoid by tumbling over them a few times. Teach him to jump rope, to swing weights, to raise his body by his arms, and to mingle, as far as possible, in the rough sports of the older students.

—Samuel Gridley Howe (1841)

This statement was made by the first director of Perkins Institution in Boston, a residential school founded in the early 1800s for children who were blind. Perkins is known for its training of Anne Sullivan Macy, the teacher of Helen Keller, and for its outstanding physical education and sport program. Most states have a residential school for children who are blind, which historically has been excellent (Buell, 1984). The trend today, however, is for children to live at home and to be educated in public schools, where resource room help is available.

Charles Buell (1912–1992), the best-known pioneer in blind sport, emphasized that children with visual impairments (VI) should be taught in mainstream settings and held to the same achievement standards as their sighted peers. Buell (1982, 1986) particularly recommended wrestling as a sport in which youth with VI can compete equitably with sighted peers (see Figure 27.1). Buell, legally blind himself, held a doctorate from the University of California and was recognized worldwide as an athlete, physical educator, coach, researcher, and a founder of the United States Association for Blind Athletes (USABA).

Founded in 1976, the USABA has showed that individuals with blindness (total or partial) can be outstanding athletes. They compete in the summer and winter Paralympics, the World Games for the Blind (held every 3 years), the National Games for the Blind (held alternate years, 2005, 2007, and so on), and in many mainstream marathons and sport events.

Definitions and Basic Concepts

Blindness and *visual impairment* are often used as synonyms, particularly in the sport world. The International Blind Sports Association (IBSA) and the U.S. Association for Blind Athletes (USABA) serve persons whose vision varies from 20/200 ft (6/18 m) to total blindness *after corrections made by glasses.* Table 27.1 shows the three sport classifications, which are based on a **Snellen chart measure** of **acuity** (sharpness of vision) and assessment of field of vision.

Field of vision refers to the area within which objects can be seen when the eyes are fixed straight ahead. A severely limited field of vision is called **tunnel vision.** To understand limitations of field of vision, look through a straw (equivalent to a 5° field of vision) or larger tubes for progressively greater fields of vision. Most persons have a field of vision of about 180°.

Educators often use different terminology than sport people to denote degrees of visual acuity. Following is an explanation of how the educational and sport classifications relate.

Table 27.1 **Sport classifications for USABA and IBSA based on vision corrected by glasses.**

Classification	Description
B1	No light perception in either eye up to light perception and inability to recognize the shape of a hand in any direction and at any distance
B2	Ability to recognize the shape of a hand up to a visual acuity of 2/60 and/or a limitation of field of vision of 5°
B3	2/60 to 6/60 (20/200) vision and/or field of vision between 5 and 20°

B1 Classification

B1 encompasses two educational classifications:

Total Blindness (lack of visual perception). Inability to recognize a strong light shown directly into the eye.

Light Perception (less than 3/200). Ability to distinguish a strong light at a distance of 3 ft from the eye, but inability to detect movement of a hand at the same distance.

B1s, as they are called in sport events, do some sports like swimming, judo, and wrestling independently. In track events, they typically run side by side with a guide. The athlete maintains contact with the guide by means of a **tether** (a rope or shoestring no more than 50 cm in length) held by each by the inside hand (see Figure 27.2A). In snow skiing, a longer tether allows a person who is blind to follow his or her guide (see Figure 27.2B). In water skiing, the rope between the boat and the skier serves as the tether.

B2 Classification

B2 encompasses two educational classifications:

Motion Perception (3/200 to 5/200). Ability to see at 3 to 5 ft what the normal eye sees at 200 ft. This ability is limited almost entirely to motion.

Travel Vision (5/200 to 10/200). Ability to see at 5 to 10 ft what the normal eye sees at 200 ft.

B2s can do many activities independently when the sunlight or indoor lights are bright. In track events, they have the option of running independently or using a guide. Tethers are optional. Obviously, individuals with travel vision have greater acuity than those with only motion vision, but the low prevalence of blindness among youth and young adults requires that these two abilities be grouped together in order to have enough competitors to hold a track meet. B2s typically wear thick glasses and can read large print with the aid of magnifying devices.

B3 Classification

B3 is the same as legal blindness, the minimal disability condition specified by law that permits special services:

Legal Blindness (20/200). Ability to see at 20 ft what the normal eye sees at 200 ft (i.e., 1/10 or less of normal vision).

B3s do not use guides, but they might require verbal assistance during night or low-vision conditions. They wear thick glasses and can read large print without magnifying devices. Some can read regular-size print by placing their faces very close to the page.

Guidelines for Interactions

At least 80% of people who are blind have some residual vision. Given good light conditions to use residual vision, their sport performance is similar to that of sighted peers when instruction and practice are equal. *They are most disadvantaged by weather (dark, rainy days) and scheduling of early or late practices*

Figure 27.2 *(A)* The tethers used in track. Harry Cordellos *(left)* with sighted partner, Randy Foederer. Both will take first step with inside foot. *(B)* Long tethers make blind skiing possible.

A

B

when the sun is not overhead. Persons often profess to see more than they do, partly because of the desire for normalcy and partly because they have no experience upon which to judge sight. Some persons, although legally blind, are very sensitive about being called *blind.*

In general, the following guidelines will facilitate interactions with people with visual impairments (VI) in social and instructional settings.

Table 27.2   Websites pertaining to persons with visual impairments and deaf-blind conditions.

American Council for the Blind	www.acb.org
American Foundation for the Blind	www.afb.org
American Association for the Deaf-Blind	www.tr.wou.edu/dblink/aadb.htm
International Blind Sports Association	www.ibsa.es/
Marla Runyan website	www.marlarunyan.com
National Beep Baseball Association	www.nbba.org
National Federation of the Blind	www.nfb.org
United States Association for Blind Athletes	www.usaba.org

Figure 27.3   Retinal detachment, which can be corrected by surgery, contraindicates contact sports.

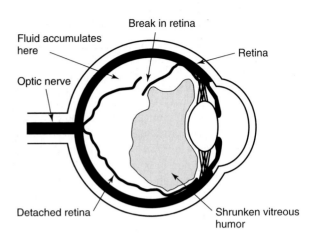

1. When starting an interaction, always state your name. Do not expect to be recognized by the sound of your voice. This is especially important in noisy settings.

2. Ask if help is needed with mobility. Do not grab the person's arm. The appropriate protocol is for the person with VI to grasp your upper arm and walk with you, side by side, unless the passage is too narrow. Give verbal cues, indicating steps (up or down), changes in surface (holes, inclines), and doors to be opened (in, out; push, pull). Ask for feedback on how you can improve your technique.

3. When suggesting places to go, indicate the anticipated level of noise. When the goal is conversation, select quiet settings where you can be heard.

4. When serving food, indicate the location of food on the plate (e.g., meat at 12 o'clock, salad at 3 o'clock, potatoes at 6 o'clock). Provide bread or a cracker to be used as a pusher.

5. When providing learning material, ask whether the person prefers large print, braille, or audiotapes. Check the technology offered by your library or other nearby resources in terms of specially designed computers that can read print and speak.

For additional information on interacting with persons with visual impairments, see Table 27.2.

Prevalence of Blindness and Visual Impairment

Blindness and VI are largely problems of old age. Approximately a half-million persons in the United States are legally blind, and countless others have serious visual problems. At least two thirds of these persons are over 65 years of age.

The statistics concerning VI among school-age children vary with the definition used. Approximately 23,000 children with VI between the ages of 3 and 21 are receiving special education services. However, VI affects fewer children than any other disability, with the exception of the deaf-blind classification.

Causes of Blindness and Activity Contraindications

Most blindness in school-age persons is attributed to birth defects (congenital cataracts, optic nerve disease, retinopathy) or retinopathy of prematurity (ROP), previously called retrolental fibroplasia. **ROP** occurs when oxygen is poorly regulated in incubators. Excessive oxygen damages the retina and sometimes causes mild brain damage and learning problems.

Most VI conditions have no activity contraindications, but three conditions require particular attention: retinal detachment, retinitis pigmentosa, and glaucoma. The **retina,** or inner lining of the eyeball, is an expansion of the optic nerve that contains the sensory receptors for light rays. **Retinal detachment** is a break or tear in the retina that causes fluid to seep between the retina and the cells that supply its nutrition (see Figure 27.3). As cells die, vision is lost. No pain is involved. The presence of a retinal tear or detachment contraindicates contact sports and other activities that might jar the head and increase damage.

Retinitis pigmentosa is an inherited, progressive degeneration of the retinal cells. Its name comes from scar tissue that is **pigmented** (i.e., looks like footprints of a bird). The degeneration gradually restricts the vision field, eventually causing tunnel vision and night blindness. The condition most often occurs in childhood and adolescence. Sport participation in low-light conditions is contraindicated.

Glaucoma is a condition in which the pressure inside the eyeball rises to a point where it damages the optic nerve, first affecting peripheral vision and later causing central vision blindness. An early sign is complaints that lights appear to have halos around them. There are several types, some of which cause considerable pain. Contraindications are isometric activities, swimming underwater, inverted body positions, excess fluid intake, use of antihistamines, and other practices that may increase eye pressure.

About 4% of visual disorders in children are caused by a genetic disorder called **albinism,** a congenital absence of pigment in the skin, hair, and eyes. These persons have very fair skin, platinum blond hair, and blue eyes. Related visual problems are myopia, predisposition to sunburn, **photophobia** (unusual intolerance of light), astigmatism, and nystagmus. Many persons with albinism compete as Class B3 athletes in USABA.

Infectious diseases, tumors, and injuries are minor causes of blindness. *In older persons, cataracts and diabetes are leading causes.* **Cataracts** are clouded or opaque spots on the lens that gradually increase in size and diminish vision, particularly in low-light conditions. When night driving, sensitivity to the glare of oncoming lights is a symptom. Cataracts are easily removed by surgery or laser beam. Within 10 years of the onset of diabetes, 50% of individuals have pathological changes of the retina, called **diabetic retinopathy.** *Between the ages of 20 and 65, diabetes is the leading cause of blindness.*

 For a great description of an older woman living with diabetic retinopathy, read Kissing the Virgin's Mouth *(2001) by Donna M. Gershten.*

Motor Development and Performance

Motor development is delayed in blind infants, particularly in mobility- and locomotion-related behaviors (Adelson & Fraiberg, 1974; Fraiberg, 1977; Jong, 1990). The median age of walking is about 20 months. Mastery of motor milestones is in a different order from that of sighted infants. Milestones that require vision for motivation are delayed most (e.g., raising the head from prone, reaching, crawling, creeping, and walking). Object control and manipulation tend to be delayed 3 to 6 months. This, in turn, prevents proper emergence of tactile perception abilities and related problem-solving skills.

Early intervention is beneficial but does not completely remediate delays. Of particular concern are delays in development of play and social skills. Children with VI cannot progress without help to parallel or cooperative play because of lack of awareness of others' presence.

Research on the motor performance of individuals with VI reveals lower levels than sighted classmates (Skaggs & Hopper, 1996). Generally, persons with partial sight perform better than those with total blindness.

Time of Onset

VI is typically designated as **congenital** (born with) or **adventitious** (diagnosed at age 2 or 3 or later). Congenital VI is often not recognized until motor or cognitive delays appear. Age of onset should always be indicated because it gives insight into amount of time the student had for developing space and form perception, visualization skills, and locomotor and object con-

trol patterns. The younger children are when they develop blindness, the more likely they are to be overprotected.

Overemphasis on Academics

Reading and other academic skills require more time than average for individuals with VI. As a result, such children often spend time in study that others use for leisure and large muscle activity. This not only deprives them of skill and fitness but also interferes with making and keeping friends. With age, deficits in social competence become more and more obvious.

Unless helped with social development, the life experiences of persons with VI differ considerably from those of peers. This eventually may interfere with job success. Most jobs are lost, not because of inadequate vocational skills, but because of inability to get along with other workers.

Stereotyped Behaviors and Appearance

Stereotyped behaviors or **stereotypies** (previously called blindisms) are mannerisms like rocking backward and forward, putting fist or fingers into eyes (see Figure 27.4), waving fingers in front of face, whirling rapidly round and round, and bending the head forward. These same behaviors may be observed among sighted persons with emotional problems, autism, or limited opportunities to move. They can be prevented or at least minimized through the provision of vigorous daily exercise. Some persons like Ray Charles become quite successful in spite of stereotypies, but most need help in making appearance as acceptable as possible. Verbal correction often causes anxiousness and self-consciousness. A good approach is to agree on a tactile cue like a hand on the shoulder as a reminder to stop.

Persons with VI should be taught self-monitoring in relation to appearance, postures, and facial expressions. VI limits ability to imitate, thereby spontaneously learning appropriate behaviors and responses as do sighted persons. Verbal instructions are needed in many areas that individuals with sight take for granted.

Physical and Motor Fitness

Most research shows that persons with VI have lower fitness than sighted peers (Lieberman & McHugh, 2001; Skaggs & Hopper, 1996; Winnick, 1985; Wyatt & Ng, 1997). This is generally attributed to lack of instruction and practice, inactive lifestyles, and overprotection. Degree of VI, age, and sex affect fitness scores. The more severe the VI, the lower the fitness; this is probably because overprotection increases with severity. The performance gap between males and females with VI is greater than for sighted peers; presumably this is because girls are more overprotected than boys. Boys improve steadily from ages 6 to 17, whereas girls plateau at about age 13 or 14.

Of the 14 items used to assess and compare fitness of youth with and without blindness, the greatest discrepancy was in throwing, running, and jumping (Winnick, 1985). These findings partially support the work of Buell (1982), which showed greatest weakness in running and throwing events.

Most research also shows that persons with VI have greater skinfold thicknesses than sighted peers (Winnick,

Review this excellent film if you can find a copy and/or read one of Cordellos's several books.

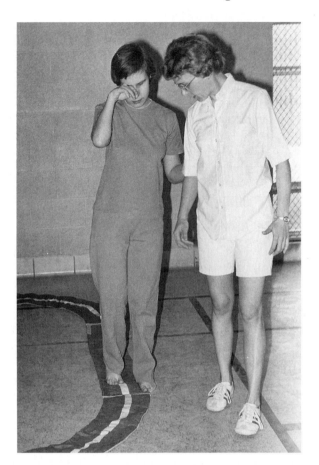

1985). There is also a tendency toward shorter heights (Lee, Ward, & Shephard, 1985).

In general, youth with VI can take the same fitness tests as sighted peers. In health-related fitness, distance runs require a partner. Otherwise, few adaptations are needed except in motivation. Whereas sighted persons are challenged to personal bests by seeing others succeed, VI limits the motivational value of social comparison. Verbal input should be substituted.

VI also limits social comparisons of height and weight, the amount that others are eating, and exercise habits. Whereas we may see someone jogging on the other side of the street and be motivated to follow suit, persons with VI are more dependent on internal motivation. Whereas we can run, cycle, or drive to an exercise site at will, persons with VI must be assertive in finding companions.

Studies on cardiorespiratory fitness of persons with VI have shown fitness levels either equal to sighted persons or low fitness levels that significantly improve as a result of treadmill and bicycle ergometer training. Harry Cordellos, marathon runner who is blind and an American Alliance for Health, Physical Education, Recreation, and Dance (AAHPERD) honor award recipient, has such outstanding fitness that he is the subject of an ongoing longitudinal study at the Cooper Aerobic Institute in Dallas. A film featuring Cordellos, entitled *Survival Run,* is available (Cordellos, 1983).

When persons with VI are navigating unfamiliar areas, gaits become mechanically less efficient. This, in turn, contributes to early fatigue. Good fitness is needed to combat both fatigue and stress. B1 and B2 sprinting patterns are less mechanically efficient than those of B3. Long-distance runs that require a sighted partner heighten stress because of the required adjustment to new people.

Role Models

Models with VI help individuals with VI to realize what is possible. For sighted persons, models with VI help to change attitudes and dispel misconceptions. While live models are best, books and videotapes are also helpful.

The autobiographies of such persons as Harold Krents (1972) and Tomi Keitlen (1960) indicate that persons with VI have been participating in mainstream sport for several decades. Krents recalls step-by-step how his brother taught him to catch a regulation football and to bat a 10-inch playground ball—skills he could have been taught by a physical educator but was not. In high school physical education, he was allowed to play touch football with his sighted classmates but was admonished to "Keep out of the way." The anecdotes leading to his acquisition of the nickname "Cannonball" make the book well worth reading. Tomi Keitlen describes in detail her first attempts at swimming, golf, horseback riding, fencing, and skiing after becoming totally blind at age 33. In addition to valuable accounts of how such sports can be learned and enjoyed without sight, Keitlen describes the problems of adjusting to blindness. The greatest battle, she stresses, is to avoid being segregated and labeled as different from sighted persons.

James Mastro, a B1 international athlete, has been active in USABA since its inception in 1976, repeatedly winning gold medals in wrestling, judo, shot put, and discus. Mastro was born with one eye sightless and injured the other while fencing with curtain rods in late childhood. In spite of countless surgeries, he lost all vision but light perception by age 18. This did not deter his becoming a member of the university wrestling team and eventually becoming an Olympic wrestler. A broken arm in the last qualifying bout kept him from winning and becoming a member of the U.S. Olympic Team, but he was named an alternate.

Since completing his doctorate in adapted physical education at Texas Woman's University, Dr. Mastro has achieved tenure at Bemidji State University in MN, been president of the National Beep Baseball Association, and conducted workshops throughout the world (see Figure 27.5). He is also a prolific researcher (see Sherrill, 1990b, for a review of his work). Dr. Mastro is the first totally blind person to earn a doctorate in physical education and is a strong model for others.

Marla Runyan, in 2000, was the first legally blind athlete to compete in the Olympic Games; she achieved eighth place in the 1,500 meters, a personal best that surpassed times of the sighted Americans in the race. Marla also made news when she entered her first marathon (the New York City Marathon)

Figure 27.5 Dr. James Mastro teaching judo at Camp Abilities in New York; this is Dr. Lauren Lieberman's camp.

Figure 27.6 Marla Runyan, B3, passing another competitor. Runyan is the only person with VI to ever race in the Olympics.

and took fifth place with a time of 2:27:10. Marla, in her early 30s, had previously competed mostly at the Paralympics and in USABA and IBSA events (see Figure 27.6). Marla, a B3, had good sight until about age 8 when her macula began degenerating; at age 9, she was diagnosed with Stargardt's disease. Today, her sight is limited to about 15 feet.

Read Marla's autobiography, No Finish Line, *and/or interact with her via her website* (www.marlarunyan. com). *Many international level athletes, with and without disabilities, have websites. Try to find others. Share with your class.*

Harry Cordellos (1976, 1981, 1993) is another strong model whose autobiographies *Breaking Through* and *No Limits* are filled with sport stories. Cordellos, born with glaucoma and a heart murmur, was partially sighted throughout childhood but so overprotected by his parents and teachers that he never engaged in vigorous play. In spite of 14 operations, he was totally blind by age 20. Fortunately, he outgrew his heart problems. At age 20, he was introduced to sports via water skiing (see Figure 27.7), and subsequently he dedicated his life to athletic training and educating the sighted world about the potential of persons with VI. Cordellos has run over 100 marathons; he does this with a sighted partner. His best time in the Boston Marathon is 2 hr, 57 min, 42 sec. Cordellos has run 50 mi in less than 8 hr and has competed in the Iron Man Triathlon in Hawaii (swimming 2.4 mi, biking 112 mi, and running 26.2 mi). He has demonstrated that there is no physiological reason why persons with VI cannot excel in sports.

Erling Stordahl, of Norway, now deceased, is also an outstanding model. The creator of the world-famous sport center (Helsesportsenter) in Beitostølen, he broadened the horizons of persons with and without disabilities. He was particularly known for leadership in winter sports and innovations that permit persons with VI to ski.

Charles Buell, described in the opening section of this chapter, is another model. Until age 80, he continued to work out daily and to encourage mainstream acceptance of people with VI.

Physical Education Instruction

General class physical education placement is recommended for students with VI (Nixon, 1988, 1989), but consultant help is often needed. Except for ball-handling activities, students with VI can participate with few adaptations. Their success depends in large part on the ability of the physical educator to give precise verbal instructions. Like other students, they strive to fulfill their teacher's expectations. Falls, scratches, and bruises should be disregarded as much as possible to allow the dignity of recovering without oversolicitous help.

When activities are practiced in small groups, the teacher should ascertain that students with VI know the names of their classmates, the approximate space allocated to each, their place in the order of rotation if turns are being taken, and the direction of movement. Sight is not required for success on the trampoline, parallel bars, and other pieces of apparatus; for tumbling, free exercise, and dance; for weight lifting, fitness activities, swimming; or for many other sports.

Especially recommended activities for persons with VI are wrestling, tumbling, gymnastics, bowling, swimming, weight training, judo, dart throwing, dance, roller skating, ice skating, shuffleboard, horseback riding, tandem cycling, hiking, camping, fishing, rowing, waterskiing, surfing, and most winter sports. These sports require little or no adaptation for students with VI to participate with the sighted (see Figure 27.8).

Community facilities, like schools, need to make materials available in braille (see Figure 27.9), in large-size print, and on audiotapes. Physical educators are responsible for promoting the use of community resources and encouraging better communication.

Figure 27.7   Harry Cordellos performing on one ski.

Figure 27.8   Athletes who are blind compete in tandem cycling. The pilot (first cyclist) is sighted. Here, pilot Natalie Kelly and Julie Werner compete in USABA Nationals.

Adaptations of Equipment and Facilities

Teachers and parents of children with VI should contact the American Foundation for the Blind for catalogs of special equipment. Each year, improvements are made in sound-source balls and audible goal locators that facilitate the teaching of ball skills. Electronic balls with beepers are gradually replacing balls with bells. *Balls should be painted orange or yellow for persons with partial sight.* In most primary school activities, beanbags with bells sewn inside are preferred over balls, which are harder to recover.

Outside softball diamonds should be of grass with mowed baselines or should have wide asphalt paths from base to base and from the pitcher's mound to the catcher. Inside, guidewires can be constructed from base to base. Boundaries for various games are marked by a change in floor or ground surfaces that can be perceived by the soles of the feet. Tumbling mats, for instance, can be placed around the outside periphery of the playing area to mark its dimensions.

Braille can be used on the swimming pool walls to designate the changing water depths. It can also be used on gymnasium floors and walls as aids in determining the colors, shapes, and sizes of targets.

Portable aluminum bowling rails are available through the American Foundation for the Blind. These rails are easily assembled and broken down for transportation to different bowling alleys.

For the most part, however, equipment does not need to be adapted for individuals with VI. The play area should be quiet enough to facilitate use of sound and well lighted to enhance use of residual vision.

Guidewire Activities

Students with VI and blindfolded friends should be provided with a **guidewire** stretched from one end of the playfield or gymnasium to the other to enable them to meet such challenges as "Run as fast as you can," "Roller skate as fast as you can," or "Ride a tricycle or bicycle as fast as you can." The students can hold onto a short rope looped around the guidewire (see Figure 27.10). *Gliding fingers directly over the wire can cause burns.* Window-sash cord stretched at *hip height* is probably best for running practice. A knot at the far end of the rope warns the runner of the finish line. Students can improve their running efficiency or master a new locomotor skill *by grasping the upper arm of a sighted partner,* but the ultimate goal should always be self-confidence in independent travel.

Spatial Awareness and Body Image Activities

In spatial awareness training, objectives are tactile identification of objects, orientation to stable and moving sounds, spatial orientation, improvement of movement efficiency, and mobility training. **Brailling** is the term for tactile inspection of an object (see Figure 27.11).

Children with VI need special training in recognizing the right-left dimensions of objects that are facing them (Cratty,

Figure 27.10 **B1 adolescent uses a guidewire to practice running skills at Camp Abilities.**

Figure 27.9 **Standard English braille alphabet.**

a	b	c	d	e	f	g	h	i	j	k	l	m

n	o	p	q	r	s	t	u	v	w	x	y	z

Figure 27.11   B1 child brailles her medal.

1971b). Not capable of seeing, they have never received a mirror image; hence, the concept of someone facing them is especially difficult.

Children with VI must be provided with opportunities for learning about their own body parts as well as about those of animals and other human beings. This can be accomplished, at least partially, by tactual inspection. Three-dimensional figures must be available to teach similarities and differences between different body builds, male and female physical characteristics, and postural deviations. Movement exploration based on modifications of the dog walk, seal crawl, mule kick, and the like is meaningless unless the child can feel, smell, and hear the animal about to be imitated.

The following are other activities that help individuals with VI to organize and learn about space:

1. Practice walking a straight line. Without sight, persons tend to veer about 1.25 inches per step or walk a spiral-shaped pathway.

2. Practice facing sounds or following instructions to make quarter, half, three-quarter, and full turns.

3. Practice reproducing the exact distance and pathway just taken with a partner.

4. Take a short walk with a partner and practice finding the way back to the starting point alone.

5. Outside, where the rays of the sun can be felt, practice facing north, south, east, west. Relate these to goal cages and the direction of play in various games.

6. Practice determining whether the walking surface is uphill or downhill or tilted to the left or right; relate this to the principles of stability and efficient movement.

7. Practice walking different floor patterns. Originate novel patterns and then try to reproduce the same movement.

These and other space explorations offer fun and excitement for sighted youngsters who are blindfolded as well as for children with VI. Remember, however, that the blindfolded child is at a greater disadvantage than persons who have had several years to cope with spatial problems.

Sound Usage Activities

Students with VI can be grouped with individuals who have auditory perception deficits for special training in recognizing and following sounds. A continuous sound is better than intermittent ones. Whenever possible, the sound source should be placed in front of the student so that he or she is moving directly toward it. The next best position is behind the person so that he or she can proceed in a straight line away from it. Most difficult to perceive and follow are sounds to the side. A progression from simple to difficult should be developed. After success with a single sound source, students should be exposed to several simultaneous sounds, with instructions to pick out and follow only the relevant one.

Try the following activities, using a blindfold, to get an idea of competencies that must be developed for success in sport:

1. Discriminate between the bouncing of a small rubber ball for playing jacks, a tennis ball, a basketball, and a cageball.

2. Judge the height of the rebound of a basketball from its sound and thus be able to catch a ball bounced by you or by another.

3. Perceive the direction of a ground ball and thus be able to field or kick one being rolled toward your left, right, or center.

4. Discriminate, in bowling, the difference between sounds of a ball rolling down the gutter as opposed to the lane and also the difference between one bowling pin versus several falling.

5. Recognize, in archery, the sound of a balloon bursting when it is hit by an arrow or of an arrow penetrating a target made of a sound-producing material (see Figure 27.12).

6. Recognize the difference between the center of the trampoline and its outer areas by the sound of a ball attached to its undersurface.

7. Walk a nature trail or participate in a treasure hunt by following sounds from several tape cassettes located about the area.

Figure 27.12   Balloons attached to the target enable the child who is blind to hear a bull's-eye.

8. Follow a voice or bell as you swim and dive in an open area.

9. Perceive the rhythm of a long rope alternately touching the ground and turning in the air so that you know when to run under and jump the rope.

Orientation and Mobility Training

Comprehensive physical education programs include units on orientation and mobility (O and M). Many children with VI are overprotected prior to entering school and hence need immediate help in adjusting to travel within the school environment. The physical educator must orient young children to the playground equipment as well as to space. Bells may be attached to playground swings to warn of danger. Children who are blind often excel in climbing and hanging feats. Unable to see their distance from the ground, they seem fearless in the conquering

of great heights and enjoy the wonder and praise of sighted classmates.

An appropriate goal for many children with VI is to demonstrate functional movement skills in safe play with one or more friends on playground equipment. Related objectives might be the following:

1. Demonstrate how to play safely on all equipment.
2. Tell safety rules and reasons for each.
3. Display a cooperative attitude and express a willingness to learn.
4. Walk a hand ladder (arm-swing from rung to rung).
5. Use the legs to pump while swinging (in a sitting position).
6. Climb to the top of both 8- and 14-ft slides alone and slide down feet first.
7. Perpetuate a tilted merry-go-round by swinging out on the downside and leaning in on the upside.
8. Play simple games on the jungle gym.
9. Use a seesaw safely with a companion.

 These objectives are not written correctly. Rewrite them in a form acceptable to an IEP team.

Haptic Perception Teaching Model

In general, the pedagogy in this section is a *haptic teaching model.* **Haptic perception** refers to the combined use of tactile sensations and kinesthesis.

When planning movement exploration activities, the physical educator must realize that space is interpreted unconventionally by haptic-minded persons. Whereas the visually oriented child perceives distant objects as smaller than those nearby, *the child with VI does not differentiate between foreground and background.* The size of objects is not determined by nearness and farness, but rather by the objects' emotional significance and the child's imagination.

Children with VI experience difficulty in conceptualizing boundaries. Having no visual field to restrict them, their space is as large as their imagination. They tend, however, to think in parts rather than wholes since concepts are limited to the amount of surface they can touch at any given time. To familiarize themselves with the gymnasium, they may move from one piece of apparatus to another, feel the walls, discover windows and doors, and creep on the floor. They are, however, never completely certain how the unified whole feels or looks.

Three-dimensional models (similar to dollhouses) of the gymnasium, swimming pool, playground, campsite, and other areas are helpful. Miniature figures can be arranged on the simulated playground to acquaint students with playing positions, rules, and strategies. Dolls can also be used to teach spatial relationships among dancers in a group composition, cheerleaders in a pep squad demonstration, and swimmers in the assigned lanes of a meet. Unless dolls with movable joints are taken through such movements as forward rolls, cartwheels, and skin-the-snake on a parallel bar, the student with VI finds it difficult to conceptualize the whole prior to attempting a new activity.

USABA and Sport Competition

An understanding of national and international sport opportunities gives insight into programming for individuals with VI. Although persons with VI can participate in many integrated activities, they should be given optimal training in areas where they are most likely to excel.

Sports have been well organized within the residential school network for years, but the movement gained new impetus with the formation of USABA in 1976. In 1977, USABA sponsored its first national championships. Summer games are now held on alternate years (1997, 1999, etc.). Winter sports are held annually. Sanctioned sports for the national games include power lifting, judo, swimming, track and field, wrestling, goal ball, women's gymnastics, winter sports (downhill and cross-country skiing), tandem cycling, and others as selected by the USABA board. Under consideration are crew rowing, sailing, archery, and competitive diving. The rules for these sports are based on those used by such national governing bodies as the U.S. Gymnastics Federation (USGF), the National Collegiate Athletic Association (NCAA), and the National Federation of State High School Associations (NFSHSA).

Track-and-Field Events

Three systems enable individuals to excel in track: guide runners with tethers, callers, and guidewires. In the United States, guide runners are favored. Track events include 100, 200, 400, 800, 1500, 3000 (women) 5000 (men) 10,000 meters 4 × 100 Relay, 4 × 400 Relay, and the Marathon conducted separately for B1, B2, and B3 athletes. B1 runners must use guide runners, B2 runners may or may not use guide runners, and the use of a tether is optional. B3 runners require no assistance. When guides are used, the person with VI must always precede the sighted partner.

Field events include the long jump, triple jump, high jump, shot put, javelin, pentathlon, and discus. Regulation throwing implements are used. Callers at the end of a runway may help athletes jump in the right direction. These activities should be practiced from elementary school on (see Figure 27.13).

Goal Ball

A game created in Europe especially for veterans blinded in World War II, goal ball is played under the rules of the International Blind Sport Association (IBSA). The only required equipment is a bell ball. Each team consists of three players wearing knee and elbow pads and blindfolds. The playing area is the same for males and females (see Figure 27.14). Very important is the regulation that all field markings be 5 cm in width and made of a distinctive texture for easy player orientation.

Games are 14 min in duration, with 5-min halves and 2 min between halves. Each team tries to roll the ball across the opponent's goal while the other team tries to stop them (see Figure 27.15). A thrown ball may bounce, but it must be rolling before it reaches the opponent's throwing area or it becomes an infraction. The entire team helps with defense. The arriving ball can be warded off in a standing, kneeling, or lying position with any body part or the whole body.

Figure 27.13   Jumping with a sighted cross-age tutor or teacher helps establish rhythm and the feeling of flight.

Figure 27.14   Playing area for goal ball (18 × 9 m).

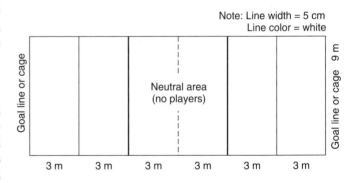

Because all team members are required to wear a blindfold, goal ball places persons with VI on equal terms with sighted peers and thus can be used in mainstream physical education. Rules are available through USABA (see Appendix C), or from physical educators at residential schools. Many adapted games and drills of this nature can be designed to give mainstream students a novel experience as well as excellent training in auditory perception (Davis, 2002). Goal ball is suitable for all age groups, beginning in about the third or fourth grade.

Figure 27.15   **In goal ball, three teammates work together to stop a bell ball from rolling across the goal line. There is no goalie.**

Beep Baseball

Although not a USABA regulation sport, beep baseball is played by many persons with VI. Its rules are governed by the National Beep Baseball Association, which was founded in 1976. These rules are different from the original game, invented by Charlie Fairbanks in 1964.

Current rules call for a regulation-size baseball diamond with grass mowed to an approximate height of 2 inches (see Figure 27.16). Grassy areas are used because they provide optimal safety and comfort for players who often dive onto the ground to field balls. The ball is a regulation softball 16 inches in circumference, with a battery-operated electronic sound device inside. A regulation bat is used. Bases are 48 inches tall, with the bottom part made of a 36-inch-tall pliable plastic cone and the top part made of a long cylinder of foam rubber. An electronic buzzer is installed in each base.

A team is comprised of six blindfolded players and two sighted players who act as pitcher and catcher when their team is up to bat and act as spotters when their team is in the field. As spotters, their role is to call out the fielder's name to whom the hit ball is coming closest. Only one name is called, for obvious safety reasons.

Batters are allowed four strikes and one ball (1991 rule change). Except on the last strike, fouls are considered strikes. Batters must attempt to hit all pitched balls, with the option of letting one go by without penalty. When a fair ball is hit, the umpire designates which one of the two buzzing bases shall be activated. *A run is scored if the batter gets to the designated base before the ball is fielded.* Games are six innings, with three outs an inning. Teams have both male and female players.

Other Games and Sports

Many other excellent activities are described in a book by Lieberman and Cowart (1996). Lieberman, at the State University of New York at Brockport, spent many years teaching at

Figure 27.16   **Playing field for beep baseball. The circular foul line between 1st and 3rd bases is a constant distance of 40 ft from home plate. A batted ball must travel over this line to be considered *fair*. The pitcher stands 20 ft from home plate. The distance between home plate and each base location is 90 ft. The base is 10 ft outside the baseline.**

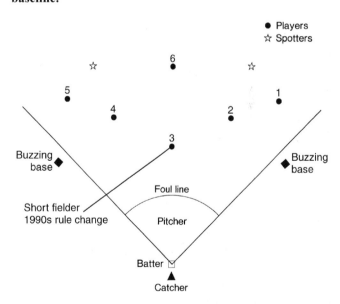

Perkins, possesses skills for working with all kinds of sensory impairments, and is available as a consultant (see Figure 27.17).

Deaf-Blindness

Deaf-blind means a combination of auditory and visual impairments that results in severe communication and other needs that require supplementary educational assistance beyond that provided in special education for one disability.

Figure 27.17 Dr. Lauren Lieberman, coauthor of *Games for People With Sensory Impairments,* communicates with an athlete who is deaf-blind.

Figure 27.18 Two ways to converse with a person who is deaf-blind. *(A)* Fingerspelling in palm of hand. *(B)* Use of a telecommunication device for the deaf (TDD) with braille output.

A

B

Athletes who are deaf-blind compete under the auspices of the USABA. Illustrative of such athletes is the 16-year-old boy in Figure 27.18 A & B, who lost his vision as a toddler and then progressively lost all hearing by the age of 15. He was, however, an excellent competitive swimmer and practiced with a local swim team. At a recent Paralympics, he carried a small, portable TDD (a **telecommunication device for the deaf,** see Chapter 26) with him so that persons could type in communication, which he read via a braille tape output and then answered. He also could understand fingerspelling when hand positions for the various letters were made in the palm of his hand (see Figure 27.18). Unfortunately, few team and staff members had fingerspelling skills of sufficient speed to maintain his interest. His greatest problem thus was communication. Embedded in this was the need for sensory stimulation and companionship, especially for people to take the time to talk to him via the TDD or fingerspelling.

A considerable body of literature on physical education and recreation for deaf-blindness was developed in the 1960s and 1970s, and the pedagogy therein remains relevant. Information can be accessed through the ERIC computer network or by contacting 1 of the 10 regional offices of the Helen Keller National Center for Deaf-Blind Youths and Adults.

Deaf-blindness, of course, seldom results in total loss. Diagnosis aims at determining amount of residual vision and hearing and prescribing education, eyeglasses, hearing aids, and communication devices that will enable optimal function.

Prevalence and Causes

Approximately 1,600 students, ages 6 to 21, are documented as receiving special education services for deaf-blindness. Because the widespread rubella epidemics of the early 1960s resulted in more deaf-blindness than any other factor, most persons with this condition are adults (an estimated 8,000).

Deaf-blindness can be hereditary or acquired. Prenatal and perinatal conditions that affect the nervous system often damage both vision and hearing. Drug and alcohol abuse, sexu-

ally transmitted diseases, and maternal infections are associated with multiple disability. Childhood diseases linked with deaf-blindness are meningitis, rubella, and scarlet fever. In the hereditary category, **Usher's syndrome** is the leading cause. It is a genetic condition resulting in congenital deafness and a progressive blindness known as **retinitis pigmentosa,** which first appears in the early thirties. Usher's syndrome affects 3 of every 100,000 persons.

Coactive Movement Model

The coactive movement model is an instructional model that works well with toddlers and young children who are blind or deaf-blind and was popularized by Van Dijk of the Netherlands in the 1960s and incorporated into instructional programs throughout the world. The purpose of this model is to develop communication skills through movement instruction that progresses through several stages (Leuw, 1972; Van Dijk, 1966).

In the initial stage, the teacher sits with legs extended on the floor, places the child on his or her lap, and seat-scoots across the floor. Arms, legs, and trunks of the teacher and child touch so that body part movements are in unison. This **coactive movement pattern** is used also for creeping, with the teacher's chest touching the child's back and all eight limbs plastered against one another.

Surfaces of the two bodies are in as much contact as possible as new patterns (knee-walking, walking, rise-to-stand, stair climbing, and the like) are tried in a variety of environments: on mats, water beds, moon walks, trampolines, floors with carpets of various textures, grass, and wading pools. The teacher talks, sings, hums, or whistles the name of the activity throughout the coactive movement. If the child has no residual hearing, fingerspelling or a tactual cue is used before, during, and after the movement.

In the second stage, the child and teacher cooperatively move together, but the distance between their bodies is gradually increased so that the action becomes mirroring or imitation. When the child links language with movement, then cues can be given to promote independent body action. Subsequent stages resemble **perceptual-motor programming,** with emphasis on imitation of total body movements, then limb actions, then hand gestures, and finally, fingerspelling and sign language. For children who have residual hearing, learning to follow verbal commands is stressed.

Deaf-Blind Role Models

The best known of persons with deaf-blindness was Helen Keller (1880–1968), who was disabled by an illness at 19 months of age. Helen Keller graduated *cum laude* from Radcliffe, mastered five languages, and wrote three books. Her autobiography (Keller, 1965) is among the classics that everyone should read. Her story has also been immortalized in a play and film called *The Miracle Worker.*

Still another deaf-blind person, Robert J. Smithdas, who suffered cerebral spinal meningitis at age 5, has gained recognition via an autobiography and his work as a public relations counselor and lecturer. At age 32, after completing a master of arts degree at New York University and working in a salaried position for several years, Smithdas wrote,

> Loneliness was continually present in my life after I became deaf and blind. And even now, in adulthood, I find it with me despite all my adjustments to social living. Loneliness is a hunger for increasing human companionship, a need to be part of the activity that I know is constantly going on about me. . . . To share my moments of joy with someone else, to have others sympathize with my failures, appreciate my accomplishments, understand my moods, and value my intelligence—these are the essential conditions that are needed for happiness. (Smithdas, 1958, p. 259)

 OPTIONAL ACTIVITIES

1. Practice leading a blindfolded person in different environments, including up and down stairs and through doorways. Be sure the blindfolded person holds on to the upper arm of the sighted person, not vice versa. Have snacks that involve use of paper cups and plates at the end of the session. Take turns being blindfolded.

2. Plan and conduct an activity session in which some persons are blindfolded and some are wearing old glasses that have been modified to permit simulation of different vision losses. Encourage persons with limited or no sight to perform locomotor and object control activities. If time, try some goal ball or beep baseball activities.

3. Several USABA athletes and individuals like Harry Cordellos do freelance lecturing to supplement their income. Ask your faculty if you might have an athlete with VI to come speak to your class or do a workshop.

4. Volunteer for weekend or summer experience at a camp (mainstream or separate) that serves children and youth with VI. One such resource is Camp Abilities, organized by a leading adapted physical education professor, Dr. Lauren Lieberman. Contact her at State University of New York (SUNY) at Brockport or arrange to meet her at a conference.

5. Volunteer 1–2 hours a week to lead one or more persons, ages 70 and up, with VI in physical activity. This may be in their homes or in a residential center. Encourage them to talk about life in general as well as their feelings about physical activity and their diminishing sight.

CHAPTER

28

Aging and Disability

Claudia Emes

Figure 28.1   A woman in the oldest-old category, over 100 years, takes her daily walk with assistance.

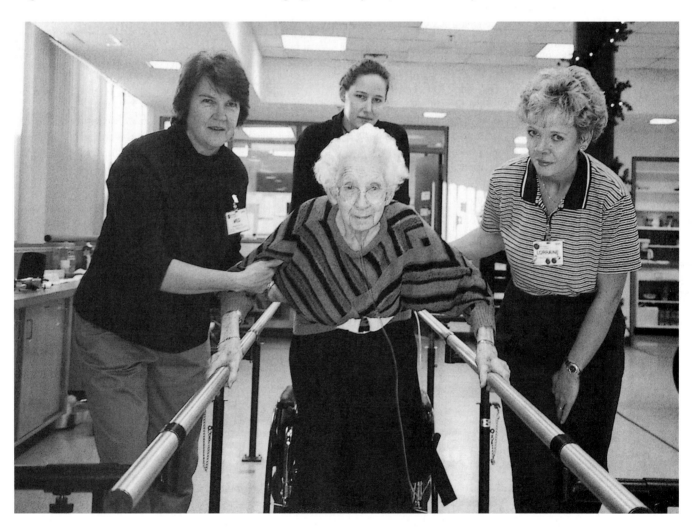

1. Consider why we rarely think about ourselves getting old; create a list of reasons. What do you think about getting old? What or who do you want to be like when you are very old?

2. Talk to your parents or another relative and ask them what they think about getting old. Write down what you heard and at a later time read it back to them and ask for their comments.

3. Review the key concepts of this chapter and answer the following questions:
   a. Why are more people living longer in today's society?
   b. What impact will aging baby boomers have on our economy, health care system, and services to people with disability?
   c. How do the issues faced by older people with disability differ from the issues of those who acquire the chronic diseases of aging?

Demography, the science of population dynamics, focuses on large and broad statistical groups within and across populations. Given past and present population structures, demography can project the future of a population (Woodruff & Birren, 1975). Demographic data of the twenty-first century reflect the accelerating increase of older people in today's society. In 2000 the proportion of people over 65 was approximately 12%. Projections forecast that by 2020 this figure will increase to 20% or 51 million people. In 2011 the first wave of **baby boomers** (born between 1946 and 1960) will turn 65, an era that will impact every aspect of growing old in today's society. While the proportionate number of people over 65 is increasing, so too is the number of people over 85; estimates project that their number in the United States will reach 8 million by 2030 (Fowles, 1991).

Why Persons Age

Differences in the way we age are unique to each individual. A person of 45 may feel and look like a person of 60, whereas a person of 80 may feel as young and be as active as someone who is 60. **Gerontology** is the scientific study of aging that examines individual differences including biological, psychological, and sociological perspectives. It attempts to explain how the 45-, 60-, and 80-year-old are similar and why they are different. To describe and discuss aging, gerontologists divide people into categories according to **chronological age** (i.e., the number of years or months since birth). Spirduso (1995) proposed the following descriptors: The term **older or old** refers to persons 65 years and more. Within that frame **young-old** are between 65 and 74, **old** are 75 to 84, **old-old** are 85 to 99, and the **oldest-old** are 100 years and older (see Figure 28.1).

Can we all expect to reach the category of oldest-old? Not likely, because many variables intervene. **Life expectancy,** or the average number of years of life remaining, differs depending on heredity, age, **cohort** (a group of people who have experienced similar conditions or events), gender, geographic location, and ethnic background. It is also influenced by environmental factors such as disease, accidents, nutrition, stress, substance abuse, and physical activity. This complex of variables also influences our health and the quality of our life as we age. The absence of health is called **morbidity,** a term describing people who, due to physical or mental disability or chronic disease, require care by others.

Despite our individual differences and the many factors that affect how we will age, everyone shares one aspect of aging. The strongest and most **ubiquitous** feature of aging, that is, one that is seen everywhere, is behavioral slowing. Both declining reaction speed and movement affect the slowing of response. Reaction time is used as an index of the effects of aging on the integrity of the CNS; however, slower nerve conduction accounts for less than 4% of deterioration in response time. In part, movement time slows because of factors such as joint stiffness and muscle power (Wright & Shephard, 1978). The greatest slowing, however, can be attributed to biological changes of the brain that affect information processing. Based on observed structural and functional changes in both central and peripheral nervous systems, Spirduso (1995) describes changes that affect the ability to code, retrieve, compare, and select information based on biological factors. These include a decline in (a) cerebral blood flow, (b) neuroreceptor structures, and (c) neurohormonal function as well as changes in enzyme activity.

With your class peers consider the evidence of behavioral slowing that you may have witnessed in older people while you were shopping or driving. Compare your experiences and discuss the impact of technology and our "instant service" culture on people who are elderly and their ability to function efficiently in today's society. What adaptations can be made to facilitate easier execution of relevant skills?

As the population of people who are older rapidly increases, overall health appears to be increasing as well. According to the National Institute on Aging (NIA) disability rates are declining. *Despite the declining rates of disability, 78% of people 70 years and older have at least one of the following chronic diseases: arthritis, cancer, diabetes, hypertension, heart disease, respiratory disease, and stroke.* The remainder of this chapter examines chronic diseases, mental and physical disability, and service delivery in physical activity within the context of older age categories. As a point of reference for this chapter, the benefits of engaging in physical activity as we grow old that have been outlined by the World Health Organization are presented in Table 28.1.

Chronic Diseases of Aging

Aging persons are most at risk for arthritis, cancer, diabetes, heart and blood diseases, and osteoporosis. Following is information for physical activity specialists.

Table 28.1   Benefits of engaging in physical activity in the older years.

Psychological Benefits

Immediate Benefits

Relaxation: Appropriate physical activity enhances relaxation.

Reduced stress and anxiety: There is evidence that regular physical activity can reduce stress and anxiety.

Enhanced mood state: Numerous people report elevations in mood state following appropriate physical activity.

Long-Term Effects

General well-being: Improvements in almost all aspects of psychological functioning have been observed following periods of extended physical activity.

Improved mental health: Regular exercise can make an important contribution in the treatment of several mental illnesses, including depression and anxiety neuroses.

Improved cognitive function: Regular physical activity may help postpone age-related declines in central nervous system processing speed and improve reaction time.

Motor control and performance: Regular activity helps prevent and/or postpone the age-associated declines in both fine and gross motor performance.

Skill acquisition: New skills can be learned and existing skills refined by all individuals regardless of age.

Social Benefits

Immediate Benefits

Empowered older individuals: A large proportion of the older adult population voluntarily adopts a sedentary lifestyle, which eventually threatens to reduce independence and self-sufficiency. Participation in appropriate physical activity can help empower older individuals and assist them in playing a more active role in society.

Enhanced social and cultural integration: Physical activity programs, particularly when carried out in small groups and/or in social environments, enhance social and intercultural interactions for many older adults.

Long-Term Effects

Enhanced integration: Regularly active individuals are less likely to withdraw from society and more likely to actively contribute to the social milieu.

Formation of new friendships: Participation in physical activity, particularly in small groups and other stimulating social environments, stimulates new friendships and acquaintances.

Widened social and cultural networks: Physical activity frequently provides individuals with an opportunity to widen available social networks.

Role maintenance and new role acquisition: A physically active lifestyle helps foster the stimulating environments necessary for maintaining an active role in society, as well as for acquiring positive new roles.

Enhanced intergenerational activity: In many societies, physical activity is a shared activity that provides opportunities for intergenerational contact thereby diminishing stereotypical perceptions about aging and the elderly.

Note: The WHO Guidelines have been placed in the public domain and can be freely copied and distributed (WHO, 1997).

Arthritis

There are over 100 different forms of **arthritis** or joint inflammation, and in most cases the cause is unknown. The answer probably is a combination of genetics, infection or insult to the body, and lifestyle. Common to most forms of arthritis are joint soreness, pain, and stiffness. In this chapter only two types of arthritis, osteoarthritis and rheumatoid arthritis, are discussed.

Osteoarthritis

An estimated 20.7 million Americans have **osteoarthritis,** one of the most common forms of arthritis. This type of arthritis most commonly affects women over 45. It is characterized by the breakdown of the joint cartilage. As the cartilage deteriorates, adjoining bones begin to rub against each other and, as a result, the joints become stiff and painful. Most frequently osteoarthritis occurs in the hands and the weight-bearing joints (knees, hips, and spine).

Treatment of osteoarthritis focuses on decreasing the levels of pain and improving joint movement. Pain is controlled with different medications. **Corticosteroids** offer rapid relief from swelling, pain, stiffness, fatigue, and loss of appetite. The use of corticosteroids is usually restricted to managing flare-ups because of the potential negative side effects associated with long-term use (osteoporosis, infection, and peptic ulcer disease).

Nonsteroidal anti-inflammatory drugs (NSAIDs) are used in long-term management, and in cases that are not responsive to NSAIDs, glucocorticoids are injected into the inflamed joints. Heat/cold therapy offers temporary pain relief, but many older people choose surgery to find relief of chronic pain. Protecting the joints from strain, including weight control to prevent extra stress on weight-bearing joints, is helpful in the long term. Diet control and non-weight-bearing exercises such as aquatic activities are excellent starting points for managing arthritis. However, most exercises that increase mobility, keep joints flexible, and improve related muscle strength are suitable for osteoarthritis.

Rheumatoid Arthritis

The most distinctive feature of **rheumatoid arthritis** (RA) is chronic inflammation of the synovia or lining of multiple joints. It is a systemic disease that affects the entire body and is one of the **autoimmune diseases.** This means that the body's natural immune system does not operate properly and as a result the immune system attacks healthy joint tissue. The unpredictable, progressive nature of RA impacts physical function and well-being, as well as psychological and social well-being. It affects primarily people over 50, and the impact on society is staggering. An estimated 64.8 billion U.S. dollars per year in medical expenses and time lost from work is attributed to RA (Yelin & Callahan, 1995).

The cause of rheumatoid arthritis is unknown; however, it is known that the inflammatory cells of the synovia release enzymes that may digest bone and cartilage and damage the joint. In addition to joint inflammation, other symptoms of RA are fever, loss of appetite, anemia, loss of energy, and appearance of rheumatoid nodules or lumps that appear under the skin (usually in area where there is pressure, e.g., elbows). It is on the basis of these overall symptoms and X rays of the joints that RA is diagnosed.

Treatment for RA starts with NSAID drugs that provide both rapid suppression of the inflammatory process and control of pain. They do not affect the progression of the disease. Second-line drugs, disease-modifying antirheumatic drugs (DMARDs), lessen joint inflammation and slow or prevent further damage to joint structures. In addition to drug treatment, a balance of rest and exercise is recommended.

 Frequently asked questions regarding exercise and arthritis include the following:

Should people with arthritis exercise?

How does exercise fit into a treatment plan for people with arthritis?

What types of exercise are most suitable for someone with arthritis?

How does a person with arthritis start an exercise program?

How often should people with arthritis exercise?

What type of strengthening program is best?

Are there different exercises for people with different types of arthritis?

How much exercise is too much?

Should someone with rheumatoid arthritis continue to exercise during a general flare? How about during a local joint flare?

Are researchers studying arthritis and exercise?

Where can people find more information on arthritis and exercise?

Go to www.niams.nih.gov/hi/topics/arthritis/arthexfs.htm#2 to learn the answers.

Cancer

In Chapter 19, cancer is discussed in terms of children and with reference to participating in physical education. It is important to include cancer in this chapter because it is the second-leading cause of death in older people. The greatest risk for most cancers is increasing age, and more than half of all adult cancer incidents are among people over 65 years.

Most people are aware of the seven warning signs of cancer. The following signs should prompt a visit to the doctor: (a) change in bowel or bladder habits, (b) a sore that does not heal, (c) unusual bleeding or discharge, (d) thickening or lump in the breast or elsewhere, (e) indigestion or difficulty swallowing, (f) obvious change in wart or mole, and (g) nagging cough or hoarseness. Remembering these signs and attending immediately to any of the related changes is important because the key to overcoming cancer is early detection and treatment. In this chapter adult cancers with the highest mortality rate are reviewed. Lung cancer is the most common fatal cancer in men (31%), followed by prostate (11%), and colon/rectum (10%). In women, lung (25%), breast (15%), and colon/rectum (11%) are the most frequent causes of cancer death (American Cancer Society [ACS], 2002).

Lung Cancer

The leading cause of cancer death is lung cancer. It occurs most often in people between the ages of 55 and 65, and upon diagnosis most people die within one year. The greatest risk factor is smoking. For example, a person who smokes two packs a day has a risk that is 60 to 70 times greater than a nonsmoker of the same age. It is the most lethal cancer and the most preventable cancer; yet the smoking incidence in females has increased over the last two decades. Cessation of smoking reduces risk; 10 years after stopping, the risk of developing lung cancer drops to nearly the same rate as those who have never smoked. However, people who don't smoke are also at risk, as environmental hazards such as asbestos, chemical toxins, and secondary smoke also cause cancer. Current policies in North America to restrict smoking in public places such as restaurants, airlines, offices, and institutions are designed to protect nonsmokers from the adverse effects of secondary smoke.

Early symptoms of lung cancer include a chronic cough, shortness of breath, chest pain, recurrent episodes of pneumonia that won't respond to treatment, and blood-tinged phlegm. Advanced symptoms include loss of appetite, loss of weight, nausea and vomiting, hoarseness, bone pain, and neurological symptoms. Lung cancer frequently spreads to the lymph glands, bone and bone marrow, and the brain (Ciesielski, 1992).

Lung cancer causes the largest number of deaths, but the incidence of breast and prostrate cancer is higher.

Breast Cancer

The most common form of cancer in women is breast cancer. About 1 in 10 women develop breast cancer, most frequently after the age of 50, but many young women contract cancer as early as 20 years. Usually, but not always, it appears first as a painless hardening or dimpling of breast tissue. Most lumps are benign, but if a biopsy detects a malignancy, then treatment begins by removing the lump. Depending on the stage of development, either a **lumpectomy** is performed where the lump and surrounding lymph nodes are removed, or a **mastectomy** where the breast and surrounding lymph nodes are removed. Chemotherapy following surgery increases survival, and generally the survival rate is about 75% (National Cancer Institute of Canada, 2002).

Treatment of breast cancer can be a difficult and frightening experience. As a result depression and low self-esteem can be an outcome of the disease. This, in turn, has a negative impact on the quality of life of women living with breast cancer. Courney and Friedenreich (1997) identified a link between physical activity and enhanced quality of life in breast cancer survivors. Their findings indicated that while participating with other breast cancer survivors in an activity program, women received comfort and understanding and were encouraged to adhere to the exercise routine. It was a time for socializing where fears and anxieties could be discussed, but it also made participants feel more in control of their health status. They also experienced a sense of accomplishment and normalcy. This research also speaks to the need for enabling and supportive physical and social environments. Survivor groups develop a special bond, and this might be a reflection of high adherence rates to exercise programs.

The risk of breast cancer is reduced by physical activity. Friedenreich and Rohan (1995) found that two thirds of 28 epidemiological studies reported reduced risks of breast cancer among those women who were the most physically active. In half of the studies, the risk reductions were statistically significant. Friedenreich (1999) suggests that physical activity may delay onset of menarche, onset of regular ovulatory cycles, and earlier age at menopause. Other factors associated with a reduced risk of breast cancer that may be affected by physical activity include reduced postmenopausal obesity and weight gain over a lifetime and reduced levels of circulating estrogens, progesterone, and luteinizing and follicle-stimulating hormones.

Prostate Cancer

The greatest risk factor for prostate cancer is increasing age. After 50 the rate increases rapidly; 70% of all prostate cancers are diagnosed in men over the age of 65. It is still unclear why the increase of prostate cancer occurs with age (ACS, 2002). This type of cancer starts in the prostate gland, which is about the size of a walnut and is situated just below the bladder and in front of the rectum. The urinary tract (urethra) runs through the prostate. The fluid produced by the prostate gland adds bulk to semen and enhances the motility and fertility of sperm. Nerves found next to the prostate take part in causing an erection of the penis, and treatment of this cancer that removes or damages these nerves can cause problems with erection (impotence). Usually prostate cancer grows very slowly. In cases where it grows quickly, it can spread to the lymph system and lymph nodes and from there to other organs of the body. Warning signs include frequent urinations at night, weak or interrupted flow of urine, inability to urinate or difficulty starting or stopping the flow of urine. Other symptoms include blood in the urine or pain in the lower back and thighs. Early detection and prompt treatment are key to minimizing the spread of cancer.

Cancer of the Colon and Rectum

The term **colorectal cancer** refers to the two cancers, colon and rectum, combined. Colorectal cancer represents the third most common form of cancer in both men and women. When detected early and treated promptly, almost all cases can be cured; yet only 37% of cases are diagnosed while still localized (ACS, 2002). Over 90% of colorectal cancer is found in people over 50. Early warning signs include rectal bleeding, blood in stools, and changes in bowel habits.

Early detection and prevention are the best approaches to reducing the incidence of prostate and colorectal cancers. Diet may have an important role to play, and the ACS (2002) recommends reducing fatty foods and red meat and increasing fruits, vegetables, and grains.

You can examine your diet in relation to recommended eating patterns by going to www.cancer.org and clicking on Nutrition for Risk Reduction and then clicking on the nutrition and activity quiz.

If it hasn't already, cancer will likely touch you or someone you know. Getting involved is a way to learn more, and it is also a form of advocacy. By volunteering to assist in an activity like Making Strides, Relay for Life, or Susan B. Komen walks, you will learn more about cancer, and you will have an opportunity to become an advocate. **Making Strides** *is a noncompetitive walk designed to raise awareness, foster camaraderie, and raise funds for breast cancer research, services, patient education, and advocacy.* **Relay for Life** *is a fun-filled overnight event designed to celebrate survivorship and raise money for cancer research. During the event, teams of people gather at schools, fairgrounds, or parks and take turns walking or running laps. Each team tries to keep at least one team member on the track at all times. To volunteer for these activities visit the ACS site www.cancer.org.*

Diabetes

Two forms of diabetes, Type 1 and Type 2, impair glucose utilization, but the mechanisms are different. In Chapter 19, Type 1 diabetes is emphasized: usual onset before age 25 and insulin dependent. Type 2 is noninsulin dependent and usually occurs in overweight and obese adults over 40. It is also linked to inactivity, family history of diabetes, and ethnic heritage. Ninety percent of diabetes in North America is Type 2 or adult-onset diabetes.

Treatment of Type 2 diabetes is through weight reduction, following a sensible diet, exercise, and in some cases antidiabetic oral medication to control glucose. A sensible diet is one in which approximately 50% of total daily calories come from carbohydrates, 15 to 20% from protein, and less than 30% from fat sources (American Diabetes Association, 2002). Losing weight and adopting a healthy lifestyle of exercise in conjunction with an appropriate diet is the key to preventing the complications of diabetes. These include heart disease (diabetics are at twice the risk as nondiabetics) and long-term complications such as kidney disease, eye problems, blindness, and nerve damage.

Many adults with Type 2 diabetes can manage their diabetes by diet and exercise alone; others need oral pills, medications, or insulin. Exercise offers an important contribution of improving blood glucose levels or blood sugar. It reduces insulin resistance. This is particularly relevant because that is, in part, the cause of Type 2, resistance to insulin. *Exercise helps the body use insulin appropriately.* It also offers all the standard health benefits described in Table 28.1 that produce an overall sense of well-being. Recommended levels of exercise are a minimum of 30 minutes, 3 to 5 times a week. To maximize benefits, longer duration and increased frequency are required.

> *To test your knowledge of exercise in relation to diabetes complete either the exercise crossword puzzle or the exercise quiz found at www.diabetes.org/main/health/exercise/games.jsp.*

Diseases of the Heart and Blood Vessels

Hypertension, heart attack, and stroke are discussed in this section. Weight control and exercise are important in reducing the risk of these conditions.

Hypertension

The incidence of high blood pressure increases with age. Currently 50 million Americans have hypertension. It is a serious health problem, called the *silent killer* because it has no obvious symptoms. The only way to determine if you have hypertension is to have your blood pressure measured. High blood pressure can lead to cardiovascular complications such as strokes, heart attacks, heart failure, heart rhythm irregularities, and kidney failure. Blood pressure in a healthy young person is under 120/80. The National Heart, Lung, and Blood Institute revised its blood pressure guidelines in 2003, specifying a new diagnostic category called **prehypertension.** This high risk condition is diagnosed whenever systolic pressures are between 120–139 and diastolic pressures are between 80–89. Prehypertension is managed the same way as hypertension. Blood pressure levels above 140/90 place a person at risk for stroke and cardiovascular disease. The longer the duration of hypertension, the greater the risk.

Management of hypertension is threefold: diet, exercise, and medication. A diet high in grains, fresh fruits, and vegetables and low in salts and fat, coupled with an exercise/physical activity program, is a critical part of a healthy lifestyle.

Aerobic exercises such as jogging, walking, bicycling, and swimming are recommended. Even with a healthy lifestyle, medication to combat hypertension may be required as a person grows older.

Diuretic drugs (furosemide, sironolactone, and hydrochlorothiazide) increase the normal kidney action by removing excessive fluid from the blood, producing **diuresis.** This lowers blood pressure by reducing total volume of blood. This can lead to **postural hypotension**, a condition where the blood pressure drops and dizziness or light-headedness occurs. Therefore, it is important during exercise to make sure not only that persons taking diuretics have the opportunity to go to the bathroom but also that they are well hydrated following exercise.

Three types of medication are prescribed for hypertension. **Beta blockers** reduce the force of the heartbeat and can also inhibit the dilation of the blood vessels surrounding the brain. This reduces the workload of the heart. **Calcium channel blockers** help relax the muscles surrounding the blood vessels, reducing constriction. Both beta blockers and calcium channel blockers help to control angina. *Since the beta blocker reduces heart rate, heart rate is not a good measure of exercise intensity. Instead, a rating of perceived exertion (RPE) is preferred.* **Angiotension converting enzyme** inhibitors block enzyme activity in the blood vessels, which allows the blood vessels to dilate.

Heart Attack

"Coronary heart disease (CHD) is the leading cause of death for both men and women in the United States. CHD, which is caused by a narrowing of the coronary arteries that supply blood to the heart, often results in a heart attack" (National Heart, Lung, and Blood Institute, 2002). Men over 45 and women over 55 are at increased risk of a heart attack. Controllable factors that contribute to increased risk are smoking, overweight/obesity, high blood pressure, high cholesterol, sedentary lifestyle, and diabetes. Unfortunately, other factors such as a family history of CHD increase risk as well. In Chapter 19 the events of CHD are described, and cardiac rehabilitation is presented. Refer to that chapter to complete your reading on heart attacks.

Stroke

In addition to heart disease, hypertension can lead to stroke. During a stroke, blood flow to the brain is suddenly interrupted (**ischemic**) or a vessel ruptures and blood flows into the surrounding brain cells (**hemorrhagic**). As a result, brain cells are damaged either from lack of oxygen or from the sudden bleeding. However, these damaged cells can be saved by timely treatment. Every 53 seconds someone in the U.S. has a stroke; that is 600,000 people in one year, and there are about 4.5 million survivors living today (American Stroke Association, 2002).

Warning signs of a stroke incident can be crucial because treatment provided immediately after a stroke is more effective than delayed treatment.

Sudden numbness or temporary weakness of the face, an arm, or a leg.

Sudden difficulty with or loss of speech or trouble understanding speech.

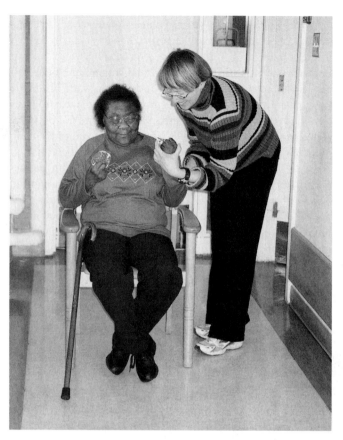

Sudden temporary dimness or loss of vision, particularly in one eye.

Sudden episode of double vision.

Sudden dizziness or unsteadiness.

Sudden change in personality or mental ability.

Sudden severe headache without cause.

When one or more signs occur, medical attention must be sought immediately. The speed of recovery from stroke depends on the area of the brain that was damaged, the amount of brain tissue that was destroyed, the rehabilitation services available, and the attitude of the person who had the stroke. After a stroke, treatment focuses on recovery, rehabilitation (Figure 28.2), and preventing another stroke. Prevention strategies include following a low-fat, low-cholesterol, calorie-controlled diet; regularly checking blood pressure; monitoring blood sugar; exercising regularly; and conducting routine blood tests to identify other problems.

Osteoporosis

"Osteoporosis and low bone mass are a major public health threat for almost 44 million U.S. women and men aged 50 and older" (National Osteoporosis Foundation [NOF], 2002). This strikingly large number represents approximately 55% of the people in the United States who are over 55 years. Of them, ap-

proximately 80% are women. These figures are expected to rise to 61 million people by 2020. Osteoporosis is not a normal part of aging and may be largely preventable by adopting a healthy lifestyle and investing in early treatment.

You can learn more about osteoporosis by visiting the NOF website at www.nof.org. Here you will find access to video and audio segments that discuss a vast array of topics relevant to the risks, cause, diagnosis, treatment, and prevention of osteoporosis.

Osteoporosis is characterized as a loss of bone mass and microarchitectural deteriorations of bone tissue. As a result, bones become fragile and are at increased risk for fractures. The most common sites of fragility fractures are the wrist, spinal vertebrae, and hip. With advancing age, the incidence of wrist fractures declines while those of the vertebrae and the hip increase exponentially (Prentice, 2002). Fractures cause the vertebrae to compress over time and may lead to notable loss of height and dowager's hump. Osteoporetic fractures are a major cause of disability in older people, and hip fractures can lead to premature death. **Osteopenia** is a term frequently used in conjunction with osteoporosis. Shephard (1997) explains the difference: "investigators distinguish osteopenia (a loss of bone mass—for example 2.5 SD below the reference standard for a young adult) from osteoporosis (a combination of osteopenia with a mechanical failure of the skeleton)" (p. 79).

The World Health Organization provides diagnostic risk categories. Using dual-energy X-ray absorptometry (DXA) of several sites, including the lumbar spine and the proximal femur, quantitative measures of bone mass reduction are calculated. These are compared with young adult reference values to determine increased risk of bone fracture (Dalsky, 1996).

Several factors are commonly associated with the risk of developing osteoporosis. Take the One Minute Risk test to determine your possible level of risk by visiting www.osteofound.org.

Prevention and treatment of osteoporosis often use the same approach. These focus on diet, exercise, and hormone replacement therapy (HRT). The latter (HRT) became controversial around 2002–2003. Diets that are rich in calcium (broccoli, oysters, salmon, and most dairy products) and vitamin D (milk) are recommended. Exercise that is weight-bearing (walking) is highly recommended (see Figure 28.3). Spence and Humphries (2001), in a quantitative review of exercise interventions for osteoporosis, concluded that aerobic or weight-bearing activities are effective in promoting bone growth in pre- and postmenopausal women, whereas there is less consensus about the effectiveness of resistance training (stretch bands) on bone strength.

More than 40 million women are over age 50 in the United States, 38% among those who are postmenopausal use HRT (Fletcher & Colditz, 2002). Early clinical trials such as the Postmenopausal Estrogen/Progestin Interventions Trial (PEPI) of HRT focused on its effects on the risk factors associated

Figure 28.3 Weight-bearing and dumbbell exercises can help prevent bone mineral loss.

Figure 28.4 Balance exercises improve stability and can help reduce the risk of falls.

with various diseases. It was followed by HERS (Heart and Estrogen-Progestin Replacement Study) designed to examine whether HRT would prevent a second heart attack or other coronary event. Although PEPI results were somewhat positive with regard to cholesterol levels and possible protection against uterine cancer, the HERS results *showed an increased risk of heart attack during the first year of HRT.* Risk declined after that but there was also an increased risk for blood clots (U.S. Dept. of Health and Human Services, 2003).

More recently a national study on the risks for heart disease, the Women's Health Initiative (WHI), was launched in 40 centers throughout the country to examine the effects of HRT, diet, and supplements on the incidence of osteoporotic fractures and colorectal cancer relative to the risks of breast cancer, uterine cancer, and blood clots. It found that generally *the benefits* of HRT, mainly fewer hip and other fractures and colorectal cancer, *were outweighed by the risk of breast cancer, heart attack, stroke, and blot clots* (U.S. Dept Of Health and Human Services, 2003). On May 31, 2002, the WHI study, which was to have continued until 2005, was stopped. "Overall health risks exceeded benefits from use of combined estrogen plus progestin for an average 5.2 year follow-up among healthy postmenopausal U.S. women." (Women's Health Initiative, 2002). Although the estrogen plus progestin study has ended, the estrogen-only segment continues. For example, Prestwood (2003) found that lower

doses of estrogen replacement therapy can strengthen bones apparently without adverse effects. The risk/benefit ratio of HRT is not definitive in most areas; therefore women should seek medical advice if they are considering HRT.

Falls and Posture Training

One fear that older people share more than any other is the fear of falling. This fear is well founded. For people with bone fragility, falling can have serious consequences. Within a year of falling, most fallers who are over 80 die. Okada, Hirakawa, Takada, and Kinoshita (2001) found that this fear leads to a sedentary lifestyle. This is unfortunate because physical activity can help improve strength, reaction, and balance (Figure 28.4). As strength and steadiness build, confidence also improves and older people are more likely to increase the amount of physical activity in their life. Increased leg strength and aerobic fitness associated with faster walking speed and a longer stride are also associated with reduced risk of falling (Wolfson, Whipple, Amerman, & Tobin, 1990).

The most common cause (47%) of falls is tripping (Overstall, Exton-Smith, Imms, & Johnson, 1977). Exercise and training can help prevent some falls such as those triggered by stumbling on an uneven floor, a misplaced object, or a slippery surface. By learning fall techniques and better reaction and

recovery, bodies resist the force of falling (O'Brien Cousins & Goodwin, 2002). Tripping types of fall can be absorbed or avoided by people with stronger and more agile (good reaction time) bodies. In addition to building strength and agility, postural exercises are important to stability and balance. Activities that improve balance like dance (Figure 28.5) and focus on recovery can help older people particularly when they fall forward.

Drop attacks (12%) are the second most common cause of falling (Overstall et al., 1977) and are more common after age 75. **Postural hypotension** results when blood pressure drops, causing light-headedness or dizziness followed by a fall. Other balance-related factors that cause falls include medications, joint pathologies of arthritis, and disabilities such as Parkinson's disease.

Alzheimer's Disease

Before you begin this section, take a minute to complete the following quiz: "try the quiz" at www. mygeneration.org/departments/2001/health/0905_a.html.

We all have changes in our memory as we grow older, but people with Alzheimer's disease (AD) experience severe problems that interfere with their ability to function well (Alzheimer's Association, 2001). Early signs of **dementia,** or loss of memory and other intellectual capacities, include difficulty performing familiar tasks such as making a cup of tea; problems with language that are reflected in forgetting words for objects or describing events; constant repetition of the same phrases; and unintelligible conversations. Judgment is affected and often is evident in the way a person dresses (e.g., wearing winter gloves and a heavy jacket on a nice warm day). Misplacing things such as putting a kettle in the trunk of the car or

putting shoes in a tea towel drawer is often coupled with hoarding or pack-rat behavior such as stuffing pockets with cookies or putting handfuls of facial tissues inside a coat or vest. Rapid mood swings and changes in personality are common. It is not unusual for someone with AD to become easily frustrated or to have an outburst of anger that appears to be out of character for that person. Last, they become less interested in things and show an increasing loss of initiative.

The rate of AD increases dramatically with age. AD is not a normal part of the aging process; however, 10% of people over 65 have AD, and the rate doubles to 50% for those over 85. An estimated 4 million Americans have AD. Loss of functional ability progresses differently in different people, but generally the progression period is between 8 and 20 years. Decline is associated with loss of neurons of the frontal cerebral cortex, the hippocampus (the associative center that converts short-term to long-term memory), and the amyloid-containing plaques of degenerating neurons throughout the cerebral cortex. A deficiency in the neurons of the cerebral cortex affects acetylcholine for synaptic transmission. Also present are intracellular tangles and neurofibrils. The result is a gradual shutdown of the brain that leads to loss of cognition, physical function, and social skills. The exact cause is unknown; however, research is addressing several factors.

Although compliance can be an issue when engaging a person with AD in an activity program, exercise during early-stage AD can have a positive impact. For example, Namazi, Zadorozny, and Gwinnup (1995) provided a light exercise program for 40 minutes, 7 days a week for 4 weeks, to persons with AD in a nursing home. The leader encouraged active participation rather than perfection. During the study, program staff documented sleep patterns; the results indicated that a moderate amount of exercise each day could help persons to sleep soundly at night and also reduce the amount of restless behavior. Other research has reported that exercise is effective for reducing aggressive incidents in nursing home residents who are cognitively impaired (McGrowder-Lin & Blatt, 1988; Meddaugh, 1987). More recent research has confirmed that walking programs improve ambulatory status and walking endurance (Koroknay, Werner, & Cohen-Mansfield, 1995; McCrae, Asplund, Schnelle, & Braun, 1996). Attempts to determine the effects of a walking program on communication have produced mixed results. Friedman and Tappen (1991) examined the impact of a combined walking and talking program and found improved communication performance. Cot, Dawson, Sidani, and Wells (2002) did not find any significant change in communication skills; however, they offered a possible explanation that the participants were in an advanced disease state.

Generally speaking, exercise can contribute to aerobic capacity and cerebral circulation that will enhance functioning of neurons that activate muscle fibers. It will also increase the regional cerebral blood flow, thus attenuating the naturally occurring reductions in blood flow to specific areas of the brain. Exercise can increase physical and mental arousal that contributes to attention processes. In addition to basic exercises, dancing and tossing objects such as balls, Nerf Frisbees, plastic horseshoes, and beanbags can be pleasing and enjoyable activities.

The American Council on Exercise (ACE) (1998) offers guidelines for delivering activity programs to people with early-stage dementia:

1. *Patience.* Be understanding and sensitive to the anguish the person is experiencing due to memory loss. Provide moral support and make reminder phone calls before each class.
2. *Dropout Prevention.* Depression is common in this cohort and may lead to higher dropout rates. Regular contact and reminders to their caregivers about the importance of exercise will help.
3. *Simplify.* Replace complex exercise routines with simpler activities. Focus on walking, stationary cycles, and basic stretches and eliminate weights, treadmills and other equipment that requires steady control of the body. It could be dangerous to people with AD.
4. *Praise.* It may be difficult to keep participants interested; therefore use lots of verbal praise and positive reinforcement to encourage adherence.
5. *Maintain Frequency.* The intensity of the exercise is not as important as doing it frequently and for sustained periods of time. It is recommended that the program run 5 days a week. Morning is best as participants can be more agitated and fatigued as the day progresses.

Later-stage dementia presents new challenges, and the ACE (1998) offers the following guidelines:

1. Be aware of behavior that has nothing to do with you or the program. It is not unusual for people with AD to have sudden outbursts that are symptoms of the disease and not in their control. They do not know what or why they are saying or doing in their outburst. If they are part of a group activity, remove them by speaking softly and soothingly and allow them to calm down before returning

to the activity. People with AD respond best to a quiet, reassuring approach. Raising your voice or trying to manage them using physical force will just heighten their agitation and increase their frustration.

2. As memory loss progresses, the participant may have to leave the group setting and switch to individual training.
3. The primary caregiver should be present at the exercise program. Individuals with AD often refuse to be left alone with anyone except the person they are most familiar with.
4. Keep the program structured with little variation. New activities may confuse participants.
5. Wandering is common among people with AD. Never leave them alone.
6. Playing music, particularly from their generation, can be a good way to keep them interested in the program.

Parkinson's Disease

Parkinson's disease is a progressive neurological disorder that is most commonly seen in individuals older than 50. Degeneration of neurons in a region of the brain that controls movement creates a shortage of **dopamine,** a chemical responsible for transmitting messages across nerve pathways in the brain. Voluntary movement is affected, and the result is the shaking or tremor-type movement that characterizes Parkinson's disease. It usually appears in people over 60, and the incidence increases for people in their 70s and 80s. Initially, trembling is isolated to the hands, but over time the impact is apparent in other movements such as rising from a chair, walking, and initiating new movements.

There is no cure for Parkinson's disease, but drug treatment for severe symptoms is available in the form of levodopa (L-dopa) and similar drugs that help restore the brain's level of dopamine. Transplants into the brain of healthy dopamine-producing tissues are being tested, while research attempts to determine how to prevent dopamine-producing brain cells from dying (National Institute of Neurological Disorders and Stroke, 2001).

Exercise can offer much in the management of Parkinson's. For example, neuromuscular relaxation exercises can help reduce tremors, and flexibility exercises will help stretch tightened muscles. Balance can be a problem, but by exercising on mats on the floor and by engaging in aquatic exercises, the risk of falling can be eliminated. Breathing exercises to strengthen respiratory muscles should also be part of an exercise program.

Depression

Depression is not a normal part of aging, and the majority of older people age without having episodes of depression. However, late-life depression does affect older people who have medical conditions including stroke, heart disease, cancer, Parkinson's, and hormonal changes. The physical change associated with many chronic diseases can affect mood and make a person apathetic and uninterested in his or her own self-care. This type of depression illness is **comorbid,** meaning that it exists alongside another disease. Loss or stressful change can also trigger a depression illness.

Many incidents of depression go unreported or undiagnosed, especially in men; it is estimated that there are 3 to 4 million men in the United States with depression illness. Women are more likely than men to become depressed. Serious depression can lead to suicide, and the rate of suicide among men is four times that of women. Suicide increases for men over 70 and peaks around 85 (National Institute of Mental Health, 2002).

Incidence of depression increases significantly with age, but research suggests that this increase may be due in part to declining levels of physical activity as we age (Parent & Whall, 1986). Exercise can contribute to an improved mood and is recommended for both the physical well-being outcomes and social well-being outcomes that can contribute to general psychological well-being (see Table 28.1).

Vision and Hearing

Aging is associated with a steady decline in visual and auditory acuity. Structural changes to the eye associated with aging can reduce the visual field and impair focusing on near objects. Hearing loss is associated with deterioration in the structures of the middle and inner ear and the auditory cortex. By 65 approximately one third of older people have noticeable hearing loss; by 80, the number has risen to over half.

Macular Degeneration

The leading cause of blindness in Americans over 55 is macular degeneration. Between 10 and 12 million adults are affected by this disease, which is characterized by deterioration of the macula, the central portion of the retina that records the images we see and relays them to the brain via the optic nerve. Gradually vision deteriorates and the ability to read, drive a car, or recognize faces and colors is lost. Factors that should be modified after a diagnosis of macular degeneration include diet (low fat, low cholesterol), protection of the eyes (sunglasses and avoiding smoking and/or secondhand smoke), and vitamin supplements (E and C).

Cataracts and Glaucoma

Cataracts and glaucoma are both described in Chapter 27. Cataracts are common in elderly people, and they are the leading cause of blindness worldwide; however, removal of cataracts is the most common surgery for Americans over the age of 65. Over a million operations are successfully performed each year. The risk of glaucoma increases over 60; however, glaucoma can also be successfully treated. Drugs and eye drops can effectively lower pressure in the eye.

Considerations for exercise and activity programs that include persons with declining vision and hearing include basic adaptations to the environment and adjustments when speaking to participants. For example, use brightly colored tape or markings that have sharp contrast to mark objects. Keep the floor area clear of all objects to prevent falls. Use equipment that requires sitting rather than standing. Always face the participant and give clear verbal instructions along with demonstrations. Consistently keep equipment in the same place to avoid confusion. Keep your hands away from your face so that everyone can see your lips. Speak in a normal tone.

Aging With Disability Acquired When Young

Aging is very individualistic regardless of the presence or absence of disability. However, people with disability experience unique changes associated with the nature of their physical disability.

Spinal Cord Injury

McColl, Charlifue, Glass, Savic, and Meehan (2002) summarized five categories of age-related changes that occur in older people with spinal cord injury (SCI). The first are problems associated with the prolonged duration of SCI such as shoulder deterioration, chronic bladder infections, and postural problems. Second are the secondary complications associated with the original lesion such as posttraumatic **syringomyelia** (presence of fluid cavities in the substance of the spinal cord) and autonomic dysreflexia. Trieschmann (1987) noted in the same report that several interviewees complained that they were more susceptible to pressure sores than in their youth. The third category includes pathological processes not related to the SCI, such as hypertension and heart, respiratory, and cerebrovascular disease. The fourth category includes degenerative changes of aging such as arthritic joints, loss of visual and auditory acuity, and connective tissue problems. The fifth category encompasses environmental factors such as societal, community, and cultural issues. This suite of changes suggest the need for services that address new challenges associated with the aging process in persons with SCI.

McColl et al. (2002) compared the quality of life and health outcomes of older people with and without SCI. In America there were fewer psychological problems, less depression, less fatigue, and more life satisfaction than in other countries. In Britain fewer persons reported joints affected by pain, whereas in Canada there were more specific health complaints, bowel problems, pain, and fatigue. Differences were attributed to the sociopolitical environments that govern the provision of services. The Americans with Disabilities Act has ensured wide-ranging provisions that are not as easily accessed in other countries.

Congenital or Childhood Onset Disabilities

Individuals with cerebral palsy (CP), spina bifida, and other acquired physical disabilities tend to have aging problems with the musculoskeletal system. These include soreness of joints, pain and weakness in muscles, and decline in energy.

Gajdosik and Cicirello (2001) summarized research on secondary conditions that impact quality of life during the aging process of individuals with CP. Musculoskeletal conditions such as scoliosis worsen over time. Overuse syndromes such as carpal tunnel syndrome have been reported, and osteoarthritis is frequently present. Osteoporosis is also present and results in fractures more frequently than in non-CP. In a retrospective study of adults with CP, Andersson and Mattson (2001) found that 90% of the respondents had lost their ability to walk. In most cases, this happened before age 35. In contrast, 19% reported improved walking as a result of regular physical training. The largest number, over one third, reported that their walking ability had declined. Other problems frequently cited were contractures in four to six joints and daily pain. Despite the problems, it is important to note the number of people who were engaged in physical training (60%) and their high levels of motivation to exercise based on the assumption that exercise will improve their walking and wheelchair management.

Loss of independent walking is not unusual (Curran, Sharples, White, & Knapp, 2001). With increasing age, persons with CP and spina bifida will give up walking because it becomes less efficient or because of chronic pain. Curran et al. (2001) describe physiological burnout and the fear of falling due to postural instability to explain why some adults with CP stop walking. We need to focus on the challenges of aging for adults with CP and spina bifida. Gajdosik and Cicirello (2001) point to the necessity to understand that the damage to the CNS is static, but that function and ability change. Physical abilities are tenuous and must be preserved. Rather than demanding more from the body in their youth, persons with CP should consider conserving in order to slow functional loss in later adulthood.

Mental Retardation

In a survey, Hand (1994) found that 52% of people with a lifelong intellectual disability had at least one major chronic physical problem, such as musculoskeletal, cardiovascular, respiratory, digestive, or endocrinological problems, or cancer. General health problems are similar to the older population as a whole: vision and hearing loss, loss of mobility, tendency to fall, and incontinence.

Provision of services for aging adults with mental retardation was first explored on a national basis by Seltzer and Krauss (1987). They identified 327 community-based and 202 institutionally-based programs that serve people with developmental disability over 55 years. They pointed out that about half of the programs were modifications of existing programs, and half were designed specifically for this population. The largest category of community-based residential living was group homes where the average age of residents was 62 years and most were women (53%). Within the area of physical recreation, they offered several program options such as swimming, bowling, exercise, and yoga, but they tended to be center based. Leisure and outreach services were the least likely of all activities to use generic seniors programs.

A national study conducted in New Zealand identified needs in the area of social and support services (Hand, 1994) and determined that leisure education was the second highest ranking need (21%) behind budgeting and money training (22%). They also determined a need for professional training programs. Meeting the needs of older people with mental disability will require greater attention in the future. Our current inclusive practices in education and community programs may influence future trends in service delivery; however, in the interim, previous practices of segregation have created social issues. For example, for many older adults with intellectual disability, their only friends are their parents, and the loss of their primary caregivers and closest friends can be devastating. Resulting behavioral changes can be problematic to manage because of the difficulties associated with diagnosing the difference between dementia, depression, and behavioral problems (Harper & Wadsworth, 1990). Long-term planning is an important aspect of service delivery.

Recall from Chapter 21 that trisomy 21 or Down syndrome (DS) results from a chromosome anomaly, having an extra chromosome. AD neuropathology is universally present in adults with Down syndrome, which strongly suggests a link between chromosome 21 and early onset Alzheimer's. Autopsies have revealed that brain changes in adults with DS are indistinguishable from AD (Brookbank, 1990). Neuronal tangles and plaques begin appearing around ages 35 to 40 and, for many, a rapid aggressive form of AD develops. Day and Jancar (1994) reviewed the literature on level of incidence and found rates varied (6–45%) but increased with age to 70% at age 60. The average age of onset is 54 years. The duration of AD, compared to an overall average of 8 years for persons without DS, is much shorter at 4–6 years. Clearly the expression of AD symptoms occurs after neuropathological changes in the brain.

The search for the cause of AD and its relationship to DS has overshadowed to some extent the study of other health changes associated with aging in DS. Research has revealed twice the rate of vision loss and three times as many incidents of auditory loss compared with other people with mental disabilities (Haveman, Maaskant, & Sturman, 1989). The same study also found higher rates of osteoporosis, epilepsy, motor disabilities, and chronic lung disease. Adults with DS tend to have a lower frequency of depression but higher rates of diabetes and stroke than those with non-Down syndrome.

Before reading the section on interacting with older people, think about two people who you know who are in the old-old age category. Set up an opportunity to speak to each of them separately. Ask about the types of activities or sports they played when they were young. Find out about the things they liked doing when they were your age. What are their hobbies or pastimes now? Enjoy your conversations with them and let each conversation flow in any direction. Later write down what struck you about each person. How were they alike? How were they different? Do you ever have any of the same feelings they expressed? What was your overall impression?

Interactions With People Who Are Older

Chapter 2 describes stigmatization and stigma theory that focuses on one-to-one interactions and how interactions can be strained, based on assumptions and stereotyping of people with disabilities. This situation can be twice as difficult for older people who have to deal with **ageism,** or prejudice against a person based on old age, and a disability. Research by Giles, Fox, and Smith (1993) examined intergenerational attitudes and how these were perceived in a continuing care facility for elderly. Based on stereotyped expectations rather than the reality of older persons, communication can deteriorate between younger and older people. Younger people may start using patronizing speech or secondary baby talk. Giles et al. (1993) explored this phenomenon in a survey of nursing home residents. The residents were asked if this kind of talk actually happened.

Over half believed that older people in general received secondary baby talk, and over half responded that they personally had received it. Their feelings in response to baby talk were generally consistent; they felt patronized, irritated, angry, and inferior. When it was used, residents viewed the patronizer as less competent and even less intelligent than people who use a neutral style of talk. By thinking about the person you are interacting with, and not his or her age and whether or not he or she has a disability, you are more likely to avoid stigmatizing and stereotyping people. You will be less likely to fall into bad habits such as using secondary baby talk.

Interacting with older people should not be very different than with others. Remember that just as you like to be treated with respect and listened to when you have a concern or a question, so, too, do elderly people. Many are very wise, and there is much to be learned from them if you are willing to listen. Most important, relax and enjoy what they have to offer.

 ## OPTIONAL ACTIVITIES

1. Sign up for a practicum where you will work with people who are older. Practicum experiences are wonderful opportunities to expand your knowledge by applying the theory of the classroom to practice in the field. By journaling your experience you will begin to reflect more thoughtfully about learning. You can guide your practicum experience by using the *Adapted Physical Activity Practicum Manual* (Emes & Velde, 2004).

2. Undertake a media watch. Create an inventory of portrayals of older people in the media. Build your inventory around the type of media—TV, radio, or print. Assign the portrayals as either stereotypical or realistic. For example, look for older character roles on your favorite TV show. Note any stereotypes that you see being perpetuated through the media and/or describe media depictions that are realistic or appropriate. Write brief notes about the differences within the types of media and between stereotypical and realistic depictions.

3. Visit one of each type of facility that provides exercise and activity programs for people who are older. Take a notebook with you and record the types of programs you saw and the different levels of activity that were provided and who were the participants in each facility. Types of facilities could include the following: community center, seniors center, semi-independent living facility, long-term care facility, and/or nursing care facility.

4. See films that include persons who have had strokes or who are living with advanced old age. Discuss such films as the following with persons of different ages:

On Golden Pond (1981)
The Gin Game (1984)
Cocoon (1985)
Whales of August (1987)
Driving Miss Daisy (1989)
Strangers in Good Company (1991)
Grumpy Old Men (1993)
Space Cowboys (2000)
It Runs in the Family (2003)
Second-Hand Lions (2003)

Federal Law Definitions of Disabilities

1. **Autism** means a developmental disability significantly affecting verbal and nonverbal communication and social interaction, generally evident before age 3, that adversely affects a child's educational performance. Other characteristics often associated with autism are engagement in repetitive activities and stereotyped movements, resistance to environmental change or change in daily routines, and unusual responses to sensory experiences. The term does not apply if a child's educational performance is adversely affected primarily because the child has a serious emotional disturbance.

2. **Deaf-blindness** means concomitant hearing and visual impairments the combination of which causes such severe communication and other developmental and educational problems that they cannot be accommodated in special education programs solely for children with deafness or children with blindness.

3. **Deafness** means a hearing impairment that is so severe that the child is impaired in processing linguistic information through hearing, with or without amplification, and this adversely affects a child's educational performance.

4. **Emotional disturbance** is defined as follows:
   (i) The term means a condition exhibiting one or more of the following characteristics over a long period of time and to a marked degree that adversely affects a child's educational performance:
      A. An inability to learn that cannot be explained by intellectual, sensory, or health factors
      B. An inability to build or maintain satisfactory interpersonal relationships with peers and teachers
      C. Inappropriate types of behavior or feelings under normal circumstances
      D. A general pervasive mood of unhappiness or depression
      E. A tendency to develop physical symptoms or fears associated with personal or school problems
   (ii) The term includes schizophrenia. The term does not necessarily apply to children who are socially maladjusted, unless it is determined that they have a serious emotional disturbance.

5. **Hearing impairment** means an impairment in hearing, whether permanent or fluctuating, that adversely affects a child's educational performance but that is not included under the definition of deafness in this section.

6. **Mental retardation** means significantly subaverage general intellectual functioning existing concurrently with deficits in adaptive behavior and manifested during the developmental period that adversely affects a child's educational performance.

7. **Multiple disabilities** means concomitant impairments (such as mental retardation–blindness, mental retardation–orthopedic impairment, etc.) the combination

of which causes such severe educational problems that they cannot be accommodated in special education programs solely for one of the impairments. The term does not include deaf-blindness.

8. **Orthopedic impairment** means a severe orthopedic impairment that adversely affects a child's educational performance. The term includes impairments caused by congenital anomaly (e.g., clubfoot, absence of some member, etc.), impairments caused by disease (e.g., poliomyelitis, bone tuberculosis, etc.), and impairments from other causes (e.g., cerebral palsy, amputations, and fractures or burns that cause contractures).

9. **Other health impairment** means having limited strength, vitality, or alertness, as due to chronic or acute health problems such as asthma, attention deficit disorder or attention deficit hyperactivity disorder, diabetes, epilepsy, a heart condition, hemophilia, lead poisoning, leukemia, nephritis, rheumatic fever, and sickle-cell anemia; and that adversely affects a child's educational performance.

10. **Specific learning disability** means a disorder in one or more of the basic psychological processes involved in understanding or in using language, spoken or written, that may manifest itself in an imperfect ability to listen, think, speak, read, write, spell, or do mathematical calculations. The term includes such conditions as perceptual disabilities, brain injury, minimal brain dysfunction, dyslexia, and developmental aphasia. The term does not apply to children who have learning problems that are primarily the result of visual, hearing, or motor disabilities, mental retardation, emotional disturbance, or environmental, cultural, or economic disadvantage.

11. **Speech or language impairment** means a communication disorder such as stuttering, impaired articulation, a language impairment, or a voice impairment that adversely affects a child's educational performance.

12. **Traumatic brain injury** means acquired injury to the brain caused by an external physical force, resulting in total or partial functional disability or psychosocial impairment, or both, that adversely affects a child's educational performance. The term applies to open or closed head injuries resulting in impairments in one or more areas, such as cognition; language; memory; attention; reasoning; abstract thinking; judgment; problem solving; sensory, perceptual, and motor abilities; psychosocial behavior; physical functions; information processing; and speech. The term does not apply to brain injuries that are congenital or degenerative, or brain injuries induced by birth trauma.

13. **Visual impairment including blindness** means an impairment in vision that, even with correction, adversely affects a child's educational performance. The term includes both partial sight and blindness.

Source: 34 C.F.R., Section 300.7.

Prevalence and Incidence Information

Prevalence

Prevalence is the number of cases with a specific condition in the population at a given time. For prevalence statistics to be meaningful, we must know the total number of people in the population. Consider the following:

1. The United States population is 281.4 million. Of this total, 45 million individuals (over 16%) have disabilities.
2. Of this 45 million, about 10% are children and adolescents, about 30% are young and middle-aged adults, and about 50% are persons over the age of 65.
3. The U.S. Department of Education, Office of Special Education Programs, documents services to about 5 million individuals from birth through age 21. This is only

about 2% of this age group, although most sources indicate that 10 to 12% of individuals in the birth-to-age-22 group have disabilities and could benefit from special education services, including physical education.

Incidence

Incidence is the frequency of occurrence of a condition in relation to the population. Incidence varies by age groups (e.g., muscular dystrophy affects 1 out of 500 children but only 3 out of 100,000 persons when all age groups are combined).

Table B.1 gives insight into conditions of high, moderate, and low incidence. Sources vary considerably on incidence statistics, so remember that the figures in the table are estimates.

Table B.1   Incidence of selected conditions for all age groups combined.

High-Incidence Conditions (Based on 1,000 Persons)		Moderate-Incidence Conditions (Based on 10,000 Persons)		Low-Incidence Conditions (Based on 100,000 Persons)	
Amputations	2	Achondroplasia	1	Apert's syndrome	0.5
Anorexia nervosa	4[a]	Arthrogryposis	3	Cri-du-chat	5
Arthritis	150	Asperger's syndrome	3	Friedreich's ataxia	2
Asthma	3–6	Blindness	2	Galactosemia	2.2
Autism	1.5	Cooley's anemia	9	Guillain-Barré	1
Cancer	250	Cornelia de Lange syndrome	1	Huntington's disease	6.5
Cerebral palsy	3.5	Cretinism	1.7	Hurler's syndrome	1
Cleft palate and/or lip	1	Hemophilia	1	Marfan's syndrome	5
Clubfoot (Talipes)	1.5	Neurofibromatosis	3	Muscular dystrophy	3
Congenital heart defects	6–10	Prader-Willi	1–2	Osteogenesis imperfecta	3
Congenital hip dislocation	1–3	Rett's syndrome	1	Perthes' condition	4–5
Convulsive disorders	5	Rubella syndrome	1	Phenylketonuria	7
Cystic fibrosis	1	Tourette's syndrome	4–5	Reye's syndrome	1
Deafness	9	Trisomy 18	3	Spinal cord injury	5
Depression	120	Turner's syndrome	1[a]	Tuberous sclerosis	1
Diabetes	30	Williams syndrome	0.5		
Down syndrome	1				
Fetal alcohol syndrome	2				
Fragile X syndrome	1				
Hard of hearing	32				
Klinefelter syndrome	1[b]				
Learning disabilities	3–20				
Mental illness	200				
Mental retardation	30				
Multiple sclerosis	1				
Noonan syndrome	1				
Obesity	200				
Parkinson's disease	4				
Schizophrenia	10				
Sickle-cell anemia	2[c]				
Spina bifida	1–3				

[a]Females only
[b]Males only
[c]Blacks only

Addresses of Sport Organizations

Table C.1   Multisport governing bodies and programs.

International Paralympic Committee (IPC)
Adenauerallee 212-214
53113 Bonn
Germany
Phone: 49 228-2097-200
Fax: 49-228-2097-209
E-mail: info@paralympic.org
Website: www.paralympic.org

National Disability Sports Alliance
25 West Independence Way
Kingston, RI 02881
Phone: 401-792-7130
Website: www.ndsaonline.org

Turning POINT (Paraplegics
On Independent Nature Trips)
403 Pacific Avenue
Terrell, TX 75160
972-524-4231 / pointntl@aol.com /
www.turningpoint1.com

American Association of
Adapted Sports Programs
Project ASPIRE
Phone: 404-294-0070
Fax: 404-294-5758
Website: www.aaasp.org

Canadian Wheelchair Sports Association
#200-2460 Lancaster Road
Ottawa, Ontario K1B 4S5,
Canada
Phone: 613-523-0004
Fax: 613-523-0149
Website: www.cwsa.ca

Casa Colina Center for
Rehabilitation
255 East Bonita Ave
Pomona, CA 91769
Phone: 909-596-7733
Fax: 909-596-0153
E-mail: rehab@casacolina.org
Website: www.casacolina.org

United States Olympic
Committee (USOC)
1750 East Boulder Street
Colorado Springs, CO 80909-5760
Phone: 719-578-4818
Fax: 719-578-4976
Website: www.usoc.com

Courage Center
3915 Golden Valley Road
Golden Valley, MN 55422
Phone: 1-888-846-8253
Fax: 763-520-0577
E-mail: courageinfo@courage.org
Website: www.courage.org

Rehabilitation Institute of Chicago (RIC)
345 E. Superior Street
Chicago, IL 60611
Phone: 1-800-354-7342
Fax: 312-908-1051
E-mail: webmaster@rehabchicago.org
Website: www.rehabchicago.org

Blaze Sports Clubs of America
1775 The Exchange
Suite 540
Atlanta, GA 30339
Phone: 770-850-8199
Website: www.blazesports.com

Table C.2   Major disability sport organizations by disability.

Amputations and Les Autres Conditions

Disabled Sports/USA
451 Hungerford Drive, Suite 100
Rockville, MD 20850
Phone: 301-217-0968
Fax: 301-271-0963
E-mail: dsusa@dsusa.org
Website: www.dsusa.org

International Sports Organization for
the Disabled (ISOD)
Idrottens Hus
Storforsplan 44
12387, Farsta
Sweden

Blindness and Visual Impairment

U.S. Association for Blind Athletes
33 North Institute Street
Colorado Springs, CO 80903
Phone: 719-630-0422
Fax: 719-630-0616
E-mail: usaba@usa.net
Website: www.usaba.org

International Blind Sports Association
Jose Ortega y Gasset, 18
28006 Madrid, Spain
Phone: 34-1-589-4537
E-mail: ibsasecretary@fibertal.com.ar
Website: www.ibsa.es

Canadian Blind Sport Association
7 Mill Street, Lower Level
Almonte, ON KOA 1AO
Canada
Phone: 613-748-5609
Fax: 613-256-8759
E-mail: cbsa@istar.ca
Website: www.canadianblindsports.org

Ski for Light
1455 West Lake Street
Minneapolis, MN 55408
Phone: 612-827-3232
E-mail: info@sfl.org
Website: www.sfl.org

Table C.2   Continued.

**Cerebral Palsy, Stroke,
Traumatic Brain Injury**

National Disability Sports Alliance
25 West Independence Way
Kingston, RI 02881
Phone: 401-792-7130
Website: www.ndsaonline.org

Cerebral Palsy International Sports
and Recreation Association (CP–ISRA)
Secretariat CP-ISRA
PO Box 16
6666 ZG HETEREN
The Netherlands
Phone: 31-26-47-22-593
Fax: 31-26-47-23-914
E-mail: cpisra_nl@hotmail.com
Website: www.cpisra.org

Canadian Cerebral Palsy Sports Association
1010 Ploytek St, Unit #2, 2nd Floor
Gloucester, Ontario
Canada, K1J 9H9
Phone: 613-748-1340
Fax: 613-748-1355
E-mail: ccpsa@cyberus.ca
Website: www.ccpsa.ca

Traumatic Brain Injury
Contact NDSA
www.ndsaonline.org

Deafness

USA Deaf Sports Federation
102 North Krohn Place
Sioux Falls, SD 57103-1800
TTY: 605-367-5761
Phone: 605-367-5760
Fax: 605-367-5958
E-mail: homeoffice@usadsf.org
Website: www.usadsf.org

Gallaudet University
800 Florida Avenue NE
Washington, DC 20002-3625
Phone: 202-651-5000
E-mail: webmaster@gallaudet.edu
Website: www.gallaudet.edu

National Center on Deafness
California State University,
Northridge
18111 Nordhoff Street Maildrop 8267
Northridge, CA 91330
Phone: 818-677-2611 V/TDD
Fax: 818-677-4899
E-mail: ncod.tech@csun.edu
Website: www.ncod.csun.edu

Canadian Deaf Sports Association
4545 Ave. Pierre-De Coubertin
C.P. 1000, Succ. M
Montreal, Quebec
Canada, H1V 3R2
Phone: 1-800-855-5111
Fax: 514-252-3213
E-mail: office@assc-cdsa.com
Website: www.assc-cdsa.com

Dwarf

Dwarf Athletic Association of America
418 Willow Way
Lewisville, TX 75067
Phone: 972-317-8630
E-mail: daaa@flash.net
Website: www.daaa.org

Mental Retardation

Special Olympics International
1325 G Street, NW, Suite 500
Washington, DC 20005
Phone:202-628-3630
Fax: 202-824-0200
E-mail: info@specialolympics.org
Website: www.specialolympics.org

International Federation for Sport
for Persons with Intellectual
Disabilities (INAS-FID)
Contact IPC
info@paralympic.org

Spinal Paralysis

Wheelchair Sports, USA
10 Lake Circle, Suite G19
Colorado Springs, CO 80906
Phone: 719-574-9840
Fax: 719-574-9840
E-mail: wsusa@aol.com
Website: www.wsusa.org

International Stoke Mandeville
Wheelchair Sports Federation
Stoke Mandeville Sports Stadium
Olympic Village,
Guttmann Road Aylesburg
Bucks HP21 9PP
United Kingdom
Phone: 44-0-01296-436179
Fax: 44-0-01296-436484
E-mail: info@wsw.org.uk
Website: www.wsw.org.uk

Canadian Wheelchair Sports
Association
2460 Lancaster Road, Suite 200
Ottawa, Ontario
K1B 4S5
Canada
Phone: 613-523-0004
Fax: 613-523-0149
E-mail: info@cwsa.ca
Website: www.cwsa.ca

Table C.3   Sport organizations/contact for one sport.

Basketball

National Wheelchair Basketball Association
8245 Charles Crawford Lane
Charlotte, NC 28262
Phone: 704-547-0176
Fax: 704-446-4999
Website: www.nwba.org

Canadian Wheelchair Basketball
Association
Suite B2-2211 Riverside Drive
Ottawa, Ontario K1H 7X5, Canada
Phone: 613-260-1296
Fax: 613-260-1456
E-mail: cwba@cwba.ca
Website: www.cwba.ca

International Wheelchair
Basketball Federation
189 Watson Street #109
Winnipeg, Manitoba, R2P 2E1
Canada
204-632-6475 / morchard@mts.net /
www.iwbf.org

Boccia or Bocce

Capper Foundation
3500 SW 10th Avenue
Topeka, KS 66604-1995
Phone: 913-272-4060
Fax: 913-272-7912

National Disability Sports Alliance
25 West Independence Way
Kingston, RI 02881
Phone: 401-792-7130
Website: www.ndsaonline.org

Bowling

American Wheelchair
Bowling Association
2912 Country Woods Lane
Palm Harbor, FL 34683
727-734-0023 / www.awba.org

American Blind Bowling
Association
315 N. Main
Houston, PA 15342
Phone: 724-745-5986

Golf

Association of Disabled American
Golfers
PO Box 2647
Littleton, CO 80161-2647
Phone: 303-922-5228
E-mail: adag@usga.org
Website: www.adag.org

U.S. Golf Association
Resource Center for Individuals
with Disabilities
PO Box 708
Far Hills, NJ 07931
719-471-4810 ext.18
aphipps@usgafoundation.org

National Amputee Golf Association
11 Walnut Hill Road
Amherst, NH 03031
1-800-633-6242
www.nagagolf.org

Horseback Riding

North American Riding for the
Handicapped Association
PO Box 33150
Denver, CO 80233
Phone: 1-800-369-7433
Fax: 303-252-4610
E-mail: narha@narha.org
Website: www.narha.org

Quad Rugby

United States Quad Rugby
Association
1667 Auburn Road
Swedesboro, NJ 08085
Phone: 856-241-2440

Racquet Sports

International Tennis Federation
(Wheelchair Tennis Department)
Bank Lane, Roehampton
London SW15 5XZ, England
(011) 0044-(0)208-878-6464
0044-(0)208-392-4744 (fax)
www.itftennis.com
wheelchairtennis@itftennis.com

United States Tennis Association
70 W. Red Oak Lane
White Plains, NY 10604
914-696-7000
Fax: 696-7029
www.usta.com

United States Racquetball
Association
1685 West Uintah
Colorado Springs, CO 80904
Phone: 719-635-5396
Fax: 719-635-0685
E-mail: usragen@webaccess.net
Website: www.usra.org

Road Racing & Handcycling

U.S. Handcycling Federation
721 N. Taft Road
Ft. Collins, CO 80521
E-mail: info@ushf.org
Website: www.ushforg.org

Wheelchair Track and Field-USA
(WFTUSA)
2351 Parkwood Road
Snellville, GA 30039
770-972-0763 / 985-4885 (fax)

Shooting

National Wheelchair Shooting
Federation
102 Park Avenue
Rockledge, PA 19046
215-379-2359 / 663-9662 (fax)

NRA Disabled Shooting Services
11250 Waples Mill Road
Fairfax, VA 22030
Phone: 703-267-1495
Fax: 703-267-3941
Website: www.nra.org

Swimming/Aquatics

Aquatics Council/AAHPERD
c/o Sue Grosse
7252 Wabash Avenue
Milwaukee, WI 53223
Phone: 414-354-8717
sjgrosse@execpc.com

Council for National Cooperation in
Aquatics
c/o Louise Priest
901 W. New York Street
Indianapolis, IN 46202
Phone: 317-638-4238

USA Swimming
One Olympic Plaza
Colorado Springs, CO 80909
Phone: 719-578-4578
E-mail: ussinfo@usa-swimming.org
Website: www.usa-swimming.org

Table C.3   Continued.

U.S. Wheelchair Swimming, Inc.
c/o Wheelchair Sports, U.S.A.
3595 E. Fountain Boulevard, Suite L-1
Colorado Springs, CO 80910
719-574-1150 / 574-9840 (fax)

Water Skiers With
Disabilities Association
1251 Holy Cow Road
Polk City, FL 33868
1-800-533-2972 / 863-324-4341 /
325-8259 (fax) / www.usawaterski.org

Access to Sailing
6475 E. Pacific Coast Highway
Long Beach, CA 90803
562-881-0576 / 437-7655 (fax) /
atssailing@aol.com /
www.access2sailing.org

American Canoe Association
7432 Alban Station Blvd., Ste. B-232
Springfield, VA 22150
703-451-0141 / 451-2245 (fax) /
www.acanet.org

Handicapped Scuba Association
1104 El Prado
San Clemente, CA 92672
949-498-4540 / 498-6128 (fax) /
hsa@hsascuba.com /
www.hsascuba.com

U.S. Rowing Association
201 S. Capitol Avenue, Ste. 400
Indianapolis, IN 46225
317-237-5656 / 237-5646 (fax) /
www.usrowing.org

Softball/Baseball

National Wheelchair Softball
Association
1616 Todd Court
Hasting, MN 55033
Phone: 651-437-1792
Website: www.wheelchairsoftball.com

Challenger Baseball
Little League Headquarters
PO Box 3485
Williamsport, PA 17701
Website: www.littleleague.org/programs/
challenger.htm

National Beep Baseball
Association
4427 Knottynold
Houston, TX 77053
E-mail: info@nbba.org
Website: www.nbba.org

Weightlifting/Power lifting

U.S. Wheelchair Weightlifting Federation
39 Michael Place
Levittown, PA 19057
Phone: 215-945-1964
Fax: 215-946-2574
Website: www.wsusa.org/weightrule

NDSA Power lifting
25 W. Independence Way
Kingston, RI 02881
Phone: 401-792-7130
Website: www.ndsaonline.org

Winter Sports

Skiing for All
Disabled Sports USA
451 Hungerford Drive, Ste. 100
Rockville, MD 20850
310-217-0960

United States Ski and Snowboard
Association: Disabled Home Page
E-mail: ljohnson@ussa.org
www.usskiteam.com/disabled/disabled

National Sports Center for the Disabled
PO Box 1290
Winter Park, CO 80482
Phone: 970-726-1540
Fax: 970-726-4112
E-mail: info@nscd.org
Website: www.nscd.org

International Paralympic Committee
Sledge Hockey
www.paralympic.org/sports/sections/sledge
hockey.asp

U.S. Sled Hockey Association
710 N. Lake Shore Dr., 3rd Floor
Chicago, IL 60611
312-908-4292 / 908-1051 (fax)
www.sledhockey.org
info@sledhockey.org

Ski for Light, Inc.
1400 Carole Lane
Green Bay, WI 54313
920-494-5572 / 492-5821 / 492-5877 (fax)
pagsj@aol.com / www.sfl.org

Addresses of Other Organizations and Agencies

Note. Most e-mail addresses for content of this Appendix are embedded in the text.

Table D.1   Professional associations.

Adapted Physical Activity Council,
American Association for Active Lifestyles
and Fitness (AAALF), AAHPERD
c/o Dr. Janet Seaman
1900 Association Drive
Reston, VA 22091
1-800-213-7193, ext. 431
E-mail: jseaman@aahperd.org
Website: www.aahperd.org/aaalf

Adapted Physical Education
National Standards
(APENS); National Certification Exam
Dr. Tim Davis
Cortland State University
Cortland, NY 13077
Website: www.davist@cortland.edu
also www.cortland.edu/APENS

American College of Sports Medicine
PO Box 1440
Indianapolis, IN 46206-1440
317-637-9200
Fax: 317-634-7817
Website: www.acsm.org/index.asp

American Dance Therapy Association
2000 Century Plaza, Suite 108
Columbia, MD 21044
410-997-4040
Website: www.adta.org

American Occupational
Therapy Association
4720 Montgomery Lane
PO Box 31220
Bethesda, MD 20824-1220
1-800-377-8555
Website: www.aota.org

American Kinesiotherapy Association
PO Box 614
Wheeling, IL 60090-0614
1-800-296-AKTA
Website: www.akta.org

American Physical Therapy Association
1111 North Fairfax Street
Alexandria, VA 22314
1-800-999-2782
Website: www.apta.org

American Psychological Association
750 First Street NE
Washington, DC 20002
Website: www.apa.org

American Therapeutic
Recreation Association
PO Box 15215
Hattiesburg, MS 93404-5215
1-800-553-0304
www.atra-tr.org/atra.htm

Canadian Association for Health, Physical
Education, and Recreation (Suite 606)
1600 James Naismith Drive
Gloucester, Ontario K1B 5N4, Canada
Website: www.cahperd.ca/e

Council for Exceptional Children (CEC)
1110 N. Glebe Road, Suite 300
Arlington, VA 22201-5704
1-888-232-7733
Website: www.cec.sped.org

International Federation of
Adapted Physical Activity (IFAPA)
Contact Dr. Claudine Sherrill, President
11168 Windjammer Drive
Frisco, TX 75034
E-mail: csherrill1@earthlink.net
Website: www.IFAPA.net

National Association of
State Directors of Special Education
1800 Diagonal Road, Suite 320
Alexandria, VA 22314
703-519-3800
Website: www.nasdse.org

National Center on Physical Activity
and Disability (NCPAD)
University of Illinois at Chicago
1640 West Roosevelt Road, Suite 711
Chicago, IL 60608-6904
E-mail: ncpad@uic.edu
Website: www.ncpad.org

National Consortium for Physical Education
and Recreation for Individuals with
Disabilities (NCPERID)
(Address changes every 2 years with
new president)
Contact Dr. Daniel Webb
NCPERID Newsletter Editor
North Carolina A&T State University
Dept. of Human Performance and
Leisure Studies
Greensboro, NC 27411
336-334-7712
E-mail: dwebb@ncat.edu
Website: www.ncperid.usf.edu

National Dance Association
1900 Association Drive
Reston, VA 22091
Website: www.aahperd.org/nda/
nda-main.html

National Rehabilitation Association
633 S. Washington Street
Alexandria, VA 22314
Website: www.nationalrehab.org

National Therapeutic Recreation Society
2775 S. Quincy Street, Suite 300
Arlington, VA 22206
1-800-626-6772

Rehabilitation International USA
25 East 21st Street
New York, NY 10010
Website: www.rehab-international.org

TASH
29 W. Sesquehanna Avenue, Suite A210
Baltimore, MD 21204
1-800-482-8274
Website: www.tash.org

VSA Arts
John F. Kennedy Center for Performing Arts
1300 Connecticut Avenue NW, Suite 700
Washington, DC 20036
1-800-933-8721
Website: www.vsarts.org

Table D.2   Nonsport associations related to disabilities.

Autism

Autism Society of America
7910 Woodmont Avenue, Suite 650
Bethesda, MD 20814
1-800-3-AUTISM
Website: www.autism-
society.org/site/PageServer

Blind

American Foundation for the Blind
11 Penn Plaza, Suite 300
New York, NY 10001
1-800-232-5463
Website: www.afb.org

Association for the Education and
Rehabilitation of the Blind and Visually
Impaired—Bulletin for Physical Educators
206 N. Washington Street, Suite 320
Alexandria, VA 22314
Website: www.aerbvi.org

**Cerebral Palsy and
Traumatic Brain Injury**

American Academy for Cerebral Palsy and
Developmental Medicine
6300 N. River Road, Suite 727
Rosemont, IL 60018
708-698-1635
Website: www.aacpdm.org/home.html

Brain Injury Association
1776 Massachusetts Avenue NW, Suite 100
Washington, DC 20036-1904
202-296-6443
www.biausa.org/Pages/splash.html

National Easter Seal Society, Inc.
230 West Monroe Street, Suite 1800
Chicago, IL 60606
1-800-221-6827
Website: www.easter-
seals.org/site/PageServer

United Cerebral Palsy Associations
1660 L Street NW, Suite 700
Washington, DC 20036
1-800-872-5827
Website: www.ucp-utica.org

Dwarf

Little People of America
PO Box 9897
Washington, DC 20016
1-800-24-DWARF
Website: www.lpaonline.org

Deaf

Alexander Graham Bell Association
for the Deaf
3417 Volta Place NW
Washington, DC 20007
Website: www.agbell.org

Gallaudet College
800 Florida Avenue NE
Washington, DC 20002-3625
202-651-5000
Website: www.gallaudet.edu

Helen Keller National Center for
Deaf-Blind Youths and Adults
111 Middle Neck Road
Sands Point, NY 11050
Website: www.helenkeller.org

National Association of the Deaf
814 Thayer Avenue
Silver Spring, MD 20910
301-587-1788
Website: www.nad.org

Learning Disabilities

Council for Learning Disabilities
PO Box 40303
Overland Park, KS 66204
913-492-8755
Website: www.cldinternational.org/

Learning Disability Association of
America (LDA)
(formerly ACLD)
4156 Library Road
Pittsburgh, PA 15234
412-341-1515
Website: www.ldanatl.org

Mental Retardation

American Association on
Mental Retardation
444 N. Capitol Street NW, Suite 846
Washington, DC 20001-1512
1-800-424-3688
Website: www.aamr.org

The ARC (formerly Association for
Retarded Citizens)
1010 Wayne Avenue, Suite 650
Silver Spring, MD 20910-5638
1-800-433-5255
Website: www.thearc.org

National Down Syndrome Congress
1605 Chantilly Drive, Suite 250
Atlanta, GA 30324
1-800-232-6372
Website: www.ndsccenter.org

National Down Syndrome Society
666 Broadway
New York, NY 10012
1-800-221-4602
Website: www.nads.org

National Fragile X Foundation
1441 York St., Suite 303
Denver, CO 80206
1-800-688-8765
Website: www.fragilex.org/home.htm

Physical Disabilities

Muscular Dystrophy Association (MDA)
3300 East Sunrise Drive
Tucson, AZ 85718
520-529-2000
Website: www.mdausa.org

National Spinal Cord Injury Association
545 Concord Avenue, No. 29
Cambridge, MA 02138
1-800-962-9629
Website: www.spinalcord.org

Paralyzed Veterans of America
801 18th Street NW
Washington, DC 20006
1-800-424-8200
Website: www.pva.org

Spina Bifida Association of America
4590 MacArthur Boulevard NW, Suite 250
Washington, DC 20007
1-800-621-3141
Website: www.sbaa.org

Table D.3   Voluntary health organizations.

American Disabilities Act
1-800-514-0301
www.usdoj.gov/crt/ada/adahom1.htm

American Cancer Society
1599 Clifton Road NE
Atlanta, GA 30329
www.cancer.org/docroot/home/index.asp

American Diabetes Association
PO Box 25757
1660 Duke Street
Alexandria, VA 22314
www.diabetes.org/main/application/
commercewf

American Heart Association
7272 Greenville Avenue
Dallas, TX 75231-4596
214-373-6300
Website: www.americanheart.org

American Lung Association
1740 Broadway
New York, NY 10019
Website: www.lungusa.org

American Red Cross
17th and D Streets NW
Washington, DC 20006
Website: www.redcross.org

Arthritis Foundation
1314 Spring Street NW
Atlanta, GA 30309
Website: www.arthritis.org

Asthma and Allergy Foundation of America
1125 15th Street NW, Suite 502
Washington, DC 20005
1-800-7-ASTHMA
Website: www.aafa.org

American Stroke Association
7272 Greenville Ave.
Dallas, TX 75231
Phone: 1-888-4-STROKE (478-7653)
Fax: 214-706-5231
Website: www.StrokeAssociation.org

Cystic Fibrosis Foundation
6931 Arlington Road, No. 200
Bethesda, MD 20814
Website: www.cff.org

Epilepsy Foundation of America
4351 Garden City Drive
Landover, MD 20785
Website: www.epilepsyfoundation.org

National Hemophilia Foundation
110 Greene Street, Room 406
New York, NY 10012
Website: www.hemophilia.org

National Multiple Sclerosis Society
733 Third Avenue
New York, NY 10017
Website: www.nmss.org

Table D.4   Federal government agencies that determine policies, make grant awards, and monitor compliance with laws.

1. Office of Special Education and Rehabilitative Services (OSERS)
   www.ed.gov/offices/OSERS/
   Highest-level office within the Department of Education focused on improving results and outcomes for individuals with disabilities of all ages. Has three subcomponents, as follows:

   (a) Office of Special Education Programs (OSEP)
       www.ed.gov/offices/OSERS/OSEP/
       OSEP administers IDEA. Provides leadership and financial support to assist states, and through them, local school districts. Responsible for individuals with disabilities from birth through age 21.

   (b) National Institute on Disability and Rehabilitation Research (NIDRR)
       www.ed.gov/offices/OSERS/NIDRR/
       NIDRR generates, disseminates, and promotes new knowledge to improve options available to individuals with disabilities through grant awards. Its research focus includes such areas as health and function, independent living and community integration, employment, and technology for access and function.

   (c) Rehabilitation Services Administration (RSA)
       www.ed.gov/offices/OSERS/RSA/
       RSA administers the Vocational Rehabilitation Act of 1973, expected to be reauthorized in 2003. Provides grants to state vocational rehabilitation (VR) agencies to provide employment-related services for individuals with disabilities, helps to support independent living centers, transition, and such supports as job training, counseling, and medical and psychological services.

2. National Institutes of Health (NIH)
   www.nih.gov/
   NIH is the highest-level office within the Department of Health and Human Services' Public Health Service. It oversees the medical and behavioral research and policies for the nation.

3. Office of Civil Rights (OCR)
   www.ed.gov/offices/OCR or ocr@ed.gov
   OCR is one place to file complaints for IDEA, Section 504, and ADA violations. Contact information for 12 regional OCR offices is available in Siegel (2002).

Addresses for Purchasing Journals and Materials

Table E.1   **Books, journals, and videos.**

McGraw-Hill Higher Education
2460 Kerper Boulevard
Dubuque, IA 52001
1-800-338-5578
Publishes several textbooks
Website: www.mhhe.com

Challenge Publications Ltd.
P.O. Box 508
Macomb, IL 61455
309-833-1902
Publishes **Palaestra**
Website: www.chall-pub.fsnet.co.uk/
index.htm

Charles C Thomas
2600 S. First Street
PO Box 19265
Springfield, IL 62794-9265
1-800-258-8980
Fax: 217-789-9130
Website: www.ccthomas.com

Front Row Experience
540 Discovery Bay Boulevard
Discovery Bay, CA 94514-9454
1-800-524-9091
Website: www.frontrowexperience.com

Holcomb Hathaway, Publishers
6207 N. Cattle Track Road, Suite 5
Scottsdale, AZ 85250-4681
480-991-7881
Website www.hh-pub.com
Publishes adapted physical education texts

Human Kinetics Publishers
Box 5076
Champaign, IL 61825-5076
1-800-747-4457
Website: www.humankinetics.com/
Publishes **Adapted Physical Activity Quarterly** and several textbooks

Paralyzed Veterans of America/
Sports 'N Spokes
211 East Highland, Suite 180
Phoenix, AZ 85016
602-224-0500 or 1-888-888-2201
Publishes **Sports 'N Spokes,** which is a major information source for purchase of wheelchairs and products used by people in wheelchairs
www.sportsnspokes.com
Also publishes **PN/Paraplegic News**
www.pn-magazine.com

Paul H. Brookes
P.O. Box 10624
Baltimore, MD 21285-0624
Phone: 1-800-638-3775
Fax: 410-337-8539
Website: www.brookespublishing.com

Pro•Ed
8700 Shoal Creek Boulevard
Austin, TX 78757-6897
512-451-3246
Publishes **Academic Therapy, Focus on Autism and Other Disabilities, Journal of Learning Disabilities, Topics in Early Childhood Special Education,** and other journals
Website: www.proedinc.com/

Research Press
Behavior Management Videos
Box 31775
Champaign, IL 60820
Website: pubs.nrc-cnrc.gc.ca/
rp2_home_e.html

SPORT Database
1600 James Naismith Drive
Gloucester, Ontario K1B 5N4, Canada
Produces comprehensive reference lists and computerized data

Venture Publishing, Inc.
1999 Cato Avenue
State College, PA 16801
814-234-4561
Website: www.venturepublish.com
Publishes recreation and leisure books

Table E.2   Equipment and Music Companies.

Equipment

Abilitations
One Sportime Way
Atlanta, Georgia 30340
Phone: 1-800-850-8602
Fax: 1-800-845-1535
Website: www.abilitations.com

Athletic Stuff
PO Box 1769
Nipomo, CA 93444
Phone: 1-877-406-0607
Fax: 1-805-929-6014
Website: www.athleticstuff.com

FlagHouse (and Project ASPIRE)
601 FlagHouse Drive
Hasbrouck Hts., NJ 07604-3116
Phone: 1-800-793-7900
Fax: 1-800-793-7922
Website: www.flaghouse.com

GOPHER
220 24th Ave. Northwest
PO Box 998
Owatonna, MN 55060-0998
Phone: 1-800-533-0446
1-507-451-7470
Fax: 1-800-451-4855
1-507-451-4755
Website: www.gophersport.com

NASCO
901 Janesville Ave.
PO Box 901
Fort Akinson, WI 53538-0901
Phone: 1-800-563-2446
Fax: 920-563-8296
Website: www.eNASCO.com

Omnikin, Inc.
PO Box 45009
CHARNY (QC) G6X 3R4
Canada
Phone: 1-800-706-6645
Fax: 418-832-6932
Website: www.omnikin.com

Polo Sports
11711 South Austin Ave.
Alsip, IL 60803
Phone: 1-800-233-5484
Fax: 1-877-800-5973
Website: www.polosport.com

S & S Worldwide
PO Box 513
Colchester, CT 06415-0513
Phone: 1-800-937-3482
Fax: 1-800-566-6678
Website: www.ssww.com

Sport For All
NASPE
1900 Association Drive
Reston, VA 20191-1598
Phone: 1-800-213-7193 ext. 483
Fax: 1-703-476-8316
Website: www.sportforall.net

Sportime International (APAC, AAALF
Sponsor)
1 Sportime Way
Atlanta, GA 30340
Phone: 1-800-283-5700
Fax: 1-800-845-1535
Website: www.sportime.com

U.S. Games
PO Box 117028
Carrollton, TX 75011-7028
Phone: 1-800-327-0484
Fax: 1-800-899-0149
Website: www.us-games.com

Music Resources

Kimbo Educational
Department F
PO Box 477
Long Branch, NJ 07740
Phone: 1-800-631-2187
Fax: 732-870-3340
Website: www.kimboed.com

Educational Activities, Inc.
PO Box 392
Freeport, NY 11520
Phone: 1-800-645-3739
Fax: 1-516-623-9282
Website: www.edact.com

Melody House
819 NW 92nd Street
Oklahoma City, OK 73114
Phone: 1-800-243-9228
Fax: 1-405-840-3384
Website: www.melodyhousemusic.com

Music for Little People
PO Box 1460
Redway, CA 95560-1460
Phone: 1-800-346-4445
Fax: 1-707-923-3241
Website: www.mflp.com

Wagon Wheel Recording & Books
16812 Pembrook Lane
Huntington Beach, CA 92649
Phone: 714-846-8169
Fax: 714-846-8169

Table E.3   Aquatic Supplies and Equipment.

**Websites with Links
to Equipment Vendors**

What You Need to Know About Swimming
swimming.about.com/mbody.htm
Search for "equipment."

Yahoo Sports: Swimming and Diving
dir.yahoo.com/Recreation/Sports/
Swimming_and_Diving/
Click on "shopping and services."

SwimInfo
www.swiminfo.com
Go to "swim shop" and select the
equipment of interest.

Selected Websites for Equipment Vendors

Kiefer On-Line Swim Shop
www.kiefer.com
Excellent source of lifeguarding and safety
equipment, as well as aquatic exercise,
learn-to-swim, and competitive swimming
equipment.

Recreonics
www.recreonics.com
Great source of swimming pool equipment
such as pool lifts and safety equipment.

Danmar Products
www.danmarproducts.com
Specialized flotation devices for persons
with disabilities. Click on "customer
catalog," then "swimming aids."

Table E.4   Test and curriculum materials.

American Guidance Service (AGS)
P.O. Box 99
Circle Pines, MN 55014-1796
800-328-2560
Website: www.agsnet.com
**Bruininks-Oseretsky Test and Body
Skills: A Motor Development Curriculum**

Paul H. Brookes Publishing Company
P.O. Box 10624
Baltimore, MD 21285
(800) 638-3775
Website: www.brookespublishing.com
**Bricker's Assessment, Evaluation,
and Programming System; Carolina
Curriculum; Transdisciplinary
Play-Based Assessment and Curriculum**

Council for Exceptional Children (CEC)
1110 N. Glebe Rd., Suite 300
Arlington, VA 22201-5764
(888) 232-7733
Website: www.cec.sped.org
Special education assessment materials and
curricula

Canadian Association for Health, Physical
Education, and Recreation
1600 James Naismith Drive
Gloucester, Ontario K1B 5N4, Canada
www.cahperd.ca/e
**Moving to Inclusion Curriculum; PREP
materials, Canadian fitness tests**

Cooper Institute for Aerobics Research
12330 Preston Road
Dallas, TX 75230
(800) 635-7050
www.fitnessgram.net
www.activitygram.net
FITNESSGRAM and ACTIVITYGRAM
materials

Denver Developmental Materials, Inc.
Ladoca Publishing
5100 Lincoln St.
Denver, CO 80216
**Denver Developmental Screening Test;
Denver II**

President's Council on Physical
Fitness & Sports
200 Independence Ave. SW,
Washington DC 20201
www.presidentialchallenge.org
**Free PCPFS Research Digest quarterly
Presidential Active Lifestyle Award
(PALA) materials**

Pro•Ed
8700 Shoal Creek Boulevard
Austin, TX 78757-6897
(512) 451-3246
Website: www.proedline.com
I CAN physical education materials, **Test of
Gross Motor Development (TGMD 1 and
2),** data-based gymnasium materials,
behavior management and social skills
curricula

Psychological Corporation
19500 Bulverde Rd.
San Antonio, TX 78259
(800) 872-1726
Website: www.psychcorp.com
Movement ABC; TOMI revisions; **Bayley
Scales II**

Special Olympics International
Sports Training Curricula
Attn: Finance/Publications
1325 G Street NW, Suite 500
Washington, DC 20005-4709
(202) 628-3630
Website: www.specialolympics.org
Sports skills program guides for all major
summer and winter sports, applicable to all
disabilities

Western Psychological Services (WPS)
12031 Wilshire Boulevard
Los Angeles, CA 90025
(800) 222-2670
Self-concept and personality inventories;
counseling materials; Ayres sensory
integration tests
www.wpspublish.com

Important Events in Special Education, Adapted Physical Activity, and Disability Sport

Early 1800s Roots of special education can be traced mostly to France, England, and Switzerland. Early corrective physical education came mostly from Sweden.

1817 The first residential schools established in the United States were for deaf students: the American School for the Deaf in Hartford, CT, and the New York School for the Deaf in White Plains, NY, founded in 1817 and 1818, respectively. Thomas Hopkins Gallaudet is credited with founding the school in Connecticut. In 1856, the institution now known as Gallaudet University, Washington, DC, evolved through the efforts of philanthropist Amos Kendall.

1830 The first residential schools for individuals with blindness in the United States were founded between 1830 and 1833 in Boston, New York, and Philadelphia. Only one of the early residential facilities, the Perkins Institution in Boston, provided physical education for its students.

1847 *The American Annals of the Deaf,* first published in 1847, is the oldest educational journal in the United States still in existence.

1848 The first residential institution for persons with mental retardation in the United States was organized in Massachusetts.

1863 The earliest residential facilities for persons with physical disabilities bore such names as Hospital of the New York Society for the Relief of the Ruptured and Crippled (1863) and Home for Incurables in Philadelphia (1877).

1864 Edouard Seguin's classic book *Idiocy and Its Diagnoses and Treatment by the Physiological Method* was translated into English. This book provided the framework for the earliest attempts to train persons with mental retardation. Seguin was a student and

protégé of Jean-Marc Itard, of France known for his work with Victor, the "Wild Boy of Aveyron," in the early 1800s.

1876 Establishment of the American Association on Mental Deficiency (AAMD). First president was Edouard Seguin. One of its original goals was to promote the development of residential facilities. During the first decade of AAMD's existence, 20 states created residential schools for persons with MR.

1885 Formation of the Association for the Advancement of Physical Education, the forerunner of AAHPERD. First president was Edward Hitchcock, MD. Almost all the early members were physicians.

1885 Baron Nils Posse of Sweden introduced Per Henrik Ling's medical gymnastics into the United States. This was the beginning of corrective physical education (now called adapted physical activity service delivery).

1895 The National Education Association (NEA) organized a Department of Physical Education.

1899 Public schooling for persons with disabilities had begun, with the earliest documentation citing 100 large cities with special education classes. Among these were Boston, Chicago, Cleveland, Detroit, New York, and Milwaukee.

1902 The National Education Association organized a Department of Special Education. Alexander Graham Bell, pioneer in deaf education, spearheaded this recognition.

1905 Therapeutic Section of the American Physical Education Association (APEA) began with Baroness Rose Posse as chair. *This date is often used to mark the beginning of the adapted physical activity profession.*

1906 Formation of the Playground Association of America, the forerunner

of National Recreation and Park Association (NRPA), of which the National Therapeutic Recreation Society (NTRS) is a subdivision. First president was Dr. Luther Halsey Gulick.

1912 Establishment of Children's Bureau in Washington, DC, to promote the welfare of children and to prevent their exploitation in industry.

1917 Origin of the National Society for the Promotion of Occupational Therapy, the forerunner of the American Occupational Therapy Association (1921). First president was William Rush Dunton, Jr., now considered the "father of OT."

1919 National Easter Seals Society for Crippled Children and Adults founded. It is still operative.

1920 The National Civilian Vocational Rehabilitation Act, a forerunner of the Social Security Act, passed.

1921 Origin of forerunner of American Physical Therapy Association. First president was Mary McMillan, who strongly influenced early leaders in corrective physical education who were also physical therapists: George Stafford and Josephine Rathbone.

1922 Establishment of Council for Exceptional Children (CEC), the first organization to advocate for all groups with disabilities. First president was Elizabeth Farrell.

1928 First textbooks to use the term *corrective physical education* were published:

Stafford, G.T. (1928). *Preventive and corrective physical education.* New York: A.S. Barnes.

Lowman, C., Colestock, C., & Cooper, H. (1928). *Corrective physical education for groups.* New York: A.S. Barnes.

1930 Historic White House Conference on Child Health and Protection. The Committee on the

Physically and Mentally Handicapped wrote the often-quoted Bill of Rights for Handicapped Children.

1935 Social Security Act passed.

1944, 1952, also **1915–17** Major epidemics of poliomyelitis, which left thousands of persons paralyzed. In 1952 alone, 57,628 cases of polio were reported.

1944 Sir Ludwig Guttmann, a neurosurgeon, established the Stoke-Mandeville Hospital for treatment of spinal cord injuries and began experimenting with sport as rehabilitation.

1945 Formation of the American Athletic Association for the Deaf (AAAD). This was the first special population in the United States to form its own sport organization.

1946 Association for Physical and Mental Rehabilitation (APMR) established, the forerunner of American Kinesiotherapy Association (AKA). Name changed to American Corrective Therapy Association in 1967 and to AKA in 1983.

1949 Formation of the National Wheelchair Basketball Association (NWBA). Founder and first commissioner was Timothy Nugent, University of Illinois.

1950 The National Association for Music Therapy, Inc. (NAMT) formed.

1950 The National Association for Retarded Citizens (NARC) founded. Name changed in 1979 to Association for Retarded Citizens (ARC). In 1992, ARC became the name rather than the initials for words.

1952 Terminology officially changed from *corrective physical education* to *adapted physical education*. First definition of adapted physical education published by AAHPER.

1954 First textbook entitled *Adapted Physical Education* published. Author was Arthur Daniels of the Ohio State University.

1955 Salk vaccine recognized as 80 to 90% effective against paralytic polio.

1956 Formation of National Wheelchair Athletic Association (NWAA). Name changed to Wheelchair Sports, USA in 1994.

1958 National Foundation for Infantile Paralysis became The National Foundation—March of Dimes and turned attention to birth defects and genetic counseling.

1958 PL 85-926 was passed, authorizing grants for training personnel in mental retardation. This legislation represents the beginning of the federal government's commitment to the rights of persons with disabilities.

1959 Pioneer research on mental retardation and motor development by Francis and Rarick published, which reported that children with MR were 2 to 4 years behind nondisabled peers.

1960 First Paralympic Games held in Rome (only athletes with spinal paralysis competed). This was the first time that the International Stoke-Mandeville Games were held in conjunction with Olympic Games.

1961 Kennedy appointed the first President's Panel on Mental Retardation.

1963 PL 88-164 amended 1958 legislation to encompass all handicapped groups that required special education.

1964 Civil rights legislation (PL 88-352) passed.

1964 Association for Children with Learning Disabilities (ACLD) formed. Name changed in 1980 to ACLD, Inc. (An Association for Children and Adults with Learning Disabilities) and in 1990 to LDA (Learning Disability of America).

1965 PL 89-10, the Elementary and Secondary Education Act (ESEA), passed. Included Titles I to IV. Illustrative funded programs were Vodola's Project ACTIVE in New Jersey and Long's Project PEOPEL in Arizona.

1965 Eunice Kennedy Shriver was keynote speaker at AAHPER conference in Dallas. Her challenge to professionals was the beginning of awareness of needs of people with mental retardation.

1965 The AAHPER Project on Recreation and Fitness for the Mentally Retarded was formed with a grant from the Joseph P. Kennedy, Jr. Foundation.

This project was the forerunner of the Unit on Programs for the Handicapped, directed by Julian U. Stein, which served AAHPERD members from 1968 to 1981.

1966 American Dance Therapy Association, Inc. (ADTA) founded in New York City.

1966 Bureau of Education for the Handicapped (BEH) created by PL 89-750 within the Office of Education of HEW. BEH, which became the Office of Special Education Programs (OSEP) in 1980, is the agency that funds university training programs in physical education and recreation for persons with disabilities.

1966 Hollis Fait of University of Connecticut began battle concerning name of the profession by changing title of his textbook from *Adapted Physical Education* (1st ed., 1960) to *Special Physical Education*. This battle ended in late 1980s. Fait lost the battle.

1967 Formation of the National Handicapped Sports and Recreation Association (NHSRA), which governs winter and amputee sports. Name changed to National Handicapped Sports (NHS) in 1992 and to Disabled Sports/USA in 1995.

1967 ESEA amended under PL 90-170, Title V, Section 502, to support training, research, and demonstration projects in physical education and recreation for individuals with disabilities.

1967 National Therapeutic Recreation Society (NTRS) created as a branch of the National Recreation and Park Association.

1968 AAHPER Unit on Programs for the Handicapped approved. This replaced Project on Recreation and Fitness for the Mentally Retarded. Director until 1981 was Julian U. Stein.

1968 Special Olympics founded by Eunice Kennedy Shriver. AAHPER-Kennedy Foundation Special Fitness Awards established. First director of Special Olympics was Frank Hayden of Canada.

1968 First master's degree specialization in adapted physical education established by Joseph

Winnick at State University of New York (SUNY) at Brockport.

1969 First doctoral programs in adapted physical education established at several universities with help of federal funding (PL 90-170).

1970 Title VI, Public Law 91-230, Education of the Handicapped Act (EHA), passed. This was the first major legislation leading to the subsequent passage of PL 94-142 in 1975.

1970 Series of institutes sponsored by BEH held on the Development of AAHPER Guidelines for Professional Preparation Programs for Personnel Involved in Physical Education and Recreation for the Handicapped. Report published by AAHPER in 1973.

1972 Information and Research Utilization Center (IRUC) in Physical Education and Recreation for the Handicapped funded by BEH and established in conjunction with AAHPER Unit on Programs for the Handicapped. Julian U. Stein was director.

1972 Title IX legislation (PL 92-318) passed.

1972 AC/FMR (Accreditation Council for Facilities for the Mentally Retarded) issued standards, including recreation services, which all residential and intermediate care facilities must implement in order to receive accreditation. New AC/FMR standards are issued periodically.

1973 Section 504 of Rehabilitation Act (PL 93-112) enacted, mandating nondiscrimination in programs and facilities receiving federal funds. Not implemented, however, until 1977, when rules and regulations were published in the *Federal Register*.

1973 National Ad Hoc Committee on Physical Education and Recreation for the Handicapped formed by BEH project directors at Minneapolis (AAHPER) conference. This was the forerunner of the National Consortium (see 1975).

1973 International Federation of Adapted Physical Activity founded by Clermont Simard and colleagues in French-speaking Canada and Belgium. First symposium held in Montreal in 1977.

1974 At the annual conference in Anaheim, California, AAHPER was reorganized as the American Alliance for Health, Physical Education, and Recreation with seven independent associations. Three of these included programs for people with disabilities: ARAPCS (Association for Research, Administration, Professional Councils and Societies), NASPE (National Association for Sport and Physical Education), and AALR (American Association for Leisure and Recreation).

1974 Formation of the American Association for the Education of the Severely/Profoundly Handicapped (AAESPH). In 1980, the name of this organization changed to The Association for the Severely Handicapped (TASH) and the title of its journal became *JASH, Journal of Association for Severely Handicapped*.

1975 National Consortium on Physical Education and Recreation for the Handicapped (NCPERH) evolved from National Ad Hoc Committee. First president was Leon Johnson, University of Missouri. Name changed in 1992 to National Consortium for Physical Education and Recreation for Individuals With Disabilities (NCPERID).

1975 PL 94-142 enacted. Called the "Education for All Handicapped Children Act," it stated specifically that *instruction in physical education* shall be provided for all children with disabilities.

1976 Formation of the U.S. Association for Blind Athletes (USABA).

1976 The Olympiad for the Physically Handicapped held in Canada in conjunction with the Olympic Games. This was the first time that athletes with blindness and amputations were recognized and allowed to participate.

1976 White House Conference on Handicapped Individuals (WHCHI) held. The final report included 420 recommendations, several of which pertained to recreation and leisure.

1977 First National Championships, U.S. Association for Blind Athletes.

1977 Regulations to implement Section 504 of PL 93-112, the Rehabilitation Act of 1973, published in May 4 issue of *Federal Register*.

1977 Regulations to implement PL 94-142 published in the August 23 issue of the *Federal Register*. (See Chapter 4.)

1977 First Annual National Wheelchair Marathon held in conjunction with the Boston Marathon (26.2 mi).

1978 Formation of the National Association of Sports for Cerebral Palsy (NASCP). Name changed in 1986 to U.S. Cerebral Palsy Athletic Association and in 2001 to National Disability Sports Alliance (NDSA).

1978 PL 95-606, the Amateur Sports Act, recognized the sport organizations of athletes with disabilities as part of the U.S. Olympic Committee structure.

1979 The U.S. Olympic Committee (USOC) organized a Committee for the Handicapped in Sports, with Kathryn Sallade Barclift elected as its first chairperson. This committee brought together for the first time representatives from the five major sport organizations for athletes with disabilities. Later named Committee on Sports for the Disabled (COSD) and dissolved in early 2000.

1979 PL 96-88 changed the status of the old U.S. Office of Education within the Department of Health, Education, and Welfare (HEW) to a Department of Education. Shirley M. Hufstedler was appointed its first secretary. HEW was disbanded.

1979 AAHPER's name officially changed to AAHPERD (American Alliance for Health, Physical Education, Recreation, and Dance), thereby giving recognition to dance as a discipline separate from physical education.

1980 Reorganization completed for the two new departments replacing HEW. These new structures are the Department of Education (ED) and the Department of Health and Human Services (HHS). Within ED's seven principal program offices, the **Office of Special Education and Rehabilitative Services** (OSERS) relates to people with disabilities. Principal components of OSERS are Office of Special Education Programs (OSEP), which replaces BEH; Rehabilitation Services Administration (RSA); and National

Institute on Disability and Rehabilitation Research.

1981 New AAHPERD guidelines (competencies) on adapted physical education published. Edited by Julian U. Stein.

1981 Declared the "International Year of the Disabled" by the United Nations.

1981 January 19 issue of *Federal Register* (Vol. 46, No. 12) devoted to IEPs, including clarifications for physical education.

1981 Formation of the U.S. Amputee Athletic Association (USAAA). Dissolved in 1990.

1982 First UNESCO-sponsored international symposium on physical education and sport programs for persons with physical and mental disabilities. Leader was Julian U. Stein.

1984 International Games for the Disabled (blind, cerebral palsied, amputee, and les autres) held in Long Island, NY, with approximately 2,500 athletes competing. Seventh World Wheelchair Games (spinally paralyzed) held in England.

1984 *Adapted Physical Activity Quarterly* first published by Human Kinetics. This was first professional journal to be devoted specifically to adapted physical activity. Geoffrey Broadhead was founding editor.

1984 *Palaestra: Forum of Sport, Physical Education & Recreation for Those With Disabilities* first published. This was a specialized journal for adapted physical activity, sport, and recreation. David Beaver remains founder/owner/editor.

1985 Merger completed within AAHPERD of NASPE Adapted Physical Education Academy and ARAPCS Therapeutic Council. The new structure was called the Adapted Physical Activity Council and was housed within ARAPCS. See 1993 for current names.

1986 Canadian adapted physical activity movement was stimulated by Jasper Conference on Strategies for Change.

1986 *Sport and Disabled Athletes,* the proceedings of the Olympic Scientific Congress, published by Human Kinetics. This was the first published source of information on all disability sports. Editor was Claudine Sherrill.

1988 Paralympics held in Korea. This was the first time that all athletes with physical disabilities competed at the same site (i.e., athletes with spinal paralysis (see 1960 and 1984) joined athletes with other physical disabilities).

1989 Revitalization of International Federation of Adapted Physical Activity (IFAPA) with symposium in Berlin directed by Gudrun Doll-Tepper. Marks beginning of international era.

1990 Americans with Disabilities Act (PL 101-336) enacted.

1990 Individuals With Disabilities Education Act (PL 101-476) enacted. Person-first philosophy and terminology established. Rules and regulations published in September 29, 1992, *Federal Register.*

1990 PL 101-613 established the National Center for Medical Rehabilitation Research (NCMRR) as part of the National Institute of Child Health and Human Development (NICHD) at the National Institutes of Health (NIH) of the U.S. Department of Health and Human Services in Bethesda, Maryland. The mission of NCMRR is to enhance quality of life for people with disabilities through the support of research on restoration, replacement, enhancement, or prevention of the deterioration of functions. This broad mission encompasses physical activity for health and wellness.

1991 European Master's Degree Program in Adapted Physical Activity (EMDAPA) established in Leuven, Belgium. Director remains Herman Van Coppenolle.

1992 Montreal Symposium on Adapted Physical Activity conducted by Greg Reid. Planning for a North American regional affiliate of IFAPA began.

1992 National Consortium on Physical Education and Recreation for Individuals with Disabilities (NCPERID) received 5-year grant from federal government to develop adapted physical education national standards (APENS) and a national certification exam. Project director was Luke Kelly.

1992 Paralympics held in Barcelona, Spain. This was the first time that integrated classifications were used.

1993 First quadrennial International Special Olympics Meet held outside of USA. World Winter Games in Salzburg, Austria.

1993 AAHPERD's ARAPCS was changed to the American Association for Active Lifestyles and Fitness (AAALF). This is the AAHPERD structure that adapted physical activity personnel join because it contains the Adapted Physical Activity Council (APAC). Janet Seaman is director.

1994 *Adapted Physical Activity Quarterly* became the official journal of the International Federation of Adapted Physical Activity (IFAPA).

1994 North American Federation of Adapted Physical Activity (NAFAPA) founded as a regional affiliate of IFAPA at symposium directed by Gail Dummer at Michigan State University. Dale Ulrich was first president.

1994 First federally-funded conference on the Health of Women with Physical Disabilities conducted by NCMRR of NIH. See resulting book edited by Krostoski, Nosek, and Turk (1996).

1995 Adapted Physical Education National Standards (APENS) authored by NCPERID published by Human Kinetics. APENS specifies knowledge related to 15 standards to be tested by the national certification exam.

1995 Deaf sport group withdrew from Paralympic movement.

1996 Paralympics held in Atlanta. This was first Paralympics to include athletes with mental disabilities at the same competition site and events.

1996 Gudrun Doll-Tepper elected president of the International Council of Sport Science and Physical Education (ICSSPE), an indicator of acceptance of adapted physical activity by the other sport science associations.

1997 Adapted physical activity included as one of the nine basic sport science disciplines in textbook, *The History of Exercise and Sport Science,* edited by John Massengale and Richard Swanson. Considered evidence that adapted physical activity was accepted by other academic disciplines as an emerging scholarly discipline worthy of equal coverage.

1997 IDEA Amendments 1997 (PL 105-17) passed but regulations not printed until 1999.

1997 First cohort of adapted physical educators ($N = 219$) took APENS examination and began to use the acronym CAPE (Certified Adapted Physical Educator) after their names.

1998 Olympic and Amateur Sports Act (PL 105-277) enacted. This gave the United States Olympic Committee (USOC) total responsibility for Paralympics.

1999 Regulations published for IDEA Amendments 1997.

1999 American Athletic Association for the Deaf (AAAD) changed name to USA Deaf Sports Federation (USADSF).

2000 Paralympics (summer) held in Sydney, Australia. International Paralympic Committee (IPC) held elections, and presidency changed from Robert D. Steadward of Canada to Philip Craven of Great Britain. Craven (a wheelchair basketball leader) is first top leader since movement began in 1960 to come from the ranks of elite athletes with disabilities.

2001 World Health Organization (WHO) published revised version of the *International Classification of Impairments, Disabilities, and Handicaps (ICIDH)*.

2001 National Disability Sports Alliance (NDSA) became the new name of the United States Cerebral Palsy Sport Association (USCPAA). NDSA extended services to more disabilities and assumed governance of sports formerly under governance of the United States Les Autres Association, which was dissolved.

2001 No Child Left Behind Act (PL 107-110) enacted.

2001 September 11 memorialized as day to remember worldwide in the global fight against terrorism.

2002 *Special Olympics Get Into It,* a free curriculum that provides K–12 teachers with materials to teach *all students* to appreciate the uniqueness of every person, no matter his or her ability, was disseminated throughout the USA and later to 50 other countries.

2002 APENS responsibility for examinations and certifications passed from Ron French at Texas Woman's University to Timothy Davis at State University of New York, Cortland.

2002 American Association on Mental Retardation (AAMR) issued revision of 1992 definitions, classification, and systems of supports manual.

2003 IDEA Amendments expected to be enacted.

2003 Rehabilitation Act Amendments expected to be enacted.

2003 IFAPA celebrated its 30th birthday in Seoul, Korea, in conjunction with its Fourteenth Symposium of Adapted Physical Activity. Over 500 professionals from 30 countries attended.

2003 Special Olympics International celebrated its 35th birthday; held its 11th World Summer Games in Dublin, Ireland (first time outside of the United States); and announced that it provides sports training and competition in over 150 countries, thereby serving more than 1.2 million persons with mental retardation.

2003 The President's Council on Physical Fitness and Sports (PCPPS), in partnership with AAHPERD and the Cooper Institute for Aerobics Research, announced its new Presidential Active Lifestyle Award (PALA) program. For information about PALA, visit www.presidentschallenge.org.

2004 Paralympic Summer Games in Athens, Greece.

2005 Fifteenth symposium of IFAPA held in Pavia and Verona, Italy.

2006 Paralympic Winter Games in Torino, Italy.

Glossary

Note: For terms not included in this glossary, and for more extensive explanations, please check the index.

ABA Acronym for *applied behavior analysis.* A series of procedures used in behavior management pedagogy.

Abilities-based approach Beliefs, attitudes, intentions, and actions that emphasize strengths, aspirations, and effort rather than weaknesses and problems.

Accommodations "... supports or services provided to help students progress in the general education curriculum and demonstrate their learning. These do not mean big changes in the instructional level, content, or standards" (CEC, 1999, p. 43). *Testing accommodations* are changes in ways that a test is administered or responded to.

Accommodation plan Legal document specifying accommodations required under Section 504 for individuals who meet the eligibility criterion of an impairment that substantially limits one or more major life activities. Accommodations are intended to equalize opportunity for persons with and without disabilities.

ACSM Acronym for the *American College of Sports Medicine,* the organization to which most exercise scientists belong. ACSM certification enhances the overall value of adapted physical activity services. ACSM publishes many books and journals pertaining to exercise and fitness of persons with and without disabilities.

ADA Acronym for *Americans with Disabilities Act,* enacted in 1990.

Adaptation The art and science of assessing, prioritizing, and managing variables (i.e., person-environment interactions) to facilitate the changes needed to achieve desired outcomes. May be done by self or others. Also an umbrella term for accommodation, modification, and other change strategies made by qualified professionals to facilitate success.

Adaptation theory An emerging metatheory that enables the synthesis of the many ideas, theories, philosophies, and practices that guide everyday critical thinking about the beliefs, attitudes, intentions, and actions associated with adapted physical activity.

Adapted physical activity Service delivery, pedagogy, coaching, training, or empowerment conducted by qualified professionals, in mainstream and special settings, to enhance physical activity goal achievement of individuals of all ages with movement limitations and/or societal restrictions (i.e., attitudinal and environmental barriers); also the term for a profession, an academic specialization, a scholarly discipline, a service delivery system, or a program.

Adapted Physical Activity Council (APAC) The organization within the American Association of Active Lifestyles and Fitness (AAALF) of the American Alliance for Health, Physical Education, Recreation and Dance (AAHPERD) that professionals join and support.

Adapted Physical Activity Quarterly (APAQ) The official journal of the International Federation of Adapted Physical Activity, published since 1984.

Adapting Specially designed instruction, as appropriate to the needs of an eligible child . . . the content, methodology, or delivery of instruction to address unique needs that result from the child's disability and to ensure access to the general curriculum so that he or she can meet state or national educational standards for all children (IDEA, Sec. 300.26). The definition of *adapting* is modified for different ages, life activity areas, and service delivery professions.

Adaptive behavior Dimension II of the multidimensionality of mental retardation; "the collection of conceptual, social, and practical skills that have been learned by people in order to function in their everyday lives" (AAMR, 2002, p. 41).

Advocacy Working to change beliefs, attitudes, intentions, and behaviors of others to support a cause: action aimed at promoting, maintaining, or defending human rights. Tasks involved are the five Ls: *look at me* (modeling, setting an example); *leverage* (consumerism, media, lobbying, demonstrations); *literature* (all forms of writing); *legislation* (law); *litigation* (law suits, court cases).

Aides Shortest term for paraprofessionals or paraeducators.

Alternate assessment An assessment used in place of a state's or school district's regular achievement test because of severe disability; must be approved by the student's IEP team.

Alternative assessment Alternatives to traditional short-answer, timed tests (e.g., portfolios, work samples, teacher and peer observations, self-ratings with justifications, videotaped documentation of performance). Linked with authentic assessment and multiple measures.

APA Acronym for *adapted physical activity, American Psychological Association,* and *American Psychiatric Association.*

APAM Acronym for *American Psychological Association Publication Manual,* the style manual required by APAQ and used in most journals and books pertaining to adapted physical activity.

APENS Acronym for Adapted Physical Education National Standards and the national examination that determines whether a professional meets these standards. APENS testing is governed by the National Consortium for Physical Education and Recreation for Individuals with Disabilities (NCPERID).

Assessment Data collection, interpretation, and decision making about person-environmental interactions (barriers or enablers) and health functioning as defined by the World Health Organization (WHO, 2001).

Assistive technology (AT) device Any item used to increase, maintain, or improve the functional capabilities of an individual with disability (IDEA, Sec. 300.5). See definition of *functional capabilities.*

Attitude An enduring set of evaluative beliefs, charged with feelings and emotions, that predispose persons to certain kinds of intentions and behaviors: the key to inclusive, accepting behaviors toward individual differences.

Attitude-behavior link The assumption that beliefs lead to attitudes, attitudes lead to intentions, and intentions lead to behaviors, practices, and habits. Associated with reasoned action theory and planned behavior theory.

Authentic assessment models Performance assessment and portfolio assessment approaches in which a profile of children's abilities is documented by observing real-life tasks (Losardo & Notari-Syverson, 2001).

Behaviors Single acts or sets of acts that occur under certain conditions, toward a specific target, for a specified period of time that can be observed and assessed.

Benchmarks Alternatives to *short-term objectives,* introduced in IDEA 1997. Broader statements than short-term objectives, but both serve as intermediate steps to reach the long-range goals and must be measurable and concrete. *Example:* Amy will be able to participate in three lead-up games that require running and change of position skills by May.

BIP Acronym for behavioral intervention plan, which IDEA requires to be written and approved by the IEP committee for students with behavioral problems.

CAPE Acronym for certified adapted physical educator, the title given to professionals who pass the APENS examination.

Characteristics A term used incorrectly in adapted physical activity as a synonym for diagnostic criteria, behaviors, descriptors, and performance indicators or needs. A *characteristic* is a highly stable quality, a constituent or trait that is difficult or impossible to change (e.g., gender, race, age). Inasmuch as the purpose of both education and activity is positive change, the term *characteristics* (as well as *attributes*) simply should not be used to describe or to make generalizations about persons with disabilities. It is correct, however, to identify *characteristics of things* (a good or bad plan, program, or system), but *criteria to be met* would probably be better.

Community-based instruction Learning skills in the community rather than a school classroom.

Concrete mental operations Piaget's descriptor for highest-level thought processes during ages 7 to 11; processes include problem solving, cause-effect linkages, and generalizing to identical situations and things of a tangible nature.

Contact theory The body of knowledge that supports carefully planned and executed *direct contact* between persons who perceive themselves as different from others as a pedagogy to achieve inclusive behaviors and environments. Contact conditions that must be present are interactive, pleasant, focused on common goals (cooperative), meaningful, promoting respect, equal status, frequent, and of long duration.

Context "the interrelated conditions under which people live their everyday lives . . . an ecological perspective" (AAMR, 2002, p. 47). **Situational context** is the specific person-environment interactions affecting a particular situation, problem, success, or decision.

CTAPE Acronym for Competency Test for Adapted Physical Education used by the Louisiana Department of Education to refer to content-referenced test with criteria to determine if students in Grades K through 12 meet minimum state standards for retention in general physical education.

CBS Acronym or mnemonic device for remembering the three parts of a short-term objective: *c*onditions, *b*ehavior, and *s*uccess criteria. Sherrill prefers this to ABCD of Jansma and French (1994), in which A refers to audience (meaning child), B to behavior, C to conditions, and D to degree of success in measurable terms.

Developmental disability "A severe, chronic disability of an individual 5 years or older" that (a) is attributable to a mental and/or physical impairment; (b) is manifested before age 22; (c) is likely to continue indefinitely, (d) results in functional limitations in three or more of seven areas of major life activity; and (e) reflects needs for services, supports, and assistance that are of lifelong or extended duration (Developmental Disabilities Assistance and Bill of Rights Act of 2000, PL 106-402). See also definition of *major life activity* under functional capabilities.

Disability A limitation in performing an activity, not a medical condition, a different appearance, or a defect of some kind (World Health Organization, 2001). A legal classification that makes an individual with activity limitations eligible for aid.

Disability sport Any sport (club, community, interscholastic, intercollegiate, Paralympic) conducted primarily for people with disabilities. Term is not used in *Special Olympics,* which is a worldwide program for people with mental disabilities. In the United States, sport generally refers to competitive activities; in most of the world, sport can be competitive, recreational, or health and encompasses all forms of physical activity.

DSM Acronym for *Diagnostic and Statistical Manual of Mental Disorders* published periodically by the American Psychiatric Association and used in the United States as the equivalent of the International Classification of Functioning, Disability, and Health (ICFDH).

Due process Constitutional guarantee that fair and impartial treatment procedures will be followed whenever life, liberty, or property rights are challenged or removed. Comes from Fifth and Fourteenth Amendments.

Ecological assessment Data collection, synthesis, and interpretation about interactions between the environment and the individual rather than assuming the problem is in the individual.

Ecological task analysis (ETA) A systematic top-down process of critical thinking about all of the variables in the ecosystem that influence learning a particular task or function as demonstrated by a measurable outcome.

Ecosystem An individual in continuous interaction with his or her environment (both physical and psychosocial).

Empowerment Process by which individuals (typically members of social minorities) gain control over their lives, a sense of power equitable with that of others, and a feeling of responsibility for self, others, and the environment. Also a goal or mission, an outcome.

Equal/equality (exactly the same); **equitable, equity** (fairness, social justice) Terms frequently used and confused in disability sport, advocacy, and mainstream adaptations and supports.

Equal-status relationships Collaborations in which both parties share power, benefit to the same extent (although perhaps in different ways), respect and value each other, and experience mutual satisfaction and enjoyment in being together.

Evaluation Data collection, synthesis, and decision making about programs, service delivery systems, products of art or science, consumer satisfaction, and the like. Not usually applied to individuals except by the federal government (IDEA, 504, etc.), which uses evaluation as an umbrella term and does not distinguish between *assessment* and *evaluation.*

FAPE Acronym for *free appropriate public education* as assured by IDEA.

FIE Acronym for *full individual evaluation,* the term that IDEA gives the written document that reports the results of comprehensive, multidisciplinary testing conducted as part of the IEP process.

FIT Acronym for *frequency* (number of sessions), *intensity or intimacy* (amount of effort to be exerted by self and/or others), and *time* (duration in minutes) used as a device for remembering conditions of a behavioral intervention or an exercise prescription. If FIT is applied to social inclusion intervention, the concept *intimacy* (amount of closeness) may be substituted for *intensity.*

Formal mental operations Piaget's descriptor for the level of cognitive processes typically achieved from ages 11 on; these processes include inductive and deductive logic, ability to think about abstractions, and skill in simultaneously processing many cause-effect relationships.

Functional abilities Refers to residual potential after impairment imposes permanent imitations (e.g., paralysis of a certain muscle, loss of a body part). In disability sport, functional ability is an estimate, made by highly qualified classifiers, of personal best performance which cannot be altered by training, practice, or motivation (i.e., a Class 1 is always a Class 1, if properly classified). Functional abilities can, however, be altered through the use of assistive devices and environmental adaptations.

Functional assessment   Top down, starting at the chronological age of the individual and assessing competencies appropriate to that age.

Functional capabilities   Life activity tasks a person can still perform after impairment or disability. Performance must be observable and measurable. Not the same as *functional abilities.* Major areas of life activity are defined as " (i) self-care, (ii) receptive and expressive language, (iii) learning, (iv) mobility, (v) self-direction, (vi) capacity for independent living, and (vii) economic self-sufficiency" (Developmental Disabilities Assistance and Bill of Rights Act of 2000, PL 106-402). Best synonym is probably *present level of performance,* a term used in IEPs.

Functioning, Human   Person-environment interactions along a continuum of ability (or capability), depending on whether the perspective is estimated potential or actual performance. ICF identifies underlying concepts as health condition, body function and structures, activities, participation, and contextual factors. AAMR indicates that the dimensions of functioning are intellectual abilities; adaptive behavior; participation, interactions, and social roles; health; and context.

ICF   Acronym for *International Classification of Functioning, Disability, and Health* (2001, published by the World Health Organization), which replaces the *International Classification of Impairments, Disabilities, and Handicaps* (ICIDH, 1980). The ICF provides contemporary definitions and perspectives related to health and disability for most of the world's service delivery systems.

ICF Model of Human Functioning and Disability (2001)   Uses *functioning* as an umbrella term for neutral or nonproblematic states of functioning and *disability* as a term for problems in functioning. However, the widely disseminated ICF figure does not mention *disability* or *handicap*; its key words are *health condition, body functions and structures, activities, participation,* and *contextual factors.* ICF text links body functions and structures to *impairments,* activity limitations to *disabilities,* and participation restrictions to *handicaps.* See Figure 2.8.

IDEA   Acronym for *Individuals with Disabilities Education Act,* first enacted in 1990 as a replacement for PL 94-142, and subsequently reauthorized every 3-5 years.

IEP   Acronym for *individualized education program,* the legal document required by IDEA that is developed by an IEP team that includes parents and, when appropriate, the student; is based on multidisciplinary assessment; and indicates eligibility for special services in subject matter areas of weakness.

IFSP   Acronym for *individualized family service plan,* the legal document required by IDEA for infants and toddlers, ages 0 through 2, at risk for disability or with disability.

Inclusion   A controversial term with many meanings; can refer to philosophy, process, or product. Typically refers to the process of educating students with and without disabilities in the general physical education environment; this definition does not necessarily encompass *social inclusion,* which refers to reciprocal social acceptance and direct contact with everyone present and specific social behaviors like knowing and using each other's names, sharing power and resources, cooperating, offering support and praise, and appreciating and respecting diversity.

Inclusive environment   One that offers tasks that are equally accessible, interesting, meaningful, and engaging to all individuals; requires attention to physical, psychosocial, and temporal environments and specially designed goals, objectives, and interventions.

Inclusive placement   Compliance with IDEA's requirement that all students be served in the general education setting (with supports, accommodations, adaptations) unless such placement is determined by the IEP committee to *not* meet the criterion of least restrictive.

IPEP   Acronym for *individualized physical education program,* the term created by adapted physical educators to indicate the part of the IEP that refers specifically to physical education assessment findings and services. Often used to refer to the separate document that adapted physical educators prepare to guide programming for students with special needs; includes the same components as the IEP.

Individual differences   Person-environment interactions that cause persons to be perceived as having *unique needs* that require special services or *unique strengths* that deserve recognition.

ITP   Acronym for *individualized transition plan.* A part of the IEP or the IFSP, agreed on by their respective teams, that specifies the process for moving infants and toddlers into preschool programs and students age 14 on into community-based programs.

Least restrictive environment (LRE)   A legal requirement concerning placement and provision of services that, to the maximum extent possible, children with and without disabilities are educated together and that separate classes shall not be provided unless the nature or severity of the disability is such that education in general classes *with the use of supplementary aids and services* cannot be achieved satisfactorily.

Mirroring   Imitating (reflecting) another's movement to show understanding and acceptance.

MOBILITEE   Acronym for *Movement Opportunities for Building Independence and Leisure Interests through Training Educators and Exceptional Learners.* Used to refer to an Ohio-based curriculum-referenced test for students with moderate and severe mental retardation in Grades 1 through 12.

Modifications   Changes in curriculum, instructional level, or standards that require formal justification and subsequent changes in assessment and evaluation procedures. Changes in "content and performance expectations for what a student should learn" (CEC, 1999, p. 43).

Motor abilities   "General traits or capacities of an individual that underlie the performance of a variety of movement skills. These traits are assumed to *not* be easily modified by practice or experience and to be relatively stable across an individual's lifetime" (Burton & Miller, 1998, p. 366).

Movement skill foundations (MSFs)   "Not movement skills themselves, but all aspects of a person—physical, mental, and emotional—that facilitate or limit his/her performance of movement skills" (Burton & Miller, 1998, p. 367).

Mnemonic devices   Games, tricks, or gimmicks to aid memory. For example, *first letter mnemonics or acronym* like IDEA for Individuals with Disabilities Education Act or *rhyme mnemonics* like "i before e except after c." Meta-analyses by Kavale and Forness (1999, p. 74) indicated that this was one of the best ways of enhancing academic performance of special education students.

National Consortium for Physical Education and Recreation for Individuals with Disabilities (NCPERID)   An organization founded in 1973 by university personnel committed to advocacy and grant writing as a means of improving service delivery, professional preparation, and research. The governing body for APENS and the voluntary national testing and certification of adapted physical education teachers.

Nonacademic and extracurricular services and activities   In IDEA, defined as including counseling services, athletics, transportation, health services, recreational activities, special interest groups, or clubs. Same definition in Rehabilitation Act of 1973, Section 504.

National Center of Physical Activity and Disability (NCPAD) In Chicago, the first federally funded national center to disseminate information on research and practice for promotion of healthy lifestyles for persons with disabilities.

North American Federation of Adapted Physical Activity (NAFAPA) A branch of the International Federation of Adapted Physical Activity (IFAPA) that brings professionals from Canada and the United States together to share research every 2 years.

Normal The state or trait of being average (i.e., like the dominant social majority). Historically, considered a desirable state, but this thinking is being challenged by scholars in disability studies.

Normative beliefs Beliefs (expectancies) of one's significant others, sometimes perceived as social pressures. Important term in reasoned action and planned behavior attitude theories.

Normalization The theory and practice of making opportunities and conditions enjoyed by the dominant social majority (the norm) accessible to persons with disabilities. Popular from the 1960s through the 1990s, now being challenged by scholars who reject the idea that opportunities and conditions should be based on what is *normal* for the *dominant social majority* (i.e., able-bodied, white, male, heterosexual).

Organizing centers An alternative term in APENS for *frame of reference,* an approach to education or treatment that is based on philosophy and theoretical knowledge. Encompasses *functional* (top-down), *developmental* (bottom-up), and *interactional* (ecological) approaches to organizing curriculum.

PAP-TE-CA Acronym for the *services (job tasks)* comprising adapted physical activity service delivery. PAP-TE-CA refers to Planning; Assessment; Paperwork and Meetings; Teaching, Counseling, and Coaching; Evaluation; Consulting; Advocacy.

Paralympics Worldwide training and competition for elite athletes with disabilities, considered the equivalent of Olympics, and governed by the International Paralympic Committee (IPC). Includes sports for all disability categories except the Deaf.

Procedural safeguards Due process procedures for parents and children, specified in IDEA, and involving process standards for consent, evaluation, and personally identifiable information for each student.

Person-first language Placement of the noun (*individual or person*) before the descriptive phrase (*with disabilities*) to conceptualize the whole person with many abilities and disabilities rather than emphasizing disabilities.

PDR Acronym for *Physicians' Desk Reference,* published every year, that provides comprehensive information on medications.

Preoperational mental operations Piaget's descriptor for the highest level of cognitive function between ages 2 and 7. Thought that is tied to perception rather than logic and is limited by language, memory, and attention capabilities.

Related services Transportation and such developmental, corrective, and other supportive services as are required to assist a child with disability to benefit from special education, including physical education (IDEA, Sec. 300.24). Many of these are listed and defined in IDEA (e.g., OT, PT, recreation).

Reliability Characteristic of a good measurement related to either stability or internal consistency.

Responsivity disorders Behaviors described as *hyper* (over, above, too much), *hypo* (under, too little), or *fluctuating* (inconsistent or labile).

Rubrics Criteria (standards) used on checklists, rating sheets, or task analyses to specify the elements of performance and/or interactions between individual and environment that will be used in assessing strengths and weaknesses.

Self-determination "The capacity to choose and to act on the basis of those choices . . . requires that the young person be provided with the knowledge, competency, and opportunities necessary to exercise freedom and choice in ways that are valuable to him or her" (Wehman, 2001, p. 29).

Self-direction A frequently mentioned *adaptive skill* included in the conceptual category along with language, reading and writing, and money concepts (AAMR, 2002).

Sensorimotor mental operations Piaget's descriptor for the highest level of cognitive processes achieved during ages 0 to 2; these processes are translation of sensory input (e.g., visual, auditory, tactile) into initial meanings that form the basis of inner language and later cognitive, affective, and psychomotor function.

Sport classification A system of ecological, criterion-based assessment that groups persons with disabilities with others of similar functional capacity so as to facilitate fairness in determining who should compete against another in individual and team sport events.

Sporting identity The sense of who we are in the sport world, according to interactionist theory (modified from Coakley, 2001, p. 38); "a consistent, coherent, and recognizable self-package" (Fox, 1997, p. xii) that develops as a person integrates and constructs herself or himself as an athlete or a retired athlete.

Sport socialization Lifespan *interactive* process of becoming involved and staying involved in sport; learning sport behaviors, roles, ethics, and values; and acquiring a sporting identity; this is an interactionist theory definition. *Interactive* is the key word and encompasses interactions with the physical, social, and media environments. Now mostly outdated is functional theory that defines socialization as "a process through which we develop the social characteristics that enable us to fit into society and contribute to its operation." (Coakley, 2001, p. 82)

Supplementary aids and services Aids, services, and supports that are provided *in general education classes* to enable students with disabilities to be educated with nondisabled peers to the maximum extent appropriate. Supplementary services include itinerant or resource room adapted physical education instruction in conjunction with general education instruction (IDEA, Sec. 300.26, Sec. 300, 551).

Supports Resources and strategies that aim to promote the development, education, interests, and personal well-being of a person and that enhance individual functioning (AAMR, 2002). Concept of *functional supports* first used in Vocational Rehabilitation Act (VRA) of 1986, of personal dignity and natural supports in VRA of 1992. *Sources of supports* are oneself, other people, technology, and services (AAMR, 1992) or *natural* (including oneself and other people who are typically available) and *service-based* (provided by people or equipment not typically part of a person's natural environment, AAMR, 2002).

Supports areas Also called *life activity areas.* Includes human development, teaching and education, home living, community living, employment, health and safety (i.e., exercise, nutrition, medications), behavioral, social, and protection and advocacy (AAMR, 2002, p. 155).

Supports intensities Intermittent or on as-needed basis; *limited* as in time-limited helping; *extensive* characterized by regular involvement (e.g., daily) in some environments; and *pervasive,* provision across environments, potentially life-sustaining nature.

Supports model See AAMR (2002, p. 148) or this text, Figure 21.3.

Teaching styles Numerous instructional approaches described by Mosston and Ashworth (1994) and based on the belief that adaptation of teachers' pedagogy to students' needs is a vehicle to better learning. Also an important part of the APENS content on teaching.

Transitions to adulthood Major lifestyle changes that must be successful for persons to pass into a stable adulthood, such as employment, living arrangements, getting around the community, financial independence, making friends, sexuality, self-esteem, and having fun (Wehman, 2001, p. 24). Physical education, in adolescence, should be shown to contribute to these lifestyle changes.

Validity *Measurement validity*—meaningfulness, appropriateness, and usefulness of the specific inferences made from test scores. *Experimental validity*—evidence that research findings occurred as the result of an intervention or treatment. *Ecological validity*—findings that are applicable to everyday life.

World Health Organization (WHO) An agency of the United Nations, with headquarters in Geneva, Switzerland, concerned with improving the health of the world's people.

REFERENCES

Ablon, J. (1988). *Living with a difference: Families with dwarf children.* New York: Praeger.

Active Living Alliance for Canadians with a Disability. (1994). *Moving to inclusion.* Gloucester, Ontario: Author.

Adams, M., Bell, L. A., & Griffin, P. (Eds.). (1997). *Teaching for diversity and social justice: A sourcebook.* New York: Routledge.

Adams-Mushett, C., Wyeth, D. O., & Richter, K. H. (1995). Cerebral palsy. In B. Goldberg (Ed.), *Sports and exercise for children with chronic health conditions* (pp. 123–133). Champaign, IL: Human Kinetics.

Adelson, E., & Fraiberg, S. (1974). Gross motor development in infants blind from birth. *Child Development, 45,* 114–126.

Ainsworth, B. E. (2000). Issues in the assessment of physical activity of women. *Research Quarterly for Exercise and Sport, 71* (supplement to No. 2). 37–42.

Ajzen, I. (1985). From intentions to actions: A theory of planned behavior. In J. Kuhl & J. Beckmann (Eds.), *Action-control from cognition to behavior* (pp. 11–39). Heidelberg: Springer.

Ajzen, I. (1991). The theory of planned behavior. *Organizational Behavior and Human Decision Processes, 50,* 179–211.

Ajzen, I., & Fishbein, M. (1980). *Understanding attitudes and predicting social behavior.* Englewood Cliffs, NJ: Prentice-Hall.

Allport, G. W. (1954). *The nature of prejudice.* Cambridge, MA: Addison-Wesley.

Alter, M. J. (1996). *Science of flexibility and stretching* (2nd ed.). Champaign, IL: Human Kinetics.

Altman, B. (1996). Causes, risks, and consequences of disability among women. In D. M. Krotoski, M. A. Nosek, & M. A. Turk (Eds.), *Women with physical disabilities* (pp. 35–55). Baltimore: Brookes.

Alzheimer's Association. (2001). Retrieved 2002 from http://www.alz.org/AboutAD/10signs.htm.

American Alliance for Health, Physical Education, Recreation and Dance, and Cooper Institute for Aerobics Research. (1995). *You stay active.* Dallas: Cooper Institute for Aerobics Research. Now out of print.

American Association for Active Lifestyles and Fitness/American Alliance for Health, Physical Education, Recreation and Dance (AALF/AAHPERD). (1996). *Adapted aquatics: A position paper.* Reston, VA: Author.

American Association on Mental Retardation (AAMR, 1992). *Mental retardation: Definition, classification, and systems of supports* (9th ed.). Washington, DC: Author.

American Association on Mental Retardation (AAMR). (2002a). *Mental retardation: Definition, classification, and systems of supports* (10th ed.). Washington, DC: Author.

American Association on Mental Retardation (AAMR). (2002b). Symposium: What's in a name? Eight articles. *Mental Retardation, 40,* 51–80.

American Cancer Society (ACS). (2002). Retrieved 2002 from www.cancer.org.

American College of Sports Medicine (ACSM). (2000). *ACSM's guidelines for exercise testing and prescription* (6th ed.). Philadelphia: Lippincott, Williams, & Wilkins.

American College of Sports Medicine (ACSM). (2001). *ACSM's resource manual for guidelines for exercise testing and prescription* (4th ed.). Philadelphia: Lippincott, Williams, & Wilkins.

American College of Sports Medicine (ACSM). (2003). *Exercise management for persons with chronic diseases and disabilities.* (2nd ed.). Philadephia: Lippincott, Williams, & Wilkins.

American Council on Exercise. (1998). *Exercise for older adults.* Champaign, IL: Human Kinetics.

American Dance Therapy Association (2002). Retrieved from www.adta.org.

American Diabetes Association. (2002). Retrieved from http://care.diabetesjournals.org/cgi/content/full/25/suppl 1/s50.

American Psychological Association (2001). *Publication manual of the American Psychological Association.* (5th ed.). Washington, DC: Author.

American Psychiatric Association. (2000). *Diagnostic and statistical manual of mental disorders* (5th ed.). Washington, DC: Author.

American Red Cross. (1992). *Swimming and diving.* St. Louis, MO: Mosby Lifeline.

American Red Cross. (1996). *Safety training for swim coaches.* St. Louis, MO: Mosby Lifeline.

American Red Cross. (1997). *Sport safety training handbook.* St. Louis, MO: Mosby Lifeline.

American Stroke Association. (2002). Retrieved from http://www.strokeassociation.org/presenter.jhtml?identifer=1200037.

Amir, Y. (1969). Contact hypothesis in ethnic relations. *Psychological Bulletin, 71,* 319–342.

Andersson, C., & Mattsson, E. (2001). Adults with cerebral palsy: A survey describing problems, needs, resources, with special emphasis on locomotion. *Developmental Medicine & Child Neurology, 43*(2), 76–82.

Apfel, N. H., & Provence, S. (2001). *Infant-Toddler and Family Instrument (ITFI) & manual.* Baltimore: Brookes.

Arendt, R. E., MacLean, W., & Baumeister, A. (1988). Critique of sensory integration therapy and its application in mental retardation. *Mental Retardation, 92*(5), 401–411.

Arunovic, D., & Pantelic, Z. (1997). Comparative analysis of the physical development and abilities of pupils with damaged and pupils with normal sense of hearing. *Facta Universitatis: Series IV, Physical Education-Nis 1*(4), 29–36.

Ashman, R. M. (2000). The effects of cooperative learning on students with learning difficulties in lower elementary school. *Journal of Special Education, 34,* 19–37.

Ashton-Shaeffer, C., Gibson, H. J., Autry, C. E., & Hanson, C. S. (2001). Meaning of sport to adults with physical disabilities: A disability sport camp experience. *Sociology of Sport Journal, 18,* 95–114.

Asperger, H. (1944). Autistic psychopathology in childhood. Translated by U. Frith. In U. Frith (Ed.). (1991). *Autism and Asperger's syndrome* (pp. 37–92). Cambridge, England: Cambridge University Press.

Aufderheide, S. (1983). ALT-PE in mainstreamed physical education classes. *Journal of Teaching in Physical Education, 1,* 22–26.

Auxter, D., Pyfer, J., & Huettig, C. (2001). *Principles and methods of adapted physical education and recreation* (9th ed.). Boston: McGraw-Hill.

Axelson, P. (1986). Facilitation of integrated recreation. In C. Sherrill (Ed.), *Sport and disabled athletes* (pp. 81–89). Champaign, IL: Human Kinetics.

Ayers, A. J. (1972). *Sensory integration and learning disorders.* Los Angeles: Western Psychological Services.

Ayers, A. J. (1989). *Sensory integration and praxis tests.* Los Angeles: Western Psychological Services.

Bagnato, S. J., Neisworth, J. T., & Munson, S. M. (1997). *Linking assessment and early intervention.* Baltimore: Brookes.

Baker, B. L., Blacher, J., Crnic, K. A., & Edelbrock, C. (2002). Behavior problems and poverty stress in families of three year-old children with and without developmental delays. *American Journal on Mental Retardation, 107*(6), 433–444.

Balan, C., & Davis, W. (1993). Ecological task analysis: An approach to teaching physical education. *Journal of Physical Education, Recreation, and Dance, 64*(9), 54–61.

Bandy, W. D., & Sanders, B. (2001). *Therapeutic exercise: Techniques for intervention.* Philadelphia: Lippincott, Williams, & Wilkins.

Bandura, A. (1977). Self-efficacy: Toward a unifying theory of behavioral change. *Psychological Review, 84*(7), 191–215.

Bandura, A. (1986). *Social foundations of thought and action: A social cognitive theory.* Englewood Cliffs, NJ: Prentice-Hall.

Bandura, A. (1997). *Self-efficacy: The exercise of control.* New York: W. H. Freeman.

Baranowski, T. (1988). Validity and reliability of self-report measures of physical activity: An information processing perspective. *Research Quarterly for Exercise and Sport, 59*(4), 314–327.

Bard, C., Fleury, M., & Hay, L. (1990). *Eye-hand coordination across the life span.* Columbia: University of South Carolina Press.

Barker, R. (1968). *Ecological psychology.* Stanford, CA: Stanford University Press.

Barkley, R. A. (1998). *Attention-deficit hyperactivity disorder: A handbook for diagnosis and treatment.* New York: Guilford Press.

Barnes, J. T., Pujol, T. J., & Elder, L. (2002). Exercise consideration for patients with rheumatoid arthritis. *Strength and Conditioning Journal, 24*(3), 46–50.

Bartlett, L. P., Weisenstein, G. R., & Etscheidt, S. (2002). *Successful inclusion for educational leaders.* Columbus, OH: Merrill Prentice-Hall.

Basmajian, J., & Wolf, S. (Eds.). (1990). *Therapeutic exercise* (5th ed.). Baltimore: Williams & Wilkins.

Bates, B. (1983). *A guide to physical examination* (3rd ed.). Philadelphia: J. B. Lippincott.

Beardsley, D. S. (1995). Hemophilia. In B. Goldberg (Ed.), *Sports and exercise for children with chronic health conditions* (pp. 301–310). Champaign, IL: Human Kinetics.

Beasley, C. R. (1982). Effects of a jogging program on cardiovascular fitness and work performance of mentally retarded persons. *American Journal of Mental Deficiency, 6,* 609–613.

Beitchman, J. H., Wilson, B., Douglas, L., Young, A., & Adlaf, E. (2001). Substance use disorders in young adults with and without LD: Predictive and concurrent relationships. *Journal of Learning Disabilities, 34,* 317–332.

Bennett, D. R. (1995). Epilepsy. In B. Goldberg (Ed.), *Sports and exercise for children with chronic health conditions* (pp. 89–108). Champaign, IL: Human Kinetics.

Best, C., Lieberman, L., & Arndt, K. (2002). Effective use of interpreters in general physical education. *Journal of Physical Education, Recreation and Dance, 73*(8), 45–50.

Berkeley, S. L., Zittel, L. L., Pitney, L. V., & Nichols, S. E. (2001). Locomotor and object control skills of children diagnosed with autism. *Adapted Physical Activity Quarterly, 18,* 405–416.

Beyer, R. (1999). Motor proficiency of boys with attention deficit hyperactivity disorder. *Adapted Physical Activity Quarterly, 16,* 403–414.

Bhambhani, Y. (2001). Bridging the gap between research and practice in Paralympic sport. In G. Doll-Tepper, M. Kröner, & W. Sonnenschein (Eds.). *New horizons in sport for athletes with a disability* (pp. 5–26). Lansing, MI: Meyer & Meyer Sport (UK) ltd.

Biddle, S. (1997). Cognitive theories of motivation and the physical self. In K. R. Fox (Ed.), *The physical self* (pp. 59–82). Champaign, IL: Human Kinetics.

Biddle, S., Page, A., Ashford, B., Jennings, D., Brooke, R., & Fox, K. (1993). Assessment of children's physical self-perceptions. *International Journal of Adolescence and Youth, 4,* 93–109.

Biersdorff, K. K. (1994). Incidence of significantly altered pain experience among individuals with developmental disabilities. *American Journal on Mental Retardation, 98*(5), 619–631.

Biery, M. J., & Kauffman, N. (1989). The effects of therapeutic horse-back riding on balance. *Adapted Physical Activity Quarterly, 6*(3), 221–229.

Biesold, H. (1998). *Crying hands: Eugenics and deaf people in Nazi Germany.* Washington, DC: Gallaudet Press.

Birenhaum, A. (2002). Poverty, welfare reform, and disproportionate rates of disability among children. *Mental Retardation, 40,* 212–218.

Bitcon, C. H. (1976). *Alike and different: The clinical and educational use of Orff-Schulwerk.* Santa Ana, CA: Rosha.

Bleck, E., & Nagel, D. (Eds.). (1982). *Physically handicapped children: A medical atlas for teachers* (2nd ed.). New York: Grune & Stratton.

Block, G., Hartman, A., Dresser, C., Carroll, M., Gannon, J., & Gardner, L. (1986). A data-based approach to diet questionnaire design and testing. *American Journal of Epidemiology, 124*(3), 453–469.

Block, M. E. (1991). Motor development in children with Down syndrome: A review of the literature. *Adapted Physical Activity Quarterly, 8,* 179–209.

Block, M. E. (1995a). Americans with Disabilities Act: Its impact on youth sports. *Journal of Physical Education, Recreation and Dance, 66,* 28–32.

Block, M. E. (1995b). Development and validation of the Children's Attitudes Toward Physical Education-Revised Inventory. *Adapted Physical Activity Quarterly, 12,* 60–77.

Block, M. E. (1996). Implications of U.S. federal law and court cases for physical education placement of students with disabilities. *Adapted Physical Activity Quarterly, 13,* 127–152.

Block, M. E. (2000). *A teacher's guide to including students with disabilities in general physical education* (2nd ed.). Baltimore: Brookes.

Block, M. E., & Conaster, P. (2002). Adapted aquatics and inclusion. *Journal of Physical Education, Recreation and Dance, 73,* 31–34.

Block, M. E., & Davis, T. D. (1996). An activity-based approach to physical education for preschool children with disabilities. *Adapted Physical Activity Quarterly, 13,* 230–246.

Block, M. E., & Zeman, R. (1996). Including students with disabilities in regular physical education: Effects on nondisabled children. *Adapted Physical Activity Quarterly, 13,* 38–49.

Bloom, B. (Ed.). (1956). *Taxonomy of educational objectives. Handbook 1: Cognitive domain.* New York: David McKay.

Bobath, B. (1985). *Abnormal postural reflex activity caused by brain lesions.* (3rd ed.). Rockville, MD: Aspen Systems.

Bobath, K. (1980). *A neurophysiological basis for the treatment of cerebral palsy.* Philadelphia: J. B. Lippincott.

Borg, G. A. (1998). *Borg's perceived exertion and pain scales.* Champaign, IL: Human Kinetics.

Boss, P. G., Doherty, W. J., LaRossa, R., Schumm, W. R., & Steinmetz, S. K. (1993). *Sourcebook of family theories and methods.* New York: Plenum Press.

Boswell, B. (1989). Dance as creative expression for the disabled. *Palaestra, 6*(1), 28–30.

Bouffard, M. (1990). Movement problem solutions for educable mentally handicapped individuals. *Adapted Physical Activity Quarterly, 7,* 183–197.

Bouffard, M., & Wall, A. E. (1990). A problem-solving approach to movement skill acquisition: Implications for special populations. In G. Reid (Ed.), *Problems in movement control* (pp. 107–131). Amsterdam: North-Holland.

Bouffard, M., Watkinson, E. J., Thompson, L. P., Causgrove Dunn, J., & Romanow, S. K. E. (1996). A test of the activity deficit hypothesis with children with movement difficulties. *Adapted Physical Activity Quarterly, 18,* 61–73.

Bracken, B. A. (1996). Clinical applications of a context-dependent, multidimensional model of self-concept. In B. A. Bracken (Ed.), *Handbook of self-concept: Developmental, social, and clinical considerations* (pp. 463–504). New York: Wiley.

Bracken, B. A. (1992). *Multidimensional self-concept scale.* Austin, TX: Pro•Ed.

Brasile, F. (1984). A wheelchair basketball skills test. *Sports 'N Spokes, 9*(7), 36–40.

Brasile, F. (1986). Do you measure up? *Sports 'N Spokes, 12*(4), 42–47.

Brasile, F. (1990). Wheelchair sports: A new perspective on integration. *Adapted Physical Activity Quarterly, 7*(1), 3–11.

Brasile, F. (1992). Inclusion: A developmental perspective. A rejoinder to "Examining the Concept of Reverse Integration." *Adapted Physical Activity Quarterly, 9*(4), 293–304.

Bricker, D. (Ed.). (2002). *Assessment, evaluation, and programming system (AEPS) for infants and children (2nd ed.). Volumes 1 and 2 for birth to three years; Volumes 3 and 4 for three to six years.* Baltimore: Brookes.

Bricker, D., & Associates (1999). *Ages and Stages Questionnaires (ASQ-revised).* Baltimore: Brookes.

Bricker, D., & Woods-Cripe, J. J. (1998). *An activity-based approach to early intervention* (2nd ed.). Baltimore: Brookes.

Brigance, A. (1999). *Brigance Diagnostic Instrument.* (rev.) North Billerica, MA: Curriculum Associates, Inc. (First edition, 1978).

Broadhead, G., & Bruininks, R. (1982). Childhood motor performance traits on the short form Bruininks-Oseretsky Test. *Physical Educator, 39,* 149–155.

Brookbank, J. W. (1990). *The biology of aging.* New York: Harper & Row.

Bruininks, R. H. (1978). *Bruininks-Oseretsky Test of Motor Proficiency: Examiner's manual.* Circle Pines, MN: American Guidance Service.

Brunner, B. (Ed.). (2001). *Time Almanac 2002.* Boston: Information Please.

Buell, C. (1973). *Physical education and recreation for the visually handicapped.* Washington, DC: American Alliance for Health, Physical Education and Recreation.

Buell, C. (1982). *Physical education and recreation for the visually handicapped* (2nd ed.). Washington, DC: American Alliance for Health, Physical Education, Recreation and Dance.

Buell, C. (1984). *Physical education for blind children* (2nd ed.). Springfield, IL: Charles C. Thomas.

Buell, C. (1986). Blind athletes successfully compete against able-bodied opponents. In C. Sherrill (Ed.), *Sport and disabled athletes* (pp. 217–223). Champaign, IL: Human Kinetics.

Bulger, S. M., Townsend, J. S., & Carson, L. M. (2001). Promoting responsible student decision-making in elementary physical education. *Journal of Physical Education, Recreation and Dance, 72*(7), 18–23.

Bulgren, J. A., & Carta, J. J. (1992). Examining the instructional contexts of students with learning disabilities. *Exceptional Children, 59*(3), 182–191.

Burd, R., & Grass, K. (1987). Strapping to enhance athletic performance of wheelchair competitors with cerebral palsy. *Palaestra, 3,* 28–32.

Burgeson, C. R., Wechsler, H., Brener, N. D., Young, J., & Spain, C. G. (2001). Physical education and activity: Results from the school health policies and programs study of 2000. *Journal of School Health, 7,* 279–293.

Buros, O. (1938–1978) *Mental measurement yearbooks* (all editions through 1978). Lincoln: University of Nebraska Press.

Burton, A. W. (1990). Assessing the perceptual-motor interaction in developmentally disabled and nonhandicapped children. *Adapted Physical Activity Quarterly, 7,* 325–337.

Burton, A. W., & Miller, D. (1998). *Movement skill assessment.* Champaign, IL: Human Kinetics.

Burton, A. W., & Rodgerson, R. W. (2001). New perspectives on the assessment of movement skills and motor abilities. *Adapted Physical Activity Quarterly, 18,* 347–365.

Butterfield, S. (1991). Physical education and sport for the deaf: Rethinking the least restrictive environment. *Adapted Physical Activity Quarterly, 8*(2), 95–102.

Butterfield, S., Lehnhard, R., Martens, D., & Moirs, K. (1998). Kinematic analysis of a dynamic balance task by children who are deaf. *Clinical Kinesiology, 52*(4), 72–77.

Byra M. (2000). A review of spectrum research: The contributions of two eras. *Quest, 32,* 229–245.

Byra, M., & Karp, G. G. (2000). Data collection techniques employed in qualitative research in physical education teacher education. *Journal of Teaching in Physical Education, 19,* 246–266.

Byrd, D. E. (1990). Peer tutoring with the learning disabled: A critical review. *Journal of Educational Research, 84*(2), 115–118.

California Department of Education (2001). *Adapted physical education guidelines in California schools.* Sacramento: Author.

Campanella, R. (1959). *It's good to be alive.* New York: Little, Brown.

Campbell, E., & Jones, G. (2002a). Sources of stress experienced by elite male wheelchair basketball players. *Adapted Physical Activity Quarterly, 19,* 82–99.

Campbell, E., & Jones, G. (2002b). Cognitive appraisal of sources of stress experienced by elite male wheelchair basketball players. *Adapted Physical Activity Quarterly, 19,* 100–108.

Campion, M. (1985). *Hydrotherapy in pediatrics.* Rockville, MD: Aspen Systems.

Canada Fitness Survey. (1986). *Physical activity among activity-limited and disabled adults in Canada.* Montreal: Author.

Canadian Society for Exercise Physiology (Ed.). (1998). Recommendations for the fitness assessment, programming, and counseling for persons with a disability. *Canadian Journal of Applied Physiology, 23,* 119–130.

Cantell, M., & Kooistra, L. (2002). Long-term outcomes of developmental coordination disorder. In S. A. Cermak & D. Larkin (Eds.). *Developmental coordination disorder* (pp. 23–38). Albany, NY: Delmar.

Cantell, M., Smyth, M. M., & Ahonen, T. P. (1994). Clumsiness in adolescence: Educational, motor, and social outcomes of motor delay detected at 5 years. *Adapted Physical Activity Quarterly, 11*(2), 115–129.

Caron, K. L., & Henry, A. (2002). *The everyday meal planner for Type 2 diabetes.* New York: Contemporary Books.

Castagno, K. S. (2001). Special Olympics unified sports: Changes in male athletes during a basketball season. *Adapted Physical Activity Quarterly, 18,* 193–206.

Casteñeda , L. D. (1997). *Perceived outcomes of participation in challenger baseball.* Unpublished thesis, Texas Woman's University, Denton.

Casteñeda, L., & Sherrill, C. (1999). Family participation in challenger baseball: Critical theory perspectives. *Adapted Physical Activity Quarterly, 16,* 372–388.

Causgrove Dunn, J. L., & Watkinson, E. J. (1994). A study of the relationship between physical awkwardness and children's perceptions of physical competence. *Adapted Physical Activity Quarterly, 11*(3), 275–283.

Causgrove Dunn, J. (2000). Goal orientations, perceptions of the motivational climate, and perceived competence of children with movement difficulty. *Adapted Physical Activity Quarterly, 17,* 1–19.

Cermak, S. A. (1988). Sensible integration. *Mental Retardation, 92*(5), 413–414.

Cermak, S. A., & Larkin, D. (2002). *Developmental coordination disorder.* Albany, NY: Delmar.

Chace, M. (n.d.). *Dance alone is not enough.* From mimeographed materials distributed by St. Elizabeth's Hospital and Chestnut Lodge in Washington, DC.

Chad, K., Jobling, A., & Frail, H. (1990). Metabolic rate: A factor in developing obesity in children with Down syndrome. *American Journal on Mental Retardation, 95*(2), 228–235.

Challem, J., Berkson, B., & Smith, M. D. (2000). *Syndrome X.* New York: Wiley.

Charlton, J. I. (1998). *Nothing about us without us: Disability oppression and empowerment.* Berkeley: University of California Press.

Cheatum, B. A., & Hammond, A. A. (2000). *Physical activities for improving learning and behavior: A guide to sensory motor development.* Champaign, IL: Human Kinetics.

Chen, A. (1998). Meaningfulness in physical education: A description of high school students' conceptions. *Journal of Teaching in Physical Education, 17,* 285–306.

Chen, S. (2002). A modified tai chi program for individuals with physical disabilities. *Palaestra, 18,* 43–47.

Chen, S., Zhang, J., Lange, E., Miko, P., & Joseph D. (2001). Progressive time delay procedure for teaching motor skills to adults with severe mental retardation. *Adapted Physical Activity Quarterly, 18,* 35–48.

Chesler, M., & Chesney, B. (1988). Self-help groups: Empowerment attitudes and behaviors of disabled or chronically ill persons. In H. E. Yuker (Ed.), *Attitudes toward persons with disabilities* (pp. 230–245). New York: Springer.

Ciesielski, P. F. (1992). *Wellness: Major chronic diseases.* Guildford: CT: The Duskin Publishing Group.

Cioni, M., Cocilovo, A., DiPasquale, F., Rillo Araujo, M. B., Rodriguez Siqueria, C., & Blanco, M. (1994). Strength deficit of knee extensor muscles of individuals with Down syndrome from childhood to adolescence. *American Journal on Mental Retardation, 99*(2), 166–174.

Clandinin, D. J., & Connelly, F. M. (1994). Personal experience methods. In N. K. Denzin & Y. S. Lincoln (Eds.), *Handbook of qualitative research* (pp. 413–427). Thousand Oaks, CA: Sage.

Clark, J. E., & Whithall, J. (1989). Changing patterns of locomotion: From walking to skipping. In M. H. Woollacott & A. Shunway-Cook (Eds.), *Development of posture and gait across the lifespan* (pp. 128–154). Columbia: University of South Carolina Press.

Clarke, L. (1973). *Can't read, can't write, can't takl too good either.* New York: Walker & Company.

Clements, R., & Kinzler, S. (2003). *A multicultural approach to physical education.* Champaign, IL: Human Kinetics.

Cluphf, D., O'Connor, J., & Vanin, S. (2001). Effects of aerobic dance on the cardiovascular endurance of adults with intellectual disabilities. *Adapted Physical Activity Quarterly, 18,* 60–71.

Coakley, J. (2001). *Sport in society: Issues and controversies* (7th ed.). Boston: McGraw-Hill.

Collier, D., & Reid, G. (1987). A comparison of two models designed to teach autistic children a motor task. *Adapted Physical Activity Quarterly, 4,* 226–236.

Colwin, C. M. (2002). *Breakthrough swimming.* Champaign, IL: Human Kinetics.

Committee on Adapted Physical Education. (1952). Guiding principles for adapted physical education. *Journal of Health, Physical Education, and Recreation, 23,* 15.

Conaster, P., Block, M., & Gansneder, B. (2002). Aquatic instructors' beliefs toward inclusion: The theory of planned behavior. *Adapted Physical Activity Quarterly, 19,* 172–187.

Connolly, M. (1994). Practicum experiences and journal writing in adapted physical education: Implications for teacher education. *Adapted Physical Activity Quarterly, 11,* 306–328.

Connor, F. (1990). Physical education for children with autism. *Teaching Exceptional Children, 23,* 30–33.

Connor-Kuntz, F. J., Dummer, G. M., & Paciorek, M. J. (1995). Physical education and sport participation of children and youth with spina bifida myelomeningocele. *Adapted Physical Activity Quarterly, 12*(3), 228–238.

Connor-Kuntz, F., & Dummer, G. M. (1996). Teaching across the curriculum: Language-enriched physical education for preschool children. *Adapted Physical Activity Quarterly, 13*(3), 302–315.

Conroy, D. E. (2001). Fear of failure: An exemplar for social development research in sport. *Quest, 53,* 165–183.

Cooney, T. P., & Thurlbeck, W. M. (1982). Pulmonary hypoplasia in Down syndrome. *New England Journal of Medicine, 307*(9), 1170–1173.

Cooper Institute for Aerobics Research. (1999a). *ACTIVITYGRAM, Part of the FITNESSGRAM 6.0 software package.* Champaign, IL: Human Kinetics.

Cooper Institute for Aerobics Research. (1999b). *FITNESSGRAM test administration manual.* Champaign, IL: Human Kinetics.

Cooper Institute for Aerobics Research. (1999c). *The FITNESSGRAM technical reference manual.* Dallas: Author.

Cooper, K. H. (1968). *Aerobics.* New York: M. Evans.

Cooper, K. H. (1982). *The aerobics program for total well-being.* New York: Bantam Books.

Cooper, R. (1988). Racing chair lingo…or how to order a racing wheelchair. *Sports 'N Spokes, 13*(6), 29–32.

Corbin, C. B., Lindsey, R., Welk, G. J., & Corbin, W. R. (2002). *Concepts of fitness and wellness: A comprehensive lifestyle* (4th ed.). St Louis: McGraw-Hill.

Cordellos, H. (1976). *Aquatic recreation for the blind.* Washington, DC: American Alliance for Health, Physical Education and Recreation.

Cordellos, H. (1981). *Breaking through.* Mountain View, CA: Anderson World.

Cordellos, H. (1983). *Survival run.* Videotape available through Harry Cordellos, 1021 Second Street, Unit B, Novato, CA 94945.

Cordellos, H. C. (1993). *No limits.* Waco, TX: WRS Publishing.

Corker, M. (1999). Differences, conflations, and foundations: The limits to accurate, theoretical representation of disabled people's experiences. *Disability and Society, 14,* 627–642.

Cornett, R. O. (1967). Cued speech. *American Annals of the Deaf, 112,* 3–13.

Costill, D. L., Maglischo, E. W., & Richardson, A. B. (1992). *Swimming.* Oxford, England: Blackwell Science.

Cott, C. A., Dawson, P., Sidani, S., & Wells, D. (2002). The effects of a walking/talking program on communication, ambulation, and functional status in residents with Alzheimer disease. *Alzheimer Disease and Associated Disorders, 16,* 81–87.

Council of Administrators of Special Education, Inc. (CASE, 1999). *Section 504 and the ADA: Promoting student access* (2nd ed.). Reston, VA: Author.

Council for Exceptional Children (CEC, 1999). *IEP team guide.* Reston, VA: Author.

Council for Exceptional Children (CEC, 2002). *Performance-based standards for beginning special education teachers.* Reston, VA: Author.

Council of Europe (1975). *The European Sport for All Charter.* Geneva: Author.

Courney, K. S., & Friedenreich, C. M. (1997). Relationship between exercise during treatment and current quality of life among survivors of breast cancer. *Journal of Psychosocial Oncology, 15*(3/4), 35–37.

Cowden, J. E. (1980). *Administrator inservice training for program implementation in adapted and developmental physical education.* Unpublished doctoral dissertation, Texas Woman's University (ERIC #ED204–29B).

Cowden, J. E., & Megginson, N. (1988). Opinion and attitude assessment: The first step in changing public school service delivery. In C. Sherrill (Ed.), *Leadership training in adapted physical activity* (pp. 227–256). Champaign, IL: Human Kinetics.

Cowden, J. E., Sayers, L. K., & Torrey, C. C. (1998). *Pediatric adapted motor development and exercise: An innovative multisystem approach for professionals and families.* Springfield, IL: Charles C. Thomas.

Cowden, J. E., & Torrey, C. C. (1995). A ROADMAP for assessing infants, toddlers, and preschoolers: The role of the adapted motor developmentalist. *Adapted Physical Activity Quarterly, 12*(1), 1–11.

Crain, W. (1992). *Theories of development* (3rd ed.). Englewood Cliffs, NJ: Prentice-Hall.

Crase, N. (1990). Winning: Randy Snow. *Sports 'N Spokes, 15*(5), 8–12.

Cratty, B. J. (1967*)*. *Development sequences of perceptual motor tasks.* Long Island, NY: Educational Activities.

Cratty, B. J. (1971a). *Active learning.* Englewood Cliffs, NJ: Prentice-Hall.

Cratty, B. (1971b). *Movement and spatial awareness in blind children and youth.* Springfield, IL: Charles C. Thomas.

Cratty, B. J. (1972). *Physical expressions of intelligence.* Englewood Cliffs, NJ: Prentice-Hall.

Cratty, B. J. (1986). *Perceptual and motor development in infants and children* (3rd ed.). Englewood Cliffs, NJ: Prentice-Hall.

Cratty, B. J. (1990). Motor development of infants subject to maternal drug use: Current evidence and future research strategies. *Adapted Physical Activity Quarterly, 7,* 110–125.

Crocker, P. R. E. (1993). Sport and exercise psychology and research with individuals with physical disabilities: Using theory to advance knowledge. *Adapted Physical Activity Quarterly, 10*(4) 324–335.

Cruickshank, W. (1967). *The brain-injured child in home, school, and community.* Syracuse, NY: Syracuse University Press.

Crutchfield, C. A., & Barnes, M. R. (1995). *Motor control and motor learning in rehabilitation* (2nd ed.). Atlanta: Stokesville.

Curran, A. L., Sharples, P. M., White, C., & Knapp, M. (2001). Time costs of caring for children with severe disabilities compared with caring for children without disabilities. *Developmental Medicine and Child Neurology, 43,* 529–533.

Curtis, K. A. (1981). Stretching routines. *Sports 'N Spokes, 7*(3), 16–18.

Curtis, K. A. (1991). Sport-specific functional classification for wheelchair athletes. *Sports 'N Spokes, 17*(2), 45–48.

Cypcar, D., & Lemanske, R. F. (1995). Exercise-induced asthma. In B. Goldberg (Ed.), *Sports and exercise for children with chronic health conditions* (pp. 149–166). Champaign, IL: Human Kinetics.

D'Angelo, L. J. (1995). Chronic blood-borne infections. In B. Goldberg (Ed.), *Sports and exercise for children with chronic health conditions* (pp. 187–196). Champaign, IL: Human Kinetics.

Dalsky, G. P. (1996). Guidelines for diagnosing osteoporosis. *The Physician and Sports Medicine, 24*(7), 96–100.

Daly, D. J., Malone, L. A., Smith, D. J., Vanlanadewijck, Y., & Steadward, R. D. (2001). The contribution of starting, turning, and finishing total race performance in male Paralympic swimmers. *Adapted Physical Activity Quarterly, 18*(3), 316–333.

Daniels, L., & Worthingham, C. (1986). *Muscle testing: Techniques of manual examination* (5th ed.). Philadelphia: Saunders.

Dattilo, J. (2002). *Inclusive leisure services: Responding to the rights of people with disabilities* (2nd ed.). State College, PA: Venture.

Davis, L. J. (1995). *Enforcing normalcy: Disability, deafness, and the body.* London: Verso.

Davis, R. D., & Braun, E. M. (2003). *The gift of learning: Proven new methods for correcting ADD, math & handwriting problems.* New York: Perigee.

Davis, R. W. (2002). *Inclusion through sports.* Champaign, IL: Human Kinetics.

Davis, W. E. (1983). An ecological approach to perceptual-motor learning. In R. L. Eason, T. L. Smith, & F. Caron (Eds.), *Adapted physical activity: From theory to application* (pp. 162–171). Champaign, IL: Human Kinetics.

Davis, W. E., & Broadhead, G. D. (Eds.). (in preparation). *Ecological task analysis: Looking back, Thinking forward.* Champaign, IL: Human Kinetics.

Davis, W. E., & Burton, A. W. (1991). Ecological task analysis: Translating movement behavior theory into practice. *Adapted Physical Activity Quarterly, 8,* 154–177.

Day, K., & Jancar, J. (1994). Mental and physical health and aging in mental handicap: A review. *Journal of Intellectual Disability Research, 38,* 241–256.

DeBettencourt, L. U. (2002). Understanding the differences between IDEA and Section 504. *Teaching Exceptional Children, 34*(3), 16–23.

Deci, E. L., & Ryan, R. M. (1985). *Intrinsic motivation and self-determination in human behavior.* New York: Plenum Press.

DeJong, C. G. A. (1990). The development of mobility in blind and multiply handicapped infants. In A. Vermeer (Ed.), *Motor development, adapted physical activity, and mental retardation* (pp. 56–66). Basel, Switzerland: Karger.

De Knop, P., & Oja, P. (1996). Sport for all. In J. D. Halloran, P. V. Komi, H. G. Knuttgen, P. De Knop, P. Oja, & F. Roskam (Eds.), *Current issues of sport science.* (pp. 15–37). Schorndorf, Germany: Verlag Karl Hofmann.

DeLorme, T., & Watkins, A. (1948). Techniques of progressive resistance exercise. *Archives of Physical and Medical Rehabilitation, 29,* 263–273.

DePaepe, J. L. (1985). The influence of three least restrictive environments on the content motor ALT and performance of moderately mentally retarded students. *Journal of Teaching in Physical Education, 3,* 34–41.

DePauw, K. P., & Doll-Tepper, G. (1989). European perspectives on adapted physical education. *Adapted Physical Activity Quarterly, 6,* 95–99.

DePauw, K. P., & Doll-Tepper, G. (2000). Toward progressive inclusion and acceptance: Myth or reality? The inclusion debate and bandwagon discourse. *Adapted Physical Activity Quarterly, 17,* 135–143.

DePauw, K. P., & Gavron, S. J. (1995). *Disability and sport.* Champaign, IL: Human Kinetics.

Dewey, J. (1933). *How we think* (rev. ed.). Chicago: Henry Regnery.

Dishman, R. K. (Ed.). (1994). *Advances in exercise adherence.* Champaign, IL: Human Kinetics.

Dishman, R. K., Ickes, W., & Morgan, W. (1980). Self-motivation and adherence to habitual physical activity. *Journal of Applied Social Psychology, 10,* 115–132.

Dissanayake, C., & Crossley, S. A. (1996). Proximity and sociable behaviors in autism: Evidence for attachment. *Journal of Child Psychology and Psychiatry, 37*(2), 149–156.

Dobbins, D., Garron, R., & Rarick, G. S. (1981). The motor performance of EMR and intellectually normal boys after covariate control for differences in body size. *Research Quarterly for Exercise and Sport, 52*(1), 1–8.

Dollinger, M., Rosenbaum, E. H., Tempero, M., & Mulvihill, S. J. (2002). *Everyone's guide to cancer therapy* (4th ed.). Kansas City, MO: Andrews McMeel Publishing.

Doren, B., Bullis, M., & Benz, M. R. (1996). Predicting arrest status of adolescents with disabilities in transition. *Journal of Special Education, 29,* 363–380.

Dorris, M. (1989). *The broken cord.* New York: Harper & Row.

Doty, A. K., McEwen, I. R., Parker, D., & Laskin, J. (1999). Effects of testing context on ball skill performance in 5-year-old children with and without developmental delay. *Physical Therapy, 79,* 818–826.

Dougherty, N. J., Auxter, D., Goldberger, A. S., & Heinzmann, G. S. (1994). *Sport, physical activity, and the law.* Champaign, IL: Human Kinetics.

Downing, J. E. (2002). *Including students with severe and multiple disabilities in typical classrooms.* (2nd ed.). Baltimore: Brookes.

Driscoll, J. (2000). *Determined to win.* New York: Barnes & Noble.

Duchane, K. A., & French, R. (1998). Attitudes and grading practices of secondary physical educators in regular education settings. *Adapted Physical Activity Quarterly, 15,* 370–380.

Dummer, G. M. (1999). Classification of swimmers with physical disabilities. *Adapted Physical Activity Quarterly, 16*(3), 216–218.

Dummer, G. M. (2001). Including athletes with disabilities. In V. Seefeldt, M. A. Clark, & E. W. Brown (Eds.), *Program for athletic coaches' education* (3rd ed., pp. 21–26). Traverse City, MI: Cooper Publishing Group.

Dummer, G., & Bare, J. (2001). *Including swimmers with a disability* (Series of five brochures). Colorado Springs: USA Swimming.

Dummer, G., Ewing, M., Habeck, R., & Overton, S. (1987). Attributions of athletes with cerebral palsy. *Adapted Physical Activity Quarterly, 4,* 278–292.

Dummer, G., Haubenstricker, J., & Stewart, D. A. (1996). Motor skill performance of children who are deaf. *Adapted Physical Activity Quarterly, 13,* 400–414.

Dummer, G. M., & Heusner, W. W. (1996, September). *Stroke technique characteristics of elite swimmers with disabilities.* Paper presented at the North American Federation on Adapted Physical Activity, Banff, Alberta, Canada.

Duncan, S. C., Duncan, T. E., Strycker, L. A.. & Chaaumeton, N. R. (2002). Neighborhood physical activity opportunity. *Research Quarterly for Exercise and Sport, 73,* 457–463.

Dunkin, M. J., & Biddle, B. J. (1974). *The study of teaching.* New York: Holt, Rinehart & Winston.

Dunn, J., Morehouse, J., & Fredericks, H. (1986). *Physical education for the severely handicapped: A systematic approach to a data-based gymnasium.* Austin, TX: Pro•Ed.

Dunn, L., McCartan, K., & Fuqua, R. (1988). Young children with orthopedic handicaps: Self-knowledge about disability. *Exceptional Children, 55*(3), 249–252.

Dunn, R. (1990). Bias over substance: A critical analysis of Kavale and Forness' report on modality-based instruction. *Exceptional Children, 56*(4), 357–361.

Dyer, S., Gunn, P., Rauh, H., & Berry, P. (1990). Motor development in Down syndrome children: An analysis of the motor scale of the Bayley Scales of Infant Development. In A. Vermeer (Ed.), *Motor development, adapted physical activity, and mental retardation* (pp. 7–20). Basel, Switzerland: Karger.

Dykens, E. M., Hodapp, R. M., & Evans, D. W. (1994). Profiles and development of adaptive behavior in children with Down syndrome. *American Journal on Mental Retardation, 98*(5), 580–587.

Dykens, E. M., Hodapp, R. M., & Leckman, J. F. (1994). *Behavior and development in fragile X syndrome.* Thousand Oaks, CA: Sage.

Eddy, J. (1982). *The music came from deep inside: Professional artists and severely handicapped children.* New York: McGraw-Hill.

Edgerton, R. B. (1967). *The cloak of competence: Stigma in the lives of the mentally retarded.* Berkeley: University of California Press.

Eichstaedt, C., & Kalakian, L. (1987). *Developmental/adapted physical education* (2nd ed.). New York: Macmillan.

Eichstaedt, C., & Lavay, B. (1992). *Physical activity for individuals with mental retardation: Infant to adult.* Champaign, IL: Human Kinetics.

Eichstaedt, C., Wang, P., Polacek, J., & Dohrmann, P. (1991). *Physical fitness and motor skill levels of individuals with mental retardation, ages 6–21.* Normal, IL: Illinois State University.

Eidson, T. A., & Stadulis, R. E. (1991). Effects of variability of practice on the transfer and performance of open and closed motor skills. *Adapted Physical Activity Quarterly, 8,* 342–356.

Elliott, R. O., Dobbin, A. R., Rose, G. D., & Soper, H. V. (1994). Vigorous, aerobic exercise versus general motor training activities: Effects on maladaptive and stereotypic behaviors of adults with both autism and mental retardation. *Journal of Autism and Developmental Disorders, 24*(5), 565–576.

Elliott, S. N., Braden, J. P., & White, J. L. (2001). *Assessing one and all: Educational accountability for students with disabilities.* Arlington, VA: Council for Exceptional Children.

Ellison, P., Browning, C., Larson, B., & Denny, J. (1983). Development of a scoring system for the Milani-Comparetti and Gidoni methods of assessing neurological abnormality in infancy. *Physical Therapy, 63*(9), 1414–1423.

Emes, C. G., & Velde, B. (2004). *Adapted physical activity practicum manual.* Champaign, IL: Human Kinetics.

Emes, C. G., Longmuir, P., & Downs, P. (2002). An abilities-based approach to service delivery and professional preparation in adapted physical activity. *Adapted Physical Activity Quarterly, 19,* 403–419.

Englebert, R. H., Gutmans, V. A., Uiterwaal, C. S., & Helders, P. J. (2001). Osteogenesis imperfecta in childhood: Perceived competence in relation to impairment and disability. *Archives of Physical Medicine and Rehabilitation, 82*(7), 943–948.

Ennis, C. D., Cothran, D. J., Davidson, K. S., Loftus, S. J., Owens, L., Swanson, L., & Hopsicker, P. (1997). Implementing curriculum within a context of fear and disengagement. *Journal of Teaching in Physical Education, 17,* 52–71.

Erikson, E. H. (1950). *Childhood and society.* New York: W. W. Norton.

Erikson, E. H. (1968). *Identity: Youth and crisis.* New York: W. W. Norton.

Etscheidt, S. K., & Bartlett, L. (1999). The IDEA amendments: A four step approach for determining supplementary aids and services. *Exceptional Children, 65,* 163–174.

Fawcett, J., & Downs, F. S. (1992). *The relationship of theory and research* (2nd ed.). Philadelphia: F. A. Davis.

Federal Register, March 12, 1999, PL 105–17, IDEA 1997.

Federal Register, May 4, 1977, PL 93-112, The Rehabilitation Act of 1973, Section 504.

Federal Register, August 23, 1977, PL 91-142, The Education for All Handicapped Children Act.

Federal Register, June 22, 1989, PL 99-457, The Education of the Handicapped Act.

Federal Register, September 29, 1992, Vol. 57, No. 189, The Individuals with Disabilities Act.

Feil, E., Severson, H., & Walker, H. (1998). Screening for emotional and behavioral delays: The early screen project. *Journal of Early Intervention, 21,* 252–266.

Fernhall, B., Tymeson, G., & Webster, G. (1988). Cardiovascular fitness of mentally retarded individuals. *Adapted Physical Activity Quarterly, 5,* 12–18.

Ferrara, M., Dattilo, J., & Dattilo, A. (1994). A crossdisability analysis of programming needs for athletes with disabilities. *Palaestra, 11*(1), 32–42.

Ferro, J., Foster-Johnson, & Dunlap, G. (1996). Relation between curricular activities and problem behaviors of students with mental retardation. *American Journal on Mental Retardation, 101*(2), 184–194.

Festinger, L. (1954). A theory of social comparison processes. *Human Relations, 7,* 117–140.

Festinger, L. (1957). *A theory of cognitive dissonance.* Stanford, CA: Stanford University Press.

Fetterman, D. M., Kaftarian, S. J., & Wandersman, A. (Eds.). (1996). *Empowerment evaluation.* Thousand Oaks, CA: Sage.

Fiorentino, M. (1963). *Reflex testing methods for evaluating C.N.S. development.* Springfield, IL: Charles C. Thomas.

Fiorentino, M. (1981). *A basis for sensorimotor development-Normal and abnormal.* Springfield, IL: Charles C. Thomas.

Fiorini, J., Stanton, K., & Reid, G. (1996). Understanding of parents and families of children with disabilities. *Palaestra, 12*(2), 16–23, 51.

Fishbein, H. D. (2002). *Peer prejudice and discrimination: The origins of prejudice* (2nd ed.). Mahwah, NJ: Erlbaum.

Fisher, A. (2001). *Critical thinking: An introduction.* Cambridge, UK: Cambridge University Press.

Fisher, A. G., Murray, E. A., & Bundy, A. C. (1991). *Sensory integration: Theory and practice.* Philadelphia: F. A. Davis.

Fisher, S. V., & Gullickson, G. (1978). Energy cost of ambulation in health and disability: A literature view. *Archives of Physical Medicine and Rehabilitation, 59,* 124–132.

Fishler, K., & Koch, R. (1991). Mental development in Down syndrome mosaicism. *American Journal on Mental Retardation, 96*(3), 345–351.

Fitt, S., & Riordan, A. (Eds.). (1980). *Dance for the handicapped—Focus on dance IX.* Reston, VA: American Alliance for Health, Physical Education, Recreation and Dance.

Fletcher, G. F., Balady, G., Froelicher, V. F., Hartely, L. H., Haskell, W. L., & Pollock, M. L. (1995). Exercise standards: A statement for healthcare professionals for the American Heart Association. *Circulation, 91,* 580–615.

Flodin, M. (1991). *Signing for kids.* New York: Putnam.

Folio, M., & Fewell, R. (1983). *Peabody Developmental Motor Scales.* Hingham, MA: Teaching Resources.

Folio, M., & Fewell, R. (2000). *Peabody Developmental Motor Scales* (2nd ed.). Austin, TX: Pro•Ed.

Folsom-Meek, S. L., & Rizzo, T. L. (2002). Validating the Physical Educators' Attitude Toward Teaching Individuals with Disabilities III (PEATID III) Survey for Professionals. *Adapted Physical Activity Quarterly, 19*, 141–154.

Folsom-Meek, S. L., Nearing, R. J., Groteluschen, W., & Krampf, H. (1999). Effects of academic major, gender, and hands-on experience on attitudes of preservice professionals. *Adapted Physical Activity Quarterly, 16*, 389–402.

Ford, B. A. (Ed.). (2001). *Multiple voices for ethnically diverse exceptional learners 2000.* Arlington, VA: Council for Exceptional Children.

Fowles, D. G. (1991). The numbers game: Pyramid power. *Aging, 2*, 58–59.

Fox, K. R. (1990). *The Physical Self-Perception Profile manual.* DeKalb, IL: Northern Illinois University, Office for Health Promotion.

Fox, K. R. (Ed.). (1997). *The physical self: From motivation to well-being.* Champaign, IL: Human Kinetics.

Fox, K. R., & Corbin, C. B. (1989). The physical self-perception profile: Development and preliminary validation. *Journal of Sport and Exercise Psychology, 11*, 408–430.

Fraiberg, S. (1977). *Insights from the blind: Comparative studies of blind and sighted infants.* New York: New American Library.

Francis, R. J., & Rarick, G. L. (1959). Motor characteristics of the mentally retarded. *American Journal of Mental Deficiency, 63*, 792–811.

Frank, G. (2000). *Venus on wheels: Two decades of dialogue on disability, biography, and being female in America.* Berkeley, CA: University of California Press.

French, R., Kinnison, L., Sherrill, C., & Henderson, H. (1998). Relationship of Section 504 to physical education and sport: Revisited. *Journal of Physical Education, Recreation and Dance, 69*(7), 57–63.

French, S. (1994). 'Can you see the rainbow?' The roots of denial. In J. Swain, V. Finkelstein, S. French, & M. Oliver (Eds.), *Disabling barriers—Enabling environments* (pp. 69–77). London: Sage.

Friedenreich, C. (1999). Physical activity and risk of breast cancer. *Research Update* 6:4. Retrieved 2002 from http://www.centre4activeliving.ca/Research/ResearchUpdate/1999/cancer jun 99 htm.

Friedenreich, C., & Rohan, T. E. (1995). A review of physical activity and breast cancer. *Epidemiology, 6*(3), 311–318.

Friedman, R., & Tappen, R. M. (1991). The effect of planned walking on communication in Alzheimer's disease. *Journal of the American Geriatric Society, 39*, 650–654.

Gajdosik, C. G., & Circirello, N. (2001). Secondary conditions of the musculoskeletal system in adolescents and adults. *Physical and Occupational Therapy in Pediatrics, 21*(4), 49–68.

Gallahue, D. L., & Ozmun, J. C. (1998). *Understanding motor development* (4th ed.). Boston: McGraw-Hill.

Garbarino, J., & deLara, E. (2002). *And words can hurt forever: How to protect adolescents from bullying, harassment, and emotional violence.* New York: The Free Press.

Garber, S., Ridgely, M. S., Bradley, M., & Chin, K. W. (2002). Payment under public and private insurance and access to cochlear implants. *Archives of Otolaryngology-Head and Neck Surgery, 128*(10), 1145–1152.

Gelinas, J. E., & Reid, G. (2000). The developmental validity of traditional learn-to-swim progressions for children with physical disabilities. *Adapted Physical Activity Quarterly, 17*(3), 269–285.

Gershten, D. M. (2001). *Kissing the virgin's mouth.* New York: HarperCollins.

Gibbs, J. (2001). *Tribes: A new way of learning and being together.* Windsor, CA: Center Source Systems.

Gibson, J. J. (1979). *The ecological approach to visual perception.* Boston: Houghton Mifflin.

Giles, H., Fox, S., & Smith, E. (1993). Patronizing the elderly: Intergenerational evaluations. *Research on Language and Social Interaction, 26*(2), 129–149.

Glaser, R. (1989). Arm exercise training for wheelchair users. *Medicine and Science in Sports and Exercise, 21*(5, Suppl.), S149–S153.

Goffman, E. (1959). *The presentation of self in everyday life.* New York: Doubleday.

Goffman, E. (1963). *Stigma: Notes on the management of spoiled identity.* Englewood Cliffs, NJ: Prentice-Hall.

Gold, M. W. (1980). *Try Another Way training manual.* Champaign, IL: Research Press.

Goldberger, M. (1992). The spectrum of teaching styles: A perspective for research on teaching physical education. *Journal of Physical Education, Recreation and Dance, 63*(1), 42–46.

Golding, L. A., Myers, C. R., & Sinning, W. (1989). *Y's way to physical fitness.* Champaign, IL: Human Kinetics.

Goodman, J., & Hopper, C. (1992). Hearing impaired children and youth: A review of psychomotor behavior. *Adapted Physical Activity Quarterly, 9*(3), 214–236.

Goodman, S. (1995). *Coaching athletes with disabilities. General principles.* Belconnen, ACT: Australian Sports Commission.

Goodwin, D. L. (2001). The meaning of help in PE: Perceptions of students with physical disabilities. *Adapted Physical Activity Quarterly, 18*, 289–303.

Goodwin, D. L., & Watkinson, E. J. (2000). Inclusive physical education from the perspective of students with physical disabilities. *Adapted Physical Activity Quarterly, 17*, 144–160.

Gorely, T., Jobling, A., Lewis, K., & Bruce, D. (2002). An evaluative case study of a psychological skills training program for athletes with intellectual abilities. *Adapted Physical Activity Quarterly, 19*, 350–363.

Gossett, J. (1981). *Movement opportunities for building independence and leisure interests through training educators and exceptional learners (MOBILITEE).* Hillsboro, OH: Hopewell Special Education Regional Resource Center.

Gottlieb, B. W., Gottlieb, J., Berkell, D., & Levy, L. (1986). Sociometric status and solitary play of LD boys and girls. *Journal of Learning Disabilities, 19*(10), 619–622.

Gould, D., Feltz, D., & Weiss, M. (1985). Motives for participating in competitive youth swimming. *International Journal of Sport Psychology, 16*, 126–140.

Govaerts, P. J., De Beukelaer, C., Daemers, K., De Ceulaer, G., Yperman, M., Somers, T., Schatteman, I., & Offeciers, F. E. (2002). Outcome of cochlear implantation at different ages from 0 to 6 years. *Otology & Neurotology: Official Publication of the American Otological Society, American Neurotology Society [and] European Academy of Otology and Neurotology, 23*(6), 885–890.

Government of Canada. (1987). *Canadian standardized test of fitness, interpretation, and counseling manual.* Ottawa: Fitness Canada.

Grandin, T. (1995). *Thinking in pictures.* New York: Vintage.

Grandin, T., & Scariano, M. (1986). *Emergence: Labeled autistic.* Navato, CA: Arena.

Green, A. (1992). *Coaching methods when working with swimmers with a disability.* Canberra, ACT: Australian Sports Commission.

Green, J. S., & Miles, B. (1987). Use of mask, fins, snorkel, and scuba equipment in aquatics for the disabled. *Palaestra, 3*(4), 12–17.

Greendorfer, S. L., & Lewko, J. H. (1978). Role of family members in sport socialization of children. *Research Quarterly, 49*, 146, 153.

Griffin, P., & McClintock, M. (1997). History of ableism in Europe and the United States—Selected timeline. In M. Adams, L. E. Bell, & P. Griffin (Eds.), *Teaching for social justice: A sourcebook* (pp. 219–227). New York: Routledge.

Grineski, S. (1996). *Cooperative learning in physical education.* Champaign, IL: Human Kinetics.

Grossarth-Maticek, R., Eyesenck, H. J., Uhlenbruck, G., Rieder, H., Freesemann, C., Rakic, L., Gallasch, G., Kanazir, D., & Liesen, H. (1990).

Sport activity and personality as elements in preventing cancer and coronary heart disease. *Perceptual and Motor Skills, 71,* 199–209.

Grosse, S. (1987). Use and misuse of flotation devices in adapted aquatics. *Palaestra, 4*(1), 31–33, 56.

Grosse, S. (1996). Aquatics for individuals with disabilities: Challenges for the 21st century. *ICHPER-SD Journal, 33*(1), 27–29.

Grosse, S., & Gildersleeve, L. (1984). *The Halliwick method: Water freedom for the handicapped.* Unpublished material available from sjgrosse@execpc.com

Guilford, J. (1952). *A factor analytic study of creative thinking.* Report from the psychological laboratory, No. 8, University of Southern California.

Guralnick, M. J. (Ed.) (2001). *Early childhood inclusion.* Baltimore: Brookes.

Guthrie, S. R., & Castelnuovo, S. (2001). Disability management among women with physical impairments: The contribution of physical activity. *Sociology of Sport Journal, 18,* 5–20.

Hall, S. (1996). Introduction: Who needs identity. In S. Hall & P. Du Gay (Eds.), *Questions of cultural identity* (pp. 9–27). London: Sage.

Hallahan, D., & Cruickshank, W. (1973). *Psychoeducational foundations of learning disabilities.* Englewood Cliffs, NJ: Prentice-Hall.

Hamilton, M., Goodway, J., & Haubenstricker, J. (1999). Parent-assisted instruction in a motor skill program for at-risk preschool children. *Adapted Physical Activity Quarterly, 16,* 415–426.

Hand, J. E. (1994). Report of a national survey of older people with lifelong intellectual handicap in New Zealand. *Journal of Intellectual Disability Research, 38,* 275–287.

Hannaford, C. (1995). *Smart moves: Why learning is not all in your head.* Arlington, VA: Great Oceans.

Hannula, D., & Thornton, N. (2001). *The swim coaching bible.* Champaign, IL: Human Kinetics.

Hansen, K., & Fuller, L. (2003). Varsity wheelers. *Sports 'N Spokes, 29*(1), 34–38.

Hansen, R., & Taylor, J. (1987). *Rick Hansen: Man in motion.* Vancouver: Douglas & McIntyre.

Hanson, M., & Carta, J. (1995). Addressing the challenges of families with multiple risks. *Exceptional Children, 62*(3), 201–212.

Hareli, S., & Weiner, B. (2002). Social emotions and personality inferences: Scaffold for a new direction in the study of achievement motivation. *Educational Psychologist 37*(3), 183–193.

Harper, D. C., & Wadsworth, J. S. (1990). Dementia and depression in elders with mental retardation: A pilot study. *Research and Developmental Disabilities, 11,* 117–198.

Harris, K. R., & Pressley, M. (1991). The nature of cognitive strategy instruction: Interactive strategy construction. *Exceptional Children, 57*(5), 392–404.

Harrison, L. (2001). Understanding the influence of stereotypes: Implications for the African American in sport and physical activity. *Quest, 53,* 97–114.

Hart, E. A., Leary, M. R., & Rejeski, W. J. (1989). The measurement of social physique anxiety. *Journal of Sport and Exercise Psychology, 11,* 94–104.

Harter, S. (1985). *Manual for the Self-Perception Profile for Children.* Denver: Author.

Harter, S. (1988). *Manual for the Self-Perception Profile for Adolescents.* Denver: Author.

Harter, S., & Pike, R. (1984). The pictorial scale of perceived competence and social acceptance for young children. *Child Development, 55,* 1969–1982.

Harvey, W. J., & Reid, G. (2003). Attention-deficit/hyperactivity disorder: A review of research on movement skill performance and physical fitness. *Adapted Physical Activity Quarterly, 20,* 1–25.

Hastie, P. (1995). An ecology of a secondary school outdoor adventure camp. *Journal of Teaching in Physical Education, 15,* 79–97.

Hastie, P. (2000). An ecological analysis of a sport education season. *Journal of Teaching in Physical Education, 19,* 355–373.

Haveman, M. J., Maaskant, M. A., & Sturman, S. F. (1989). Older Dutch residents of institutions with and without Down's syndrome: Comparisons of mortality and morbidity trends and motor/social functions. *Australia and New Zealand Journal of Developmental Disabilities, 15,* 241–255.

Heath, G. W., Pratt, M., Warren, C. W., & Kann, L. (1995, Fall). Physical activity patterns in American high school students. *Canadian Journal of Health, Physical Education, Recreation, and Dance,* 35–39.

Hedrick, B., Byrnes, D., & Shaver, L. (1989). *Wheelchair basketball.* Washington, DC: Paralyzed Veterans of America.

Hedrick, B., & Morse, M. (1991). Getting the most from roller training. *Sports 'N Spokes, 16*(6), 81–83.

Heikinaro-Johansson, P., & Sherrill, C. (1994). Integrating children with special needs in physical education: A school district assessment model from Finland. *Adapted Physical Activity Quarterly, 11*(1), 44–56.

Heikinaro-Johansson, P., Sherrill, C., French, R., & Huuhka, H. (1995). Adapted physical education consultant model to facilitate integration. *Adapted Physical Activity Quarterly, 12,* 12–33.

Heikinaro-Johansson, P., & Vogler, E. W. (1996). Physical education including individuals with disabilities in school settings. *Sport Science Review, 5*(1), 12–25.

Hellebrandt, F., & Houtz, S. (1956). Mechanisms of muscle training in man: Experimental demonstration of the overload principle. *Physical Therapy Review, 36,* 371–383.

Hellison, D. R. (1995). *Teaching responsibility through physical activity.* Champaign, IL: Human Kinetics.

Hellison, D. R., & Templin, T. J. (1991). *A reflective approach to teaching physical education.* Champaign, IL: Human Kinetics.

Hellison, D. R., & Walsh, D. (2002). Responsibility-based youth programs evaluation: Investigating the investigations. *Quest, 54,* 292–307.

Henderson, K. A., Bialeschki, M. D., Hemingway, J. L., Hodges, J. S., Kivel, B. D., & Sessoms, H. D. (Eds.). (2001). *Introduction to recreation and leisure services* (8th ed.). State College, PA: Venture Publishing.

Henderson, S. E. (1986). Some aspects of the development of motor control in Down's syndrome. In H. T. A. Whiting & M. G. Wade (Eds.), *Themes in motor development* (pp. 69–92). Boston: Martinus Nijhoff.

Henderson, S. E. (1994). Editorial: Developmental coordination disorder issue, *Adapted Physical Activity Quarterly, 11*(2), 111–114.

Henderson, S. E., & Henderson, L. (2002). Toward an understanding of developmental coordination disorder. *Adapted Physical Activity Quarterly, 19,* 12–31.

Henderson, S. E., & Sugden, D. A. (1992). *Movement assessment battery (ABC) for children.* London: Psychological Corporation.

Hernandez, D. J. (1994). Children's changing access to resources: A historical perspective. *Society for Research in Child Development Social Policy Report, 8*(1), 1–23.

Hershey, P., Blanchard, K. H., & Johnson, D. E. (2001). *Management of organizational behavior: Leading human resources* (8th ed.). Upper Saddle River, NJ: Prentice-Hall.

Hettinger, T., & Müller, E. (1953). Muskelleistung and muskeltraining. *Arbeitphysiologie, 15,* 111–126.

Hilgenbrinck, L. C. (2001). *Physical education programs: Perceptions within the Texas Youth Commission.* Unpublished dissertation, Texas Woman's University, Denton.

Hiser, E. (1999). *The other diabetes: Living and eating well with type 2 diabetes.* New York: William Morrow.

Hockenberry, J. (1995). *Moving violations: War zones, wheelchairs, and declarations of independence.* New York: Hyperion.

Hodge, S. R., Davis, R., Woodard, R., & Sherrill, C. (2002). Comparison of practicum types in changing preservice teachers' attitudes and perceived competence. *Adapted Physical Activity Quarterly, 19,* 156–171.

Hodge, S. R., & Jansma, R. (1999). Effects of contact time and location of practicum experiences on attitudes of physical education majors. *Adapted Physical Activity Quarterly, 16,* 48–63.

Hodge, S. R., Murata, N., Block, M. E., & Lieberman, L. (2003). *Case studies in adapted physical education: Empowering critical thinking.* Scottsdale, AZ: Holcomb, Hathaway.

Holland, L. J., & Steadward, R. D. (1990). Effects of resistance and flexibility training on strength, spasticity/muscle tone, and range of motion of elite athletes with cerebral palsy. *Palaestra, 6*(4), 27–31.

Hollowood, T., Salisbury, C., Rainforth, B., & Palombaro, M. (1994). Use of instructional time in classrooms serving students with and without severe disabilities. *Exceptional Children, 61*(3), 242–252.

Hoover, J. H., & Wade, M. (1985). Motor learning theory and mentally retarded individuals: A historical review. *Adapted Physical Activity Quarterly, 2,* 228–252.

Hoover, J. H., & Horgan, J. S. (1990). Short-term memory for motor skills in mentally retarded persons: Training and research issues. In G. Reid (Ed.), *Problems in movement control* (pp. 217–239). Amsterdam: North-Holland.

Hopkins, H. (1988). Current basis for theory and philosophy of occupational therapy. In H. Hopkins & H. Smith (Eds.), *Willard and Spackman's occupational therapy* (7th ed., pp. 38–42). Philadelphia: Lippincott.

Hopper, C. (1988). Self-concept and motor performance of hearing impaired boys and girls. *Adapted Physical Activity Quarterly, 5*(4), 293–304.

Houston-Wilson, C., Dunn, J. M., van der Mars, H., & McCubbin, J. (1997). The effect of peer tutors on motor performance in integrated physical education classes. *Adapted Physical Activity Quarterly, 14,* 298–313.

Howe, S. G. (1841). *Perkins report.* Watertown, MA: Perkins Institute for the Blind.

Howley, E. T., & Franks, B. D. (1997). *Health fitness instructor's handbook.* Champaign, IL: Human Kinetics.

Hsu, P., & Dunn, J. M. (1984). Comparing reverse and forward chaining instructional methods on a motor task with moderately mentally retarded individuals. *Adapted Physical Activity Quarterly, 1*(3), 240–246.

Huber, J. H. (1996). Boston: The 100th marathon and the wheelchair athlete. *Palaestra, 12*(2), 33–37.

Hughes, C. (1996). Planning problems in autism at the level of motor control. *Journal of Autism and Developmental Disorders, 26*(1), 99.

Hughes, J. (1979). *Hughes basic gross motor assessment manual.* Yonkers, NY: G. E. Miller.

Hutzler, Y., & Bar-Eli, M. (1993). Psychological benefits of sports for disabled people: A review. *Scandinavian Journal of Medical Science and Sports, 3,* 217–228.

Hutzler, Y., Fliess, O., Chachman, A., & Van den Auweele, Y. (2002). Perspectives of children with physical disabilities on inclusion and empowerment: Supporting and limiting factors. *Adapted Physical Activity Quarterly, 19,* 300–317.

Idol, L., Nevin, A., & Paolucci-Whitcomb, P. (1994). *Collaborative consultation* (2nd ed.). Austin, TX: Pro•Ed.

Individuals with Disabilities Education Act (IDEA) Amendments of 1997, 20 U.S.C. 1400 et seq.

Individuals with Disabilities Education Act (IDEA) of 1990, 20 U.S.C. 1400 et seq. (West 1993).

Irons, P. (2002). *Jim Crow's children: The broken promise of the Brown decision.* New York: Viking.

Ittenbach, R., Abery, B., Larson, S., Spiegel, A., & Prouty, R. (1994). Community adjustment of young adults with mental retardation: Overcoming barriers to inclusion. *Palaestra, 10*(2), 32–42.

Jacobson, E. (1970). *Modern treatment of tense patients.* Springfield, IL: Charles C. Thomas.

Jamison, K. R. (1993). *Touched with fire: Manic-depressive illness and the artistic temperament.* New York: Free Press.

Jamison, K. R. (1995). *An unquiet mind: A memoir of moodness and madness.* New York: Alfred A. Knopf.

Jankowski, K. A. (1997). *Deaf empowerment: Emergence, struggle, and rhetoric.* Washington, DC: Gallaudet University Press.

Jankowski, L. W. (1995). *Teaching persons with disabilities to SCUBA dive.* Montreal: Quebec Underwater Foundation.

Jansma, J., Decker, J., Ersing, W., McCubbin, H., & Combs, S. (1988). A fitness assessment system for individuals with severe mental retardation. *Adapted Physical Activity Quarterly, 5*(3), 223–232.

Jansma, P., & French, R. (1994). *Special physical education: Physical activity, sports, and recreation* (2nd ed.). Englewood Cliffs, NJ: Prentice-Hall.

Jay, D. (1991). Effect of a dance program on the creativity of preschool handicapped children. *Adapted Physical Activity Quarterly, 8,* 305–316.

Jenkins, J., & Jenkins, L. (1981). *Cross-age and peer tutoring: Help for children with learning problems.* Reston, VA: Council for Exceptional Children.

Jenkins, J., Speltz, M., & Odom, S. (1985). Integrating normal and handicapped preschoolers: Effects on child development and social interaction. *Exceptional Children, 52*(1), 7–17.

Jensen, E. (2000). *Learning with the body in mind: The scientific basis for energizers, movement, play, games, and physical education.* San Diego, CA: The Brain Store, Inc.

Jensen, E. (1998). *Teaching with the brain in mind.* Alexandria, VA: Association for Supervision and Curriculum Development.

Johnson, C. M., Catherman, G. D., & Spiro, S. H. (1981). Improving posture in a cerebral palsied child with response-contingent music. *Education and Treatment of Children, 4*(3), 243–251.

Johnson, D. W., & Johnson, R. (1975). *Learning together and alone: Cooperation, competition, and individualization.* Englewood Cliffs: NJ: Prentice-Hall.

Johnson, D. W., Johnson, R., Holubec, E., & Roy, P. (1984). *Circles of learning: Cooperation in the classroom.* Alexandria, VA: Association for Supervision and Curriculum Development.

Johnson, L., & Londeree, B. (1976). *Motor fitness testing manual for the moderately mentally retarded.* Washington, DC: American Alliance for Health, Physical Education and Recreation.

Johnson-Martin, N. M., Jens, K. G., Attermeier, S. M., & Hacker, B. J. (1991). *The Carolina curriculum for infants and toddlers with special needs (CCITSN),* (2nd ed.). Baltimore: Brookes.

Jones, J. A. (1988). *Training guide to cerebral palsy sports* (3rd ed.). Champaign, IL: Human Kinetics.

Jones, R. L. (Ed.). (1984). *Attitudes and attitude change in special education: Theory and practice.* Reston, VA: Council for Exceptional Children.

Jones, V., & Prior, M. (1985). Motor imitation abilities and neurological signs in autistic children. *Journal of Autism and Developmental Disorders, 15,* 37–46.

Jong, C. G. A. (1990). The development of mobility in blind and multiply handicapped infants. In A. Vermeer (Ed.), *Motor development, adapted physical activity, and mental retardation* (pp. 56–66). Basel, Switzerland: Karger.

Kaardal, K. (2001). *Learning by choice in secondary physical education: Creating a goal-directed program.* Champaign, IL: Human Kinetics.

Kahrs, N. (1974). *Swimming teaching for the handicapped.* Oslo, Norway: Statens ungdoms-Og idrettskontor.

Kallen, E. (1989). *Label me human: Minority rights of stigmatized Canadians.* Toronto: University of Toronto Press.

Kallstrom, C. (1975). *Yellow brick road manual.* Garland, TX: R&K Out of print.

Kalyanpur, M., & Harry, B. (1999). *Culture in special education.* Baltimore: Brookes.

Kalyvas, V., & Reid, G. (2003). Sport adaptation, participation, and enjoyment of students with and without physical disabilities. *Adapted Physical Activity Quarterly, 20,* 182–199.

Kamps, D. M., Dugan, E. P., Leonard, B. R., & Daoust, P. M. (1994). Enhanced small group instruction using choral responding and student interaction for children with autism and developmental disabilities. *American Journal of Mental Retardation, 99*(1), 60–73.

Kanner, L. (1943). Autistic disturbances of affective contact. *Nervous Child, 2,* 217–250.

Kaplan, N. M. (1990). *Clinical hypertension* (5th ed.). Baltimore: Williams & Wilkins.

Kaplan-Mayer, G. (2003). *Insulin pump therapy demystified.* New York: Marlowe & Company.

Karper, W. B., & Martinek, T. J. (1985). The integration of handicapped and nonhandicapped children in elementary physical education. *Adapted Physical Activity Quarterly, 2*(4), 314–319.

Kasser, S. L. (1995). *Inclusive games: Movement for everyone.* Champaign, IL: Human Kinetics.

Kaufman, B. (1994). *Son-rise: The miracle continues.* Tiburon, CA: H. J. Kramer.

Kavale, K. A., & Forness, S. R. (1999). *Efficacy of special education and related services.* Washington, DC: American Association on Mental Retardation.

Kavale, K. A., & Mattson, P. D. (1983). One jumped off the balance beam: Meta-analysis of perceptual motor training. *Journal of Learning Disabilities, 16,* 165–173.

Keitlen, T. (1960). *Farewell to fear.* New York: Avon Books.

Keith, K. D., & Schalock, R. L. (2000). *Cross-cultural perspectives on quality of life.* Washington, DC: American Association on Mental Retardation.

Keller, H. (1965). *The story of my life.* New York: Airmont.

Kellner, M. H., & Tutin, J. (1995). A school-based anger management program for developmentally and emotionally disabled high school students. *Adolescence, 30*(120), 813–825.

Kelly, L. E., & Gansneder, B. (1998). Preparation and job demographics of adapted physical educators in the United States. *Adapted Physical Activity Quarterly, 15,* 141–154.

Kelly, L. E., & Rimmer, J. (1987). A practical method for estimating percent body fat of adult mentally retarded males. *Adapted Physical Activity Quarterly, 4,* 117–125.

Kelso, J. A. S. (1996). *Dynamic patterns: The organization of brain and behavior.* Cambridge, MA: MIT Press.

Kennedy, R. (2002). *Nigger: The strange career of a troublesome word.* New York: Pantheon Books.

Kephart, N. C. (1971). *The slow learner in the classroom* (2nd ed.). Columbus, OH: Charles E. Merrill.

Keyser-Marcus, L., Briel, L., Sherron-Targett, P., Yasuda, S., Johnson, S., & Wehman, P. (2002). Enhancing the schooling of students with traumatic brain injury. *Teaching Exceptional Children, 34*(4), 62–67.

Killian, K., Joyce-Petrovich, R., Menna, L., & Arena, S. (1984). Measuring water orientation and beginner swim skills of autistic individuals. *Adapted Physical Activity Quarterly, 1*(4), 287–295.

Kimball, J. G. (2002). Developmental coordination disorder from a sensory integration perspective. In S. A. Cermak & D. Larkin (Eds.), *Developmental coordination disorder* (pp. 210–220). Albany, NY: Delmar.

Kiphard, E. (1983). Adapted physical education in Germany. In R. Eason, T. Smith, & F. Caron (Eds.), *Adapted physical activity: From theory to application* (pp. 25–32). Champaign, IL: Human Kinetics.

Kisor, H. (1990). *What's that pig outdoors? A memoir of deafness.* New York: Penguin Books.

Kitaha, K. (1984). *Daily life in physical education for autistic children: Volume III.* Boston: Nimrod Press.

Klass, C. S. (1996). *Home visiting: Promoting healthy parent and child development.* Baltimore: Brookes.

Klein, J. T. (1990). *Interdisciplinary: History, theory, and practice.* Detroit, MI: Wayne State University.

Kleinert, H. L., & Kearns, J. F. (2001). *Alternate assessment: Measuring outcomes and supports for students with disabilities.* Baltimore: Brookes.

Knop, P. D., & Oja, P. (1996). Sport for all. In J. D. Halloran, P. V. Komi, H. G. Knuttgen, P. D. Knop, P. Oja, & F. Roskam (Eds.), *Current issues of sport science* (pp. 15–43). Schorndorf, Germany: Verlag Karl Hoffman.

Kobberling, G., Jankowski, L., & Leger, L. (1989). Energy cost of locomotion in blind adolescents. *Adapted Physical Activity Quarterly, 6*(1), 58–67.

Kohlberg, L. (1984). *The psychology of moral development: The nature and validity of moral stages.* San Francisco: Harper & Row.

Koroknay, V. J., Werner, P., Cohen-Mansfield, J., & Braun, J. V. (1995). Maintaining ambulation in the frail nursing home resident: A nursing administered walking program. *Journal of Gerontological Nursing, 21*(11), 18–24.

Kottke, F. (1990). Therapeutic exercise to maintain mobility. In F. Kottke & J. Lehmann (Eds.), *Krusen's handbook of physical medicine and rehabilitation* (4th ed., pp. 436–451). Philadelphia: W. B. Saunders.

Kottke, F. J., & Lehmann, J. (1990). *Krusen's handbook of physical medicine and rehabilitation* (4th ed.). Philadelphia: W. B. Sanders.

Kowalski, E. M., & Rizzo, T. L. (1996). Factors influencing preservice student attitudes toward individuals with disabilities. *Adapted Physical Activity Quarterly, 13,* 180–196.

Kowalski, E., & Sherrill, C. (1992). Modeling and motor sequencing strategies of learning-disabled boys. *Adapted Physical Activity Quarterly, 9*(3), 261–272.

Kozub, F. M., Sherblom, P. R., & Perry, T. L. (1999). Inclusion paradigms and perspectives: A stepping stone to accepting learner diversity in physical education. *Quest, 51,* 346–354.

Kraus, H., & Hirschland, R. (1954). Minimum muscular fitness tests in schoolchildren. *Research Quarterly, 25*(2), 177–188.

Krebs, P. L., & Block, M. E. (1992). Transition of students with disabilities into community recreation: The role of the adapted physical educator. *Adapted Physical Activity Quarterly, 9,* 305–315.

Krents, H. (1972). *To race the wind.* New York: Putman.

Krotoski, D. M., Nosek, M. A., & Turk, M. A. (1996). *Women with physical disabilities: Achieving and maintaining health and well-being.* Baltimore: Brookes.

Krueger, D. L., DiRocco, P., & Felix, M. (2000). Obstacles adapted physical education specialists encounter when developing transition plans. *Adapted Physical Activity Quarterly, 17,* 222–236.

Kudláček, M., Válková, H., Sherrill, C., Myers, B., & French, R. (2002). An inclusion instrument based on planned behavior theory for prospective physical educators. *Adapted Physical Activity Quarterly, 19,* 280–299.

Kugler, P. N., Kelso, J. A. S., & Turvey, M. T. (1982). On coordination and control in naturally developing systems. In J. A. S. Kelso & J. E. Clark (Eds.), *The development of movement control and coordination* (pp. 5–78). New York: Wiley.

Laban, R. (1960). *The mastery of movement* (2nd ed.). London: MacDonald & Evans.

Laban, R. (1975). *Modern educational dance.* London: MacDonald & Evans.

Labat, J., & Maggi, A. (1997). *Weight management for Type II diabetes: An action plan.* New York: Wiley.

Lagorio, J. (1993). *Life cycle.* Tucson, AZ: Zephyr Press.

LaMaster, K., Gall, K., Kinchin, G., & Siedentop, D. (1998). Inclusion practices of effective elementary specialists. *Adapted Physical Activity Quarterly, 15,* 64–81.

Lambert, N., Nihira, K., & Leland, H. (1993). *AAMR Adaptive Behavior Scale-School and Community.* Austin, TX: Pro•Ed.

Landry, G. (1989). *AIDS in sport.* Champaign, IL: Leisure Press.

Landrus, R., & Mesibov, G. (1985). *Preparing autistic students for community living: A functional and sequential approach to training.* Chapel

Hill, NC: University of North Carolina, Department of Psychiatry, Division TEACCH.

Lange, L. (1919). *Uber funktionelle amprassurig.* Berlin: Springer-Verlag.

Langendorfer, S. J., & Bruya, L. D. (1994). *Aquatic readiness: Developing water competence in young children.* Champaign, IL: Human Kinetics.

Larkin, S. A., & Gurry, S. (1998). Brief report: Progress reported in three children with autism in Daily Life Therapy. *Journal of Autism and Developmental Disorders, 28*(4), 339–342.

Larkin, D., & Parker, H. E. (2002). Task-specific intervention for children with developmental coordination disorder: A systems view. In S. A. Cermak & D. Larkin (Eds.), *Developmental coordination disorder* (pp. 234–247). Albany, NY: Delmar.

Lavay, B., French, R., & Henderson, H. (1997). *Positive behavior management strategies for physical educators.* Champaign, IL: Human Kinetics.

Lazarus, J. C. (1990). Factors underlying inefficient movement in learning-disabled children. In G. Reid (Ed.), *Problems in motor control: Advances in psychology series* (pp. 241–282). Amsterdam: North-Holland.

Lazarus, R. S., & Folkman, S. (1984). *Stress, appraisal, and coping.* New York: Springer.

Leavitt, R. L. (1999). *Cross-cultural rehabilitation: An international perspective.* Philadelphia: W. B. Sanders.

Lee, M., Ward, G., & Shephard, R. J. (1985). Physical capacities of sightless adolescents. *Developmental Medicine and Child Neurology, 27,* 767–774.

LeFevre, D. N. (2002). *Best new games.* Champaign, IL: Human Kinetics.

Leitschuh, C. A., & Dunn, J. M. (2001). Prediction of the gross-motor quotient in young children prenatally exposed to cocaine/polydrugs. *Adapted Physical Activity Quarterly, 18,* 240–256.

Lepore, M., Gayle, G. W., & Stevens, S. (1998). *Adapted aquatics programming: A professional guide.* Champaign, IL: Human Kinetics.

Leuw, L. (1972). *Co-active movement with deaf-blind children: The Van Dijk model.* Videotape made at Michigan School for the Blind. Available through many regional centers for the deaf-blind.

Levine, P., & Edgar, E. (1994). An analysis of gender of long-term postschool outcomes for youth with and without disabilities. *Exceptional Children, 61*(3), 282–300.

Levitt, S. (1995). *Treatment of cerebral palsy and motor delay* (3rd ed.). Boston: Blackwell Scientific.

Lewin, K. (1936). *Principles of topological psychology.* New York: McGraw-Hill.

Lewin, K. (1951). *Field theory in social science.* New York: Harper.

Lieberman, L. J., & Cowart, J. F. (1996). *Games for people with sensory impairments.* Champaign, IL: Human Kinetics.

Lieberman, L. J., Dunn, J. M., van der Mars, H., & McCubbin, J. (2000). Peer tutors' effects on activity levels of deaf students in inclusive elementary physical education. *Adapted Physical Activity Quarterly, 17,* 20–39.

Lieberman, L. J., & Houston-Wilson, C. (2002). *Strategies for inclusion: A handbook for physical educators.* Champaign, IL: Human Kinetics.

Lieberman, L. J., Houston-Wilson, C., and Kozub, F. M. (2002). Perceived barriers to including students with visual impairments in general physical education. *Adapted Physical Activity Quarterly, 19,* 364–377.

Lieberman, L. J., & McHugh, E. (2001). Health-related fitness of children who are visually impaired. *Journal of Visual Impairment and Blindness, 95,* 272–287.

Lienert, C., Sherrill, C., & Myers, B. (2001). Physical educators' concerns about integrating children with disabilities: A cross-cultural comparison. *Adapted Physical Activity Quarterly, 18,* 1–17.

Linder, T. W. (1993a). *Transdisciplinary play-based assessment.* Baltimore: Brookes.

Linder, T. W. (1993b). *Transdisciplinary play-based intervention.* Baltimore: Brookes.

Linschoten, R., Backx, F., Mulder, O., & Meinardi, H. (1990). Epilepsy and sports. *Sports Medicine, 10*(1), 9–19.

Littlejohn, S. W. (1999). *Theories of human communication* (6th ed.). Belmont, CA: Wadsworth.

Lockette, K. F., & Keyes, A. M. (1994). *Conditioning with physical disabilities.* Champaign, IL: Human Kinetics.

Long, E., Irmer, L., Burkett, L., Glasenapp, G., & Odenkirk, B. (1980). PEOPEL. *Journal of Physical Education and Recreation, 51,* 28–29.

Longmuir, P. E., & Bar-Or, O. (2000). Factors influencing the physical activity levels of youths with physical and sensory disabilities. *Adapted Physical Activity Quarterly, 17,* 40–53.

Loovis, E. M. (1985). Evaluation of toy preference and associated movement behaviors of preschool orthopedically handicapped children. *Adapted Physical Activity Quarterly, 2,* 117–126.

Losardo, A., & Notari-Syverson, A. (2001). *Alternative approaches to assessing young children.* Baltimore: Brookes.

Louisiana Department of Education. (2001). *Competency Test for Adapted Physical Education (CTAPE).* Baton Rouge, LA: Author.

Lovaas, I. (1981). *The me book.* Austin, TX: Pro•Ed.

Low, L. (1992). *Prediction of selected track, field, and swimming performance of dwarf athletes by anthropometry.* Unpublished doctoral study, Texas Woman's University, Denton.

Low, L., Knudsen, M. J., & Sherrill, C. (1996). Dwarfism: New interest area for adapted physical activity. *Adapted Physical Activity Quarterly, 13*(1), 1–15.

Lowman, C. L. (1937). *Techniques of underwater gymnastics.* Los Angeles: American Publications.

Lowman, C. L., & Roen, S. (1952). *Therapeutic use of pools and tanks.* Philadelphia: W. B. Saunders.

Lowman, C. L., & Young, C. H. (1960). *Postural fitness.* Philadelphia: Lea & Febiger.

Lubin, E., & Sherrill, C. (1980). Motor creativity of preschool deaf children. *American Annals of the Deaf, 125,* 460–466.

Luckasson, R., Coutler, D., Polloway, E., Deiss, S., Schalock, R., Snell, M., Spitalnik, D., & Stark, J. (1992). *Mental retardation: Definition, classification, and systems of supports* (9th ed.). Washington, DC: American Association on Mental Retardation.

Lucyshyn, J. M., Dunlap, G., & Albin, R. W. (Eds.) (2002). *Families and positive behavior support: Addressing problem behavior in family contexts.* Baltimore: Brookes.

Lund, J. L. (2000). *Creating rubrics for physical education.* Reston, VA: NASPE Publications, AAHPERD.

Lytle, R. K., & Collier, D. (2002). The consultation process: Adapted physical education specialists' perceptions. *Adapted Physical Activity Quarterly, 19,* 261–279.

Macdonald, D., Kirk, D., Metzler, M., Nilges, L. M., Schempp, P., & Wright, J. (2002). It's all very well, in theory: Theoretical perspectives and their applications in contemporary pedagogical research. *Quest, 54,* 133–156.

MacMillan, D. L., Gresham, F. M., & Siperstein, G. N. (1995). Heightened concerns over the 1992 AAMR definition: Advocacy versus precision. *American Journal on Mental Retardation, 100*(1), 87–97.

Mackelprang, R., & Salsgiver, R. (1999). *Disability: A diversity model approach in human service practice.* Pacific Grove, CA: Brooks/Cole.

Magill, R. A. (2001). *Motor learning: Concepts and applications* (6th ed.). Boston: McGraw-Hill.

Maglischo, E. W. (2003). *Swimming fastest.* Champaign, IL: Human Kinetics.

Malina, R. M. (2001). Adherence to physical activity from childhood to adulthood: A perspective from tracking studies. *Quest Academy Papers, 53,* 346–355.

Malina, R. M. (2001, September) Tracking of physical activity across the lifespan. *Research Digest, President's Council on Physical Fitness and Sport, 3,* 14, 1–8.

Manjiviona, J., & Prior, M. (1995). Comparison of Asperger syndrome and high-functioning autistic children on a test of motor impairment. *Journal of Autism and Developmental Disorders, 25*(1), 23–39.

Mannell, R. C., & Kleiber, D. A. (1997). *A social psychology of leisure.* State College, PA: Venture Publishing.

Margalit, M. (1984). Leisure activities of learning disabled children as a reflection of their passive lifestyle and prolonged dependence. *Child Psychiatry and Human Development, 15*(2), 133–141.

Marino, B., & Pueschel, S. M. (Eds.). (1996). *Heart disease in persons with Down syndrome.* Baltimore: Brookes.

Marlowe, M. (1980). Games analysis intervention: A procedure to increase peer acceptance of socially isolated children. *Research Quarterly for Exercise and Sport, 51,* 422–426.

Marsh, H. W. (1997). The measurement of physical self-concept: A construct validation approach. In K. R. Fox (Ed.), *The physical self* (pp. 27–58). Champaign, IL: Human Kinetics.

Marsh, H. W., Richards, G. E., Johnson, S., Roche, L., & Tremayne, P. (1994). Physical self-description questionnaire: Psychometric properties and a multitrait-multimethod analysis of relations to existing instruments. *Journal of Sport and Exercise Psychology, 16,* 270–305.

Marshall, J. D., & Bouffard, M. (1994). Obesity and movement competency in children. *Adapted Physical Activity Quarterly, 11*(3), 297–365.

Martens, R. (1977). *The sport competition anxiety test.* Champaign, IL: Human Kinetics.

Martens, R., Burton, D., Vealey, R. S., Bump, L A., & Smith, D. E. (1990). The competitive state anxiety–2 (CSAI-2). In R. Martens, R. S. Vealey, & D. Burton, *Competitive anxiety in sport* (pp. 117–190). Champaign, IL: Human Kinetics.

Martin, J. J. (1999). Predictors of social physique anxiety in adolescent swimmers with physical disabilities. *Adapted Physical Activity Quarterly, 16,* 75–85.

Martin, J. J., & Smith, K. (2002). Friendship quality in youth disability sport: Perceptions of a best friend. *Adapted Physical Activity Quarterly, 19,* 472–482.

Martin, J. L. (1996). *Overview of legal issues involved in educating students with autism and PDD under IDEA.* Paper presented at the Fifth Annual State Conference on Autism, Corpus Christi, TX.

Martinek, T., & Hellison, D. (1997). Service-bonded inquiry: The road less traveled. *Journal of Teaching in Physical Education, 17,* 107–121.

Maslow, A. (1954). *Motivation and personality,* New York: Harper & Row.

Maslow, A. (1970). *Motivation and personality* (2nd ed.). New York: Harper & Row.

Mastro, J., Burton, A. W., Rosendahl, M., & Sherrill, C. (1996). Attitudes of elite athletes with impairments toward one another: A hierarchy of preference. *Adapted Physical Activity Quarterly, 13*(2), 197–210.

Matter, R., Nash, R., & Frogley, M. (2002). Interscholastic athletics for student-athletes with disabilities. *Palaestra, 18,* 32–38.

Maurer, H. M. (1983). *Pediatrics.* New York: Churchill Livingstone.

Maurice, C. (1993). *Let me hear your voice: A family's triumph over autism.* New York: Fawcett Columbine.

McBee, F., & Ballinger, J. (1984). *The continental quest.* Tampa, FL: Overland Press.

McCall, R. M., & Craft, D. H. (2000). *Movement with a purpose.* Champaign, IL: Human Kinetics.

McColl, M. A., Charlifue, S., Glass, C., Savic, G., & Meehan, M. (2002). International differences in aging and spinal cord injury. *Spinal Cord, 49,* 128–136.

McCracken, B. (2001). *It's not just gym anymore: Teaching secondary school students how to be active for life.* Champaign, IL: American Fitness Alliance.

McCrae, P. G., Asplund, L. S., Schnell, J. F., Ouslander, J. R., & Abrahamse, A. (1966). A walking program for nursing home residents: Effects on walk endurance, physical activity, mobility and quality of life. *Journal of the American Geriatric Society, 44*(2), 175–180.

McGrowder-Lin, R., & Blatt, A. (1988). A wanderer's lounge program for nursing home residents with Alzheimer's disease. *Gerontologist, 28,* 607–609.

McKenzie, T. L. (2001). Promoting physical activity in youth: Focus on middle school environments. *Quest Academy Papers, 53,* 326–334.

McKenzie, R. T. (1909, 1915, 1923). *Exercise in education and medicine.* Philadelphia: Saunders.

McKiddie, B., & Maynard, I. W. (1997). Perceived competence of school children in physical education. *Journal of Teaching in Physical Education, 13,* 324–339.

Meddaugh, D. (1987). Exercise to music for the abusive patient. In T. L. Brink (Ed.), *The elderly uncooperative patient* (pp. 47–54). London: Haworth Press.

Mender, J., Kerr, R., & Orlick, T. (1982). A cooperative games program for learning disabled children. *International Journal of Sports Psychology, 13,* 222–233.

Messer, B., & Harter, S. (1986). *Manual for the Self-Perception Profile for Adults.* Denver: Authors.

Meyer Rehabilitation Institute. (1992). *Milani-Comparetti motor development screening test for infants and young children: A manual.* Omaha: Author.

Milani-Comparetti, A., & Gidoni, E. (1967). Pattern analysis of motor development and its disorders. *Developmental Medicine and Child Neurology, 9,* 625–630.

Miller, N., Merritt, J., Merkel, K., & Westbrook, P. (1984). Paraplegic energy expenditure during negotiation of architectural barriers. *Archives of Physical Medicine and Rehabilitation, 65,* 778–779.

Miller, P. D. (Ed.). (1995). *Fitness programming for physical disabilities: A publication for disabled sports.* Champaign, IL: Human Kinetics.

Miller, S. E., & Schaumberg, K. (1988). Physical education activities for children with severe cerebral palsy. *Teaching Exceptional Children, 20*(2), 9–11.

Missiuna, C., & Mandich, A. (2002). Integrating motor learning theories into practice. In S. A. Cermak & D. Larkin (Eds.). *Developmental coordination disorder* (pp. 221–233). Albany, NY: Delmar.

Miyahara, M. (1994). Subtypes of students with learning disabilities based on gross motor functions. *Adapted Physical Activity Quarterly, 11,* 368–382.

Molnar, G. (1978). Analysis of motor disorder in retarded infants and young children. *American Journal of Mental Deficiency, 83,* 213–221.

Montagu, A. (1971). *The elephant man.* New York: Ballantine.

Montgomery, D. L., Reid, G., & Seidl, C. (1988). The effects of two physical fitness programs designed for mentally retarded adults. *Canadian Journal of Sport Sciences, 13*(1), 73–78.

Mon-Williams, M. A., Pascal, E., & Wann, J. P. (1994). Opthalmic factors in developmental coordination disorder. *Adapted Physical Activity Quarterly, 11*(2), 170–178.

Moore, B., & Snow, R. (1994). *Wheelchair tennis: Myth to reality.* Dubuque, IA: Kendall/Hunt.

Morgan, W. P. (2001). Prescription of physical activity: A paradigm shift. *Quest academy papers: Adherence to exercise and physical activity, 53,* 366–382.

Morgan, W. P., & Dishman, R. K. (Eds.). (2001). Adherence to exercise and physical activity: The Academy Papers, *Quest, 53,* (3) 277–399.

Morris, J. (1991). *Pride against prejudice: Transforming attitudes to disability.* Philadelphia: New Society Publishers.

Morris, G. S. D. (1976). *How to change the games children play.* Minneapolis: Burgess.

Morris, G. S. D., & Stiehl, J. (1999). *Changing kids' games* (2nd ed.) Champaign, IL: Human Kinetics.

Mosston, M. (1966). *Teaching physical education.* Columbus, OH: Merrill.

Mosston, M. (1992). Tug-o-war, no more: Meeting teaching-learning objectives using the spectrum of teaching styles. *Journal of Physical Education, Recreation and Dance, 63*(1), 27–31, 56.

Mosston, M., & Ashworth, S. (1986). *Teaching physical education* (3rd ed.). Columbus, OH: Merrill.

Mosston, M., & Ashworth, S. (1990). *The spectrum of teaching styles: From command to discovery.* White Plains, NY: Longman.

Mosston, M., & Ashworth, S. (1994). *Teaching physical education* (4th ed.) Columbus, OH: Merrill.

Moucha, S. (1991). The disabled female athlete as role model. *Journal of Physical Education, Recreation and Dance, 62*(3), 37–38.

Murata, N. A. (2003). Language augmentation strategies in physical education. *Journal of Physical Education, Recreation and Dance, 74*(3), 29–32.

Murray, M. T. (1994). *Diabetes and hypoglycemia.* Roseville, CA: Prima Publishing.

Myers, D. G. (2000). *A quiet world: Living with hearing loss.* New Haven: Yale University Press.

Namazi, K. H., Zadorozny, C., & Gwinnup, P. B. (1995). The influences of physical activity on patterns of sleep behavior of patients with Alzheimer's disease. *International Journal of Aging and Human Development, 20*(2), 145–153.

Nash, S. (2002). Youth force. *Sports 'N Spokes, 28*(6), 54–57.

National Association of Sport and Physical Education (NASPE). (1995). *NASPE standards for physical education.* Reston, VA: Author.

National Cancer Institute of Canada, (2002). Retrieved from http://www.ncic.cancer.ca.

National Center on Educational Outcomes (1999). *Participation of students with disabilities.* Minneapolis: Author. http://www.coled.umn.edu/NCEO.

National Consortium for Physical Education and Recreation for Individuals with Disabilities (NCPERID). (1995). *Adapted physical education national standards (APENS).* Champaign, IL: Human Kinetics.

National Disability Sports Alliance. (2002). *NDSA sports rules manual* (6th ed). Kingston, RI: Author.

National Heart, Lung, and Blood Institute. (2002). Retrieved from http://www.nhlbi.nih.gov/health/public/heart/other/chdfacts.htm.

National Institute of Neurological Disorders and Stroke. (2001). Retrieved from http://www.ninds.nih.gov/health and medical/pubs/parkinson's disease backgrounder.htm.

National Institute of Mental Health. (2002). Retrieved from http://www.nimh.nih.gov/publicat/depression.cfm#ptdepl.

National Osteoporosis Foundation. (2002). Retrieved from www.nof.org.

Neemann, J., & Harter, S. (1986). *Manual for the Self-Perception Profile for College Students.* Denver: Author.

Neistadt, M. E., & Crepeau, E. B. (1998). *Willard & Spackman's occupational therapy* (9th ed.). Philadelphia: Lippicott, Williams, & Wilkins.

Newman, J. (1976). *Swimming for children with physical and sensory impairments.* Springfield, IL: Charles C. Thomas.

NICHCY. (1995, December). *Helping students develop their IEPs: Technical assistance guide.* Washington, DC: Author. (Address is NICHCY, P. O. Box 1492, Washington, DC 20013).

Nicholls, J. G. (1989). *The competitive ethos and democratic education.* Cambridge, MA: Harvard University Press.

Nickel, R. E., & Desch, L. W. (Eds.). (2000). *The physician's guide to caring for children with disabilities and chronic conditions.* Baltimore: Brookes.

Nideffer, R. M. (1977). *Test of attentional and interpersonal style.* San Diego, CA: Enhanced Performance Associates.

Nihira, K., Weisner, T. S., & Bernheimer, L. P. (1994). Ecocultural assessment in families of children with developmental delays: Construct and concurrent validities. *American Journal on Mental Retardation, 98,* 551–566.

Nirje, B. (1969). The normalization principle and its human management implications. In R. Kugel & W. Wolfensberger (Eds.), *Changing patterns in residential services for the mentally retarded* (pp. 179–195). Washington, DC: President's Committee on Mental Retardation.

Nirje, B. (1980). The normalization principle. In R. J. Flynn & K. E. Nitsch (Eds.), *Normalization, social integration, and community services* (pp. 31–49). Baltimore: University Park Press.

Nixon, H. L. (1988). Getting over the worry hurdle: Parental encouragement and the sports involvement of visually impaired children and youths. *Adapted Physical Activity Quarterly, 5,* 29–43.

Nixon, H. L. (1989). Integration of disabled people in mainstream sports: Case study of a partially sighted child. *Adapted Physical Activity Quarterly, 6,* 17–31.

Obiakor, F. E. (1999). Teacher expectations of minority exceptional learners: Impact of "accuracy" of self-concepts. *Exceptional Children, 66,* 39–53.

O'Brien, F., & Azrin, N. H. (1970). Behavioral engineering: Control of posture by informational feedback. *Journal of Applied Behavior Analysis, 3,* 235–240.

O'Brien-Cousins, S., & Goodwin, D. (2002). Balance your life! The metaphors of falling. *WellSpring, 13*(3), 607.

O'Connor, J., French, R., & Henderson, H. (2000). Use of physical activity to improve behavior of children with autism—Two for one benefits. *Palaestra, 16*(3), 22–26, 28–29.

O'Connor, J., Sherrill, C., & French, R. (2001). Information retrieval and pedagogy in adapted physical activity. *Perceptual and Motor Skills, 92,* 937–940.

O'Leary, K. D., & Schneider, M. R. (1980). *Catch 'em being good: Approaches to motivation and discipline* [film]. Champaign, IL: Research Press.

Okada, S., Hirakawa, K., Takada, Y., & Kinoshita, H. (2001). Relationship between fear of falling and balancing ability during abrupt deceleration in aged women having similar habitual physical activities. *European Journal of Applied Physiology, 85*(6), 501–506.

Olenik, L., & Sherrill, C. (1994). Physical education and students with HIV/AIDS. *Journal of Physical Education, Recreation and Dance, 65*(5), 49–52.

Oliver, C., Murphy, G., Hall, S., Arron, K., & Leggett, J. (2003). Phenomenology of self-restraint. *American Journal on Mental Retardation, 108,* 71–81.

Oliver, M. (1990). *The politics of disablement.* London: Macmillan.

Orlick, T. (1978). *The cooperative sports and games book.* New York: Pantheon.

Oskamp. S. (Ed.). (2002) *Reducing prejudice and discrimination.* Mahwah, NJ: Erlbaum.

Ottenbacher, K. J. (1988). Sensory integration-Myth, method, imperative. *Mental Retardation, 92*(5), 425–426.

Overstall, P. S., Exton-Smith, A. N., Imms, F. J., & Johnson, A. L. (1977). Falls in the elderly related to postural imbalance. *British Medical Journal 1,* 261–264.

Overton, T. (2003). *Assessing learners with special needs: An applied approach* (4th ed.). Columbus, OH: Merrill Prentice-Hall.

Owen, E. (1982). *Playing and coaching wheelchair basketball.* Champaign: University of Illinois Press.

Owens, M. F. (1974). *Every child a winner.* Ocilla, GA: Irwin County Schools.

Paciorek, M. J., & Jones, J. A. (2001). *Disability sport and recreation resources* (3rd ed.). Traverse City, MI: Cooper Publishing Group.

Painter, M. A., Inman, K. B., & Vincent, W. J. (1994). Contextual interference effects in the acquisition and retention of motor tasks by individuals with mild mental handicaps. *Adapted Physical Activity Quarterly, 11*(4), 383–395.

Papolos, D., & Papolos, J. (2002). *The bipolar child* (rev. ed.). New York: Broadway Books.

Parent, C. J. & Whall, A. L. (1986). Are physical activity and self-esteem and depression related? *Journal of Geriatric Nursing, 10,* 8–11.

Parish, L. E., & Treasure, D. C. (2003). Physical activity and situational motivation in physical education: Influence of the motivational climate and perceived ability. *Research Quarterly for Exercise and Sport, 74,* 173–182.

Parker, M., & Hellison, D. (2001). Teaching responsibility in physical education: Standards, outcomes, and beyond. *Journal of Physical Education, Recreation and Dance, 72*(9), 25–33.

Parks, B. A. (1997). *Tennis in a wheelchair* (rev. ed.). New York: United States Tennis Association.

Parten, M. (1932). Social participation among preschool children. *Journal of Abnormal and Social Psychology, 27,* 243–269.

Pate, R. R., Pratt, M., Blair, S. N., Haskell, W. L., Macera, C. A., Boucard, C., et al. (1995). Physical activity and public health: A recommendation from the Centers for Disease Control and Prevention and the American College of Sports Medicine. *Journal of the American Medical Association, 273,* 402–407.

Pellett, T. L., & Lox, C. L. (1997). Tennis racket length comparisons and their effect on beginning college players' playing success and achievement. *Journal of Teaching in Physical Education, 16,* 490–499.

Pennington, B. F., & Ozonoff, S. (1996). Executive functions and developmental psychology. *Journal of Child Psychology and Psychiatry, 37*(1), 51–87.

Pensgaard, A. M., & Sorensen, M. (2002). Empowerment through the sport context: A model to guide research for individuals with disability. *Adapted Physical Activity Quarterly, 19,* 48–67.

Petrofsky, J. S., Brown, S. W., & Cerrel-Baxo, H. (1992). Active physical therapy and its benefits in rehabilitation. *Palaestra, 8*(3), 23–27, 61–62.

Pfeiffer, D. (1993). Overview of the disability movement: History, legislative record, and political implications. *Policy Studies Journal, 21,* 724–734.

Physician's Desk Reference. (published annually). Oradell, NJ: Medical Economics.

Piaget, J. (1936). *The origins of intelligence in children.* (M. Cook, translator). New York: International Universities Press, 1974.

Piaget, J. (1952). *The origins of intelligence in children.* New York: International Universities Press.

Piaget, J. (1962). *Play, dreams, and limitation in childhood.* New York: W. W. Norton.

Pianta, R. C., & Cox, M. J. (2000). *The transition to kindergarten.* Baltimore: Brookes.

Pickett, A. L., & Gerlach, K. (Eds.). (1997). *Supervising paraeducators in school settings.* Austin, TX: Pro•Ed.

Pitetti, K., Jackson, J., Stubbs, N., Campbell, K., & Battar, S. (1989). Fitness levels of adult Special Olympics participants. *Adapted Physical Activity Quarterly, 6,* 354–370.

Pitetti, K., Fernandez, J., & Lanciault, M. (1991). Feasibility of an exercise program for adults with cerebral palsy: A pilot study. *Adapted Physical Activity Quarterly, 8*(4), 333–341.

Pivik, J., McComas, J., & Laflamme, M. (2002). Barriers and facilitators to inclusive education. *Exceptional Children, 69,* 97–107.

Place, K., & Hodge, S. R. (2001). Social inclusion of students with disabilities in general physical education: A behavioral analysis. *Adapted Physical Activity Quarterly, 18,* 389–404.

Plake, B. S., Impara, J. C., & Spies, R. A. (Eds.). (2003). *The fifteenth mental measurements yearbook.* Lincoln, NE: University of Nebraska Press. See related resources from www.nebraskapress.unl.edu.

Pliszka, S. R. (2000). Patterns of psychiatric morbidity with attention-deficit/hyperactivity disorder. *Child and Adolescent Psychiatric Clinics of North America, 9,* 525–540.

Porretta, D. L., Nesbitt, J., & Labanowich, S. (1993). Terminology usage: A case for clarity. *Adapted Physical Activity Quarterly, 10,* 87–96.

Porretta, D. L., & O'Brien, K. (1991). The use of contextual interference trials by mildly mentally retarded children. *Research Quarterly for Exercise and Sport, 62,* 244–248.

Porretta, D. L., Surburg, P. R., & Jansma, P. (2002). Perceptions of adapted physical education graduates from selected universities on attainment of doctoral competencies: 1980–1999. *Adapted Physical Activity Quarterly, 19,* 420–434.

Porter, S., Heynie, M., Bierle, T., Calwell, T. H., & Palfrey, J. S. (Eds.). (2001). *Children and youth assisted by medical technology in educational settings* (2nd ed.). Baltimore: Brookes.

Powers, S. K., & Dodd, S. L. (2003). *Total fitness and wellness* (3rd ed). San Francisco: Benjamin Cummings.

Prentice, A. (2002). *Annex 7: The scientific basis for diet, nutrition and the prevention of osteoporosis. Background paper for the Joint WHO/FAP Expert Consultation on diet, nutrition and the prevention of chronic diseases.* Geneva: World Health Organization.

President's Council on Physical Fitness and Sports (PCPFS). (1987). *Get fit: A handbook for youth ages 6–17.* Washington, DC: Author.

President's Council on Physical Fitness and Sport (PCPFS). (1997). *President's challenge* (rev.). Washington, DC: Author.

President's Council on Physical Fitness and Sport (PCPFS). (2003). *Presidential Active Lifestyle Award (PALA).* Washington, DC: Author.

Priest, E. L. (1996). *Adapted aquatics.* Kingwood, TX: Jeff Ellis and Associates.

Promis, D., Erevelles, N., & Matthews, J. (2001). Reconceptualizing inclusion: The politics of university sports and recreation programs for students with mobility impairments. *Sociology of Sport Journal, 18,* 37–50.

Provus, M. (1971). *The discrepancy evaluation model.* Berkeley, CA: McCutchan.

Pueschel, S. M., Linakis, J. G., & Anderson, A. C. (Eds.). (1996). *Lead poisoning in childhood.* Baltimore: Brookes.

Purnell, L. D., & Paulanka, B. J. (1998). *Transcultural health care: A culturally competent approach.* Philadelphia: F. A. Davis.

Purvis, J. (1985). A new description of corrective therapy. *American Corrective Therapy Journal, 39*(1), 4–5.

Quill, K. (1989). Daily Life Therapy: A Japanese model of educating children with autism. *Journal of Autism and Developmental Disorders, 19*(4), 625–635.

Rafter, D., & Crase, N. (1998). Living history [Wheelchair tennis]. *Sports 'N Spokes, 24*(8), 32–38.

Rainforth, B., & York-Barr, J. (1997). *Collaborative teams for students with severe disabilities* (2nd ed.). Baltimore: Brookes.

Ramm, P. (1988). Pediatric occupational therapy. In H. Hopkins & H. Smith (Eds.), *Willard and Spackman's occupational therapy* (7th ed., pp. 601–627). Philadelphia, J. B. Lippincott.

Rarick, G. L. (1980). Cognitive-motor relationships in the growing years. *Research Quarterly for Exercise and Sport, 51*(1), 174–192.

Rathbone, J., & Hunt, V. V. (1965). *Corrective physical education* (7th ed.). Philadelphia: W. B. Saunders.

Reber, R., & Sherrill, C. (1981). Creative thinking and dance/movement skills of hearing impaired youth: An experimental study. *American Annals of the Deaf, 26*(9), 1004–1009.

Reeve, C. (1999). *Still me.* New York: Random House.

Reeve, C. (2002). *Nothing is impossible.* New York: Random House.

Reeve, D. (2002). Negotiating psycho-emotional dimensions of disability and their influence on identity constructions. *Disability and Society, 17,* 493–508.

Reid, G. (Ed.). (1980). *Problems in movement control.* New York: North Holland Elsevier Science Publishing.

Reid, G. (1986). The trainability of motor processing strategies with developmentally delayed performers. In H. T. A. Whiting & M. G. Wade (Eds.), *Themes in motor development* (pp. 93–107). Dordrecht, Holland: Martinus Nijhoff.

Reid, G. (1987). Motor behavior and psychosocial correlates in young handicapped performers. In D. Gould & M. R. Weiss (Eds.), *Advances in pediatric sport sciences* (Vol. 2, pp. 235–258). Champaign, IL: Human Kinetics.

Reid, G., & Collier, D. (2002). Motor behavior and the autism spectrum disorders: Introduction. *Palaestra, 18*(4), 20–27, 44.

Reid, G., & Collier, D. (2003). The autism spectrum disorders: Preventing and coping with difficult behaviors. *Palaestra, 19*(3), 36–45.

Reid, G., Collier, D., & Cauchon, M. (1991). Skill acquisition by children with autism: Influence of prompts. *Adapted Physical Activity Quarterly, 8,* 357–366.

Reid, G., Seidl, C., & Montgomery, D. (1989). Fitness test for retarded adults: Tips for test selection, subject familiarization, administration, and interpretation. *Journal of Physical Education, Recreation and Dance, 60*(6), 76–78.

Reid, G., Montgomery, D. L., & Seidl, C. (1990). *Stepping out for fitness: A program for adults who are intellectually handicapped.* Gloucester, Ontario: Canadian Association for Health, Physical Education, and Recreation.

Renick, M. J., & Harter, S. (1988). *Manual for the Self-Perception Profile for Learning Disabled Students.* Denver: Authors.

Research and Training Center for Independent Learning (2000). *Guidelines for reporting and writing about people with disabilities* (rev. ed.). Lawrence: University of Kansas.

Reynolds, G. (1973). *A swimming program for the handicapped.* New York: Association Press.

Richter, K. J., Gaebler-Spira, R., & Adams-Mushett, C. (1996). Sport and the person with spasticity of cerebral origin. *Developmental Medicine and Child Neurology, 38,* 867–870.

Riggen, K. J., Ulrich, D. A., & Ozmun, J. C. (1990). Reliability and concurrent validity of the Test of Motor Impairment-Henderson Revision. *Adapted Physical Activity Quarterly, 7,* 249–258.

Rimmer, J. H. (1994). *Fitness and rehabilitation programs for special populations.* Dubuque, IA: Brown & Benchmark.

Rimmer, J. H., Braddock, D., & Fujiura, G. (1993). Prevalence of obesity in adults with mental retardation: Implications for health promotion and disease prevention. *Mental Retardation, 31*(2), 105–110.

Rimmer, J. H., Connor-Kunz, F., Winnick, J. P., & Short, F. X. (1997). Feasibility of the target aerobic movement test in children and adolescents with spina bifida. *Adapted Physical Activity Quarterly, 14, 147–155.*

Rink, J., & Mitchell, M. (2002). High stakes assessment: A journey into unknown territory. *Quest, 54,* 205–223.

Rintala, P., Lytinen, H., & Dunn, J. M. (1990). Influence of a physical activity program on children with cerebral palsy: A single subject design. *Pediatric Exercise Science, 2,* 46–56.

Rippe, J. M., & Ward, A. (1989). *The Rockport walking program.* New York: Prentice-Hall.

Rizzo, T. L. (1984). Attitudes of physical educators toward teaching handicapped pupils. *Adapted Physical Activity Quarterly, 1,* 267–274.

Rizzo, T. L. (1995). *The Physical Educators' Attitude Toward Teaching Individuals with Disabilities—III.* Unpublished instrument. Available from Dr. Terry Rizzo, California State University at San Bernardino, 5500 University Parkway, San Bernardino, CA 92407-2397.

Rizzo, T. L., Broadhead, G. D., & Kowalski, E. (1997). Changing kinesiology and physical education by diffusing information about individuals with disabilities. *Quest, 49,* 229–237.

Rizzo, T. L., & Kirkendall, D. R. (1995). Teaching students with mild disabilities: What affects attitudes of future physical educators? *Adapted Physical Activity Quarterly, 12*(3), 205–216.

Rizzo, T. L., & Vispoel, W. P. (1991). Physical educators' attributes and attitudes toward teaching students with handicaps. *Adapted Physical Activity Quarterly, 8*(1), 4–11.

Rizzo, T. L., & Vispoel, W. P. (1992). Changing attitudes about teaching students with handicaps. *Adapted Physical Activity Quarterly, 9*(7), 54–63.

Roach, E. F., & Kephart. (1966). *Purdue perceptual-motor survey.* Columbus, OH: Charles E. Merrill.

Robinson, J. (1986). *Scuba diving with disabilities.* Champaign, IL: Human Kinetics.

Roeser, R., & Downs, M. (1988). *Auditory disorders in school children* (2nd ed.). New York: Thieme Medical.

Rogers, C. R. (1951). *Client-centered therapy.* Boston: Houghton Mifflin.

Rogers, C. R. (1969). *Freedom to learn.* Columbus, OH: Merrill.

Rohnke, K. (1997). *Cowstails and cobras: A guide to ropes courses, initiative games, and other adventure activities.* Hamilton, MA: Project Adventure.

Roper, P. (1988). Throwing patterns of individuals with cerebral palsy. *Palaestra, 4*(4), 9–11, 51.

Rose, E., & Larkin, D. (2002). Perceived competence, discrepancy scores, and global self-worth. *Adapted Physical Activity Quarterly, 19,* 127–140.

Rosenthal, R., & Jacobsen, L. (1968). *Pygmalion in the classroom.* New York: Holt, Rinehart & Winston.

Roswal, P. M., Sherrill, C., & Roswal, G. M. (1988). A comparison of data-based and creative dance pedagogies in teaching mentally retarded youth. *Adapted Physical Activity Quarterly, 5,* 212–222.

Rothenberg, M., & White, M. (1985). *David: Severely burned by father.* Old Tappen, NJ: Fleming H. Revell.

Rotter, J. B. (1966). Generalized expectancies for internal versus external control of reinforcement. *Psychological Monographs: General and Applied, 80*(1), 1–28.

Rowe, J., & Stutts, R. M. (1987). Effects of practica type, experience, and gender on undergraduate physical education majors toward disabled persons. *Adapted Physical Activity Quarterly, 4,* 268–277.

Rubin, A. L. (2002). *High blood pressure for dummies.* New York: Wiley Publishing Inc.

Runyan, M. (2001). *No finish line: My life as I see it.* New York: G. P. Putnam's Sons.

Ryan, A. L., Halsey, H. N., & Matthews, W. J. (2003). Using functional assessment to promote desirable student behavior in schools. *Teaching Exceptional Children, 35,* 8–15.

Sacks, O. (1989). *Seeing voices: A journey into the world of the deaf.* Berkeley: University of California Press.

Sacks, O. (1995). *An anthropologist on Mars.* New York: Vintage.

Sacks, S. Z., & Silberman, R. K. (1998). *Educating students who have visual impairments with other disabilities.* Baltimore: Brookes.

Samples, P. (1990). Exercise encouraged for people with arthritis. *Physician and Sportsmedicine, 18*(1), 122–127.

Savelsbergh, G., & Netelenbos, J. B. (1992). Can the developmental lag in motor abilities of deaf children be partly attributed to localization problems? *Adapted Physical Activity Quarterly, 9*(4), 343–352.

Sax, C. L., & Thoma, C. A. (2002). *Transition assessment: Wise practices for quality lives.* Baltimore: Brookes.

Sayers, L. K., Cowden, J. E., & Sherrill, C. (2002). Parents' perceptions of motor interventions for infants and toddlers with Down syndrome. *Adapted Physical Activity Quarterly, 19,* 199–219.

Sayers, L. K., Cowden, J. E., Newton, M., Warren, B., & Eason, B. (1996). Qualitative analysis of a pediatric strength intervention on the developmental stepping movements of infants with Down syndrome. *Adapted Physical Activity Quarterly, 13,* 247–268.

Sayers, L. K., Shapiro, D. R., & Webster, G. (2003). Community-based physical activities for elementary students. *Journal of Physical Education, Recreation and Dance 74*(4), 49–54.

Sayers, S. P. (2000). The role of exercise as a therapy for children with Duchenne muscular dystrophy. *Pediatric Exercise Science, 12*(1), 23–33.

Schack, F. (1991). Effects of exercise on selected physical fitness components of an ambulatory quadriplegic. *Palaestra, 7*(3), 18–23.

Schilling, S. (1990). *My name is Jonathan (and I have AIDS): Teacher's edition*. Denver: Prickly Pair.

Schleien, S. J., Meyer, L. H., Heyne, L., & Brandt, B. (1995). *Lifelong leisure skills and lifestyles for persons with developmental disabilities*. Baltimore: Brookes.

Schmidt, R. A., & Wrisberg, C. A. (2000). *Motor learning and performance* (2nd ed.). Champaign, IL: Human Kinetics.

Schmitz, N. B. (1989). Children with learning disabilities and the dance/movement class. *Journal of Physical Education, Recreation and Dance, 60*(9), 59–61.

Schoel, J., Prouty, D., & Radcliff, P. (1988). *Islands of healing*. Hamilton, MA: Project Adventure, Inc.

Scott, C. Z. (1988). Dwarfism, *Clinical Symposia, 40*(1), 2–32.

Screws, D. P., & Surburg, P. R. (1997). Motor performance of children with mild mental retardation after using imagery. *Adapted Physical Activity Quarterly, 14*(2), 119–130.

Seaman, J. A. (Ed.). (1995). *Physical Best and individuals with disabilities: A handbook for inclusion in fitness programs*. Reston, VA: AAHPERD, American Association for Active Lifestyles and Fitness.

Seefeldt, V., Ewing, M., & Walk, S. (1992). *An overview of youth sports programs in the United States*. Washington, DC: Carnegie Council on Adolescent Development.

Seidl, C., Reid, G., & Montgomery, D. L. (1987). A critique of cardiovascular fitness testing with mentally retarded persons. *Adapted Physical Activity Quarterly, 2,* 106–116.

Seligman, M. (1975). *Helplessness: On depression, development, and death*. San Francisco: W. H. Freeman.

Selsky, C., & Pearson, H. A. (1995). Neoplasms. In B. Goldberg (Ed.), *Sports and exercise in children with chronic health conditions* (pp. 311–322). Champaign, IL: Human Kinetics.

Seltzer, D. G. (1993). Educating athletes on HIV disease and AIDS: The team physician's role. *Physician and Sports Medicine, 2*(1), 109–115.

Senne, T. A., & Rikard, G. L. (2002). Experiencing the portfolio process during the internship: A comparative analysis of two PETE portfolio models. *Journal of Teaching in Physical Education, 21,* 309–336.

Shakespeare, T. (Ed.). (1998). *The disability reader: Social science perspectives*. New York: Cassell.

Shapiro, D. R., & Sayers, L. K. (2003). Who does what on the interdisciplinary team: Regarding physical education for students with disabilities. *Teaching Exceptional Children, 35*(6), 32–39.

Shapiro, D. R., & Ulrich, D. A. (2002). Expectancies, values, and perceptions of physical competence of children with and without learning disabilities. *Adapted Physical Activity Quarterly, 19,* 318–333.

Shapiro, J. P. (1993). *No pity: People with disabilities forging a new civil rights movement*. New York: Times Books Random House.

Shaver, L. (1981). *Wheelchair basketball: Concepts and techniques*. Marshall, MN: Southwest State University Press.

Shaywitz, S. (2003). *Overcoming dyslexia*. New York: Alfred A. Knopf.

Shephard, R. J. (1990). *Fitness in special populations*. Champaign, IL: Human Kinetics.

Shephard, R. J. (1997). *Aging, physical activity, and health*. Champaign, IL: Human Kinetics.

Shephard, R. (2003). Boosting of performance in the athlete with high-level spinal injury. *Adapted Physical Activity Quarterly, 20,* 103–117.

Sherborne, V. (1987). Movement observation and practice. In M. Berridge & G. R. Ward (Eds.), *International perspectives on adapted physical activity* (pp. 3–10). Champaign, IL: Human Kinetics.

Sherrill, C. (1972). Learning disabilities. In H. Fait, *Special physical education* (3rd ed., pp. 168–182). Philadelphia: W. B. Saunders.

Sherrill, C. (Ed.). (1979). *Creative arts for the severely handicapped* (2nd ed.). Springfield, IL: Charles C. Thomas.

Sherrill, C. (1986). *Adapted physical education and recreation* (3rd ed.). Dubuque, IA: Wm C. Brown.

Sherrill, C. (Ed.). (1988). *Leadership training in adapted physical education*. Champaign, IL: Human Kinetics.

Sherrill, C. (1990a). Interdisciplinary perspectives in adapted physical education. In G. Doll-Tepper, C. Dahms, B. Doll, & H. Von Selzam (Eds.), *Adapted physical activity: An interdisciplinary approach* (pp. 23–28). New York: Springer-Verlag.

Sherrill, C. (1990b). Psychosocial status of disabled athletes. In G. Reid (Ed.), *Problems in motor control* (pp. 339–364). Amsterdam: North-Holland.

Sherrill, C. (1994). Least restrictive environments and total inclusion philosophies: Critical analysis. *Palaestra, 10*(3), 25–35.

Sherrill, C. (1997a). Adaptation theory: The essence of our profession and discipline. In I. Morisbak & P. E. Jorgensen (Eds.), *Quality of life through adapted physical activity. 10th ISAPA Symposium Proceedings* (pp. 31–45). Omslag, Norway: BB Grafisk.

Sherrill, C. (1997b). *Adaptation theory: Epistemological perspectives*. Presentation at the International Symposium on Adapted Physical Activity, Quebec City, Quebec, Canada.

Sherrill, C. (1997c). Disability, identity, and involvement in sport and exercise. In K. R. Fox (Ed.), *The physical self: From motivation to well-being* (pp. 257–286). Champaign, IL: Human Kinetics.

Sherrill, C. (1998). *Adapted physical activity, recreation, and sport: Crossdisciplinary and lifespan* (5th ed.). Boston: Wm C. Brown/McGraw.

Sherrill, C. (1999). Disability sport and classification theory: A new era. *Adapted Physical Activity Quarterly, 16,* 206–215.

Sherrill, C., & DePauw, K. P. (1997). Adapted physical activity and education. In J. D. Massengale & R. A. Swanson (Eds.), *History of exercise and sport science* (pp. 39–108). Champaign, IL: Human Kinetics.

Sherrill, C., & McBride, H. (1984). An arts infusion intervention model for severely handicapped children. *Mental Retardation, 22*(6), 316–320.

Sherrill, C., & Megginson, N. (1984). A needs assessment instrument for local school district use in adapted physical education. *Adapted Physical Activity Quarterly, 1,* 147–157.

Sherrill, C., & Oakley, T. (1988). Evaluation and curriculum processes in adapted physical education: Understanding and creating theory. In C. Sherrill (Ed.), *Leadership training in adapted physical education* (pp. 123–138). Champaign, IL: Human Kinetics.

Sherrill, C., & Williams, T. (1996). Disability and sport: Psychosocial perspectives on inclusion, integration, and participation. *Sport Science Review, 5*(1), 42–64.

Sherrill, C., Heikinaro-Johansson, P., & Slininger, D. (1994). Equal-status relationships in the gym. *Journal of Physical Education, Recreation and Dance, 65*(1), 27–31, 56.

Sherrill, C., Rainbolt, W., Montelione, T., & Pope, C. (1986). Sport socialization of blind and of cerebral palsied elite athletes. In C. Sherrill (Ed.), *Sport and disabled athletes* (pp. 189–195). Champaign, IL: Human Kinetics.

Sherrill, C., Silliman, L., Gench, B., & Hinson, M. (1990). Self-actualization of elite wheelchair athletes. *Paraplegia, 28,* 252–260.

Sherrill, C., Hinson, M., Gench, B., Kennedy, S., & Low, L. (1990). Self-concepts of disabled youth athletes. *Perceptual and Motor Skills, 70,* 1093–1098.

Shogan, D. (1998). The social construction of disability: The impact of statistics and technology. *Adapted Physical Activity Quarterly, 15,* 269–277.

Shoham-Vardi, I., Davison, P. W., Cain, N. N., Sloane-Reeves, J., Giesow, V., Quaijano, L. E., & Houser, K. D. (1996). Factors predicting re-referral following crisis intervention for community-based persons with developmental disabilities and behavioral and psychiatric disorders. *American Journal on Mental Retardation, 101*(2), 109–117.

Short, F. X., & Winnick, J. P. (1986). The performance of adolescents with cerebral palsy on measures of physical fitness. In C. Sherrill (Ed.), *Sport and disabled athletes* (pp. 239–244). Champaign, IL: Human Kinetics.

Shumway-Cook, A., & Woollacott, M. H. (2001). *Motor control: Theory and practical applications* (2nd ed.). Philadelphia: Lippincott, Williams, & Wilkins.

Sidorenko, A. (1999). 1999-The International year of the older person. *Journal of Aging and Physical Activity, 7,* 1–2.

Siedentop, D. (1983). *Developing teaching skills in physical education.* Palo Alto, CA: Mayfield. (2000, new ed. by Siedentop, D., & Tannehill, D.)

Siedentop, D. (1994). *Sport education: Quality PE through positive sport experiences.* Champaign, IL: Human Kinetics.

Siedentop, D. (1996). Physical education and recreation reform: The case of sport education. In S. J. Silverman & C. D. Ennis (Eds.), *Student learning in physical education: Applying research to enhance instruction* (pp. 247–268). Champaign, IL: Human Kinetics.

Siedentop, D. (2002a). Ecological perspectives in teaching research. *Journal of Teaching in Physical Education, 21,* 427–440.

Siedentop, D. (2002b). Lessons learned. *Journal of Teaching in Physical Education, 21,* 454–464.

Siedentop, D. (2002c). Sport education: A retrospective. *Journal of Teaching in Physical Education, 21,* 409–418.

Siegel, L. M. (2002). *The complete IEP guide: How to advocate for your special ed child* (2nd ed.). Berkeley, CA: Nolo.

Siller, J. (1984). Attitudes toward the physically disabled. In R. L. Jones (Ed.), *Attitudes and attitude change in special education: Theory and practice* (pp. 184–205). Reston, VA: Council for Exceptional Children.

Silliman-French, L., French, R., Sherrill, C., & Gench, B. (1998). Auditory feedback and time-on-task of postural alignment of individuals with profound mental retardation. *Adapted Physical Activity Quarterly, 15,* 51–63.

Siperstein, G. N. (1980). *Instruments for measuring children's attitudes toward the handicapped.* (Unpublished, available from Dr. Gary Siperstein, Center for the Study of Social Acceptance, University of Massachusetts, Boston, MA 02125).

Skaggs, S., & Hopper, C. (1996). Individuals with visual impairments: A review of psychomotor behavior. *Adapted Physical Activity Quarterly, 13,* 16–26.

Skordilis, E. K., Koutsouki, D., Asonitou, K., Evans, E., Jensen, B., & Wall, K. (2001). Sport orientations and goal perspectives of wheelchair athletes. *Adapted Physical Activity Quarterly, 18,* 304–315.

Skrotsky, K. (1983). Gait analysis in cerebral palsied and nonhandicapped children. *Archives of Physical Medicine and Rehabilitation, 64,* 291–295.

Slininger, D., Sherrill, C., & Jankowski, C. M. (2000). Children's attitudes toward peers with severe disability; Revisiting contact theory. *Adapted Physical Activity Quarterly, 17,* 176–196.

Smith, B. T., & Goc Karp, G. (1998). Adapting to marginalization in a middle school physical education class. *Journal of Teaching in Physical Education, 16,* 30–47.

Smith, L. G., & Thelen, E. (Eds.). (1993). *A dynamic systems approach to development: Applications.* Cambridge, MA: MIT Press.

Smithdas, R. J. (1958). *Life at my fingertips.* New York: Doubleday.

Smyth, M. M., & Anderson, H. I. (2000). Coping with clumsiness in the school playground: Social and physical play in children with coordination impairments. *British Journal of Developmental Psychology, 18,* 389–413.

Snell, M. E., & Janney, R. (2000). *Social relationships and peer support.* Baltimore: Brookes.

Sobsey, D. (1994). *Violence and abuse in the lives of people with disabilities: The end of silent acceptance.* Baltimore: Brookes.

Solomon, M. A., & Lee, A. M. (1991). A contrast of the planning behaviors between expert and novice adapted physical education teachers. *Adapted Physical Activity Quarterly, 8,* 115–127.

Soneral, L. M. (1999). *The Type 2 diabetes cookbook* (2nd ed.). Los Angeles: Lowell House.

Sonstroem, R. J. (1978). Physical estimation and attraction scales: Rationale and research. *Medicine and Science in Sports, 10,* 97–102.

Sonstroem, R. J. (1997). The physical self-system: A mediator of exercise and self-esteem. In K. R. Fox (Ed.), *The physical self* (pp. 3–26). Champaign, IL: Human Kinetics.

Sorensen, M. (1999). Physical activities for individuals with disabilities: Sensory impairments and psychosocial problems. In F. G. Garcia (Ed.), *La Psicologia del deporte en Espana al Final del Milenio* (pp. 71–88). Las Palmas: Universidad de las Palmas de Gran Canaria.

Sova, R. (1999). *Essential principles of aquatic therapy and rehabilitation.* Port Washington, WI: DSL, Ltd.

Sova, R. (2000). *Aquatics: The complete reference guide for aquatic fitness professionals.* Port Washington, WI: DSL, Ltd.

Special Olympics International. (1980s, most revised in last 5 years). *Sports skills program guides.* Washington, DC: Author.

Special Olympics International. (1989). *Special Olympics motor activities training guide.* Washington, DC: Author.

Special Olympics International. (1992). *Aquatics: Special Olympics sports skills program.* Washington, DC: Author.

Special Olympics International. (2002). *Official Special Olympics summer sports rules: 2000–2003 revised edition.* Washington, DC: Author.

Spence, J. C., & Humphries, B. (2001, September). The effect of resistance training on bone strength in women: A quantitative review. *Research Update, 8*(5). Retrieved from http://www.centre4activeliving.ca.

Spicer, R. L. (1984). Cardiovascular disease in Down syndrome. *Pediatric Clinics of North America, 31*(6), 1331–1344.

Spirduso, W. W. (1995). *Physical dimensions of aging.* Champaign, IL: Human Kinetics.

Sprenger, M. (1999). *Learning and memory: The brain in action.* Alexandria, VA: Association for Supervision and Curriculum Development.

Stanish, H. I., McCubbin, J. A., Draheim, C. C., & van der Mars, H. (2001). Participation of adults with mental retardation in a video- and leader-directed aerobic dance program. *Adapted Physical Activity Quarterly, 18,* 142–155.

Stanley, K. (2001). *Diabetic cooking for seniors.* Alexandria, VA: American Diabetes Association.

Staum, M. (1988). The effect of background music on the motor performance recall of preschool children. *Journal of Human Movement Studies, 15,* 27–35.

Stebbins, R. A. (2002). *The organizational basis of leisure participation: A motivational exploration.* State College, PA: Venture.

Stewart, D. A. (1991). *Deaf sport: The impact of sport within the deaf community.* Washington, DC: Gallaudet University Press.

Stewart, D. A. (2001). The power of IDEA: Kling vs. Mentor School District. *Palaestra, 17,* 28–32.

Stewart, D. A., & Ammons, D. (2001). Future directions of the Deaflympics. *Palaestra, 17,* 45–49.

Stewart, D. A., Dummer, G., & Haubenstricker, J. (1990). Review of administration procedures used to assess the motor skills of deaf children and youth. *Adapted Physical Activity Quarterly, 7,* 231–239.

Stirling, D. (2000). *Character education connections.* Port Chester, NY: National Professional Resources.

Stokes, J. (Ed.). (1999). *Hearing impaired infants: Support in the first 18 months.* Baltimore: Brookes.

Stott, D. H., Moyes, F. A., & Henderson, S. E. (1972). *The Test of Motor Impairment.* San Antonio: Psychological Corporation.

Stotts, K. M. (1986). Health maintenance: Paraplegic athletes and nonathletes. *Archives of Physical Medicine Rehabilitation, 67,* 109–114.

Stratford, B., & Ching, E. (1983). Rhythm and time in the perception of Down syndrome children. *Journal of Mental Deficiency Research, 27,* 23–38.

Strohkendl, H. (1986). The new classification system for wheelchair basketball. In C. Sherrill (Ed.), *Sport and disabled athletes* (pp. 101–112). Champaign, IL: Human Kinetics.

Strohkendl, H. (1996). *The 50th anniversary of wheelchair basketball: A history*. New York: Waxmann.

Strong, W. B., & Alpert, B. S. (1982). The child with heart disease: Play, recreation, and sports. *Current Problems in Pediatrics, 13*(21), 1–34.

Stroot, S. A. (Ed.). (2000). *Case studies in physical education: Real world preparation for teaching*. Scottsdale, AZ: Holcomb Hathaway.

Sugden, D. A., & Keogh, J. (1990). *Problems in movement skill development*. Columbia, SC: University of South Carolina Press.

Sugden, D. A., & Wright, H. C. (1998). Motor coordination disorders in children. In A. E. Kasdin (Series Ed.) *Developmental Clinical Psychology and Psychiatry Series* (pp. 1–129). Thousand Oaks, CA: Sage.

Surburg, P. R. (1986). New perspectives for developing range of motion and flexibility for special populations. *Adapted Physical Activity Quarterly, 3*(3), 227–235.

Surburg, P. R., Poretta, D. L., & Sutlive, V. (1995). Use of imagery practice for improving a motor skill. *Adapted Physical Activity Quarterly, 1,* 217–227.

Sutherland, G., & Anderson, M. G. (2001). Can aerobic exercise training affect health-related quality of life for people with multiple sclerosis? *Journal of Sports Medicine and Physical Fitness, 41*(4), 421–432.

Swain, J., Finkelstein, V., French, S., & Oliver, M. (Eds.). (1993). *Disabling barriers-Enabling environments*. London: Sage.

Takken, T., van der Net, J., & Helders, P. (2001). Do juvenile idiopathic arthritis patients benefit from an exercise program? A pilot study. *Arthritis Care & Research, 45*(1), 81–85.

Tan, S. K., Parker, H. E., & Larkin, D. (2001). Concurrent validity of motor tests used to identify children with motor impairment. *Adapted Physical Activity Quarterly, 18,* 168–182.

Tannock, R. (1998). Attention deficit hyperactivity disorder: Advances in cognitive, neurobiological, and genetic research. *Journal of Child Psychology and Psychiatry, 39,* 65–99.

Tarr, S. J., & Pyfer, J. L. (1996). Physical and motor development of neonates/infants prenatally exposed to drugs in utero: A meta-analysis. *Adapted Physical Activity Quarterly, 13*(3), 269–287.

Task Force on Blood Pressure Control in Children. (1987). Report on the task force. *Pediatrics, 79,* 271.

Taylor, M. J. (1987). Leisure counseling as an integral part of program development. *Canadian Association for Health, Physical Education, and Recreation Journal, 53,* 21–25.

Temple, V. A., & Walkley, J. W. (1999). Academic learning time-physical education (ALT-PE) of students with mild disabilities in regular Victorian schools. *Adapted Physical Activity Quarterly, 16,* 64–74.

Teplin, S. W., Howard, J. A., & O'Connor, M. J. (1981). Self-concept of young children with cerebral palsy. *Developmental Medicine and Child Neurology, 23,* 730–738.

Thelen, E., & Smith, L. B. (1994). *A dynamic systems approach to the development of cognition and action*. Cambridge, MA: MIT Press.

Thiboutot, T. (2002). Snow rules, Gimp doesn't. *Sports 'N Spokes, 28*(2), 66.

Thousand, J. S., Villa, R. A., & Nevin, A. I. (Eds.) (2002). *Creativity and collaborative learning: The practical guide to empowering students, teachers, and families* (2nd ed.). Baltimore: Brookes.

Thurstone, L. L. (1931). The measurement of attitudes. *Journal of Abnormal and Social Psychology, 26,* 249–269.

Tiefenbacher, W. (Ed.). (1999). *Deaf girls rule*. Washington, DC: Gallaudet Press.

Tiller, J., Stygar, M. K., Hess, C., & Reimer, L. (1982). Treatment of functional chronic stooped posture using a training device and behavior therapy. *Physical Therapy, 11,* 1597–1600.

Torrance, E. P. (1962). *Guiding creative talent*. Englewood Cliffs, NJ: Prentice-Hall.

Trent, J. W. (1994). *Inventing the feeble mind: A history of mental retardation in the United States*. Berkeley: University of California Press.

Trieschmann, R. B. (1987). *Aging with a disability*. New York: Demos Publications.

Tripp, A. (1988). Comparison of attitudes of regular and adapted physical educators toward disabled individuals. *Perceptual and Motor Skills, 66,* 425–426.

Tripp, A., & Sherrill, C. (1991). Attitude theories of relevance to adapted physical education. *Adapted Physical Activity Quarterly, 8,* 12–27.

Tsand, T. (2000). Let me tell you a story: A narrative exploration of identity in high performance sport. *Sociology of Sport Journal, 17,* 44–59.

Tsangardiou, N., & O'Sullivan, M. (1997). The role of reflection in shaping physical education teachers' educational values and practices. *Journal of Teaching in Physical Education, 17,* 2–25.

Turkington, C., & Sussman, A. E. (2000). *Living with hearing loss*. New York: Checkmark Books.

Turnbull, A. P., & Ruef, M. (1996). Family perspectives on problem behavior. *Mental Retardation, 34*(5), 280–293.

Turnbull, H. R. (1986). Appropriate education and Rowley. *Exceptional Children, 52*(4), 347–352.

Turnbull, H. R., & Turnball, A. (2000). *Free appropriate public education: The law and children with disabilities* (6th ed.). Denver, CO: Love.

Turney, S., French, R., Pyfer, J., & Kinnison, L. (2000, July 14). *Assessment practices used by certified adapted physical educators*. Presented at conference of the National Consortium for Physical Education and Recreation for Individuals with Disabilities (NCPERID), Washington, DC.

Tuttle, D. W., & Tuttle, N. R. (1996). *Self-esteem and adjusting with blindness* (2nd ed.). Springfield, IL: Charles C. Thomas.

Ulrich, B. D., & Ulrich, D. A. (1995). Spontaneous leg movements of infants with Down syndrome and nondisabled infants. *Child Development, 66,* 1844–1855.

Ulrich, D. A. (1985). *The Test of Gross Motor Development*. Austin, TX: Pro•Ed.

Ulrich, D. A. (1988). Children with special needs-Assessing the quality of movement competence. *Journal of Physical Education, Recreation and Dance, 59*(91), 43–47.

Ulrich, D. A. (2000). *The Test of Gross Motor Development-2*. Austin, TX: Pro•Ed.

Ulrich, D. A., Ulrich, B. D., Angulo-Kinzler, R. M., & Yun, J. (2001). Treadmill training of infants with Down syndrome: Evidence-based developmental outcomes. *Pediatrics, 108,* 1–7.

United Nations Educational, Scientific, & Cultural Organization (UNESCO, 1978). *The International Charter of Physical Education and Sport*. Geneva: Author.

United States Census Bureau. (2000). *Census report*. Washington, DC: Government Printing.

United States Code (U.S.C.) (no date, continuously updated as laws are codified) Washington, DC: Government Printing Bureau.

U.S. Department of Health and Human Services. (1996). *The surgeon general's report on physical activity and health*. Washington, DC: Author.

U.S. Department of Health and Human Services. (2000). *Healthy People 2010*. (Conference edition in two volumes). Washington, DC: U.S. Government Printing House.

Vallerand, R. J., & Reid, G. (1990). Motivation and special populations: Theory, research, and implications regarding motor behavior. In G. Reid (Ed.), *Problems in movement control* (pp. 159–197). Amsterdam: North Holland.

Van Dijk, J. (1966). The first steps of the deaf-blind child towards language. *International Journal for the Education of the Blind, 15*(1), 112–115.

Van Reusen, A. K., & Box, C. S. (1994). Facilitating student participation in individualized education programs through motivation strategy instruction. *Exceptional Children, 60*(5), 466–475.

Varela, A. M., & Pitetti, K. H. (1995). Heart rate response to two field exercise tests by adolescents and young adults with Down syndrome. *Adapted Physical Activity Quarterly, 12*(1), 43–51.

Verderber, J., & Payne, V. G. (1987). A comparison of the long and short forms of the Bruininks-Oseretsky Test of Motor Proficiency. *Adapted Physical Activity Quarterly, 4*(1), 51–59.

Verderber, J., Rizzo, T. L., & Sherrill, C. (2003). Assessing student intention to participate in inclusive physical education. *Adapted Physical Activity Quarterly, 20*, 26–45.

Vodola, T. (1976). *Project ACTIVE maxi-model: Nine training manuals.* Oakhurst, NJ: Project ACTIVE.

Vogler, E. W., Koranda, P., & Romance, T. (2000). Including a child with severe cerebral palsy in physical education: A case study. *Adapted Physical Activity Quarterly, 17*, 161–175.

Vogler, E. W., van der Mars, H., Cusimano, B., & Darst, P. (1992). Experience, expertise, and teaching effectiveness with mainstreamed and nondisabled children in physical education. *Adapted Physical Activity Quarterly, 9*, 316–329.

Vogler, E. W., van der Mars, H., Darst, P., & Cusimano, B. (1990). Relationship of presage, context, and process variables to ALT-PE of elementary level mainstreamed students. *Adapted Physical Activity Quarterly, 7*, 298–313.

Waksman, S., Messmer, C. L., & Waksman, D. D. (1988). *The Waksman social skills program.* Austin: Pro•Ed.

Walker, H. M., McConnell, S., Homes, D., Todis, B., Walker, J., & Golden, N. (1988). *The Walker Social Skills Curriculum. The ACCEPTS Program.* Austin: Pro•Ed.

Wall, A. E. (1982). Physically awkward children: A motor development perspective. In J. Das, R. Mulcahy, & A. Wall (Eds.), *Theory and research in learning disabilities* (pp. 253–268). New York: Plenum Press.

Wall, A. E., Bouffard, M., McClements, J., Findlay, H., & Taylor, M. J. (1995). A knowledge-based approach to motor development: Implications for the physically awkward. *Adapted Physical Activity Quarterly, 2*(1), 21–43.

Ward, D. S., & Bar-Or, O. (1990). Use of the Borg scale in exercise prescription for overweight youth. *Canadian Journal of Sport Science, 15*(2), 120–125.

Watkinson, E. J., & Wall, A. E. (1982). *The PREP play program: Play skill instruction for mentally handicapped children.* Ottawa: Canadian Association for Health, Physical Education, and Recreation.

Watkinson, E. J., Causgrove Dunn, J., Cavaliere, N., Calzonetti, K., Wilheim, L., & Dwyer, S. (2001). Engagement in playground activities as a criterion for diagnosing developmental coordination disorder. *Adapted Physical Activity Quarterly, 18*, 18–34.

Watson, N. (2002). Well, I know this is going to sound very strange to you, but I don't see myself as a disabled person: Identity and disability. *Disability and Society, 17*, 509–527.

Webb, R., & Koller, J. (1979). Effects of sensorimotor training on intellectual and adaptive skills of profoundly retarded adults. *American Journal of Mental Deficiency, 83*, 490–496.

Weber, R. C. (1993). Physical education for children with Prader-Willi syndrome. *Palaestra, 9*(3), 41–47.

Weber, R. C. (1994). Physical activity for children with Apert syndrome. *Palaestra, 10*(2), 13–18.

Weber, R. C., & Thorpe, J. (1989). Comparison of task variation and constant task methods for severely disabled in physical education. *Adapted Physical Activity Quarterly, 6*, 338–353.

Webster, G. E. (1987). Influence of peer tutors upon academic learning time-Physical education of mentally handicapped students. *Journal of Teaching in Physical Education, 6*, 393–403.

Webster, G. E. (1993). Effective teaching in adapted physical education: A review. *Palaestra, 9*(3), 25–31.

Webster, J. B., Levy, C. E., Bryant, P. R., & Prusakowski, P. E. (2001). Sports and recreation for persons with limb deficiency. *Archives of Physical Medicine and Rehabilitation, 82*(3), Supplement 1, S38–S45.

Wehman, P. (2001). *Life beyond the classroom: Transition strategies for young people with disabilities* (3rd ed.). Baltimore: Brookes.

Wehmeyer, M. L., Kelchner, K., & Richards, S. (1996). Essential characteristics of self-determined behavior of individuals with mental retardation. *American Journal of Mental Retardation, 100*(6), 632–642.

Weiner, B. (1972). *Theories of motivation from mechanism to cognition.* Chicago: Markham.

Weiner, B. (1992). *Human motivation: Metaphors, theories, and research.* Newbury Park, CA: Sage.

Weiss, M. R. (1987). Self-esteem and achievement in children's sport and physical activity. In D. Gould & M. R. Weiss (Eds.), *Advances in pediatric sport sciences* (Vol. 2, pp. 87–119). Champaign, IL: Human Kinetics.

Weiss, M. R., McCullagh, P., Smith, A. L., & Berlant, A. R. (1998). Observational learning and the fearful child: Influence of peer models on swimming skill performance and psychological responses. *Research Quarterly for Exercise and Sport, 69*, 380–394.

Weld, E. M., & Evans, I. M. (1990). Effects of part vs. whole instructional strategies. *American Journal of Mental Deficiency, 94*(4), 377–386.

Wellman, M., & Flinn, J. (1995). *Climbing back* [book] and *No barriers* [videotape]. Available from Eric Perlman Productions, P.O. Box 8636, Truckee, CA 96162. Phone 800–726–7003.

Wells, C., & Hooker, S. (1990). The spinal injured athlete. *Adapted Physical Activity Quarterly, 7*, 265–285.

Wendell, S. (1996). *The rejected body: Feminist philosophical reflections on disability.* New York: Routledge.

Werder, J. K., & Bruininks, R. H. (1988). *Body skills: A motor development curriculum for children.* Circle Pines, MN: American Guidance Service.

Wessel, J. (1976). *I CAN—Primary Skills.* Northbrook, IL: Hubbard.

Wessel, J. (Ed.). (1977). *Planning individualized education programs in special education.* Northbrook, IL: Hubbard.

Wessel, J. (1980). *I CAN implementation guide for preprimary motor and play skills.* East Lansing: Michigan State University, Marketing Division, Instructional Media Center.

Wessel, J., & Kelly, L. (1986). *Achievement-based curriculum in physical education.* Philadelphia: Lea & Febiger.

Wessel, J. A., & Zittel, L. L. (1995). *Smart Start: Preschool movement curriculum designed for children of all abilities.* Austin, TX: Pro•Ed.

Wheeler, G. D., Malone, L. A., VanVlack, S., Nelson, E. R., & Steadward, R. D. (1996). Retirement from disability sport: A pilot study. *Adapted Physical Activity Quarterly, 13*, 382–399.

Wheeler, G. D., Steadward, R. D., Legg, D., Hutzler, Y., Campbell, E., & Johnson, A. (1999). Personal investment in disability sport careers: An international study. *Adapted Physical Activity Quarterly, 16*, 219–237.

Whinnery, K. W., & Barnes, S. B. (2002). Mobility training using the MOVE curriculum: A parent's view. *Teaching Exceptional Children, 34*, 44–50.

White, R., & Cunningham A. M. (1991). *Ryan White: My own story.* New York: Dial Books.

White, R. W. (1959). Motivation reconsidered: The concept of competence. *Psychological Review, 66*, 297–333.

Whitehead, J. R. (1995). A study of children's physical self-perceptions using an adapted physical self-perception profile questionnaire. *Pediatric Exercise Science, 7*(2), 132–151.

Wilens, T. E., & Spencer, T. J. (2000). The stimulants revisited. *Child and Adolescent Psychiatric Clinics of North America, 9*, 573–603.

Williams, F. (1972). *Total creativity program.* Englewood Cliffs, NJ: Educational Technology Publications. Now available through Pro•Ed (see Appendix E).

Williams, H. G. (1983). *Perceptual and motor development.* Englewood Cliffs, NJ: Prentice-Hall.

Williams, H. G. (2002). Motor control in children with developmental coordination disorder. In S. A. Cermak & D. Larkin (Eds.), *Developmental coordination disorder* (pp. 117–137). Albany, NY: Delmar.

Williams, P. J. (2000). *Lives in progress: Case studies in early intervention.* Baltimore: Brookes.

Williams, T. (1994). Disability sport socialization and identity construction. *Adapted Physical Activity Quarterly, 11,* 14–31.

Wing, L. (1997). The autistic spectrum. *Lancet 350,* 1761–1766.

Winnick, J. (1985). The performance of visually impaired youngsters in physical education activities: Implications for mainstreaming. *Adapted Physical Activity Quarterly, 2*(4), 292–299.

Winnick, J. (1995). Personalizing measurement and evaluation for individuals with disabilities. In J. A. Seaman (Ed.), *Physical best for individuals with disabilities: A handbook for inclusion in fitness programs* (pp. 21–31). Reston, VA: American Alliance for Health, Physical Education, Recreation and Dance.

Winnick, J. (Ed.). (2000). *Adapted physical education and sport* (3rd ed.). Champaign, IL: Human Kinetics.

Winnick, J., & Short, F. (1984). Test item selection for the Project UNIQUE physical fitness test. *Adapted Physical Activity Quarterly, 1*(4), 296–314.

Winnick, J., & Short, F. (1985). *Physical fitness testing of the disabled: Project UNIQUE.* Champaign, IL: Human Kinetics.

Winnick, J., & Short, F. (1986). Physical fitness of adolescents with auditory impairments. *Adapted Physical Activity Quarterly, 3,* 58–66.

Winnick, J., & Short, F. (1991). A comparison of the physical fitness of nonretarded and mildly mentally retarded adolescents with cerebral palsy. *Adapted Physical Activity Quarterly, 8,* 43–56.

Winnick, J., & Short, F. (1999). *The Brockport Physical Fitness Test Manual.* Champaign, IL: Human Kinetics.

Wolfensberger, W. (1972). *The principle of normalization in human services.* Toronto: National Institute on Mental Retardation.

Wolfensberger, W. (2000). A brief overview of social role valorization. *Mental Retardation, 38,* 105–123.

Wolfson, L., Whipple, R., Amerman, P., & Tobin, J. N. (1990). Gait assessment in the elderly: A gait abnormality rating scale and its relation to falls. *Journal of Gerontology, 45,* M12–M19.

Woodruff, D. S., & Birren, J. W. (1975). *Aging: Scientific perspectives and social issues.* New York: D. Van Nostrand.

Woolley, M. (1993). Acquired hearing loss: Acquired oppression. In J. Swain, V. Fickelstein, S. French, & M. Oliver (Eds.), *Disabling barriers-Enabling environments* (pp. 79–84). London: Sage.

World Health Organization. (1947). Constitution of the World Health Organization. *Chronicle of WHO, 1,* 1–2.

World Health Organization (1993). *The international statistical classification of disease and related health problems* (ICD-10). Geneva, Switzerland: Author.

World Health Organization. (1997). The Heidelberg guidelines for promoting physical activity among older persons. *Journal of Aging and Physical Activity, 5,* 2–8.

World Health Organization (WHO). (2001). *International classification of functioning, disability, and health (ICF).* Geneva, Switzerland: Author.

Wright, B. A. (1960). *Physical disability: A psychological approach.* New York: Harper & Row.

Wright, B. A. (1983). *Physical disability: A psychosocial approach* (2nd ed.). New York: Harper & Row.

Wright, G. F., & Shephard, R. J. (1978). Brake reaction time-effects of age, sex, and carbon monoxide. *Archives of Environmental Health, 33,* 141–150.

Wright, H. F., & Barker, R. G. (1950). *Methods in psychological ecology.* Lawrence, KS: University of Kansas Press.

Wright, J. W. (Ed.). (2001). *The New York Times Almanac 2002.* New York: Penguin Publishing.

Wu, F. H. (2002). *Yellow: Race in America beyond black and white.* New York: Basic Books.

Wu, S. K., & Williams, T. (1999). Paralympic swimming performance, impairment, and the functional classification system. *Adapted Physical Activity Quarterly, 16,* 251–270.

Wyatt, L., & Ng, G. Y. (1997). The effect of visual impairment on the strength of children's hip and knee extensors. *Journal of Visual Impairment and Blindness, 91,* 40–46.

Xiang, P., Lowry, S., & McBride, R. (2002). The impact of a field-based elementary physical education methods course on preservice classroom teachers' beliefs. *Journal of Teaching in Physical Education, 21,* 145–161.

Yelin, E., & Callahan, L. (1995). The economic cost and social and psychological impact of musculoskeletal conditions. *Arthritis and Rheumatism, 38,* 1351–1362.

Yilla, A. (1994). Full inclusion—A philosophical statement. *Palaestra, 10*(4), 18.

Yilla, A., & Sherrill, C. (1994). Quad rugby illustrated. *Palaestra, 10*(4), 25–31.

Yilla, A., & Sherrill, C. (1998). Validating the Beck Battery of Quad Rugby Skills Tests. *Adapted Physical Activity Quarterly, 15,* 155–198.

Yilla, A. (2000). Enhancing wheelchair performance. In J. P. Winnick (Ed.), *Adapted physical education and sport* (2nd ed., pp. 419–432). Champaign, IL: Human Kinetics.

YMCA of the USA. (1987). *Aquatics for special populations.* Champaign, IL: Human Kinetics.

Yuker, H. E. (1988). The effects of contact on attitudes toward disabled persons: Some empirical generalizations. In H. E. Yuker (Ed.), *Attitudes toward persons with disabilities* (pp. 262–274). New York: Springer.

Yun, J., & Ulrich, D. A. (2002). Estimating measurement validity: A tutorial. *Adapted Physical Activity Quarterly, 19,* 32–47.

Zhang, J., Horvat, M., & Gast, D. (1994). Using the constant time delay procedure to teach task analyzed gross motor skills to individuals with disabilities. *Adapted Physical Activity Quarterly, 11,* 347–358.

Zhang, J., Joseph, D., & Horvat, M. (1999). Marketable features of the adapted physical activity career in higher education. *Adapted Physical Activity Quarterly, 16,* 178–191.

Zhang, J., Kelly, L., Berkey, D., Joseph, D., & Chen, S. (2000). The prevalence-based need for adapted physical education teachers in the United States. *Adapted Physical Activity Quarterly, 17,* 297–309.

Zittel, L. L. (1994). Gross motor assessment of preschool children with special needs: Instrument selection considerations. *Adapted Physical Activity Quarterly, 11,* 245–260.

Zittel, L. L., & McCubbin, J. A. (1996). Effect of an integrated physical education setting on motor performance of preschool children with developmental delays. *Adapted Physical Activity Quarterly, 13*(3), 316–333.

Zuckoff, M. (2002). *Choosing Naia: A family's journey.* Boston: Beacon.

CREDITS

LINE ART, TABLES, TEXT

Figure 2.1. Adapted from unpublished work of Duncan Wyeth, Michigan Department of Education.
Excerpts (p. 33–35), from G. Frank. (2000). *Venus on wheels: Two decades of dialogue on disability, biography, and being female in America* (pp. 1–4, 104, 162). Berkeley, CA: University of California Press.
Figure 2.8. Adapted from World Health Organization (WHO). (2001). *International classification of functioning, disability, and health (ICF)* (p. 18). Geneva, Switzerland: Author.
Excerpt (p. 37), from Research and Training Center for Independent Learning. (2000). *Guidelines for reporting and writing about people with disabilities* (rev.). Lawrence, KS: University of Kansas.
Table 2.1. By permission of Dr. Terry Rizzo, California State University, San Bernardino.
Table 2.3. Adapted from D. L. Goodwin & E. J. Watkinson. (2000). Inclusive physical education from the perspective of students with physical disabilities. *Adapted Physical Activity Quarterly 17,* 150, permission of D. L. Goodwin and Human Kinetics.
Table 2.4. Adapted from M. Adams, L. A. Bell, & P. Griffin (Eds.). (1997). *Teaching for diversity and social justice: A sourcebook* (p. 73). New York: Routledge.

Table 5.5. Adapted from M. Hanson. (1965). Unpublished dissertation.
Table 5.6. From D. W. Johnson, R. T. Johnson, E. J. Holubec, & P. Roy. (1984). *Circles of learning: Cooperation in the classroom* (p. 10). Alexandria, VA: Association for Supervision and Curriculum Development.
Tables 5.9 and 5.10. Adapted from concepts of Janet Wessel's *I CAN* and *ABC,* federally funded projects in the 1970s and 1980s.
Figure 5.10. Developed from concepts of A. Maslow. (1970). *Motivation and personality* (2nd ed., pp. 15–510) New York: Harper & Row.
Figure 5.12. Based on concepts presented in A. Bandura. (1977). Self-efficacy: Toward a unifying theory of behavioral change. *Psychological Review 84*(7), 191–215.
Figure 5.13. Based on concepts of I. Ajzen & M. Fishbein. (1980). *Understanding attitudes and predicting social behavior.* Englewood Cliffs, NJ: Prentice-Hall.

Figures 6.2 and 6.3. Courtesy Dr. Lisa Silliman-French for Denton ISD.
Table 6.2. Courtesy Dr. Dale Ulrich and Pro•Ed Company.
Table 6.3. Courtesy The Cooper Institute for Aerobics Research, Dallas.
Table 6.5. Content from Test of Gross Motor Development-2 (2001) by D. A. Ulrich, Pro•Ed, 8700 Shoal Creek Blvd., Austin, TX 78758.
Figure 6.8. From G. S. D. Morris. (1980). *How to change the games children play* (2nd ed.). Minneapolis: Burgess.
Figure 6.9. Reproduced with permission of American Guidance Service, Inc. Bruininks-Oseretsky Test of Motor Proficiency by Robert N. Bruininks. Copyright 1978. All rights reserved.
Figures 6.15 through 6.21. Courtesy Dr. Lisa Silliman-French, based on Denton ISD forms, but original and anonymous for this chapter.

Figure 7.11. From P. Heikinaro-Johansson, C. Sherrill, R. French, & H. Huuhka. (1995). Adapted physical education consultant model to facilitate integration. *Adapted Physical Activity Quarterly 12*(1), 12–33.
Table 7.12. Based on unpublished dissertation of N. Megginson. (1982). Unpublished dissertation, Texas Woman's University, Denton, TX.

Figure 8.4. From K. R. Fox. (1988). The self-esteem complex and youth fitness. *Quest 40,* 233, 237.
Tables 8.3 and 8.4. From S. Harter, *Manual for the Self-Perception Profile for Adolescents,* 1988. Reprinted with permission.
Table 8.5. From K. R. Fox. (1990). *The Physical Self-Perception Profile Manual.* Office of Health Promotion, Northern Illinois University, DeKalb, IL 60115.
Figure 8.9. Based on content in M. R. Weiss, B. Bredemeier, & R. Shewchuk. (1985). An intrinsic/extrinsic motivation scale for the youth sport setting. *Journal of Sport Psychology 7,* 75–91.
Figure 8.10. From "Attributions of Athletes with Cerebral Palsy" by G. Dummer, M. Ewing, R. Habeck, & S. Overton. (1987). *Adapted Physical Activity Quarterly, 4,* p. 282. Reprinted with modification with permission.

Figure 9.5. From *Cowstails and Cobras: A Guide to Ropes Courses, Initiative Games, and Other Adventure Activities* (pp. 34, 36, 41, and 43) by Karl Rohnke, 1997, Hamilton, MA: Project Adventure, Copyright 1977 by Project Adventure. Reprinted with permission.
Table 9.5. Permission from Martin E. Block.
Table 9.6. From G. N. Siperstein. (1980). *Instruments for measuring children's attitudes toward the handicapped.* (Unpublished, available from Dr. Gary Siperstein, Center for the Study of Social Acceptance, University of Massachusetts, Boston, MA 02125)

Figure 10.5. Adapted from G. Sage. (1977). *Introduction to motor behavior: A neuropsychological approach* (p. 106). Reading, MA: Addison-Wesley.
Figure 10.24. Reprinted by permission of A. Milani-Comparetti and E. A. Gidoni, Italy. Reproduced by permission from Norris G. Haring, *Developing Effective Individualized Education Programs for Severely Handicapped Children and Youth.* Columbus, OH: Special Press, 1977, p. 79.
Figures 10.6, 10.28, 10.29, and 10.31. From John W. Hole, Jr., *Human Anatomy and Physiology,* 2nd ed. Copyright © 1985 Wm. C. Brown Communications, Inc., Dubuque, Iowa. All Rights Reserved. Reprinted by permission.
Figure 10.32. From Sylvia S. Mader, *Inquiry Into Life,* 4th ed. Copyright © 1985 Wm. C. Brown Communications, Inc., Dubuque, Iowa. All Rights Reserved. Reprinted by permission.

Figure 11.17. Adapted from *Fundamental Movement: A Developmental and Remedial Approach,* by Bruce A. McClenaghan and David L. Galluhue. Copyright © 1978 by W. B. Saunders Company.
Figures 11.18(c) and (d) and 11.19 (d) and (e). Courtesy Mr. Jeffrey A. Jones, Rehabilitation Institute of Chicago.
Figure 11.20. Adapted from M. Wild, *Research Quarterly,* AAHPERD, 1938; redrawing from C. Corbin, *A Textbook of Motor Development,* 2nd ed. Copyright © 1980 Wm. C. Brown Publishers, Dubuque, Iowa. All Rights Reserved. Reprinted by permission.
Figure 11.22. Table portion from G. S. D. Morris. (1980). *How to change the games children play* (2nd ed.). Minneapolis: Burgess.
Excerpts from Test of Gross Motor Development-2, 2000, by Dale A., Ulrich Pro•Ed, 8700 Shoal Creek Blvd., Austin, TX 78758.

Figure 13.3. © Cooper Institute for Aerobics Research.
Figure 13.5. Adapted from R. Detrano & V. F. Froelicher. (1988). Exercise testing: Uses and limitations considering recent studies. *Progress in Cardiovascular Diseases, 31*(3), 173–204. Figure on p. 178.
Figure 13.9(b). From Carl C. Seltzer and Jean Mayer, "A Simple Criterion of Obesity," *Postgraduate Medicine 38* (August 1965), A101–107.
Figure 13.12(a). Courtesy Mr. Jeffrey A. Jones, Rehabilitation Institute of Chicago.
Figure 13.14. From Edward L. Fox, Richard W. Bowers, and Merle L. Foss, *The Physiological Basis of Physical Education and Athletics,* 4th ed. Copyright © 1989 Wm. C. Brown Communications, Inc., Dubuque, Iowa. All Rights Reserved. Reprinted by permission.

Figure 14.2. Reprinted by permission of Reedco Incorporated.

Figures 15.8 through 15.27, Tables 15.4 through 15.12. Used by coauthor R. W. Davis with permission from Human Kinetics. From R. W. Davis. (2002). *Inclusion Through Sports.* Champaign, IL: Human Kinetics.

Figure 18.3. Redrawn from M. M. Shirley. "The First Two Years" in *Child Welfare Monograph* 7, 1933. © 1933, renewed 1960, University of Minnesota Press, Minneapolis.
Figure 18.5. From *The Cerebral Cortex of Man,* by Penfield and Rasmussen © 1985 by Macmillan Publishing Co.

Figures 19.3 (center), 19.7, 19.8 (left), 19.12, 19.22, and 19.24. From John W. Hole, Jr., *Human Anatomy and Physiology,* 5th ed. Copyright © 1990 Wm. C. Brown Communications, Inc., Dubuque, Iowa. All Rights Reserved. Reprinted by permission.
Figure 19.3 (top left/bottom right). From Charles B. Corbin and Ruth Lindsey, *Concepts of Physical Fitness,* 7th ed. Copyright © 1990 Wm. C. Brown Communications, Inc., Dubuque, Iowa. All Rights Reserved. Reprinted by permission.
Figure 19.5. From *American Heart Association Heartbook.* New York: E. P. Dutton, p. 176. Reproduced with permission. *American Heart Association Heartbook,* 1980. Copyright American Heart Association.
Figure 19.6. From "Natural History of Human Atherosclerotic Lesions" by H. L. McGill, J. C. Geer, and J. P. Strong. In *Atherosclerosis and Its Origins* (p. 42) by M. Sandler and G. H. Bourne (Eds.), 1963, New York: Academic Press. Copyright 1963 by Academic Press. Reprinted by permission.
Figures 19.8 (right) and 19.9. From *American Heart Association Heartbook.* New York: E. P. Dutton, pp. 243–246. Reproduced with permission. *American Heart Association Heartbook,* 1980. Copyright American Heart Association.
Figure 19.10 (left). From Stuart Ira Fox, *Laboratory Guide to Human Physiology,* 5th ed. Copyright © 1990 Wm. C. Brown Communications, Inc., Dubuque, Iowa. All Rights Reserved. Reprinted by permission.
Figure 19.11. From Herbert A. de Vries, *Physiology of Exercise for Physical Education and Athletics,* 4th ed. Copyright © 1986 Wm. C. Brown Communications, Inc., Dubuque, Iowa. All Rights Reserved. Reprinted by permission.
Figure 19.20. From Sylvia S. Mader, *Inquiry Into Life,* 4th ed. Copyright © 1985 Wm. C. Brown Communications, Inc., Dubuque, Iowa. All Rights Reserved. Reprinted by permission.

Table 20.2. From American Psychiatric Association. (1994). *Diagnostic and Statistical Manual IV,* pp. 83–84.

Figure 21.3. From American Association on Mental Retardation (2002). *Mental retardation: Definition, classification, and systems of supports,* p. 148.
Figures 21.8(a) and 21.9. From John W. Hole, Jr., *Human Anatomy and Physiology,* 5th ed. Copyright © 1990 Wm. C. Brown Communications, Inc., Dubuque, Iowa. All Rights Reserved. Reprinted by permission.
Figure 21.11. Redrawn from D. A. Dobbins, R. Garron, & G. L. Rarick. (1981). The motor performance of educable mentally retarded and intellectually normal boys after covariate control for differences in body size. *Research Quarterly for Exercise and Sport, 58,* 1–8.
Figure 21.12. From A. E. Wall, M. Bouffard, J. McClements, H. Findlay, & M. J. Taylor (1995). A knowledge-based approach to motor development: Implications for the physically awkward, p. 32, *Adapted Physical Activity Quarterly, 2*(1), 21–42.
Figure 21.14. From Special Olympics International. *Athletics Sports Skills Program.* Reprinted by permission.
Table 21.15. From E. J. Watkinson and A. E. Wall. *PREP: The Play Program: Play Skill Instruction for Mentally Handicapped Children,* pp. 14 & 21. Copyright 1982 by Canadian Association for Health, Physical Education, and Recreation.
Table 21.2. Adapted from Ruth C. Webb, "Sensory-Motor Training of the Profoundly Retarded." *American Journal of Mental Deficiency, 74* (September, 1969), 287.
Tables 21.3 and 21.4. From Special Olympics International (1989). *Special Olympics Motor Activities Training Guide.* Reprinted with permission.

Figure 23.3(a). From John W. Hole, Jr., *Human Anatomy and Physiology,* 5th ed. Copyright © 1990 Wm. C. Brown Communications, Inc., Dubuque, Iowa. All Rights Reserved. Reprinted by permission.
Figure 23.4. From G. G. Williamson (1987). *Children with Spina Bifida: Early Intervention and Preschool Programs* (p. 2). Baltimore, MD: Paul H. Brookes Publishing Co. Reprinted with permission.
Figure 23.10. From M. L. Barr & J. A. Kiernan. (1988). *The Human Nervous System: A Medical Viewpoint* (5th ed.). Hagerstown, MD: Harper & Row. By permission of J. P. Lippincott, Philadelphia.

Figure 25.11. Redrawn from *Handling the Young Cerebral Palsied Child at Home,* 2nd ed., by Nancy R. Finnie. Copyright © 1974 by Nancy R. Finnie, F. C. S. P., additions for U.S. edition, copyright © by E. P. Dutton and Company, Inc.

Figure 26.7. From J. L. Northern & M. P. Downs (1991). *Hearing in Children* (4th ed.). Baltimore: Williams & Wilkins Co., p. 17. © Williams & Wilkins Co.

Table 28.1. From World Health Organization (1997). These guidelines have been placed in the public domain and can be freely copied and distributed.

PHOTOGRAPHS

Figures 1.2 and 1.10. Courtesy Dr. Lisa Silliman-French.
Figure 1.7. Courtesy Dr. Deborah Buswell.
Figure 1.8. Courtesy Dr. Joseph P. Winnick.

Figure 2.3. Courtesy Linda Thibault.
Figure 2.5. Courtesy Dr. Lisa Silliman-French.
Figures 2.6 and 2.18. Courtesy Dr. Abu Yilla.
Figure 2.7. Courtesy Rae Allen.
Figure 2.15. Courtesy Mary Carol Peterson, Action Top End, Invacare Corporation.
Figure 2.19. Courtesy Dr. Terry Rizzo.

Figure 3.4. Courtesy Leslie Waugh.
Figure 3.8. Courtesy Linda Thibault.
Figure 3.10. Courtesy Lupe Casteñada.

Figure 5.2. Courtesy Barbara Cadden, Valdez Public Schools, Alaska.
Figure 5.3. Courtesy Dr. Joe Nolan.
Figure 5.7. Courtesy Dr. Deborah Buswell.
Figure 5.11. Courtesy *Denton Record Chronicle.*

Figure 6.6. Courtesy Cosom Games and Athletic Goods Company, Minneapolis, MN.

Figure 7.1. Courtesy Rae Allen.
Figure 7.2. Courtesy Dr. Patricia Paulsen Hughes.
Figure 7.4. Courtesy Dr. Lauriece Zittel.
Figure 7.6. Courtesy Leslie Waugh.
Figure 7.9. Courtesy Dr. Deborah Buswell.
Figure 7.10. Courtesy Dr. Lisa Silliman-French.

Figures 8.1(a) and (c), 8.3, 8.5, and 8.8. Courtesy Dr. April Tripp.

Figures 9.1, 9.2, and 9.8. Courtesy Dr. April Tripp.

Figure 10.7. Courtesy Dr. Patricia Paulsen Hughes.

Figures 13.1 and 13.2. Courtesy Dr. Deborah Buswell.

Figure 15.1. Courtesy Mary Carol Peterson, Action Top End, Invacare Corporation.

Figure 16.9. Courtesy Barron Ludlam, *Denton Record Chronicle.*

Figure 17.1. Courtesy Judy Newman.
Figures 17.10 through 17.16. Courtesy Dr. Gail Dummer, Michigan State University.

Figures 18.8 and 18.12(a). Courtesy Dr. Lisa Silliman-French.
Figure 18.10. Courtesy Dr. Lauriece Zittel.
Figure 18.11(a). Courtesy Dr. Jo Cowden.
Figure 18.11(b). Courtesy Dr. Dale Ulrich.

Figure 19.1. Courtesy Rae Allen.
Figure 19.2. Courtesy Fonda Johnstone.
Figures 19.13 and 19.14. Courtesy Dr. April Tripp.

Figures 20.2 and 20.3. Courtesy Barbara Wood, Homer Public Schools, New York.

Figure 21.7. Courtesy Dr. Katie Stanton, University of Indiana at Indianapolis.
Figure 21.13. Courtesy Lupe Casteñada.

Figures 22.4 and 22.7. Courtesy Linda Thibault.
Figures 22.5 and 22.6. Courtesy Dr. Lisa Silliman-French.

Figure 23.1. Courtesy Dr. Deborah Buswell.
Figure 23.7. Courtesy Dr. David Beaver, *Palaestra*; photographer Jim David, *The Boston Globe.*
Figure 23.9. Courtesy Dr. Abu Yilla.
Figure 23.13. Courtesy Dr. Patricia Paulsen Hughes.
Figures 23.14 through 23.16. Courtesy Mary Carol Peterson, Action Top End, Invacare Corporation.
Figure 23.18(a). Courtesy Beneficial Designs, Inc., Santa Cruz, CA.
Figure 23.18(b). Courtesy Dr. David Beaver, *Palaestra*; photographer Randy Anderson.
Figure 23.8(c). Courtesy Dr. David Beaver, *Palaestra*; photographer Curt Beamer.

Figures 24.1(b) and (c), 24.3, and 24.28. Courtesy Dr. Patricia Paulsen Hughes.
Figure 24.4. Courtesy Marilyn Butt, Ontario, Canada.
Figures 24.5 and 24.6. Courtesy University of Texas Medical School at Dallas, Department of Medical Art.
Figure 24.13. Courtesy Dr. Jo Cowden, University of New Orleans.
Figures 24.16 and 24.34. Courtesy Dr. David Beaver, *Palaestra.*
Figure 24.20. Courtesy David Chen Bo-I and Jang-rong Cheen.

Figure 26.2. Courtesy Dr. Stephen Butterfield, University of Maine.
Figure 26.11. Courtesy Dr. Gail Dummer, University of Michigan.

Figure 27.1. Courtesy Steve Edmonds.
Figures 27.2(b), 27.6, and 27.8. Courtesy Dr. David Beaver, *Palaestra,* and USABA.
Figures 27.5, 27.9, and 27.13. Courtesy Linda Thibault.
Figures 27.10 and 27.11. Courtesy Christian Record Braille Foundation; photos by Robert Shelton.
Figure 27.15. Courtesy Dr. Eugenia Scott, Butler University, Indianapolis.

Figures 28.1 through 28.5. Courtesy Dr. Claudia Emes, University of Calgary, Canada.

Skiing, adaptive, 644
Skills, closed and open, 39
Skills cross-reference table (by Davis), 421t
Skinfolds, 376f, 377f
Skinner, B. F., 206–207
Sledge competition, 438, 439f, 638
Slipped femoral epiphysis, 661
Slosson Intelligence Test, 562
Smith, Jaronnie, 357
Smith, Jean Kennedy, 71
Smithdas, Robert J., 727
Snellen chart, 714
Snowballs game, 236
Soccer
  ambulatory, 690
  indoor wheelchair, See Wheelchair
    soccer, indoor
Soccer competition, 437
Social acceptance, 251
Social cognitive theory, 254–255, 382
  Bandura's, 136–137
Social comparison, 231–232
Social competence, 38, 118, 498
Social criteria, 98
Social desirability effect, 227
Social inclusion competence, 241, 251
Social interaction, 250
Social learning theory, 255
Social minority disability model, 27–30
Social role valorization theory, 55
Social science, 20–21
Social skills curriculums, 251–253
Sociograms, 259–260
Soft signs, neurologic, 676–678
Softball, teaching perceptual motor tasks in, 354–355
SOI. See Special Olympics International
Space reduction, principle of, 558
Spasticity. See Hypertonia (spasticity)
Spatial awareness, 339
  in learning disabilities, 551
Speaking, guidelines for, 37
Special education, 12, 19–20, 549
  adapted physical education and,
    advocacy issues, 100
  criterion for justification of, 13
Special education director, 63
Special education personnel, in services
    delivery, 67
Special Olympics, 45, 103, 560
  creation of, 16, 560
  curriculum model of, 130
  sports of, 45
Special Olympics International (SOI), 45t
  Unified Sports model of, 246, 248
Special Olympics Motor Activities Training
    Program, 587–588
Special Olympics Sports Skills Program, 130,
    168, 580
Specialist(s), 10, 13
Specialist competencies, 22–25
Specific gravity, 464
Specificity, principle of, 378
Speech augmentation, 502
Speechreading, 699
Spina bifida, 618–619
  and aging, 738
  cognitive functioning in, 621
  developmental activites in, 620
  gait in, 310f
  hydrocephalus in, 621, 622f
  and latex allergy, 620
  posture in, 621–622
  sport socialization in, 622
  strabismus in, 621
  types of, 618–619, 619f
Spinal column curves, 391, 392f
Spinal cord, 293–294
Spinal cord injuries, 622–623
  and aging, 738
  physical activities in, 623–624
Spinal cord tracts, 263–264
  pyramidal and extrapyramidal, 296
Spinal muscle atrophy, 649
Spinal nerves, 617f
  cutaneous distribution of, 626f
Spinal paralysis, 615
  acquired, 618, See also Postpolio
    syndrome; Spinal cord injuries
  autonomic dysreflexia in, 627
  blood pressure control in, 627
  body temperature control in, 625
  boosting in, 627
  catheterization in, 626
  congenital, 618, See also Spina bifida
  functional electrical stimulation in, 618
  heart and circulatory function in, 627
  injuries causing, 617
  latex allergy in, 626
  limb atrophy in, 625
  muscle contraction and stretching in, 625

Spinal paralysis—Cont.
  osteoporosis in, 627–628
  paraplegic, 632–636
  quadriplegic, 629–632
  sensation and skin breakdown in, 624
  severity of, 617–618
  sexual function in, 626
  spasms in, 625
  urinary and fecal elimination in, 626
  walking potential in, 617–618
  weight management in, 627–628
Spinocerebellar tract, 263
Spirit, 107t
Spirometer, 529
SPMTC. See Sherrill Perceptual Motor Tasks
    Checklist
Spondyloepiphyseal dysplasia, 657
Sport(s), 6, 17, 415
  able body, 45
  advocacy for, 104
  deaf, 45
  definition of, 44–45
  disability, 45–46, See also Disability
    sport
  mainstream, 44–45
  organizations of, international and
    United States, 45t
  paralympics, 45
  recreational, 45–46
  reverse mainstream, 45
  Special Olympics, 45
  wheelchair, 45–46, 46–47
Sport chairs, 48
Sport classification systems, 98–99
  assessment and, 151
Sport commitment, 232–233
Sport education model, 6
Sport organizations, 46t
  disability, 44–45
  paralympic, 46
Sport skills, 118
Sport Skills Program Guides, 168
Sport socialization, 48, 79, 193–194, 499
  in active leisure, 415–416
Sporting identity, 56–57
Sports medicine credentials, 14
Sports 'N Spokes, 50, 107t, 416, 499,
    632–633
SPPLD. See Self-Perception Profile for
    Learning Disabled Students
Stair climbing/descending skill, teaching,
    316–317
Standard deviation (SD), 171
Standard score(s), 171
  z and T conversions, 172–173
Standardized tests, 152
Stanford-Binet Intelligence Scale, 562
Stanine bar graph, 174f
Stanine score, 173
State law(s), 114
Status asthmaticus, 527
Staunton, Katie, 512
Stein, Julian, 18, 20, 367
Stepping Out for Fitness program, 581, 583
Stepping reactions, 287
Stereoagnosia, 269
Stereotypes, 54
Stereotypies, 264t, 274, 718
Stewart, David, 43–44, 696, 708
Stigma, 28
Stigma theory, 28–29
Stigmatized social minority, 52
Stimming, 608, 610–611
STNR. See Symmetrical tonic neck reflex
Stoke Mandeville Center, 45–46, 104
Stordahl, Erling, 719
Strabismus, 273, 329
Strategies, 107t
Strauss, Alfred, 549
Strauss syndrome, 549
Stress, and coping theory, 239
Stretching exercises, 382
Strohkendl, Horst, 629
Strohkendl Basketball Function Tests,
    629, 630f
Stroke, 516, 674–675. See also under
    Cerebral palsy
  behavioral indicators of, 676–678
  motor disorders in, 678–681
Structure, principle of, 558
Structured alternative response format, 225
Student behaviors, 198
Sturge-Weber disease, 566
Subcortical disorders, 266
Subscapular skinfold, 377f
Substance-related disorders, 592–593
Substantive due process, 105–106
Substitution, definition of, 56–57
Success, and failure, 223–224
Suicide, 591
Summary, of lesson, 193

Summative evaluation, 132
Supination, 410
Support services, 7, 65–66
  for children with mental retardation,
    563–565
  prescribed in Individuals with
    Disabilities Education Act,
    65–73, 414
  in school district curriculum, 122
Supports, 62–63
  human, 7
  nonhuman, 7–8
Suprailiac skinfold, 377f
Survey of Adapted Physical Education Needs
    (SAPEN), 215, 215t
Swimming
  competitive, 476–477, 691
  movement direction in, 471–472
  propulsion in, increasing, 471
  resistance reduction in, 469–471
  shoulder/hip roll in, 470, 470f
  skill development for, 476
  stroke techniques for, 469–472
    adaptations of, 473t–475t
    teaching, 472
  synchronized, 466–469
Swimming competition, 437
  for amputees, 670–671
Symbols, meaning of, 30
Symmetrical tonic neck reflex (STNR), 275t,
    277, 277f
  assessment of, 278
  physical education activities for,
    281, 282
Symptomatic clinical status, 367–368
Synapses, 292
Syndactylism, 411, 411f
Syndrome X, 510
Systems theory, 191, 299
T scores, 173
Table tennis competition, 437
Tachycardias, 518
Tactile defensiveness, 611
Tactile integration, and problems assessment,
    268–269
Tag, 96–97
Tag agnosia, 269
Tai chi, 452–453
Target Aerobic Movement Test, 364
Target heart rate zone, 364
TASH: The Association of Persons with
    Severe Handicaps, 584
Task, 7
Task analysis, 11. See also Ecological task
    analysis
Task cards, 204
Task orientation, 138, 223
TDD. See Telecommunication Device for the
    Deaf
TEACCH program, 606–607
Teacher expectancy motivation theory, 237
Teaching, 189–216. See also Adapted
    physical educator(s); Physical
    education, and adapted physical
    activity; Physical educator(s)
  acronyms and mottos used in, 191t
  behavior management in
    strategies of, 206–212
  and consulting, 213–215
  contextual interference in, 201–204
  and counseling, 210–212
  creativity in, 202–203, 203t
  definition of, 190
  ecologically valid activities in, 198–200
  effective, indicators of, 190
  flexibility in, 202–203
  fluency in, 202–203
  inclusive, 32, 124, 244–249
  individualized instruction in, 195,
    203–204
  inputs that influence, 191–194
  learning climate in, 195
  and lesson plan development, 193–194
  models of, 190–191, 192t
  and out-of-school time, 193
  outcomes of, 194–195
  practice variability in, 201–204
  principles of, 195–213
  self-confidence and self-concept
    enhancement through, 232–236
  Sherrill's model of, summary, 211–212
  and sport socialization, 193–194
  strategies and techniques in, 204–205
  style of, and adaptations, 205–206,
    207t, 208t
  time management in, 200
  time-on-task in, 199–201
  traditional, 124
  variability, 203–204
Teaching Exceptional Children, 107t
Teaching/testing progressions (TTPs), 304

Teamwork, 6. See also Service delivery
    system(s)
  case studies of, 78–79
  for child under age three, case study,
    62–63
  for children, ages 3–9, case study, 63–65
  collaborative, 74–75
  communication in, 75–77
  cross-cultural communication in, 76, 77
  crossdisciplinary, 73–74
  family relationship considerations, 76–77
  home, school, community, 61–62
  interdisciplinary, 73–74
  models for, 60–61
  multidisciplinary, 73–74
Telecommunication Device for the Deaf
    (TDD), 707, 726
Temperature concerns, in physical
    activity, 383
Temporal awareness, 339
Temporal lobe, 265, 293
Tennis chair, 49
Terman-Merrill Scale, 562
Test(s). See Assessment instruments
Test of Gross Motor Development (TGMD-
    2), 151, 152, 152t, 164
  description of, 164, 166
  ordering information for, 164t
  of running skills, 316
Test of Motor Impairment (TOMI), 346, 347
Testing accommodations, definition of, 145
Tetraplegia, 47
TGMD-2. See Test of Gross Motor
    Development
Thalamus, 265, 295
Theory, 8, 85
Thibeault, Linda, 205
Thomas heel shoes, 410f
Thoracic-lumbar-sacral orthosis (TLSO), 401
Thoreau, Henry David, 235
Throwing and catching motor skills, teaching,
    325, 327f, 328f
Tibia vara, 407
Tibial torsion, 409, 409f
Tic disorder, 595–596
Tiltboards, 343f
Tilting reactions, 285–287, 286f
Time delay intervention, 575
Time of onset, of injury, 48
Time-on-task, 197–201
  definition of, 197
  individual, 197
  student behavior and, 198
Tinnitus, 706
Title IX (Education Amendments Act of
    1972), 102
Toddlers. See also Infants, toddlers, early
    childhood
  age definition of, 485
Toeing inward, 409–410
Toeing outward, 410
Token(s), 209
TOMI. See Test of Motor Impairment
Tonic labyrinthine reflex (TLR)-prone, 275,
    275f, 275t
  assessment of, 277
  physical education activities for,
    280–281
Tonic labyrinthine reflex (TLR)-supine, 275,
    275t, 276f
  assessment of, 277
  physical education activities for,
    280–281
Tonic neck reflex, 87
Tosado, Eric, 40
Total self, 222
Tourette's disorder, 595–596
Toxoplasmosis, 705
Track and field competition
  for amputees, 668–670
  for blind and visually impaired, 724
  for cerebral palsied persons, 690–692
  Paralympic, 435–438
Track and racing chairs, 48, 634f, 636
Track and racing events, paraplegic, 633–634
Tracts. See Spinal cord tracts
Traditional teaching style, 124
Trampoline, movement exploration on, 321
Transactional stress model, 239
Transdisciplinary Play-Based Intervention
    (TPBI), 494
Transfer test, 202
Transient ischemic attacks (TIAs), 516, 675
Transition services, 12, 44–51, 63–65
  to community sport, 414, 420–423, See
    also Active leisure; Teamwork
Transporation services, 68
Triceps skinfold, 376f
Triplegia, 47
Tripp, April, 234
TTPs. See Teaching/testing progressions

Tuberculosis, 540–541
Tuberous sclerosis, 566
Turner syndrome, 658
Turtle tag, 96–97
Tutors, peer and cross-age, 244
Ulrich, Beverly, 299, 495
Ulrich, Dale, 63, 299, 495. *See also* Test of
    Gross Motor Development
Underlying abilities approach, 262
Unified Sports in Special Olympics, 47,
    246, 581
Uniqueness, 5–6
United States Association for Blind Athletes
    (USABA), 46t, 90, 714
    sport classification in, 714–715, 714t
    sport competition of, 724–725
United States Code (USC), 4, 109
United States Congress, structure of, 108
United States Congressional representatives,
    locating, 110
United States Department of Health and
    Human Services, 358
United States Disabled Ski Team, 644
United States Olympic Committee (USOC),
    46, 113, 615–616
United States Special Olympics Committee, 46
Urinary tract, anatomy of, 536f
Urinary tract conditions, 535–536
    and physical education, implications,
        536–537
USA Deaf Sports Federation (USADSF), 46t,
    696–697
    sports organized by, 697t
Usher's syndrome, 726
Valorization, 55
Valsalva effect, 380, 398
van Beethoven, Ludwig, 704
Van Dijk, J., 727
Variability, measure of, 171
Variable(s), 7, 37, 86, 94
Vascular disease, 733–734
Verbal rehearsal, 555, 576, 610
Verderber Inventory of Students' Intention to
    Participate in Inclusive Physical
    Education (VISIPIPE), 257–258
Very Special Arts, 71
Vestibular integration, and problems
    assessment, 270–272

Vestibular system, 270, 271f
Videotapes, as teaching tools, 204
Visceroptosis, 397
Visual impairment, 46
    communication in, 88
Visual perception, 339
    assessment of, 272–274
    and motor skills, 359
Visualization, 610
VO2max, 367–368
Volleyball
    four corners, 96
    teaching perceptual motor tasks in,
        352, 354
Volleyball competition, 437
    for amputees, 670
Volpentest, Tony, 665, 666f
Waksman Social Skills Program, 251
Walker(s), 51
Walker, Kenny, 696
Walker Social Skills Curriculum,
    251–252
Walking, 306
    assessment checklist for, 313t
    developmental levels in,
        310–312, 310f
    functional, 47
    and individual gait analysis, 314–316
Walking quads, 47
Wall, Tedd, 579
Washington, Wayne, 658–659
Webb, Ruth, 585
Webster, Gail, 345
Wechsler Intelligence Scale for Children-
    Revised, 562
Weight, guidelines for, 506t
Weight reduction programs, 509–510
Weiner, Bernard, 238
Welch, Steve, 660
Wellness, definition of, 359
Wells, Ken, 113
Werder, Judy, 129–130
Werner, Julie, 720
Wessel, Janet, 10, 128–129
Wheelbase, 48
Wheelchair(s)
    armrests and footplates of,
        handling, 51

Wheelchair(s)—*Cont.*
    brakes on, handling, 51
    component parts of, 636, 637f
    medical model, 51
    motorized, 50–51, 69
    opening and closing, 51
    pushing, skills for people, 51
    sport, 636–638
        for physical education classes,
            637–638
    techniques for sport, 636–637, 648f
    track and racing, 48, 634f, 636
    types of, 48, 49
Wheelchair basketball, 46, 57, 104, 423,
    634–635
    ball retrieval game for moderate/high
        functional level in, 427
    bounce spin game for moderate/high
        functional level in, 426–427
    Challenger, 47, 78–79
    competition in, 437
    functional profiles for, 422t
    integrated, 46
    passing game for low functional level in,
        425–426
    rules at a glance, 422t
    shooting game for low functional level
        in, 426
    skills for, 423–425, 426f, 427f
Wheelchair dance, 445
Wheelchair dance sport, 445
Wheelchair rugby, 629
Wheelchair slalom, motorized,
    431–432, 690
    figure eight turn game for low functional
        level in, 434
    reverse turn game for low functional
        level in, 433
    rules at a glance for, 432t
    skills for, 432–433, 433f,
        433t, 434f
Wheelchair soccer, indoor, 429, 690
    court layout for, 429f
    functional profiles for, 430t
    rules at a glance in, 428t–429t
    shot-blocking game for low functional
        level in, 431
    skills for, 429, 430f, 430t

Wheelchair soccer, indoor—*Cont.*
    throw-in game for low functional level
        in, 431
Wheelchair sports, 45–47, 615–616,
    632–636. *See also* Wheelchair
        basketball; Wheelchair rugby;
        Wheelchair soccer; Wheelchair tennis
    assessment of function and skill for, 629
    fitness assessment for, and
        programming, 638–642
    medical and functional classifications in,
        628–629, 628f
    motorized, 50–51, 69, 630–631
    for paraplegics, 632–636
    for quadriplegics, 629–632
    rotator cuff injuries in, 618, 641–642
    winter, 638, 639f
Wheelchair Sports, USA, 46t, 615
Wheelchair tennis, 635–636
Wheelchair tennis competition, 437–438
White, Ryan, 542
Whole method, 195
Williams, Montel, 647
Winged scapulae, 393, 403, 404f
Winnick, Joseph, 18, 20, 367
Winter sports, 438–439, 638, 639f, 671
Withdrawal, 29
Wolfensberger, Wolf, 55
Woodson, Andrea, 67
Working jointly, 74
World Health Organization (WHO), 36
    classification of disability by,
        357–358
Wright, Beatrice, personal meaning theory of,
    135–136
Writing, guidelines for, 37
WS, USA. *See* Wheelchair Sports, USA
Wyeth, Duncan, 27–28
Yachting competition, 438
Yellow Brick Road, The, 162
Yilla, Abu, 35, 206, 625
Yoga, 452
You Stay Active curriculum model, 130
Z scores, transformation of,
    172–173, 172f
Zero reject, 107
Zittel, Lauriece, 202, 495
Zoerink, Dean, 106